D0302772

WITHDRAWN FROM
THE LIBRARY

UNIVERSITY OF
WINCHESTER

KA 0390453 9

The Princeton Companion to Atlantic History

The Princeton Companion to Atlantic History

Editor

Joseph C. Miller
University of Virginia

UNIVERSITY OF WINCHESTER
LIBRARY

Associate Editors

Vincent Brown
Harvard University

Jorge Cañizares-Esguerra
University of Texas at Austin

Laurent Dubois
Duke University

Karen Ordahl Kupperman
New York University

PRINCETON UNIVERSITY PRESS
PRINCETON AND OXFORD

UNIVERSITY OF WINCHESTER

03904559 | 909.
| 09821 MIL

Copyright © 2015 by Princeton University Press
Published by Princeton University Press, 41 William Street, Princeton,
New Jersey 08540
In the United Kingdom: Princeton University Press, 6 Oxford Street,
Woodstock, Oxfordshire OX20 1TW

press.princeton.edu

Jacket Art: Detail from *Burning of the Town of Cap-Français, Saint-Domingue (Haiti)*, 1795 (color engraving), French School (18th century).
Private Collection/Archives Charmet/The Bridgeman Art Library.

The research for the entry "Livestock" by Eva Botella-Ordinas was made
possible thanks to the following: Epistemología Histórica: Historia de las
emociones en los siglos XIX y XX' MICIN, FFI2010–20876 (subpro-
grama FISO), and: "Repensando la identidad: la Monarquía de España
entre 1665 y 1746", MICIN REF. HAR2011–27562.

Parts of the entries "Creolization" and "Maroons" by Richard Price have
been previously published in other web and print sources.

All Rights Reserved

Library of Congress Cataloging-in-Publication Data

The Princeton companion to Atlantic history / editor, Joseph C. Miller,
University of Virginia ; associate editors, Vincent Brown, Harvard
University, Jorge Cañizares-Esguerra, University of Texas at Austin,
Laurent Dubois, Duke University, Karen Ordahl Kupperman, New York
University.
    pages cm
  Includes bibliographical references and index.
  ISBN 978-0-691-14853-3 (hardcover : alk. paper)
  1. Atlantic Ocean Region—History—Encyclopedias.   I. Miller,
Joseph Calder, editor.
D210.P936 2014
909'.09821—dc23   2014010013

British Library Cataloging-in-Publication Data is available

This book has been composed in Adobe Garamond Pro and Myriad Pro

Editorial and Project Management Services by Valerie Tomaselli/MTM
Publishing

Printed on acid-free paper. ∞

Printed in the United States of America

10 9 8 7 6 5 4 3 2 1

Contents

Preface

At the beginning of the fifteenth century, the peoples inhabiting Africa, the Americas, and Europe were largely separated by the watery medium of the seas, but by the turn of the nineteenth century, their connections around the Atlantic had transformed history—not just the history of the regions bordering it, but of the world as well. The study of these interactions—of maritime exploration, of commercial engagement, of human migration and settlement, of plants and pathogens, of cultural exchange and production, of political realignment and upheaval—is the Atlantic history that this volume considers.

The Princeton Companion to Atlantic History is the first encyclopedic reference work to examine this history. The *Companion* takes into account the multiple perspectives that the Atlantic World embodied, with an accent on its dynamics of change. Following a prologue that sets the stage for these engagements around the Atlantic World, introductory essays in part one outline the dynamics distinctive to each of four century-long chronological periods, beginning with the early to mid-fifteenth century and continuing into the mid-nineteenth century, each viewed through the lenses of the regional components contributing to the world of the Atlantic and the forces of exchange and conflict among them that shaped these periods. These chronological essays are followed by a set of some 120 entries in part two, in A-to-Z format, examining the specific regions, strategies, and groups central to understanding the complexities of these encounters in the Atlantic World. Written by an international team of scholars, the essays in part two fill in the contours and add human actors, details of their strategies, and analytical implications to the synthetic essays in part one. These shorter entries present seemingly familiar topics—the Seven Years' War or trading companies, for instance—in unfamiliar and provocative ways, as well as unfamiliar topics—such as family networks or imperial planning—in accessible terms. The result, we hope, is a work that mediates among the specific academic cultures of the varied disciplinary and regional fields involved in studying the Atlantic World in an effort to integrate Atlantic history as a coherent and distinctive field of knowledge and understanding.

The *Companion* thus offers undergraduate and graduate students, as well as practicing scholars, the first comprehensive reference guide to this growing field, in an epistemologically challenging historical examination of concepts critical to it. It aims to help readers confront the distinctiveness of the field in ways not yet offered in the growing literature on Atlantic history, still often Eurocentric and rooted in the conceptual underpinnings of our modern era rather than in the perspectives and motivations of the varied peoples of the past who made it happen.

We now understand the world in terms of the modern social sciences—the efforts to aggregate behaviors in terms of statistical descriptions and to analyze human life in terms of societies, economies, and the formally constituted politics of nation-states. Today politicians must create abstract ideologies, particularly of nationhood, to mobilize and motivate masses of strangers to coordinated action. But none of these modern premises existed at the start of the distinctively open history of the Atlantic in the later fifteenth century. The familiar concepts of the modern social sciences thus offer little to further our understanding of the motivations and the strategies that people brought to the Atlantic World. Europeans no less than Native Americans and Africans thought and acted in terms of their relationships to one another; they lived in small communities of familiarity and trust, of kinship and faith thought of as enduring and stable, or in similarly mutually responsible relationships of patronage and loyalty.

Thus, the historians of the Atlantic World who have written for this volume explore the details of these communities, the interactions among the peoples in them, and the strategies individuals developed as they encountered the unexpected realities of the New World. So it is that Atlantic history focuses not on overarching abstractions but on human experiences and the deep historical processes created from them. While the *Companion* certainly considers abstract concepts—gender, race, sovereignty, and even modernity itself—it concentrates on the complex detail and texture of all the component parts of the Atlantic Era.

The field of Atlantic history is inherently challenging, owing to the several, to-date-largely isolated regional perspectives that it brings together. The literatures on all of them have become sufficiently dense and complex to contribute substantively to the integrated treatment found in the *Companion*, and in turn to benefit from the contextualization offered in this volume. Research in this area—begun tentatively in the 1970s, though with antecedents dating back to the 1950s, cohering in an active field since the 1990s—has also grown to a critical mass. Journals focusing on more specialized subjects are publishing special issues considering the implications of Atlantic history for their readers. The existing literature includes mostly collections of essays considering a range of questions still from the perspective of the regional components, and many others relate to the definitions, boundaries, and emergent historiography of the field. Monographs in a range of fields have increasingly viewed their targeted topics through Atlantic lenses. The first large historical surveys have recently appeared, considering the early-modern period through the interconnections inherent in the Atlantic World.

The purpose of *The Princeton Companion to Atlantic History* is to present what the field has achieved after 30 years of work in an intellectually coherent historical structure. It aims to create a suitably compound presentation of an inherently composite subject. By bringing together scholars engaged in the many components of the field, we hope the *Companion* will help carry Atlantic history beyond its formative stages toward intellectual maturity.

Part One

As the essays in part one trace the elongated outlines of Atlantic history, they explore the historical strategies and processes that defined the Atlantic Era—economic consolidation, human migration, military expansion, technological progress, environmental change, and cultural diffusion. In the sixteenth century, improving European maritime technology—such as navigation and shipbuilding—extended Europeans' reach across the open ocean and helped to yield inflows of gold and silver from Africa and the Americas to Europe, satisfying the shortages of the specie needed to feed growing commercialization. Domestic slaving in the Mediterranean, as mentioned in the essay on the sixteenth century, was extended into the Atlantic and redefined to treat human beings as legal collateral for commercial production of commodities in the Atlantic, notably sugar. On all continents unsustainably costly militarization created complementing needs for the new resources that the opening of the Atlantic provided.

Across the seventeenth century, continued advances in maritime and geographical knowledge—maritime technology and mapmaking, for instance—made crossing the ocean more viable and settlement in the New World more feasible, leading to increasing economic activity on all shores of the Atlantic and to militarization of the seas. Commodities established new connections, seeded with the imbalances of power that would come to characterize many Atlantic World engagements that grew out of them, some extreme. The new commodities, as noted in the essay on the seventeenth century, transformed European lifestyles: furs, sugar, tobacco—all became luxury goods that fed a growing consumerism in the British Isles and on the continent. The sugar trade, initially developed in Brazil but spreading northward through the Caribbean, spurred the transatlantic slave trade to new heights, and western African polities consolidated military power as they intensified their involvement in fueling the trade in captives enslaved to labor in the Americas. Religious conflict in Reformation Europe drove voluntary migration as well, bringing Europeans across the Atlantic as the century proceeded.

In the eighteenth century the slave trade strongly shaped the contours of an increasingly integrated Atlantic World—demographically, culturally, economically. The forced movement of Africans across the ocean reached new heights and was overwhelmingly responsible for the demographic composition of the commodity-producing regions of the New World. As noted in the essay on the eighteenth century, enslaved peoples from Africa composed more than three-quarters of all migrants to the Americas between 1500 and 1820. This trade in humans also undergirded the economic networks that consolidated the Atlantic Basin in the eighteenth century. Capitalism would flourish, along with the globalized warfare that supported it, and solidify its hold on economic life. At the same time, political upheaval would intensify, laying out the framework for the emergence of the modern nation-state.

While the specific chronological dimensions of the Atlantic World are hard to delineate—a challenge considered directly in the essay on the nineteenth century—the processes that had come to define the Atlantic Era yielded outcomes that were being consolidated by the mid-1800s. The political upheavals begun in the previous century yielded national independence throughout the Americas. The abolition of the slave trade was intimately connected to these political transformations and ultimately to the burgeoning investment by European powers, primarily Britain, in economic expansion and military imperialism in Africa and Asia. At the same time as the British were looking southward and eastward, the United States was looking west, gaining in territory, in technological and military capacity, and economic strength, representing a consolidation of at least hemispheric geostrategic influence on the west side of the Atlantic. This drive for settlement and sovereign expansion across the Americas, north and south, became the leading edge of the transition to the nation-state, which would engender a profound transfer of allegiance from family, community, and individual patron-client relationships to the more abstract associations of modern political identities. These abstractions of identity and political relations—revolving around inclusion and exclusion—echo well into the modern era. As the essay on the nineteenth century suggests, this longer-term influence of Atlantic outcomes—in the twentieth and twenty-first centuries—makes a case for an extended chronological definition of the modern world created in the Atlantic: that we are still living in it, though on increasingly global scales.

Part Two

The components woven through the panoramic views in the essays of part one are disentangled in the granular coverage of the shorter part two entries, which examine specific participants and strategies central to the dynamics of the Atlantic World as a whole. These shorter entries gloss both concepts and themes relevant to the chronological periods and others elucidating overarching processes and trends spanning the centuries under consideration.

In selecting these topics, we considered the full range of concepts, events, and trends embodying the major areas of development in the Atlantic World, including economic, political, and military contexts; movements of people; technologies and science; environmental contexts; and cultures and communities. However, our intention in part two was not to be comprehensive in the sense of a gazetteer; rather, we aimed to design entries around concepts that are analytically significant for the historical dynamics of the Atlantic World. As seen from the examples below, some of the topics—such as commercialization and language—span the long-term periods considered in the chronological essays of part one, while others are more targeted—covering, for instance, specific wars, political upheavals, commodities, or contributors to events.

Economic Contexts. Systems of labor, production, trade, and financing were critical mechanisms of change in the Atlantic World. These processes are explored in entries on the economies and economic strategies of the regions bordering the Atlantic, as well as in entries on leading commodities, practices, and areas of production (such as in Furs and Skins, Livestock, and Marine Resources) and methods of trade (such as in Trading Companies, Trading Diasporas, and Specie). Among labor systems, several entries explore the Atlantic trade in enslaved Africans and its suppression, as well as slavery and its abolition.

Movements of People. The A-to-Z entries also highlight the more voluntary movements of Europeans across the Atlantic as one of the primary components of Atlantic encounters, including a general entry on Emigrants and a specific note on Family Networks. The strategies used to force emigration—beyond the slave trade—are also featured in such entries as those on Impressment, Kidnapping, and Panyarring, and Native American Removals. Others, such as Family and Family Production and Blended Communities, explore the economic, cultural, and demographic characteristics of the people who moved throughout the Atlantic regions.

Political and Legal Contexts. Political transformations and upheavals were critical markers of the changes in the Atlantic World. These processes are illuminated in a range of ways. Several entries dissect the specific legal strategies involved in European engagements across the Atlantic, including Canon Law and the Law of Nations, for instance. The intimate sources of political and economic power in the Atlantic World are explored in such entries as Royal Liberties and Patron-Client Networks. The unique political structures of Native American and African polities are examined in such entries as African Political Systems and Paramount Chiefdoms. Consideration of the independence struggles that ended the European legal and military efforts in the Americas can be found in entries on Haiti, the Hispanic Americas, the United States, and France.

Military Contexts. The military context of the struggle for U.S. independence is considered in a separate entry on the War for U.S. Independence. Other military encounters are also examined in such essays as the Seven Years' War, African Wars (Slaving and Others), Napoleonic Wars, and in an umbrella entry on the early Wars of Conquest. The strong general trend toward militarization of the Atlantic space is also covered; see for instance Military Mobilization and Navies and Naval Arming.

Technologies and Science. Technologies enabled more than military engagements. This aspect of the practical knowledge enabling Atlantic history is covered in such entries as Cartography and Navigation and Nautical Sciences. Scientific knowledge as a product of encountering the Atlantic World is also examined in such essays as Natural History and Geography. Knowledge and techniques of healing are also explored in several entries covering the distinct practices of the Atlantic communities—Africans, African Americans, Europeans, and Native Americans.

Environmental Contexts. Related to these entries are those that consider the physical features of the Atlantic World with which the people who entered the Atlantic worked, both as obstacles and as opportunities. A general entry on Environments is included, as are more specific examinations of Climate and Weather, Forest Resources, and River Systems. An entry on Agricultural Production reflects the varying regional potentials. The Columbian Exchange of Old World and New World plants, animals, and pathogens is examined in a general entry and in such specific aspects as Diseases and Foods and Diets.

Cultures and Communities. Cultural aspects of Atlantic encounters are found in several sets of essays. Literary and visual representations, as well as ideological constructions, of the various peoples of the Atlantic can be found in such entries as Visual Representations, Captivity Narratives, and Travel Narratives and Compilations. Essays on religions and religious practices are included, as well as entries on how Christianity in various Atlantic contexts was hybridized, in such entries as Adaptations of Christianity in Africa and Native American Appropriations of Christianity. More specific religious strategies are covered as well; see for instance, Missionary Orders and Communities and the Prophetic Movements (in Native American contexts).

Conceptual Approaches. While we did not focus extensively on conceptual issues and historiography, it seemed useful to frame the more specific entries with coverage of concepts and methodological approaches important in the scholarly backdrop of Atlantic history. These entries on ways of conceptualizing the field include, among others, Center-Periphery Analysis and Underdevelopment. Other essays introduce key abstract concepts now considered standard categories of analysis in the modern social sciences, such as Class, Empire, Ethnicity, and Race, while exploring—and sometimes questioning—their relevance to the historical strategies of an Atlantic World that its creators often understood in other terms of their own, earlier times.

The beginning of the volume includes a topical list of A-to-Z entries to help readers identify articles that touch on specific areas of interest. They may find several articles, each highlighting a different aspect of the topic they seek, as the resources, participants, and strategies delineated in part two are not discrete or mutually exclusive; in the complex, multiple processes of Atlantic history they overlap and converge. From one viewpoint, Forest Resources, for instance, in an article of that title, may be seen as an economic concept; from another it is a feature of the physical environment. An entry on Furs and Skins covers another aspect of the same territory, but in a more targeted way, as these specific commodities become the primary engine of exchange and encounter between Native North Americans and European traders in the early Atlantic period. The entry on Capitalism also explores the role furs and skins play in the growing Atlantic system of capital accumulation and consumer-driven production. The topical list of entries is followed by a regional listing, which also enables readers to locate material that targets their specific needs and interests.

The various disciplines and viewpoints brought together in the *Companion* may result in variations among some historical details, such as dates of events. For instance, differing years are given for the War of the Spanish Succession, as individual scholars bring the perspectives of their geographic specialties to the analysis of this international and transoceanic conflict: Does the end of the war come with the Treaty of Utrecht in 1713, or does it extend further as some parties to the conflict continued fighting or did not ratify the peace immediately? Since we did not apply dogmatic answers to these questions in the pursuit of a false consistency, the vigilant reader will see such seeming incongruities.

In fact, the *Companion* embraces this diversity. The multiplicity of this history is represented in the plural format of part two, with its compound perspectives and many points of entry and in the eclectic range of imaginative scholars who have contributed them. The historical fabric thus produced has been woven from infinite threads, of every hue visible to the human eye, that readers of this volume may then weave together for themselves as a whole.

Alphabetical List of Entries

Topical List of Entries

Commodities
Conceptual Approaches
Cultures and Communities
Economic Strategies
Environmental Contexts
Labor Recruitment
Legal Strategies
Military Strategies and War
Movements of People
Political Strategies
Regional Focus
Religions
Slaving
Technologies and Science

Gender
Literary and Visual Expressions, African
    American
Literary Genres: Captivity Narratives
Literary Genres: Travel Narratives and
    Compilations
Mami Wata
Modernity
Nation
Race
Religions, African, Historiography of
Underdevelopment
Utopias
Visual Representations
World/Global History
World-Systems Theory

Commodities

Commodities
Forest Resources
Furs and Skins
Livestock
Marine Resources

Conceptual Approaches

Center-Periphery Analysis
Class
Colonies and Colonization
Cornucopias
Creolization
Democratic Revolutions, Age of
Economic Cycles
Frontiers

Cultures and Communities

See also Religions
Blended Communities
Creolization
Death and Burial
Diasporas
Family and Family Networks
Emigrants
Ethnicity
Foods and Diets
Freed People
Healing, African
Healing, African American
Healing, European
Healing, Native American

Movements of People

Blended Communities
Creolization
Diasporas
Emigrants
Family and Family Networks
Freed People
Impressment, Kidnapping, and
    Panyarring
Indentured Contracts
Maroons
Native American Removals
Penal Transportation
Slaving, in Africa
Slaving, European, from Africa
Slaving, European, of Native Americans
Slaving, Muslim, of Christians
Trading Diasporas

Political Strategies

Captivity, Native American
Colonies and Colonization
Democratic Revolutions, Age of
Emancipations
Empires
Ethnicity
Freed People
Government, Representative
Imperial Planning
Independence: Haiti
Independence: Hispanic Americas
Independence: United States
Monarchies and Agents
Nation
Native American Removals
Paramount Chiefdoms
Patron-Client Networks
Penal Transportation
Political Systems, African
Political Systems, Collective
    Consensual
Prophetic Movements
Revolts, Slave
Revolutions, National: France
Slave Trade, Suppression of Atlantic
Weapons of the Weak

Regional Focus

The following entries focus explicitly on regions
and regional actors; any not listed here are pan-
Atlantic in orientation.

Africa

Christianity, Adaptations in Africa of
Economic Strategies, African
Economies, African
Healing, African
Islam in Africa
Political Systems, African
Political Systems, Collective Consensual
Religions, African
Religions, African, Historiography of
Slaving, European, from Africa
Slaving, in Africa
Slaving, Muslim, of Christians
Technologies, African
Wars, African: Slaving and Other

Americas, African

Christianity, African American
Emancipations
Freed People
Healing, African American
Independence: Haiti
Literary and Visual Expressions, African
    American
Maroons
Muslims, African, in the Americas
Religions, African, in America
Revolts, Slave

Americas, European

Economies, American: Brazil
Economies, American: Caribbean
Economies, American: North America
Economies, American: Spanish Territories
Frontiers
Independence: United States
Missionary Orders and Communities
Seven Years' War
Slavery, U.S.
Slaving, European, of Native Americans

Contributors

Ida Altman
Professor, History Department, University of Florida
   Cornucopias

Jennifer L. Anderson
Associate Professor, Department of History, State University of New York, Stony Brook
   Forest Resources

Kenneth J. Andrien
Edmund J. and Louise Kahn Chair in History, Southern Methodist University
   Economies, American: Spanish Territories

Ralph A. Austen
Professor Emeritus, Department of History, University of Chicago
   Economies, Africa

Kenneth J. Banks
Assistant Professor, History Department, Wofford College
   Contraband; Monarchies and Agents

Juliana Barr
Associate Professor of History, University of Florida
   Captivity, Native American

Robert M. Baum
Associate Professor, Department of Religion, Dartmouth College
   Religions, African

Sven Beckert
Laird Bell Professor of American History, Harvard University
   Commodities

Aviva Ben-Ur
Associate Professor, Department of Judaic and Near Eastern Studies, University of Massachusetts, Amherst
   Jewish Communities

Celeste-Marie Bernier
Professor of African American Studies, Faculty of Arts, University of Nottingham
   Literary and Visual Expressions, African American

Kristen Block
Associate Professor, Department of History, Florida Atlantic University
   Patron-Client Networks

W. Jeffrey Bolster
Associate Professor, Department of History, University of New Hampshire
   Marine Resources

Eva Botella-Ordinas
Associate Professor of the Department of Early Modern History, Universidad Autónoma de Madrid
   Livestock

John P. Bowes
Associate Professor, Department of History, Eastern Kentucky University
 Native American Removals

Kathleen J. Bragdon
Professor, Department of Anthropology, College of William & Mary
 Languages

Holly Brewer
Burke Chair of American History and Associate Professor, Department of History, University of Maryland
 Law, Constitutional

Vincent Brown
Charles Warren Professor of American History and Professor of African and African American Studies, History Department, Harvard University
 The Eighteenth Century; Death and Burial

Trevor Burnard
Professor and Head of School, School of Historical and Philosophical Studies, University of Melbourne
 Colonies and Colonization

Amy Turner Bushnell
Adjunct Associate Professor, Department of History, Brown University
 Center-Periphery Analysis

Judith A. Carney
Professor, Department of Geography, Institute of the Environment and Sustainability, University of California, Los Angeles
 Columbian Exchange

Vincent Carretta
Professor, Department of English, University of Maryland
 Literary Genres: Captivity Narratives

Jill H. Casid
Professor of Visual Studies, Department of Art History, University of Wisconsin-Madison
 Visual Representations

Andrew Cayton
University Distinguished Professor, History Department, Miami University
 Wars of Independence, American

Timothy J. Coates
Professor, Department of History, The College of Charleston
 Penal Transportation

Peter A. Coclanis
Director of the Global Research Institute and Albert R. Newsome Professor, Department of History, University of North Carolina-Chapel Hill
 Economies, American: North America

John Collins
Lecturer, History Department, Eastern Washington University
 Law, Military

Duane Corpis
Assistant Professor, Department of History, Cornell University
 Christianity

Samuel Willard Crompton
Professor, History Department, Holyoke Community College
 Military Mobilization; Military Technologies; Navies and Naval Arming

Christian Ayne Crouch
Assistant Professor, Historical Studies Department, Bard College
 Seven Years' War

Enrico Dal Lago
Lecturer in American History, Department of History, National University of Ireland, Galway
 Underdevelopment; World-Systems Theory

John Donoghue
Associate Professor, Department of History, Loyola University of Chicago
 Class

Seymour Drescher
Professor, Department of History, University of Pittsburgh
 Abolition of Atlantic Slave Trade

Henry John Drewal
Evjue-Bascom Professor of African and African Diaspora Arts, Departments of Art History & Afro-American Studies, University of Wisconsin-Madison
 Mami Wata

Laurent Dubois
Marcello Lotti Professor of Romance Studies and History, Department of Romance Studies, Duke University
    The Nineteenth Century; Emancipations; Revolts, Slave

Chris S. Duvall
Assistant Professor, Geography and Environmental Studies, University of New Mexico
    Geography

Jordana Dym
Associate Professor, History Department, Skidmore College
    Independence: Hispanic Americas

Pieter C. Emmer
Institute for History (emeritus), Leiden University
    Economies: European

Robbie Ethridge
Professor, Department of Sociology and Anthropology, University of Mississippi
    Economic Strategies, Native North American

Roquinaldo Ferreira
Vasco da Gama Associate Professor, History, Portuguese and Brazilian Studies, Brown University
    Slave Trade, Suppression of Atlantic

Charles R. Foy
Assistant Professor, History Department, Eastern Illinois University
    Maritime Populations

Zephyr Frank
Associate Professor, Department of History, Stanford University
    Economies, American: Brazil

Niklas Frykman
Assistant Professor, Department of History, University of Pittsburgh
    Impressment, Kidnapping, and Panyarring

Alan Gallay
Lyndon B. Johnson Chair of U.S. History, Department of History and Geography, Texas Christian University
    Slaving, European, of Native Americans

John D. Garrigus
Associate Professor, Department of History, University of Texas at Arlington
    Independence: Haiti

Noah L. Gelfand
Adjunct Professor, History Department, University of Connecticut at Stamford
    Judaism

Malick W. Ghachem
Associate Professor, History Department, Massachusetts Institute of Technology
    Liberties, Royal

Michael A. Gomez
Professor, Department of History, New York University
    Muslims, African, in the Americas

Pablo F. Gómez
Assistant Professor, Department of History and Geography, Texas Christian University
    Healing, African American

Eliga H. Gould
Professor and Department Chair, Department of History, University of New Hampshire
    Law of Nations

Karen B. Graubart
Associate Professor, Department of History, Notre Dame University
    Ethnicity

Toby Green
Lecturer, Departments of History and Spanish, Portuguese and Latin American Studies, King's College, London
    Diasporas

Allan Greer
Professor and Canada Research Chair in Colonial North America, Department of History and Classical Studies, McGill University
    Christianity, Native American Appropriations of

Keila Grinberg
Associate Professor, History Department, Universidade Federal do Rio de Janeiro
    Manumission

Jane I. Guyer
George Armstrong Kelly Professor, Department of Anthropology, Johns Hopkins University
    Economic Strategies, African

Jonathan Todd Hancock
Assistant Professor, History Department, Hendrix College
    Prophetic Movements (co-author)

Walter Hawthorne
Professor, Department of History, Michigan State University
    Technologies, African

Gad Heuman
Professor Emeritus, Department of History, University of Warwick
    Freed People

M. H. Hoeflich
Kane Distinguished Professor of Law, University of Kansas, School of Law
    Law, Roman, in the Americas

Woody Holton
McCausland Professor of History, History Department, University of South Carolina
    Independence: United States

James Horn
Vice President, Research and Historical Interpretation, Colonial Williamsburg Foundation
    Indentured Contracts

John M. Janzen
Professor, Department of Anthropology, University of Kansas, Lawrence
    Healing, African

David S. Jones
A. Bernard Ackerman Professor of the Culture of Medicine, Faculty of Arts and Sciences and the Faculty of Medicine, Harvard University
    Healing, Native American

Martin A. Klein
Professor Emeritus, Department of History, University of Toronto
    Wars, African: Slaving and Other

Wim Klooster
Professor and Chair, Department of History, Clark University
    Economic Strategies, European

Karen Ordahl Kupperman
Silver Professor of History, New York University
    The Seventeenth Century

Paul S. Landau
Associate Professor, Department of History, University of Maryland
    Political Systems, African

Kris Lane
Professor, History Department, Tulane University
    Raiders

Pier M. Larson
Professor, Department of History, Johns Hopkins University
    Slaving, in Africa

Kimberly Lynn
Associate Professor, Department of Liberal Studies, Western Washington University
    Law, Canon

Wyatt MacGaffey
J. R. Coleman Professor Emeritus in Social Anthropology, Haverford College
    Religions, African, Historiography of

Ken MacMillan
Professor, Department of History, University of Calgary
    Law, Monarchical

Anouar Majid
Vice President for Global Affairs, University of New England
    Slaving, Muslim, of Christians

Elizabeth Mancke
Professor and Canada Research Chair in Atlantic Canada Studies, University of New Brunswick
    Modernity

Bertie Mandelblatt
Assistant Professor, Department of History and Program in Caribbean Studies, University of Toronto
    Foods and Diets

Jane E. Mangan
Associate Professor and Department of History Chair, Latin American Studies Program, Davidson College
Family and Family Networks

Armin Mattes
Gilder Lehrman Research Fellow, Robert H. Smith International Center for Jefferson Studies at Monticello
Government, Representative

Alexander Mikaberidze
Associate Professor, Department of History and Social Sciences, Louisiana State University, Shreveport
Wars, Napoleonic

Joseph C. Miller
T. Cary Johnson, Jr. Professor, Corcoran Department of History, University of Virginia
Prologue; The Sixteenth Century; Political Systems, Collective Consensual

Cary J. Mock
Professor, Department of Geography, University of South Carolina
Climate and Weather

Michelle Molina
John W. Croghan Associate Professor, Department of Religious Studies, Northwestern University
Missionary Orders and Communities

Christopher Morris
Associate Professor, History, University of Texas at Arlington
River Systems

Melanie Newton
Associate Professor, Department of History, University of Toronto
Gender

Stephan Palmié
Professor, Department of Anthropology, University of Chicago
Religions, African, in the Americas

Gabriel Paquette
Assistant Professor, Department of History, Johns Hopkins University
Imperial Planning (co-author)

Mark Peterson
Professor, Department of History, University of California, Berkeley
Capitalism

William A. Pettigrew
Reader, School of History, University of Kent
Commercialization; Law, Commercial

Steve Pincus
Bradford Durfee Professor of History, Yale University
Empires

Geoffrey Plank
Professor of Early Modern History, University of East Anglia
Wars of Conquest

Richard Price
Professor Emeritus, American Studies, College of William & Mary
Creolization; Maroons

James D. Rice
Professor, Department of History, State University of New York, Plattsburgh
Paramount Chiefdoms

David Richardson
Professor, Department of History, University of Hull
Slaving, European, from Africa

Sophia Rosenfeld
Professor, Corcoran Department of History, University of Virginia
Revolutions, National: France

Brett Rushforth
Associate Professor, Lyon G. Tyler Department of History, College of William & Mary
Furs and Skins

Dominic M. Sachsenmaier
Professor, Department of History, Jacobs University
World/Global History

David Harris Sacks
Richard F. Scholz Professor of History and Humanities, History Department, Reed College
Utopias

Neil Safier
Associate Professor, Department of History,
University of British Columbia, Vancouver
    Cartography

Richard Salvucci
Professor, Department of Economics, Trinity
University
    Economic Cycles

Alison Sandman
Associate Professor, Department of History, James
Madison University
    Navigation and Nautical Sciences

Calvin Schermerhorn
Associate Professor, Faculty of History, Arizona State
University
    Slavery, U.S.

Londa Schiebinger
The John L. Hinds Professor of History of Science,
History Department, Stanford University
    Natural History

Christopher Schmidt-Nowara
Professor of History and Prince of Asturias Chair in
Spanish Culture & Civilization, Department of
History, Tufts University
    Democratic Revolutions, Age of

James F. Searing (deceased)
University of Illinois, Chicago
    Brokers

Erik R. Seeman
Professor, History Department, State University of
New York, Buffalo
    Diseases

Jon F. Sensbach
Professor, Department of History, University of
Florida
    Christianity, African American

Jason T. Sharples
Assistant Professor, Department of History, Catholic
University
    Weapons of the Weak

James Sidbury
Andrew W. Mellon Distinguished Professor of
Humanities and Director of Graduate Studies,
History Department, Rice University
    Race

Frederick H. Smith
Associate Professor, Department of Anthropology,
College of William & Mary
    Economies, American: Caribbean

Patrick Spero
Assistant Professor, Department of History, Williams
College
    Frontiers

Philip J. Stern
Associate Professor, Department of History, Duke
University
    Sovereignty; Trading Companies

Fionnghuala Sweeney
Senior Lecturer, School of English Literature,
Language, and Linguistics, Newcastle University
    Literary Genres: Travel Narratives and Compi-
    lations

John Wood Sweet
Associate Professor, Department of History,
University of North Carolina
    Prophetic Movements (co-author)

Andrew Toebben
Independent Scholar
    Imperial Planning (co-author)

Dale Tomich
Professor, Department of History, State University of
New York, Binghamton
    Agricultural Production

John Tutino
Professor, Department of History, Georgetown
University
    Family Production and Commercial Labor

Thomas M. Truxes
Clinical Associate Professor, Department of History,
New York University
    Trading Diasporas

Cécile Vidal
Lecturer, L'École des Hautes Études en Sciences Sociales
    Nation

Jelmer Vos
Assistant Professor, Department of History, Old Dominion University
    Christianity, Adaptations in Africa of

Rudolph T. Ware III
Assistant Professor, Department of History, University of Michigan
    Islam in Africa

David Weiland
Professor, Department of History, Collin College
    Specie

David Wheat
Assistant Professor, Department of History, Michigan State University
    Blended Communities

Samuel White
Assistant Professor, Department of History, Ohio State University
    Environments

Kelly Wisecup
Assistant Professor, English Department, University of North Texas
    Healing, European

Marianne S. Wokeck
Chancellor's Professor of History, Department of History, Indiana University—Purdue University, Indianapolis
    Emigrants

Maps

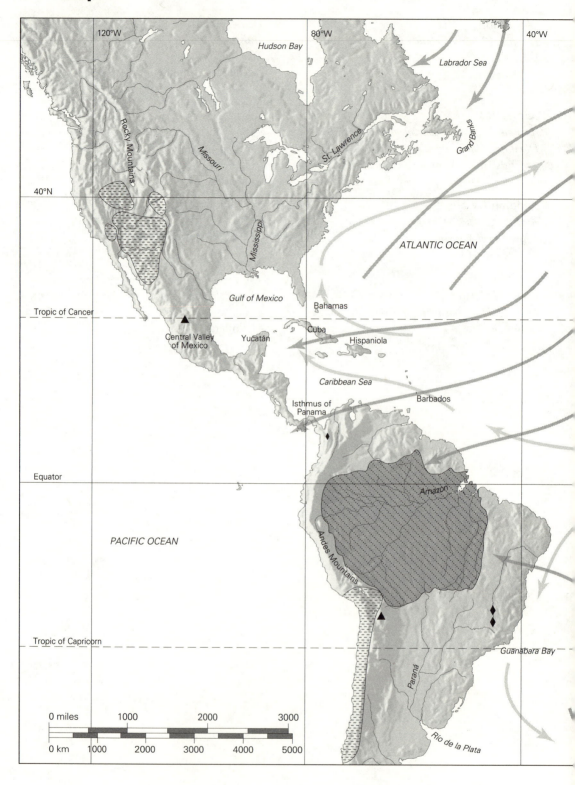

Map 1. Winds, Currents, and Major Physical Features of the Atlantic World.

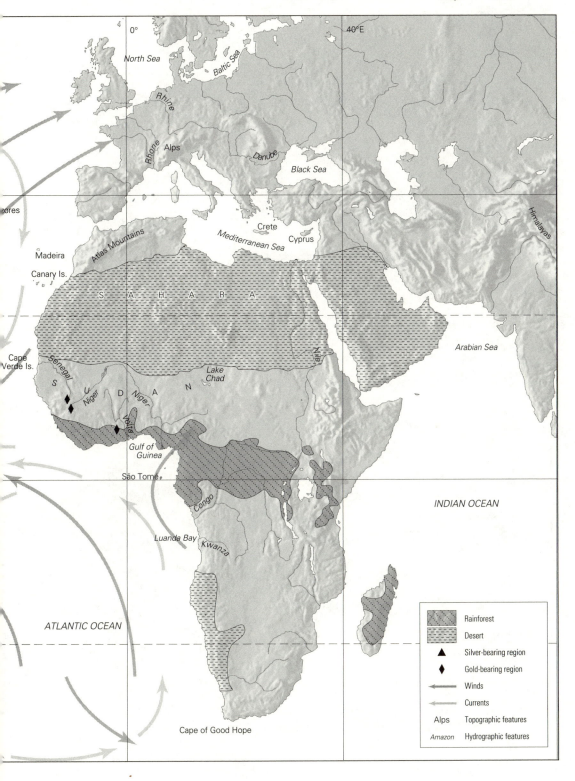

0°
40°E

North Sea
Baltic Sea
Rhine
Rhône
Alps
Danube
Black Sea
Crete
Mediterranean Sea
Cyprus
Himalayas

Azores

Madeira
Canary Is.
Atlas Mountains

S   A   H   A   R   A

Cape
Verde Is.
Senegal
S   U
Niger
D   A   N
Niger
Volta
Lake
Chad
Nile
Arabian Sea

Gulf of
Guinea
São Tomé

Congo
INDIAN OCEAN

Luanda Bay
Kwanza

ATLANTIC OCEAN

Cape of Good Hope

	Rainforest
	Desert
▲	Silver-bearing region
♦	Gold-bearing region
←	Winds
←	Currents
Alps	Topographic features
Amazon	Hydrographic features

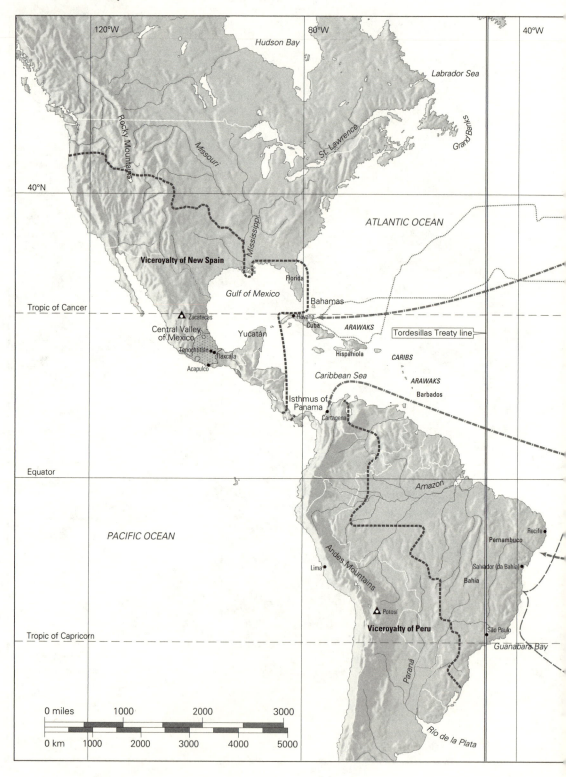

120°W

Hudson Bay

80°W

Labrador Sea

40°W

Rocky Mountains

Missouri

St. Lawrence

Grand Banks

40°N

ATLANTIC OCEAN

Viceroyalty of New Spain

Mississippi

Florida

Gulf of Mexico

Bahamas

Tropic of Cancer

△ Zacatecas

Havana

Cuba

ARAWAKS

Tordesillas Treaty line

Central Valley of Mexico

Yucatán

Tenochtitlán ● ● Tlaxcala

Hispaniola

CARIBS

Acapulco

ARAWAKS

Caribbean Sea

Barbados

Isthmus of Panama

Cartagena

Amazon

Equator

PACIFIC OCEAN

Recife

Pernambuco

Andes Mountains

Lima ●

Salvador (da Bahia) ●

Bahia

△ Potosí

Tropic of Capricorn

Viceroyalty of Peru

São Paulo

Paraná

Guanabara Bay

0 miles   1000   2000   3000

0 km   1000   2000   3000   4000   5000

Río de la Plata

Map 2. Sixteenth-Century Atlantic World.
Map shows only features relevant to the historical processes of the century.

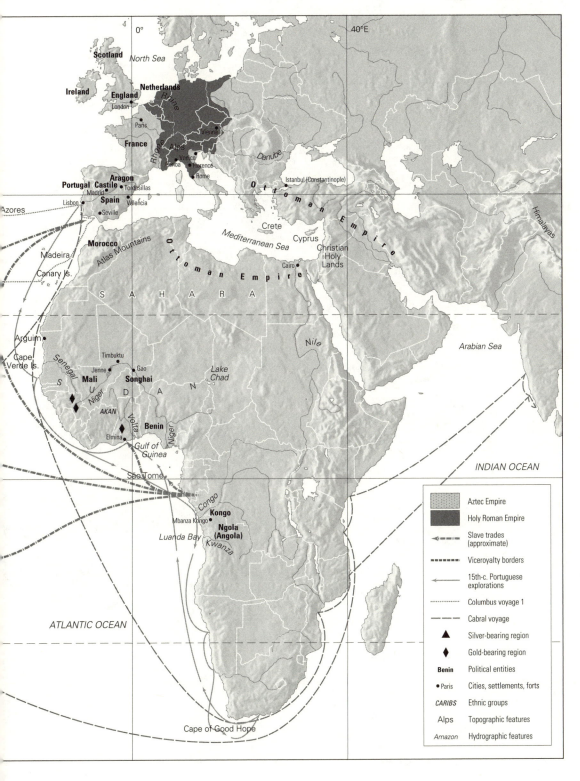

0°

40°E

Scotland

North Sea

Ireland

Netherlands

Rhine

England

London

France

Paris

Vienna

Alps

Genoa

Venice

Florence

Rome

Portugal **Castile** **Aragon**

Tordesillas

Madrid

Danube

Istanbul (Constantinople)

O t t o m a n   E m p i r e

Spain

Azores

Lisbon

Valencia

Seville

Morocco

Atlas Mountains

O t t o m a n   E m p i r e

Mediterranean Sea

Crete

Cyprus

Christian
Holy
Lands

Himalayas

Madeira

Canary Is.

S A H A R A

Cairo

Arabian Sea

Arguim

Cape
Verde Is.

Senegal

S
U
D
A
N

Timbuktu

Jenne

Gao

Mali

Niger

Songhai

AKAN

Volta

Lake
Chad

Nile

Elmina

Benin

Niger

Gulf of
Guinea

São Tomé

INDIAN OCEAN

Congo

Mbanza Kongo

Kongo

**Ngola
(Angola)**

Luanda Bay

Kwanza

ATLANTIC OCEAN

Cape of Good Hope

▦	Aztec Empire
■	Holy Roman Empire
◀━ ■ ■ ■ ■	Slave trades (approximate)
▪▪▪▪▪	Viceroyalty borders
←	15th-c. Portuguese explorations
⋯⋯	Columbus voyage 1
— — —	Cabral voyage
▲	Silver-bearing region
◆	Gold-bearing region
Benin	Political entities
• Paris	Cities, settlements, forts
CARIBS	Ethnic groups
Alps	Topographic features
Amazon	Hydrographic features

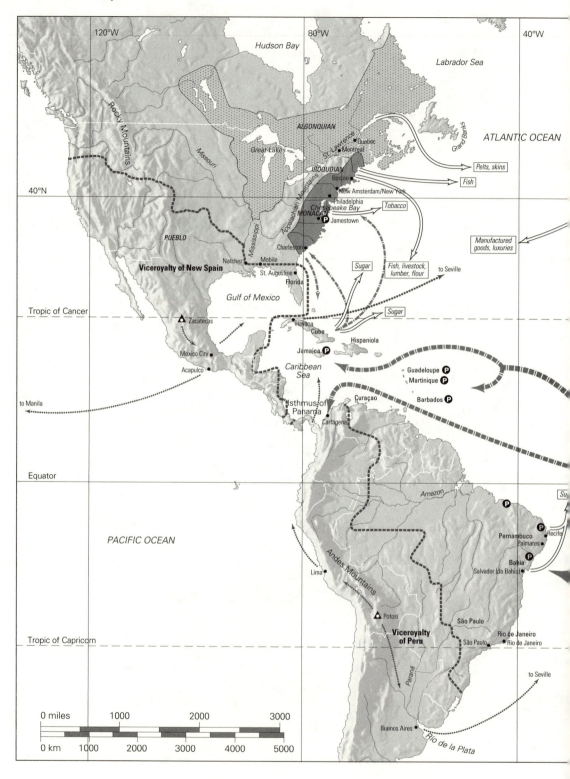

Map 3. Seventeenth-Century Atlantic World.
Map shows only features relevant to the historical processes of the century.

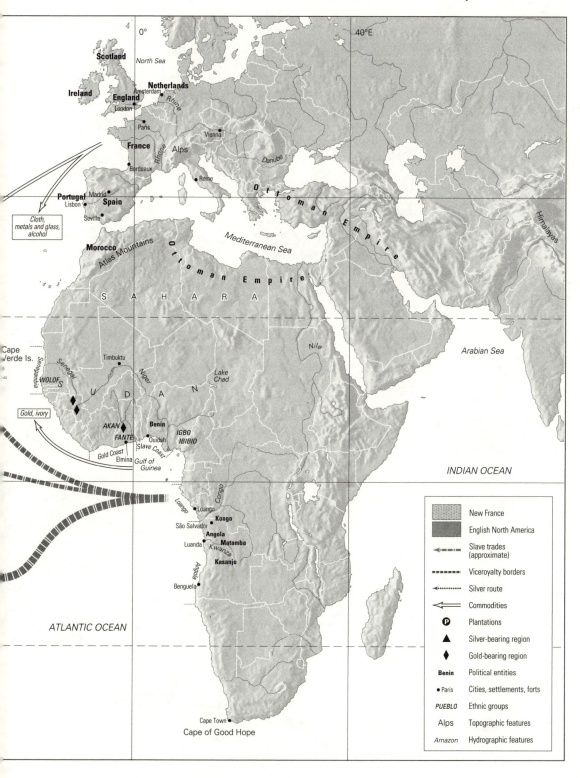

0°

40°E

Scotland

North Sea

Ireland

Netherlands
Amsterdam

England
London

Rhine

Paris

France

Vienna

Alps

Rhône

Bordeaux

Rome

Danube

Portugal
Lisbon

Madrid

Spain

Seville

**Cloth,
metals and glass,
alcohol**

Morocco

Atlas Mountains

Mediterranean Sea

O t t o m a n   E m p i r e

O t t o m a n   E m p i r e

S A H A R A

Nile

Arabian Sea

Cape
Verde Is.

Timbuktu

Senegal

Senegambia

WOLOF S

Niger

*Lake
Chad*

S   U   D   A   N

Gold, ivory

AKAN

Benin

*IGBO
IBIBIO*

FANTE
Ouidah

Gold Coast *Slave Coast*
Elmina *Gulf of
Guinea*

INDIAN OCEAN

Loango
Loango

Congo

Kongo

São Salvador

Angola

Matamba

Luanda

Kwanza

Kasanje

Angola

Benguela

ATLANTIC OCEAN

Himalayas

Cape Town

Cape of Good Hope

	New France
	English North America
◄--■-■-	Slave trades (approximate)
-------	Viceroyalty borders
◄••••••••	Silver route
◄────	Commodities
℗	Plantations
▲	Silver-bearing region
◆	Gold-bearing region
Benin	Political entities
• Paris	Cities, settlements, forts
PUEBLO	Ethnic groups
Alps	Topographic features
Amazon	Hydrographic features

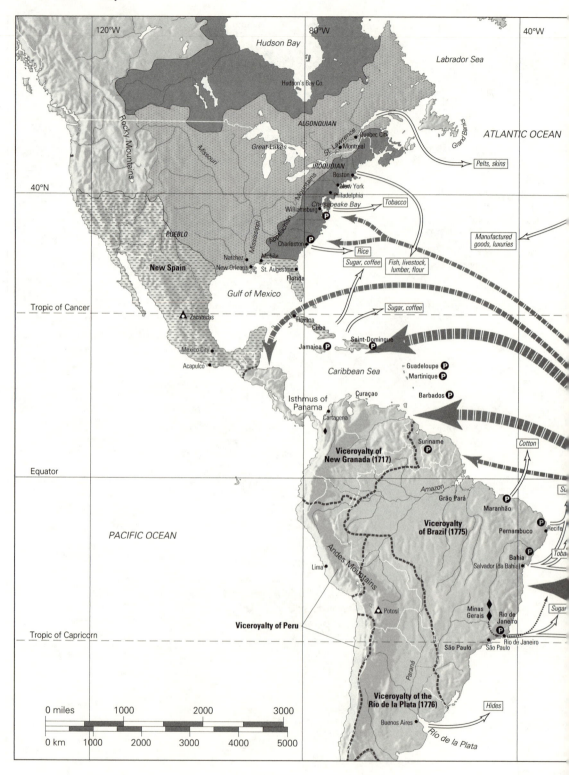

Map 4. Eighteenth-Century Atlantic World.
Map shows only features relevant to the historical processes of the century.

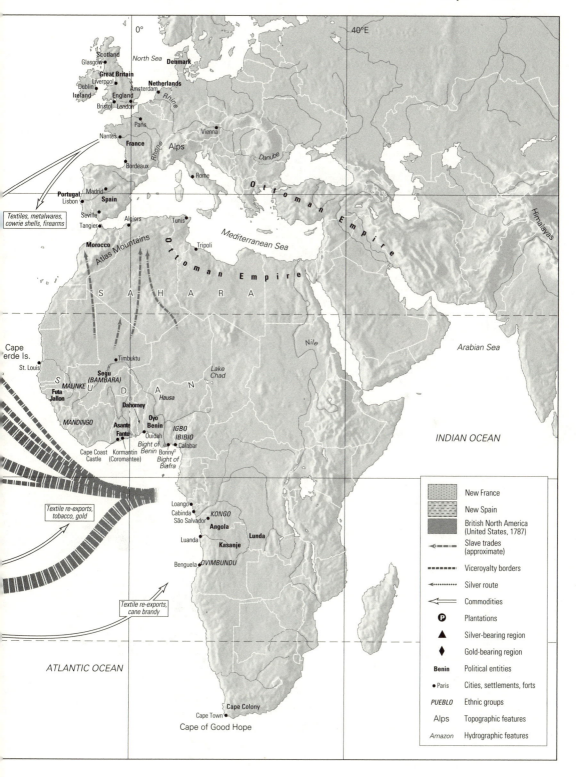

0°

40°E

Scotland
Glasgow
Great Britain
Liverpool
Denmark
North Sea
Netherlands
Amsterdam
Dublin
England
Ireland
Bristol
London
Rhine
Paris
Vienna
Nantes
France
Alps
Danube
Rhône
Bordeaux
Rome
Madrid
Portugal
Lisbon
Spain
Seville
Algiers
Tunis
Tangier
Morocco
Atlas Mountains
Tripoli
Mediterranean Sea
O t t o m a n   E m p i r e
O t t o m a n   E m p i r e
Himalayas

Textiles, metalwares,
cowrie shells, firearms

S A H A R A

Nile
Arabian Sea

Cape
Verde Is.
St. Louis
Timbuktu
*Lake
Chad*
**Segu
(BAMBARA)**
S
MALINKE
U
D
A
N
**Futa
Jallon**
Hausa
MANDINGO
Dahomey
**Asante
Fante**
**Oyo
Benin**
IGBO
Ouidah
IBIBIO
Cape Coast
Castle
Kormantin
(Coromantee)
*Bight of
Benin*
Bonny
Calabar
*Bight of
Biafra*

INDIAN OCEAN

Textile re-exports,
tobacco, gold

Loango
Cabinda
São Salvador
KONGO
Angola
Luanda
Lunda
Kasanje
Benguela
OVIMBUNDU

Textile re-exports,
cane brandy

ATLANTIC OCEAN

Cape Colony
Cape Town
Cape of Good Hope

	New France
	New Spain
	British North America (United States, 1787)
⊸■■■◂	Slave trades (approximate)
-------	Viceroyalty borders
◂······	Silver route
⟵	Commodities
Ⓟ	Plantations
▲	Silver-bearing region
◆	Gold-bearing region
Benin	Political entities
• Paris	Cities, settlements, forts
PUEBLO	Ethnic groups
Alps	Topographic features
Amazon	Hydrographic features

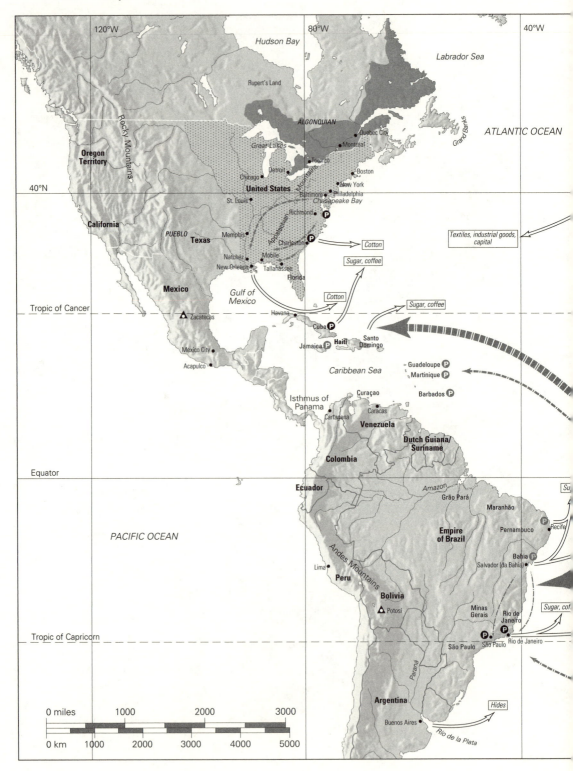

Map 5. Early Nineteenth-Century Atlantic World.
Map shows only features relevant to the historical processes of the century.

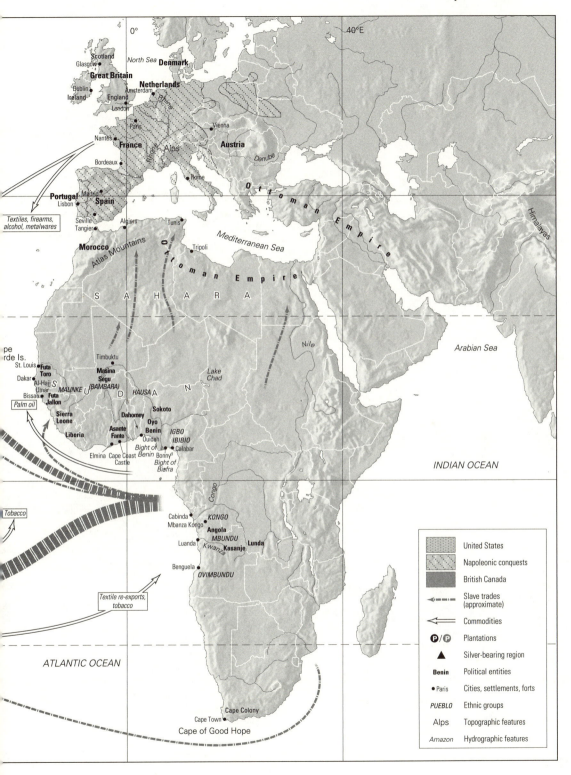

0°
40°E

Scotland
Glasgow●
Great Britain
●Dublin
Iceland   England
          London●

North Sea   **Denmark**

Netherlands
Amsterdam●
Vienna●

Nantes●
France   Alps
         Rhône

Bordeaux●

Rome●

Portugal Madrid●
Lisbon● **Spain**

Seville●
Tangier● Algiers●   Tunis●

Morocco   Tripoli●

Atlas Mountains   *Ottoman Empire*

Ottoman Empire

Mediterranean Sea

S A H A R A

Paris●

Austria

Danube

Himalayas

Textiles, firearms,
alcohol, metalwares

Nile

Lake
Chad

Arabian Sea

pe
rde Is.
St. Louis●**Futa**
       Toro
Dakar●
●Al-Hajj
  Umar *MALINKE* **Masina**
Bissau●   **Ségu**
Futa   *(BAMBARA)*
Jallon   *HAUSA*
Palm oil U
          D
Sierra   **Sokoto**
Leone   **Dahomey**
          Oyo
Liberia **Benin**
      Asante *IGBO*
      Fante *IBIBIO*
       Ouidah● ●Calabar
Elmina● Cape Coast Bonny●
      Castle *Bight of*
      Bight of *Benin*
      Biafra

Timbuktu●

S   U   D   A   N

INDIAN OCEAN

Congo

Tobacco

Cabinda●   *KONGO*
Mbanza Kongo●
      Angola
      MBUNDU
Luanda● **Lunda**
      Kwanza **Kasanje**
Benguela●
      OVIMBUNDU

Textile re-exports,
tobacco

ATLANTIC OCEAN

Cape Town● Cape Colony●
Cape of Good Hope

	United States
	Napoleonic conquests
	British Canada
⬅	Slave trades (approximate)
⬅	Commodities
P/Ⓟ	Plantations
▲	Silver-bearing region
Benin	Political entities
●Paris	Cities, settlements, forts
PUEBLO	Ethnic groups
Alps	Topographic features
Amazon	Hydrographic features

Part One

Prologue
Historical Dynamics of Change

Joseph C. Miller

The opening century of the four hundred years of Atlantic history explored in this volume can be understood historically only in terms of the cards that the entrants into it brought to the table. The hands they held were similar—in fact global—in Europe, Africa, and the Americas. The historical dynamics that motivated and enabled the players in all three regions revolved around very long-term struggles among powerful military interests, who thrived by conquest of accessible lands and the populations living on them. Other, commercial, interests were also at play in Afro-Eurasia. Merchants thrived by moving through the surrounding uninhabited spaces—often deserts—and also on the seas and oceans.

The customary perspective on these processes tends to celebrate "civilizations"—expansive "empires" and the luxuries supported by the wealth appropriated through conquests—thus taking militarism and commerce for granted. This volume balances this familiar story with the more local perspectives of small communities in most of Africa and Native America, as well as more of the ordinary villages in Europe and small communities in the Americas. It also historicizes the triumphs of conquest by emphasizing the costs of achieving them, and even more of maintaining them through time. There is nothing stable about history: continuity is fragile and requires effort to achieve.

Taking a very long-term view, the military conquests prominent in the history of Eurasia were costly and destructive and in the long run tended to burn the aggressors out. On this millennial scale, merchants, on the other hand, tended to accumulate wealth in enduring forms and to grow in financial strength. They invested their excess assets in military regimes that were reaching the logistical limits of plundering and in agricultural and other producers, as well as in more remote, and independent, communities. These relatively isolated communities, in turn, extracted commodities of value to visiting traders, and did so—without abandoning their own strategies of mobility, diversity, and mutual obligations—to invest in productive, but immovable and costly, infrastructure.

Militarists and merchants thus drew similarly on resources external to the structured cultural or political domains within which they competed. The balances among the strategies of local communities, merchant commerce, and military conquest varied by region—Africa, the Americas, and Europe—and within each region as well. This prologue sketches specifics of these variations relevant to what motivated European merchants and militarists to venture out into what became a fast-changing Atlantic World. The results everywhere were enabling for some, if also at the expense of others. But these initial Atlantic-oriented successes eventually proved overwhelmingly effective, enriching, and empowering, primarily for the partnership of merchants and militarists unique to northwestern Europe.

Backgrounds—Lands, People, and Seas

In the second half of the fifteenth century, the open waters of the Atlantic Ocean became historical spaces exploited by humans as relatively marginal players in Europe nosed their ways west beyond the horizons of coast-hugging maritime transportation networks known since ancient times. From Europe, the strong Canary Current flowing south and then west off the desert shores of northwestern Africa carried mariners sponsored by minor members of Portugal's late-medieval military aristocracy. They probed the barren Saharan coasts in search of fabulous wealth in gold reported to exist in regions beyond the desert, inhabited by people whom Muslims in North Africa distinguished from themselves as "black," a term also differentiating them as enslaveable unbelievers. Mariners seem to have been aware of these ocean winds and currents, and even the mid-Atlantic Azores archipelago, as early as the first half of the fourteenth century. The modern name for what we now see as an ocean, the Atlantic, comes from the eastern Mediterranean perspective of those ancient eras and alludes implicitly to the mysteries of the open sea among European literati: the word is an adjectival Greek form (*atlantikos*) referring to the Atlas Mountains in modern Morocco, thus to the endless waters beyond the Pillars of Hercules (Strait of Gibraltar).

Beyond this fanciful vision of the Atlantic in European-written scholarship, practical mariners and pirates had for centuries ranged widely through the northeastern Atlantic, and a few even out to its closer western shores. Portuguese fishermen are reputed somehow to have crossed the north-flowing Gulf Stream to reach the Grand Banks off modern Newfoundland, where they found greater interest in teeming schools of cod and haddock in the sea itself than in the land or its inhabitants. These northerly latitudes had been well known to Norse mariners, who had settled then-uninhabited Iceland as early as the 800s and in the 900s had reached western Greenland and, at least occasionally, even the North American mainland.

For fourteenth-century Christian Europe, commercial prospects to the east loomed much larger. The sophistication of China became legendary upon Marco Polo's return in 1295 from his venture along Central Asia's Silk Road, under the sponsorship of Kublai Khan (1215–1294). The Christian holy lands in the eastern Mediterranean had even earlier become targets of pious late Middle-Age European chivalry, culminating in the Crusades, a series of intermittent raids and military occupations by European knights between 1096 and 1272. It is no wonder that the ocean initially attracted primarily interests who were relatively marginal within Europe at the time.

The people along the other shores of the Atlantic cared even less about open waters. Western Africans were oriented internally toward interpersonal relationships of obligation and trust and exploited the ocean only in accessible tidal estuaries, shallow bays, and an extensive network of lagoons running east from the mouth of the Volta River (in modern Ghana) through the vast delta of the Niger River and on to modern Cameroon. Their maritime technologies centered on offshore fishing with nets in long canoes, and fishing communities occupied the shores of sheltered inlets and dried their catches to exchange with inland neighbors for grains, tubers, and other products. One shallow bay in Central Africa harbored a distinctive small bivalve with a shell (*nzimbo*) that Kikongo-speaking communities in adjacent inland regions circulated as a kind of regional currency. Beyond the nearby horizons of these shoreline communities, the red-dening sun set over an Atlantic underworld of ancestors, Kalunga in the word of the Kongo. Neither evidence nor apparent historical motivation supports a conjecture, sometimes heard, of ancient African ancestors of the Olmecs in Mesoamerica, and a report of a massive fleet dispatched from Senegambia to the west in the fourteenth century is no less legendary.

Native Americans were similarly landlubbers, although they also harvested the shell-fish and crustaceans of the shorelines and dried the salt from sometimes elaborately constructed tidal pans to trade with inlanders. Also like Africans, they found their ways out to islands accessible with their canoes. The rich marine resources of the shallow Caribbean waters, including manatees, sea turtles, and reef fishes, had long ago attracted settlers from the mainland of Central America, the overspill of populations growing around maize agriculture. They had been followed somewhat later by cassava-cultivating arrivals from northern South America, later called Arawaks from a word for the starchy tuber domesticated in Amazonian forests that they cultivated.

These smaller communities of most of Africa and Native America were efficient, in the sense of sustaining themselves at relatively low cost through the vagaries of varying climates and occasional momentary concentrations of individual authority. The low maintenance required of such small communities, and their consequent durability and ubiquity (not only in the Americas and Africa but also throughout the world, including Europe), derived from the flexible coordination that they achieved without the burdens of the permanent infrastructure of coercion. In contrast, the Eurasian strategies of monu-mental construction and military destruction, although generally understood as "civiliza-tion," came with considerable costs. These very expensive investments are significant historically—that is, in the sense of motivating change—because conquests could be maintained only with often-coerced, and eventually profound, modifications in the lives of the villagers compelled to support the military and ceremonial aristocracies who man-aged them.

The historical perspective of this volume treats change as a challenge. History is about change, of course, but a historicized account of the Atlantic (or any past) starts from the premise that innovation takes creative effort and resources, that novelty presents chal-lenges for humans to seize as opportunity rather than to resist. Arrangements worked out in the past are the only tools that humans have to draw on to compete for success in the emergent circumstances of the present. They create simplified, highly selective, usually self-interested versions of the past as guidelines used in the present to confront the yawn-ing unknown of an incipient future. History, taking full account of the ephemerality and uncertainties of life, is contingent; outcomes are more accidental than intended.

Understanding the historical Atlantic therefore requires a suspension of the comfort-able, optimistic visions that typically construct the European past as progressive. Though civilization in Western societies is based on militarization and material wealth, most Africans and Native Americans lived by less costly standards of achieving and maintain-ing human community; hence, they were less in need of the external resources of the Atlantic to sustain them. An inclusive, balanced consideration of the regions around the Atlantic in the fifteenth century thus understands the great stone structures; the modest-sized urban concentrations of people in Europe, the Americas, and (less commonly in) Africa; and in particular the horse-based extreme militarization unique to the Eurasian background not only as "dynamic" but also as unstable, costly anomalies sustainable only by constant innovation to reach and absorb ever-more-distant resources. For particular parties on four continents the Atlantic became such a resource, in differing ways.

Europe with Its Back to the Water

The dynamics of military consolidation in Eurasia had revolved for 3,000 years around the vast spaces of the continent's temperate latitudes, from the Ukraine to Mongolia, especially the speed and power of the horses bred there. Horse-based raiding from the steppes had long before spilled southward into densely populated agrarian valleys from the Yellow River to Mesopotamia and eventually the lower Nile. In the millennium following Roman domination masses of mounted invaders had repeatedly punctuated the history of western Europe, raising the military costs of defense to the limits supportable within its relatively confined spaces.

Although the military aristocrats of Europe invested heavily in defensive redoubts—the dramatically perched castles and walled villages atop hills that now attract tourists—they survived by contracting in scale, and they multiplied accordingly in numbers. Christian prohibitions on lending money at interest had favored Jewish merchants as the creditors of choice among Europe's military aristocrats, but merchants in Venice, Florence, and Siena, relatively free of landed military competition, used the wealth generated from Mediterranean commerce to take control of these cities as republics. They were distinctive in Europe in the liquidity that they could mobilize for investment in artisan processing—especially glass in Venice and woolen textiles in Florence—and eventually also in banking and credit for the military aristocrats. The major riverine arteries of central Europe—the Rhone, Rhine, and Danube—similarly supported commercial consolidation of liquid wealth in the hands of the great banking families of the Germanic-speaking areas, not least in the low country around the channels where the Rhine emptied into the North Sea.

Merchants represented potential challenges to military power everywhere in Eurasia. Conquest was cheap, but the costs of consolidating military rule tended to escalate beyond the capacities of the local populations called upon to sustain them. Thus the conquerors' dynastic heirs sustained the initial grandeur paid for through plundering by slipping into debt to merchant bankers. Merchants and bankers, unlike military rulers who supported themselves through destruction of opponents and exploitation of the survivors, accumulated wealth in durable, relatively low-maintenance forms—coins, jewels, transport and storage facilities, and inventories. They then, even more profitably, leveraged these relatively fixed assets by lending against their cash values for higher returns in the future. The formal proscriptions against lending money at interest by Christian authorities in Europe at some level reflected awareness of the long-term promise—and power—of investing capital at interest. Literally with their backs up against the Atlantic coastline, they could not afford the geostrategic division characteristic of parts of Asia—that is, between the military aristocracies ruling over populated territories and merchant networks investing their growing commercial assets in traversing desert wastelands and empty seas.

By the fifteenth century, growing commercial sectors of the European economy were straining the available quantities of the specie that underlay their commercialized transactions. This shortage of monetized bullion was intensified by a persistent drain of silver into the giant Asian world economy, integrated under Islamic law and stretching from Senegal, Andalusia, and eastern Africa's Swahili Coast to Central Asia and the Philippines. European aristocrats competed to acquire and display the spices, silks, and fine porcelains of the East, but they had little of comparable quality to offer in return.

In a pattern to be duplicated later in the Atlantic, Italian merchants found markets for their modest products among the Slavic-speaking agricultural populations along the Adriatic and around the Black Sea, selling their goods to them on credit. Indebted Slav buyers ended up repaying their Venetian creditors in captives and dependents, mostly girls and women, whom the Italians sold as slaves to service the wealthy merchant households of port cities around the Mediterranean, from Venice to Barcelona. These Slavic-speaking females were gathered in numbers sufficient to provoke public notice. The ethnonym "Slavs" denigrating them, and eventually also males, as outsiders eventually came to refer also to their status as captives, that is, as "slaves" in English and cognate terms in most European languages. Thus captive Slavs, and a few Africans, became visible in the Christian Mediterranean as ethnicized outsiders, not as the legal category of *servus* (for slave) inherited from Roman law.

The legal standing of the enslaved on both Mediterranean shores, Muslim and Christian, was instead largely urban and domestic, in contrast with the later public standing of commercialized slaves as productive assets in the Atlantic. That is, though some captives transited public spaces, the ports and marketplaces, they did so only incidentally as they moved into the private households of the urban families wealthy enough to buy them. Households often acquired them or disposed of them through personal relationships of inheritance or marriage or as donations among friends that did not involve currencies or public markets. Within households they were secluded from monarchical law or the public regulations of other recognized corporate bodies—or "orders" or estates. Under the law of the Catholic Church their masters and mistresses were responsible for their spiritual welfare. Under similar Muslim domestic laws of familial responsibility for persons, slaves were *'abd*, or similarly beholden to the heads of the households within which they lived. Outside households, governments—primarily the seaport municipalities around the Mediterranean through which captives passed—were involved primarily as buyers and not as regulators. Christian and Muslim authorities alike raided their confessional rivals on the opposing shores of the inland sea for captives and held them for ransoms in cash or employed them for urban services or as galley slaves to move goods through their harbors.

Rural estates could not compete with the prices that prospering households of Mediterranean cities paid for captives. The Christian manors of the medieval Mediterranean, generally too poor to buy enslaveable outsiders or to generate demand for labor in excess of what local populations could offer, therefore made do with the resident peasant labor generally characteristic of Europe. European military aristocrats' confinement in Eurasia's western extremity also denied them the access to remote and alien populations that had brought reliable numbers of captives into Muslim domains, from sub-Saharan Africans and Circassians to non-Muslim populations of South Asia and the outlying islands of the Indonesian archipelago. And just as Muslims' monotheistic community of faith forbade enslaving other believers, so were Christians in western Europe prohibited from enslaving fellow communicants.

The personal politics of monarchical sovereignty in Europe further inhibited slaving. The aspiring Christian monarchs of Europe were seen as benevolent patrons enmeshed in intricate personal relationships of loyalty—lord to liege and on out to villagers living on the estates of the aristocracy—and patronage and protection in return. These mutual responsibilities contrasted with the entirely one-sided power gained in Asia by military conquests. The sovereign authority of monarchy in Europe was thus comprehensive and exclusive within territorially defined domains, and increasingly direct. As fifteenth-century military aristocrats managed slowly to define and implement claims to the singular sovereignty of monarchy, to the exclusion of all competitors for claims on their local populations, they had little room to tolerate the exclusive loyalty to masters that enslavement entailed. Significant retinues of slaves, beyond the reach of monarchical authority, posed potential threats to supreme royal power.

The royal legal codes in thirteenth-century Europe, from Scandinavia to Iberia, promoted significant assertions of dynastic sovereignty beyond the persons of the kings proclaiming them. These codes only exceptionally recognized competing private rights of individuals over captives. Recruitment of personnel by slaving thus withered away in most of Christian Europe. This was not the case, however, in "Reconquista" Iberia or the independent cities of the Mediterranean. In this context, the increasing commercial, and thus publicly visible, transactions in Slavic-speakers in the fifteenth century prompted creation of the ethnic label that the subsequent distinctively commercialized context of the Atlantic turned into a designation of personal property, and thus a financial asset, with profound consequences for the non-Christians whom Europeans acquired there.

Commerce and Militarization in Africa

The small, flexible communities along the coasts of Africa were relatively self-sufficient. In the interior, communities of traders—pivot points in the extensive regional economies in the northwestern bulge of the continent—had dispersed in diasporas of small settlements linked by their shared Islamic monotheism, literacy employed in contracts and communication over distances, and accompanying Muslim commercial law. With these unifying strategies they moved Saharan salts and other minerals in significant quantities over considerable distances between the desert and the processing and artisan industries of the more populous savanna lands to the south. On their return to the north, the diasporic traders carried grain and other products of the agricultural latitudes, as well as commodities extracted from the margins of the forests beyond, notably oils from palms and nuts from the kola trees found there.

The dramatically contrasting wet and dry seasons of western Africa shifted in latitudes through century-long (or longer) cycles of droughts, which were transformative in intensity and duration. Cultivators favored mobile, flexible strategies of production. They abandoned plots exhausted through cultivation within a generation or so and opened new ones. In these circumstances, it made no sense to invest in permanent, improved fields. Cultivators also favored similarly adaptable methods of political integration. People lived in small communities, where personal familiarity and multiple ongoing relationships defined by mutual commitments lasted through generations. Local village-centered communities understood themselves in terms of reproduction, using the relevant concepts of kinship—genealogies, generations, and marriage alliances—to exchange fertile women among communities defined by descent.

Significant urban concentrations of artisans, merchants, and groups servicing the traders, some of them stable over centuries, marked the latitude at which the desert traders offloaded their camels and donkeys. The trading diasporas carried on to the south with caravans of men bearing packets of salt and other desert commodities on their heads. The fertile alluvial floodplains of the rivers, which rose and fell annually with the strong concentration of rains in the few months of the summer, supported the larger and more enduring of these cities from the valley of the lower Senegal River in the west, east to Lake Chad (and further east to the Upper Nile). The most enduring were Jenne-Jeno in the vast inland delta, or floodplain, of the northeastward-flowing upper course of the Niger River and Gao on the river's southeasterly middle course.

The best known of these towns, at least in Europe, were the most northerly outposts, the jumping-off points for the long trek across the desert to Mediterranean markets. An early one, an outpost on the very edge of the Sahara since the tenth century or so, had intercepted Muslim traders arriving from Mediterranean North Africa in search of gold from the headwaters of the Niger and Senegal rivers to the south. The market authority in charge of monitoring (and taxing) these exchanges loomed as a mighty "king" in the militarized style of Asia and Europe for Muslim traders arriving there, at the limit of their resources in this remote and strange "land of the blacks" (*sudan*, in Arabic). However, in Africans' terms—to the network of communities harvesting the gold for trade northward in exchange for imported goods, which they distributed through their own local alliances—he was not. This figure, known as the *ghana*, exercised personal authority primarily over the vulnerable visitors from the north. The *ghana*, in effect, quarantined the Muslim outsiders to insulate the southern communities, integrated around distribution and sharing of material wealth, from the greedy material accumulation of the commercial world of the Mediterranean.

The regional trading diasporas, as well as artisan guilds in the towns, extended the intimate language of kinship and descent to keep their distinctive, and thus valuable, specialized knowledge, skills, and contacts to themselves. They dressed, behaved, and spoke in distinguishing ways that highlighted themselves and thus what they had to offer to neighbors who lacked their unique and stylized products and services. They acknowledged the diverse "others" around them with collective ethnonyms, which Europeans learned as they sought partners suitable for doing business. Though Europeans exoticized these characteristics for Africans as "tribal," these names for the occupational groups in African towns differed little from the similarly ethnicized foreign trading "nations" of towns in Europe.

Distributed and differentiated complementing powers, like the differentiated communities, were characteristic of the political systems of Africa. They were composites, or networks, of the local reproducing communities of kin. However, a centuries-long dry phase in western Africa after about 1100 had dramatically corroded this balance. The desiccation severely distressed the so-called Berbers living in the desert, herders of livestock—donkeys, horses, camels—and masters of the oases. They rallied around an intense reformist vision of Islam, identifying themselves as *al-murabitun*, or Almoravids, and survived by deploying their horses in a wave of militarization and plundering toward the north, through Morocco, to overrun the southern Iberian peninsula, where they became known as "Moors" (in English, *Moros* in Spanish). In the background of the Christian "Reconquista," the far-western Mediterranean was a part of the historical dynamics of Africa.

At the same time, south of the desert the militarization brought Sudanic Africa into the Greater Mediterranean sphere of large-scale and continuing warfare. Conflicts in tropical Africa, previously lacking horses, had been fought primarily on a flexible, ad hoc, relatively low-cost, militia-like basis consistent with the dispersed composition of the region's political systems. But as drought spread in the twelfth century, some of the agricultural communities south of the desert imported horses to save themselves by mobilizing militarily for plunder. In the thirteenth century they extended the range of costly Mediterranean-style cavalry raiding to the populous valley of the upper Niger. The victims of their raiding there defended themselves by rallying behind the banners of mounted warriors of their own, who had adopted Islam to consolidate their connections with the commercial sources of their overwhelming cavalry power in the Islamic north. These warriors of the resulting so-called "Mali empire"—more likely a highly contested military composite—paid for their mounts with the gold that, by the fourteenth century, made the region truly legendary, even among Christians, and in the following century drew the Portuguese south along Africa's Atlantic coastline.

But the costs of the escalating militarization eventually exceeded the gold available to pay for the imports, and the horsemen of the western Sudan covered the deficits in their balance of trade with the Mediterranean by deploying the speed, range, and force of their

mounts to raid for captives, whom they sold to their North African creditors. They justified this slaving as pious Muslims defending their faith against infidels, thus confirming
under Islamic law their possession of the captives they seized and sold. Traders, also
cultivating their Muslim commercial contacts, followed in their wake, moving south into
the forests beyond the savanna-bound range of the horses. There they worked with Akan-
speaking populations to exploit gold-bearing strata exposed along river banks. These
Akan mining communities became the sources for the Portuguese of the precious metal
toward the later fifteenth century, fortifying a promontory west of the Volta River's
mouth as a trading castle called São Jorge da Mina ("the mine"), or Elmina.

To the east and south of the Volta ran a series of lagoons and the intricate deltaic
channels through which the Niger River seeped into the Gulf of Guinea. One defensive
reaction in this area to the militarization of the savanna was a more permanently structured military regime there known as Benin. Benin was a populous forested area filled
with refugees from the cavalry assaults of the savannas, as well as a center of textile weaving. Beyond the Niger Delta a thousand miles of densely forested and lightly populated
coast eventually gave way to more open terrain near the estuary of the Zaire (later Congo)
River, beyond the equator. In the highlands south of the river a network of regional chiefs
connected the coast to the vast forested basin of the river in the interior. The Portuguese
later recognized this network, a political composite of the sort characteristic of most of
Africa, by the title of the official charged with representing it to outsiders, and thus to
them: the *mani* (master) Kongo.

This Kongo network distributed copper (the prestige metal of Africa) from local
sources, the *nzimbo* shells from Luanda Bay and salt from adjacent coastal pans, and
elaborate textiles woven from dyed fibers of the raffia palm growing on the fringes of the
equatorial forest in the interior. The local communities composing the network competed among themselves—probably not always peacefully—for the lucrative right to
represent the network to external contacts. Unlike Benin, the regime was not militarized,
though it could mobilize local militia if challenged by outsiders or to contest the succession to the position of the *mani* Kongo. African composite polities like the Kongo network were not dissimilar to the early monarchies of Europe in their moderate degrees of
effective political centralization.

Militarization by Terror in Mesoamerica

The Native peoples of the Atlantic seaboard of both North and South America resembled Africans in their separation and dispersal of specific responsibilities for the welfare
of their communities. Neither recognized power as singular, or inhering in individuals,
and thus inherently competitive. To the extent that individuals held sway, they acted as
custodians of specified kinds of expertise, imbued with powers attributed to distinct,
abstract, "spiritualized" forms: ancestors, spirits of localized resources, the rains, techniques of healing and hunting, valor in conflict, and other differentiated powers. Authority in each sphere, rather than dominating, contributed to the whole and in turn
depended on the complementing specialized powers of others.

Also like Africans, they devoted themselves primarily to reproduction, managing marriages among neighboring groups and raiding more remote communities for women and
children when reproduction failed. In times of widespread crisis, great warriors or healers
seemingly successful in overcoming the tensions arising from hard times might achieve
personal recognition among large numbers of grateful local groups. These prophet-like
leaders—really, healers of community discord—might also leave enduring legacies that,
in localities favored by rich resources and riverine transport, the survivors honored and

sustained with tombs of sizes impressive even by European standards. In temperate woodlands these monuments appeared as earthen mounds; in rocky deserts and mountains, appreciative heirs assembled stones in layers built on the rubble of earlier monuments honoring previous leaders. The resulting pyramidal forms sometimes grew to truly imposing proportions, even though they were atypical and undoubtedly costly to sustain. The Maya of the many regimes in the Yucatán, for instance, elevated fierce dedication to military valor and manipulation of mighty cosmic forces to noted extremes of monumental expression in the soft limestone of the peninsula.

In Mesoamerica in about the thirteenth century, warriors from the northern deserts had entered the fertile and populous valley of what is now central Mexico, by then heir to a tradition of grandiose stone monumentality. These Mexica warriors gradually made places for themselves as mercenaries in continuing struggles among the valley's paramount chieftaincies—networks of communities recognizing a single chief for such collective interests as war—and militarized the area. After a century or so, their heirs emerged as more or less equal partners, charged with the military aspects of the partnership, in a composite polity formed with the two surviving regional regimes. During a period of severe drought and starvation after 1446, a Mexica chief claimed power independent of, and superior to, the representatives of the two local regimes. A return of the rains in 1455 seemed to confirm his powers after a frenzy of human sacrifices to beseech the war gods of the Mexica.

The resulting Aztec military regime aimed to maintain the power of the moment despite the fact that the crisis it had seemed to divert had faded. The inhabitants of the valley, without a life-threatening predicament to motivate them, had no immediate reason to meet the enormous demands for human lives, wealth, and labor to support the Aztec authorities' grandiose displays of superiority. The Aztecs, like the military regimes of Eurasia, faced the dilemmas of consolidating the gains of conquest, or maintaining loyalties conceded in moments of acute distress, by erecting imposing edifices, ideological indoctrination through continued brutality (including human sacrifices), and intensified demands for tribute and labor. The costs of maintaining permanently armed polities were high, in the long run unsustainably so.

These strategies of political consolidation by violence differed principally in their cultural idioms from the no less demanding military regimes of contemporaneous Asia and Sudanic western Africa. Though the mounted warlords in Afro-Eurasia could assert their power with the speed and force deliverable astride a horse, in the Americas the absence of horses placed the burden of dominating on daunting—indeed terrifying—displays of wanton cruelty. The subsequently legendary Spanish stories of beating hearts plucked from sacrificial victims placed atop pyramids testify not only to the enormous political power of terrorism but also to the extremes required to transcend the limits of the loyalty that local populations were willing to cede to warrior outsiders. The brittleness of Aztec power among the populations of the central valley seems evident also in the massive effort demanded of them to build a relatively siege-proof citadel, Tenochtitlán, on an island in the large lake in the valley floor. This complex of temples was accessible only by a single, defensible causeway, and the population clustered there could be fed only with hyper-intensive cultivation of artificial ("floating") gardens. The sort of grandeur usually acclaimed as "imperial" had its price.

Like their Afro-Eurasian counterparts, the Aztec chief-priests—in effect warlords—also undertook expansive military campaigns to obtain the plunder, and population, needed to sustain so costly a form of forceful overrule. They reduced local communities, otherwise integrated around reproduction and descent, to regimented tribute-paying wards, and they stationed warriors to occupy and intimidate the more remote territories

UNIVERSITY OF WINCHESTER
LIBRARY

conquered. By the late sixteenth century, they had reached both the Pacific and Gulf coasts, where the Spaniards just then exploring the area learned of them. Although a failed military campaign had revealed the probable overextension of this systematic violence as early as 1481, Montezuma, the able warleader who eventually met Hernán Cortés, had regained the military momentum. However, the tenuousness of the regime remained apparent in its inability to subdue large valley populations, even ones near the central valley, such as Tlaxcala, who joined Cortés to assault their overlords at Tenochtitlán.

* * *

The Atlantic thus appeared as an opportunity to actors pressured by the growing costs of militarization on all continents—Africa, the Americas, and not least in Europe, where competing warlords were converting the explosive force of the Chinese mixture of charcoal, sulfur, and potassium nitrate from spectacle to munitions. Although the long history of uneasy partnerships between military rulers and merchant venturers in Eurasia had settled into an array of shifting balances in their competing claims to local populations, merchants as a group there had gained on the military regimes. Militarism was expensive and destructive. Victorious conquerors paid for their conquests with the booty they seized but left their successors with the considerable costs of occupation. In contrast, merchants accumulated assets in enduring forms—inventories, transport equipment, specie, and debt—and leveraged them by providing goods or services on credit to support or obligate suppliers, including outlying communities. Merchants in Europe needed only specie to join in financing the military costs of the monarchies on its maritime fringe, in varying opportunistic partnerships with interests in Africa and the Americas who had their own local reasons for seeing them as opportunities. The Atlantic, as it turned out in the following four centuries, provided the precious metals needed, in quantities that proved catalytic in the changes they financed all around the Atlantic.

The Sixteenth Century
Specie, Sugar, and Slaves

Joseph C. Miller

Europeans entered the Atlantic systematically in the later part of the fifteenth century. Those who put out to sea were relatively marginal competitors within the confined, fragmented politics of their region, reacting to the shortages of specie as the costs of intensifying militarization escalated. The Ottoman Turkish capture in 1453 of Byzantium, the gateway to the Black Sea and keystone of Venetian commercial prosperity in the eastern Mediterranean, amplified these costs.

Bankers and investors in central Europe and in Genoa, until then only marginally competitive in Mediterranean commerce, looked west, toward the Atlantic. So did the monarchs of the kingdoms on the Iberian Peninsula, still consolidating domains reconquered from Muslim rulers there. The military aristocracies of Castile and Portugal extended their campaigns south along the Atlantic shores of Morocco. Castile consigned the Canary Islands, and their Guanche residents, to the mercies of conquistadors, and the Portuguese House of Avis awarded other uninhabited islands in the eastern Atlantic, first Madeira and then the Cape Verde islands, to their military captains.

Implementing formal claims to sovereignty overseas, however, would prove demanding throughout Atlantic history. Shortages of capital relative to the costs of trying to operate on transoceanic scales remained significant challenges of implementing initial legal claims. Transatlantic territories, like all military conquests, were cheap to declare and costly to develop and defend. Effective occupation, even of small uninhabited islands in the eastern Atlantic, therefore proceeded through a series of incremental, affordable steps, each building on prior efforts as modest initial successes attracted further capital.

The typical sequence began with minimal investment—ships leaving livestock to breed for hunting by the crews of later vessels. This passing presence would then intensify to extraction of natural resources—timber from Madeira or Brazil, salt from the Cape Verdes—and then to settling families who would support themselves by clearing, cutting, and farming. When the more successful of these settlers moved on to smallholder agriculture—tobacco, cotton, and indigo, as later in Barbados—commodities then attracted outside investors to consolidate land ownership, which they leveraged for capital to invest in larger-scale improvements, such as irrigation channels on drier islands. The principal commercial agricultural opportunity of the time was sugar cane, and estates producing raw sugar emerged on the islands early in the century as the commodity gained a seemingly limitless market in Europe and attracted significant investment.

Some accounts have attempted to trace the complex of large slave-worked sugar plantations of the Americas, which in the second half of the seventeenth century became the economic center of the Atlantic, back to the Renaissance Mediterranean. However, the same scarcity of commercial capital that drove the Portuguese quests for African gold meant that generations of Europeans assembled the elements of this classic Atlantic system through an extended series of incremental steps. Christian Crusaders in Palestine had learned about saccharine crystals, dried from the concentrated juices of a southeast Asian reedy grass. Medieval Italian manors on Crete, Cyprus, and Sicily had added small-scale plantings of the cane to their grain agriculture, employing resident peasant labor to plant and harvest and using heavy stone milling wheels to crush the sweet juice from the freshly cut cane. They then boiled down the juices to a dark brown syrupy mush. Once they drained its liquid content off as molasses, the remaining moist crystalline *mascavado* was chemically stable enough to pack in kegs for shipment to refineries in the European cities that were the principal markets for the dry white sugar finally produced. Refining and distribution, just as in modern commodity supply chains, were the profitable nodes in the extended sequence from manor to market.

The final sales of refined sugar thus produced the currency returns that attracted merchants and bankers to invest in the earlier links in the chain, so that relatively marginal players, even merchants excluded from owning lands in Europe, could borrow to invest in production of sugar on the empty islands of the eastern Atlantic. Commercial credit and sugar became the driving engines of the Atlantic economy, and in turn of Atlantic history. But in the sixteenth century sugar was Plan B. The lure of gold from beyond the Sahara had first drawn Iberian interests to Africa in the fifteenth century, and until 1700 gold remained Europeans' primary acquisition in Africa. In the sixteenth century, Ferdinand and Isabella, rulers of landlocked Castile and Mediterranean-dependent Aragon, speculating on a seemingly fanciful western shortcut to Asia by sea, found sources of specie in the Americas even greater than the riches of India they had sought.

The risks of lending capital to minor military aristocrats from Portugal, who were growing cane on Madeira, and ambitious Spanish conquistadors of similarly limited creditworthiness in the Canaries made it prudent for investors to demand collateral. As viable collateral must be reasonably liquid, land and heavy processing equipment on the islands, bound up by medieval laws entailing real property, disqualified the major assets of sugar's production system.

The small islands that had become the initial locations of cane cultivation were uninhabited, or—in the case of the Canaries—systematically depopulated, with the survivors enslaved. To cultivate cane there it was necessary to populate them with people to do the work. The enslaved status of Africans brought there for that purpose was the financial key, as the commercial laws of personal—that is, fungible, moveable—property already gave secure title to human beings acquirable through purchase. As it happened, first the Guanche of the Canaries and then people from the adjacent African mainland were available through capture and purchase at little additional cost of investing in market organization. Portuguese ventures searching for gold in the vicinity of Cape Verde simply diverted captive Africans already being taken to the cities of Muslim North Africa from the agricultural regions south of the Sahara.

Enslaved personnel were thereby suitable as the collateral that would-be planters on the islands needed to secure loans to build new cane estates. A commercialized extension of Mediterranean methods of recruiting personnel for urban households, without having to wrest labor away from local landed competitors, became the primary strategy of populating the transatlantic domains that Europeans claimed to produce commodity exports to pay for them.

Luso-Africans in Upper Guinea

On the African mainland, ethnicized groups formed around the warriors (Mande), the traders (Juula), the miners (Akan), and various refugees fleeing the escalating militarization of the time. There was no shortage of captives to retain as personnel at the large warrior courts, or to deploy in cultivation and other services of these regimes, or—for that matter—to bear the salt and other commodities moving through the region's thriving commercial networks.

With militarization and commercial integration in western Africa accelerating around slaving, the Portuguese ventures along the coast had little difficulty in finding captives to fill space available on ships returning otherwise lightly laden with gold. They would be able to sell captives in Madeira for liens on the sugar they would produce, which when sold in Lisbon would bring the cash to cover the funds loaned. On both sides slaving was a backup strategy. On the part of the Europeans, it was ancillary to the king's search for gold. For the Africans, sales into the Atlantic were an extension of warriors' quests for retainers to support escalating militarization, and, with gold sufficient to cover their modest purchases from the Europeans, the Africans succeeded in their primary purpose—retaining the people whom they captured. The initial steps toward momentous changes were small.

Off western Africa's shores, New Christians—Jews forcibly converted in Spain and Portugal and then expelled at the end of the fifteenth century—and other marginalized Portuguese developed local trades from bases on the Cape Verde Islands. They worked through a string of trading factories scattered along the bays and river mouths of the mainland from the Senegal to Elmina (in today's Ghana). These individuals arbitraged the European currency values of the goods they sold against the quite different African systems of converting values among commodities, artisan wares, and people. Goods cheap in Europe became valuable in Africa, and Africans could acquire them without significant investment in productive infrastructure by extracting the natural resources—ivory, gold, wild beeswax, tree resins, and melegueta pepper (known in Europe as *grains of paradise*)—that Europeans bought as valuable commodities.

Although the modest scale of the commercial resources introduced by the European traders on the African coast added only a minor Atlantic component to the much vaster resources that the trading diaspora of the mainland had built up over generations, some African suppliers gained from, and became correspondingly dependent on, collecting and selling them. They engaged the Jews and Christians living on the coast through marriage alliances, the same strategy they had long used to consolidate relationships of trust with the Muslim trading diasporas in the interior. The generations to be born of these marriages constituted the human collateral that enabled the traders to secure returns on goods they advanced from their inventories to prospective suppliers on credit. European credit was vital in efforts to integrate African-European exchanges along the coast.

The representatives of the Portuguese crown and ships' officers passing through these trading settlements condemned the Portuguese and their Luso-African descendants as renegades gone native. However, these initial engagements on Africans' terms succeeded so well that, by the middle of the sixteenth century, communities had grown up around the trading sites. The settlements were African in their ability to speak local languages and their integration into local trading circuits but flexibly also Portuguese in their family connections to the Cape Verde islands and their nominal inclusion of Catholicism in their uses of the spirit-based powers of their African kin. The creolized language that they created to facilitate these contacts—African in grammar, with many Portuguese words—became the language of trade all along the western African coast.

To the south, the first Portuguese to reach the mouth of the Zaire River in 1483 were directed, according to the conventions of the Kongo network there, to the *mani* Kongo of the time. Without a standing army of his own, this representative of the collective welfare welcomed them and in 1491 accepted the blandishments of the clergy, who accompanied every Portuguese venture, to accept Catholicism. The *mani* Kongo would have understood Christian rituals in the additive manner of African political ideologies, situational in scope, supplementing but not replacing, for instance, their relations with spiritized ancestors. The priests, on the other hand, saw only conflict between the exclusive truth of Catholicism and ignorant superstition.

The emissaries of the Portuguese king treated the *mani* in similarly European terms, as sovereign of a rank equal to, and thus capable of negotiating legally with, their own. Aside from their inability to comprehend the multiplicity of power in Africa, the Portuguese tended to recognize authorities they encountered there as "rulers" capable of entering into binding agreements that secured Portuguese interests in their domains to the exclusion of rival Europeans. The "kingdoms" they thus attributed to Africans denoted standing in European law more than they described the political composites they encountered. The documentation created from these arrangements has left a limiting legacy among historians today, who often misunderstand African compound polities in European terms as centralized "kingdoms."

Treasure and Tributaries in the Indies

The exclusionary legal strategies of the Portuguese in Africa became more sensitive in 1492, owing to Spanish discoveries on what proved to be the opposite shores of the Atlantic. In the meanwhile, in 1488, another Portuguese captain, Bartolomeu Dias, had reached the southern tip of the continent in search of a sea route to the spices, silks, and other luxuries of the East. With news of Dias's opening to the Indian Ocean, Ferdinand of Castile and Isabella of Aragon underwrote a risky, though not entirely unprecedented, scheme to sail west in hopes of reaching India. Christopher Columbus, a Genoese navigator and entrepreneur who had gained his open-ocean sailing experience with the Portuguese in the waters off western Africa, rode the westward swing of the Canary Current to end up at an archipelago of low islands, now the Bahamas. His small flotilla of three vessels, wondering where they might have landed, reconnoitered on what is now Cuba and also on a second large island to the east that Columbus named Española (the "Spanish Island," anglicized as Hispaniola) in honor of his sponsors in Madrid.

Ferdinand and Isabella, like the Portuguese in Africa, then moved to exclude European competitors from access to the western region that Columbus insisted must be the Indies that he had sought. Since the pope in Rome held legal authority over Latin Christians' relationships with others, he could grant earthly dominion over, and impose corresponding religious responsibilities for, previously unknown peoples on other shores of the ocean. By the terms of a treaty confirmed at Tordesillas in Spain in 1494, the Portuguese retained their contacts in Africa, and its gold, as well as the recent promise of maritime access to the Indies, east of a longitude line declared to exist 370 dubiously measurable leagues (or 1,110 miles, 46° 37' W) beyond the Azores archipelago, roughly halfway to Bermuda in the mid-Atlantic.

No one then suspected a continent to the west so massive that, at equatorial latitudes far to the south of Colombus's initial probings, it might extend well east (35° W) of the declared meridian. But in 1500 a Portuguese voyage, led by Pedro Álvares Cabral, followed up on Dias's discovery of the Cape of Torments, renamed the Cape of Good Hope, and sought to avoid the strong north-flowing currents along Africa's southwestern coast by sailing well out to the west. The expedition made unexpected landfall, east of the agreed longitude, on what proved to be the northern coast of Brazil. The European political geography of the Americas was thus divided between the two Iberian monarchies. Since conquest as a legal concept conveyed sovereignty over the conquered, Portuguese authorities extended their military mode to the other shore of the Atlantic by awarding the lands to minor aristocrats as military captains.

These extensions of royal sovereignty were free of the complications of multiple jurisdictions in Europe. Agents authorized to act in the monarch's stead could offer Christian salvation and military protection to peoples found in new lands claimed. Any who resisted forfeited their right to life itself or, if captured in wars fought to defend the Catholic faith, deemed "just" by canon law, became subject to enslavement. Other beings regarded as savage, or lacking human souls salvageable for Jesus, could be enslaved legally by default. And so piously ambitious warriors for Christ repeatedly condemned as cannibals the (reported) enemies of the people with whom they allied, thus justifying—and establishing legal title to the spoils of—the opportunistic raiding that they pursued.

In Spain's Indies across the Atlantic, at first constituting only the Caribbean islands and adjacent shores of the Gulf of Mexico, conquistadors sought glory and quick riches in precious metals. Columbus, experienced with the Portuguese off the Gold Coast, had been obsessed with finding gold. He was able to buy just enough gold from the inhabitants of the islands of the Caribbean, whom he designated "Indios," to confirm his own illusions of the wealth attributed to Asia. The agents of the Spanish crown who followed Columbus set out in earnest to strip the islands' inhabitants of treasures they had accumulated and then forced the Indios themselves to pan the streams for more of the precious metal. The small communities of Arawaks in the main islands quickly succumbed to these pressures and to the contagious diseases of the invaders—measles, chicken pox—to which they had no immunities. This same fate befell the Arawaks' enemies in the mostly southeasterly islands: they had been castigated as "cannibals," or "Caribs" in Taino, which also qualified them for capture and enslavement. The massive mortality depopulated the Caribbean islands within a generation, forcing the growing numbers of single-minded military aristocrats from Castile who flocked to the reported gold rush to look toward the coasts of what was taking shape as a mainland of significant proportions. One of these, Juan Ponce de León, unexpectedly found Florida lying west of the Bahamas in 1511 and claimed it for the king of Spain as a conquest.

As the Arawak and Carib populations of the islands succumbed to viruses and violence, slaving became the hallmark of the first cohort of conquistadors, who dispersed along other Caribbean mainland coasts quite beyond the control of their nominal sovereigns in Spain. The small, scattered Native communities along the coasts of both American continents were organized politically in paramount chiefdoms—composite networks not unlike those in Central Africa. These networks were similarly low in costs of maintenance and flexible in time of need, but they therefore also teemed with ambitious component communities who welcomed potential allies from outside the system—gods, ancestors, or, as it turned out, Europeans with muskets and horses—to support their struggles with other groups in expediting successions to chieftaincies. The conquistadors heated the simmering tensions to the boiling point, making away with plunder and captives and leaving their erstwhile patrons and partners exhausted, scattered, and vulnerable. Native politics thus significantly multiplied the effectiveness of the Spaniards' own modest military presence.

Contests for Control on the Mainland

By the 1510s these opportunistic interventions in the politics of the mainland, and outright raiding, constituted a systematic strategy of capturing people to work the declining yields of gold in Hispaniola and Cuba, and also to cultivate sugar cane in vain attempts to extend their successes in the Canaries, and those of the Portuguese in Madeira. Hernán Cortés achieved the definitive, and subsequently paradigmatic, success of this strategy in 1521: a force he led to the mainland fought off a rival conquistador with the assistance of the army of a large paramount chiefdom, Tlaxcala, in one of the valleys leading up to the more populous valley of the Mexica, the Aztec military regime in the center of the mainland.

The Aztec armies at the time of Cortés's arrival, under the leadership of Montezuma, had only just succeeded in cutting off supplies to the area of Tlaxcala in hopes of bringing the resistant regime there to its knees. A renewed sign that the gods were backing Montezuma would have maintained his military momentum. Cortés, even with only 500 men of his own, also brought horses and firearms that might well have inspired godlike shock and awe, superior even to the terrorizing tactics of the Aztecs. Some 150,000 to 200,000 Tlaxcalan warriors, along with Cortés's small force, besieged the island citadel of Tenochtitlán, already weakened by an epidemic in 1511–1512, to exploit its vulnerability. They eventually captured and killed Montezuma and leveled the island's monumental structures as they plundered them for the treasures they contained.

From the rubble Cortés claimed victory for Spain but, recognizing the military efficiency of the Aztec system, restored the underlying composite structure of the regime he had decapitated by awarding Spanish titles of aristocracy to his allies among the regional authorities in the valley. Cortés's Spanish successors, in alliance with their Native partners, then resumed the military campaigns of their Aztec predecessors, although the combined forces required nearly 60 years to disarm the last resisters in the northern deserts. The Maya, meanwhile, had dealt with other Spanish conquistadors rampaging through the forests of Yucatán by retreating from direct confrontations with mounted Spaniards armed with muskets and fighting back with guerrilla tactics. For over a century they did not realize that they had been subjected to the "conquests" that ambitious conquistadors reported to their king to provide legal cover for their monarch's claims to sovereignty in the Americas and to advance their own careers.

By the 1530s Spain was in control of the mainland primarily from the point of view of the Portuguese, less so from the perspectives of many Native Americans, and problematically from the standpoint of a Habsburg dynasty in Madrid, which was still straining to consolidate its primacy in Iberia and distracted by dynastic responsibilities elsewhere in Europe. Carlos V, who had succeeded Ferdinand and Isabella in 1516, found himself relying on freewheeling armed bands of countrymen operating thousands of miles away in the Americas with Native allies and retinues of captives independent of royal resources from Spain. As the limits of the gold to be found there became evident, the wealth of the Indies came to consist primarily of its inhabitants. The Spanish monarchs thus drafted the services of the populations conquered through medieval grants of rights to them, the so-called "allocation" (*repartimiento*) system.

Carlos V soon also confronted the challenge of imposing restraint on feuding warlords on the American mainland by invoking his predecessors' charge from the pope to save the souls of the inhabitants of these lands. He dispatched legions of missionaries to guide his conquered wards to the Catholic salvation that they merited as his direct subjects. The king entrusted native souls to several different orders of regular (monastic) clergy, whose worldly ambitions he could play against each other to royal advantage. He thus sent Franciscans in 1523, Dominicans in 1525, and Augustinians in 1533. He also used his political strength as patron of the ecclesiastical administration of the Church itself: his bishops and parish priests concentrated their efforts on Spaniards and, eventually, the growing mixed (*casta*) populations of the towns.

Other conquistadors raised the stakes of both riches and royal control yet again in the early 1530s by intruding similarly on the contested politics of the Inca military regime in the Andean highlands to the south. In 1535 Carlos V extended his own legal personage across the Atlantic by appointing a viceroy over a vast jurisdiction of New Spain, covering all of the Americas north of Panama. The legal framework for which this viceroy would be responsible followed in 1542 with the issuance of "New Laws" that declared Native inhabitants exempt from the conquistadors' slaving, rampant up to that point, and replaced the *repartimiento* system's allocations of souls with trusteeships (*encomiendas*) over the lands, not people, within the legal authority of the monarch's conquests. This complex, and contested, framework of partial jurisdictions and royally awarded personal privileges extended the compound legal background of Iberia to the New World, with specific privileges awarded to military orders, municipalities, and regional high courts (*audiencias*) exercising independent jurisdiction under royal law. Native communities under local authorities were incorporated in an overarching *república de indios*. This pastiche of overlapping legal constraints handicapped the powerful within any one of them, again using local historical dynamics to multiply the efficacy of remote royal initiatives from Spain. The maze of alternative legal avenues also allowed weaker parties to evade the pressures of the powerful.

Gold from Africa

In the eastern Atlantic, although gold until the eighteenth century remained the principal commodity (as measured by monetary value) that Europeans took from Africa, slaving grew around it in a series of incremental steps. The short-term European financing that the Portuguese invested in their African suppliers in the sixteenth century tended over time to deplete readily accessible supplies of extracted resources. Depletion provoked the suppliers to resort to violence to preserve gains from a trade that they saw eroding. Like the Spanish warriors in the Americas, but more subtly, the Portuguese thus exacerbated the tensions of local politics in Africa. The conflicts they exploited yielded captives who could be sold as slaves, in effect turning extraction of commodities into extractions of people.

This process, critical to slaving, centered on the primary interest of Portuguese royal officials: the gold from the Akan region that they acquired through their fortified post at Elmina. They stimulated further extraction by providing additional labor for the gold fields. At first the Portuguese exploited diplomatic contacts in the Benin polity to acquire captives, but the well-established military regime there needed manpower for its own purposes and moved to suppress the tendencies toward uncontrollable violence that accompanied the Portuguese quest for captives. They therefore expelled Catholic missionaries in 1516 and forbade further sales of slaves.

The Central African Kongo leader Afonso was in a more vulnerable position. He had become a strategic convert to Catholicism, baptized in 1506 by the Portuguese as "king," and had received Portuguese missionaries and military advisers. These moves used the outsiders to assert a personal authority dubious in his domain of networked communities, as it challenged the practice of rotating responsibility for the political collective among its component communities. The Portuguese military officers on the scene, not unlike Spanish conquistadors in the composite polities of the Americas, enlisted with

Afonso as mercenaries and roamed the area in search of precious metals. The region turned out to offer no gold. The disappointed Portuguese military men then turned to the factional politics of the Kongo network, which Afonso was attempting to defy, and the politically threatened local communities welcomed other Portuguese for their own purposes, assaulting rivals and paying off the Portuguese in shares of the captives they seized. Composite African polities were as vulnerable to outsiders as were their counterparts in the Americas.

By 1516 the resulting flows of prisoners, destined to be sold at Elmina for Akan gold, had strained the modest maritime capacities of the Portuguese in the Gulf of Guinea. Overcrowding aboard the craft that carried them from the mouth of the Zaire (Congo) River to the Gold Coast provoked Lisbon to attempt to regulate food, water, and other shipboard conditions. The Portuguese in the Gulf of Guinea thus took the first step in learning to carry large numbers of people over long distances on the open ocean.

Among the ad hoc measures that these slavers introduced to reduce mortality among the captives on board was to call en route at the small equatorial, originally uninhabited island of São Tomé. Since discovering the volcanic peak in the 1470s, Lisbon authorities had struggled to maintain a tiny population of cast-offs from Portugal. As it lay on the direct course from Kongo to Elmina, by the 1520s residents were building a business out of provisioning the passing vessels, taking captives in payment and presumably using them as labor to produce the provisions they were selling. But the volcanic soils of the island and its ample equatorial rains also made it competitive with Madeira or the Canaries as a producer of cane for the growing sugar markets in Europe. Captive Africans destined for Elmina and held on the island to recuperate could be used initially at little additional cost as field labor to cultivate cane. São Tomé prospered so sufficiently that by the 1550s the island had become the largest supplier of Europe's sugars. They also built up the largest force of enslaved field workers yet employed in producing sugar, numbering in the tens of thousands.

The planters found additional captives to sustain this booming growth by developing a slaving network of their own on the mainland south of Kongo, intruding on the sources of the shells, the key Kongo-area currency, at Luanda Bay, and using the Kwanza River to contact the relatively populous Kimbundu-speaking communities of the inland plateaus that it drained. The lower Kwanza watershed was passing through a phase of militarization, as a conquering warleader, known by his title as the *ngola*, integrated the area militarily. Captives from these wars, or raids, were readily available. Also in the 1560s, the Christian dynasty of successors to Afonso in Kongo was driven out, evidently by local opponents, possibly instigated by the planting interests on São Tomé in need of captives. Word of these obscure events surfaced only two decades later, depicting them as an invasion by mysterious "cannibal Jaga." This characterization condemned the opponents of the Christian dynasty as enslaveable savages, which would have justified whatever captives an expedition sent in 1569 to restore the Christian dynasty might have taken. The Portuguese intensification of the dynamics of Africa's composite politics was bearing bitter fruit to nourish São Tomé's satisfaction of Europeans' sweet tooth.

Silver and Sovereignty

The Spaniards found a "mountain of silver" at Potosí in upper Peru, at more than 13,000 feet in altitude, and mining began officially in 1545. The cornucopia of gleaming metal, though oriented geographically toward South America's Pacific coast, added a much more direct Spanish royal presence in the Atlantic, to channel the long-sought treasure from the Americas back to Spain. The value of this wealth, minted in coins valued at eight Spanish *reales* (crowns) or *pesos de ocho* ("weights of eight," or "pieces of eight"), overwhelmed gold from Africa as the financial core of the Atlantic.

This wave of precious metal swept the history of the second half of the sixteenth century in the Atlantic along in its wake. In Spain the silver financed Habsburg dynastic ambitions as rulers of the central European Holy Roman Empire, which was severely challenged since 1453 by Ottoman advances. Forces under Sultan Mehmed II subsequently drove up the Danube River toward the heartland of Western Christianity, culminating in 1529 in a failed siege of Vienna. At the same time, the robes of the Catholic Church enveloping England were fraying, as King Henry VIII (r. 1509–1547) attempted to destroy the institution in the 1530s in the course of disposing of a succession of wives by whom he had hoped (in vain) to bear a legitimate male heir. Dutch revolt against Habsburg rule followed in the 1550s and 1560s. The opening of other mines in northern New Spain after 1548 augmented the swelling tide of silver from Potosí, and this increasing wealth enabled the Habsburg ruler, Philip II (r. 1556–1598), to invest in the military forces needed to renew the historic defense of the Church against all opponents, their numbers growing fast to include, beyond "Turks" and "savage" tribes in the Indies, also Anglicans, Calvinists, and Lutherans.

Elizabeth, daughter of Henry VIII and Queen of England (r. 1558–1603), mounted the principal challenge in the Atlantic. She sent the legendary privateers John Hawkins (1532–1595) and Francis Drake (1540–1596) to raid Spain's Indies and steal the silver en route to Spain. Using the private resources of the ambitious lords of Elizabeth's realm, as well as the prospect of plunder, they elevated piracy, which had plagued the (literally) lawless high seas since the Portuguese first returned from Africa bearing gold, to a state enterprise. Philip II spent his silver on launching a royal armada of warships, which first battled Ottoman fleets in the Mediterranean and then, in 1588, turned against England. This Atlantic expedition ended in the famous defeat by Elizabeth's assemblage of opportunistic privateers, aided by a fortuitous tempest.

By the end of the sixteenth century the Atlantic was becoming a sphere in which European monarchs expanded their legal responsibilities outside the borders of their realms to establish direct monarchical authority, often military, unhindered by the corporate politics of the Church and competing military aristocrats—dukes, counts, and other titled interests—in their home territories. The Habsburgs of Spain, the Tudors and Stuarts (and their successors) in England, and the Bourbons in France used resources from the Atlantic to move toward the formal legal absolutism of Louis XIV (r. 1643–1714) and his counterparts in England and Spain. Spain initially spent the silver on military escalation, but England and the Netherlands countered later by investing in partnerships with commercial interests, while continental France, much larger, was initially involved more marginally.

The merchant networks of the Portuguese and Spanish Atlantic were closely linked combinations of families. Merchants operated in a world of occasional exchanges of material goods with strangers, clearly distinct from the ongoing communities of mutual obligation and trust then prevailing in Africa and the Americas. But the merchant-bankers of Florence, Genoa, and central Europe, as well as the Jewish trading and financial networks, achieved commercial coherence and trust over significant distances by extending family connections. They contracted with monarchs to manage royal revenues overseas, paying into the king's treasury in advance, in return for authority to collect fees and duties from smaller operators, keeping whatever excess they accumulated over the contract price as profit. These contractors functioned less as traders than as investors, leaving the considerable risks of early business in the Atlantic to less well-funded merchants and traders. Africans' and Americans' dynamic responses to the still-slight resources that sixteenth-century investors could bring to bear in the Atlantic further multiplied the effects of these investments. Europeans did not "expand" into the Atlantic so much as they opportunistically skimmed the by-products of the historical dynamics of the regions that they encountered.

Silver and Slaves in the Americas

Merchants in the Atlantic nonetheless, unencumbered by the landed, ecclesiastical, and military interests that confined them in Europe, took the profound and enabling step of moving for the first time beyond their limited economic sector—transportation and market organization—into land ownership and production. The abundant silver from the Indies, which did not all find its way into the hands of the agents of the Spanish monarchy, indirectly financed the extension of commercial sugar enterprises and slaving from the small islands of the eastern Atlantic to the much vaster spaces of the Americas.

The likely significant amount of bullion that remained in the cities of the Spanish Main (the land encompassing the Caribbean and Gulf of Mexico under Spanish control) financed substantial purchasing power there for products of Iberian artistry, for textiles, for comfort foods from home, for the services of craftsmen skilled in producing the prestige goods and architecture of the era, and for the mercury and equipment needed to refine the silver. The significant demand for skilled artisans and domestic servants generated in American cities, though met in part by voluntary emigrants from Iberia, also drew enslaved Africans, whom the Portuguese had been carrying to Seville since the late fifteenth century.

A massive escalation in the supplies of captives brought directly from Africa followed in the 1580s, resulting from the convergence of barely related events on every shore of the Atlantic and beyond. This wave of captives was destined for the cities of the Spanish Indies, and not for the struggling Portuguese military captaincies in Brazil. The Portuguese in Brazil faced a dilemma. The tropical soils, abundant rains, and accessible forests in the northeastern captaincies of Pernambuco and Bahia, which produced the wood needed for fuel to reduce raw cane sap into concentrated molasses, could produce sugar in far greater amounts than the small islands of the eastern Atlantic. However, the financial resources required to take advantage of these natural resources increased correspondingly. Lacking these, struggling cane planters in Brazil, like the early Spanish conquistadors in the Caribbean, turned for affordable labor to the Native Americans in the region, hunting them down like animals. But the Native workers succumbed to European diseases and fled into their familiar forests. Portuguese efforts to use locally enslaved Native Americans to repeat the successes of sugar in Madeira and São Tomé were foundering.

Potosí glittered on the horizons of Europeans everywhere in the Atlantic at the time. Military men in the less accessible inland Brazilian captaincies to the south ranged far into the interior in search of precious minerals, principally from a base at São Paulo. When they failed to find gold or silver they seized people. These Paulistas (or *bandeirantes*, named for the banners flown by the bands of mounted raiders roaming the interior) delivered some of the captives they seized to Bahia and Pernambuco to supplement labor shortages on the struggling sugar plantations there. They kept others in the coastal plains around Guanabara Bay (later Rio de Janeiro) to cultivate manioc (or cassava) to feed the Native workers enslaved in the northeast to cultivate cane.

Parallel dreams of an African Potosí glimmered also on the other side of the Atlantic, just inland from the sandy coastlands of Kongo and the Kwanza River valley. A belated would-be conquistador gained a royal order to occupy and fortify the inviting headland above Luanda Bay, arriving in 1575 with a small contingent of Portuguese army troops. They were nominally sent to conquer the "mountains of silver" reputed to rise inland, in the *conquista* proclaimed "Angola" after the *ngola* title of the Mbundu warlord there, whom they attempted to defeat. As it happened, the contingent arrived at a moment when the region, already distressed by two decades of slaving wars, was entering a period of sustained severe drought. As conflicts intensified among the cultivators of the area, the small force of Portuguese, dwindling in numbers as tropical fevers took their toll, survived by offering their services as mercenaries in the spreading local conflicts. In return they received some of the captives taken.

To the north, Portugal's ambitious and incautious young King Sebastião (1554–1578) embarked on an ill-advised conquest in Morocco in 1578 and died in a climactic defeat at Alcazarquivir (El-Ksar el-Kebir or al-Cácer Quibir). With no heir, the throne in Lisbon fell to Philip II of Spain to claim as yet another component of his scattered Habsburg domains. This dynastic accident turned the Portuguese in Africa into Spanish subjects and thus integrated the two shores of the Atlantic divided by the Treaty of Tordesillas. Under a series of commercial contracts known as *asientos*, he authorized the Portuguese to deliver Africans as slaves to the Indies. These deals gave Portuguese merchants access to Spain's zealously restricted trade in silver by extending the trade in enslaved people moving through the Gulf of Guinea across the ocean to the Americas.

Among the casualties of the drought in Central Africa were bands of young men who had abandoned their homes and kin in higher, drier elevations to survive by pillaging the surviving cultivators in the better-watered river valleys. These bandit gangs multiplied their effectiveness with a campaign of terror, in which they presented themselves as driven by fanatically demanding, bloodthirsty spirits, in effect operating as witches who "consumed," by enlisting, the young men of every community they encountered. They called themselves Imbangala, but the Portuguese incorporated their reputation for ferocity into the image of the alleged cannibalistic invaders of Kongo in the 1560s and labeled them "Jaga."

Communities of cultivators dispersed when crops failed and tried to survive by foraging; the Imbangala rounded up the vulnerable refugees from the drought, in effect extending the economics of extraction to humans adrift in the tide of violence of the time. As these Imbangala bands marauded in the better-watered terrain near the Atlantic coast, they found the struggling Portuguese—themselves, like all Europeans in Africa, reputed also as "cannibals"—eager to collaborate in disposing of the starving captives they seized. Embarkations of these captives at Luanda, as recorded under the *asiento* contracts of the 1590s, rose by a full order of magnitude to more than 10,000 per year.

The history of the Americas would not have become the success story—or certainly not as quickly—of slave-based commodity production that it did in the following century without the sudden rush of starving captives, purchased at derisory cost, and the prospect of selling them in Cartagena (in modern Colombia) for *pesos de ocho*. The initial American markets for captive Africans, though, did not significantly involve sugar. Rather, some of the Africans carried off across the Atlantic remained in Cartagena, the main port city in the Spanish Indies, to serve as municipal and harbor workers and domestics. Others were sent to the nearby Cauca River valley to open gold mines, and some went to Mexico City. Still others were herded across the Isthmus of Panama south to Lima, Peru, the access point for the silver from Potosí. More than a few went to Havana for deployment in government construction and other work throughout the Caribbean, by then all but depopulated of its Amerindian populations. The work of the Africans initially enslaved in the Americas extended the urban-centered employments of their predecessors in the Mediterranean.

The classic integrated American sugar plantation—with enslaved Africans driven to cultivate, cut, and crush cane and boil its juice down—emerged only in the seventeenth century with the introduction of financial resources developed by then in the Netherlands and England. Earlier plantings in Madeira and São Tomé, or in Cuba and Hispaniola before the mainland conquests and silver rush, were smaller and less integrated. The same separation of functions continued into the halting beginnings of cane cultivation in northeastern Brazil. Even as late as the 1620s investors there concentrated on the milling and boiling complex, the *engenhos* ("machine" or "engine"), that produced the semi-refined product they could sell in Europe for currencies to pay off the credit extended to build them. Cultivation of the cane, and ownership of the risky, flight-prone, and dying enslaved Native people working in the canebrakes, were distributed among tenant farmers of lesser means. They seem unlikely competitors for the enslaved Africans on board the *asiento* ships from Angola aiming for the silver of Potosí.

Such early Brazilian purchases of Africans as slaves, like the dubious "cannibal invasion" in the 1560s in Kongo, are not evident in the official record, but against the backdrop of Spain's careful regulation of trade to its Indies and its interest in taxing the value of the enslaved Africans reaching its own ports in the Americas, one suspects a thriving black market for the slavers' human cargoes in Brazil. It was widely alleged that captains arriving in Spain's New World holdings smuggled significant numbers of their enslaved charges past government customs inspectors. Although the specific locations of the smuggling are murky, northeastern Brazil would be among the suspects.

The possibility becomes more likely under the challenges that Portuguese slavers faced in working out viable technologies of providing food and water for the unprecedentedly large numbers of weakened captives they were carrying on the long course from Angola to Cartagena. The transatlantic passage was many times the distances in the already strained slaving technologies of the eastern Atlantic. As captains flocked into the trade in the 1590s, they boarded more enslaved Africans than they expected to land alive, and the captives in the holds paid the cost in high mortality—reportedly 25 percent and more—on the ensuing voyages. It would have made sense for them to make unauthorized, and unrecorded, calls at the ports of northeastern Brazil to reprovision and restore their captive cargoes for the remainder of the passage.

The quiet provisioning in Brazil, along with the exceptionally low costs of acquiring the refugees from drought in Angola, and the eventual sale of the survivors for silver, would have reduced the start-up costs of bringing enslaved Africans to cultivate sugar in the Americas to the point of initial affordability, even in the failing captaincies of Brazil. The succeeding stages of creating the large slave-worked plantations in the Caribbean that made sugar the driving force of the Atlantic in the seventeenth and eighteenth centuries awaited only Dutch and then English capital investment to finance them.

Catalytic Combinations

Practices familiar in all the regional components of the Atlantic produced consequential results when extended into the sixteenth-century Atlantic and combined there in new ways. Aspiring monarchs in maritime Europe, unhindered on the ocean and overseas by the complex compromises with which they were struggling at home, extended dynastic diplomacy and militarization to claim their resources. Merchants found parallel and complementary, though different, openings. In Africa the Portuguese worked with Genoese merchants, who found opportunities denied them in Europe to invest directly in production of what became a prime commodity, sugar, using slaves as necessary collateral. For the Africans, the Portuguese probing slowly along the coasts offered initially unthreatening new means to pursue local ends, some commercial, others advantageous to contenders in the continent's composite political systems. Native Americans, with similarly competitive political structures, also viewed Spanish military aristocrats as opportunities.

Europeans ruled the waves of the Atlantic, but in Africa and the Americas in the sixteenth century they subsisted on the historical dynamics of the populations they contacted there. To describe the resulting process as a unilateral "expansion" of Europe would obscure the multilateral historical dynamics of how parties on all the shores of the Atlantic gained new resources for disposition and advantage within their ongoing struggles at home, efficacious in local political and commercial integration, and—in Europe—also finance. The depopulated lands of the Americas, momentarily surplus labor in drought-stricken West-Central Africa, and concentration of capital in Europe provided a catalytic combination, sparked by the openness of the ocean.

The Seventeenth Century
Expansion and Consolidation

Karen Ordahl Kupperman

As the seventeenth century opened, the four continents bordering the Atlantic increasingly oriented themselves toward the ocean. All four had centered trade on their interiors, with goods and people moving along great river systems such as the Amazon, Paraná, and Mississippi in the Americas and the Rhine, Tagus, and Danube in Europe, across the inland Caribbean and Mediterranean seas, and the Sahara, itself a huge sea of sand. As ocean travel became more feasible, and innovations in ship design made long-distance voyages possible, exchange moved increasingly to the coasts. One result of this shift was growing accumulation of military and economic power among previously marginal people bordering the sea. By the century's end, all four continents had been transformed by the growth of transatlantic interactions and the increasing flow of people, products, and ideas around and across the ocean.

Africa had long been engaged across the Sahara and the Mediterranean in trade with Europe, where gold, ivory, and captives were prized commodities. Western Europe had been looking for an entrée into the rich trade with Asia through the eastern Mediterranean; the revolutions in mathematics, navigation, and ship design that finally allowed western Europeans to engage in that commerce came through Africa. Islamic and Jewish scholars in North Africa had made crucial advances in mathematics, and knowledge from China and India also came to western Europe through Africa. As the Atlantic increasingly became a focus of activity, Africa's western coasts assumed a key position. European merchants early on attempted to engage in trading activity there. Islamic merchants and clerics, drawn from Africa's interior, set up small commercial communities in the continent's Atlantic territories. Muslim merchants, because of their knowledge of the Qur'ān and Islamic law, often functioned as judges as they traveled.

Portugal, capitalizing on its proximity both to North Africa and to the ocean, had been the first to venture into the Atlantic toward the south. Columbus's feat of crossing the ocean to the west was relatively easy in comparison to the tricky proposition of navigating the winds and currents along the African coast. In the first decade of the seventeenth century venturers from northern Europe began to try to break into Portugal's rich commerce there by establishing trading posts of their own on the African coast. They were on a steep learning curve, however. Throughout the seventeenth century, sailors from farther north along the European coast often swung far out into the Atlantic and then back to the West African coast rather than attempt the problematic coastal route that was beyond their skills.

Spain had soon joined Portugal in Atlantic enterprises, focusing attention on the Caribbean islands and the mainland to their south and west. The death of the Portuguese king Sebastião, along with much of the Portuguese nobility, at the battle of Alcazarquivir (El-Ksar el-Kebir or al-Cácer Quibir) in Morocco in 1578 meant that Spain, building on a dynastic claim, was in control of Portugal and its knowledge resources as the seventeenth century began.

By this time Spain had organized extensive American colonies into great viceroyalties with bureaucracies spread throughout the territories. The tremendous wealth in precious metals that flowed into Spain from the Indies made this high level of organization possible. In the last decades of the sixteenth century, when Spain took control of Portugal, the ousted Portuguese claimant to the throne, Dom António, and the royal geographers had fled to Paris, giving northern European countries new access to Portuguese mathematical and navigational knowledge. Richard Hakluyt, who dedicated himself to collecting and publishing accounts of foreign lands, was appointed chaplain to the English ambassador to France so that he could confer with the Portuguese geographers and learn from them. Unlike the Portuguese and Spanish colonies, which were created and controlled by their governments, ventures from northern European countries were private commercial enterprises. Governments provided licenses and sometimes personnel and ships, but the overseas ventures were all funded, and therefore controlled, by trading companies of merchants.

Transatlantic Commodities

Northern European projects initially focused attention on the northern coast of North America, especially Newfoundland and northern New England. Mariners were attracted first by the rich fisheries created there by the underwater banks, where upswelling of the currents forced the fish and the nutrients on which they relied closer to the surface. How early Europeans may have reached these fisheries is a matter of dispute; some scholars have argued that regular transatlantic voyages by fishermen predated Columbus's first venture. No matter when the European exploitation of these fisheries actually began, each summer of the seventeenth century saw an international community of fishermen from Europe, including Basques, French, and English, along with some Spanish and Portuguese, converge on the Newfoundland Grand Banks. Dried fish from America provided much-needed protein for Europe's population, which was experiencing a period of dramatic growth that coincided with the opening of the Atlantic. Although the value of these catches is difficult to calculate, historians have argued that the fish from the northern coast of North America was equal to or greater than the value of the precious metals imported from America. Fish joined other American foods—cacao, maize, manioc, sweet potatoes—that from the beginning of transatlantic contacts provided calories for European and African populations.

French, Dutch, and English venturers also looked south at the end of the sixteenth century and the beginning of the seventeenth, as ships from these northern European countries sought to divert through privateering some of the wealth Spain was gathering from its colonies. Privateering was state-sponsored piracy in the Caribbean and the Atlantic; merchants who could make plausible claims for having been injured by Spanish agents could apply for royal licenses to recover their losses by attacking Spanish ships. These licenses made merchants independent contractors, and monarchs, who took a sizeable portion of the proceeds, found privateering a cheap way to strike at the Spanish with the possibility of deniability if things went wrong. For the English and Dutch, rivalries were intensified by the Reformation and the division of Europe into Protestant and Roman Catholic countries. Protestants argued that Spain was using its newfound wealth to try to turn back the Reformation, so privateering could be construed as a principled defense of religion. These tensions culminated in the devastating Thirty Years' War that tore much of Europe apart between 1618 and 1648.

England and France were able to create permanent presences in North America in the first decade of the seventeenth century, a century after Spain. Earlier efforts along the southern coast—France's Charlesfort (Parris Island, South Carolina), Fort Caroline on Florida's north Atlantic coast, and England's Roanoke in the Outer Banks of North Carolina—had failed. In 1607 English entrepreneurs founded Jamestown in the southern part of Chesapeake Bay, and in 1608 a French party led by Samuel de Champlain founded Quebec on the St. Lawrence River in the north. At about the same time, a Spanish expedition from New Spain traveled north to create the settlement of Santa Fe, in what is now New Mexico.

In the 1620s English Puritans who had first sought refuge in the Netherlands crossed the Atlantic to found Plymouth colony in New England, and a Dutch company established New Netherland on the Hudson River. Maryland, an English Roman Catholic refuge on Chesapeake Bay, and Massachusetts Bay, a Puritan colony, were both founded in the 1630s. And in 1638 a Swedish company created a settlement on the Delaware River, which was absorbed by New Netherland in 1655.

French engagement with the north had grown out of the fishing trade there. American Indians, who were interested in acquiring the manufactured goods that Europeans brought, approached French fishermen with the possibility of involving them in the fur trade, an extremely lucrative commerce. Indian leaders organized and controlled acquisition of furs from a vast network of hunters in the continent's northern interior; French merchants were involved only in the final exchanges on the coast. American beaver pelts were used to create the lustrous felt for the large hats worn by fashionable and wealthy Europeans. On the American side, the high level of organization required to manage the trade and control of the flow of manufactured products to Indian trappers and processors in the interior led to consolidation of powerful American nations.

Other commodities transformed life on both sides of the Atlantic. As with the beautiful felt hats made from beaver pelts, many of the seventeenth-century imports involved luxury goods, or at least products not essential to maintaining life. In this way, transatlantic trades contributed to increased levels of consumerism in Europe.

Tobacco was another luxury commodity. American production of tobacco grew enormously in the seventeenth century. English planters in Virginia developed a crop that was acceptable to European consumers, and tobacco farming spread through the region and to Barbados in the Caribbean. Tobacco from Spanish colonies around the Caribbean had been a luxury product in the sixteenth century; by the 1620s tobacco from the English colonies was on its way to becoming an item of mass consumption in Europe. As with many American goods, it was first greeted as a potential medicine, thought able to rid the body of noxious humors with the expulsion of smoke.

Sugar was an even bigger commodity, and its implications were enormous. Portuguese developers, having learned the secrets of sugar production through sources in the eastern Mediterranean and North Africa, had built plantations on their islands in the Atlantic and then in Brazil. Spain also had sugar plantations on its Caribbean islands, and by the middle of the seventeenth century English entrepreneurs were turning Barbados and Jamaica into great sugar-producing centers. France created settlements and plantations on the islands of Martinique and Guadeloupe and, in 1665, in the western portion of Hispaniola, which they named Saint-Domingue (today's Haiti). The island of St. Kitts was divided between French and English colonies. Dutch adventurers founded colonies on St. Eustatius and Curaçao and seized Suriname on the mainland in mid-century. As cane production increased, prices dropped, and Europeans of all economic ranks began to consume sugar in quantity. Sugar was valuable not only as a sweetener, but also as a preservative. In an era before antibiotics, sugar was also applied to wounds and sores to slow the growth of bacteria. Molasses was distilled into rum, creating another major commodity of Atlantic exchange. Sugar production fostered creation of a huge integrated transatlantic system.

Transatlantic Movements of People

The transatlantic slave trade began in earnest with the creation of sugar plantations in Brazil, and the numbers of enslaved Africans carried into lifetime servitude across the Atlantic grew steadily through the seventeenth century. Africans forced into slavery across the ocean constituted two-thirds of the total migration into the Americas between 1600 and 1700. The proliferation of sugar and tobacco plantations in the colonies absorbed huge numbers of laborers, but enslaved people could be found in the seventeenth century in all regions colonized by Europeans from the far north to the tip of South America. Merchants from the Netherlands, France, and England moved to break the Portuguese control of the supply of enslaved Africans early in the seventeenth century, and in the second half of the century England came to dominate the transatlantic commerce in human beings. Europeans involved in the trade in Africa were restricted to the coast. Capture of those destined for slavery took place in territories controlled by Africans, and chains of middlemen linked the regions in the interior where raids took place to the coast. These increasingly systematic extractions of people involved great and growing violence, with the spread of wars conducted largely for the purpose of acquiring captives. The growing enslavement of African populations was opposed by Islamic clerics in Africa, sometimes violently, but Christian doctrine of the time stated that it was lawful to enslave those taken in a "just war."

As with other Atlantic trades, commerce in human beings enriched leaders and merchants on the west coast of Africa who controlled the transactions. The kingdom of Kongo was already well-established at the century's opening, with links to Europe through missionaries and diplomacy. Trade in gold and ivory with Europe had contributed to consolidation of increasingly politicized and militarized networks that taxed and regulated European traders along Africa's Atlantic coast. The imported products received by those in authority in exchange for captives enhanced the lives of their relatives and clients, helping to cement new loyalties to the traders and raiders exploiting the Atlantic trade. Europeans saw these larger groupings as ethnicities, such as "Igbo" or "Angola," formed along language and religious lines. Political consolidation along the coast facilitated expansion into the interior, as people living away from the ocean sought imported goods. Warfare for the purpose of enslavement of populations spread.

Flows of Europeans across the ocean also increased in the seventeenth century. Chain migration, a pattern in which early migrants sent home for relatives, neighbors, and coreligionists in Europe to join them, fueled settlement throughout the colonies. Castilian law required that male migrants send for their wives as soon as they were established in the Indies, and parts of New Spain were settled by such chains from specific Spanish villages and regions. Spanish authorities encouraged emigration but also regulated these flows in an attempt to make sure that only Roman Catholics went to the colonies.

Religion played a major role in motivating and structuring Atlantic migrations throughout the Americas. Conflict between Roman Catholics and Protestants in France, the Netherlands, and central Europe meant that emigration, with all its uncertainties, appeared to offer more security than remaining at home, especially after the start of religious wars in 1618. The Reformation, with its emphasis on the priesthood of all believers and translation of the Bible into vernacular languages, ensured heated controversy over interpretation even in Protestant countries such as England. English Puritans saw American settlements as a way to ensure that they could worship according to their own lights. That New England was deemed a far less promising place for settlement than more southerly regions settled a century earlier by the Portuguese and Spanish was a plus, as there they would not be troubled by non-Puritans trying to intrude on them. Later in the seventeenth century the logic of evolving Biblical interpretation led to the founding of Quakerism, whose followers took the dramatic step of arguing that believers could access the truth of God within themselves, thereby threatening the centrifugal growth of new beliefs. Moravians from central Europe also began emigrating to North America in the seventeenth century, and in the next century this migration became a flood. Moravian missionaries, who demonstrated their commitment by living among the American Indians and enslaved Africans they sought to convert, were active on the eastern North American mainland and in the Caribbean.

Most European migrants to seventeenth-century colonies went as servants. In early-modern Europe servitude was a stage of life; prospective servants left home in early adolescence to enter into one-year contracts with masters who, they hoped, would teach them skills necessary to their future lives. Annual contracts meant that both masters and servants had a degree of control over the relationships into which they were entering. As servitude became a way of populating American colonies, it was transformed. Many embarked because they found Europe offered little in the way of opportunities for people coming of age and seeking to set themselves up as adults. Servants, many of whom were illiterate, signed indenture contracts before they embarked. Usually these contracts were then sold when the ships arrived. Contracts called for "freedom dues" when the years of servitude were up, but meanwhile servants had little control over their situations.

Environmental Stress

Europe's population explosion was one reason why opportunities there seemed diminished; ecological stress was another. Transatlantic interactions began in a period of environmental challenge. The Little Ice Age, as the period has come to be called, was marked by cold temperatures, shorter growing seasons in the north, and widespread drought. Historians' impression of colder temperatures derived from the writing of people in the period has now been confirmed by scientific readings of glacial, lake, and ocean bed cores and by tree ring studies. Dramatic weather events may have been intensified by unusually severe occurrences of El Niño, the periodic appearance of warm water off the Peruvian coast; El Niño interacts with weather systems all over the world. Colder temperatures and attendant drought created hardships for indigenous people on all four continents bordering the Atlantic as well as for newcomers trying to establish themselves in America.

Extreme environmental conditions formed one context for the religious confrontations posed by the attempts of Christians to convert Africans and American Indians. Conversion was a stated priority of all colonizing nations in the seventeenth century. According to the European sources, people they encountered around the Atlantic attributed the extreme drought conditions to a failure of their relationship to their own deities. Jamestown was founded near the beginning of the worst Chesapeake-area drought in the last 770 years; extreme conditions lasted seven years. In 1612, Captain

John Smith wrote in his *Proceedings of the English Colony in Virginia* that the "honest, proper, good promis-keeping king" of the Quiyoughcohannocks in Virginia sent the colony's governor "manie presents to praie to his God for raine, or his corne would perish, for his Gods were angrie."

Extreme weather conditions created a continuity of approach across Christian denominations. Although Protestants and Roman Catholics almost always saw themselves as occupying opposing theological positions, their response to Little Ice Age conditions was remarkably similar as they sought to demonstrate the power of the Christian God and of those who believed in him. Puritans in New England invited Indians to pray with them in the drought of 1623. Jesuits in New France promised Indians deep snow to aid in the moose hunt if they would pray to the Christian God, and Jesuits accompanying a 1601 Spanish expedition under Juan de Oñate staged a dramatic demonstration of divine control over nature as they entered northern New Spain with the goal of founding a settlement. Because drought and extreme cold affected Europeans and Native peoples alike, asking for and receiving a demonstration of God's power was interpreted as divine approval of the Christians' presence and activities as well as support for their conversion efforts.

Africa was profoundly affected by recurrent droughts during the Little Ice Age. Drought conditions and the excessive drying of the Sahara region forced populations to intrude on the wetter lands of neighbors to the south, and the resulting conflict created refugees who ended up as captives forced into Atlantic enslavement. Dutch trader Pieter de Marees, who made several trips to the coast of West Africa in the early seventeenth century, recorded a positive reception among the Africans he encountered, arguing that they were interested in the Christian God because they believed he could bring life-giving rain.

Transatlantic Knowledge and Administration in the Americas

Increasingly from the later sixteenth century, navigational knowledge became a commodity to be traded just as sugar, tobacco, and other commodities were. Venturers from European nations that were less involved in creating permanent American settlements engaged in the information business. In particular, Dutch operators seemed to be omnipresent in the Atlantic, and for a suitable consideration they were willing to impart intelligence about resources, navigation issues, and political arrangements. Sephardic Jews, who had been welcomed in the Netherlands after their expulsion from the Iberian Peninsula in the later fifteenth century, similarly traded in commercially valuable information. Sephardim were often allowed to create settlements within European colonies but were never assured of permanence, and so they found ways to make themselves essential to international commerce.

Dutch entrepreneurs were credited with giving English settlers in Barbados the technical knowledge to grow and process sugar. Dutch planters knew about sugar production because they had seized Pernambuco in Brazil from the Portuguese in the 1630s and had occupied it for two decades. Portugal resumed control of Pernambuco in 1654, and in the next decade England seized New Netherland from the Dutch, renaming it New York. A series of wars between the Dutch and English in the later seventeenth century was prompted largely by their rivalries in Atlantic trades. Although the Dutch West India Company continued settlements in the Caribbean, Dutch entrepreneurs largely focused on control of the flow of knowledge and commodities.

The Portuguese expulsion of the Dutch from Pernambuco and the English conquest of New Netherland signaled a new phase in Europe's relationship with the Americas.

Overall, European nations with American involvements tried to reconstruct their colonial governments in order to make them more regular and controlled in emulation of Spain's highly structured administration of its colonies. By the middle of the seventeenth century, northern European nations had accepted that they could not replicate Spain's discovery of rich caches of precious metals and mines from which further riches could be extracted. But they believed they could achieve the same kind of administration, the complicated and highly organized bureaucratic structure under the viceroyalties of New Spain and Peru, that Spain had instituted from the beginning.

The Spanish administrative model was based on extensive research of the American geologic, geographic, and demographic landscape. Spain's monarch pored over reports from American territories and had sent officials to investigate and questionnaires to gather specific sorts of information. Officials in every district were responsible for finding out the answers to the questions and for producing maps and other kinds of documents in response to the Spanish government's desire to know as much as possible about the colonies' populations and resources. The resulting *Relaciones geográficas*, which incorporated Native knowledge, were the envy of other, far less well-informed, European colonizers.

In Brazil, Portugal moved to extend control, especially after gold and diamonds were discovered at the end of the seventeenth century. With the expulsion of the Dutch from Pernambuco in 1654 and repulsion of French attempts to establish a foothold, consolidation was deemed necessary. Not only were European rivals attempting to encroach, but the restriction of European settlements to areas largely on or near the coast also meant that enslaved people who were able to escape their bondage could move into the interior, where they formed large communities of Africans and Indians called *mocambos* from the Kimbundu (Angolan) word for "hideout," according to an early seventeenth-century report. The largest was Palmares in the southern part of Pernambuco. These communities replicated many African forms of worship and administration. In response, Jesuits created missions in regions where Portuguese government authority had been lacking, and sought to extend the European presence among largely autonomous Indian polities.

Jesuits were also important in New France north of the St. Lawrence River and in most of the Great Lakes region and the upper Mississippi Valley. The fur trade, and its control by powerful Indian nations, meant that large-scale migration of Europeans was not encouraged. Displacement of essential Native allies was seen as counterproductive. The French Ministry of Marine assumed administrative authority for the colonies in the early 1660s, and the king's chief minister Jean-Baptiste Colbert hatched plans to create more permanent and extensive settlements, but the principal effect of the French presence was to carry European trade goods and wampum produced by coastal Indians from shells found on the Atlantic coast far into the North American interior. Political consolidation in this case was among Native polities. Those who managed the vast networks of hunters, processors, and traders assumed a degree of power hitherto unknown in the region.

England, whose entry into American colonization had been most ragged, made great efforts in the later seventeenth century to bring a degree of coherence to its presence. Political change at home wrought by the English Civil War and the return of the Stuart monarchy in 1660, led to an intensive examination of the plantations. Each colony, formed by a private company with a government license, had its own form of government and procedures. Although the charters all had clauses saying that colonial laws must conform to the laws of England, this stipulation had meant little in daily practice. Moreover, because of the variety of jurisdictions and the extensive lands that they covered, dissidents found ample room to move away from established settlements and create their own new communities on lines of their own choosing. The restored monarchy decided it was time to take control.

Although individuals and private groups had sent out questionnaires since the 1620s to try to find out as much as possible about what was going on in some colonies, in the later seventeenth century, the newly created Lords of Trade and Plantations (1675), later to become the Board of Trade (1696), consciously emulated Spanish practice by sending detailed questionnaires to each colony's governor. Like the Spanish government, they also began to send bureaucrats who, because they were not connected to the colonists and their specific interests, were expected to gather information untainted by local concerns.

At the same time, as the third generation of English settlers began to emerge in North America, American Indians began actively to resist the colonies' growth and the way that the Europeans increasingly impinged on indigenous culture and economies. In the mid-1670s, Virginia and the New England colonies, the longest-established English plantations, engaged in major Indian wars. Bacon's Rebellion in Virginia involved resistance on the part of more recent immigrants to the colonial government in the east, but their principal grievance involved perceived threats from Indians and the rebellion became a war against the region's Native people. In King Philip's War in New England a coalition of Native armies attempted to reverse the spread of English settlements. In both conflicts the European Americans emerged victorious, although badly shaken. In northern New Spain, by contrast, the 1680 Pueblo Revolt that sought to shake off Christianity and resume Native religious practices succeeded in pushing Spanish soldiers and their families as well as Roman Catholic priests out of their territories. Although the Spanish returned a decade later, their control thenceforth was less secure.

The two Indian wars of the 1670s cemented the English government's growing conviction that it was time to act. Beginning in 1684, the Privy Council attempted to reverse the perceived disorder and variety of governments in their mainland colonies by creation of viceroyalties on the Spanish model. As a first step all the colonial charters from New York north were revoked, and the colonies were organized into the Dominion of New England with its headquarters in New York. The Puritan New England colonies were required to recognize the Church of England, and broad religious toleration was enacted. The new government was beginning to examine land grants issued by the now-defunct colonial governments when England's Glorious Revolution (1688) removed King James II, the force behind many of these centralizing changes even while his brother was king, and replaced him with the Dutch William of Orange and his wife Mary, daughter of James II. The Dominion of New England was dissolved, and the colonies eventually received new charters, but with much less room for maneuver. Only Connecticut, which had contrived to hide its charter from the royal authorities, was allowed to resume its original government.

Governments' quests for accurate information and development of knowledge-gathering techniques were matched, and sometimes abetted, by intellectuals' desire to know intimately the new kinds of people, plants, animals, and environments revealed by overseas travel. Inherited lore, such as that of the Ancients, no longer sufficed. The Ancients had known nothing of America, so their authority was discredited or at least questioned. Experience now became the source of true understanding. Many European scholars traveled to Africa and the Americas in order to learn firsthand about lands that had been little understood in the past. Jean Mocquet traveled extensively, including in the Amazonian forests of South America, on behalf of his employer, the French king. John Tradescant, gardener to the king of England, even signed on as a soldier in order to join expeditions where he could gather rare plants. Others crafted techniques, including questionnaires, that colonists could use either in their own researches or in interviewing Native people to learn about their medicinal practices, and the strange plants and animals of newly revealed lands.

People throughout Europe were fascinated by specimens and individuals brought from abroad and flocked to early museums, called cabinets of curiosities, such as Tradescant's in London and Ole Worm's in Copenhagen. Shakespeare played on this fascination with Atlantic exotica when Trinculo in *The Tempest* exclaimed at how much he thought people would pay to see a dead Indian.

European scholars gathered to study reports of new discoveries and to craft new questions to be sent out. The Academy of Linceans in Rome (1603) adopted the goal of cataloguing all the world's species. England's Royal Society and the French Academy of Sciences, both founded in the 1660s when their governments were seeking better control of their colonies, sought information and organized it into scientific analyses. In fact, membership in scientific societies and government agencies often overlapped. All this activity led to the breakthroughs in mathematics, astronomy, medicine, physics, and biology that collectively came to be known as the Scientific Revolution.

***

The seventeenth century opened with the beginnings of large-scale European settlement in mainland North America north of the Rio Grande. Previously, this vast area had not been seen as worth the trouble and expense of permanent settlement. The fishing and fur trades were seasonal and did not require year-round habitation. The one exception was Spain's St. Augustine in Florida founded in 1565, the region's first permanently occupied city, which protected Spanish ships exiting the Caribbean on their homeward voyage from privateers.

Proliferation and consolidation of settlements were the keynotes as the century progressed. Northern European nations began to establish and defend colonies on Caribbean islands as they learned the methods of sugar planting and processing. Portugal regained its independence from Spain in 1640, and sugar production soared in Brazil after the expulsion of the Dutch in the 1650s. With the growth of sugar plantations, the transatlantic trade in enslaved Africans also grew rapidly. Northern Europeans had sought a share in the African trades from the beginning of the century, and by century's end England became dominant. Colonies along North America's east coast grew rapidly; many Europeans were prepared to emigrate as the Thirty Years' War intensified policing of religious beliefs even as newly formed Protestant groups proliferated. Spain's and England's colonies both grew through chain migration.

Europeans and Africans, even those without direct Atlantic connections, became Atlantic citizens as they consumed foreign products. Some American foods, such as maize, cassava (manioc, tapioca), and potatoes, had been transplanted to Europe and Africa so long ago that they had lost their exotic associations. In Africa, the clearing of rain forest to facilitate planting these new crops meant that environmental change had followed their introduction. Tobacco and cacao from the mid-Atlantic region joined the fish and furs that had been coming in from the north. Sugar, introduced to Atlantic islands centuries earlier by Portuguese and Genoese entrepreneurs from South Asia via Africa, spawned the most technically sophisticated industrial plants in the seventeenth century. The product of these plantations was consumed in various hues of sugar and molasses, and also in the form of rum. The huge expansion of production meant wide availability and falling prices so that items that had been luxuries for the wealthy few in 1600 quickly became broadly available across the social spectrum. New dyes meant that drab garments could, at least on occasion, be supplemented by richly colored ones. European pharma-copeia expanded to include new medicines, especially purgatives and laxatives. Toward the end of the century, coffee was introduced, and American mahogany began to feed a new vogue for highly polished furniture. Some of these products continued to be luxuries for the few, but most added calories and variety to diets across the social spectrum. Coffee and tobacco led to creation of new venues for sociability. In these and many other ways, Atlantic connections forged in the seventeenth century transformed lives around the ocean and into continents' interiors, a process that would intensify in the next century.

The Eighteenth Century
Growth, Crisis, and Revolution

Vincent Brown

A geographic imaginary doesn't always link to a particular time period, but the iconic outlines of the Atlantic World frame the fundamental transformations of the eighteenth century. The slave trade, the demographic contours of North, Central, and South America, militarized capitalism under the banner of free trade, global imperial warfare, and national revolution all fermented in the eighteenth-century Atlantic. None of these things were exclusive to that century or oceanic region, of course, but no other century and place bind them all so closely in the historical imagination.

The transatlantic slave trade reached its apogee during this period, in terms of numbers of captives, in its reach throughout the whole of the Atlantic Basin, and in its close association with the leading forces of global change. The slave trade also provided the fundamental spur to the peopling of the Americas and their cultural efflorescence. Between 1500 and 1820, enslaved Africans made up more than three-quarters of all immigrants to the Americas. Capitalism and its attendant ideologies grew and entrenched themselves as a dominant form of economic life, while Europeans extended local conflicts into global conflagrations. Finally, in the last quarter of the century, the Age of Revolution set the stage for the birth of the post-imperial nation-state. Each of these processes resulted from integrating the energies of people on four continents, all of whom developed new strategies of their own to negotiate the rapidly transforming world they were creating. Many of these innovations, only dimly discernible even in retrospect, altered and accelerated the changes taking place around them and had profound and far-flung consequences that no one could have foreseen.

The processes consolidated in the eighteenth century mark the region's imagined cohesion down to the present, a framing perspective on social and political change that still resonates in racial politics, increasing inequality, perpetual warfare, and the specter of revolution. The eighteenth century was in this way a temporal index for the origins of Atlantic modernity. By this period, the networks that had been extended across the Atlantic from Europe and Africa were no longer inchoate, and the entire region had become a dense and regionally differentiated labor system joining the European, African, and American continents in a complex symbiosis. It was also a political system on the verge of upheaval, one that would dramatize the deepest divisions and embody the most fervent hopes of Atlantic peoples, leaving paradoxical legacies of idealism and exploitation.

Africans

The transatlantic slave trade lay at the base of fundamental developments in economic, cultural, military, and political history in the Atlantic World. Over its entire duration the trade drained about 12.5 million men, women, and children from the African continent and made the mining and plantation enterprises of the Americas profitable, providing the impetus for incessant conflict between European powers, between settlers and Native peoples, and between slaves and slaveholders, even as it also facilitated a massive cultural diaspora.

Although transatlantic slaving had begun centuries before, the trade expanded dramatically in the eighteenth century, when its numbers reached new heights and integrated more territories than in any other time period. European enterprise in the Americas flourished when and where enslaved African labor was most exploited. Slavery made the Americas valuable to Europe, and slaves were the most significant commodities and the most vital producers of good and services. The importance of the slave trade to commerce was clear enough by the early eighteenth century, when the political arithmetician and novelist Daniel Defoe argued: "The case is as plain as cause and consequence: Mark the climax. No African trade, no negroes; no negroes no sugars, gingers, indicoes, etc; no sugars etc no islands, no islands no continent; no continent no trade" (Defoe quoted in Earle, 131).

An early inter-American trade in enslaved Native Americans diminished by the late seventeenth century, even as imports of captive Africans ballooned. Of the 11 million slaves who survived their journeys across the Atlantic during the entire course of the slave trade, more than half, nearly 6 million, made the passage between 1700 and 1800. The sugar industry, which consumed more slaves than any other economic sector in the Americas, had expanded in the seventeenth century from northeastern Brazil to the Caribbean. To feed the plantations, French and English traders joined Portuguese and Dutch slavers plying the African coast for captive workers. Monarchies chartered monopoly companies to conduct most of the European trading operations until after 1698, when the English ended the privileges of the Royal African Company and threw the trade open to private ventures. This liberalization facilitated the rise of English—and then British—merchants, who surpassed the Portuguese to become the most prolific slavers in the Atlantic. Increasing demand for Caribbean sugar and rising prices for commoditized humans encouraged intense competition on the Atlantic coast of Africa. European slavers were keen analysts of African markets, taking advantage of regions where local political institutions facilitated foreign exchange, or where sudden disruptions of wars or droughts provided windfall opportunities. Before long, Africa's Atlantic coast was crawling with slave ships.

Although African traders in the Senegambia and Angola regions had supplied slaves to the European traders from the mid-sixteenth century, in the later seventeenth century the four-hundred-mile stretch of West African coastline known to Europeans as the Gold Coast and Slave Coast entered the trade, reaching deep into the interior of Atlantic Africa for the captives sold. Just as importantly, the slave trade came to dominate African overseas commerce. By European calculations, captives had made up about half of Europe's trade with Africa in 1680; however, by 1780 that figure was 90 percent (Eltis and Jennings). During the eighteenth century "slaving states" proliferated. Atlantic trade was not African elites' only concern, but as various merchants, middlemen, and renegades recognized the increasing scope of Atlantic opportunities, they found ways to turn the slave trade to their advantage. The process was dramatically embodied by the highly militaristic centralized states—such as Dahomey, Oyo, and Asante inland from the Gold and Slave Coasts; Segu in the valley of the upper Niger; and Lunda in the heart of Central Africa—that incorporated trade with Europeans into their wars of expansion. As the privations and chaos of war made ever more refugees available for capture and sale, these strong militarized regimes imposed a brutal order on the land. Elsewhere, decentralized trading networks such the Aro behind the Bight of Biafra or the Vili behind the Loango Coast (north of the mouth of the Congo River) grew more dense and prolific as the Atlantic trade increased.

African migration to the plantation core of the American economy dwarfed that of Europeans. Over the century, nearly 2 million Africans arrived in Brazil alone, with another 1.8 million landing in the British Caribbean. The eighteenth-century French Caribbean captured nearly another 1 million, while the Dutch West Indies and Guianas took just under 300,000. Added to those numbers were 300,000 Africans landed in British North America, and 70,000 each to the Danish Caribbean and Spanish America. Demographically, the 1700s were the African century in America.

Europeans and Native Americans

The slave trade, though the most significant, was not the only great movement in the peopling of the early-modern Americas. The great slave majorities in America's commercial center—in the plantations of the South Atlantic—diverted European populations to areas where slavery was limited. Settlers and sojourners from Europe responded to the opportunities presented elsewhere by the burgeoning Atlantic trade. By the time of the War of American Independence in the 1770s, some 700,000 people from England, Scotland, and Ireland had arrived in British America. Despite the large concentrations of American Indians on the Spanish mainland, nearly 700,000 emigrants from Spain came to assume family obligations, look for work, or find refuge. Though New France (later Canada) drew only 70,000 or so migrants from Europe, nearly 400,000 had come by 1760 to the French islands in the Caribbean (Bailyn, 93).

Differentiated epidemiological conditions continued to concentrate European settlement in the higher latitudes, leaving the tropics to Africans with higher levels of immunities to pathogens that killed significant portions of the Europeans who ventured there. In the northern regions of North America, mortality rates had fallen dramatically, and white settler populations burgeoned. Even in the continent's mid-Atlantic and southern regions, by the mid-eighteenth century native-born populations of both whites and blacks began to surpass immigrants. But in the tropical Caribbean and much of South America, massive immigration was required to sustain populations of Europeans.

In the Spanish and Portuguese territories large groups of American Indians had been absorbed into colonial society or, as in the case of the Amazonians, remained beyond its reach. Indians within colonial Latin America generally occupied the low social status of conquered peoples, and bodily signs of Native American descent or affiliation marked even culturally assimilated individuals for discrimination. Waves of disease that came with immigrants from the Old World, the destruction of habitats, and the continual flood of European material goods put steady pressure on Native Americans far beyond colonial societies. In the dizzying variety of cultural practices in play, it cannot be said that European culture displaced others in any smooth or linear way. But over time, the Europeans' military and commercial advantages gave them a shaping power in American cultures, aiding the advance of missionary Christianity, European styles of governance, and acquisitive economic practices. Where Native Americans had survived contact and conquest in significant numbers, fewer Africans and Europeans were needed to maintain European colonial ventures. Still, throughout the Americas, in the eighteenth century the European colonial presence expanded to reshape American economic and social life.

Patterns of cultural creativity reflected the demography, as Africans recreated or reinvented religious and social practices to suit their new circumstances, Europeans adapted institutions from the Old World, and Native Americans responded to the increasing consolidation of the Eurafrican societies. As Europeans and Africans in America jostled with each other, they recreated familiar cultural patterns as best they could, while under pressure from the growth of black and white populations, Native Americans made desperate adjustments in a world that was rapidly slipping out of their control.

Commercialization

The outlines of an integrated Atlantic economic system were clear by the late seventeenth century. Opportunities for steady accumulation coalesced around planting, even as the Spanish continued to extract as much silver as they could from their mines. Sugar, tobacco, indigo, and lesser commodities grown by enslaved labor offered great profits to their owners and stimulated ancillary markets in lumber and shipbuilding, fishing to feed plantation laborers, and wine and luxury imports from Europe. With the plantation economies as the engine of the system, European capital moved into American agricultural production.

Meanwhile, England was well on its way to supplanting Spain, the Netherlands, and France as the preeminent trading power in the Atlantic. A series of Acts of Trade and Navigation aimed to secure the benefits of British trade to the exclusion of foreigners, while *l'exclusif* was supposed to accomplish the same for France. Historians have debated at length the question of how integral the profits from the Atlantic economy were to the concentration of capital in Europe, but there can be no doubt that the growth of Atlantic networks of trade, migration, and association offered new opportunities for accumulation, new stimulants to manufacturing, and created new and expanded classes of consumers in Europe.

Europeans, Africans, and Native Americans all over the region responded in their own ways to the growing commercial integration of the Atlantic. Early on, as Toby Green explains in the entry on Trading Diasporas in this volume, local traders with close cultural ties began to seek new regions like seeds on the wind, transcending their places of origin as commerce followed their movements out across the early-modern Atlantic. Merchant families, religious networks such as the Quakers, or such African linguistic groups as the Mbundu and Kongo of Angola, Akan from the Gold Coast, or Igbo from the area east of the lower Niger River flowed through the Atlantic in multiple "ethnic diasporas." By the eighteenth century, however, an emerging Atlantic capitalism served European government officials, great navies and armies, and wealthy merchants.

While the eighteenth century witnessed the decline of the trading companies chartered by European monarchies and the emergence of more open networks of private trade, metropolitan finance, backed by royal navies, guaranteed the system. Government treasuries still hoped to obtain precious metals, though by less direct means. Again, the African trade offers an instructive example. The first European "factories" along the West African coast were built to try to control the trade in gold. Following the Spanish windfall of silver from the Americas, other European governments sought precious metals to finance their growing military ventures. As the plantation system developed and the value of slaves surpassed that of gold from Africa (by about 1700), slave trading came to provide an indirect route to the mineral wealth of the Americas. Merchants competed for the *asiento*, the monopoly contract to supply slaves in the New World to the Spanish, who had been forbidden by the Vatican to trade directly in Africa. By selling slaves to Spanish America, merchants of other European nations obtained Spanish bullion. Or, as the British did during the first half of the eighteenth century, they could sell textiles and grains to Portugal to access the bullion sent to Lisbon from the gold boom in Minas Gerais in Brazil. Many other trading networks proliferated around the core economies of the Caribbean and South Atlantic with the slave trade at their base.

New financial arrangements supported these denser networks of trade, more powerful militaries, more elaborate administrative regulation, and better communication. The British gained on their rivals by developing sophisticated systems of finance to offer credit on liberal terms in Africa and flooding American markets with inexpensive manufactured goods, squeezing the profits of merchants in the colonies. In North America, for example, British merchants dominated imports of manufactured goods for the burgeoning population. Still, throughout the Atlantic Basin, the rising tide of capitalist accumulation lifted new classes of wealthy elites in formerly obscure port towns such as Liverpool, Bristol, Nantes, and Bordeaux in Europe; Providence, New York, Charleston, Kingston, Cap Français, or Rio de Janeiro in the Americas; and Luanda, Bonny, New Calabar, and Anomabu, among others, in Africa.

African merchants and political authorities had generally valued the agglomeration of networks of partners and dependents over accumulation of material goods. They deployed the textiles, currencies, and weapons that they acquired from the Atlantic in building and managing arrays of connections among people with diverse kinds of expertise, people who could contribute to the viability of their kin groups and polities. But as Jane Guyer maintains in the entry on African Economic Strategies, priorities often shifted from the diversification of networks to the amassing of wealth as the Atlantic trade peaked during the eighteenth century. Accumulation in Atlantic Africa led to a great expansion in numbers of wives and slaves, an extension of alliances, and a growth in the scale of warfare. With the swelling of African social networks came a terrific expansion of debt, and so, unlike the commodities taken by Europeans—slaves who were used as factors of production—Africans could not convert the currencies they received into stores of increasing value but instead resorted to capturing people in the short term to cover what they owed.

European credit created even greater problems for Native American borrowers. While large numbers of Native Americans had been incorporated into the colonial societies of Latin America, the English in eastern North America had few or no places for them. There, as Robbie Ethridge explains in the entry on Native North American Economic Strategies, by 1680 Native Americans lived on the margins of an expanding, commercially competitive, and belligerent colonial society populated mostly by Africans and Europeans. The strategy of the Native nations in North America was to play Europeans off against one another, using the animal skins and human captives they provided to them for both economic and diplomatic leverage. But they too were ensnared by the flood of goods proffered by Europeans, especially by those of the British. Balanced exchanges gave way to dramatic differences in wealth, prestige, and power. As guns became ever more important in Native American warfare, military conflict was increasingly tied to commercial European credit, plentiful in quantity but offered on strict terms for repayment. As in Atlantic Africa, as Ethridge notes, competitive wars led to a "vicious cycle of slaving, trading, warfare, weapons escalation, and debt."

Militarization

Though wars in Europe, Africa, and America had preceded Atlantic capitalism, in the eighteenth century they drew nourishment from its growth. The routine violence of military occupation and brutal exploitation of colonial workers led to murders, revolts, and massacres. But the extensions in the scope and scale of commerce encouraged a parallel increase in militarism, both to protect investments and for the tax revenues derived from them. What had been frontier incidents developed into titanic struggles over the fate of empires. Ritual combat that intended to establish symbolic dominance and political tribute turned into more frequent armed conflicts aimed at exterminating the enemy. Naval competitions to control sea lanes and to establish strategic enclaves mushroomed into wars that stretched across the ocean to multiple continents.

When you enslave people, noted the eighteenth-century abolitionist and former slave Olaudah Equiano, "you compel them to live with you in a state of war" (Equiano, 111). By implication, in Equiano's accounting, entire Atlantic societies were organized around violence and defense against retaliation. Militant resistance by the enslaved to the everyday brutality of slavery was frequent, if generally doomed to failure. No territory with a great concentration of slaves failed to witness a serious revolt, and the intensity of insurrection grew in the eighteenth century as the plantation system reached its apogee. The Spanish had contended with slave insurrections from the sixteenth century. Brazil had seen fugitives create and maintain Palmares, a maroon community in Pernambuco, for most of the seventeenth century. In the British, Danish, and French Caribbean, and in North America, revolts in the eighteenth century followed the growth of slavery there. In the 1730s the English even feared loss of Jamaica to maroon warriors in the mountains of the island, who forced them to sue for peace. The colony was rocked again in the 1760s by insurrections among Coromantees from Africa's Gold Coast, who killed more than 60 whites and cost planters more than a quarter million pounds in lost property. In each case, the scale of the revolts grew throughout the eighteenth century with the increasing intensity of exploitation.

Native Americans in North America adapted to European settlement when and where they could, by alternating between careful diplomacy and militant resistance. Where pressure on their lands grew too intense and alliances were infeasible, they responded with attacks on outlying English and French settlements. Attempting to play one European country off another, they enlisted in European wars, hoping the outcomes would increase their leverage and room for maneuver. In eighteenth-century North America, Queen Anne's War (1702–1713), the Tuscarora War (1711–1715), Father Rale's War (1722–1725), the French and Indian War (1754–1773), Pontiac's War (1763–1764), and Lord Dunmore's War (1774) all saw American Indians joining in the fighting among Europeans to establish land claims, resist incursions, or liberate their territories from occupation. In the Andes of South America, where Native Americans were more incorporated into Spanish administrative structures, the indigenous uprising in 1780 led by Túpac Amaru II aimed to correct abuses by Spanish authorities and colonists. The transformations of the eighteenth century expanded the scale of Native American resistance from local to regional and, with the Seven Years' War—the French and Indian War as it was known in British North America—indigenous politics led to the outbreak of a global confrontation touching European claims in Asia and Africa.

The growth of the Atlantic system fueled militarization of vast areas of Africa behind the coast. Warfare increased in scale, and entire societies came to celebrate militarism with great public displays of brutality. The powerful slaving regimes were dominated by military aristocracies, who in many cases had come to power by turning processes of political integration away from efforts to build networks linking local communities and toward the exploitation of Atlantic commerce. Whether these warrior regimes used cavalry, like Oyo and Segu in the open grasslands south of the Sahara, or infantry like Asante and Dahomey in the forests where horses gave no military advantage and did not survive, these slaving regimes engaged in regular campaigns to plunder the populations of uncontrolled regions for captives or to raid weakened polities that could no longer protect their people. The captives could be retained to swell their armies or be sold to Europeans for guns, which only deepened the spiraling vortex of violence.

These expansive wars in Africa were part of the pan-Atlantic trend toward the integration of smaller-scale conflicts to transoceanic proportions. The greatest of the European slaving nations, the United Kingdom, developed into a bellicose "fiscal-military state" capable of conducting overseas warfare on unprecedented scales and mobilizing the massive financial resources required to pay for it. Cognizant of the synergy between war and commerce, Britain waged a long campaign in the eighteenth century to make the world safe for its private traders.

By the end of the seventeenth century, even European powers that had benefited greatly from piracy, like England, recognized that freebooting raiders on the high seas threatened the steady accumulation of wealth produced by plantation agriculture. Aggressive campaigns against Atlantic pirates aimed to clear the oceans for civilian commerce—most importantly in human and agricultural commodities. France cleared the buccaneers, pirate bands based on the western third of Hispaniola, from the island and turned the region, renamed Saint-Domingue (now Haiti), into the most profitable plantation colony in the world, followed by its other Caribbean possessions in Martinique and Guadeloupe. As ever, wealth invited war, and France replaced the Netherlands as the United Kingdom's fiercest competitor in the Atlantic.

Dynastic conflicts on the European peninsula became Atlantic wars through a domino effect, in which a conflict in one theater provoked retaliation in another across the ocean. The War of the Spanish Succession (1702–1713), though fought primarily in Europe, in North America pitted Spain and France against England under the name of Queen Anne's War. The War of Jenkins' Ear (1739–1748), which took its name from the mutilation of a British merchant captain by Spanish naval patrollers, offered the British an excuse to pry open the trade to Spanish America, and from 1742 the American conflict merged into the wider War of the Austrian Succession.

In 1754, with British colonial settlements pushing ever deeper into the North American continent, a territorial dispute with the French and their Indian allies in the Ohio backcountry sparked a conflict that would last until 1763 and eventually encompass the globe, with theaters in North America, the Caribbean, South America, West Africa, India, and the Philippine Islands. Enslaved rebels took advantage of the imperial conflict to wage battles of their own, as in the Mackandal conspiracy in Saint-Domingue in 1758, when enslaved workers poisoned hundreds of their owners, or the Coromantee revolt in Jamaica in 1760. The Seven Years' War, as it came to be known, ended with the Treaty of Paris in 1763 in an overwhelming victory for the United Kingdom, including formally establishing Britain's dominance in eastern North America. But the war left the British, as well as the French and Spanish, financially exhausted. As colonies had grown bigger and more complex, the costs of defending and governing them were becoming unsustainable.

Political Disintegration

Before long, these ballooning costs had serious consequences for the governing strategies of all the major Atlantic powers. Two great wars in the last quarter of the eighteenth century shook the Atlantic empires of Great Britain and France. The North American (1775–1789) and Haitian (1789–1804) struggles against European rule threw the imperial powers in the Atlantic into chaos, killing and dislocating tens of thousands, depriving European powers of prized American territories, disrupting established patterns of commerce, and, finally, allowing two independent nation-states to emerge. These rebellions grew out of the tensions created by the very forces that had integrated the Atlantic World: fiscal-military governance overseas; the massive movements of African populations and the racial hierarchies of the slave system; the growth of European settler populations with local aspirations; and the spread of liberal ideas of governance and human rights that found expression in amplified political turmoil.

For Great Britain the high cost of winning the Seven Years' War, the challenge of managing the vast territories acquired from it, and recognition that the unauthorized actions of colonial settlers could drag the empire into further spiraling engagements overseas convinced policymakers in London to undertake a sweeping tightening of controls over the government and trade of all the colonies. A series of acts of Parliament mandated the enforcement of trade laws, maintenance of a permanent military garrison in North America, and new taxes. Colonists resented these restrictions on their customary activities, which they perceived as guaranteed liberties, and reacted angrily.

Organizing initially in 1765 to demonstrate against abridgment of what they viewed as "rights of Englishmen" laid down in the English revolutions of the seventeenth century, colonists staged a decade of protest that moved steadily toward a radical political theory articulated by John Locke: that the people were sovereign over their government, with its officials elected and accountable to their will. Of course, few of those asserting these rights were willing to extend them beyond free white men of property, especially given the importance of slavery, which denied civic standing and even the most elementary human respect to the enslaved, to the economy. Even John Locke, celebrated as "the philosopher of freedom," had briefly held stock in the Royal African Company, which had provided the African captives to build plantation sugar in Barbados and Jamaica.

And more was at stake than abstract principle. Colonial merchants and planters chafed at their debts to metropolitan creditors, and settlers with growing families strained against new restrictions on occupying turbulent Indian lands that they coveted. When it appeared that the British might be willing to arm slaves in order to suppress the rebellion budding among their masters, many southern colonists came to agree with the more tumultuous New Englanders that it was time for Britain's colonies to part ways with their king. Thirteen of Britain's North American colonies broke away, with the help of the French, who had been eager to avenge the loss suffered during the Seven Years' War, although thirteen others, mostly in the Caribbean, remained within the imperial framework that financed their operations, supplied their slaves, provided markets for the sugar they produced, and defended them from foreign invasions and domestic insurrections.

With withdrawal of British military forces from North America, confirmed in 1783 by the Treaty of Paris, the sponsoring French had scored a pyrrhic victory over the British. The finance ministry in France had prosecuted the war by borrowing heavily at high rates of interest, adding to domestic financial strain. The French monarchy was bankrupt. To address this fiscal crisis the government embarked on its own sweeping political and economic reorganization, thus providing the catalyst for the revolution in Paris in 1789. Both the French and American upheavals drew on the language of "natural, inalienable, and sacred rights," in direct contravention of the "divine right" enjoyed by persons of royal birth, military prowess, or religious ordination. But unlike the principles affirmed in the North Americans' Declaration of Independence and the Virginia Bill of Rights in 1776, the French Declaration of the Rights of Man and Citizen provided a fundamental framework for governance, establishing that the legitimacy of the state stemmed from its guarantee, by law, of individual rights. For the monarchies of the rest of Europe, the overthrow of the monarchy in France and the abolition of aristocratic privilege were massive provocations that sparked new wars across the peninsula lasting into the middle of the nineteenth century.

Merchants and planters in France's colonies in the Caribbean had followed the political liberation of North America with some envy. Without the representative assemblies developed in the British colonies, French colonists lacked any representation in their own governance, and traders chafed against the restrictions of *l'exclusif* even more than the British Americans had resented the Navigation Acts. When revolution in France began in 1789, colonists in Saint-Domingue hoped it would result in government-guaranteed rights similar to those recently secured by the formerly British North Americans in their constitution of 1787 and its first 10 amendments (1789). Yet a large population of free people of color, many of them property holders, thought the Declaration of the Rights of Man and Citizen should bring an end to racial discrimination, or—as they styled it— "the aristocracy of the skin."

Meanwhile, the hundreds of thousands of the enslaved awaited their opportunity to rise against the divided and weakened power of their masters. Slaves constituted 90 percent of the population of Saint-Domingue in 1790, and the overwhelming majority of them—more than 300,000—had come from Africa within the previous decade and a half. Many of these Africans had been deeply involved in wars in Africa, and they arrived in the Caribbean with military skills and political aspirations of their own. They put these to effective use when they joined the revolution in 1791. A long and complex struggle with many shifting alliances resulted in the banning of racial discrimination in the French Empire in 1792, the abolition of slavery in 1794, and ultimately in 1804, independence for the new nation of Haiti.

* * *

The American and Haitian revolutions, viewed together, highlight the themes characteristic of the eighteenth century. Both resulted from crises of governance brought on by growth in the Atlantic trading system: the surpassing of Spain's silver by production of agricultural commodities, which depended on the labor of commodified humans drawn from war-torn Africa; the inability of Europeans to muster the financial resources to manage vast populations of colonists, slaves, and Native groups; the catalytic effect of imperial warfare; and the unpredictable appeal of radical political ideas. These consequences of the extension and integration of Atlantic networks made by statesmen, traders, warriors, workers, and myriad other commoners were beyond the control or foresight of any of them.

The forces they unleashed did not dissipate with the end of the century. Political independence followed in Spanish America, and the United States expanded its international influence, while that of Haiti dwindled. With the Industrial Revolution capitalism expanded. Racial hierarchy became scientific dogma. The scope of empire and war increased further. Indeed many of the Atlantic World's most distinctive and enduring phenomena—racial politics, African American cultural styles, churning capitalism, the fiscal-military way of war, and the idealistic struggle for freedom—had all coalesced in the eighteenth century.

References

Bailyn, Bernard. *Atlantic History: Concept and Contours*. Cambridge, MA: Harvard University Press, 2005.

Brown, Vincent. *Slave Revolt in Jamaica, 1760–1761: A Cartographic Narrative*. Hewitt, TX: Axis Maps, 2013. Available at http://revolt.axismaps.com.

Earle, Peter. *The World of Defoe*. New York: Atheneum, 1977.

Eltis, David, and Lawrence C. Jennings. "Trade between Western Africa and the Atlantic World in the Pre-Colonial Era." *The American Historical Review* 93, no. 4 (October 1988): 936–959.

Equiano, Olaudah. *The Interesting Narrative and Other Writings*. Edited by Vincent Carretta. New York: Penguin Classics, 1995 [1789].

Holton, Woody. *Force Founders: Indians, Debtors, Slaves, and the Making of the American Revolution in Virginia*. Chapel Hill: University of North Carolina Press, 1999.

O'Shaughnessy, Andrew Jackson. *An Empire Divided: The American Revolution and the British Caribbean*. Philadelphia: University of Pennsylvania Press, 2000.

Rediker, Marcus. *Villains of All Nations: Atlantic Pirates in the Golden Age*. Boston: Beacon Press, 2005.

Reid, Richard J. *Warfare in African History*. Cambridge, UK: Cambridge University Press, 2012.

The Nineteenth Century
Consolidation and Reconfiguration

Laurent Dubois

When was the Atlantic World—what time frame defines it? That historical question, as critical as the geography of the Atlantic World might be, is the difficult but central one taken up throughout this volume. The assumption made in the underlying approach of the *Companion*, and borne out in the many contributions to it, is that the relevant historical contexts moved on from Atlantic scales toward global proportions sometime in the first half of the nineteenth century. But the parameters that determine the "closing" of the Atlantic Era considered in this essay are multifaceted.

One answer to the question of chronology would define a closing moment for the historical processes that defined the Atlantic World as the "Age of Revolution," that is, the independence movements of the early nineteenth century. Alternatively another answer might be the ending of the slave trade after 1807 and, though only gradually, also of slavery itself in a growing number of the new American republics. The other extreme would be to argue that in many ways we are still living in an Atlantic World, that the forms of transregional and transatlantic connections that defined that early-modern world are still very much at play, although in today's modern world reconfigured and reordered. In either case, the challenge is the same: to think through the specific aspects of the analysis used to define the Atlantic World: economic structures . . . forms of governance . . . cultural circulation? The chronologies of these processes—all part of a complex, intertwined whole—differ. A viable response to the question of chronology then is "also/and" rather than "either/or": the Atlantic nineteenth century was an era of transitions and of continuities across a wide range of variables.

Historians love to stretch out calendrical centuries to claim them for the themes they emphasize, or alternatively to contract them, since historical processes do not run in round numbers. A "long nineteenth century," for instance, might stretch from 1789 to 1914 from France's struggle to integrate the republican legacies of the Revolution with the imperial impulses of Louis XIV and Napoleon. From the perspective of Haitians declaring their independence, the century might have begun in 1804. The Louisiana Purchase and the opening of the trans-Mississippi West in 1803 marked a new national era for U.S. president Thomas Jefferson. But for many British North Americans, it may have instead started in 1776 with the Declaration of Independence or in 1783 with European recognition of a confederation of 13 independent states.

In coastal Africa the key to a chronological mapping of the century might be the abolition of the slave trade by Britain in 1807 or later with gradual suppression of Portuguese, Brazilian, and Spanish slaving; however, in the Sudanic regions of western Africa a century of militant Islamic conquests and conversions intensified after 1804. Republicans and military claimants to Spain's colonies throughout the southern and central Americas began a century of struggles in the 1810s, but relative political continuity prevailed in Brazil, where an heir to the Portuguese monarchy claimed independence as emperor. Although these, and other, differing chronologies describe the particular novelties that people on the several shores of the Atlantic experienced around the beginning of the nineteenth century, together they form several core—and coordinated—processes and moments that indicate the extent to which the four continents had become an integrated historical space. This consolidation of the earlier regional histories marked the ending of the Atlantic Era.

Political Independence

First among these processes were the struggles for political independence throughout the Americas in the late eighteenth and early nineteenth centuries: starting in the north and heading south, they resulted in the colonial populations on the North American Atlantic seaboard, followed by Haiti and then by Spain's Latin American colonies, transforming themselves into independent republics. That epochal political change stripped monarchies in Europe of Atlantic means key to the balance of powers there—both interdynastically and between the royal palaces and the subject populations—and created a broader crisis of republican national reconfigurations in France, Spain, and Portugal in the early decades of the nineteenth century. The decline of resources from the Atlantic opened up opportunities for landlocked regions in central Europe, especially German-speaking principalities that had not been involved directly in the Atlantic. For some countries, notably Spain, the rather sudden loss of an entire colonial empire in the 1820s had long-standing consequences for both political and economic structures. For England, Spain's withdrawal opened new opportunities for economic expansion in Latin America.

For certain Native Americans of North America the independence of the United States reduced the possibilities for negotiation and resistance as it decreased opportunities for playing imperial interests off one another, removing what historian Richard White famously dubbed the "Middle Ground"—between France and Britain in the Ohio Valley and the Great Lakes, between Britain and Spain in the Southeast, and among all three in the lower Mississippi Valley. Native communities in the new Spanish-speaking republics lost the protections of the crown in Madrid but became the objects of recruitment by politicians seeking the support of the majority populations of their countries in their feuds with one another or in the international wars that developed in the nineteenth century. Native groups in the interior of the continent became targets of exploitation, where weak new national governments allowed foreign, often British, investors to recruit them as workers producing tropical commodities.

The Slave Trade

Intertwined in these political processes—in fact, the other side of the same coin—was the abolition of the slave trade from Africa and of slavery in the new American republics, which came belatedly in the United States (1863), Cuba (1886), and Brazil (1888). The leading British proponents of abolishing the Atlantic trade originally asserted their campaign as an altruistic, even economically self-destructive, affirmation of national moral purpose on behalf of humanity on a global scale. But this expansive humanistic rhetoric blossomed throughout the remainder of the century to characterize, or even disguise, the growing commercial investments in Africa, and eventually beyond in the Victorian "age of imperialism" to the southern and eastern shores of the Mediterranean and maritime Asia, which in turn triggered the military interventions of the 1870s and 1880s. These commercial changes and armed interventions in Africa and Asia represented the end of the Atlantic Era. But they also extended its historical dynamics, and indeed returned on even larger scales to the types of unsustainable costs of military protection and legal claims that had ultimately undermined the viability of the Atlantic empires themselves.

Britain began this strategy of covering commercial interests with military intervention and national virtue by ending its subjects' Atlantic slaving in 1808. The new United States, in the same year only by coincidence, prohibited further imports as a way of lessening its dependence on British suppliers and protecting the value of the rapidly growing native-born enslaved populations of the eastern seaboard. Both strategies were viewed as a necessity since the supply of slave labor was outstripping demands for it in the declining tobacco plantations of the Chesapeake and among the rice producers of the Carolina Lowcountry. The collapse of French sugar and coffee production in Saint-Domingue in the chaos of the Haitian independence struggle after 1791 created opportunities, particularly in Brazil and then in Cuba, Spain's principal remaining American territory, to continue the earlier Atlantic pattern of dependency on Africa for labor. Nineteenth-century Atlantic slaving consequently thrived in the southern Atlantic, provoking the British to an extended campaign of diplomatic negotiations and naval interventions until the Brazilian Empire terminated imports in 1850. Spain, more and more dependent on Cuba's sugar and coffee, relented only in 1867 after revolts among the massive numbers of Africans enslaved on the island seemed to threaten a new Haiti.

West Africans adjusted to the ending of slave exports that had financed the militarization and commercialization of the Atlantic Era by replacing the captives who had produced the American consumer commodities of the Atlantic, led by sugar and tobacco, with commodity exports, mostly vegetable oils (peanuts and palm oil) to illuminate and lubricate the factories and cities of industrializing Europe. In Africa, the "three C's" of the European nineteenth century—Christianity, commerce, and (modern) civilization—meant that slaving intensified as military regimes organized around capturing people to sell and commodity producers restructured themselves around retaining captives to tend palm plantings or fields of peanuts. By the later nineteenth century, the focus on palm and peanuts turned to refined petroleum (literally "rock" or mineral oil). While abolitionists celebrated this growing European investment in slave-produced African palm oil and peanuts as "legitimate trade"—a supposed means of combatting slavery in the Americas—African political regimes became as dependent on slaves as were the plantation-dependent areas of the Americas.

In the Americas the abolition of slave trading on the Atlantic and emancipation of the enslaved were correspondingly interdependent. They were not coterminous in timing, except in the case of Haiti, where a single, concerted revolutionary process ended both together. Though the abolition of the slave trade in Britain in 1808 helped to spur diplomatic and naval campaigns to end other Europeans' slaving in the 1810s and 1820s, London emancipated the slaves in its overseas territories only in the 1830s. In the United States an even longer period separated the two steps in what was everywhere a slow process of gradual emancipation, owing to the revitalization of plantation production in the southern states that followed the invention of the cotton gin in 1793. This mechanical solution to the bottleneck in moving raw cotton from field to factory made southern slavery a major—and divisive—component of the consolidation of the new nation and culminated in the violent imposition of union in the Civil War.

In Brazil and Cuba the Atlantic slave trade and slavery continued intertwined through much of the nineteenth century, with imports to Brazil ending effectively in 1850 and trickling down in Cuba only in 1867. In Cuba emancipation followed a generation later in 1886, and in Brazil in 1888. Latin American republics haltingly ended enslavement of their African-descended populations but saw the emergence of various new forms of coercion and control, notably through "tutelage" arrangements for the children of Native American communities, through which families were pressured to accept forms of forced adoption, schooling, or apprenticing. The Spanish, French, and British in the Caribbean imported indentured Asian laborers through their growing economic and military presence in India and China, as well as indentured Africans, in efforts to maintain the plantation system of the Atlantic Era as the emancipated survivors of slavery refused to labor under coercion.

The Emerging Power of the United States

A third process, also rooted in the political and economic openings brought by withdrawal of European military and fiscal controls in the central and southern Americas, was the emergence of the United States as an economic force and ultimately as a new American military empire. With the U.S. purchase of Louisiana from the French during the presidency of Thomas Jefferson in 1803, as Napoleon attempted to cover the costs of yawning military losses in the final stages of the Haitian war of independence, the small, barely "united states" on the Atlantic seaboard of North America gained access to an entire continent. The Monroe Doctrine and the Panama Congress of 1826 declared U.S. strategic interests in the Americas to the south off-limits to powers in Europe. U.S. armed forces invaded independent but politically divided Mexico in 1835 and in 1845 seized its northernmost territories beyond the Rio Grande River. The parallel rise in economic power of the British in Latin America also provoked, and also limited, U.S. assertiveness throughout the Western Hemisphere. London investors, in the name of "free trade," financed the construction of railroads to move commodities—coffee from Brazil, beef from Argentina, and later rubber from the Amazon—to Atlantic seaports where British shippers could buy them. They also invested in the processing industries linked to these commodities.

British investment in transportation infrastructure in the United States, including railroads and canals, was no less significant, with industrialization in England (and New England) accelerating through mechanized weaving of slave-grown cotton from the U.S. South into textiles exported to the world. This reconfiguration of Atlantic exchange from production of commodities for consumption—tobacco, rum, and coffee—to raw materials for industrial production and export was central in securing Britain's economic and political power in the nineteenth century. Neither the French nor the Spanish had the wealth to match Britain's Atlantic investments in North America, the independent Spanish-speaking republics, and the Caribbean, or its military expansion in Africa and Asia that followed after the 1870s. These African and Asian markets conveniently distracted the noble attentions of British abolitionists and missionaries away from the continuing slavery in the Americas, on which they depended, and that they supported financially.

As European interests grew in Africa and Asia the centrality of the Atlantic Ocean decreased as a field for geostrategic military competition and commercial integration. Though Atlantic trade remained vital, the transition from the legal forms and military defense of transoceanic commercial systems to a system based on "free trade" among independent nation-states loosened the relationship of merchant networks to sponsoring governments. Though investors and merchants would of course continue to depend on and cultivate links to states, and would depend on colonial military support, they also increasingly cultivated connections that crossed national boundaries and their imperial extensions. This internationalization of trade deepened and consolidated the many forms of inter-imperial trade that had existed since the beginning of Atlantic integration, though often against the laws of metropolitan governments. The decoupling of trade from military control, as well as the increasing investment in strategic mineral resources, empowered corporate investors in relation to sovereign nations.

The gradual ending of the Atlantic slave trade removed what had long been the heart of the system that connected Europe to Africa and Africa to the Americas but also opened new contexts for cultural circulation and production among the formerly excluded, as Paul Gilroy showed in his classic *The Black Atlantic*. The broad cultural exchanges and creations—linguistic, religious, and musical—that had emerged through the removals and mixtures of Africans in slavery laid the foundation for many of the shared, and ultimately global, forms of culture that would come to shape life not only in the Americas and Africa but also far beyond.

Looking Inward and Transcontinental Connections

Finally, the United States gradually shifted during the nineteenth century away from an almost exclusively Atlantic-focused economic orientation to one oriented inland to the west. African American slaves found their generations-deep families and communities on the eastern seaboard devastated by this transformation, since, in the absence of a legal Atlantic import system of enslaved Africans, the need for plantation labor in Alabama, Mississippi, and the area of the Louisiana Purchase was satisfied by selling enslaved African Americans "down the (Ohio) river" to western regions. The popular song "Oh, Susanna!," perhaps the most important hit in the history of U.S. popular music, probably goes back to a slave lament about being sold westward.

For Native American communities in the U.S. West, the nineteenth century represented a period of renewed warfare and genocide. The Spanish and mixed settler communities in far-northern Mexico—modern California, Arizona, New Mexico, and Texas—were absorbed into the United States on disablingly unequal terms. This expansion of the imperial power of the United States throughout the continent and into the Caribbean and Central America ultimately was also the foundation for incorporation of the Pacific as a "rim" of U.S. trade and strategic power. In this sense, the European political and military control born out of the Atlantic World of the eighteenth century expanded to the global proportions that would define the twentieth century.

Fossil-fuel-powered technologies drove these growing quests for political and military control of resources. On the slave plantations of Louisiana, Cuba, and Brazil coal-fired steam-powered mills expanded production of sugar. Cuba's nineteenth-century slave economy combined cutting-edge industrial technology with massive imports of captives from Africa, belying the common narrative (based on an inaccurate version of the history of the United States) that slavery was a primitive form of economic organization doomed to extinction in competition with the superior scale and speed of modern mechanized industry. The explosive growth of slavery in nineteenth-century Cuba highlights the extent to which an integrated Atlantic, or in the nineteenth century an increasingly globalized, economic system, both built upon and in other ways upended the industrial consolidation of the commercial investments of the preceding centuries.

Technology had perhaps its most profound impact in the realm of fossil-fuel-powered transportation, specifically the railroad and the steamship. These fast and efficient means of moving commodities and people shrank geopolitical and economic spaces. When the steamship came into regular use by the middle of the nineteenth century, it freed maritime military, geopolitical, and economic strategies from dependence on indirect oceanic currents and wind patterns. Naval and merchant vessels could plot their courses more directly and reliably. The greater speeds of steamships linked new production regions to remote markets: by the late nineteenth century tropical bananas, for instance, which could not be shipped successfully to temperate-latitude markets on slower and less dependable sailing vessels, became a key product tying Central America and the Caribbean to North America. The higher capital costs of these vessels opened the way for larger shipping conglomerates to overtake the smaller-scale merchant shipping that, from the beginnings of European shipping in the Atlantic, had carried the bulk of commodities. North American investors worked hard to establish shipping links that connected different regions of the Americas and to gain monopolies over trade within regions like the Caribbean.

From a military perspective, the steamship was both a strategic advantage and a logistical challenge. Though steamers freed navies and merchants from the fickle, but ultimately free, power of wind and currents, they needed coal to fire their boilers, and as they moved longer distances they needed more of it. For European states with global interests, such as France and Britain, refueling military vessels posed little difficulty, since they could establish coaling stations on the remote territories that they controlled. The United States, a power of only hemispheric proportions, faced greater difficulties, since it did not have ports around the world where its navy could refuel its vessels. The search for coaling stations was in fact one of the drives for various U.S. diplomatic strategies, such as the repeated attempts in the late nineteenth century to acquire the protected bay and port facilities at Môle St. Nicholas in Haiti.

Since the mid-sixteenth-century Spanish mule trains that moved people and goods across the Isthmus of Panama, the dream of a Central American canal had tempted imperial planners in Europe, but steam technology made needs for a canal more pressing. Many of the people from the Atlantic seaboard of the United States who filled the western territories of the continent did not cross the prairies in wagons but rather traveled by sea, heading through the Caribbean and then over the Isthmus by donkey-back or on foot, and finally on to ships on the Pacific side. The digging of a canal was the next step toward assuring speedier and more reliable oceanic movements of goods and people. Such strategic investments in turn brought enduring forms of indirect and sometimes direct U.S. military control in Central America and the Caribbean.

Railroads throughout the Americas integrated vast interior regions into the maritime transport networks of the Atlantic. And through the intensive and often deadly work of building tunnels, often with convict labor and immortalized in such classic folk songs as "John Henry," mountain ranges like the Appalachians ceased to constitute barriers. Until the nineteenth century water had been the fastest and by far the cheapest way of connecting most places on the planet, so that oceans and rivers had been the keys to transport, and islands and sheltered bays and estuaries the most connected of places. The European Atlantic had become the prime example of the accelerated economic integration enabled by maritime mobility. The oceans continued to be the leading means of moving commodities and people, and seaports did not entirely lose their importance as economic and cultural nodes, but the slow conversion from riverboat to rail left rivers less vital for inland transport.

Geography was critical, as railroads were much cheaper and easier to build through flat areas like the Great Plains or the Río de la Plata basin than through mountains. Railroads enabled settlement and uses of the flatter and more open parts of Latin America, notably Argentina, as well as in the plains draining the greater Mississippi, for agriculture and livestock-raising. Once the obstacle of tunneling through the Appalachian Mountains was overcome, expansion accelerated across the center of the United States. This technological, economic, and labor deployment combined to transform an effectively eastern-seaboard Atlantic polity into a transcontinental one, opening onto two oceanic networks. Railroads also enabled new phases of conquest and removal of Native American communities in these regions.

The British companies that built most of the railroads in Latin America also brought cultural consequences: it was British railway engineers who spread their national working-class game of football in Latin America, so that by the late nineteenth century people in Brazil and Uruguay were taking over the game as their own, drawing together around international rivalries on the pitch more than through often-divided national politics. Football today, not only in Latin America but also in Africa, the Caribbean, and Asia, can be viewed as a trace element of the intricate and unpredictable ways in which local peoples drew on transoceanic connections of the nineteenth century to produce emblems of their new communities and nations. By the end of the century the game had become one among many forms of performance and consumption critical to the imagining of strongly differentiated "national" cultures.

Practices of daily material life throughout Europe and the Americas became centered on consumption of new material goods like porcelain, musical instruments, and decorative arts, as well as cultural products, such as blackface minstrelsy in the United States and beyond. Although community-building entertainments and commercial goods had circulated in earlier centuries, the pace and variety of their production and consumption multiplied in the nineteenth century from the practices and meanings left behind from the long period of Atlantic empires.

Inclusion, Exclusion, and the New Nation-State

Abandonment of the personal politics of patronage and clientage, as well as the economic configurations of community and family, left aggregates of marginalized vulnerable individuals, who gradually grouped themselves in new, more abstract ways to make new claims upon the national regimes that excluded them. The proclaimed political principles of inclusiveness and equality—essentially an imagined homogenous nation—that guided and justified struggles for popular political sovereignty and independence in the late eighteenth and early nineteenth centuries thus paradoxically generated new forms of racial and social exclusion. National ideologies proclaimed equality and inclusion in part because they needed to draw citizens together out of the great diversity—ethnic, racial, religious, and regional—of communities that had gathered in the New World.

The small groups of the wealthy and powerful who led these American nation-states—the landed, military commanders, but not the clergy, who were marginalized by the animating political theory of liberal humanism—defined them according to standards to which all might aspire, at least in the longer term. In the shorter run of historical experience, propertied white Protestant males in nations of British heritage and landed aristocrats of Spanish backgrounds and military leadership in the independence wars excluded women, Native populations, and freed people of African descent. With industrialization, native-born investors in factories distinguished themselves from the immigrants from Europe, as well as from local rural farming communities, who arrived to operate the machines. The ideal of the homogeneity of the nation-state united its citizens against outsiders, whether distant monarchs or neighboring republics, but it highlighted the differences among new abstract categories of strangers that transcended the personal rivalries of family, community, and faith.

These new impersonal groups deployed the national rhetoric justifying and consolidating independence against these exclusions, many of them successfully, though often only over the very long term. Wars created critical opportunities for demands for inclusion, since they required mobilization of every human resource in the nation against a shared enemy, regardless of class, race, or gender. New forms of mass production and consumption of their standardized output as markers of participation in a national economy did so as well.

The nineteenth-century struggle over compensation of industrial laborers and the political rights through which they might negotiate also emerged from the struggle at the end of the eighteenth century over the end of slavery. The hardships of early industrial work were condemned as a kind of "wage slavery." Modern class and race, slavery and free labor, the plantation and the factory: all were co-constructed in disparate areas linked across the Atlantic. The nineteenth century saw many of these differentiating processes come to a head around powerful forms of political organizing, including labor unions and various forms of socialist visioning to extend the proclaimed political equality of liberalism into economic welfare.

No less paradoxically, the liberal humanism of politics in Europe and North America was intimately intertwined with Africa and parts of Asia through brutal military occupation. That seeming contradiction is one of the many ironies of the nineteenth century that historians and current intellectuals (including some who continue to fetishize the "West" as the world's unsullied bearer of democracy and progress toward supporting universal human dignity) have to confront. In France the Third Republic, begun in 1870, saw the nation's revolutionary legacy of democracy and equality institutionalized but was also the motor for the country's greatest and most violent period of colonial expansion in Africa and Asia. The paradoxical pairing of liberalism in Paris and racist brutality overseas paralleled the contradictions embedded in the burgeoning military expansionism of the United States and Britain's economic domination of the economies of the smaller Spanish-speaking republics in the Americas.

In the wakes of the earlier leaders (Portugal, Spain, and the Netherlands), these three had emerged as the winners of the long-term competition around the Atlantic. Seen in this way, the legacy of the period of Atlantic confrontations with and domination of "others" was critical, as the Iberian reliance on specie and the Dutch carrying trade had supported the more militarily powerful monarchies in financing their control of Atlantic territories. The racialized thinking of the nineteenth century converted the proud and devout religious and ethnic differentiation cultivated in the Atlantic from the sixteenth century into confrontations. These convictions justified even violent extermination, as the openness of the Atlantic yielded to the confined spaces produced by faster communications and greater investments, which competed to acquire materials for the gaping maw of European industrial production.

The discriminatory standards of a universal humanism—which confused one's own way of doing things with the only way to do things that others do quite well in many other ways—left the modern world divided between Europe and parts of the Americas built from Atlantic resources and the rest of the peoples of the Atlantic who had provided those resources, human, mineral, and agricultural. The northern Atlantic nations became the norms, if not the requirements, of civilization; by those standards everyone else was deficient in civilized accomplishment, if not also in body and in spirit.

* * *

These exclusionary standards of inclusion in modernity itself drew a veil over the histories of Africans, Native Americans, Muslims, and Catholics. And this makes it vital to conclude with an alternative view on modernity, one derived from the areas that the imperial center condemned as "peoples without history"—Africa and Brazil around the Atlantic, and also their Asian counterparts in Japan, India, and China—and that even today continue to be described as "emergent" from some unstated condition of backwardness. In fact, all Atlantic regions in the nineteenth century engaged, in varied ways, in processes of social and political construction that may yet prove to be the defining historical forces of the twenty-first century. Even within a geopolitical context dominated by European capital and military force, individuals and communities, religious institutions and political structures, and social orders and discursive landscapes engaged in reconstruction and reimagination. Inherited cultural tropes and values were codified to engage globalization. In some instances whole communities were invented: the "Yoruba" people of modern southwestern Nigeria were born in Atlantic contexts in Sierra Leone and Brazil; narratives about the history of the Native peoples of the Americas were collected and crafted; national visions about the ways the complex cultural amalgam of Brazil brought together Africans, Europeans, and Native Americans began to be articulated by a wide range of voices in literary and intellectual circles. Twentieth-century moves toward national independence tapped these nineteenth-century forms of imagination and possibility.

Fully Atlantic perspectives allow us to begin to see Europe in its global historical context, including the multiple and diverse perspectives of the peoples eventually subjected to its industrial armaments and, though less so, capital investment. Atlantic perspectives also reveal long-term cultural and intellectual trajectories that place European conquest and colonization within its historical limits, that is, as a relevant but not determining process, one component of an increasingly integrated set of much longer and deeper local and regional histories. This balanced perspective is still difficult to maintain, for we are not yet finished with the necessary task of exposing the nineteenth-century rationalizations that obscured the crimes of twentieth-century colonialism. With the passage of time histories can be written that capture, sufficiently if only in part, the multiplistic essence of an Atlantic World in which people acted in the ways that made their futures with very imperfect knowledge of their own times, with consequences that they could not anticipate and did not intend.

All these patterns marked a new, modern consolidation of a wide range of phenomena birthed in the Atlantic Era: vast geographical scales, mobility of persons and of products, abstract forms of political identity and economic participation, and industrial mass production in and around the Atlantic empires in the seventeenth and eighteenth centuries. At their outset these patterns had been tendencies on the margins of other, earlier social, economic, legal, and military strategies. In the nineteenth century and into the twentieth they emerged to marginalize the lingering residues of earlier strategies in rural Europe, on American frontiers, in surviving intact Native American communities, and in Africa.

Part Two

Abolition of Atlantic Slave Trade

Transcontinental networks for the long-distance transfer of enslaved captives existed on all continents long before the transatlantic slave trade, girded by customary, legal, and religious systems. A distinctive political and ideological project to end the slave trades emerged only in the seventeenth and eighteenth centuries, out of the most recent global slaving network in the European Atlantic. It took shape in the most dynamic orbits of slavery late in the eighteenth century—the British and French political systems in the 1780s. These two systems together accounted for 80 percent of the sugar consumed by Europeans and 70 percent of the enslaved Africans transported to the Americas.

Why were these European empires—the last to get into the trade—the first to exit from it and then to prohibit others also at the peak of their productivity? A crucial novelty had appeared in the relationship between northwestern European monarchies and their slave systems in the Americas. They had entered the Atlantic system when they had declared their own realms to be juridically "free soil" for any enslaved person who entered them. In the eighteenth-century world, this political principle of freedom, and not slavery, was the "peculiar institution"—an anomaly that created a latent contradiction. In these free-soil metropolitan territories, slavery was from the start the colonial exception to the northwestern European exception. In a metropole without slaves it was possible to imagine, in the long run, an empire without slaves. Trading in slaves could more easily be envisioned as alien, immoral, and ultimately criminal.

A final contrast, this time between the two northwestern European Atlantic political cultures, proved crucial in the abolition of slave trading. The British and French polities crossed the threshold to the formation of national abolitionist organizations almost simultaneously at the end of the eighteenth century, but the two movements differed in popular participation. In 1787 the founders of British abolitionism had immediate recourse to long-standing political mechanisms to enter a developed public sphere and to appeal to a stable, elected parliamentary regime. French abolitionists in 1788 operated in a monarchical regime that severely inhibited civil associations, public meetings, and an autonomous press. With the wider popular political participation at their disposal by that time, British abolitionists quickly found themselves at the head of a pioneering model of the modern social movement, mobilizing mass public petitions and meetings and eliciting an unprecedented outburst of printed agitation. The organizers could incorporate voices and signatures on vast scales that forced even their opponents to concede the overwhelming support of "public opinion."

In this initial decade of abolitionism, French intellectuals appeared to be outpacing their neighbors across the English Channel in terms of concept and commitment. But their lead was brief. The small band of French abolitionists was outmaneuvered by a proslavery countermobilization in French slaving ports and among planters in the colonies. After the revolution of 1789, neither the first French republican constitution (1791) nor its more radical successor (1793) even mentioned slavery or the slave trade, much less intimated a desire to limit the futures of either. The overwhelming consensus among legislators in Paris was that the colonial system, based on slave-grown sugar in Saint-Domingue and other Caribbean islands, was simply too important to the financial survival of a bankrupt home government and a turbulent metropolitan society to be subjected to interference. The major impetus toward abolition came from the great slave revolution in Saint-Domingue (1791), and then was expanded in 1794 by the French Convention to a decree of general emancipation throughout the empire.

By the decade's end the revolutionary societies on both sides of the French Atlantic had been subjected to militarized states, at the cost of the civil and political liberties they had proclaimed. In 1802, Napoleon Bonaparte made France the first and only European nation to reopen an abolished slave trade and to reenslave tens of thousands of men and women who had been living in Martinique and Guadeloupe as fellow citizens. In the following year Napoleon's army of reconquest in Saint-Domingue suffered a disastrous defeat, ending in the creation of Haiti, a nation largely of ex-slaves and without slavery. Napoleon's concurrent suppression of civil and political associations in France ensured that both his restoration of slavery and his loss of Saint-Domingue occurred without manifest disapproval, or approval, in the metropole. Henceforth, France would be a reluctant follower on the trail being blazed in London, ending its own slave trade in the early 1830s.

After the British abolished their own slaving in 1807, London remained at the forefront of the international movement, though it took six more decades before the last British ship with a cargo of enslaved people left Africa. A combination of civil, naval, and diplomatic mobilization fueled the engine of British anti–slave trade policy. Subsequent waves of British popular political mobilization, each more massive than the last, continued to spur authorities at home and abroad to expand and internationalize their campaign against Atlantic slaving. British governments pursued slave-trade abolition relentlessly over half a century. British abolitionism's own social base expanded, incorporating supporters from all British classes, religious denominations, sexes, and ages. Propaganda and individual agents dispatched by British abolitionists made their way to cities receiving enslaved Africans throughout the Americas, from the United States to Brazil, and along the eastern shores of the Atlantic from the Netherlands to Morocco.

With the prohibition of the slave trade in 1808 by the United States—domestic trading in enslaved people in the United States remained legal—the locus of the traffic, and hence British efforts to abolish it, swerved from the northern to the southern Atlantic. The Ibero-American empires recov-

ered their initial preeminence in Atlantic slaving, and so, as with their Anglo-French predecessors, the roaring Spanish and Luso-Brazilian slave trades were also assaulted at their heights. Unlike in their northern counterparts, however, the major sources of pressure to close down their involvement came from outside their own imperial orbits, from the British. Even more than in the French case, organized abolitionism, after the initial phase of the South American wars of independence against Spain, found barely an echo in Iberia or in independent (after 1821) Brazil; it was swept into the vortex of British imperial abolition.

At the Congress of Vienna, in the 1815 treaty ending the Napoleonic Wars in Europe, an article condemning the slave trade as contrary to the supposed universal principles of religion and humanity was the only mention of the world beyond the Continent. British wartime campaigns against enemy (French) and foreign (Portuguese) trades, begun immediately after Britain's own abolition act had taken effect, were continued by a long postwar sequence of treaties, some offering financial incentives. The Royal Navy obtained the right to search vessels of other nations for the victims and tools of slaving. A system of international courts was erected on both shores of the Atlantic to adjudicate seizures of ships caught with slaves or slaving equipment on board. An ever-expanding network of bilateral anti–slave trade treaties always included Great Britain as one of the signatories.

Britain's exercise of "hard power" in pursuit of international abolition was an extension of its naval domination of the world's oceans. The Royal Navy's largest armed action against the slave trade actually occurred in the Mediterranean rather than the Atlantic. Its bombardment of Algiers in 1816 is little noted in most histories of abolition. This action, more costly to British seamen than Lord Nelson's celebrated triumph over France at Trafalgar, liberated thousands of mainland European Christians enslaved in North Africa—but not one white Briton nor one black African among them. Both intimidation and military action could also be used against the less powerful European participants in the Atlantic slave trade. Portugal was threatened with a virtual declaration of war. West African coasts were raided. The most successful British naval action against the slave trade was in Brazil. A major naval action off its coast in 1850 precipitated

Brazil's abandonment of Atlantic slaving and produced the largest single drop in the transatlantic slave trade in its three centuries, exceeding even the reduction that the Anglo-American withdrawal in 1808 had produced. Massive antislavery mobilizations would occur in the Ibero-Atlantic orbit, but they would be directed against the institution of slavery itself rather than the trade. The American Civil War and uninhibited United States intervention at the end of the 1860s finally accelerated the ending of the great forced migration of Africans to Latin America.

On the eastern side of the Atlantic, abolition of the transatlantic slave trade ensured that Europe's colonization of Africa in the 1880s and 1890s was carried out under the antislavery banner. At the 1884–1885 Berlin Conference, which laid out the rules for carving up Africa, the British proposed a resolution in the treaty calling for the suppression of ongoing slaving within the continent. The ensuing (1890) antislavery treaty of Brussels more formally incorporated abolition as an obligation of imperial sovereignty in Africa. One of the requisites for non-Europeans wishing to enter the circle of recognized civilization and political autonomy was to seek a forum in which they could affirm unequivocal hostility to slave trading. Six decades later, Article 4 of the United Nations Universal Declaration of Human Rights (1948) placed abolition of the slave trade and slavery at the top of its list of member nations' commitments to the welfare of their, and other nations', citizens.

SEYMOUR DRESCHER

Bibliography

Bethell, Leslie. *The Abolition of the Brazilian Slave Trade: Britain, Brazil and the Slave Trade Question*. New York: Cambridge University Press, 1970; reprint 2009.

Brown, Christopher. *Moral Capital: The Foundation of British Abolitionism*. Chapel Hill: University of North Carolina Press, for the Omohundro Institute of Early American History and Culture, 2006.

Drescher, Seymour. *Abolition: A History of Slavery and Antislavery*. New York: Cambridge University Press, 2009.

Eltis, David. *Economic Growth and the Ending of the Transatlantic Slave Trade*. New York: Oxford University Press, 1987.

Kielstra, Paul Michael. *The Politics of Slave Trade Suppression in Britain and France, 1814–48: Diplomacy, Morality, and Economics*. New York: Palgrave Macmillan, 2000.

Martinez, Jenny S. *The Slave Trade and the Origins of International Human Rights Law*. New York: Oxford University Press, 2012.

Agricultural Production

The great French historian Fernand Braudel wrote that "Europe . . . neither discovered America and Africa, nor first penetrated the mysterious continents. . . . Europe's own achievement was to discover the Atlantic and to master its difficult stretches, currents and winds" (Braudel, 62–63). Braudel's emphasis on the Atlantic as a historical space created by European domination of the ocean shifts our attention away from the discoveries and conquests of unknown (for Europe) territories. Braudel instead asks us to reflect on the creation of social and material dependencies that integrated previously disparate continents into a coherent economic region of the European world economy. In contrast to Europe's predominantly mercantile relations with Asia and Africa, the Americas emerged as a dynamic zone of commodity production. Extractive and agricultural frontiers remade the landscapes of the Atlantic World. Agriculture—together with mining, lumbering, the fisheries, and the fur trade—widened, deepened, and accelerated integration of the Americas into the European division of labor as these commodities flowed across the Atlantic region.

European expansion, conquest, and colonization were driven by the search for valuable commodities, of which silver, sugar, and slaves were the most significant. At the same time, the making of the Atlantic World entailed the broader interaction of distinct agrarian civilizations under the unequal conditions of conquest, military-authoritarian control, and a world market financed from Europe.

We may begin to understand the character of Atlantic agriculture by comparing food cultures of the Americas, Europe, and Africa. In the Americas and Europe, diet was generally constructed around the cultivation of a particular complex carbohydrate supplemented by other plant foods and by meat, fowl, fish, and seasonings. In the Americas maize was the dominant staple starch and was cultivated across a variety of environments and social formations. Under the proper conditions, it was capable of supporting dense populations and hierarchical social structures. Over the long term it made possible the development of the monumental civilizations of Mesoamerica and the Andes.

In Europe, a complex of livestock and grains, especially wheat, shaped the organization of land tenure, population distributions, and societies. Wheat had a low yield and was hard on the soil. It was generally grown in combination with other supplementary cereals (rye, oats, barley). Domesticated animals were a distinguishing feature of European agriculture, and livestock not only supplied a meat-rich diet but also provided draft animals for traction and manure that increased cereal yields. At the same time, however, cereals and animals competed with one another for land. Braudel refers to these major food crops (together with rice) as "plants of civilization" because they sustained highly differentiated material, social, and cultural systems over long periods. In contrast, tropical Africa, though home to skilled farmers and husbandmen, had no similar integration of high-yield staple cultivation and animal traction capable of supporting dense populations and concentrated specializations in urban centers. African societies relied upon complementary but separate cultivation of diverse plants, pastoralist herding of livestock (mostly cattle), and hunting and gathering in a wide variety of combinations for their food supply.

The making of the Atlantic as a historical region of the European world economy involved movements of people, plants, and animals that brought these three agricultural systems into sustained contact with one another. In the Americas their interactions created three distinct but interrelated productive frontiers. The densely populated highland zone, running from Mexico through Bolivia and Peru to northern Chile, was organized on the basis of mineral extraction, most notably of silver, preserving indigenous communities for labor. The tropical and subtropical coastal lowlands from Maryland through the Caribbean basin to São Paulo in Brazil were home to plantation agriculture using coerced, predominantly slave, labor to produce staples for the world market. Finally, the temperate zones of both North and South America became sites of European settlement and family farms. Greater and lesser degrees of interrelation among these distinctive agricultural regimes—with products, technologies, and forms of social organization particular to each—integrated the Americas into the Atlantic economy.

Highland America

Maize is indigenous to the Americas, where centuries of human invention created a high-yield, nutritious plant capable of supporting large populations. Intensive cultivation of maize in the valleys of Mexico and Central America, the jungles of Yucatán, and the terraced hillsides of Peru and Bolivia supported large cities and state structures capable of tapping the resources of extensive territories and diverse populations. Maize not only produced extraordinarily high yields, but its cultivation required as little as 50 work days per year, leaving populations dependent on it available for other tasks to support the architectural, engineering, and military achievements of the Aztecs, Maya, and Incas.

Spanish conquest transformed the economy of this zone from monuments to mining. Metals precious to Europeans, especially silver, were sources of individual and national wealth and were fundamental to commercial integration of the European world economy. Through various systems of compulsion, Spanish authorities drafted indigenous populations to provide the bulk of the labor force needed to work the mines they opened to obtain the precious metal. At the same time, the Spanish did not adopt the indigenous corn culture but rather imported wheat agriculture in accordance with their own dietary preferences. Spanish conquerors were awarded extensive grants of land in prime agricultural areas and rights to exploit the labor of the populations resident on them. They also brought horses, cattle, sheep, and pigs, and converted the best lands to the cultivation of wheat and to stock raising. Wherever conditions were suitable, they established vineyards. The integrated hacienda emerged, producing grain and livestock for regional markets in the growing cities and mining centers. The hacienda initially relied upon compulsory labor drafts but eventually was able to thrive on the labor of Indians uprooted from their home communities. Because the Spanish colonies reproduced metropolitan agriculture in the New World, they became self-sufficient in key foodstuffs and less dependent on imports from Spain. This high degree of self-sufficiency was the source of tensions with Spain but also contributed to the stability of the American colonies after the mining economy declined in the late eighteenth century. The Spanish in the New World could feed themselves.

The imposition of Spanish crops, practices, and institutions on indigenous societies created a two-tiered agricultural system. Although maize was core to the diets of the native populations, the Spanish considered it an inferior grain, with a place in the Spanish household primarily as animal feed. The best lands were reserved for wheat production and cattle ranching, and Indian cornfields were victims of wandering herds of Spanish livestock. Maize yields were nonetheless abundant and provided a cheap and nutritious staple starch that allowed demographic recovery from the population collapse that had followed the conquest in the sixteenth century. Maize supported a numerous but impoverished population of Native Americans who provided the Spanish colonies with an exploitable labor force.

The Lowland Plantation Zone

The tropical and subtropical lowlands of the Americas were largely inhospitable to the temperate-latitude crops of Europe. These regions had had low population densities before Europeans arrived, with economies based on hunting, gathering, and migratory "slash-and-burn" agriculture, in which the heavy vegetation was periodically burned to enrich infertile soils with ash. These dispersed populations consequently supported few urban or centralized political systems. Yet these regions became home to perhaps the most radical and innovative kind of agriculture in the Atlantic: the production of tropical commodities for the world market. Here the products, the form of labor (racialized slavery), and the plantations themselves were artifacts of the emerging Atlantic economy.

The classic plantation commodities—sugar, coffee, cacao, and tobacco—are stimulants and to one degree or another addictive. Their availability and growing popularity shaped new cultures of consumption in Europe, especially among the emerging urban middle and working classes. The coffeehouse emerged as the emblematic site for sociability around shared consumption of these energizing products.

Sugar was the most important of the plantation crops and paradigmatic of the integration of the expanding plantation frontier. Each step in the expansion of the sugar economy exploited new territories on larger scales. The plantation mobilized land, labor, and capital for monocropping of high-value export commodities for world markets. Production was organized through more complex divisions of labor within and between cultivation and processing. New milling and refining technologies were developed, and reliance on slave labor increased. The Atlantic trade in enslaved Africans became a major branch of commerce in its own right. Increasingly extensive and rationalized monoculture was destructive of both local environments and available labor and so encouraged further geographical expansion. The intensive concentration of land, labor, and capital for production of export commodities meant that plantation zones had to import food and other supplies—manufactured goods, grains, livestock for work and consumption, lumber, fisheries—from elsewhere around the Atlantic.

Europeans had first encountered sugar in the Levant during the Crusades. Beginning in the twelfth century, European sugar production moved westward across the Mediterranean. Columbus took sugar west with him on his second voyage, and the first sugar industry in the Americas was established on the Spanish island of Hispaniola. However, production of sugar in the Spanish Caribbean collapsed for a variety of reasons, and the origins of the Atlantic sugar industry can instead be traced to the Portuguese. They established the first Atlantic sugar colony, in Madeira, by 1450. Holdings were relatively small, and a mixture of Italian sugar masters, Portuguese farmers, and African slaves cultivated and cut the cane. Technological advances in milling and boiling converted the raw cane juice to chemically stable crystals that would survive shipment to Europe for refining. Sugar production in Madeira was linked to Genoese and Flemish capital, and the island surpassed the levels of production attained by the Mediterranean sugar industry.

After 1500, however, Madeira declined owing to deforestation of wood to fuel the boilers, and gave way to heavily forested, equatorial São Tomé. This Portuguese island colony off the coast of Africa was the first sugar plantation monoculture worked entirely by African slaves. But São Tomé, too, went through the cycle of expansion and decline characteristic of sugar and was unable to keep pace with growing European demand. By 1520, sugar cultivation had begun also in Brazil, where, after a halting beginning, it became securely established by the end of the sixteenth century. Brazilian mill owners and cane farmers extended sugar cultivation across the fertile *massapé* (clay) soils of the Bahian and Pernambucan littorals. The relatively sparse indigenous population of this zone proved unsuitable for plantation labor, and after 1570 planters' demands were met by enslaved Africans. Henceforth the Atlantic plantation systems and the African slave trade were to grow in the closest interdependence.

The extensive scale of Brazilian cane production made sugar accessible to new groups of consumers in Europe and secured its position as the most valuable commodity in Atlantic trade, exceeded in value only by silver as specie. Atlantic sugar production and consumption took another leap forward after 1640, when the Dutch, who had seized the plantation zones of Brazil, were expelled. They took sugar plants, refining technology, slaves, and credit to the islands of the English and French Caribbean, then inhabited by a European yeomanry engaged in small-scale production of tobacco, offering the colonists the right to trade as citizens of Amsterdam and Rotterdam. The Dutch investments triggered a plantation revolution in the Caribbean that marginalized European farmers and tobacco. However, the English and French governments asserted control over their respective islands and imposed mercantilist policies to expel the Dutch. The West Indian sugar industry developed under the direct control of the most dynamic metropolitan powers of the day. The plantation monopolized land, the slave trade grew steadily, and the West Indies were transformed into "sugar islands," populated with preponderant majorities of enslaved Africans. Sugar made them the richest colonies in the world and the objects of intense colonial rivalry. By the eighteenth century even the poorest sectors of the population in Britain consumed sugar in some form, while reexports of colonial commodities—led by sugar—allowed French foreign trade to compete with that of Britain.

Temperate Zones of European Settlement

The temperate regions of both North and South America remained zones of European settlement of the sort that sugar had eliminated from the tropics. However, the agricultural regimes of the two hemispheres developed in quite different directions. North America had no agricultural products of obvious commercial value to Europeans. The first export commodities—furs, timber, fish—were obtained from Native American extractive frontiers beyond the zone of European settlement. Attempts to establish large-scale commercial agriculture were on the whole unsuccessful; instead the family farm predominated. The immigrant European populations wanted land to support themselves and were inspired by an ideal of family economic self-sufficiency. There was always more land than labor to work it, and the condition of development for this region was the attraction of continuous cheap lands on the frontiers of settlement, matched by a chronic shortage of labor.

The settlers brought their northern European patterns of mixed farming—grain and stock raising—but they had to adapt to North American crops and climatic conditions. Those in Canada, New England, and the Middle Colonies had to learn to farm successfully despite short growing seasons, dense forests, often thin and rocky soils, and frontier lack of infrastructure. The Native Americans' maize was particularly important in securing survival for both man and beast. Settler families also ate native squash, pumpkins, and beans. Native American methods of cultivation were employed initially, as they produced a sufficient yield without requiring clearance of the forest. North American forage crops were inadequate, and cattle, horses, and swine simply ran loose in the woods. With gradual clearance of the land and the adoption of plows, corn yields increased, and wheat, barley, and oats were also grown. Pastures were cleared, and more attention was paid to fodder crops and the selection and care of stock.

The geography of eastern Canada was even less supportive of commercial agriculture than that of New England and the Middle Atlantic colonies, where fertile river valleys and coastal plains encouraged both commercial family farming, some of it involving small numbers of slaves, and the development of cities. The Hudson Valley, New Jersey, Pennsylvania, Delaware, and Maryland developed quickly into agricultural hinterlands for New York, Philadelphia, and Baltimore, while the rocky soils of New England gave Boston a less productive hinterland, leaving the city more oriented toward the sea. With commercialization of agriculture, wheat became the dominant crop, and greater attention was given to stock raising. Maize, despite its nutritious character, was increasingly regarded as an "inferior" grain to be used as a feed crop—more profitable in the hog than as a commodity in its own right.

Although there was no demand for the agricultural commodities of these temperate zones in Europe, the settlers developed an important trade with the tropical West Indian slave-plantation colonies. Commodities including wheat and other grains, salt beef, pork, fish, and horses, along with forest products—timber, pitch, tar—provided the settler colonies with favorable balances of trade. By the eighteenth century the tobacco and rice plantations of the southern mainland colonies developed growing markets as well. After 1800, pioneer farmers pushed westward across the Alleghenies, and commercial farming extended through southern Pennsylvania, up the Mohawk Valley in central New York, and along the shores of Lake Ontario. Agricultural development in the west, especially in the Ohio Valley, was tied to the availability of transport. By the 1820s the Erie Canal linked Ohio farmers to eastern seaboard markets, while the Ohio and Mississippi rivers, especially after the appearance of the steamboat, made southern and West Indian markets also accessible. The wheat frontier moved westward, and in the same decades corn and pork from the upper Midwest supported the opening of the Cotton South.

In Spanish America, the presence of large towns and mining centers, a monetized economy, abundant land, and a subordinate indigenous labor force supported the development of agriculture in the temperate zones. Urban demand radiated out over broad hinterlands from Chile to northern Mexico, and Spanish settlers produced for urban markets as well as for their own subsistence. The temperate zones of central Chile and southern Peru supplied wheat and wine to Lima and other Peruvian cities.

Tucumán supplied mules, draft animals, and hacienda products to the legendary mines at Potosí (modern Bolivia). Production of wheat and other provisions developed in close proximity to Buenos Aires, but the vast grasslands of far-southern temperate South America presented a formidable obstacle to commercial agriculture. However, enormous herds of cattle and horses, introduced by the Spanish, flourished on the pampas well before the region was settled. The Spanish had practiced open-range ranching in the Old World, and the favorable conditions of the New World allowed them to develop a cattle economy centered on hides, tallow, and dried meat on unprecedented scales, not only for Spanish America but also for Europe. Similarly Portuguese settlers in São Paulo and Paraná in southern Brazil raised huge herds of mules for draft animals and transportation, and they also supplied corn, manioc, rice, beans, dried beef, and pork for the mines and plantations in neighboring districts. Farther south, Rio Grande do Sul produced dried and salted beef (*charque*) on commercial scales to feed the enslaved workers of the tropical plantation and mining zones.

The "Other" Atlantic Agricultural Economy

Atlantic history focuses on the major export commodities of the Americas. But another category of products—the staple starches—was also of fundamental importance in the formation of the Atlantic economy. These crops were too bulky and of values too low to be produced for international trade, although they were often produced commercially for local or regional markets. Cultivation of American maize, manioc, and potatoes spread eastward throughout the Atlantic. They provided cheap, abundant, and nutritious complex carbohydrates, which underwrote the demographic growth and social divisions that sustained the formation of the Atlantic economy. These cheap starches provided sufficient nutrition to sustain impoverished rural and urban laboring populations throughout the Americas, in Africa, and in Europe. They lowered the costs of supporting larger families, who were often left with less or poorer land, and thus made available pools of cheap labor for colonial employers.

We have already seen how maize subsidized marginalization of the native populations of Mesoamerica and the Andes. In the tropical lowland plantation zones, the indigenous root crop, manioc (or cassava), became the dietary staple of the enslaved populations, supplemented by corn, beans, yams, and sweet potatoes. Old World imports, including rice, bananas and plantains, mangos, ackee, and breadfruit also found their ways into the slave diet. Conversely, corn and manioc were widely adopted in Africa, readily integrated into the prevailing multicrop economies. These new dietary staples provided increased nutritional inputs, helping African populations to recover from the disruptions and demographic losses of the slave trade. Because corn was durable and could withstand the humid ocean air, it was also consumed extensively on the ships of the transatlantic slave trade; indeed, some of the first large-scale commercial agriculture carried on by Africans developed around the slaving centers on the coast, supplying grain for the ships filled with captives. Meanwhile, corn and potatoes became mainstays of the diet of Europe's laboring poor, both in the countryside and in towns. The potato was more prevalent in northern Europe, while corn was grown more widely in the south.

The End of the Atlantic Food Regime

Production, commercial distribution, and mass consumption of the agricultural commodities of the Atlantic created complex, uneven, overlapping interdependencies across environmental zones, political boundaries, and class, ethnic, and cultural divisions. These relations were simultaneously formative of, and formed by, the Atlantic region as part of an integrated world economy. However, by the nineteenth century, a new cycle of material and economic expansion brought changes. Production of the tropical commodities of the American plantation zone spread to Africa, the Indian Ocean, Asia, and the Pacific and expanded beyond foods and drugs for personal consumption to industrial raw materials: fibers, vegetable oils, and wild rubber. Dissociated from their Atlantic origins, they became embedded in global geographical and social patterns of industrial production and consumption.

Perhaps more importantly, mechanization of agriculture and cheap transportation provided by railroads and steamships made the basic dietary staples—the complex carbohydrates—objects of in-

ternational trade. Wheat, beef, and pork to feed industrializing Europe arrived not only from North and South America but also from Australia. Even though maize took second place to wheat as a grain, its cultivation became more widespread, and with the introduction of refrigerator ships in the second half of the century, corn-fed fresh beef and pork became important exports. Even as the Atlantic was superseded in a New World economic division of labor, the products that had distinguished Atlantic agriculture became integral to a New World food regime and dietary hierarchy. With the availability of new and mass-produced foodstuffs, the dietary choices of upper and middle classes became more varied. Cheap and simply produced starches and stimulants, as well as new opium-based drugs, lowered the standards of living and increased the economic dependency of the world's poor and laboring populations, whether peasants or any of the many victims of coerced or semi-coerced labor.

DALE TOMICH

Bibliography

Braudel, Fernand. *Civilization & Capitalism, 15th–18th Century.* Vol. I, *The Structures of Everyday Life.* New York: Harper & Row, 1979.

Crosby, Alfred. *The Columbian Exchange: Biological and Cultural Consequences of 1492.* Westport, CT: Greenwood Press, 1972.

Friedmann, Harriet, and Philip McMichael. "Agriculture and the State System: The Rise and Decline of National Agricultures, 1870 to the Present." *Sociologia Ruralis* 29, no. 2 (1989): 93–117.

Galloway, J. H. *The Sugar Cane Industry: An Historical Geography from Its Origins to 1914.* Cambridge: Cambridge University Press, 1989.

Kiple, Kenneth F. *A Movable Feast: Ten Millennia of Food Globalization.* Cambridge: Cambridge University Press, 2007.

Luna, Francisco Vidal, and Herbert Klein. *Slavery and the Economy of São Paulo, 1750–1850.* Stanford, CA: Stanford University Press, 2003.

Mintz, Sidney W. *Sweetness and Power: The Place of Sugar in Modern History.* New York: Penguin, 1985.

Moore, Jason W. "Sugar and the Expansion of the Early Modern World-Economy: Commodity Frontiers, Ecological Transformation, and Industrialization,"

Review (Fernand Braudel Center) 23, no. 3 (2000): 409–434.

Salaman, Redcliffe. *The History and Social Influence of the Potato.* Cambridge: Cambridge University Press, 1970, repr.

Schivelbusch, Wolfgang. *Tastes of Paradise: A Social History of Spices, Stimulants, and Intoxicants.* New York: Vintage Books, 1992.

Warman, Arturo. *Corn & Capitalism: How a Botanical Bastard Grew to Global Dominance.* Chapel Hill: University of North Carolina Press, 2003.

Art

See Literary and Visual Expressions, African American; Visual Representations.

Blended Communities

From the fifteenth through the early nineteenth centuries, members of very dissimilar communities came into sustained contact with one another on an unprecedented scale in port towns, centers of trade, colonial capitals, and on imperial peripheries all around the Atlantic Basin. Their social and economic engagements gave rise to polycultural, ethnically mixed communities that traditional empire-centered histories represent only poorly. European imperial histories typically skew their depictions of the early-modern era by foregrounding European rulers' objectives and metropolitan perspectives on the peoples they encountered overseas. National histories, though less reluctant to address cross-cultural exchanges, tend to obscure the contexts of the times in favor of romanticized narratives. Rather than dismissing culturally heterogeneous peoples as mere flotsam and jetsam littering the wake of European overseas expansion, or as mere figureheads for modern multicultural national identities, scholars increasingly view diverse European African, Amerindian European, and African Amerindian groups as historical actors in their own right, as both products and creators of an Atlantic World, even as emblematic of its inherent and animating plurality.

Many of the blended communities of the early-modern Atlantic World originated in sexual unions between European men overseas and the African or Amerindian women they met there. Discussions of these encounters often focus on the extremely unequal power relations within European colonies in the Americas—for example, plantation overseers' sexual abuse of enslaved women—in which the men drew on dense economic and political networks while enslaved women had no kin or lineage groups capable of protecting them. In other contexts, where men alone or few in number lived among the women's kin, however, the European outsiders adopted the laws and customs of their partners' societies, and cross-cultural sexual unions channeled transatlantic commerce. For European men far beyond the reach of any imperial authority, African and Amerindian women provided not only sexual companionship but also valuable information, social and political capital, and access to regional markets. For example, the famous Portuguese merchant in sixteenth-century Senegambia, Ganagoga, "man of many languages," built his success by marrying the daughter of one of the important military authorities in the region. In similar fashion, French traders in eighteenth-century North America, known as *coureurs de bois* ("wood runners"), relied heavily on their Amerindian wives and their extended family networks. Unions like these generated enduring mixed communities of so-called *lançados* in Upper Guinea and *métis* in the Red River valley and what is now the area of Winnipeg in the northern plains. The iconic association of the English planter at Jamestown, John Rolfe, and Pocahontas, daughter of the Native chief of the region, though parallel in its promise, left no similar blended community.

On the other side, some African and Amerindian leaders made similar initiatives and adaptations, accepting Catholic baptism (as in Kongo) or sending their children to Europe for education. Others forged alliances with European men by offering them daughters or other females as wives to confirm long-term commercial commitments. For African and Amerindian elites, these relationships could facilitate international trade and diplomacy, opening up new possibilities for economic prosperity and military security. In Peru, Inca noblewomen's marriages to Spanish conquistadors gave them distinctive voices in the highest circles of colonial society, at the same time conferring the legitimacy of formal affiliation on Spanish invaders. Intermarriage with Hispanic immigrants in central Mexico probably aided Tlaxcalan noble families' efforts to preserve aspects of their former status throughout the colonial period. From the fifteenth-century arrival of Portuguese mariners and traders along the coasts of Upper Guinea, sub-Saharan African women formed comparable sexual and economic partnerships with Portuguese men. Known to the Portuguese by the respectful term *senhoras* or *nharas* (sources of the better-known French cognate, *signares*), these women came to wield considerable influence, becoming powerful as independent merchants themselves. While European traders and administrators may have treated their relationships with African or Luso-African women as temporary, the unions were clearly beneficial for both parties. Furthermore, many *nharas* retained and built their prestige and economic clout long after the deaths or departures of their European "husbands."

The children of these cross-cultural unions grew up in pluri-cultural milieus and thrived at the interfaces of European, African, and Amerindian commercial networks. The Portuguese and Cape Verdean traders known as *tangomãos* or *lançados* stayed in Africa for many years, adopting African customs; virtually all had African wives and culturally mixed families. Their Eurafrican descendants usually identified themselves as "Portuguese" and "Christian" in their engagements with officials from Europe, and, sometimes recognized as respected business partners, proved invaluable to later European merchants as intermediaries, interpreters, and pilots in intricate coastal waterways. Individuals of mixed European and Amerindian descent in the Americas likewise found respected places as go-

betweens and diplomats. Like the *lançados* of Upper Guinea, they moved through the borderlands of European settlements, near enough to Europeans to profit from their commerce but far enough away to lead non-European lives when they chose. Domingo Fernandes Nobre traveled into the interior of sixteenth-century Brazil to procure Amerindian slaves for Portuguese colonists at the coast; he wore body paint and feathers, practiced a hybrid religion, and took the indigenous name Tomacaúna. Two centuries later, along the Gulf of Mexico's northern rim, multiethnic statesmen like the Upper Creek leader Alexander McGillivray used their cultural skills in the struggle to maintain Amerindian sovereignty in the contested region of what is now southeastern Texas, Louisiana, Mississippi, Alabama, and Georgia, and which was alternately claimed by Spain, France, Britain, and the United States.

Blended communities formed throughout the early-modern Atlantic World around the nodes of commercial exchange between Europeans and local populations, but others were formed independently by exiles and refugees from Europe. Imperial histories tend to ignore these cross-cultural sexual unions because the European men (and occasionally women) who formed them were frequently coerced or semi-coerced migrants, excluded from official recognition and viewed in their own homelands as marginal. European military and administrative systems commonly relied on criminal exiles (*degredados, forzados, forçats*) as unpaid soldiers, convict laborers, or galley oarsmen. In various overseas colonies they would work alongside enslaved Africans, Amerindians, Roma people ("gypsies"), prisoners of war, and anyone else authorities could press into service in far-flung outposts. Convicts and orphans were sent to live with African or Amerindian communities to learn their languages for future service as interpreters. Orphan boys were sailors in Spanish, French, and Portuguese fleets. Female orphans, prostitutes, and other unmarried, impoverished women were sent to Angola, Barbados, Louisiana, and elsewhere as ostensible future spouses for European colonists. Religious minorities, too, became involuntary or ambiguous agents of European empires. In the 1490s Jewish children in Portugal were taken from their parents, forcibly baptized, and sent to São Tomé, while by the early seventeenth century—contemporary with

Puritan migration to New England—Sephardim and crypto-Jews managed to practice their faith openly as *tangomãos* in western Africa, beyond the reach of Iberian authorities.

If imperial histories centered on metropolitan control tell us little of the Europeans exiled, they tell even less of blended communities formed by Africans and Amerindians during the same era. The conventional history of empires also marginalizes the Africans carried into exile and service in the Americas as slaves. Dwarfing both free and coerced migration from Europe until well into the nineteenth century, this flow of over 10 million women, men, and children from Africa to the Americas between the early 1500s and the 1860s was one of the largest forced migrations known to history. While sub-Saharan African peoples had ample prior experience of long-distance trading and cross-cultural interactions, Africans first came into widespread contact with Amerindian peoples during the era of the transatlantic slave trade. In the Spanish Americas, African slavery initially overlapped with the widespread enslavement of Amerindians. While Spain outlawed the latter in its Indies during the 1540s, following the precipitous decline of the indigenous populations of the circum-Caribbean, multiple forms of Amerindian compulsory service persisted, including *encomienda* labor, the *mita*, and the *boga*. Elsewhere, from Brazil to French Louisiana, and from Dutch Guiana to New England, Amerindian slavery remained common until the late-1700s. Social relations between Africans and Amerindians rapidly spread beyond the realm of shared labor, extending also to sexual unions, marriages, and the formation of families, with African-Amerindian children described in various European languages as *zambahigos*, *cafuzos*, and *griffes*, or simply dubbed *mulatos*. Extant sacramental records in French, Portuguese, and Spanish Catholic regions also reveal Africans serving as godparents for Amerindians, and vice versa. Unsurprisingly, some European colonial administrations employed African and African-descended interpreters of Amerindian languages.

Shared experiences of servitude and a common need for survival invited further African-Amerindian interaction on the outskirts of Euroamerican population centers. Africans who escaped from slavery came into contact with autonomous or semiautonomous Amerindian groups, who sometimes incorporated the escaped slaves into their communities. In the same manner as some European castaways, escaped or shipwrecked slaves like Alonso de Illescas in sixteenth-century Esmeraldas (present-day Ecuador) managed to integrate themselves into Amerindian communities with marked success; the modern Garifuna (Belize) trace their origins to similar circumstances in the eastern Caribbean. When larger numbers of Africans and people of African descent fled slavery, forming independent maroon towns, their position in relation to neighboring Amerindian peoples varied considerably over time and place. Nearly indomitable maroon federations such as Bayano in sixteenth-century Panama and Palmares in seventeenth-century Brazil have been described as "African kingdoms," but even Bayano (and perhaps Palmares) incorporated Amerindians, especially women. In some cases, maroons are known to have raided Amerindian polities, murdering men and abducting women, while in others, maroon settlements developed in peaceful coexistence with nearby Amerindian towns. In the late 1700s and early 1800s, Florida's black Seminoles provided an example of an African–Amerindian political alliance, with former slaves and their families initially living in towns scattered among other Seminole towns.

During the same centuries that witnessed the growth and consolidation of western Europe's overseas military conquests, Africans, Amerindians, and some Europeans formed new blended communities, often on the borders of the areas under European control, and sometimes within them. While the vast majority of these groups came into being either directly or indirectly as a result of European expansion, "in-between" peoples provide evidence of ways that global interaction extended beyond the reach of European imperial authorities. Their stories also provide insight into African and Amerindian influences on European processes of establishing control and on the European migrants themselves involved. These communities highlight the historical contingency of individual and group identities throughout the early-modern Atlantic Era, in which racial, political, and religious identities were often far more fluid than imperial and national histories would lead us to believe.

DAVID WHEAT

Bibliography

Berlin, Ira. "From Creole to African: Atlantic Creoles and the Origins of African-American Society in Mainland North America." *William & Mary Quarterly*, 3rd ser., 53, no. 2 (April 1996): 251–288.

Brooks, George E. *Eurafricans in Western Africa: Commerce, Social Status, Gender, and Religious Observance from the Sixteenth to the Eighteenth Century*. Athens: Ohio University Press, 2003.

Metcalf, Alida C. *Go-Betweens and the Colonization of Brazil, 1500–1600*. Austin: University of Texas Press, 2005.

Restall, Matthew, ed. *Beyond Black and Red: African-Native Relations in Colonial Latin America*. Albuquerque: University of New Mexico Press, 2005.

Sleeper-Smith, Susan. *Indian Women and French Men: Rethinking Cultural Encounter in the Western Great Lakes*. Amherst: University of Massachusetts Press, 2001.

Brokers

The cross-cultural contacts of commerce in the Atlantic World, and the epidemiological challenges that Europeans faced in tropical disease environments, frequently led to the emergence of powerful local brokers in African port towns, who served as intermediaries between European seaborne merchants and the Africans who supplied the commodities they purchased, whether ivory, gold, or gum arabic, or the human captives they purchased as slaves. Although brokers appeared in other regions as well, they were arguably more common in Africa than in other parts of the Atlantic World because of the responsiveness of African suppliers to European demand for captives and commodities. Both the disease ecology and the linguistic diversity of Africa raised the costs of creating trade networks under European control. As a result, the economic benefits of relinquishing local commercial responsibilities to African brokers were considerable, even if Europeans frequently complained about the resulting independence of these semiautonomous brokers. Brokers in this sense, then, gained leverage over social or commercial transactions as go-betweens necessary for two other groups or individuals to engage as buyers and suppliers. They were middlemen, or intermediaries, who benefited materially and socially from performing these services. However, when one group simply contracted with agents or hired employees to represent it, it contacted buyers or sellers on the other side who were not brokers in the full autonomous sense of the term.

Brokers in Africa were most often coastal merchants who supplied exports to Europeans, paying African producers or merchants with imports they obtained from them in return. The most successful brokers operated on river systems or other well-defined trade routes and typically dominated at least one link in these trading systems, allowing them to interpose themselves as obligatory at those key transit points. Brokers of this kind received early attention from African historians, beginning with Kenneth O. Dike's *Trade and Politics in the Niger Delta 1830–1885*, which was followed by important works on the so-called canoe house system of the Niger Delta, including G. I. Jones's *Trading States of the Oil Rivers: A Study of Political Development in Eastern Nigeria*. While these early works focused on the commodity trades of the nineteenth century, they paved the way for later studies of earlier African merchants in the era of the slave trade. Such brokers, often women—called *signares*, or *nyaras* (also *nharas*), from *senhora*, or "lady" in the Portuguese-based trade language of the coast—accumulated significant capital in the form of urban houses, slaves, and boats, as well as cultural capital as translators and cross-cultural negotiators. Relations between European merchants and African brokers were based on trust and credit, despite cultural differences and frequent tensions.

Robert Harms applied a similar analysis to the Middle Congo, upriver from Malebo Pool, where Bobangi canoemen emerged as brokers between land-based merchants on the lower river and upriver suppliers. Because of the efficiency, and the effective power, of these intermediaries, Europeans never ventured very far inland or abandoned initial efforts at direct trade. A network controlled by the *signares* and *habitants* (local residents) emerged on the Senegal River by the 1740s, when Europeans learned the advantages of outsourcing the river trade to Africans. Using these brokers spared the lives of European sailors and merchants, otherwise exposed to horrendous rates of mortality from yellow fever and malaria. Brokers allowed Atlantic commerce to reach far into the African continent, even though European traders remained largely confined to the coast. African middlemen operating on the rivers of Atlantic Africa relied heavily on slaves to serve as sailors or canoemen to transport cargo and to protect their property. In almost all cases, skilled slaves had some opportunity to trade on their own accounts and to accumulate wealth, with the result that some purchased their freedom and became traders in their own right.

Brokers who worked on the river systems of Atlantic Africa, such as on the Lower Niger and the Senegal, occupied the middle segment in a classic three-part network of exchange. The traders of the Niger Delta relayed imports that they obtained from Europeans on credit to middlemen traders like the Aro, who moved throughout the Igbo-speaking hinterland of the Delta in search of captives, and later palm oil and other commodities. The network maintained by the Senegal *signares* and *habitants* connected French and British merchants to Muslim trading networks at river ports on the Upper Senegal. While these Muslim networks were often nearly invisible to Europeans, they in turn reached far inland, linking to Atlantic traders on the Senegal, the upper Gambia River, and the hinterland of the Gold Coast.

Another approach to understanding these African brokers stresses their intermediary role from the point of view of the enslaved. For captive Africans catching their first—often terrifying—view of the coast and European sailing ships, these "Eurafricans" or "Atlantic Creoles" introduced them to the alien and baffling world of Atlantic commerce. This more cultural approach to these intermediaries emphasizes how they brokered trade across the boundary between African and Atlantic cultures by virtue of belonging to both, or having knowledge of both. Although some of these brokers were the children of European traders or sailors and women of the communities of their African trading partners, a focus on their mixed racial backgrounds is unwarranted. The *lançados* (in Upper Guinea) and *pombeiros* (in Angola) were men of Portuguese origin, often criminals or New Christians, that is, nominal Jewish converts, and other outcasts who lived in local communities and had adopted African ways, married and produced mixed-race descendants who served as intermediaries in trade with Europeans. But the fortunes of these families were often volatile

and did not generally lead to stable, self-financed networks because they were unable to establish control over either the land or oceanic trade routes. While people of mixed race may have sometimes possessed the cultural skills required to broker cross-cultural trade, their knowledge was not conferred by their racialized identity.

The ports of West Africa, and the trade networks behind the coastal brokers, were full of people of other backgrounds who possessed similar skills. Many of these urban dwellers were slaves and worked for merchants, but they were not Eurafricans. Other variants of this interpretation focus on the so-called Atlantic Creoles and their knowledge of Christianity, European languages, technologies, and ways of thinking, often by virtue of living in an African port of trade. However, it is not clear why Africans with these skills are described as Creoles, except to contrast them with an erroneous stereotype of an unchanging Africa. A significant body of scholarship on Africans in the Atlantic has used the phrases "Atlantic Creoles" and "realization" to denote people in Africa who adopted European cultural practices or technologies (language, religion, and guns), sometimes including broad swaths of the populations, especially in West-Central Africa before the latter third of the seventeenth century. The patterns of at least partial conversion to Christianity cited in support of this interpretation in fact reflected the quite localized politics of the Kongo kingdom there and the unsuccessful efforts of its Christian elite to act as brokers in the region's trade with Europeans on the coast. In fact, Kongo's—and perhaps others'—incorporation of aspects of European culture did not meet the technical definition of *creolization*, which refers to the construction of a new culture rather than the perhaps strategically selected addition of foreign elements to an ongoing—in this case African—cultural tradition.

Political brokerage in Atlantic Africa, like that in Kongo, was rarely successful over the long run. When political authorities—whether the military regimes often called "kingdoms," the coastal composites of African trading houses known as "city states," or dispersed federations of trading communities resident among suppliers (or trading diasporas)—tried to broker trade with the Atlantic World by monopolizing it, the typical result was war. The African authorities who did try to use military power to establish monopolies or near-monopolies on trade with Europe, as in the early Kongo kingdom, or Alladaand (later) Dahomey trading through Ouidah (modern Benin), found their efforts challenged by more flexible rivals and opportunists. Rebecca Shumway's study *The Fante and the Transatlantic Slave Trade* illustrates these hazards through the experiences of a local federation that attempted to monopolize and broker trade between the Gold Coast and its hinterland. While these Fante merchants succeeded for a time, they paid a heavy price by provoking war with their highly militarized Asante suppliers of captives farther into the interior, leading eventually to invasion and defeat. The same dilemma was found at the port of Ouidah in the slave-trade era, illustrated in Robin Law's history. Ouidah was conquered by Dahomey, another strong inland military power, and the merchants who operated through the port struggled to maintain autonomy from their political overlords. They nevertheless played an important role in brokering Dahomey's sale of its own war captives, until the militarists there ran out of populations to raid and themselves became brokers in a transit trade in slaves from even farther inland, when they weren't defending themselves from military rivals.

Powerful brokers in Atlantic Africa succeeded through their control of strategic trade routes to and from the coast, not by force but through efficient transportation of imported goods toward the interior and returns of slaves and commodities to the Europeans. These economics of market organization explain why river-based brokers were the most successful. Entry into such a role required mobilization of considerable resources—boats, slaves, protection—as well as cross-cultural contacts. Networks of this kind, once established, endured for considerable periods of time. River-based traders did not try to control territory and paid duties for crossing boundaries maintained by military rulers who did. Rival political rulers, since the brokers posed no threats to their power, found them also useful as negotiators. Attempts to establish control of land-based trade routes were much more costly and uncertain. The most successful merchants carefully maintained political neutrality. When military authorities tried to broker trade, they blocked it, and the usual result was war and failure.

The prominence of commercial brokers in Atlantic Africa contrasted with their relative rarity in the Americas. Disease environments in the temperate latitudes of North America favored Europeans more than the native inhabitants, who had no immunities to Old World pathogens. With little constraint on European mobility and local residence, trade tended to be extensions of the Atlantic networks controlled by Europeans. The "Indian Trader" was usually a European living in Indian society, or a person of mixed origins. While the French created a "middle ground" between Europeans and Algonquians in the Great Lakes region of North America, to use the term of the author of the original study of these connections, where intermarriage was relatively frequent, powerful local merchant brokers did act as intermediaries in the fur trade or other trades of the region. The French, and later British, made gifts to Indian leaders, but trading was decentralized, and the costs of entry were low. It therefore operated through direct exchanges between European importers and the suppliers of the extracted commodities they sought.

JAMES F. SEARING

Bibliography

Dike, Kenneth O. *Trade and Politics in the Niger Delta 1830–1885.* Oxford: Oxford University Press, 1956.

Harms, Robert. *River of Wealth, River of Sorrow: The Central Zaire Basin in the Era of the Slave and Ivory Trade, 1500–1891.* New Haven, CT: Yale University Press, 1981.

Heywood, Linda M., and John K. Thornton. *Central Africans, Atlantic Creoles, and the Foundation of the Americas, 1585–1660.* New York: Cambridge University Press, 2007.

Jones, G. I. *The Trading States of the Oil Rivers: A Study of Political Development in Eastern Nigeria.* London: Oxford University Press, 1962.

Law, Robin. *Ouidah: The Social History of a West African Slaving Port, 1727–1892.* Athens: Ohio University Press, 2004.

Searing, James F. *West African Slavery and Atlantic Commerce: The Senegal River Valley, 1700–1850.* New York: Cambridge University Press, 1993.

Seibert, Gerhard. "Creolization and Creole Communities in the Portuguese Atlantic: São Tomé, Cape Verde and the Rivers of Guinea in Comparison." In *Brokers of Change: Atlantic Commerce and Cultures in Pre-*

Colonial Western Africa, edited by Toby Green, 29–52. New York: Oxford University Press, 2012.

Shumway, Rebecca. *The Fante and the Transatlantic Slave Trade*. Rochester, NY: University of Rochester Press, 2011.

Capitalism

"Ism" is the problem. Capital was everywhere. Capital made the Atlantic World go 'round, from the ships that moved people and goods from one coast to another, to the silver dug from the mountains of Mexico and Peru and minted into coins, to radically commodified labor in the form of enslaved persons, forcibly transported from distant places and turned en masse to producing commodities from which their alienation was total. The Atlantic World was made with capital, but where in all this was capital*ism*?

This essay borrows a rather neutral, not to say anodyne, definition of that loaded term from the *Oxford English Dictionary*: ". . . an economic system in which private capital or wealth is used in the production or distribution of goods and prices are determined mainly in a free market; the dominance of private owners of capital and of production for profit." Capitalism is easy enough to define (most reference works and textbooks offer something similar), but its emergence as historical practice is far more elusive. From the late Middle Ages the word *capital* (in English) was in common usage as a synonym for *stock,* the accumulated goods or wealth with which a merchant began a commercial venture. But the term *capitalism* denoting an economic system or a habitual set of practices and beliefs is a coinage of the late nineteenth century, emerging only at the end of the period this volume addresses. Adam Smith, whose *Wealth of Nations* (1776) is often seen as the manifesto of an emergent capitalism, used the word *capital* frequently, but never *capitalism.* By the time *capitalism* became common in European languages, it had already acquired negative connotations—money-loving, self-serving, antisocial, ruthless, oppressive. In the mid-nineteenth century, Karl Marx wrote of the capitalist as the worker's enemy, but not until later, in *Das Kapital* (1867), did he speak of capitalism as such. Even there he used the term only twice, though "capitalist" mode of production appears frequently.

Given this linguistic trajectory, it is plausible to suggest that capital made the Atlantic World, while the Atlantic World in turn made capitalism. This supposition is not intended as a whole-hearted embrace of the famous thesis of Eric Williams (1911–1981), a mid-twentieth-century critic of Britain's history of slaving and economic dominance in the Caribbean region, later prime minister of Trinidad and Tobago. Williams argued that the surplus value appropriated from the labors of West Indian slaves had formed the capital basis for Britain's industrial takeoff. Even today modified forms of Williams's pioneering study remain an active pursuit within the scholarly community. But this essay, rather than joining this ongoing quest to trace the gradual accumulation of capital in various centers of power, as if that were all that was necessary for the emergence of capitalism, aims instead to illuminate the Atlantic dimensions of the emergence of capitalism as a widespread system of beliefs as well as practices.

We may thus trace a series of interrelated shifts taking place gradually across the Atlantic World, and at varying rates in different locations, regarding the forms of use, ownership, control, and distribution of capital and its inherently related elements—natural resources, labor, and markets—that played important roles in the making of modern Western capitalism as a coherent ideology, for better or worse. These changes include first, a shift from merchant capital to productive or industrial capital; second, a shift from local and particular markets for high-value goods to large and widespread mass markets for standardized commodities; third, a shift from localized labor forces, heavily encumbered with mutual obligations between lord and liege, artisan and apprentice, master and servant, toward the prospect of free, mobile, unencumbered wage labor—with race-based slavery as a key and telling exception to this general development; and fourth, a general shift from government to private ownership of wealth, with the royally chartered corporation playing a critical intermediary role in the transition.

Although they are treated separately here, none of these four elements was independent of the others, and in many ways the roles they played were mutually constitutive. While this essay emphasizes the power of these elements in combination it does not propose an inevitable, evolutionary progression toward capitalism's triumph. Rather, each of these shifting controls over capital and its uses was shaped by contingent historical conditions in and around the early-modern Atlantic—differing soils, climates, and diseases; varying distances and the flexible development of technologies and transport systems; widely varying governmental structures and population dynamics; and uneven distributions of natural resources across space and time—particularities that gave these developments a peculiarly Atlantic cast.

Merchant Capital and Productive Capital

The beginnings of an Atlantic World lay at least in part in the long-standing interests of European merchants and the monarchies that sponsored them to bring goods that were rare, exotic, and expensive in Europe from faraway places where they were plentiful and cheap. Europe's elite consumers would get the luxuries they wanted—spices, currants, silks, cotton, porcelain—and merchants would get rich, so long as the costs and hazards of transport did not consume the profits. These risky ventures were not capitalism in the sense of investment in long-term productive infrastructure. They were just trade, and not very different from long-standing exchanges within Europe, such as the trade taking Bordeaux wines to Bristol. In Shakespeare's *Merchant of Venice*, Antonio's money is tied up in voyages to Tripoli, England, "the Indies," and Mexico—a telling indication of how the first Atlantic trade routes in the sixteenth century simply extended older Mediterranean, European, and Levantine patterns. These older luxury trades were profitable for very small numbers of merchants and made a few elite customers happier but did not transform the ways most people experienced their economic lives. However, the high costs and increased risks of exploring new routes to the Indies—both the southern and eastern route around Africa and the western route across the Atlantic—required greater capital investments in ships, provisions for crews, and risk management than shorter, well-integrated Mediterranean or European coastal trades.

The capital to support longer Atlantic ventures was already present in the Mediterranean commercial world, provided by the merchant banking houses of Venice and Genoa. However, Genoese merchants made a momentous turn to the production of sugar, which was in decline in the eastern Mediterranean, as a way to invest profits from their trading ventures. Before entering the Atlantic they had financed its development in Sicily, Castile, and southern Portugal and so were positioned to extend the cultivation of cane to the eastern Atlantic islands near Africa. They were also prepared to supply these integrated production systems, forerunners of plantations, with enslaved labor acquired in their wide-ranging trade routes, from the Black Sea to the coast of Morocco. The profits that these sugar factories—in effect a network of commercial colonies—generated for Genoa became a source of capital to which the competing kingdoms of the Iberian Peninsula—Castile, Aragon, and Portugal—turned at the end of the fifteenth century as they developed their own political economies. But the drive for expansion, especially in Portugal, grew as much from the crusading and chivalric ideology of its ruling family, seeking noble and honorable occupations for the crown princes and the heavily militarized aristocratic orders, as it did from commercial interests.

Portugal's location west of the Strait of Gibraltar, together with its resource-poor landscape, encouraged military adventures by its crusading warrior classes into northwest Africa and the nearby Atlantic islands, which Genoese bankers were happy to finance. As the military ventures hopscotched down the African coast in the mid-fifteenth century toward Senegambia, the Niger Delta, and beyond, the royal family claimed spiritual authority and seigneurial privileges over the lands they "discovered." But they licensed trading monopolies to Genoese or Portuguese merchants interested in the gold, pepper, ivory, and slaves made available in these regions by African merchants. This pattern of monarchical initiative, making way for commercial development and depending on the revenues it generated, became the model for Portugal's continuing expansion all the way down the coast of Africa to Kongo, Angola, and around the Cape of Good Hope into the Indian Ocean, culminating in the creation of the Estado da India under the military authority of the crown, through an appointed viceroy.

The implicit claim by the crown of Portugal to sovereignty over a discontinuous set of territories overseas—a maritime network of trading factories under the nominal political and spiritual authority of a European feudal ruler—protected the extension of Mediterranean-style merchant capital investment halfway around the world. The Atlantic coast of Africa and the shores of the Indian Ocean became for Portugal what the Mediterranean and Black Sea had been for Venice—not a landed empire in the Roman sense so much as a network of trading factories where people from a wide range of places congregated and became Portuguese in language, sometimes also in religion, and always in at least nominal political fealty, even if they never laid eyes on Lisbon.

The Spanish version of this military and commercial project, following upon the somewhat later "discoveries" of Columbus in the Western Hemisphere, was remarkably similar to Portugal's African and Asian initiatives in its balance of royal military and private, often foreign, commercial initiatives. The very different populations of the Americas and the diseases that ravaged them, however, made it possible for Spain to claim sovereignty over vast tracts of land and its residents—something more like the Roman Empire—that the commercial integration of Africa and Asia not only denied to the Portuguese but also made unnecessary. For both Spain and Portugal, though, and for the northern European kingdoms that followed their leads, the initial benefits of trade in the wake of conquest involved access to whole new worlds of luxury goods. The Americas offered exotic furs, tobacco, chocolate, and dyes from cochineal and logwood, as well as new tropical lands for producing familiar commodities such as sugar, rice, indigo, and, of course, unprecedented quantities of gold and silver.

Older forms of merchant capital investment remained the dominant model for many of these commodities. Furs, for instance, required the skilled labor of Native American hunters and curers of the pelts to produce the beaver and other animal hides highly desired in European luxury circles, depleting an inherently limited supply of these natural resources. Merchants invested in inventories of European-made trade goods—such as textiles, metal tools, and ceramics—to exchange with Native producers for furs but could in no way take control over the process itself, which required local knowledge, skill, and access to the lands of the continent's interior monopolized by Native Americans. These exchanges, too, were extensions of "just trade" from the European merchants' point of view, though they instigated new relationships between Native Americans and animal resources, geared toward production for exchange rather than for use.

However, within these emerging Atlantic trade networks, European merchants and the governments that supported them began to discover prospects for extending their investments, in much greater quantities and over much longer terms, into production. Sugar provides the prominent example. The commodity itself and the technologies for its production were broadly familiar to the Old World. But its transplantation across the Atlantic by the Portuguese in Brazil, and its subsequent development by Dutch, English, French, and Spanish successors in the Caribbean, thrived on two fundamental new factors that dramatically increased production. The first was the extensive tracts of land suitable for cultivation of the crop, land that was rapidly depopulated by Old World diseases and therefore appropriated by European conquerors at low cost. The second was the availability of large supplies of enslaved labor from Africa at prices affordable in the initial stages of investing in sugar. By sheer happenstance, Portuguese military contingents and merchants were present in Angola, in West-Central Africa, in the 1580s and 1590s when severe drought produced tens of thousands of starving refugees for purchase and shipment to the Spanish Americas and to Brazil at very low cost. It was this fortuitous indirect subsidy that eased the costly transition to intensive capital investment in sugar production on an unprecedented scale. Over the following century, with the addition of Dutch and then English commercial capital, the mature "plantation complex" emerged in the Caribbean, with sugar at the forefront of a general shift toward investment in production, as well as trade, in the Atlantic World.

Sugar was not the only example of an Atlantic World shift from mercantile- to production-oriented capital investment. The vast reserves of precious metals that Spanish conquistadors located in the mountains of Mexico and Peru—often imagined as a kind of windfall, a money tree on which Spain's fortunes grew—actually gave rise to an extraordinarily complex and capital-intensive system of industrial production of silver coinage. The development of mercury-based processes for separating silver from baser elements in the ore required large investments of capital in mining operations for both mercury and silver, and in the technical infrastructure for bringing the two together and conducting the mercury amalgamation process, then minting the purified ore into coins. Similarly larger investments can be found in other locations with respect to other commodities. Tobacco, rice, and indigo production in the southern parts of British America, for example, mimicked on smaller scales the plantation-complex model of sugar production. All shared in the growing prospects that steadier, less risky, more reliable profits could be made from expanding the production of desirable commodities and taking in smaller profit margins on larger volumes of production, as a substitute for the less reliable windfall profits sometimes acquired through risky long-distance trade.

The Rise of Mass Markets for "Luxury" Goods

The initial commodities that had lured merchant expansion into the Atlantic World were luxury items for wealthy elites well known to the merchant community: royalty and aristocrats with the highly developed tastes and sufficient wealth to command silks and spices, of which cane sugar was initially also an example. Such limited markets could not support production on industrial scales. Therefore the rise of mass markets of anonymous buyers at lower, accessible prices for what had once been strictly luxury goods marked a second major shift in the economic system of the emerging Atlantic World.

Sidney Mintz's classic study *Sweetness and Power* (1985) described this transition from personal economics to abstract markets supported by capital with respect to the marketing of sugar in Britain,

where a luxury good gradually became a daily necessity, even for the poorest of Britons. But other commodities, such as tobacco and wine, followed similar trajectories into ordinary homes, and, equally important, these mass markets spread to remote corners of the Atlantic World.

Thus long-distance traders no longer handled only luxury items destined for consumption by rulers and elites in a few centers of power—in the major cities and the courts of European kingdoms and African rulers, and at the wealthy urban centers of Mexico and the Andes. For instance, David Hancock has demonstrated how merchants and distributors worked with producers, consumers, and government authorities in the years between 1640 and 1815 to develop mass markets for Madeira wines across all of eastern North America and the Caribbean. Similarly, in the fifteenth century fine cotton goods from India had been luxury imports for European aristocrats, but by the eighteenth century European merchants used them as key components in the "bundles" of goods they sold for slaves in Africa. Nascent British textile mills found corresponding mass markets for their cheap but inferior cotton textiles among poor and enslaved workers and indigenous peoples throughout the Americas. A mass market for rum emerged in Africa, most of it produced in Brazil and shipped directly to Angola in exchange for enslaved Africans, allowing the direct trade between these ostensible colonies of Portugal to bypass entirely the Portuguese homeland. New England distillers produced smaller quantities of rum from molasses that local merchants bought with food and timber products they sold in the West Indies. Even mass markets for precious metals, in the form of coins, developed throughout the Atlantic World, as the millions of pesos minted at Potosí and Zacatecas worked their way into the pockets and purses of ordinary consumers, such as the New England farmers who used the "Pine Tree" shillings, half-shillings, threepence and twopence coins that the Massachusetts government minted from Spanish silver as the small change for everyday transactions.

In a similar sense, it might also be said that the indentured servants and enslaved persons at the core of American commodity production were themselves "produced" for a growing mass market. In the early days of the trades in bound labor, a perceived superabundance of workers in one place, such as the "masterless men" of Elizabethan and Jacobean England, made bound labor cheap, while the heavy demand for workers in the booming tobacco economy of the Chesapeake across the Atlantic made these laborers worth the considerable cost and risks of transporting them. Indentured servants were thus a labor variation on the early trades in luxury commodities: find something cheap in one place, expensive in another, and hope you can get it from point A to point B without too much transit cost. In much the same way, the momentary population surplus created by drought in late sixteenth-century Angola provided an opportunity for Brazilian sugar plantations to acquire affordable labor, even from Africa.

But as the scale of the plantation economies in the Americas grew, what had begun as niche markets grew into mass markets for productive labor. Like wines differentiated and defined by region and methods of production, or cloth woven in distinctive colors, patterns, and textures to brand it by its artisan producers, different "varieties" of enslaved persons, native to different regions of Africa or sold by merchants working through different trading forts or "castles," were marketed as having specific qualities desirable in the eyes of differing buyers. Owners of a relatively few sugar plantations in Brazil and the Caribbean could be counted on to purchase enslaved Africans in very large numbers, while large numbers of small tobacco farmers in the Chesapeake could be counted on to purchase enslaved Africans in very small lots. This insatiable demand meant that the "production" of captives in Africa through the warfare and indebtedness created by African merchant capitalists investing deeper and deeper into the African interior, as well as the distribution of these captives' labor through the Atlantic slave-trading networks dominated first by Portugal, then the Dutch, and later the English and French, could and did take place on unprecedented scales, comparable to the mass marketing of American commodities and European (and Asian) manufactures.

The development of reliable mass markets, in which the locations of high-investment commodity production were separated from the places of their consumption over oceanic distances, increased the anonymity of production, the expansion of production for exchange rather than for use, and the alienation of the producers from the returns on their labor—all significant aspects of the gradual transformation of capital and its investment from linking local producers and consumers into the "market" integration eventually understood as "capitalism."

The Rise of "Free" Wage Labor and the Invention of Slavery as an Anomaly

When Iberian expansion inaugurated the Atlantic World in the fifteenth century, working people, whether in Europe, Africa, or the Americas, were generally not compensated with money. Cities and towns, where merchants and skilled artisans worked and currencies circulated, were exceptions that proved the rule. Most work was rural, and in most (rural) places work tended to be governed by rules of mutual obligation, whether within the family or beyond. Masters, lords, or nobles who depended on the products and efforts of others often demanded long-term control of land, persons, or both, while in turn guaranteeing workers' access to land, protection, and sustenance in times of need. If labor for the lord produced surpluses sold on the market, the money gained might enrich the lord and buy luxury goods for his use, but little of it found its way into workers' hands. In one sense, the enslavement regimes of the Atlantic plantation complex represented simply the most extreme version of this general pattern of nonmonetized employment. Owners of slaves claimed permanent—and complete—control over their workers, and provided only the barest of subsistence goods in return, but owner and worker were still bound by a strict, if brutally stripped down, mutual obligation, a skewed version of the traditional "moral economy" as this reciprocal bond has been termed (Scott), in which peasants might be heavily taxed but also counted on the patronage and protection of their lords.

The gradual proliferation of capital investment in commodity production and the rise of mass markets for its products attenuated ancient norms of master-servant reciprocities, most noticeably in those Atlantic World locations where large-scale plantation slavery did not take hold. For example, in seventeenth-century New England, where investment in the slave system of English America was weakest, the local agricultural economy turned rapidly toward family farms for production of foodstuffs and timber to sell to West Indian plantation markets. Nonfamily servants who lived and worked within the household were often paid wages, sometimes in specie and sometimes, when hard money was scarce, recorded as book credits. But by the eighteenth century, with New England's growing engagement as both producer and consumer in the proliferating mass markets for Atlantic commodities (including money itself), it became increasingly possible for even unskilled workers to live independently on wages as compensation for their work. As money became more plentiful, and as other necessities of life (clothing, food and drink, land and housing) became available for purchase or rent with currency, it became thinkable for unskilled laborers to live without, or beyond, the bounds and bonds of mutual personal obligation.

Devotion to the illusion of the personal "freedom" associated with wage labor, often cast in political terms, was in part a direct result of the disappearance of these bonds of obligation. But it was also a function of the commodities' alienation from their producers and distance from their places of production. For instance, it was difficult for a free wage worker in the urban economies of Britain or North America to recognize that enslaved workers across the ocean in the West Indies were both producing surplus value that their owners claimed as profit and consuming the commodities generated in the farms of America and produced in the factories of Britain. Yet the monetary profits generated by slave labor and the commodities that slaves consumed were key elements in spurring the generation of money for wages and the proliferation of commodities that wages could purchase in Britain; slave labor on a grand scale in the tropical Americas made wage labor on a grand scale possible in parts of Europe and North America.

As the "free" (white) wage-work model emerged in some places as a viable alternative for employers and workers, forms of bound labor other than slavery—indentured servitude, for instance—gradually gave way. By paying workers in cash, masters and owners could avoid the heavy burdens of obligation that had required them to feed, clothe, and house workers over long periods, regardless of the quality or quantity of work performed or the varying seasonal needs for their efforts. They found it cheaper to leave workers to fend for themselves in the open market. The wage workers, so long as they were

relatively scarce and wages were high, as was often the case in North America before the mid-nineteenth century, gained the advantages of mobility to seek out the best rewards for their time and abilities—alternatives to the stability they had lost.

Free wage labor came to predominate in growing centers of economic production and political power on both shores of the Atlantic, such as London and the English Midlands or the booming port cities of British America and their hinterlands. With the rise of wages came an emerging sense that money was the new norm for engaging labor, accompanied by the gradual disappearance of indentured servitude, compulsory apprenticeships (abolished in England in 1814), and other vestigial forms of feudal labor relations. In this context of normalizing labor paid with cash wages, the slave-plantation system of the Americas appeared increasingly anomalous, rather than simply the more extreme end of a spectrum of forms of labor as a personal bond. If free labor now appeared to be the foundation of an independent element within the larger system of political economy, separate from and potentially opposed to the interests of capital, enslaved labor remained simply a form of capital, as fully owned and controlled by the master as any other element of production. As productive capital, slaves were the largest asset category in most of the Americas.

As consumers, the enslaved were completely alienated from money and its power to enable individual choice in consumption, an especially ironic exclusion considering how heavily banking relied on slaves as collateral for the credit that backed circulating notes and other securities. Banknotes in the American South commonly depicted slaves at work in the fields, which meant that workers in northern "free" states often carried pictures of slaves on the money in their pockets. By the eve of the American Civil War, a conflict over which of these two systems would prevail, free wage labor and slave labor had become the opposite ends of what had once been a labor continuum whose middle terms—forms of labor relationships between masters and workers that included mutual obligations and rights on both sides—had been hollowed out by the rise of mass production and mass markets. Yet despite their seemingly oppositional character, wage and slave labor were complementary parts of an integrated broader system of capital, in which enslaved human beings produced the commodities and secured the credit that financed the relative economic autonomy of the "free."

Ownership and Control: State, Corporate, and Private

As early as the fourteenth century, Europe had already possessed a remarkable example of industrial-scale mass production—the famous arsenal of Venice, with its assembly-line system that could turn out a fully equipped Venetian galley (a rowed warship) in a day. But the Venetian state—a council of the commercial city's leading patricians—operated this forerunner of Fordism to produce ships for the maritime power and glory of the most serene republic, not for the private profit of the arsenal's owners. Much of the early expansion by Mediterranean powers into the Atlantic World followed a similar combination of government power and private investment. In both Portugal's Estado da India and Spain's New World viceroyalties, crown legal sponsorship and military protection made investments in trade and production possible and profitable for private interests, and the crowns demanded major shares of the income from these ventures in return, such as the *quinto*—the Spanish monarch's claim to a fifth of all the gold and silver mined within its domains. The governments' military might and growing bureaucracy established forts and trading factories, and licensed royal monopolies that allowed producers and traders to develop the transatlantic economies.

Among the northern European colonial powers, the Dutch Republic, England's Tudor and Stuart dynasties, and—though to a lesser extent—France, often relied on chartered corporations of private investors rather than direct crown control as a means to finance and administer trading empires, especially in their earlier ventures. By the sixteenth century the royally chartered corporation was already an ancient form, a legal delegation of delimited sovereign powers to a defined group of subjects who promised to perform the crown's business within the rules of their charter, and in return could reap rewards in the form of profits or power or the pursuit of an ideal; medieval universities had been corporations chartered to protect the purity of knowledge, as it was understood at that time. The Dutch East and West India companies, together with the English East India Company, were the initial primary examples of extending this delegation of defined legal powers into the Indian Ocean and then also the Atlantic. They held broad powers to govern the regions consigned to them and possessed strong military arms to enforce their decisions and defend their interests.

In the Atlantic Ocean, perhaps because of the lesser potential for stunning windfall trading profits, the Dutch West India Company failed to establish the lasting powers of its Indian Ocean predecessor. Similarly, England's Royal African Company, established in 1672 as a royal monopoly by Charles II after the Restoration, failed to meet the booming demand for enslaved labor in England's growing plantation colonies in the Caribbean. A great deal of contraband trade and piracy emerged in the interstices of these competing corporations and government claims to territory in the Americas at the end of the seventeenth century, so much so that its volume and value may have rivaled or surpassed that of the chartered, legitimate trade. Ostensibly state-controlled enterprises—such as the *asiento* granted by the Spanish crown to a series of private investors, all foreign, to supply enslaved Africans to Spain's cities in the New World—were systematically exploited to conduct contraband trade in otherwise forbidden territories. In this competitive and only loosely administered context, smaller, more mobile private partnerships, family enterprises, or networks of coreligionists could maximize profits by operating across the porous margins of nominal legal regimes.

The large, state-chartered corporations with monopoly rights over Atlantic trade were giving way by the eighteenth century to private investment in commerce, the so-called mercantilist system, which tried to keep its profits within the taxable domains of monarchies. Only Spain, in the Americas, and Portugal, in Africa, continued to work through state monopolies until after midcentury, when both abandoned what had become losing bets. But to colonial merchants and commodity producers in North America, even Britain's indirect regulation through customs duties and navigation laws appeared increasingly oppressive and became one of the defining causes in the rebellion in the 1770s that sundered its empire. Capital assets under private ownership had outgrown the need for the government sponsorship that had protected the start-up phases of investments in the Atlantic, creating a growing sense of conflict between the interests of the crown and the interests of its most enterprising subjects.

In the wake of the War of American Independence, the chartered corporation experienced a resurgence as a business model, but in a form that separated government power and private capital, the two parties to the marriage of convenience that had previously integrated the Atlantic economy. The justification for the private privileges that had accompanied royal charters under the old regime had been that the corporation would perform some service for the public good that the crown itself, or private subjects without corporate privileges and powers, could not or would not do. In effect, the charter acknowledged the inability of early-modern monarchies to extend their effective reach beyond, and sometimes even within, their own home territories.

The new governments of the independent United States at the end of the eighteenth century were similarly weak, at both the state and federal levels. Struggling state legislatures accordingly granted corporate charters to private citizens for similar purposes—to build a bridge, a turnpike, a canal, a manufactory, or other infrastructure that would benefit the public constituencies to whom electoral politics had made them immediately and continuously accountable. But as the American economy recovered from war, and the democratic politics and legal framework of the new nation became more viable, citizen challenges gradually undermined the monopolistic privileges of private companies. Instead of eliminating corporate privilege altogether (the more democratic thing to do), state governments shifted from making occasional grants of corporate monopolies to creating general laws of incorporation, in effect opening the privileges of corporate personhood and power, formerly the gift of monarchs, to any private person or persons with the capital resources to use them. Similar measures in the legal regimes of other nations in the nineteenth century privatized the privileges that had once been tools employed by crowns to reward their favorites and made them widely available to the possessors of commercial, and increasingly industrial, capital. This transformation left modern economies in the hands of privileged private wealth, implicitly in competition with "free" waged workers, who were in fact highly dependent on its possessors for employment, and also opposed to government competition for investment in infrastructure and to the welfare of citizens unable to find work under conditions of employment that they control—all defended ideologically as systemic capitalism.

Conclusion

The general shifts traced separately in the four preceding sections may appear to have been linear developments over time from one end of an abstract spectrum to the other: merchant capital to industrial capital; niche markets to mass markets; bound labor to free wage labor; government ownership and control of capital to private ownership and control of capital. In reality, the process was never so simple or direct. Forms of economic enterprise could move back and forth, and historical conditions in any given place could create several different and perhaps even conflicting versions at the same time.

For instance, the merchant families of New England at the end of the eighteenth century, after generations of earning marginal profits by dealing in inexpensive local commodities, suddenly lurched back into the old-fashioned luxury trades to exploit new global markets, shipping Pacific Northwest furs to Canton and returning with silks and porcelains for the urban elites of Boston and New York, and ranging widely through the Indian Ocean trades formerly denied them under British monopoly restrictions. Yet within a very few years, thanks in large part to the vacillating course of the Napoleonic Wars and the inconsistent reactions of the U.S. government to them, these merchants converted their windfall profits in the China trade into capital-intensive textile mills at home in New England, owned on a corporate model and operated by waged workers turning out cheap cotton clothes for enslaved field workers in the Cotton South and the thriving sugar plantations of Cuba. The point is not that Boston's traditional merchant families became industrial capitalists overnight, rather that the proliferation of investment in production, mass markets, mobile and uprooted laborers, and flexible forms of private ownership made "capitalism" easy to latch onto anywhere in the Atlantic World by those with the resources to do so, and increasingly impossible for everyone else to avoid.

MARK PETERSON

Bibliography

Bakewell, Peter. *Silver Mining and Society in Colonial Mexico, Zacatecas 1546–1700.* 1971. Reprint, Cambridge: Cambridge University Press, 2002.

Coclanis, Peter, ed. *The Atlantic Economy in the Seventeenth and Eighteenth Centuries: Organization, Operation, Practice, and Personnel.* Columbia: University of South Carolina Press, 2005.

Dalzell, Robert. *Enterprising Elites: The Boston Associates and the World They Made.* New York: W. W. Norton, 1993.

de Vries, Jan. *The Industrious Revolution: Consumer Behavior and the Household Economy, 1650 to the Present.* New York: Cambridge University Press, 2008.

Eltis, David. *The Rise of African Slavery in the Americas.* Cambridge: Cambridge University Press, 1999.

Hancock, David. *Oceans of Wine: Madeira and the Emergence of American Trade and Taste.* New Haven, CT: Yale University Press, 2009.

Klooster, Wim. *Illicit Riches: Dutch Trade in the Caribbean, 1648–1795.* Leiden: KITLV Press, 1998.

Levy, Barry. *Town Born: The Political Economy of New England from Its Founding to the Revolution.* Philadelphia: University of Pennsylvania Press, 2009.

Miller, Joseph C. *Way of Death: Merchant Capitalism and the Angolan Slave Trade, 1730–1830.* Madison: University of Wisconsin Press, 1988.

Mintz, Sidney W. *Sweetness and Power: The Place of Sugar in Modern History.* New York: Penguin, 1985.

Morgan, Kenneth. *Slavery, Atlantic Trade, and the British Economy: 1660–1800.* Cambridge: Cambridge University Press, 2001.

Newitt, Malyn. *A History of Portuguese Overseas Expansion, 1400–1688.* New York: Routledge, 2005.

Schwartz, Stuart, ed. *Tropical Babylons: Sugar and the Making of the Atlantic World, 1450–1680.* Chapel Hill: University of North Carolina Press, 2003.

Scott, James C. *The Moral Economy of the Peasant: Rebellion and Subsistence in Southeast Asia.* New Haven, CT: Yale University Press, 1977.

Williams, Eric. *Capitalism and Slavery.* Chapel Hill: University of North Carolina Press, 1944. Fiftieth anniversary edition with new introduction by Colin A. Palmer. Chapel Hill: University of North Carolina Press, 1994.

Captivity, Native American

Practices of captivity in the pre-Columbian Americas must be understood as aspects of Native social and political systems and should not be conflated with European slaving systems introduced after 1492. Indian captive taking was neither a preliminary stage of modern slavery nor a hinterland offshoot of an Atlantic complex of commercial slavery. Diverse Native American captive practices had contexts, histories, origins, meanings, and purposes of their own. This essay distinguishes Native captive taking from European chattel slavery and explores overarching patterns of captivity within the geographic and cultural diversity of the Americas. Native forms of captivity evolved alongside European systems of bondage, but at its root Native captivity bore no similarity to European systems of coerced labor.

Native societies in different regions of the Americas held individuals captured in war, primarily women and children, as social, political, and cultural capital. Captives might possess a variety of open-ended and mutable social statuses but never ones that their children inherited. The fate of war captives ranged from ritual torture and sacrifice (usually limited to men), to use in prisoner exchanges, adoption as kin, or obligatory service to their captors. Yet, though their labor might be valued for its contribution to the household, family, or community, production was not the purpose of their capture, nor was capture aimed at gaining bodies to sell. The function of captives was not economic, but rather psychological and social.

Indigenous societies took captives in warfare to avenge or replace kin who had been killed or captured. Captivity might be an alternative to death on battlefields, offering captured men the opportunity for an honorable end through ritual torture and sacrifice. More often, captive taking targeted women and children, seeking those best suited for adoption and marriage, and thus for full assimilation into the captors' circles of kinship and community. Adoption functioned as a form of social rebirth, with the captive assuming a new identity within the captor's clan. Oftentimes, in matrilineal societies, female heads of clans held the authority to call for raids, to fulfill obligations of vengeance and mourning, and then to determine the fate of captives brought back from war. Some captives might also represent a variant to "gifts" of individuals given among leaders in expectation of reciprocal exchanges and alliance; they might have been the product of war but were also a currency of diplomacy. All captives came from groups deemed outsiders, strangers, or enemies of the captor's society—those with whom political bonds were absent but desired. Thus, captivity represented a violent extreme along a spectrum of exchanges of personnel among groups that had adoption and marriage at its other, pacific end and involved women and children in the politics of alliance.

Captive taking among Indian nations was limited in scale and, unlike in Africa, never involved long distance trade across the American continent, commercial or otherwise. Battlefield victory, revenge, and mourning were not measured in the numbers of captives taken; one or two might be sufficient to address the social or political exigencies of the moment. This held true among indigenous groups throughout the Americas, except for larger political systems like those of the Aztecs and Inca. In those empires, a combination of warfare, cosmology, and sacrificial complexes demanded the capture of prisoners of war, often in large numbers, for human sacrifice of the imposing magnitude required to maintain cosmic order. These military regimes demanded tribute in the form of obligatory service as a separate function, to keep people in subsidiary or allied nations in place. Yet, even for captives destined for sacrifice, kinship shaped the relationship of captor and captive—proscribing the involvement of the captor in any sacramental cannibalism, owing to the mystical familial bond presumed between the two. Similarly, among the Tupí in Brazil, marriage of a captive (male or female) to a member of a captor's family was not uncommon, as captives might become assimilated members of the household for extended periods of time before sacrifice.

Native American practices of captivity changed with European invasion, but even as Europeans bought captives to hold or sell as slaves, Native systems did not become subsumed into this European practice. Native "captives" became "slaves" only when sold to Europeans. Captive raiding in southeastern North America dramatically increased in scale as British traders commodified Native war captives to use and sell in labor regimes there and in the Caribbean. Some Indian groups, like the Westos in western Virginia, pursued capture and trading as a form of territorial expansion as they migrated into South Carolina, seeking new lands. For most other indigenous communities, trade incentives, escalating debt, and fear of their own enslavement led to systematic raiding and selling of enemy captives to their British trade partners. British agents thereby expanded the volume and reach of indigenous captive taking in the second half of the seventeenth century, tied it to European slave trading, and sent 30,000 to 50,000 Indians to brutal enslavement, primarily in the West Indies. For Native populations, this extension of captive taking into systematic slaving put communities on the move (both those raiding and fleeing, as well as the resulting captives and refugees) and, in turn, created conditions that enabled the spread of European epidemics and paved the way for massive Native depopulation. These disasters created a geopolitical opening essential to subsequent European settlement and territorial expansion, as well as to the plantation system and enslavement of Africans in North America.

Yet even the levels of raiding in the Southeast that ultimately tied Native communities to Atlantic slave systems involving both Indians and Africans might still be seen as rationalized extensions of strategies of captive taking. As Native systems of bondage allowed for the assimilation of enemy captives, these practices guided Native decisions regarding the later incorporation of Africans into their communities as outsider kin rather than chattel.

In the Northeast, members of the Iroquois Confederacy—known to Europeans as the "Romans of the Native world" for their devotion to warfare and capture of enemies—were not tempted to sell captives into European slaving systems, even as they incorporated French and English fur traders into the networks connecting them with Atlantic World economies. The presence of European traders exacerbated the spread of diseases, and the resulting demographic losses reinforced the Iroquois practice of taking captives to stabilize declining populations. Captive raids increased in the seventeenth century, targeting Iroquoian-speaking neighbors who might be assimilated into their communities as full-fledged members and kin, then waned in the eighteenth century. Others throughout North America similarly found captives a source of demographic stability, even expansion. Comanches on the southern plains took aim at Indian and Hispanic populations in New Mexico and northern Mexico as sources of additional wives and children needed in economies built around horse pastoralism and the production of buffalo hides.

In the Great Lakes region and the Southwest, where Spaniards and French stimulated Native practices of warfare and captive taking, one sees the strongest evidence of Native economic and political systems controlling European captive exchange. Indeed, practices in these interior regions indicate that Indian trading partners or geopolitical rivals had the power to demand that Europeans model their behavior to fit the demands of their societies.

In New France (eastern Canada and the Great Lakes region), Indian nations used exchanges of captives—their most prized possessions—as hostages to seal pacts that gained them trade with the French. Even within French communities, however, custodians of these captives enjoyed no security of ownership, nor did captives face the permanent status of slaves. Standards of native diplomacy meant there was always that possibility of further return or exchange. Moreover, even as the French in the colony of New France held captives as "slaves," their military and trade dependence on Native allies prevented such bondage from becoming racialized, because individuals of only certain nations—enemies of the Frenchmen's Native allies—could be taken to confirm a pact. In Louisiana and the Great Plains, French traders viewed the purchase of female captives much as they did marriages with female relatives of their trading partners: as a means of gaining kinship standing with their counterparts, as well as securing sex and familial reproduction. The French thus adopted Native systems of kinship regarding female captives.

In the Southwest, powerful Navajo and Comanche nations expanded their assimilation of captives for domestic purposes as the Spanish presence accelerated their sheep and horse pastoral economies. Spaniards responded in kind when they, too, absorbed captives into their own society. Spanish

colonists took Native prisoners of war and ransomed captives from their Indian neighbors, declaring these prisoners and captives *criados* ("those raised up"), who owed service within their owner's household. Indian captives thereby became integrated into Spanish households as servants to be instructed in Christianity and Spanish "civilization." In the process, the *genízaro* population (from the Turkish word for janissary, *yeniçeri*, referring to servants trained as soldiers) became independent frontier settlers and military auxiliaries, owning their own lands and gaining a modicum of recognition within colonial society. Ultimately, *genízaros* made up one-third of the inhabitants of the New Mexico colony.

The fates of "white" captives in the hands of Indian captors also followed the rules of previous Native practices, though it might be argued that prisoner exchanges as part of diplomatic strategies increasingly outweighed considerations of adoption and assimilation. Women and children remained the primary targets of such captive taking, and could be incorporated into Native communities and families through adoption and marriage. Europeans often refused to recognize such kinship ties, however, always considering Europeans and Euroamericans living among Indians to be "captives" and failing to accept their refusals to return to white society. More pointedly, they labeled as "rape" any relationship that resulted in white women giving birth to children by Indian men, because they could not fathom the possibility of a consensual relationship qualifying as marriage across the line they believed separated "civilized" from "savage."

Yet attributed kinship mitigated the possibility of sexual abuse: because captives were to be adopted into families, no Native captor would risk an act that would amount to incest. Kinship ties were sometimes hard for European observers to deny. In an infamous moment, Pontiac's War ended in 1764 with British treaty demands that Shawnees and Delawares return all English captives taken in the previous ten years of warfare, resulting in heartbreaking resistance as the "captives" sobbingly fought to remain with their Native "captors," and their English "rescuers" had to tie them to their horses to thwart escapes. Several of the women succeeded in fleeing back to their Indian families. On the other hand, Euroamericans were not often desirable targets of adoption, especially by the late eighteenth and early nineteenth centuries. Even as Comanche captive raiding increased steadily over that time, so that adopted captives came to represent 20 percent of their population, that group was made up primarily of Indians (60 percent) and Spanish Mexicans (40 percent). Anglo-Americans like Cynthia Ann Parker, who became the wife of a Comanche leader and the mother of Chief Quanah Parker, who guided Comanches in their transition to reservation life, were rarities despite the popularity of white-captivity narratives based on them.

Native captivity was rationalized by kinship, not race. It sought to meet political and social needs rather than labor and economic ones. Instead of resulting in bondage in perpetuity through an enslaved woman's children, it culminated in adoption of captives and the integration of their children into the families and communities of the captors. Grounded as it was in social, cultural, political, and religious imperatives, captivity found its greatest importance in maintaining order on cosmological, political, and familial scales. Only with European invasion did Native systems of captive taking become tied to those of Atlantic slavery, and only in the hands of Europeans were Native "captives" transformed into "slaves."

JULIANA BARR

Bibliography

Brooks, James. *Captives and Cousins: Slavery, Kinship and Community in the Southwest Borderlands*. Chapel Hill: University of North Carolina Press, 2002.

Gallay, Alan, ed. *Indian Slavery in Colonial America*. Lincoln: University of Nebraska Press, 2010.

Kelton, Paul. *Epidemics and Enslavement: Biological Catastrophe in the Native Southeast, 1492–1715*. Lincoln: University of Nebraska Press, 2007.

Rushforth, Brett. *Bonds of Alliance: Indigenous and Atlantic Slaveries in New France*. Chapel Hill: University of North Carolina Press, 2012.

Whitehead, Neil L. "Indigenous Slavery in South America, 1492–1820." In *The Cambridge World History of Slavery, Volume 3, AD 1420–1804*, edited by David Eltis and Stanley L. Engerman, 248–271. New York: Cambridge University Press, 2011.

Cartography

When Benjamin Franklin decided to reveal his growing understanding of the warm current that connected the eastern seaboard of Britain's American colonies with northern Europe, he did so by publishing a curious chart of the "gulph stream": a printed map that showed a thick strip of dark water flowing up the coast of North America, jetting into the wider Atlantic toward the British Isles, and another similarly shaded zone returning in a southerly fashion, circling back to tie these two continents together like a transoceanic wedding band. Franklin's utilitarian impulse, on land and on sea, was of course notorious, and he hoped this map would convince the British postmaster general that ships could save two weeks on their transatlantic journey by following currents that simple American fishermen—whalers, for the most part—had already known about for decades, if not centuries. In Franklin's day, it was hard to imagine the concept of a connected Atlantic Ocean without recourse to a map; in this case, the Euroamerican cartographic vision that Franklin put forward owed much to mariners' knowledge that had not previously been codified through a cartographic representation.

The reigning concepts in studies of the Atlantic World in Franklin's day, as in our own, have often been depicted through cartography. Bringing continents, oceans, and the flows of peoples, commodities, and waterways together under a single umbrella term was an impulse that correlated to the ability, beginning in the late fifteenth century if not before, of European states and their agents to conceptualize particular natural, cultural, and political phenomena within a visual frame. Often such visualizations came in the form of elegant sheets of lambskin, parchment, or paper, produced with stunning visual imagination in the commercial print shops of Italy and the Low Countries, which in turn thrived on the ever-increasing popular thirst for this new and entertaining mode of understanding places otherwise unimaginable. Following the earliest fleets to reach newly discovered continents across an ocean-sea from Europe, the Portuguese and Spanish already understood that their posses-

Figure 1. "A Chart of the Gulph Stream," published by Benjamin Franklin in the late 1700s.

sions in the Old and New worlds—connected by water—could be conceived as a unified and interdependent community and drawn as such.

This fact, dramatically portrayed in the margins of the earliest maps they produced, which showed spouting sea monsters, exuberant tropical birds, and colorful scenes of plumed Amerindians at work and play, came to life in the expansive cartographies of the Cantino Planisphere (1502), the Miller Atlas (1519), and Sebastian Münster's *Cosmographia* (1544). As demand for raw materials changed and monoculture came to the fore, Europeans became less dependent on indigenous labor and subsequently more reliant on enslaved Africans. Consequently, such terms as the *Ethiopic Sea* occurred with greater frequency within cartographic representations, demonstrating the increasing importance of the southern part of the Atlantic and its connections to Africa. These images, whether in atlases or loose-leaf maps, pulled together a world that lay beyond Europe and that had previously been imagined in less spatial, and indeed more imaginative, veins, a world as much of geographical uncertainty as littoral specificity.

Nevertheless, the very tangible connections that developed in the centuries that followed European engagement with the Atlantic World were at least conceptually dependent on this early understanding of a unified geographical space, as articulated in the maps that were produced largely in early-modern Europe's geographically ambitious political and military centers. Maps were central for the conceiving of this space, but the cartographic articulation of an Atlantic World—especially for the Portuguese and Spanish—emerged as a result of very early practical engagement with the geographical features of Europe, the African coast, and the plantation cultures of the Caribbean, none of them predicted, including the northeastern coast of South America. Centuries later, the scholarly impulse to study Africa, the Americas, and Europe from interconnected perspectives of this kind emerged also, by and large, as a result of political engagements, especially within the Anglo-American world, whose historians—including such twentieth-century luminaries as Herbert Baxter Adams and Herbert Bolton—sought to place the historical narrative of the United States into this broader frame. The

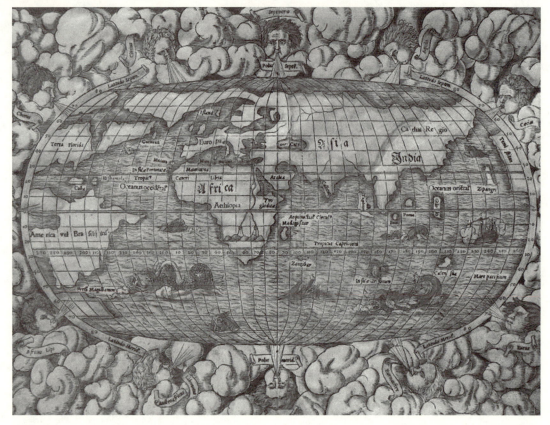

Figure 2. Map of the world printed in Sebastian Münster's 1544 *Cosmographia*, an example of the pictorial representations typical of the period.

model received an even stronger impetus in the wake of World War II and the establishment of institutions such as the Atlantic Council of the United States, the North Atlantic Treaty Organization (NATO), and other military alliances privileging connections across the North Atlantic.

This geopolitically motivated interest in a North Atlantic history grew out of an earlier, more general interest in imperial history—an approach that followed the colonizing programs of several European powers. This occasionally nostalgic celebration of nineteenth-century economic ambitions would end up dividing the Atlantic conceptually into separated imperial Atlantics: Spanish, Portuguese, Dutch, English, or French. In turn, this privileging of Atlantic worlds defined linguistically or politically neglected the underlying integrating geography of a maritime core and the connections that it enabled to the interior of surrounding continents,

such as the trans-Appalachian west in North America, or the Andes or Amazon regions in South America, or especially to other oceanic spaces, including the Pacific and Indian oceans.

Since representing the Atlantic region as a set of separate linguistic or imperial "Atlantics" obscures the interlinked historical processes built out of its geographical position as connector among the various strands of local and regional histories, we might, as John Brian Harley and other historians of cartography have cogently argued, recognize that our conventional maps—with their neat arrangements of continental masses around an empty blue block of water—frequently functioned in the service of empire. Against this panoptically derived Atlantic, and instead tracing geographical contours following historical actors themselves, we might rather see multiple connections at different scales: from mixing along the docks of port cities to commodities that traversed the oceans and individuals—in bondage or not—who circulated on the high seas. Emphasizing itineraries—the movement of peoples, commodities, and ideas across imaginary geopolitical and linguistic boundaries—enables Atlantic history to achieve its proper aim of connecting regions that anachronistic categories have rendered separate and distinct. The result is a more historical and cosmopolitan, and less teleological and nationalistic, Atlantic space, one that accommodates the fine-grained stories that broader and more abstract perspectives tend to efface.

Avoiding the abstract, and often ahistorical, boundaries imposed on an open and fluid Atlantic World allows historical actors—animate and inanimate, including winds and currents—to follow their own courses, just like Franklin's meandering Gulf Stream, and provides an invitation to historians of other oceanic spaces—the Pacific, the Indian Ocean, and the Arctic, for instance—to see the Atlantic region as a model for other interconnections. In addition, focusing on individuals allows scholars to include radically different African and Native American perspectives on geography in the production of cartographic knowledge. Among European forms, the use of individual perspectives includes literary mapping and the use of texts as forms of graphic devices. Traversing the Atlantic World along the itineraries of its makers enables historians to consider spatial representations as social creations expressed in colonial-era legal papers and other texts that reformulated space in the process of encountering collaborators formerly unknown. These new geographies emerged in spaces removed from the ocean itself but nonetheless projected from processes created by its existence.

Such was the case in the Andes, physically nearer to—and approached by Europeans from—South America's Pacific coast than to the Atlantic Ocean, but nonetheless a geographical region that Spanish silver mining integrated into transatlantic commerce, political claims, and military coercion. Indigenous scribes, notaries, and artists using the spatial and alphabetic literacies of the Inca (Quechua-speaking) masters of those mountains produced a series of hybrid map-grids, artistic frescoes, and traditional scripted texts different from those proposed by the religious and secular logics of the arriving Spaniards. The Relaciones Geográficas,

a series of questionnaires sent out in 1577 by Philip II in order to acquire geographical knowledge of Spain's newly conquered territories in America, also integrated local knowledge systems and communal representations of New World geography.

These geographical concepts of indigenous peoples of the Americas entered the historical record as parts of European cartographic representations, frequently without acknowledging their Native sources. In the Rio Branco region of the Brazilian Amazon, for instance, when the Luso-Brazilian naturalist Alexandre Rodrigues Ferreira (1756–1815) encountered an Amerindian on his way from the Atlantic port city of Belém do Pará, he obtained a map from his indigenous source that he passed along to one of the primary mapmakers of the Portuguese. Through mental maps, lived experience translated orally to Europeans, and other forms of spatial understanding such as stick-charts and ephemeral drawings, indigenous peoples from throughout the Americas conceptualized geographic space alongside their European interlocutors, although only some of this knowledge ever ended up being placed on European maps or even described in accounts of European exploration, despite a keen attention throughout the early-modern period to indigenous practices that were represented as icons, toponyms (place-names), narrative descriptions, and cartouche (small oval-framed) depictions.

While only a small minority of Africans made any use of Atlantic coastal waters before the arrival of Europeans, their experience and geographical knowledge also influenced European perceptions of the broader Atlantic World. Angola and Brazil, for instance, were connected in the era of the slave trade by direct mercantile and sociocultural links centered along an axis across the southern seas, which supplements the European fulcrum for triangular transatlantic economic engagements. The eighteenth-century itinerary of an African-born man, who became known as Domingos Álvares, from Benin to Pernambuco and on to Portugal, is a telling example of how human geography can be told through the prism of African healing: his medical practices in Africa and Brazil yielded an "ability to collapse time and space into a unity of human and spiritual power," which in turn challenged Western ideas about history as "chronologically ordered and geographically bound" (Sweet, 231). These alternative epistemologies of time and space lead us to question exclusively European, and geostrategic, representations of Atlantic geography and point in the direction of exploring new ways of thinking about mapping and charting the maritime and terrestrial worlds connected by human movements and perceptions as well as by currents and commodities.

NEIL SAFIER

Bibliography

Bailyn, Bernard. *Atlantic History: Concept and Contours.* Cambridge, MA: Harvard University Press, 2005.

Carney, Judith, and Nicholas Rosomoff. *In the Shadow of Slavery: Africa's Botanical Legacy in the Atlantic World.* Berkeley: University of California Press, 2011.

Ferreira, Roquinaldo. *Cross-Cultural Exchange in the Atlantic World: Angola and Brazil during the Era of the Slave Trade.* New York: Cambridge University Press, 2012.

Greene, Jack P., and Philip D. Morgan, eds. *Atlantic History: A Critical Appraisal.* New York: Oxford University Press, 2009.

Rappaport, Joanne, and Tom Cummins. *Beyond the Lettered City: Indigenous Literacies in the Andes.* Durham, NC: Duke University Press, 2011.

Safier, Neil. "The Confines of the Colony: Boundaries, Ethnographic Landscapes, and Imperial Cartography in Iberoamerica." In *The Imperial Map: Cartography and the Mastery of Empire*, edited by James Akerman. Chicago: University of Chicago Press, 2009.

Sweet, James H. *Domingos Álvares, African Healing, and the Intellectual History of the Atlantic World.* Chapel Hill: University of North Carolina Press, 2011.

Center-Periphery Analysis

The sociologist Edward Shils first used the concept of center and periphery to analyze systems composed of unequal parts in an influential interpretive essay published in 1961. Premodern societies, he contended, consisted of a center with a well-formed and charismatic system of values and authority, but that authority was attenuated by distance. Lacking sufficient coercive resources, the center was unable to impose its values upon the distant peripheries, which became pockets of independence within a loosely organized polity. This analytical approach has been prominent among the ways that scholars have thought about the relationships among the regions composing the Atlantic World.

In the 1980s, Jack P. Greene applied Shils's framework to the study of constitutional arrangements in the early-modern British Atlantic, emphasizing the agency of the peripheries in negotiating those arrangements. Also in the 1980s, the historical geographer D. W. Meinig used the concepts of center, core, periphery, and distance decay to depict the organization of the emerging Atlantic World. Meinig saw the Atlantic World as an integrated sequence: first, the European core regions, which had their industrial hinterlands, Atlantic ports, and outports; these core regions had parallel communities overseas, which were divided into colonial ports, frontier entrepôts or trading centers, and inland outposts; and these in turn were linked to Indian core areas of powerful intermediary tribes, which had hinterlands of their own, for hunting and trading with partners even more remote from the European cores.

In the late 1990s historians of Atlantic empires further expanded this framework, comparing the processes of secondary colonization by which colonial peripheries developed peripheries of their own. For example, A. J. R. Russell-Wood used the geographic concepts of Umland (hinterland) and Vorland (areas contiguous to a trading center) to describe direct contact between Portuguese Brazil and Portuguese Africa as a linkage of periphery to periphery. Amy Turner Bushnell complicated the typology of peripheries by distinguishing the settled ecumene from the trading sphere of influence and from the ephemeral cartographic claim to sovereignty and by applying the differentiating concepts of strategic or nonstrategic, internal or external, and significant or insignificant to margins and frontiers.

One of the most influential uses of the center and periphery concept was that of historical sociologist Immanuel Wallerstein. In his schema, strong European core-states with complex economies and systems of waged labor presided over an emerging world economy that in turn dominated a semi-periphery of unpaid sharecropping and tenancy and a more distant periphery of weak or no states, simple economies, and systems of forced labor.

Although Wallerstein's concept of a world-system made its way quickly into the language of scholarship, historians of his peripheries—Africa, Latin America, Asia—and semi-peripheries—eastern and southern Europe—faulted the conceptual scheme for granting too much power to the cores, echoing the accent on initiatives beyond the core that Greene had proposed in his initial application of Shils's sociological model. Steve J. Stern concluded in 1998 that world-system analysis had arrived too late for Latin America and the Caribbean, where a well-worked "dependency" theory was already in place, providing an alternative political-economic explanation of peripherality and underdevelopment, and where a general "crisis of theory" was causing local intellectuals to reject any theory that did not take regional particularities into consideration.

In the early years of the new millennium, however, center-periphery theory informed understandings of relationships among the peripheries. Introducing the concept of "entangled" empires, Eliga H. Gould pointed out that the English-speaking Atlantic World originated as a Spanish periphery. Lauren Benton related European law and sovereignty to the geography of empire. Juliana Barr and Kathleen DuVal showed that Indian history could be written from an Indian and continental perspective instead of the Atlantic World model, which is inherently centered on European cores. Brian DeLay, mining archives in both the United States and Mexico, disregarded the political boundaries of the early-modern metropoles and the succeeding modern nation-states to frame the southwestern borderlands from the perspectives of the Comanches and Apaches. Anthropologist Robbie Ethridge, working on the southeastern "shatter zone" of indigenous slavery, demonstrated that world-system analysis retains its value. Center-periphery theory has proven to be a fertile approach to the Atlantic World, illuminating the historical processes that linked its distant centers and peripheries and comprehending their multiple perspectives.

AMY TURNER BUSHNELL

Bibliography

Barr, Juliana. *Peace Came in the Form of a Woman: Indians and Spaniards in the Texas Borderlands*. Chapel Hill: University of North Carolina Press, 2007.

Benton, Lauren. *A Search for Sovereignty: Law and Geography in European Empires, 1400–1900*. New York: Cambridge University Press, 2010.

Bushnell, Amy Turner. "Indigenous America and the Limits of the Atlantic World, 1493–1825." In *Atlantic History: A Critical Appraisal*, edited by Jack P. Greene and Philip D. Morgan, 191–221. New York: Oxford University Press, 2009.

Daniels, Christine, and Michael V. Kennedy, eds. *Negotiated Empires: Centers and Peripheries in the Americas, 1500–1820*. New York: Routledge, 2002.

DeLay, Brian. *War of a Thousand Deserts: Indian Raids and the U.S.-Mexican War*. New Haven, CT: Yale University Press, 2008.

DuVal, Kathleen. *The Native Ground: Indians and Colonists in the Heart of the Continent*. Philadelphia: University of Pennsylvania Press, 2006.

Ethridge, Robbie. *From Chicaza to Chickasaw: The Transformation of the Mississippian World, 1540–1715*. Chapel Hill: University of North Carolina Press, 2010.

Gould, Eliga H. "Entangled Histories, Entangled Worlds: The English-Speaking Atlantic as a Spanish Periphery." *American Historical Review* 112, no. 3 (June 2007): 764–786.

Greene, Jack P. *Peripheries and Center: Constitutional Development in the Extended Polities of the British Empire and the United States, 1607–1788*. Athens: University of Georgia Press, 1986.

Meinig, D. W. *The Shaping of America: A Geographical Perspective on 500 Years of History*. 4 vols. New Haven, CT: Yale University Press, 1986, 1993, 1998, 2004. Volume I, 258–267.

Shils, Edward. "Centre and Periphery." In *The Logic of Personal Knowledge: Essays Presented to Michael Polanyi*, 117–130. London: Routledge & Kegan Paul, 1961.

Stern, Steve J. "Feudalism, Capitalism, and the World-System in the Perspective of Latin America and the Caribbean." *American Historical Review* 93, no. 4 (October 1988): 829–872, and Stern's exchange with Wallerstein in the same issue, 873–897.

Wallerstein, Immanuel. *The Modern World-System*. 3 vols. New York: Academic Press, 1974, 1980, 1989.

Christianity

European Christianity framed many intercultural encounters, exchanges, and conflicts in the fifteenth century, as Europeans began venturing more systematically into the Atlantic World. The Roman Catholic Church had already had a long history with non-Europeans and non-Christians beyond its Mediterranean core. The papacy, as the divinely appointed head of the universal Church, claimed the authority to dictate Christians' relations with polities and populations outside of Christendom—from its militant support of the Crusades, including the "reconquest" of the Islamic emirates of Iberia, to its diplomatic and missionary engagements extending into China.

For this reason, the fifteenth-century popes felt responsible for issuing bulls defining the territorial claims and duties of their favored Catholic monarchs. For example, Dum Diversas (1452) authorized the kings of Spain and Portugal to conquer and enslave Muslims and pagans. Although the papacy had in mind Islamic rivals in Iberia and the Mediterranean, the bull tacitly facilitated Iberian naval expeditions and the incipient trade in enslaved Africans, already by the 1440s established in Portugal. Impressed with Portuguese successes in the Azores, North Africa, and the coast of West Africa, the pope issued Romanus Pontifex (1455), which reaffirmed King Afonso's right to wage "just" wars in defense of the faith against so-called infidels and to enslave them. Although Sixtus IV's Aeterni Regis (1481) granted Portugal possession of all territories they might find south of the Canary Islands, Spanish influence on the papacy grew after Columbus's voyage, especially under Pope Alexander VI (1483–1498), who hailed from Valencia.

In 1493 Alexander VI issued a series of pronouncements collectively known as the Bulls of Donation. The two most important of these were Inter Caetera, which specifically commanded the monarchs of Castile and Aragon, Ferdinand and Isabella, to conquer and convert the "barbarous nations" of the world, and Dudum Siquidem, which sanctioned Spanish territorial expansion west of a vaguely defined line beyond the Azores, despite earlier papal guarantees given to Portugal. The diplomatic controversy generated by Columbus's voyages and these new papal bulls led the Spanish and Portuguese monarchs to negotiate the Treaty of Tordesillas (1494), which imposed a line of demarcation along a meridian 370 leagues west of Cape Verde. According to this treaty, the Spanish had a claim to lands and oceanic routes west of this line, while the Portuguese secured their claims to the east.

The popes' authority to define the terms of Iberian activities beyond the confines of Christendom rested upon the medieval model of a universal monarchy, developed to legitimize the papacy's call for the Crusades, its direct confrontations with the Holy Roman Emperor, and its independent diplomatic engagements with the Byzantines, Mongols, and Ottomans. Yet papal power had begun to weaken in the fourteenth century during the Avignon Papacy and the crisis of competing claimants to the throne during the Western Schism (1378–1417). The papacy, restored to Rome, would be dealt another serious blow in the early sixteenth century by the evangelical militants of the Reformation. Protestants rejected papal jurisdiction over Christendom and the realms beyond, and even some loyal Catholics questioned the more extreme claims of the popes to universal sovereignty. Nevertheless, how Europeans understood the geopolitics of the Atlantic World owed much to how the popes first divided this space, even before they apprehended the Americas as a New World.

The repeated reference in these bulls to "Saracens" indicates the degree to which the pope viewed Portugal's and Spain's exploratory projects in the light of Christendom's political and religious rivalries with Islam. European Christians exported this anxiety from the Mediterranean into the Atlantic World. Spanish conquistadors and missionaries carried the triumphalism of the Spanish "Reconquista"—completed with the fall of the last Muslim emirate in Andalusia in the same year that Columbus sailed—to the New World, even referring to the Indians they encountered as "Moors" and to Mesoamerican temples as "mosques." Several contemporary Spaniards compared the customs and fashions of Native Americans with Muslims in Spain. European attempts to absorb the strange New World into a comprehensible cosmology and geography also involved another non-Christian rival familiar from the Old World, the Jew. Thus, some European Christians explained the existence of an entire new continent populated by peoples unknown in either Scripture or classical texts by asserting that Native Americans had descended from the lost tribes of biblical Israel.

This epistemological assimilation also reinvigorated theological debates in Spain about the nature of Christian salvation, specifically whether those who lived outside of the sacramental community governed by the Church (indeed, beyond knowledge of Christ and the Gospels) but who nevertheless abided by natural law would be saved by a more inclusive, merciful God or condemned by a more exclusionary, punitive deity. These debates were as old as the early Apostolic Church. In the fourth century, the debate had crystallized around the arguments of Pelagius (fl. c. 390–418), who said that humans could achieve a "natural sanctity" by living a moral life in accord with natural law through their own free will, and of Augustine of Hippo (354–430), who rejected Pelagian free will, emphasizing the necessity of God's grace and the institutional Church for salvation. The debate reached some degree of resolution when Pelagius was condemned for heresy and Augustine's stricter God became mainstream doctrine.

The encounter with New World populations raised the question of the requirements for salvation once again, revisiting the language of the early Church. Some sixteenth-century Catholic theologians like Juan de Palacios Rubios (1450–1524) defended the possibility that God would spare from eternal damnation those New World pagans who had not yet heard the Gospels but nevertheless lived virtuously according to the dictates of natural law. Such positions, voiced by other theologians as well, opened a possibility of limited toleration of Indians and of their pagan practices, at least insofar as some Catholics embraced Indians as members of a broader human community. This tolerance by no means precluded the Catholic missionary impulse to proselytize and convert. For authors like the Dominican friar Bartolomé de Las Casas (1484–1566), who decried the conquest and enslavement of Indians, conversion was legitimate only through persuasion, which necessarily presumed that Indians possessed a reasonable soul capable of understanding Christian truths. But even for Las Casas, bringing New World indigenes into the Catholic Church remained the ultimate justification for Spanish claims to authority in the Americas.

This attitude of patient tolerance was increasingly foreclosed, in no small part owing to the explosive European politics of the Protestant Reformation. Confronted with heterodox dissent in Europe, Catholic authorities in the New World saw little room to accommodate religious diversity and disunity among the new peoples under their tutelage. The emergence of militant Counter-Reformation Catholicism after the Council of Trent (1545–1563) reinforced Augustine's theological precept that no person could attain salvation outside of the Church. Furthermore, influenced by Tridentine reforms, Catholic political thinkers argued that the political unity and legitimacy of monarchical authority demanded the religious conformity of all subjects.

The process of appropriating Native American religion into a historical, cultural, and theological narrative consistent with this more militant Catholicism involved a brutal decision to literally demonize Native religion, rejecting the possibility that Indians and their beliefs could exist in accordance with natural law. Increasingly, Catholic theologians claimed that Lucifer and his legion of devils had long ago infiltrated the New World, masquerading as gods to dupe its inhabitants. Manifestations of the Indian supernatural, whether Aztec gods like Huitzilopochtli or Quechua spirits inhabiting local sacred sites (*huacas*), were, in fact, demons that misguided the gullible and ignorant.

Since Iberian Catholics in the Americas presumed that Indians were prone to diabolical influences, it was no great leap for them to imagine indigenous forms of popular magic—no matter how inflected by the cults of the Virgin Mary or the saints—as demonic in origin and hence a form of witchcraft. The colonizers' tendency to demonize Native culture and to see the Indian healer or sorcerer as a witch contrasted sharply with the perspective of the metropolitan Spanish Inquisition, which had largely resisted the witch hysteria found in other parts of Europe. In addition to fears of Indian diabolism, concerns plagued Catholic missionaries that Native American converts readily reverted to pagan ways; these led to "extirpation of idolatry" campaigns that continued through the eighteenth century.

Despite the Church's attempts to discipline and police indigenous religious beliefs and practices, the local clergy could not destroy Indian traditions or impose a form of Christianity fully in line with Roman Catholic expectations. Rather, new modalities of Christian praxis rooted in local conditions and Native American culture began to emerge. In North America, Indians converted by Jesuit missionaries merged Christian practices with their own customs and cultural expectations, while the Jesuits themselves projected their (often negative) interpretations of European festive culture—such as Carnival's exuberant popular excesses—onto native festivities and celebrations. Local inflections emerged wherever European Catholics introduced their version of Christianity. Catholic missionaries in the Kongo in Central Africa, for example, faced constant hybridizations of Catholic and Kongo notions of spiritual power and religious authority, and this hybridized Catholicism traveled with at least some enslaved Kongo across the Atlantic to the Americas.

The Church encouraged enslaved and free people of African descent in Spanish America and Brazil to be baptized in the faith and even to organize their own religious confraternities, although these groups were often policed. Because Catholic priests sanctioned and performed marriages between enslaved African women and men, they also discouraged slaveholders from maliciously separating couples married in the Church. In this context, enslaved and free Africans often mingled African and European cultural practices within a Catholic system of sacraments, rites, and beliefs. Although Catholic clergymen encouraged Africans to convert, and even occasionally criticized slaveholders' maltreatment of enslaved Africans, the Church did not disavow slavery, and some high-ranking clerics actively defended the trade.

Whether Catholic clergymen reacted with patience, anxiety, or hostility to the religious diversity and cultural resilience of African and American populations in the early Atlantic World, they managed great success in imposing Catholic institutional infrastructures in vast stretches of Central and South America and parts of the Caribbean. In part, this success grew out of the mobilization of missionary orders in Europe—especially Franciscans, Dominicans, and Jesuits who worked assiduously to instruct and convert non-Christians in the Americas, Africa, and farther afield in Asia and the Pacific. But also important was the transplantation of an episcopal hierarchy and parish structure as

Catholicism expanded in the Atlantic. A Kongo prince was elevated to bishop in 1521, and a bishopric for the Atlantic coast of Africa was established in São Tomé in 1534.

In Spanish America, archbishoprics were established first in Santo Domingo, Mexico City, and Lima in the 1540s. In Portuguese Brazil, the first two bishoprics were established in São Salvador da Bahia (1552, elevated to archdiocese in 1676) and then much later in São Sebastião (Rio de Janeiro, 1675, elevated to archdiocese in 1893). Further, the Spanish monarchy also introduced the Holy Office to police orthodoxy in Lima (1570), Mexico City (1571), and Cartagena (1610), although the Native populations were exempted from its jurisdiction. It must be noted that, as in Catholic Europe itself, the interests of the episcopate, regular clergy, Inquisition, and secular authorities overlapped but at times differed strongly, leading to conflict and competition among the various representatives of Catholic Christianity throughout America.

While the Spanish and Portuguese transplanted Catholic ecclesiastical institutions in the regions of the Atlantic they controlled, European Protestants relied less on Church structures, largely because the fragmented Protestantism in the European metropoles diversified even further in the broader Atlantic. Despite the attempts of the English crown to establish the Anglican Church across the Atlantic as the official public church, various dissenting groups and religious minorities—including Puritans, Presbyterians, and Quakers—settled in Providence Island and Bermuda and throughout the North American colonies to escape religious restrictions and intolerance at home. While Congregationalists dominated the governance of Providence Island, Bermuda, and Massachusetts Bay, the Quaker colony of Pennsylvania and the dissenter colony of Providence Plantation (in modern Rhode Island) promised religious tolerance. English Catholics escaped the religious struggles in England and Scotland and carved a space for themselves in Maryland.

Archbishop of Canterbury William Laud (1573–1645) tried to prevent dissenters from moving to the colonies, where they could worship beyond the reach of Anglican ecclesiastical discipline, by forcing all emigrants to take a loyalty oath to king and church, but this policy failed. Indeed, Laud's expanded restrictions on English religious minorities in the 1630s exacerbated discontent and resulted in a substantial exodus of dissenters to continental Europe, especially the Netherlands, as well as to the Atlantic colonies. In addition to the many reform-minded clergymen who led the Puritan communities across the Atlantic, the nonconformist Anne Hutchinson (1591–1643) sailed in 1634 to the Massachusetts Bay Colony, where she became a center of controversy for her dissenting beliefs.

Beyond the relative autonomy of dissenters in the colonies, Anglican clergy and parishioners there also gained a degree of independence from Canterbury. However, dissenting denominations had an advantage in winning local autonomy, for most organized their communities (and their particular forms of church discipline) along congregational lines, free of higher levels of doctrinal authority. Thus, Puritan communities, for example, could carefully police membership, organization, and orthodoxy on the local level. As a result, Puritans paradoxically often reinstitutionalized the religious intolerance they had sought to escape by leaving England, as they built energetically exclusionary communities of the godly based on their own particular visions.

The circulation of European Protestants around the Atlantic World was often tied to Europe's fraught and violent confessional politics, exemplified by disruptive policies of religious reform or official acts of outright religious intolerance. Aside from the English Protestants who escaped Archbishop Laud's restrictive policies by emigrating across the Atlantic, some Huguenot families fled from their homes in Catholic France to the continent or overseas to Florida, New Netherland and New York, Charleston, and other New World locations, as well as to the Dutch East India Company station at the Cape of Good Hope. Huguenots were among the French colonizers who briefly established a foothold in 1555 in Guanabara Bay, Brazil (modern Rio de Janeiro). The Portuguese destroyed the colony in 1560, and when the Huguenots gave the victorious Catholics a declaration of their religious principles, known as the Guanabara Confession of Faith, they were killed as heretics. In 1598 French king Henry IV issued the Edict of Nantes, which granted the Huguenots limited toleration in the kingdom, reducing the pressure on them to emigrate. In 1685, however, Louis XIV revoked this edict, and Hu-

guenot emigration exploded around Europe and to the broader Atlantic.

Similarly, a group of Lutherans known as the Salzburg émigrés fled their home in 1732 when the Archbishop of Salzburg forced crypto-Protestant communities there to either convert or leave his domains. In the years following, as many as 30,000 Salzburg exiles relocated to Protestant polities across the Holy Roman Empire and beyond. The German minister Samuel Urlsperger (1685–1772), with the help of the London-based (Anglican) Society for Promoting Christian Knowledge (SPCK), helped relocate fewer than a hundred Salzburgers to the English colony of Georgia, where, despite their small numbers, they established a successful community in New Ebenezer. The Salzburgers were part of a broader "Pietist" Atlantic, which included communities in Pennsylvania and North Carolina built by German Lutherans from Halle and Moravians from the Herrnhut village community organized under the leadership of Count Nikolaus Ludwig von Zinzendorf (1700–1760).

In many respects, Protestant understandings of religious reform, which ranged from reconstructing society as a whole to reconstituting the soul of each individual Christian, found fertile soil across the Atlantic, since the New World's distance from European metropoles opened spaces where minority religious communities could experiment with their own models of religious life. Protestants projected providential and even eschatological expectations onto the New World, referring to their projects as a New Jerusalem, a godly commonwealth, or a city upon the hill (from Matthew 5:14).

One short-lived French Protestant mission to Brazil in the 1550s, documented in Jean de Léry's *History of a Voyage to the Land of Brazil*, demonstrates how, like Iberian Catholics, Protestants absorbed their encounters with New World denizens into their own theological and religious frameworks. Just under the surface Léry's discussions of Tupinambá customs and practices, which included cannibalism, lay his concerns with Eucharistic debates between Catholics and Protestants in sixteenth-century Europe (since some Protestants referred to Catholic transubstantiation as cannibalistic), as well as the sectarian violence that marked the French religious wars.

Léry was not alone in his appropriation of Native Americans into Protestant theology. Protestants wondered where Native Americans came from, where they fit in providential history, and what they signified morally and religiously. One master's thesis at Harvard University in 1773 asked, "Were the aborigines of America descended from Abraham?" The answer given was affirmative. But most debates about the origins of Europeans, Indians, and Africans traced the question back to Noah and the postdiluvian repopulation of the earth. Always implicit in these Old Testament genealogies was a hierarchy that positioned white Protestant Europeans above non-European peoples. Reinforcing such hierarchies, some Protestant colonists agreed with their Catholic rivals in the New World that Indian religion involved worship of the Devil, and they feared the diabolical nature of the power that Native religious leaders wielded.

But the Atlantic was not just a stage for competition between Europeans with their Christian confessions and non-Europeans with other religious traditions. It was also a stage upon which the believers in variant forms of European Christianity imagined and pursued their own rivalries. As Protestant colonizers and missionaries expanded their foothold in the Atlantic world during the seventeenth and eighteenth centuries, their anti-Catholic rhetorical justifications even deployed the arguments of Catholics like Bartolomé de Las Casas, citing his critiques of early Spanish mistreatment of Indians as evidence that greed rather than piety motivated their popish rivals. Most English royal charters establishing colonies in the Americas included such rhetoric to legitimize their intrusion onto a continent consigned by the pope to Spain, before its proportions were even vaguely known.

Spreading the Gospels, displacing Catholicism, and absorbing the heathen spiritual threat into Christendom—whatever the combination of motives, Protestant missions to Native Americans were a variegated lot. At first, the English colonies generally possessed only enough clergymen for pastoral care of the local parishes or congregations. Thus, in practice, the missionary impulse was much attenuated. In this sense, the much more lavishly endowed Catholic missionary orders offered Catholicism a major advantage in converting the indigenous populations of the Americas. For example, Catholic authors had already translated catechisms into Native American languages in the sixteenth century and published a Kikongo catechism in 1624. In contrast, the first Protestant catechism in a Native American language was composed later, in the 1640s, by a Swedish Lutheran minister stationed on the banks of the Delaware River.

English initiatives would follow a bit later, especially under the leadership of Puritan minister John Eliot (1604–1690), whom Cotton Mather called the "Apostle to the Indians." Eliot gave his first sermon in an Indian language in 1646 and began establishing small communities called Praying Indian Villages. Arguably, Native Americans joined such villages in some part as a defensive response to protect the collective integrity of their communities in the face of English colonial expansion, and to some extent to preserve their cultural practices, which they often fused with Christian elements. In 1698, the Anglicans joined the fray with the Society for Promoting Christian Knowledge, which focused on the publication of religious tracts and the distribution of funds for missionary enterprises. As evidenced by the SPCK's work with pietist Lutherans like Samuel Urlsperger (1685–1772), the Society demonstrated an ecumenical, if wholly Protestant, spirit.

The many paradoxes of conversion are especially evident in the Protestant attitude toward converting enslaved Africans. On one hand, many Protestant slave owners felt that converting their slaves would undermine the legitimacy of slaveholding, since Christians generally disdained owning other Christians. In addition, they feared that Christianized slaves, especially those taught to read and write, might equate the Protestant concept of Christian freedom with worldly manumission and use their acquired knowledge to challenge racial hierarchies.

On the other hand, some Protestant clergymen found the conversion of slaves a greater moral good. The Massachusetts Puritan minister Cotton Mather (1663–1738), himself a slaveholder, advocated baptism of African and African-descended slaves in the beginning decades of the eighteenth century, and his book *The Negro Christianized* (1706) circulated widely around the Anglophone Atlantic World. In the eighteenth century, Moravians sent missionaries to preach among enslaved Africans around the Atlantic as well as to communities on the African mainland, with their greatest successes in the Danish Caribbean island colonies of St. Thomas, St. Croix, and St. John. But while Moravian belief in the spiritual equality of Europeans, Africans, and Indians led early missionaries to critique the abuses of slavery, over time Moravians compromised by defending a regressive distinction between humanity's universal spiritual equality, on one hand, and the natural, even divinely ordained, inferiority of Africans' intelligence and character, on the other.

For many Protestants, Scripture revealed that God had sanctioned slavery. Furthermore, some Christian defenders of slavery expanded and reworked the "curse of Ham" inflicted by Noah upon Canaan (or Cham) in the Book of Genesis (9:25) into a racialized narrative, in which the descendants of Ham were cursed with black skin and eternal subjugation by others. Finally, some thought slavery might even bring inferior heathens to knowledge of Christ through the workings of divine providence. This latter position appeared repeatedly among Protestants who challenged slaveholders' refusal to baptize the enslaved but refused to condemn slavery itself. The Quakers, in contrast with many other Protestant denominations, had already developed a consistent opposition to slavery in the seventeenth century, and they would become leaders in the transatlantic antislavery movement of the eighteenth century.

European Christianity in the Atlantic World always had direct ties to the confessional and secular affairs of Europe, but Christians overseas also reacted to local cultural, social, and political contingencies. Indeed, it has become nearly impossible to discuss Christianity in Europe without some consideration of the wider world. The Christian impulse to reach across the Atlantic during the fifteenth through the eighteenth centuries was driven by two motives. At first with the Catholic missions in Africa and the New World and then later with Protestants, most Christians expected to spread their particular truths across the global landscape in order to bring salvation to non-Christian heathens. This often aggressive impulse was itself a reflection of confessional rivalries in Europe, for success at converting non-Europeans would become polemical fodder in Reformation struggles at home between the Catholic Church and Protestant faiths. Beyond these missionary aspirations, longing for religious self-preservation in the face of intolerance at home led many dissenting Christians to take flight across the Atlantic. Whether looking outward to convert the world or inward to preserve their own communities—and often both simultaneously—European Christians shaped the transatlantic networks that connected Europe, Africa, and the Americas.

DUANE CORPIS

Bibliography

Cervantes, Fernando. *The Devil in the New World: The Impact of Diabolism in New Spain*. New Haven, CT: Yale University Press, 1997.

Kidd, Colin. *The Forging of Races: Race and Scripture in the Protestant Atlantic World, 1600–2000*. Cambridge: Cambridge University Press, 2006.

Pestana, Carla Gardina. *The Protestant Empire: Religion and the Making of the British Atlantic World*. Philadelphia: University of Pennsylvania Press, 2009.

Schwartz, Stuart B. *All Can Be Saved: Religious Tolerance and Salvation in the Iberian Atlantic World*. New Haven, CT: Yale University Press, 2008.

Sensbach, Jon F. *A Separate Canaan: The Making of an Afro-Moravian World in North Carolina, 1763–1840*. Chapel Hill: University of North Carolina Press, 1998.

Soares, Mariza de Carvalho. *People of Faith: Slavery and African Catholics in Eighteenth-Century Rio de Janeiro*. Durham, NC: Duke University Press, 2011.

Thornton, John. *The Kongolese Saint Anthony: Dona Beatriz Kimpa Vita and the Antonian Movement, 1684–1706*. Cambridge: Cambridge University Press, 1998.

Christianity, Adaptations in Africa of

Missionaries often traveled with the Portuguese sailors who opened the African continent to the world of Atlantic commerce in the course of the fifteenth and sixteenth centuries, exposing African rulers and their subjects to a new religion, Christianity. Africans' responses to the evangelizing work of these missionaries varied from outright rejection to partial or full acceptance and incorporation of the Gospel into their own political and social agendas. These reactions were always conditioned by historically and regionally specific circumstances, but wherever and whenever Christianity took root, it did so because Africans were able to give meanings of their own to alien religious concepts and materials.

Africans were generally open to new beliefs and practices, including ones originating elsewhere. They repeatedly looked for fresh sources of supernatural power in their enduring quest to eliminate evil from all domains of their lives. Elites often adopted new cults to enhance their political powers, which everywhere had strong spiritual dimensions. Despite a common impression that Europeans and Africans held fundamentally incompatible worldviews, a strong case can be made for the commonalities between early-modern European and African cosmologies—beliefs in lesser spirits or saints, nature spirits, spiritual mediators or priests, witchcraft for both, and supernatural intervention in everyday life generally. In view of these underlying similarities, it is perhaps remarkable that by the early 1800s, after more than three centuries of intense commercial interaction between the Atlantic coast of Africa and Europe, only the people of Kongo in West-Central Africa had embraced Christianity as a "national religion," beyond their ongoing embrace of ancestral and other local spirits.

The kingdom of Benin in West Africa was a case where African rulers, initially interested in Christianity, soon rejected the entreaties of Portuguese missionaries. Portugal established diplomatic relations with Benin in 1486 and made military support for its rulers conditional on their conversion to Catholicism. Part of Benin's ruling group converted in the 1510s, instigated by the king (*oba*) who "sought the combined power of the firearms and the spiritual force behind them" (Northrup, 33). This openness to religious innovation should not be seen as mere opportunism. Both parties—Catholics and Africans—believed that political strength relied on spiritual blessing; the commanders of Benin's armies therefore expected the missionaries to employ their spiritual powers on their battlefields. By the late 1530s, however, they had not blessed Benin's military campaigns sufficiently to sustain belief in the white priests' magical powers, and the Portuguese effort to Christianize the people of Benin halted. Later attempts by Spanish and Italian missionaries to reintroduce Christianity in Benin met only with resistance.

Seventeenth-century Jesuit missionaries left a longer Christian legacy in the region of Guinea-Bissau, even if their converts remained limited in numbers. Here, practitioners of the Catholic faith were mostly concentrated in fortified towns (*praças*), like Bissau, Cacheu, Farim, and Geba, which were nominally overseas territories of Portugal. The free residents of these towns, known as *moradores*, claimed dual Christian and Portuguese identities. They typically worked as brokers in the trade between Atlantic merchants and local communities, supplying the merchants with slaves. A few *moradores* had been born in Portugal, but most were Luso-Africans (locally born people of mixed descent, often several generations deep), while others were black African converts. As a distinct social group, they never counted more than a few thousand. Despite their professed Catholicism, the *moradores* often mixed Christian and local religious beliefs, frequently making offerings at traditional shrines as well as attending mass.

Since the Guinea-Bissau region was composed of many small polities, chiefs who converted lacked the ability to impose Christianity on their neighbors. Nevertheless, just as *moradores* dabbled in local religious practices, many Africans living in the vicinity of the *praças*, without becoming Christian themselves, also participated in Christian rites such as baptism, Mass, and marriage, and recognized the power of Catholic clergy. They maintained a similar openness toward Islamic influences coming from inland. Some members of African communities in the region identified themselves as Christian since they could increase their opportunities for trade and employment in the Atlantic economy by attaching themselves to the Christian community of Luso-African merchants. A Christian identity furthermore provided at least a minimal level of protection against enslavement. Finally, these Africans saw Christian rites and symbols as alternative means to protect themselves against evil forces, which troubled humanity with diseases, poor harvests, and other kinds of misfortune, and increasingly by slave raids. For them, typically Christian icons like saints, the Cross, and Catholic churches and priests did not look so different from local charms, shrines, and healers.

Guinea-Bissau was a rare case of enduring conversion to Christianity in Atlantic Africa. There were few Christians outside the small world of the Luso-African merchant community, itself a peculiar product of the Portuguese presence in the Atlantic. For these Christians, moreover, their religious identity was also a matter of claiming standing as Catholic Portuguese rather than Africans. More importantly, however, this case—like the history of Kongo Catholicism, as outlined below—suggests that when the Catholic faith took root, it was not because of the presence of European missionaries or attractions inherent to Christianity but rather because Africans saw benefits in converting elements of the new faith into their own religious practices.

In Kongo, the governing class converted to Christianity in the late fifteenth century. The country at large quickly responded to an African laity, who taught local elites as well as commoners the rudiments of the faith and the main Catholic prayers. In the meantime, white missionaries—Jesuits at first, then mostly Capuchins after 1645—administered the sacraments of the Church. For the Kongo, Christianity became part of a political identity on scales exceeding those of villages and regions that had composed the fifteenth-century polity. They thus integrated Christianity on their own terms, according to their own needs, and drawing on the adaptability of Christian practices to their own. Baptism was the most popular sacrament, probably because the baptismal salt was thought to deter witches. Confession was another form of the purification rituals that they had always practiced, as breaking the consensus of the community, or in Catholic terms rule-breaking or "sin," was believed to cause disease. In African terms, Catholicism was a healing cult, or—as ethnographers term these ubiquitous practices—a "cult of affliction."

Elites accepted the ideal (though rarely the practice) of canon-law marriage, which they perceived as a special kind of blessing on the fertility of a union and a way to strengthen marital alliances between noble families. Kongo nobility furthermore adopted the Portuguese aristocratic Order of Christ, an order of nobility symbolized by the Cross, as a cult to regulate trading contacts among people otherwise strangers to one another. They also adapted the Christian calendar to organize public rituals of the polity as a whole. For example, All Saints' Day was turned into an opportunity to pay respect to the ancestors. In the western province of Soyo, St. Luke's Day was appropriated to celebrate the defeat of Portugal at the battle of Kitombo on October 18, 1670. But the most important holiday was St. James's Day, when people flocked to their provincial capitals, Mbanza Kongo

and Mbanza Soyo, to hear Mass, pay tribute, and commemorate Kongo's second Christian king, Afonso I (c. 1456–c. 1542), who had overthrown a pagan brother through the claimed miraculous intervention of St. James, the warrior saint of the Iberian "Reconquista." Christian Kongo authorities, in short, appropriated the church holidays to underwrite their political power.

Christianity in Kongo was predominantly a royal political cult, and from the start it was therefore rivaled by alternative cults, some of them millenarian versions of Catholicism itself. After the mid-seventeenth century, the central cult of Catholicism lost some of its attraction because of the dispersal of political and economic power. Around 1700, when warfare between rival political factions ravaged the country, a young woman named Dona Beatriz Kimpa Vita, who had been initiated as a traditional healer (*nganga*) and claimed to be possessed by St. Anthony, started a purification movement aiming to restore the political harmony for which Christianity stood. As she denied the power of the Cross, she was a threat to Kongo's nobility, but large segments of the populace accepted her for promising not only peace but also to cure infertility. Although Beatriz was burned at the stake and peace was restored without her, the civil wars of the late seventeenth and early eighteenth centuries seriously undermined the allure of the Kongo Christian cult. By 1850, nevertheless, crosses still signaled chiefly authority along the trade routes to the historic seat of Christianity, Mbanza Kongo, where the *mani* Kongo (king) was still the only mediator of the highest spirit, called Desu (from the Portuguese *Deus*, God). Throughout the region, Catholic symbols coexisted with non-Christian charms. Christianity was, indeed, an integral part of Kongo's religious outlook and politics.

In sum, conversion in Africa entailed both Christianization of African religious practices and Africanization of Christianity. Conversion should therefore not be read as assimilation into European culture. African absorption of Christian concepts and symbols is often wrongly described as syncretism, a conscious attempt to create a distinct religious amalgam, which implies incompatibility of the parts combined. Perhaps the Antonian movement of Dona Beatriz was a case of syncretism, as she intentionally bypassed the sacraments, charms, and priesthood of the Catholic Church, rewrote the

Ave Maria and Salve Regina prayers, and attributed a Kongolese origin to the Church. Although she drew on both traditional concepts of witchcraft and healing and the Christianized version of that tradition, not all Christian Kongo identified with her movement. It was particularly unpopular in Soyo, whose ruling elites had been molded in Catholic confraternities and considered themselves part of the universal Catholic Church.

Conversions to Christianity in Africa were elements in larger processes of eager cultural borrowing, including fashions for Western commodities, weaponry, and technology. The Atlantic slave trade was central to introducing these novelties, whether material, spiritual, or ideological. The rulers of Benin converted because they were interested in exchanging slaves for guns with Portugal. In Guinea-Bissau, primarily Luso-African slave traders identified as Christian, and they protected fellow Christians from enslavement. Kongo slave-trading elites solidified their alliances through Christian marriages and controlled their trade through membership in the Order of Christ. But conversion was also a genuinely religious experience, achieved through fundamental belief in Christian rites and materials. It matters little that European missionaries were often doubtful about Africans' knowledge of Christianity, as the missionaries understood it, and the sincerity of conversions that combined Catholic practices with beliefs in other spiritualized powers. "Inevitably the Gospel carries implications which transcend the understanding of those who proclaim it" (Gray, 1). Like the many Kongo Christians who ended up enslaved in the Americas, African converts' interpretations of Christianity demonstrated the creativity that made a religion of universal pretensions also global in practice.

JELMER VOS

Bibliography

Gray, Richard. *Black Christians and White Missionaries.* New Haven, CT: Yale University Press, 1990.

Hawthorne, Walter. *From Africa to Brazil: Culture, Identity, and an Atlantic Slave Trade, 1600–1830.* New York: Cambridge University Press, 2010.

MacGaffey, Wyatt. *Religion and Society in Central Africa: The BaKongo of Lower Zaire.* Chicago: University of Chicago Press, 1986.

Northrup, David. *Africa's Discovery of Europe, 1450–1850.* 2nd ed. New York: Oxford University Press, 2009.

Thornton, John K. *The Kongolese Saint Anthony: Dona Beatriz Kimpa Vita and the Antonian Movement, 1684–1706.* Cambridge: Cambridge University Press, 1998.

Christianity, African American

Christianity was a fundamental element of the religious heritage of Africans and their descendants in the Americas. With ancient roots in northeast Africa, Christianity made inroads in fifteenth-century western Africa well before European colonization of the Americas. The transatlantic slave trade created a vast and permanent zone of African engagement with that religion on both sides of the Atlantic. African American Christianity was thus in some sense an extension of pre-Columbian African Christianity.

Africa

For more than two hundred years, African encounters with Latin Christianity almost exclusively involved Roman Catholicism, beginning in the 1440s with the first contacts by Portuguese mariners and traders in West Africa. In subsequent decades, as the Portuguese established mercantile and political relationships with African rulers along the coast, Christianity became an important factor in cementing these bonds. African authorities in Elmina (in modern Ghana), Benin, and elsewhere accepted baptism as a token of political alliance, giving rise by the 1470s to small African Catholic enclaves; these later declined in the sixteenth century as Portuguese influence in Upper Guinea and the Gold Coast eroded. But these early connections fostered the transportation of several thousand slaves to Portugal and Spain, where many converted to Catholicism, spawning an African Christian community in southern Europe.

This early embrace of Catholicism in western Africa and Iberia was a prelude to the more intensive relationship farther south forged between the Portuguese and the political authorities in Kongo, in West-Central Africa. In 1491 the conversion of the head of Kongo, Nzinga a Nkuwu, began a widespread adoption of Christianity in that region, which intensified with the miraculous succession to his position of his son, Afonso, in 1506 on the angelic wings of the warrior saint of the "Reconquista" in Iberia, James (Iago). Afonso sent several dozen of the converts he sponsored to Portugal to train for the priesthood. The resulting native Kongo clergy and the construction of numerous churches and schools in provincial capitals introduced Catholic Christianity throughout the region, with reported mass conversions. Kongo Catholicism was characterized by a syncretic blend of Catholic and local beliefs. Though scholars debate the balance of this fusion, Kongo Christianity in effect became an indigenous African religion. To the south of Kongo, after two generations of conflict between the Portuguese military, based at Luanda on the coast, and the Ngola regime in the interior, the heir to this political tradition, Queen Nzinga, likewise embraced Christianity with her baptism in 1656 as part of the peace settlement with Portugal. Thus, Christianity became at least a political convenience and perhaps also a source of communal strength in a significant portion of war-torn West-Central Africa just as European colonization in America and the transatlantic slave trade gathered momentum.

Catholic Americas

Many thousands of Kongo and Angolan Christians, in fact, were among the approximately 12 million captive Africans sent to the Americas during the nearly four centuries of Atlantic slaving, particularly in its earliest phases focused on Spanish Cartagena and Lima. Many were captives taken in civil wars and sold through African brokers to slave-trading ports on the coast, particularly to Luanda. The Church sanctioned the enslavement of baptized Africans, though it sought to direct sales of them to Catholic colonies in America. The later bulk of the enslaved Christians went via the Portuguese trade to sugar plantations and towns in Brazil, where they continued to practice a blend of Catholicism and African rituals. Dutch traders, meanwhile, pried their way into these Portuguese trades in the early 1600s, capturing their ships and taking their human cargoes, including many enslaved African Christians, to English, Dutch, Spanish, and French colonies in the Caribbean and

mainland North America. West-Central African Catholics were thus distributed in varying degrees throughout slave societies in America—numbering, for example, among the famous first "20 and odd Negroes" sold in 1619 from a Dutch vessel in Virginia. Portuguese-speaking Angolan or Kongo Catholics turned up later, in 1739 in Stono, South Carolina, among the slave rebels who attempted to flee to freedom, or at least Catholicism, in Spanish Florida. More Kongo Catholics took part in the massive slave uprising in 1791 in Saint-Domingue.

In addition to those Africans who entered enslavement in the Americas as Christians, many more from other parts of western Africa were baptized into the Catholic faith throughout Latin America. In some of these colonies majorities of the population of Catholics were of African descent. Though the Church defended slavery and made clear that baptism into the community of the faithful did not bring manumission from secular masters, it did forge a policy derived from papal bulls, natural law, and the Bible that the fellowship of Christianity should be open to the enslaved. Masters were required to catechize and instruct their slaves in the faith, to make baptism accessible, to respect the sacrament of marriage, and to ensure attendance at Mass. Church doctrine held master and slave to be spiritual equals, bound by mutual obligation as brothers and sisters in Christ. This acknowledgment of slaves' human souls put the fear of God into the hearts of masters, or offered at least doctrinal protection from extreme forms of abuse. In practice, church enforcement of these safeguards was uneven, and baptized slaves on large sugar plantations often found church membership no protection against mistreatment. The seventeenth-century Jesuit Antonio Vieria deplored the "inhumanity and brutality of the exorbitant punishments" with which Afro-Brazilians were "tyrannized . . . or martyrized" (Conrad, 173). Inquisition records report severe beatings, even execution, of slaves convicted of practicing African "sorcery," committing marital transgressions, and other behaviors condemned as sinful.

Still, enslaved Catholics throughout Latin America took advantage of baptism to surround themselves with protective layers of the Christian family. In cities like Recife, Rio de Janeiro, and Mexico City, blacks formed lay brotherhoods, often chapters devoted to Our Lady of the Rosary, that fostered communal fellowship, religious self-sufficiency, and Catholic burials and remembrance of the dead that masters were not inclined to provide. Through *compadrazgo* (Spanish) or godparenthood, black Catholics built elaborate networks of spiritual kin for themselves and their children, often choosing respected authority figures in the slave community as baptismal sponsors, as well as white and free-black patrons who might be in positions to advocate on their behalf. Enslaved Catholics used the Church's administrative structure to protect themselves by filing complaints against abusive masters, petitioning against the sale of spouses, and even seeking manumission. In Mexico, relatively high numbers of successful freedom suits gave rise to one of the largest free populations of African descent in the Americas.

Protestant Americas

Because the northern European Protestant political authorities were slower to build up large numbers of slaves, Africans had only limited encounters with reformed religion on either side of the Atlantic through the end of the seventeenth century. In contrast to the Catholic Church, Protestants had few clear legal or theological precedents regarding baptism of enslaved Africans. The main ambiguity was the question of whether religious fellowship, in communities often formed around considerations of faith, also brought political standing as protected subjects of European monarchs. English common law forbade one Christian to enslave another, an injunction that the first Africans in Virginia exploited to claim, and win, the liberties of Englishmen upon baptism. To close the Christian loophole to admission to the political community, the Virginia assembly departed from English law in 1663 by writing its own statute that "the conferring of baptisme doth not alter the condition of the person as to his bondage or freedome" (Hening, 260). This radical secular juridical closure, along with similar laws passed at about the same time in Maryland, Barbados, and Jamaica, marked an essential step in separating Christian communion from legal standing, separating church from state, and basing chattel slavery on racial difference.

Despite such clear legal exclusions, planters harbored lingering doubts about the connection between Christian communion and English liberties,

and they remained reluctant to expose their slaves to Christianity, even though the Church of England officially encouraged instruction and baptism. Planter suspicions, combined with enslaved Africans' disdain for the religion that sanctioned their captivity, meant that few slaves embraced Protestantism. The new mission organization of the Anglican Church, the Society for the Propagation of the Gospel in Foreign Parts, founded in 1701, was allowed to make a few converts in South Carolina and Barbados, where it owned a plantation and slaves. By the 1730s the pace of missionary proselytization picked up slightly as more planters gave in to pressure to allow baptism for their slaves. One Virginian, James Blair, reported in 1729 that the "Negroes themselves in our neighbourhood are very desirous to become Christians" (Parent, 258). Still, only a tiny fraction of enslaved Africans in English or Dutch colonies gained formal standing in Protestant denominations.

Independent Black Churches

A series of evangelical revivals in British America between the 1730s and 1770s, collectively known as the Great Awakening, animated Protestants to open their Christian fellowship more broadly to the enslaved. Led both by famous itinerant preachers such as George Whitefield and by lesser-known lay exhorters, many of them religious dissenters, the intense emotional revivalists' message of egalitarian spiritual embrace resonated powerfully with slaves. Whitefield traveled up and down the Atlantic seaboard from Georgia to New England for 30 years in a series of barnstorming revival tours, making a particular impact among Africans and African Americans in the South Carolina Lowcountry. Like most white evangelicals of his day, he was careful not to attack slavery itself, but he castigated plantation masters for withholding Christianity from their enslaved laborers. In Virginia, Presbyterian "New Light" minister Samuel Davies's mission likewise achieved broad appeal in the 1750s among black listeners, despite opposition from planters who feared that the spiritual strength of Christianity would breed insurrection among enslaved converts. Throughout the colonies black and white Baptists and Methodists worshiped together in biracial congregations, transcending—and perhaps undermining—the legal dichotomy between slave and free.

In several Caribbean outposts of the Awakening, Moravian missions on the Danish islands of St. Thomas, St. Croix, and St. John, as well as in the British colonies of Antigua and Jamaica, brought thousands of African converts to Christianity.

A distinguishing feature of many of these revivals was the prominence of black lay preachers, both men and women, who often foretold of a coming day of judgment against the slave masters and in the slave quarters spoke of Christianity as God's weapon against human oppression. Early black congregations, mostly associated with Baptists, formed in the 1770s and 1780s in Silver Bluff, South Carolina; Savannah, Georgia; and Williamsburg, Virginia, thus generating black congregational life among the enslaved. The 1790s saw the rise of independent African Methodist Episcopal congregations in Philadelphia, New York, and other mid-Atlantic and northern cities, comprising mostly free black members under the leadership of ordained African American pastors. These churches became centers for social and political organization and antislavery activism in urban black communities throughout the North.

African American and European evangelical Christians spread the inspiration of their religious convictions to disparate points around the Atlantic. In the mid-eighteenth century, several African-born evangelists who had been raised and educated in Europe—such as the Anglican Philip Quaque, the Dutch Reformed Jacobus Capitein, and the Moravian Christian Protten—returned on missions to their birthplaces on the Gold Coast. None were particularly successful. Of far greater impact were the black preachers and congregants among the Loyalists who gained freedom and evacuated the United States with the British at the end of the American War of Independence. The black Baptist congregation at Silver Bluff produced several of these evangelists, including George Liele, who founded a Baptist church in Jamaica, as well as Boston King and David George, who ministered to the new free-black settlement of Loyalists at Birchtown, Nova Scotia. From there, King and George departed in the 1790s with a contingent of black settlers from London destined for Sierra Leone, the new British Province of Freedom intended as a West African outpost for Christian evangelism. Though the settlers became embroiled almost immediately in disputes with imperial administrators, their effort was part of a nascent pan-evangelical African movement to link the fortunes of all people of African descent in disparate points of the Protestant Atlantic together under the banner of Christianity as God's chosen people.

African American and black Atlantic Christianity were entwined inseparably with slavery and the slave trade. Christianity provided new ties of community, kinship in the family of Christ, to people whose families the slave trade had splintered. Through it, people of African descent asserted their spiritual equality and claims to human rights, challenged the morality of slavery, and fashioned a theology of divine redemption from their captivity.

JON F. SENSBACH

Bibliography

Bennett, Herman. *Africans in Colonial Mexico: Absolutism, Christianity, and Afro-Creole Consciousness, 1570–1640*. Bloomington: Indiana University Press, 2005.

Conrad, Robert Edgar, ed. *Children of God's Fire: A Documentary History of Black Slavery in Brazil*. Princeton, NJ: Princeton University Press, 1983.

Frey, Sylvia R., and Betty Wood. *Come Shouting to Zion: African American Protestantism in the American South and British Caribbean to 1830*. Chapel Hill: University of North Carolina Press, 1998.

Hening, William Waller, ed. *The Statutes at Large; Being a Collection of All the Laws of Virginia, from the First Session of the Legislature in the Year 1619*. 13 vols. Richmond, New York, and Philadelphia, 1809–1823.

Heywood, Linda M., and John K. Thornton. *Central Africans, Atlantic Creoles, and the Foundation of the Americas, 1585–1660*. New York: Cambridge University Press, 2007.

Parent, Anthony S. *Foul Means: The Formation of a Slave Society in Virginia, 1660–1740*. Chapel Hill: University of North Carolina Press, 2003.

Raboteau, Albert S. *Slave Religion: The "Invisible Institution" in the Antebellum South*. New York: Oxford University Press, 1978.

Sensbach, Jon F. *Rebecca's Revival: Creating Black Christianity in the Atlantic World*. Cambridge, MA: Harvard University Press, 2005.

Sweet, James H. *Recreating Africa: Culture, Kinship, and Religion in the African-Portuguese World, 1441–1770*. Chapel Hill: University of North Carolina Press, 2004.

Christianity, Native American Appropriations of

Christianity arguably became the most important religion of the Atlantic World with its acceptance by large numbers of Native Americans. Indian peoples encountered Christianity as an aspect of contact, conquest, and colonization. However, viewing Indian engagement in Christianity only as something done to indigenous people rather than by them ignores an essential feature of religious change in the Atlantic World: the agency of Native peoples in appropriating an Old World religion, incorporating selected elements into their own evolving cultural forms, and adapting these to their purposes.

When Native American adoptions of Christianity are viewed as episodes in their own histories, rather than as a chapter in the triumphal history of European missions, familiar vocabulary and the conceptual apparatus begin to fail. The term *conversion,* with its implications of wholly renouncing one religion in favor of another, becomes problematic in view of the evident differences between New and Old World religions. For example, doctrines of truth and dogmatic creed were central to monotheistic European definitions of religion, but these categories were foreign to Native American spirituality. Much in European Christianity—such as sin, the state of grace, and free will—also revolved around a particular conception of the human person as individual in soul and mind, whereas Indians generally had a very different, more relational sense of the self. The term *syncretism* is also problematic, since the notion that a portion of one religion can be added to a portion of another to produce a new, stable set of beliefs also rests on a false sense of commensurability. The premise that religion can be captured in theological terms is at odds with the experiential and experimental character of most Native American spirituality.

Although millions of Native people in the early-modern Americas came to see themselves as Catholics or, less frequently, Protestants, it is far less clear that they thought of themselves as "converts." Indigenous historical memory, as recorded in settings ranging from Andean Peru and the Amazon to northern British Columbia, later spoke of Native American pasts, stretching back to earliest times, long before contact with Europeans, as Christian; Indians were essentially good Christians, and missionary priests played at best a modestly helpful function in "reminding" the people of what their ancestors had known God expected of them.

Christianization was always complex and varied, enmeshed in specific local circumstances of contact and colonization. In Mesoamerica and the Andes, where indigenous political regimes had been brutally eliminated and their peoples forced to accept Spanish military domination, they experienced the Catholic Church as a central agency of colonial rule. Indians there, for the most part, accepted baptism as an unavoidable gesture of political submission if not a way to personal salvation. Underground currents of independent community religions, with overtones of resistance, were the inevitable accompaniment to so oppressive a church-state regime. Occasionally, when the state threatened the underlying communities, these solidarities boiled to the surface as anti-Christian, as when the Pueblos of New Mexico rose in revolt in 1680, killing Franciscan missionaries and filling their chapels with ordure. Yet, in this and many other instances of overt conflict, Indian rebels frequently carried elements of Christian belief and ritual into their struggles against the colonial state. Native American communities had so integrated society, politics, and religion that there was no going back to their precontact condition in any complete sense; in any event, given the fact that Native religions had always been in dynamic flux, they had no stable precolonial religion to which they might return.

While mission zealotry provoked open revolt against the Church in only a few instances in the centers of Spain's Catholic American empire, suspicious priests worried that a vast anti-Christian underground lurked beneath the appearance of Native American piety. A generation or two after the conquest, clerical investigators began to unearth alarming signs of "idolatry" in Christian Indian communities: statuettes and amulets buried under church altars, accusations that people were consulting shamans to cure their ills, and offerings of food buried with deceased ancestors. These revelations, interpreted as signs of disguised devil worship rather than Native communities' sense of compatibility with the Catholicism of their conquerors, set off waves of repression. In the 1560s, the Franciscan Diego de Landa unleashed a campaign of imprisonment, torture, and execution among the Maya of Yucatán in his efforts to identify and stamp out covert idolatry. Later investigations uncovered widespread community-religious practices surviving among the Indians of Peru and central Mexico.

Although some scholars have found in the archives of such repression evidence of deliberate concealment of pre-conquest religion under a veneer of Christian conformity, others more recently have become convinced that the reports of idols behind the altar suggest instead a gradual, ongoing process of Christianization—always incomplete, uneven, and uncertain, as Native groups adapted Catholicism to the changing challenges of maintaining their communal integrity. Indians of the Andes scandalized priests by making secret offerings to the bones of their ancestors, a form of piety characteristic of Inca times, but in some cases they also removed their ancestors' remains from remote locations to inter them in or near local churches: in effect, they wanted to bring their dead relations, and thus themselves as the living trustees of their ancestors' legacies, into the Catholic fold. Recent scholarship suggests that Andean Native peoples were doing their best to make themselves Christian in the only way they could—within the terms of their own culture, which, though rooted in the ancient past, was in rapid evolution, and not exclusively through contact with Spanish culture.

Nahua (central Mexican), Maya (Central American), and Quechua (Andean) peoples incorporated aspects of Christianity into the fabrics of their daily lives. A village church, the ringing of its bells, the annual cycle of Catholic processions and festivals, and the cults of local patron saints helped to restore and reinforce community in the wake of the dislocations of the conquest period. A Spanish priest might be enlisted into an essentially shamanic role to fend off an epidemic or summon rain in time of drought. The Andean writer Guáman Poma de Ayalla (c. 1535–c. 1615) and other Native Americans deployed Christianity's ideals of universality and justice to argue for an updated unifying connection between Indians and Spaniards and to articulate protests against abuses of the responsibilities they attributed to colonial power. Indians under Spanish rule thus asserted a viable version of Christianity of their own, excluded as they were on racial grounds from the clergy and from the women's religious orders.

Across North America and in most of South America, far from the Aztec, Inca, and Spanish centers of missionary and legal authority, Native Americans encountered Christianity piecemeal rather than as an integrated, authoritarian whole. In seventeenth-century New England, for example, many Indians lived in prolonged contact with English settlers but independently of Puritan congregations. Others—typically fragments, lineages, and factions of Algonquian societies—showed interest in the religion of the Puritans and gravitated to new Native "praying towns." Scholars suggest that such "conversions" could originate in desires to build connections with the English settlers; their hopes, at least in some cases, also included moderating the pressures of dispossession of their lands; in other cases, ambitious sachems, or chiefs, looked to Christian connections to strengthen their positions vis-à-vis rivals. In the fast-moving currents of colonization, depopulation, and war, Christianization could be of interest as a strategy for protecting Algonquian interests and furthering Algonquian purposes.

Enacting conversion was particularly challenging in the Puritan setting, however, since Protestants placed so much emphasis on the written word and on the individual conscience; much more than Catholicism, theirs was a religion of language rather than ritual. A massive effort of translation and transposition was required of Indians who sought membership in a church. Indigenous traditions of storytelling had to be adapted to the demands of the "conversion narrative," as oral performances through which aspirants gave proof of inner conviction. Grasping the opportunity to expand their narrative repertoire by incorporating Christian performance, Algonquian Protestants also found new techniques for supplicating the supernatural forces in their own lives; in Puritan "practices of the self" revolving around the notion of sin, praying Indians may also have discovered personal psychological resources for coping with the pressures and tragedies of colonial life.

A somewhat fuller picture of the religious lives of Algonquian and Iroquoian people who accepted Catholic baptism in seventeenth-century New France, or in much of the upper Middle West and eastern Canada, can be found in the writings of French Jesuit missionaries. As in the New England case, these Native Americans incorporated Christianity within larger patterns of economic and political connections with the French. Though the Indians of New France maintained a high degree of independence, Native Catholic villages that sprang up near Quebec and Montreal cemented community identities in masses, religious processions, and ceremonies; these rituals also articulated diplomatic links among various Indian nations and to the French. Though Native Catholicism can be approached in terms of these political and social functions, it also needs to be understood as a genuinely religious phenomenon. Long before Europeans appeared on the scene, Algonquian and Iroquoian peoples had appropriated healing rituals, sacred objects, and other spiritualized practices from other strangers. Their religions were experimental and undogmatic; they tolerated a wide range of beliefs and behaviors. Accordingly, missionaries had little difficulty securing acceptance of Christian legends, prayers, and precepts; persuading Native peoples to reject all other beliefs and practices was much more difficult.

The emergence in the 1670s of an Iroquois version of Catholic mystic-asceticism among recent converts at the New France missions shows how serious Native Americans, especially women, could be about claiming the spiritual content of Christianity for themselves. Fasting, praying, flagellating themselves, and alternately burning their flesh and immersing their bodies in freezing waters, these new Christians were hardly seeking clerical approval, as they did all this in secret; instead their aim appears to have been to surpass the priests in the experience of piety and to circumvent the latter's monopoly over access to the sacred. Indian Catholicism in this case sought direct contact with the sources of European spiritual power. This behavior was extreme, by definition rare, but it illustrates a larger point about Native American Christians of the colonial period: they were not passive victims of religious colonization, but rather active, even aggressive, appropriators.

ALLAN GREER

Bibliography

Greer, Allan. *Mohawk Saint: Catherine Tekakwitha and the Jesuits*. New York: Oxford University Press, 2005.

Griffiths, Nicholas, and Fernando Cervantes, eds. *Spiritual Encounters: Interactions between Christianity and Native Religions in Colonial America*. Birmingham, UK: University of Birmingham Press, 1999.

Mills, Kenneth. *Idolatry and Its Enemies: Colonial Andean Religion and Extirpation, 1640–1750*. Princeton, NJ: Princeton University Press, 1997.

Silverman, David J. *Faith and Boundaries: Colonists, Christianity, and Community among the Wampanoag Indians of Martha's Vineyard, 1600–1871*. New York: Cambridge University Press, 2005.

Vilaca, Aparecida, and Robin Wright, eds. *Native Christians: Modes and Effects of Christianity among Indigenous Peoples of the Americas*. Burlington, VT: Ashgate, 2009.

Class

Class—crucial for understanding how social hierarchies form and how the relationships among groups within a hierarchical system explain their unequal access to economic resources, social privilege, and political power—is one lens through which to analyze the profound historical shifts that define the Atlantic World. By the late sixteenth century, traditional landed European elites—and the aspiring business elites with whom they competed—had recognized that the accumulation of capital at home and in colonies had become indispensable to the health of the military state and to the propertied classes of civil society. The capitalist innovations that they pursued around the Atlantic World generated new classes and new relationships of unequal exchange among Europeans, Native Americans, and Africans, a process that cannot be looked at apart from the accompanying emergence of modified and invented gender and racial hierarchies. These new relationships formed in tandem with the advent of European imperial political economies. Fueled by capitalist modes of finance, commerce, and agricultural production, they concentrated power in upper-class hands, with historically unrivaled, often dislocating rapidity, by depriving the lowest classes of the wealth their labor created.

In early-modern Europe, most particularly in Britain, the capitalist revolution in agriculture, striving to increase commercial production of food-stuffs and wool for national and international markets, depended upon government support for the private enclosure of lands formerly held in common and for the abolition of customary rights of families to remain on land that they had worked for generations. While titled aristocrats participated in this process, new gentry and yeoman classes, who prospered in relative contrast to the new class of wage-earning rural workers they exploited for profit, led the way in expropriating the commons and terminating rights to tenancy.

Trade legislation and seemingly ceaseless imperial wars also facilitated the expansion of commercial capitalism around the Atlantic and the world over. Merchant classes involved in overseas trade as well as in wholesale and retail commerce grew in Europe, Africa, and the Americas. Some of these merchants were members of the old aristocratic class, while others ranked among a loosely defined "middling sort" that also included master craftsmen with apprentice workers engaged in artisanal manufactures as well as capitalists investing in the early mechanized production of arms, ceramics, textiles, ships, and spirits. Merchants did not themselves move the goods produced in ever-greater quantities overseas: mariners did. Although seamen's labor increased mercantile wealth, merchants increased their own take by paying fixed wages to sailors rather than giving them their traditional shares in the profits of a voyage. Agricultural and merchant capitalism thus created new classes of wage laborers, both on land and on the sea.

Merchants also created another new class of commodified human beings by sponsoring the transatlantic trade in servants and slaves. In Africa, European and African slave traders collaborated to produce a new class of permanently enslaved workers bound for Atlantic markets. A spectrum of lower-class workers served as slave catchers and labored at coastal slave-trading installations called *factories*. European governments enabled this human commerce—or trafficking in humans—by incorporating joint-stock slave-trading companies and granting contracts to merchants to ship members of marginalized ethnic groups, orphans, convicts, political prisoners, and poor people to the colonies, where they were forced to labor as indentured servants. In the colonies of the Americas, they sold both servants and slaves as differing species of chattel property.

Additional classes emerged around the early-modern Atlantic through the evolution of the plantation and *encomienda* systems. The plantation system, which the Portuguese built from late-medieval beginnings in the Mediterranean through extensions in the Atlantic off the west coast of Africa, was driven by the emergent planter class's pursuit of maximal profits through the unpaid labor of a brutally disciplined, highly organized, unfree workforce. This newly constituted class of laborers, most of them enslaved Africans, worked primarily to produce cash crops for export in imperial and international markets. Although planters in the Iberian, Dutch, and French Atlantics directly adopted the Portuguese model, British planters moved to it only after first experimenting with indentured servants, whose conditions in the colonies resembled those of slaves more than those of servants in Britain and Ireland.

Wherever the plantation system in the Atlantic thrived, slave societies did as well, with legally enshrined class hierarchies prescribed along racial lines and justified by patriarchal or paternalistic pretensions. In the Iberian Atlantic, the state-sponsored *encomienda* system, transplanted to the Americas after Christian consolidation of Iberian lands seized from Muslim owners during the "Reconquista," granted the first generation of conquistadors the right to exploit Indian laborers in mining, ranching, and agricultural production. After abolition of the *encomienda* in 1542, landowners and artisans in Spanish America continued to control Native laborers through such legal devices as clientage, debt, and vagrancy laws, so that mixed-race *castas* labored alongside Indians and African slaves in mines, on ranches, and on haciendas.

The history of class formation throughout the early-modern Atlantic reveals the human agency behind the construction of social inequalities. Classes are not existential reflections of the human condition, nor products of natural economic forces. The creation of upper classes (and capital accumulation) depended upon the willingness of powerful elites to tear asunder moral obligations that stemmed from medieval notions of humanity's common origins, so as to exclude both foreigners and the lower orders of their own societies. This broken circuit transformed traditional notions of sin, or transgressions against community, into the virtues of competitive individual accumulation. Exploitation of workers for private profit, which Christian tradition perceived as a sign of humanity's fallen nature, was recast as capitalism, a supposedly civilizing pathway to the betterment of humankind. Many from the growing ranks of the middling classes tacitly accepted or actively endorsed this view as an opportunity, even invitation, to join the elite themselves.

On the other hand, those who ended up laboring within the most exploited classes in the early-modern Atlantic found little in the way of virtue in their situations. Through whatever means at hand, they tried to ameliorate their conditions through calculated displays of deference, appeals to religious traditions of social justice, petitions to upper-class patrons and to political authorities, and nonviolent demonstrations of collective strength. Gender and racial hierarchies, however, made for unequal and sometimes oppressive relationships, as men of European descent often embraced the limited opportunities masculinity and whiteness afforded them to secure their own interests at the expense of the others among whom they lived.

Working-class people also collectively resisted their political subjugation, personal humiliation, and material deprivation, often surmounting racial and ethnic barriers in the process. They broke down enclosures converting common lands to private property, sabotaged their employers' workplaces, staged slowdowns and stoppages, ran away from plantations, and fought whip-wielding overseers. They also staged mass uprisings that while largely unsuccessful became endemic, destabilizing features of early-modern Atlantic history, among them the Midlands Rising (England, 1607), Bacon's Rebellion (Virginia, 1676), the Pueblo Revolt (New Spain, 1680), black-flag piracy (1713–1726), the New York City slave risings (1712, 1741), Tacky's Revolt (Jamaica, 1760), the White Boy movement (Ireland, 1760s), the London Port Strike (1768), the rebellions of Túpac Amaru II (Peru, 1780) and Túpac Katari (Bolivia, 1781), the French peasant revolts (1788–1789), the Haitian Revolution (1791–1804), and the Malê Revolt (Brazil, 1835). Both violent and nonviolent forms of politicized, class-conscious protest reveal how early-modern working-class people, from well before the nineteenth-century

Industrial Revolution, organized collective action to modify or abolish the imperial and capitalistic institutions that had led to social marginalization, economic exploitation, and political oppression.

JOHN DONOGHUE

Bibliography

Berlin, Ira. *Many Thousands Gone: The First Two Centuries of Slavery in North America*. Cambridge, MA: Belknap Press of Harvard University Press, 2000.

Donoghue, John, and Evelyn Jennings, eds. *Building the Atlantic Empires: The State, Unfree Labor, and the Rise of Global Capitalism, 1500–1945*. Leiden: Netherlands: Brill, 2014.

Linebaugh, Peter, and Marcus Rediker. *The Many-Headed Hydra: Sailors, Slaves, Commoners, and the Hidden History of the Revolutionary Atlantic*. Boston, MA: Beacon, 2000.

Lockhart, James, and Stuart B. Schwarz. *A History of Colonial Spanish America and Brazil*. New York: Cambridge University Press, 1983.

Climate and Weather

The term *weather* refers to day-to-day variations of the atmosphere. *Climate* is defined as "average weather," with interest focused on greater, though varying, lengths of time. Generally, climatologists use 30-year periods, but some paleoclimatologists study climate over longer timeframes, such as the last 2,000 years. Copious conventional meteorological records cover roughly the last century and a half. The earlier climate record comes mostly from documentation and from "proxy data," natural phenomena that vary with changing climates (for example, tree rings, lake sediments, and ice layers).

Climate variations can occur on hemispheric or global scales, resulting from broad controls such as incoming solar radiation and wind and atmospheric circulation systems. Or, variations can occur dramatically within short distances (for example, within eastern Virginia) owing to topographic diversity and such elements as localized land-sea breezes. At the geographic scales of the Atlantic Basin, westerly winds with traversing mid-latitude cyclonic storms dominate in the winter half of the year in the Northern Hemisphere, with the trade winds (moving from east to west) confined to the deep tropics within about 20 degrees latitude of the equator. In the summer season, the "Bermuda High" system dominates the central North Atlantic Ocean. Winds around this high-pressure system flow clockwise, transporting southerly humid air from the Caribbean along much of the southeast coast of North America and bringing the warmer moist air that keeps western Europe relatively mild. Generally from June to November, hurricanes can be guided from east to west by the trade winds in the tropics and occasionally migrate northward, steered by the circulation along the western edge of the Bermuda high system. Eastern North America also falls under the influence of cold continental air masses in the winter and warm Gulf flows in the summer, thus normally experiencing a wider range of climate extremes (warm/cold, dry/wet) than the same latitudes in Europe.

The climate of the Southern Hemisphere's Atlantic-Basin is more maritime and experiences fewer weather extremes than that of the Northern Hemisphere, owing to the much smaller coverage by land area. Westerly winds dominate south of 30 degrees latitude. A major feature of the climate of tropical western Africa is the annual oscillation of the Inter-Tropical Convergence Zone (ITCZ), in which the northeast and southeast trade winds at the surface converge to cause uplifting and create belts of monsoonal precipitation as the warm, moist surface air rises, cools, and produces sometimes torrential rainfall. The ITCZ migrates, although unevenly, northward and southward with the positions of maximum solar radiation. Persistent lack of the ITCZ in an area can lead to severe drought. Tropical cyclones are extremely rare in the southern Atlantic Ocean due to colder ocean temperatures. The desert regions of both northern and southern Africa (the Sahara and the Kalahari, respectively) remain under the influence of high-pressure systems along the Tropics of Cancer and Capricorn throughout most of the year, thus receiving little precipitation, if any at all.

Historians of climate change, dating back to the pioneering work by historical climatologist Hubert Lamb in the 1970s, are interested in both general trends of climate, over timescales encompassing the last millennium, and the frequencies of climate extremes. Generally, the signals of long-range global warming from increased human-induced carbon dioxide have been observed over much of the Atlantic Basin since the early twentieth century, particularly in the last few decades. However, decadal variations extending centuries back, not directly related to the carbon-dioxide signal, are related to the North Atlantic Oscillation, a dominant mode of atmospheric circulation over the Atlantic Ocean indicative of the Bermuda High and Icelandic Low. The strength of the North Atlantic Oscillation varies, but it has mostly been in a higher phase since the later twentieth century, which correlates with more storms in northern and central Europe and cold and dry conditions on the North American east coast. A low North Atlantic Oscillation can lead to fewer storms in Europe and more cold-air outbreaks in eastern North America.

Generally, from about 1500 to 1850, much of western Europe and parts of eastern North America experienced a persistent oscillation known as the Little Ice Age, in which summer cooling generally took place, although it was not consistent every year or everywhere. Some extreme years of the Little Ice Age are prominent in the historical climate literature, such as the "Year without a Summer" in 1816 for Europe and eastern North America. The Little Ice Age was also characterized by higher climate variability for some locations in the Atlantic Basin, as with the warm weather during the Great Fire in London in 1660 and the "Year without a Winter" for the eastern United States in 1828. Some scholars link cold extremes of the Little Ice Age with increased volcanic activity, although eruptions and the sun-blocking ash they distribute around the globe at high altitudes cannot alone explain all cold events. Some scholars also emphasize the importance of the North Atlantic Deep Water, a great marine conveyor belt that normally transports heat to the North Atlantic. When it is weaker, that can lead to colder climate episodes, perhaps like those of the Little Ice Age. Weather extremes and hazards, such as the Great Snow of 1717 in New England, pervasive drought in the American Southeast during the late 1500s and early 1600s, and increased Caribbean hurricanes in the late 1700s, are also evident, although, again, these did not persist throughout the Little Ice Age.

Decade- or two-decade-long periods of drought, tending to recur toward the ends of centuries, seem to have framed epochal changes in the history of

Africa. The militarization of the southern fringes of the Sahara Desert in western Africa coincided with dry conditions in the eleventh century, following several hundred years of relatively moist environments. Population dispersals and violence during a period of severe drought in the 1580s and 1590s converted coastal Angola into a northerly extension of the Kalahari and produced refugees, raiding, and captives in the large numbers that raised European slave trading in the Atlantic from its irregular early levels to the mass transportation scheme it became in the seventeenth century. Also at the end of the seventeenth century, the sale of captives generated by drought in both western and central Africa fed rapid increases in the volume of the trade throughout the eighteenth century, peaking in the 1780s and 1790s during yet another return of extended failures of rain. The calamitous epidemics, animal die-offs, and raiding of the next great drought, in the 1880s and 1890s, are well documented, owing to its not incidental concurrence with European military conquest.

Historians are interested in linking climate change with societal impacts through time, as well as explaining the contributions of weather extremes to major historical events. Older and more simplistic concepts in this field of study include *climate determinism*, originating with Ellsworth Huntington, which suggests that particular sets of climate characteristics can be linked directly to sets of societal types, and that the characteristics of such impacts have remained largely unchanged through time. An early version of climate determinism was the belief that climates are constant at equal latitudes and that this stability, persisting for at least a few centuries, has had determinative impacts on early settlement patterns in the New World.

Climate determinism is viewed today as unlikely, nor can the method be broadly generalized, although in the new millennium it has enjoyed a revival, with many earth scientists studying climate with regard to selected historical events. The extinction of the Norse settlements in Greenland occurred in the early part of the Little Ice Age, and protracted drought and famine in fifteenth-century Mexico preceded the arrival of the Spaniards and the ensuing epidemiological collapse. The hardships of the early Jamestown settlement in the early 1600s are well known, and the numerous eighteenth- and nineteenth-century yellow fever epidemics in the American Southeast may be linked with the El Niño phenomenon in the Pacific Ocean. Severe droughts in Brazil during colonial times may also be linked with major El Niño episodes.

Disciplines in the social sciences and the humanities have inverted the imputed causation of climate determinism to emphasize societal adaptations to climate changes. Such ideas have varied from broad, simplistic approaches, such as testing a *lessening hypothesis*—which assumes that society can adapt to minor climatic stress through time—to a *catastrophe hypothesis*, which adds the idea that societies adapting according to the lessening hypothesis gradually become more vulnerable to major climatic events. Some scholars study the interactions of climate and society with a *globalization* perspective that integrates political and economic aspects to explain both climate vulnerability and historical adaptations. Mike Davis, in *Late Victorian Holocausts* (2000), describes elegantly how extreme climate events in the late nineteenth century can be correlated with global famine, including in Brazil, and major social stresses in the areas that fell to European military power at the time. Some studies have contrasted *climate reality* with *climate perception*, that is, climate as measurable in scientific terms and climate as experienced, as understandings of the atmosphere have changed at different times in the past. Other new cultural perspectives include changes in the ways scholars view climate change and its impacts over time, as well as the effects of natural variations on fire as a Native American tool of environmental management. Opportunities and challenges involving collaboration among experts from the natural and physical sciences, social sciences, and the humanities await study toward understanding links between climate and history in the Atlantic World.

CARY J. MOCK

Bibliography

Davis, Michael. *Late Victorian Holocausts: El Niño Famines and the Making of the Third World*. New York: Verso, 2000.

Dupigny-Giroux, Lesley-Ann, and Cary J. Mock, eds. *Historical Climate Variability and Impacts in North America*. New York: Springer, 2009.

Endfield, Georgina H. *Climate and Society in Colonial Mexico: A Study in Vulnerability.* Malden, MA, and Oxford: Blackwell, 2008.

Lamb, Hubert H. *Climate: Present, Past, and Future.* London: Methuen, 1977.

Wigley, T. M. L., M. J. Ingram, and G. Farmer, eds. *Climate and History: Studies in Past Climates and their Impact on Man.* Cambridge: Cambridge University Press, 1981.

Colonies and Colonization

Empire was always more than a matter of economic exploitation and political control. It also involved profound social and cultural processes that changed both the colonizers and those colonized. The essential political corollary to "imperial thinking" was a "colony": the notion of imperialism as dominance was complemented by the notion of "colonialism as dependency." Both were statements of fact and also states of mind. It is worthwhile to emphasize this conceptual binary: understanding the relationship between colonies and colonialism is, above all, about establishing contrasting and mutually excluding categories. A colony was different from an autonomous political entity as power over a colony resided in another place—in the case of the Atlantic generally in Europe—and because colonists often aspired to ape the culture of an imperial center that, ironically, tended to exclude them. Understandably, colonial resentment often followed.

In the Americas, the colonial elites, most of whom were the descendants of emigrants from Europe, aspired to share the exalted qualities attributed to the imperial center—to claim its heritage as theirs. Although colonial elites often developed their own variants of metropolitan culture, a process called *creolization*, they remained oriented toward the imperial center. Indeed, many chosen place names—such as New England and New Amsterdam—reflect as much. Devotion to the imperial homeland was also manifested in political and religious rituals, clothing, and culture. But the imperial center seldom accepted colonists' claims that they had created close imitations of the metropolis and continued to treat colonial elites as inferior, capable only of mimicry, rather than genuine cultural and political emulation. One of the principal reasons for the War of American Independence—above all else a colonial revolt against disliked imperial overlords—was that officials in London refused to accept American assertions that they had shown themselves equal to Britons through their services to the motherland in war and through their development of an elite American society that corresponded to the best in Britain. Britons thought of American colonials as subordinates, not equals.

The American colonies were the only part of the Atlantic World where relationships between Europe and overseas people were conceived of in colonial terms. In Africa, both Europeans and Africans understood their relationships as based upon mutual economic advantages but carrying few or no political or cultural implications, at least before the mid-nineteenth century. One of the great themes in the history of the American colonies is how settlers, usually through armed revolt, forced the metropolis to recognize their rights to the independent social and political existence that Africans had maintained. The end of political colonialism in the Americas in the early nineteenth century did not necessarily mean an end to colonial emulation of European values: well after political dependence ended, the American heirs to colonial elites tended to emulate cultural practices emanating from the imperial center.

Most of all, colonialism represented the institutionalization of difference. It involved a recognition that whatever happened in colonial settings needed to be mediated against a larger and normative social and political standard set by metropolitan opinion and power. At the same time, colonialism was also about incorporation. Consider, for example, the tattooed Cherokee chieftain wearing European dress; the Spanish American nationalist speaking the language of the imperialists from whose control he sought liberation; and the Native American woman living with an imperial official or merchant, bearing his children, and raising them in the culture of their father.

Colonialism and Atlantic history, however, have a complicated relationship: the latter was in part created to escape the confines of empire-colony dichotomies. Atlantic historians recognized that the relationship between imperial center and colonial periphery was not a simple process of the center dictating and the periphery receiving. Some colonials—notably elite Europeans resident in the Americas and a few Africans in charge of economic activities along the West African coast—succeeded in defying imperial military power. Indeed, in the United States in the nineteenth century the former colonists became themselves imperialists. And settlers in Australia became imperialists in the same century, while themselves remaining colonials. Colonization was thus never a fixed relationship between the parties contrasted. The United States, in particular, complicates theories of colonialism and post-colonialism: while clearly a post-colonial state, it is also the nation against which other post-colonial peoples construct their identities and political positions. Nevertheless, colonialism is something with which Atlantic historians continue to engage, as they analyze the development of processes of acceptance, emulation, and resistance against imperial cultural hegemony. Indeed, Atlantic places were deeply imbued with colonialist prejudices and attitudes born out of a common colonial condition.

Thus, Atlantic history both embraces and rejects colonialism as a governing paradigm. It mainly does so due to its particular conception of spatial relationships: a colonial bond is usually conceived of as that between a dominant center and a subordinate periphery. Empires command; colonies obey. A criticism sometimes made about Atlantic history is that it seems to concentrate on relatively insignificant places, emphasizing initiatives emanating from overseas. Historians have argued that it is at the peripheries that the true lineaments of Atlantic history can be discerned—there, the collision between various worlds took place. The whole of these connections, Atlantic historians contend, is greater than the sum of their parts, so that even if the parts are inconsequential in themselves, taken together they reveal significant patterns. The Atlantic World was a complex, plural, and largely self-motivated adaptive system. That the center does not hold conceptually is something to be celebrated rather than lamented. In this respect, Atlantic history sees colonials and imperialists as engaged in a delicate dance, in which neither side was politically, culturally, or economically dominant.

TREVOR BURNARD

Bibliography

Chatterjee, Partha. *The Black Hole of Empire: History of a Global Practice of Power*. Princeton, NJ: Princeton University Press, 2012.

Lake, Marilyn, and Henry Reynolds. *Drawing the Global Colour Line: White Men's Countries and the International Challenge of Racial Equality*. Cambridge: Cambridge University Press, 2008.

McCoy, Alfred W., and Francisco Scarano, eds. *Colonial Crucible: Empire in the Making of the Modern American State*. Madison: University of Wisconsin Press, 2009.

Stoler, Ann Laura, and Frederic Cooper. *Tensions of Empire: Colonial Cultures in a Bourgeois World*. Berkeley and Los Angeles: University of California Press, 1997.

Columbian Exchange

Columbian Exchange is a term used to illuminate the two-way intercontinental transfers—intended and unintended, seen and unseen—of living species that followed the voyages of Columbus. Historian Alfred W. Crosby introduced the idea and the term in his landmark *The Columbian Exchange*, published in 1972, in which he created a new paradigm for understanding these movements as a key biological aspect of world history.

The concept of the exchange elucidates the transoceanic movements of plants, pathogens, and animals that accompanied European maritime expansion between the fifteenth and nineteenth centuries. Old World sugarcane transformed the New World tropics, while European livestock—brought to a continent without cattle, sheep, goats, pigs, or horses—launched the fabled ranching economies of the Americas. Conversely, Amerindian food staples were transported eastward, where they radically changed the diets and altered the agricultural systems and landscapes of Europe, Africa, and Asia. Maize, white and sweet potatoes, manioc, tomatoes, peanuts, and chili peppers contributed to the "Americanization" of three continents. Before the Columbian Exchange, none of these crops were grown outside the Americas. By the 1840s, the peasant population of Ireland had become utterly dependent on the potato (with devastating consequences during the Great Famine). Italy's poor similarly adopted the tomato, which ultimately became a defining ingredient of Italian cooking. West African and Asian cuisines owe their celebrated piquancy to the New World's chili peppers. Maize found new footing as a fast-growing staple along West Africa's coast, in China, and in Italy as polenta. The peanut also made an early appearance in West Africa, and later was taken up in China. New World chocolate and tobacco, Asian tea, and African coffee enlivened the salons and public houses of Europe.

Set against these intentional transfers were the accidental biological introductions of the Columbian Exchange. These include the insects, weeds, microbes, and other opportunistic stowaways that were unknowingly carried in European ships. Most notable were the Old World diseases that decimated Amerindian populations: smallpox, measles, influenza, malaria, yellow fever, typhus, and bubonic plague killed millions who had no prior exposure or immunity. As the substantial body of scholarship on the Columbian Exchange makes clear, European hegemony was built not only on firearms and military dominance but also on the plants, livestock, and pathogens European ships transplanted around the globe.

The settlement of new lands—not merely their conquest—was a prime mover of Columbian Exchange biota. Crosby, in his second book, *Ecological Imperialism* (1986), and other historians have underscored the importance of human contributions to the environmental histories of selected regions around the globe. Ordinary emigrants carried their Old World crops and animals to the new lands where they settled. With these familiar species, immigrants deliberately transformed distant and exotic outposts into landscapes resembling the ones they had left behind. In this way, ordinary people—not only plutocrat planters—remade the environments of New England, Australia, New Zealand, and South African as facsimiles of their birth countries, what Crosby calls *Neo-Europes*.

Among these broader initiatives, Africa's contributions to the Columbian Exchange have been largely diminished or ignored. This is not wholly surprising, given long-standing narratives of a continent dependent on agriculture and animal husbandry that developed in other world regions. However, recent research on Africa and Africans in the Atlantic World belies the perception of Africa as a passive recipient with few contributions of its own. Discoveries in archaeology, historical linguistics, and genetics reveal Africa as an ancient cradle of plant and animal domestication and a wellspring of improvements to crops and breeds. From this work a new portrait of the dynamic past of Africa emerges, that of a continent of creative, expert farmers and herders.

Africans independently domesticated cattle and developed breeds adapted to humid tropical climates. The guinea fowl and hair sheep, the latter bred for meat rather than for wool, contributed important food animals to Atlantic and global tables. Africa's indigenous agricultural revolution, which began some 7,000 years ago, added sorghum, pearl and eleusine millets, African ("red") rice, yams, and black-eyed peas to tropical diets. Scholarship on these foods now places Africa centrally within ancient Indian Ocean botanical exchanges that expanded Old World tropical repertoires in the millennia prior to European maritime expansion. As African sorghums and millets diffused to India, Africans adopted Asian bananas and plantains, developing them over time into more than 120 new cultivars. By the seventeenth century African plants, animals, and pathogens had crossed the Atlantic and taken root in the Americas. Just like the other transfers of the Columbian Exchange, the African biota were carried to new lands aboard European vessels. In this case, however, the vessels were slave ships, and the migrants they carried were not ordinary Europeans but enslaved Africans.

Between the sixteenth and nineteenth centuries Europeans forced the migration of more than 12 million Africans to New World plantations and mines. In fact, until the beginning of the nineteenth century, Africans made up three-quarters of all immigrants to the Americas. By then, slave ships had completed more than 35,000 voyages. To feed their captives as they crossed the Middle Passage, captains took onboard foods grown at their African ports of embarkation. These included the Amerindian crops introduced there—maize, manioc, and peanuts—as well as the continent's own principal dietary staples: sorghum, millet, rice, yams, and plantains. Within a century of Columbus's voyages, many of Africa's principal food crops had found new footings in the Americas.

These introductions make it possible to identify a distinctly African component of the Columbian Exchange, in which slave ships conveyed people, plants, and even food animals from Africa to the New World. Although the literature on the transatlantic slave trade and plantation slavery in the Americas emphasizes the commercialized commodities at the heart of the Atlantic economy—the Africans who were made chattel and the export crops they produced for European markets—African plant transfers underscore the importance of subsistence agriculture even on the plantations: the foods slaves preferentially grew for themselves in dooryard gardens, provision grounds, and plantation food plots.

The presence of African food staples in these early subsistence sites illustrates a component of the Columbian Exchange that was inadvertent and opportunistic rather than intentional. These transfers were accidental only in the minds of the Europeans, because slave victuals left over from the Atlantic crossings lost their utility to captains and crews when ships reached their New World destinations. The viable seeds and tubers remaining among these provisions, on the other hand, created opportunities for anonymous appropriation and appreciation by the enslaved.

These African components of the Columbian Exchange were principally food plants of the Old World tropics. They were well suited to the growing conditions of tropical and subtropical America where plantation economies evolved and where most enslaved Africans were settled. Some of these African introductions, such as yams and plantains, required little labor to plant and process; in this regard they had advantages over such more demanding New World root crops as manioc (or cassava). Others, especially sorghum and millet, were well adapted to semi-arid climates and poor soils. As these labor-saving and versatile cultigens found favor in slave food plots, they enabled Africans in the New World to recover familiar dietary preferences in trying and unfamiliar circumstances.

The African farmers and herders whom the slave ships carried were experienced in tropical agriculture and animal husbandry. The New World tropi-

cal and subtropical environments in which they found themselves would not have seemed entirely alien. Present, for instance, were plant species from pantropical botanical families also found in Africa, which slaves likely recognized and used. They would also gain familiarity with the foods and medicines of Amerindians, who often shared their fates in plantation fields, mines, or maroon hideaways. In the Caribbean enslaved Africans inherited the ethno-botanical knowledge of Amerindian inhabitants and became its living repositories when the Native populations vanished.

In the slaves' food plots and dooryard gardens European naturalists and slaveholders first encountered many foods and medicinal remedies new to them. A few even recognized that slaves had introduced these species. Confronted with novel tropical plants for which they had no names, Europeans borrowed the words slaves gave them. In this way, New World colonial languages gained words for *yam, okra, ackee* (the national fruit of Jamaica), *benne* (sesame), *banana, goober* (peanut), *callalou* (a popular pan-Caribbean stew), and *gumbo*. For some species already known to be African, Europeans affixed the geographical descriptor *guinea*, creating such vernacular names as guinea corn (*Sorghum vulgaris*), guinea squash (*Solanum aethiopicum*), guinea sorrel (*Hibiscus sabdariffa*), and even the guinea fowl (*Numida meleagris*). The creolized food assemblages in the subsistence plots of the enslaved eventually shaped the dishes that enslaved cooks prepared for slaveholder tables. Indeed, African ingredients have remained the defining culinary signatures of former plantation societies. Okra, black-eyed peas, palm oil, plantains, rice, the broad emphasis on greens, fritters, sesame confections, and one-pot stews, all are among the African hallmarks of modern Atlantic foodways.

The African contributions to the Columbian Exchange also included animals. African cattle invigorated the gene pool of the livestock populations that came to thrive in New World tropical lowlands. Slaves raised the African guinea fowl, introduced at an early date to plantation societies, in their dooryard gardens and sacrificed them in religious rituals. The food animals brought from Africa were provisioned for the Atlantic crossing with fodder and bedding cut from Native African grasses. These chance arrivals of guinea grass (*Panicum maximum*), Angola (Pará) grass (*Brachiaria mutica*), Bermuda grass (*Cynodon dactylon*), and other African species found new environmental niches in the emergent livestock economies of the New World tropics. These nutritive pasture grasses spearheaded a botanical invasion that environmental scientists have described as the "Africanization" of the New World tropics.

The Atlantic World was a time and place where people from all its continents—Native Americans, Europeans, and Africans—populated new landscapes with the crops, animals, and microbes transferred among them. A multiplicity of semiautonomous historical initiatives, at both regional and transregional scales, catalyzed the processes that shaped the environments in three continents, creating a compound Atlantic biome that all participants in the Atlantic World helped to create.

JUDITH A. CARNEY

Bibliography

Alpern, Stanley B. "The European Introduction of Crops into West Africa in Precolonial Times." *History in Africa* 19 (1992): 13–43.

Carney, Judith, and Richard Rosomoff. *In the Shadow of Slavery: Africa's Botanical Legacy in the Atlantic World.* Berkeley: University of California Press, 2009.

Crosby, Alfred W. *The Columbian Exchange: Biological and Cultural Consequences of 1492.* Westport, CT: Greenwood Press, 1972.

Crosby, Alfred W. *Ecological Imperialism: The Biological Expansion of Europe, 900–1900.* New York: Cambridge University Press, 1986.

Magee, D. A., C. Meghen, S. Harrison, C. S. Troy, T. Cymbron, C. Gaillard, A. Morrow, J. C. Maillard, and D. G. Bradley. "A Partial African Ancestry for the Creole Cattle Populations of the Caribbean." *The Journal of Heredity* 93, no. 6 (2002): 429–432.

McCann, James C. *Maize and Grace: Africa's Encounter with a New World Crop: 1500–2000.* Cambridge, MA: Harvard University Press, 2007.

McNeill, J. R. *Mosquito Empires: Ecology and War in the Greater Caribbean, 1620–1914.* Cambridge: Cambridge University Press, 2010.

Norton, Marcy. *Sacred Gifts, Profane Pleasures: A History of Tobacco and Chocolate in the Atlantic World.* Ithaca, NY: Cornell University Press, 2010.

Commercialization

Commerce became the central medium of the economies that developed and defined the Atlantic World. Although this characterization of the deep underlying dynamic in Atlantic history might appear to be a pure tautology within the framework of modern liberal economics, which defines itself in terms of commercialized exchanges—monetized, price-setting aggregates of demands and supplies—these arm's-length or contractual negotiations among strangers began as small sectors of much larger economies of production and consumption in late-medieval Europe, as well as (and more pervasively) in the Americas and in Africa. In these earlier economies, people sought what they wanted through ongoing personal relationships, directly from producers or from patrons in possession of what they needed or desired. Wealthy patrons, or skilled producers, in turn built relationships with clients by offering what they desired as obligating "gifts." Economies of this more general sort are sometimes termed *domestic* to emphasize the family-like personalism of the relationships through which material products flowed. Only through an artificially theorized limitation of "economy" to exchange, or commercial, transactions, can they be termed—rather negatively—"barter" or "subsistence." They were not simple. In them, complicated transactions stimulated and distributed substantial surpluses of commodities and artisan production over significant distances.

Commercialization can be defined as the intensification of the economic, social, and ethical connotations of exchange-based interactions among strangers, led by mercantile groups invested in inventories—and eventually financial interests in inventories and infrastructure—more than in personal relationships. The vast scale of the Atlantic World did much to promote commercialization as the defining process of transregional economic interaction. The features of commercialization originally distinctive to the Atlantic became standardized around the world toward the end of the twentieth century, broadly speaking, in the contemporary notion of globalization. Commercial law records the political aspects of commercialization as authorities rooted in earlier, more personalistic sorts of influence attempted to regulate and tax the enormous wealth arising from transatlantic economic integration in commercial terms. Commercialization represented an altogether broader process with cultural, political, and ideological, as well as economic, determinants and connotations.

Economic theorizing aside, though without discounting its great value in understanding human affairs, the historian concerned with human intentions and abilities to act might well guard against the temptation to view commercialization as a self-interpreting phenomenon. Atlantic commercialization offers an instructive case study showing how changes measurable in terms of economic variables depended upon structural and ideological changes embedded in the political realm and how commercial growth both stimulated and financed efficacious responses in social, ethical, and intellectual aspects of life. Focus on commercialization also helps to replace conventional nationalist teleologies, which interpret selected political strategies of the era as directly ancestral, if not equivalent, to later frameworks of empire and modern nation-states, with narratives demonstrating the more efficacious networks of small-scale, atomized commercial practices, initiated by all the leading participants in the economy of the Atlantic World. Atlantic history notes the centrality of commerce to the competition, mutual constitution, reciprocation, hybridization, and creolization of many hundreds of communities into an integrated whole that cannot be reduced into prototypical nation-states. Quite the opposite: in fact, commercial actors created and exploited new political frameworks to advance their economic initiatives. Commerce knew few boundaries, in spite of political efforts to impose them. Pan-Atlantic family networks—Jewish, Quaker, Huguenot, and others—led this commercialization, and the Dutch in the seventeenth century systematically exploited the monarchical domains of others. Commercialization in the Atlantic World was a process with as many political, intellectual, and ethical aspects as purely economic ones.

Commercialization accelerated in the Atlantic World primarily under European financial initiative, but the Europeans succeeded only with the intercession, negotiation, and influence of Africans and Native Americans. Trading practices and interests on the west coast of Africa, as well as on the Hudson River, framed the mechanics of Europeans' exchanges in both places. The anonymity of commercialization provided the practical framework for interactions among strangers from differing cultures. The delays, risks, and great expense of regular commercial interactions across an entire ocean placed financial capital at the center of the process. Capital as credit to finance initiatives produced indebtedness, which gave increasing political power to lenders, who were always in Europe. Overall, commercialization in the Atlantic World led to massive aggregate outflows of capital from Europe into the Americas and to Africa. Much of this investment credit remained unpaid, and this accumulated debt surfaced in the transatlantic political struggles that marked the Atlantic World in the half century after 1776. Although commercialization generated a distinctively dynamic Atlantic economy, which produced economic growth for all of the cultures on the Atlantic rim, Europe became the creditor region, with the Americas and Africa massively leveraged in its debt.

Management by Monarchy

The ideologies, institutions, and geography of commercialization shifted dramatically from the fifteenth century to the nineteenth century. Over the long term, Atlantic commercialization eroded the power of European monarchs. In the medieval period, outsiders had financed European monarchs, especially Florentines (for the Portuguese and for the Papacy) and the Augsburg Fuggers (for the Habsburg Holy Roman emperors in central Europe). More commercialized economies, first in the Netherlands and then in England, provided a means for these maritime powers to become self-financing. Commerce, unlike conquest, generated assets in cumulative and low-maintenance forms, so that by the sixteenth century merchants began to rival militarists as backers of public institutions. The ethic (and the end) of sixteenth- and seventeenth-century European polities remained largely monarchical because of the escalating demand for military materiel, but the means became commercial, and the most important domain for that commerce became increasingly Atlantic.

Early sixteenth-century extensions of European political authority into the Atlantic, especially by Spain, used the evangelical impulses of Catholicism to cover the quest for trade with conversions of their trading partners to Christianity. The commercially energizing return, however, was precious metals, gold from Africa in the fifteenth century and then much greater wealth in silver from the Americas. The Habsburg monarchs in Madrid succeeded in engrossing this unprecedented wealth to buttress their sole control in Iberia and to fund military adventures throughout most of Europe. Protestant competitors, the Dutch and then the English, sought to intrude on their Atlantic sources of specie (gold and silver coin) and succeeded sufficiently to start to fund commercial economies based on investments in the tropical Americas, in production of artisan goods in England exported to settler populations in temperate North America, on increasingly mechanized metallurgy for the militarization, especially naval, that accompanied these commercial initiatives, and in slaving in Africa to staff the commercial core of these strategies in the American plantations.

Commercialization—investment of monetized credit in production, in captives in Africa, in commodities in the Americas, and in consumer goods and military infrastructure—became the most efficacious strategy of growing Protestant intrusion into the formerly Iberian world of the Atlantic, Spain in the Americas, and Portugal in Africa. Northern Europeans thus shifted the economic center of gravity of the Atlantic from the Mediterranean, Iberia, and the Southern Ocean to the North Sea and the Baltic and North Atlantic. This recentering had been completed by the early years of the eighteenth century and had yielded returns sufficient to fund private trade without the umbrella of royal charters or military cover that had shielded earlier start-up phases of the process. Independent traders could make the case for removal of the privileges of the English Royal African Company (founded in 1672), for example, in ways more persuasive than opponents of England's East India Company's monopolistic charter in the Indian Ocean. Private merchants could operate with far greater success on the smaller scales of the Atlantic, and—particularly—did not face the competition of Asian economies more skilled and productive than their own.

Pervasive commercialization entailed institutional innovations, including developments in capital, finance, and trade. Two innovative practices—bills of exchange and the commission system—stand out as enabling and integrating. The bill of exchange was a note binding a merchant to pay a stated sum of money to another at a determined date in the future. It thus transferred needed sums without requiring huge and risky shipments of bulky specie—as the Spaniards had done in the sixteenth century—to the considerable benefit of English and Dutch privateers. These private notes, like modern financial derivatives, circulated beyond the specie-based and government-backed paper currencies emerging at the same time (for example, the sterling-based English pound) and became a significant source of liquidity—increasing the amount of monetary instruments in circulation faster than production of goods to buy—and thus contributed to inflation, the elemental corollary of commercialization. The commission system worked hand-in-glove with bills of exchange and reflected the improving capital positions of planters in the western Atlantic. Under this arrangement, planters shipped their commodities, retaining ownership, to commission agents in Europe. For a small commission the agent would land, warehouse, and market their crops, arrange return cargoes with the proceeds of selling them, and hold remaining balances for the planters to spend or invest in Europe or America via bills of exchange drawn on their accounts. The commission system enabled intensification and growth of commercial interactions across the Atlantic by allowing centripetal accumulations of capital in the Americas to contribute to the rapid rates of growth of commercialization centered in Europe.

The Atlantic World was both the source of the financial capital and the locale for its application in commerce. The process produced a new integration of the institutional realms previously separated as political—personal loyalties and protections—or economic—material exchanges beyond the sphere of mutual moral responsibility. In the Mediterranean and central Europe, trade and banking had developed as private family "houses." In the Atlantic, royal authorities gradually seized control, converting credit to pay for the crushing debts left by late-medieval monarchs' military ambitions into a source of revenue to fund the even greater costs of militarizing the early-modern Atlantic. Observers around Europe agreed that the liberalizing Dutch merchants of the sixteenth and seventeenth centuries, once freed of Habsburg taxes, worked out the legal form of "companies," which limited the liabilities of wealthy merchants and thus enabled them to assume the considerable risks of trading overseas. Wealth accumulated from the Atlantic—African gold through the Royal African Company, silver from the Spanish Americas, and a strategic royal marriage in Portugal—allowed the British to succeed the Dutch as leaders of commercialization in the eighteenth century.

Although African gold and American silver had funded the consolidation of monarchy in Portugal and Spain in the sixteenth and seventeenth centuries, the royal houses remained allied more closely with the Catholic Church than with commercializing merchants and spent these economic rewards, at least initially, for displays of piety and on military power. As they became dependent on these commercial sources of revenues, and on loans from merchant-bankers, princes began to jealously control domestic and international trade to protect the positions they had gained. However, they conflated wealth with precious metals and perceived exchange as a zero-sum game, that is, as yielding gains only at the expense of one's trading partners. Wars were aimed at seizing the assets of rival powers to pay for the conflicts themselves and to increase the prestige of the victor relative to that of the loser. As long as politics was territorially based and focused on personal power and prestige, and as long as commerce was dismissed as an unworthy—but increasingly necessary—pursuit of the ignoble, ethnic minorities, and foreigners, court intellectuals and their royal patrons viewed land and the producers resident on it as the natural vessel for wealth. Gold and silver were for hoarding and display rather than for circulation as currency. Wealth thus remained as finite as power.

The England of James I (r. 1603–1625), followed by Louis XIV (r. 1643–1715) in France and Charles II (the English monarch who restored the Stuart line in 1660), turned to commercial investment in the Atlantic. These monarchs used trading companies chartered with exclusive access (within their realms) to overseas resources. They meant to project their own power relative to that of dynastic rivals in remote spaces that were legally less defined than the hotly contested territorial domains within Europe. Covering private merchants with royal patronage proposed to concentrate political authority in the monarchy and to govern overseas territories and the royal agents in them—like the Dominion of New England (1686–1689)—with the collaboration of home merchants managed by councils—the Lords of Trade and Plantations in London (1621, as a temporary committee of the king's Privy Council) and the French Navy. Atlantic commerce became the material buttress for the royal prerogative.

Economics as Opportunity

Such monarchical control sat ill at ease with a growing number of merchants who also looked to Atlantic commerce as a source of wealth. Commercialization required cultural, intellectual, and legal framing expressed in the form of the new "science" of political economy, which contemplated the institutional arrangements that could gloss the dubious propriety of exchange with the ethical legitimacy of politics. By the end of the seventeenth century a distinctive, liberal Atlantic political-economic ideology emerged to celebrate and defend Atlantic commercialization as increasing the wealth of merchants and financiers, particularly in England. Commercialization was what the great political economists—John Locke (1632–1704), John Law (1671–1729), Adam Smith (1723–1790), and others—defined it as throughout the eighteenth century: the surest route to a civilized society.

These ideas proved too much for European monarchs' prerogative-sponsored attempts to monopolize the benefits of commerce. The accumulation of financial capital through commercialization in the Atlantic World far outpaced seventeenth-century attempts by political authorities in Europe to siphon tax revenues into the coffers of the government by regulating trade. Growing awareness, by the final third of the seventeenth century, of the difficulties of regulating commerce in far reaches of the Atlantic World, and broader participation in its benefits by private merchants in London and other ports, produced a growing consensus in England that economic success overseas resulted from the absence of monarchical interference. This new political economy delineated separate, though interrelated, spheres of economy and polity. Commercialization in the Atlantic proceeded best without government patronage. As Adam Smith appreciated, European exploitation of American resources created economic opportunities for new groups—mostly those, like John Locke (born in the maritime southwest of England), whose lives bordered the Atlantic. These ideas developed Dutch precedents articulated by Hugo Grotius, who had argued that maritime trade ought not be the property of a single nation. They then inspired mid-eighteenth-century French physiocrats like François Quesnay (1694–1774) who championed a more generalized notion of *laissez-faire* for domestic and international commerce but remained loyal to an economy based on agriculture, managed by monarchy, and stimulated by royal subsidies that were the belated equivalents of the chartered monopolies the Dutch and English had made outmoded by the middle of the eighteenth century.

The western coasts of Europe and their ports facing the ocean, especially Bristol, Glasgow, Nantes, Zeeland, and Liverpool, became the greatest relative beneficiaries of the growing Atlantic economy. By the seventeenth century new, liberal political ideas circulated that urged denying access to this Atlantic wealth to metropolitan trading monopolies and the Stuart dynasty's centralizing political strategies. The English beneficiaries of Atlantic trade created the movements against the monopoly companies in the 1620s; contributed to the republican cause during the English civil war (1642–1651); attempted to exclude the Catholic Duke of York from succession to the crown between 1679 and 1681; and most importantly, became the agents of economic growth and liberal politics after the Glorious Revolution of 1688 definitively installed commercial interests behind the throne. During the first half of the eighteenth century antimonopoly movements in France and in the Netherlands deployed similar rhetoric. All thrived on the new resources of wealth and power produced by commercialization in the Atlantic.

Commercial political economy presented the political right to assert individual economic self-interest as collectively (i.e., politically) virtuous ("efficient"). Pamphleteers began to celebrate how rationally calculated material self-interest could substitute for the morality of interpersonal equivalents and condemned such pernicious human passions as carnal lust and megalomania. Politics became less

concerned with justice in a moral sense and more concerned with guaranteeing personal autonomy to pursue one's own economic self-interest, including the right to act politically as groups formed around common material pursuits. Accommodating such interest-driven activity within the political system came to be viewed as fluid political activity itself rather than as a threat to politics seen as stable authority. Intellectuals and policy makers, but mostly Atlantic traders themselves, began to erode the authority of theory with their own empirical experience of trading in the Atlantic. They endorsed politics' jettisoning of theologically based "just" order by expunging morality from the commercial political economy of interest. As with political theory, they continued to invoke the teachings of the ancients by incorporating the republican stricture that civic responsibility—or personal virtue—was the lifeblood of politics. It was the consequential intellectual achievement of this Atlantic political economy to eclipse the earlier pan-European, humanist, republican belief that individual wealth corrupted society.

Jeffersonian Republicans in the new United States of America sought to keep the humanist flame alive by promoting a society grounded on the inherent virtues of an agrarian citizenry. This vision could not withstand the attractions, to government and the indivdual, of an economy and society integrated by capital and commerce, which was the brainchild of Alexander Hamilton. As a result, wealth replaced personal virtue in legitimizing government policy. The advocates of individual enterprise began to argue that commercial markets displayed systematic, autonomous, and reliably observable opportunities and that it was folly to intervene politically in these inherently beneficial processes. Deregulation of both domestic and overseas markets became a cause célèbre of the eighteenth century. In an extended monarchical network held together by trade, individual material interests chafed against centralized control of commercial initiative. It was no small historical irony that the political economy of interest, developed to support monarchy in Europe, first eroded that monarchical authority, then became a refrain that later justified limiting the mother country's power over its outposts in North America.

Commercialization altered institutions as well as ideas across the Atlantic. New structures deferred the formulation of policy to merchant practitioners who understood and had experienced Atlantic commercialization. From 1696, the English Board of Trade, for example, without access to constitutional means to act unilaterally, became an information-gathering body. It then became a sounding board, within a parliamentary framework, for participants in the economy, predisposing itself toward the cause of deregulation and indeed operating as an alternative to the old state-sponsored monopoly companies themselves. During this period, Atlantic merchants developed the political means to resist metropolitan attempts to restrict their commercial economy and centralize their political institutions. These means of resistance included and complemented the institution of colonial agencies in London and the shift from direct trade—in which merchants purchased colonial produce in America—to the commission system that allowed American producers to sell their commodities in Britain. Both allowed Atlantic merchants access to European correspondents who also represented the interests of their vendors within the metropolitan political process. Trading formats adapted to the need to defend, uphold, and advance their economic interests, using new political strategies at a time when such means multiplied.

Atlantic commerce thus integrated formerly separated political and economic spheres—both the institutions and the ideas that rationalized and legitimated them. In the early eighteenth century this new synthesis of politics and economies stressed their interdependence, but by the time of Adam Smith it had come to stress their interchangeability, their virtual identity, and, by the early years of the nineteenth century and the triumph of the ideology of free trade, was embracing the neoclassical view espoused by David Ricardo that politics and economics ought to be considered entirely separately. These ideas dissociated commercial exchange from political responsibility and created the need to define the separate sphere of modern liberal economics. By the nineteenth century, finance had so outpaced the monarchies who had sought, from the fifteenth century, to siphon the power of commerce that it began to supplant monarchical and aristocratic prestige in the form of "bourgeois revolutions." These political upheavals brought political power into line with a redistribution of wealth in society reflecting that accumulated from Atlantic commerce. The pervasive commercialization of so-

ciety, so much the outcome of the development of transatlantic markets and industrial manufacturing, saw republican and humanist traditions challenged by the distinctive liberal doctrine of a sovereign domain of economics.

WILLIAM A. PETTIGREW

Bibliography

Brenner, Robert. *Merchants and Revolution: Commercial Change, Political Conflict, and London's Overseas Traders, 1550–1653*. Princeton, NJ: Princeton University Press, 1993.

Hirschman, Albert O. *The Passions and the Interests: Political Arguments for Capitalism before Its Triumph*. Princeton, NJ: Princeton University Press, 1976.

Hont, Istvan. *Jealousy of Trade: International Competition and the Nation-State in Historical Perspective*. Cambridge, MA: Harvard University Press, 2010.

Pettigrew, Wlliam A. *Freedom's Debt: The Royal African Company and the Politics of the Atlantic Slave Trade, 1672–1752*. Chapel Hill: University of North Carolina Press, 2013.

Pocock, J. G. A. *The Machiavellian Moment: Florentine Political Thought and the Atlantic Republican Tradition*. Princeton, NJ: Princeton University Press, 2003.

Steele, Ian K. *The English Atlantic: An Exploration of Communication and Community*. New York: Oxford University Press, 1986.

Commodities

The unfolding of capitalism rested on the transformation of the global countryside, in Europe, throughout the Atlantic World, and beyond—a massive change to turn rural cultivators into the producers of commodities for metropolitan markets. While such transformations were important to the surge of capitalism within Europe, reallocations of the land and labor involved proved difficult to effect in the face of deeply entrenched social orders at home and in Africa. On a most basic level, such restraints were lacking in the Americas, and this relatively open field gave Europe the key to economic development. Whereas in Europe landowners engaged in drawn-out struggles with rural cultivators, and budding urban capitalists with feudal landlords, and whereas in Africa flexible local communities absorbed European commercial capital, in vast swaths of the New World enterprising Europeans entered lands emptied of Native populations, decimated on massive scales by contacts with the newcomers, who were then able to invent a radically new world of commodity production, with low initial costs and huge profits.

This violent and radical transformation of the social structure and ecology of the American countryside was thus one of the most important factors in Europe's rise toward global economic supremacy by the nineteenth century. In many ways, the roots of what has been called "the Great Divergence" (Pomeranz), as maritime Europe pulled ahead of China and other parts of Asia in wealth, technologies, and productivity, can be found in the mines and on the plantations of the Americas. Mines provided resources, principally gold and silver, to tap the manufacturing bounty of Asia and to fund Europe's nearly permanent state of war—which, in turn, created the greatly enhanced capabilities of the fiscal-military state that would become the framework of global domination. The plantations produced the foodstuffs, fibers, and drugs to overcome the resource constraints of a small, politically divided peninsula of western Eurasia. Atlantic commodities became the core resource feeding European economic growth.

This growing commodity-producing complex in the Americas unfolded in three distinct steps. First, in the sixteenth, seventeenth, and early eighteenth centuries, the combination of expropriated American lands and enslaved African labor fed specie and commodities into parts of maritime Europe. Spanish silver and Brazilian, then Caribbean, sugar were at the center of this first phase, and the core institutional innovation that made possible the exploitation of the resources of the Americas was enslaved labor. In many ways the transatlantic trade in captive Africans became the central channel in the flows of Atlantic commerce, the trade in commodified humans on which all other commodity trades rested. Mobilizing slave labor on expropriated lands, building on earlier ventures on the Atlantic islands along the African coast, allowed Europeans to produce bulk commodities at great geographic distances from processing industries and final consumers in Europe. The Atlantic World helped Europe escape the ecological constraints of its small

size by putting much more land at the disposal of Europeans wanting to produce calories, textile fibers, and drugs. For the first time in human history, local resource constraints were overcome by organizing production on an extracontinental scale. Atlantic expansion also overcame local constraints on the availability of labor in Europe, much of it locked into supporting ecclesiastical and aristocratic rural domains. Such sudden and radical reallocations of resources on transoceanic scales were possible only because of the great commitment of European military powers and private investors to violence, and their ability to deploy it by sea.

The second phase of commodity production in the Americas spanned the late eighteenth and first half of the nineteenth centuries. As industrialized processing and fabrication emerged in pockets of Europe and North America, manufacturing and the expanding class of nonagricultural workers drew increasingly on the Atlantic World's resources for food, as well as for raw materials. For the first time Africa, the Americas, and Europe were integrated into a single, vast production complex. Faster communication and transportation technologies, and enhanced military force, also allowed for control of hinterlands far beyond the port cities, which in turn provided access to new raw materials such as cotton in the West Indies, Brazil, and especially the United States; rubber and coffee in Brazil; and increasing quantities of sugar from new producers, such as Cuba. That dynamic integration of plantation commodities and metropolitan manufacturing rested on vast intensification of slavery in the Americas, and access to labor from the African continent remained at the center of the Atlantic economy into the 1850s and 1860s.

In a third phase, beginning in the mid-nineteenth century, the Americas expanded the commodity-production complex through the work of sharecroppers, family farmers, and wage workers. For the first time, new administrative capacities of the state were able to transform the countryside without resorting to slavery and other forms of outright expropriation.

A surprisingly narrow range of undifferentiated bulk commodities (products not distinguished by traits qualitatively valued in the marketplace) dominated these processes. Precious metals came first, followed by extracted fish, fur, and woods, and then investments in producing sugar, tobacco, indigo, rice, and—by the early nineteenth century—also cotton and coffee. By the nineteenth century, the Americas became a significant provider also of hides, wheat, wool, and meat to feed and clothe consumers in Europe, and eventually of copper, rubber, and petroleum for industrialized production and transportation.

Categorizing these Atlantic commodities by how they were produced highlights the accumulating capital invested in producing them. By far the most significant system of production in the Atlantic World was based on force: expropriated lands and enslaved Africans working under high degrees of coercion. It was indeed the unique ability of Europeans to use the power of capital in conjunction with the military power of the state to empty vast territories and then repopulate them with Africans deported and made to labor under violent supervision. Sugar, indigo, rice, cotton, and coffee were first and foremost the products of enslaved labor, explaining why four times as many Africans as Europeans arrived in the New World between 1491 and 1830. White planters grew wealthy on the commodities slaves produced for European consumers, along with the merchants and bankers involved in financing the costly productive infrastructure. Indeed, Atlantic investors were among the very wealthiest Europeans of their times. Until well into the nineteenth century the plantation economies of the South produced the greatest wealth in North America and the Caribbean. The "great divide" in North America was between a wealthy South and a less prosperous North. Slavery was the institutional tool that intensified production most effectively.

A second set of commodities was secured by trade with indigenous producers, even though the importance of these commodities paled in comparison with the commodities enslaved laborers produced. Already in the sixteenth and seventeenth centuries, Europeans began exchanging goods for commodities that Africans and Native Americans extracted. Within Africa the core of such merchant-mediated trade, without significant investment in productive capacity, was the purchasing of captives, essentially extracted humans, enriching local warrior-rulers and European merchants, while devastating large swaths of the African countryside. In the Americas, one of the most significant extractive trades took place in the northern forests, where Na-

tive hunters and trappers secured large quantities of animal pelts and furs that would provide the raw material for increasingly fashionable styles of dressing in Europe. European settlers in these regions began to specialize in ice, wood, and salted fish to provide the plantation economy of the Caribbean and the American South with urgently needed foods and other supplies.

Commodity extraction and exchanges remained marginal within the Atlantic economy as a whole, but they laid the foundations for a third kind of industrial capitalism in North America in the nineteenth century, based on household food farming, mercantile pursuits, and wage-labor manufacturing. This group of agricultural commodities began dominating Atlantic trade in the last third of the nineteenth century as the administrative, scientific, and bureaucratic abilities of the state grew, increasingly able to transform the countryside to producing commodities for world markets without resorting to slavery. Perhaps the first wave of modern commodities hit the Atlantic in the 1850s, when massive wheat exports from North America began to reach European ports. With the emancipation of slaves in the United States in 1865, cotton grown by sharecroppers and wage workers also arrived in Liverpool, Le Havre, and Bremen markets, to be followed later in the century by barely "free labor" coffee and sugar. By the late century, new regions of the Atlantic, especially Argentina, Uruguay, and Paraguay, also became major suppliers of hides and meat by drawing on nonslave labor; Brazil became a major exporter of coffee. Central America eventually also gained a place in Atlantic commodity production, primarily through the export of bananas to North American and European markets, made possible by the advent of refrigerated shipping.

The commodity trades of the Atlantic laid the foundations of modern capitalism by extracting land and labor by violence, by accumulating capital as a result, and by enabling well-financed merchants to create globally integrated networks of production, using innovations in finance, insurance, banking, bookkeeping, and personnel management. These Atlantic, and eventually global, commodity markets also financed the fiscal-military states that would become increasingly important to the unfolding of industrial capitalism in Europe itself. By creating an export-oriented service economy in New England and the Middle Atlantic region of the United States, it also laid the groundwork for the industrial development of these parts of North America. It has been argued, persuasively, that Europe's incorporation of the Americas and Africa into its network of capital investment was the core innovation that created the modern world of global commercial integration. It was certainly the basis of the tremendous economic growth in England after 1780, and also—though rather later—on the continent, in France and Germany, and Europe's eventual economic, military, and cultural domination of the larger world.

SVEN BECKERT

Bibliography

Beckert, Sven. *The Empire of Cotton: A Global History.* New York: Alfred A. Knopf, 2014.

Mintz, Sidney. *Sweetness and Power: The Place of Sugar in Modern History.* New York: Viking, 1985.

Pomeranz, Kenneth. *The Great Divergence: China, Europe, and the Making of the Modern World Economy.* Princeton, NJ: Princeton University Press, 2000.

Contraband

Contraband and its associated terms (smuggling, illicit trade, and *commerce étranger*), although defined slightly differently among the early-modern European principalities, is rooted in the legal concept of a neutral power continuing to trade with an enemy during a period of declared war. While contraband has always been the bane of centralized authorities, sovereign powers in Europe regarded as illegal many of the new commercial axes that were critical components for integrating the Atlantic World.

From the late-medieval period until well into the mid-nineteenth century, smuggling in western and central Europe and the Mediterranean world consisted of a plurality of regional, largely bilateral, exchanges across adjacent terrestrial political boundaries or within delimited maritime frontiers by organized gangs of resident peasants, villagers, or mariners. These smugglers dealt either in luxury goods, such as brandy or silk, or bulk items, such as salt and tobacco, to evade heavy taxes that authori-

ties imposed on them to raise revenues, such as the French *gabelle* (salt tax), or that they imposed to protect particular home industries, or both. Smugglers and their buyers justified evading such duties with a moral, or "just-price," economic argument. In practical terms, distributing smuggled goods also supplemented meager seasonal agricultural or artisanal earnings.

The vast scale and formative openness of the Atlantic World created opportunities for European merchants and shipmasters, and some non-Europeans as well, to invest systematically in contraband trades that spanned thousands of miles across the open ocean and crossed contentious and poorly defined or policed jurisdictional boundaries. Smugglers dealt in every item imaginable, from onions to furs to molasses, and even humans. As emerging European monarchies attempted to pay for their growing military commitments during the eighteenth century, they expanded the size and increased the efficiency of customs bureaucracies and licensing houses meant to enforce the transatlantic boundaries they were demarcating and contesting. At the same time, justifications by Atlantic merchants for evading these intensifying regulations also became more concise, well-articulated, and shrill. These arguments centered on the inability of the home monarchies to provide adequate goods and labor to their overseas possessions, as well as their suppression of the ability of their subjects, whom they claimed to protect, to earn reasonable livelihoods honestly.

As Wim Klooster has noted, the Atlantic economy grew from its mid-sixteenth century roots in the intrusions of principally Protestant merchants on the exclusionary trade laws of Catholic Spain's Casa de la Contratación (founded in Seville in 1503), which guarded Spain's trade in silver from its American colonies. This form of contraband was transatlantic in scale and semi-piratical in operation. One famous example was the English adventurer John Hawkins's landing of enslaved Africans in Santo Domingo and New Spain (in three voyages, 1555–1565) to sell for the silver circulating within these Spanish domains.

After the union of the two Iberian crowns (1580–1640), Portuguese merchants quickly established agents in all the major Spanish ports on both sides of the Atlantic, acquiring the license (*asiento*) to sell enslaved Africans in Spain's American colonies and then using it to undermine the *Casa*'s regulations and official trading fleets by introducing other prohibited goods as well. In theory, the *asiento* granted licensees the right to land European products and African slaves from a single giant, 500-ton ship; in practice any combination of ships totaling the tonnage could be sent legally. Both France and England vied for the *asiento* during the late seventeenth century, with French merchants acquiring it by 1701 and English merchants succeeding them after the War of the Spanish Succession (1702–1713). This exploitation of government authorization to smuggle additional goods, always in pursuit of Spanish silver, remained a contentious issue and even prompted war between Great Britain and Spain by 1739, and differed only due to its legal framing from nineteenth-century treaties that opened the new Spanish American republics and independent Brazil to British "free trade."

From the mid-seventeenth century, a collection of regular trade axes began to link major European ports with distinct colonial regions, which were in turn linked to one another. These axes were at first focused on the huge Spanish American market. Dutch merchants promoted the island of Curaçao, lying just off the northern coast of South America, as a supplier of European products and slaves to the Spanish Main in violation of the royal monopoly held by the merchants of Seville. Jamaica served the same purpose for the English after they captured the island from the Spanish in 1655. The emergence of these contraband trade axes, the success of private Dutch merchants in the nominal domains of France and England, and the growing dependence of European monarchies on trade with their American territories led both England and France to create closed systems of legitimate trade (often referred to as *mercantilism*) that became the economic cores of a growing rhetoric of empire as the eighteenth century proceeded.

In England Parliament had begun to pass major regulations, known collectively as the Navigation Acts, in 1651, 1660, and 1696. These acts reserved trade with and among the crown's Atlantic domains for English subjects to be carried in English-registered ships manned by largely English crews, and established the rudiments of a colonial customs service. As a result, Anglo-American producers could not develop markets of their own in continental Europe. Related laws beginning in 1663 required "enumerated commodities" from the New World territories meant for continental markets to be landed first in English ports in order to apply duties, even on goods subsequently re-exported. While initially aimed at wresting Atlantic trade from Dutch merchants, the laws effectively gave birth to trans–English-Atlantic contraband as merchants from England, quickly joined by their Anglo-American associates, easily circumvented laws that were more declarations of intent than implementable in practice.

The French, less prepared financially to compete through private trade, used a series of poorly coordinated, government-sponsored commercial companies to build an overseas commercial system, starting with the Compagnie des Indes Occidentales in 1664, and turned to military methods to root out the Dutch and English who had filled the gaps in meeting the needs of French traders and planters in the New World. These military interventions included expeditions led by the Marquis de Tracy to enforce the king's law in all French American colonies from Cayenne to New France in 1665–1666, and Jean du Casse's attacks on Dutch posts and coastal African towns in 1677–1679. As French mercantilist laws transferred trade from Dutch to French holds, Dutch merchants transferred their smuggling to the Caribbean entrepôts of Curaçao and especially St. Eustatius. Moreover, unlike the smooth American evasion of English restrictions on Atlantic trade, French enforcement of monopolistic company practices and pricing sparked spontaneous major popular revolts by colonists in Saint-Domingue in 1670 and 1722–1723, Guadeloupe in 1715, and Martinique in 1717 (the *Gaoulé*).

As Atlantic trades grew in the first half of the eighteenth century, both England and France expanded the scope of their restrictions. The French introduced a controlling set of laws in 1727 (the *Exclusif*) that reserved all colonial trade to 16 French ports. In turn, the British Molasses Act of 1733 slapped a very high tariff on sugar and derivatives reaching England or its territories from the foreign (mostly French) Caribbean. However, these laws were progressively circumvented by the French and consistently ignored by Anglo-American captains until the Seven Years' War (1756–1763), helping spur a rapid growth in both legal and illegal French Caribbean trade. The application of all these laws in the colonies was always tenuous: coastlines were poorly patrolled, collusion among all levels of colonial society with officials posted to control them was rampant, and shortages of basic necessities, particularly after natural disasters such as hurricanes and droughts, made strict enforcement unrealistic.

From the last years of the seventeenth century, an intra-American dimension of Atlantic contraband emerged to profit from continuing Spanish mining of silver and the spectacular rise elsewhere of plantation monoculture. In South America, this new axis of illicit trade centered on exchanges between Portuguese Brazil and the Spanish Río de la Plata region, siphoning significant amounts of the silver from the fabulous mines of Potosí south to Buenos Aires and Colonia de Santiago (founded in 1680). In the Northern Hemisphere, a contraband trade axis grew between New England and the French Lesser Antilles during the same era. After the end of the War of the Spanish Succession in 1713, a second, parallel, and eventually larger Anglo-French trade axis developed between the Anglo-American colonies of New York and Pennsylvania and French Saint-Domingue (today's Haiti).

These Anglo-French exchanges rested on the inability of merchants in the authorized ports in France to supply French planters in the Antilles with the assortments, competitive prices, and volumes of foodstuffs, manufactured items, animals, and slaves that Anglo-American merchants could provide. At the same time, French planters, similarly restricted to limited markets in France, had an overabundance of sugar and sugar by-products, especially molasses, which French merchants eschewed but which Anglo-American ship captains bought eagerly in defiance of the 1733 Molasses Act. As early as 1730, planters in Barbados lamented the smuggling of French sugar by-products—commonly referred to as the "pernicious trade"—complaining to Parliament that "the foreign colonys are daily improving while your Majesty's Sugar Colonies are apparently declining" (Southwick 1951, 392). French sources supported such assertions. According to the governor-general of Martinique, more than 200 small ships from that small island alone engaged in illicit foreign trade by 1750.

Other axes of smuggling peripheral to the central flows of the Atlantic economy, legally favored

in order to regulate them in the interest of milking revenues for expanding and expensive governments in Europe, emerged in the late seventeenth century. These contraband trades included a thriving business in wines from Portuguese Madeira to England and New England; an extensive illegal fur trade that linked New France (Canada) with Anglo-Dutch New York via Iroquois intermediaries; a growing trade between British Jamaica and small-scale black Creole merchants and indigo planters in southern French Saint-Domingue; a minuscule trade from French New Orleans with Spanish Havana; and trade between Anglo-American Boston with the "free port" of Louisburg in New France (modern Nova Scotia). Dutch ships also smuggled enslaved Africans, either from trading-post factories around the Bight of Benin to Curaçao and then to Spanish American ports, or directly from Angola to Portuguese Bahia (northeastern Brazil) or Spanish Buenos Aires.

The Seven Years' War between Great Britain and France proved decisive in promoting contraband trade in the Atlantic. Private trade between the territories of the two belligerents reached levels never again equaled and prompted a tightening of the customs administration in North America that provoked open revolt as early as 1772. While the French islands of Guadeloupe and Martinique in the eastern Caribbean withered under British naval attacks, French ports on Saint-Domingue, as well as the nominally Spanish port of Monte Christi on Hispaniola, emerged as major contraband entrepôts. British conquests of French and Spanish colonies in the Caribbean, beginning with Guadeloupe in 1759, helped to create a temporary "free trade zone" under British law, with lower British duties secured by the Royal Navy. The imprint of this access to British markets was never overcome, for immediately after the war the French crown designated the contraband ports it recovered as "freer ports" of trade with modest duties. The British responded by opening the Caribbean islands they had acquired in the war, while Spain's King Charles II, for the first time in two and a half centuries, allowed trade between Spanish and colonial ports within the empire beginning in 1765.

This "free-port system" set the stage for the War of American Independence (1775–1783). Beginning with the Revenue Act of 1764 (less formally known as the Sugar Act), the British Parliament attempted to enforce the imperial cohesion emerging from the Seven Years' War and increase revenues to pay for the heavy costs of the conflict by collecting duties on colonial trade more effectively, and reserving British West Indian trades for British home merchants. Enhanced customs collections alienated colonial merchants, ship captains, and their customers and suppliers, and they turned prosecutions of accused smugglers, such as the famous James Otis trial in Massachusetts in 1761, which supposedly spawned the resonant slogan of "no taxation without representation," into popular protests over the use of arbitrary power by metropolitan-appointed officials and ideological objections over the curtailing of "natural" trade.

The War of American Independence furthered the previous violations of British imperial restrictions, diverting Anglo-American trade throughout the Caribbean from the remaining British colonies there to the island holdings of France, Spain, and the Netherlands. France supported the rebel colonies with arms, ammunition, and markets, suspending existing restrictions on trade with the former British colonies in 1778, and Bourbon Spain followed suit. But no entrepôt played a more important role in promoting the economic independence of the North Americans than Dutch St. Eustatius, which not only fired the first salute that acknowledged American independence but more importantly also served as the major overseas supply channel for the rebels. The thriving Dutch contraband drew the ire of the Royal Navy, which raided the port in 1781, seizing over 140 ships and more than £3 million in goods.

The transformed ideological Atlantic World after 1790—composed of human rights, national independence, and free trade—elevated existing opportunities in illicit trade and ushered in a plethora of new ones. British merchants poured into Havana and Buenos Aires; New Orleans prospered as a regional center of illicit exchange; efforts by the Royal Navy to suppress the slave trade after 1811 launched a new, hideous era in smuggling human beings from Angola to Brazil, as well as to Cuba to launch the island's sugar and coffee plantation industries. Most important, Napoleon's "Continental System," established in 1805, prohibited French and French-conquered territories in Europe from trading with Britain. The subsequent bottling up of European ports by the British blockade in 1806 not only ele-

vated regional maritime smuggling within Europe but also invited violations throughout the Atlantic. The ships of neutrals, particularly from the new United States, breached the blockade of French markets on the continent, prompting a multitude of high-seas confrontations with the Royal Navy. In turn, an embargo imposed in 1807 by the United States on trade with both Britain and France created major hardships at home, renewed and intensified customs violations, and led to a second major war with Great Britain in 1812.

Little was new: contraband remained the strategy by which competitors marginalized by European efforts to control the initiatives that built the Atlantic economy intruded on the opportunities created by these very successes. The new element in the early nineteenth century was the ideological reformulation of these formerly illicit commercial axes as legal free trade. These liberal trade policies had grown in favor after 1807, together with the emergence of multiple nation-states in the Americas and in western and central Europe. After the Treaty of Vienna ended the century-long struggles between France and Britain in 1815, commodities and manufactured goods flowed openly and legally, leaving smuggling in the Atlantic World centered on trading in enslaved Africans conducted in violation of a growing web of international treaties outlawing it. With growing diplomatic recognition of powers elsewhere in the world and protectorates and other extensions of European legal authority into Asia, new regional contraband trade axes emerged, such as the British East India Company's smuggling of opium from Bengal into China.

KENNETH J. BANKS

Bibliography

Grahn, Lance. *The Political Economy of Smuggling: Regional Informal Economies in Early Bourbon New Granada*. Boulder, CO: Westview Press, 1997.

Karras, Alan L. *Smuggling: Contraband and Corruption in World History*. Lanham, MD: Rowman & Littlefield, 2009.

Klooster, Wim. "Inter-Imperial Smuggling in the Americas, 1600–1800." In *Soundings in Atlantic History: Latent Structures and Intellectual Currents, 1500–1830*, edited by Bernard Bailyn and Patricia L. Denault, 141–180. Cambridge, MA: Harvard University Press, 2009.

Southwick, Albert B. "The Molasses Act: Source of Precedents." *The William and Mary Quarterly,* 3rd ser., 8, no. 3 (July 1951).

Truxes, Thomas. *Defying Empire: Trading with the Enemy in Colonial New York.* New Haven, CT: Yale University Press, 2008.

Cornucopias

As Europeans moved beyond their perceived borders, motivated by scarcity and hopes for enrichment, the ostensible and real possibilities offered by the hitherto unknown (to them) territories of the Americas at times became embodied in persons or places that drew on legends of the past, even as they reflected the realities at hand. El Dorado, the Seven Cities of Cibola, lands of the Amazons, and the Fountain of Youth exemplify these fantasies. Notably, they took shape not in the first phases of European contact with indigenous Americans and Africans but rather during a second stage, when a good deal more about the new lands and peoples was known. Columbus, although visionary to the point of delusional, sent real gold back to the Spanish court as early as 1493, and a gold rush took place in the larger islands of the Caribbean during the next 20 or 30 years. Pearl fishing also got under way almost immediately, and the enormous treasure demanded by Francisco Pizarro from the captive Inca ruler Atahualpa in 1532 was divided up among Spaniards just 40 years after Columbus made his first voyage across the Atlantic. Virtually from the outset Europeans found substantial amounts of treasure and precious metals, if not the legendary wealth of "India" that Columbus hoped to encounter. Why, then, did these visions of cornucopias emerge only after the first Europeans in the Americas had already experienced significant success in their exploitations? And why did these cornucopias fascinate subsequent generations arguably more than they did the mostly pragmatic seekers of wealth or betterment who flocked to the Indies in the first decades following Columbus's first voyage?

These fantasies perhaps had as much to do with thwarted ambitions and competition for precedence as they did with realistic expectations. Hernán Cortés saw and hoped to seize Montezuma's treasure, although ultimately it disappeared without a trace. His later-arriving rival, Nuño de Guzmán, whose first governorship of Pánuco yielded only the limited profits to be made from slave-taking, undertook the conquest of western and northern present-day Mexico in some part to seek the fabled Seven Cities of Cibola. The legend of Cibola may have dated back to the Middle Ages—with classical precedents dating some 2,000 years before—and to tales linked to the eighth-century Muslim invasion of the Iberian Peninsula. Some Christians ostensibly fled westward across the Atlantic in search of "Antilla," which the Florentine Toscanelli—correspondent of Columbus—linked to the "Island of Seven Cities," as had others before him. Thus the cities, or island, of Antilla, became a gateway to old (or new?) worlds, and Antilla (or Antilles) became one of the names applied to the islands of the Caribbean.

This tale of medieval origins fails to suggest, however, how the fabled Seven Cities came to be associated with the ostensibly wealthy peoples whom Álvar Núñez Cabeza de Vaca and his companions thought they would find in the arid north when they finally reached Mexico in 1528. In any case, the utter failure of Francisco Vázquez de Coronado's 1540–1542 expedition into North America to find the seven golden cities put a definitive end to any subsequent aspirations to find them. Thus the outcomes of these quests seem to have reflected a progressive diminution of the arenas of ignorance in which the ambitious could contend based on promise more than on performance, while in contrast the actual trajectories of more pragmatic searches for wealth soon yielded real bonanzas of precious metals with the opening of silver mines at Potosí (Peru, 1545) and Zacatecas (Mexico, 1546).

In reviewing the chronicles and reports of early European forays into the interior of Colombia, geographer John Hemming has concluded that the legend of El Dorado—the gilded Native king, the land that he ruled, or the imaginary great lake associated with his people—emerged after those expeditions took place, although they may have motivated the frustrated search for La Canela, the land of cinnamon, by Gonzalo Pizarro, a half-brother of the conqueror of the Inca. The legend of El Dorado

Figure 1. An interpretation of the legend of the Fountain of Youth painted in 1546 by German artist Lucas Cranach the Elder.

lingered on, possibly to inspire Sir Walter Raleigh's ill-fated early seventeenth-century voyages to Guiana. Juan Ponce de León's equally frustrated ventures to Florida in the 1510s actually had nothing to do with a search for the Fountain of Youth. Like the elusive El Dorado, promises of immortality flowed only from the pens of later chroniclers.

Parallel fantasies of lands of gold—as well as of huge lakes imagined as the inland sources of rivers known only at their outlets into the sea—had lured the Portuguese down the Atlantic coast of Africa in the 1400s. For several centuries before the fifteenth, a "golden trade of the Moors" had been delivering the precious metal across the Sahara Desert from the sources of the Niger River—in an area then thought to be Mali—to Italians at the Muslim ports on the southern shores of the Mediterranean. Columbus himself learned to navigate Atlantic waters with Portuguese mariners seeking the real riches of the Gold Coast (modern Ghana). The European image of the Christian ruler of Ethiopia combined reputed piety of biblical proportions

with fabulous wealth as Prester (priest) John. The Portuguese were repeatedly disillusioned in Africa. Even the gold of Great Zimbabwe, inland from the golden coast on the Indian Ocean known to Muslim traders as Sofala, or land of gold, was exhausted by the time of their arrival in the early sixteenth century. If the reputed riches of Africa lay perhaps in the background of Spanish dreams of golden cities in the Americas, the reality of silver at Potosí, discovered in the 1540s, might have in turn inspired Portugal's utterly illusory dreams of mountains of silver in Central Africa, one of the motivating considerations in sending the expedition in the 1570s that claimed the captaincy and *conquista* of Angola.

When Europeans intruded into worlds beyond the Atlantic they attempted to recast the traditions and cultures of the peoples they encountered into familiar forms. Dazzled by gold, emeralds, and pearls—but not by the prized, intricate, and revered featherwork of Mesoamericans or the elaborate textiles of the Andeans—the legends they pursued privileged their own fantasies of wealth in the form of precious metals. Yet for most Europeans expectations of a better life took more realistic forms, as expressed time and again in letters written to relatives and friends back home emphasizing that, with hard work, one could do well in the new lands.

Did European fantasies of glittering metallic wealth affect the expectations of other peoples forced into the expanding Atlantic World? The millenarian hopes that emerged among American groups that resisted European domination suggest that they might have done so, at least in a negative sense. It is difficult to separate an indigenous longing for a world free of Europeans from visions of abundance that they might have derived from earlier legends. To take one example, following the massive insurrection in northwestern Mexico that has become known as the Mixton war (1540–1542), the viceroy Antonio de Mendoza reported that the rebels preached a new order in which their ancestors would revive, they all would be immortal, the fields would flourish without being cultivated, and bows and arrows would never break. These visions of abundance hinged on elimination of the Christians, and indigenous testimony seemed to place greater emphasis on reuniting with ancestors and the predicted deaths of Christians than on prospects of material plenty. In central Africa, the Atlantic itself—called Kalunga—was known as a Land of the Dead, since Africans saw the boundary between the living and their ancestors as permeable, similar to the surfaces of bodies of water.

Given how limited was the impact of these wild hopes and the occasional quests for fabled wealth, their staying power has been striking. Perhaps their appeal—from the utopian refuge of Antilla or Cibola to the dazzling spiritual and material potential of Prester John or promised immortality of the Fountain of Youth—lies in their promise of extraordinary achievement. Finding such a person or place, such incalculable riches, could place one forever beyond the strivings of the known world and ordinary humans. For Europeans who sought fortune and fame in the unknown territories of Africa and the Americas, dreams of enormous rewards that might fulfill their greatest ambitions perhaps made the extreme risks they undertook to pursue them worth the while, in spite of the reality of frequent, devastating failures.

IDA ALTMAN

Bibliography

Altman, Ida. *The War for Mexico's West: Indians and Spaniards in New Galicia, 1524–1550.* Albuquerque: University of New Mexico Press, 2010.

Hamdani, Abbas. "An Islamic Background to the Voyages of Discovery." In *The Legacy of Muslim Spain*, edited by Salma Khadra Jayyusi, 273–306. Leiden: Brill, 1992.

Hemming, John. *The Search for El Dorado.* London: Phoenix Press, 1978.

Isichei, Elizabeth. *Voices of the Poor in Africa.* Rochester, NY: University of Rochester Press, 2002.

Creolization

Creolization is a term that describes the process by which people, flora and fauna, ideas, and institutions with roots in the Old World were born, grew, and prospered in the New. As early as the sixteenth century, people were speaking of "creole" pigs and chickens; they were soon also referring to people born in the New World but of at least partial Old World ancestry as Creoles, but the term *creolization* was first used in English to refer to cultural as opposed to biological processes in 1928. During the course of the twentieth century it moved from the field of natural history to linguistics and thence to anthropology, history, and cultural studies. In the 1960s linguists and anthropologists began applying it to the unusual processes of rapid cultural change that first took place in the violent colonial cauldron of the early New World, where it replaced previous scholars' models such as "acculturation" (Melville J. Herskovits), "transculturation" (Fernando Ortiz), and "cultural interpenetration" (Roger Bastide).

Many anthropologists and historians of the Americas, following the lead of an essay by Sidney W. Mintz and Richard Price originally written in 1976, came to depend on "creolization" as the marker for what they saw as the almost "miraculous" process by which enslaved and self-liberated Africans, against all odds, created new institutions—languages, religions, legal systems, and more. The term also came to refer to the ways that these peoples, coming from a diversity of Old World societies, drew on their knowledge of homeland institutions to create new ones that they could call their own and pass on to their children, who elaborated them further.

That essay, which built on and extended the ideas of Herskovits, emphasized that creolization involved rupture and loss, creativity and transformation, and celebration as well as silencing of cultural continuities. For the study of slavery across the Americas, for instance, it tried to lay out the kinds of constants (e.g., the realities of power differences) and the kinds of variables (e.g., demographic, cultural, geographic specificities) that merited scholars' attention. It assumed that, despite certain commonalities based on relations of power, slavery in nineteenth-century Virginia, for example, was in significant ways a different institution from slavery in seventeenth-century Mexico or slavery in eighteenth-century Saint-Domingue, and it tried to point to the kinds of specific historical contexts that brought about these differences. The clarion call of that essay was historicization and contextualization.

The Mintz and Price essay sought an answer to certain kinds of questions, still hotly debated today, as a way of getting at more general sociocultural processes. How "ethnically" homogeneous, or heterogeneous, were the enslaved Africans arriving in a particular locality—to what extent was there a clearly dominant group—and what were the cultural consequences? What were the processes by which these imported Africans became African *Americans*? How quickly and in what ways did Africans transported to the Americas as slaves, and their African American offspring, begin thinking and acting as members of new communities—that is, how rapid was creolization? In what ways did the African arrivants choose, and were they able, to continue particular ways of thinking and of doing things that they brought from the Old World? What did "Africa," that is, its subregions and peoples, mean at different times to African arrivants and their descendants? How did the various demographic profiles and social conditions of New World plantations in particular places and times encourage or inhibit these processes?

By the millennium, the concept of creolization was under attack from two directions. Cultural studies scholars (such as James Clifford, Ulf Hannerz, and the *créoliste* movement in Martinique) were claiming that it was best used in a much broader sense to describe a worldwide con-temporary phenomena of mixing, blending, and hybridization, whether in Tokyo, Lagos, or New York City—the ways in which consumers of culture were creatively adapting new offerings, transforming the global into the local and thereby indigenizing the global. At the same time, some Africanist historians (such as Paul Lovejoy and John Thornton) were claiming that these processes were endemic in Africa and in fact long predated the beginning of the transatlantic slave trade, rendering the Americanist emphasis on the distinctiveness of the cultural creativity of enslaved Africans misguided. Today, a number of Caribbeanists (such as Mintz, Stephan Palmié, Price, and Michel-Rolph Trouillot) continue to argue for the historical specialness of the early Caribbean because of the extraordinary social circumstances that were unmatched in "normal" conquests, mixings, and the like, such as those in Africa or elsewhere in the modern world. The linguist Dell Hymes argued that creolization, compared to "normal" kinds of linguistic change, is best used to refer to a very particular sociohistorical nexus, representing "the extreme to which social factors can go in shaping the transmission and use of language" (Hymes, 5). From this perspective, creolization could be said to describe a precise and unusual set of sociohistorical circumstances in which individuals from diverse societies and cultures are suddenly thrust together and create new social and cultural institutions under conditions of vastly unequal power.

These conditions certainly prevailed in the post-Columbian Caribbean, which constituted a tumultuous stage for an unlikely and varied set of actors, from European pirates and buccaneers through African and African American maroons to Caribs deported from the islands and large numbers of Native Indians. In this colonial arena, unspeakable greed, lust, and conquest rubbed shoulders with heroic acts of resistance and solidarity. Millions of human beings were killed outright by enslavement, forced labor, and disease. Yet in many parts of the region, vibrant new societies and cultures emerged from the ashes. Within this prototypical space of death—indeed, often within the complex interstices that divided it internally—displaced Africans, a motley crew of Europeans, and what remained of Native American populations forged new, distinctively American modes of human interaction. Together, through the complex processes of negotiation between such individuals and groups, they created whole new cultures and societies.

Studies of North American slavery, like African Americanist research more generally, remain enmeshed in the realities of North American racism. Studies of historical creolization are no exception and continue to be deeply affected by scholars' ideological and political positions in the present. Nowhere is this influence of the present on the interpretation of the past clearer than in considerations of the role of African "ethnicities" in the development of African American culture and society. Many Africanist historians writing about the Americas (such as Michael Gomez and John Thornton) tend to emphasize the persistence of African ethnicities, while Americanist historians (such as Ira Berlin and Philip Morgan) tend to stress the malleability of identities and the importance of cultural creativity on the part of the enslaved in their new lives under slavery. Nonetheless, most recent studies agree that, because of the diversity of labor regimes and the demographic mixes they brought with them, creolization proceeded in different ways at different times in North America and that everywhere African ideas and practices were constantly reshaped according to the immediacies of local North American life. Whether they take as their focus the development of slave institutions—material life, work in the fields, skilled labor, exchanges between whites and blacks, family life, religious life, and so forth—or the comparison of regions through time, the best of these studies suggest that African ethnicity was important at certain moments in certain places but was a variable that tended to fade relatively quickly, in terms of the slaves' own identity politics.

Given the variety of historical circumstances in which New World creolization took place and the weight on the field of presentist ideological concerns, the best strategy might be to insist on some combination of careful historical contextualization and broader comparisons across the Americas. After all, speakers of diverse languages meet and communicate; languages don't. Human beings engage one another; cultures don't. Individuals who claim multiple identities interact with one another; ethnicities don't. Creolization remains an abstraction from the ways that diverse individuals historically

interacted and individually and together made meaning of these encounters.

RICHARD PRICE

Bibliography

Hymes. Dell. *Pidginization and Creolization of Languages: Proceedings of a Conference Held at the University of the West Indies, Mona, Jamaica, April, 1968*. London: Cambridge University Press, 1971.

Mintz, Sidney W., and Richard Price. *The Birth of African American Culture*. Boston: Beacon Press, 1992 [orig. 1976].

Price, Richard. *Travels with Tooy: History, Memory, and the African American Imagination*. Chicago: University of Chicago Press, 2008.

Stewart, Charles, ed. *Creolization: History, Ethnography, Theory*. Walnut Creek, CA: Left Coast Press, 2007.

Yelvington, Kevin A, ed. *Afro-Atlantic Dialogues: Anthropology in the Diaspora*. Santa Fe, NM: SAR Press, 2006.

Death and Burial

In the late seventeenth century, the British naturalist Sir Hans Sloane remarked soberly upon some Native American tombs in Jamaica: "I have seen in the woods, many of their bones in caves, which some people thought were of such as had voluntarily inclos'd or immured themselves, in order to be starved to death, to avoid the severities of their Masters" (Sloane, iv). He was, of course, allowing his readers to indulge in the Black Legend of the ruthlessness of Spanish conquest, which the British used as an alibi for the brutality of their own imperial ambitions. But he was also describing a connection between burial rites, sometimes seen only as an expression of cultural values, and the political history of empire and slavery. Sloane's remark is a reminder that, while Native Americans, Africans, African Americans, and Europeans drew upon myriad ideas for burying and remembering the dead, their methods of doing so were never disconnected from the historical transformations of the Atlantic Era.

To begin with, catastrophic demography reconstituted the deathways of early-modern Atlantic peoples. High mortality rates have been widely recognized as a pervading feature of the emerging Atlantic World, from the genocidal conquest of Native America, through the grindingly morbid mining and plantation operations of the Caribbean and South America, to the epidemics that followed along new circuits of trade, warfare, and migration. Diseases brought by Europeans and Africans to the Americas, against which Native Americans had few to no immunities, were among the chief agents of conquest. The implantation of European empires established networks of contacts among peoples that would serve as vectors of contagion, while brutal labor regimes and hardscrabble conditions kept people in marginal health at the best of times, vulnerable to the frequent provisioning disruptions brought by disastrous weather and wars.

Of course, there were important regional differences. In the tropics, Europeans died in droves. Although the very first settlers to New England faced severe mortality rates, by the end of the seventeenth century their births exceeded deaths by wide margins, and their population boomed. English settlers farther south in the Chesapeake region had to await the mid-eighteenth century for their populations to stabilize, while the great plantation zones of the Carolina Lowcountry, the Caribbean, and Brazil, and the mining lands of New Spain and the Andes remained death traps well into the nineteenth century. Short life expectancies tended to prevail in the most productive and populous territories. The closer one was to the major centers of power and profit, the quicker one's passage to the afterlife.

Death and the dead weighed heavily in everyone's considerations. In the activities that joined the living with the dead, survivors in Atlantic societies could make the transcendent available for use in worldly conflicts, wrestling awesome questions of spiritual existence into temporal social struggles. People interpreted and expressed material life in concrete efforts to resist the transience and entropy of Atlantic life.

Organizing burials, commemorating the departed, and making communities of the living upon landscapes overrun with the dead were among the most urgent initiatives. Majorities of the Europeans adapted ideas and rituals from their Old World religious heritages to the material conditions of the Americas, with churches remaining the locus of burial and remembrance in towns, especially for the wealthy and well connected, and families playing a greater role in rural areas. Native Americans continued their death rites as best they could, when the collapse of social institutions in the areas of demographic catastrophe and colonization did not wipe out entire systems for managing relations between the living and dead. Africans and their descendants, whose transcendent communities had been disrupted by the slave trade, struggled to establish new deathways out of idioms they already shared, learned from one another, or had forced upon them by slaveholders. Meanwhile, in Africa, the fortunes amassed by families with Atlantic interests added to the extravagance of their ceremonies, even as conscription and slaving generated new forms of sorcery, ghost stories, monsters, and healing cults to account for the interdependency of wealth and death.

Death rites in the Americas provided opportunities for people to express and enact social values, to articulate their visions of what it was that bound communities together, made their members unique, and separated them from others. Although everyone acknowledged that the dead carried great meaning for the living, mortuary ideas and customs specific to different groups could be potent sources and arenas of conflict. Partisans disputed uses of sacred symbols and drew upon communal experiences of loss and group memories to make claims on social institutions. Among Protestants, for example, burial rites expressed a continuing need to distinguish themselves from Catholics and to play out internal civil and religious tensions. For their part, Catholics aspired to universal incorporation, offering the laity space for burial societies, which served as crucial mutual-aid associations, while arguing over the terms of inclusion.

Enslaved people organized and managed funerals largely without the intervention of their masters, as long as their ceremonies did not interfere with labor regimes. In American towns and plantations, various groups of Africans and African Americans—Christians, Muslims, and adherents to myriad traditional and innovative faiths—worked out appropriate funeral ceremonies. Fearing the harmful consequences of negligence toward the deceased, they drew upon ideas about the crossings between the worlds of the living and dead, and about the words, rhythms, melodies, and dances that could bind participants in ritual communion. African burial societies were organized into "nations" demarcating the limits of affiliation and exclusion at ceremonies for the dead, while whites, to varying degrees, delineated and underscored the distinction they supposed between themselves, "mulattoes," and blacks, as well as that most important secular division between free and enslaved. Rites of death thus gave enduring forms and patterns to social life, shaping its terms of interaction by providing frequent occasions for people to assert and affirm group boundaries and to act out their visions of the ideal social order.

Atlantic worlds of death were transformed with changes in governance, migration, population, and religion. Europeans gathered strength in the Americas, extending and expanding their churches, whose missions reached out to convert those they dubbed "heathens." Shrinking populations of Native Americans reacted to conquest and the westward expansion of colonial societies by adapting their traditions to an enveloping Christianity. Similarly, Africans and ever-growing numbers of African Americans responded first to Catholic universalism and then to Protestant Evangelicalism by synthesizing familiar practices with imperial Christianity. By the nineteenth century these processes had significantly expanded the scope of Christendom, while exponentially multiplying the diversity of its practice. The contacts among disparate peoples, the circulation of migrants and ideas about their behaviors, and the development of oceanic networks contributed to the emergence of novel deathways that were simultaneously local, regional, and Atlantic in scope. Their particularities arose from the precise local ways that they were embedded within an integrated Atlantic history.

VINCENT BROWN

Bibliography

Brown, Vincent. *The Reaper's Garden: Death and Power in the World of Atlantic Slavery*. Cambridge, MA: Harvard University Press, 2008.

Reis, João José. *Death Is a Festival: Funeral Rites and Rebellion in Nineteenth-Century Brazil*. Chapel Hill: University of North Carolina Press, 2003.

Seeman, Erik R. *Death in the New World: Cross-Cultural Encounters, 1492–1800*. Philadelphia: University of Pennsylvania Press, 2010.

Sloane, Sir Hans. *A Voyage to the Islands Madera, Barbados, Nieves, S. Christophers and Jamaica . . .* London: The British Museum, 1707.

Democratic Revolutions, Age of

The concept of an Age of Democratic Revolutions, covering roughly the 1770s to the 1790s, arose from efforts to link—both ideologically and causally—the American and French revolutions as popular uprisings, and represented an early approach to Atlantic history by bringing together North America and Europe. The paradigm continues to shape historical periodization, but with two significant, perhaps opposing, qualifications. First, historians have considerably expanded chronological, spatial, and social contours of the concept; second, they have placed greater emphasis on imperial crises than on popular insurgencies as the motive forces that created contexts for conflicts that later proved revolutionary.

The Age of Democratic Revolutions is strongly associated with the post–World War II scholarship of R. R. Palmer and Jacques Godechot, historians of the French Revolution, who argued that the American and French revolutions, as well as others in Europe, derived from unique features of an integrated "Atlantic civilization," democratic and anti-aristocratic in spirit. Palmer's two-volume study, which spoke of a single pan-Atlantic "Democratic Revolution," rather than national revolutions, surveyed events and ideas in British North America and Europe from the antecedents of the American Revolution until the rise of Napoleon Bonaparte in France. In his view, a frustration among ordinary subjects with inherited privilege and unresponsive institutions ran through all the many revolts of the era: "revolutionary aims and sympathies existed throughout Europe and America. They arose everywhere out of local, genuine, and specific causes; or, contrariwise, they reflected conditions that were universal throughout the Western world. They were not imported from one country to another. . . . There was one big revolutionary agitation . . ." (Palmer, 1:7).

Though Palmer and Godechot's emphasis on an inspired pan-Atlantic spirit have remained influential, contemporaries rejected their ideas from various political and nationalist perspectives. On the one hand, critics on the left dismissed Palmer and Godechot as apologists for the Atlantic Alliance during the Cold War, even as mouthpieces for the CIA. On the other, many French and American historians, and scholars of other European revolutions, preferred to emphasize the national peculiarities of their revolutionary histories rather than commonalities with others. While the denunciations of Palmer and Godechot were overstated, the Cold War preoccupations with the future of democracy were nonetheless apparent in their work. As Palmer admitted: "the successful and threatening revolution of our own time, 'the revolution' *par excellence*, is the one represented by communist parties, soviet republics, and, at least allegedly, the social doctrines of Karl Marx. To this revolution, most readers of this book, as well as the author, feel a certain lack of cordiality" (Palmer, 1:9).

Since the Cold War ended in 1989, other criticisms have emerged, especially concerning Palmer and Godechot's neglect of the world beyond the northern Atlantic. For instance, they both left the Iberian empires out of their accounts. If the story ended with the rise of Napoleon Bonaparte after 1804, the revolutions temporarily tamed, the old regime in the Iberian Peninsula and the vast Atlantic empires remained intact. However, expanding the chronology to take in the Napoleonic Wars and the struggles over restoration and constitutional government that lasted until the middle of the nineteenth century, the end point of E. J. Hobsbawm's global survey of the era (discussed below), then the struggle against the Old Regime in Europe takes on an important Iberian and Latin American complexion. One of the most central revolutionary documents of the period, Spain's 1812 Constitution of Cádiz, written during the resistance to France's occupation of the Iberian Peninsula, exerted tremendous influence throughout Latin America and the Mediterranean well into the 1820s and 1830s.

Historians such as Robin Blackburn have also called attention to the major role played by social groups left out of Palmer's account of intellectual currents and political leadership. Democratic revolutions are now understood as liberation from various forms of domination, not only from the formal political institutions of empire, bulwarks of aristocratic privilege, at the heart of Palmer's study. As a result, it is impossible to discuss the Age of Democratic Revolutions without considering the participation of slaves and the conflicts over slavery beginning with the American Revolution, when the British liberated the thousands of slaves who fled to their lines, and continuing through the Haitian Revolution and the multiracial struggles for independence in Spanish America. The fight for liberty and democracy, when seen through the lens of slavery, now looks more partial because slavery and slave trafficking formed the core of new regimes in the United States and Brazil. But it also appears more radical because the Haitian revolutionaries who overthrew slavery and colonial rule inspired revolutionaries and abolitionists in other corners of the Atlantic World.

Historians have thus retained a conceptualization of the Atlantic as a whole resembling Palmer and Godechot's, while considerably revising the spatial, temporal, and social boundaries of the mutual influences and causes behind the revolutionary movements that reverberated around the Atlantic during the era. Palmer's criticism of "work . . . carried on in national isolation, compartmentalized by barriers of language or the particular histories of governments and states" (Palmer, 1:8) is resonant today. However, in placing greater emphasis on imperial crises, as opposed to revolutionary insurgencies, scholars have highlighted the ironies of European attempts to consolidate and defend claims to pan-Atlantic territorial control: "inter-imperial warfare called for reforms, which exposed the foundations of empires and jeopardized their existence by revealing and exacerbating enduring social, political, and ethnic inequities" (Klooster, 2). Or, in a cogent formulation of revolution and independence in the Iberian empires: "anticolonialism and its corollary, nationalism, were the effects, not the causes, of a broader imperial collapse" (Adelman, 177). The revolutions of the era appear more accidental, localized, and inconclusive to many contemporary historians, the sources of regime change less unified and intentional, more subject to the vagaries of imperial ambitions and warfare, than in Palmer's account of shared, almost inevitable, ideas and yearnings.

Moreover, from this new imperial perspective, the "Age of Revolution" in the Atlantic begins to look less distinctive. Warfare and the institutional and ideological crises it brought in its wake were not only transatlantic in scale but also global in this era. The Seven Years' War saw the British overwhelm the French in North America and also in South Asia. Bonaparte waged war not only in central Europe and the Iberian Peninsula but also in Egypt. British and French losses in the Americas were simultaneous with gains in Africa and Asia.

This global approach to the era also has intellectual roots in the Cold War. Hobsbawm's seminal *The Age of Revolution, 1789–1848* explored the tensions within what he saw as a "dual revolution," the Industrial Revolution in Britain and the political and ideological revolution in France: "the twin upheaval which took place in those two countries, and was propagated thence across the entire world" (Hobsbawm, 2). Hobsbawm minimized the American Revolution, as well as those in Spanish America and Brazil, arguing that they failed to challenge the Old Regime: "the results of the American revolutions were, broadly speaking, countries carrying on much as before, only minus the political control of the British, Spaniards, and Portuguese," (Hobsbawm, 54), a characterization of continuity that few historians would now accept.

Hobsbawm's Europe-centered view of global change has remained influential, although historians working in this vein also emphasize the era's enhancement of state power through economic change and constant imperial warfare. C. A. Bayly's studies, speaking of an "industrious revolution" rather than the Industrial Revolution, signal the consolidation of newly predatory military states, especially the British and French, that preyed upon weaker European neighbors, such as Portugal and Spain, as well as non-European states, especially in Africa and Asia. Fiscal-military regimes of unrivaled efficiency gained an edge over previously unassailable sovereigns in such places as South Asia, Algeria, and, in certain respects, China. The new state of the late eighteenth and early nineteenth centuries "grew gargantuan in its ideological ambitions, its global reach, and its demand for military and civilian labor. Its appetite stretched across continents. Before the impact of the steam engine or the electric telegraph had been registered, the European state, its soldiers and bureaucrats, became hyperactive in what was an 'axial age' for world history" (Bayly, 83). Thus, even as war and revolution weakened or destroyed authoritarian rule in the Atlantic World, Britain and France found themselves at the forefront of an unprecedented European ascendancy on a global scale. An era of European global conquest and subjugation arose in tandem with an age of democratic revolutions in the Atlantic.

CHRISTOPHER SCHMIDT-NOWARA

Bibliography

Adelman, Jeremy. *Sovereignty and Revolution in the Iberian Atlantic*. Princeton, NJ: Princeton University Press, 2006.

Bayly, C. A. *The Birth of the Modern World, 1780–1914: Global Connections and Comparisons*. Malden, MA: Blackwell, 2004.

Blackburn, Robin. *The Overthrow of Colonial Slavery, 1776–1848*. London: Verso, 1988.

Godechot, Jacques. *France and the Atlantic Revolution of the Eighteenth Century, 1770–1799*. Translated by Herbert H. Rowen. New York: The Free Press, 1965.

Hobsbawm, E. J. *The Age of Revolution, 1789–1848*. 1962. Reprint, New York: Vintage Books, 1996.

Klooster, Wim. *Revolutions in the Atlantic World: A Comparative Perspective*. New York: New York University Press, 2009.

Palmer, R. R. *The Age of the Democratic Revolution: A Political History of Europe and America, 1760–1800*. 2 vols. Princeton, NJ: Princeton University Press, 1959–1964.

Diasporas

Central to the early-modern Atlantic system was the surmounting of a vast oceanic barrier. The strategies of purveying desired products across this boundary produced networks of dispersed trading communities, known as *diasporas*, resident in the territories of their trading partners. The Atlantic, although different from previous such diasporic theaters owing to the vastness of the distances separating its nodes, was first integrated more through networks of traders, marked ethnically by their distinctive (often religious) customs, than through military or administrative controls centered in Europe.

Focus on Atlantic diasporas prompts analysis of who constructed these transoceanic communities, and how. One cannot read features of modern diasporas from the current era of technocratic globalization back into the Atlantic past. Early-modern Atlantic diasporas were not protonational anticipations of modern political and cultural identities. In the early-modern period it was not the discrete aspects of diasporas—with internal coherence and homogeneity—that mattered but rather how the multiple outlying components were connected with one another, for example how the Yoruba Diaspora in Brazil, emanating from Africa, connected to its Brazilian counterparts, or how Iberian diasporas in the North American borderlands were "entangled" with their English counterparts in the region, as well as with the Native American diasporas, and also other diasporas in Africa. These interconnections yielded the efficacy of these networks in consolidating what eventually became a pan-Atlantic trading economy, and the model for today's global order.

Early-modern diasporas offered an efficient method of initiating economic contacts due to their low operational costs: bonds of trust founded on common descent and shared practices, as well as the solidarity born of their standings as outsiders, made diasporic networks more efficient at long-distance trade than monopolies enforced by military operations or by centralized administrations. During the Atlantic Era, capital, know-how, and communications technologies necessary for centrally directed operations had not yet been developed. Indeed, in spite of the emphases on the administrative and military aspects of "formal" empires in conventional historiography, conquest and formal structures of trade were colossally expensive and inefficient to operate. Military intervention in both Africa and the Americas generally succeeded only through the collaboration of local allies—be they Imbangala who aided the marginal Portuguese military presence in Angola, Inca lords who joined Pizarro in the Andes, or Cortés's Tlaxcalan allies in

his attack on the Mexica city of Tenochtitlán. In this way, locally embedded groups of culturally linked traders integrated economic systems transcending the economic particulars of different nodes of the early-modern Atlantic World.

Dispersed and embedded diasporic trading networks throughout the world long predated the early-modern Atlantic. Thus, a trans-Saharan framework of Muslim Wangara merchants had linked North Africa to goldfields in western Africa since the thirteenth century. Although this diasporic strategy has been featured in studies of the African past, the contributions of the Wangara and other internal African networks have been underemphasized in Atlantic history. In fact, the Sahara Desert was one of the largest geographical spaces anywhere integrated by diasporic trade networks at the time the Portuguese entered the Atlantic, and the diasporic patterns of settlement, lineages, and marriages that emerged following their arrival were essential in allowing early Europeans to gain footholds in Atlantic Africa.

This integration of various diasporas began around 1500 when New Christians (converted Jewish families, related to the Sephardim expelled from Iberia) from Cape Verde and Portugal settled on the coast of Upper Guinea (present-day Senegambia and Guinea-Bissau). These New Christians soon had family connections also in Spanish America, so that by 1600 their diasporic networks, originating in Iberia, linked Lisbon, Cape Verde, Guinea-Bissau, Cartagena (modern Colombia), and Lima. Their commerce flowed through shared transatlantic cultural practices, and by the early seventeenth century such African products as kola nuts and *barafulas* (blue and white cloths woven on Cape Verde) were readily available in Cartagena.

In the southern Atlantic, from the 1550s at the latest, transoceanic commercial and cultural connections had also been connecting Brazil and the West-Central African regions of Kongo, Loango, and Angola. The dried-manioc meal *farinha de guerra* ("battle rations") used by the Tupinambá in Brazil was imported to West-Central Africa from around this time, and the transatlantic links intensified with the foundation of the Portuguese military base at Luanda in 1575. The Angolan-Brazilian mercantile community was reinforced by administrative links appointed from Portugal, but these informal diasporic networks, cemented by personal connections, enabled the formal administrative structures to operate.

Personal ties and religio-cultural identities built around shared ritual practices underpinned the success of these diasporas during the sixteenth and seventeenth centuries. Islam and Islamic commercial law were essential to the trans-Saharan diasporas, and crypto-Judaism (Judaic practice at home, hidden behind a public veneer of Catholicism) was a central "faith of memory" in the New Christian diasporas of the early African and Iberian Atlantic. Similarly important, especially in the southern Atlantic, were shared agricultural practices and religious beliefs that West-Central Africans carried to Brazil and recreated in such sites as the seventeenth-century community of fugitives from enslavement in Palmares in Pernambuco. Native American diasporas also developed in the sixteenth century, with a network of converted members of the Nahua (central Mexican) aristocracy, who mixed Spanish Christianity and rituals from their Mexica heritage as they dispersed to integrate themselves into the new hybrid cultural worlds of the cities of colonial Spanish America.

The diasporic strategies of opening an Atlantic World continued with the entry of the northern European Protestant powers from the 1620s onward. Inquisition trials of the 1630s and 1640s destroyed the New Christian networks linking West Africa and Spanish America, but others survived to connect Amsterdam with the Dutch colonies of Curaçao and Suriname, both of which had strong Jewish communities and developed intra-Caribbean networks tying the Dutch islands to English Barbados and Jamaica and to Sephardic communities in England, Italy, and the Netherlands. Linguistic connections followed, with Papiamento Creole emerging on Curaçao by 1700 from roots in the Cape Verde vernacular Kriolu spoken by this time; the language also followed traders dispersing from the islands to the coasts of modern Colombia and Venezuela.

By the eighteenth century the Atlantic was crisscrossed by multiple ethnic diasporas characterized by flowing mobility of personnel and evolving shared practices. The best known of these later diasporas were the Quaker commercial networks linking the planters of the northern Atlantic and the Caribbean with economically booming Britain. Other English merchant communities extended their operations to the middle and southern Atlantic through involvement in the Madeira wine trade, connecting other diasporic groups in the southern and northern Atlantic. Sailors from Bermuda linked producers on the North American seaboard with markets in the Caribbean. Meanwhile, with available land on Barbados growing scarce in the late seventeenth century owing to the consolidation of plantation sugar on the island, many early settlers departed for South Carolina. They brought with them hard-bitten ideologies of slavery and the economic promise of plantations on which to produce Atlantic commodities—in their instance, eventually rice. A diaspora of enslaved Upper Guineans steeped in the intricacies of rice production brought their agricultural know-how to this Barbadian–South Carolinian connection, building the most important rice-growing colony in North America in the Carolina Lowcountry. Indeed, South Carolina offers a classic example of the interlocking diasporas of the early Atlantic, with the Upper Guineans interacting with Anglo-Caribbeans to produce a new context of culture and production.

In the southern Atlantic, Luso-Brazilian merchant families in Rio de Janeiro and their trading partners based in the Angolan port of Benguela built another strong network in the eighteenth century. The trading connections among these families, often cemented through marriage alliances, satisfied the demand for slaves to work the gold and diamond mines of Minas Gerais in Brazil. In the West-Central African interior, these diasporic connections linked to other diaspora traders in the Lunda polity in the heart of the continent, and from there back west to Luanda and to Loango, on the Atlantic coasts, and north almost as far as the Equator. Loango, well north of the Congo River estuary, was the base of another set of dispersed communities of traders known as Vili (or Mubire).

The efficiency of these diasporic networks—African, Iberian, Native American, or English—arose from the fact that they were embedded in the same local contexts. And the commercial fabric of the early-modern Atlantic emerged through these interconnections. Bonds of trust rooted in cultural practices shared across great distances ensured the longevity of these connections. The Euro-American military and legal institutions, often in the foreground of historians' narratives of Atlantic history, not only depended on these networks but often represented attempts to disrupt the independent, politically transcending commercial initiatives flowing through diasporic corridors. As the Atlantic commercial economy grew in the seventeenth century, these merchant diasporas channeled the shift in the accumulation of capital from Iberia to northern Europe, with Dutch Sephardim and English Quakers supplanting the New Christian Iberians. Thus "empires," commerce, and diasporas were fundamentally interconnected, and all three were necessary to the development of one another.

The fact that diasporas had bridged environmental boundaries and connected remote populations elsewhere in the world—not just by land in Afro-Eurasia but also in the archipelagos of the Indian and Pacific oceans—dissipates the illusion of the uniqueness of European expansion in the Atlantic and places the process of integrating the Atlantic economy well within the contours of world history as a whole. In fact, the Atlantic diasporas merely extended familiar strategies into a new geographical context. However, this extension into the Atlantic was novel in the interconnections of its multiple diasporas: most earlier dispersed trading networks had acted as single bridges between two geographical regions, but the multiple connections in the Atlantic catalyzed a greater range and speed of exchanges and played their part in the construction of global modernity. Africans, Native Americans, and Europeans all played complementing roles in the complex diasporic web of the early Atlantic, interacting in the creation of a shared cultural framework of commerce that brought Tupinambá and Yoruba in Brazil, English in North America and the Caribbean, and Papiamento-speakers and Sephardim in Suriname, Curaçao and New Netherland, together.

TOBY GREEN

Bibliography

Curtin, Philip. *Cross-Cultural Exchange in World History.* New York: Cambridge University Press, 1984.

Ferreira, Roquinaldo. *Cross-Cultural Exchange in the Atlantic World: Angola and Brazil in the Era of the Slave Trade.* New York: Cambridge University Press, 2012.

Green, Toby. *The Rise of the Trans-Atlantic Slave Trade in Western Africa, 1300–1589.* New York: Cambridge University Press, 2012.

Diseases

If the history of the Atlantic World is the story of the increasingly entwined fates of the region's peoples, then little demonstrates those engagements more concretely than the transmission of diseases among them. It is common knowledge that in the three centuries after 1492, Old World diseases felled American Indians by the millions. But even though the epidemics that decimated Native peoples are the best-known consequence of diseases in the Atlantic World, they are only part of the story. At least one New World disease—syphilis—caused untold suffering in the Old World, while other diseases set the stage for the exploitation of African labor that defined the plantation economy in the Americas, helped the Spanish hold on to their colonies longer than they otherwise would have, and allowed the slave rebels in Saint-Domingue to form the independent republic of Haiti. Diseases thus played a central role in creating the Atlantic World.

An Atlantic history of diseases begins with Columbus, or more precisely with his second voyage (1493), since no evidence exists that his first voyage introduced disease among the Tainos he encountered in the Caribbean. When Columbus and his enormous second fleet of 17 ships and 1,500 men landed on the island of Hispaniola (present-day Dominican Republic and Haiti) in November 1493, they met a thriving Taino civilization numbering in the hundreds of thousands. But Columbus's men had brought diseases from Europe, and they soon communicated those illnesses to the island's indigenous residents. A "virgin-soil epidemic" ensued from the new pathogens introduced into a population with no immunity, or even partial resistance, to them. The accounts of these specific illnesses are too vague to allow for precise identification of them, but the most common diseases that are thought to have been brought by Europeans to the New World were smallpox, measles, bubonic plague, influenza, and typhus. Lack of immunity was not the only factor in the rapid spread of diseases, however. Malnutrition increased the toll of diseases imported from Europe, as did political disruptions and other societal breakdowns brought on by colonization, which undermined the support structures used by Native peoples in times of stress.

Thus began the rapid depopulation of Hispaniola: within three decades the island was nearly devoid of Tainos. The rest of the indigenous Caribbean was soon to follow.

Hispaniola's demographic collapse was repeated not just in the Caribbean but throughout the Americas from Hudson Bay to Tierra del Fuego, sometimes even before Europeans arrived, as viruses traveled faster than colonists. The epidemics helped clear the way for European conquest and colonization, though their devastation was greatest on the islands of the Caribbean; on mainland North and South America, initial losses were often followed a generation or two later by stability and even modest recovery, though never to precontact levels. Nonetheless, without virgin-soil epidemics, European colonization in the New World might have looked more like that which emerged in Africa, India, and China: tiny European populations huddled in trading ports amid the enormous indigenous populations.

Although the rapid decline of Native populations was the most important consequence of disease transmissions in the Atlantic World, American diseases also afflicted Europeans. Columbus's men returned to Europe with syphilis—a disease that struck at the most intimate encounters. Although the question of whether syphilis originated in the Americas once provoked controversy among historians, scientific studies of human remains on both sides of the Atlantic have largely settled the issue. Observers first reported syphilis in Europe in 1493, and the disease spread rapidly from western Europe all the way to eastern Asia. Everywhere the local names for the disease suggested import from somewhere else: in England it was called the French disease, in Poland the German disease, in India the disease of the Franks—that is, western Europeans (Crosby, 124–125). One of the leading sixteenth-century treatments for syphilis was mercury, a disadvantage of which was its high toxicity. Another treatment was derived from guaiacum, an extraordinarily hard wood from the New World. This therapy was considered to be more advantageous than mercury, because it was associated with the place from which syphilis was thought to have been transmitted: many people believed that God provided local cures for local diseases. Europeans thus quickly recognized the New World's contributions to both diseases and their antidotes, thereby facili-

tating the intellectual creation of an integrated Atlantic World.

Back in the Caribbean and other tropical regions of the Americas, diseases shaped the organization of labor in the plantation economy that emerged in the late sixteenth and early seventeenth centuries. The diseases of these regions felled many residents there, whatever their epidemiological backgrounds. But two of the most lethal diseases—yellow fever and malaria—had less severe consequences for Africans, because these mosquito-borne sicknesses were imports from Africa. Many West Africans therefore carried the sickle-cell gene, which provides partial immunity to malaria's symptoms, and most had experienced bouts of yellow fever in childhood, thus retaining the lifelong immunity it confers on survivors. Although the emergence of race-based slavery in the Americas had many causes, resistance to yellow fever and malaria rendered Africans more reliable plantation laborers than American Indians or Europeans.

By contrast, tropical diseases limited the European presence in Africa. West Africa was widely considered a "white man's grave" during the era of the transatlantic slave trade, with Europeans suffering frequent bouts of malaria, yellow fever, dysentery, and smallpox. The most reliable figures suggest that 20 percent of Europeans living in West Africa died each year. As a result, Europeans mostly confined themselves to slaving forts and ships lying just offshore, and no large settler population arrived to challenge African control in the region. Resistance to disease was one factor that allowed for the growing presence of locally born individuals with mixed African and European parentage, who came to play important roles as merchants and slave traders in brokering the trade between the mobile populations and commercial cultures in the Atlantic and resident communities in Africa.

Even as the slave trade and the tropical plantation complex expanded in size and scope, in the seventeenth century Europeans pushed into regions of mainland North and South America that had yet been spared virgin-soil epidemics. The Wendat (Huron) Indians of present-day Ontario, for example, seem to have suffered their first major outbreak of European disease as late as 1634. Measles, strep infection, and smallpox then struck in rapid succession, so that by 1640 the population of the Wendat Confederacy had plummeted from 24,000 to 9,000. The ubiquity of death led French Jesuit missionaries and Wendats to use mortuary rituals as an initial means of communication, gaining some cross-cultural understanding in this encounter of death practices. Jesuits "admired" the Wendat Feast of the Dead, a dramatic ritual in which hundreds of individuals were reburied in a communal ossuary. But, in a pattern repeated by missionaries throughout the Americas, Jesuits used their knowledge of Wendat mortuary rituals to attempt to convert the Native peoples to Christianity. Disease thus helped tie many indigenous peoples into an Atlantic system of religious and material connections.

Diseases were even more central to the history of the tropics, where yellow fever and malaria facilitated Spanish domination of the greater Caribbean through most of the eighteenth century. Once these new diseases became endemic in the Caribbean, residents of both African and Afro-European descent had some resistance to malaria—Europeans had not been able to evolve over many centuries the protective sickle-cell gene through infection—and those who had survived a bout with the dreaded "yellow jack" would have acquired a lifelong immunity to it. When European powers tried to use their troops to conquer islands held by their Caribbean rivals, particularly after the Seven Years' War (1756–1763), the invading forces suffered virgin-soil epidemics of their own. The British attempt to seize Spanish Cartagena, on the Caribbean coast of present-day Colombia, is a textbook example of the epidemiological costs of conquest. The British Admiral Edward Vernon sailed into Cartagena Bay in March 1741 with 186 ships and 29,000 men, "possibly the largest amphibious assault force yet assembled in world history" (McNeill, 154). Yet this massive naval force could not defeat the residents and garrison of this city, numbering only 10,000, largely because yellow fever tore through the British troops while sparing local Spanish forces.

The same dynamic helped revolutionary political movements succeed throughout the Americas in the late eighteenth and early nineteenth centuries. Slaves on the French sugar island of Saint-Domingue launched a massive revolt in 1791 that resulted in the hemisphere's second independent republic, but they probably could not have created Haiti, roughly a decade later, without the protection of acquired immunity to yellow fever. The French sent some 60,000 to 65,000 troops to Saint-Domingue in hopes of ending the revolution; 80 to 85 percent of them died, mostly from disease (McNeill, 258). In the revolt against British rule in North America, the local disease profile likewise aided the Creole patriots against the foreign invaders, especially in battles in the Carolinas in 1780 and 1781. Resistance to tropical diseases also aided subsequent revolutionaries in the Spanish American republics. It is not a stretch to say that the modern Atlantic, born in revolution at the end of the eighteenth century, gestated in the womb of the epidemiological encounters of earlier eras.

Although the Atlantic World was not hermetically sealed off from the rest of the globe, disease provides a particularly clear example of historical processes cohering around a distinct Atlantic narrative. It is true that some of the diseases in the Atlantic World—bubonic plague, for example—originated in Asia, and syphilis was carried from the Americas to Europe and thence to India and China. But Old World diseases uniquely favored European and African populations in the Americas. The millennia of separation between the peoples of the Old World and the New led to the devastating virgin-soil epidemics of the Americas, which allowed European settler populations to flourish in temperate North America and enslaved Africans to become the basis of tropical colonial possessions in a manner seen virtually nowhere else on the globe. The European slave trade, which imported not only 11 million captive Africans, but also two deadly mosquito-borne diseases, created a distinctively Atlantic conjunction of populations, slavery, and republican political ambitions.

ERIK R. SEEMAN

Bibliography

Cook, Noble David. *Born to Die: Disease and New World Conquest, 1492–1650.* New York: Cambridge University Press, 1998.

Crosby, Alfred W., Jr. *The Columbian Exchange: Biological and Cultural Consequences of 1492.* Westport, CT: Greenwood Press, 1972.

McNeill, J. R. *Mosquito Empires: Ecology and War in the Greater Caribbean, 1620–1914.* New York: Cambridge University Press, 2010.

Seeman, Erik R. *Death in the New World: Cross-Cultural Encounters, 1492–1800.* Philadelphia: University of Pennsylvania Press, 2010.

Economic Cycles

If we are to speak about economic cycles in the Atlantic World between 1450 and 1850, we must explain what we mean. In an economic sense, a *cycle* is a repeated phenomenon of change of generally predictable frequency and amplitude. Historians, however, tend use the term more casually to mean the coalescence, maintenance, and replacement of the innovative and productive strategies characteristic of specific eras. These usages are very different in their degrees of precision. The discussion here focuses on the former.

In 1450, there were no economic cycles in a modern sense, but by 1850 these cycles not only existed but had become the subject of formal analysis. Modern economic cycles, as the economist Nikolai Kondratieff observed, were based on significant accumulations of fixed capital. With nineteenth-century investments in industrial technology it took lengthy periods of time to plan, finance, construct, and employ the productive assets and infrastructure of innovation. Factories, canals, railroads, or other investments in production and transportation are durable: they are not consumed as soon as they are produced. As late as 1800, even in advanced economies in England and France, the share of fixed capital was no more than 6 to 7 percent of economic activity (Gross Domestic Product, or GDP). In 1450, on the other hand, although there had been fixed capital, economies were basically agrarian—hand to mouth, one might say. Agricultural goods are generally consumed more or less at once by the same people who produce them. Hence, "classical" economists placed little emphasis on long investment cycles. They thought, as Say's Law (1803) said, that supply created its own demand.

At an informal level, commodity cycles in the Atlantic World, such as the Brazilian sugar cycle of the seventeenth century or the gold cycle of the eighteenth century, should also be considered. These were episodes of production of new consumer commodities. There could also be lengthy periods of demographic growth and decline, or even prolonged contrasting periods of war and peace, as were common in the sixteenth and seventeenth centuries for political and religious reasons.

These changing dynamics may have had economic components, economic motivations, or economic consequences, but they were not economic cycles in the formal sense, generated by the timings of investments and returns.

This ambiguity in casual use of the term makes describing cycles in the Atlantic World more challenging, and not only because historians and economists use the word differently. As the "wealth of nations" grew in Europe over the period from 1450 to 1850, these historical "cycles" of economic growth were changing in their dynamics, and cycles generated in the *economic* sense were making their appearance as well, and increasingly so. Economic cycles, in turn, were related to these expansions of trade and the growth and spread of markets in the modern sense—including investments in transportation and inventories—in regions that had formerly operated on more local scales. The consumer markets, mostly in Europe, in turn reflected the rise of commodity production overseas, such as tobacco and sugar, the diffusion of these plantation commodities, the growing monetization of the international economy, and the growth of the transatlantic slave trade. These processes occurred simultaneously and were all aspects of the broad economic integration accelerating all around the Atlantic.

Market integration was already under way at the beginning of this Atlantic integration. The well-known rise in price levels in western Europe, or the "Price Revolution," had begun around 1460, or nearly a century before the decisive discovery of silver in Peru and New Spain. The increase in supply of American silver, drawing on earlier technological developments in central European silver mines, outstripped European demand, driving up agricultural prices in western Europe as quantities of silver flowed into Europe faster than Europeans could increase local agricultural production—more money chasing fewer commodities—until the mid-seventeenth century. The expansion of the transatlantic slave trade after 1650 coincided with the leveling off of European price inflation. As inflation results from an excess in supplies of currency over demand for it, this moderation in prices perhaps reflected the growing deflection of money to finance the purchase of slave ships, trade goods, and the enslaved Africans themselves. By 1700, then, this diversion of investments to integrate an expanding new economy of the Atlantic Basin was well underway, and through the growing plantation system, so too was industrial-scale production of sugar, tobacco, coffee, rice, and, increasingly, raw cotton. Investment in these agricultural commodities, extensions of the food-based economies of the past, represented the first phase of the investments in modern productive infrastructure that would grow to drive modern economic cycles.

Economic cycles had a complex relation to the spread of markets, the expansion of trade, and the European consolidation of military and political control overseas. In West Africa, where the impact of the transatlantic slave trade was most intensely felt, the initial effect of the trade was an increase in the demand for money to finance development of commercial infrastructure. After 1650, however, almost precisely the opposite occurred: the disruptive violence of slaving reduced productivity, and market development receded. In western Europe, on the other hand, growing monetization and commercial development were reflected in a decline of over two-thirds in the range of prices (minimum versus maximum) recorded for wheat between 1400 and 1760, with the only conspicuous exception coming, not unexpectedly, during the Thirty Years' War (1618–1648). In other words, markets in Europe tended to work more efficiently. In the Americas, the pattern of integration into an increasingly capitalized Atlantic economy was different yet again. The catastrophic decline of the Native American population—virtually complete in the Caribbean and the Brazilian littoral, but with a surviving core in the Mesoamerican and Andean highlands—retarded economic growth until the European settlers and the indigenous peoples adapted to the radically changed endowments of land and labor: unknown plenty of the former and inhibiting scarcities of the latter.

Generalizations across the Atlantic Basin are impossible until the political and territorial readjustments of the Seven Years' War and the Napoleonic Wars were fully realized, such as the transfer of sovereignty over Louisiana and Guyana, which became large producers of sugar and significant consumers of slave labor. In the nineteenth century, industrialization in both Great Britain and the United States built up the asset base that generated modern economic cycles. Growth became self-sustaining in the northern Atlantic on the basis of capital accumulation and corresponding growth in productivity. Abandonment of mercantilist restrictions lowered barriers to trade in the plantation zones of the remaining colonial empires. Comparative advantage on transoceanic scales finally came to govern allocation of resources in the production of tropical commodities. The areas that could produce commodities most profitably did so. The agricultural zones of Brazil, Cuba, and the North American South continued to employ increasingly costly African slave labor because the international competition of open trade reduced commodity prices to their costs of production. On the other hand, in the British islands of the West Indies, where slavery was abolished by the 1830s, economic growth based on free labor stalled.

In a final example of the complex relations among markets, trade, and commodity and modern economic cycles, in the 1840s, the status of foreign slave-produced sugar in British markets, where plantation slavery had been abolished, was controversial as the British economy moved toward free trade in agricultural commodities. Even though British abolitionist statesmen argued that slave-produced sugar from Cuba, Louisiana, or Brazil would inevitably find its way to British consumers, the connection between the price of Havana sugar, the prices of sugar in British markets, and the demand for slaves on the island of Cuba remained widely divergent, and in the early 1840s the importation of African slaves into Cuban markets had begun to decline precipitously for want of markets for the sugar they might produce.

It was not until Lord John Russell's bill admitting slave-grown sugar into British markets in July 1846 that British and Havana sugar prices finally converged. At the same time, the moribund market for slaves in Cuba, which had practically disappeared in 1846, suddenly went into high gear.

News of the admission of Cuban sugar directly into Great Britain was greeted in Havana, it was said, with great rejoicing, and the prices of slaves and land there promptly began to recover. Even more to the point, the price difference between Havana and British plantation sugar, which had averaged 13 shillings per ton in the early 1840s, narrowed in 1847 to about half that and by the end of 1847 was no more than 2 shillings per ton. Moreover, prices for sugar in Havana and London moved almost in parallel. An integrated market, in short, had emerged.

Economic cycles, defined in terms of capitalized production for integrated remote markets, had been impossible in 1450. By 1850, Atlantic markets displayed every characteristic of modern price series. The mobility of capital, the breakdown of mercantilist restrictions on commodity trades, and, ironically at best, the transatlantic slave trade had produced modern economic cycles in the nineteenth century.

RICHARD SALVUCCI

Bibliography

Eltis, David. *Economic Growth and the Ending of the Transatlantic Slave Trade.* Oxford: Oxford University Press, 1987.

Stein, Stanley J., and Barbara H. Stein. *Apogee of Empire: Spain and New Spain in the Age of Charles III.* Baltimore, MD: Johns Hopkins University Press, 2003.

Zahedieh, Nuala. *The Capital and the Colonies: London and the Atlantic Economy, 1660–1700.* Cambridge: Cambridge University Press, 2010.

Economic Strategies, African

Africa is a continent of enormous riches, which have inspired the innovations of its own people and attracted the commercial ambitions of outsiders over very long periods of time. The center of concern for the outsiders' strategies was the output of the land (including minerals, crops, animals, and people as commodities), mobilized through capital, for extraction, and money, for trade. Indigenous strategies, however, rested largely not on "labor" simply as a factor of production. More important, rather, was the human factor "in motion" in a more encompassing sense—as a source of continuously differentiating expertise and reproductive power—and on relationships as a mode of short- and long-distance communication on a continent where wheeled vehicles, traction livestock, and literate commercial recording were not widely available before the twentieth century. For ecological reasons, and because of the cultivated capacities of the population for human forms of transport, record-keeping, and communication, long-distance mobility and trade were feasible and efficient without these Eurasian technologies.

From 1400 to 1850, before the imposition of colonial borders and European regimes, Africans continued what we must infer, from linguistic and archaeological evidence, to have been a millennia-long peopling of the continent involving migration, innovation, domestication of new environments, and extracting preexisting resources (see Miller). The so-called Bantu expansion, one of the great migrations of human history, comprised thousands of small and large, local and regional movements whose variety has encouraged scholars to see "the African frontier" of an open horizon of resources as a continuous and central theme in culture, society, politics, and economics. Breakaway groups, advance forays, refugee populations, colonizers, and trading expeditions recurred, even across major ecological boundaries, as from savanna to forest, low to high altitudes, and across deserts. African economic strategies have always included an orientation toward innovation: in tools and techniques, accommodation of new neighbors, and openness to novelty introduced from outside, whether in crops, currencies, or ideas.

Mobility and Wealth in Human Form

The pervasiveness of mobility means that, although provisioning was adapted to local conditions in varied ecological zones, African economies are better considered as centered on the networks of transfers and communication than on the demographics and agro-ecology of the producers. The absence of long-distance wheeled transport, limited literate communication, and the dangers of tropical diseases that parasites posed for draft animals placed great prominence on expertise in water navigation, on caravans of camels in Saharan regions, and on the human capacity to carry goods over long distances. The Swahili coast and Indian Ocean, the Atlantic coast, the Niger, Nile and Congo basins, and the Great Lakes (Victoria and others at the sources of the Nile) are all at the heart of zones of economic communication defined by techniques of navigation. The oases of the Sahara and the circum-Sahara savannas formed a vast zone in which currencies circulated in a seasonal pattern and bulky goods were moved by camel caravans. The great forests and Guinea savannas were traversed by long lines of human porters, whose efficiency in carrying heavy loads on their heads over long distances has been proven by scientific study.

Where multiple innovations and human-powered transport, far more than land and capital, are the key resources, strategies for economic success focus on the human factor. Large networks of partners and many dependents were universally valued before the recent rapid rise of urban density, which had made impractical—due to new rates and kinds of mobility—one of the classic forms of human collectivity, the large and diverse household. However, the principles of value-in-people persist in the present: in the cultivation of kinship, associations, political clientage, religious congregations, and settlement diasporas near and far, some circling the globe. Scholars have termed this human networking a strategy of *wealth-in-people*. Ambition is based on quality—the diversity and skills—of this human factor, as well as quantity. Diversity led to success even where a primary concern was with protection, as for the maroons and other refugees from the slave trade who developed intensive cultivation in mountainous and otherwise inaccessible regions. Bringing complementary capacities together is better thought of as "composition" than "accumulation"; wealth-in-people entails forms of management that go beyond simply amassing "more," as in accumulation based on individual ownership and deployment of land (feudalism) or money (capitalism).

This compositional dynamic makes building models of strategic behavior more difficult than where they are based on the quantifiable factors: land, labor (as simply abstracted labor *power*), and capital. Indeed, Africa scholars have been reluctant to formalize a model comparable with the conventional "firm" and "household" because of the wide variation in forms and ideologies. The human factor can be analyzed in socioeconomic units ranging from the great houses and complex courts of the slave-trading polities of the eighteenth century to the lineage diasporas of, for example, fishers along the coasts, trade networks along the rivers, and—today—such occupations as kin-organized automobile spare-parts manufacturers and dealers across entire urban hinterlands. In West Africa, associations formed around religious convictions mediate financial transactions across national borders. Along the eastern seaboard and the western desert and savanna, Islam fosters economic institutions particular to itself: frameworks for contracts, hostels for travelers, apprenticeships in trades, and principles for community giving (*zakat*). Particular practices, such as numbering and accounting, pass from one to another.

Human Skills in Composition

Valued skills change as historical and ecological-economic environments shift. Metallurgy, focusing on copper, gold, and iron, has been highly developed for centuries. The skills of the smith respond to demand, from the gold-weight currency technologies of the Ashanti to the multi-bladed throwing knives for display, hunting, and warfare of the equatorial region. Crop development and the domestication of New World cultigens to African microenvironments have long been intensely active, to the degree that Africans from particular crop areas (for example, rice cultivators from Sierra Leone and the Gambia) were especially in demand in the Atlantic slave trade. Raffia-cloth and cotton textiles of distinguishing variety were distributed through vast regions of Central and West Africa, respectively. Experiments with fishponds along the Congo were replicated. Healing was highly valued, as were skills in the arts that celebrated spiritual and political ideologies.

Fostering these skills, controlling access to them, and employing them in production and trading systems was a management skill all its own. Economic units are communities best thought of as composed—by marriage and reproduction, by descent, by attracting others with varied skills through alliances or apprenticeships, and by the acquisition

UNIVERSITY OF WINCHESTER
LIBRARY

of slaves and other dependents through debt systems (see Miller; Lovejoy). Famous "houselike" units include the *gida* of the Hausa kolanut, cattle, and other commodity traders of northern Nigeria and its diasporas (see Cohen; Baier); the house-settlements of the Central African forest (see Vansina); and the trading houses of the Niger Delta (see Horton). The great royal lineages, such as the Ashanti, operated more like large versions of houses with administrative responsibilities than exclusionary aristocratic families of feudal regimes in Europe, in that able children of members acquired in servile roles had ways of becoming full and contributing members. In some systems the house was a literal structure, or physical complex of buildings, bringing in strangers from alliance networks as temporary guests and attached workers as resident dependents.

Internally, roles were differentiated by aptitudes and skills, while in many areas of the African Atlantic World houses themselves were identified with specialties. These artisan communities were found particularly in occupations that demanded spiritual guardianship as well as high levels of technical expertise. Metalwork of all kinds, from the smelter to the smithy, required "medicines" and supplication of deities. Music and oratory could be embodied in house groups that were defined genealogically as responsible for performances of the collective ritual cycle and for guardianship of the oral-history corpus. Ownership of the masquerades, which were essential for the legal and spiritual welfare of wider social groups, was often held by house units. Building strong units of this kind involved finesse in management strategies: to protect specialist occupations; to attract enough members to assure ongoing reproduction; to send members out to claim new land or pastures; to connect to the wider world through social alliances and exchange networks; and to grow in relation to advantages on the "frontier," in whatever forms the frontier presented itself at different historical moments. People crossed from one ecology to another and from one language to another (on a continent with 2,000 languages); people created bridges between spiritual beings and worlds (in a context characterized by polytheism); and people approached the future through the divination of possibilities rather than prediction of trends or fates.

Frontier Strategies

The pervasiveness of borders and thresholds meant that some commonalities in strategies normalized margins of all kinds as centers of social and commercial life. Many institutional complexes were focused on transitions across the thresholds, from one place to another, from one social status to another, from states of affliction to states of health, or from one value scale to another. It is not accidental that the anthropology of "rites of passage" has been so developed in African studies.

There are two structural components to these economic movements. First, the skills and specialties can be best thought of as employing the ecological concept of the "niche" (see Guyer 1997), in that communities and concepts were constantly in both competition and collaboration with others as novel opportunities appeared. For example, new crops could allow the colonization of new lands, while also colonizing their own spaces in the existing agro-ecology, plant classification, cuisine, and pharmacopeia. In Central Africa, where music mediated access to the spiritual world, associations of musicians created novel dances through competitions. New crops and dances alike edged aside others, became a focus of new expertise and organization, but also became complementary to the existing repertoire. Similar processes applied in many other technologies, conceptual elements, and social forms. The modern world has invented a new word—*coopetition*—to depict this kind of dynamic, where firms' successful access to market space is gained through collaboration rather than through mechanisms assumed in the free-market model of outright competition. Africa has had markets, trade, and currencies for centuries. These have been combined with modes of dividing skills and commodities into named categories so that they could be identified, managed by associations, and composed or disaggregated situationally in ways not dissimilar to the dynamics of wealth-in-people itself. In the Congo Basin in the era of the slave trade, different groups created many differently shaped metal currencies that they exchanged against others in varying ways, in response to supplies of and demands for specific trade items. Specific commodities, such as salt, could occupy a niche in a regional system, where its consumption and use as a kind of currency changed with the seasons and with the politics of trade routes.

A dynamic property of niche economies is that the framework for flexibility and a diversity of options to embrace novelty is already set up. One needs only a name, a "good," and the capacity to build an organization, like a house or a guild, by applying social principles of replication, adaptation, and insertion into local and regional market "coopetition." This historical dynamism works even at the microeconomic level. A master craftsman trains dependents from his own house but eventually sends many of them off to social or geographical frontiers to replicate units of their own. These new independent units characteristically both compete for market share with their erstwhile masters and collaborate to adjust to shifts in overall economic conditions. From the perspective of conventional decision theory, this kind of arrangement cannot reduce easily to household and industrial-workshop models where microeconomic decision-making is an optimal allocation of its own, currently held, scarce resources. By contrast, African frontier strategies facilitate continual adjustment across the thresholds of time, space, and social organization.

The second property of the economic dynamic of the African frontier is the multiplicity of its value scales and associated physical currencies, which proliferated with particular rapidity in the era of the slave trade (see Guyer 2004; Zeleza). Atlantic trade brought in currency in large amounts and a variety of forms. Cowries were imported from the Indian Ocean via the great ports of Europe. Copper rings or bracelets, or *manillas*, were manufactured, for example in Birmingham. Copper—Africa's prestige metal—and its alloys were introduced in large quantities into the Congo Basin as well, where an ancient smelting industry had already fostered the manufacture of a great array of distinguishing objects, such as *croisettes* in the shape of St. Andrew's crosses. The iron crafts of Africa met iron imports. Textiles—worn to distinguish their wearers by individual status, family membership, occupation, ethnicity, and according to occasion—differentiated further as Indian cottons came in from the coast. The home-manufactured strip cloth of the Tiv of central Nigeria, for example, may have gone into a growth spurt as it became a standard of value and medium

for regional exchanges. It has been argued that the import of such currency-objects as cowries facilitated a rapid growth in African markets and trade over longer ranges in many commodities that until then had not reached such distant communities directly (see Hogendorn and Johnson). This multiplicity of currencies meant that brokering among them across borders became a vast field of creativity: in the institutions of exchange, in the creation of value scales, in numeration and memory skills, and in the differential deployment of several currencies within house-settlement organizations that has been termed "spheres of exchange."

In spheres of exchange, the currencies are not denominations of a single scheme. They circulate in differentiated registers, and there are losses and gains made at their borders. In the classic version (see Bohannan), the differences include moral values and status: one converts "up" or "down" when one changes one currency into another, or uses one currency to purchase goods assigned to the sphere of another. Bargaining in material tokens becomes a social and political process, having to do with composition of qualities arranged in hierarchies of value, rather than a strictly "economic" process, to do with accumulation of undifferentiated quantities.

The concept of spheres of exchange, which originates in ethnographic work on the Tiv of central Nigeria in the 1950s, is considered one of the main contributions of African economics to general economic theory. Skill in dealing with margins of all kinds—between currencies, among peoples or language groups, and into or out of spheres of exchange—has been highlighted (see Guyer 2004) in ways found potentially important for the novel multiplicity of the current global world in the twenty-first century (see Callon). The classic functions of money—as a homogenizing medium of exchange, means of payment, standardized unit of account, and store of fungible wealth—may be precipitating out, each into its own specialized currency medium, in our present economic world. Some officially recognized but low-value national and alternative currencies circulate quickly but locally and fluctuate in value; these are known as *soft currencies*, distinguished from *hard currencies*, which hold value over time and are used to store value. Some (derivatives; proposed units of international account) are purely fictional, while others (gold; the dollar) function highly selectively for some populations as pools of stored wealth. The ways in which the functions of money have been managed through multiplying their forms, as money-in-circulation grows very rapidly, makes African economic strategies in the era from 1400 to 1850 a particularly important case for study and possible extrapolation to newly emergent conditions.

Accumulation: Wealth-in-Things? Investment?

There were obvious ways in which wealth-in-people could shift from diversifying to accumulative modes. In some places, the era of Atlantic trade encouraged the expansion of numbers of wives in high-status polygynous marriages. Community members could be pledged to others within the community, against advances of monetary or material wealth. This practice extended to debt pawning, which provided labor in the expanding productive and sumptuary economies and gained warriors as the foundation of military capability. In other smaller institutions of dependency the practice also contributed to urban growth in political centers and trade entrepôts. The logic was impeccable for investing material gains in rights-in-people, in which obligations could be maintained without incurring the costs of policing that would be entailed in massing sheer numbers of people. Diverse skills could open up new productive and commercial opportunities, as by developing transport technologies on rivers and coasts with new kinds of boats and larger fleets. Forests could be cleared for cultivation when labor could be mobilized for felling the giant trees of the tropics. New relations of dependency created by tribute or purchase could create new armies of the kind that—everywhere in the world—contribute to production by facilitating primitive accumulation, seizing resources such as herds, land, mineral fields, and transport routes. Storage of wealth is not a major problem in a system based on wealth-in-people, so long as inexpensive daily practices, such as niche economies of differentiation and relational authority, allow maintenance of control.

The question of accumulating wealth in things, however, does remain. Proliferation and diversity could coexist with such accumulation. Throughout the Atlantic area—given the physical deterioration characteristic of tropical climates and the African commitment to mobility—there are commentaries on, and cultural enactments of distrust of, excessive volumes of many things: gold body adornments, bowls, cloth, decorative arts featuring imported cowrie shells and glass beads, and even house styles (the number of roofs is a poetic allusion to wealth). In the desert and border areas of the Sahara, compilations of religious manuscripts have also survived in large number. Consonant with the prominence of wealth-in-people, it is possible that the heterogeneity of these things was itself valued, since the logic of diversity would fine-tune the intricacies of complementing relationships rather than create a simple class or caste system of differential access to material resources (see Meillassoux).

Looking more deeply into "thingness," linguistic sources suggest that the primary distinction in African expressions is between things that reproduce by their own powers and things that do not. But the lexicons and artistic representations of wealth-in-things are complex, continually reverting to the specifics of their deployment for access to particular forms of wealth-in-people whether as labor power, reproductive potential, and/or "wealth in knowledge" (see Guyer and Eno Belinga). The incommensurability of the systems of valuation in Africa and Europe contributed to the terrible asymmetries of the Atlantic slave trade. Europe took out the commodities it valued as factors of production and stores of value—primarily gold, slaves, and extracted primary products—and poured in the equivalent of what became, in the twentieth century, soft currencies with no convertibility and limited capacity as stores of value beyond seasonal fluctuations and life-cycle stages. The wealth of Africa in the rising capitalist era was only a factor of production, as labor and capital, when the proceeds were exported. Joseph Miller has argued that what was left in Africa was vastly expanded debt, amplified by the succession and expansion of new currencies as media of exchange to which not all people had access all of the time, or on the calendars required.

Such a system originated in the interface between contrasting African and European economic strategies, with the results in money wealth being held largely in the reserve currencies of the Atlantic that were hardly used within Africa. Their conversion into the African soft-currency economy has two main effects. On the one hand it fosters the dependency aspects of the wealth-in-people dynamic, because only certain people hold the stores of value. And on the other, it fuels the skill/wealth-in-knowledge mode of ordinary people, particularly within the shorter-term horizons fostered by the instability and rapid circulation of soft currency. These days, promissory notes proliferate as these people try to pursue the innovative dynamics of the niche model, mediated by currencies whose values and exchange rates have become chronically unstable, which may add its own power to the debt mode. The denomination of debt over time, when soft-currency value fluctuates against hard currencies, can intensify problems of repayment, which may endanger the mutual commitments in the "coopetition" model of the modern niche economy and put a premium on cultivating dependency on access to stores of value. Tracing out the moral economy of debt (in quantities of money, timed on calendars) and promises (untimed, in terms of on-going mutual commitments) urgently awaits research in the twenty-first-century version of Africa's niche economies.

JANE I. GUYER

Bibliography

Alagoa, E. J. *Jaja of Opobo: The Slave Who Became King*. London: Longman, 1970.

Baier, Stephen. *An Economic History of Central Niger*. Oxford: Clarendon, 1980.

Bohannan, Paul. "Some Principles of Exchange and Investment among the Tiv." *American Anthropologist* 57, no. 1 (1955): 60–70.

Callon, Michel. "Il n'y a d'économie qu'aux marges: A propos du livre de Jane Guyer (*Marginal Gains. Monetary Transactions in Atlantic Africa*. Chicago: University of Chicago Press, 2004)," *Le Libellio d'Aegis* 4, no. 2 (2008):1–18.

Cohen, Abner. *Custom and Politics in Urban Africa: A Study of Hausa Migrants in Yoruba Towns*. Berkeley: University of California Press, 1969.

Guyer, Jane I. *An African Niche Economy: Farming to Feed Ibadan, 1968–88*. Edinburgh: Edinburgh University Press and the International African Institute, 1997.

———. *Marginal Gains: Monetary Transactions in Atlan-tic Africa*. Chicago: University of Chicago Press, 2004.

Guyer, Jane I., and S. M. Eno Belinga. "Wealth in People as Wealth in Knowledge: Accumulation and Composition in Equatorial Africa." *Journal of African History* 36, no. 2 (1995): 91–120.

Hogendorn, Jan S., and Marion Johnson. *The Shell Money of the Slave Trade*. Cambridge: Cambridge University Press, 1986.

Horton, Robin. "Stateless Societies in the History of West Africa." In *History of West Africa*. Edited by J. F. A. Ajayi and Michael Crowder. New York: Columbia University Press, 1973.

Kopytoff, Igor, ed. *The African Frontier: The Reproduction of Traditional African Societies*. Bloomington: Indiana University Press, 1987.

Lovejoy, Paul. *Caravans of Kola: The Hausa Kola Trade, 1700–1900*. Zaria, Nigeria: Ahmadu Bello University Press, 1980.

Meillassoux, Claude. *The Anthropology of Slavery: The Womb of Iron and Gold*. Chicago: University of Chicago Press, 1991.

Miller, Joseph. *Way of Death: Merchant Capitalism and the Angolan Slave Trade, 1730–1830*. Madison: University of Wisconsin Press, 1988.

Vansina, Jan. *Paths in the Rainforest: Toward a History of Political Tradition in Equatorial Africa*. Madison: University of Wisconsin Press, 1990.

Zeleza, Paul Tiyambe. *A Modern Economic History of Africa*. Vol. 1, *The Nineteenth Century*. Dakar, Senegal: CODESRIA, 1996.

Economic Strategies, European

As a historical process, economic success—that is, strategies of change—depends on the emergence of new opportunities and the financial resources to respond quickly to them. The Atlantic presented vast new resources, and eventually markets, to potential investors in Europe. This essay emphasizes the marginality of the economic actors at home who entered the Atlantic, how they raised the funds—implicitly lacking to merchants on the margins of European wealth invested in land, aristocratic privilege, and sanctity—to do so, the financing built on African and American bullion, and the changing forms of collateral developed to support the enormous pyramid of debt behind nineteenth-century industrialization in Europe and the commerce of truly global proportions that supported it.

Interest Groups

European trade in the Atlantic World got its start in the archipelagoes of the eastern Atlantic. The Portuguese began to exploit the previously uninhabited islands of Madeira, the Azores, and Cape Verde in the 1420s, 1440s, and 1460s, respectively, while Portuguese and Spanish merchants and their crowns hotly contested control of the Canary Islands until Spain's victory in the colonial war, fought from 1475 to 1479. Although the Iberians thus sponsored Atlantic trade, the Genoese largely financed their ventures. In the early fourteenth century, a Genoese captain and his crew discovered the Canaries, and the Genoese subsequently provided financial and commercial expertise to both Iberian powers as they developed their Atlantic outposts. These ventures were not confined to the archipelagoes but soon arose also in Africa and later again in the Americas. Portuguese merchants exploring the coast of West Africa in the mid-fifteenth century laid the foundation for long-lasting European commercial ties with the continent from Senegal to Angola. Columbus, the Genoese captain in Spanish service, then opened up the New World. It was not this famous first transatlantic voyage, but his third of 1498, that caught the Old World's attention, as Seville's merchants responded eagerly to the discovery of pearls on the coast of Venezuela.

Merchants in northern European ports were quick to join their Iberian counterparts in sending ships to test commercial possibilities on the far side of the Atlantic, but members of the old landed and aristocratic elites, who were well-placed to take advantage of potential new markets, were less eager. Josef Schumpeter's claim that economic elites are not usually the ones to introduce innovations offers an illuminating framework in which to analyze and understand the opening of Atlantic commerce. In Schumpeter's analysis, the new does not grow organically out of the old but comes into existence alongside it and in time succeeds in driving established interests out of existence. This dynamic of innovation from the margins would suggest that

adventurers responsible for opening up the Atlantic World were members of new groups, men willing to take enormous risks because they were marginal to safer opportunities closer to home.

The great lengths of sea voyages to transatlantic shores, prevailing winds and ocean currents, and the dearth of information on overseas prices, goods, and routes made most Atlantic ventures hazardous undertakings compared to the familiar trades of Europe and the Mediterranean. The early-modern period was one in which traders routinely lost fortunes, yet time and again others fitted out more ships to parts of Africa and the New World known and unknown, even to areas where previous ventures or colonizing schemes had utterly failed. The mercantile pioneers of the Atlantic World were not alone in their willingness to take on high-risk commercial adventures. As Theodore K. Rabb has argued, the "proclivity for taking large risks, against heavy odds, was a fundamental characteristic of the early-modern merchant. It was entirely in keeping with his outlook that he should have approached overseas enterprise in an almost reckless frame of mind" (Rabb, 679).

The Schumpeter thesis can be demonstrated clearly for England and the Dutch Republic. In the last quarter of the sixteenth century, when England's overseas expansion took off, the great London merchants dominated its trade. Not all of them shunned the chancy commerce of the Atlantic, so long as they could reduce the uncertainties and delays by organizing their businesses in companies they formed to spread the risks and operating under the shelter of legal privileges. The initial English company set up to develop American commerce, the Virginia Company, was organized as a joint-stock venture in imitation of the seemingly secure East India Company chartered to tap the fabled riches of Asia. The failure of the Virginia Company to attract many investors was not due to a lack of funds: merchants of the City of London and members of the landed gentry poured massive amounts of money into the East India Company in the same years that its Virginia counterpart struggled. Investor reluctance can be attributed to the larger outlays foreseen in opening up the Americas in comparison with Asian exploits. The Virginia Company not only sought trade with resident populations, as was the case with the vast and skilled artisan production of Asian peasants, but also aimed to set up and maintain productive plantations of its own, which required large and frequent injections of capital over a long period. The merchants of London also withdrew their support from the contemporaneous Newfoundland Company, as its investments in settlement and plantation infrastructure left only a minute margin of profit for the extractive, and thus much less costly, local fisheries. Barring the minor and insular exceptions of the Puritan-led Bermuda and Providence Island Companies, established English merchant capital looked elsewhere for cheaper opportunities.

Men marginal to the mercantile or political elites filled the Atlantic vacuum. Sons of the minor gentry and well-to-do yeomen, many of them had not even been Londoners. The prior pursuits of these former shopkeepers and ship captains did not particularly qualify them for exploiting distant colonies, and yet many of them succeeded, as they were willing to accept small and irregular profits from businesses of new types, open to novices and innovators, that involved expensive colonization as well as trade. Whether emigrating to the nascent colonies or remaining in London, they engaged the potential markets not monopolized by chartered, more established interests. Through ties of extended kinship and ad hoc partnerships, they accumulated impressive capital resources as well as knowledge of markets and products, thus reducing risks and transaction costs.

In the Netherlands, the vast majority of the Amsterdam merchants prior to the beginning of Dutch commercial expansion in the 1590s continued to invest in the traditional European maritime trades, importing Baltic grain and Iberian salt or dealing with Norway for salted herring, and the city's major markets in northern Germany. But, as in England, a few of the old merchants were willing to take the risks of trading with new markets in the Atlantic and elsewhere around the globe. While members of the old trading families used their political clout as city burgomasters to use their gains to speculate locally in land, its limited availability in a small country turned their searches for profitable investments to the Atlantic. They also joined forces in chartered companies, including the West India Company, founded in 1621, to coordinate trade and warfare against their recent Habsburg rulers in Spain

throughout the Atlantic Basin, with themselves as directors.

Joining them in pioneering Dutch transatlantic trade were two groups of newcomers: merchants from the southern Netherlands and "men of the Portuguese Nation." The latter group, largely made up of Sephardic Jews expelled from Iberia (nominally converted as New Christians, but secretly observing Mosaic laws), distinguished themselves by their drive to innovate, to take risks. They collaborated with business associates to whom they were not related or whom they did not know, diversified their trades, experimented with new routes and products, and integrated distant locales, trade routes, and products. They may not have brought large amounts of capital to these ventures, but their variety of contacts with fellow Portuguese around the quite well-integrated Iberian Atlantic gave them significant advantages in contacts and information. The other group of outsiders—merchants hailing from Antwerp and adjacent areas in the southern Netherlands—operated as cogs in well-oiled international networks and were far greater in number than the Amsterdam investors. However, the economic significance of the Amsterdam elite lies in their endowing the city with an important money and capital market to raise the large sums required in Atlantic ventures.

The demise of the restrictive chartered English Virginia Company in 1626 and the attendant triumph of new merchants who championed "free trade," open to less well-connected associates, was paralleled across the English Channel in the termination of the government monopolies granted to the Dutch West India Company. Ideally, the argument ran, a large, government-chartered organization possessed the political and even military capacities needed to establish a permanent infrastructure overseas, protecting investments against intrusions (by establishing an administrative staff resident overseas), extending military protections, organizing regular transport, and constructing warehouses, depots, shipyards, and forts. When the balance sheet for New Netherland (the colony set up at the mouth of the Hudson River at the present-day site of Manhattan) showed that expenditures were much higher than anticipated—five years into its existence—the Company directors allowed for private capital to make the colony profitable. New Amsterdam traders gained the right to trade along the entire eastern seaboard, while non-Company merchants in the Dutch Republic could also freely dispatch their goods to them. Before long, the Company monopolies in the trade with the Portuguese sugar-producing areas in northeastern Brazil, which the Company had seized, were also abandoned.

Though these new merchants took key initiatives in creating and exploiting overseas opportunities, older interests did not entirely neglect the possibilities of the Atlantic. However, they required government subsidies in the form of monopolies to undertake the costly and risky investments in commercial infrastructure and, eventually, even more to enter commodity production in the Americas. The financial demands and lack of reliable military protection eventually made most of them abandon the risky and costly new arena of the Atlantic World to newcomers marginal to the interests well-established in Europe.

Extending Existing Strategies and Resources

Not all Atlantic destinations were sufficiently remote to be left to the innovators. The Genoese and others in the fifteenth century had simply extended coastal circuits of intra-European trade. A sixteenth-century ship could complete a voyage to the Azores in the mid-Atlantic, the Canaries, and Madeira off Africa's Atlantic coast, virtually all of the Caribbean islands, the African coast itself as far as Elmina (on the Gold Coast, in modern Ghana), and the easterly corner of the Americas, that is, northern Brazil in six months' time. These voyages—compared to more distant trade undertakings—did not require technical resources or investments of prohibitive scales; their relative short durations made it possible to use 70 to 80 percent of the ships' carrying capacity for economic objectives rather than for the logistics of the voyage itself. They were therefore alluring to merchants whose roles in European and Mediterranean commerce were minor.

The early trading initiatives in eastern and mid-Atlantic outposts in the fifteenth century thus did not represent a break with familiar strategies and commodities. Genoese merchants relied on their prior experience in the slave trade in the Mediter-

ranean as they helped the Spanish crown in colonizing the Canary Islands (beginning in 1402) and its American Indies (after 1492). They also supported the initial Portuguese Atlantic investments in producing sugar on the islands adjacent to Africa and the trade in brazilwood—one of the main early imports from the New World. In keeping with their time-honored role as financiers, the Genoese also took the lead in Atlantic maritime insurance and in financing transatlantic shipping. French merchants experienced in the salt and fish trades from Iberia branched out to North America, while those with expertise in selling northern European linen textiles tried their luck offering the cloth in African markets. The seventeenth-century London shopkeepers, sea captains, or domestic traders who became England's new colonial merchants likewise extended their older operations to trade with Africa and the New World, sometimes taking advantage of new commercial opportunities in Europe. The English search for Newfoundland salt cod, for example, was encouraged by the shift in English trade from Antwerp to Spain and the Mediterranean and the consequent need to find new goods to sell in these established markets for salt fish from northern latitudes. And what motivated the Protestant Dutch to capitalize on salt deposits around the Atlantic Basin was their exclusion by the Catholic Spanish kings, with whom they were at war, from their traditional sources of the mineral in the Iberian peninsula.

Merchants from Rouen in northern France were among the first non-Iberians to discover that the linen cloth and grain they had always sent to Spain also found ready markets in Spain's Canary Islands and then the burgeoning Spanish populations in the Americas. Yet, in the sixteenth and early seventeenth centuries, trade with Spanish America remained largely a Spanish monopoly, in the sense that all trade to the Indies took place by means of ships licensed by Spain and departing from Seville. From the 1560s through the mid-eighteenth century, the main form of Spanish Atlantic commerce was a system called the *carrera de Indias*, made up of highly regulated fleets that sailed from Seville to the Mexican and Peruvian viceroyalties and exchanged European manufactures for American silver and other commodities at officially authorized trade fairs. To a large extent, this fleet system was self-financing: the silver on the inbound fleet paid for the next outbound one. One profitable strategy of Spanish merchants specific to this fair-based system was to delay their purchases of American commodities, expecting that once the ending date of the fair was declared, local suppliers would lower their prices considerably in order to dispose of their inventories.

Foreign investors in the Spanish Atlantic fleets, led by the French, steadily increased their roles by using Spanish figureheads to consign their goods to Spanish shippers. The French merchants sailed themselves as supercargoes (in charge of the cargos carried by Spanish vessels) or sent commission agents to the Indies to supervise sales and arrange safe returns of the proceeds in silver. These arrangements transported the goods sent across the Atlantic at the expense and risk of the foreigners. By competing with Spanish merchants attempting to sell goods in the regulated New World markets, these foreigners disabled their strategy of keeping prices for their goods high by limiting supplies.

Although foreign merchants could reap handsome profits in both trade and finance in the existing markets of Spain's Indies, some began to bypass the Spanish fleets entirely, to avoid the multiple taxes and costs of trading through the *carrera de Indias*, in particular the inability to claim redress against the shippers in case something went wrong. By sending vessels of their own to the Americas, aiming for vertical integration, they cut costs by gaining direct access to American suppliers and producers. Bypassing local networks had been a central strategy of integrating late medieval markets and so represented another extension of older practices to integrate the new Atlantic trading economy.

Independent northern European trade with the tropical and subtropical areas of the Atlantic similarly tended to grow organically out of these early Iberian apprenticeships. The "men of the Portuguese Nation," no friends of the Spanish rulers who had expelled their ancestors from the Iberian peninsula, just as they had been among the pioneers of Dutch trade with Africa, developed commercial access to Brazil in tandem with their native Dutch partners, sparking the two Dutch invasions of the Portuguese colony in 1624 and 1630. However, northern Europeans resorted only very rarely to costly military conquests of the American colonies

of the Iberians. Instead, they developed more efficient commercial contacts with Ibero-America by sending ships cruising from port to port, exploring a variety of markets during lengthy voyages, their holds filled with large and diverse cargoes, to be sold in complex transactions according to local demands left unmet by the bulky regulations of distant governments in Europe. Even though individual ventures were often unsuccessful, multiple investors in these complex voyages spread their risks and could often reap handsome profits. The major objective of subsequent intercolonial trade between northern European colonies and those of Spain was to obtain the precious metals of New Spain (Mexico) and Peru. The silver bullion of Spain's mainland viceroyalties ended up mostly on Dutch and English East India ships bound for Asia and the Baltic Sea and made only modest contributions to launching the northerners' more costly mid- to late seventeenth-century investments in plantation agriculture in the Caribbean. In addition, the quantities of silver leaving Spanish America diminished precisely as these needs for financing commodity-producing plantations grew.

There were other ways to obtain American bullion through Atlantic commerce. One was by trading with Africa, where until around 1700 the value of European purchases of gold exceeded that of human cargoes. Merchants seeking bullion could also gain access to American silver by contracting or subcontracting the *asiento*, the monopoly charter that Spain used to supply slaves, paid for in pieces of eight, to its New World enterprises. The companies—almost invariably non-Spanish—that signed these agreements with the Spanish government exploited the authorized deliveries of enslaved Africans by filling the holds of their ships with all kinds of commodities for Spain's colonial markets and crowding their human cargoes into minimal remaining spaces on board. One of these firms was the South Sea Company, a British joint-stock company chartered in 1711, whose shares shot up so high in response to rumors about the potential silver to be gained in American waters that it collapsed by 1720, leaving many investors ruined.

Gold became available in the Portuguese Atlantic from 1700 through 1760, and the British moved in. By way of Portugal, London merchants obtained a wealth of bullion by sending the light woolen and worsted textiles in which British producers specialized to Lisbon, which re-exported the bulk of these goods to its American colony. The British merchants were paid mostly in gold. The Portuguese were largely sidelined from the trade between Lisbon and Brazil but used their foothold in the slave-exporting colony of Angola, and assistance from government-chartered corporations, to export large quantities of second-rate goods that had originated from all over the Portuguese Empire. They were paid not in slaves, whom Angolan and Brazilian traders used only to transfer account balances among themselves in the southern Atlantic, but in merchant notes of credit, valuable in Europe because they were payable in Brazilian gold, sugar, and coffee. Merchants marginal in Europe thus, once again, invested in the specie and commodities of the Atlantic World to carve out places for themselves at home.

Capital and Credit in Trade and Production

Capital resources had obviously been instrumental in launching transatlantic trade. For a long time, the bottomry loan—using the ship itself as collateral—was the preferred credit mechanism for commercial ventures of all sorts. In this arrangement, an investor would lend the ship's owner a sum of money to fit out and load the ocean-going vessel and would be repaid the amount advanced after the ship's safe return, as well as an additional markup that had been agreed upon before sailing. If the ship was wrecked or captured, the investor lost the capital secured by the vessel.

Although this single-venture mechanism was suited to the average merchant, the very costly investments in infrastructure and plantation production that England and the Dutch Republic undertook in the seventeenth-century Atlantic demanded a larger-scale solution: joint-stock companies, which assembled resources from several or many investors to cover heavy startup costs. The open market for shares of such companies guaranteed the requisite long-term investments in goods, warehouses, and general commercial infrastructure, since they removed dependency on the short-term fortunes of any particular merchant or group. Credit, obtained from joint-stock companies or other established sources in Europe, accelerated the three connected processes critical to the startup years of northern European colonies in the Caribbean and the Chesapeake: acquiring enslaved labor, assembling equipment and facilities, and improving lands.

Joint-stock companies with monopoly contracts, such as the Dutch West India Company, enabled new countries to move into the Atlantic slave trade before their infant colonies in the Americas gained the wherewithal to pay for themselves. They flourished as traders in the early and middle decades of the seventeenth century but provided no permanent solution to the ever-growing need for funds to invest in infrastructure and in production itself, on plantations. Sooner or later, these companies faltered because they tied up too much capital, for too long, in the slow-paying start-up phases of complicated and costly plantation agriculture. By the turn of the eighteenth century, however, as Caribbean plantations were becoming productive, private traders, sensing the coming payoffs, inherited their commercial contacts, shipping practices, and credit arrangements.

A new form of credit, the bill of exchange, eventually became the norm. Through this type of financial instrument, the American commodity producer, say an indebted Caribbean sugar planter or a Chesapeake tobacco grower, told his merchant-agent-banker in Europe, to whom the American sugar or tobacco was consigned for sale, to use the proceeds from selling the commodities to pay the merchant who had originally financed goods sent from Europe on credit to the American planter. This transfer of the financing of Atlantic trade from merchants in Europe to producers in the Americas leveraged significant new assets, beyond American bullion, to fund its great expansion in the eighteenth century.

Private British merchants dominated the transatlantic trade thereafter. Many of the successful ones had first worked as resident agents, or factors, for the chartered corporations in the colonies, acquiring valuable experience, capital, and personal connections. Liberal extensions of European merchant credit were key to succeeding in the colonies. After 1745, British merchants used their credit resources to achieve complete control of increasing exports of manufactured consumer goods to the rapidly growing populations of the North American colonies. They abandoned consigning goods to their own factors in the colonies and enabled shopkeepers to buy goods directly by extending credit to them. Another strategy that metropolitan merchants employed to gain control of American consumer markets was selling goods in bulk with very low markups through inexpensive auctions.

In some colonies, creditors in Europe were authorized by law to seize debtors' crops, agricultural implements, livestock, and slaves to obtain payment. Other colonies were a debtor's paradise, where creditors could claim only cash crops. French law protected Caribbean planters to such a degree that metropolitan merchants had no choice but to keep extending credit even to slow-paying debtors, thereby financing the fast-growing production of sugar in Saint-Domingue, as well as from Martinique and Guadeloupe. The French Revolution of 1789 led to no relief for creditors, as the new National Assembly feared that a law benefiting creditors in France would spark secession in the deeply indebted Antilles. Metropolitan commercial capital thus sustained French plantations throughout the colonial era. The broad trend for European capital to move increasingly into American production can be observed also in the British colonies, both in the Caribbean and North America. The shift came about smoothly, as an extension of the merchants' experience in the colonies, where they had gained knowledge of markets as factors.

The era of political revolutions from 1775 to 1824 that ended European military control in the mainland Americas did not terminate European investment in the overseas Atlantic. British merchants conducted a flourishing trade with their former colonies in the United States and in Central and South America switched from smuggling to the informal imperialism of free trade. With the notable exception of Saint-Domingue, independent as Haiti, Europeans lost none of their island colonies in the Caribbean. Nonetheless, European imports of sugar and coffee from them declined as European capital moved into domestic industrial trade and production. The relatively minor merchants driven out of Atlantic slaving with the suppression of the trade after 1807 turned to Africa, buying vegetable oils and other commodities for industrializing home economies. From the perspective of European investors, therefore, the increasingly populous Americas gradually changed from sources of bullion and agricultural commodities to markets for industrial goods and direct investments in the spreading transportation infrastructure of rails and canals.

WIM KLOOSTER

Bibliography

Bakewell, Peter. *Silver and Entrepreneurship: The Life and Times of Antonio López de Quiroga in Seventeenth-Century Potosí*. Dallas: Southern Methodist University Press, 1995.

Bernal, Antonio Miguel. *La financiación de la Carrera de Indias (1492–1824): Dinero y crédito en el comercio colonial español con América*. Sevilla: El Monte & Banco de España, 1992.

Brenner, Robert. *Merchants and Revolution: Commercial Change, Political Conflict, and London's Overseas Traders, 1550–1653*. Princeton, NJ: Princeton University Press, 1993.

Brunelle, Gayle K. *The New World Merchants of Rouen, 1559–1630*. Kirksville, MO: Sixteenth Century Journal Publishers, 1991.

Eltis, David. *The Rise of African Slavery in the Americas*. Cambridge: Cambridge University Press, 2000.

Hancock, David. *Citizens of the World: London Merchants and the Integration of the British Atlantic*. Cambridge: Cambridge University Press, 1995.

Klein, Herbert S. *The Atlantic Slave Trade*. Cambridge: Cambridge University Press, 1999.

Lesger, Clé. *The Rise of the Amsterdam Market and Information Exchange: Merchants, Commercial Expansion and Change in the Spatial Economy of the Low Countries, c. 1550–1630*. Aldershot, UK: Ashgate, 2006.

Miller, Joseph C. *Way of Death: Merchant Capitalism and the Angolan Slave Trade, 1730–1830*. Madison, WI: University of Wisconsin Press, 1988.

Price, Jacob M. "Multilateralism and/or Bilateralism: The Settlement of British Trade Balances with 'the North', ca. 1700," in idem, *Overseas Trade and Traders: Essays on Some Commercial, Financial and Political Challenges Facing British Atlantic Merchants, 1660–1775*. Aldershot, UK, and Brookfield, VT: Variorum, 1996.

Rabb, Theodore K. "The Expansion of Europe and the Spirit of Capitalism." *The Historical Journal* 17, no. 4 (December 1974).

Stein, Robert Louis. *The French Sugar Business in the Eighteenth Century*. Baton Rouge and London: Louisiana State University Press, 1988.

Zahedieh, Nuala. *The Capital and the Colonies: London*

and the Atlantic Economy, 1660–1700. Cambridge: Cambridge University Press, 2010.

Economic Strategies, Native North American

In the first hundred or so years after 1492, Indian participation in Atlantic World economics took the form of sales of slaves and skins in return for acquisitions of guns. In the beginning this trade proceeded through integration of indigenous reciprocal economic systems with the commercial system of the European Atlantic; however, these engagements still resulted in widespread disruptions of the community-based systems of Native Americans in favor of the competitive individualism driving Europeans. And as individual Indian entrepreneurs became tied to the nexus of global trade at the heart of the Atlantic World they not only transformed their own economic and political systems but also helped build the commercial economic scaffolding of the Atlantic.

The Creation of Shatter Zones

The myriad transoceanic connections between the New World, Europe, and Africa during the Atlantic Era were generated, in part, out of initiatives emanating from two contrasting worlds: the emerging commercial world of Europe and its American colonies and the well-integrated domestic economies of American Indians. In 1500 Indians in North America lived on resources of their own; by 1680 they lived on the edges of an expanding and conflict-ridden domain of commercial competition and in a new social landscape filled increasingly with Europeans and Africans. Engagements between these two worlds were not peaceful or orderly; rather, they were marked by warfare, violence, struggle, disease, and hardship for all involved. Although the Europeans eventually prevailed over the Indians, their meeting also opened new opportunities, new possibilities, and new ways of doing things for both Native groups and newcomers.

The first 180 years of European colonization, from about 1500 to 1680, disturbed Indians' lives. The archaeological and documentary evidence attests to movements of people into tightly compacted and heavily fortified towns, a dramatic loss of life, multiple migrations and splinterings of groups, the coalescence of new confederations, and the dissipation of many others. Despite such disruptions, Indians did not disappear. Instead, they reconfigured their lives, including their economic systems, in order to gain what they could from the changing colonial circumstances and new economic opportunities presented to them. In some cases, disparate peoples coalesced into large political and social groups, even gaining control over new trade systems by brokering alliances with Europeans and vanquishing their Indian competitors.

Although engagements with the Europeans played out differently for specific Indian polities and social groups, one widespread process has come to be known as the *Mississippian shatter zone.* This was a large region of instability in southeastern North America between the late sixteenth and early eighteenth centuries, brought about from the combined conditions of (1) the political fragility of precontact Indian polities (known as Mississippian chiefdoms); (2) the serial disease episodes and loss of life following the introduction of Old World pathogens; (3) Europeans' commercial financing of trade in Indian slaves and animal skins; and (4) the intensification of violence and warfare throughout the new Indian trade system, especially through militaristic Native slaving societies, which emerged to seize larger shares of the European trade. The violence of and disruptions within the Mississippian shatter zone exemplified the general patterns of domestic Native American economic strategies as they struggled to absorb the commercial wealth of the dynamic Atlantic commercial economy. The concept of a shatter zone provides a framework for understanding the reformation of Native societies from the Mississippi Valley to the Atlantic region as they became engaged in the Atlantic economy. This Mississippian shatter zone was one particular case of instability that may exemplify general patterns in the engagement of domestic economic strategies with the commercial strategies that thrived as the Atlantic consolidated into a new and dynamic economy.

The Trade in Skins and Captives

When early Spanish conquistadors and missionaries introduced Old World diseases and cultural exchanges, the resulting epidemics and adaptations were not transforming in and of themselves. Not until Native peoples engaged the Atlantic economy commercially through subsequent contacts with English, French, and Dutch traders did they use their gains from these engagements to revamp their social, political, and economic orders. The first Europeans who came to eastern North America during the age of colonialism hoped to gain easy wealth and corresponding prestige. They quickly grasped how to involve Native populations in trade, especially through the sale of armaments, and they recognized the commercial values of the extracted commodities, that is, deer and beaver skins, that the Indians offered in return. Early European traders also developed a brisk trade in Indian slaves.

The initial exchanges closely resembled indigenous diplomatic gift-giving, wherein two parties exchanged gifts—including captives—as symbolic gestures of alliance, compared with the later, more commercialized arm's-length trade between strangers. However, gift-giving was not the only form of exchange in Native North America. Indian people for centuries had maintained far-flung trade networks through which itinerant traders carried specialized products over long distances or through long chains of personal connections: trade in the sense of acquiring valuable exotic materials was nothing new to Indian people. In addition, Native people had utilized "debt" through delayed reciprocation of goods offered neighbors and kin. When transient Europeans arrived from afar, wanting to buy skins and slaves, Indian people had little difficulty recognizing and engaging in these transactions to acquire guns, ammunition, and other goods. Furthermore, when Europeans offered to give their goods to their Indian partners on credit, expecting commodities in return within a prescribed time, this obligation, too, conformed to Indian notions of reciprocity, wherein two or more people established enduring relationships of sharing.

Nor was slaving completely new to North American Indians, as most Native groups sometimes put war captives into bondage. However, captive taking on the large scales of the seventeenth and early eighteenth centuries had most likely not been conducted before the commercial resources of the Europeans financed raiding for the capture of prisoners. Warfare and captive taking thus served as the mechanism by which North American Indians could engage the capitalist economy within their own rules of war and peace.

The fates of the captives, though, changed radically with commercial slaving. In precontact days male captives had often been killed and their women seized and retained, but with European markets for commercial labor available, both warriors and noncombatants were taken as captives and sold. Indian captors also continued former practices in assigning other captives they retained—often women and children—to forced labor, adopting them into kin groups, marrying them, obtaining ransoms for them, or using them in prisoner exchanges to forge political alignments. But they sold the vast majority of their captives to Europeans.

Indians also supplied beaver, deer, and other animal skins to European entrepreneurs in North America. Because of the versatility of these leathers they were in high demand in European manufacturing centers, which used them to produce any number of items—from hats, gloves, and coats to saddles, horse tack, bookbindings, trunks, and furniture coverings. These finished goods often circulated across the globe, and even back into North America. Two aspects of the trade in animal skins made it lucrative to Europeans. In addition to the fact that extracting skins had a low acquisition cost, the trade did not require any significant investments in infrastructure. American Indians already had intricate trail and trade networks in place, through which they moved both goods and people. Indian males were trained as expert hunters and trackers and thus easily made the transition from subsistence to commercial hunting. However, women's efforts increased to support the trade in animal skins: they devoted considerably more time than their mothers and grandmothers had to tanning and dressing hides for sale. That said, both men and women could devote additional time to hunting and dressing skins because commercial hunting was seasonal (fall and winter) and did not appreciably disrupt the complementing summer labor demands of agriculture, dwelling maintenance, politics, and war. Within a decade or so of Europeans arriving in North America, the newcomers were buying thousands of skins from Indians, especially in the Northeast. Over the following 150 years, these quantities increased substantially, making the trade in skins the economic mainstay of most French and English colonies in North America, seriously depleting populations of beaver and deer across the eastern woodlands, and provoking violence like that of the Mississippian shatter zone as hunting bands ranged out into the lands of other Native communities.

Indian slaves also entered the circuits of global trade, with some being sold and resold as far away as present-day China. Mostly, though, European slavers shipped captive Native North Americans to work on the plantations of the West Indies and in the mines of South America. Closer to home, in New England, French Canada, and French Louisiana, they were used as domestic servants, concubines, urban laborers, and small-scale agricultural laborers. Scores were also sold to tobacco and rice planters in Jamestown, Charleston, and Savannah. There, Indian slaves blended into labor forces staffed primarily with enslaved Africans.

The Spread of Violence

The concept of the shatter zone centers on the violence through which Native peoples engaged with the relative wealth of capitalist enterprises. The colonial trade in slaves required high levels of force, whereas trading in furs or skins did not necessarily involve warfare. Certainly warfare had pervaded Indian life throughout North America before contact, so much so that conflict may have been the accepted state of affairs in most Indian polities. However, as Native warfare became tied to pursuing commercial gains, indigenous mechanisms for mitigating war and brokering peace collapsed. An initial result of integration into the market economy was the consolidation of militaristic Indian societies that held control of the trade, such as the Iroquois of the Eastern Great Lakes region. In addition, Europeans exploited the hostilities resulting from Indian rivalries by favoring one side over the other as suppliers of skins and by buying the captives taken in the ongoing conflicts and even instigating Indian conflicts in order to acquire Indian slaves. The result was the creation of shatter zones across large regions, resulting in widespread dislocation, migration, amalgamation, and, in some cases, the disappearance of Native communities as the survivors were dispersed into the larger, more successful groupings or sold as slaves to the Europeans.

The disturbances attending integration with the Atlantic spread west beyond the Mississippi River. For example, whole peoples such as the Hurons, Shawnee, and others fled westward from the turmoil in the eastern woodlands. Such movements often involved violent encounters with the residents of the areas the migrants entered. In other cases, migrants coalesced with resident groups, thereby forming new, powerful militarized entities, such as the Ojibwes and Illinois on the upper Mississippi River and the Osage in present-day Arkansas, Missouri, and eastern Kansas, all of whom controlled trade across vast areas. In southeastern North America, every Native polity that had existed at the time of contact fell by 1730, and the survivors regrouped into such powerful coalescent societies as the Creek Confederacy, the Cherokee, the Choctaw, and the Chickasaw. In the course of these movements, European goods, especially guns, made their way deep into the continent through Indian middlemen. The militarized groups used the firearms to vie for access to ever more remote regions to raid and to gain control of the trading routes back to the coast.

The reasons why Native populations fell into this cycle of spreading violence—and depleted the wild animals they hunted—lurk in the high values they found in the European goods they obtained in return for their skins and human captives. They bought metal objects in particular—brass and copper objects, steel knives, fishhooks, iron hoes, and axes—as well as objects of distinguishing adornment and hospitality—beads, bells, and alcohol. Indian women expected their husbands, brothers, and fathers to purchase cloths, metal cooking pots, and sewing implements. Only munitions outpaced cloths as the commodity in highest demand (measured in European currency values). Scholars divide over why Indians wanted firearms, especially since it is unclear whether the muskets available through the early trade gave a significant military edge to their purchasers. Some reason that these weapons, no matter how poorly made or ineffective, would still have revolutionized Indian warfare; others propose that Indian men sought them more as status symbols within their own communities than as implements to combat others. For whatever reasons, Indian people went to extraordinary lengths to acquire guns and created an escalating militarization that left the survivors of the violence dependent on acquiring still more muskets to defend themselves and to pursue the furs and captives that had become necessary for survival in the shatter zones.

Indian warfare became inexorably tied to commercial strategies based on European commercial credit. Europeans demanded that debts be paid in predetermined quantities of slaves and skins. In the case of the slave trade, the Indian debtors, armed with European weapons, raided rivals for captives. In the case of the trade in animal pelts, well-armed Indians launched wars against competing hunting groups and forced them to flee in order to open up the abandoned regions for commercial hunting. Warfare escalated in both cases because members of the unarmed groups had to acquire guns with which to defend themselves, and they in turn would fight for slaves and skins in order to pay for the armaments given them initially on European credit. The result was a vicious cycle of slaving, trading, warfare, weapons escalation, and debt.

Transformations

Even though the Indians engaged with capitalism through their own systems of exchange, in which material values articulated enduring personal obligations, the capitalist system of the Atlantic worked through relatively fleeting and impersonal contacts between strangers. Native American communities may not have reorganized themselves around the individual materialism of the capitalist mind-set until over a century later, but from the beginning the individuals engaged with the Atlantic became more dependent on European manufacturing, production, and lines of credit. Diplomatic gift-giving, sharing, and other forms of Indian exchanges continued throughout the following century or two, but by the end of the eighteenth century differences in wealth, prestige, and power emerged within Indian social orders to restructure intracommunity relations. Gender relations, too, became less reciprocal, as men devoted themselves to market pursuits outside their communities, and women sought to participate through marriages to Europeans and through expanding their own domestic economies. European commercial trade also promoted factionalism within indigenous political institutions and redefined the bases of power and authority—from succession through kinship and religious sanction to economic prowess and diplomatic contacts with powerful Europeans. It also transformed social relationships based on kinship and collaboration into competitive roles that promoted internal factionalism. However, the individualism that strained Indian communities was also useful for brokering relationships with competing European powers, and thus became the foundation for many Indian political and military successes over the eighteenth and nineteenth centuries.

Native Americans' involvement with European traders also transformed the Atlantic World. Throughout the seventeenth and eighteenth centuries, North American skins and captives extracted at low costs of investment made entry into Atlantic trade affordable for marginally financed Europeans and similarly contributed cheap labor for the start-up phases of the plantation economies that would form the commercial core of the Atlantic World. Direct raiding of the Native populations of southern South America supported the initial phases of sugar production in northeastern Brazil and then production of the crops that fed later captive African laborers there. Most historians of the Atlantic World focus on these commercial processes, acknowledging the North American Indian trade system only briefly and incidentally. But the initial formation of the Atlantic World took place through the reliability of Native Americans in supplying skins and slaves on minimal European commercial investment.

ROBBIE ETHRIDGE

Bibliography

Edmunds, R. David, Frederick E. Hoxie, and Neil Salisbury. *The People: A History of Native America*. Boston: Houghton Mifflin, 2007.

Ethridge, Robbie. *From Chicaza to Chickasaw: The European Invasion and the Transformation of the Mississippian World, 1540–1715*. Chapel Hill: University of North Carolina Press, 2010.

Gallay, Alan. *The Indian Slave Trade: The Rise of the English Empire in the American South, 1670–1717*. New Haven, CT: Yale University Press, 2002.

White, Richard. *The Middle Ground: Indians, Empires, and Republics in the Great Lakes Region, 1650–1815*. Cambridge: Cambridge University Press, 1991.

Witgen, Michael. *An Infinity of Nations: How the Native New World Shaped Modern North America.* Philadelphia: University of Pennsylvania Press, 2011.

Wolf, Eric. *Europe and the People without History.* Berkeley: University of California Press, 1990.

Economies, African

The opening of the Atlantic frontier in the mid-fifteenth century initiated a major new phase of Africa's economic history, although one with precedents in earlier intracontinental markets as well as external trade across the Indian Ocean and the Sahara Desert. At the coastal sites of Atlantic exchange, African merchants operated independently of European political control and received steadily higher prices for their exports. But the fact that Africans exchanged raw materials and, eventually, human captives in return for manufactured imports indicates at least an asymmetry in this commercial system, and probably a destructive effect on internal African economic development.

Before 1400: The Pre-Atlantic African Economy

Unlike the American regions discovered via Iberian voyages to the western shores of the Atlantic, tropical Africa was an integral part of the Old World, and had long been in commercial contact with both Europe and Asia. However, sub-Saharan Africa produced and traded under a number of geographic and demographic handicaps compared with these adjoining continents, as well as with the portions of its own landmass to the north on the Mediterranean. Agriculture had to be undertaken on thin layers of topsoil, leached by a combination of high temperatures and seasonally intensive rainfall. Transportation suffered from river basins interrupted by major cataracts at points of juncture between coastal and interior zones and from coastlines that contained no deep indentions suitable for sheltering maritime vessels. The woodland zones covering much of the region harbored sleeping sickness—inducing trypanosomes that prevented the use of large animals for overland transport. All of these conditions kept African population densities well below the levels of Asia and Europe, fur-

ther inhibiting the deployment of labor and the concentration of markets.

Despite these handicaps, tropical Africa played a major role in the medieval world-economy, especially as a source of gold needed both for coinage systems in Europe and the Middle East and to balance accounts in the wider trade of these regions with the rest of Asia. Africa's second major export was slaves. Although never reaching the proportions or playing the vital role in this era that it did in the later Atlantic economy, the export of captives nonetheless set a precedent for sustained long-distance traffic in human beings.

The large-scale supply of slaves from such an underpopulated region remains one of the great paradoxes of African history. In attempting to explain this contradiction, scholars have described a political economy where labor is the scarce factor of production in relation to both land, which is abundant, and fixed capital—whether permanent equipment or technologies—not highly developed due to limits on intensive cultivation of poor soils and epidemiological barriers to the use of animal power. As a result, Africans viewed people, assembled and retained in coherent groups, as their primary form of wealth. African labor for internal purposes thus had to be recruited by force, and these same captives, usually strangers brought from some distance, could also be offered to non-Africans in exchange for goods not available locally, goods whose distribution in exchange for personnel and loyalties also enabled the further accumulation of human capital.

Slave procurement always involved some level of violence, and the value received for captives in trans-Saharan trade is usually represented as horses, used here as animate instruments of war and raiding rather than for commercial transport. Moreover, this Mediterranean traffic continued and probably even increased after 1400, so its consequences in the Atlantic period must be added to those of the Atlantic slave trade. On balance, however, pre-Atlantic commerce probably did more to stimulate African development of productive capacities than damage them. Contacts across the Indian Ocean, for instance, mitigated a geographical limitation on agriculture in Africa. Since the biological gradations of the continent aligned latitudinally, that is, in a series of east-west zones varying across a north-south range, its ecologically incompatible zones, such as the temperate Mediterranean and tropical sub-Saharan portions of the continent, inhibited the diffusion of cultigens from north to south; however, the Indian Ocean linked Africa latitudinally to tropical regions in Asia and brought at least one valuable food crop, the plantain banana.

North-south contrasts between desert, savanna, and forest did encourage internal trade across these ecological frontiers, which in turn supported urbanization in the Upper Niger River basin in the tropical western Sudan even before commercial contacts with the Mediterranean. With growing Mediterranean interest in the gold of the region, Sudanic cities continued to thrive on the resulting trans-Saharan commerce, becoming bases of both indigenous merchant networks extending into the forests to the south and artisanal industries that exported textiles and leather goods into and across the Sahara.

After 1400: Africa in the Atlantic Economy

When Portuguese navigators first felt their way along the Atlantic coast of Africa, they sought the same commodities that trans-Saharan caravans had delivered to the Mediterranean world, primarily gold and slaves. Between these two African exports, gold initially took precedence, and the most imposing structure that the Portuguese built along the coast in the fifteenth century was the massive fortress named Elmina (the Mine), in a region known correspondingly as the Gold Coast (now Ghana). The Portuguese also purchased slaves along the African coast, but their numbers did not exceed those of the existing trans-Saharan trade, and their employments in Europe remained irregular and largely urban rather than intensive and rural, as in the later American plantations. Slaves were even brought to Elmina from elsewhere in Africa to sell for gold.

African supplies of gold proved limited given the range of available mining technologies, even in the productive Volta region feeding Elmina, to say nothing of the exhausted alluvial sources in (modern) Zimbabwe that the Portuguese seized and the wholly imaginary silver mines they pursued in Angola. In any case, the massive exports of New World specie (mainly silver) soon overshadowed Africa as a source of bullion for both Europe and Asia.

European demands for commercial labor grew instead. From the mid-fifteenth century, the Portuguese and Spanish began to experiment with growing sugar on islands off Africa's Atlantic coast, and soon recruited African slaves as the main field workers in this industry. From the 1570s, when the nascent sugar-plantation system was extended to Brazil, the numbers of African emigrants forced across the Atlantic each year rose to entirely unprecedented levels, reaching a peak of close to 100,000 in the second half of the eighteenth century, according to Voyages: The Transatlantic Slave Trade Database, and continuing at close to 75,000 until 1850.

The first half of the nineteenth century also marked the beginning of what abolitionists optimistically labeled "legitimate" African trade, meaning nonhuman commodities, mainly vegetable oils extracted from either the fruit of oil palm trees or peanuts, originally an import from the Americas. This new commerce not only provided at least as much African export revenues as sales of slaves but also increased domestic demand for captive labor to cultivate, transport, and guard the routes along which the new commodities moved to the coast. Thus southeastern Nigeria and many other regions witnessed no decrease in levels of violence.

On the numerous trading castles erected before 1800 along the then Gold Coast, the guns pointed outward, toward the Atlantic and potential European rivals, rather than inward toward the African populations. Especially in the coastal regions that provided the greatest numbers of slaves for the Atlantic trade—Dahomey/Benin (the "Slave Coast"), the Bight of Biafra east of the delta of the Niger River, and the southward-running Congo-Angola regions beyond—Europeans traded from relatively lightly defended locations and, most often, directly from the decks of their anchored ships. With the exception of a few coastal towns in Senegal and northern Angola (along with Mozambique on the Indian Ocean side of the continent), Africa's Atlantic trade in the slaving era took place on territory controlled by Africans, who negotiated the prices of export commodities and captives based on both European demand and their costs of supply, almost always involving chains of middlemen reaching well into the interior of the continent.

The autonomy and resulting bargaining power of African exporters help explain the consistently positive terms of trade they enjoyed; that is, prices for slaves and later vegetable oils went up consistently. Most obviously, such favorable conditions resulted from an ever-growing need in the rest of the Atlantic World for the people and commodities that Africans provided. European buyers of these goods also raised prices by competing with one another. Not only did they represent a variety of European monarchies, especially Portuguese/Brazilian, British, and French, but these states' early attempts to organize the African commerce of their own subjects along monopolistic lines had collapsed by the early 1700s. Thus, in another paradox, slave dealing was, for everyone involved but the captives themselves, a "free trade" that benefited both African sellers and New World planters.

The asymmetry of this market also contributed to the positive terms of trade enjoyed by African exporters. Whatever the movements in external demand, the costs of the goods that Europeans used to buy African captives and commodities went down consistently during this period, due to advances in the transport technology, financial institutions, and marketing organization of European-dominated international trade. Up until the late 1700s Indian-produced cotton textiles remained the dominant manufactured component of European exports to Africa, but with the subsequent Industrial Revolution, Europeans mastered and further lowered prices in even this sector of Atlantic exchange. African merchants were clearly able to turn these international factors to their immediate advantage, but the extent to which the internal economies of the continent benefited or suffered from this engagement within the Atlantic World remains open for debate.

After 1400: The Atlantic Economy in Africa

The massive slave exports throughout this period of Africa's engagement with the Atlantic suggest that the impact on internal African economies was largely negative. However, for coastal regions that received captives from the interior, such commerce did develop capacities for organizing both long-distance trade and agriculture using increased inputs of dependent labor, if seldom more intensive technology. That said, slaves were mainly procured by violence, in the interior of the continent. Thus many of the imported goods—including but not restricted to the guns and other weapons demanded

in every transaction—were invested in military formations designed for coercion rather than to increase agricultural or artisanal production. Moral repugnance against the sustained inhumanity of slave trading played a negative economic role even within Africa, where individual material gain became suspect as the dangerous outcome of greedy accumulators standing independent of the strong ethos of community, in which gains of any one person were seen as coming at the expense of others; this zero-sum calculus was seen as witchcraft threatening the social reproduction of the group.

At the same time, European development during this period centered around "fiscal-military states," and a "Second Hundred Years' War" (1689–1815) between Britain and France coincided with the high point of Atlantic slaving in Africa. With abolition in the nineteenth century and industrialization in Europe, African economies adapted to the demands of "legitimate" trade in raw materials. African military regimes like the Asante Empire or Dahomey in West Africa or even the less-stable political regimes of Central Africa, where exports of slaves and equally rapacious ivory trading continued well past 1850, might also have eventually used their power to encourage the development of greater economic capacities; but their opportunity to do so was cut off by the imposition of European colonial rule from the late 1800s. The demographic losses of sending out over 12 million people (plus the additional deaths among captives en route to the Atlantic) were balanced somewhat by the biological contributions of the New World as a second tropical contact. The Americas provided Africa with three major new food sources: maize, manioc (cassava), and peanuts. Of the goods regularly exchanged by Europeans for slaves and African commodity exports, some stimulated local economies as intermediary goods—such as bars of pig iron, replacing smelting as supplies of African hardwoods for iron furnaces dwindled—or as currencies to facilitate small-scale transactions—such as cowrie shells from the Indian Ocean.

However, just as slave exports increased at the end of the seventeenth century, a greater proportion of imports shifted to firearms and, above all, cotton textiles. These cloths supported existing African production of textiles in a number of ways, including the demonstration of new patterns and provision of colors not otherwise available in yarns that were rewoven to local tastes. The weaving and dyeing enterprises of inland Sudanic cities also survived, due to their protection by the high costs of overland transport. Nearer to the Atlantic coasts, however, imports of cloth on greatly enlarged scales undermined the potential intensification of African cotton cloth production, which had shown some potential for artisanal integration into Atlantic circuits of merchant capital.

After 1850: Epilogue

Africa's engagement with the Atlantic economy increased further in the second half of the nineteenth century, but on much less advantageous terms. The Atlantic slave trade came to an end around 1860, but shortly afterwards global prices for its commodity substitutes, mainly vegetable oils, took a sharp drop. The subsequent imposition of colonial regimes produced transport infrastructure that overcame previous barriers between the Atlantic and the interior of the continent, but the ensuing stream of new mineral and agricultural exports fluctuated with world commodity prices and never gave Africa the significance in the modern world-economy that it had enjoyed (or suffered) through its earlier Atlantic Era provision of gold and slaves.

RALPH A. AUSTEN

Bibliography

Austen, Ralph A. "The Moral Economy of Witchcraft: An Essay in Comparative History." In *Modernity and Its Malcontents*, edited by Jean and John L. Comaroff, 89–110. Chicago: University of Chicago Press, 1993.

Austin, Gareth. "Resources, Techniques, and Strategies South of the Sahara: Revising the Factor Endowments Perspective on African Economic Development, 1500–2001." *Economic History Review*, 61, no. 3 (2008): 587–624.

Eltis, David, David Richardson, Stephen D. Behrendt, and Manolo Florentino. The Transatlantic Slave Trade Database, http://www.slavevoyages.org. 2007.

Inikori, Joseph. "English versus Indian Cotton Textiles: The Impact of Imports on Cotton Textile Production in West Africa." In *How India Clothed the World: The World of South Asian Textiles, 1500–1850*, edited by

Giorgio Riello and Tirthankar Roy, 85–114. Leiden: Brill, 2009.

———. "Transatlantic Slavery and Economic Development in the Atlantic World: West Africa, 1450–1850." In *The Cambridge World History of Slavery*. Vol. 3, *AD 1420–AD 1804*, edited by David Eltis and Stanley L. Engerman, 650–676. Cambridge: Cambridge University Press, 2011.

Kriger, Colleen E. *Cloth in West African History*. Lanham, MD: Altamira Press, 2006.

Miller, Joseph C. *Way of Death: Merchant Capitalism and the Angolan Slave Trade, 1730–1830*. Madison: University of Wisconsin Press, 1988.

Nwokeji, G. Ugo. *The Slave Trade and Culture in the Bight of Biafra: An African Society in the Atlantic World*. New York: Cambridge University Press, 2010.

Economies, American: Brazil

By any measure, Brazil's economy was quintessentially Atlantic from the first years of European contact through the mid-nineteenth century. Yet, over this broad scale of time and space, the Atlantic in Brazil and Brazil in the Atlantic were deeply marked by shifting regional factors, reflecting the diversity of a continental space containing regionally distinctive environments, settlement patterns, economies, and a vast oceanic arena crisscrossed with shifting lines of commerce and sovereignty. Brazil's economy was tied both to the northern Atlantic, as a market for commodities, and to the southern Atlantic, via the slave trade and subsidiary exchanges of other commodities. This dual orientation explains the rise of sugar production, particularly along the northeastern littoral around Salvador (Bahia) and in Pernambuco. Demand for sugar centered in Europe; land fit for growing cane was abundant in the northeast of Brazil. As for labor, after a brief experiment with indigenous workers, plantation owners came to rely on African slaves. By 1630 there were approximately 350 sugar mills (*engenhos*, the paradigmatic "engines" that drove the economy) in all of Brazil, making the colony a target of the imperial ambitions of rival powers, including the Dutch, who organized their West India Company in part to finance the conquest of the sugar-producing zones of the northeast, holding Pernambuco between 1630 and 1654, and taking Luanda, in Angola, between 1641 and 1648.

This story of combining European demand (and capital), Brazilian land and supply, and transplanted and coerced African labor was repeated in other regions of Brazil: to produce gold in Minas Gerais in the eighteenth century and coffee in the nineteenth century in Rio de Janeiro and São Paulo. The flows of enslaved Africans across the Atlantic to these different regions marked the scales and timing of this secular process. Nearly 650,000 captives were sent during the seventeenth century to Bahia and Pernambuco, primarily destined to work in sugar production; in the course of the 1700s, the stream shifted toward the southeast, especially to Minas Gerais with its gold, carrying nearly 850,000 Africans; the flow to the southeast continued in the first half of the nineteenth century, with nearly 1.5 million additional captives transported, primarily to Rio, São Paulo, and southern Minas Gerais, where coffee was king. The relative economic preeminence of the northeast and southeast, by this measure of external trade, reversed over these three centuries.

The story is not merely that of the insertion of Brazil into an abstract Atlantic economy in response to European demand for its commodity exports; it is also the story of local and regional historical processes. These practices included expropriation (or extraction), coercion, and exchange. The practices associated with access to and occupation and ownership of land centered on expropriation and its legal framing, the establishment of personal rights in property. Coercion is at the root of slavery, which emerged as the dominant labor regime in the Brazilian economy, particularly in its Atlantic dimensions. Finally, commercial exchange was the motivation for these practices of appropriation in land and labor. The accumulation of commercial wealth through exchange provided most of the capital mobilized in economic development in the regions touched directly or indirectly by the broader economy of the Atlantic World. Land in America, labor from Africa, and capital from Europe (though the Brazilian contribution to labor and capital stocks tended to increase over time) provided the fundamental building blocks of the economy.

Expropriation and Land

Brazil's economy suffered a major imbalance in these endowments from the perspective of European settlement. Land was plentiful, but labor relatively scarce. The indigenous populations of the forests and woods of eastern South America, for the most part, did not reside in large, settled communities like their counterparts in the core regions of Spanish America, where they were susceptible to control by conquest and direct coercion. Patterns of expropriation in Brazil therefore tended to result in enslavement of indigenous peoples or their eradication, or both. Capture, flight, and epidemic diseases in the sixteenth century reduced Native populations along the Atlantic coast, and the pattern of near extinction moved inland in the eighteenth century, when the discovery of gold shifted Euro-Brazilian settlement toward the mountainous mining districts of Minas Gerais.

Expropriation of land through conquest had been the common denominator in Iberia during the struggle of its Christian kingdoms with the Moors, and this pattern was extended to the far shore of the Atlantic in Brazil. The Avis dynasty in Portugal had consolidated its control in the fourteenth century during the so-called "Reconquista" by making substantial land grants to the nobility and to the religious orders. Later in the fifteenth century, on the Atlantic islands of Madeira and São Tomé, similar royal land grants were extended to sugar production and slavery in a kind of dress rehearsal for the economic complex that would eventually transform the Brazilian littoral, particularly the northeast, on vastly greater scales.

The practice of expropriating the best land and exploiting it with coerced labor was ingrained by the 1540s when settlement in Brazil was under way in earnest. The practice of awarding large land grants (sesmarias) to well-connected settlers with military commissions resulted in the creation of large holdings, which were subdivided and rendered more overlapping over time through the vagaries of partible inheritance and local responses to economic opportunities. Although the wealthy few controlled the largest areas, land remained abundant, and so small and medium holdings existed alongside the largest estates.

Because most Native peoples fled or went into

dramatic demographic collapse in advance of European settlement, grants of land, not people, predominated in the earliest years of occupation. Large-scale commercial agricultural production tied to Atlantic markets thus depended primarily on acquiring the scarce factor—labor, not land—which meant that the dominant class came to control the economy through slaveholding rather than by exploiting resident populations. Meanwhile, from the very beginning, many Europeans arriving in Brazil had a preference for town living, settling in nucleated cities along the coast rather than dispersing into the vast interior, where transport was virtually nonexistent and where Amerindians retained de facto political control. Most coastal towns depended on Atlantic commerce for their prosperity. As merchants made fortunes in the trade of goods and people across the Atlantic, the towns grew around rather splendid residences (*casas grandes,* the "big houses") and the urban infrastructure to support them, with large populations of slaves and freed people living in sprawling neighborhoods of shacks (*senzalas*). This urban growth stimulated demand for food and locally manufactured cloth. In this broad sense, the Atlantic economy pervaded Brazilian towns and their hinterlands, even when the goods and commodities produced and exchanged never left American shores.

Coercion and Labor

The quickening pace of the broader Atlantic economy in Brazil, first based on sugar, particularly in the northeast beginning in the sixteenth century, then based on coffee in the southeast from the end of the eighteenth, intensified a second practice characteristic of the Atlantic: slavery. European demand for stimulants—tobacco, sugar, and coffee—generated a regime based on the enslavement of Africans along the entire Atlantic seaboard of the Americas, extending from the Chesapeake down to Buenos Aires. Labor practices in Brazil, as with patterns in appropriating land, were modified from European antecedents. The enslavement of sub-Saharan Africans, though not on a large scale, had a long history predating Portugal's development of what was to become Brazil. What changed was the locations and magnitudes of the flows of captured labor, from a sixteenth-century northward drift toward the islands of the eastern Atlantic and Lisbon to a westerly avalanche oriented toward Recife (Pernambuco) and Salvador (Bahia) in the seventeenth century, and later in the eighteenth century to Rio de Janeiro and Minas Gerais.

In the prime rural zones connected with Atlantic trade, slaves toiled in large numbers under brutal regimes of discipline and control. Hundreds of sizable communities of escapees (maroons or *quilombos*), pursued by private armies of slave-catchers, testify to the tensions this coercive regime generated in regions where control of land remained incomplete. Sex ratios among slaves arriving from Africa tilted strongly toward males; birth rates were relatively low, and mortality was high. As a result, with the possible exception of Minas Gerais by the late eighteenth century, enslaved populations in Brazil did not increase naturally. Slaving and slavery themselves thus created unceasing demands for more slaves, fueling a vast slave trade from Africa, the largest and most enduring in the Atlantic, as well as engendering distinctive slave cultures in Brazil with remarkably strong and persistent ties to Africa.

Markets, Exchange, and Capital in an Atlantic Perspective

The contrasting ecologies and economics of producing sugar and coffee, the two great export crops that connected Brazil to the economy of the Atlantic World led to differing practices associated with slavery in the two zones. Coffee required less investment than sugar in labor and capital; in the nineteenth century it made the most of land, the relatively abundant factor of production. It was therefore land-hungry and fueled waves of land expropriation in an internal "frontier" of plantation production. Its growth in scale was faster, and it arguably generated more sustained economic expansion than sugar, its predecessor. Sugar required more skilled labor, particularly in processing the cane juice to raw sugar, and more capital in fixed equipment and buildings, the famous *engenhos*—mills and boiling houses. With greater fixed investment, the sugar economy expanded (and contracted) more slowly and tended to remain rooted in the coastal regions where it had started.

Although the sugar in northeastern Brazil and the coffee in the southeast both involved practices of land tenure and coerced labor that can be traced directly to their positions in the broader Atlantic economy, the economic trajectories of the two regions were quite distinct. Coffee in the nineteenth century ultimately offered more opportunities for continued growth and for adaptation to free labor, via the *colono* system, based on free immigrant workers from Italy and elsewhere. Moreover, Brazil's market share of sugar exports to Europe was never as high as its share of coffee exports. It was only with coffee (and, for a brief time at the end of the century, with wild-rubber production in northern equatorial regions) that Brazil held significant power in global markets. The later timing of the coffee boom also favored Brazil. The rise of coffee in the southeast was a phenomenon of the nineteenth-century era of expanding trade throughout the world, beyond the Atlantic. The nineteenth century was also an era of expanding foreign investment, particularly from Britain. British direct investments, primarily in Brazilian railroads concentrated in the coffee-producing regions of the southeast, increased by an order of magnitude between 1840 and 1875, then doubled again in value by 1885. Finally, the nineteenth century was an era of mass immigration of free labor from Europe to everywhere in the Americas, with its Brazilian component settled in the south and southeast, drawn by the economic opportunities created first by coffee and later by incipient industrialization.

Trade in the oceanic arena is the most common point of departure for histories of Atlantic economies, and the Atlantic is a useful way to think of Brazil's economy. On this basis Lisbon, Luanda in Angola, and Rio de Janeiro shared a common Atlantic orientation. But the local practices of markets and consumption, just like the local manifestations of land tenure and labor, can also be understood as Atlantic stories.

If expropriation of land eliminated resident populations for the purpose of enabling new property relations, and if slavery concentrated and bound labor to regimes of production owned by others, then exchange enabled accumulation across the interface between the local and the transoceanic: in Africa, expropriation of people, not land; in Brazil, expropriation of land and the binding of people to a coercive labor regime; across the ocean, accumulation in the exchange.

Brazil's integration of land, labor, and capital was a particularly Atlantic story, rather than one of local or global dimensions. The changing patterns of trade across the ocean help to explain the rise and fall of Brazil's three major regional economies. But there was also an Atlantic in Brazil. In the interior of Minas Gerais, long after gold ceased to fuel exchanges with the oceanic arena, land expropriation and slavery persisted. This interiorized commercial Atlantic was also found in the northeast, far from the sugar mills of the coast, where cattle production expanded inland, leading to expropriation of locals' lands, to settlement, and to production keyed to markets that were in turn connected with the larger Atlantic economy through production of export commodities—sugar and hides, but also cotton and cacao in significant volume—and with the slave trade as an engine of economic production. Brazil's interior Atlantic had a dynamism all its own, and it is pointless to try to find the economic equivalent of a continental divide, where the country's economy lost its Atlantic accents and found its own dynamic.

ZEPHYR FRANK

Bibliography

Adelman, Jeremy, ed. *Colonial Legacies: The Problem of Persistence in Latin American History*. New York: Routledge, 1999.

Engerman, Stanley, and Kenneth Sokoloff. *Economic Development in the Americas since 1500: Endowments and Institutions*. Cambridge: Cambridge University Press, 2012.

Prado Júnior, Caio. *História econômica do Brasil*. 1945. Reprint, São Paulo: Editora Brasiliense, 1977.

Schwartz, Stuart, ed. *Tropical Babylons: Sugar and the Making of the Atlantic World, 1450–1680*. Chapel Hill: University of North Carolina Press, 2004.

Economies, American: Caribbean

The island chain in the Caribbean stretching from the Bahamas to Trinidad, as well as the continental enclaves of Suriname, (British) Guyana, and French Guiana, coheres as a modern economic unit owing to the region's shared history of colonialism and plantation slavery. Yet in political terms the Caribbean has been a fractured arena—split by the competing colonial powers that claimed the different islands of the region. The Caribbean is a construct of empire, and while its riches in exports of sugar significantly shaped the political-economic structure of the modern Atlantic World, its linguistic, cultural, ethnic, religious, and political diversity has been an obstacle to regional economic unity and to the formation of an integrated post-slavery economy. Islands within sight of one another were, and in many cases still are, as distant economically as the markets of Europe and Asia. Yet in spite of this fragmentation, the economic impact of the Caribbean region on the Atlantic economy cannot be overstated. This chain of tropical satellites—sustained by a coerced indigenous labor force, followed by indentured Europeans, climaxing with enslaved Africans, and eventually surviving with contracted South Asians—filled the shelves of Atlantic markets with exotic plantation commodities and sparked the development of industry in Europe and North America.

The Native Caribbean, before c. 1500

The first migrants into the islands were hunters and gatherers who used stone-tool technologies and traveled throughout the region by canoe. The initial occupants came from Belize or the Yucatán peninsula perhaps as long as 6,000 years ago, and about 1,000 years later a second wave of settlers entered the eastern Caribbean—the small islands of the Lesser Antilles—from the Orinoco delta region of mainland South America. These migrants exploited the abundant flora and fauna of the islands, hunting land mammals, such as sloths, and marine resources, such as sea turtles, manatee, and reef fishes. A little more than 2,000 years ago a further wave of immigrants—horticulturalists from the Orinoco—also arrived in the Caribbean. Although they hunted land mammals and exploited the rich marine environments, the staple of their diet was cassava cakes, made from the starchy root of the manioc plant. Paddling their canoes up the island chain they displaced some of the hunters and gatherers they met, and merged with groups of others. These cultivators reached the large islands of the Greater Antilles—Cuba, Hispaniola, Jamaica, and Puerto Rico—and after centuries established a politically complex set of chiefdoms.

These Amerindians became known as the Taino, and they were the people who greeted Columbus in 1492 when he arrived in Hispaniola. By that time the peoples of the Caribbean had established trade networks that stretched from the Orinoco in the south to the Bahamas in the north, and perhaps also to Florida and Central America. Greenstone amulets, shell beads, and gold and copper ornaments from the South American mainland, for example, have been recovered from the sites of their former villages. Salt, honey, pottery, stone, and numerous other commodities moved throughout this system. But Spanish colonization marked the beginning of the end of the trade networks that had linked the Amerindian peoples of the Caribbean.

The Era of the Spanish, c. 1500–1650

When Columbus sailed west from Castile in 1492, his intent was to gain direct access to the great markets of the Far East, or the "Indies." While the New World blocked his access to the artisanry of Asia, Spanish colonists coerced the Native peoples of the islands to extract the region's deposits of gold, especially on the island of Hispaniola. European-introduced diseases and conflict weakened the social structures of the Taino and left them susceptible to Spanish control. However, the gold was quickly depleted, and the small islands of the Lesser Antilles offered few natural resources valuable to the Spanish. The people there, whom the Spanish knew as Caribs (after a Spanish distortion of a Taino word for them, taken to mean "cannibal") lived in small villages and often violently resisted Spanish incursions. These Caribs grew tobacco and cotton, however, and Spanish ships occasionally traded with them for these products, especially on the islands of Dominica and Guadeloupe.

Subsequent discoveries of gold and silver deposits in mainland South America led to an exodus of Spanish colonists, and after the 1520s a general decline in Spanish settlement and economic progress, in the Caribbean region. Few Native people remained, owing to maltreatment and European diseases. The islands became a sleepy Spanish colonial backwater, dotted with small farms and cattle ranches, except for the port city of Havana in Cuba. A few small sugar mills operated in the sixteenth century in Hispaniola, but in general economic development stalled.

However, the Caribbean took on strategic importance as the passage followed by Spanish ships laden with gold and silver from South America. These silver fleets were vulnerable to attacks from foreigners, especially from English and Dutch corsairs and privateers in search of Spanish treasure. In response to these attacks, Spain instituted a fortification and convoy system based at Havana to help stave off its foreign foes. Ships would assemble in the Havana harbor before heading across the Atlantic together to Spain. A surrounding network of fortifications helped generate a settlement pattern of small urban centers surrounded by agricultural lands growing food and supplies for these garrison ports. The military organization of these settlements maintained the convoy system and preserved Spain's foothold in the region.

Commodities and the Rise of Atlantic Markets, c. 1650–1830

Though the Spanish did little to stimulate local production for Atlantic markets in these early years of Caribbean colonization, the region's contributions to the Atlantic economy grew enormously in the seventeenth century as Spain's European rivals shifted from raiding shipping to seizing and settling island territories. The sixteenth-century incursions of English, French, and Dutch privateers had done little more than disrupt Spanish shipping and engage in small-scale smuggling. In the early seventeenth century, however, they began to challenge Spain's territorial claims to the region. In the 1620s the English established settlements in the Lesser Antillean islands of St. Kitts, Nevis, and Barbados, safely remote from the Spanish garrisons in the Greater Antilles to the west. The French, too, began grabbing territory, most notably the small islands of Martinique and Guadeloupe. In the 1650s, the British were confident enough in their military capabilities to attack Spain's more central settlements in Hispaniola and to wrestle the island of Jamaica out of Spanish hands. The French would eventually take the western half of Hispaniola, which they later called Saint-Domingue.

The Caribbean economies that the English and French built were defined by the tropical agricultural commodities cultivated in them and exported to Atlantic markets. Bananas in Martinique, limes in Dominica, nutmeg in Grenada, tobacco in Cuba, and coffee in Saint-Domingue, among other commodities, are examples of the classic Caribbean plantation production produced by massive majorities of enslaved workers, supplemented by small peasantries engaged in provision gardening. Sugar was by far the dominant commodity of the Caribbean economy, and for good reason. Desired initially by Europe's elite and later a staple of overworked laboring classes during the initial phases of the Industrial Revolution, sugar generated enormous revenues that accelerated the expansion of European merchant capitalism and the emerging Atlantic economy.

Sugar production was revolutionary. It altered the social, political, environmental, and economic landscapes of the Caribbean from small European farms to massive plantations. In Barbados, in 1627, for example, British colonists established small farms on the wooded island's coasts that produced a few commercial crops, especially tobacco. Labor was largely performed by indentured Europeans, who expected to receive small plots of their own at the end of their contracts, usually in three to five years. Yet the Barbadians could not compete with their tobacco-growing colonial cousins in the Chesapeake. Despite the increasing popularity of tobacco in England, the Barbadian economy struggled.

However, the introduction of sugarcane in the 1640s transformed the island almost overnight. Large planters swallowed up small farms and cut down ancient rain forests to turn the entire island into dense canebrakes. Moreover, the intensive nature of sugarcane cultivation required more labor than planters could assemble from the relatively small numbers of European indentured servants. With expansion of the English presence along the coasts of western Africa, Barbadian planters increasingly turned to enslaved Africans for labor. By the end of the seventeenth century, the ratio of blacks to whites in Barbados was nearly three to one. Barbados became the most valuable English colony in the seventeenth century, and by the eighteenth century it, along with Jamaica, generated huge revenues from sugar that filled the pockets of planters and investors, as well as the royal coffers.

Indeed, the intensive nature of cultivating sugarcane, as well as of the production of other tropical agricultural commodities, led to the distinctively coercive labor systems that defined Caribbean economies. The voracious consumption of laborers led to the transport to the Caribbean of millions of people from three continents, beginning with successive waves of indentured European workers in the seventeenth century, then millions of enslaved Africans in the eighteenth century, and finally indentured laborers from South Asia after the end of slavery in the middle of the nineteenth century. The racial and ethnic diversity of the Caribbean today is largely a product of the demands that sugarcane agriculture created for imported laborers.

No scholar has done a better job of unraveling the transatlantic political-economic dimensions of sugar in the Caribbean than Sidney W. Mintz. His book *Sweetness and Power* showed how human biological desires for sucrose and the attempts of the British working class to emulate elite foodways bound enslaved Africans and Afro-Creoles on the plantations in the Caribbean to the industrial workers in Europe. In a parallel connection, Eric Williams attributed the rise of Europe's Industrial Revolution, at least in part, to Caribbean plantations' needs for equipment, provisions, and supplies. Ceramic molds for processing sugar, iron billhooks for cutting sugarcane, copper kettles for boiling sugarcane juice, textiles for enslaved workers, and lumber for barrel staves were just some of the many components of producing Caribbean sugar that spurred industrial development in Britain. The mutually stimulating relationship between European metropole and colonial satellite made the Caribbean central to the Atlantic economy—in fact, the region became the Atlantic's pivot. Every European power, save Portugal with its parallel investments in sugar in Brazil, anchored its Atlantic ventures there.

Rum

While sugar connected the Caribbean islands with their respective European centers, rum, a byproduct of sugarmaking, connected it with other regions in the New World. Unlike sugar, which was shipped almost exclusively to European markets,

the primary market for Caribbean rum was the Caribbean and North America, especially in the early years of its distilling and distribution. Rum is truly a creolized product of the mixed cultures of the Caribbean—one that was produced first in the early to mid-seventeenth century in Barbados and Martinique. The rise of sugarmaking in those two islands coincided with increasing knowledge of distilling alcohol from surplus grains in Europe, and European colonists and enslaved Africans were no doubt pleased to have easy access to drink that would help them cope with the many anxieties of unfamiliar surroundings of the Caribbean frontier. The production of rum also underscores the efficiency of the early sugar planters, who turned the waste products of sugar factories into a profitable commodity. To ship granular sugar in a chemically stable form to Europe, producers boiled raw cane juice to a viscous brown mash and then drained off the liquid, as molasses, to leave moist granular *mascavado* to pack in barrels for shipping. The molasses would go to waste if not distilled to produce high-proof alcohol. Planters doled out large amounts of this rum to the workers on their estates as part of their weekly rations. It was also a central component of plantation medicine and a reward for hard work. The order and security of village life, whether in England, the Gold Coast, or the indigenous Caribbean, were washed away by the energy of Atlantic capitalism, and high-alcohol rum offered a temporary means of escape from the anomie of the Caribbean plantation system.

In the eighteenth century, Barbados and Jamaica emerged as the leading rum-making colonies in the Caribbean, and British North America was one of their main markets. Planters sold rum to North Americans in exchange for much-needed provisions and supplies from their forests and family farms. New Englanders, however, began importing molasses to distill their own variety of rum, much of which they exported to West Africa to fuel a notorious trade in slaves, whom they carried across the Atlantic to Caribbean planters so as to buy more molasses.

New Englanders also bought cheap molasses from the French Caribbean to make rum. The French planters, owing to the successful lobbying efforts of wine and brandy interests in France, had no market for their rum in Europe, and so had plenty of molasses available for New England distillers. The importation of French Caribbean molasses lowered the value of British Caribbean rum, thus raising the costs of their plantation supplies. In 1733, the British Parliament passed the Molasses Act, which imposed a repressive tax on foreign molasses entering the ports of British North America. However, New Englanders found ways of circumventing the tax through bribes and smuggling, and the act was rarely enforced. The ensuing Sugar Act of 1764 strengthened enforcement of the Molasses Act. The continental colonists' reaction was to boycott all British imports. Although the Sugar Act was repealed within a few years, its restrictions stoked the flames of revolutionary sentiment in British North America and helped spark the American Revolution.

Post-Emancipation and Peasantries

Abolition of slavery in Haiti (1804), the British islands of the Caribbean (1834–1838), and the remaining French islands (1848) coincided with, and accelerated, a general decline in the profitability of Caribbean sugar production. Although many former slaves rejected plantation work, those in some of the smaller islands with limited amounts of arable land, such as Barbados, were forced to return to plantations as low-paid wage laborers. In other islands, independent peasantries emerged, often with the aid of Christian missionaries seeking to proselytize the former slaves. In Haiti and Jamaica, for example, former slaves produced provisions, as well as such commercial crops as bananas for export markets. Large-scale production of sugar continued, but by turning to British India for workers brought to the Caribbean under contracts of indenture and worked under slavery-like conditions.

FREDERICK H. SMITH

Bibliography

Dunn, Richard S. *Sugar and Slaves: The Rise of the Planter Class in the English West Indies, 1624–1713.* New York: W. W. Norton, 1972.

Higman, Barry W. "The Sugar Revolution." *Economic History Review* 53 (2000): 213–236.

Mintz, Sidney W. *Sweetness and Power: The Place of Sugar in Modern History.* London: Penguin, 1985.

Ortiz, Fernando. *Cuban Counterpoint: Tobacco and Sugar.* Translated by H. de Onis. 1947. Reprint, Durham, NC: Duke University Press, 1995.

Rouse, Irving B. *The Taino: Rise and Decline of the People Who Greeted Columbus.* New Haven, CT: Yale University Press, 1992.

Smith, Frederick H. *Caribbean Rum: A Social and Economic History.* Gainesville: University Press of Florida, 2005.

Williams, Eric. *Capitalism and Slavery.* Chapel Hill: University of North Carolina Press, 1944. Reprint, Chapel Hill: University of North Carolina Press, 1994.

Wilson, Samuel M. *The Archaeology of the Caribbean.* Cambridge: Cambridge University Press, 2007.

Economies, American: North America

Although economic life in many parts of pre-Columbian North America was relatively sophisticated—marked, for example, by ample food surpluses and trade networks over long distances—the arrival of Old World populations in the sixteenth century began a new chapter in the economic history of the continent. Small groups of Europeans had arrived earlier, beginning with the Vikings in the late tenth century CE, but it was not until the sixteenth century that the presence of populations from the Old World began to matter in North America. Over time, Old World populations under European control transformed economic life in North America for everyone involved, Native Americans and immigrants alike.

European economic strategies around the Atlantic differed from one another in countless ways, but they shared a number of characteristics that facilitated general economic transformation. Broadly, the behavior of the Europeans was highly commercialized, and the colonizers shared conceptions of property based on private ownership and on credible legal and political protections of it. These behaviors contrasted with Native Americans' general commitments to collective welfare on local scales of community and to conceptions of wealth centered more on people than on material possessions. In time the European commercial strategy won out in North America, at once enabling and promoting maximizing behavior that facilitated rising economic productivity and increasingly large material surpluses, vented or sold, to greater and greater degrees in market settings, including those on pan-Atlantic and eventually global scales. Over time, integration of the European colonies in North America into these broader factor and product markets rendered them increasingly efficient, enabling these colonies and considerable, though varying, proportions of the populations living in them to grow quite wealthy by early-modern standards. At the same time, the European-sponsored colonies in North America and other parts of the Western Hemisphere contributed significantly to the wealth both of the political jurisdictions—eventually nation-states—that begat them, and, more generally, to the prominence of western Europe relative to other world regions.

The North American economies continued to develop in the nineteenth century, marked by rising levels of income and wealth, increasingly democratic politics, and more and more creative intellectual and cultural expressions. Their histories were also marked by many developments about which their free populations might have been less proud—racial slavery, most notably. From 40,000 feet, mainstream economic historians today would accept this general view of "progress," although they would disagree about specifics. Some economic historians, for example, prefer protonational narratives of the seventeenth and eighteenth centuries—in the U.S. case, keeping their focus firmly on the Thirteen Colonies—and some interpret virtually every development in early American history teleologically, as a harbinger of modern democratic capitalism.

Many social and cultural—and even some political—historians, however, would find this narrative of progress unconvincing and would take issue with its strong emphasis on economic growth but relative inattention to the costs of attaining it, human as well as economic. Beginning 30 or 40 years ago, many such historians also shifted their focus—at least at the margin—from the benefits of commercial markets (particularly extraregional ones) to effects seen as pernicious. In economic terms, they moved their interests and empathies from market "winners" to market "losers."

In addition, numerous scholars, including some economic historians, have complained over the last two decades about the traditional fixation on imperial boundaries in studying North America. These European-based parameters allowed for little attention to Native Americans and often led researchers to neglect important cross-border economic transactions and to omit consideration altogether of economic processes occurring in adjacent and entangled imperial jurisdictions. To remedy such problems, scholars have increasingly stressed the need to analyze the economies of all of the populations of North America and the ways in which the diverse populations there interacted with other economic actors—whether in Europe, other parts of the Americas, Africa, and even Asia—to forge the continent's economy. The argument that follows is consonant with many of these recent tendencies to contextualize the economies of North America as broadly as might be relevant.

* * *

European-led groups—whether statal, para-statal, or private—in the early sixteenth century began to probe, establish beachheads on, and acquire (sometimes accurate) reconnaissance relating to North America. These initiatives were generally tentative, opportunistic "one-offs" with few long-term effects. But despite the relatively faint imprint, early on, of Old World human populations, microbes accompanying Europeans and Africans to North America had no hesitation in establishing themselves among the populations native to the region. Native peoples lacked previous exposure, and thus any immunities, to many of the diseases such microbes caused, leading at times to "virgin-soil" epidemics with terrifying demographic losses. Not infrequently, these microbes began killing Native Americans before they encountered Europeans and Africans in person.

Old World "footprints" became more pervasive during the seventeenth century. Between 1565 and the late 1630s, the Spanish, English, French, Dutch, and Swedes all established small settlements and a few fortified positions fronting the Atlantic. The Spanish also launched a series of territorial initiatives to the north of Mexico City to extend their viceroyalty of New Spain into the southwestern part of the North American landmass.

By the turn of the eighteenth century the English had carved up most of the Atlantic seaboard of North America into legal jurisdictions populated largely with dependent labor of one type or another, most notably English indentured servants and African slaves. By that time, the English had also established a far-northern base of operations on Hudson Bay—contested by the French until 1713—while Spain had intensified its occupation of the Southwest and the Florida peninsula, and France had increased its footholds in the upper and lower valley of the Mississippi and to the north-northeast of the Great Lakes and St. Lawrence River to a significant presence. Native Americans retained the upper hand in several areas of the interior, including those in which European "parchment" claims—those more substantial on paper than in presence on the ground—served as legal attempts to exclude other Europeans. Gradually, however, European military and economic power in these areas was projected more forcefully. The lure of European goods and chains of merchant credit attracted products that Native Americans extracted from their woodlands and plains—primarily deerskins and beaver pelts. Over time, burgeoning trade links and credit chains reoriented Native demand patterns toward imported goods and integrated many Native populations more tightly into broader, indeed intercontinental, markets.

Europeans engaged these Native economies in large part because the colonies they had planted in North America left them with the hard work of paying for them. In general, an initial "pioneer" phase of economic experimentation—still often ad hoc, frequently desultory, and occasionally desperate—gradually gave way to more routinized, sometimes even systematic, efforts to pursue "development strategies" based, if only implicitly, on a vague sense of comparative advantage, well before political economist David Ricardo (1772–1823) laid out the concept formally in the early nineteenth century. The early engagements with extractive Native economies had offered affordable low-investment (if also high-risk) start-up strategies. North American enterprises attracted significant long-term investments only after a sufficient amount of capital—broadly defined to include tools, equipment, infrastructure, financing, local knowledge, and so forth—had been amassed, often through an initial phase of primitive accumulation by raiding and capturing, supplementing, then destroying, and fi-

nally replacing the contributions of the Native economies.

As European investments grew the investors were able to concentrate their resources more and more on each colony's "comparative advantage"— the marketable goods it could produce more efficiently (with less expenditure of resources) and more profitably than other goods. In most cases, the costs of discovering, let alone implementing, a particular strategy were high and borne largely by groups of subaltern laborers, mostly the enslaved, at first Native Americans, then overwhelmingly Africans. The aggressive, entrepreneurial, commercially minded, and financially far better equipped Europeans and European Americans who controlled and benefited from these investments did not rest, however, until they had found and begun successfully to exploit a given colony's comparative advantage.

In North America—a vast landmass with a diverse array of abundant resources—specific comparative advantages, under prevailing technologies and levels of market integration, came in various forms. In the Southeast, the principle of comparative advantage favored production of agricultural staples for export to extraregional markets, mainly in Europe and the West Indies. In the Chesapeake region, tobacco was the staple of choice, supplemented after 1750 or so by wheat. Rice carried the day in coastal South Carolina and Georgia, supplemented for periods of varying lengths by indigo and long-staple (Sea Island) cotton. The vast majority of these staple crops was grown on large, heavily capitalized units (plantations) worked primarily by enslaved Africans and, later, African Americans. Smaller family production units, using labor of European descent, either indentured or free, were of some importance in producing Chesapeake tobacco and wheat.

Production of rice for export in South Carolina and Georgia was, almost from the start, all but limited to plantations and enslaved African and African American labor. The grain grew best in irrigated marshlands near the coast. These areas were swamped by mosquitoes, one genus of which (*Anopheles*) proved an efficient vector for transmission of malaria, one of the dangerous microbial migrants brought to America via the so-called Columbian Exchange. Malaria, which caused debilitating fevers, often resulting in death, was endemic in parts of West Africa, and so many West Africans had long experience with the disease through the generations. As a result, enslaved individuals in the Carolina Lowcountry often possessed sufficient inherited and/or acquired immunity to it to survive in the region's mosquito-infested rice paddies. Few whites and no Native Americans had similar immunities, which left Africans and their American-born children the most viable labor force for the region's economy. They were also more desirable—and efficient—because nearly all of them were experienced agriculturalists; indeed some were knowledgeable specifically in risiculture. Increasing numbers of scholars believe, in fact, that West Africans helped to lay the foundation for production and milling practices in the rice region by transferring elements of their rice technology to South Carolina and Georgia. Among immediate economic circumstances supporting Lowcountry rice, the profit possibilities were sufficiently high to allow planters to bid away expensive African labor that might have been employed instead in the sugarcane fields of Barbados or Jamaica, the economic drivers of the British Atlantic economy during the entire eighteenth century.

By the end of the eighteenth century it was becoming clear that climatic and soil conditions in the interior of what came to be called the South were suitable for the production of other plantation staples, most notably short-staple cotton and in a few places sugarcane. These crops, in great demand in the Atlantic World, brought prices sufficient to sustain the use of increasingly high-cost slave labor. The plantation complex established earlier along the tobacco and rice coasts was found to be reasonably "portable," as economic historian David Weiman puts it, to convert to producing cotton and other crops. Thus, by the middle of the nineteenth century economic life in large portions of the southern part of North America—from the Atlantic seaboard to eastern Texas—revolved around the production of cotton, often on sizable units, with slave labor. Crops of cotton and other southern agricultural staples were destined largely for extraregional markets, most of which were in Atlantic Europe. Indeed, throughout the nineteenth century cotton was by far the leading export from the United States. In the mid-1800s, cotton, rice, and tobacco, all three of which were all but exclusively southern crops, accounted for well over half of the total value of U.S. exports.

Although African and African American (as well as Native American) slaves were present in the more northerly colonies in North America by the eighteenth century, sometimes in considerable numbers, the uses to which slave labor could be put in these regions were not sufficiently remunerative to base these economies on slaves. Rather, at most, slaves supplemented family agriculture and served as artisan apprentices, waged or leased workers in growing manufactories, and casual day laborers.

To be sure, other regions of North America became organized around their own respective comparative advantages, such as they were. Quebec and Atlantic Canada, for example, benefited from animal staples—fish, furs, and skins—rather than agricultural staples, as in the South. They found export markets but not ones remunerative enough to bear the cost of working large numbers of slaves to extract them. Concentrated labor forces were, in any case, unnecessary in these very low-yield (land-extensive and mobile) extractive systems, as they did not require high fixed investment, such as was typical in plantations, and the relatively higher returns from bonded labor used to finance such investments.

The "Middle Colonies"—New York and Pennsylvania—and New England made the most out of their *lack* of clear-cut advantages in resources, developing instead entrepreneurship and an ever-evolving portfolio of varied economic niches. For these areas, necessity was the mother of invention. More specifically, these regions provided rapidly changing mixes of exports comprising local (and imported) agricultural products and the "Three Fs" of extracted natural resources—fish, furs, and forest products—as well as processing activities, handicraft manufacturing, and what economists call market organization: shipping, commercial, and financial services. Philadelphia, New York, and Boston owed much of their prominence, and still do even today, to this early concentration on commercial services, economic flexibility, and entrepreneurial activity.

These early pursuits of comparative advantages defined the principal economic regions of North America. The economic agents in all of these regions—or, more accurately, their free populations—

specialized in activities in which their efficiency was superior to possible competitors in other regions. The comparative advantage in the southern colonies grew out of agricultural staples; Massachusetts, New York, and Pennsylvania, less well endowed with natural resources, concentrated on entrepreneurship and on servicing the productive activities of other regions, most notably the South and the British Caribbean. The wealth produced through such strategies was not evenly distributed regionally, since by most measures the free inhabitants of the slave economies were far wealthier by the late colonial period than their counterparts farther north. The "Spanish" Southwest and Native lands in other parts of the "frontier" West lagged far behind in terms of capital accumulation. But in 1820 North America and western Europe, taken as wholes, were the two wealthiest regions in the world, by a wide margin, according to Angus Maddison, the leading authority on the subject.

The South replicated, over and over again, its initial economic strategy based on production for export of a narrow range of agricultural staples—or even a single commodity, cotton—on large plantations worked by slave laborers. This monocultural focus exposed southern producers and investors to the vagaries of international commodity markets, intense competition, periodic crises, and eventually to commodity hell, wherein the growing number of competitors in Atlantic and global markets and the fungibility of the most important agricultural commodities greatly diminished the region's pricing power. The more diversified and agile economies of the Middle Atlantic and New England, based as they were on liquid assets and flexible entrepreneurship, provided options that enabled long-term capital accumulation. As the nineteenth century wore on and the cutting edge of economic activity moved westward, the South was left with row after row of cotton and little else.

In contrast, entrepreneurs in New England and the Middle Atlantic states successfully integrated the Midwest, the upper Mississippi Valley, and the Great Lakes into an emerging agro-industrial economy that eventually constituted the "manufacturing belt" comprising the entire northeastern quadrant of North America, east of the Mississippi and north of the Ohio River, through southern Ontario. The Plantation South eventually begat

Faulkner and the blues, but the rest of the country between 1850 and 1950 become the most dynamic economic region in the world. To the early "losers" went the long-term economic spoils. Or, as Drew McCoy memorably put it long ago, the South expanded across *space*, while the North developed through *time*, becoming more advanced economically in so doing.

The economic trajectories of both the northern and southern regions of the United States—indeed, the trajectories of Canada and the Spanish Southwest as well—diverged markedly between the early sixteenth century and the early nineteenth century. Although the economies in each of these areas came to be organized around their respective comparative advantages and, in the most economically important parts of the continent, around strategies of export-led growth, the long-term results were very different. In particular, the type of export-based growth pursued in New England and the Middle Colonies gradually gave way to a "balanced" approach focusing not merely on exports but on local and regional markets as well. Over time this flexible strategy proved more sustainable and more successful than those pursued elsewhere in North America.

PETER A. COCLANIS

Bibliography

Canny, Nicholas, and Philip Morgan, eds. *The Oxford Handbook of the Atlantic World c. 1450–1850*. New York: Oxford University Press, 2011.

Coclanis, Peter A. "Atlantic World or Atlantic/World?" *William and Mary Quarterly*, 3rd ser., 58 (October 2006): 725–742.

———. "Tracking the Economic Divergence of the North and the South." *Southern Cultures* 6 (Winter 2000): 82–103.

Crosby, Alfred W., Jr. *The Columbian Exchange: Biological and Cultural Consequences of 1492*. Westport, CT: Greenwood, 1972.

Engerman, Stanley L., and Robert E. Gallman, eds. *The Cambridge Economic History of the United States*. Vol. 1, *The Colonial Era*. New York: Cambridge University Press, 1996.

Engerman, Stanley L., and Kenneth L. Sokoloff. *Economic Development in the Americas since 1500: En-*

dowments and Institutions. New York: Cambridge University Press, 2012.

Maddison, Angus. *Contours of the World Economy, 1–2030 AD: Essays in Macro-Economic History.* New York: Oxford University Press, 2007.

Matson, Cathy, ed. *The Economy of Early America: Historical Perspectives & New Directions.* University Park: Pennsylvania State University Press, 2006.

McCoy, Drew R. *The Elusive Republic: Political Economy in Jeffersonian America.* Chapel Hill: Published for the Institute of Early American History and Culture by the University of North Carolina Press, 1980.

McCusker, John J., and Russell R. Menard. *The Economy of British America, 1606–1789.* Chapel Hill: Published for the Institute of Early American History and Culture by the University of North Carolina Press, 1985. Reprinted 1991, with a supplementary bibliography.

Taylor, Alan. *American Colonies.* New York: Viking, 2001.

Weiman, David F. "Staple Crops and Slave Plantations: Alternative Perspectives on Regional Development in the Antebellum Cotton South." In *Agriculture and National Development: Views on the Nineteenth Century,* edited by Lou Ferleger, 119–161. Ames: Iowa State University Press, 1990.

Economies, American: Spanish Territories

Spain dominated the first stage of European overseas expansion into the Americas, contributing to the forging of an Atlantic World over the period from the fifteenth to the mid-nineteenth centuries. Gold and silver, the bases of the modern monetary system, funded this expansionary impulse. Mercantilist thinkers in Europe emphasized the link between monarchical power and large reserves of bullion, and shortages of both metals in Europe and Asia in the fifteenth century encouraged the search for new mines. Christopher Columbus mentioned gold over 60 times in the diary of his first voyage, for example, and the crown outfitted his second voyage primarily to explore the new lands he had found for precious metals. Later Spanish conquistadors and settlers found plentiful supplies of the metals, which gave European merchants a commodity to penetrate rich markets in the Far East, particularly in China, where they exchanged silver for silk, porcelain, and other luxury goods. As Spain claimed its fabulously rich overseas possessions, Britain, France, and the Netherlands sought to gain access to supplies of American precious metals by raiding Spanish shipping and later by establishing outposts of their own. Such competition sparked wars in both Europe and the Americas between Spain and its rivals. This struggle to control the New World's vast resources, particularly gold and silver, shaped the course of Atlantic empires, tied the Atlantic World to vibrant Asian markets, and provoked the enslavement of millions of Africans and Native Americans.

The Age of Gold and Silver in the Spanish Atlantic World, 1492–1640

Spain began its overseas expansion with the conquest of the eastern Atlantic islands of the Canary archipelago in the fifteenth century and expanded rapidly into the Americas following the first voyage of Christopher Columbus in 1492. Spanish expansion into the New World (which they called the Indies) spread from a few Caribbean islands to include Mexico as the forces of Hernán Cortés and his indigenous allies overthrew the Aztec (Mexica) Empire and later moved southward to annex the Maya domains in southern Mexico and Central America. Within a decade the spectacular victories of Francisco Pizarro brought down the vast Inca Empire (Tawantinsuyu) in the Andes, giving the Spaniards control over the extensive human and material resources (especially gold and silver) in both North and South America.

To police smuggling and control the fractious conquistadors who had established Spain's claim to these rich lands, the Spanish crown set up an extensive bureaucracy in the New World. This administration was headed by a viceroy in each of the two major political units, New Spain (including portions of the southwestern United States, Mexico, Central America, and the Caribbean) and Peru (encompassing territory from Panama to the southern tip of South America, excluding Portuguese Brazil). Within these massive territories, the crown created a series of courts (*audiencias*) and numerous regional magistracies, city councils, and treasury offices to govern, tax, and oversee the provision of indigenous laborers and mercury (used in the refining of silver) for Spain's mineral-rich New World possessions. The crown paid the salaries of this extensive colonial bureaucracy with taxes levied on local production, sales, and especially the *quinto* (the fifth), a flat 20 percent tax on the output of gold and silver mines in the Indies. No other European monarchy gained resources sufficient to establish so extensive a governmental apparatus in the New World.

This bureaucracy annually shipped large quantities of gold and silver to metropolitan Spain. As the decade-by-decade totals of officially registered bullion output in table 1 indicate, gold production outstripped that of silver until the 1540s, when silver mining began to dominate. The gold came first from the Caribbean, and later from Chile, Ecuador, and Colombia. Silver lodes discovered in both the viceroyalties of New Spain and Peru (particularly in Potosí in modern Bolivia) by the mid-sixteenth century led to this dramatic rise in output (see figure 1). From a low of 340,000 pesos of silver mined in the 1520s, silver production rose to over 100 million silver pesos in the 1580s, reaching a peak of 128,600,000 pesos in the 1630s. Gold production during that period rose steadily until the 1530s to over 11 million pesos, but then it declined for two decades to the 1550s, and then fluctuated between 10,180,000 and 12,750,000 pesos during the next 80 years, when gold output began to fall. In the period when silver dominated the production of precious metals, the output of Spain's New World silver mines accounted for between 76 percent and 96 percent of all New World mining production. Gold remained the far-scarcer metal, totaling 132,790,000 pesos during the entire period 1492 to 1640, while silver output reached 918,150,000 pesos, seven times as much, over the same span. These official figures do not account for contraband, which contemporaries estimated at 17 to 20 percent of the total mined annually. Legal and contraband gold and silver by the 1640s allowed Spaniards to penetrate Asian markets more successfully through their colony at Manila in the Philippine Islands and to pursue an aggressive foreign policy in Europe, leading to a series of expensive and ultimately unsuccessful wars with European rivals.

The discoveries of precious metals led to an accelerated expansion and integration of market economies in the Spanish Indies. In New Spain the principal avenue for market exchanges extended from the port city of Veracruz on the Caribbean coast to Mexico City and then moved northward to the major mining towns, particularly Zacatecas. Lesser market centers emerged southward to Oaxaca and Guatemala, east to the Yucatán, and west to Acapulco on the Pacific coast. This western port city was connected to Manila in the Philippines by the Manila galleon, a large royally chartered vessel that sailed annually from Acapulco. A substantial Chinese merchant colony resident in Manila connected this Spanish Pacific outpost to China. In the Viceroyalty of Peru the principal market exchanges emanated from the capital city of Lima, first by sea to Arica and then inland through Arequipa and the populous indigenous centers of Bolivia to the famous silver mines at Potosí. Lesser lines of market exchanges extended north to Quito, south to Chile, and east to Cuzco. The produce of these markets, principally silver, went by sea to Panama, where it was carried by river and overland to Portobelo on the Caribbean shore of the isthmus. Silver produced in the Pacific trading zone thus became a vital component of the emerging Atlantic economy.

Diversified Economic Order in the Spanish Atlantic World, 1641–1730

The output of New World silver and gold mines declined unevenly between 1641 and 1730. As table 1 indicates, silver production dropped in value from 102,830,000 pesos in the 1640s to 85,730,000 pesos in the 1660s. It then recovered to over 100 million pesos from 1671 to 1690, but fell again until 1720, before rallying to over 112 million pesos by 1730. New Spain became the principal silver producer, as discoveries of new deposits and more abundant supplies of mercury contributed to this overall increase. Meanwhile, production in the Viceroyalty of Peru declined, particularly at Potosí, from 69,330,000 pesos in the 1640s to a low of 27,410,000 pesos in the period from 1711 to 1720. As a result, by the 1680s silver production in New Spain surpassed Peru for the first time, and thereafter the output of New Spain's silver mines would remain higher than in the southern viceroyalty.

Although silver production slowed, the output of New World gold mines increased, particularly from the late seventeenth century. As the data in table 1 indicate, gold production fell in value to 4,540,000 pesos in the 1670s, but from the 1690s

Table 1. New World Gold and Silver Output in Pesos of 272 Maravedis, 1492–1810

Years	Silver	Gold	Total
1492–1500	0.00	0.70	0.70
1501–1510	0.00	8.20	8.20
1511–1520	0.00	7.21	7.21
1521–1530	0.34	3.92	4.26
1531–1540	7.55	11.12	18.67
1541–1550	28.12	8.73	36.85
1551–1560	42.71	10.64	53.35
1561–1570	56.05	8.85	64.90
1571–1580	71.47	13.00	84.47
1581–1590	100.19	10.18	110.37
1591–1600	113.40	11.91	125.31
1601–1610	121.81	12.75	134.56
1611–1620	124.28	10.43	134.71
1621–1630	123.63	9.91	133.54
1631–1640	128.60	5.24	133.84
1641–1650	102.83	6.72	109.55
1651–1660	92.16	6.73	98.89
1661–1670	85.73	4.74	90.47
1671–1680	100.02	4.54	104.56
1681–1690	109.85	5.85	115.70
1691–1700	92.80	8.24	101.04
1701–1710	78.25	33.24	111.49
1711–1720	92.61	37.05	129.66
1721–1730	112.45	74.25	186.70
1731–1740	130.65	99.12	229.77
1741–1750	147.94	108.73	256.67
1751–1760	174.58	90.41	264.99
1761–1770	166.72	95.41	262.13
1771–1780	216.55	104.65	321.20
1781–1790	241.88	102.27	344.15
1791–1800	289.94	102.59	392.53
1801–1810	279.46	82.06	361.52

Source: John J. TePaske, *A New World of Gold and Silver*, edited by Kendall W. Brown (Leiden and Boston: Brill, 2010), table 1.2, p. 20.

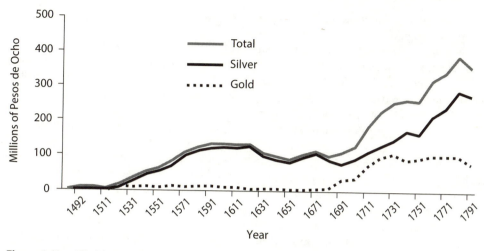

Figure 1. New World registered silver and gold output, 1492–1810.

output soared. By the eighteenth century gold production had shot upward in value to over 37 million pesos from 1711 to 1720 and by 1730 output more than doubled again, to 74,250,000 pesos. Although gold mines in New Granada remained productive, with output fluctuating from 2 to 5 million pesos, the bulk of the increase came from new gold strikes in Minas Gerais in Brazil. Production at these Brazilian placer mines rose twentyfold from 2,790,000 pesos in the 1690s to 66,610,000 pesos in the 1720s, accounting for nearly 90 percent of the New World's gold production. Although gold always remained a less important metal than silver, by the 1720s it accounted for nearly 40 percent of the value of precious metals produced in the New World.

The Spanish Atlantic economy underwent a period of consolidation and diversification between 1640 and 1730, despite the declining productivity of the silver mines. The indigenous populations slowly recovered from epidemic diseases of the previous century, immigration from Europe continued, and large numbers of African slaves were imported to work in the cities, in placer gold mines, and in burgeoning plantation economies. The market economy expanded apace, and although silver mining remained important in the central regions of New Spain and Peru, colonial economies became more diverse and integrated. Investment capital (provided primarily by colonial merchants and clerical institutions) flowed from mining enterprises to other prosperous economic sectors, such as

agriculture, grazing, textile manufacturing, and artisan production. Population centers shifted, and commercial exchanges became more widespread as formerly frontier provinces (Chile, Buenos Aires, Colombia, and Venezuela in South America, and Guanajuato and Guadalajara in northern New Spain) rose to prominence. Intercolonial trade links in legal and contraband goods also expanded throughout the Indies. The beleaguered Habsburg monarchy in Spain, desperate for money to fund a series of disastrous wars in Europe, sold appointments to key colonial offices, and these corrupt officeholders remitted less in tax revenues to Spain, instead retaining more money in the Indies to support local defenses and the salaries of crown bureaucrats. Overall, as regional economies in the Indies experienced cycles of growth and contraction, they became more politically and economically independent of the metropolis.

The Age of War and Reform: The Return of Gold and Silver, 1730–1810

By the eighteenth century, crown ministers in Madrid recognized the need to regain control over Spain's Atlantic empire. From the mid-seventeenth century foreign contrabandists plied trade routes with the Spanish Indies, and merchants from rival European powers carried much of the merchandise in the legal trading system under a series of unequal treaties. Ministers of the new Bourbon dynasty in Spain (after 1700) attempted to curb contraband commerce, regain control over the legal transatlantic trade from foreign merchants, modernize state finances, establish stronger political control within the empire, and raise new taxes and collect existing levies more effectively to fill depleted royal coffers throughout the Spanish Atlantic World.

A principal objective of reformers in Madrid was to stimulate the output of precious metals in the Indies and thus increase remittances of tax revenues to the metropolis. The Madrid government achieved this goal by cutting the *quinto* to a tenth (*diezmo*), introducing new mining technologies, and increasing supplies of mercury, all of which increased the volume of production. According to the data in table 1, silver production more than doubled from 130,650,000 pesos in the 1730s to 279,460,000 pesos between 1800 and 1810. The Viceroyalty of New Spain expanded its domination of the silver industry in the Indies, producing between 62 percent and 72 percent of the New World total. Production also rallied in Peru, which accounted for most of the remaining output of silver. Gold production (largely from Brazil) increased from the previous period, rising to 108,730,000 pesos and then fluctuating between 90,410,000 (1751–1760) and 104,650,000 in the 1770s. It dipped below 100 million pesos only in the first decade of the nineteenth century. Increased bullion production, more efficient tax collection, new levies, and greater liberalization of trade within the empire all paid for the Bourbon expansion of the colonial bureaucracy, which also oversaw the shipment of escalating remittances to Spain.

Napoleon's invasion of the Iberian Peninsula in 1807 led ultimately to the dissolution of the Spanish Atlantic World. Despite large remittances of precious metals, Spain was unable to sustain its overseas empire. Napoleon forced the Spanish monarchs, Charles IV and Crown Prince Ferdinand, to abdicate, creating a constitutional crisis that seriously disrupted relations with the Indies. Moreover, from the 1790s, war in Europe had disturbed trade with the colonies, curtailing dramatically the shipments of silver and gold needed to fight the French invaders at home. In the end, the wars of empire and for European hegemony in the late eighteenth and early nineteenth centuries consumed the lion's share of the bullion and other resources husbanded by a century of reform, but they were not enough to save Spain's Atlantic empire.

* * *

From the foundation of the Spanish Atlantic economy in the late fifteenth century to its dissolution in the 1820s, the mining of precious metals played a fundamental role. Gold and silver promoted a market economy oriented toward the Atlantic and Spain, which transformed indigenous modes of production and led to the forced migration of African slaves. Precious metals also supported a colonial bureaucracy, large for its day, to curtail smuggling, to levy taxes on mining and other economic sectors, and to provide the labor and mercury that kept the mines operating. Moreover, bullion encouraged the crown to embark on ongoing, expensive conflicts with its rivals over hegemony in Europe and access to American markets, particularly to supplies of precious metals. When silver production declined in the seventeenth century, colonial economies began to diversify beyond the export-led model built around mining, and the mining revival in the eighteenth century further stimulated local economic autonomy. The Bourbon reformers attempted with some success to regain tight fiscal and economic control over the increasingly self-sufficient colonial economies, but once again, war with Spain's rivals intervened, culminating in the French invasion of Iberia in 1807 and the dissolution of Spain's Atlantic economy.

KENNETH J. ANDRIEN

Bibliography

Andrien, Kenneth J. *Crisis and Decline: The Viceroyalty of Peru in the Seventeenth Century.* Albuquerque: University of New Mexico Press, 1985.

Bakewell, Peter J. "Registered Silver Production in the Potosí District, 1550–1735." *Jahrbuch für Geschichte von Staat, Wirtschaft, und Gesellschaft Lateinamerikas* 12 (1975): 67–103.

Lockhart, James. "Trunk Lines and Feeder Lines: The Spanish Reaction to American Resources." In *Transatlantic Encounters: Europeans and Andeans in the Sixteenth Century,* edited by Kenneth J. Andrien and Rolena Adorno, 107–110. Berkeley and Los Angeles: University of California Press, 1991.

Stein, Stanley J., and Barbara H. Stein. *Silver, Trade, and War: Spain and America in the Making of Early Modern Europe.* Baltimore, MD: Johns Hopkins University Press, 2000.

TePaske, John J. *A New World of Gold and Silver.* Edited by Kendall W. Brown. Leiden and Boston: Brill, 2010.

Economies, European

The effects on Europe of its expansion in the Atlantic have fascinated historians and economists, as well as the public at large, for centuries. After 1492, Europe created a new economy in the Atlantic based on the mining of precious metals in South America and on plantations worked by African slaves, as well as on the large-scale settlement by European colonists, while the Amerindians, the autochthonous population of the New World, were marginalized. In Asia, on the other hand, the Europeans had far less of an impact and remained for the most part just another trading community. No wonder that for a long time the prevailing popular and, to some extent scholarly, opinion suggested that the Atlantic had made the difference in world history and that in exchange for a few trinkets European traders had been able to rob Africans and Amerindians of their wealth. Moreover, as this line of thinking goes, this unequal exchange explains the present dominant economic position of the West and the blatant poverty of Africa and of parts of South America and the Caribbean. As the evidently destructive consequences of European expansion on Africa and much of the New World were so dramatic, it seemed obvious that it must have been correspondingly beneficial to Europe. Therefore, historians began to look for possible links between the growth of trade and investments in the Atlantic and the growth and subsequent industrialization of the European economy.

Trade

The discussion regarding the effects of early intercontinental commerce has centered on Great Britain, where the growth of the Atlantic trade, particularly in slaves and sugar, was more pronounced than in any other European country, especially during the course of the eighteenth century. In the second half of that century, Great Britain became the first nation in the world to start to industrialize, while at the same time Britain was the most important carrier of slaves in the Atlantic as well as the owner of an increasing number of wealthy plantation colonies based on slavery. As early as 1944 Eric Williams, a West Indian historian later to become the prime minister of Trinidad and Tobago, published the classic *Capitalism and Slavery*, in which he argued that the slave trade and plantation slavery in the New World provided re-investable profits essential to the financing of capitalist growth.

Yet subsequent research has not been very successful in substantiating the claim that profits from the slave trade and slavery "provided one of the main streams of that accumulation of capital in England which financed the Industrial Revolution" (Williams, 52). In fact, the quantitative effects of the profits of the slave trade on the British Industrial Revolution, according to scholars such as Stanley L. Engerman, were negligible. As D. Richardson pointed out in a 1987 essay, the slave trade depended on European demand for sugar, which itself was a function of prior economic growth in the sugar-consuming economies in western Europe. And as R. Findlay noted three years later, in the absence of the Atlantic slave trade and slavery, Britain would have had to drink bitter tea, but it still would have had an Industrial Revolution, if perhaps at a marginally slower pace.

Subsequent research into the history of European expansion abroad, and of industrialization at home, has shown time and again: (1) that the profitability of Europe's activities in the Atlantic was not out of the ordinary; (2) that during the first phase of the Industrial Revolution, the captains of industry had only a tenuous connection with colonial trade; (3) that investments in the first stages of industrialization were small and easily obtainable at home; and (4) that endogenous factors of development, such as growing volumes of domestic commerce and the increasing size of national markets, played key roles in making industry a permanent and growing sector of the European economy.

Moreover, for the adherents of the thesis that Atlantic trade was instrumental in financing nascent industry in Europe, it is sobering that a considerable time lag existed between the start of Europe's expansion into the Atlantic on the one hand, and the beginnings of industrialization in Europe on the other. The first countries to profit from Atlantic trade, the mining of precious metals, the slave trade, and slave labor were Portugal and Spain. However, these two countries were among the last in western Europe to industrialize. Similarly, the volume of French colonial trade far exceeded that of the United Kingdom, yet France started to industrialize only belatedly in the middle of the nineteenth century, at least a half century later than Britain, and even later than the heyday of French expansion into the Atlantic. Both Germany and Belgium, two non-imperial economies, were among the earliest industrializers on the Continent, whereas the Netherlands, a small country with a large colonial empire overseas, lagged behind.

The historiography has thus moved beyond mono-causal and linear explanations of the process of Europe's industrialization, and it now seems an outdated idea that commerce from the Atlantic and in particular the profits from slavery and the slave trade might have been at the root of Europe's development. First of all, engagements with the Atlantic differed greatly from nation to nation. Atlantic trade was most pronounced in Great Britain and France, where it constituted around 40 percent of the total trade of these countries towards 1800, according to analysis in 2010 by Jan de Vries, while the Atlantic then accounted for only 15 percent of Dutch trade. In a political sense, it has been argued by historians such as D. Acemoglu, S. Johnson, and J. Robinson in 2005, that the Atlantic ports in Europe experienced an extraordinary growth rate between 1500 and 1800 and contributed disproportionately to the development of economic and democratic institutions there. However, the economic consequences of Atlantic trade should not be exaggerated. Trade contributed at most 10 to 15 percent to the GNP of any European country, and usually intercontinental trade in all regions of the world constituted only a minor part of that. In addition, none of the goods imported from outside Europe were vital to the European economies at the time. Sugar provided only a small share of all calories consumed, and cotton became important to the British textile industry only *after* industrialization.

Migration

However difficult it might be to measure the impact of Atlantic trade on the economies of Europe, emigration from Europe to the New World is easier to quantify, as the transatlantic migrations have been well studied. In spite of the fact that European emigration has given the Atlantic its distinct character, before 1800 the yearly number of emigrants was not impressive, and the effect of migration on European economies would not be felt until the latter half of the nineteenth century, when transatlantic migration considerably increased.

During the 300 years after Columbus, about 2 million Europeans moved across the Atlantic. Thus, during the period between 1500 and 1800, the population loss to Europe amounted to approximately 6,500 migrants on average per year. Assuming that the maritime regions of western Europe were home to populations of about 20 million, Europe lost only 0.3 per thousand of its population, while the demographic growth in Europe between 1500 and 1800 has been estimated to be at least a hundred times greater, and perhaps much more: 40 per thousand per year. Basic demographic rates thus suggest that before the middle of the nineteenth century the emigration into the Atlantic could have reduced European population growth by a very minor degree.

Another remarkable feature of European emigration into the Atlantic is the uneven distribution of the migrants over time, by geographical origins, and in relation to the sizes of the sending populations (see table 1). The two extreme examples are Portugal and the Dutch Republic. Both had home populations of about 2 million between 1500 and 1760 and in that period directed 532,000 and 20,000 migrants respectively into the Atlantic. An even greater order of magnitude marked the difference in the propensities to emigrate from Britain (6 million inhabitants around 1750) and France (22 million), sending respectively 750,000 (12.5 percent) and 100,000 (0.05 percent) migrants across the Atlantic.

Why the numbers of Atlantic migrants differed so dramatically from country to country remains largely unexplained. One of the contributing factors might have been differing rates of mobility within the countries of departure. England stood out in that respect, as almost half the population there did not die in the places where they were born. Another stimulus for overseas migration was the availability of contracts of indenture allowing poor emigrants to cover the costs of crossing the

Table 1. Emigration from Europe to the New World, 1500–1760 (in thousands)

	Spain	Portugal	France	Dutch Rep.	Britain	Total
Before 1580	138	93	0	0	0	231
1580–1640	188	110	4	2	126	430
1640–1700	158	50	45	13	248	514
1700–1760	193	270	51	5	372	891

Source: David Eltis, *The Rise of African Slavery in the Americas* (Cambridge: Cambridge University Press, 2000), p. 9.

Atlantic. In these contracts employers in the New World advanced the costs of the passage, to be repaid by the migrants during the first years after their arrival. The number of indentured servants was highest among the migrants going to the British colonies in America, according to my analysis published in 1999, while indentured servitude was completely absent among Spanish and Portuguese migrants.

These figures lead to the conclusion that transatlantic emigration had only limited demographic effects on Europe. The growth of the European populations in both North and South America were impressive, but migration across the Atlantic had little to do with their growth before 1850; after 1850, the increase in migration would have its impact not just on population, but on economics as well.

The Atlantic Impact

Around 1500 both Portugal and Spain were the two most advanced countries in Europe. They were the first to expand into the Atlantic, they had first choices of the overseas territories, and, as a result, they seemed to have assembled a particularly promising collection of colonial assets. Spain conquered the most developed parts of the New World—the Mesoamerican areas possessing plenty of local labor and easily exportable precious metals. Portugal developed Brazil's rich soils into the world's major sugar producer. Yet after three centuries of colonial exploitation, the economies of both Portugal and Spain ranked among the most backward in western Europe. The impact of Spanish trade with the New World on the Iberian economy was limited, as the range of export products

from Spain was confined to textiles and alcoholic beverages, and even some of these were re-exports from economically more advanced countries elsewhere in Europe and paid for by the silver imported from the Americas.

Another interesting contrast is presented by the parallel initiatives of the Dutch Republic and England, with sharply differing outcomes. The Dutch conquest and colonization of part of Brazil (1630–1654) was short-lived and bankrupted the Dutch West India Company because of the high costs of the expeditionary army sent to drive out the Portuguese, who in the end retook the colony. In the following century, the Dutch invested far too much money in their Caribbean plantation colonies, resulting in a crash on the Amsterdam stock exchange. As a result, the volume of the Dutch slave trade to the Caribbean declined dramatically towards the end of the eighteenth century, while the slaving of all other European nations increased dramatically. Britain, on the other hand, continued to enjoy the benefits of the growing imports of sugar from its West Indian island possessions, in spite of a temporary decline during the War of American Independence. In addition, Britain derived some profit from settlement colonies in North America, albeit that the North Americans themselves constantly increased their own share in the Atlantic trade, especially after the independence of the United States in 1783.

On the continent, the Dutch were not alone in seeing their Atlantic commerce decline. Had there been no intercontinental trade at all, France's national income would have been lowered by a mere 1.5 to 2 percent. French trading and shipping firms used the colonial markets as substitutes for the more competitive markets in Europe where they could not compete. In the long run, avoiding competition turned out to be detrimental to French shipping and trade. Industrialization triggered by overseas trade remained limited to a few port cities, and these port cities were not well connected to the rest of the French economy. And what applied to France and the Netherlands was even truer for the Nordic countries, where the impacts of colonial and overseas trade on the economy remained extremely marginal.

* * *

The Atlantic empires fell apart around 1800 because of the decolonization of part of British North America, the French loss of Saint-Domingue, and the sale of French Louisiana; Spanish and Portuguese America soon followed these examples. What was left of the colonial empires in the Atlantic were the plantation colonies in the Caribbean, and even their commercial value to their mother countries weakened as liberalization of trade during the nineteenth century allowed the colonies to sell their products wherever they found the highest rewards, often outside their European mother countries. Furthermore, the productive capacities of the plantation economies were adversely affected by abolition of the slave trade and of slavery.

The abolition of protectionist legislation was clearly reflected in the geography of British overseas trade, for example. Toward the end of the eighteenth century Europe had accounted for 37 percent of British exports, the West Indies for 12 percent, Canada and the United States for 23 percent, Latin America for 0 percent, and Africa for 3 percent. A century later, the figures were as follows: Europe 39 percent, West Indies 1 percent, Canada and the United States 12 percent, Latin America 11 percent, and Africa 8 percent. Trade with Asia increased from 15 percent to 21 percent. Britain was the European economy most oriented to markets outside of Europe, as it was the only power for which Continental markets constituted only 35 percent to 40 percent of the imports and exports. In the international trades of France, Spain, and Portugal, European markets accounted for more than 70 percent.

Europe brought Africa under colonial rule at the end of the nineteenth century, but that hardly had an impact on trade or migration in the Atlantic. At the same time, the Atlantic experienced a dramatic increase in European emigration and investments, providing the emigrants and investors with higher incomes than at home. Perhaps the most beneficial effect of the nineteenth-century Atlantic on Europe was the lowered growth rate of its population due to emigration, as some 55 million migrants left Europe between 1840 and 1940, of whom 65 percent migrated to the United States—more than 40 times the number of migrants than in the three centuries before 1800. This massive human outflow helped to improve the ratios between land and investment and the labor in Europe, presumably providing those who stayed behind with higher incomes. It seems that the Atlantic started to make a difference, keying on the human component of the European economies, long after the colonial era in the Atlantic had ended.

PIETER C. EMMER

Bibliography

Acemoglu, D., S. Johnson, and J. Robinson. "The Rise of Europe: Atlantic Trade, Institutional Change, and Economic Growth." *American Economic Review* 95 (2005): 546–549.

de Vries, Jan. "The Limits of Globalization in the Early Modern World." *Economic History Review* 63 (2010): 729.

Eltis, David. *The Rise of African Slavery in the Americas.* Cambridge: Cambridge University Press, 2000.

Emmer, Pieter C. "The Dutch and the Slave Americas." In *Slavery in the Development of the Americas*, edited by David Eltis, Frank D. Lewis, and Kenneth L. Sokoloff, 70–86. Cambridge: Cambridge University Press, 2004.

———. "Europäische Expansion und interkontinentale Migration." In *Überseegeschichte: Beiträge der jüngeren Forschung. [Festschrift anlässlich der Gründung der Forschungsstiftung für vergleichende europäische Überseegeschichte 1999 in Bamberg]*, edited by Thomas Beck, Horst Gründer, Horst Pietschmann, and Roderich Ptak. Stuttgart: Franz Steiner, 1999.

Emmer, P. C., O. Pétré-Grenouilleau, and J. V. Roitman, eds. *A Deus ex Machina Revisited: Atlantic Colonial Trade and European Economic Development.* Leiden and Boston: Brill, 2006.

Engerman, Stanley L. "The Slave Trade and Capital Formation in the Eighteenth Century: A Comment on the Williams Thesis," *Business History Review*, 46, no. 4 (Winter 1972): 304–332.

Findlay, R. *The "Triangular Trade" and the Atlantic Economy of the Eighteenth Century: A Simple General Equilibrium Model*. Princeton, NJ: Princeton University Press, 1990.

Hatton, Timothy J., and Jeffrey G. Williamson, eds. *Migration and the International Labor Market, 1850–1939*. London: Routledge, 1994.

Pétré-Grenouilleau, Olivier. *Les traites négrières: Essai d'histoire globale*. Paris: Gallimard, 2004.

Richardson, D. "The Slave Trade, Sugar, and British Economic Growth, 1748–1776." *Journal of Interdisciplinary History* 17 (1987): 739–769.

Williams, Eric. *Capitalism and Slavery*. Chapel Hill: University of North Carolina Press, 1944.

Emancipations

Speaking to Kenneth Bilby in Jamaica in 1978, a man named Charles Bernard told a short story about the most famous of his maroon ancestors: "White man say, 'you fe work.' Grandy Nanny say, 'me not working!' And she tek the river, follow river! She follow river." These four sentences powerfully evoke both an individual journey and the much larger struggle of the enslaved for emancipation, one that stretched out over hundreds of years and involved the complex interplay of actors throughout the Atlantic World. The process ranged from the self-emancipations of individuals and communities through *marronage*, to the massive insurrectionary emancipation carried out during the Haitian Revolution, to processes of imperially or nationally decreed emancipation in the British and French Caribbean, in all of the mainland Spanish-speaking republics, eventually in the United States, and finally by Cuban and Brazilian governments in the late nineteenth century.

Writing the history of the various currents swirling in this broader river of relief from bondage requires thinking about this process from the perspective of the enslaved and highlighting the consistent and critical roles they played in the course of emancipating themselves by winning legal recognition of their presence. Traditionally the authors of emancipation are usually understood to be those free political leaders—Victor Schoelcher in France, Abraham Lincoln in the United States—who at critical moments propelled the legal abolition of slavery. And yet emancipation as a process was something much fuller and more complex than laws releasing people from enslavement. Emancipation was a broad struggle for social inclusion and human dignity, a struggle that some of our greatest historians—most notably Thomas Holt in his work *The Problem of Freedom* (1992)—have shown long remained, and in many ways still remains, unfinished.

Self-Emancipations

If refugee maroons represented the most powerful and direct strategy of self-emancipation, other enslaved individuals also worked or bargained their way to manumission granted by their masters, sometimes through self-purchase or as a reward for military service with the opponents of their masters. Such liberation was rarely a purely individual achievement: family members and friends, both enslaved and free, often participated in an individual's pursuit of manumission. Once freed, former slaves struggled to find places for themselves in both colonial and national societies. By gaining education, practicing professions, and becoming owners of land and slaves, they often challenged the racial boundaries of the social order. At the same time, in certain societies—notably Saint-Domingue—free people of African descent became pillars of local militias and police forces, whose role was to protect the plantation system. In the longer term, the first to escape slavery often became the founders of long lineages who continued to struggle, in various ways, to realize full emancipation for others, as historians Rebecca Scott and Jean Hébrard have recently shown in *Freedom Papers* (2012), a riveting transgenerational story of a family that begins in Saint-Domingue and carries on in later generations in Cuba and New Orleans.

In the second half of the eighteenth century, a series of larger-scale attacks on the entire structure took place throughout the Atlantic World. Abolitionism was remarkable for the transcontinental reach of its networks and their ability to mobilize people across regions, faiths, and social situations. Indeed, open political abolitionism in many ways created the vocabulary and strategies of much modern political activism, blending arresting visual and literary propaganda with the force of mass meetings, petition campaigns, and at times violent resistance. In addition to free abolitionists, however, the concerted action of the enslaved—sometimes individually, quietly, and strategically, sometimes more openly or violently—was both strategically and ideologically a central part of the conjoined struggles for emancipation. Allies were sometimes local, and could be relatively powerless, but at times included elites and governors with the capacity to shape policy directly, as some great and celebrated abolitionists did. The history of Atlantic emancipation is the story of the deliberate, risky crossings of the boundary between individuals and communities otherwise divided by slavery.

Emancipations by Violence

The insurgency launched in 1791 by the great majority of the enslaved in French Saint-Domingue was one of the largest, and certainly the most immediately successful, of abolitionist movements. Within two years, by the summer of 1793, it secured emancipation, an achievement that resonated broadly within France and in French territories around the world. When, a decade later, Napoleon Bonaparte threatened this release from slavery, a movement that had begun as a slave insurrection became a military and political movement for independence, achieved in 1804. Haiti thus became a sovereign state founded on the principle of antislavery, and a country whose rural cultural and economic institutions—created by exslaves, the majority of them African-born—were organized around the pursuit and protection of emancipation.

In the United States, the War of American Independence had provided an earlier, but more limited, opportunity for emancipation than the Haitian independence would offer 15 years later. Yet there, too, the first significant political moves toward emancipation, within particular states, had emerged from a moment of political upheaval and war. Vermont outlawed slavery in its original constitution in 1777, and other northern states with larger slave populations—notably Rhode Island and Massachusetts—initiated processes of gradual emancipation. Southern states faced the prospect of massive defections when the British offered the promise of individual freedom to any of the en-slaved who joined their effort to end the colonists' fight for political independence. And these states emerged from the war more strongly committed to slavery than ever.

The contrasting policies of the states in the free North and the slave South (along with general emancipation in British Canada) offered the enslaved growing opportunities for self-emancipation through flight. Frequent escapes from the South to freedom in the North were the foundation for the tradition of slave narratives that became a critical vehicle for mobilizing popular antislavery sentiment in the antebellum years by articulating powerful aspirations for full emancipation for those left behind. The tensions inherent in a political order in which regions differed on the most basic matters of law and politics created the impasse settled only by the cataclysmic U.S. Civil War. An ill-fated, but ultimately politically successful, raid on a federal government arsenal led by John Brown partly precipitated the resort to war; Brown had been inspired in planning his action by tales of the emancipatory revolution in Haiti.

Historian Stephen Hahn has argued that the Civil War itself can be interpreted as a massive slave revolt, in this sense the largest in history. In terms of the numbers of enslaved people involved, that assessment is probably true, though the struggle differed critically from the events in Haiti in that the latter were initiated by and largely led by enslaved and then freed people of African descent, who constituted the majority in the struggle. In the U.S. Civil War, many of the enslaved joined in the service of the Union army and accordingly found themselves after the war dependent on—and eventually betrayed by—a Federal government that ultimately abandoned the policies of political equality instituted through Reconstruction. In Haiti, meanwhile, the struggle over the meaning of freedom between the masses of former slaves and a new elite sometimes took parallel forms of betrayal of the powerless by the powerful. Yet thanks to an independence in Haiti that guaranteed much greater cultural and social autonomy than people of African descent enjoyed elsewhere, nineteenth-century Haitians were broadly successful in constructing what Jean Casimir calls a "counter-plantation" system, even in the face of political hostility and new forms of foreign economic control.

The comparison between the U.S. Civil War and the revolt and subsequent wars leading to Haitian independence serves as a reminder that the actions of the enslaved were at the center of the pan-Atlantic process of emancipation. Hahn's emphasis on the contributions of the enslaved to the eventual Union victory is vital, for it prompts us to connect Haiti and the United States through this pan-Atlantic perspective.

Emancipations by Decree

Between these two instances of extremely violent emancipation came the more orderly legal processes of British and French emancipations, histories quite different but no less intertwined on a scale extending across the Atlantic and even beyond. Abolition of the slave trade—begun in 1808 by Great Britain and the United States, and belatedly and reluctantly joined by France—and then the abolition of slavery itself in the British West Indies in 1833–1838 and in 1848 in the French Antilles were decreed from the imperial centers and spurred on by domestic abolitionist movements. The anti-slavery movements in England (like those in North America) had a broad popular base, rooted in church communities and an emerging industrial working class. Their French counterparts were both more elite and more policy-oriented. Yet abolition ultimately arrived in the seats of political power in both London and Paris through popular activism.

Other popular events in the Americas, particularly in the Caribbean colonies, shaped the progress and strategies of abolitionist movements in the political centers in Europe. The early nineteenth century saw a series of large revolts by the enslaved in the British West Indies: Barbados in 1816, Demerara in 1823, and Jamaica in 1831. Each of these revolts derived inspiration from, and in turn inspired, the progress of political abolitionism in England, with slave insurgents responding to rumors—usually rooted in fact, but also infused with hope for more rapid change than was actually on offer—as they mobilized for change. The revolts were all brutally suppressed. In the case of the Baptist War in Jamaica in 1831, which was a largely nonviolent protest, more of a strike than a war, the death toll was almost entirely from executions of enslaved people accused of participating in the revolt. The French Caribbean saw fewer revolts but more open activism on the part of freed people of African descent, who at times allied with those still in slavery. The specter of the Haitian Revolution always haunted discussions of abolition in France, as it had in the United States, shaping the considerations of the Republicans who rapidly decreed emancipation after they took power in Paris in 1848.

The processes of emancipation in Latin America were the most complex and layered of all. They stretched from the constitution of independent maroon communities in Brazil and other parts of the continent in the seventeenth century, through the gradual government abolitions brought about largely through slave participation in the wars of independence in the early nineteenth century, and led, though gradually, to the complete elimination of slavery in the Latin American republics. The last country to abolish slavery was Brazil in 1888. By the time of the formal abolition of slavery there, however, the size of the slave population had shrunk considerably through processes of manumission driven by social and cultural changes, as well as a context of war with Paraguay in which enslaved people gained freedom in return for military service.

The Atlantic Context of Emancipations

These interlinked stories of emancipation, which can be understood only in a pan-Atlantic frame, were the result of the actions, visions, and discourses of varied actors in Africa, Europe, and the Americas. Before, during, and after the government decrees of emancipation, the broader struggle was to infuse social, cultural, and economic realities with individual autonomy, sovereignty, dignity, and liberty.

The struggles for emancipation defined these ideals of the emerging modern nation-state, shaping music, literature, and art throughout the Americas. In this sense, emancipation is everywhere in our cultural and intellectual reflexes, even as the many traces of its incompleteness lurk in continuing forms of racial exclusion, economic inequality, and hierarchy. The multiplicity of histories of Atlantic emancipation shows how far the river of freedom has flowed and also reminds us of how far it still has to go.

LAURENT DUBOIS

Bibliography

Bilby, Kenneth M. *True-Born Maroons*. Gainesville: University Press of Florida, 2005.

Casimir, Jean. *La Culture opprimée*. Port-au-Prince, Haiti: Imprimerie Lakay, 2001.

Clavin, Matthew J. *Toussaint Louverture and the American Civil War: The Promise and Peril of a Second Haitian Revolution*. Philadelphia: University of Pennsylvania Press, 2010.

Cooper, Frederick. *From Slaves to Squatters: Plantation Labor and Agriculture in Zanzibar and Coastal Kenya, 1890–1925*. New Haven, CT: Yale University Press, 1980.

Dubois, Laurent. *Avengers of the New World: The Story of the Haitian Revolution*. Cambridge, MA: Belknap Press of Harvard University Press, 2004.

———. *Haiti: The Aftershocks of History*. New York: Metropolitan Books, 2012.

Hahn, Steven. *The Political Worlds of Slavery and Freedom*. Cambridge, MA: Harvard University Press, 2009.

Holt, Thomas C. *The Problem of Freedom: Race, Labor, and Politics in Jamaica and Britain, 1832–1938*. Baltimore, MD: Johns Hopkins University Press, 1992.

Scott, Rebecca J., and Jean M. Hébrard. *Freedom Papers: An Atlantic Odyssey in the Age of Emancipation*. Cambridge, MA: Harvard University Press, 2012.

Turner, Mary. *Slaves and Missionaries: The Disintegration of Jamaican Slave Society, 1787–1834*. Urbana: University of Illinois Press, 1982.

Viotti da Costa, Emília. *Crowns of Glory, Tears of Blood: The Demerara Slave Rebellion of 1823*. New York: Oxford University Press, 1994.

Emigrants

Before the 1830s, the Europeans who settled permanently in the Americas by choice varied in character and were few in number compared with those who were compelled to settle there. Emigrants from Europe gained disproportionately because they and their American-born descendants built distinctly American communities—those from Spain in combination with Native populations, others from Britain and Portugal with Africans they bought as slaves, and smaller communities of French and Dutch in the Americas—and then redefined themselves as citizens of independent nation-states after 1787 in North America, often to the exclusion of the majorities of the others among whom they lived. In these communities of descendants the perspective was reversed with regard to later groups who relocated across the Atlantic: from European *e*migrants to American *im*migrants.

The Voluntary Character of Emigration

Emigrants played no role in the early phases of Europeans' discovery, exploration, and occupation of the Americas. The adventurers who undertook long, perilous, and expensive journeys across thousands of miles of open water did so for gain and glory upon returning home. Similarly, those who arrived in the employ of European governments or as missionaries of the Catholic Church considered their stays to be temporary—a way of extending the Christian world they had known at home. Africa, reputed as a "white man's grave" throughout the Atlantic Era, attracted mostly maritime traders; there were virtually no voluntary emigrants with intent to stay, few missionaries, and only skeletal military postings, entirely Portuguese. Most, if not all, of these men believed that success overseas would enable them to return home to make their mark with riches from abroad, and consequently arranged that their children were educated in their respective lands of origin. Even the minority of travelers who managed to survive in tropical disease environments and eventually prospered in the Americas often remained in the colonies only unintentionally. With no little irony, these unintended emigrants, who were nearly all men, became the models of successful colonists for successors who settled in family groups.

In the seventeenth and eighteenth centuries, emigrants to North America intending to settle and build communities tended to be religious congregations, families of exiles who sought to escape the faith-based conflagration of Reformation Europe, in North America mostly Protestants and other dissenters. The English-managed Virginia Company initiated an underfunded commercial enterprise in the Chesapeake region, expecting its colonists to grow in numbers to support themselves and company enterprises through long-term, if not permanent, settlement. If emigrants landed as single men, as was sometimes the case at first, or if their families followed later, the children born to the married women among them grew up with only their parents' memories and some customs from their places of origin but had no direct experience of, and few personal connections to, the homelands the older generations had left. The early males who had remained overseas had often found women locally, sometimes married them, and usually left children with their mothers. These succeeding generations, particularly on the coast of Africa, identified themselves with their mothers and were excluded from the ranks of later family emigrants from Europe and their descendants.

Until the mid-nineteenth century, two-thirds of the Africans and Europeans who landed on the Atlantic's western shores were bound laborers, transported against their wills. The number of voluntary emigrants from Europe grew only slowly and unevenly in most of the colonies in the Americas over the course of the seventeenth and eighteenth centuries, increasing especially in English (later British) North America as a result of complementing developments on both sides of the Atlantic. Foremost was the shift from the men streaming to the tropics in the beginnings of European engagement with the Atlantic to migrations to more temperate latitudes in North America that included women and children. These family dependents may have had little choice but to comply with their husbands' or fathers' decisions to emigrate; the patriarchal aspects of their emigration complicate the conventional distinction drawn between these communities and the indentured servants, captives of wars in Europe, convicts, and others forced into exile abroad. Nonetheless, these women played crucial roles in turning small settlements of European-born emigrants into growing communities of American-born descendants with distinctly local economic interests, family roots, and community cultural values and customs.

In addition, information about the Atlantic World became more available to ordinary people in Europe, who came to see the colonies as not only abundant in the hallmarks of material success but also far removed from local authorities and circumstances that constrained their lives in Europe. Stories about the exploits of transatlantic voyagers increased the familiarity of distant places in alluring ways, sparking the imaginations of Europeans hard pressed to make decent livings at home. Direct contact with returning travelers became more common, and diverse promotional literature to recruit not just poor but also more affluent emigrants for colonial settlement schemes circulated more widely and made westward emigration an accessible option for people intent on improving their lives.

If imagining the New World as an opportunity rather than a fallback was one prerequisite for growing voluntary emigration, the resources needed to execute so demanding and expensive a move were another, and even more difficult, challenge. While some emigrants, such as supercargoes (ships' officers responsible for the cargoes and passengers they carried) and agents of European trading houses, had the connections and means to finance their moves to and start-up in America, many would-be emigrants were unable to come up with funds to cover these considerable costs. By the eighteenth century fewer British boys and young men were hard pressed enough to end up as servants in the American colonies, but the legal mechanisms already in place for transferring interests in indentured servants and transporting them proved useful to mostly German-speaking young, single men looking overseas for opportunities. These emigrants agreed, largely voluntarily, to contracts of indenture in colonial America and played active parts in negotiating their terms, which usually equaled about one year's wages of a skilled worker and better prospects at the end of their service than they could expect at home, often including homesteads with land and tools to work them. Even those emigrants who could afford to pay up front depended on the services of merchants, shippers, and their agents along the way. By the late seventeenth century advances in transport and communication also contributed to more frequent and cheaper transatlantic passages, and the commercial networks that linked the major European and American ports and financial centers provided all manner of services for emigrants. However, even well-off and highly skilled emigrants could not succeed in making new lives in the Americas without credit.

Those who eventually came out on top—and then sent back trustworthy information about their good fortune to family and friends—inspired others to follow in their footsteps. Established settlers, in becoming models for kin, coreligionists, and former neighbors, were in positions first to enhance their local standing by extending personal financial assistance and later to recruit more broadly among members of their own countries in order to meet their growing needs for additional labor. What started out as informal support presented merchants and shippers with profit-making opportunities—for example, using space available on transatlantic vessels returning with various commodities for transportation of passengers on the outbound passages. Since the profit of each westward voyage depended on the number of passengers on board, merchants sought to augment their returns by increasing the number of passengers, balancing the proportions of emigrants who could pay fares with others who pledged to redeem their passages by contracting as indentured servants. In the course of the eighteenth century this "redemptioner" system expanded into a routine trade.

Emigrants into Immigrants

As government-supported European agents established the territorial legal domains within which families might settle, prosper, and reproduce, thriving market towns and port cities offered newcomers as well as Native-born residents opportunities for making a living. All newcomers were bound by the authority of colonial governments, and emigrants who came from other jurisdictions, even if officially released from obligations to their former governments, needed permission to settle, own land, or trade. These requirements were designed to favor emigrants with capital, or with personal sponsors, and kept their numbers relatively small. However, both governments and private speculators had invested in land, and they needed settlers to defend or improve it. They often attracted settlers with promises of free or nominally priced land and low taxes. The chance at prosperity in the Americas changed the face of the typical emigrant, replacing fugitives from failures or hardships in Europe with opportunity-seeking volunteers.

Although the shift toward voluntary emigrants began in the later-seventeenth century, most of the privately recruited and funded emigrants crossed the Atlantic in the eighteenth century and settled in British North America. This new wave of eager volunteers in the late 1700s was the first designated by the term *emigrant* itself, as seeing the Americas as an attractive option for personal advancement took firm hold of the European imagination. The bases for a perception of opportunity across the Atlantic

evolved owing to more settled economic circumstances at home, which allowed more people to accumulate the financial resources needed to move, as well as improved communication, better transportation, lower costs of relocation, and a variety of options for financing travel to, and a start in, the Americas. As the eighteenth century progressed, more and more emigrants relocated, especially to British North America, and, building on their successes, attracted not only additional kin, former neighbors, and people from their own countries but also strangers to join them in communities that, while distinctly local in nature, also reimagined and redefined their traditions from the Old World. Succeeding generations grew up as firmly established settlers, and their perspectives shifted from memories and models of home to planning for, and investing in, futures in America.

Those communities of Americans soon claimed political standing consistent with their shared viability and growing autonomy. The British colonies in North America, in which both free and enslaved populations had grown substantially, and which had recruited settlers from beyond the boundaries of their British origins, were first in declaring and gaining independence; Mexico, Brazil, and other European populations of growing American descent declared other new republics in the nineteenth century. Economic growth in the United States, and later in Brazil and the Spanish-speaking republics, profited from the human and financial capital of emigrants. As a consequence, and again tellingly introducing a new term in the early nineteenth century, the Europeans who left their homelands permanently for opportunities including citizenship in formative nation-states across the Atlantic were called *immigrants*.

Conclusion

The transformation from those who traveled from Europe to the coasts of Africa and the Americas in the early Atlantic phase without intending to stay to emigrants, whose bleak prospects at home left them with little choice but to try their luck in the colonies, to families who immigrated voluntarily with resources and in increasing numbers in pursuit of overseas opportunities not only marks shifting perspectives but also expands the focus of Atlantic history. The narrative broadened from static political frameworks centered on their mother countries to the histories of the emigrants themselves—their improving circumstances, the reduced risks and costs of moving, and their growing contributions of hard work and entrepreneurial ambition in the emergent nation-states of the Americas.

MARIANNE S. WOKECK

Bibliography

Altman, Ida, and James J. Horn, eds. *"To Make America": European Emigration in the Early Modern Period.* Berkeley: University of California Press, 1991.

Bailyn, Bernard. *The Peopling of British North America: An Introduction.* New York: Vintage, 1988.

Eltis, David, ed. *Coerced and Free Migration: Global Perspectives.* Stanford, CA: Stanford University Press. 2002.

Games, Alison. *Migration and the Origins of the English Atlantic.* Cambridge, MA: Harvard University Press, 1999.

Empires

Empires have a bad name in the history of the Atlantic World for both historical and historiographical reasons. Ever since post–World War II and decolonization, empires have been understood as instruments of oppression. While a number of voices have dissented in recent years—both among those who see empires as bringing benefits to the conquered and others who see empires as a plausible political alternative to the nation-state—empires remain broadly lamented as an unfortunate alternative to more liberating political forms. Historiographically, empires are even more problematic. Historians of North America and their colleagues who study former French, Portuguese, and Spanish colonies have long fought against a version of imperial history that understood developments in the Western Hemisphere to have been determined by decisions made in Europe. The response by a wide range of scholars, who agree about little else, has been to argue that most of the action in the development of the Atlantic World occurred on the peripheries rather than in the metropolitan center.

This essay offers an alternative to this emerging-consensus critique of imperial determinism by placing European transoceanic initiatives more firmly in dialogue with the regional histories of the parts of the Atlantic World that Europeans claimed. First, imperial relationships mattered fundamentally in all early-modern Atlantic regions. The British Empire was not an outlier characterized by an unusually liberal and permissive attitude toward its colonies. British imperial institutions were just as robust as the tight bureaucratic administration usually attributed to Spain. Second, the imperial politics of transatlantic connections in the seventeenth and eighteenth centuries was not a politics dictated from the European center. Rather it was a politics mutually constituted by developments in both the colonies and in the traditional centers. Political alignments in the fierce debates that characterized the period were shaped less by geography than by ideologies that transcended the ocean. Finally, what set the British Atlantic empire apart from its rivals was not the absence of an imperial state but rather openness of the connected popular and public imperial dialogue on both sides of the Atlantic. British imperial politics involved a wide range of social classes and a vast array of publications circulating the competing positions and making information about the empire widely available for discussion, and ultimately action. Britons in both hemispheres discussed and debated the issues of empire.

The centrality of Castilian-based institutions of control to the history of the Spanish Atlantic is well known. The Catholic monarchs Ferdinand and Isabella, concerned by reports of abuses by the first generations of conquistadors after 1492, turned to the archdeacon of Seville, Juan Rodriguez de Fonseca, to oversee colonial affairs as part of the Council of Castile. By 1523 this grouping responsible for expanding American interests was formalized as the Council of the Indies. The new Council of the Indies quickly took control over trade, justice, and services in Spain's overseas possessions. It worked alongside the Casa de la Contratación, which regulated the trade connecting Spain to the Americas. In the 1530s and 1540s the Council moved swiftly to ensure that neither the conqueror of Mexico, Hernán Cortés, nor the conqueror of Peru, Francisco Pizarro, could establish quasi-autonomous feudal possessions. Instead the Castilian government established crown-appointed judicial courts, or *audiencias*, to bring their vast new possessions under the control of officers obedient to Spain. The Spanish rulers consolidated their royal presence, and hence authority, in their new holdings by appointing viceroys, in New Spain (Mexico) in 1535 and in Peru in 1542.

The Portuguese Empire followed a similar pattern of extending royal authority, if with a later chronology and through institutions elaborated from the military authority of the king. In the 1530s the Portuguese monarchy created donatary captaincies in Brazil. These under-financed initiatives quickly proved failures, outside of Pernambuco and São Vicente. As a consequence King João III determined in 1548 to create a centralized chain of command like the Spanish viceroyalties. The first royal governor, Tomé de Sousa (1549–1553), set up a new capital at Salvador in the captaincy of Bahia. The Portuguese had established a Casa da India in the fifteenth century to register its overseas trade in Africa and into the Indian Ocean but set up a separate council to regulate governance in the overseas territories, the Conselho Ultramarino, only in 1642 upon breaking free of the 60-year union under the crown of Spain (1580–1640).

The Spanish and Portuguese had initiated their Atlantic ventures through private-public partnerships, but the two crowns steadily asserted firmer royal control. The Tudor and early Stuart monarchs of England, by contrast, played a less direct role in sixteenth-century overseas enterprises of their subjects. The results were disastrous. Again and again, underfinanced and grudgingly supported English colonial ventures failed. Sir Walter Raleigh's aspirations to create English settlements in Guiana (1595) barely got off the ground. But even those enterprises that lasted longer should not be seen as success stories or indeed forebears of the later integrated British Empire of the eighteenth and nineteenth centuries. The Virginia Company, which established Jamestown in 1607, had gone bankrupt by 1624. The Providence Island Company, founded in 1629 by critics of King Charles I, managed to set up a small island colony off the Central American coast in the 1630s, only to have their base overrun by the Spanish in 1641. The Massachusetts Bay Company, founded the year before at Providence Island by those with similar sentiments, is usually viewed as a success, but its population and wealth were risible compared to the

mineral-rich possessions of the Spanish in the Americas and the Portuguese in Africa. Had the English state not become directly involved in the Massachusetts Bay enterprise in the mid-century, the significance of the colony would surely now be seen in a less favorable light. Since the English crown failed to develop institutions to supervise the overseas ventures of its subjects prior to the middle of the seventeenth century, England had a tiny, fragile, and ephemeral presence in the Atlantic prior to the establishment of the English Republic in 1649.

The experience of civil war and the emergence of new radical ideas of governance fundamentally transformed the English state and then created an imperial state after the middle of the seventeenth century. During the English Civil War (1642–1647), both the Royalists and Parliamentarians raised standing armies and developed permanent navies. In order to pay for these costly new military forces, the succession of English governments had to develop a new financial infrastructure. Oliver Cromwell and his Council of State (1649–1653) immediately deployed this new fiscal and military capacity in the Western Design launched in 1655 against Spanish Hispaniola. The English amphibious invasion force not only broke the Spanish monopoly in the Caribbean but also created the first institutions of an English imperial state. The Council of Trade and the Council of the Americas, both created in 1655, were designed to centralize control over England's disparate New World possessions and to rationalize English commercial activities in the Atlantic. Cromwell and his supporters sought to take over the Spanish Empire in the New World by mimicking Spanish imperial institutions.

Institutions even more clearly framed British endeavors overseas in the eighteenth century. After the Restoration of the monarchy (1660), Charles II (r. 1660–1685) continued to devote a great deal of energy to colonial settlement and governance. But the committees and councils that dealt with colonial affairs were once again offshoots of the Privy Council, the private and personal advisors of the king. They performed similar functions to Cromwell's Council of State, but they were in fact appointed and consulted at the king's personal pleasure rather than operating as continuing administrative bodies. Charles II had tried to impose a model of royal authority overseas much closer to the Spanish monarchy's exclusive control in the Indies. However, the primacy of the monarchy in England's Atlantic territories ended in 1696, when Parliament sanctioned the Board of Trade, the council that would oversee imperial governance and commercial regulation throughout much of the eighteenth century. Many Britons explicitly understood their new imperial authority to be modeled on the Spanish Council of the Indies, which for over a century had yielded wealth of legendary magnitudes.

Although councils in Europe organized and rationalized early-modern connections between European states and their overseas territories, they did not dictate what was going on in the colonies. American-born subjects of the Iberian, French, and British crowns provided the vital information that advisers in Europe needed to plan, placed limits on what they would accept in terms of European direction, and responded to growing and increasingly complex local concerns with varying degrees of authority of their own. Though institutions coordinated these debates and interactions, both in Britain and in the continental European monarchies, they did not and could not determine the outcomes. Instead they made it possible for groups on both sides of the Atlantic to coalesce around competing imperial visions. Within the shared framework of royal sovereignty, no political distinction emerged dividing core from periphery. Divisions, when they occurred over political economic priorities, split factions in Europe as they did in Europeans' Atlantic possessions.

Although the British Empire was not a loose collection of colonies conventionally contrasted with institutionally integrated continental rivals, the empires did diverge along differing economic and political trajectories. The vast wealth of Portuguese, Spanish, and, by the mid-eighteenth century, French possessions contrasted with the relatively modest profitability of the mainland possessions of Great Britain. Politically, a large swath of North America successfully sought independence from the British crown. The cataclysmic events of the French Revolution and the Napoleonic wars effectively orphaned Spanish America and put significant pressure on Portuguese and French America as well. Was there then anything distinctive about the British state in comparison with the Atlantic domains of the French and Iberians?

In fact, though transatlantic policies in Spain, Portugal, and France were deeply informed by advice and information from their various colonies and often subjected to intense scrutiny and profound debate, decisions in the continental regimes invariably took place in private, in the relative anonymity of royal councils. In Britain and its colonies, by contrast, imperial issues were debated in public and by increasingly popular audiences, eventually leading to significant public participation and influence. The Board of Trade, created in 1696, submitted its reports to a representative body, Parliament. English, Scottish, Irish, North American, and West Indian newspapers reported on and criticized military and fiscal strategies and imperial policies. After 1688 the post-revolutionary English state—Parliament working alongside the crown—created a range of new financial institutions that allowed a wide variety of investors in government annuities and bonds to fund a national debt. That is, the British public invested in the British state, giving a deep and abiding interest in the success of overseas ventures that generated the dividends from their investments to a wide range of relatively modest people. As a consequence, in Britain, unlike on the continent, imperial policies became popular politics.

Ideological—and, in Britain, also political—disagreements over imperial policies anywhere in Europe, especially over the best ways to promote economic development, have usually been obscured by the assumption that all early-modern European governments attempted to implement a common set of economic ideas, known as *mercantilism*, limiting the commercial activity of subjects of the various crowns to Atlantic ports subject to taxation in efforts to support growing fiscal-military states. In fact no mercantilist consensus existed; there was no agreement on the political economic goals that Atlantic trade and American territorial claims should support. From the middle of the seventeenth century, if not earlier, Europeans in councils of state, company committee rooms, and in the popular press debated vociferously the best ways both to generate more state revenue and improve the quality of life of their subject populations. They discussed a breathtaking range of issues and recommended varying policies to solve them. Some argued, for example, that colonial wealth should be used to finance European state activity. Spanish silver and eventually Portuguese gold served exactly that function. Others argued that European states and their overseas possessions should function as a single, large market in which the Atlantic possessions would be conceived as yet another region filled with potential consumers, no different from Aragon, the Bordelais, or Yorkshire.

One of the fundamental fissures in European thinking about growing Atlantic commerce and its potential yields for Europe was over the nature of property, the assets on which revenues might be earned, and taxes levied. Some argued that property was material, primarily in land, and thus necessarily finite. In this model, the best way to ensure prosperity was to maximize the quantities of raw materials that one possessed. Proponents of this view argued that the most important of these raw materials were precious metals. The proper aim of acquiring territories, according to this way of thinking, was to control areas containing gold and silver; Spain's Andean and northern Mexican holdings, as well as Portugal's Brazil, were prototypical wealth. Others argued, on the contrary, that value in property was created by human labor and was thus potentially infinite. In this reading, more prominent in Britain, governments should promote manufactures and look abroad for markets in which to sell these goods. The decision about which of these models to pursue was a political question—a choice based on contrasting interests and interpretations of those interests—that cut right across Europe. They were not distinguished along the political boundaries of the paradigmatic contrast.

The continental European polities also reoriented their imperial strategies repeatedly, further diminishing the viability of contrasts made in "imperial" terms. Portuguese thinking about the purposes of attempting to control territories overseas changed in the late sixteenth century as a consequence of an ideological and fiscal crisis at home. As a result, they changed their focus from the East Indies to Brazil. The Portuguese revolt against Spanish rule in the 1640s and 1650s, which eventually reestablished a sovereign dynasty in Portugal, was motivated in part by opposition to the Spanish political economic system imposed on the Portuguese during the preceding union of the two Iberian crowns (1580–1640). Revenues from taxing the trade in Brazilian sugar and the slave trade from Africa helped to finance the war. Similarly a profound debate over the benefits and dangers of freer intra-imperial trade in both the Spanish and Portuguese empires resulted in profound mid-eighteenth century reforms.

After the Treaty of Utrecht, which concluded the War of the Spanish Succession in 1713, the French regency government became enmeshed in a vitriolic debate about the relationship between overseas possessions and royal finance that culminated in the Mississippi Bubble and French financial collapse of 1720. Half a century later the massive French debts generated by the Seven Years' War (1756–1763)—a war fought in large part over Atlantic possessions—gave birth to new political economic controversies fought out between moderate fiscal reformers and defenders of aggressive overseas territorial expansion that ultimately helped spawn the French Revolution. Political-economic contestation and political choice, rather than mercantilist consensus, shaped how early-modern monarchies attempted to distribute the spoils of their Atlantic networks of trade and territories. In continental Europe these discussions were largely restricted to the private chambers of royal councils. Public opinion and popular sentiment mattered very little.

In Britain, by contrast, the robust restored monarchy of the early eighteenth century brought a new public into being on both sides of the Atlantic. Britons in the Americas as well as in the home islands invested heavily in the growing national debt, were recruited into the British army and navy in ever-larger numbers and paid taxes to an increasingly efficient revenue service. A variety of pamphlets, newspapers, and broadsides widely circulated information about colonial affairs on both sides of the Atlantic. The positions proclaimed in these publications were the stuff of conversations in taverns and coffeehouses from Bombay to Edinburgh, from Dublin to Kingston, and from London to New York. These debates raged with such public intensity because popular sentiments ran high and mattered politically. The nature of taxes and revenues, the value and danger of further territorial expansion, and the nature of political representation were all discussed in legislative institutions with public representation—in colonial assemblies as well in the parliaments of Westminster and Dublin—and in the committee rooms of corporations with public investors, such as the Bank of England, the East India Company, and the South Sea Company.

The political debates over commercial direction played themselves out in British colony after British colony. Jamaicans debated whether the island's economic future lay in continued exclusive reliance on sugar plantations or in developing and fostering trade of manufactured goods with Spanish America in pursuit of silver. Alexander Spotswood initiated a debate in Virginia (where he was governor, 1710–1722) as to whether or not the colony should move away from its tobacco monoculture to develop such manufacturing as an iron industry. Politicians from upland and lowcountry South Carolina disagreed vociferously in the early eighteenth century as to whether the colony should focus its energies exclusively on plantation production of rice or develop manufactures of various naval stores. Scottish and Irish politicians also debated actively over the prospects and means to develop manufactures.

In Britain, from the tumultuous years leading to the Revolution of 1688–1689 through the concession of American independence in 1783 and beyond, party politics coalesced around competing visions of empire within institutions like the Board of Trade, the Society for the Propagation of the Gospel, the Royal African Company, the East India Company, and the Royal Navy. They produced new institutions, such as the Anglican commissary, the South Sea Company, and the various agencies designed to communicate the local needs and desires of individual colonies to the Westminster parliament and British public. Although these competing visions were expressed in different ways at different moments, robust communication networks and well-developed forms of party organization made it possible for these policy debates to be both vitriolic and coherent across the vast distances of the Atlantic.

These British institutions of public outreach increasingly structured life in the American colonies and dependent kingdoms of Scotland and Ireland throughout the late seventeenth and the eighteenth centuries. Those in the colonies—in the West Indies, in North America, and to a lesser extent in India—used these institutions to advance agendas of their own. They petitioned the Board of Trade and lobbied the South Sea, East India, and Royal African companies. They dispatched agents to present their arguments to Parliament in Westminster in forms that were consciously tailored to appeal to metropolitan opinion. They also sought to reform those very institutions to pursue their own interests. The institutions of pan-Atlantic integration were dynamic and the overseas participants in the processes contributed significantly to modifying them.

A multilateral politics of imperial integration shaped the cultural, intellectual, and economic contours of the European Atlantic World, involving parties on both sides of the Atlantic. The institutions of empire were not conduits of power in which Europeans unilaterally imposed their wills on subject colonials. Rather, ideas and information flowed in both directions. The British developed imperial institutions as robust as those of the Spanish, French, and Portuguese. What distinguished Britain from its European counterparts and competitors was that its imperial institutions were uniquely subject to a politics that became both public and broadly participatory by the end of the seventeenth century. This robust popular discussion on transatlantic governance in the 1760s and 1770s enabled North Americans who claimed relief from a new set of taxes and political restrictions to attract immediate and significant support from partisan allies in England, Scotland, and Ireland. In the Spanish and French empires, by contrast, it was only the implosion of the European center that made necessary the creation of independent republics.

STEVE PINCUS

Bibliography

Adelman, Jeremy. *Sovereignty and Revolution in the Iberian Atlantic*. Princeton, NJ: Princeton University Press, 2006.

Bethencourt, Francisco. "Political Configurations and Local Powers." In *Portuguese Oceanic Expansion, 1400–1800*, edited by Francisco Bethencourt and Diogo Ramada Curto, 197–254. Cambridge: Cambridge University Press, 2007.

Elliott, J. H. *Empires of the Atlantic World: Britain and Spain in America 1492–1830*. New Haven, CT: Yale University Press, 2006.

Pincus, Steve. *1688: The First Modern Revolution*. New Haven, CT: Yale University Press, 2009.

———. "Rethinking Mercantilism." *William and Mary Quarterly* 69, no. 1 (2012): 3–34.

Robertson, John. *The Case for Enlightenment*. Cambridge: Cambridge University Press, 2005.

Schaub, Jean-Frederic. *Le Portugal au temps du Comte-Duc d'Olivares*. Madrid: Casa de Velazquez, 2001.

Schwartz, Stuart. "The Iberian Atlantic to 1650." In *The Oxford Handbook of the Atlantic World*, edited by Nicholas Canny and Philip Morgan. Oxford: Oxford University Press, 2011.

Steele, Ian. *Politics of Colonial Policy: The Board of Trade in Colonial Administration 1696–1720*. Oxford: Clarendon Press, 1968.

Subrahmanyam, Sanjay. *The Portuguese Empire in Asia 1500–1700*. New York: Longman, 1993.

Environments

The story of the early-modern Atlantic involves not only trade and empires but also germs, seeds, plants, animals, and soils. From 1450 to 1850, environmental factors profoundly shaped Atlantic history, and humans in turn reshaped Atlantic environments. New exchanges of people, microbes, flora, and fauna across the ocean set off a wave of changes that went well beyond the immediate impacts of the Columbian Exchange. At the same time, a burgeoning Atlantic economy drove new frontiers of settlement, agriculture, and commodity extraction that left enduring changes in the landscapes of the Americas.

Even before 1492, humans on all four continents had substantially altered their environments. Western European populations, recovering from losses in the Black Death, were clearing new land, digging mines, building cities, and searching out new sources of fish, timber, and other commodities in eastern Europe and on the seas. African populations, although limited by tropical diseases such as malaria, had developed agricultural and pastoralist systems in difficult environments. In the Americas, too, humans had transformed the land they lived on. Modern archaeology and ethnography have dispelled the "pristine myth" of tall, healthy Indians living lightly on lands they worshiped. Amerindians reworked their environments, too, through fire, hunting, and farming practices—not only in populous regions such as those of the Maya, Aztec, and Inca, but even in remote rain forests and grasslands.

The Columbian voyages brought together populations separated by thousands of years of history; they also began to integrate microbes, plants, and animals that had evolved differently over millions of years of continental drift and tens of millennia of human domestication and cultivation. For more than a century after Columbus, wave after wave of European infections—most acquired from European livestock—reduced Amerindians to a fraction of their former numbers. Old World pigs, sheep, cattle, weeds, and grasses invaded and transformed New World landscapes. European conquests and settlement in the Americas typically followed in the wake of deadly epidemics and ecological disturbances. The collapse of New World populations left an opening for Old World people, plants, and animals.

In the long term, commercial exchange proved as transformative in the Atlantic landscape as the biological exchanges. Throughout the sixteenth and seventeenth centuries, Atlantic shipping forged a vast new transoceanic market. Resource demands and commercial opportunities created revolutionary pressures to extract commodities, clear land, plant cash crops, and introduce new sources of labor.

In some cases, Atlantic markets turned local goods into global commodities almost overnight. Peruvian silver—for the Native Inca just a decorative metal—became the lifeblood of international trade once the Spanish opened the world's largest mines at Potosí, in present-day Peru, in the 1540s. North American Native peoples who had once hunted beaver and white-tailed deer for subsistence soon became suppliers in a competitive international market for furs and hides, as European consumers developed tastes for felt hats and buckskin gloves. By the eighteenth century, both species had been driven to near extinction in some regions. Cod off Newfoundland became a substantial protein supply for European consumers by the 1600s, driving colonial ventures and a major fishing industry, until the fishery collapsed in the twentieth century. A highly prized tropical red wood for dyes even gave the country of Brazil its name—and contributed to the early deforestation of its once-extensive Atlantic forest.

More consequential still was the rise of a far-reaching "plantation complex" combining European capital, African labor, and American land to produce cash crops for Atlantic markets. Even before 1492, colonists had imported indentured or slave labor to islands in the eastern Atlantic to produce high-value commodities, including sugar. The conquest and depopulation of the Americas opened vast new lands for cash crops difficult or impossible to produce in Europe. By the mid-1600s, African slaves had entirely replaced the Native Arawak and Carib populations, and some Caribbean islands had become virtual sugar monocultures, with significant loss of biodiversity. Virginia planters had turned almost exclusively to tobacco, and relied increasingly on slave labor to clear and cultivate the new lands that plant continuously demanded. Over the following two centuries, cotton, coffee, and a host of lesser cash crops would drive the importation of millions of African slaves and the clearance of millions of acres of woodlands, and consumers in Europe and around the world would come to depend on the calories, clothing, and comforts of American plantation products.

The recourse to African slaves had both environmental causes and consequences. Africa's endemic tropical diseases left many Africans with immunities and gave planters the impression they could better endure the harsh demands of the plantation regimen. The continent's low population density also meant that many African societies placed more emphasis on control of labor rather than of land, and Atlantic merchants could aggravate and exploit an already present trade in slaves. In time, the Atlantic Middle Passage transported not only African labor but African plants and pathogens as well. Africans brought new crops and agricultural techniques, including wet rice, which shaped the diets and landscapes of much of the New World. In the meantime, African malaria and yellow fever became endemic to the Americas and created a disease environment that only Africans and locally born Creoles could easily survive. One legacy of the slave trade was thus a mosquito-borne environmental defense that repeatedly limited the efficacy of European military invasions—first in Spanish America and then, later, in revolutionary Haiti and in the southern British colonies in North America.

Well beyond the tropical and subtropical plantation zones, Atlantic commerce and colonies brought profound environmental consequences. Following a difficult period of learning and adjustment, most settler populations in temperate regions grew rapidly from the start—some, as in Quebec and New England, more than doubling every generation. Land hunger and European demands for extracted commodities, especially for naval stores and furs, drove rapid frontier expansion, forest clearance, and habitat loss, especially in eastern North America. In more arid regions, such as northern Mexico, Argentina, and the American Southwest, settler and mestizo populations also created extensive new ranching economies based on introduced horses, sheep, and cattle.

Atlantic commerce and colonies grew at a time of global cooling known as the Little Ice Age. In Europe, cold wet summers and freezing winters killed animals and ruined crops, triggering frequent hunger, epidemics, and unrest, especially in the late sixteenth and seventeenth centuries. These climate-related disasters at home encouraged new colonial ventures abroad, especially from Britain. However, the Little Ice Age proved just as severe across the Atlantic, and early North American settlements, particularly Jamestown, suffered high mortality in extreme winters and dry summers. Over the same period, parts of Latin America and the American Southwest suffered severe droughts linked to strong phases of the El Niño southern oscillation, a periodic shift in temperatures and pressures over the Pacific Ocean with effects in the Americas. In Africa too, particularly Angola and the Sahel, the Little Ice Age brought more frequent droughts and famines, which contributed at times to political instability and slave raiding. In the 1780s, a massive volcanic eruption in Iceland and a strong El Niño event created harvest failures and shortages on both sides of the Atlantic, which contributed to stresses and thus played a part in revolutionary movements in both Europe and Latin America.

Finally, the early-modern Atlantic left its mark on the history of environmental thought. The first contact with new worlds shook up the mental map of Renaissance Europeans (and no doubt also of Americans and Africans, though they have left us fewer accounts). The narrow medieval worldview of the fifteenth century had to accommodate previously unknown peoples, flora, and fauna, and early settlers struggled to adapt to unfamiliar environments. Over the following centuries, Atlantic experiences—from Alexander von Humboldt's South American explorations (1799–1803) to Darwin's voyage on the *Beagle* (1831–1836)—would inspire major revisions in natural history. By the mid-nineteenth century, the sharp contrast between the Americas' frontiers of resource extraction and the depopulated Amerindian lands beyond also left observers, such as U.S. scholar and statesman George Perkins Marsh (1801–1882), with the strong impression of a once unspoiled "wilderness" degraded by human encroachment—a powerful concept in the emergence of American environmentalism.

By the mid-nineteenth century, the Industrial Revolution was bringing about a new age in not only Atlantic, but also global, environmental history. New industrial technologies—railroads, steamships, telegraphs, and even quinine (as a treatment for malarial fevers)—were fast opening new regions and new populations to Western military intrusions and global commodity markets, which supported growing industrial cities. Africa, Asia, and the Pacific world, as well as the Atlantic, were further transformed by rapid biological invasions, mass migrations, and plantation agriculture. The early-modern Atlantic experience had launched these processes of exchange and commodification and thus proved a portent for the environmental consequences of globalization in the industrial age.

SAMUEL WHITE

Bibliography

Cronon, William. *Changes in the Land: Indians, Colonists, and the Ecology of New England*. New York: Hill and Wang, 1983.

Crosby, Alfred. *Ecological Imperialism: The Biological Expansion of Europe, 900–1900*. New York: Cambridge University Press, 2004.

Dean, Warren. *With Broadax and Firebrand: The Destruction of the Brazilian Atlantic Forest*. Berkeley: University of California Press, 1995.

Mann, Charles. *1491: New Revelations of the Americas before Columbus*. New York: Alfred A. Knopf, 2005.

McNeill, John R. *Mosquito Empires: Ecology and War in the Greater Caribbean, 1620–1914*. New York: Cambridge University Press, 2010.

Ethnicity

Ethnicity is an elastic term in Atlantic history, used not only as a way of recognizing existing groups who were to be reimagined under the weight of colonization and slavery but also as a way to represent the collective responses of the peoples being so categorized and constructed. The concept of *ethnogenesis,* or the invention and reproduction of a sense of collective self, has emerged as a powerful tool for describing the building and rebuilding of cultures in response to the movements of people and inventions of new institutions that marked the Atlantic World. It serves in analyzing how enslaved and free individuals, colonizers and colonized, invented collective places in formative societies. While indigenous Americans, Europeans, and Africans had all devised collectivities based upon shared spaces, languages, cultures, spiritual practices, and kinship (real and fictive) long before their encounters in the Atlantic World, they radically reformulated these linkages as they moved along Atlantic paths. Observing ethnicity in formation offers one route for demonstrating how diverse peoples from four continents became Atlantic in new communities of, and claims to, identification and exclusion.

Defining Atlantic ethnicities is more complicated in practice than in principle. While modern historians tend to reject biological race as a fiction, some substitute ethnicity, which they associate with the idea of unchanging "traditional" cultures. However, communities, ethnic or racialized, seen as permanent still remain part of historical analysis. Some observers, including historians, simply reinscribe the colonial binary of superior/inferior on the static cultures they associate with ethnicity. Also, ethnicity is even more likely to collapse into meaningless uses of racialized concepts because the documentation on which scholars draw—from colonial and imperial planners and the official records they designed—labels the colonized in ways that reflect the logic of race-based colonial legal and economic systems rather than expressing the beliefs and strategies of the people so categorized.

One step toward locating ethnicity as a creative strategy would be observing how people used the commonalities they asserted through it to organize the social, institutional, and economic networks in which they lived. These networks were also the interfaces through which their creators—subalterns, that is, individuals in relatively weak positions—connected with larger and dominant elements of society. Such uses of ethnicity to make claims on resources or exclude others from access to them were an Atlantic-wide phenomenon, but the specific ethnic strategies developed depended upon local historical contexts and institutional structures.

Within the near-universal displacements of people from their home communities that marked the Atlantic World, ethnicity emerged as a prominent means for reconstituting claims of belonging, and through it individuals often demanded the rights correlated with those claims. In the early-modern world, membership in communities followed upon the unimpeded ability to exercise certain rights, as well as upon the performance of responsibilities for or compliance with duties imposed by central political authorities. Collective forms like ethnicity were less expressions of firm identity than they were strategic claims of identification and access in specific historical contexts. This essay examines ethnicity as flexible claims-making and as a response to institutional opportunities by members of each of the main groups formed by participants in the Atlantic World: indigenous Americans, Europeans, and African peoples. The primary examples focus on the specifically Iberian forms, rising where both law and the Catholic Church provided particular outlets through which local communities asserted themselves in ethnicized forms. Other legal and religious regimes in Africa, the Americas, and Europe gave rise to differing expressions of ethnicity, but the conditions of change, movement, and confrontation that brought about the need for local collectivities to claim them were similar across the Atlantic World.

Homogenizing Distinctions

Historians of the indigenous Americas have noted a "flattening" of intricate indigenous ethnic differentiation as a prominent side effect of European conquests. With regard to the Hispanic Americas, on which this essay focuses much of its analysis, this homogenization took two forms. First, the legal and fiscal aspects of colonial military rule drew upon Spain's corporate political form and thus granted indigenous peoples their own, singular, corporate identity, that of the "Indian," in exchange for payments of tribute; this abstract legal category ignored the diversity of Native communities formed around multiple distinctions. Second, even

when the state recognized specific indigenous ethnicities, it generally did so only at crude levels, for example by reducing the variety of Native communities in the Caribbean to "Caribs" and "Arawaks," or by negotiating special status with groups who performed exceptional services for the crown.

Yet these conceptual flattenings were not simply reductive. Within Spanish law, "Indianness" was inevitably about adapting local practices to serve the needs of colonial administration. The Spanish monarchy thus governed through subsidiary corporate bodies and depended upon semiautonomous local political structures to carry out the basic functions of governance. The so-called *república de indios* was the legal grant of corporate status to indigenous communities, requiring them to deal with issues internal to their own affairs, short of heinous criminal acts, through their customary laws. While local governance was far from independent (even the most basic right—the appointment of local rulers—was subject to the discretion of the Spanish authorities), it was not inconsequential. Tribute payment and compliance with forced-labor demands were parts of the crown's strategy in recognizing "Indianness"; but ethnic belonging was a counterclaim made by the Native communities affected—it represented their collective claims to participatory governance and access to land and kin, and it specified particular forms of compliance with Spanish legal demands for forced labor and tribute.

European-Based Iberian Communities

While Spanish conquerors dispersed many of the ethnic groupings they encountered, sometimes traumatically, the survivors immediately created new forms of ethnicity. Elites negotiated with the colonial state in order to claim ethnicity-based status—such as those of "Incas" in Peru or "Tlaxcalans" in Mexico—that flourished, especially since they bore attendant privileges like exemption from demands for tribute payments. These earlier ethnicized contrasts proved key to the Spanish conquest: the 1524 conquest of the K'iche' Maya of Guatemala, for example, was carried out predominantly by their Mesoamerican rivals of the moment, as allies of the Spaniards. Some of the privileges that such allies requested were personal rewards, but many of them sought, and received, collective favors as ethnicized groups. The courts were famously congested with communities litigating their collective standings with their conquerors and also against neighbors. Since scarce resources were so often tied to kinship and community, Spanish legal recognition of ethnic collectivity served as an instrument for claiming them.

Iberians in the New World, too, found themselves creating and recreating ethnic communities. Their senses of community were tied not only to local birthplaces but also to law, as the right to emigrate to and trade with the New World was given only to natives of the Spanish kingdoms. For this reason, a Spanish "nativeness," common across the empire, was legally created in the late sixteenth century, corresponding to the *república de españoles*, the legal structure establishing royal jurisdiction over most peoples of European descent in the Spanish Americas; a popular sense of a single community of Spaniards did not form beyond this abstract legal standing until the eighteenth century. Instead, regional allegiances to local places of origin in Iberia resonated even as immigrants from Europe enjoyed general privileges in the Americas relative to indigenous and African peoples.

In some cases, emigration from Iberia to the Americas was built around existing local communities, families, parishes, villages, or artisan guilds. Many European monarchs relocated whole families from one end of the empire to another, often populating and securing colonial claims with the empire's poor. In 1778 the Spanish crown issued an edict offering to transport the most impoverished Galicians to the Río de la Plata, as part of a strategy to colonize Patagonia. Two hundred families made the long and difficult journey; the monarchy supplied food, housing, and a small stipend. They found themselves in the remotest parts of the Americas, as much Galicians as they were Spaniards. Similarly ethnicized settlements, sometimes with religious characters, prevailed in the diverse British colonies in North America.

Ethnic-like ties of origin and distant kinship in Europe continued to matter in the Americas, especially to newcomers who arrived as individuals and depended upon established predecessors to assist them in the name of local solidarity. Residents of the city of Brihuega in Castile immigrated to Puebla, Mexico, en masse as their textile economy declined, and in so doing they transferred their intricate Castilian social network to Mexico. Even more important, emigrants used these kin connections to establish themselves economically and socially. Indeed, while Puebla was already producing textiles in the mid-sixteenth century, it was the later arrival of experts from Brihuega that pushed the city into regional leadership in textile production.

The tendency of emigrants from Europe to maintain at least some ethnic-like connections based upon places of origin is made evident by the ease with which they called upon those who had known them and their forebears at home, despite difficulties of travel and communication. Applicants to the Franciscan monastery at Puebla, Mexico, established the "purity of blood" standard required for admission by calling on local witnesses who could testify to their ancestors' freedom from illegitimacy, heresy, slavery, or conversion from Judaism or Islam. Candidates in Mexico originally from the Iberian Peninsula had little trouble rounding up witnesses; even an applicant from the Canary Islands produced three compatriots, two of whom had known his parents, and a third who had made his acquaintance only recently in Mexico City.

However, this kind of ethnic affiliation drawing on common origins could be more exclusionary and less benign. The Spanish chronicler Arzáns tells of the bloody battles that took place in early seventeenth-century Potosí, Upper Peru, between the Vicuñas (those born in Potosí or in Andalusía) and the Vascongados (those from the Basque country in present-day northern Spain). Despite sharing the American status of *vecinos*, that is, citizens, and a growing sense of quasi-racialized ethnic identification distinct from Native Americans, other colonists of European descent often chose to worship and live peacefully in proximity to others sharing their ancestral homelands and to preserve inherited markers of inclusion, particularly through in-marriages, intended to shore up their local standings collectively.

The production of new ethnic communities among immigrants to the Atlantic colonies of all the European kingdoms remains insufficiently studied. This neglect may well reflect the fact that many European immigrants were looking to leave behind encumbering pasts and benefited from the creation of racialized whiteness that allowed any person of European descent to claim superiority to those who could not, regardless of backgrounds. Creoles—the generations of purported European ancestry born in Spain's New World colonies—carried out a strong form of ethnogenesis by the late eighteenth century, carving out differences between themselves and their counterparts of recent Peninsular origin. Their emphasis on their own American indigenousness opened the way to constructing national identities in the late eighteenth century that included romantic evocations of extinguished Native cultures, albeit excluding their living descendants. They also participated in the production of the emerging racial science that elevated them biologically above both the European-born and the African-descended and Native American populations with whom they shared living space. But even these protonationalist discourses had limited currency, and some have argued that republican nationhood throughout Latin America was the result of the movements for independence of the early nineteenth century rather than their cause.

African-Based Communities

Perhaps the least transparent transformations—to the modern historian—of ethnicity in the Atlantic World took place among the Africans enslaved there, since our sources rarely speak of self-identification and depend so deeply on the limited, often hostile, perceptions of people other than the enslaved. In modern Africa, ethnonyms—the names given to specific ethnic groups—are often epithets bestowed by others. Studies of the diasporic identities of enslaved peoples have depended in great part on supposed ethnic origins in Africa as recorded in shipping records and in notarial and ecclesiastical documents in the Americas. In the Iberian Atlantic, such reportage was intended to meet the needs of slave traders and owners, the church, and other authorities rather than the needs of the enslaved themselves for community. A sophisticated literature exists critiquing the meanings of such labels, which often pointed to invented and generic New World categories rather than to home communities in Africa.

Nonetheless, in slavery studies ethnicity has been a central concern, as it seems to be one of the very few means of recognizing the humanity of the people enslaved, otherwise treated as nameless commodities. Certainly Africans traveled with historical memories and cultural tools that they called upon selectively when seeking community in their new American environments; yet cultural heritages from Africa by no means conferred community in these radically different circumstances. Conversely, people of differing communities in Africa collaborated in the Americas by adopting elements of one another's ancestral cultures. Atlantic ethnicities were specifically negotiated responses to Atlantic circumstances; sometimes one's coreligionists and colinguists were the most advantageous group through which to organize—but not always, or even often, given the radical dispersal and isolation of the individuals captured in Africa.

The Iberian world provided a set of voluntary institutions intended for mutual aid that people of African descent utilized widely for purposes of their own: Catholic confraternities (or lay brotherhoods) and African *cabildos de nación*, which were parallel associations not affiliated with the Catholic Church and drawn along the lines of similar types in West and Central Africa. Confraternity populations were sometimes mandated by agents of the Church; for example, the Dominican order created separate Rosary confraternities for Spaniards, Indians, blacks, and mulattoes in Spain, Portugal, their American possessions, and parts of Africa. Groups of Catholics in all of these populations also organized themselves and then petitioned the Church for formal recognition. Some of these latter groups were self-consciously ethnic, claiming kinship through origin in a Spanish or American city or an African *casta*, or ethnic group; others came from shared occupations or personal devotion to a particular saint.

For African Catholics, ethnic collectivity also raised questions of rights and exclusivity. Confraternities collected fees from members and alms from the wider community and spent those funds on public and private festivities, on funeral services, and on charitable assistance for members and their larger constituency. On religious feast days black confraternities marched in procession with all of the city's other confraternities, acting out colonial hierarchies but also demonstrating the solemn Catholic form of being racialized as black. *Cabildos* hosted dances that notoriously aroused the suspicions of Spanish authorities.

The confraternity of Nuestra Señora de los Reyes in Lima had a *banco*, or subgroup, for "Biafarans," which paid for funerals for dead slaves, abandoned by their masters, from whatever parts of the African coast their Portuguese buyers had designated by that name (probably modern southeastern Nigeria). These associations enabled free and better-off Africans to extend support to the newly arrived and less connected. There was ambivalence about membership: many confraternities made no ethnic claims, some created multiple ethnic *bancos*, and others exercised dramatic exclusivity. The constitution of Lima's confraternity of San Bartolomé in 1699 excluded all "who were not of the *casta* Luanga" and required that members not collect alms for another brotherhood. A member of San Bartolomé (a "Luanga") had been caught collecting alms for the Mosanga brotherhood and was to be expelled. Loango was, roughly, the western African coast north of the mouth of the Congo River, named from a trading polity there that shipped slaves from catchment regions like Mosanga (possibly modern Sangu of Gabon), likely just to its north; the dispute reminds us that the clear lines drawn between alleged groups might well have hidden actual ambivalences and multiple possibilities of ethnic belonging in Africa.

Forming new communities of Africans in the diaspora did not exclude continuing connections with communities of origin, however distant. Some of the Mahi—from one of the areas in West Africa (modern Benin) ravaged by Dahomean slavers— living in Rio de Janeiro not only sought to reconstruct community within a Catholic confraternity but also expressed ongoing concern for the state of the souls of their beleaguered kin in Africa. On the other hand, the members of the confraternity of San Juan de la Buenaventura in Lima expelled a portion of their membership in 1607: the founders called themselves "blacks of the Bioho *casta* born in Guinea," and they removed a subgroup of Bioho born in Panama because of their supposed poor behavior, drunkenness, and disrespect. Shared origins, actual or merely claimed strategically in the Americas, did not always merit continued alliance.

***

Peoples of the early-modern Atlantic World experienced change and continuity in very modern ways. The majority of Atlantic residents could trace radical migration patterns in their recent past, often many times, over several generations, and with varying degrees of their own volition. In addition to physical dislocations, denizens of the Atlantic also experienced institutional shifts—new political, legal, and religious regimes. Ethnicity provided a collective language for strangers to join together to make powerful claims amid these changes, and the institutional frameworks of the Iberian Atlantic provided them with opportunities to express themselves collectively, acquire corporate rights, and join in negotiating obligations. While the specific forms of ethnic expression would be particular to the differing European legal and religious frameworks, the impulse and even some of the language of these claims traveled across empires, as active strategies, often borrowing from discourses of race and political subjugation, creating the forms that we now term *ethnicity*.

KAREN B. GRAUBART

Bibliography

Altman, Ida. *Transatlantic Ties in the Spanish Empire: Brihuega, Spain, and Puebla, Mexico, 1560–1620*. Stanford, CA: Stanford University Press, 2000.

Cañizares-Esguerra, Jorge, and James Sidbury. "Mapping Ethnogenesis in the Early Modern Atlantic." *William and Mary Quarterly*, 3rd ser., 68, no. 2 (April 2011): 181–208.

Canny, Nicholas, and Anthony Pagden, eds. *Colonial Identity in the Atlantic World 1500–1800*. Princeton, NJ: Princeton University Press, 1987.

Graubart, Karen B. "'*So color de una cofradía*': Catholic Confraternities and the Development of Afro-Peruvian Ethnicities in Early Colonial Peru." *Slavery and Abolition* 33, no. 2 (March 2012): 43–64.

Owensby, Brian. *Empire of Law and Indian Justice in Colonial Mexico*. Stanford, CA: Stanford University Press, 2008.

Soares, Mariza de Carvalho. *People of Faith: Slavery and African Catholics in Eighteenth-Century Rio de Janeiro*. Durham, NC: Duke University Press, 2011.

Family and Family Networks

Everyone who set foot on a ship to cross the Atlantic Ocean came from and remained part of a family. Yet travelers and their personal connections across a vast watery divide often have been studied apart from their families and instead in conjunction with abstract themes such as piracy, conquest, or religion. Families have accordingly been underrepresented as enabling strategies in the historiography of the Atlantic World. This essay explores the significant extent to which families, through networks of emigrants, facilitated the integration of the early-modern Atlantic. They increased European populations in the New World, created new markets, and communicated elements of their American experiences back to relatives in the realms of Europe. Examples from the transatlantic connections between Spain and Peru also show how families tried to advance their own fortunes through transatlantic exchanges. They gathered family finances to send members across the Atlantic, profited from trading through family links in the Americas and Africa, and transferred money across the ocean. Through these social connections and economic transactions, families formed central networks that moved people through the European spaces of the Atlantic.

Emigrants who traveled to the New World worked hard to maintain their ties to home. Through ships and passengers, families stayed connected, provided material goods and news to one another, counseled children, and cared for members of extended families. Indeed, family networks provided the rationale for traveling, the funds to travel, and the preparations for a successful voyage.

Family ties in the New World served as a major motivation to leave Europe. In the 1540s and 1550s, husbands in Lima, at the prompting of a Spanish royal decree, called for their wives to travel to the New World. Spouses sent money through trusted third parties to help make the women's trips as comfortable as possible. Parents invited grown children to move to the Indies and assist them in business or to care for them in old age. Uncles and aunts wrote to nephews with news of good opportunities for making names for themselves.

These family connections were equally significant in terms of securing the necessary documentation, a travel license from the House of Trade, or Casa de la Contratación, in Seville, to travel to Spain's Indies. In one letter presented to the crown to justify the royal favor to move, a mother wrote to tell her son that she was recently widowed. With no one to look after her estate, lest it dwindle to nothing, she begged him to board the first ship destined for Peru. Siblings also served as sponsors for sisters or brothers who wished to travel. When Juan de Ayala wanted to go to Peru, he attested that his brother Pedro had lived for more than fifteen years with his wife and children in Lima (Protocolos Notariales, Signatura 6743). On the same day, Juan's nephew Pedro, son of the elder Pedro, followed the same procedure, asking for a license to visit his parents in Peru. Witnesses in Spain testified to the presence of the Ayalas in Peru based on their hearing Pedro's letters read aloud. Given the tight-knit colonial society, Pedro Ayala's established life in Lima offered his brother and son a home and sufficiently promising connections for employment to impress royal officials and justify the would-be emigrant's license to embark.

Fathers and mothers seeking licenses to travel to the Indies also made explicit reference to the possibilities for good marriage matches for their daughters. The large numbers of males, supported by the opportunities opened to them by plunder and in silver in sixteenth-century Peru, were reputed to make the marriage market there better than that in Spain, and family connections that could secure a potential groom in the New World constituted good reasons to send a daughter across the Atlantic.

Family connections that helped to move relatives from Europe to the New World also moved money. Individuals frequently entrusted kin with their petty trade negotiations. Diego de Segura took 1,000 pounds of olive oil to the Indies to sell for his aunt, the widow Francisca Segura (Protocolos, Signatura 7764). Other passengers fulfilled requests from relatives to carry goods for small-scale trade opportunities onboard ships from Spain. Relatives in the New World specified exactly what goods they desired, such as items of clothing. At times, these items might have been for private consumption, but in other instances they were goods destined for sale. The transit of trusted relatives between Iberia and the Indies opened up the possibility of family profit.

Families with a history of traveling between Peru and Spain built their knowledge of the transatlantic terrain into more substantial business endeavors. In 1580 Pedro de Mollinedo and Diego de Mollinedo, his *hijo natural* (full brother), appeared before a Sevillian notary to arrange that Diego would serve his father in Lima as clerk for selling merchandise and collecting payments. Diego noted that the pair could count on assistance in the New World, "because," he said, "I have a rich mother in Peru and we assume and have understood that when I go there she will favor me" (Protocolos Francisco de Almonte). The Mollinedos counted on these ties to Diego's mother, even in the absence of a formal marriage between his parents. Her expected financial contribution served as extra motivation and justification to cross the Atlantic again.

The archival records showing these family strategies—mostly notarial records preserved in the Archivo Histórico de Protocolos (Seville)—privilege Spaniards with families in Iberia, but they also hint at parallel Afro-Iberian and mestizo networks. In Lima, a free Afro-Sevillian woman named a sister back in Spain as heir in a will that left a dry goods store and slaves. In multiple cases, indigenous women in Peru sent money to their mestizo sons and daughters who had joined their fathers in Spain. These might be token sums, but in some instances they amounted to hundreds of silver pesos that could pay for an education, a dowry, or entry into a convent. In the era of conquest, sons born to indigenous women and Spanish men became important assets for their Spanish fathers (or uncles or brothers) in conducting business in Iberia. Juan Martínez was born in Cuzco to an indigenous mother and Spanish father and eventually lived in Spain. But in 1557, Martínez's father, the merchant Manuel Martín, sent Juan back to Peru as his agent. Non-Spaniards used networks similar to those of Spaniards for social and economic purposes.

Family connections also pervaded the networks of royal officials often oversimplified as "empire." Christopher Columbus's appointment of his brothers to political positions in Hispaniola in the 1490s is emblematic of how elite family networks dominated the political, economic, and social structure of Spanish settlements in the Indies. The island's Iberian elite maintained close ties and sailed frequently between Spain and the islands to consolidate adventure and potential riches for single men. But the family networks functioning in the Atlantic World shifted by the 1540s to less itinerant and more settled patterns, as men and women came to Peru and elsewhere to live and work in cities and to reunite their families. As the economy of Iberian Spain sank into challenging times at the dawn of the seventeenth century, petitions to secure licenses to the Indies rocketed in numbers.

Migrations in the sixteenth- and seventeenth-century Iberian Atlantic patterns flowed through calculated emigration by individuals and family groups. Indentured servitude or government-sponsored migration schemes, common drivers of migration in other contexts, did not dominate in this instance. Although Spanish authorities desired to settle their American territories with European families as models for indigenous populations to follow, the transatlantic family networks of the sixteenth and seventeenth centuries generally operated below the radar of government policies and commercial networks. Individual family initiatives prompted much of the travel between Europe and the New World. Family communications from one side of the Atlantic to the other offered incentives and means for travel. Relatives offered strategic information about how and when to travel. Parents and siblings allocated funds for their journeys. These small-scale, highly personal actions were resilient threads in the grand transatlantic tapestries of kings.

JANE E. MANGAN

Bibliography

Altman, Ida. *Transatlantic Ties in the Spanish Empire, Brihuega, Spain and Puebla, Mexico, 1560—1620*. Stanford, CA: Stanford University Press, 2000.

Archivo Histórico de Protocolos (Seville), Protocolos, Signatura 5383, Francisco de Almonte, Oficio 8, fol. 470, October 11, 1570.

Archivo Histórico de Protocolos (Seville), Protocolos Notariales, Signatura 6743, Francisco Roman, Oficio 11, fol. 636, March 9, 1560.

Archivo Histórico de Protocolos (Seville), Protocolos, Signatura 7764, Francisco Diaz, Oficio 13, fol. 148v, 1570. Testamento de Francisca Segura.

Otte, Enrique. *Cartas privadas de emigrantes a Indias, 1540–1616*. Mexico: Fondo de Cultura Económica, 1996.

Pearsall, Sarah. *Atlantic Families: Lives and Letters in the Later Eighteenth Century*. Oxford: Oxford University Press, 2008.

Family Production and Commercial Labor

Around 1500, families organized most of the world's production. They sustained themselves, traded locally, and also supported those who ruled and led worship. Expanding maritime trade, however, exerted pressure on family production in the sixteenth century and after, particularly in the Atlantic. The incorporation of the Americas into global trade networks in the sixteenth century radically increased the demand for trade goods and for the labor to make them. Silver mined in Spanish America fueled trade spanning the globe; the sugar harvested in the Atlantic colonies of America drew goods from Europe and people from Africa, who were sold as commodities, into expanding commercial systems. In time, other commodities— from tobacco in the Chesapeake to cochineal dye in Oaxaca in southern Mexico—entered oceanic trade, creating arrangements in which people worked for the profit of others in distant markets. This long transition—from sustenance-oriented production to labor supporting trade and profit— reshaped the Americas and the Atlantic into a commercialized world.

Profit-seeking entrepreneurs promoted the production for trade that pulled workers into the commercial economy. Seeing sources of revenue for colonial regimes, monarchs, as well as their representatives in local arenas, backed those efforts. Though Amerindians, Africans, and their diverse descendants were pressed to labor in the emerging commercial world, they often preferred to limit their involvement in work for profit-driven, distant markets. Production for use and local markets enhanced the autonomy of families and communities, allowing them meaningful control over everyday needs and an ability to resist or negotiate the demands of those who ruled and aimed to profit from their efforts. The history of the Americas after 1500 revolved around these ongoing tensions between powerful interests promoting trade and labor for others and families seeking to maintain capacities for autonomous production.

Contact with Europeans

Before 1492 people across the hemisphere organized their lives in diverse ways. States, including the Inca regime that dominated the Andes, and the Aztecs and other military powers that competed to rule Mesoamerica (now southern Mexico and Guatemala), built armies, religious institutions, and exchange systems by extracting goods and labor service from local cultivating communities that also sustained themselves. Along Atlantic coasts villagers grew crops to feed families, less subject to exactions from mostly local and limited powers. And across vast continental interiors, mobile groups of hunters and gatherers (often also cultivators) lived off the land—sustaining families and clans.

Europeans arrived expecting to rule and to profit. Yet early on they lacked the local knowledge and coercive capacity to force radical change in established approaches to production and to control it. During the early decades of contact Europeans depended on Native leaders as intermediaries and on indigenous forms of extraction to gain access to labor and commodities. In the Caribbean from the 1490s, Spaniards relied on Arawak notables to gain food and natural resources, as well as for access to gangs of workers who would pan for the gold that funded the colonial enterprise. During the ensuing conquests of Mesoamerica and the Andes, grants to receive tribute goods and labor service from indigenous communities were sanctioned as *encomiendas*—which transferred to Europeans precisely what indigenous overlords had previously claimed. Spaniards imagined that they ruled over Native subjects, but Native lords saw their relationships with the powerful newcomers as useful if uncertain alliances, while production, sustenance, tribute goods, and labor services all depended on continuing household production.

Beyond the Caribbean, Mesoamerica, and the Andes, only the Portuguese on the coasts of Brazil kept contacts with indigenous peoples in the sixteenth century. Beginning in 1500, the Portuguese traded with the Tupí and their neighbors, delivering hatchets, cutlery, and other metal wares that facilitated cultivation, hunting, and gathering in exchange for brazilwood (a red dyestuff valued in Europe). These exchanges linked relative equals, although Europeans resisted recognizing the limits of their own powers along with their reliance on indigenous trading partners and Native production within households and communities.

These early and relatively balanced relationships broke down everywhere within a half century. In the Caribbean, Mesoamerica, and the Andes, smallpox, plague, typhus, and other diseases imported across the Atlantic devastated Native populations, leaving them incapable of sustaining existing production, tribute, and labor services—and ironically leaving surviving families, who had lost so many kin and neighbors, with ample land for production on their own. In coastal Brazil, disease diminished indigenous populations and productive capacity, and in midcentury most remaining Tupí had all the hatchets, knives, and bowls they could use. They saw no gain in continuing to cut brazilwood for Europeans—and refused to trade, thwarting an early European attempt to convert family production to extracting surpluses for remote markets.

Two Commodities

Around 1550, as the first European ways of taking surpluses via collaborations with Native lords and trade with indigenous producers collapsed, silver and sugar, the two great commodity economies that would shape the Americas into the nineteenth century, began to develop. Silver and sugar produced for global markets generated profit for Europeans and transformed the lives of Native peoples and newcomers across the Americas. Labor—defined as dependent production of goods owned by an entrepreneur, merchant, or master—became a way of life for growing numbers of Native Americans and throngs of enslaved immigrants taken from Africa. Still, household producers adapted and persisted, sustaining families, communities, and many of the laborers (including slaves) who worked to supply rising global trades.

Gold and silver were native to the Americas, mined in small quantities, and used mostly for aristocratic artistic display. Across Europe and Asia, however, the same metals served as money. When the Europeans arrived in the Americas, therefore, these metals took on new commercial meaning, increasing demand for them and consequently their value. Before 1550 the Spaniards commandeered Native workers to mine gold in small quantities in the Caribbean and Mesoamerica; silver as well as gold was found in the Andes. Radical change came after 1551, when the emperor of Ming China decreed silver to be the only valid money in the world's largest population and economy. The price of silver doubled just as Europeans learned of literal mountains of the metal at Potosí, high in the Andes, at Taxco and Pachuca in Mesoamerica, and at Zacatecas and Guanajuato in northern New Spain (now Mexico).

The silver boom—from 1550 to 1650—started first at Potosí. From 1550 to 1570, mines were near the surface, worked by Native populations using indigenous smelting techniques. In the 1570s, surface ores became scarce, and Spanish miners turned to veins deep underground. Tunneling, draining shafts, and refining less-rich ores by amalgamation with mercury required growing numbers of workers—some skilled, most needing only strong bodies, and all facing the risks of labor underground or exposure to mercury's toxicity. Such workers were mobilized by combinations of regime mandates and employers' incentives. Early Native miners, if they survived disease and danger, might stay on as skilled producers. Larger numbers came via the *mita*, the Inca draft that viceroy Francisco de Toledo reasserted to provide laborers to Potosí beginning in the 1570s. Under the Incas, the *mita* had drawn rotating work gangs, seasonally, for major building projects—palaces, temples, and roads, usually near workers' communities. The Inca draft thus presumed that its temporarily conscripted workers were sustained by family and community production. The Spanish *mita*, however, drew villagers far from home to work for a year. They received low wages when they worked as conscripts and no payments during periods of "rest"—when they usually toiled "outside" the draft, seeking substitute wages from other employers to sustain themselves. Over the decades, many worked for a year at Potosí and returned to home communities and family production; others stayed on to become skilled laborers, paid well for assuming deadly risks.

The century-long boom in silver depended on family production in Native villages, rotating labor by men drafted from designated communities, and a growing core of skilled workers living permanently at the mines. Urban markets for food, firewood, fibers, and other supplies grew as Potosí became a city of over 100,000, and Lima approached 50,000 as the center of Spanish administration, finance, and trade. Early on, the urban populations were fed and clothed by household producers in Andean communities reconstituted as indigenous republics. *Kurakas* (Native lords) and *encomenderos* (Spanish overlords) took surpluses from villagers to sell in the cities. In time, mining and urban demand stimulated the development of irrigated commercial estates along the coast of Peru; as Native populations there died of disease, the estates came to depend on enslaved Africans. Shipyards appeared at Guayaquil, also worked by African slaves. Large textile shops employed Native workers at Quito. Chile produced wheat, wine, and olive oil—mostly through the work of Hispanic tenant families on commercial estates. Livestock came north to Potosí from regions now in northwest Argentina, tended by African and mixed herders. Underlying everything, family producers—most in Native communities, others as estate tenants—produced the food and clothing required by all and provided reservoirs of laborers for the commercial economy.

A silver economy developed simultaneously around the city of Mexico. There, as in Peru, Spanish entrepreneurs mined underground and refined ores with mercury—creating growing demand for workers. Skilled permanent laborers were mostly free men of mixed origins, paid well to face the daily dangers. Less-skilled workers rotated weekly from nearby communities in the *repartimiento* draft—a replication of the Aztec *coatequil*. Sustenance for mining centers and the growing city of Mexico, approaching 70,000 residents around 1600, came from Native communities again reconsolidated legally as semiautonomous republics and from new commercial estates raising wheat and grazing cattle, hogs, and sheep on lands vacated by depopulation. Mexico City and the estates that supplied it relied on permanent workers who were enslaved Africans or free people of mixed origins—and on the seasonal labor of men and boys from landed indigenous communities.

Family production on community lands remained foundational to the silver economy in Mesoamerica, too. There, however, Native power centered on local councils of community notables, not on regional lords (like Andean *kurakas*) whose power might extend to wider polities. And in Mesoamerica, conscripted workers labored for a week, not a year (as in the Andes)—allowing continuing participation in family and community production. When the *repartimiento* draft collapsed in the 1630s, community residents continued to cultivate the land and supply urban markets. They also labored at mines, cities, and estates—for cash wages, often in gangs led by village labor brokers. To the south and southeast, across Oaxaca, Yucatán, Chiapas, and Guatemala, limited silver curtailed commercial production, leaving family producers in indigenous republics as the basis of the entire economy.

The challenges of building a silver economy in northern Mexico at Zacatecas and Guanajuato proved greater. The northern mines were surrounded by independent, mobile, hunting, gathering, and cultivating peoples the Mesoamericans called Chichimecas. They had no tradition of providing surpluses to rulers—and no interest in working for the profit of Spaniards. Chichimeca attacks delayed mining development from the 1550s to the 1590s. Before and during those wars, Otomí communities from areas north of Mexico City drove farther north to claim lands and build communities around Querétaro. They and other Mesoamericans joined Spaniards in the fight against Chichimecas;

Otomí Querétaro provided a base of family production to sustain the war and the silver economy that soared after 1590. Chichimecas who survived war and disease took refuge in mountain enclaves or settled in the mission communities founded to establish them in families and convert them.

After the wars, the region around Querétaro, Guanajuato, and Zacatecas—called the Bajío—built a mining economy that in some ways paralleled earlier developments in the Andes and Mesoamerica. Men of mixed ancestry did most mine labor and were paid ore shares and high wages to compensate for the risks they faced. Towns focused on crafts and making cloth, with household producers living side by side with large workshops using permanent workers. Some of these workers were African slaves; growing numbers were of mixed ancestry, free and employed for salaries. Grazing properties relied on African slaves, who over the years became free mulatto *vaqueros* ("cowboys"). Commercial estates worked by salaried laborers and seasonal hands who were paid day wages fed almost everyone—except the family tenant producers who sustained themselves and sent sons to estate fields, mines, and cities to work for wages.

Although the combination of commercial and family production that developed in the Bajío mirrored the similar balance in the Andes and Mesoamerica, important differences also marked social relations there—and on the plateaus stretching north. Across Spanish North America, almost everyone was an immigrant: Europeans, Africans, and Mesoamericans; entrepreneurs, workers, and cultivators. Family production was rarely a right of community membership; it depended on leasing lands from estate owners, who always claimed to be Spanish, yet often were mulattoes a few generations out of slavery. From the late sixteenth to the early eighteenth centuries, the silver economy of the Bajío and Spanish North America rose and receded in generally upward waves, while population remained sparse. Mine workers, cloth makers, artisans, and estate residents—both workers and tenants—survived well enough. However, after 1770, silver production, the commercial economy, and population growth soared, and the resulting demographic pressures made a majority without rights to land "expendable." Salary and wage cuts, evictions, and unemployment stalked the Bajío. Tensions escalated in the most commercial silver economy in the Atlantic World as family production was eviscerated.

Sugar Economies

After 1550, while the silver economies surged across Spanish America, the first vast sugar and slave economy developed in Brazil. With the collapse of the brazilwood trade, Portuguese colonizers and their Genoese financiers looked for a new source of profit. Sugar had been raised by Italians and Spaniards (using bound Muslim slaves as workers) in the Mediterranean since the Crusades; growing markets had led Genoese investors to introduce cane on eastern Atlantic islands, where African slaves predominated as labor. The rich clay soils of Brazil's coast welcomed the crop, but Africans were costly to transport across the Atlantic. Although a few skilled slave artisans came from the islands of the eastern Atlantic, early Brazilian growers forced Native workers to produce their cane. The crown and Jesuit missionaries gathered Native inhabitants along the coast into villages to learn Christianity and settle as cultivators—they would become family producers who supported themselves and provided seasonal harvest labor at nearby plantations. To capture more permanent workers, planters sent armed expeditions into the interior, offered Christianity (in Portuguese) to startled Native peoples, and used their rejection as a ruse to enslave them as enemies of the faith. The two ways of taking Native labor grounded the early plantation system: bound workers labored permanently, and mission villagers cut cane seasonally for wages (while a few African slaves brought the skills of cultivating cane and refining sugar from the Atlantic islands). The first great plantation colony in the Americas grew by drawing key workers seasonally from communities of indigenous family producers.

By the late sixteenth century it was clear that sugar could be made in Brazil on a large scale. Expanding markets in Europe made it profitable to do so. But with Native peoples living among Europeans, imported contagious diseases spread, and the Native bondsmen and villagers who had built the first sugar economy of Brazil vanished just as opportunities for profits soared. To sustain the sugar economy after 1600, African slaves became the primary laborers at Brazilian plantations, and at all others that developed subsequently across the tropical Americas. Yet family production did not disappear, even in the sugar-and-slave economy that shaped Atlantic America from 1550 to the 1880s. To cut costs and give slaves a precious bit of autonomy, many planters in Brazil and the Caribbean permitted provision grounds where slaves, often living as families, used "free" time to grow food for themselves. Planters and port towns also bought food from family growers, some of them just inland from Jamaican plantations, others from as far away as villages in New England. The more the balance of sugar production in the tropics shifted toward the full-time work of slaves, the more family producers remained essential to the highly specialized commercial sugar economy. In a parallel development, as Chesapeake planters in the late seventeenth century turned to slaves to grow tobacco, they depended on English "yeoman" family producers to sustain the populations of Virginia and Maryland.

Spain's silver economy in the Americas declined briefly after 1650; Andean primacy gave way after 1700 to New Spain (now Mexico), where output rose to unprecedented heights. Sugar shifted from Brazil to flourish in the British Caribbean, then to soar after 1750 in French Saint-Domingue. Production and labor regimes forged before 1650 carried on, adapting to new regions and market conditions. In the silver economies, family producers everywhere supported permanent and seasonal labor—indigenous and Hispanic. In sugar economies, slaves were sustained in part by the produce of family farmers in New England villages and in part by their own efforts on provision grounds.

Resurgent Family Production

The land rights granted to the indigenous republics in Spanish America allowed Andean and Mesoamerican villagers the autonomy to negotiate limited independence—and in the Andes to mount insurrection in the 1780s, when a sputtering silver economy, rising Spanish demands for taxes, and the needs of a growing population could not be reconciled. When Saint-Domingue sugar production and slavery reached new heights, also in the 1780s, slaves approached 90 percent of the population just as Paris revolutionaries proclaimed liberty and equality. Conflicts in Saint-Domingue escalated into a Haitian revolution that by 1804 ended

slavery, French rule, and plantation production on the western end of the island. Armed ex-slaves took over the abandoned plantations for family cultivation. Their reclamation of family autonomy anticipated the strategies of ex-slaves on other Caribbean islands when the British (1838) and the French (1848) finally ended slavery on plantations there.

A parallel transformation—from intense commercial development to family production—occurred by 1820 in the Bajío, the most dynamic silver mining, textile, and agricultural region of New Spain. Workers without land rights had faced population pressure, falling incomes, rising rents, and evictions as silver production soared after 1770. They struggled on until Napoleon's invasion of Spain in 1808 loosened the grip of local authorities; many joined the political revolt begun in the region led by Padre Miguel Hidalgo in 1810. That uprising, though soon crushed, opened the way for ten years of popular insurgency across the Bajío, resulting in a collapse of mining in Guanajuato and a family takeover of cultivation in the countryside. Just before Mexico became an independent republic in 1821, an armed rural majority took control of the region that had led the world in silver production and commercial cultivation for a century. They converted its rich bottomlands to family production and maintained that preferred way of life for decades into the National Era.

Family production sustained Europeans, indigenous Americans, and enslaved Africans across vast regions of the Americas throughout the early-modern Atlantic Era. Families supported commercial production and labor in silver, sugar, and other commodities. Production for sustenance proved the preferred way of life for many among the growing numbers of people who worked in the most commercial eighteenth-century economies: Haitian (and other) slaves, along with laborers and tenants in the Bajío, found working for the benefit of others—taken to exploitative extremes—wanting. Amid political conflicts in the Atlantic World, families worked to rebuild their productive capacities—some taking arms and risking their lives to do so. In the process of taking down the leading American engines of the first global economy, New Spain's silver and Saint-Domingue's sugar, they exemplified the way that the most dynamic American economy of the nineteenth century also would grow. While cotton and slavery expanded across the

U.S. South to sustain industries in England and New England, farm families committed to household production settled western regions of the United States. The contradictions among slave labor, free labor, and family production culminated in a devastating Civil War that ended slavery, enabling family farmers to become central protagonists in the national myth of the richest nation in a new industrial world.

JOHN TUTINO

Bibliography

Bakewell, Peter. *Miners of the Red Mountain: Indian Labor in Potosí, 1545–1650.* Albuquerque: University of New Mexico Press, 1984.

Dubois, Laurent. *Avengers of the New World: The Story of the Haitian Revolution.* Cambridge, MA: Harvard University Press, 2005.

Graham, Richard. *Feeding the City: From Street Market to Liberal Reform in Salvador, Brazil, 1780–1860.* Austin: University of Texas Press, 2010.

McCusker, John, and Russell Menard. *The Economy of British America, 1607–1789.* Chapel Hill: University of North Carolina Press, 1991.

Sauer, Carl. *The Early Spanish Main.* Berkeley: University of California Press, 1966.

Schwartz, Stuart. *Sugar Plantations in the Formation of Brazilian Society: Bahia, 1550–1835.* Cambridge: Cambridge University Press, 1985.

Tutino, John. *Making a New World: Founding Capitalism in the Bajío and Spanish North America.* Durham, NC: Duke University Press, 2011.

Zulawski, Ann. *"They Eat from Their Labor": Work and Social Change in Colonial Bolivia.* Pittsburgh, PA: University of Pittsburgh Press, 1995.

Foods and Diets

The profound and permanent shifts in global dietary patterns during and after the large-scale transatlantic traffic and migrations of Europeans and Africans following 1492 were felt nowhere as quickly and deeply as in the Atlantic World itself—the four regions that are today North and South America (including the Caribbean), Europe, and Africa. These new patterns of food consumption followed from the transatlantic circulation of crop varieties and domestic livestock, supplanting or complementing local ones, and from critical changes in land use, triggered by colonization and the clearing of timber for plantations and for the construction and maintenance of large maritime vessels.

Markets for foodstuffs, buoyed by new consumption practices, expanded to include complex transoceanic trade networks connecting Ireland, Nantes, and Martinique, for example, as well as such regional entrepôts as Louisbourg in Nova Scotia and St. Eustatius in the Caribbean. At local levels in the Americas, autonomy and starvation often characterized early settlements and developing plantations. However, broader markets emerged in the late seventeenth and eighteenth centuries as these regions began to produce agricultural surpluses. Both small farmers and slave populations often depended on food produced both within plantation grounds and on adjacent marginal plots. Itinerant food sellers, often women, emerged as key marketers in the Caribbean and in urban Brazil. As transatlantic commerce increased, markets in urban centers throughout the Atlantic World began to offer foodstuffs previously unknown.

North America

At the end of the fifteenth century, Amerindian diets throughout North America centered on mixtures of maize, beans, and squash, supplemented by game, shellfish, and other seafood. Maize, originating in Mesoamerica, had reached the eastern seaboard and the upper Mississippi and Ohio valleys by 1100 CE; certain varieties were cultivated up to 50° north latitude throughout the St. Lawrence River valley and the Great Lakes. Beans of a far wider variety than existed in Europe were cultivated and consumed in North America, and squash, unknown in Europe, constituted a third basic element of this diet.

European colonists introduced a wide variety of Old World crops—including wheat, rye, peas, melons, citrus fruits, cabbage, and lettuce—in attempts to replicate their own backgrounds and expertise. They were also responsible for introducing both sweet potatoes and potatoes, native to the Caribbean and South America, to North America. The diets of early colonists were monotonous, consisting largely of rye-and-maize bread, salted meat, and game. Only from the mid-eighteenth century onward did autumn harvests last the whole year or did diets expand to include more vegetables and fresh meat. Catholic missionaries in the borderlands of southwestern North America were more successful in cultivating wheat for their bread (and for the Eucharist) and grapes for wine. In the southern colonies, plantation slaves consumed a diet of pork and maize and also cultivated and consumed African varieties of rice alongside the Asian variety cultivated in the Carolinas for export. Trade with the Caribbean brought large quantities of molasses into the northeastern colonies, and by the mid-eighteenth century rum distilled from these syrups was produced for local and regional consumption on a proto-industrial scale, as well as for export to Africa for slaves. By this time, the French fur trade had already introduced distilled alcohol (mostly French brandy) to populations in the interior of the continent.

Caribbean

Amerindians in the Caribbean also consumed maize, although of a soft variety, and their diets were dominated by such starchy tubers as manioc (cassava), sweet potato, and arrowroot and by seafood, marine animals, and reptiles such as tortoise. Europeans began introducing nonnative crops and a host of domesticated livestock (pigs and cattle in particular) for their own consumption immediately upon arrival. The European practice of crop and livestock introductions took on particular resonance with the development of the transatlantic slave trade. The growth of plantations, especially in the Caribbean, specializing in the production of commodities for export and reliant on enslaved labor forces resulted in populations dependent for their subsistence on others. The Spanish introduced bananas and plantains, which were of Asian origin, to Hispaniola via the Canary Islands (1516), in addition to melons and citrus fruit; they also brought millet and taro (dasheen, a tuber) from West Africa. Higher-yielding African varieties of yams arrived with slaving voyages and quickly overtook consumption of native Caribbean yams. Andean (white) potatoes reached the Caribbean indirectly, from Europe. The practice of introducing new foodstuffs to meet the food crises exacer-

bated by slavery continued until the end of the eighteenth century, when the French brought mangoes to Martinique from Mauritius in the Indian Ocean (1782), and the British brought ackee (a fruit, 1778) from equatorial Africa and breadfruit (1793) from islands in the Pacific Ocean to the West Indies. North Atlantic salt cod and European (and later North American) salt beef were also essential, although minor, components of the diets of the enslaved, testifying to the complexity of the transatlantic networks of foodstuffs. Colonists of European origin consumed European food when possible, relying on transatlantic shipments of wheat flour for their bread (as wheat did not grow in the Caribbean), olive oil, dried fruit, salt beef, wine, and brandy; they resorted to locally cultivated food mostly when European food was too expensive or unavailable.

Meso- and South America

Aztecs and other Amerindians in Mesoamerica had complex diets differentiated by social hierarchies of consumption. Their basic diet was built around the triumvirate of maize, beans, and squash, supplemented by a wide range other foodstuffs, such as amaranth (both leaves and seeds as a grain), tomatoes, chilies, chocolate, and such fruits as guava and avocado; they obtained protein from domesticated rabbits and dogs, wild game, lizards and amphibians, insects, freshwater fish, and marine resources such as shellfish and other seafood. After the introduction of European fruits and vegetables and the rapid proliferation of the domesticated sheep, cattle, and pigs brought by Spanish and Portuguese colonists, Amerindians adapted their food habits to include European wheat flour, beef, pork and pork fat, and citrus fruits, as well as other Mediterranean staples such as olive oil, chickpeas, eggplant, and onions.

In the Andean highlands, the potato was the staple crop, cultivated since between 3000 and 2000 BCE. The Incas developed sophisticated storage techniques based on drying and freezing, by which means the nutritional value of the tuber could be retained for several years. This foodstuff was the basis of the diet of enslaved and conscripted Amerindian miners, dragooned by the Spanish in the sixteenth and seventeenth centuries to work in the silver mines in Potosí. The large-scale availability of Spanish cattle, slaughtered for their hides more than their meat, meant that slaves in South America consumed far more fresh beef than slaves elsewhere in the Atlantic World. The diets of the enslaved in South America were also characterized by imports from Africa such as palm oil, peas, beans, and African varieties of rice and yams.

Europe

European diets saw no-less-dramatic changes as transatlantic voyages brought new food crops and new patterns of consumption. Portuguese, French, and English fishermen brought salted codfish from the northern Atlantic to northern Europe, where its intense popularity in the sixteenth century predated the establishment of European colonies in the northeastern part of North America. Diets in the Balkans and in eastern and central Europe rapidly integrated Mesoamerican chilies, beans, squash, and maize introduced—unexpectedly—by Ottoman Turks during their westward military campaigns in the first half of the sixteenth century. The Ottomans had most likely come into contact with these crops in Portuguese colonies in India. The Spanish also introduced the Andean potato to Spain, although it was cultivated only in the northwestern part of the Iberian peninsula, where it became part of Basque shipboard rations for their fishing expeditions to the northern Atlantic. Basque fishermen, in turn, brought the potato to Ireland in the first half of the seventeenth century. By that date, potatoes were already being consumed in Italy and in central and northern Europe, as they had accompanied the sixteenth-century overland military campaigns of the Spanish Habsburgs. Although the tomato arrived in Europe with the returning Spanish, it did not enter into European diets until the end of the eighteenth and early nineteenth century, as it was a member of the deadly nightshade botanical family and was believed to be poisonous.

European consumption practices were transformed also by integration of the key tropical stimulants, sometimes characterized as "drugs," cultivated in the Americas and exported across the Atlantic: sugar (and sugar by-products such as molasses and rum), coffee, and chocolate. By the sixteenth century, sugar refineries had been established in northwestern Europe (Antwerp, London, the

Loire Valley) to make the myriad sugary confections that larger production from the sugar islands of the eastern Atlantic, from Madeira to São Tomé, had developed from earlier modest-scaled and expensive Mediterranean production for use as a spice, as medicine, and as decoration. Consumption exploded when Brazilian and then Caribbean plantation sugar appeared in the last decades of the sixteenth and into the seventeenth century, and, as the price came down, sugar was used as a preservative for fruits and a sweetener for an entirely new form of preparation (desserts). In addition, sugar assisted the growth in consumption of the new tropical stimulants, in themselves bitter and unpleasant to European palates. Chocolate was popular in Spain by 1590, and coffee expanded greatly in popularity in the seventeenth century. The population of Great Britain had the highest sugar consumption in Europe, tripling between 1700 and 1800, when it reached 12 pounds per person per year.

Africa

The diets of the populations located along the western coasts of Senegambia, the Gulf of Guinea, and southwestern Africa were the first to undergo upheavals brought about by European traffic across the Atlantic Ocean, although all of Africa was eventually affected. The transatlantic expansion in the trade in African captives, which in the sixteenth and seventeenth centuries was conducted primarily by Portugal, brought American maize and manioc to the comparably tropical latitudes of the Old World. Africans carefully added these foodstuffs to their diets, driven particularly by the population displacements and other hardships caused by the spread of slaving. Manioc was much more laborious than local yams to prepare, owing to the poisonous qualities of the raw root, which had to be removed by leaching, but the quick-growing tubers in the ground survived both raids and droughts. African populations, sustained by these high-caloric crops, declined only slightly and for brief periods, despite the losses to the slave trade. Other New World foodstuffs, such as sweet potatoes and groundnuts, were integrated into African diets sooner. Distilled alcohol, in the form of wine-based French brandy and sugarcane-based Brazilian and Caribbean rums (or, in Brazil, *gere-*

bita, today *cachaça*) became important imports used to buy slaves; before the sixteenth century, fermented millet beers and palm wine (the sap from a West African variety of palm tree) had been the most significant forms of alcohol consumed in Africa.

In the other direction, African foodstuffs fed the human cargoes of the slave ships heading for the Americas. In Senegambia, African staples such as millet, sorghum, and palm oil rapidly became standard provisions on European slaving vessels. Farther south and east along the coast, African varieties of rice (west of the Côte d'Ivoire) and yams (along the Gold Coast and in the Niger River Delta) crossed the Atlantic in this way, as did vegetables and seasonings that made these staples palatable: okra, malaguetta pepper, and ackee. Maize, cultivated along the coasts of the Gulf of Guinea as early as the mid-sixteenth century, had also become a slaving-vessel staple by the 1670s.

Conclusion

Although crop varieties have accompanied human migrations on a global scale from the Neolithic period, shipping and trade across the Atlantic Ocean after the end of the fifteenth century transformed diets on intercontinental dimensions. European colonies in the Americas, linked through culture and trade to their metropoles, extended European food tastes to extra-European settings. Conversely, European involvement in the Americas integrated different American staples to both Africa and Europe and introduced tropical commodities into European diets. European relations with Amerindians were paradoxically both dependent and exclusionary in the realm of food. Although hostilities complicated the creation of syncretic dietary habits, the majority of post-contact colonial and Amerindian food practices combined elements of both native and nonnative diets, depending in many cases on the mobility and density of Amerindian populations. That is, European incursions affected the diets of small bands of fast-moving plains hunters located in the interior later and to lesser degrees, but larger woodland coastal communities established direct trading relations with Europeans in the sixteenth and seventeenth centuries, and their eating practices shifted as a result. Lastly, the specifically transatlantic trade in African captives that underlay plantation slavery in the Americas was responsible for the transoceanic diffusion of a whole host of foodstuffs that profoundly changed food habits on both sides of the Atlantic and led to the creation of an African diasporic food culture. While these transatlantic exchanges certainly contributed to and linked up with wider circles of global connections, the specific patterns of Atlantic commerce between the sixteenth and nineteenth centuries set in motion a series of traceable shifts in food consumption in the regions directly connected through trade.

BERTIE MANDELBLATT

Bibliography

Carney, Judith. *Black Rice: The African Origins of Rice Cultivation in the Americas*. Cambridge, MA: Harvard University Press, 2001.

Crosby, Alfred. *The Columbian Exchange: Biological and Cultural Consequences of 1492*. Westport, CT: Praeger, 2003.

Debien, Gabriel. "La nourriture des esclaves sur les plantations des Antilles françaises aux XVIIe et XVIIIe siècles." *Caribbean Studies* 4, no. 2 (1964): 3–27.

LaFleur, James D. *Fusion Foodways of Africa's Gold Coast in the Atlantic Era*. Leiden: Brill, 2012.

McCann, James C. *Stirring the Pot: A History of African Cuisine*. Athens: Ohio University Press, 2009.

McMahon, Sarah. "A Comfortable Subsistence: The Changing Composition of Diet in Rural New England, 1620–1840." *William and Mary Quarterly*, 3rd ser., 42, no. 1 (1985): 26–65.

Mintz, Sidney. *Sweetness and Power: The Place of Sugar in Modern History*. New York: Viking, 1985.

Norton, Marcy. "Tasting Empire: Chocolate and the European Internalization of Mesoamerican Aesthetics." *American Historical Review* 111, no. 3 (2006): 660–691.

Forest Resources

Forest resources were employed in almost all aspects of daily life in the early-modern period, so maintaining reliable supplies was a matter of great importance to people on every continent surrounding the Atlantic. A wide range of extracted forest resources—including many different types of timber, nuts, barks, roots, leaves, fibers, saps, and resins—was used in everything from construction, manufacturing, and transportation to cooking, medicine, and clothing. (Other vital materials processed from wood included tar, turpentine, charcoal, and some dyes, which are addressed more fully in other essays in this volume). Beginning in the early-modern period, vast quantities of forest resources were transported from one part of the Atlantic World to another in order to replace diminishing local supplies, to secure materials with particularly useful properties, and to cater to the emerging consumer market for exotic woods.

An active timber trade was already underway within Europe by the late sixteenth century, particularly from heavily forested Scandinavia to deforested areas such as England, the Netherlands, and the Mediterranean. European expansion into the Americas significantly increased the volume and geographical scope of this trade as colonizing powers sought to meet their need for wood. England, France, Spain, and the Netherlands all cited the need for additional forest resources as among their primary motivations for seeking out new territories. Although European colonizers initially sought familiar types of trees to fill existing needs, they were also open to the possibility of discovering new species with virtues as yet unknown, and demand for such novelties grew steadily.

As European monarchies claimed territories in the Americas, however, settlers' first priority was usually to clear lands for agriculture, a laborious task of cutting and burning that took precedence over establishing commercial logging enterprises. In many areas, the forests were so extensive that thousands of trees had to be felled in order to open sufficient acreage for planting, and only a relatively small portion of the resulting timber was consumed. Whatever was not immediately utilized in the building of colonial infrastructure was burned or left rotting in the fields.

Because forest resources were harvested from the wild, however, they offered a readily available and immediate source of revenue requiring little investment other than labor. As farms and plantations began to be carved out of forests, colonists in some areas began to export increasing quantities of wood and wood-derived commodities to the metropolitan centers of Europe. Logging was a very labor

intensive and hazardous endeavor; indeed, it is still considered among the most dangerous of human occupations today. Nevertheless, from New England to the West Indies and Amazonia, massive trees were cut down by hand, usually by men wielding broad axes or long, two-handled saws.

Whether for local use or for sale in distant locales, the heavy logs had to be hauled out of the forest by hand or by draft animals or, where possible, floated out along inland waterways to embarkation points at the rivers' mouths. In New England, many family farmers supplemented their incomes with small-scale logging during the snowy winter months when logs could be more easily hauled across frozen ground. In many areas, especially in the American South, the Caribbean, and Brazil, enslaved Africans provided all or part of the necessary labor for logging. In each locality, the potential value of forest resources always had to be weighed against the expense of labor needed to extract, transport, and process them. With some exceptions, moreover, the profits to be made on such commodities usually were less than for plantation produce, such as West Indian sugar.

Imported forest resources were especially vital to Europe's seafaring nations, which required large supplies of timber and naval stores to build and maintain their fleets. Spain, for example, imported large quantities of timber from Cuba before establishing a shipbuilding industry on the island itself. The British Royal Navy likewise relied on timbers, tars, and resins extracted from forests in New England, South Carolina, and later Georgia; exceptionally tall pine trees, for example, were reserved by the crown to serve as masts on the navy's warships on the high seas. The tropical forests of Brazil made it the center of Portuguese naval construction and supported a maritime commerce that grew to exceed that of Portugal itself.

During the precontact period, long before European colonization, the scale and composition of American forests were shaped by many nonhuman ecological factors as well as by the actions, intentional and unintentional, of human beings; there never was, in William Cronon's words, any "timeless wilderness in a state of perfect changelessness, no climax forest in permanent stasis" (Cronon, 11). Forest environments were transformed by diseases, droughts, fires, climate change, and natural selection from among competing species. In addition,

Native Americans made extensive use of forest resources. Indigenous people in woodland regions collected fruits and nuts for food, stripped bark off trees for housing and textile fibers, hunted numerous birds and mammals, made wooden implements and ornaments for personal use or trade, and felled and hollowed out tree trunks to make canoes. Many Indian groups also managed and manipulated forests, most notably through controlled burning, to improve their accessibility and productivity. On the eastern seaboard of North America, for example, many Indian groups routinely set fires to clear underbrush, making the woods easier to traverse, clearing openings for agriculture, and improving hunting conditions. In some cases, human-made meadows were later mistaken by European newcomers as providential clearings readied for their use by God.

While indigenous populations reshaped natural environments in myriad ways, their utilization of forests tended to remain at sustainable levels, since their practices were less invasive and their populations smaller than those of later European immigrants. In areas where they relied on extensive slash-and-burn agriculture, however, the cumulative result (although more gradual than clear-cutting) was the destruction of significant areas of forest as they felled and burned trees to fertilize the soil and provide sunlight for crops. Though briefly enriched with wood ash, land cultivated in this fashion typically yielded only a few years of productivity before the soil was exhausted, leading to renewed slashing and burning. In the wake of this mode of agriculture, which was vital to many woodland peoples, forests often were permanently diminished, or at minimum, suffered a loss of diversity: even after worn-out fields were abandoned and secondary forest allowed to spring up, the ecological conditions sometimes were so altered that the original mix of species did not grow back. Such human-driven ecological transformations became much more pronounced, however, with the expansion of European colonization.

In some places indigenous people, such as the Mosquito Indians on the southeastern coast of Central America, initially entered into the broader circum-Atlantic trade by gathering readily extractable forest resources, such as dyewoods, for sale to European traders. Likewise, Indians in the northeast and southeast of North America reorganized

their whole ways of life during the early colonial period to capitalize on European demand for such natural products as beaver furs and deerskins. As they veered away from their independent modes of sustaining themselves, indigenous peoples became dangerously reliant on the imported goods that international trade brought to them, even as several animal species were decimated by overhunting. Reduced populations of dam-building beavers and grazing deer, in turn, changed the ecology of their native woodlands.

Nevertheless, European colonizers often learned about native trees unfamiliar to them from Indians or, as was the case in the circum-Caribbean, from enslaved Africans more familiar with neotropical settings. Extensive experimentation also revealed the valuable properties of the diverse species composing American forests. European settlers in North America made ample use of the many local woods, including oak, walnut, maple, pine, birch, butternut, ash, hickory, and cherry, among others. Although colonial joiners continued to prefer oak and walnut, traditionally used in European furniture making, into the late seventeenth century, they increasingly employed a much wider range of North American species. In the Greater Antilles, tropical hardwoods, such as cedar, mahogany, and lignum vitae, were readily adopted by Europeans in the late seventeenth century for shipbuilding because they were found to be extremely strong, durable, and resistant to the rot and insect damage that plagued wooden vessels sailing in the tropics. These tropical hardwoods were especially preferred for warships because they did not shatter as easily when pummeled with cannonballs. By the early eighteenth century, cabinetmakers in Europe and colonial North America, especially those in more urban areas, began to fabricate furniture out of imported tropical woods, notably mahogany, cedar, and later rosewood, often in combination with local secondary woods.

Over time, many sugar-producing islands in the Caribbean were deforested and became net importers of timber. As the plantation complex developed, sugar planters cleared extensive forests for cane but still required large supplies of wood for construction, fuel, and other purposes. Reluctant to divert their enslaved African workers from sugar production to logging, West Indian planters instead imported increasing quantities of timber from North

America, especially New England, including various kinds of pine, maple, and white and red oak. The latter, in particular, became a preferred material for making sugar barrels, since many tropical woods, like mahogany and lignum vitae, were too hard for coopering or, like cedar, so aromatic that they imparted an unwanted flavor to their contents. Thousands of oak staves were sent in bundles from the northern colonies to the Caribbean to be assembled into barrels on-site, packed with sugar, and then shipped back to North America or on to European destinations.

The main reason wood imports became so important in the Caribbean, however, was that by the late seventeenth and eighteenth centuries, many sugar-producing islands had followed the same pattern of deforestation that began on the island of Madeira in the eastern Atlantic; named (in Portuguese) for the heavy woods that once covered it, the island today remains all but treeless since canebrakes replaced its forests in the sixteenth century. Indeed, throughout the Atlantic, wherever woodlands competed with other forms of land use such as agriculture and early industrialization, high degrees of deforestation typically resulted. Facing wood shortages and the depletion of particularly desirable species, a few colonies attempted to regulate logging or implemented early conservation programs to curb the destruction of forests, but usually with limited success. In North America, deforestation did not become a significant concern until the mid-eighteenth century, and then mainly around the more urbanized stretches of the Atlantic coast, where city dwellers needed wood for heating, cooking, and building. Forests along the western frontier remained abundant, and settlers there continued to employ fine hardwoods in ways that others at the time regarded as profligate, such as for fencing and fuel. Where waterways or other transportation networks allowed, however, commercial logging for both domestic use and export steadily drew these interior areas into the Atlantic economy. In many of these locales, deforestation eventually exacerbated the displacement of indigenous peoples who relied on forest resources and slash-and-burn agriculture to subsist. Similar disruptions are being caused by logging in Amazonia today.

The Atlantic timber trade was also tied into the developing slave trade between dryland western Africa and the Americas. As trees suitable for fueling iron smelting were depleted in the regions adjacent to the Sahara Desert, people had difficulty fabricating essential tools such as those used in agriculture. Some scholars have argued that their interest in importing iron bars—and selling people to get them—arose from shortages of wood for fuel to achieve the high temperatures required by their iron industry. Rather than transport bulky shipments of timber, American and European slave traders supplied them with soft iron bars that could be reshaped at lower temperatures. In what became a vicious cycle, African merchants imported iron bars, paid for them by selling captive people, and then waged war against neighboring realms to acquire more slaves to buy more iron.

With a few exceptions, the Atlantic timber trade entailed shipping an unwieldy commodity over long distances, often with relatively small margins of profit. Yet the basis of this international trade in forest resources was that it allowed consumers to take advantage of each wood's distinctive characteristics—varying degrees of density and strength, straight or figured grains, unique colors or patterns, and useful resins or aromatic oils—that were suitable for different commercial purposes. Meeting these varied needs in the international marketplace meant that some colonies became both importers and exporters of differing forest resources—they logged and sold the trees native to their region or climate zone while acquiring desirable nonnative species, sometimes at considerable expense. As trees and their derivative products were commodified and circulated among the tropical, temperate, and more northerly reaches of the Western Hemisphere, they added to the complex patterns of exchange that characterized the Atlantic period.

JENNIFER L. ANDERSON

Bibliography

Bowett, Adam. *Woods in British Furniture Making 1400–1900: An Illustrated Historical Dictionary*. Chicago: University of Chicago Press, 2012.

Cronon, William. *Changes in the Land: Indians, Colonists, and the Ecology of New England*. New York: Hill and Wang, 1983.

Dean, Warren. *With Broadax and Firebrand: The Destruction of the Brazilian Atlantic Forest. Berkeley: University of California Press, 1995.

Funes Monzote, Reinaldo. *From Rainforest to Cane Field in Cuba: An Environmental History since 1492.* Translated by Alex Martin. Chapel Hill: University of North Carolina Press, 2008.

Grove, Richard. *Green Imperialism: Colonial Expansion, Tropical Island Edens, and the Origins of Environmentalism, 1600–1800.* Cambridge: Cambridge University Press, 1995.

Krech, Shepard. *The Ecological Indian: Myth and History.* New York: W. W. Norton, 1999.

Miller, Shawn. *Fruitless Trees: Portuguese Conservation and Brazil's Colonial Timber.* Stanford, CA: Stanford University Press, 2000.

Silver, Timothy. *A New Face on the Countryside: Indians, Colonists, and Slaves in South Atlantic Forests, 1500–1800.* New York: Cambridge University Press, 1990.

Watts, David. *The West Indies: Patterns of Development, Culture, and Environmental Change since 1492.* Cambridge: Cambridge University Press, 1987.

Freed People

Freed people is a term used—interchangeably here with *free people of color*, *free coloreds*, and *free blacks*—to indicate individuals of African descent who lived in slavery in the Americas, but who were subsequently freed; it also refers to the descendants of these individuals. Freed people were an important element in the slave societies of the Atlantic World. With close links personally and culturally to the enslaved, free people of color were an unintended by-product of bringing millions of Africans, including many women, under the arbitrary control of European owners. Many free coloreds were the offspring of liaisons between white males and enslaved black women. Their white fathers sometimes freed the children of these unions, as well as the slave mothers who produced them. The resulting free-colored population was predominantly female and of mixed backgrounds.

The proportions of freed people, relative to the enslaved population, varied across the Americas. They were particularly numerous, and eventually majorities, in Latin America. For example, in Brazil, by the nineteenth century free coloreds significantly outnumbered the enslaved population: in 1872, 4.2 million free people of color—compared with a total of 1.5 million slaves—lived in Brazil. In Mexico, the figures favored the free colored even more: in 1810 only 10,000 enslaved people lived there, compared with approximately 300,000 free people of color. The proportion of freed people in the Caribbean and in the United States, however, was much smaller. In Saint-Domingue and the Upper South states of Maryland, Virginia, and North Carolina, free people of color made up just over 5 percent of the nonwhite population when slavery ended.

The free-colored population occupied differing positions in the New World, depending on the societies in which they lived. Free coloreds and free blacks had separate and distinct militia companies, for instance, in a range of areas across the Americas, including Brazil, Martinique, and Saint-Domingue, although they were excluded from bearing arms in the United States. Also, people of color in the Spanish Caribbean, according to some observers, were classified into 25 different ethnoracial categories. Though it is unlikely that these many different categorizations were very significant for the social status of freed people, it is true that the free coloreds in Jamaica, who were nearly white, enjoyed all the rights of whites. It also sometimes mattered how free people of color had attained their freedom. In Jamaica, people of color born free were treated more favorably in the courts than those who were newly manumitted.

Despite these differences in status, freed men and women everywhere throughout the Atlantic World faced legal obstacles and personal discrimination. Free coloreds in early seventeenth-century Mexico were required to pay special taxes, were restricted from studying in universities, and were barred from a variety of professions. Elsewhere, sumptuary laws identified free blacks and coloreds by imposing limitations on the clothing or bodily adornments they might wear in public. Freed people in the mid-eighteenth-century Danish West Indies had to wear badges or cockades and were not allowed to have clothing made of silk or gold. In many parts of the Americas, free people of color could not participate in politics and could not sit on juries or give evidence against whites. Their economic possibilities were also sharply curtailed; thus, in Jamaica, the House of Assembly passed legislation in 1761 restricting whites from leaving real or personal property worth more than £1,200 to any free person of color. Freed people in New Orleans, as elsewhere in the Americas, were excluded from a wide range of jobs reserved for whites.

In light of these restrictions, freed people generally lived in towns rather than on plantations. There, the greater diversity of jobs opened niches for them between the upper ranks of domestic slaves and the lower class of whites. Free male coloreds worked primarily as artisans—especially as carpenters, masons, tailors, and shoemakers—but also as barber-surgeons. On the other hand, free colored women had a smaller range of occupations open to them, working as seamstresses, washerwomen, domestics, and midwives. Some, however, kept taverns, and one, Rachel Pringle-Polgreen, gained considerable notoriety in Bridgetown, Barbados, as the owner of a hotel and brothel in the 1770s and 1780s. Unlike most free colored women, she died wealthy, leaving 19 slaves and considerable property.

Although most freed people were relatively poor, a small number prospered as planters. This was especially the case in Saint-Domingue, where free coloreds such as Julien Raimond inherited land and slaves from his French father in the middle of the eighteenth century. By the 1780s, Raimond was one of the wealthiest free men of color in the Atlantic World, owning over 200 slaves. After the Haitian Revolution (1791–1804), many free coloreds in Saint-Domingue fled to the United States, especially New Orleans, where some succeeded as entrepreneurs. In Brazil, the wealthiest free woman of color was Chica da Silva. Born about 1732 an enslaved woman, da Silva became the mistress of a diamond merchant in Minas Gerais and eventually owned over 100 slaves before she died in 1796.

Chica da Silva and Julien Raimond, wealthy and both of partial white descent, were exceptions. The kind of acceptance they experienced in colonial society did not create broader links between freed people and whites. The vast majority of freed people could not socialize with whites. Many, if not most, public institutions were segregated, with free people of color compelled to sit apart from whites. Theaters sometimes held separate performances for whites and freed people, and each group usually had burial grounds of its own.

Yet these public discriminations could not be enforced in private. Sexual relations between whites and freedwomen fell well outside the usual conventions of separation. While some of these relationships were casual, others were longer-term liaisons. One of the most prominent of these in the Caribbean involved Peter von Scholten, the governor-general (1827–1848) of the Danish West Indies, and the freedwoman Anna Heegard. Heegard and von Scholten lived together for 20 years; moreover, Heegard participated with von Scholten in formal social events.

These more permanent relationships were often formally recognized in rituals or contracts. In nineteenth-century New Orleans, for example, white men agreed to provide their free colored mistresses with property in *plaçage* agreements. Some whites agreed to pay large sums of money to their colored mistresses if the men abandoned the relationship. Such arrangements often provided a measure of security for the freedwoman as well as for any resulting children.

But most freed people in the Atlantic World lived closer to the world of the enslaved than to that of the whites, especially in towns where freed people and the urban enslaved mixed freely. Free coloreds and slaves not only lived in close proximity but also worked together as artisans, shopkeepers, or hucksters. Freed people frequently participated in the social networks of the enslaved, attending their funerals and religious activities, as well as weekend dances. They often had kin in common; some freed people owned slaves who were their kin and whom they were seeking to manumit or protect from separation by other owners intent on selling them. Manumitted former slaves, then, reinforced the family ties between the enslaved and freed people.

The wealthier freed people who owned plantations and slaves had much to lose from the abolition of slavery in the nineteenth century, and some supported slavery's continuation. Earlier, across the Americas south of the United States, free-colored men served in militias that sought to arrest escaped slaves and return them to their owners. In addition, free people of color joined whites to help put down slave rebellions.

The majority of freed people, though, fought vigorously for the abolition of slavery. The most famous of these was Toussaint L'Ouverture (1743–

1803), leader of the Haitian Revolution after 1791. Prominent freed men among the abolitionists in the United States included Frederick Douglass, Martin Delaney, and David Walker. The leading men of color in Jamaica, Edward Jordon and Robert Osborn, corresponded with British abolitionists and were visited in Jamaica by representatives of the antislavery societies. Osborn and Jordon established a newspaper in Kingston, *The Watchman*, which advocated the ending of slavery.

Even prominent and outspoken freed men such as Osborn and Jordon struggled against legal limitations and discrimination. Across the Anglophone Caribbean in the early nineteenth century, freed people petitioned local assemblies for increased rights and also sought to influence officials in the British Colonial Office in London. Parliament granted freed people full civil rights a year before the British abolition of slavery in 1834. Once able to participate in politics, free-colored politicians generally adopted a humanitarian stance in opposition to the local plantocracy.

In the process, freed people demonstrated their significant political presence in Atlantic history. They were a Creole group—one of many with roots in the Old World, in Europe as well as Africa, but remade in the Americas through adaptations and accommodations—who were increasingly conscious of themselves as distinctive and separate from the rest of the population. Unlike the enslaved, they were not from Africa; unlike the whites, they were not from Europe. They were committed to their own hybrid Atlantic communities while also linking the worlds of the enslaved and the free.

GAD HEUMAN

Bibliography

Cohen, David W., and Jack P. Greene. *Neither Slave Nor Free: The Freedmen of African Descent in the Slave Societies of the New World.* Baltimore, MD: Johns Hopkins University Press, 1972.

Garrigus, John. "Free Coloureds." In *The Routledge History of Slavery.* Edited by Gad Heuman and Trevor Burnard. London: Routledge, 2011.

Heuman, Gad J. *Between Black and White: Race, Politics, and the Free Coloreds in Jamaica, 1792–1865.* Westport, CT: Greenwood, 1981.

Frontiers

The frontier has loomed large in North American historiography. Historians have spent countless pages debating the meaning and import of this expansive zone, seen from the Atlantic seaboard looking west. Frederick Jackson Turner sparked this discussion with his seminal 1893 essay "The Significance of the Frontier in American History," which located "the frontier" as the heart of the nation's identity. While novelists and popular historians such as James Fenimore Cooper and Francis Parkman had written about frontiers before then, Turner—a Wisconsinite by birth who was trained to be a professional historian at Johns Hopkins—brought a more scholarly and analytical approach to understanding the historicity of such zones. Turner argued that the process of settling the American frontier—or an accessible "area of free land" according to Turner's simplest definition—helped create the political institutions of the United States and gave rise to a democratic and individualistic national character. His argument that domesticating the "wild" West was formative for the United States shook a field dominated by historians trained in elite eastern universities who had focused their scholarly attentions on the Atlantic seaboard and located the cultural origins of the country in its transatlantic ties to European traditions. Turner forced these easterners to turn their collective gaze both westward and inward.

Turner's thesis has influenced scholarship on the history of the United States ever since. For a time, his thesis reigned supreme, even influencing Franklin Delano Roosevelt's New Deal policies. With the closure of the frontier and its landed opportunities, Roosevelt argued, the government needed to establish a safety net to replace it as nurturer of the nation. Even when historians questioned certain aspects of Turner's argument, like his claim that the "free land" of frontier regions served as a safety valve for eastern urban discontent, his thesis nonetheless framed the questions scholars asked about the significance of the frontier. By the 1980s, however, the framework of Turner's thesis came under sustained and withering assault. Rather than take issue with specific parts of his analysis, new critiques questioned the fundamental premise of Turner's ethnocentric assumption of inevitable conquest, which failed to account for the experiences of the many peoples (particularly Native Americans) who were not agents of the United States' "civilizing" mission. They pointed out that the land was not "free" and that the violence and destruction of expansion often looked decidedly uncivil. Others criticized Turner's use of the term as being too all-encompassing to have any specific meaning. Indeed, the flaws that this cohort of critics exposed led some historians to question the term's analytical usefulness altogether. As Patricia Limerick, one of Turner's most vocal critics, put it, "the frontier is . . . an unsubtle concept in a subtle world" (Limerick, 25). Another reviewer noted that Turner's thesis had become "a shibboleth, denoting a triumphalist and Anglocentric narrative of continental conquest" (Adelman and Aron, 814).

The frontier as an analytical concept survived this onslaught, however, because historians have inherited—even embraced—another essential component of Turner's thesis. Turner had defended the term frontier as "elastic" and not in need of "sharp definition" (Turner, 3). Recent historians, while often rejecting Turner's glorified conception of the North American frontier, have nonetheless embraced his understanding of its elasticity. For many scholars, *frontier* remains useful as an analytical term because they have redefined its significance to meet the changing interests of the field of history. Fredrika Teute and Andrew Cayton, editors of an influential anthology on the early American frontier east of the Mississippi, offer an example of this recasting. They adopted "a revisionist notion" of the frontier by defining it as a zone of "kinetic interactions among many peoples, which created new cultural matrices distinctively American" (Teute and Cayton, 2). This reconceptualization of frontiers as zones of engagement among multiple, diverse historical actors gave the term, in the words of Jeremy Adelman and Stephen Aron, "a new historiographical lease on life" (Adelman and Aron, 814). In this new formulation, the frontier became connected to the eastern seaboard and to the rest of the globe through the Atlantic Ocean, as peoples crossed the ocean and came into contact with one another and with Native Americans on the land frontiers of North America. The diverse cultural groups that inhabited these frontier zones often ex-changed commodities and goods originating from oceanic trade or fought over lands whose value for Europeans rested in their ability to provide commodities for global markets.

The etymology of *frontier* suggests that the malleability of the concept is historical as well as intellectual. The term originates from *frons*, the Latin word for "front." In Old French, *frontier* referred to the front line of an army. This usage continued in Middle English, but by the fifteenth century *frontier* had evolved from a technical military term to refer to specific communities and towns that "fronted" an armed and hostile rival. As early-modern monarchies developed territorial parameters in the seventeenth century, theorists trying to describe this new political entity further refined the meaning of frontiers, envisioning them as the metaphorical limbs of the body politic, able to protect the heart of the state by warding off attack.

By the eighteenth century, the term *frontier* had incorporated these changes to become a zone—often a specific community—that was vulnerable to invasion, and not only in the Americas. A London dictionary published in 1776 provides a good working definition: "Frontier: the border, confine, or boundary of a kingdom or province, which the enemies find in the front when they are about to enter the same" (Bailey, 229). Frontiers were thus stable defensive zones exposed to assault. As the site of a potential invasion, they also held strategic importance to the larger state. Failure to fortify frontiers adequately meant that enemies could breach a polity's borders, putting the heart of the state in danger. Those who inhabited such zones lived in far greater states of fear than those in the core. Though few scholarly works have taken these historical meanings of the word seriously, putting them in the contexts of their times sheds new light on the culture of the seventeenth- and eighteenth-century Atlantic World, on the coming of the American Revolution, and ultimately, on the transition of frontiers from militarized, potentially contracting defensive zones in the long eighteenth century into an expanding arena offering the opportunities associated by the late nineteenth century—Turner's era—with free (not occupied) land and limited (rather than intense) government involvement.

While scholars can trace the etymological shifts in the meanings of the term, for most historical actors, however, its definition remained static for the durations of their lives. That was certainly the case for most English-speaking inhabitants of the Atlantic World in the seventeenth and eighteenth centuries. As English men and women crossed the Atlantic Ocean to settle new lands in the seventeenth century, perceived culturally and construed legally as empty, they carried with them a vocabulary to help them describe their positions in these territories. *Frontier* was one such word. Colonists deployed the term to explain their geopolitical landscape soon after establishing their polities, and colonial legislatures regularly passed laws that identified specific places as military frontiers and tried to regulate such zones in order to defend themselves from intruders, whether other Europeans or the Native peoples, who were—in spite of legal doctrines of *terra nullius*—very much and threateningly present.

Those tasked with managing the zones treated in this defensive sense as frontiers imported policies developed first in Europe, though they sometimes took on new form in the North American setting. Boston printers reproduced English military dictionaries that outlined the proper treatment of frontiers, and, as war loomed, the Massachusetts Bay government reprinted as easily disseminated proclamations the specific instructions for conduct that these guides contained for people living on frontiers. These European ideas also directly influenced the laws Massachusetts Bay passed for regulating the ways that individuals living on frontiers should act. Many English governments also encouraged people to settle on such frontiers by reducing the cost of land there, under the theory that promoting settlement would provide greater protection. Some colonies reduced the tax burdens for frontier regions to entice those who ventured out into frontier zones to remain. Settlers living in these areas also argued that because they were going into these areas, they deserved special support from their government for taking such risks. Moreover, European settlers, who were very much aware of their geopolitical position within their polity, often believed that living on frontiers meant that they, inhabiting a war zone, were bound by fewer social restraints, which could lead to increased violence among the many people who inhabited these zones. Though there was no uniform frontier policy throughout North America because the English and then British imperial policies delegated frontier

defense to the militias of each of its overseas provinces, the collective efforts of these individual polities had a common effect. Frontiers—though cast and treated as defensive zones in need of protection—seemed to push settlement farther inland and increase the likelihood of conflict, often in ways that served expansionist interests.

By examining where people located a "frontier," we can see whom Europeans considered to be their probable enemies. In the earliest phase of settlement on the North American seaboard, frontier zones were often inland and reflected the settlers' concerns about war with neighboring Native American groups who were trying to stop European intrusions on their territories. As European control in North America expanded and imperial rivalries with France and Spain simmered, English colonies began to reconsider where they might position their frontiers. The growing hostility among European powers in the eighteenth century led many colonial governments to label their exposed seacoasts as frontiers and consider European rivals as likely an invading force as Indians. In 1734, for instance, the governor referred to Boston as the colony's "principal maritime frontier" (Belcher, np) as he prepared for the possibility of a naval war. In the 1740s, Georgians who worried about a Spanish seaborne invasion wrote of their "large and extended frontier towards the sea" (Force, 16). That colonists considered Atlantic coasts as frontiers shows how far Turner's emphasis on the West as the American frontier had moved from seventeenth- and eighteenth-century ideas about frontiers, both in geographic placement and in the activities that characterized them.

Indeed, colonists often envisioned their communities and their frontiers within much larger, global geopolitical frameworks, and there is no evidence that they envisioned the frontier toward the west as in any way distinctive. Instead, government officials discussed, and colonial newspapers often reported on, the status of frontiers in continental Europe. This shared concern about others' frontiers, both local and distant, helped bind the Euro-Atlantic World together. These connections did not last, however. In the wake of the Seven Years' War (1756–1763), this shared understanding of Britain's global frontiers became contested as inhabitants on the eastern and western shores of the Atlantic developed different perceptions of where such zones existed within this transoceanic domain. This division helped spur a split in the 1770s between the king and Parliament in Britain and their subjects in North America.

Frontiers, defined as zones vulnerable to invasion and in need of military support, placed specific demands upon governments, often of the most fundamental nature. When people believed they lived in a frontier, they turned to their governments—local, colonial, and imperial—for protection. Governments with frontiers managed themselves without much controversy for most of the seventeenth and eighteenth centuries. That relative ease disappeared in the aftermath of the Seven Years' War, which removed the French from all of North America east of the Mississippi. As colonists and government officials tried to come to terms with their greatly expanded North American domain, a dispute developed over the geopolitical situation of this territory. Many colonists in western areas, especially from the Middle Colonies, who had—in their own words—"become" a frontier during the conflict, continued to believe that they still lived upon a frontier threatened by the Native Americans who had fought with the French. British officials held a different view: they wanted to open trade, restore alliances, and keep peace with most Native groups. This policy of maintaining an "open road" to Indian country, they hoped, would help them bring order to the West and integrate Indian trade goods within their economic plan for their global empire.

The two conflicting visions called for government policies that were inherently incompatible. Colonists who continued to refer to themselves throughout the 1760s and 1770s as "frontier inhabitants" living in "frontier counties" felt that they faced potential invasion from inherent, permanent Indian enemies. At the same time and in strong contradistinction, government officials were trying to integrate the same groups within their larger imperial schema. In the colonists' eyes, frontiers—defensive zones that faced a potential invader—should not be sites of open and free trade with perceived enemies. This geopolitical dispute appeared clearly in a 1765 petition in which the authors described themselves as "the distressed people of the frontiers" who lived in fear of an "Indian war." They complained that those "remote from danger, sit at ease and know not what we feel." In their view, the government officials—securely "remote from dan-

ger"—were ignoring the fundamental duty of protection they owed to British subjects ("Petition from Cumberland County [Mar. 1765]" 1951–1994, 777–779). In the 1770s, as settlers in other regions of eastern North America mobilized around shared senses of betrayal in other aspects of their relationships with their king and government, these western complaints became intertwined with eastern seaboard complaints about Parliament's taxation and regulation of trade, culminating in Thomas Jefferson's Declaration of Independence in 1776, in which he cited George III's treatment of "the inhabitants of our frontiers" as one of the causes of just rebellion.

After victory in the ensuing War for American Independence, the more democratic governments of the new United States began to incorporate areas previously considered frontiers into their polities. Western areas, often underrepresented in colonial legislatures, gained seats. Moreover, those in the east had come to understand the complaints of western inhabitants against the British Empire. On a more practical level, sales of western lands—areas often described as frontiers—provided a means of procuring revenue for the fledgling nation-state. As the new nation turned inward, away from Atlantic entanglements, and westward, frontier zones became synonymous with these incorporative attitudes toward western lands. Citizens increasingly saw Indians as inherent enemies, whose very presence marked a territory as a dangerous frontier zone. The process of establishing policies for these areas in the new nation-state changed the definition of frontiers from one that was defensive to one that was offensive. As one prominent western citizen declared in 1794, the defensive definition of frontiers would be "a help but no effectual defense" because it would amount to nothing more than defending against a continuous invasion; "watching the beasts of prey who come against our folds." Instead, he argued that "the best defense is offense" and that the new nation needed to take measures to "penetrat[e] the forests, where they haunt, and extirpat[e] the race" (Brackenridge, 41). By the early nineteenth century, the singular, distinguishing "frontier" displaced the more common pluralized use of the word "frontiers," signaling the growing consolidation of the nation-state in the wake of the War of 1812. This consolidation fostered among American citizens a shared sense of a common frontier line in the West. By Turner's time, the success of the nation's frontier policy—culminating in Indian deportations starting with President Jackson's Indian Removal Act of 1830—would make the American frontier appear to be an expansive area of free land that offered hope and opportunity for whites.

Historicizing the term *frontier* thus helps us to understand the lived experiences and motivations of many colonists, the roots and course of Britain's imperial crisis of the 1770s, the strategies of forming the young United States, and, ultimately, the development of the better-known Turnerian definition of the late nineteenth century. The fears of invasion, militarization, and warfare that defined frontiers in the seventeenth and eighteenth centuries created a process that produced Turner's later, very different conception of opportunity.

PATRICK SPERO

Bibliography

Aron, Stephen, and Jeremy Adelman. "From Borderlands to Borders: Empires, Nation-States, and the Peoples in between in North American History." *American Historical Review* 104, no. 3 (1999): 814–841.

Bailey, Nathan. *The New Universal Etymological English Dictionary: . . . To which Is Added, a Dictionary of Cant Words.* London, 1776.

Belcher, Jonathen. "Speech of Jonathen Belcher, February 22, 1733." *Boston News-letter,* February 28, 1733/1734.

Billington, Ray Allen, ed. *The Frontier Thesis: Valid Interpretation of American History?* New York: Krieger, 1966.

Brackenridge, Hugh Henry. *Incidents of the Insurrection.* New Haven, CT: Rowman and Littlefield, 1972.

Force, Peter, ed. "A State of the *Province of Georgia,* Attested upon Oath, in the Court of Savannah, Nov. 10, 1740." In *Tracts and Other Papers Relating Principally to the Origin, Settlement, and Progress of the Colonies in North America from the Discovery of the Country to the Year 1776.* Washington, DC: P. Force, 1836.

Hofstadter, Richard, ed. *Turner and the Sociology of the Frontier.* New York: Basic Books, 1968.

Juricek, John. "American Usage of the Term 'Frontier' from Colonial Times to Frederick Jackson Turner." *Proceedings of the American Philosophical Society* 110, no. 1 (1966), 10–34.

Klein, Kerwin Lee. "Reclaiming the 'F' Word, or Being and Becoming Postwestern." *Pacific Historical Review* 65, no. 2 (1996): 179–216.

Limerick, Patricia. *The Legacy of Conquest: The Unbroken Past of the American West.* New York: W. W. Norton, 1987.

Nobles, Gregory. "Breaking the Backcountry: New Approaches to the Early American Frontier, 1750–1800." *William and Mary Quarterly* 46, no. 4 (1989): 641–670.

"Petition from Cumberland County [Mar. 1765]." *Papers of Henry Bouquet.* Harrisburg: Pennsylvania Historical and Museum Commission, 1951–1994, 6: 777–779.

Teute, Fredrika, and Andrew Cayton, eds. *Contact Points: American Frontiers from the Mohawk Valley to the Mississippi, 1750–1800.* Chapel Hill: University of North Carolina Press, 1998.

Turner, Frederick Jackson. "The Significance of the Frontier in American History." In *The Frontier in American History,* edited by Ray Allen Billington. New York: Rinehart and Winston, 1962.

Furs and Skins

Trade in pelts and skins drew Europeans and Amerindians into a complex array of relationships that spanned North America and lasted more than 400 years, making it one of the earliest and most enduring transatlantic encounters. Although the trade began modestly and remained intensely local in many respects, it grew into a major component of Native and European economies that shaped cultural practices all around the Atlantic. Unlike other extractive enterprises like mining or fishing, production of furs and skins thrived only when controlled by Native peoples. Well into the nineteenth century, North America remained predominantly Indian country, in no small measure because Native peoples set the terms of millions of face-to-face commercial exchanges with European colonizers. Yet these exchanges came at a high price for many communities, emptying their lands of valuable resources and creating cycles of debt and obligation that bound them to the intruders. All too often, too, hunts for furs and skins morphed into raiding for human captives, providing immediate benefits to the Native captors while embedding them in systems of violence that in the longer run would prove devastating.

Encounters

Extracted animal products dominated North American commerce during the first decades of sustained contact between Amerindians and Europeans. Although cod dwarfed pelts in quantity and in commercial value throughout the sixteenth century, it was the modest trade in furs that created incentives for cultural engagements between the peoples of Europe and North America. The earliest exchanges were mostly incidental, as locals offered a handful of skins and pelts to fishermen or whalers in exchange for European manufactured goods. Most of this bartering was undocumented, but it was frequent enough to create patterns. During a 1524 voyage along the North American coast, Giovanni da Verrazano encountered many people who seemed already accustomed to trading with European ships, following elaborate protocols and expressing clear preferences for particular goods. A decade later, when Jacques Cartier entered the Gulf of St. Lawrence, people turned out in numbers, "holding up to us some skins on sticks," communicating in a nervous pantomime that they wanted to trade. Despite Cartier's initial hostility, the Native traders persisted and ended up exchanging skins for "knives and other iron goods . . . to such an extent that all went back naked without anything on them" (Cook, 20–21).

By midcentury, Basque, French, English, and Portuguese seafarers occupied only a few whaling stations and seasonal fishing camps in what are now New England and the Canadian Maritimes, yet the region's inhabitants had developed a small but sustained trade in furs and skins by incorporating the newcomers into existing trade systems. They also developed a discriminating taste for European goods, though they often repurposed them in ways that surprised their European suppliers. They broke apart copper kettles and worked the fragments into arrowheads or amulets. They used iron knives and axe heads until they were dull and then wore them on necklaces. They adopted glass beads for personal adornment but also attached them to sacred bundles and bags. Europeans did much the same thing, reworking leather robes into shoes, book covers, or tools and turning beaver pelts into ornamental

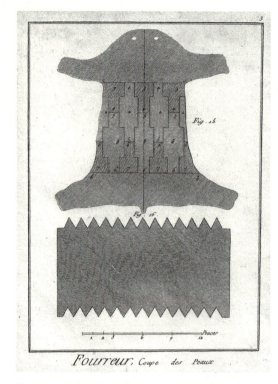

Figure 1. Pattern for a fur garment. Printed in *Encyclopédie, ou dictionnaire raisonné des sciences, des arts et des métiers (Encyclopedia, or a Systematic Dictionary of the Sciences, Arts, and Crafts)*, edited by Denis Diderot and first published between 1751 and 1765.

headwear that was symbolically important in Europe for its origin in a distant new world. By the end of the sixteenth century, consumer demand on both sides of the Atlantic influenced what goods were offered in these exchanges, leading Native hunters to target specific animals (beaver, marten, moose, deer, seal) and European manufacturers to produce larger quantities of the items desired in North America (glass beads, knives, axes, kettles, wool). Merchants across Europe organized companies to meet this demand; taking note, European governments started searching for ways to siphon revenues from merchants in exchange for trade protections.

Cultural Innovations

One-time bargains could be struck with minimal effort and required little knowledge of the trading partner's language or culture. But sustained trade and predictable supplies of goods required more stable relationships, facilitated by linguistic and cultural knowledge and often structured by extended kin networks. As European settlements began to dot North America's eastern seaboard in the seventeenth century, the drive for longer-term trade relationships brought Indians and Europeans into dialogue. Fur traders were the first Europeans to learn Native languages, marry Native women, and negotiate stable relationships with Native communities. Everyone from missionaries to colonial officials depended upon these intercultural brokers to translate not only the words of their Amerindian partners but also their cultural practices.

Native hunters used their ties to European traders and the valuable manufactured goods they offered to bolster their position within their own communities. Nothing cemented a Native family's relationship with merchants more effectively than marriage. Rather than a mere function of colonial policy or a measure of European racial attitudes, marriage was an indigenous strategy of alliance that Native traders used to channel European goods into their networks of kin. Over time, marriages "in the custom of the country" became one of the more common ways to mediate conversations across cultures and the trade that made that dialogue necessary. After a generation, assigning the descendants of these unions to the communities of either their European or Amerindian parents was both beyond possibility and beside the point.

Centers of this multicultural trade emerged quickly, often around indigenous sites that had long drawn diverse collections of peoples. The names of these attest to their Native origins: Tadoussac, Penobscot, Michilimackinac, Natchez. A number of European trading towns arose to channel the furs and hides into Atlantic markets: Detroit in the Great Lakes area and Mobile in the South, Schenectady and Albany in New York, Springfield in Massachusetts, and Casco Bay in southern Maine.

Sites of trade became crossroads of cultural integration and innovation. Because Europeans and Amerindians brought different expectations to their exchanges, to build a lasting partnership required mutual compromise and adaptation. Even the most basic issues like pricing, or the method and timing of payment, were open to misunderstanding. Amerindians, for example, did not sepa-

rate the act of trade from broader rituals of generosity associated with political alliances, making it hard for Europeans to distinguish what they offered as gifts from the payments they expected or to differentiate between specialized agreements to trade and comprehensive pacts implying military support. For Europeans, debt and credit functioned as abstracted values on a balance sheet, where the obligation was limited to the amount owed in commodities or currencies. Native traders, who carried more personal and relational notions of debt and obligation, found demands for such precise payment insulting. But with time and experience, a new set of shared practices developed, not as a series of concessions tipping to one side or the other, but as a new cultural idiom in its own right that both sides worked out together. The material culture at trade sites attests to these cultural combinations. Native people increasingly wore clothes bought with, rather than made from, skins and furs. Settlements like those near Fort Toulouse, a center of the deerskin trade in modern Alabama, blended Native and French elements in revealing ways: clay wine bottles and dinner platters mingled with ceremonial pipes topped with imported metal tobacco bowls.

The Amerindian Atlantic

Although Native traders held the upper hand in most individual exchanges, selling beaver pelts or deerskins tied them to an increasingly integrated system of Atlantic commerce that linked villages in the North American interior with agents in the colonies, in turn to suppliers in European port cities, and eventually to consumers all across Europe and in Africa. The fur trade exploded in the seventeenth century, responding to superheated demands in Europe for American furs and in North America for European metal and cloth goods. The northern fur trade, centered on beaver pelts, had its heyday in the mid-seventeenth century but remained important well into the eighteenth. The deerskin trade dominated in warmer southern climates, thriving from the 1670s to the 1770s. European demand for pelts gave leverage to Native suppliers, who could play one empire against another as they sought not only merchandise but also the political and military alliances they associated with trade relationships. A Great Lakes Indian could choose whether to sell his pelts to the French at Montreal or the English at Albany; a deerskin trader could truck with Charleston or Mobile. Knowledge of that competition encouraged Europeans to bargain. But as the seventeenth century shaded into the eighteenth, Indians throughout North America's eastern woodlands found that, as important as it was to have a choice between empires, the option to remain aloof from the Europeans was fading quickly.

Intensifying cycles of competition among Native hunters and trappers often led to warfare that melded the trade in skins and furs into hunting for human captives to sell as slaves. In the Mississippi Valley and eastern Great Plains, French and Amerindians channeled captured enemies into fur-trade networks, enslaving them in part to prevent them from entering into competing trade with English merchants. The deerskin trade in the Southeast in the late seventeenth and early eighteenth centuries was tied even more closely to slaving, as skins and captives flowed simultaneously into places like Charleston. Although slaving was profitable for the slavers in the short run, raiding ultimately brought violent reprisals and destabilized commodities trades, including that in deerskins. Slave raids and forced migration also spread disease, and by encouraging the selling of captives, rather than their adoption, accelerated demographic decline. The deerskin and slave trades also funded initial English investments in plantation agriculture, to disastrous effect. Many of South Carolina's rice plantations were built with profits from exported hides and slaves, and a number of prominent Virginia planter families used revenues from Indian trade to invest in land and enslaved Africans; as colonial planting expanded, pressure built to force Indians from the lands involved.

In the seventeenth-century Northeast, European demand for beaver pelts seemed almost limitless, leading some Amerindian groups to hunt fur-bearing animals at a reckless pace. Territories that had sustained hunting for generations when demand was low could not possibly supply enough animals to satisfy a growing global export market. In parts of New England, New York, and Canada beavers were hunted to virtual extinction; Native hunters were forced to go farther afield to find them, which often took them toward (and into) enemy territory. Deer populations in the Southeast

also thinned quickly, fueling the cycles of competition, warfare, and slaving that so destabilized the region in the early eighteenth century.

The fur and skin trades also brought technological innovations to Native towns, especially metal tools, processed cloth, and firearms. But however welcome these goods were, their very utility created dependencies. Even if Native people could live without European goods, they had restructured their farming practices, sartorial customs, and ways of warfare so thoroughly that it was no longer practical to disengage. European traders manipulated these needs, extending credit and exploiting addictive substances like alcohol to deepen Indians' dependency. Colonizers were dependent, too, unwilling to forego the profits of the fur and skin trades and unable to survive without the military alliances that accompanied commerce.

Despite these challenges, and also in part because of them, the trades in furs and skins endured for generations, remaining influential as European and Euroamerican traders pushed westward and northward throughout the nineteenth century. American and British trading companies competed for the furs of the Old Northwest and then the Pacific Northwest, extending the cultural and commercial practices developed over the previous three centuries. But as the United States colonized and depopulated much of western North America, the fur trade declined in tandem with the Native independence that had sustained it.

BRETT RUSHFORTH

Bibliography

Cook, Ramsay. *The Voyages of Jacques Cartier*. Toronto: University of Toronto Press, 1993.

Cronon, William. *Changes in the Land: Indians, Colonists, and the Ecology of New England*. New York: Hill and Wang, 1983.

Merrell, James H. *The Indians' New World: Catawbas and their Neighbors from European Contact through the Era of Removal*. Chapel Hill: University of North Carolina Press for the Omohundro Institute of Early American History and Culture, 1989.

Sleeper-Smith, Susan. *Indian Women and French Men: Rethinking Cultural Encounter in the Western Great Lakes*. Amherst: University of Massachusetts Press, 2001.

Trigger, Bruce. *Natives and Newcomers: Canada's "Heroic Age" Reconsidered.* Montreal: McGill-Queens University Press, 1985.

White, Richard. *The Middle Ground: Indians, Empires, and Republics in the Great Lakes Region, 1650–1815.* Cambridge and New York: Cambridge University Press, 1991.

G

Gender

The Atlantic World came into existence through the European conquest of aboriginal America, the establishment and expansion of commodities trades between Europe, Africa, and the Americas, and the Atlantic slave trade. What usually began as relatively peaceful and balanced relations between Europeans on one hand, and Africans and indigenous Americans on the other, were everywhere transformed between the fifteenth and twentieth centuries into forms of European domination. Policies and practices that violently imposed a binary categorization of people according to their bodies as "male" and "female" and assumed the superiority of the people designated "men" over the others marginalized as "women" were integral to the processes of trade and conquest that extended European power across the Atlantic World. The heteronormative and patriarchal gender order that accompanied the consolidation of Atlantic World colonialism never entirely undermined more diverse—sometimes radically different and more egalitarian—understandings of the relationship between sexed bodies and the body politic. Nevertheless, the imposition of the political, legal, and socioeconomic frameworks of European patriarchy is one of the defining features of the history of the Atlantic World.

Patriarchal norms became entrenched in European societies during the turbulent processes of centralization that shaped medieval Christian, Jewish, and Islamic warfare and politics. The concept of *limpieza de sangre* (purity of blood) in medieval Iberia, based in part on the violent regulation of women's sexuality, was key to the maintenance of religious and ethnic segregation and informed the sociopolitical order of the Iberian Catholic monarchies that launched Europe on the path of Atlantic expansion. Iberian rule spread these crude but highly adaptable binary conceptions of gender difference across the Atlantic. The fifteenth- and early sixteenth-century Canary Islanders, the indigenous peoples of the northern Caribbean, and the Aztecs were among the first Atlantic peoples to experience violent remaking of their more heterogeneous and inclusive gender orders after the arrival of Iberian conquistadors. The inherently exclusionary concept of *limpieza de sangre* became fundamental to post-1492 justifications for enslavement and dispossession of Africans and indigenous Americans.

Racialized concepts of blood purity coexisted with strategies encouraging heterosexual intercourse across boundaries of racial difference, so long as such relations reinforced European male sovereignty. The early-colonial Spanish and Portuguese inaugurated a policy, later adopted by their northern European rivals for power in the Atlantic, of pursuing their colonizing interests by "invading" the bodies of aboriginal women (Stolcke, 1994). European conquerors engaged in systematic sexualized violence as a weapon of war against indigenous people, including the forced impregnation of indigenous women and girls. Later, romanticized stories of conquerors' mistresses and wives, such as La Malinche (c. 1496 or c. 1505–1529), the woman given to Hernán Cortés by his aboriginal allies, later his mistress and mother of his son, and Virginia's Pocahontas (c. 1595–1617), daughter of Powhatan and wife of the Englishman John Rolfe, illustrate how European men used sexual relations with women as a means of undermining the autonomy of aboriginal societies. Colonial narrators cloaked the violent context of such unions in metaphors of seduction and used them as evidence of indigenous Americans' wider "consent" to European conquest.

Between the fifteenth and eighteenth centuries the Atlantic World was consolidated through law codes and systematized labor regimes and forms of commercial exchange that legitimated a potentially limitless sovereignty for propertied, Christian, European men over both the domestic and emerging public realms. Elite masculine European sovereignty found its ultimate expression in the legalized enslavement of others, whose degrees of "enslaveability" were mapped on the bodies of women. Adult males formed the largest age and sex cohort of Africans transported across the Atlantic, in part because the slave trades across the Sahara Desert and internal to the continent enslaved primarily women. Slave traders penned narratives that justified the enslavement of Africans by sexualizing and dehumanizing African women's bodies. Texts and images likening black women to breeding animals mirrored legal structures in the Americas that classified men and women alike as property. African women who crossed the Atlantic, even as a minority, brought with them knowledge of agricultural technology that proved crucial to the economies of American slaveholding societies.

Between the seventeenth and mid-eighteenth centuries, American slaveholding jurisdictions and European legal theorists adopted the principle that the owner of an enslaved woman also owned her children, regardless of the legal status, social rank, or race of the father. This principle, known in Roman law as *partus sequitur ventrem* ("the offspring follows the condition of the mother"), became the legal mechanism for reproducing commercially valuable human property in the Atlantic World, making slave women chattel whose wombs "increased" their owners' wealth. For most African-born or Afro-Creole women in the plantation Americas, enslavement meant a lifetime consigned to physically destructive forms of labor in the fields. Even though poor nutrition and devastating work environments left most women on sugar plantations unable to bear children, by the time of emancipation in the nineteenth century the majority of field laborers were women and girls. There was therefore a contradiction between the exploitation of enslaved women's bodies beyond the point of producing offspring and the legal claim to women's reproductive capacities as the basis for chattel slavery. As a result, most enslaved populations in the Americas grew via importing more bodies rather than through births of children. Major exceptions to this pattern were the Chesapeake region of North America, the island of Barbados by the end of the

eighteenth century, and the declining agricultural economy of post–gold rush (1770s) Minas Gerais in central Brazil.

The intersections between gender, sexuality, and the development of Atlantic colonialism passed through discernible historical phases. In the initial frontier phase, most colonists were white men seeking quick fortunes. The few European women present—who were often extremely poor and sometimes penal exiles—were generally derided by male colonial authorities as prostitutes. Sexual unions between white men and indigenous and African women were the norm. Indigenous and African women might have viewed these unions as committed marriages, but European men often saw them as temporary and informal, eventually to be superseded by legitimate marriage to a Christian woman of European descent, with property passing exclusively to her children. Nevertheless, not all such relationships reinforced European power and wealth. In areas of the Atlantic World where small European outposts coexisted on terms of relative equality with indigenous American and African communities, such unions could end with Christian marriage and the full legitimation of the couple's children, or with the de-Europeanization of the men and their full adoption into indigenous communities. In some instances the women in these arrangements accumulated local property, including urban real estate and slaves; the wealthy female women traders, or *signares*, of Senegambia, the Upper Guinea Coast, and Luanda in Africa became managers of the trade with the Atlantic.

As the frontier quality of these settlements gave way to formal structures of European governance, colonial authorities grew concerned about the absence of "respectable" European wives who could produce legitimate white heirs rather than the mestizos or mulattoes born to local women, Native American or African. The mid-seventeenth-century administrators of New France, like many of their counterparts in British North America and the Caribbean, invested heavily in schemes to promote emigration of white females to the colonies. Seventeenth- and eighteenth-century colonial regimes increasingly sought to restrict marriages between European men and non-European women. The 1685 French Code Noir—the law governing slavery across the French Empire—penalized male colonists for engaging in sexual relations with enslaved women by forcing the men to marry them and free both the women and any children of the couples. This regulation was intended to reframe such marriages as lifelong punishment for men who diluted the "purity" of French blood through such *mésalliances*. The provision was never actually enforced, and later versions of the Code entirely banned marriages between free Frenchmen and "blacks."

The Code Noir reflected the exclusionary impact that slavery and the racialization of relations between Europeans, Africans, and Americans had on Euro-Atlantic marriage laws. Roman, Islamic, and medieval European laws regulating marriage for enslaved women had sometimes offered freedom to those who bore children to their masters. By the eighteenth century the slave codes of the Americas universally rejected the premise of eligibility by maternity for manumission. If an enslaved woman had a child by a free man, she and the child remained slaves, unless the father/owner later voluntarily manumitted either one or both of them. By contrast, Euro-Atlantic laws of marriage and inheritance made white women's bodies the principal means for reproducing free status. This racist instrumentalization of women's reproductive capacities created a legal community of "rights-bearing" subjects of European maternity who could travel the Atlantic without fear of enslavement. By contrast, even freeborn people of color from the slaveholding Americas who could not prove that they were descended from free women ran the risk of being condemned to chattel slavery, especially if they were of African ancestry.

Although Atlantic World gender hierarchies victimized women in these and many other ways, viewing the experiences of women exclusively through the lens of victimhood does not capture the complex intersections of gender, race, and legal status. Analyses of gender in nineteenth-century African societies suggest striking similarities across the Atlantic World in the dynamics of heterosexual interactions. For example, indigenous and enslaved women could consciously and deliberately use sexual relations with white men as a means of personal advancement. Across the Americas, aboriginal women used sexual relations with white men as a means of consolidating political alliances between their nations and Europeans, often at the expense of rival indigenous peoples. Phibba, the mistress of the notorious sexual predator Anglo-Jamaican

plantation overseer Thomas Thistlewood used his affection for her to secure a better life and legal freedom for herself and their son. The *signares* of West Africa used sexual relations with white men to consolidate their trading interests. Regardless of race, the women of slave-based domestic units—plantation houses in the Americas and the compounds of African towns—were heavily invested in maintaining their power over their enslaved counterparts in disparate Atlantic locations. High-status Muslim women, secluded in patriarchal households, avoided domestic drudgery and participated in trade beyond the walls of the compounds where they lived by relegating lower-status menial labor and movement through the streets to enslaved women.

Enslaved women, free women of color, and indigenous women found many ways to survive, even thrive, within the severely restrictive, gendered, and racialized class stratification of the Americas. In the Caribbean, northeastern Brazil, and the U.S. South, for example, enslaved and free women of color crossed the legal boundaries of slavery to create a vibrant system of small-scale artisan production, gardening and food preparation, and marketing, supplying essential food items and services on which other colonial residents, especially urban dwellers, came to depend. Afro-Atlantic and Afro-indigenous spiritualties such as Brazilian Candomblé, Vodou in French Saint-Domingue, and some black Christian churches could be spaces of comparatively equitable gender dynamics, exhibiting through the worship of female ancestral deities the respect and authority that these religious communities accorded to female members. French Saint-Domingue's free elite of color included women who were significant owners of property in their own right, some of whom had wealthy sons who championed the free-colored cause in the French and Haitian revolutions at the end of the eighteenth century.

At the same time, the idealization of white women as virtuous wives produced secure lives of privilege for very few female colonists. In areas of the Americas where free wage laborers significantly outnumbered enslaved workers, the working poor often included majorities of white women. In the slaveholding societies of the Caribbean, white women appeared disproportionately on lists of paupers, since most forms of wage labor were off-limits to them. Few white females owned plantations, and female members of wealthy planter families were extremely vulnerable to the consequences of their often-indebted male relatives' financial mismanagement. Death rates among white male colonists were extremely high, and white women tended to outlive white men, not least because of a culture of white Creole masculinity based on displays of profligacy. Wealthy planter wives frequently ended as pauper widows.

From the late eighteenth to the early twentieth centuries, a few women crossed the boundary of masculine militarism to take part in revolutionary struggles as combatants, spies, and messengers. Other women of all socioeconomic backgrounds converted their domestic roles to harbor revolutionary troops in the popular movements that led to independence and emancipation in continental America and the Caribbean. Popular abolitionism in the nineteenth century brought black and white women onto otherwise male political stages in unprecedented public ways. The antislavery mobilization of women in the United States, Britain, and France in many ways launched modern Western feminism as a movement for public participation equal to men's. Yet nowhere in Europe or the Americas did abolitionism, successful anticolonial struggle, or emancipation lead directly to the political enfranchisement or economic autonomy of women. By 1807 the original thirteen colonies of the United States explicitly denied women the right to vote. Haitian independence led to the establishment of a highly militarized and masculinist state that excluded women from full citizenship and limited landownership by females to a tiny number of privileged women. Even in the Reconstruction-era United States, the suffrage movement split over the question whether the vote should be extended to black men before it was extended to women. Many prominent white suffragists actively supported racial segregation and opposed the enfranchisement of blacks.

Historians should neither romanticize life in the circum-Atlantic regions before the emergence of an Atlantic World as a time of gender equity, nor should they assume that modern conceptions of gender are appropriate for the study of earlier societies in Europe or other parts of the world. European, African, and indigenous people did not simply yield to colonial patriarchy; sometimes they (re) created cultures and communities that exhibited equitable and complementary, rather than exclusionary, relationships. Nevertheless, Atlantic World history exemplifies the often-violent interplay among militarism, enslavement, and patriarchal structures in the making of the modern global system. The history of the Atlantic World reveals that the basic contours of heteronormative European gender roles remained remarkably durable in the face of the dramatic upheavals of the fifteenth and nineteenth centuries. Gender thus became a fundamental—and still insufficiently examined—pillar of the social, legal, and economic order, as well as the dynamics of everyday life, in the Atlantic World.

MELANIE NEWTON

Bibliography

Aubert, Guillaume. "The Blood of France: Race and Purity of Blood in the French Atlantic World." *William and Mary Quarterly* 61, no. 3 (2004): 439–478.

Carney, Judith. *Black Rice: The African Origins of Rice Cultivation in the Americas*. Cambridge, MA: Harvard University Press, 2001.

Cooper, Barbara M. "Slavery, Seclusion and Female Labor in the Maradi Region of Niger in the Nineteenth and Twentieth Centuries." *Journal of African History* 35, no. 1 (1994): 61–78.

Eltis, David, and Stanley L. Engerman, "Fluctuations in Sex and Age Ratios in the Transatlantic Slave Trade, 1663–1864." *Economic History Review* 46, no. 2 (1993): 308–323.

Glymph, Thavolia. *Out of the House of Bondage: The Transformation of the Plantation Household*. New York: Cambridge University Press, 2008.

Lovejoy, Paul E. "Concubinage and the Status of Women in Early Colonial Nigeria." *Journal of African History* 29, no. 2 (1988): 245–266.

Mathurin Mair, Lucille. *A Historical Study of Women in Jamaica, 1655–1844*. Jamaica, Barbados, and Trinidad and Tobago: University Press of the West Indies, 2006.

Morgan, Jennifer L. *Laboring Women: Reproduction and Gender in New World Slavery*. Philadelphia: University of Pennsylvania Press, 2004.

Nirenberg, David L. *Communities of Violence: Persecution of Minorities in the Middle Ages*. Princeton, NJ: Princeton University Press, 1996.

Paton, Diana, and Pamela Scully, eds. *Gender and Slave*

Emancipation in the Atlantic World. Durham, NC: Duke University Press, 2005.

Stolcke, Verena. "Invaded Women: Race, Sex and Class in the Formation of Colonial Society." *Journal of European Development Research* 6 (1994): 7–21.

Geography

The Atlantic World is a geographic region centered on the Atlantic Ocean, encompassing primarily Europe, North America, Africa (including North Africa and sub-Saharan Africa), and South America (including Central America and the Caribbean). The center of the Atlantic Ocean on its north-south axis is the Equatorial Countercurrent that flows from northern South America toward West Africa, at about 5°N. This current separates the circulation systems of the North Atlantic and South Atlantic oceans. The east-west axis is the Mid-Atlantic Ridge, a divergent tectonic-plate boundary.

Since 1492 humans have understood the Atlantic as dividing the Old World (Europe, Africa, and Asia) from a New World (the Americas), but the nomenclature reflects a historical distinction rather than the relative ages of the two continental landmasses. Physically, the Atlantic World extends to the continental watersheds of the Atlantic Basin, including its seas. In the Old World, the Mediterranean, Black, and Baltic seas extend the Atlantic eastward; in the New World, the Caribbean Sea, Gulf of Mexico, and Hudson Bay extend it westward. The Atlantic receives many major rivers, including South America's Amazon, Orinoco, and Río de la Plata; Africa's Congo, Niger, and Senegal; Europe's Rhine; and North America's Mississippi, Rio Grande, and St. Lawrence. In the New World, the Atlantic watershed extends to the Continental Divide of the Americas, continuing northeasterly to the Hudson Bay watershed; in the Old World, the Atlantic watershed includes those of the Norwegian, Baltic, Mediterranean, and Black seas, extending south through the central and southern African highlands. In human geography, the Atlantic World may extend to locations that exert sustained influence within the basin from beyond its physical watershed. For instance, sources of silver in western Central America and South America are located in the Pacific Ocean basin but have been important in the history of the Atlantic World. The Atlantic merges in the north with the Arctic Ocean and in the Southern Ocean with the Pacific and Indian oceans, although no distinct boundaries delimit the polar ends of the Atlantic World.

Geologically, the Atlantic originated during the Mesozoic Era, 251 to 65 million years ago (MYA), when the ancient supercontinent Pangaea fragmented into Africa, Europe, North America, South America, and the other continents of historical times. North America and Europe share geologies as residual components of the pre-Pangaean continent Laurasia; Africa and South America were components of Gondwana. At the beginning of the Age of Reptiles, during the Triassic period (251–206 MYA), the proto-Mediterranean developed as tectonic rifting separated Europe and Africa. Rifting continued southwest during the Jurassic (206–142 MYA), splitting North America and Africa and creating the proto-Caribbean between North and South America. The Mid-Atlantic Ridge developed fully in the Cretaceous (142–65 MYA), as Laurasia and Gondwana rifted internally to create the North and South Atlantic basins. The modern continents reached their current relative locations 3 MYA. However, new oceanic crust continually erupts along the Mid-Atlantic Ridge, pushing the eastern and western Atlantic shorelines apart 2–3 cm annually, or about 13 meters since 1492.

Hominids occupied Atlantic shores in the Old World for much of the Pleistocene (which began 1.8 MYA), but the humans descended from them reached the New World fewer than 20,000 years ago. Modern humans developed seafaring in several Atlantic coastal locations, mostly in the early Holocene (which began 12,000 years ago), or in the warming wake of the last glaciation. Norse sailors made the first certain crossing of the Atlantic Ocean about 1000 CE. However, sustained contact across the ocean did not begin until Columbus's voyage in 1492. Portuguese sailors first transited the Atlantic into the Indian Ocean in 1497 and into the Pacific in 1520. Exploration into the Arctic Ocean has mostly occurred since 1553. Undersea exploration did not begin substantially until the mid-1900s.

This land and ocean exploration uncovered the broad geographic patterns that have served to organize knowledge about the Atlantic World. First, the north-south orientation of the Atlantic means that it provides maritime access to contrasting latitudinal climate zones, produced through global atmospheric circulation, ranging from polar to equatorial in both the North and South Atlantic basins. The most salient distinguishing climate features have been temperature, precipitation, and the directions of prevailing winds and associated ocean currents, which were especially important during the European Age of Sail (1400s–1850). The equatorial band has warm, wet climates and weak winds (historically lamented by sailors as the doldrums); tropical areas have hot, seasonally humid climates and easterly winds (the trade winds); subtropical areas have hot climates and weak winds (the horse latitudes); midlatitude areas have temperate climates and westerly winds; subpolar areas are cold, wet, and stormy; and polar climates are dry and frigid. Within these latitudinal climate bands, terrestrial physical geographic processes produce regional variation. For instance, elevation creates relatively cool highland climates, and the ocean creates relatively warm, moist maritime climates.

The wind and ocean currents helped determine historical trade routes, particularly those of the Triangular Trade—actually a circle around the Northern Hemisphere's mid-Atlantic zone of persistent high atmospheric pressures—that supported the Atlantic slave trade between Europe, Africa, and the Americas. Climate and particularly the presence of transatlantic bioclimatic zones are important in some aspects of post-Columbian economic and settlement history. Examples include crop transfers between Africa and the tropical Americas, and migration between temperate Europe and the Neo-Europes in settlement colonies of the Americas.

A second discovery helping to structure observers' understanding of the Atlantic involves plate tectonics, which separated ancient geological features shared on opposite shores of the ocean. Since the 1500s, scholars have theorized continental drift based on the matched shapes of eastern and western Atlantic shorelines. In fact, first-order relief (shapes of tectonic plates) in the South Atlantic often illustrates plate-tectonic theory in geoscience textbooks. The Atlantic World has weak second-order relief (topography produced by plate movements), except regionally, as in the European Alps and other ranges extending southeast into Asia; along the Continental Divide of the Americas (including the Rocky, Sierra Madre, and Andes mountains); and North America's Appalachians and North Africa's

Atlas Mountains (which formed together in Laurasia). Second-order relief also appears as islands along the Mid-Atlantic Ridge (outcropping as eight island groups, including Iceland, the Azores, St. Helena, and Ascension) and volcanic hot spots (island arcs in the Gulf of Guinea; the Lesser Antilles; and the North Atlantic, particularly the Canary, Cape Verde, and Madeira islands). Other island groups are exposed continental crust, including the Falkland/Malvinas Islands and Cuba and portions of the small Caribbean tectonic plate (the southern Greater Antilles and southern Central America). Coral islands are important in the low-latitude western Atlantic (especially in the Bahamas). Geologically and climatically similar sites may have similar third-order relief (topography produced by surface processes), including sandstone mesas in the humid tropical highlands of Guiana (northern South America) and Guinea (West Africa), and red sandstone hills in central Europe and the Canadian Maritimes.

A third discovery affecting analysis of the Atlantic World centers on biological evolution, which has produced global, hence transoceanic, biomes in broad latitudinal bands, as well as genetic dissimilarities between the regions ultimately separated by water. From the North Pole to the Equator the biomes are: icecap, polar tundra, subpolar forests, temperate forests and woodlands, subtropical deserts, tropical grasslands and woodlands, and tropical humid forests. The subpolar forest is absent in the truncated continents in the Earth's Southern Hemisphere. Laurasian and Gondwanan landmasses share broad biogeographic similarities, particularly the transatlantic presence of certain botanical families, including the annona family (flowering shrubs in the pawpaw/sugar apple family), found in both Africa and South America. Nonetheless, the four Atlantic continents represent distinct biogeographic realms that developed through post-Pangaean evolutionary history. Convergent evolution has produced ecologically and morphologically similar but unrelated organisms in transatlantic bioclimatic regions, including American cactuses and African cactiform euphorbias. Many species have crossed the ocean naturally through long-distance dispersals, especially on surface currents. These transatlantic plants and animals have been noted by many throughout the Atlantic World's history, including eleventh-century Norse settlers in Newfoundland, scholars since the 1500s, African slaves on American plantations, and twentieth-century European immigrants to the United States.

Human activities have transformed environmental conditions in essentially all the land areas in the Atlantic World. The cultural landscapes of the Atlantic reflect their distinctive evolutionary and human histories. From 10,000 to 2,000 years ago, Native peoples of the four Atlantic continents independently developed agriculture, which transformed large areas. After 1492, European expansion led to the Columbian Exchange of organisms between Old World and New World, which muted the distinctiveness of the biogeographic regions of the Eastern and Western hemispheres through habitat destruction, extinctions of locally endemic organisms, and introductions of others. Since 1492, introduced species, not least humans, have widely established robust populations, providing common material elements to otherwise distant cultural ecologies.

Three broad genetic groups of humans initially occupied the Atlantic World: peoples of sub-Saharan Africa, the Americas, and North Africa and Europe. Modern humans originated in sub-Saharan Africa some 200,000 years ago, inhabited North Africa 70,000 years ago, and moved into Europe 45,000 years ago; ancestral Native Americans colonized the Americas from Asia less than 20,000 years ago. The Atlantic's three broad human groups are genetically and culturally diverse, mostly isolated from one another for long periods of independent evolutionary and historical change; nearly 100,000 years separated African and Native American populations before 1492. Genetic distances between humans are slight, but physical differences among long-isolated groups have aligned with significant sociocultural differences. For instance, Native Americans, Africans, and Europeans developed different material cultures and belief systems before 1492, and these cultural differences gained historical significance when racial theories arose out of their Atlantic encounters to explain between-group variation in pigmentation and physiognomy.

Atlantic cultural regions today reflect differences produced through pre- and post-Columbian physical and human geographies. After 1492, cultural diversity and distributions changed substantially, especially in the New World, through European expansion and consequent decimation of popula-tions, involuntary emigration of enslaved Africans and some Asians, and mostly voluntary emigrations from Europe. Since 1492, European and Neo-European polities have dominated the Atlantic World, particularly those of Portugal, Spain, France, Great Britain, and the United States. The dominant European polities appropriated natural resources—including humans—outside Europe, which produced economic underdevelopment in Central and South America, the Caribbean, and Africa.

CHRIS S. DUVALL

Bibliography

Carney, J. A., and R. N. Rosomoff. *In the Shadow of Slavery: Africa's Botanical Legacy in the Atlantic World*. Berkeley: University of California Press, 2009.

Diamond, J. M. *Guns, Germs, and Steel: The Fates of Human Societies*. New York: W. W. Norton, 1997.

George, W., and R. Lavocat, eds. *The Africa–South America Connection*. Oxford: Clarendon, 1993.

Meinig, D. W. *The Shaping of America: A Geographical Perspective on 500 years of History*. 4 vols. New Haven, CT: Yale University Press, 1986–2004.

Government, Representative

"The Independence of America," Thomas Paine wrote in the midst of the French Revolution, "would have been a matter but of little importance, had it not been accompanied by a revolution in the principles and practice of government" (Paine, 548). The most momentous result of this revolution, he continued, was the emergence of the "system of representative government." In this new system, which Paine described in his famous *Rights of Man* (1791), government derived its authority from the governed rather than from God or king and was legitimated by their voluntary consent. Magistrates were chosen through regular elections and were accountable to their constituents. In short, representative government constituted a means to implement and operate the principle of popular sovereignty.

While Paine was right to point to the fledgling North American states as the first to have adopted this notion of government by representatives of the governed, they were building on older forms of representative institutions. A British-born revolutionary presenting the American example to the French, Paine symbolizes a crucial aspect of its development: the adaptation of European institutions and ideas in a New World environment and their advancement in a constant dialogue—and often conflict—with theoretical developments, on the eastern side of the Atlantic, regarding royal power and representation.

At the end of the Middle Ages, representative institutions had been ubiquitous in the emergent European monarchies. Although late-medieval kings based their rule on divine right, they lacked resources, had no developed state apparatus, and were operating according to medieval notions of the contractual nature of lord-vassal relationships. They thus had to rely on local nobles, church officials, and municipal elites to comply with and implement their policies. These elites, in turn, joined together in corporate bodies to represent their collective interests. Hence, the Holy Roman emperor had to cooperate with a diet of representatives of the principalities of the realm, the Estates-General advised French kings, the kingdoms on the Iberian peninsula had their Cortes, and in England Parliament represented both Lords and Commons. Around 1500 the actual powers of these representative institutions varied considerably, but during the early-modern period, when European monarchs embarked on what historians describe as the building of the "fiscal-military state" and, often successfully, centralized authority in the royal court, most of them lost much of their authority.

The major exception to this declining prominence of representation of the governed was the English (British, after the Act of Union of 1707) Parliament. Parliament had early on secured the crucial right to levy taxes, and it subsequently used this privilege to secure an ever-more-important role in the politics of the realm. Its rise, however, was not uncontested. Especially during the seventeenth century, English kings, taking the centralizing efforts of their French counterparts as a model, attempted to stop the ascendancy of Parliament and to reinforce royal authority. The ensuing tensions resulted in two major crises, the English Civil War (1642–1651) and the Glorious Revolution of 1688, which ended in the execution of one king (Charles I in 1649) and the deposition of another (James II in 1688). The victory of the parliamentary forces in these struggles constituted a milestone in the preservation of representation in European governments. The English Bill of Rights (1689) stipulated limits to the powers of the crown and specified the rights of Parliament, thus effectively turning England into a constitutional monarchy.

In these conflicts between monarch and Parliament originated also the connection of representative government to the notion of popular sovereignty. The Diet, Cortes, Estates-General, and even the English House of Lords had all represented hereditary privilege. In order to legitimate royal claims to superior authority, advocates of the crown routinely stressed the divine source of the kings' prerogatives. To counter this argument, parliamentarians during the English Civil War increasingly contended that while all governmental power came ultimately from God, it was the people in whom divine authority resided. In practice, however, this turn to the subjects of the realm did not yet mean the kind of popular sovereignty that Paine would extol 100 years later. Rather, when English parliamentarians in the middle and late seventeenth century invoked the sovereignty of the people, they did so to buttress their own positions as its custodians, thus preparing the ground for the system of representation that in the eighteenth century would claim absolute sovereignty for the oligarchic British Parliament throughout British dominions, at home and overseas.

It was against this background of growing royal, and in Britain also aristocratic parliamentary, power that representative institutions, and ultimately new ideas about representing a sovereign people in government, emerged in British America. The turn toward representative assemblies of local interests in the British American colonies was no foregone conclusion. Regardless of whether a colony was founded by a chartered company (as were Virginia and Massachusetts) or by a designated proprietor (as were Maryland and Pennsylvania), all derived their authority directly from the king. But the English kings of the seventeenth century—already locked in a power struggle at home with a representative assembly—had little interest in creating similarly recalcitrant institutions in their domains overseas. Thus, when Virginia in 1624 became a royal colony, the king moved to discontinue its House of Burgesses, created in 1618–1619 as the first popular assembly in North America. Colonial resistance, however, and the recognition in the metropolis that colonies 3,000 miles away could not be governed without participation of their populations, ensured the failures of this and similar attempts (most importantly, the Dominion of New England, in 1686–1689) to assert direct royal authority. Subsequent British administrations were still bent on tightening control over the colonies, but after the Glorious Revolution (1688) it was clear that politics in the colonies—as in the mother country—would be conducted within a framework of government that included representatives of their residents.

Representative government in the American colonies was not democratic in a modern sense. The American assemblies modeled themselves more and more after the House of Commons and thus imitated the nature of that body. By the time of the French and Indian War (1754–1763), the assemblies in virtually all colonies were controlled by a relatively small and cohesive propertied elite, committed to upholding its predominance. Appeals to the people at large in the early stages of the imperial crisis leading up to the War of American Independence thus came largely from the top down.

The resistance of colonial assemblies to metropolitan imposition of taxes and other burdens in the 1760s and 1770s differed from earlier struggles in pitting representatives of the people in the colonies not against the crown but against Parliament, the institution that claimed to represent the people of the entire British Empire. The result was a clash between ultimately irreconcilable visions of representation. Parliament asserted that it "virtually" represented colonists, but Americans insisted on the necessity of "actual" representation, by men chosen by those represented. This demand enabled American patriots to combat Parliament's claim to absolute sovereignty with the idea that sovereignty rested in the people. Basing their fight for local rather than remote representation on the notion of popular sovereignty helped American revolutionaries to unite large segments of the colonial populations across class lines and political boundaries.

The intimate link North Americans forged between representative government and popular sovereignty turned traditional top-down government on its head. Besides providing for frequent elections to ensure the accountability of the representatives to their constituents, Americans also experimented, by erecting independent states and a continental union, with new means to prevent their representatives from following the path of Parliament, toward setting themselves up as the absolute sovereign. Their most important innovations were written constitutions, drafted by specially elected conventions and, at least in some cases, also ratified popularly. The advantages of a constitution adopted by explicit consent of the governed were that it embodied authority higher than did ordinary acts of legislation, and that it turned not only the legislature but all branches of government into representatives of the people.

A very important—and divisive—issue regarding representative government was who should be represented and in what manner. This question generated heated debates as to whether the legislature should be unicameral (a single chamber) or bicameral and balanced. Most Americans agreed that even in a bicameral system, both houses derived their power from the same constituents and did not represent different classes or social orders. The uncontested acceptance of "the people" as the constituent power in the United States government made its basis very different from that of the three contrasting "estates"—clergy, nobility, and commoners—at the commencement of the French revolution in the late 1780s.

The existence of entrenched privileged orders such as the church and the nobility made the issue of who might be represented in government central when the Estates-General convened in early 1789. The debate centered around two opposing conceptions: The first maintained that the classes into which French society had long been divided should be represented separately, while the second argued for representation on the basis of a single, indivisible French nation. Advocates of corporate representation took the continental heritage—and especially the British mixed constitution—as their model, whereas adherents of a single nation looked to the form of popular sovereignty that had just emerged in America. Accordingly, the two factions were dubbed *anglomanes* and *amèricanistes*. The *amèricanistes* prevailed in the early stages of the

French Revolution and transmitted the idea of representative government as the sovereignty of a single people throughout the Atlantic World.

The ideas of representative government as they had evolved in the United States and the French Republic did not immediately inspire universal demands for similar forms in other Atlantic World political communities. Yet when Napoleon (1769–1821) invaded Spain in 1808 and transferred its crown to his brother, liberal-minded segments of the Spanish opposition used the ensuing civil war to press ahead with reform of the Spanish Empire along representative lines. The result of these efforts was the Constitution of 1812, which provided for relatively widespread suffrage and—while uniting the entire Spanish Empire in a single transatlantic nation-state—also established a more decentralized regime with strong local, representative institutions. The Constitution of 1812, however, was short lived; upon his reinstatement in 1814, Ferdinand VII (1784–1833) abolished it and strove to reassert the traditional royal prerogative. But he, as well as his Portuguese counterpart John VI (1767–1826), had to recognize that absolute prerogative was no longer viable. Both the Spanish and Portuguese empires disintegrated during the wars of independence in Latin America and liberal revolutions at home.

While Brazil opted for a constitutional monarchy with authority divided between an emperor and a General Assembly, after attaining independence in 1822 the newly independent states in Spanish America generally followed the example set in the Constitution of 1812 and elected representative governments based on popular sovereignty. Unlike in the United States, however, domestic regional and racial tensions in many cases resulted in the authoritarian leadership of a military *caudillo* instead of a government representing citizens. In

the early nineteenth century, representative government as a means of popular sovereignty had thus not (yet), as Thomas Paine had hoped, replaced monarchy or more oligarchic forms of representative government throughout the Atlantic World. Yet the spread of representative government based on popular sovereignty in the British American context, its subsequent appearance in the French Revolution, its adaptations in Latin America, in France after the restoration of the monarchy (1814), and in Great Britain (especially after the Reform Act of 1832) illustrates the flow of ideas and the interconnectedness of events they inspired in the larger Atlantic World from the early-modern to the modern eras.

ARMIN MATTES

Bibliography

Elliott, John H. *Empires of the Atlantic World: Britain and Spain in America, 1492–1830*. New Haven, CT, and London: Yale University Press, 2006.

Morgan, Edmund S. *Inventing the People: The Rise of Popular Sovereignty in England and America*. New York and London: W. W. Norton, 1988.

Paine, Thomas. *Collected Writings*. Edited by Eric Foner. New York: Library of America, 1995.

Rodriguez O., Jaime E. *The Independence of Spanish America*. New York: Cambridge University Press, 1998.

Yirush, Craig. *Settlers, Liberty, and Empire: The Roots of Early American Political Theory, 1675–1775*. New York: Cambridge University Press, 2011.

Healing, African

To see "healing" in the African side of the Atlantic story presupposes an affliction—a disaster, an undesirable, threatening situation, an adverse condition—that was thought to require collective resolution. And communities in Africa experienced such disruptions brought about by Atlantic mercantilism, which was experienced often as a threat to their integrity. Responses to these threats can best be traced in the rise of the *min'kisi*, consecrated medicines or techniques that Africans created to address them. The story of *min'kisi*, which begins in the sixteenth century, can be found in the primary evidence of African culture, including outsiders' accounts of institutions and practices, pivotal historical events and personalities, and firsthand accounts by African actors. Scholars also unearth knowledge about *min'kisi* from key verbal concepts in the history of African languages. Such sources combine to yield a picture of the distinctive social healing that responded to the displacements and disruptions of the Atlantic trade.

Min'kisi

N'kisi (singular) is an untranslatable term in the Kongo language of West-Central Africa meaning technique, knowledge, and expertise in the physical and social worlds; material artifacts; social processes surrounding the efficacious uses of these materials; and initiation to the specialized knowledge of them. The term also refers to the consecrated legitimation of—that is, general belief in—the whole conceptual system. Terms cognate with *n'kisi* are found in Bantu languages spoken on the Atlantic coast from Gabon to Angola and inland across the rain forest and southern savanna to the eastern Congo and Zambia—more or less the area of Central Africa engaged with Atlantic commerce. The term thus reflects a thousand years of Western-Bantu languages and cultures, with varying local adaptations. *Min'kisi* originate in visions by individuals facing adversity or challenge. Techniques, the specific materials employed, applications, strict codes of applying them, and prohibitions to be observed by owners of the material and its users are all parts of the *n'kisi*, and the original and complete set of procedures must be observed to preserve its efficacy. As consecrated knowing, the *n'kisi* has features in common with the Western conventions of patenting of knowledge and scholarly referencing; it is also similar to the *hadith* (stories, parables) authenticating Islamic memory of the Prophet.

Min'kisi inventories that particular communities used to heal themselves socially are classified by the types of authorized users—that is, for individual, household, or collective application (the last composed and "drummed up" in public song-dance ceremonies). They are also categorized by their associations with the cosmic—we would say "natu-ral"—sources of power in the world: water, land, and sky; and they are also distinguished according to their utility for protective or aggressive purposes. The clustered features of specific *min'kisi* are sometimes given agency by and integrated into carved anthropomorphic or mammalian figures, which are brought to life and engaged in action through a skilled *nganga* (trained specialist). The *nganga* might verbally address and spit at the figures, smear them with the blood of a sacrificed animal, or drive wedges into them. The specialists also might simply combine ingredients from contrasting categories in animating the objects. Such figurines with cavities, packs, and attachments—beloved, if also badly misunderstood, by art collectors and museums—or calabashes, pots, and sacks functioned only as the containers that held the active substance of the *n'kisi*. Plants, or suggestive parts of animals, birds, or earth, are combined and alluded to in formulae that engage the *n'kisi* in its assigned task. Thus, in a historical example, the aromatic *nsaku-nsaku* plant was incorporated into an *n'kisi*'s medicine to bless (*sakamuna*) the owner or action; a cluster of plants, including *lemba-lemba*, was mixed to sedate or calm (*lembikisa*) an agitated or deranged individual.

Medicines for Mercantilism

In the seventeenth century Dutch travelogue publisher Olfert Dapper offered an inventory of Loango coast *min'kisi* that included those used in relation to the coastal trade. *N'kisi* Bossi-Batta was contained in a large lionskin bag and two calabashes, which were taken along on trading expeditions and also kept on a shelf over the door of the merchant's house. Upon the merchant's return, as he unpacked the goods he had purchased, the *nganga* (priest or expert) of Bossi-Batta would unpack the *n'kisi* and go into a trance, giving himself up to the energy or spirit of the *n'kisi*. The ingredients of the large pack—bits from various creatures of nature and technology (iron ore and slag), and hair, nails, and teeth from albinos and other anomalous (hence powerful) creatures—represented the cosmological realms of water, land, and sky and powers derived therefrom. One of the calabashes had a mouthlike orifice into which wine was poured to activate the *n'kisi*, to give it life. Another *n'kisi* in Dapper's Loango inventory, Kikokoo, protected the dead against theft of their souls by witches who would drag them off to slavery and forced labor beyond Kalunga, the watery land of the dead, readily associated with the Atlantic. Yet at the same time Kikokoo also assured the safe arrival of the European ships bringing merchandise.

Both of these *min'kisi* reflected the profound ambivalence that coastal Kongo of the seventeenth century felt toward Atlantic mercantilism: they desired trade goods for the wealth in people—clients, wives, slaves—that they could obtain with them, but they also feared being somehow polluted by personal success, having their spiritual power weakened or their ancestors' souls and family members abandoned and taken off into slavery. The dominant theme of these *min'kisi* is protection from a rising threat to well-being, the social dimension of a healthy community. Engagement in commercial trade with outsiders, like Europeans, who were widely depicted as "cannibals," or the witches who secretively gnawed away at community integrity, created the same potential for corrosive individual power through personal wealth, leaving African communities to create *min'kisi* to heal themselves.

By the eighteenth century, *n'kisi* Lemba, on the other hand, not only provided individual and household protection for Africans engaged in Atlantic trade but also addressed the need for regional economic integration resulting from the numerous caravan routes between the coastal ports of Boma, Ngoyo, Kakongo, and Loango and the huge market in the interior at Malebo Pool (above today's Kinshasa). Originally an *n'kisi* to protect the king of Loango, ruler of the largest trading port in the region, simultaneously dependent on and contaminated by the commerce of the Atlantic, Lemba was adapted by wealthy merchants across the largely decentralized communities of the region north of the lower Congo River to promote trade, markets, and caravan routes and to foster the prosperity and fertility of their households and lineages. The communities brought into contact through competitive trading were prone to break out in difficult-to-resolve feuds that would engulf multiple villages, resulting in deaths, destruction of homes, and disruption of the commerce that simultaneously united and divided them. Adjudicatory *min'kisi*, such as N'kondi, were common in this area to prevent or resolve such trade feuds. The centerpiece of Lemba's "medicine" was a marriage ceremony that consecrated alliances between neighboring land-owning lineages along the trade routes.

The physical manifestation of Lemba consisted of a chest with effigies of the Lemba father, Lemba son, and wives, associated in their symbolism with trade objects, the power of ironworking, the domains of earth, sky, water, and the graves of ancestors. Each Lemba household owned a special Lemba drum used in the initiatory and celebratory ceremonies. Lemba gave its initiates the ability to move across the region unhindered by local affiliations. Initiatory costs were very high, both befitting wealthy merchants and limiting membership in the network. Some of the animals slaughtered in the feasts, and goods distributed during them, amounted to ritual allocations of valuable trade goods—to those who would otherwise envy the merchants' wealth and influence—thereby stilling the spirits of disunion that might otherwise cause disease.

* * *

This social mode of healing made possible the preservation of mutual interdependencies, although in altered forms, in the face of the highly individuating and thus destabilizing personal riches of Atlantic trade. It addressed the contradiction between kin-based societies that valued the mutuality of lineages and extended households and the great wealth that Atlantic commerce made available to individuals. Throughout Atlantic Africa other communities developed parallel strategies of social healing, always derived from their own local cultural resources. Because of the massive removal of people from the region to the other side of the Atlantic, some of the features of these healing practices Africans developed to deal with strangers reemerged, in yet-again-altered forms, in the radical alienation of enslavement in the New World.

JOHN M. JANZEN

Bibliography

Janzen, John. *Lemba 1650–1930: A Drum of Affliction in Africa and the New World.* New York: Garland, 1982.

Vansina, Jan. *Paths in the Rainforests: Toward a History of Political Tradition in Equatorial Africa.* Madison: University of Wisconsin Press, 1990.

Healing, African American

It could be argued that diseases condemned millions of Africans to live in bondage: the collapse of Native American populations caused by epidemics of influenza, smallpox, typhus, and bubonic plague, among others, spurred the emergence of the transatlantic slave trade. However, corporeal afflictions also provided a rich space in which people of African descent shaped American cultures and societies. Human bodies functioned throughout the Atlantic Era as one of the central stages for the deployment of African ideas about the nature of the world and the contestation of ideologies of European imperial and cultural dominance. Early-modern Atlantic people from all origins faced worlds populated by people and plagues of the likes they had never seen. Like Europeans, Africans and African American communities in Africa and the Americas strove within their own intellectual frameworks to compile, catalogue, and transmit understandings of the myriad uncanny bodies, diseases, and medical treatments that appeared in front of them.

Afro-Atlantic healers—*ngangas, babalawos,* and *jabacouses,* among others—occupied prominent religious, political, and social positions in communities on both sides of the Atlantic. They were the intellectual forces modeling systems of beliefs about the body, not only in Africa but also in the many American locales where they arrived. These ritual specialists, however, lacked licenses from European authorities and did not offer "sanctioned" healing procedures. Their holistic concepts of corporeality and healing were closer to what today would be considered preventive medical care and were based largely on beliefs about the social origins of health and disease. Forces that Europeans viewed as spiritualized figured largely in Afro-Atlantic conceptualizations of disease causation. Consequently, rites aimed at appeasing or manipulating ancestors and other spirits were essential parts of the therapeutic arsenals of Afro-Atlantic ritual specialists. These practitioners, in seeking cures, also resorted to a vast ethnobotanical armamentarium accumulated in West and West Central Africa over many generations. In the Americas, African ritual specialists would look for therapeutic elements similar to those they had used in the Old World, while incorporating new materials they found in the different places where they lived. Although deployed in American locales by practitioners of African descent, it would be misleading to call these practices "African American." Though largely based on the incorporative traditions of West and West-Central African cultures, African Atlantic healing practitioners in the Americas eagerly appropriated practices coming not only from other African cultures, but also from European, Islamic, Asian, and Native American healing systems. For centuries before the arrival of Portuguese mariners in the fifteenth century, Africans had been engaged in rich interchanges of knowledge about healing techniques. These dynamics were only amplified by the tumultuous explosion in commercial exchanges of people and goods in the three centuries that followed.

People of African descent developed extended networks of information about healing practices that linked distinct locales in Africa, Europe, and the Americas. The historical record shows startling similarities in rites that black ritual specialists practiced in places as distant as Havana, Salvador da Bahia, Lisbon, and Luanda. Afro-Atlantic rituals such as sucking, cutting and cupping, and ritual objects such as Mandinga bags (amulets of Islamic origin) and horns retained powerful symbolic and instrumental meanings recognizable to Africans living on both sides of the Atlantic. While these wide distributions seem to betoken continuities in meanings, they also underscore the flexibility with which African ritual specialists adapted their knowledge and procedures to specific local concerns. In fact, pragmatic malleability underlay their ubiquity in the Atlantic World. Black healers were sought after not only by slaves, free blacks, and people of mixed descent but also by members of the European elite, including ecclesiastical authorities. In the competitive therapeutic marketplace of the New World, African ritual specialists transformed rites and materials to conform to the multicultural communal scenarios in which they worked.

Afro-Atlantic healing systems were shaped by the particular socioeconomic systems in different American regions and the origins and numbers of the Africans arriving in them. The same regional factors also influenced the relative visibility and cultural diffusion of black healing practices. Spanish and Portuguese colonial societies provided spaces for the consumption of Afro-Atlantic healing procedures that the British or French did not. In cities and towns in Brazil, Cuba, and the New Kingdom of Granada (Spanish colonies in northern South America), Afro-Atlantic healing practices were in full display among the resident majorities of African origin in complex and durable forms that were empirically sound in addressing individual and social ills. These practices were less widespread in British colonies, where Africans lived in relative isolation, formed smaller percentages of the populations, and had limited social spaces for enacting their rites. However, even within the constraints of classic British or French chattel slavery in Jamaica or Saint-Domingue, African ritual practitioners gained recognition among the enslaved as powerful and effective health practitioners.

Removed from modern understandings about the biological nature of disease, corporeal individuality, and the intimacy of medical practices, Afro-Atlantic rituals of healing were closely associated with social and political circumstances and can be understood only within these collective frameworks. Healers operated within local public imaginaries and depended on adequate readings and translations of the social, cultural, and political contexts of their clients. Parallel in these ways to the community coherence achieved in modern contexts by beliefs termed religious, Afro-Atlantic healing practices were integral parts of Afro-Atlantic religions such as Candomblé, Santeria, Vodou, or Obeah. Healing practices also offered black practitioners in the Americas unique opportunities for social and economic advancement and cultural penetration. For black communities they worked as effective instruments to restore personal and collective wholeness in the context of ubiquitous disruptions through disease, death, discipline, and sales, while at the same time functioning as powerful tools to elaborate and publicly display alternative narratives about the "truthfulness" of the world. The widespread effectiveness of Afro-Atlantic healing practices evidences the porous borders of supposedly separate areas of knowledge secluded in the numerous cultures of the Atlantic World. By creating alternative visions of American spiritual, human, and physical landscapes, they functioned as powerful instruments to question the validity of Western discourses of imperial dominance.

PABLO F. GÓMEZ

Bibliography

Fett, Sharla M. *Working Cures: Healing, Health, and Power on Southern Slave Plantations.* Chapel Hill: University of North Carolina Press, 2002.

Sweet, James. *Domingos Alvares, African Healing, and the Intellectual History of the Atlantic World.* Chapel Hill: University of North Carolina Press, 2011.

Healing, European

European colonists in the Americas and in Africa developed healing practices not by comprehensively transporting Old World ideas, plants, and procedures to the New World but by adapting those familiar practices to unfamiliar diseases and climates. These adaptations must be understood in the context of concerns regarding the medical risks and opportunities of transatlantic travel and settlement. While some Europeans promoted the New World as a site of medicinal wealth, colonists also worried that tropical climates, whether in the Americas or in Africa, would disease and alter their bodies. Such anxieties motivated travelers and settlers to seek new remedies and to investigate the medical knowledge of Native Americans and Africans.

Medicinal Wealth across the Atlantic

Travel across the Atlantic seemed initially to promise great medical benefits. Searching for herbal remedies as much as for gold, travelers in the fifteenth, sixteenth, and seventeenth centuries described America as a treasure trove of medicinal riches. Colonial promoters argued that tobacco, an herb that Native Americans employed in religious and political ceremonies, was a panacea, a universal cure that would heal many illnesses in many places. Popular compilations of herbal remedies, such as *Historia medicinal*, compiled by Spanish physician Nicolás Monardes (c. 1512–1588), described the benefits for Europeans of indigenous medicines in Spanish America. *Historia medicinal* was translated into multiple languages and republished several times, attesting to the universal European interest in herbal medicines from the Americas. New World remedies—from sassafras or guaiacum to cure the great pox, or syphilis, now known to be an American disease, to Peruvian bark, from which quinine is derived, to treat malarial fevers—entered not only Europeans' print culture but also their everyday medicinal practices.

Deadly Travel, Healing Strategies

Despite their hopes for medicinal wealth, colonists also feared the consequences of travel across the Atlantic. Early-modern theories of disease posited connections among place, body, and mind, and by extension suggested that the climatological environment determined dominant physical and mental characteristics as well as one's ideal state of health. Europeans had defined their own respective environments as best-suited for producing healthy bodies and rational minds: as a consequence, travel to the tropics threatened to disease and degrade both. In particular, Europeans worried that they would take on the mental and physical attributes of the people whom they found living in, and presumably adapted to, hot climates—an alleged condition in all of the Americas owing to their supposed locations in latitudes south of Europe. Traditionally, such attributes of residents in hot climates included superstition, laziness, and irrationality. Colonists who were born in or who had adapted to the American climate thus faced suspicions that their mental and physical constitutions were compromised.

Colonists responded to the dangers they perceived in their encounters beyond the Atlantic by documenting local strategies for resisting the ill effects of American climates. In medical tracts such as the 1672 *American Physitian,* William Hughes (fl. 1665–1683), an English horticultural writer who had visited the Caribbean, advised his countrymen living there to avoid eating heavy meats that would cloud the mind with heavy vapors. Experienced colonists frequently offered advice regarding the clothing and building materials needed to protect new arrivals from the contagions of the climate. Medical practitioners likewise urged colonists to limit their exposure to New World hazards, such as tropical air found in its lower latitudes, and they drew upon remedies from Europe to cure dietary maladies and fevers.

In contrast with the herbal cures that America could offer, Africa's climate was legendary for its heat and fevers. In the sixteenth century, Portuguese and English travelers to Guinea feared that the sun near the Equator would burn them to death, as articulated in travel narratives collected by Richard Hakluyt (c. 1552–1616), an English geographer. By the eighteenth century, colonists, soldiers, and slave traders focused on the dangerous fevers, particularly yellow fever and malaria, for which Africa's west coast became infamous as "the white man's grave." Bleeding and purging were the primary therapies for these fevers before physicians and surgeons began in the seventeenth century to prescribe Peruvian bark, which gave rise to quinine as a treatment for malaria—an example of the many directions in which transatlantic exchanges moved. European fatalities in Africa ultimately were used to support theories of scientifically based racism, as Europeans interpreted their susceptibility to fevers as a sign of their bodies' temperate nature, and they argued that Africans' immunity to the same fevers signaled an innate propensity for hard labor in tropical conditions.

Medical Exchanges

Colonists also turned to the medical knowledge of Native Americans and Africans in order to maintain their own health. British colonists in North America frequently commented on how remarkably healthy Native Americans appeared compared to people in England—even despite contact-era epidemics of European diseases that reduced Native populations by 90 to 95 percent. Colonists often attributed Indians' fitness to their herbal knowledge, and they sought to discover the specific plants they employed. John Josselyn (1608–1700?), an English Royalist with botanical interests, noted in his 1674 *Two Voyages to New-England* that his Native informants often chose to keep their remedies secret, even though he also gathered information regarding many New England herbs. In the eighteenth century, colonists in the Caribbean noted Africans' secretive medical and religious practices, which they called Obeah, to heal bodies as well as to poison people for purposes of revenge or justice. While most colonists dismissed Obeah as superstition, some colonial physicians acknowledged the practices as curative. Similarly, they depended upon Africans' abilities to treat yaws, an extremely contagious skin disease akin to smallpox, greatly feared by Europeans.

Colonists often represented the natural, epistemological, and spiritual contexts in which Indians and Africans had employed the herbs and roots that they described. Certainly, colonists sometimes effaced the processes of exchange and translation by which they obtained knowledge of Native and African healing practices when they adapted them to their own cures or to present them to European scientific societies; however, colonists did not completely erase the transatlantic origins of their knowledge. They frequently retained Native and African names for plants unknown in Europe, and they highlighted the Native or African origins of medical practices in order to emphasize their exotic nature. In Boston, for example, minister Cotton Mather (1663–1728) emphasized that he had learned of inoculation—a preventive treatment for smallpox in which live smallpox virus was inserted into patients' bloodstreams—from his African slave Onesimus, rather than from the publications of the British Royal Society.

* * *

The Atlantic World—having been integrated by, in part, the circulation of humans, medicines, diseases, and medical knowledge—inspired new healing practices and medical writings even as it endangered colonists' health. While people's travels and settlement throughout the Atlantic were seen as dangerous, these explorations and migrations motivated searches for, and resulted in discoveries of, new remedies. And encounters among Europeans, Native Americans, and Africans enriched both European practices and oral and print communications about healing and health.

KELLY WISECUP

Bibliography

Crosby, Alfred. *The Columbian Exchange: Biological and Cultural Consequences of 1492*. Westport, CT: Greenwood, 1972.

Handler, Jerome S. "Slave Medicine and Obeah in Barbados, Circa 1650 to 1834." *New West Indian Guide* 74, nos. 1 & 2 (2000): 57–90.

Parrish, Susan Scott. *American Curiosity: Cultures of Natural History in the Colonial British Atlantic World*. Chapel Hill: University of North Carolina Press, 2006.

Wey-Gómez, Nicolás. *The Tropics of Empire: Why Columbus Sailed South to the Indies*. Cambridge, MA: MIT Press, 2008.

Healing, Native American

As Europeans and Africans moved throughout the Atlantic Basin in the sixteenth and seventeenth centuries, they brought the populations of three continents into sustained physical contact for the first time. Historians have focused on the causes and consequences of the ensuing exchange of pathogens and diseases. Important exchanges also took place between the therapeutic systems of all the peoples involved. The history of Native American healing demonstrates the range of fates of therapeutic practices, from displacement to persistence and pragmatic adaptation.

With nearly 2,000 languages spoken in the Americas in 1490, it is likely that an equal number of distinct therapeutic systems existed, all in ongoing pragmatic elaboration. Scholars have used several sources to reconstruct these diverse healing beliefs and practices. Much has been learned by studying Indian therapeutic systems that remain in use today, though current therapies reflect centuries of further adaptation and assimilation. Historians have also mined written accounts left by European explorers, missionaries, soldiers, traders, and scientists. The Dutch, English, French, Portuguese, and Spanish were all eager to learn how Indians managed disease. Their writings, read with care, provide revealing glimpses.

Native Americans had long responded to the challenge of disease by turning to self-treatment or engaging a wide assortment of diagnosticians and healers. Their diagnoses gave social meanings to individual symptoms and assigned blame and responsibility accordingly. Beyond obvious wounds, diseases were attributed to poisoning, or to such spiritualized causes as soul stealing. Diagnoses thus often pointed beyond the afflicted individuals to tensions in their communities. Herbal remedies, bloodletting, sweating, incantations, and other healing ceremonies relieved symptoms and indirectly addressed underlying physical causes. Many drugs derived from Indian botanical knowledge remain in use today, including nicotine, capsicum (from species of peppers, including the piquant varieties), coca, quinine, curare (a paralyzing poison), and ipecac (a purgative). Scholars have often contrasted the empirical-rational aspects of herbal medicine with the superstitious-magical practices of religious healing, but such distinctions are misleading. With tight ties between medicine and religion, episodes of illness had social significance far beyond an individual's physical symptoms.

Contacts with Europeans and Africans confronted Indians with both new stresses and new opportunities for their therapeutic systems. How did they evaluate the therapeutic practices of these others? How did Indian healers respond to European intrusions and epidemics? Many individuals were pragmatic. Native Americans often dabbled in European healing. Wampanoags and Massachusetts sought help for diseases as varied as constipation and smallpox from the English. Indians in Maine tried European remedies based on bran, molasses, and licorice. When French and Spanish missionaries opened hospitals in Quebec and Mexico, they were inundated with Indian patients. This embrace of European therapies extended beyond herbal remedies into European spirituality. Many Indians converted to Christianity and prayed for relief from their sufferings.

European explorers, meanwhile, turned to Native American medical knowledge as they searched the Americas for plants of scientific, commercial, or medicinal value. European botanical texts often included stories about how Indians treated diseases with specific plants. Their interests were not just academic. European colonists frequently relied on Indian healing and remedies. Locked in ice in the St. Lawrence River in 1536, Jacques Cartier's crew used a local remedy to treat scurvy. Jesuits in Quebec and physicians in Virginia respected the power of Indian remedies derived from tobacco or sassafras. One Carolina farmer even agreed—grudgingly—to drink an Indian potion and take a defanged rattlesnake into his bed to cure (successfully) a distemper. Whether motivated by respect, curiosity, or desperation, colonists understood that if they were going to live in the Americas, they would suffer American diseases and would need to learn American remedies. Africans, brought to the Americas against their will, also sought knowledge of Indian medical practices that could help them survive the extreme stresses in their world of bondage.

Europeans condemned other aspects of Indian healing, especially the practices they saw as religious. European accounts—and not just those by missionaries—derided them as superstitions, antics, and devilish practices, labeling Indian shamans and other healers as sorcerers, knaves, and imposters. Their disdain was not simply because the practices seemed magical or religious. After all, European and African healing systems alike at the time made extensive use of treatments we now see as magical and religious. Instead, the judgments focused on the non-Christian aspects of Indian healing and on the suspicion that some Indian healers were charlatans who knowingly defrauded credulous patients with meaningless practices—a critique also often made of European physicians.

Among the emerging European biomedical treatments that crossed the Atlantic, vaccination against smallpox was surely the most important. Brought to England initially from Asia (via the Ottomans) as inoculation, the procedure was refined to vaccination in 1796 by Edward Jenner. Thomas Jefferson vaccinated a delegation of Miami chiefs in 1801. British and Spanish officials launched vaccination campaigns in 1803. The Expedition de la Vacuna, for instance, claimed to have vaccinated 100,000 people, many of them Indians, from South America to New Mexico. Representatives of the Five Nations in Canada even sent Jenner a string of wampum and thanked the Great Spirit for bestowing wisdom on him.

Did the willingness of Indians to accept European medicine indicate that they had lost faith in their own medicine and religions? Many historians have said yes, arguing that the inability of Indian healers to provide effective remedies for epidemics of smallpox and other European diseases demonstrated their impotence. According to this theory, disillusionment led to the abandonment of traditional cultural practices and facilitated acculturation into European colonial regimes. However, significant examples also demonstrate the resilience and adaptability of Indian healing systems. Creek and Cherokee healers and religious leaders, for instance, developed new beliefs and practices to cope with smallpox. They quarantined sufferers to reduce the risk of transmission and offered new, specific healing ceremonies to those who fell sick. Although the epidemics challenged Indian medical beliefs and practices, Indian healers maintained their respected roles during the struggles of colonization.

The Atlantic World made possible exchanges of therapeutic systems as well as diseases among Indians, Africans, and Europeans. Into the eighteenth century, curiosity and awareness of shared susceptibility fostered exchanges grounded in pragmatic open-mindedness. Over time, however, Europeans became increasingly confident about the superiority of both their bodies and their knowledge of healing as physical medicine. Their new sense of supremacy guided subsequent encounters as they extended their colonial regimes beyond the Atlantic World.

DAVID S. JONES

Bibliography

Chaplin, Joyce E. *Subject Matter: Technology, the Body, and Science on the Anglo-American Frontier, 1500–1676*. Cambridge, MA: Harvard University Press, 2001.

Jones, D. S. *Rationalizing Epidemics: Meanings and Uses of American Indian Mortality since 1600*. Cambridge, MA: Harvard University Press, 2004.

Kelton, Paul. "Avoiding the Smallpox Spirits: Colonial Epidemics and Southeastern Indian Survival." *Ethnohistory* 51 (Winter 2004): 45–71.

Vogel, Victor J. *American Indian Medicine*. Norman: University of Oklahoma Press, 1970.

Imperial Planning

A great deal of Atlantic history, and the histories of the European empires that conventionally compose it, may be rewritten to emphasize unplanned, improvised processes. Such historical contingencies—resulting from unforeseen events—were amplified in the Atlantic in at least two distinct ways. First, encounters with unknown cultures generated unanticipated, in some cases unprecedented, outcomes, from cultural hybridity and religious syncretism to the inadvertent Columbian Exchange of flora and fauna. Second, much "empire building"—construed narrowly as establishing legal rights to, and military control over, remote territories and their populations—was undertaken by agents acting independently of governments, whether Jesuits, itinerant traders, swashbuckling *bandeirantes* in southern Brazil, or Portuguese *lançados* ("castaways") integrated into communities in Africa. These individuals and groups sometimes acted with the authorization or even sponsorship of monarchical authorities in Europe, but more often they operated without their knowledge or support. Only later would their scattered presence become incorporated into government claims to formal dominion and be portrayed retrospectively as parts of carefully planned and executed master strategies originating in royal chanceries.

The success or failure of imperial efforts in the Atlantic World depended on local dynamics, which meant that the ability of European authorities to impose their wills (even when a coherent vision existed) was extremely limited. Local collaborators and partners, themselves acting with their own projects, aspirations, and priorities in mind, were indispensable to Europeans—to both states and independently operating agents alike throughout the process often mischaracterized as early-modern "imperial expansion." In the face of these local partnerships, relationships of dependence and relative weakness, there would seem to be little place for planning in the making of eventual claims to empire. Moreover, belying claims to the internal "national" character of their claims, European monarchies remained reliant on private, often foreign, finance to undertake even minor enterprises beyond their home borders. The spectacular dissolution of the eventual military and legal claims in the name of "empires" in the late eighteenth and early nineteenth centuries reveals the limits of imperial planning and its attendant, emergent ideologies.

Although imperial strategies accordingly changed over time and differed depending on the European monarchies engaged in this dangerously expansive competition, the historical processes they generated converged in three aspects. First, dynamic, semiautonomous, quasi-official interests mounted the initial maritime and transoceanic ventures into the Atlantic. That is, monarchs, courtiers, and other personal representatives of royal prerogative played only the minor roles that they could afford at the time, mostly taking legal responsibility to defend the claims they made from European intruders similarly sponsored by rival monarchies. Protection from the peoples they engaged in the Americas or in Africa was not the primary issue, as most of these engagements were more collaborative than hostile or, when conflictive, successful only in combining European firearms with local allies. Church militants, military adventurers, and merchants with goods to attract local people as trading partners took the lead. Authorities with scant capacity to impose their will unilaterally even within Europe were loath to devote precious resources to far-fetched ventures overseas, preferring to compete "on the cheap." They were content to skim the prospective profits of their vassals' risky ventures by imposing guaranteed advance payments for licenses in exchange for implied promises of protection in case of need. Planning was less common than spasmodic opportunism, with domestic competitors and dynastic rivals in Europe more in mind than systematic possession of, not to say productive uses of, remote peoples or places.

Where uncontrolled private interests managed to succeed nonetheless, monarchical sponsors found themselves committed to degrees that forced them to invest in costly military protection, inflated legal claims, and public defenses of the funds required to continue. Central government planning thus increased as much from domestic politics as from transatlantic policies, making construction of ideological justifications necessary. Crown agents exerted royal authority in remote corners of the Atlantic, often at the expense of the local decision-making institutions through which earlier, more limited royal involvements had been extended. One example of this trend is the rise of the crown-appointed intendant in Spanish America after the mid-eighteenth century, limiting American-born subjects' participation in local governance and administration as part of a broader consolidation of Bourbon dynastic authority in Spain. The contemporaneous expulsion of Jesuits from both Portuguese and Spanish domains (in 1759 and 1767),

whose earlier exemptions from crown oversight had allowed them to build devout followings and business enterprises stronger than those of the Iberian crowns, formed part of a belated broad extension of direct European monarchical control throughout the Americas. At the same time, the Anglo-French Seven Years' War (1756–1763) represented a parallel initiative on the parts of the militarily waxing monarchies of northern Europe. The rationalizing strategies necessary to sustain the growing investments in military control and royal prestige also manifested themselves in the establishment of councils, and later ministries, devoted exclusively to affairs overseas. Such a deliberately centralized approach brought the monarchies' Atlantic interests from secondary concerns of the broader state to the forefront of its planning, at correspondingly increased costs.

The Ibero-Atlantic empires thus moved discernibly from conceiving of their overseas claims as extensions of the royal personage (as viceroyalties or colonies governed by royal governors) to crucial components, not extraneous appendages, of the European monarchies themselves. As these overseas provinces became more complex, benign neglect of them no longer remained an option. Furthermore, the wealth extracted from these possessions became an essential prop of the emergent early-modern fiscal-military monarchy, and dynastic rivals' competition for existing extra-European territories required greater levels of planning and investment to make them "profitable" and stable. Coastal fortifications, closely monitored local militias and standing European armies, tax collection, and improved record keeping became the norm after the middle of the eighteenth century. Enlarged bureaucracies and more sophisticated planning began to make sense of and manage such complexity.

New sciences of administration and political economy (such as cameralism, a German theory of economic management through maximizing the revenues of the state; English mercantilism, the parallel—and today more familiar—theory of maximizing trade flows among dispersed economies; and French physiocratic faith in the generation of wealth from agriculture), building on advances in the natural sciences and cartography, made possible for the first time something that approached policy making in the modern sense, in its precision and potential for prescription. Emergent systematic forms of empirical knowledge, protoethnography, cartography, natural history, more refined techniques of quantification and accounting, and improved navigation, combined with intensifying flows of commodities and manufactures, enabled imperial planners to have a clearer sense of what was happening across the ocean, "on the ground," and to attempt to rationalize it. Planners received a further boost from political ideologies favorable to the centralization of authority as the ambitions of absolute monarchs peaked, which made administration less diffused, less dependent on collaboration with indigenous and Creole elites, and less subject to the whims of "men on the spot." Empire was acquiring an operational dimension, beyond its origins in theories of *imperium,* in international law and the uses of legal theory to cover the scattered initiatives of the subjects of European crowns.

Imperial planning, as it was elaborated in the second half of the eighteenth century, was Atlantic in perspective. Planners in the metropole sought to distill lessons with general applicability from the variety and complexity of events they encountered, formerly managed ad hoc according to local particularities. In earlier eras, they had sometimes deferred to local agents owing to the heterogeneity inherent on Atlantic scales. The Spanish formula, "I obey, but do not execute," accommodated the local needs of imperial agents in remote lands to metropolitan demands until the middle of the eighteenth century. After 1700, many imperial planners possessed firsthand experience in different parts of the Atlantic World. In the Portuguese Atlantic, for example, it was common for a single administrator to serve, in the course of a career, on three continents. But by the end of the 1700s they increasingly aspired to legislate for their territories as coherent wholes, according to sets of regular rules. Homogeneity, to the extent possible, was the goal to which they aspired. Planning always occurred in the context of rivalry with other European monarchies, often in emulating others' successful practices or by attempting to avoid their mistakes. Wary, sometimes hostile, mutual observation and "policy learning" from unanticipated experiences thus moved European governments toward closer, but also more costly, integration into increasingly pan-Atlantic political and economic systems.

GABRIEL PAQUETTE
ANDREW TOEBBEN

Bibliography

Bethencourt, Francisco, and Diogo Ramada Curto, eds. *Portuguese Oceanic Expansion, 1400–1800.* Cambridge: Cambridge University Press, 2007.

Weber, David. *Bárbaros: Spaniards and Their Savages in the Age of Enlightenment.* New Haven, CT: Yale University Press, 2005.

Impressment, Kidnapping, and Panyarring

Millions of people were extracted forcefully from European and African societies during the seventeenth and eighteenth centuries and moved west across the Atlantic to build, maintain, and secure the plantation economy of the Americas. Overall, the largest numbers of captives, by far, were African prisoners of war, but substantial numbers of both Africans and Europeans also ended up in colonial bondage as a result of finding themselves ensnared in debt, individual and collective, which in turn legalized the use of force to transport them overseas. England (later Britain) in particular relied on these mechanisms to recruit labor for its colonies.

In Africa, the English referred to the seemingly random seizure of captives destined for the Atlantic commercial economy as *panyarring,* a term of Portuguese origin (from *apanhar,* "to seize or grab"), which in one sense meant to distrain or simply plunder an enemy's land. The term described indigenous African practices that allowed creditors to seize debtors' property—or, crucially, the wealth of debtors' communities, including their members as slaves—if payments of obligations were not forthcoming when demanded. Before the era of the Atlantic slave trade, claims for repayment of debts were relatively rare, as debts and counterdebts were maintained to cement bonds of trust between different individuals, kinship groups, and polities, often over several generations. With the influx of European commercial capital, however, debt as a symbol of ongoing mutual commitments was rapidly transformed into enforced obligations, and it eventually became an important mechanism for justifying large-scale seizures of slaves. European slave traders on the coast would advance goods to African slave dealers in return for human hostages, or "pawns"; the slave dealers in turn passed along the goods they had borrowed, sometimes in the form of forced loans, to a series of debtors into the interior, until finally they reached areas where they could be exchanged for captives and other people, who then were passed back along the chains of debt all the way into the holds of waiting slave ships at the coast. The trade, however, worked this smoothly only in theory, for the pressure from ship captains only briefly anchored along the coast and eager to depart for the Americas for repayment to fill orders quickly was considerable all along the chain, and the wastage produced by high mortality among the enslaved created an almost constant need to make up for defaults through panyarring, thus degrading the original trusting connotations of debt and making it a significant motivator of random, illegitimate seizures of bystanders.

European Christians occasionally became victims of panyarring in Africa, usually in retaliation for illegal seizures of slaves along the coast, though their numbers were dwarfed by those of their core-ligionists who were captured in and around the Mediterranean and held for ransom by corsairs sailing out of Tunis, Tripoli, and Algiers, the so-called Barbary States of North Africa. Hundreds of Europeans in the Americas were also seized by Native people, among whom there were long-standing practices of capturing outsiders as hostages whom they used in a range of strategies: to establish negotiable relationships among otherwise wary neighbors, to reestablish or increase population levels in the aftermath of wars and epidemics, or in some cases to pay off debts to European traders similar to those incurred in Africa.

However, it was in Europe itself that Europeans ran the greatest risk of falling victim to kidnapping, a term that entered the English language at almost the exact same time as panyarring, and in very similar circumstances. To meet growing early seventeenth-century demands for servants in the English Americas, initially to work alongside African slaves, and by the late seventeenth century to supervise and brutalize them, metropolitan labor recruiters ensnared thousands of desperately poor rural migrants to port towns in debt bondage, forced them aboard ships, and eventually sold their time overseas as indentured servants. Outright kidnapping, though far from unheard of, was comparatively rare. More commonly, well-organized recruitment gangs descended on the bulging slums of the cities, offered food and shelter to likely victims, flattered them with promises of a better life in the colonies, seduced them with drink, and then presented a steep bill that they could pay conveniently by signing an indenture contract of servitude in parts beyond the seas, usually for seven years. By the time the victims realized what they had done, they usually were already onboard a servant ship, whose captain had purchased their indenture and thus forced them into his debt. Few then had much hope for escape. The numbers of those who fell victim to such fraudulent and coercive recruitment will most likely never be known, but indications are that a majority of indentured servants were taken to the colonies against their will. It is moreover suggestive that kidnapping quickly became a synonym for the servant trade as a whole, regardless of the victims' ages and whether or not they had signed indenture contracts.

Kidnapping in this original meaning of the term disappeared by the turn of eighteenth century and was replaced by the more orderly, government-run convict transportation systems. The recruitment of manpower for the British Royal Navy, however, continued chaotically and violently for another century. Most likely, the practice of rounding up seamen by force for service in the king's fleet had its roots in the Saxon period (fifth to eleventh centuries), but the term *impressment* had come into use only after the Norman conquest of 1066. Initially, "prest" men (from French *prêt*, meaning "ready") were a form of naval reserve, seafarers who had been paid in advance to stand ready for service, if called upon, aboard the king's ships.

The system never worked very well, as men were happy to take the money but often failed to show up for service, and by the time England commenced its seventeenth-century Atlantic conquests, advance payments had been replaced by the king's shilling, a small token payment issued after a seaman had been captured and forced aboard ship, thus securing the man's labor by symbolically putting him into the king's debt. Additionally, service in the fleet was ideologically constructed as a duty owed to their king by all English seafaring subjects, an obligation that had the peculiar and often infuriating result that foreign-born men pressed by mistake could be freed by writ of habeas corpus whereas English (later British) subjects could not. Despite massive resistance, primarily in the form of riots that at times tipped over into urban insurrections, the Royal Navy continued to rely on impressment throughout the age of sail—usually between half and two-thirds of all men were pressed—and phased it out only when the end of the Napoleonic Wars and the advent of steam shipping drastically reduced naval requirements for manpower.

Panyarring, duplicitous inducements of indentured servitude, and naval impressment were all well-established practices in recruiting manpower long before the growth of Europe's transatlantic empires dramatically increased the frequency and scale of their use. These debt-based mechanisms enabling and legalizing the massive coercive population transfers involved in overseas colonization reflected the need to supplement capital, scarce in the rapidly commercializing economy of the Atlantic World, with force. It was a development that radically delegitimized all three institutions, transforming their specific meanings into broad synonyms for the varied systems of extreme labor exploitation experienced by millions of Native, African, and European commoners in the Americas. Panyarring emphasized the randomness of the victims, kidnapping their innocence, and impressment the force and violence that propped up the whole system of transatlantic capital accumulation.

NIKLAS FRYKMAN

Bibliography

Linebaugh, Peter, and Marcus Rediker. *The Many-Headed Hydra: Sailors, Slaves, Commoners, and the Hidden History of the Revolutionary Atlantic*. Boston: Beacon, 2000.

Lovejoy, Paul E., and Nicholas Rogers, eds. *Unfree Labor in the Development of the Atlantic World*. New York: Routledge, 1994.

Miller, Joseph C. *Way of Death: Merchant Capitalism and the Angolan Slave Trade, 1730–1830*. Madison: University of Wisconsin Press, 1988.

Indentured Contracts

From the early seventeenth century until the opening years of the nineteenth, hundreds of thousands of Europeans crossed the Atlantic to work in the American colonies under some type of labor contract. Indentured servitude was the most common form of these contractual arrangements and developed as an institutionalized means of transporting masses of poor laborers to the New World in response to the rapid growth of interdependent Atlantic economies, connecting western Europe and Africa to the Caribbean and mainland America. In the course of financing this growth, merchant investors and transporters imposed harsher terms than those accepted by servants in Europe, which in their severest forms approached the strict discipline and material deprivations imposed on enslaved Africans and Native Americans.

The evolution of indentured servitude was a pragmatic approach to organizing and financing the costly transportation of laborers to American colonies. In return for the costs of their passage across the Atlantic, board and lodging, and certain "freedom dues," servants contracted to work for specified periods, usually between four and seven years. Generally, they signed printed documents that had spaces left blank for the names and occupations (and sometimes ages) of the servants, names of the ship's captains or contracting parties, the servants' destinations in America, lengths of service contracted, and freedom dues on completion of the agreed term. The document was dated, signed by the servant, witnessed, and registered before city officials or magistrates of the local court. Ships' captains or merchants would buy the indenture contracts, transport the servants to America, and then sell their contracts to masters or mistresses in the colonies at a profit. The new masters would have full rights over the servants' labor for the stipulated term as recompense for the purchase of the contract, the servants' board and lodging during the contracts' terms, and freedom dues at its conclusion. Although the great majority of indentured workers served four or seven years, those who were skilled or literate might be able to negotiate better rates in the form of shorter terms or more generous freedom dues.

Individuals who arrived in the colonies without indentures served according to the "custom of the country," a series of laws left to local courts to codify. These differed from one colony to another and over time, but the basic formula was the same. Courts would judge the servant's age and set an appropriate term of service. In the Chesapeake colonies of Virginia and Maryland during the seventeenth century, for example, servants over 20 would serve four years, those over 16 between six and eight years, and those under 16 until age 24, more than eight years. Freedom dues conformed similarly to the "custom of the country" and usually consisted of differing combinations of personal property: clothing, tools, provisions, a small sum of money or equivalent value in goods, and in some cases a musket. Land was rarely included, especially after the initial period of European settlement.

Another category of indentured contract was the redemptioner system, which applied during the eighteenth century almost entirely to German-speaking immigrants from the Rhinelands—notably from the Palatinate, Hesse, and Württemburg—as well as the Swiss cantons. Redemptioners contracted to redeem the costs of their passage when they reached their destination by working for an employer who would pay their fare. The system gave settlers flexibility in raising the money to pay off their debts and in negotiating the terms of the ensuing labor obligations. Friends, kin, or coreligionists in America might cover the value of the contracts, or the immigrant might raise the money by selling goods brought from home. Otherwise, settlers would seek an employer and contract to work for a negotiated period.

The great majority of indentured servants in the New World ended up in the British plantation colonies of North America and the Caribbean. In South and Central America, enslaved Native Americans provided plentiful local labor for Spanish settlers, while in Portuguese Brazil enslaved Africans supported the development of sugar plantations. French servant immigration to the West Indies—St. Christopher (St. Kitts), Martinique, and Guadeloupe—was modest throughout the period, perhaps 20,000 to 30,000 between 1650 and 1775. Earlier, by contrast, in the British colonies of the Chesapeake, Lower South, and West Indies, indentured servants were crucial in building and sustaining an affordable labor system. Without them the rapid growth of production for local consumption and the transatlantic trade in tobacco, sugar, and rice in those years would have been impossible. During the seventeenth century, 70 to 80 percent of the approximately 350,000 British settlers who immigrated to the Chesapeake and Caribbean arrived as indentured servants, two-thirds of whom went to the Caribbean islands. In the eighteenth century, up to the War of American Independence, the proportion of indentured servants among immigrants to British colonies fell nearer to 50 percent, and their primary destinations shifted from the Caribbean to the mainland, particularly the Middle Colonies, Chesapeake, and Lower South.

Historians have pointed to traditional labor arrangements in England as providing the legal framework for indentured servitude in British colonies. In the home country, young men and women hired themselves, usually for a year, as "servants in husbandry" in rural areas or as domestic servants in comfortable urban households. In more formal arrangements, youths might take on an apprenticeship to learn a skilled trade or profession. But conditions experienced by indentured servants in the colonies were frequently far worse than those servants or apprentices experienced in England. Covering the considerable costs of oceanic transportation required an up-front investment repaid through longer terms of service, contractual arrangements to enable one master to transfer the investment in a servant to another at will, and private punishments for servants who violated their obligations to their creditors—by, for example, running away or becoming pregnant—were harsh. Although local courts provided some protections against cruel or "unchristian-like" treatment, everyday relations between masters and servants were largely beyond the reach of the law and thus, like relations between masters and slaves, largely under the control of masters, good or bad. Servants—young, poor, and generally from the lower ranks of society—were often viewed as little better than vagrants or criminals swept up from the streets of London and other major ports. Although the evidence is inconclusive, it appears that only a small minority of them ever succeeded in becoming significant landowners and respected members of their communities; the majority exchanged urban poverty in Europe for its rural equivalent in America.

Indentured servitude emerged as a specific response to the enormous requirements of labor in New World colonies and the high costs of transporting workers during the seventeenth and eighteenth centuries. The financing and organization of the servant trade evolved as an integral part of Atlantic commerce and colonial economies, just as the trade in enslaved Africans developed across the same period on much larger scales. Indentured servitude coexisted with slavery in the British plantation colonies as a relatively low-cost strategy for investors (that is, sea captains, merchants, and planters), which was employed in a wide range of economic sectors—notably the Chesapeake, Lower South, and British West Indies. It developed as one form on a spectrum of bound labor that built the Atlantic World.

JAMES HORN

Bibliography

Altman, Ida, and James Horn, eds., *"To Make America": European Emigration in the Early Modern Period*. Berkeley: University of California Press, 1991.

Galenson, David. *White Servitude in Colonial America: An Economic Analysis*. Cambridge: Cambridge University Press, 1981.

Morgan, Kenneth. *Slavery and Servitude in Colonial North America: A Short History*. New York: New York University Press, 2000.

Tomlins, Christopher. *Freedom Bound: Law, Labor, and Civic Identity in Colonizing English America, 1580–1865*. Cambridge: Cambridge University Press, 2010.

Independence: Haiti

Though long ignored by historians, the complex events known as the Haitian Revolution (1791–1804) are now recognized as pivotal in Atlantic history, demonstrating the power of enslaved people of African descent to define their own destiny in the Americas, while also destroying a highly profitable slave economy. Antislavery forces, including enslaved people throughout the hemisphere, found inspiration, while slavery's advocates huddled in fear. The general alarm forced a ripple of change throughout the Atlantic economy, driving up the prices of plantation commodities and thereby increasing demand for enslaved workers. Saint-Domingue, as prerevolutionary Haiti was known, by winning its independence showed republicans in Latin American colonies that European powers could no longer easily dominate their New World

territories. On the other hand, Haiti's example also suggested that nonwhite majority populations in Latin America would not necessarily follow the colonial-era elite. For France, the loss of Saint-Domingue marked a fundamental turning point toward an ostensibly new and safer kind of settler colonialism, without slavery.

Emancipation and Equality

Eugene Genovese, a distinguished historian of U.S. slavery, proposed that the slave revolt that led to Haiti represented a dividing point in the history of slave resistance in the New World. In *From Rebellion to Revolution* (1979), he claimed that before the consolidation of Haiti, slave revolts in the Americas had most often been led by Africans who imagined replacing white colonial societies with African-style kingdoms. But, Genovese argued, after the mid-1790s the freedom and civil equality won by rebels in Saint-Domingue inspired fighters among the enslaved with similar emancipatory goals for their uprisings. From that moment, enslaved people who rose up in the British, Spanish, and Dutch Caribbean, as well as in Virginia, South Carolina, Louisiana, modern-day Colombia, Venezuela, and Brazil, aimed not to kill whites but to force them to recognize the slaves' human dignity.

A number of circumstances have subsequently cast doubt on the specifics of Genovese's model. In some regions, slave owners were so worried about a Haitian-style uprising that they imagined slave conspiracies that historians believe never existed. Where revolts or conspiracies did occur, it is difficult to prove they were directly inspired by events in Haiti. As David Geggus observes, it is quite possible that many rebels in the 1790s and early 1800s were taking advantage of the reductions in colonial military forces drawn away by the Napoleonic wars in Europe.

The revolutionary image of the events in Haiti was more clearly an inspiration, though, to free people of color. After 1794 French authorities in revolutionary Guadeloupe sent mulatto and black soldiers into nearby St. Lucia, Dominica, and St. Vincent to raise local people against the British governors of those islands. In Grenada, a revolt led by the free-colored coffee planter Julien Fédon took control of the island for sixteen months in 1795 before falling to a British counterattack. In 1799 Saint-Domingue's black revolutionaries sent emissaries to the trading islands of Dutch Curaçao and Danish St. Thomas as well as to nearby Jamaica.

The leaders of the independent Haitian state (1804) insisted they had no plans to attack the slave regimes remaining all around them. But, as Ada Ferrer argues, this declared policy of coexistence did not prevent some of them from making a "robust intervention in global anti-slavery" (Ferrer, 43). In 1816 Alexander Pétion, president of the Haitian Republic, declared that any enslaved person who reached his territory would be free. Those who could not reach Haiti's shores were nevertheless deeply impressed with what political violence had achieved there. In Cuba in 1814, authorities charged the free-black carpenter José Aponte with plotting to overthrow the regime, after hearing of the book he had made with pictures of black Haitian leaders in uniform. Free-colored militiamen as far away as Rio de Janeiro were reportedly wearing portraits of the Haitian leader Jean-Jacques Dessalines in 1805, the year after he had declared Haitian independence.

Even if Haitian leaders did not deliberately export the antislavery philosophy to other societies, Matthew Clavin has shown that the historical memory of the Haitian Revolution shaped discussions of slavery's future in the United States among whites and blacks right up to the Civil War.

Slavery

One of the ironies of the Haitian revolt is that it ended slavery in Saint-Domingue but strengthened the institution in many other parts of the Americas. By dramatically reducing exports of sugar and coffee, the violence in Haiti made those commodities scarcer on the world market. The resulting higher prices increased the profitability of plantation slavery elsewhere. In the early 1700s, competition from the Caribbean, led by fast-growing Saint-Domingue, had made it difficult for Brazilian sugar to compete in Europe; in the early nineteenth century, the higher prices following the revolt in Haiti restored Brazil's sugar exports and resulted in the expansion of sugar cultivation into new regions. Estimates of imports of captive Africans to Brazil show an increase from 114,191 in the five years from

1786 to 1790 to 237,110 in 1816–1820. Though never previously a coffee exporter, Brazil picked up this crop from the Caribbean and bought Africans to grow and harvest the beans; it went on to supply coffee to the world throughout the nineteenth century.

Spain's colonies in the Caribbean, Cuba and Puerto Rico, also both became significant exporters of sugar and coffee and importers of slaves. Estimated imports of enslaved Africans to Cuba and Puerto Rico rose nearly eightfold from 11,633 in the years 1786–1790 to 92,449 in the years 1816–1820. In 1780 Cuba exported 18,000 tons of sugar; by the late 1820s this had grown to 70,000 tons; Cuban imports of slaves grew until the 1860s—in spite of British efforts to suppress the trade—and production kept climbing until the late 1880s.

The United States is yet another example of how the collapse of the Saint-Domingue economy encouraged slavery to expand elsewhere. Scholars disagree on the exact relationship between the arrival of news from Saint-Domingue in Paris of the failure of Bonaparte's armies to retake the island in 1802 and his 1803 decision to sell France's Louisiana Territory to the United States. But Bonaparte's decision to focus his military efforts on central Europe, rather than the Americas, was at least partly inspired by the loss of Saint-Domingue. The Louisiana Purchase opened vast lands west of the Mississippi to cotton planting and to slavery, which underwrote both economic growth and political contestation in the new United States, culminating in civil war.

Another event connecting Bonaparte, the French loss of Saint-Domingue, and the United States occurred seven years after the Louisiana Purchase. Many French colonists and free people of color had fled to Cuba in the 1790s to escape the violence in Saint-Domingue. Some brought their enslaved workers with them and used them to expand sugar and coffee planting there. Then, in 1808, Bonaparte invaded the Iberian Peninsula, arresting the royal family in Spain and putting his brother Joseph on the Spanish throne. This decapitation of the nominal colonial master triggered a wave of independence struggles in Spain's mainland American colonies. In Cuba, proslavery authorities expelled nearly 10,000 Saint-Domingue refugees. The arrival of many of these people in New Orleans roughly doubled the population of that port city and increased even more the size of its free population of color. These new arrivals also helped introduce sugar planting in what became the state of Louisiana.

Latin America's Wars for Independence

The Haitian revolt created the first Latin American nation, for Haiti was the first independent American republic in which people of non-European descent outnumbered whites. The Haitian declaration of independence identified them as the spiritual, if not physical, descendants of the indigenous people, whom European colonization had marginalized.

However, political independence in Haiti affected the independence struggles of nearby Spanish colonies in different ways. On the one hand, early Haitian leaders reached out to support those efforts, most famously when Haiti's president Alexandre Pétion met in 1816 with Simón Bolívar, the liberation leader in what became Venezuela. Pétion supplied the future liberator with guns, supplies, and money in return for Bolívar's pledge to end slavery.

The fact that Venezuela eventually abolished slavery only much later, in 1854, might be read as an indication that Bolívar did not take this promise too seriously. Elite families in his native New Granada viceroyalty owed their wealth to enslaved or landless agricultural workers of Indian and African descent, who far outnumbered them. Bolívar and his landholding allies worried they would lose their status—or their lives—in a Haitian-style mass uprising. In the 1790s, people of color in northern New Granada were well aware of events in Saint-Domingue. In 1795, 1797, and 1799 there were Haitian-inspired conspiracies in the Coro region, in Maracaibo, La Guaira, and Cartagena, in what is now the seaboard region of northwestern Venezuela. These failed not only because of elite opposition but because rural Indians would not support the urban free people of color who rose up to claim political rights.

Bolívar understood that if he abolished slavery completely, he would lose the support of many landowners. He was also aware that antislavery whites in Saint-Domingue had lost control of local politics to black leaders such as Toussaint L'Ouverture, who could mobilize the majority of former slaves. Arriving in Venezuela from Haiti in 1816, he fulfilled his pledge to Pétion by promising citizenship to all enslaved people who joined his army. Most did not take this offer, perhaps because they recognized that Bolívar was not proposing general emancipation. Nor did pro-independence planters free their workforces to bolster Bolívar's army.

After this point Bolívar was able to attract growing numbers of free men of color into his forces. They were the single largest social group in New Granada, and Bolívar worried that he might lose their loyalty to Manuel Piar, a charismatic commander of mixed race. Some whites said Piar had a secret agreement with Haiti's Pétion, and whether or not Bolívar believed this allegation, in 1817 he accused Piar of trying to foment racial war. After a brief trial, he had the mulatto officer executed.

Despite the obvious determination of white elites in New Granada to maintain control of the independence war, the Haitian example was strong enough that lower classes came to expect some form of freedom from this struggle. Marixa Lasso suggests that the rhetoric of racial harmony that Bolívar and others adopted was not just a tactic to avoid Haitian-style insurrection but an important component of an inclusive Creole patriotism. Yet Lasso also finds Colombian white elites worrying about "race-war" into the 1830s whenever men of color tried to pressure them for reforms that would bring about greater equality.

The best-documented case of "Haitian fear" occurred in Cuba. Even though the island became a global leader in sugar production thanks to the economic decline of Haiti, the fate of Saint-Domingue's whites weighed heavily on the imaginations of Cuban planters as they imported more and more captives from Africa. Cuban nationalism grew in the 1800s, but many wealthy Cubans believed their island, whose population was descended roughly half from Europeans and half from Africans, risked racial war if they attempted to seize independence from Spain. Without the Spanish army, they feared domination by nonwhites and the racial violence they associated with Haiti. While free Cubans of color fought alongside whites and formed part of the officer cadre in the failed Ten Years' War for independence (1868–1878), for many white Cubans the "Haitian fear" prevented a united front until 1898, when the United States intervened in a second independence war that had begun three years earlier.

France

The loss of Saint-Domingue in 1804 was a clear turning point in the imperial history of France, arguably a bigger blow than the loss of Canada in 1763, for it ended the prosperity of the French Atlantic ports that had shuttled trade goods to Africa to buy slaves (Nantes) and imported sugar and coffee to supply continental Europe (Bordeaux).

If France lost this much of its lucrative Atlantic commerce in 1804, it also gained thousands of embittered former colonists. These refugees from the Americas returned to France to pressure Napoleon and the Bourbons who followed him to reclaim Saint-Domingue. Although there has been no study of how the racial and political attitudes of this group shaped nineteenth-century French politics and culture, even before Haitian independence white refugees from Saint-Domingue had played a role in writing the racial laws passed by the Bonaparte regime—for example, the prohibition on interracial marriage, which passed in 1803 and lasted until 1819.

In 1818 the Bourbon-Restoration government in Paris signed a treaty with Great Britain agreeing to prohibit the slave trade. But planters in Martinique and Guadeloupe, despite the revolution in Haiti, were determined to restore their estates to Old Regime levels of profitability. The Bourbons turned a blind eye to hundreds of French ships carrying captives from Africa to the Antilles, a commerce that ended only in 1830. As Christopher Miller remarks, in the nineteenth century many French seemed to have regarded the clandestine slave trade as "a form of insurgency and resistance to the hegemony of perfidious Albion"—that is, Britain (Miller, 199).

France put aside these fantasies of Caribbean reconquest in 1825 and negotiated a treaty recognizing Haitian independence, conditioned on the new independent government paying 150 million francs to former planters and their heirs. Five years later, in 1830, France began the conquest of Algeria, under the leadership of a number of French military veterans of the campaign to recover the colony of Saint-Domingue. In Algeria, France created a new kind of colony that could be, like Saint-Domingue, a profitable exporter of commodities—in this case, wheat and wine. Unlike Saint-Domingue, conveniently adjacent Algeria could become a settlers' colony where French colonists and indigenous people could work the land without the moral and political problems raised by the masses of slaves they had assembled across the Atlantic.

Conclusion

The revolt of the enslaved and the ensuing interventions by European armies created the second independent nation-state in the Atlantic World. The events in Haiti generated fears and economic opportunities that strengthened racism and slavery in many parts of the Americas. Hundreds of thousands more Africans crossed the Atlantic in the nineteenth century specifically because of increased plantation profits elsewhere that the economic collapse of Saint-Domingue had made possible, and even more Europeans arrived to share directly and indirectly in the prosperity that slavery sustained.

The independence of Haiti also illustrated the fragility of Europe's political hold over American populations and helped create expectations for the independence of over a dozen new republics from Spanish rule. For enslaved and free people of color in many of these places, it suggested the possibility of freedom from bondage and membership in a new kind of political community, one much more inclusive than the Neo-European political ideal of the heirs to the rebels in North America.

The Haitian example all but forced the republican heirs to the old Spanish territories to adopt the concept of "racial harmony"; white elites had to claim to celebrate their new nations' human diversity, Native American as well as African-descended, to use a term from twenty-first-century U.S. culture. Yet the violence that had led to Haitian independence also raised deep fears of "race war" that lasted into the twentieth century. In the United States, in France, and even in Haiti itself, which in 1805 proclaimed the identity of all citizens as "black," the revolution produced a nation defined by race. For France, the freeing of the citizens of independent Haiti ended neither slavery, which continued until 1848, nor imperialism. It did push Napoleon's successors to begin to build a new kind of overseas empire in North Africa, one without slavery but one still marked by the racial divisions and economic exploitation that had provoked the violent uprising in Saint-Domingue.

JOHN D. GARRIGUS

Bibliography

Clavin, Matthew J. *Toussaint Louverture and the American Civil War: The Promise and Peril of a Second Haitian Revolution*. Philadelphia: University of Pennsylvania Press, 2010.

Ferrer, Ada. "Haiti, Free Soil, and Antislavery in the Revolutionary Atlantic." *American Historical Review* 117, no. 1 (2012): 40–66.

Geggus, David P., ed. *The Impact of the Haitian Revolution in the Atlantic World*. Columbia: University of South Carolina Press, 2001.

Genovese, Eugene D. *From Rebellion to Revolution: Afro-American Slave Revolts in the Making of the Modern World*. Baton Rouge: Louisiana State University Press, 1979.

Klein, Herbert S., and Ben Vinson. *African Slavery in Latin America and the Caribbean*. 2nd ed. New York: Oxford University Press, 2007.

Lasso, Marixa. *Myths of Harmony: Race and Republicanism during the Age of Revolution*. Pittsburgh, PA: University of Pittsburgh Press, 2007.

Miller, Christopher L. *The French Atlantic Triangle: Literature and Culture of the Slave Trade*. Durham, NC: Duke University Press, 2008.

White, Ashli. *Encountering Revolution: Haiti and the Making of the Early Republic*. Baltimore, MD: Johns Hopkins University Press, 2010.

Independence: Hispanic Americas

Many consider Spanish America's independence a domino effect resulting from Napoleonic ambitions. France's 1807–1808 invasions of Portugal and Spain unleashed pent-up frustrations among elites of those two empires' American provinces. Yet Brazil and Spanish America's subsequent trajectories could not have been more different. The House of Braganza fled Lisbon for Rio de Janeiro, and in 1822 independent Brazil chose its heir, Pedro I, to moderate the transition. The forced abdi-

cation of Bourbons Charles IV and Ferdinand VII and the imposition of Napoleon's brother as Joseph I unleashed Spanish-American demands for self-government and later independence on the grounds that the people had the legitimate authority to act and govern in the absence of their sovereign. In Brazil, sovereignty remained vested in the royal family. Spanish Americans, however, "had to think seriously about substituting the authority of the people for that of the king" (Dykstra, 274).

Serious thinking during the crisis of the Spanish monarchy (1808–1814) and the ensuing power vacuum in the Americas set off a series of discussions, debates, revolts, and eventually popular movements for political independence that by 1830 resulted in republican governance for mainland Spanish America. The metropolis retained only the Spanish Antilles—Cuba, Santo Domingo, and Puerto Rico. But what explains the often-destabilizing nineteenth-century commitment to popular sovereignty in Spanish America? The conditions for Spanish-American independence, much like those of British North America, had been laid in the years leading up to these separatist movements. Spanish America had experienced a revolution in governance beginning in the 1740s under the modernizing Bourbon Reforms. While Napoleon's 1807 invasion of Spain lit the fuse that set off powder kegs from Madrid to Mexico City, both sides of the Atlantic were already ripe for change.

Under the strong leadership of Charles III (1759–1788) and the lesser efforts of Charles IV (1788–1808), reforms directed from Madrid drastically increased and sought to standardize supervision and control of royal administration, governance of territories, tax policy, and military defense. This emphasis on government from above encouraged interest in government from below, and elite Spaniards and Spanish Americans sought to revive long-defunct town councils to protect or enhance local influence and to participate in the royal service as secular, military, and religious officials. Imperial reform and Atlantic revolution also increased Spanish spending on defense, especially in the Caribbean, which not only militarized political culture but also emptied local and royal coffers.

Nonetheless, all classes found something to dislike in the monarchy's efforts to professionalize and bring uniformity to imperial governance while revamping the fiscal structure to rely more on sales and other taxes than Indian tribute. The changes themselves, along with new emphasis on imposition rather than negotiation, alienated Spanish municipalities, Indian pueblos, guilds, and other local institutions accustomed to royal policies tailored to specific places. Replacing overlapping jurisdictions also removed a buffer established by the Habsburgs that kept the different groups competing with one another rather than with the crown. The royal bureaucracy's preference for employing Peninsulars stoked Spanish-American resentment, as did crown mercantilist regulations favoring Cádiz merchants over their Spanish-American counterparts. A weak crown could not stop increased inter-American trade and smuggling with Spain's imperial rivals, especially Great Britain, or the fraying reliance between the *madre patria* and her American possessions. Educated people of color resented limits to their ability to advance within institutions, such as the clergy and the military—limitations that were due to Spanish law or, as the *pardos* of Caracas knew, Creole objections. Indigenous nobilities that traditionally mediated between crown and community, trusted by neither Spaniards nor plebeians, lost legitimacy when they could not overturn new liquor or tobacco monopolies, reforms promoting Spanish-language education, and individual labor and landholding replacing communal practices. Economic, socioeconomic, and administrative innovations unsettled cities and countryside, unleashing violent popular revolts, particularly the pan-Andean movements of Túpac Amaru and Túpac Katari in 1780–1783.

In addition to violent resistance, the top-down reordering of the relation between state and society—like similar eighteenth-century programs of the British, Portuguese, and French monarchies, which Spanish Americans saw evolve into violent political revolutions in British North America, France, and Saint-Domingue (Haiti)—stimulated debate shaped by scholastic classics and liberal Enlightenment philosophy on the nature and justice of colonial government and incited musings on the possibilities of alternate systems with greater degrees of local control and representation. The principles of natural law and rights and the importance of consent of the governed and social contracts as interpreted by thinkers from Francisco Suárez to John Locke and Jean-Jacques Rousseau worked their way into Creole libraries and university cur-

ricula, nourishing demands for greater representation, free trade, and the right to increase manufacturing capacities. Newspapers published by imperial and Creole reformers delivered the newest ideas in political economy—including suggestions to improve agriculture and learn the history and geography of local *patrias*—to the provinces where subscriptions by postmasters, priests, and royal officials ensured broad circulation. Even embargoed texts, including France's Declaration of the Rights of Man and the Citizen (1789), reached Spanish America, where Antonio Nariño's clandestine 1793 translation, published in Bogotá, led to his trial and exile but did not eliminate the document's dissemination.

Thus, the crisis of the Spanish monarchy in 1808 capped 40 years of political, economic, and social change in the Iberian Atlantic, rather than unsettling an immobile traditional society. Napoleon's imposition of an illegitimate dynasty in that year offered Creole radicals an opportunity to redress old grievances by claiming autonomy or launching independence movements, while other Creole elites leveraged their loyalty to the monarchy to gain experience in an expanded form of self-government during the power vacuum in Spain. It was less clear whether political change would lead to greater economic and social mobility for the region's Native, African, and mixed-race residents. Some, however, were avid readers of the literature of political rights and, like priest José María Morelos in Mexico, rallied thousands to reject Napoleon and overturn unwelcome Bourbon innovations in the name of loyalty to Ferdinand VII. It was a short step to removing the "mask" of Ferdinand and demanding independence. Antislavery revolts against Napoleon in Haiti inspired similar movements throughout the Caribbean and advanced the abolitionist cause throughout the hemisphere.

Constitutionalism and armed resistance would be the twin pillars of Spanish-American political independence. Seeking to harness discontent within Spain's imperial system, Joseph I introduced the Bayonne Constitution (1808), a political charter based on France's Constitution of the Year XII (1804), which underwent significant editing by an Assembly of Notables that included a half-dozen Spanish Americans. This constitution, which likely influenced Spain's 1812 constitution, kept Roman Catholicism as the national religion and provided for a hereditary constitutional monarchy. It also addressed principal Creole grievances by offering Spanish-American representation in the Council of the Indies and the Cortes, a single commercial code, and stipulations to free agriculture and industry in the overseas provinces.

This liberalizing constitution might have been received warmly in Spain and overseas had it not been proffered on the point of a French bayonet. However, over the next six years, as much of Spain and Spanish America fought the usurper, residents developed their own plans for representative government. After Madrid rose up in 1808, rebelling towns and provinces across Spain formed separate juntas (citizen-led councils), arguing that in the absence of their ruler, sovereignty should return to the people. Spanish Americans from Mexico to Quito soon followed suit, regionalizing politics and threatening to replace monarchical unity with small- and medium-sized independent jurisdictions. To prevent this disintegration, anti-Bonapartist Spanish leaders established a Supreme Central Junta in Seville (1808) and later a Regency (1809). The Central Junta formally declared war on the French emperor in June 1808 and in January 1809 followed Joseph I to decree that Spanish dominions in America were not colonies but integral parts of the monarchy.

The interim governments' initial attempts to consolidate authority during the crisis had mixed effects. Some Creoles preferred conditional loyalty to revolt, which they felt would risk inciting the mostly Indian or African populations. From Guatemala City to Bogotá to Lima, Peninsular officials, local notables, and indigenous and Afro-Hispanic organizations issued acts denouncing the French invaders and expressing their loyalty and interim sovereignty, collected funds for the war effort, held masses, and formed local militias in Ferdinand's name. Buenos Aires residents fought off British invaders on their own. Others, however, argued that the Indies owed no allegiance to either the illegitimate French or the interim Spanish regime. Between 1809 and 1811, in Caracas (Venezuela), Cartagena (Colombia), and Quito (Ecuador), juntas of local notables and *cabildos abiertos* (open town meetings) sought political independence or more limited ousters of unpopular royal officials. For legitimacy, these juntas began to include popular representation, although rarely by direct elections. Interior towns did not always participate in their provincial capitals' initiatives, insisting on regional rather than ethnic or class representation and setting the stage for future civil wars. The political turmoil in the Spanish Americas was as much antiforeign as it was anti-Spain.

If increasing incorporation of popular actors into political processes was one legacy of the imperial crisis in Spanish America, an equally enduring innovation was participation in parliamentary and constitutional deliberations. In 1810 the Regency convened a Cortes with representatives elected from Spain, the Americas, and Asia, confirming the status of American "kingdoms" as integral parts, not colonies, of Spain. Although Peninsular deputies outnumbered them three to one, the Americans influenced debates on such topics as citizenship, monopolies, and trade, gaining experience that many subsequently employed at home. Most importantly, the deputies learned about establishing representative political systems governed by constitutional charters rather than a monarch's decrees.

In March 1812 the meeting of the Cortes at Cádiz adopted the Political Constitution of the Spanish Monarchy, known by many as the "Cádiz Constitution," which local authorities implemented in New Spain, Guatemala, Peru, and other loyalist districts. This charter established a constitutional monarchy; separated legislative, executive, and judicial powers; enshrined equality before the law for citizens of European and American origin; and decreed indirect elections of local, regional, and national representatives. Spanish American deputies supported both traditional provisions, including Catholicism as the official religion, and more liberal positions, including an unsuccessful push for citizenship for free people of African origin. The combination of liberal and traditional ideals, a "genuine and original offspring of Spanish intellectual life" (Marx), was exemplified in Guatemala City's instructions to its deputy to the Cortes, written in the form of a constitution. Guatemala's preamble lightly edited the liberal French Declaration of the Rights of Man and the Citizen, while its more conservative body proposed that cities, not individuals, would continue to represent communities. The Constitution of Cádiz, adapted for republican governance, provided a blueprint for many early Spanish American foundational compacts.

That blueprint was soon needed. In 1810, juntas in Venezuela, Buenos Aires, and New Granada, although theoretically loyal to Ferdinand, deposed royally appointed governors and operated autonomously. In Mexico, priest Miguel Hidalgo began a popular rebellion in the name of Ferdinand VII that in the course of a decade, under José María Morelos and Vicente Guerrero, transitioned into an armed movement for independence that fought royalist forces to a draw. The first elected Spanish American congresses, in Venezuela (1811) and Chilpancingo, New Spain (1813), issued declarations of independence emphasizing representation and liberal ideals, although only the former implemented its Magna Carta, under the leadership of Simón Bolívar. Yet winning over all inhabitants proved impossible; tensions between provinces and leaders made the armed struggles as much civil wars as fights against Peninsular forces, offering a preview of the regionalisms that undermined many of the eventual Spanish American republics.

The insurrections did not end when Ferdinand VII recovered his throne in 1814. His immediate abrogation of the 1812 constitution exacerbated tensions with Spain's loyal American territories. Having tasted limited representation and participation, if not complete autonomy, Creoles from Mexico to Buenos Aires chafed under restored monarchical absolutism. Independence movements that started during the crisis began to triumph over both Spanish forces and internal loyalists. The military tide began to turn in favor of Bolívar in Venezuela, José de San Martín in the Río de la Plata, and Guerrero in New Spain. Popularly elected congresses issued declarations of independence, drafted and implemented their own constitutions, and governed sovereign states. With a legitimate king, the new countries justified their claims to sovereignty either as a rejection of tyranny, echoing the arguments made in 1776 by Britain's North American colonies, or—if negotiating self-rule—asserting their status as political adults no longer needing the charitable tutelage of a mother country. In July 1816 the Congress of Tucumán, composed of representatives from most districts of the former Viceroyalty of La Plata, decreed—in Spanish, Quechua, and Aymara—"solemn emancipation" from the despotism of Spanish kings and formed the United Provinces of South America. Chile, under the leadership of Bernardo O'Higgins, followed suit in 1818, with a declaration describing the nineteenth century as the time for Spanish Americans to "reclaim their rights."

In 1821 Spanish North America joined the South in de facto independence, although Spain would not recognize the new countries until the 1850s. Mexico's Creole elites, led by Agustin de Iturbide, joined forces with the popular insurrection led by Vicente Guerrero and established a short-lived empire from 1821 to 1823 before founding a republic in 1824. Central America claimed independence from Spain in 1821 and then from Mexico in 1823, establishing the Federal Republic of Central America (1824). By 1825 Bolívar and San Martín had "liberated" royalist Peru and Bolivia. By 1830, only the Spanish Caribbean—notably the slavery-dependent sugar economies of Cuba (called the "ever-faithful isle"), Puerto Rico, and Santo Domingo—remained American territories. A decade after his invasion, Napoleon's strategy and policies finally achieved the results he had desired: Spain lost most of her American empire to independent, republican, and sovereign states.

Political independence in Spanish America left a revolutionary but mixed balance sheet. In the "win" column, in the decade since the first autonomist movements, Spanish American leaders had turned from traditional institutions, such as the *cabildo abierto* and junta, to modern legislatures and the constitutional system. Popular representation, equality before the law, and individual rights and freedoms were introduced into political systems with close-to-universal male citizenship. Experiments in representative government piloted during the crisis—electing junta members or Cortes delegates or municipal councils—gave the citizens of the new states experience in republican self-government. Several of the new countries abolished slavery within a decade—notably Mexico, Chile, Uruguay, Bolivia, and Central America—with Colombia, Venezuela, Peru, and Argentina following suit by the mid-1850s.

Yet without consensus over whether to vest sovereignty in a king, the people, or individually elected or corporately selected representatives, or how to negotiate authority between colonial capitals and hinterlands, the array of contenders labeled one another in oppositional dichotomies. Calling themselves or their enemies liberal or conservative, federalist or centralist, or modern and traditional, they failed to find moderate or common positions to advance national development. Instead, for 20 years after independence, constitutional experimentation and war destroyed economies and militarized societies from Mexico through the Andes to the Southern Cone. Leaders from former colonial capitals tended to favor strong centralized governments, while those from outlying districts preferred federal structures and a weak executive. Landowners, small factory owners, and merchants differed over whether to continue imperial tariff protections or to promote free trade and whether to privatize land or protect landholding communities. Reliance on well-educated and omnipresent priests and religious orders to govern clashed with pushes to separate church and state. The damaging legacy of the independence wars, such as destruction of Mexico's mines and Venezuela's haciendas, aggravated regional competition and factionalism, while the inability of early governments to collect taxes created continuing economic deficits and defaults on internationally financed loans. Reduced global markets for commodity exports, the flight of Spanish capital and businessmen, and the arrival of sometimes-unscrupulous European military officers (some of them demobilized veterans of Napoleon's defeated forces) and British investors in their stead contributed to seemingly endemic political disorder.

Such disputes divided and eventually destroyed federations by the 1830s. Notably, Gran Colombia separated into Ecuador, Venezuela, and Colombia, and the Central American Republic left Guatemala, El Salvador, Nicaragua, Honduras, and Costa Rica to struggle as fledgling nation-states. Mexico lost Texas in 1835, and by 1850 the manifestly expansionist United States absorbed that Lone-Star republic, as well as much of Mexico's northwestern territories. By mid-century anyone consulting a map of the Hispanic Americas found the countries we know today but few democratic governments, united peoples, or economic success stories. Governments and citizens struggled to accept the political legitimacy and authority of a unitary national state, to combine popular governance with political order, and to achieve economic growth and national political integration. As Mexican historian Marco Palacios argues, the Catch-22 faced by the new countries—simultaneous rather than serial development of "the national state, industrial capitalism and democracy" (Palacios, 10)—produced a decades-long seesaw between constitutional and authoritarian governance punctuated by violent disorder, a pattern all too familiar not only in the former Spanish Americas but in the civil wars and revolutions of mid-century Europe and North America.

JORDANA DYM

Bibliography

Adelman, Jeremy. *Sovereignty and Revolution in the Iberian Atlantic*. Princeton, NJ: Princeton University Press, 2006.

Breña, Roberto, *El imperio de las circunstancias: Las independencias hispanoamericanas y la revolución liberal española*. Madrid: Marcial Pons, 2012.

Brown, Matthew. *The Struggle for Power in Post-Independence Colombia and Venezuela*. Basingstoke, UK: Palgrave Macmillan, 2012.

Brown, Matthew, and Gabriel J. Paquette, eds. *Connections after Colonialism: The Reconfiguration of Relations between Europe and Latin America in the 1820s*. Tuscaloosa: University of Alabama Press, 2012.

Costeloe, Michael. *Response to Revolution: Imperial Spain and the Spanish American Revolutions, 1810–1840*. New York: Cambridge University Press, 1986.

Dykstra, Kristin. "On the Betrayal of Nations: Jose Alvarez de Toledo's Philadelphia Manifesto (1811) and Justification (1816)." *CR: The New Centennial Review* 4, no. 1 (2004): 267–305.

Gutiérrez, José Francisco Román. *Las reformas borbónicas y el nuevo orden colonial*. Mexico City: Instituto Nacional de Antropología e Historia, 1998.

Lynch, John. *Bourbon Spain, 1700–1808*. New York: Oxford University Press, 1993.

———. "The Origins of Spanish American Independence." In *The Independence of Latin America*, edited by Leslie Bethell, 1–48. New York: Cambridge University Press, 1987.

Marx, Karl. "Revolutionary Spain." *New York Daily Tribune*, September 8–December 2, 1854. Available online at http://www.marxists.org/archive/marx/works/1854/revolutionary-spain/.

Morelli, Federica. "Entre el antiguo y el nuevo regimen: La historia política hispanoamericana del siglo XIX." *Historica Crítica* 33 (2007): 122–155.

Palacios, Marco, ed. *Las independencias hispanoamericanas: Interpretaciones 200 años después*. Bogotá: Grupo Editorial Norma, 2009.

Portillo Valdéz, José María. *Crisis Atlántica: Autonomía e independencia en la crisis de la monarquía hispana*. Madrid: Marcial Pons-Fundación Carolina, 2006.

Ricketts, Monica. "Bringing Spain and Spanish America Back Together: Towards a New Political History of Independence." In *Latin American Independence: Reinterpreting the Causes, Contingencies, and Consequences*, edited by John H. Coatsworth. National History Center/Oxford University Press, forthcoming.

Rodríguez O., Jaime E. *The Independence of Spanish America*. Cambridge: Cambridge University Press, 1998.

———. *Revolución, independencia, y las nuevas naciones de América*. Madrid: Fundación MAPFRE-Tavera, 2005.

Independence: United States

Ever since July 2, 1776, when 13 of the 26 British American colonies seceded, the War of American Independence has been viewed as transatlantic in two obvious, if also contradictory, senses: it was a rebellion against a European empire, while also drawing heavily upon a hodgepodge of European ideas. More recently, historians have drawn attention to some of the independence movement's other Atlantic ingredients. They have also examined the international aspects of the ensuing military conflict and the limits, as well as the extent, of the impact of American independence on subsequent developments in the Atlantic World.

The 13 colonies' battle for home rule was also, as Carl Lotus Becker noted in 1926, a struggle over "who should rule at home," but Becker's—and many subsequent historians'—focus on the multidimensional domesticity of the War of Independence by no means obscures its transatlantic origins (Becker, 22). In fact, setting the rebellion in its Atlantic context opens up new possibilities, especially in the search for the origins of the conflict. For example, after the Seven Years' War (1756–1763), British officials tried to reduce the London government's deficit not only by increasing revenue (eliciting colonial demands for "no taxation without representation") but also by cutting expenses, and some of these cost-cutting measures were just as infuriating to white Americans as the new taxes. Whitehall decided in 1763 that the cheapest way to head off another costly conflict against the Indians was to issue the Proclamation of 1763, which confined colonial settlement (ineffectively) and land speculation (quite effectively) to the region east of the Appalachian Mountains.

A decade later, Lord Hillsborough (1718–1793), the British cabinet secretary for America, still feared his government was headed for "a general Indian war, the expense whereof will fall on this kingdom" (Holton, 26), so Great Britain stood by the Proclamation of 1763, to the dismay of its own colonists. Free settlers identified another reason for Hillsborough's insistence upon allowing the Indians to keep their lands: he was, Benjamin Franklin (1706–1790) claimed, "terribly afraid of dispeopling Ireland" (Franklin 1766), a principal source of his rental income. Hillsborough and other British officials were indeed alarmed about the massive flow of migrants from the home islands to North America, and imperial antiemigration measures figured prominently among the list of colonial grievances in the Declaration of Independence.

Also prominent among colonial grievances was the forced transportation of Africans to North America. The denunciation of the transatlantic slave trade that the Virginia slaveholder Thomas Jefferson (1743–1826) included in his rough draft of the declaration was of course hypocritical, but he was serious about it. The Virginia House of Burgesses and three other colonial assemblies had recently tried to curtail the African trade (typically through prohibitive tariffs), only to be thwarted by George III (r. 1760–1820) and his cabinet. Jefferson and other planters believed that the further importation of enslaved laborers into North America suppressed the value of two of their commodities: tobacco (by causing overproduction) and the American-born slaves they owned. The continuation of the slave trade was also seen as posing an existential threat to white colonists, not only by increasing the enslaved portion of the population but also by bringing in men and women who had known freedom in Africa and were therefore seen as more likely to rebel than their own blacks, whom they had raised in slavery. Opponents of the African slave trade also pointed out that potential European immigrants feared not only the slaves but also their depressive effect on wages.

The rebellious British colonists, like their counterparts throughout the Americas, resented what Jefferson called the mother country's "unjust encroachment" on the settlers' right to "a free trade with all parts of the world" (Jefferson, 1774). Atlantic trade also figured in the imperial conflict more immediately. Although Massachusetts and Pennsylvania had only small enslaved populations in 1776, they were as dependent as Virginia and South Carolina upon slavery, since New England and the Middle Atlantic colonies marketed roughly half of their grain, fish, livestock, and forest products to slave-worked sugar plantations in the Caribbean, receiving molasses, sugar, and rum in return. More than half of this trade was illegal, since it was with foreign-owned islands, especially French Saint-Domingue. After the Seven Years' War, British officials began trying to obstruct this economically vital trade channel with a smuggling crackdown that culminated in the despised Sugar Act of 1764.

Twentieth- and twenty-first-century historians have discovered a host of previously overlooked sources for the ideas on which the American colonists drew to justify their radical rebellion. Nothing was more important to the explosive growth of the 1740s religious revival known as the Great Awakening than the six American visits of English minister George Whitefield (1714–1770), and the revival is now seen as having promoted individual self-confidence, a willingness to question authority, an ethic of choice, and intercolonial cooperation, all of which prepared colonists for fighting together for independence. Although ideological historians focus on Old World political thinkers such as Niccolò Machiavelli (1469–1527), John Locke (1632–1704), and Francis Hutcheson (1694–1746), the American rebels did not think their European thoughts in a vacuum. Their thwarted desire for Native American land did not prevent them from embracing Indians as exemplars of liberty—a practice that Creole patriots in Latin America would repeat. Free colonists' libertarianism was also fueled by their daily experiences of their fellow Americans' bondage; the scholar F. Nwabueze Okoye described slavery as "the nightmare of the American Revolutionaries."

African Americans would soon give their owners a nightmare of a more immediate kind. By the fall of 1774, enslaved people had begun to avail themselves of the widening chasm separating loyalists to the king from American patriots, who quickly concluded that British officials were instigating unrest in the quarters. It would be more accurate to say the slaves instigated the British, but on November 15, 1775, Lord Dunmore (1732–1809), the last royal governor of Virginia, appeared to justify white colonists' worst fears when he published the first of several British proclamations offering freedom to African Americans who left patriot masters to repair to the royal standard. In the ensuing decades, beleaguered European officials throughout the Americas would issue similar emancipation proclamations, gaining valuable recruits while further alienating white colonists.

Jefferson's denunciation of the Anglo-black alliance, which his draft of the Declaration of Independence paired with a condemnation of the African slave trade, was more than three times longer than any of the other grievances he enumerated. It was also the only one of the 24 complaints against George III that moved Jefferson to capitalize entire words and to resort to religious and emotional rhetoric. Jefferson also placed his discussion of slavery at the end of the list, which was, as every English orator knew, the proper place for the capstone grievance. But in the final draft of the Declaration, the Continental Congress limited itself to a brief and allusive denunciation of Dunmore's emancipation proclamation: "He has excited domestic insurrections amongst us." For their part, slave rebels throughout the Americas responded to their owners' secession movements by spreading the rumor that the monarch had already ordered them freed, only to have his edict thwarted by their owners. Most armies of independence, in another hemisphere-wide pattern, ended up enlisting blacks, with the exception of the colonies south of the Potomac River, where most North American slaves lived.

Fittingly, given free Americans' anger at the commercial restrictions of the mother country, the patriots often wielded trade as a weapon against Parliament. The colonists boycotted British merchandise three times between 1765 and 1774, often with the explicit intention not only of reducing mercantile profits and government revenue but also of provoking riots among out-of-work textile operatives in the English midlands. The intended benefits of these boycotts were as much pecuniary as political. George Washington (1732–1799) celebrated the "nonimportation" association that he proposed to a rump session of the Virginia House of Burgesses in May 1769 as giving indebted planters "a pretext to live within bounds"—an excuse to curtail their extravagance without damaging their social standings or credit ratings (Washington,

1769, np). Many Americans also feared that their participation in the so-called consumer revolution of the preceding decades, symbolized by a mass conversion from homespun to imported finery, had corrupted them. On the other side of the colonists' ledgers, "nonexportation" had special appeal in the Chesapeake colonies, where a recession that began in 1772 had reduced tobacco prices by 40 percent. Tobacco farmers had been searching for a pretext to withhold their crops until the market glut cleared, and Parliament's adoption of the punitive Coercive Acts in retaliation for the Boston Tea Party (1773) in the spring and summer of 1774 gave them what they wanted.

Implementation of nonexportation was delayed a year to allow tobacco farmers to take advantage of the price spike resulting from its imminent arrival, but by the end of 1775, the 13 colonies had effectively halted trade with Great Britain. The mother country disappointed patriots by turning to alternative sources of raw materials and substitute markets for British products, especially in India, and the cutoff of trade had a more damaging impact on the colonists themselves. British cloth (the colonists' principal import) and Bermudan salt (a vital nutrient for livestock and preservative for meat and fish) soon disappeared from American store shelves. Concurrently, nonexportation disabled colonists from obtaining the currency necessary to satisfy tax collectors, landlords, and other creditors in Britain. During the winter of 1775–1776, poor and middling farmers rioted to obtain salt and to prevent land seizures for nonpayment of rent. Patriot authorities began to believe the only solution to the shortages and ensuing social unrest was to reopen the ports, specifically by allowing trade with France, but the French refused either commercial relations or (overt) military aid until the colonists separated formally from Britain. Many later independence declarations (for example, Haiti's in 1804) would be intended primarily for domestic consumption, but in North America, the Continental Congress submitted its case "to a candid world" and accompanied it with appeals for foreign aid and trade.

The armed phase of the ensuing War of American Independence was no less transatlantic than the politics and rhetoric that led up to it. Four German princes rented the British army a total of 30,000 soldiers (known synecdochically as Hessians), and they made up a third of the expeditionary force sent to secure North America. To a great extent, the war was decided on the Atlantic Ocean. The mother country interdicted the rebels' international trade, a strategy that came closer to winning the war than any of its territorial successes. The French navy was of course essential to the final American victory at Yorktown, and the French army supplied half of the soldiers that trapped Cornwallis there. Indeed, the Comte de Rochambeau (1725–1807) merits credit for finally diverting General Washington from his obsession with attacking New York City instead. All told, Louis XVI played as significant a role in the Continental Army's victory in the War of American Independence as Napoleon would play 30 years later in fomenting independence movements in Central and South America.

The rebellion influenced the Atlantic World no less powerfully than the Atlantic context had helped create the conditions for North American independence. Like most of the subsequent secession movements throughout the Americas, political independence led to the abolition of the slave trade, albeit in the United States with a 20-year delay. Just as the Seven Years' War had nearly doubled the British government debt, leading to the budget-balancing measures that helped provoke the colonists, the assistance that Louis XVI provided to his British rival's rebellious colonies accelerated the deterioration in French finances that in 1787 culminated in bankruptcy. Since the outbreak of the French Revolution in 1789 paved the way for the 1791 slave revolt in Saint-Domingue, the American rebellion must be considered an essential ingredient also in the independence of Haiti (1804) (even though the direct ideological links between the independence movements in North America and Haiti appear to have been few). The revolutions in France and the revolt in Saint-Domingue in turn advanced the cause of independence in Mexico and throughout Central and South America. For example, Spain's need to defend itself against Napoleon's conversion of French revolutionary fervor to invasions on every European front led to taxes on its American colonies that fueled colonists' drive for political independence, and Haiti provided sanctuary and arms to Venezuelan rebels.

Radical Jacobins, black and white, also closed the circle of transatlantic influence by casting a long shadow over the domestic politics of the new United States. The first party system essentially pitted Jeffersonian supporters of the French Revolution against its Federalist opponents. Napoleon would never have considered selling the Louisiana Territory to Jefferson in 1803—doubling the size of the United States—if he had succeeded in recapturing Haiti in 1802. The prospect of the tide of this successful slave revolt reaching North America would inspire black southerners while haunting their owners. American independence put slavery on the path to abolition only in the states where slaves composed small portions of the population (and not even in all of those; in 1865 there were still slaves in Delaware). This pattern of emancipating only small enslaved minorities would also prevail in mainland Latin America. In the Caribbean, whites passed up the opportunity to join in the rush to independence on the mainland for fear of creating openings for the vast enslaved majorities of the populations of the islands. Only Brazil (1822) and the southern United States (1776 and again in 1861) declared independence without initiating emancipation.

The most pan-Atlantic aspect of North American independence was the diaspora of British loyalists who fled with the withdrawal of the redcoats. At least 75,000 emigrated to Britain and its remaining colonies, a figure that included about 15,000 slaves who were carried off by their owners, mostly to the Caribbean. Among the free emigrants were 8,000 to 10,000 African Americans who had fought on the British side and in return had received their freedom. They went to Nova Scotia, the Caribbean, and London; more than a thousand became founders of Sierra Leone.

The revolution also influenced the mother country to treat its remaining colonies elsewhere in the world with greater consideration, though in uneven ways. In 1782, as imperial diplomats agreed on preliminary articles of peace with the United States, parliamentary leaders granted unprecedented autonomy to Ireland, and two years later they initiated an effort to curb abuses of the power of the British East India Company in India. Other British officials took the view that the way to prevent further rebellions was to rule with an iron fist. One of the most important effects of American independence, in response to these hard-liners, was also among the most ironic: the loss of the colonies started many Britons on a quest to reclaim their pride in their homeland as a wellspring of liberty,

and this mission to rehabilitate national self-esteem culminated in British authorities leading the fight against the continuing Atlantic trade in slaves and then abolishing slavery in the remaining American colonies (and the Cape Colony in southern Africa) in the mid-1830s, three decades ahead of the United States.

No less than the North American colonies' decision to secede from Great Britain in 1776, the 13 successor states' ratification of the U.S. Constitution a decade later (1787) was an event of pan-Atlantic proportions. The federal government of the new United States would at last have the power to levy its own taxes and thus to "provide for the common defence" (Preamble, Constitution of the United States). But in the short term, at least, the strengthened American military establishment was not the most international aspect of the Constitution; after all, the new national government devoted five-sixths of its military expenditures to fighting Indians rather than enemies overseas. The immediate international effect of ratification was to attract foreign investment. By prohibiting the state legislatures from "impairing the obligation of contracts," the Constitution returned the United States to Britain's Atlantic economy by reconnecting Americans to its credit network of worthy debtors.

Another controversy that cropped up both in the drafting of the Constitution during the summer of 1787 and in subsequent struggles concerned the allocation of representatives among voting districts. No one—either at the Constitutional Convention in Philadelphia or at the Cortes that convened in Cádiz in 1811 to write a constitution for the Spanish Empire—proposed to enfranchise slaves or free people of color. But at both assemblies, delegates from areas with high proportions of Africans in their populations favored counting them when the question involved apportioning representation, to give more votes in the national legislature to their owners. For the purpose of allocating representatives in the U.S. Congress, slaves ended up being counted as three-fifths of a legal person. In Spanish America, legislative apportionment altogether excluded slaves and even free blacks.

The genesis of the War of American Independence, the war itself, and its immediate impacts all had deep Atlantic contexts. However, even this Atlantic perspective on the conventional story of patriots versus redcoats is still insufficiently broad. Parliament's decision to bail out the bankrupt East India Company in 1773 (with the Tea Act, allowing tea to be conveyed directly from China to America) was an essential goad to the uprising, and immediately after the war Americans established their own direct routes to China. Salem, Massachusetts, and other thriving seaports serving the industrial development of New England in the mid-nineteenth century grew on trading in the Indian Ocean. The loyalist diaspora set in motion by the British defeat in the War of American Independence deposited former Americans not just along the Atlantic rim but also in India (where two of Benedict Arnold's sons served in the British army) and in the Australian outback (where several black loyalists took jobs as cowboys).

WOODY HOLTON

Bibliography

Armitage, David, and Sanjay Subrahmanyam, eds. *The Age of Revolutions in Global Context, c. 1760–1840*. Basingstoke, UK: Palgrave Macmillan, 2010.

Becker, Carl L. *The History of Political Parties in the Province of New York, 1760–1776*. Madison: University of Wisconsin Press, 1909.

Brown, Christopher Leslie. *Moral Capital: Foundations of British Abolitionism*. Chapel Hill: University of North Carolina Press, 2006.

Cogliano, Francis D. *Revolutionary America, 1763–1815: A Political History*. 2nd edition. New York: Routledge, 2009.

Franklin, Benjamin. "To William Franklin, September 12, 1766." The Papers of Benjamin Franklin, http://franklinpapers.org/franklin. Accessed on February 4, 2013.

Gould, Eliga H. *Among the Powers of the Earth: The American Revolution and the Making of a New World Empire*. Cambridge, MA: Harvard University Press, 2012.

Gray, Edward G., and Jane Kamensky, eds. *The Oxford Handbook of the American Revolution*. New York: Oxford University Press, 2013.

Holton, Woody. *Forced Founders: Indians, Debtors, Slaves, and the Making of the American Revolution in Virginia*. Chapel Hill: University of North Carolina Press, 1999.

Jasanoff, Maya. *Liberty's Exiles: American Loyalists in the Revolutionary World*. New York: Alfred A. Knopf, 2011.

Jefferson, Thomas. "A Summary View of the Rights of British America, 1774." Electronic Text Center, University of Virginia Library, http://etext.virginia.edu/toc/modeng/public/JefSumm.html. Accessed February 4, 2013.

Okoye, F. Nwabueze. "Chattel Slavery as the Nightmare of the American Revolutionaries." *William and Mary Quarterly*, 3rd ser., 37 (1980): 3–28.

Pybus, Cassandra. *Epic Journeys of Freedom: Runaway Slaves of the American Revolution and Their Global Quest for Liberty*. Boston: Beacon Press, 2007.

Washington, George. "George Washington to George Mason, 5 April 1769." *The Papers of George Washington*, http://gwpapers.virginia.edu/documents/revolution/letters/mason.html. Accessed February 4, 2013.

Young, Alfred F., and Gregory Nobles. *Whose American Revolution Was It? Historians Interpret the Founding*. New York: New York University Press, 2011.

Islam in Africa

The rise of the Atlantic economic system brought a literal sea change to the Muslim societies of northwest and western Africa. In the medieval era West African Muslims had been oriented toward the Mediterranean and—through its religious communities and thriving markets—to the Red Sea and the Indian Ocean. After the fifteenth century they were increasingly integrated into a wholly different world, one dominated by the cultural, economic, and religious institutions of a Christian Europe.

Islam was a key element in the history of these vast regions of Africa. It had come to the Maghreb (for Arabic speakers, the "far west," modern Algeria and Morocco) in the seventh century, and Muslim traders plied routes south to the developed trading complexes of the peoples beyond the desert. South of the Sahara, in the *bilad al-Sudan*, or the "lands of the blacks," as the Muslims knew them, indigenous merchants adopted Muslim identities as early as the ninth century and themselves became propagators of Islam. More important for the long-term growth of the Islamic community in the region, some West Africans began in this period to develop themselves into a clerisy, focusing on teaching, proselytizing, and scholarship. Adopting merchant or clerical identities meant entering social groups that enjoyed freedom of movement within and among the political domains of the region, but it also meant military neutrality and foregoing direct involvement in politics. By the eleventh century, however, some of the rulers in the region began adopting Islam as well, though they always maintained a divide—often residential as well as social—between themselves and the specialists in religion. The large political and military regimes of the sixth through sixteenth centuries (Ghana, Mali, and Songhai) played a major role in giving Islam a political cast.

The Rise of the Atlantic and the End of Empires

In the medieval heyday of these empires, Islam was important; the Atlantic was not. It was what it had always been—a backwater at the edge of the world. One fourteenth-century Malian emperor was reported to have outfitted ships to cross the Atlantic. While some have attempted to argue—from little evidence—that those voyages succeeded and left an imprint on Mesoamericans, there are no surviving traces in Africa of that or any such expeditions. The Atlantic was opened as an avenue for significant trade only when the first Portuguese ships landed along the sandy coast of what is now Mauritania in the middle of the fifteenth century, kidnapping a handful of locals and beginning the trading of enslaved Africans to Iberia.

Enslaved persons became the central items of trade only slowly. Gold, ivory, and other commodities with high ratios of value to weight were the principal articles of Africa's exchanges with the early Atlantic. At first, Europeans had little of value to offer in return, but the ships themselves provided a decisive advantage, as Europeans could move African trade goods cheaply and quickly up and down the Atlantic coast, by the middle of the sixteenth century adding a significant coastal complement to the existing desert trade routes. Things changed dramatically as the demand for—and productivity of—slave labor in the New World grew. By the end of the seventeenth century, slaves were the only currency accepted by most European merchants in Africa and thus the sole export of many Atlantic African societies.

Over the course of the sixteenth century, perhaps one-quarter of the gold that reached Europe from beyond the Sahara was being loaded onto Iberian caravels instead of packed on camels crossing the desert. The trans-Saharan gold trade had been the centerpiece of the prosperity of the large African Muslim empires, making men such as Mali's early fourteenth-century ruler Mansa Musa among the wealthiest people in history. The shift of the trade in gold to the Atlantic almost certainly played a role in the progressive weakening of Songhai, the last of the three regimes, which fell in 1591 to invasion from Morocco.

The Problem of Slavery in Islam

Before the Atlantic Era, enslaved captives had been consequential—though not central—components of western Africa's trade with the Mediterranean world. Muslim Africans participated in this trade more as agents than as victims. There is little evidence of any significant raiding for slaves early on from across the desert. The large militarized states were unlikely targets for raiders. One eleventh-century source estimated that the ruler of Ghana could put 200,000 men in the field, 40,000 of them archers; the dubious accuracy of these numbers aside, their considerable order of magnitude accurately conveys how much this ruler impressed his merchant visitors from the north. The military dominance of Mali and Songhai over lighter-skinned populations in the desert was the general pattern before 1591, and significant portions of the Berber occupants of the desert paid tribute to Mali and Songhai.

The late sixteenth, and especially the seventeenth, centuries saw substantial increases in the intensity of slaving from the north, as the balance of power shifted decisively in favor of the desert Berbers over the savanna populations to the south. From 1600 forward, a progressive desiccation of the entire desert/sahel region put increased economic pressure on Saharans. Its Muslim Arab and Berber populations began raiding sub-Saharan African communities on a large scale, capturing people and selling them as slaves across the desert and to Europeans on the coast. The development of slave-based economies within the Sahara itself, and attendant racial ideologies of the superiority of *bidan* (whites) over *sudan* (blacks), grew apace.

Color prejudice of a sort had certainly existed in Islam—including in North Africa and probably the desert—before this growth of slaving, but it was closer to religious xenophobia than racism as the modern world would come to biologize it. For generations dark-skinned Africans had entered Muslim Mediterranean markets. They were predominantly non-Muslims, captured and sold by sub-Saharan slavers who were mostly (though not exclusively) Muslims. An association between slavery and blackness had thus grown in North Africa, where there were significant populations of dark-skinned slaves, especially in southern Morocco and Egypt. Although enslaved persons came in all colors in the Mediterranean world, sub-Saharan sources of slaves were expanding while other sources—especially of Caucasians and European Christians—were contracting. North Africans began to draw tighter and tighter associations between enslavement and blackness. The Atlantic World developed its modern racism through slaving, and so did the world of Mediterranean Islam; indeed the two might be most productively seen together as the growth of a single racism as a general aspect of modernity.

The change from enslaving non-Muslims to enslaving "blacks," regardless of their faith, did not pass unremarked. After the fall of Songhai in 1591, a number of Islamic scholars from Timbuktu, on the northern bend of the Niger River, were placed under house arrest in Morocco. One of them was Ahmad Bābā (d. 1627), who used his exile to write an important treatise on slavery, the *Mi'rāj al-Ṣu'ūd*. Bābā made strong arguments about the un-Islamic, and therefore illegal, nature of enslavement based on skin color. Like most Muslim scholars of his period, he did not revisit the rather flimsy basis for the institution in Islamic law, nor the problematic ways in which many scholars had come to rationalize it as a legitimate punishment for unbelief. Instead Bābā focused on the problem of Muslims enslaving other Muslims, an act explicitly forbidden in all understandings of Islamic law. He argued that while the blacks bought and sold as slaves in North Africa in prior eras might have been of "pagan" origin, the wholesale Islamization of the *bilad al-Sudan* in the sixteenth century had made it very unlikely that the people available for purchase in Saharan and Mediterranean markets were anything other than believing Muslims. He put the burden of proof on owners that the people they acquired as

slaves were not originally free Muslims, enslaved unjustly.

The legitimacy of the growing slaving in western Africa in the early years of the Atlantic Era became a matter of significant debate among Muslim intellectuals in North and West Africa. The increasing identification of blackness with enslaveability everywhere in the world meant that light-skinned Muslim raiders could systematically victimize their dark-skinned brethren. Indeed, powerful rulers in Morocco—at the end of the sixteenth century and again in the early eighteenth century—enforced drastic conscription schemes against their black populations on grounds that they could all be rightfully enslaved.

Transformations

While these debates unfolded among Muslim legal scholars in the Maghreb and the Saharan fringe of western Africa, the unprecedented and insatiable demand for enslaved Africans in the New World was making "black" and "slave" indistinguishable in practice throughout the entire Atlantic Basin. Africans living around sheltered bays and river mouths, previously marginal to continental history, found themselves thrust to the center of global trade. Islam was not significant in most such coastal regions; if Muslims were present at all, they were only a minority of merchants with origins in the savanna heartlands.

Among Muslim majorities, the residents of Senegambia, the region of Portugal's first contacts with people south of the Sahara in the 1440s, felt the early effects of Atlantic markets most deeply. In the century after these first contacts, Senegambian Muslims were numerous among the enslaved populations taken to Iberia or to the Andes in America. In Senegambia, coastal political authorities in Kajoor imported iron, horses, and probably also early firearms in an effort to secede from the established rulers. They succeeded in 1549 and over the next century imposed sumptuary restrictions on their subject populations and began cultivating a very un-Islamic lifestyle of taking slaves and conspicuously consuming imported tobacco, alcohol, and other Atlantic goods.

Slavery was not new there, but—in a pattern that reproduced itself throughout Atlantic Africa—a focus on slave exports led to novel and increas-

UNIVERSITY OF WINCHESTER
LIBRARY

ingly extensive uses of captives within Africa for military purposes. In Kajoor the crown trained and armed large forces of captives, known collectively as *ceddo*. With these servile armies, kings bypassed the traditional councils of electors and rival families, institutions of representation that ran through the polities of the region. By the end of the sixteenth century, a segment of the Islamic clerisy emerged as voluble critics of the increasingly violent political order and the Atlantic economy of Christian "Franks" behind it. Those who opposed the temporal order of slaving warlords became increasingly radicalized after about 1650 as these new warrior elites increasingly exposed free Muslims to enslavement and exile in both the Atlantic and Saharan trades.

Eventually, these Muslim men of letters took up arms. Abandoning regional traditions of clerical pacifism, they overthrew slave-trading kings. Long before the rise of the Atlantic trade, their clerical communities had been respected as inviolable spaces. The personal sanctity of holy men (and sometimes women), and long-established regional traditions of political neutrality, made them off-limits to worldly authorities. Secular powers were not supposed to pursue even criminals onto the holy ground of a clerical compound. As the Atlantic political economy stimulated enslavement of Muslims in greater numbers, these clerical communities first became safe havens, then sites for exploring alternative models of polity, and in the 1670s staging grounds for counterattacks under the banners of Islamic revolution.

In that decade cleric-led villagers drove out the major *ceddo* warlords of northern Senegambia. The flow of slaves to the coast slowed to a trickle. The French, who were the major European slavers in the region, quickly provided military support to help the deposed rulers reestablish the status quo. This pattern of European intervention in internal disputes recurred throughout Atlantic Africa. Europeans were rarely capable of direct military intervention to assure a regular supply of slaves, but they quite frequently cultivated leaders favorable to Atlantic slaving to promote "regime change." Often this strategy meant providing logistical, military, and tactical support to favored slaving partners in civil wars or succession crises.

Restored to power, the slaving kings of Senegambia dealt the clerics painful retribution, captur-

ing them en masse and thus violating age-old taboos against harming holy persons. Jean Barbot, a French slaver, recounted in his memoirs that one such Senegambian warlord resolved never again to suffer clerics in his land,

> but to sell all such as they should find in
> their country for slaves. I am apt to believe
> there was one of this sort among the slaves I
> purchas'd at Goeree [*sic*] in the year 1681. . . .
> This black priest was abroad for two months
> before he spoke a word, so deep was his sor-
> row. I sold him in the American Islands.
> (Hair, Jones, and Law, 131, 107)

This assault marked the beginning of a century of hardship for the clerical communities and Muslim peasants of the region. The sultan of Morocco raided the Senegal River valley extensively, as did Saharans and Europeans. So too did the African warlord kings themselves. The latter identified themselves as Muslim but also believed that their hereditary "nobility" bestowed rights of life, death, and property over their subjects, believers or not.

The Senegambian clerisy rose again in 1776, a banner year also in other parts of the Atlantic Basin. A prominent cleric, Abdul-Qadir Kan, successfully led a movement to overthrow the slave raiders then disrupting the region. Kan forbade overland passage of slaves to the coast, blockaded French vessels in the Senegal River, preventing traders from accessing slave markets further inland, and even secured the right to board French boats in the river and withdraw Muslims found aboard. When the French post on the island of St. Louis bristled at these disruptive terms he cut off the supply of food that reached the coast, attempting to starve French merchants into compliance. Word of Kan's antislaving movement spread widely, attracting the attention of still-nascent abolitionist movements in both London and Paris. The Reverend Thomas Clarkson in one of his earliest publications lauded Kan:

> [Kan] *sets an illustrious example in extirpating
> the commerce in the human race*; and when we
> consider this amiable man as having been
> trained up in a land of slavery, and as having
> had in the introduction of such a revolution
> all the prejudices of education and custom to
> oppose; when we consider him again as sacri-

ficing a part of his own revenue; as refusing the presents of Europeans; and as exposing himself in consequence of it to the vindictive ravages of the agents of the latter, he is certainly more to be respected than any of the sovereigns of Europe, inasmuch as he has made a much nobler sacrifice than they, and has done more for the causes of humanity, justice, liberty, and religion. (Clarkson, 80)

For thirty years, Kan (r. 1776–1806) warred with the idea that Muslims should ever be slaves, especially to Christians. According to some sources—including Clarkson—he also freed any enslaved person who could recite a verse of the Qur'ān.

While Kan sought to use Muslim identity as a shield against Atlantic slavery, coreligionists in the Futa Jallon highlands of what is now Guinea were instead using Islam as a sword. Another party of clerics, distant cousins to the clerisy of Futa Toro, was raiding and capturing non-Muslim populations in the neighboring forest regions. By the middle of the eighteenth century they had become the predominant slavers in the area. The sword of enslavement, however, could cut both ways. Abdul-Rahman Ibn Sori, son of the then-ruler of Futa Jallon, was captured in the late 1780s on a mission to protect the trade routes from the Futa highlands to the slaving ports at the coast. He spent most of the next 40 years of his life enslaved in Natchez, Mississippi.

Many contradictory processes were at work in Futa Jallon. The clerical class was drawn almost exclusively from speakers of Fula. These Fulani (or Peul) thought of themselves as ethnically distinct from—and superior to—their darker-skinned neighbors. This imperious attitude combined with a kind of Islamic chauvinism—and the significant incentive of Atlantic demand—to produce an aggressive campaign of raiding against unbelieving neighbors, declared a jihad to justify seizing them as slaves. They seem to have had few qualms about selling the people they captured to Christian merchants, a temptation of the Atlantic trade that Abdul-Qadir Kan in Futa Toro found particularly odious. Kan's aggressive policy of freeing all slaves who learned the Qur'ān was certainly not followed. At the same time, however, a vernacular literacy and pedagogy developed in Futa Jallon that was at least partially rooted in a desire to spread the teachings

of Islam beyond the literate clerical elite, and in some cases even to the enslaved.

In the portions of West Africa more remote from the coast, the disruptive dynamics of Atlantic slaving took longer to provoke resistance inspired by Islamic notions of justice. By the 1780s the Atlantic slave trade was becoming a significant factor in the economy and politics of the Yoruba (modern southwestern Nigeria) and Hausa (now northern Nigeria and Niger) regions. Muslims from the Hausa area were being enslaved in significant numbers and passed to the Atlantic coast and especially on to Brazil. Not unlike the *ceddo* in Senegambia, the Yoruba warlords who brokered the coastal trade were also retaining these captives as a caste of military slaves. Unlike the *ceddo*, there they were conspicuous for their Islamic identity rather than their flouting of it.

Usman dan Fodio—a Muslim cleric of Fula origin—authored a famous jihad against the Hausa warlords to end the enslavement of free Muslims by non-Muslim enemies and by their own very dubiously pious rulers. The Hausa rulers, like Senegambian *ceddo* almost 2,000 miles to the west, were selling free Muslims into the trade to gain access to Atlantic goods. While Usman found much in their moral and political comportment to reproach, he declared jihad only after they sold 300 of his Qur'ān reciters as slaves. Thus began a revolution that utterly transformed the entire region as other beleaguered peasants flocked to dan Fodio's Islamic banner, bringing into being the Sokoto Caliphate, which may have been the most populous military regime in nineteenth-century Africa.

Religious Chauvinism

Beyond these political, social, and economic consequences of African Muslim responses to the Atlantic economy, sheer religious chauvinism played a key role in structuring Muslim interactions with Christians. Christian sources of all kinds, from the fifteenth century forward, lamented that Africans had come under the influence of Islamic teaching. On the other side, many Muslims looked at Christians with distaste. Even the hard-drinking, slaving kings who held Muslim clerics in disdain felt this religious pride. One, in the middle of the nineteenth century, disparaged a request that a Christian mission be established in his lands:

If these white priests came to ask to establish themselves on my lands as merchants, they would be welcome and I would place them under my high protection, provided, of course, that they bring me my royal liquor and pay me my customs. But since they are only men of religion and prayer, tell them them there is no god but God and Muhammad is his prophet, and that far from receiving the word of God from others, it is we who teach it to the world. (Boilat, 173–174)

Yet others of both faiths were capable of overcoming such zealotry. Muslim clerics were usually the hosts and guides for Christian visitors in Senegambia—when the latter were not slaves. Many such travelers noted that their Muslim clerical patrons held decidedly ecumenical ideas, sought copies of the Christian Bible, and were deeply interested in religious dialogue. Thomas Clarkson, the British abolitionist, was a striking case among the Christians. He saw in Abdul-Qadir Kan a man of faith and principle whom sovereigns in Europe might one day emulate. Eventually they did, bringing about an abolition of Atlantic slaving that, although sometimes cynical and ineffectual, did come.

The response to the ending of European slaving among Muslim intellectuals in Futa Jallon and elsewhere in Senegambia highlights the lack of clear prescriptions in Islam for the monumental challenges posed by the rise of the Atlantic political economy. Instead, Islam presented African Muslims with sets of choices. In 1810 the imam (leader of the faithful) of Futa Jallon wrote letters in Arabic to British authorities in Sierra Leone complaining about the abolition of slavery in their "colony of freedom." The imam claimed that slavery was a core part of the religion of Islam, which could not be abolished, and that British abolition was bringing endless hardship to Muslims in Futa Jallon. A few months later the governor of British Senegambia noted that the response of Muslim clerics in the lower Senegal River valley to abolition was quite different:

It may be here necessary to remark that there has been greater facility in negotiating [sic] with [the imam] and less probability of again having disputes with him in consequence of

the abolition of the Slave Trade, *a commerce which that Prince always opposed as being contrary to the Laws of his Religion,* and the means through which several of his subjects, followers of the Prophet, were led into Captivity. (British National Archives, 1811)

Although Islamic societies in northwest and western Africa dealt with the rise of the Atlantic World in sometimes diametrically opposed ways, in all of these societies, dynamics of race, slavery, and religious identity became increasingly fundamental.

RUDOLPH T. WARE III

Bibliography

Bābā, Ahmad. *Miʿrāj al-Ṣuʿūd.* Edited and translated by John O. Hunwick and Fatima Harrak. Rabat, Morocco: Maʿhad al-Dirāsāt al-Ifrīqīyah, 2000.

Barry, Boubacar. *Senegambia and the Atlantic Slave Trade.* Cambridge: Cambridge University Press, 1998.

Boilat, David. *Esquisse sénégalaises: Physionomie du pays, peuplades, commerce, religions, passé et avenir, récits et légends.* Paris: P. Bertrand, 1853.

British National Archives, Kew. CO 267/29. "Answers to the Questions proposed to the Lieutenant Colonel Maxwell." Answer 36, January 1, 1811.

British National Archives, Kew, CO 268/8. Letters from the Imam of Foota Jalloo (1810).

Clarence-Smith, William Gervase. "A Fragile Sunni Consensus." In *Islam and the Abolition of Slavery,* 22–48. New York: Oxford University Press, 2006.

Clarkson, Thomas. *Letters on the Slave Trade and the state of the natives in those parts of Africa, which are contiguous to Fort St. Louis and Goree, written at Paris in December 1789, and January 1790.* London: James Phillips, 1791.

Hair, P. E. H, Adam Jones, and Robin Law, eds. *Barbot on Guinea: The Writings of Jean Barbot on West Africa, 1678–1712.* London: Hakluyt Society, 1992.

Hunwick, John. "Islamic Law and Polemics over Race and Slavery in North and West Africa (16th–19th Century)." In *Slavery in the Islamic Middle East,* edited by Shaun E. Marmon, 43–68. Princeton, NJ: Princeton University Press, 1999.

Lovejoy, Paul E. "Islam, Slavery, and Political Transformations in West Africa: Constraints on the Trans-Atlantic Slave Trade." *Outre-Mers: Revue d'Histoire,* nos. 336/337 (2002): 247–282.

McDougall, E. Ann. "Discourse and Distortion: Critical Reflections on Studying the Saharan Slave Trade." *Outre-Mers: Revue d'Histoire*, nos. 336/337 (2002): 195–229.

Ware, Rudolph T. III. "Slavery in Islamic Africa, 1400–1800." In *Cambridge World History of Slavery.* Vol. 3, *AD 1420–AD 1814*, edited by David Eltis and Stanley Engerman, 47–80. Cambridge: Cambridge University Press, 2011.

———. *The Walking Qur'an.* Chapel Hill: University of North Carolina Press, 2013.

Jewish Communities

Jews, because of their long and continuous experience with global dispersion, are an illuminating and provocative example in Atlantic historiography of communities variably transplanted, transformed, or created in new environments. For the two millennia preceding the rise of the Atlantic World, Jews were bound to neither territorial sovereignties nor specific locales. In the early-modern period, the dispersal of Jews throughout the Atlantic World acquired a magnitude in geographical scale and a novel marginality in New World dominions that exemplify the social, economic, and religious complexity of the region.

The major forced conversions of Iberian Jews to Christianity in 1391 and 1497 in the Spanish kingdoms and Portugal, respectively, created a population of New Christians, some of whom were sincere, others insincere, and a third group, perhaps the majority, who moved back and forth between the two faiths striving to secure spiritual, social, and economic stability. Spain and Portugal, the first European powers to lay claim to the New World, officially banned Jews from all their claimed territories until the independence movements of the nineteenth century replaced those colonies with republics. During the first century and a half following Columbus's voyages, Judaizing New Christians could be found as brokers and traders among Iberians who settled in the Ibero-Americas and in West Africa, sometimes within reach of the Spanish and Portuguese Inquisitions or their "visitors" in Lima, Cartagena, Mexico City, Maranhão in northern Brazil, the Cape Verde islands, Guinea, São Tomé, and Angola. Contrary to much of the historiography on the origins of the sugar revolution, Jews were pivotal in neither Brazil nor Barbados, where sugar works had been established long before any Jewish settlement. The men of the "Portuguese nation," as Jews of Iberian origin were known, were too small in numbers in Amsterdam around 1600 to make a difference in a sugar business well established by then in Christian circles.

Only starting in the 1630s, the period coinciding with the growth of sugar planting in the Americas, could Jews live legally as Jews in any European overseas territory. The first such instance was in Dutch Brazil (from 1630), where Jews, capitalizing on their multilingualism and transatlantic Portuguese mercantile networks, imported European textiles and hardware and African slaves and sold them for sugar, tobacco, and brazilwood. The collapse of the Dutch colony to Portuguese reconquest in 1654 created a Jewish exodus that clogged the city of Amsterdam with impoverished refugees, stimulating new Jewish trade and agricultural settlement in the circum- and insular Caribbean and smaller commerce-based communities along the Atlantic seaboard of North America. Using Amsterdam and London as launching pads, professing Jews, some of whom had lived as Christians before returning to their Jewish roots, launched Jewish settlements in Dutch-controlled Berbice, Demerara, Essequibo, Curaçao, Suriname, St. Eustatius, Tobago (disputed among various powers), and Cayenne (in what is today French Guiana). Jews also settled in New Amsterdam and in the Caribbean beyond Dutch-controlled territory—in Barbados, Jamaica, and Nevis (English since 1627, 1655, and the 1620s, respectively), and the Danish Virgin islands—as well as in New York (formerly Nieuw Amsterdam), Newport, Charleston, Philadelphia, and Savannah in North America. On the French islands, where a baptized Catholic's reversion to ancestral Judaism was criminal, Judaism was generally tolerated as an open secret, although Louis XIV expelled Jews from his Caribbean territories in 1685. The largest and hence most prosperous Jewish community in the eighteenth-century Americas was perhaps Curaçao, where elite Jewish merchants owned slightly greater interests in trade, brokerage, and insurance than their proportion in the population. The overwhelming majority of Atlantic Jewish communities were mercantile at their core for the entire Atlantic period. Suriname—Curaçao's only rival in terms of the size of its Jewish population—was exceptional in that, until the latter half of the eighteenth century, most Jews there lived not in the port city (Paramaribo) but in the agricultural hinterland, producing sugar, coffee, cacao, and timber cash crops.

Each of these communities—whether in Africa, Europe, or the Americas—consisted of Jews who were culturally and linguistically Iberian and who self-identified—and presented themselves to outsiders—as those of the "Portuguese nation." The historiography, however, generally treats these individuals as members of a religious subgroup within a political nation, a teleological legacy of the Emancipation Mandate beginning in the 1790s in republican France that created this modern distinction. The elimination of Jewish civil and political disabilities and privileges in order to accord Jews equal status with other citizens of formative republics carried over to subjects of the Dutch Caribbean colonies by the early nineteenth century. This mandate, which positioned Jews at the very center of the intense debate about political identities in the emergent nation-states of the era, required them to disassociate themselves from Jewish nationhood and to consider their Jewishness as solely a creed. The nineteenth-century Protestantization of religion also encouraged both Jews and scholars who wrote about them to reimagine Jews as a confessional group.

The primary identity of early-modern Portuguese Jews, however, more closely approximated the post–World War II concept of an "ethnic group," which combines linguistic and religious (but not political) elements. Most importantly for the Atlantic context, Portuguese Jews—whose habitual mobility defied political borders and who variably identified as New Christians or as their professing Jewish descendants—transcended both political and religious boundaries. This unhinging from rigid political and at times confessional loyalties makes it at best awkward to consider Jews alongside missionizing Catholic and Protestant dissident groups, who undertook conversionary projects within the sovereign domains of European powers, while it is equally inadequate—if not racialist—to describe Jews solely in terms of mercantile endeavors.

The border-defying characteristic of Portuguese Jews enabled covert Jews to forge transatlantic economic ties with other Portuguese Jews and with sincere New Christians, who were often family members. Because of shared languages (Portuguese and Spanish) and culture, many of the difficulties associated with opening up frontiers did not beset Jews, or their Christian relatives, whom one scholar dubs a "nation on the ocean sea." On the other hand, the most successful New Christian merchants not only established trade connections with unrelated strangers but also tended to be global entrepreneurs who built broad and integrated networks that allowed them to tap into the more lucrative branches of trade otherwise reserved for Christians. It may therefore be more useful to regard the most prosperous merchants—who brought Jewish communities their transatlantic reputation for wealth—as members of an elite entrepreneurial class rather than as members of any particular religious or national group.

Successive waves of anti-Jewish persecution, beginning with the expulsion of Jews from England in 1290 and culminating with another expulsion from Spain in 1492, followed by the mass forced conversion of Jews in Portugal in 1497, meant that Europe's Atlantic seaboard was bereft of open Jewish communities at the dawn of the Atlantic Age. But several Jewish communities, some indigenous, others exiles from the Iberian Peninsula and their descendants, populated Africa's Atlantic coast. One understudied community is that of Salé (in what is today Morocco), an important trade center whose Jews maintained close connections to Spain and Portugal and to the Portuguese Jewish community of Amsterdam.

For roughly the first two hundred years of the Atlantic Age, most of the Jewish population in the Atlantic World was of Iberian origin, and this shared provenance characterized the Jewish Caribbean for the entire Atlantic period. Only in the mid-seventeenth century did Ashkenazim (Jews of central and eastern Europe) begin to migrate to western Europe, and eventually, though to smaller extents, to North America and the Caribbean. These Jews, generally engaged in petty trade rather than transatlantic commerce, further intensified the urban character of Atlantic Jews. In most cities, such as Amsterdam, London, Willemstad, and Paramaribo, Portuguese Jews and Ashkenazim created separate communities, while in the North American colonies, both groups worshiped together and were buried in the same cemeteries. Even after Ashkenazi Jews came to form the majority of the Jewish population living along the North American seaboard (around the 1720s), Portuguese Jewish hegemony—as assessed through leadership, synagogue rites, and pronunciation of Hebrew—held sway. Interactions between the two diasporic subgroups during this era were more intensive than ever before, the result of common external pressures and influences, including geographical displacement, mercantilism, and the Enlightenment.

Jewish cultural orientation extended beyond the confines of the Atlantic World owing to shared affinities with the Land of Israel and the pan-diasporic concept of Jewish solidarity. Many Atlantic Jews requested to be buried with soil from Jerusalem strewn across their eyelids, and Jewish emissaries or individuals at large traveled from the Ottoman Empire or sent letters to Atlantic Jewish communities to raise funds for Palestinian Jewish religious institutions, impoverished Middle Eastern Jews, or Jewish captives of the Barbary pirates. That many of these letters or visitors were unwelcome attests to the importance of localism, whereby certain Atlantic Jewish communities gave priority to their own struggling congregations and individuals, privileged as "natives of the land" (*filhos da terra*, in Portuguese).

Jewish messianism also spilled over the borders of the Atlantic World. Belief that the end of days was nigh, and that a Jewish Messiah would rebuild the Temple and gather in the exiles to Jerusalem, was central to the formation of New World Jewish colonies. During the second half of the seventeenth century, various Portuguese Jews patterned their synagogue architecture after an early-modern model of Solomon's Temple and gave redemptive Hebrew names to their congregations. While the conferral of communal autonomy and unprecedented privileges of worship and commerce to Jews in Brazil and many Caribbean colonies—particularly Essequibo (modern Guyana)—may have encouraged Jews to imagine their new settlements as mini-Jerusalems, it is important not to exaggerate this messianic fervor or to extrapolate its intensity to periods beyond the seventeenth century.

Because of their legal status as a corporate group, New World Atlantic Jewish communities carefully preserved their communal archives through the generations, largely motivated by the legal afterlife of documents that ratified Jewish social, commercial, and religious privileges in the colonies where they lived. Surinamese-born physician and philosophe David Nassy was the first to realize the historiographical import of his community's archives when he published in 1788 his famous *Essai Historique* on the colony and its Jews. Atlantic Jewry's extreme devotion to manmade records also applied to their synagogues and cemeteries, which they regarded as icons of their longevity and status in a given colony, and which they strove to preserve and protect from destruction. The unintended consequence of their dedication to material heritage is that history can be told—and retold—from their perspectives.

Jews in the Atlantic World were no less mobile than other whites, as most counted themselves and were accepted, but important distinctions set them apart. Jews were among the earliest colonists in the Dutch and British colonies, but—unlike their Christian counterparts—their wealthy elites tended not to repatriate to the fatherlands after making their fortunes. As a result, Caribbean Jews acquired an "old families" status, which they leveraged in political discussions with local and metropolitan authorities, stressing their loyalty, commercial utility, and consequent entitlement to political, economic, and religious privileges. Moreover, Jews often formed sizable proportions of the white populations (a third in both Curaçao and Suriname and perhaps Dutch Brazil, a quarter of Nevis, and a fifth in St. Thomas). On the other hand, Jews were the only non-Christians in these populations, and their Jewish "otherness" reserved for them a not-quite-"white" status, as reflected in colonial censuses, where they are often distinguished as "Jews," and in their ascribed position as social inferiors to free colored people, particularly by the late eighteenth century. Even though Jews mingled vigorously, socially and commercially, with Christians of various denominations, their worlds were "largely parallel to, rather than thoroughly intertwined with" (Zacek, 109) Christians, generally drawing the boundary at marriage, which—for both Christians and Jews—was a sacrament available only to members baptized or born/converted into the community of faith. This legal or de facto barrier prevented Jews from attaining the social and financial benefits accrued though acquisition of land and capital, as well as political connections. Their exclusion from Christian militias and from holding government offices, moreover, pushed the "principal source of local prestige and patronage" out of their reach (Zacek, 111).

Their marginality among the multiethnic and multidenominational Christian populations both encouraged and discouraged Jewish alliances with the enslaved and manumitted majorities in the Caribbean and Brazil. In Curaçao and the English colonies, Jews generally shunned integrating enslaved and free Africans and Eurafricans into their communities. But by the early seventeenth century on the Senegambian coast in West Africa, and in Suriname during the latter half of the eighteenth century, a sizable Jewish Eurafrican subgroup arose, in the latter case, perhaps 10 percent of the population, confessing Jews legally recognized as such by the colonial government and by Jewish communal leaders. These Jewish Eurafricans illustrate that African spiritual traditions, Christianity, and Islam were not the only possibilities available to Africans and their free or enslaved descendants. These Eurafrican Jews are examples of both the ubiquity of new ethnicities formed in the Atlantic World—what anthropologists call *ethnogenesis*—and the strategies that people of color, as they were designated in the tropical Atlantic, employed to find acceptance, gain collective autonomy, and share first-tier status as official members of the white community.

Eurafrican Jews also remind us that Jews of European origin created both legitimate families, largely responsible for upholding the status of Jews in the colonies as "white," and extralegal clans, whose members were sometimes integrated into the Jewish community (as in Amsterdam and Suriname) or were elsewhere barred from it (as in Curaçao, where unofficial wives and children sometimes claimed rights to financial support from the families whose men had spawned them). It may be that the Eurafrican Jewish families that formed in the Senegambia region in the late sixteenth and early seventeenth centuries, some of whom migrated to Amsterdam, initiated or reinforced acceptance of patrilineal Jewish descent as a marker of Portuguese Jewishness. This acceptance partly explains both the policy of Amsterdam's Dotar Society, which dispensed dowries to impoverished females whether they traced their Portuguese Jewishness to the male or distaff sides of their families, and the inclusion of Eurafrican children in Amsterdam and Suriname who were born to mothers of African origin and Portuguese Jewish fathers. The longevity of extralegal families as an informal institution—from their emergence in the late seventeenth century, when gender ratios in the Caribbean were skewed heavily in favor of men, to later centuries when ratios evened out—indicates that parallel patri-clans were commonplace, regardless of the formation stage or size of an official Jewish community.

Jews were a tiny fraction of 1 percent of the populations of the Atlantic World and as such are statistically insignificant, even if one were to include Judaizing New Christians, whose fluid Jewish identities and the secrecy inherent in Judaizing make their numbers impossible to calculate. However, Atlantic Jews acquire meaningful prominence when one considers them "a historical-demographic laboratory" (Cohen, 156). They were overwhelmingly urban, were minorities everywhere, were more dispersed than other subgroups, and—unlike any other community—considered themselves and were considered by others as a distinct and coherent entity, regardless of their domiciles. Their identities as (former) New Christians, white but not quite, or Eurafrican placed them in the forefront of the trade and cultural brokerage that drove the historical processes of the Atlantic. Jews in the early Americas, much as in revolutionary France where they were also a tiny fragment of the population, occupied a central position in discussions about citizenship and equal rights emerging in the nineteenth century. All the major themes of Atlantic history—migration, ethnogenesis, the circulation of ideas, and struggles for emancipation—unfold within this tiny group.

AVIVA BEN-UR

Bibliography

Cohen, Robert. "Jewish Demography in the Eighteenth Century: A Study of London, the West Indies, and Early America." PhD diss., Brandeis University, 1976.

Graizbord, David L. *Souls in Dispute: Converso Identities in Iberia and the Jewish Diaspora, 1580–1700.* Philadelphia: University of Pennsylvania Press, 2004.

Israel, Jonathan. *European Jewry in the Age of Mercantilism, 1550–1750.* 3rd ed. London: The Littman Library of Jewish Civilization, 1998.

Mark, Peter, and José da Silva Horta. *The Forgotten Diaspora: Jewish Communities in West Africa and the Making of the Atlantic World.* Cambridge: Cambridge University Press, 2011.

Roitman, Jessica Vance. *The Same but Different? Intercultural Trade and the Sephardim, 1595–1640.* Leiden, Netherlands: Brill, 2011.

Studnicki-Gizbert, Daviken. *A Nation upon the Ocean Sea: Portugal's Atlantic Diaspora and the Crisis of the Spanish Empire, 1492–1640.* Oxford: Oxford University Press, 2007.

Zacek, Natalie. "'A People So Subtle': Sephardic Jewish Pioneers of the English West Indies." In *Bridging the Early Modern Atlantic World: People, Products, and Practices on the Move*, edited by Caroline A. Williams, 97–112. Surrey, UK: Ashgate, 2009.

Judaism

Early-modern Judaism rested on the Torah, Talmud, and medieval Talmudic texts, which codified the practices of the religious community. The core doctrine of this Judaism was a belief in one omnipotent God, who created the world, rewarded and punished mankind, provided the Torah from heaven, and would resurrect the dead at the time of the Messiah. The idea that Jews were a special Chosen People was also a central tenet. Two major subcultures of Judaism flourished during this period: Ashkenazic Judaism, which was observed primarily in central and eastern Europe, and Sephardic Judaism, which was based in the Iberian Peninsula, North Africa, and the Middle East. Although Ashkenazim and Sephardim adhered to the same fundamental beliefs, customary practices and interpretive differences between the two communities were often significant, ranging from their pronunciations of Hebrew letters to their prayer melodies and holiday food cultures. Like Christianity and Islam, the other main organized Western religions of this era in the Mediterranean and Europe, these subcultures expanded throughout the Atlantic World in the seventeenth and eighteenth centuries.

Sephardic Judaism was the first to spread to West Africa and the Americas, as merchants and their families moved to the developing overseas territories of Portugal and Spain, bringing with them their traditional rites and rituals. Since formal Jewish worship was illegal in both the Iberian Peninsula and its overseas outposts in the first decade of the sixteenth century, many of these immigrants converted to Christianity, becoming "New Christians," but continued their Judaic religious heritage in secret. Their descendants, termed crypto-Jews by historians, followed a remembered community form of Judaism that over time became ever more distant from the text-based rabbinic version that their ancestors had observed. This form of remembered Judaism was transmitted across far-flung multigenerational kin networks through oral family histories and a community-wide emphasis on similarities between contemporary crypto-Jewish experiences and the Exodus story.

Venice, then Amsterdam, and finally London were the sources of Sephardic Jewish community authority during the early-modern era. Rejudaizing New Christians of varying personal backgrounds faced numerous questions involving religious practices when they formed new communities. Early Sephardic leaders sought interpretive pronouncements from rabbinical authorities in Venice. The establishment and maturation of Amsterdam as a center of Jewish learning eventually made that city a source of authority for communities in the Dutch Atlantic. London assumed the same role for Jews in English territories by the mid-eighteenth century. As Judaism passed to new generations through matrilineal descent, these authorities attended to the process of forming the Jewish families at the core of every congregation. An organization headquartered in Amsterdam, called the Santa Companhia de Dotar Orfaons e Donzelas Pobres (or the Dotar Society), dispensed dowries to poor women of the Sephardic Diaspora who promised to marry and live as Jews. They typically gave out two dowries per year.

The first formal Jewish communities in the western Atlantic World—in which the synagogue was the religious, social, and administrative center—emerged during the 1630s in Recife and Mauricia, in Dutch Brazil. These communities developed under the explicit protection of the Dutch West India Company, which controlled the Pernambuco region of Brazil from 1630 to 1654. Motivated by economic opportunities and an agenda to spread Judaism to the four corners of the earth as a precursor to the messianic age, Sephardic pilgrims from Amsterdam, then a key center of western European Jewry, sought to revitalize Judaism among New Christians in Brazil by founding two congregations: Kahal Zur Israel and Magen Abraham. Normative Jewish institutions, including Talmud Torah schools, purifying ritual *mikveh* baths, and a congregation cemetery were also established. During the 1640s, rabbis Isaac Aboab da Fonseca and Moses Raphael d'Aguilar tended to the spiritual needs of Dutch Brazil's approximately 1,000 Jews. In 1654, however, a Catholic Portuguese uprising culminated in expulsion of the Dutch West India Company and a return to Portuguese rule. As Judaism once again became illegal, many Jews left Brazil to return to Europe, while others removed to nascent Jewish communities elsewhere in the Atlantic. Although a small number remained, practicing their religion secretly at great risk, Jews were not permitted to worship freely again in Brazil until 1773.

Jewish settlements in French colonies proved short lived, due to the 1685 Code Noir banning their existence, but Judaism flourished during the mid- to late seventeenth century in Dutch and English Atlantic possessions. Most notably, on the Dutch island of Curaçao, Jewish adventurers in the 1650s secured charters from the Dutch West India Company protecting their right to worship. Its first Jewish inhabitants named their congregation Mikvé Israel, which means Hope of Israel, expressing messianic dreams of imminent redemption then prevalent among both Jews and Christians and reflecting their goals in planting Judaism on the island. In 1659, the Sephardic community of Amsterdam donated a Torah, and in 1674 the congregation welcomed Rabbi Josiao Pardo to Willemstad. By Passover 1732, when the Willemstad congregation dedicated its sixth synagogue building to accommodate its growing numbers, Curaçao had become the spiritual and cultural capital of New World Jewry. Today this structure remains the oldest continually used synagogue in the Americas.

After Oliver Cromwell informally readmitted Jews to England in 1656, a small community of Sephardic Jews from Hamburg and Amsterdam, joined by New Christians from the Iberian Peninsula and France, coalesced around a synagogue located in a rented house in London's East End. In 1701, Sephardic Jews in London consecrated a new house of worship, known as the Bevis Marks Synagogue, which was modeled after Amsterdam's magnificent synagogue (completed in 1677), the home congregation for Dutch Sephardic Jews. Bevis Marks functioned similarly as a source of spiritual authority for Jews in the Anglo-Atlantic. Ashkenazic Jews also immigrated to England in the 1690s and started their own congregation in London. Both Sephardic and Ashkenazic Jews moved on to English colonies in the Caribbean, including Barbados and Jamaica. They also established communities in port cities of English North America, including New York, Philadelphia, Newport, Charleston, Savannah, and, lastly, Montreal, following the defeat of the French in the Seven Years' War.

While Ashkenazim outnumbered Sephardim in the Atlantic World by the eighteenth century, the rites and rituals of the latter continued to predominate. Relations between Sephardic and Ashkenazic Jews in Europe were often strained, and members of the two subcultures attempted to maintain separate communities, even as they lived side by side in the same cities. Tensions between Sephardic and Ashkenazi Jews occasionally flared in the Americas as well. In Paramaribo, (Dutch) Suriname, for instance, antagonisms culminated in Ashkenazic Jews establishing an independent congregation (Neve Shalom) in the early eighteenth century. More typically, Sephardic and Ashkenazi Jews in the Americas found common ground in their shared beliefs and worshipped together peaceably within their small communities. Perhaps most symbolic of this overall harmony was the 1773 marriage of the spiritual leader of Newport, Rhode Island, the Sephardic *hazzan* (cantor) Isaac Touro, to an Ashkenazic woman named Reyna Hays.

Ultimately, these Jewish settlements, although geographically dispersed and culturally diverse, drew together around a shared religious culture that transcended both religious sectarianism and the political boundaries of early-modern European dynastic rivalries. Their religious solidarity was further reinforced by business networks linking distant family members and coreligionists, as well as by their continuing ties back to the vibrant European centers of Judaism. Men and women of the Jewish Diaspora gained the confidence to establish new communities as they moved throughout the Atlantic, encountering recognizable variations of Judaism wherever they went and contributing greatly to the religious and commercial development of the Atlantic World.

NOAH L. GELFAND

Bibliography

Israel, Jonathan I. *Diasporas within a Diaspora: Jews, Crypto-Jews, and World Maritime Empires, 1540–1740.* Leiden, Netherlands: Brill, 2002.

Kagan, Richard L., and Philip D. Morgan, eds. *Atlantic Diasporas: Jews, Conversos, and Crypto-Jews in the Age of Mercantilism, 1500–1800.* Baltimore, MD: Johns Hopkins University Press, 2008.

Labor

See Impressment, Kidnapping, and Panyaaring; Indentured Contracts; Slavery, U.S.; Slaving, in Africa; Slaving, European, from Africa; Slaving, European, of Native Americans

Languages

Languages were among the richest historical and cultural products, and the most complex of "commodities," exchanged over the long period of exploration, colonization, and trade that formed the Atlantic World. Languages, complex and symbolic forms of communication, have numbered in the thousands worldwide and are products of the histories of their speakers. Languages exchanged across the Atlantic beginning in the sixteenth century include both those that have emerged as descendants of older "proto" languages, such as the

Romance languages descended from "Proto-Indo-European," or Algonquian languages descended from "Proto-Algonquian," and others that are "contact induced," communicative codes sometimes known as pidgins, jargons, or creoles. Languages of both kinds were foundational in the development of the Atlantic World.

The term *commodity* is more than just metaphoric when applied to languages: skills in the languages of the New World, as well as of Europe, Africa, and the Middle East, were valuable to entrepreneurs looking for riches to exploit, laborers to enlist or enslave, and lands to conquer and settle. Countless stories have come down to us of linguistically skilled captive people who served as guides, companions, and interpreters to European explorers; these were the people who made the sharing of separate bodies of knowledge possible, as did the many Native people of Africa, the Caribbean, and the Americas who visited Europe and the Middle East during this period. Europeans and Africans arrived in a New World populated by speakers of a wide variety of languages, resulting in a great brew of cultural syncretism and change communicated most directly through language.

Explorers' accounts, missionary records, colonial archives, and many other written and material sources from the period contain a great store of knowledge about the peoples of the Atlantic World and their languages. The beginnings of the formal study of the world's languages drew on these sources. Many early accounts of these cultural encounters were recorded in the world's first printed books and broadsides, spreading throughout Europe new ideas and new curiosity about the many kinds of languages and societies they revealed. Some of the most significant information to be found in these early sources are the reports of the linguistic encounters engendered by colonization and economic expansion and of what those encounters consisted. Trading expeditions, attempts at religious conversion, colonial expansion, and military occupation all left their traces in language. Though languages were at first commodities as vehicles of cultural ideas and experiences, for modern scholars they also preserve worlds and ways of life that were soon lost to the "maelstrom of change." Because a brief history of these encounters among speakers of many hundreds of languages in the Atlantic World is impossible, this essay examines three topics broadly characterizing the rich linguistic heritage of the Atlantic World. These are contact languages, early linguistics, and language loss and change.

Contact Languages

Maps of the languages of the Atlantic World include those spoken in all the regions connected with one another through population movements and economic integration from the fifteenth century to the postcolonial present. These languages included (but were not limited to) the language families of western Europe (including Romance and Germanic languages), West Africa (including Niger-Congo and Afro-Asiatic languages), and the indigenous language families of North, Central, and South America and the Caribbean (including Algonquian, Iroquoian, Muskogean, Siouan, Caddoan, Mayan, Uto-Aztecan, and Arawakan language families, as well as such language isolates as Tunica). Except for the isolates, which have no known linguistic relatives, most language families contained several distinct languages. For example, the Iroquoian language family includes the northern Iroquoian languages Huron/Wyandot, Laurentian, Oneida, Onondaga, Mohawk, Cayuga, and Seneca, the central Iroquoian languages Susquehannock, Tuscarora, and Nottoway, and the southern Iroquoian language Cherokee. It is difficult to determine the extent of use of most of the languages identifiable through early historical sources, for languages are encompassing frameworks and mediated locally by the communities who speak them as part of a communicative economy that includes such other codes as gesture or visual signing. Many communities today and in the past were multiglossic, with members able to speak or understand several languages and dialects. Further, in

situations of contact, the relative power or numbers of the parties involved dictated to some extent what "languages" would be spoken and shared and thus adapted and left for posterity. For example, languages learned by nonnative speakers in the course of trade or exploration differ greatly from the kinds of languages derived from long-term cohabitation or the imposition of one preferred code over a subordinated local one.

Contact languages are generally understood to be codes that emerged among peoples who had come together recently, including jargons, pidgins, and creoles. Speakers of different languages participated in varied kinds of linguistic contact. For example, speakers of the Algonquian language known as Montagnais, spoken in Newfoundland and Nova Scotia, began adopting words of Basque or Portuguese origin in the fifteenth century, when Basque fishermen and their multilingual crews visited, and presumably wintered over, along the coast. Montagnais and other Algonquian-language speakers acquired new words for things they knew well, including the Basque or Portuguese term *bacalau* (dried fish). Words of Tupí (a language of Brazil) appeared in Portuguese in the sixteenth century, as did others from the indigenous languages of the Caribbean region; a well-known Tupí word is *piranha* (toothed fish). The Taíno and Arawak languages of the Caribbean contributed many terms well known in Spanish, English, and Dutch, including *canoe* and *hammock*. The languages of West Africa likewise contributed to the vocabularies of numerous European and Native American languages as speakers of them were captured and transported during the transatlantic slave trade.

Trade jargons are often characterized by vocabulary from the "target language" of the arriving merchants and syntax from the local or "substrate" language. For example, West African Pidgin English, also called Guinea-Coast Creole English, was the lingua franca, or language of commerce, derived in large part from "nautical" English, spoken along the West African coast during the later Atlantic slave trade. Many of its terms became part of the creoles of Anglophone West Africa, the Caribbean, and the Atlantic coasts of the Americas as well. Languages such as Sierra Leone Krio and Nigerian Pidgin English all emerged from West African Pidgin English, as did Jamaican Creole and the Gullah language of coastal South Carolina and Georgia. American Indian pidgins and jargons were widespread along the Atlantic seaboard of North America, including a pidgin Delaware (Algonquian) and the Mobilian Jargon, a trade language in use at the time of contact in the Mississippi Delta and the Gulf of Mexico, said to be a pidginized version of Choctaw, Chickasaw, and other southeastern languages as well as such European languages as French. Many Native people spoke pidginized versions of European languages as well, including English, French, Spanish, and Portuguese.

Creole languages are contact languages that became the first languages of their speakers. True creoles developed out of early Atlantic pidgins and jargons include French Caribbean Creole, Papiamento (also Caribbean, from Portuguese), and Patwa (from French *patroi* in Jamaica). The Garifuna of Belize, Nicaragua, and Guatemala, whose language was sometimes known as Black Carib, is said to be influenced by Caribbean, Spanish, French, and African languages. West African languages were also influential in the development of some dialects or creoles now considered under the larger umbrella as African American Vernacular English (AAVE).

The study of loanwords in indigenous languages can richly reward the historian. Not only do these reveal language contacts, they also indicate the specific ways in which natives and newcomers acquired knowledge about one another. For example, in the New England Algonquian language spoken on Martha's Vineyard (whose descendants are known as Wampanoag), loanwords for money (*peny*), measurements (*acre*), and guns (*paskehheg*, literally, it thunders) appeared in documents that Native people wrote in their own language beginning in the late seventeenth century, marking clearly what they found significant in their relations with the English newcomers. In the languages of the North American Southeast, Spanish loanwords such as *vaca* (cow), *naranja* (orange), and *azúcar* (sugar) were adopted by the speakers of Native languages in direct contact with Spanish speakers and then passed on to speakers of other indigenous languages. For example, Spanish loanwords in Creek were taken up also by Koasati and transferred from Koasati to Alabama and from Alabama to Choctaw.

Interpreters and "culture brokers," whose linguistic skills were decisive in the success of colonial ventures on both sides of the Atlantic, are also of interest to linguists and historians of the Atlantic World. As the Portuguese worked their way slowly down Africa's Atlantic coast they seized plurilingual captives familiar with the regions to the south to interpret for them. In the New World, Sir Walter Raleigh, an advocate for English colonization in the late sixteenth century, brought speakers of Algonquian languages from Virginia and Arawakan speakers from Guyana on the northeast coast of South America to England, and facilitated their learning of English. Many of these interpreters returned to their homelands, sometimes playing the role of colonial officials but as often leading revolts against colonial governments. The Nahuatl-speaking captive woman Malinali (also known as La Malinche and Doña Marina) was given to the army of Hernán Cortés in 1519. She served as interpreter, advisor, and intermediary for the Spanish invaders and later became Cortés's lover and the mother of his first child, Martín. Her historical reputation has been controversial, but she remains a powerful symbol of Mexico's tumultuous past and its linguistic and ethnic complexity.

Colonial Linguistics and Scholarship

Linguistic studies of many of the languages of the Atlantic World began within the context of colonial missionary efforts. Among the most prolific students of these languages were the Jesuits, who followed in the footsteps of explorers, merchants, and colonists in many parts of the French Atlantic World; others reached western Africa in the wake of the Portuguese and produced the first written version of a Bantu language, a Catholic catechism in Kikongo, in 1624. Jesuit translations of numerous American Indian languages were produced in the period between 1625 and 1800. Early linguistic descriptions include John Eliot's many seventeenth-century translations of Puritan religious works into the language known as Massachusett, or Natick. The Swedish missionary John Campanius translated *Luther's Catechism* (1696) into what he called the "American-Virginian" language (Lenape); and before 1600 Spanish missionaries had described the more than 30 different indigenous languages of Mexico and southeastern North America.

Many missionaries working with new converts in Africa and in the Americas, unlike some European academic linguists still working with classical models, could afford few preconceptions in their analysis of the languages they needed to learn for purposes of elementary survival, and they thus provided many new insights into the ways that the languages of the world varied. Europeans' "discovery" of American Indian languages did much to further the nascent field of linguistics, inspiring such sixteenth-century humanists as Thomas Hariot to speculate on linguistic universals and sparking the interest of such eighteenth-century scholars as Peter Stephen DuPonceau and Albert Gallatin, who began the work of cataloguing and comparing the grammatical and syntactic and lexical features of the languages of the world.

Although Europeans, Africans, and Native Americans all regarded one another through their own cultural lenses, some languages, particularly those with long local traditions of literacy (Nahuatl and Mixtec, for example) were sometimes incorporated into religious and scholarly curricula in their own right. Several men and women of mixed African, European, and indigenous American backgrounds became highly regarded scholars, including Garcilaso de la Vega ("El Inca"), whose famous *Royal Commentaries* (1604) represented an attempt to reconcile European and Andean histories. Many other African and Caribbean peoples and American Indians contributed more anonymously to growing European knowledge about their languages, histories, and traditions, such as that encapsulated in well-known José de Acosta's *The Natural and Moral History of the Indies* (1590) and in the Florentine Codex (or "General History of the Things of New Spain," c. 1590) attributed to Bernard de Sahagún and anonymous Nahuatl-speaking authors and artists.

Language Loss, Language Shift, and Language Replacement

Estimates of the numbers of languages and language families spoken in the Americas and in western Africa during the period of the expansion of Atlantic trade and colonization are necessarily inexact; some scholars suggest that nearly 700 languages were spoken in North America in the sixteenth century; today more than 500 of these are lost or in decline. European trade in Africa did not lead to settlement or conquest, allowing for the preservation of indigenous languages there, with the addition of trade jargons. But in the Americas indigenous-language loss proceeded apace, as Native populations declined through warfare and disease, were relocated, or were subsumed within immigrant economies. Particularly along the Atlantic coast of North America, such Native languages as Narragansett, Unami, and Munsee and Virginia and North Carolina Algonquian began to be threatened as early as the seventeenth century. Other indigenous languages, such as Timucua (a language isolate in what is now Florida) were spoken long enough to be recorded by missionaries but apparently did not survive the colonial period. Although some Native people became bilingual in their own and in colonial languages, economic and social pressures caused indigenous languages to be replaced, a process that continues today in the Americas. Language shifts occurred in other cases, as Native people were displaced and forced into alliances with speakers of other indigenous languages. Examples are the adoption of the Creek language by the Apalachee and the adoption of northern Iroquoian languages by some Delaware.

Though the decline and disappearance of the indigenous languages of the Americas was only one of many outcomes of the linguistic encounters in the Atlantic, its cost was incalculable. Many forms of indigenous knowledge embedded in languages were perforce destroyed, and losing the discourses of social life inhibited the ability of Native people to conduct themselves as their ancestors might have done. Fortunately, the early twenty-first century has seen a major initiative to halt the loss of native languages and even reverse their decline. Part of this salvage effort has included language-documentation projects for several Atlantic coast indigenous languages and language revitalization efforts for others.

KATHLEEN J. BRAGDON

Bibliography

Bragdon, Kathleen. "Linguistic Acculturation in Massachusett: 1663–1771." In *Papers of the Twelfth Algonquian Conference*, ed. by William Cowan, 121–132. Ottawa, ON: Carleton University, 1981.

Goddard, Ives. "The Use of Pidgins and Jargons on the

East Coast of North America." In *The Language Encounter in the Americas, 1492–1800: A Collection of Essays*, ed. by Edward G. Grey and Norman Fiering, 61–80. New York: Berghahn, 2000.

Greenblatt, Stephen. *Marvelous Possessions: The Wonder of the New World*. Chicago: University of Chicago Press, 1991.

Mufwene, Salikoko S., and Cécile B. Vigouroux. *Colonization, Globalization and Language Vitality in Africa: An Introduction*. London: Continuum, 2008.

Silverstein, Michael. "Encountering Language and Languages of Encounter in North American." *Ethnohistory: Journal of Linguistic Anthropology* 6, no. 2 (1997): 126–144.

Law, Canon

Canon law is the set of rules and regulations that governs the Catholic Church—both as a complex institution and as a community, theoretically including all baptized Christians. From the vantage point of Atlantic History, it was between the fifteenth and seventeenth centuries one of the ordering apparatuses of European societies that royal and religious authorities brought to organize new transatlantic regimes resulting from European commercial and military ventures overseas. Inhabitants of a multitude of places around the Atlantic—including the kingdoms of France, Portugal, Castile, and Aragon; the islands of the Atlantic (Madeira, the Azores, the Canaries, Cape Verde), the Caribbean, and the Gulf of Guinea (São Tomé and Príncipe); the African polities of Kongo and Angola; as well as the colonies of Brazil, New France, and the vast Spanish viceroyalties of New Spain and Peru—encountered canon law as a central element of the religious, social, and political orders in which they lived. Accordingly, it was canon law that they, in turn, manipulated to pursue a variety of their own ends, from making claims to sovereignty to dissolving a marriage. In the emerging Atlantic arena, officials used the tools of canon law to claim authority and impose discipline; they employed canon law to found and regulate Catholic institutions and turned to its principles to try to resolve new political and religious problems created in the processes of conversion and colonization.

European Expansion and Canon Law

Alongside several bodies of secular law, canon law was systematized in a legal revolution that occurred in Europe between the twelfth and fourteenth centuries. Resting ultimately on biblical text, it drew upon excerpts from writings of the Church Fathers; it comprised primarily an ongoing accumulation of papal decrees and legislation produced in an irregular series of Church councils. As medieval popes and proponents of conciliar authority (who favored Church governance by councils) sought to expand the legal tools at their disposal, experts—known as canonists—recodified extant canon law, borrowing from Roman law to fill in perceived gaps and respond to changing legal environments. On the cusp of expansion across the Atlantic, advisors to European monarchs were drawing on canon law to build stronger structures of royal administration, even as Church authorities were using canon law to check the powers of secular authorities and preserve the autonomy of ecclesiastical finances, property, and justice.

The Portuguese and Spanish crowns, from the 1450s and the 1480s respectively, negotiated concessions from the papacy that gave them direct spiritual jurisdiction over newly encountered territories overseas. Using canon law to claim particular monarchical sovereignties, they set off debate over whether the papal bulls legitimized the exercise of temporal authority or merely conferred responsibility for evangelization; moreover, by the 1510s they had institutionalized the insertion of royal patronage into ecclesiastical matters in the form of the Portuguese Padroado Régio and the Spanish Patronato Real.

In practice, the Iberian monarchs gained the right to appoint bishops in their new lands, among other powers. They also turned to the pope as an arbitrator to delineate the boundaries of their respective claims to territory overseas immediately following Columbus's first voyages, and with the resulting papal Bulls of Donation (1493) and the Treaty of Tordesillas (1494) drew the famously misplaced mid-Atlantic line that left Brazil to Portugal and, on the other side of the globe, allocated the Philippines to Spain. The French king acquired similar rights of episcopal nomination in 1516, and so the crown largely directed religious affairs in the transatlantic colonies that the French built in the seventeenth and eighteenth centuries. The Kongo rulers—who, after the arrival of the Portuguese along Central African coasts, styled themselves as kings, converted to Catholicism in the 1490s, and built a Church infrastructure in the early sixteenth century—likewise sought to use canon law to claim authority over local political rivals and external threats, long maintaining contacts with Rome, and in 1622 even securing a papal condemnation of Portuguese incursions from Angola into their kingdom.

The Church in Rome, seeking to preserve its authority in a changing world, undertook legal reform; in the face of challenges from Protestant reformers, it defined the distinguishing features of Catholic doctrine and ecclesiastical policies and procedures via the canons and decrees of the Council of Trent (1545–1563). Papal governance was overhauled in 1588, with fifteen congregations established to oversee different branches of Church administration. The addition of the Congregation of Propaganda Fide in 1622 was in part intended to mitigate the earlier delegations of authority to Iberian crowns by reasserting direct Roman authority over missionary activity by the monastic orders (Capuchins and other Franciscans, Jesuits, Augustinians, and Dominicans, among others), outside the ordinary episcopal structures of the Church. Native converts overseas and European politics thus made the Atlantic a driving consideration in the changing legal framework of Roman Catholicism.

The Courts of a Catholic Atlantic

Canon law authorized and regulated a system of ecclesiastical justice governing matters ranging from the details of the celebration of the liturgy to the formal canonization of saints. Marriage, as one of the sacraments, became a principal concern of ecclesiastical courts. The law was used to claim jurisdiction over moral offenses (including usury, blasphemy, and sexual crimes) and over particular classes of people, such as clerics and those categorized as poor wretches meriting protection (widows, orphans, the physically disabled). It was on the latter grounds that ecclesiastical jurisdiction was extended over Native populations. Similarly, Church courts could try regular clergy (the missionary friars prominent in the Catholic Americas),

secular clergy, and sometimes even their lay affiliates, in not only religious but also civil or criminal affairs. There was a hierarchy of ordinary ecclesiastical courts: bishops' courts oversaw the parishes and monasteries in the diocese and were themselves subject to archbishops, whose districts generally corresponded to the jurisdictions of royal viceroys and governors, the secular counterparts to whose authority their powers can be likened.

From there, the Roman Rota served as the papal appellate court, a function that after 1588 largely moved to the congregations entrusted with the issues at hand. Royal patronage disrupted this chain, seeking to funnel appeals instead to royal councils. Ecclesiastical tribunals, moreover, relied on secular officials to enforce their judgments. Portuguese and Spanish administrators were often trained in canon as well as civil law, the most elite hailing from the universities of Coimbra and Salamanca, respectively. In the second half of the sixteenth century, canon law was already being taught in the new colonial universities, which were founded both in Mexico City and in Lima. The first Inquisition officials sent to Peru in 1570 brought books of canon law commentary printed in Europe.

Each new ecclesiastical foundation extended the reach of canon law. Iberian monarchs were vesting religious orders with spiritual authority over new island possessions in the eastern Atlantic as early as the 1430s. Institutions as diverse as missions, monasteries, charity hospitals, seminaries, and confraternities (lay brotherhoods) all derived their privileges from canon law. To create a diocese, moreover, was to create a new jurisdiction under canon law, and prelates around the Atlantic World used diocesan visitations to gauge compliance with canon law and impose discipline for deviations from it. In the Portuguese Atlantic, dioceses were established first in the islands: in Madeira (1514) and in the Azores, Cape Verde, and São Tomé (1533–1534). The see created in 1596 in Kongo was moved to Angola in 1624. Bahia, the first diocese in Brazil (1551), rose in importance from the 1670s into the eighteenth century and acquired supervision of eight Brazilian dioceses as well as São Tomé and Angola, furthering Brazil's commercial, administrative, and religious connections with West Africa. There were recurring shortages of clergy and seminaries, absences of bishops, and few diocesan synods or visitations; the first convent for nuns outside

Portugal was founded in Bahia only in 1677. Still, the vocabulary of canon law was diffused widely, as indicated by claims in Kongo to the right of sanctuary in churches and the use of excommunication as a potentially advantageous political tool deployed both to impose and to resist persecution.

A dense landscape of Catholic institutions and jurisdictions was rapidly established in the Spanish Atlantic, as the crown consolidated royal authority following initial occupations by military expeditions. Canon law was arguably stronger there, where the ideal was that of transplanting Castilian institutions and administrative structures to new terrain, than elsewhere in the Americas. The papacy authorized three new Caribbean dioceses in 1511. By the 1620s, there were already 36 convents for nuns in the viceroyalties of New Spain and Peru (excluding the Philippines); the same territory then had no fewer than five archdioceses and 31 dioceses. In the French Atlantic, despite significant missionary activity in New France, ecclesiastical authority was fairly weak, and royal civil law was strengthened in reforms made in the 1660s as part of the ambitious initiatives under Louis XIV (1638–1715). Quebec was not made a diocese until 1674; the first bishop sought to impose the Counter-Reformation decrees of the Council of Trent, as in founding a seminary. After 1674 the French crown assumed direct control of religious life in its increasingly valuable plantation islands in the West Indies.

Prosecution of heresy was a leading field of innovation in canon law, both in Europe and in the remote and only partially controlled Atlantic areas subject to Iberian crowns. While doctrinal conformity had long been part of the ordinary jurisdiction of bishops, in the thirteenth century heresy inquisitions were introduced as an additional, extraordinary legal apparatus, directed by the papacy, outside of episcopal control, and drawing on Roman law for the crime of treason. This aggressive judicial initiative was institutionalized in the foundations of the Spanish Inquisition (1478) and the Portuguese Inquisition (1536), in which the pope again delegated authority to Iberian monarchs. These legal institutions took on unintended permanence, further inserting royal authority into religious affairs and providing moral authority to growing royal administrations. Similarly, the papacy reorganized the Roman Inquisition in 1542, eventually placing it under the direction of the Congregation of the Holy Office.

Inquisitions were most active in the Spanish Atlantic. A tribunal presence was established in the Canary Islands in 1505. In Mexico, before 1571, indigenous converts accused of idolatry were tried in ad hoc inquisitions run by Franciscans with delegated papal authority. In part responding to complaints of excessive harshness in those trials, between 1569 and 1571 the Spanish Inquisition established two district tribunals (replicating the metropolitan structure of the institution, if often with fewer officials), in Mexico City and in Lima. The crown removed indigenous populations from the Inquisition's jurisdiction, although throughout the seventeenth century bishops (as well as secular authorities) continued to conduct "extirpation of idolatry" campaigns. A Caribbean tribunal was added in Cartagena de Indias—the primary port of arrival for enslaved Africans—in 1610. These courts prosecuted foreign merchants as Protestants and so-called New Christians accused of reverting to Judaism and investigated charges of blasphemy, bigamy, witchcraft, and other practices regarded as superstitious among the local populations of European and African origin. In the Portuguese Atlantic, by contrast, the Inquisition tribunal in Lisbon claimed jurisdiction overseas. It conducted visitations in Bahia and Pernambuco in Brazil, the Azores, Madeira, and Angola in the 1590s; other Brazilian inspections followed in the seventeenth and eighteenth centuries. Less interested in fetishes or idolatry among Brazil's huge population of Africans, enslaved and liberated, or in the Native populations of Portugal's small towns and military posts in Angola, the Portuguese Inquisition continued to pursue New Christians accused of secret Judaism into the eighteenth century, on both sides of the Atlantic. The accused were sent to Lisbon for trial, and the reports of these investigative tours were shipped across the Atlantic as well.

The intertwining of canon law with secular political constellations sometimes broadened popular access to legal personality or offered possibilities for litigation around matrimony, which could address domestic conflicts and matters of inheritance. The French monarchy had begun to assume authority over marriage law early in the sixteenth century. Although some in the more remote parts of New France (for example, Acadians) still sought dispensations for marriages violating the consanguinity prohibitions of canon law as late as in the eighteenth century, other marriage conflicts fell to civil courts. In the later seventeenth century, slave marriages were increasingly discouraged in the French West Indies. On the other hand, the strong ecclesiastical courts throughout the Spanish world frequently dealt with marital conflicts until the expansion of civil jurisdiction with the Bourbon reforms of the 1770s.

On both sides of the Atlantic, ecclesiastical courts supported brides and grooms whose families opposed their union by emphasizing the importance of individual consent to valid sacramental marriage; women and men could also litigate successfully in Church tribunals to dissolve marriages. Enslaved men and women of African origin had personal standing in ecclesiastical courts; in New Spain, they sued masters for disrupting the cohabitation of couples married canonically and used Spanish Inquisition tribunals to seek manumission from abusive owners. Not a few attempted to maneuver between Spanish ecclesiastical and civil jurisdictions. Those accused of sodomy might try to move their cases into inquisitorial courts, where they would not face the capital punishment customary under secular law; others cited the exclusion of indigenous Americans from inquisitorial jurisdiction to seek advantage in differing circumstances by claiming or disavowing indigenous identities. Throughout the Catholic Atlantic, persisting tensions over who had the power to regulate religious life were exposed in jurisdictional conflicts between metropolitan and colonial secular clergy, between secular and regular clergy, between regular orders, and between clerics and civil officials.

Canon Law and Political Thought

The cultural multiplicity, numerous jurisdictions, and great distances of Portuguese and Spanish colonization around the Atlantic were among the primary spurs to change in early-modern European political and legal thought. Monarchs and their advisors referred to the tenets of canon law to probe what might—in new circumstances—constitute just war, just conquest, and just rule. The Dominican friar and Salamanca professor Francisco de Vitoria (c. 1483–1546), a theologian, drew extensively on the canonists to support the *dominium*—the right of self-governance—of indigenous Americans, as Spanish weaponry and military expeditions overran their polities. Another Dominican friar, Bartolomé de Las Casas (1484–1566), used canon law to advocate for the indigenous inhabitants of the Americas, arguing that they fell within the jurisdictional category of *miserabiles personae*, legal minors deserving of protection. An Afro-Brazilian man turned to such principles—and the mid-sixteenth-century ruling that indigenous Americans could not be justly enslaved—to expose the atrocities of the Atlantic slave trade in the 1680s in Lisbon, Madrid, and Rome, securing condemnations of its corruption of Christian morality from the papal Congregations of Propaganda Fide and the Holy Office.

Even as arguments based on the canons of the Church often failed to prevent secular abuses, they had significance in the longer term. Legal pluralism—the availability of multiple ecclesiastical and civil fora—and its attendant, persistent, jurisdictional conflicts, intensified by the unanticipated complexities of colonial societies, contributed to building the institutions of secular governance and concepts of territorial sovereignty. Spanish academics' and clerics' sixteenth-century search for legal grounds to protect indigenous Americans contributed to the privileging of reason and natural law in the seventeenth century, which in turn became bases for emerging international law in the eighteenth and nineteenth centuries. Burgeoning commerce and evolving royal efforts to regulate it drew upon the canonistic prohibition of usury. Canon law endured even in Protestant polities that had rejected papal authority, leaving traces in courts and in continued teaching of the subject in many universities in Germany, Switzerland, and the Low Countries. Theories of resistance to unjust secular rule, elaborated especially by Protestants in the sixteenth and seventeenth centuries, as well as later constitutional thought, drew on canonistic principles about the limits of monarchical authority. The architect of international law, Hugo Grotius (1583–1645), though a Dutch Calvinist, was a doctor of both civil and canon law and applied elements of the latter to construct a method for regulating relations among sovereign authorities, even though he rejected a privileged role for the pope in diplomatic affairs.

Conclusion

European monarchies drew significantly on canon law to organize the new societies of the early-modern Atlantic World. Faced with responsibility for non-Christian populations and the desire to convert and control them, as well as the practical and moral dilemmas of ordering mobile and diverse colonial societies, Catholic authorities referred to principles of canon law to draft policies and structure institutions suited to new environments. European monarchs and their officials employed ecclesiastical institutions and the records they generated to build and legitimize their secular authority, increasing royal control over the Church throughout the early-modern era, in Europe as in Africa and the Americas. Rome nonetheless remained an important countervailing moral force in a commercializing Atlantic World. In the persistent negotiations between universal principles and local environments, personal accumulation and societal responsibility, canon law was used not only to discipline but also to dissent.

KIMBERLY LYNN

Bibliography

Benton, Lauren. *Law and Colonial Cultures: Legal Regimes in World History, 1400–1900.* Cambridge and New York: Cambridge University Press, 2002.

Bethencourt, Francisco. *The Inquisition: A Global History, 1478–1834.* Translated by Jean Birrell. Cambridge and New York: Cambridge University Press, 2009.

Brundage, James A. *Medieval Canon Law.* London and New York: Longman, 1995.

Fasolt, Constantin. "Visions of Order in the Canonists and Civilians." In *Handbook of European History, 1400–1600: Late Middle Ages, Renaissance and Reformation,* edited by Thomas A. Brady, Heiko Oberman, and James Tracy, 2:31–59. Leiden and New York: Brill, 1995.

Gray, Richard. *Black Christians and White Missionaries.* New Haven, CT, and London: Yale University Press, 1990.

Greer, Allan, and Kenneth Mills. "A Catholic Atlantic." In *The Atlantic in Global History,* edited by Jorge Cañizares-Esguerra and Erik R. Seeman, 3–19. Upper Saddle River, NJ: Pearson Prentice Hall, 2007.

Guimarães Sá, Isabel dos. "Ecclesiastical Structures and Religious Action." In *Portuguese Oceanic Expansion, 1400–1800,* edited by Francisco Bethencourt and Diogo Ramada Curto, 255–282. Cambridge: Cambridge University Press, 2007.

Muldoon, James. *Popes, Lawyers, and Infidels: The Church and the Non-Christian World, 1250–1550.* Philadelphia: University of Pennsylvania Press, 1979.

Law, Commercial

Unlike the personal relations centered on land in the background of European laws, commerce became the impersonal medium of the regional economies that developed on the four continents of the Atlantic World. Commercial law was the channel through which the conceptual, social, and technological innovations of differing worlds in America, Europe, and Africa coalesced into a single new Atlantic space. The Atlantic history of commercial law documents a novel tension between two systems of law: on the one hand, the *lex mercatoria*, an extraterritorial legal domain of medieval origin, which allowed merchant communities to adjudicate among themselves and which sought to reflect mercantile practice as much as possible; and the royal prerogative, which in the Atlantic Era innovated and intruded into the law of commerce as European monarchies sought to engross, or control, the resources of the Atlantic World and to defeat their European competitors. The processes that monarchs created by challenging the *lex mercatoria* and thereby extending the commercial remit of prerogative law also reveal the difficulties that royal authorities faced and the ways in which the Atlantic World proved to be a disproving ground for mercantilist regulation. The extension of the royal prerogative also revealed how informal, illegal economies became the default setting for Atlantic commerce, and how new, liberal political and economic ideologies formalized and legalized—immortalizing in part—informality and illegality in the founding documents of the United States.

How did commercial actors in the Atlantic World interact with Europe's legal heritages of customary, or community, and monarchical law? The Atlantic World was a space of multiple and competing legal frameworks. Ancient Roman jurists had developed a customary transnational law to govern relationships among sovereign authorities and within the Roman Empire. With the breakup of that legal sphere, an informal system of rules—a new piecemeal, practical set of understandings developed and administered by merchant practitioners, that is, the *lex mercatoria*—came to govern commercial transactions that transcended the miniature territorial jurisdictions of the political authorities of the time. The Christian Church's canon law formulated regulations covering relations between those legally presumed strangers, especially Jews excluded from the primary legal community of Christianity, defined as a noncommercial space. Islamic commercial law similarly treated Christian and Jewish merchants as internally self-governing communities.

From the fifteenth century, canon law provided a means for European monarchical authorities to legitimate subjects venturing beyond their realms, as well as those of other recognized Christian princes, and to appropriate the resources of those legally unformed territories. Warfare and rule of distant territories and their residents necessitated legal definition in Europe. For the Iberian monarchs seeking to extend sovereignty into the Atlantic World, the papacy provided support in the form of the Bulls of Donation in 1493, which granted the rulers of Castile and Aragon the right to occupy the American territories they found. The Iberian rulers attempted to domesticate legally the new territories they encountered in Mesoamerica in the fifteenth and sixteenth centuries by bringing the land and its residents within their own royal jurisdictions. The Treaty of Tordesillas of 1494 drew on papal-law precedent developed in the period of the European Crusades in the Levant in the twelfth and thirteenth centuries to define the competing transoceanic claims of Europeans in the Atlantic and beyond. Canon law voiced principles of Christian amity in language that contrasted with the conflictive aspects of competitive commercial engagements. To exclude subsequent rival European monarchies—Dutch and English in the sixteenth and seventeenth centuries—the Iberian powers defined the new Atlantic territories as foreign to them and therefore outside the conventional legal jurisdiction of Europeans prior to Spanish claims.

As northern European monarchs developed their maritime reach through the mercantile resources of investors, impersonal commercial laws (the *lex mercatoria*) began to supplement, and then substitute for, the personalism of the canon law. The law of monarchy began to assume the mediating role played by the transnational reach of papal authority. Monarchs such as Francis I of France (r. 1515–1547) and Henry VIII of England (r. 1509–1547) began to use the royal prerogative to regulate commercial contacts abroad. This celebration of the monarchs' right to control the overseas activities of their subjects derived from domestic constitutional struggles among monarchies, domestic representative institutions, and local sources of power. Monarchs in France and England cited papal precedents. To reduce reliance on domestic tax revenues, and the proportionate loss of sovereignty to rival landed aristocrats that such reliance involved, monarchs asserted their rights to the proceeds of international trade, claiming them in the form of selling legal monopolies to merchants who agreed to risk their own capital developing overseas trade. This extension of the traditional jurisdiction of the royal prerogative into the law of commerce proved to be the Atlantic World's most important legal innovation.

The Dutch West India Company, the French Senegal and Guinea companies, and the Royal African companies of England were the most successful examples. These monopolies represented legally constituted forms of property, and their control over remote markets embodied the monarchs' direct personal powers beyond the kingdoms themselves. A monarch's letters patent—along with their ancient privilege of mediating their subjects' relationships with overseas peoples—conveyed specific rights to subjects within their realms, including the charter rights of such merchant companies. Legal precedents generated during the Crusades endured into the seventeenth century and therefore justified commercial monopolies with reference to the need for companies to act as vessels of the state's sovereignty with barbaric and heathen peoples, as well as Muslims, in distant lands. These monopolistic charters made specific reference to papal precedent. Monarchs worked through legal vessels charged with representing their personal diplomatic rights—a continuity dressed as innovation. The late-medieval rise of monarchical states both created the need to establish a system of international laws and supplanted jurists' attempts to create them.

Sovereign authorities on all continents, from London to Ouidah, from the Connecticut River to the Isthmus of Panama, asserted rights to regulate commerce to extract revenue from the commercial interactions that were coming to define the Atlantic World and thus to buttress their authority at home by engaging in it. This blending of foreign merchants with internal power involved a delicate balancing act, and success proved elusive. Revenue from international commerce could allow would-be sovereign rulers to escape the reliance on powerful domestic rivals through which they had built their realms, but heavy-handed taxation would limit the scale of, and perhaps jeopardize, import and export trades and thus reduce the revenues and power they brought. Control over commercial laws therefore allowed rulers to rig the price mechanism to buttress their internal authority without disrupting the international commercial interactions of their subjects. The variety of these monarchical legal restraints and exclusions, and confusion and disputes over the differing jurisdictions, encouraged merchants to resort to alternative legal frameworks to thwart specific regulations. Merchants in Port Royal in Jamaica, for example, appealed to the common-law tradition—which often served as a vernacular version of the *lex mercatoria* in English law—to contest regulations of commercial slave trading that Admiralty courts back home in England had codified under the royal prerogative.

Protestant powers developed a model of monarchical jurisdiction linked to commerce and trade rather than to the laws of war and conquest that the Iberian powers had extended into the Atlantic from their own heritage of reconquering the peninsula from Muslim military rulers. The territorially limited, and therefore outward-looking, Dutch pioneered legal techniques and rhetoric in the early seventeenth century that asserted the universal accessibility to overseas regions for trade. Although culturally unified in opposition to Catholic Habsburg rule, the Dutch associated themselves with the late-medieval European tradition of city-state republics, such as Venice, which had used international commerce to achieve significant wealth from minute territorial bases. Motivated by Protestant zeal against imperial Catholicism, the Dutch successfully battled the Iberian powers throughout the Atlantic, in the Indian Ocean, and in East Asia. They advanced a free-trade argument, in which merchants operated in a legal domain external to both statute law and monarchical decrees, as a

means to help them engross global trading flows. The Dutch began to argue a theoretical basis for free trade to justify infringing on their Iberian rivals' claims of sovereign authority to consign Atlantic trade to chosen delegates. These Iberian controls responded to Dutch attempts to extend an early free-trade argument, the famous *Mare Liberum* by Hugo Grotius (1609), to engross world trade through their superior financial capacities. Grotius argued that a prior condition of natural liberty (including doing business) predated the "secondary" laws of sovereign monarchs (or their people, as "nations") and that this condition of natural liberty prevailed in the open waters of the world's oceans and could not be restricted by monarchical fiat. Protestant solidarity between the Dutch and the English allowed the English presence in mainland North America, especially in the company colony of Virginia.

European monarchs used prerogative law not only to manage their own overseas subjects but also to compete with dynastic rivals by defining themselves as legally competent to negotiate exclusive agreements to trade with foreign authorities. For example, throughout much of the eighteenth century French commercial law designed to improve French market share of the gum trade in Senegal stipulated the illegality of French merchants or factors trading with Dutch rivals on the African coast. But the Wolof leaders in the region at times buttressed the trading position of the Dutch to the detriment of the required French market share. On the coast of Africa, local authorities stipulated who could trade—and when and where—in many ways that prevented European legal manipulation of prices in their favor.

The competition between European monarchies for the returns on non-European resources and peoples has come to be known as *mercantilism*. The concept can be broadly characterized as royal authority over external economic transactions that was claimed in order to support the power of the monarchy. Commercial law proved to be the tool for attempting such control. The mercantile system involved a dialectic in which monarchs combined protected transatlantic—and other sea-based—commerce with military means, to finance the extension of their own authority at home. But these military means incurred costs that necessitated further taxation, which could jeopardize the monarchs' authority by compelling them to gain the consent of their subjects at home, as well as by lessening the profitability of commerce itself. By the middle of the eighteenth century, Britain emerged supreme from this commercial competition, largely because of constitutional rule: those who financed the means to protect the government's overseas interests could be assured that their control over tax revenues—enacted through their involvement in Parliament—would ensure repayment of their money. These merchants and their political connections would lobby throughout the seventeenth and eighteenth centuries to enshrine the traditional *lex mercatoria* within the increasingly prominent common-law tradition. By the early nineteenth century, they succeeded.

English concern about Dutch competition led Parliament to legislate a comprehensive mercantilist policy—the navigation system, developed in a series of statutes from the 1650s into the eighteenth century. From the later Middle Ages in England, parliamentary statutes had provided the legal mechanism for the monarchs' attempts to control overseas trade, as opposed to the royal letters patent used for mercantilist regulations by French and English monarchs in the seventeenth century. Parliament had enacted legislation to encourage English shipping as early as the late fourteenth century, during the reign of Richard II. These early attempts at regulation had focused on domestic ships. By the late fifteenth century, Parliament began to regulate shipping to foreign ports as well. Seventeenth-century navigation acts proved a remarkable regulatory achievement. Countless merchants thwarted them, but their endurance suggests the mercantile community's disapproval of the monarchy's innovating intrusion into the separate legal sphere of commerce. The first effective statute in 1660 established several changes, including (1) an English monopoly on all shipping to the colonies, (2) a rule that captains and three-quarters of the crew had to be English, and (3) another regulation that all colonial goods had to be sent to England. The royal monopoly on growing Atlantic commerce proved remarkably effective. Despite the wide contravention of the restrictions, the basic objectives of the system—to fund the enlargement of the English navy, to exclude Dutch competition, and to create a captive market for English exports in the North American continent—were attained. The acts, buttressed by further legislation in 1696, helped to weaken the Dutch competition in the short term and endured well into the nineteenth century.

In general, monarchs faced real difficulties when seeking to regulate the commerce of the Atlantic World. With sufficient constitutional power at home, though, control was possible. Louis XIV of France (r. 1643–1715) and Charles II of England (r. 1660–1685) used their navies to exclude interlopers. English high courts upheld these monopolistic privileges into the 1680s, but such regulations proved hugely controversial. Test cases questioning the monarch's right to seize interlopers' goods (that is, to use the threat of forfeiture) to enforce monopolistic companies appear from the mid-1680s. After the Glorious Revolution of 1688–1689, which brought William II of the Dutch House of Orange to the English throne, the monarch's rights in this area were severely curtailed in a 1689 decision: the judgment stipulated, with reference to the Royal African Company, that Parliament alone could create the powers needed to enforce overseas trading monopolies.

The merchant-administered *lex mercartoria* began to inform the rest of the law as a result of commercial expansion in the Atlantic. Seventeenth-century English common law became a more reliable instrument for commercial regulation—to take one example, it absorbed mercantile laws under chief justice John Holt (1689–1710)—and the royal prerogative continued to dwindle. The royally chartered monopolies became the focus of legal opposition to the power of the monarchy. In Spain, merchants resented the royal monopoly given to the merchants in Seville over trade with the Spanish New World. Bristolians and Liverpudlians in England resented the commercial primacy that Londoners achieved, believing that it derived from the monopolistic corporations of the City. These companies became the focus of considerable commercial opposition from merchants within and beyond their national legal jurisdictions. The Atlantic opportunity surged in the outports—Bristol, Liverpool, and Zeeland, among others—in a tidal wave of liberal, deregulating fervor. The monopolies nevertheless continued as prizes in protracted negotiations concluding dynastic conflicts within Europe. The British negotiated for months before the Treaty of Utrecht (1713) to secure Spain's *asiento* contract that supplied slaves used to tap the silver of its American mines. The commitment of the resulting South Sea Company to deliver captive Africans proved difficult to honor, but the contract served very efficiently as a smokescreen to conceal illicit sales of British manufactures for Spanish America's riches in pieces of eight (Spanish currency). This calculated transgression violated monarchical exclusions of the very sort that the Navigation Acts system had created for Englishmen.

With regard to interactions between Europeans and their trading partners on other shores of the Atlantic, Europeans invoked their own legal traditions as justifications for, as well as means to, exclude European rivals from access to territories overseas, while conducting trade from day to day on the less-commercialized terms of their American or African hosts. European thinkers at times condescended to the practices of indigenous cultures in ways that supported European imperial designs. John Locke argued that indigenous Americans had no laws concerning the recognition of property in the emerging European sense of individual possession and that this absence of defined personal interest in their lands justified English capture of them. Native American and African custom privileged collective rights in property. In much of Africa and in America, status and property derived from membership in a corporate body, often described in metaphors of kinship, rather than from the personal autonomy that Atlantic commerce enabled Europeans to emphasize. Africans, in particular, forced European traders to operate within their much more communal ethos.

The distinctive Atlantic conditions of multiplicity, its vast scale beyond territorially defined monarchical authority, and the resulting openness in legal terms encouraged merchants to push the long-established custom of the *lex mercatoria* into monarchy-sponsored law and helped to undermine first papal, then monarchical, definitions of commercial law as external to their communities of faith and sovereignty. The impersonal features of commercial law, which enabled ad hoc transactions between strangers, eclipsed the personalism of canon, papal, and monarchical law. Merchants rather than monarchs would come to shape commercial law as European military conquests in the

sixteenth- and seventeenth-century Atlantic laid the basis for a complex, supple, and pervasive commercial system by the end of the eighteenth century.

WILLIAM A. PETTIGREW

Bibliography

Pagden, Anthony. *Lords of All the World: Ideologies of Empire in Spain, Britain, and France, c. 1500–c. 1800.* New Haven, CT: Yale University Press, 1995.

Thornton, John. *Africa and Africans in the Making of the Atlantic World, 1400–1800.* 2nd ed. Cambridge and New York: Cambridge University Press, 1998.

Tracy, James D. *The Political Economy of Merchant Empires: State Power and World Trade, 1350–1750.* Cambridge: Cambridge University Press, 1991.

Law, Constitutional

When we consider the history of constitutions in the Atlantic World, it is easy to begin with the U.S. Constitution of 1787, the first written frame of government to bear such a formal designation. But of course constitutional law had a history long before the production of that paradigmatic document. While the word characterizes a binding framework of law more concrete than existed in any of the empires that extended from Europe into the New World and along the African coast before 1787, rules of governance existed earlier. So, too, did the word itself. While the term *constitution* represents to us a kind of immutable law, in the two centuries before 1787 it referred generally to the legal health of a sovereign domain, especially monarchies. What was its basic physical frame? While many European, Mediterranean, and arguably also such Native American alliances as the Iroquois Confederacy had constitutions of sorts, in that they had frames of government, focusing on those constitutions that had a transatlantic reach helps us to think about how European countries used law and power together as instruments to legitimate their control over vast stretches of the Atlantic realms. Still, the written constitution that the United States introduced in 1787 did bring with it a way of thinking about the law as fixed and the rights of citizens as absolute, an innovation that reverberated across the Atlantic World.

Many Europeans engaged in overseas ventures, following the leads of Portugal in Africa and Spain in the Americas and the seemingly endless riches that flowed from Atlantic trade and conquest. English, French, Dutch, and other European monarchies and merchant cities sponsored exploration and also military expeditions and settlements of their subjects. But conquest was not simply a military maneuver; once these European kingdoms claimed territories, they tried to justify their claims and also to set up legal frameworks, partly by regulating their own subjects overseas and partly by negotiating arrangements with local (indigenous) authorities in Africa and in the Americas. While of course these new legal regimes were never completely enforceable, they framed European monarchies' claims of sovereignty with regard to one another and also helped them to legitimate for themselves (internally within their own realms and structures of power) control over foreign territories. Regardless of the maps that the Europeans used to lay claim to vast swaths of the new and old territories, their actual legal reach was almost always confined to the coastlands of continents and the banks of rivers, just as was their military reach, which was primarily seaborne. Alliances with Native authorities helped them to achieve a degree of influence over larger numbers of Native peoples over time, and no doubt part of the reason that islands became favorite sites of conquest was because they were uninhabited or, if populated, more easily subdued with fewer places for Native peoples to lie in wait, gather strength, and counterattack.

The legal frameworks of the competing European kingdoms were different from one another and changed through time, though they were always in mutual conversation. Most monarchies in Europe made great efforts to ally themselves with portions of the Native peoples, and especially the elites, realizing that the limited numbers of soldiers and settlers they sent could not establish control by themselves. A primary strategy of gaining from overseas ventures was trade with Native populations for commodities they could supply. Thus the Spanish and Portuguese, as they set up various systems of local control and land ownership in most of (modern) Mexico, the Caribbean, and Central and

South America, often recognized the claims to authority of local elites, with Spanish conquistadors, for example, marrying the daughters of Indian chiefs in order to consolidate alliances and gain a measure of indirect control. The Spanish system of *encomienda*—allocations of Native communities to Spanish overlords as "trustees"—epitomized the layered nature of Spanish control, with rent payments and labor dues assessed through complex local (Native) systems. Both civil and ecclesiastical courts, many of which had ultimate appeal back to the crown in Spain, blended an older but also changing Spanish law with arrangements negotiated on the ground, in the process creating (and in many cases denying) rights for Native peoples and also for the Africans whom the Spanish transported to their colonies in the New World increasingly in the seventeenth century. Spanish law was framed at the imperial level, and most officials were appointed.

The Portuguese were the first to figure out that allying with African authorities along the continent's western coast could bring them not only gold and tropical commodities but also allow them to acquire laborers for new plantations on offshore islands, especially for the cultivation of sugar. Their system of courts and laws stretched from islands off the African coast all the way to Brazil and back again to Portugal; like the Spanish system, it was hierarchical, with an imperial network that was appointed and responsible to the king.

During the seventeenth century, the Dutch West India Company made various efforts to seize parts of the New World, from Brazil to New Netherlands (what became New York), to various colonies in the Caribbean such as Curaçao, as well as the Elmina trading "castle" on Africa's Gold Coast. To all these sites they transported Dutch law, and indeed some of the efforts to frame that law in an imperial and transatlantic context led to what came to be called the *law of nations* or the *law of the sea*, a synthesis first published by Hugo Grotius in Amsterdam in 1625. Although this was primarily about the terms by which European powers could establish claims overseas respected by others, it also included guidelines about how to treat Native peoples in the New World.

The English arrangements for extending royal authority overseas are normally considered less hierarchical and more inclusive of local subjects than the Spanish, Portuguese, or Dutch systems, embodying in practice, if not in formal law, a degree of constituted order well before the U.S. Constitution. Assemblies elected by propertied local interests in England's colonies played a crucial role in their own governance. If one focuses only on the participation of local colonial elites, the English system appears relatively contractual, as compared to Spanish authoritarian administration. However, the Spanish Empire appears far more negotiated if it includes the participation of local Native authorities, and recent scholarship has also pointed to extensive evasion of nominal Spanish royal authority. Recent scholarship has also illuminated complex mechanisms of legal control in British colonies, in which local colonial elites had to negotiate with the authorities in England, most of them under the direct control of the king.

The English framework of government authority, which was based partly on statutory law and partly on common law court decisions, was famously "unwritten" and complex. It was also far from fixed: it was fiercely disputed during the seventeenth century, which saw two political revolutions in England over how the balance of power should be drawn between the king, the nobility, and the people and what role the courts should play. The first revolution was a civil war between partisans of parliamentary authority and supporters of royalty (1642–1651). The second, the so-called Glorious Revolution (1688), removed James II, whom opponents saw as seeking absolute power by controlling judges and denying the power of parliament, with a king and queen from the Netherlands (William and Mary, the next in line for the throne) more accepting of parliamentary input and judicial independence. Parliament sought to stabilize basic political rights by passing a Bill of Rights (of 1693) and the Act of Settlement of 1701, laws that guaranteed regular elections, prohibition of cruel or unusual punishments, and limits on the king's control over judges, the main elements now associated with England's unwritten constitution. These legal protections were far from as thorough as those guaranteed in the later Constitution and Bill of Rights in the United States, and as statutes they were more malleable than a fundamental constitution, but they did establish key limits on sovereign power and embed the election of representatives of the governed. These rights of Englishmen, however, did not necessarily extend to the colonies.

The seventeenth century was also a period of struggle in England's colonies, which were technically under the direct power of the monarch but deeply inspired by these two revolutions against royal absolutism. The king could grant away his right to govern—as Charles I did temporarily with the Massachusetts Bay Colony in 1629 and Charles II did with Pennsylvania in 1681—but all colonial authorities eventually had to report directly to the monarch. Charles II and James II, between 1660 and 1688, made efforts to bring the colonies under more direct monarchical control, to the extent that they abolished most local elected assemblies in the northern colonies in 1685 by merging the existing five jurisdictions in a single Dominion of New England. James II was in the midst of creating a parallel southern dominion when revolution in 1688 swept him from power, but his plans for a Dominion of Virginia, which would have included England's colonies in the West Indies, like his Dominion of New England, were hierarchical and based on the Spanish model of governance. They vested power only in appointed officials, headed by a royal governor.

By the eighteenth century, most English territories in the Americas were royal colonies, with royally appointed governors and upper legislative houses, which also served as their highest courts, and elected assemblies that met only at the discretion of the governor. The royal governor appointed local judges, and they and most other officials held their seats only at his pleasure. All laws passed in the colonies had to be approved by the royally appointed Board of Trade and by the king's Privy Council, both in London. Technically any decision from high courts in all colonies could be appealed to the Privy Council. No colonial laws or court decisions "repugnant" to—that is, going directly against—English common law could stand. Although it is unclear how extensively laws passed by Parliament applied in the colonies, British laws directly regulated and restrained them sufficiently to provoke rebellion in North America. Thus, although the king appointed the governing officials in the colonies, Parliament and common law judges in Britain regulated them indirectly. In fact, constitutional practices of judicial review in the United States, for example, grew directly out of legal processes established during the colonial period, during which all colonial laws and high court decisions were subject to review by the king's Board of Trade and Privy Council. What shifted was the ultimate source of sovereignty: Britain's constituted legal framework centered on the sovereignty of the monarch, and the Constitution of the United States located sovereignty in the governed.

Both of the two founding documents of the American nation, the Declaration of Independence (1776) and the Constitution of 1787 were widely read and modeled in the Atlantic World. Starting with the 1791 Declaration of the Rights of Man and the Citizen in revolutionary France, many other rebels against monarchy along the Atlantic rim combined the two documents—the one a statement of principles of human rights, the other a specific framework of government to guarantee them—in ways that the United States had not. The Saint-Domingue Constitution of 1801 and Napoleon's 1804 French Constitution were two examples. But in the waves of independence movements that took place in Spain and Portugal's Atlantic possessions between 1808 and 1830 they remained separate, the rebels declaring independence in one breath and framing constitutions, if they did so, separately. Not all constitutions were products of political independence, as Spain's 1812 constitution incorporated its American territories within a single constitutional monarchy.

The U.S. Constitution of 1787 thus built on legal practices that the different colonies had used, via their charters, to negotiate power with the monarch in Britain. The idea that policy and decision making should proceed within a fixed frame of written laws was implicit in colonial charters, and appeal to common law meant that they were constantly adjudicated. However, the fixity and unassailability of the U.S. Constitution was new, albeit it contained uncertainties that still needed to be interpreted judicially. (This issue of interpretation explains why judicial independence was so important.) The separation of powers mandated by the Constitution of 1787 and the rights guaranteed in its initial ten amendments—while far from complete, and notably so in the case of equality of all persons before the law—were markedly stronger than those obtained in England after 1688 and certainly in other European Atlantic empires. The permanence of the document, and its function as a statement of guidelines for all further legislation and regulation, became a model for other nations that sought to limit the powers of monarchs and

elected assemblies alike. Whatever its imperfections, the U.S. Constitution's separation of church and state, its vesting of authority in the people, its guarantees of freedom of speech, its creation of independent judges who could not easily be dismissed by monarchs or would-be tyrants, and other reforms made it a model of how a written frame of government could undergird democratic governance.

Approaching constitutional law from a fully "Atlantic" perspective means paying attention to the interrelated issues of the extent to which the legal structures and the practices of royal governance in the Americas adhered to fixed and stable forms; the extent to which imperial authorities sought input from locals and non-elites in their practices of governance; and the balance between formal legal procedures for input as opposed to personal, relatively random processes. It also means paying more attention to British methods of controlling colonies in North America and to the origins of the written constitution of the United States, which became a model—however imperfect—for other nations from France in Europe to many new ones along the western shores of the Atlantic, even if the other experiments did not last as long as that of the United States. It also means acknowledging that even the apparent fixity of constitutionalism, and the declared guarantees of rights, had to be renegotiated through legal interpretations. One of the profound ironies embedded in the very concept of constitutional law is the tension between written and relatively unbending rules and human rights. While it is easy to assume that human rights depend upon such legal fixity, such fixity can also mask invasive corruption and inequalities.

HOLLY BREWER

Bibliography

Bilder, Mary Sarah. *The Transatlantic Constitution: Colonial Legal Culture and the Empire.* Cambridge, MA: Harvard University Press, 2004.

Brewer, Holly. *By Birth or Consent: Children, Law, and the Anglo-American Revolution in Authority.* Chapel Hill: University of North Carolina Press, 2005.

Elliot, J. H. *Empires of the Atlantic World: Britain and Spain in America 1492–1830.* New Haven, CT: Yale University Press, 2006.

Herzog, Tamar. *Defining Nations: Immigrants and Citizens in Early Modern Spain and Spanish America.* New Haven, CT: Yale University Press, 2003.

Hulsebosch, Daniel J. *Constituting Empire: New York and the Transformation of Constitutionalism in the Atlantic World, 1664–1830.* Chapel Hill: University of North Carolina Press, 2005.

Kamen, Henry. *Empire: How Spain Became a World Power, 1492–1763.* New York: HarperCollins, 2003.

Rakove, Jack. *Original Meanings: Politics and Ideas in the Making of the Constitution.* New York: Alfred A. Knopf, 1996.

Law, Military

The legal formulation of monarchical authority in the Atlantic often drew on a specific body of European military law. This legal domain, in England called *martial law* until the nineteenth century, consisted of a set of written laws, procedural rules, and disciplinary measures that commanders in the limited royal armed forces utilized primarily to maintain order within the units of the army or navy that they commanded. Secondarily, commanders used military law to punish rebels—anyone who had betrayed the monarch whose forces they commanded—and to control prisoners taken in war. As opposed to civilian communal law, a strategy meant to bind people together and promote unity and reciprocity, military law defined and enforced the categorical differences in ranks that formed the lines of command.

Commanders manifested this inequality in ordinances that specified duties for members of their forces, prescribed penalties differentiated by ranks, and above all stressed unquestioning obedience to one's superior. This pervasive differentiation paralleled other European theories of legal stratification in the civilian populations of sovereign realms. However, commanders and martial lawyers were authorized to demand more severe punishments than their civilian counterparts. Commanders used this systematized terror to coerce large groups of armed men to perform efficient and effective military maneuvers together under the extreme duress of impending death at the hands of enemies and to prevent men with lethal weapons abroad in foreign lands from marauding and terrorizing resident populations. They possessed these legal powers only over the army, and only during times of formally declared war.

In Europe, monarchs confined military law to members of their armed forces. In overseas territories royal representatives and civilian entrepreneurs such as owners of plantations lived beyond domestic constraints and, by analogy with the prevalence of martial law over armies in the field, expanded the range of military law to control subordinates—in part by terrifying alien labor forces into obedience. In the process they transformed military law into an all-encompassing jurisdiction at the disposal of monarchs, independent of the aristocratic, ecclesiastical, or popular restraints on monarchical power at home.

Some scholars have argued that military rule or martial law signified the absence or suspension of law. But this depends on defining *law* as only civilian. Martial lawyers had imported procedures from other forms of law into military law. Rank and file became subject to military jurisdiction upon taking a theoretically voluntary oath of obedience to the rules and regulations of the force in which they served. Commanders read the ordinances of war—often over 100 articles in length, with well over half prescribing death for transgressions—to new recruits. For noncapital offenses within the articles, commanders prescribed "extraordinary punishments" that included public whipping, running the gauntlet, and other creative means of inflicting physical pain to discipline offenders and presumably witnesses, as all court-martial punishments were carried out in front of the regiment on its parade day. Commanders generally delegated these legal responsibilities to military courts, which consisted of between 10 and 20 commissioned officers who heard and determined a case, assisted by a legal officer trained in Roman civil law. In some Spanish military courts, an advocate alone investigated and adjudicated cases. With considerable latitude beyond these restrictions, commanders also informally disciplined their soldiers through beatings and whippings.

European monarchs were well aware of the power of military jurisdiction and had therefore generally limited its exercise to themselves and to their closest advisers. But beginning with the Spanish reconquest of Iberia in the thirteenth century, Castilian monarchs delegated the conquered jurisdictions to warriors thus authorized as conquistadors, who were effectively independent armed entrepreneurs. The transatlantic exploration and ultimate conquest of Mexico and parts of South America only accelerated freelancing of this type. Owing to the corporate structures of Spanish society, these suddenly powerful men, often of low birth, could not only brutally punish members of their own entourages but also prevent them from being prosecuted at the king's other courts by claiming the *fueromilitar*, a corporate charter that granted soldiers exception from municipal, mercantile, and ecclesiastical jurisdictions.

These warlords of the Americas thus controlled private armies that answered only to them. The conquerors of Mexico and Peru used their martial authority to engage in imposing terror on large, hostile populations of Native Americans. These shows of violence included severing right hands, executing Native leaders, raping and killing Native women, and burning villages. Conquistadors in the fifteenth century in Iberia had perfected these practices to terrify Muslim populations into submitting to the kings of Castile. In the New World, with the approval of an increasingly powerful crown, conquistadors often employed the powers of military law to force Native Americans to work in labor camps. In the eighteenth century, the Spanish crown continued this practice by sending convicts in Europe to staff fortified *presidios* in the New World, effectively prison work camps, where they labored to build and improve fortifications.

Like their Spanish counterparts, Portuguese monarchs defined military jurisdictions under captains-general to establish royal authority in Africa and in Brazil. Also like their Spanish counterparts, these military governors used their legal power to command rather than govern their retinues. The lawyers who had crafted military law delegated discretion to commanders in the treatment of prisoners, a power deemed necessary in uncertain times of war. They could thus ransom, maintain, or even kill prisoners if they could provide legal rationales for doing so. These officers drew strategically on these rules relating to prisoners of war to justify either slaving or the extermination of Native populations as enemies of the Catholic faith, which Iberian monarchs held papal authority to propagate. Using this power, Portuguese captains in Angola in

the late seventeenth century enslaved their captives for profit and justified these actions due to their supposed "cannibalism" and "heathenism." Meanwhile, in northern Brazil, with the crown's consent, captains-general had exterminated Native men and enslaved the women. Removed from the checks of civilian jurists, the all-encompassing and terrifying powers of these officers made them effectively warlords.

In contrast with the Spanish and Portuguese reliance on military law, English and French monarchs provided the officers of the royal forces with no immunities from civilian forms of law. Yet English adventurers in the sixteenth century in Ireland, like the conquistadors, used martial law to terrify resistant civilians into obedience. English and French entrepreneurs also found military law useful as a strategy for controlling laborers. The Virginia Company in 1609, within two years of landing in Jamestown, installed a military regimen that punished civilian settlers brutally in order to force them to plant crops and build fortifications. During the middle of the seventeenth century, English commanders shipped Irish and Scottish prisoners of war to the Caribbean, where they worked for planters for a period of seven years as "bond slaves." In French areas, the crown sent prisoners of war to Mediterranean ports, where as "galley slaves" they performed the backbreaking labor of oarsmen under the supervision of military officers.

By the mid-seventeenth century, New World planters imported components of military law to systematize laws to keep growing populations of slaves, legally construed as prisoners taken in wars in Africa, in terrified obedience. Slave owners applied common military punishments to these workers, such as public whipping, dismemberment, and decimation—the practice of systematically killing one out of ten for a crime committed en masse. The provost marshal, the chief policeman and jailor in an army, became a permanent fixture as a slave-catcher in Barbados, Jamaica, and the Carolinas. A French equivalent, the *maréchaussée*, operated in Saint-Domingue. Like the application of military law to soldiers, this offered slaves only limited protection from overzealous masters.

These brutal employments of military law should not have been available to English delegated officials by the middle of the seventeenth century.

In 1628 English lawyers wanted to eliminate martial law from England, and argued that the crown could not use it unless the "courts of Westminster"—that is, Parliament—were closed. Paradoxically, this restriction allowed for innovation and creativity on the part of the crown's delegated authorities in the Atlantic space. In the 1660s, Jamaican governors simply closed down common-law courts and ruled solely by martial law. They justified this usurpation by claiming status as military officers entrusted with defending the island from Spanish attacks as reprisals for their own privateering. In order to obtain the labor force necessary to build and maintain the fortifications needed for defense, leaders of the privateering faction closed common-law courts to commandeer private property. These creative uses of martial law far from metropolitan restraints left plantation owners few options but to allow their slaves to leave their plantations and build military forts.

By the end of the eighteenth century, desperate plantation owners and crown officials throughout the Atlantic resorted increasingly to military law to subdue restive enslaved labor forces. In Europe, commanders could use military law to punish rebellion of conquered populations by death. Planters used this provision strategically to punish their laborers, labeling rebellious any collective challenge—from demonstrations to violent uprisings. Panicked planters on Saint-Domingue in the violence of the Haitian rebellion of the 1790s brutally executed their former workers in an unsuccessful attempt to maintain order. The Jamaica planter class in 1833 and again in 1865 used martial law to prevent liberated men and women from obtaining the rights they deserved as subjects of the crown. Planters in Cuba and Brazil similarly employed military laws to subdue abolitionist or slave conspiracies throughout the nineteenth century.

Royal officials in the Atlantic, in both Africa and the Americas, unfettered by the restraints of monarchical authority in Europe, expanded the domain of military law there to buy captives of war in Africa—and in Europe—and then also to contain the civil tensions in the Americas that sprang from the resulting antagonism between radically differentiated legal categories of people: masters with their slaves and indentured servants. In this permanent state of class warfare, plantation owners expanded limited military command and control toward the modern concept of comprehensive martial law in nation-states.

JOHN COLLINS

Bibliography

Alencastro, Luiz-Felipede. "South Atlantic Wars: The Episode of Palmares." *Portuguese Studies Review* 19, nos. 1–2 (2011): 35–58.

Benton, Lauren. *A Search for Sovereignty: Law and Geography in European Empires, 1400–1900.* Cambridge: Cambridge University Press, 2010.

Kostal, R. W. *A Jurisprudence of Power: Victorian Empire and the Rule of Law.* Oxford: Oxford University Press, 2008.

Law, Monarchical

Monarchical law constituted the medieval and early-modern branch of western European law that bestowed powers of independent sovereignty on kings, enabled monarchs to rule over their realms and subjects through a wide range of royal prerogative rights, and provided the legal mechanisms by which sovereign powers related to one another. In the Atlantic Era, monarchical law was used to grant and retain territory, maintain relations with colonies and subjects, and engage in diplomacy and treaty negotiations with other European Atlantic nations.

Monarchical law emerged in the late-medieval period as lawyers considered the relationship between "the prince and the law." Deriving from the Latin *princeps*, *prince* referred to all monarchs who held *imperium*, or independent authority within their realms. After the Holy Roman emperor and Roman Catholic pope sought to become involved in the internal affairs of European kings, key statements on independent sovereignty were produced by a number of writers, perhaps most importantly Thomas Aquinas (1225–1273) in *On Kingship* (1267). These authors demonstrated that although the emperor and pope were once *dominus totius mundi* (lords of all the world) in secular affairs, with the decline of the Roman Empire their powers had devolved to all monarchs in western Europe. From this devolution emerged the important maxim *rex imperator in regno suo est*—that is, "a king is emperor in his own kingdom." This doctrine meant that monarchs recognized no higher earthly authority concerning domestic matters, although some accepted that the emperor and pope continued to serve as arbitrators in disputes among such sovereigns. By the early sixteenth century, Nicolò Machiavelli in *The Prince* (1513) and Francisco de Vitoria (1480–1552) and his fellow "neo-Thomists" (followers of Aquinas) demonstrated that the universal powers of the emperor and pope had virtually disappeared. This affirmation of local sovereignty was finally confirmed in the Peace of Westphalia (1648), which placed each king firmly in control of his external affairs.

The most important sixteenth-century statement on monarchical law was Jean Bodin's *Six Books of the Republic* (1576). To Bodin, "sovereignty is the most high, absolute, and perpetual power over citizens and subjects" (Bodin, 1). This authority was complete because it was indivisible: although authority might be delegated to agents of the king—to councillors, regional governors, and legislative bodies—the monarch held all of the power the state could wield. Bodin enumerated nine marks of sovereignty that dictated the breadth and depth of monarchical law: power to give laws as "sole legislator," power of war and peace, right of final appeal, power to appoint and dismiss officers of state, power of taxation, power to pardon individuals and mitigate the severity of the law, power of life and death, power to issue coinage, and the exclusive right to receive oaths of fealty and allegiance. In most European realms, these various powers were exercised through prerogatives that enabled monarchs to discharge their responsibilities toward their subjects. Despite these vast prerogative rights, however, Bodin argued that monarchs were obliged to apply the positive (written) and customary (unwritten) laws of their realms, unless these detracted from *imperium* or were contrary to the fundamental laws of humankind. Bodin privileged these fundamental laws—commonly termed the laws of God, nature, and nations (*iure divino, naturae, et gentium*) and sometimes known as the *ius commune* (common law)—over all local, customary, and royal laws. Evidence of the general acceptance of Bodin's work may be seen, for example, in James VI of Scotland's *Trew Law of Free Monarchies* (1597), which was republished shortly after he became James I of England (1603).

In an Atlantic context, monarchical law was employed in three instances: when granting subjects the privilege of discovering, conquering, and settling territory; when determining laws and future relations between the king and his subjects beyond the existing realm; and when engaging in diplomacy and treaty negotiations with other European nations that were involved in Atlantic activities. In the first instance, bulls, charters, and patents—the chief legal instruments of Atlantic expansion—emphasized that the source of authority for these activities derived solely from the power of the monarch as an independent sovereign. Christopher Columbus's charter (1492), issued by Ferdinand and Isabella of Castile, Léon, and Aragon, stated that the voyages were undertaken by "our command." The papal bull Inter Caetera (1493), which granted the New World to Spain, was issued by Alexander VI under his "mere largesse, certain science, and the fullness of our apostolic authority." Queen Elizabeth I of England issued a charter to Humphrey Gilbert (1578) under "our especial grace, certain science, and mere motion," while Henry IV of France "ordered, commissioned, and established" the Sieur de Monts (1603) to "establish our authority" in Acadia. Each of these documents clarified that these activities were being undertaken under the direct authority of a monarch who held *imperium*, rather than by the personal desires of the charter holders or colonists, who did not possess the legal capacity to claim territory.

Whereas monarchs were usually required to respect customary and positive law, in the case of the Atlantic colonies no preexisting laws were deemed to function. This legal vacuum theoretically allowed the king to develop his own laws, provided they were consonant with the *ius commune*, or general law transcending monarchy, and thus gave monarchs greater authority in their empires than they possessed in their domestic realms. In practice, however, monarchs typically encouraged the use of the laws of their own realm, which resulted in legal inheritances from the mother countries in transatlantic territories. Monarchical law also demanded that the Atlantic colonists respond to royal orders, do nothing to lessen the king's power as the ultimate source of law, and ensure that settlers continue to respect the power of the king. Even where colonial governors, councils, and legislative assemblies existed to regulate internal colonial affairs and were bestowed with lawmaking and law-enforcing capacities, in the spirit of the Bodinic theory of indivisibility, the monarchs did not relinquish any authority, and subordinate agents of the crown operated only with delegated power and always in the name of the monarch.

The continuation of royal authority was necessary because monarchical law required, in the words of the subtitle to James VI's *Trew Law*, a "reciprocal and mutual duty betwixt a free king and his natural subjects." Drawing from the medieval feudal relationship between lords and vassals, the king had the prerogative to demand perpetual homage and allegiance from his subjects. Those who failed to give these to the king could be subjected to such remedies as civil or criminal punishments, steps taken to regain allegiance, or the king's withdrawal of sovereign responsibility, essentially sending them into exile. In exchange, subjects had the right to expect royal protection against the illegal or immoral actions of all aggressors, whether foreign (thus demanding war and diplomacy) or domestic. In such cases, the king exercised his position as the fount of justice by hearing petitions and appeals, overturning the actions of subordinates who held delegated powers, or complaining to other sovereign monarchs on behalf of his subjects in Atlantic colonies.

Because, under monarchical law, kings were expected to conform to the *ius commune*, their Atlantic activities needed to reflect these principles so that the colonies that emerged from discovery and settlement would receive formal recognition from the supranational community. Recognized sovereignty demanded that monarchs utilized a pluralistic and complex legal language—for the *ius commune* itself combined more than a dozen complementary and competing forms of law—that conformed to the methods used by their counterparts. In treaty negotiations throughout the seventeenth and eighteenth centuries, Britain, France, and Spain all cited to varying degrees the expectations that territorial claims would be recognized only if made by Christian monarchs who held *imperium*—an argument commonly used to justify the lack of Native sovereignty over Atlantic regions. Additionally, claims on territory needed to be accompanied by both the mental intention to claim land (*animus*) and the physical ability to hold it (*corpore*) in order to be respected. Each of these legal notions derived from the inheritance that European monarchs gained from the "universal monarchy" of Rome (the same source of monarchical law) and the body of positive law expressed in the sixth-century emperor Justinian's *Corpus Iuris Civilis* (Body of Civil Laws). By the early-modern period, the *Corpus* was considered to be *ratio scripta* (written reason) of the *ius commune*. It was thus, in large part, the legalities of claiming territory in the Atlantic, and the negotiations that emerged from them, that determined the future development of both monarchical and supranational—later international—law.

Despite the theoretical exercise of monarchical law throughout the Atlantic, especially to claim territory vis-à-vis other European authorities, its application was always a matter of negotiation between centers (the royal governments of Europe) and peripheries (the Atlantic colonies). The exigencies of local colonial circumstances, which could not be anticipated by royal authorities; the realities of dealing with "conquered" indigenous peoples, vast colonial regions, and complex inter-imperial states; and the difficulty monarchs had in enforcing royal policies across the vast expanse of the Atlantic Ocean all meant that the exercise of monarchical law was, in practice, complicated by transatlantic challenges. While the authority of monarchical law remained relatively strong in the Atlantic empires of France, Portugal, and Spain, which were always royal in character, its exercise became a topic of dissension in the British Atlantic World; there, the idea of settler sovereignty eventuated in revolution in the eighteenth century.

KEN MACMILLAN

Bibliography

Bodin, Jean. *On Sovereignty: Four Chapters from The Six Books of the Commonwealth.* Ed. and trans. by Julian H. Franklin. Cambridge: Cambridge University Press, 1992.

Daniels, Christine, and Michael V. Kennedy, eds. *Negoti-*

ated Empires: Centers and Peripheries in the Americas, 1500–1820. New York: Routledge, 2002.

MacMillan, Ken. *Sovereignty and Possession in the English New World: The Legal Foundations of Empire, 1576–1640.* Cambridge: Cambridge University Press, 2006.

Muldoon, James, *Empire and Order: The Concept of Empire, 800–1800.* New York: Palgrave Macmillan, 1999.

Pagden, Anthony. *Lords of All the World: Ideologies of Empire in Spain, Britain and France, c. 1500–c. 1800.* New Haven, CT: Yale University Press, 1995.

Pennington, Kenneth. *The Prince and the Law, 1200–1600: Sovereignty and Rights in the Western Legal Tradition.* Berkeley: University of California Press, 1993.

Law, Roman, in the Americas

Roman law, from the perspective of late-medieval Europeans, was the product of nearly 1,000 years of evolution and development from the earliest days of the Roman city-state until the last days of the decline of the Roman Empire in the West. In many respects it proved the greatest monument to and legacy of the ancient Roman Empire. But Roman law was also more than a historical artifact; it has had multiple afterlives, and its influence is felt in many modern legal systems, including those of the nations that now compose North, Central, and South America.

Although the Roman Empire in the West lost virtually all of its political coherence in Europe by the end of the sixth century, Roman law, particularly as it was codified in the fifth-century text of the Theodosian Code and the sixth-century *Corpus Iuris Civilis*, became a principal source for the canon law of the Catholic Church. A revival of Roman-law studies in twelfth-century Europe and a further development of Roman law in the fifteenth and sixteenth centuries led to what may be called "Romanization" of the national laws of France, Spain, Portugal, the Netherlands, and Italy, as well as Germany and Austria. This Roman legal heritage was consolidated in the Napoleonic Code in revolutionary France (1804), which became a fundamental legal source for all the countries that fell to Napoleon's armies in the following decade. Today we speak of "civil law systems" being the predominant type in western Europe, as well as in many of these countries' former colonies, meaning that these laws have been founded upon Roman law. Only England and the Scandinavian countries withstood this wave of "Romanization," although some Roman law has been incorporated even in these "common law" legal systems.

Roman law provided both substantive doctrine and philosophical framework for the national laws into which it was incorporated. In the political and constitutional realm, Roman public law from the imperial period could be translated into the newly emergent national monarchies of the European states. In the United States, Roman law of the republican period, particularly as expressed in Cicero's writings, provided inspiration for the break from the English monarchy and for the republican form of government after the Revolution. Much the same was true in the development of many private-law subjects in both Europe and the United States, particularly in the case of commercial law. In both civil- and common-law jurisdictions, much of commercial law, such as the law of bailments, or trusteeship, was borrowed directly from Roman sources and was important in the creation of modern financial and transportation services.

Laws do not cross national borders—or oceans, in the case of the Atlantic—by themselves. Events, people, and books carry them along to make order out of the disorder of rapid change. Roman law and the civil-law systems developed from it in Central and South America arrived by way of the conquest and colonization of these areas by France, Spain, and Portugal; wherever these nations established colonies, they brought their own legal systems with them. In North America, successive Spanish and French colonization of what became known as the Louisiana Purchase when Thomas Jefferson acquired the greater Mississippi Valley for the United States, and French colonization of Quebec, brought Roman law to these territories. These are today "mixed" jurisdictions, because their laws combine the civil laws brought by their first colonizers with the common law brought by the English who succeeded France and Spain. New York state still bears traces (albeit minor) of Roman law, as colonists from the Netherlands brought it to New Amsterdam before English authorities acquired the colony in 1665.

M. H. HOEFLICH

Bibliography

Hoeflich, M. H. *Roman and Civil Law & the Development of Nineteenth Century Jurisprudence.* Athens: University of Georgia Press, 1997.

Mirow, Matthew. *Latin American Law: A History of Private Law and Institutions in Spanish America.* Austin: University of Texas Press, 2004.

Palmer, Vernon Valentine. *Louisiana: Microcosm of a Mixed Jurisdiction.* Durham, NC: Carolina Academic Press, 1999.

Stein, Peter. "The Attraction of the Civil Law in Post-Revolutionary America." *Virginia Law Review* 52 (1966), 404–411, 419–420.

Watson, Alan. *Legal Transplants: An Approach to Comparative Law.* Athens: University of Georgia Press, 1974.

———. *Making of the Civil Law.* Cambridge, MA: Harvard University Press, 1991.

Law of Nations

The law of nations was a European construct and at the same time, strictly speaking, a misnomer. Although Europeans freely used the term to describe customs and conventions that Europe's rulers observed in their interactions with one another and their peoples, early-modern writers who took the general concept seriously acknowledged that this body of law lacked the coercive authority associated with domestic—or "municipal"—legal systems. Skeptics often dismissed the very notion of a common public law as high-minded cant. Talk about the law of nations, it seemed, was just talk. It was, however, talk that mattered, and it mattered both within Europe and in the Atlantic World, where Europeans encountered multiple and conflicting legal systems from the fifteenth century onward. In this legally complex space, the law of nations supplied much of the rationale for European monarchies' expansion, it helped them manage conflicts resulting from their overlapping ambitions and not always controllable agents, and it ultimately defined the terms by which the era of formal empires came to a close.

Europeans recognized several important distinctions underlying the law of nations, each of which helps to illustrate how sovereigns utilized this complex body of law. The first, and in many ways most important, distinction was between the positive law of specific treaties and the informal, often unwritten customs that European merchants, soldiers, adventurers, and diplomats observed in their day-to-day interactions across the lines of monarchical and aristocratic-republican sovereignty. In the former category were great pan-European compacts such as the treaties of Westphalia (1648), Utrecht (1713), and Vienna (1815)—agreements that, through a combination of longevity and the severity of the conflicts that they brought to a close, came to be seen as a kind of public law that could bind otherwise autonomous domains. In North America, the Treaty of Paris (1763), which concluded the Seven Years' War, eventually came to function as such a fundamental law in relations between the British—and later Canadian—government and Canada's first peoples. The Anglo-American treaty that ended the War of American Independence in 1783 is rightly seen, along with the Declaration of Independence and the Constitution of 1787, as one of the United States' three founding documents. The treaty ultimately formed a bridge between the other two documents, with the obligations that it placed on Congress and the new states forcing Americans to craft a "more perfect union" in order to win international recognition for the sovereignty that the Second Continental Congress had proclaimed in 1776.

Complementing—and, at times, conflicting with—this positive law were the informal norms and customs that people in Europe and the extra-European Atlantic also observed in their interactions with one another. Some of these, notably European diplomatic ritual and the so-called rules of war observed by regular European armies and navies, had their origins in Europe, but the customary law of nations was also profoundly multicultural, blending European norms with borrowings from the norms of the South American pampas, North Africa's Barbary Coast, the slaving principalities of West Africa, and Gaelic Scotland and Ireland. Among the more notorious—and exploitative—examples of this legal hybridity was the African slave trade. From the sixteenth century onward, writers on the law of nations, including Hugo Grotius, Samuel Pufendorf, and Emer de Vattel, justified enslavement of Africans on two related grounds: first, because, by recognized rules of war, victors everywhere had the right to enslave prisoners who would otherwise be put to death; and, second, because Africa and the Americas both lacked the legal safeguards that, jurists claimed, in Europe had largely ended the practice of executing and enslaving war captives. Thus, buying the captives of others' wars conveyed title under European law. The result was a legal system that drew on both European and non-European antecedents. Ironically, the persistence of slavery outside Europe entitled Europeans in the extra-European Atlantic to perpetuate (and vastly expand) a status of persons that the law in Europe increasingly proscribed.

A second distinction within the law of nations as Europeans used it involved their collective relationship with the rest of the world. By general agreement, although the law of nations was universal, with rules that were as binding in Africa and America as they were in Europe—with a tragic effect being to justify slaving—the authority in the outer Atlantic of the European rulers whom the law was supposed to regulate was attenuated, even undefined, and often disputed. As a result, specific treaties among powers in Europe often acknowledged distinctions between their European subjects and dominions and subjects and dominions elsewhere.

These spatial distinctions took a variety of forms. Sometimes, diplomatic agreements specified differing timetables, according to which certain provisions were to take effect immediately within Europe but later overseas, allowing colonial subjects and allies in distant localities more time to comply. On other occasions, peace treaties applied only to a stated part of the world (usually Europe) and left unresolved disputes elsewhere involving the same parties. In the century and a half after Columbus's voyages, European peacemakers and diplomats, skirting responsibilities that they could not effectively enforce in remote areas, often acknowledged this distinction by deploying so-called lines of amity, beyond which the terms of particular agreements would not apply. In the Treaty of Cateau-Cambrésis (1559), France and Spain agreed—verbally, as opposed to scribally—to allow their subjects in the Americas to remain in a state of belligerence with each other without acknowledging the resulting hostilities as acts of war binding in Europe. Eventually the rulers of Europe

abandoned such formal demarcations as their claims grew and they became increasingly capable of defending sovereignty across the seas, yet the idea that the outer Atlantic was a lawless place of chronic war and violence persisted, reinforcing the customary law that Europeans used to justify exploitation of Africans and indigenous Americans.

Finally, most authorities on the law of nations recognized a crucial distinction between rulers and the people they ruled. As the phrase *law of nations* implied, the only entities that could claim rights under Europe's public law were fully sovereign. By contrast, rebels, slaves, brigands, pirates, and renegades of all sorts—including subjects who broke faith with their lawful sovereign—were excluded from the law's protections. Although governments were free to make formal concessions to such groups (and in fact often did), the resulting agreements were, from the law's standpoint, unilateral acts of sovereignty that governments had the right to change or revoke as they saw fit, not negotiated contracts for which governments could be held accountable.

Not surprisingly, this principle of unilateral dealings with outlaws bore especially hard on the Atlantic World's enslaved and indigenous peoples; however, the implications could also be dire for Europeans. On Honduras Bay and the Mosquito Coast in the western Caribbean (modern Honduras and Nicaragua), where mixed-race communities of English adventurers and Native Americans conducted a brisk trade in logwood and mahogany, both groups lived in danger of removal at the whim of Spanish officials, who regarded them as illegal squatters in the viceroyalty of New Spain. The same was true of the French Acadians in the borderlands of Nova Scotia, who remained neutral in the Seven Years' War, and whom British and New England soldiers deported in 1755. European planters on what, until the peace of 1763, were the legally vacant "neutral islands" of Dominica, Grenada, St. Lucia, St. Vincent, and Tobago were similarly stateless and subject to arbitrary treatment at the hands of recognized authorities. From a legal standpoint, all were people without an acknowledged nation, and all were, therefore, beyond the law of nations' protection.

Given this vulnerability of stateless peoples, the Creole patriots who shattered the bonds of Europe's political control in the outer Atlantic, starting with the American Declaration of Independence in 1776, were taking significant risks. All accordingly sought acceptance as independent sovereign entities under the law of nations. In the case of the United States, the quest for recognition lasted for decades and forced North Americans to create a stronger and more centralized union—starting with the Constitution of 1787—than they had initially wanted. Eventually, European rulers responded by accepting the United States as a treaty-worthy equal. With other new "nations" on Saint-Domingue and in Spanish America, on the other hand, the Atlantic powers (including the United States by the early 1800s) proved far less welcoming. In Latin America, European and North American recognition came only in the 1820s and 1830s, while the United States waited until the 1860s to recognize the sovereignty that Haiti had proclaimed in 1804. In the free-soil enclave of Sierra Leone in Africa and in North America's Indian Country—notably among the Cherokee and the other so-called civilized nations of the southeastern United States—would-be founders of independent polities eventually had to settle for the half-empty achievement of dependent nationhood.

As the sovereign rulers in Europe asserted their own absolutism in the eighteenth century, and built the administrative and military systems to implement it, the law of nations vested so much power in their hands that members of communities lacking sovereign status, especially authorities in Africa and Indians in America, fell victims to it. In both areas, the law of nations was repeatedly used to sanction forcing such groups into positions of greater dependency on the powers it recognized. For that reason, in the United States and Brazil the achievement of independence with European recognition created local, Creole sovereignties that helped breathe new life into both slavery and the slave trade, all firmly within the law of nations. As outliers in an age of abolition, both of these slaveholding nations had every reason to accept the authority of a law that accorded them full sovereignty over their internal affairs.

Because the law of nations was as much a rhetoric of consent among authorities who accepted one another's absolute sovereign status as it was a unilaterally enforceable law—in other words, more principle than practice—it would be a mistake to give it too much emphasis in framing the transoceanic politics of the Atlantic, either before or after the establishment of independent nations in the Americas. Yet even as rhetoric, the law helps to explain the transition from the Atlantic legal space of composite European monarchies and empires to an extra-European world of Creole nations. In the epoch of political independence that followed 1776, partisans of the new order rarely questioned the framework of the public law of Europe's colonial rulers, even as they embraced new ideas of sovereignty based on personal liberty and democracy to break with the authoritarian rule of monarchy. Whatever anyone made of the internal struggles of the new nations, everyone, it seemed, could agree on the respect for internal autonomy that ought to guide relations among sovereign authorities. The collapse of Spain's American empire in the early 1820s finally brought on the crisis in which governments in Europe and North America acknowledged the new reality, but they did so mainly on the ground that the new Spanish American republics would be more effective enforcers of the law of nations than the colonial authorities whom they had overthrown. In this guise, the law of nations outlived the European empires that had created it and eventually merged into a new phase of formalization as modern international law and human rights.

ELIGA H. GOULD

Bibliography

Benton, Lauren A. *A Search for Sovereignty: Law and Geography in European Empires, 1400–1900*. Cambridge: Cambridge University Press, 2010.

Gould, Eliga H. *Among the Powers of the Earth: The American Revolution and the Making of a New World Empire*. Cambridge, MA: Harvard University Press, 2012.

Onuf, Peter S., and Nicholas Greenwood. *Federal Union, Modern World: The Law of Nations in an Age of Revolutions, 1776–1814*. Madison, WI: Madison House, 1993.

Rodríguez O., Jaime E. "The Emancipation of America." *American Historical Review* 105, no. 1 (2000): 131–152.

Liberties, Royal

Royalty and liberty, two concepts often paired in opposition to one another, were profoundly enmeshed in the early-modern Atlantic World. Royal liberties emerged in the medieval period, most typically as functional grants of monarchical authority to particular individuals in return for specified services to the crown. In that context, royal liberties did as much to constitute an emerging monarchical authority as they did to reflect an already existing set of royal powers and prerogatives. But royal liberties also took shape as collective charters limiting the king's authority, presumed otherwise sovereign, over certain groups of persons, in exchange for continued fealty and/or fiscal sustenance. In this second sense, royal liberties transferred into the Atlantic World as instruments of colonization and then morphed during the Atlantic revolutionary period into something else: the basis of independent claims against metropolitan *imperium*—even while retaining traces of the old reciprocity of privilege and duty that the revolutionary ideology of natural freedom purported to erase.

Kernels of Modern Rights in Medieval European Liberties

Three aspects of medieval society were central to the development of royal liberties: (1) the very limited practical reach of monarchical sovereignty (later pretensions to "absolutism" notwithstanding); (2) the reciprocity of the patronage relations inhering in the feudal relationship between king and lord; and (3) the ordering of society into corporate bodies (social or professional as well as local or regional) separated one from another by distinguishing charters from the monarch.

The limited reach of the monarch placed a premium on the functional delegation of discrete administrative responsibilities in a world where "kingdoms" were essentially aggrandized composites of household governments. The reciprocal character of royal patronage as both responsibility and power created opportunities for the king's subjects, primarily nobles and the practitioners of favored trades and professions, to enhance their personal status and power by committing to undertake one or another of the functional roles necessitated by the pretensions of monarchy to comprehensive control. These differentiated ties of patronage contained implicit notions of direct individualized relationships between sovereign and subjects. But that atomizing tendency was counterbalanced by a third characteristic of medieval society: the creation and maintenance of collective orders or "interest" groups. These corporate units constituted a vast social terrain upon which royal liberties could be deployed, so as to empower and discipline at one and the same time. In the case of local and regional governmental units, royal liberties encouraged the collaboration of multiple and overlapping ancient and feudal realms—manors and shires, towns and cities, and provinces both newly conquered and long since domesticated—with central royal authority, a dynamic that would prove to be integral to the processes of Atlantic colonization.

Two principal categories of royal liberties, which can be roughly contrasted as micro- and macroliberties, emerged in the Middle Ages. The first involved royal delegations of power or privilege to specific individuals. In the prototypical situation, the individuals on the receiving end of these grants were effectively contracted to carry out the administrative work of the king, whose personal authority was thereby extended via local intermediaries throughout claimed realms. These medieval "regalities" tied service to privilege and encompassed a vast range of activities: the right to claim goods cast ashore from a wrecked vessel (liberty of wreck) or to hang a manifest thief (liberty of the gallows), for example. Landholding in tenure from the king was itself a form of these liberties, and indeed the term *liberty* also described the very territory within which a privilege was exercised on behalf of royalty. The liberty known as the return of writs captured both of these dimensions simultaneously, for it authorized the bearer, in place of the sheriff as the king's representative, to execute all royal writs within a locality and thereby to achieve a measure of administrative autonomy. Autonomy of this considerable extent, and the allegation that it would be falsely invoked so as to "hinder common justice and subvert royal power" (in the words of Edward I's Articles of Inquiry of 1274), carried hints of the Atlantic republican future.

Macroliberties, by contrast, consisted of charters recognizing the self-rule of cities and regions or the corporate professional, religious, and other group identities independent of the persons in them. In France, well before the apogee of absolutism under Louis XIV at the end of the seventeenth century, royal liberties had come to define dukes and cardinals, towns and provinces, and (at the broadest level) the three royally recognized and privilege-bearing orders of nobility, clergy, and the so-called third estate (consisting primarily of the representatives of town governments). In return, the medieval and early-modern monarchs secured the monies needed to run their ever-expanding royal households and to embark upon the cycle of militarization and public debt that reflected the monarchy's absolutist pretensions, even as that cycle simultaneously undermined the capacity of the House of Bourbon to sustain itself financially.

In either context—the individual or the corporate—"all of the limits and possibilities of [royal] liberties sprang from the fundamental fact of subjecthood" (Halliday, 184). But macroliberties had one distinctive advantage for monarchs. Extended kingdom-wide, as in England, they could be deployed to contain individual aristocratic challenges, which intensified with the failures—and successes—of monarchical consolidation. Magna Carta (1215, reissued in more durable form in 1225) is the best-known example. Often misunderstood as granting English liberty in the abstract, Magna Carta was instead a grant of so many different *liberties* to all "free men" of the realm. Historians have debated whether that last phrase signified all English males, landholders, "freeholders," or all those who were not villeins (persons bound to the land and owned by feudal lords). But the specific liberties granted under Magna Carta spoke for themselves, benefiting as they did widows and Jews, barons and merchants, the residents of London, and so on. The writ of habeas corpus was not itself among these privileges—for not until the decades around 1605 did the king's judges vigorously assert their prerogative to oversee the actions of jailers—but the underlying liberty to be free from arrest or imprisonment except in accordance with law was.

The line from Magna Carta to the 1628 Petition of Rights and the 1689 Declaration of Rights—which bookended England's seventeenth-century subordination of monarchy to Parliament—was anything but straight. The kingdom-wide nature of England's macroliberties ultimately distinguished

the island from its continental counterparts. The relatively muted character and divisive diversity of specific macroliberties in the Spanish and Portuguese realms (for the feudal narrative of microliberty was a pan-European one) may have owed something to the fact that those kingdoms were "a jumble of jurisdictions" rather than a "homogeneous legislative space" of the kind framed by Magna Carta. Although neither France nor England could lay claim to functionally homogeneous status prior to the eighteenth century, those two kingdoms had come closest to that mark before the opening of the Atlantic—a circumstance that may help to account for the subsequent transformation in the Franco- and Anglo-American Atlantic worlds of medieval royal liberties into modern individual "rights."

Royal Liberties as Vehicles of Expansion

These royal liberties bore highly variegated (and, in some cases, ultimately unintended) fruit as European monarchies consolidated royal power by appropriating Atlantic initiatives that opened to them. Imperial initiatives extended the European distinction between micro- and macroliberties to the New World but also blurred the line separating them. The starting points were often the charters of commercial corporations, which typically bestowed a monopolistic franchise on merchants and administrators in exchange for their commitment to settle and develop "virgin" territory or trading relations under fealty to their royal sponsor(s). The New World charter colonies, from military captaincies in Portuguese Brazil to the proprietary Quaker settlement in Pennsylvania, were concessions of royal privileges to select groups of individuals pledged to provide the financial resources or incentives to immigration. The resulting commitments would permit the "planting" necessary to establish recognized sovereignty over spaces otherwise legally "empty" and then the "keeping" of the territories thus claimed by royal sponsors. But, as incentives to cover the associated costs, these written instruments also granted macroliberties that applied on a colony-wide basis. In some cases, as in Pennsylvania, a limited form of internal representative government was allowed. Such autonomous structures were born of a New World balance between traditional manorialism and parliamentary constitutionalist limits on royal prerogatives that distinctly favored the largest property holders.

Early-sixteenth-century Spanish America's *encomienda* system was a variation on this balance of royal authority and grantee autonomy inherent in awarding monarchical "liberties." It permitted the first generation of crown military officers—the military conquistadors—to extract both commodity tribute and labor services from the residents of the lands they claimed in the sovereign's name. In exchange for this considerable privilege, the *encomenderos* promised military service to the sovereign when needed and committed to convert the Indians in their care to the apostolic faith. After the Spanish friar Bartolomé de Las Casas (1484–1566) famously protested the brutalities perpetrated under cover of these royal warrants, Charles V promulgated the so-called New Laws of 1542–1543, which granted the Indians the direct personal protections of the crown. The seventeenth-century *amparo* petitions (applications for protective judicial orders under this liberty) brought by Indians before the royal courts in Mexico City, seeking protection for both individual and communal landholdings, highlight the Indians' persistent belief that they could claim *libertad* as a matter of royal decree.

In Brazil, the legal mechanism for colonization was a donatary royal grant, an Atlantic updating of the Portuguese medieval grant of *senhorio* (seignory). The *senhorio* delegated royal rights of taxation, justice, administration, and settlement and economic development to individual nobles. In the 1530s, on the basis of this precedent, King Dom João III (r. 1521–1557) divided the Brazilian coast into 15 hereditary territorial grants and awarded direct control over each to a *donatário*, with honorary military rank (and responsibilities) of captain. The donatarial system faded in some captaincies but remained in place in others, enabling municipal councils in later Brazilian port cities, dominated by commercial interests independent of royal authority, to exercise de facto governmental control despite formal acknowledgment of metropolitan dominion.

The French and English monarchies, relative latecomers to overseas enterprise, similarly granted discrete aspects of the growing royal prerogative to the agents they entrusted with their dynastic claims throughout the Atlantic. The terms and methods of their grants varied greatly across both time and space. Seigneurial land tenure predominated in New France (Canada). In the Caribbean, the French monarchy began by enabling and then deferring to "private" initiatives—licensing (through letters patent) privateers of noble origin to seize territory in the name of the king and chartering private corporations to provide investment and manage the process of settlement. By the late seventeenth century, the king assumed direct administrative control over the islands, granting concessions to planters (for landholding) and to merchants (for the exclusive right to carry the proceeds of plantations by ship to and from the metropole). By contrast, English royal involvement in the actual processes of colonization tended to be very limited.

For slaves and free people of color, the workings of royal authority overseas could often seem invisible. There were two major exceptions, only one of which had a clear connection to the theme of royal liberties. First, by 1705 at the latest, slaves were clearly defined as personal property under both English and French colonial statutory law, a definition that in effect licensed the colonial plantocracy to hold in bondage persons whose legal status was thenceforth a matter of royal law. Second, a provision of the French colonial slave code (article 59 of the 1685 Code Noir) guaranteed freed slaves all of the "rights, privileges, and immunities" enjoyed by the king's native-born subjects—that is, those not subjected to the incapacities visited upon alien residents, including, most notably, the inability to bequeath one's estate and property to a nonnative heir. Such a privilege was particularly important in the case of free people of color, who were anchored in the traditional absolutist social order only to the extent that they owed a residual duty of respect to their former owners. Article 59 was, in effect, a royal microliberty (it acted upon individuals), but one whose operation did not depend on the direct case-by-case intervention of the monarch, and that in time came to assume the role of a macroliberty: a privilege of equality that inhered in free people of color as a group.

Royal Liberties and the Rise of Republican Freedoms

Royal liberties were products of "a world that did not conceive liberty as a quality inhering in morally autonomous individuals" (Halliday, 7). This donatary quality of royal liberties made them ill suited as precedent for the doctrine of independent, natural, individual human rights. Nonetheless, we can trace a contradictory process of borrowing and transformation from the liberties of the medieval and early-modern eras to the revolutionary language of natural inherent rights, owing to three broad circumstances particular to the Atlantic World. First, above all on the British North American mainland, the relatively stunted character of royal authority, working with limited resources from a belated start and interrupted by regicide at a formative moment in the mid-seventeenth century, combined with the use of charters granting domain-wide macroliberties, created opportunities for colonists to assert claims of independent rights and absolute immunities. Second, as the costs of heavily militarized "absolute" monarchies grew in the eighteenth century, a powerful antipathy to the medieval world of patronage-based microliberties, aggravated by a sense of betrayal that the British crown was no longer honoring the reciprocities of the medieval patron-client model, took hold in influential colonial circles. The Seven Years' War (1756–1763) was the decisive turning point in the Caribbean and North Atlantic colonial domains of nearly every European colonizing power. Third, what remained of the tradition of royal beneficence in return for loyal subjecthood became unhinged from its feudal moorings in executing the king's pleasure vis-à-vis local governmental administration, individual landholding, tax collection, and so forth, and found a new foothold in free-floating "natural rights" of American Creole gentries building positions independent of royal privileges through merchant and plantation commerce.

Domain-wide charters of political liberties, articulated more or less independently of the monarch in British North America, appeared as early as Maryland's 1639 Act for the Liberties of the People and the 1641 Massachusetts Body of Liberties. But it was not until the aftermath of the Seven Years' War that these charters were self-consciously elaborated as frameworks for limiting the authority of an overbearing executive or legislature through the enumeration of abstract rights and privileges that operated independently of royal favor. The proliferation of constitution making during the 1760s and 1770s—culminating in the 1787 federal Constitution of the United States—was the high-water

mark of this transfer of sovereignty from monarch to former subjects. Explicit enumerations of the rights due to individuals, as themselves sovereign, either shortly predated or accompanied colonial constitutions, Virginia being a case of the former and Massachusetts of the latter. The United States Constitution adopted such enumerations by way of postscript in the Bill of Rights.

At one level, the rise of republican ideology in revolutionary America entailed discrediting the hierarchies of the personal patronage upon which monarchical authority had rested. The beneficiaries of the old royal microliberties—overwhelmingly members of the landed gentry—had been losing these immunities since the English revolution of the mid-seventeenth century. Once severed from the Old World's "hierarchical lines of patronage and influence," the gentry's "exclusive corporate charters and grants became increasingly anomalous. Even in the old society of England there had been outcries against monopoly and favoritism and complaints that such corporate grants were unfairly dispersed" (Wood, 319). Such rhetoric of personal autonomy reverberated even within the putatively private world of master-slave relations, by then expressed in terms of commercial "rights of property." The masters' personal proprietary rights, however, implied the similarly individual autonomy of the enslaved. In 1774 a group of Massachusetts slaves petitioned the governor and legislature of that colony to "cause an act of the legislative to be pessed that we may obtain our Natural right our freedoms and our children be set at lebety at the years of Twenty one" (original spelling preserved)—a vision that implicitly rejected the old Roman-law doctrine that a freed person owed his or her former master a duty of loyalty in favor of a more unconditional understanding of liberty.

As the slaves' petition suggests, what traces remained of the old mutuality of royal liberties in the Atlantic revolutionary era were then competing with individuals' claims to the collective macro- or categorical liberties once associated with royal dispensation. Within 15 years of the Massachusetts petition, free people of color in Saint-Domingue combined the "equal rights" provision of the royal slave legislation with the "free and equal" language of the 1789 Declaration of the Rights of Man and the Citizen in revolutionary France: the continuities from royal to republican liberties were clear to them, if not always to their opponents. The rhetoric of royal microliberties merged with the tradition of categorical privileges and was relaunched "at large" as natural freedom, independent of persons, patrons, or clients. The resulting ideology of civil liberties was entirely consistent with the republican reaction against exclusive and monopolistic franchises dominated by a gentry elite—notwithstanding that the creolized gentry of the British North American seaboard had itself been largely responsible for the republican catechism in the 1776 Declaration of Independence. By the end of the revolutionary era, little of the old distinction between micro- and macroliberties remained. Facilitating the workings of royal administration was no longer essential to the enjoyment of personal liberties; political and civil rights could no longer be restricted to propertied recipients of royal munificence (at least within the world of adult white males).

Ironies of Change

The process of extending royal liberties to provincial actors and territories became the fulcrum of a new world order that few had imagined. The European monarchies facilitated their own consolidation by expanding their geographic reach beyond the range of the liberties they had themselves conceded in consolidating their sovereign positions in their home realms. But the more legally amorphous arena of Atlantic dynastic competition forced them also to overextend themselves militarily and fiscally, provoking colonists who had grown confident through their independent commercial successes to seize the autonomy that undergirded the personal and collective recognition of royal liberties. The ideology of contingent liberty had thus helped to yield the theory of natural law and inherent human rights.

In another continuity with the old order, when republican citizens succeeded the subjects of monarchies, Liberty—essentialized, with a capital "L," that is, abstracted from the particularities of personal relationships and severed from the specific feudal privileges of landholding or tax farming—remained a privilege that the sovereign power confirmed, though sovereignty was now the people rather than the monarch. This guarantee was the very point of the declarations of rights that ac-companied the revolutionary constitutions, which claimed an authority grounded in natural and divine law but also spoke forcefully in the name of a strong sovereignty, of "the people," by whose authority the rights respected could also be limited or denied.

For the ideologues of the new republican regimes, it may have mattered greatly that states were no longer granting liberties but rather protecting prior "natural" rights inhering in individuals and the citizenry at large. The halting history of human rights in the two centuries since then, though, suggests that there is perhaps less to that distinction in practice than theory might discern. The republican order was, on the whole, a less arbitrary and more impersonal world than the monarchies that had passed, but it preserved, in subtle (and some not so subtle) ways, the explicit medieval acknowledgment of the interdependence of personal liberties and civic duties, individual freedoms and social discipline.

MALICK W. GHACHEM

Bibliography

Beik, William. *Louis XIV and Absolutism: A Brief Study with Documents*. Boston: Bedford/St. Martin's, 2000.
Blackburn, Robin. *The American Crucible: Slavery, Emancipation, and Human Rights*. London: Verso, 2011.
———. *The Making of New World Slavery: From the Baroque to the Modern, 1492–1800*. London: Verso, 1997.
Cam, Helen. *Liberties and Communities in Medieval England*. London: Merlin, 1963.
Halliday, Paul. *Habeas Corpus: From England to Empire*. Cambridge, MA: Harvard University Press, 2010.
Owensby, Brian P. *Empire of Law and Indian Justice in Colonial Mexico*. Stanford, CA: Stanford University Press, 2008.
Peters, Edward. *Torture*, expanded ed. Philadelphia: University of Pennsylvania Press, 1996.
Schwartz, Stuart. *Early Brazil: A Documentary Collection to 1700*. New York: Cambridge University Press, 2010.
Tomlins, Christopher. *Freedom Bound: Law, Labor, and Civic Identity in Colonizing English America, 1580–1865*. New York: Cambridge University Press, 2010.
Wood, Gordon S. *The Radicalism of the American Revolution*. New York: Alfred A. Knopf, 1991.

Literary and Visual Expressions, African American

"Am I Not a Man and a Brother?"—white British potter Josiah Wedgwood's eighteenth-century anti-slavery medallion, which pictures a black man on his knees and begging for white philanthropic up-lift—has emerged over the centuries as one of the most iconic representations of chattel slavery within the white transatlantic imaginary (figure 1). Dominating European and European American abolitionist memory from the moment it was de-signed in 1787, this decontextualized and dehu-manized silhouette purporting to represent black manhood—a similarly shackled female figure sub-sequently appeared with the revised caption, "Am I Not a Woman and a Sister?"—has fixed black hu-manity according to reductive archetypes.

Wedgwood's imagining of a half-naked enslaved figure foregrounds white spiritual redemption over and above black physical emancipation and trades not in individuals but in depersonalized types, to implore whites to liberate untold millions of en-slaved women and men in order to secure their own salvation. These supplicant and shackled figures—their torsos barely delineated, much less their phys-iognomies—took center stage not only on medal-lions designed for sale to aid the antislavery cause but also on snuff boxes, necklaces, and fine porce-lain, among many other artifacts. They functioned as representative icons of abstracted suffering but never as humanized subjects.

Appearing a few decades later, and circulating in seemingly stark contrast to Wedgwood's imagining of fettered archetypes, was European American writer and illustrator Samuel Warner's frontispiece accompanying his pamphlet, *Horrid Massacre in Virginia* (figure 2). Published in the United States in 1831 in the wake of the revolutionary activism of black enslaved freedom-fighter Nathaniel Turner in Southampton County, Virginia, the sensational de-piction of savage violence met with instant critical acclaim among whites. Black-engineered and black-imagined, Turner's acts of resistance were the an-tithesis of Wedgwood's black supplicant passively awaiting white liberation. In an event still known only in skeletal outline due to the racist biases of official archives, Turner led a small army of enslaved

Figure 1. "Am I Not a Man and a Brother?" (1787).

Figure 2. *Horrid Massacre in Virginia* (1831).

men in a war against bondage on the night of Au-gust 22, 1831, that ultimately left more black women, men, and children dead in vengeful repri-sals than the few whites slain in the event.

According to Warner's racist inversion of Wedg-wood's icon, a white man and woman take the place of the subjugated enslaved subject, as they are shown on their knees and begging for salvation before the murderous horde of caricatured black men brandishing weapons. Similar to Wedgwood's creation of generic black archetypes, Warner's individualization of the facial features of his white victims works only to exacerbate his imagining of these self-liberated men's physiognomies as bestialized and contorted: they are reduced to a homogenous mass, among whom any recognition of Turner, as their revolutionary leader, is rendered impossible.

However seemingly antithetical in emphasis, Wedgwood's and Warner's iconic representations of black enslaved subjects function as two sides of the same coin by endorsing polarized stereotypes of enslaved women, men, and children. Black subjects appeared, on the one hand, as victimized martyrs and passive spectacles available for white consumption, appropriation, and commodification, while on the other they inspired fear as bestialized, bloodthirsty, and devilish barbarians. Simultaneously hyper-*visible* as icons and hyper-*invisible* as individuals, these imaginings left the complex psychological and physical realities of the enslaved aesthetically and politically off-limits, not only in the dominant iconography illustrated here but pervasively also in white official records and mainstream literary traditions.

The racist biases at work within the white visual archive—including not only abolitionist imagery and proslavery propaganda but also popular cartoons, pseudo-scientific diagrams, and fine artworks—worked to provide further ballast to the depredations enacted against enslaved subjects in dominant white official records. There they paradoxically remained only absent-presences, as a vast range of documents—such as plantation ledgers, slave ship logs, bills of sale, scientific treatises, slave auction lists, and runaway slave advertisements—listed them solely as property. The lives of countless women, men, and children appeared only in dehumanized lists, in what formerly enslaved man turned writer, philosopher, and statesman, Frederick Douglass, denigrated as the "chattel records" of a white supremacist nation (Douglass 1853, 175). The psychological and physical realities of black lives thus remained beyond the pale of white imagining even as antislavery advocates, no less than proslavery apologists, sought to "create a white fiction of blackness" by viewing African Americans, as theorized by Henry Louis Gates Jr., through a "filter of a web of racist images" (Gates, 52).

Artistic Defiance

An African, African Caribbean, and African American literary and visual arts tradition functions as a powerful countertextual and visual archive by consisting not only of slave narratives, poetry, essays, historiographical works, oratorical discourse, religious tracts, and political essays but also of paintings, photographs, drawings, and sculpture. Constituting both a radical departure and an artistic declaration of independence, eighteenth- and nineteenth-century black authors and artists, both enslaved and free, self-reflexively sought to establish alternative formal and thematic parameters within which to put flesh onto the bare bones of a white popular transatlantic imaginary. They sought to recuperate black women, men, and children as legitimate subjects of fine art portraiture and textual reimagining by challenging formal boundaries and generic conventions. These writers' and artists' diverse modes of social, political, and intellectual resistance remained inextricable from their fight for the right to an "art for art's sake ethos" in their bid not only to reclaim their humanity but to define their right to artistry.

As Frederick Douglass emphasized, to create a "pure work of art" was a political, no less than an aesthetic, necessity for black writers and authors intent on inspiring sublime awe in white audiences unaccustomed to acknowledging black legal or political equality, let alone philosophical, intellectual, or aesthetic prowess (Douglass 1979, 460). Many black authors and artists, the vast majority of whom had been enslaved, galvanized a diverse transatlantic literary and art tradition into existence by directly signifying upon, riffing off of, and recontextualizing the skewed racist biases of the white textual and visual lexicon.

Despite the clear-cut tradition of self-reflexive acts and arts of black authorship and artistry, these black aesthetic practices have remained largely beyond the pale of scholarly investigation and popular imagination. This lack of awareness has resulted in underdeveloped and oversimplified summaries of their textual and visual archive as significant solely as political strategies rather than also as "works of art." Thus, the white legal presumption of the right to examine, inspect, and even weigh black flesh, pound by pound, to appropriate the value of black bodies as property throughout the antebellum period has had lasting effects. Its intellectual legacy can be found in a continuing penchant for measuring black bodies and souls according to a reductive schema intent upon authentication, appropriation, and commodification of their narratives, histories, and artworks.

Such intellectual disregard has generated yet more collateral damage, not only in theoretical blind spots but also in vast gaps in critical awareness of the full black diasporic visual and textual archive. The work of excavation, recovery, and even identification of the diverse works produced by black writers and authors, both enslaved and free, is ongoing, and their outpouring of diverse bodies of visual and textual works will never be fully known. Such omissions are due not only to the tendency among white record keepers to demonstrate very little interest in preserving black artworks and literatures but also to a widespread scholarly dismissal and denial of these works' aesthetic value.

The responsibility not only to read but also to engage imaginatively with the signifying dynamics at work within a multifaceted African, African American, and African Caribbean visual and textual archive lies with critics. The slave narrative, a far-from-fixed artistic genre that came to dominate the North American and British transatlantic imaginary over the centuries, provides a particularly powerful place from which to begin to theorize the complex formal techniques and thematic devices in black authors' and artists' vast bodies of work. Part picaresque adventure tale, part "trials and tribulations" narrative, part a coming-of-age narrative, part spiritual autobiography, part travelogue, part oratorical invective, and part political tract, the slave narrative genre is a hybrid and experimental literary form that has been repeatedly subjected to critical dismissal. Scholars have discounted these writers' creative uses of symbolism, metaphor, and allegorical allusion in favor of an overemphasis on their seeming sociopolitical implications. For white audiences seemingly committed to the representation of black "real-life" experiences rendered only in literal terms, these works have risen or fallen according to their presumed veracity as formerly enslaved narrators engaged in explicitly experimental and transgressive aesthetic devices to their peril.

Formerly enslaved women and men chose to defy reductive narrative templates. And by giving full reign to their imaginative capabilities and forays into artistry over and above a rigorous and reductive adherence to a factual representation of their experiences, they faced terrible consequences. One powerful example was Harriet Jacobs's decision to write her narrative, *Incidents in the Life of a Slave Girl* (1861, published under the pseudonym Linda Brent), as an eclectic and experimental work in which she juxtaposed an array of genres including the bildungsroman, the domestic and sentimental novel, the adventure tale, and the confessional autobiography, to name but a few. This radical strategy was not without its cost, as it had the powerful consequence of calling the work's authenticity into question. The work was accordingly consigned to political and cultural oblivion for over 100 years prior to its identification and recuperation in the 1980s by groundbreaking scholar, Jean Fagan Yellin.

A similar difficulty confronted Frederick Douglass while writing his second autobiographical narrative, *My Bondage and My Freedom* (1855), a work in which he chose to interrogate the problems that the antebellum white abolitionist framework presented to black narrators. Candidly admitting to tensions between black and white antislavery activists, he was frank regarding his struggle to liberate his oratorical and literary discourse not from white racist dismissal but from the advice of such white abolitionists as John Collins, who insisted, "Give us the facts," as "we will take care of the philosophy" (Douglass 1855, 361). Refusing to heed any such caution, however, Douglass was unequivocal: "it did not entirely satisfy me to *narrate* wrongs; I felt like *denouncing* them." In his radical rejection of dominant formal constraints, therefore, Douglass shared Jacobs's commitment to aesthetic independence by insisting, "I must speak just the word that seemed to *me* the word to be spoken *by* me" (361–362).

Such aesthetic independence, again, was not without consequences. Just as his white abolitionist sponsors had predicted, he met immediate difficulties on the grounds that, as Douglass himself conceded, "People doubted if I had ever been a slave. They said I did not talk like a slave, look like a slave, nor act like a slave" (362). Regardless of white pressures to the contrary, formerly enslaved men and women such as Jacobs and Douglass, and thousands of others known and still unknown, sought to wrest control over the signifying dynamics of dominant genres, including the slave narrative, as they fought to create multilayered, self-reflexive works that challenged the permissible boundaries surrounding what it meant, to whites, to "talk like a slave" or "look like a slave."

Close examinations of the slave narrative's archetypal conventions by white mainstream scholars have repeatedly attempted to adjudicate a work's successes or failures by focusing solely on a simple set of staple superficial features: an "I was born" opening, a "written by him- or herself" authentication of authorship, a coming-to-consciousness regarding enslavement, an acquisition of literacy, an emphasis upon vouchsafing black humanity according to white Western mores via a conversion to Christianity, and a determination to foreground the fundamental role played by white abolitionist-authored letters of introduction and/or signed petitions. In fact, formerly enslaved black writers, intent on countering the nefarious ways in which their commodification as objects for classification and categorization had rendered their humanity null and void, were at war against these formal and thematic constraints of the slave narrative genre. Engaging in an array of visual and textual resistance strategies, these authors shared Douglass's and Jacobs's determination to destabilize the representational strategies proliferating within the dominant white proslavery imagination by employing the literary genre in eclectic ways.

Beyond rejecting the widespread insistence that these narrators construct only what white British antislavery activist Granville Sharp identified as admissible testimonies or "iron arguments" against slavery (Sharp), they took up the additional burden of attempting to memorialize black interior realities. They fought for their freedom as authors and artists engaged in creating multilayered, ambiguous, and metaphorically complex narratives. Formerly enslaved poet Phillis Wheatley's assertion that "Ethiopians speak sometimes by simile" (Wheatley, 125) expressed the fundamental importance they found in developing an alternative framework in which to theorize the literary, no less than the visual, dynamics integral to these works.

Across their oeuvre, by both necessity and design, black writers and artists engaged in formal experimentation to cross generic boundaries and expose the failures of dominant narrative forms to cut to the heart of the realities of lives as lived in slavery. Lacunae, fragmentation, and ellipses not only signaled a powerful rejection of the seemingly omniscient and detached narrative trade in black subjects solely as representative exemplars. They relied upon aesthetic subterfuge, indirection, and a narrative poetics of withholding to accentuate a white lack of knowledge regarding enslaved subjects turned narrators and authentic individuals. Foregrounding satire, irony, and semantic play across their works, they simultaneously critiqued the ideological and formal constraints of dominant white literary conventions.

Textual and Visual Hybridity

Formerly enslaved narrators typically relied on a highly visualized use of language to inspire audiences to a visceral and cognitive engagement. Working to defy reductive claims regarding what it meant not only to "talk like a slave" but to "look like a slave," the vast majority of eighteenth- and nineteenth-century black writers strained against the limitations of the words on the page with hard-hitting graphic imagery. But the writers of slave narratives also sought to declare their independence from a no less insidious visual schema. The aesthetic and political complexities of their narratives gained force via an appreciation of the complex relationship between text and image across their bodies of work. This integral dimension of black authors' signifying practices within the slave-narrative form and across many other genres—including oratorical discourse, historiographical works, poetry, and drama—has received little to no theorization. Creating emotionally charged vignettes characterized by an aesthetics of juxtaposition, disjuncture, and fragmentation in order to compel white audiences to acts of empathetic engagement and political reform, formerly enslaved writers laid bare the psychological and physical traumas of slavery in unequivocal and highly visualized terms.

More defiantly still, many enslaved and self-emancipated writers explicitly confronted the signifying possibilities of extant literary modes by importing an array of visual artworks into their hybrid narratives. These images typically took the form of engraved frontispiece portraits of the authors and/or interior illustrations that reinforced the haunting

Figure 3. Phillis Wheatley.

and works. Tellingly, this portrait also includes a book, sitting to the left of her own half-written manuscript, thereby exulting in her act of writing as indivisible from her skill in the art of reading. Clearly, Moorhead's Wheatley is no enslaved manual laborer but rather a groundbreaking icon of black female intellectual prowess.

No less powerfully, formerly enslaved narrators also accompanied their works with numerous interior images. Thus, fugitive-turned-author Moses Roper reinforced the haunting poignancy of his work, *Narrative of the Adventures and Escape of Moses Roper, from American Slavery* (1848), with diagrammatic illustrations in which an unidentified artist powerfully juxtaposed generic—for which read *representative*—and particular—for which read *autobiographical*—instances of enslaved torture. Thus, one such drawing—captioned "A woman with iron horns and bells on, to keep her from running away" (Roper, 14)—generates haunting emotive effects through the facelessness of the generic enslaved female subject, which contrasts powerfully with the detailed representation of her clothing and of the individual bells to accentuate the gruesome realities of her physical incarceration.

More revealingly still, such a stock representation of archetypal black suffering exists in expressive contrast to the illustrator's later depiction of Roper's own torture in a drawing that reveals his own body hanging from a joist while his physiognomy is characterized by individualized facial features that render the specificity of his experiences incontestable. Opting for a slippery relationship between text and image across his narrative, Roper contrasted visual vignettes dramatizing the particularities of his own experiences with textual tableaux foregrounding the atrocities of mass suffering, so as to render his own autobiographical realities indivisible from transatlantic histories of slavery. As acts and arts of reclamation and radicalism, authors' frontispieces and/or numerous interior images signified the black author's ultimate authority in resisting their ongoing marginalization and annihilation, not only in "chattel records" but also in "chattel narratives" and even "chattel images."

A scholarly engagement with the visual archive that many of these writers chose to integrate into their works has the potential to begin to do justice to their otherwise-elided experimental literary techniques. Ultimately, formerly enslaved authors' slip-

potency of epiphanic moments in their texts. One of the most iconic eighteenth-century author portraits can be found accompanying Phillis Wheatley's *Poems on Various Subjects, Religious and Moral* (1773; figure 3).

Wheatley's portrait not only broke new ground as one of the only surviving works to have been attributed to an "African Painter"—an individual named Scipio Moorhead, about whom very little is known—but as a powerful image that exists in stark contrast to the popular circulation of black female subjects as objects of sexual violation and physical exploitation. Subverting her subservient status as a "Negro Servant," according to Moorhead's imagining, Wheatley appears here in modest attire while she adopts a contemplative pose, as accentuated by her left hand which rests upon her chin; her profiled physiognomy engages in visionary contemplation as she renders Douglass's preoccupation with art making yet more explicit by holding a quill in her right hand and as poised before a half-written page. Defying her corporeal status, she is shown literally writing herself into being as she exhibits her significance as the producer rather than the product of antislavery reform by appearing in the guise of an authoritative interlocutor of her own life pery juxtapositions of visual and textual narratives confronted the failures of dominant modes to represent a gamut of unmemorialized black experiences. The slave narrative comes to life as site of formal and thematic tension only through an active (rather than passive) and imaginative (rather than factual) engagement with this genre's multilayered dynamics. Working not only to speak the unspoken and see the unseen, they also interrogated formal boundaries in a radical determination to speak the unseeable and see the unspeakable.

Contemporary Legacies

The legacies of enslavement live painfully on in contemporary cultures all around the Atlantic. Black visual artists of African, African Caribbean, African American, and black British descent, no less than writers, continue to experiment with the same technique of recycling, revising, and resisting the iconography and textual narratives dominant within a white transatlantic imaginary. Modern black Atlantic painters, sculptors, muralists, photographers, and performance artists have continued to employ the literary motifs and visual archetypes established by formerly enslaved and self-emancipated black writers and activists in provocative and challenging ways. Imaging slavery while imagining freedom, their multifarious and hybrid works continue to transform "chattel records" into "works of art." They do so by turning the racist biases of dominant textual and visual filters of perception into self-reflexive and aesthetically experimental vignettes of the hidden factual histories—as well as the hidden inner stories—of enslavement and emancipation. Living and working in the twentieth and twenty-first centuries, contemporary authors and artists take inspiration from their antecedents in slavery via a powerful commitment to creating multi-layered and mixed-media works in which they transform white images of slavery into black visions of freedom.

CELESTE-MARIE BERNIER

Bibliography

Andrews, William L. *To Tell a Free Story: The First Century of Afro-American Autobiography, 1760–1865.* Champaign: University of Illinois Press, 1988.

Bernier, Celeste-Marie. *Characters of Blood: Black Heroism in the Transatlantic Imagination.* Charlottesville: University of Virginia Press, 2012.

Frederick Douglass. *The Heroic Slave.* In *Autographs for Freedom,* edited by Julia Griffiths, 174–239. Boston: John P. Jewett, 1853.

———. *My Bondage and My Freedom.* New York: Miller, Orton & Mulligan, 1855.

———. "Pictures and Progress" (3 December 1861). Rpt. The Frederick Douglass Papers. Series One: Speeches, Debates, and Interviews, edited by John W. Blassingame, 452–473. Vol. 3. New Haven, CT: Yale University Press, 1979.

Gates, Henry Louis, Jr. "The Face and Voice of Blackness." In *Modern Art and Society: An Anthology of Social and Multicultural Readings,* edited by Maurice Berger, 51–72. Boulder, CO: Westview Press, 1994.

Jacobs, Harriet. *Incidents in the Life of a Slave Girl.* Edited by Lydia Maria Child. Boston: Published for the author, 1861.

Rodriguez, Barbara. *Autobiographical Inscriptions: Form, Personhood, and the American Woman Writer of Color.* Oxford: Oxford University Press, 1999.

Rohrbach, Augusta. *Truth Stranger than Fiction: Race, Realism, and the U.S. Literary Marketplace.* London: Palgrave Macmillan, 2002.

Roper, Moses. *Narrative of the Adventures and Escape of Moses Roper, from American Slavery.* Berwick-Upon-Tweed: Published for the author, 1848.

Sharp, Granville. "Letter to Mr. Sergeant Davy," February 5, 1772. Quoted in Greta Gerzina, *Black England: Life before Emancipation,* 99–100. London: Allison and Busby, 1991.

Stauffer, John. *The Black Hearts of Men: Radical Abolitionists and the Transformation of Race.* Cambridge, MA: Harvard University Press, 2004.

Wheatley, Phillis. *The Poems of Phillis Wheatley* (1773). Edited by Julian D. Mason Jr. Chapel Hill: University of North Carolina Press, 1966.

Yellin, Jean Fagan, ed. *The Harriet Jacobs Family Papers.* 2 vols. Durham: University of North Carolina Press, 2008.

Literary Genres: Captivity Narratives

The captivity narrative, in which the seizure of an individual or group of people by an ethnically or culturally alien people is recounted, has a long and prestigious literary pedigree. The earliest examples, such as the capture of Odysseus by the Cyclops in Homer's *Odyssey* and the enslavement of the Jews by the Egyptians in the Old Testament, introduced the genre's central themes of physical, psychological, and spiritual suffering, as well as questions of personal, national, and cultural identities, that emerged from the sixteenth to the nineteenth centuries in Atlantic captivity narratives.

The expansion of European trade and exploration in the early-modern period greatly increased Europeans' opportunities to encounter alien cultures powerful enough militarily and politically to capture and hold them for extended periods of time. Tales of capture and return consequently became one of the most common and capacious prose forms of the era. Such narratives often incorporated tales of adventure as well as of travail. Many of the first early-modern captivity accounts told of imprisonment along the Barbary Coast or in other parts of Muslim North Africa. Captivity narratives often included ethnography as well as autobiography. They also frequently served religious and political agendas, emphasizing the purported superiority of European culture to those of others. For example, Anthony Munday's *The Admirable Deliverance of 266 Christians . . . from the Captivity of the Turks* (London, 1608) contrasts Christian Providence and English liberty with Muslim infidelity and Turkish oppression. The agendas of the early-modern captivity narratives, combined with the fact that many of them are as-told-to tales transcribed and edited by amanuenses, as well as their authors' desires to entertain their readers, frequently led them to combine facts and fiction.

Following the European discovery, exploration, and settlement of the Americas, captivity narratives became a distinctively transatlantic genre. Álvar Núñez Cabeza de Vaca published *La Relación* in Madrid, Spain, in 1542, following his release from captivity by Karankawa Indians on Galveston Island, on the Gulf Coast of present-day Texas. The best-known of the early Indian captivity narratives in English is Mary Rowlandson's *The Sovereignty and Goodness of God*, published under different titles on both sides of the Atlantic in 1682. Its account of the kidnapping of a relatively defenseless victim in a New England raiding expedition during

Figure 1. Mary Rowlandson's captivity narrative, published under various titles including the one shown in this 1773 edition, nearly a century after the work's original publication. The illustration of Rowlandson defending herself with a gun might be a marketing tactic, as she doesn't mention such a detail in the narrative.

King Philip's War (1676) and its themes—the disruption of domestic life, the temptation to identify with kidnappers, the return home, the testing of religious faith and cultural identity, and the validation of Christianity—anticipated plots and subjects typical in many subsequent captivity narratives, especially those that combined elements of spiritual autobiography.

But seeing Rowlandson's as the model captivity narrative can cause historians and literary critics to overlook the flexibility of the genre, especially from an Atlantic perspective. In *The Redeemed Captive*

Returning to Zion (Boston, 1707), John Williams elaborated the religious agenda reflected in Rowlandson's title to include an attack on Roman Catholicism within a more general political assault on France, England's imperial rival in North America. Barbary captivity narratives continued to be published, such as Susanna Rowson's drama, *Slaves in Algiers* (Philadelphia, 1795), and Royall Tyler's novel *The Algerine Captive* (Walpole, New Hampshire, 1797). These later adaptations of the genre contrast American republicanism with African despotism. Some captivity narratives had sub-Saharan African settings, increasingly adapted to the purposes of the growing abolitionist struggles against the Atlantic slave trade: Bullfinch Lambe's "Letter on Captivity in Dahomy," in William Smith's *A New Voyage to Guinea* (London, 1744); Robert Norris's *Memoirs of the Reign of Bossa Ahadee, King of Dahomey* (London, 1793); and Archibald Dalzel's *The History of Dahomy, an Inland Kingdom* (London, 1793).

The capaciousness of the captivity-narrative genre and its significance in anglophone Atlantic history are particularly evident in eighteenth-century texts by and about authors of African descent, especially those whose experience of the Middle Passage transformed their identities, first to Africans in America and eventually to African Americans or African Britons. The earliest published captivity narrative by a person of African descent was Briton Hammon's *Narrative of the Uncommon Sufferings and Surprizing Deliverance of Briton Hammon, a Negro Man* (Boston, 1760). Sailing from Boston to the Caribbean, he is captured by Indians who sell him into Spanish slavery in Cuba. He eventually escapes, joins the Royal Navy, and is providentially reunited in London with his former employer, or perhaps owner, with whom he returns to Boston. Whether Hammon was a free man or a slave remains uncertain from his own account. Published while Britain was at war with France, the story of Hammon's life follows the conventional trajectory of the religious-captivity narrative, blended with a patriotic political agenda.

Eighteenth-century accounts of captive survivors of the Middle Passage radically transformed the captivity genre by conflating it with narratives of conversion. In the as-told-to tale *A Narrative of the Most Remarkable Particulars in the Life of James Albert Ukawsaw Gronniosaw, an African Prince* (Bath, England, 1772), and the first-person spiritual autobiography and abolitionist text, *The Interesting Narrative of the Life of Olaudah Equiano, or Gustavus Vassa, the African. Written by Himself* (London, 1789), innocent Africans are victims of European kidnappers. These narratives of the civilization of pagans captured by European Christians replaced earlier accounts of European anxieties about the possibility of being assimilated into pagan cultures. Both texts, however, do so by ironically reversing earlier celebrations of Christianity. The appropriation of Christianity by Gronniosaw and Equiano renders them morally superior to their white readers. Their narratives employ the stranger-in-a-strange-land trope to enable their subjects to speak as observers and critics of societies they are in, but not of.

Although fact-based captivity stories continued to be published in the English-speaking Atlantic World during the nineteenth century, they decreased greatly in frequency and cultural significance, largely because of the growing ability of Europeans to protect themselves as they explored and settled new territories. At the beginning of the century, European countries and the United States were able to stop Muslim rulers along the Barbary Coast from kidnapping their citizens. The closing of the frontier in North America and the rapidly increasing military superiority of white Americans substantially decreased the incidence of Indian captivities. Abolition of the legal slave trade by Britain and the United States in the first decade ended Middle Passage captivity narratives. These were succeeded by a new genre, the African American slave narrative, accounts of people born into slavery. For European writers and readers, chronicles of exploration celebrating Christianity, European commerce, and modern civilization—hallmarks of nineteenth-century imperialism—became the literary order of the day.

VINCENT CARRETTA

Bibliography

Snader, Joe. *Caught between Worlds: British Captivity Narratives in Fact and Fiction.* Lexington: University Press of Kentucky, 2000.

Voigt, Lisa. *Writing Captivity in the Early Modern Atlantic: Circulations of Knowledge and Authority in the Ibe-*

rian and English Imperial Worlds. Chapel Hill: University of North Carolina Press, 2009.

Literary Genres: Travel Narratives and Compilations

Memory, autobiography, fiction, metaphor, fact? The corpus of Atlantic travel literature produced in the 350 years to the early nineteenth century presents significant critical challenges owing to difficulties of disciplinary classification, defiance of aesthetic expectation, dubious accuracy, complicity in systems of exploitation, and sometimes shameless promotion of individual or commercial interests. Nonetheless, travel writing may be considered one of the most important cultural products of the early-modern Atlantic. Inscribing complex convergences of peoples and cultures previously unknown to one another into a system of commercial, biological, and cultural exchanges, narratives of travel provide a layered resource for understanding the matrix of geohistorical relationships between the many subjectivities brought together in the Atlantic. At the same time, this literature raises fundamental questions regarding the implication of literary aesthetics in networks of political power.

Early Fantasies and Facts

Early-modern travel writing began in 1492 with Christopher Columbus's voyage from Cádiz in search of a western trade route to China. Inspired by the eastward journey of the thirteenth-century Venetian merchant Marco Polo, whose travelogue *Il Milione*, or the *Travels of Marco Polo*, had introduced the idea of Asia to Europe, this voyage was the first of four made by Columbus, and he recorded it in detail in his captain's log for later presentation to his sponsors, the Catholic monarchs of Aragon and Castile. The later-compiled *Journal of the Four Voyages*, reconstructed from surviving fragments of the log and fifteenth-century printed editions of a letter announcing his "discovery" of the Americas, now constitutes the first of many tales to emerge from, and in the following centuries to contribute to, processes of European exploration, conquest, colonialism, enslavement, a range of new

literary forms, the culture of leisured reading, and the cult of literary/commercial celebrity.

Columbus's mistaken insistence that he had reached Asia underlines the fabulous, even orientalist, nature of a disparate genre of travel and descriptive accounts that formed the bulk of American literature until around 1700. In the period between the 1490s and the 1840s, Europe looked obsessively outward, producing narratives of incorporation that also constructed lasting models of cultural difference. Travel writing, including mapping the topography of newly encountered territories, quickly became an enabling technology of military and political encroachment. For example, Bernal Diaz's *Historia verdadera de la conquista de la Nueva España* (*True History of the Conquest of New Spain* [1632]), a chronicle of the subjugation of the Aztec Empire by Hernán Cortés and 700 enlisted men, confirmed the dominion of European power, positioning the chronicler—in addition to the explorer and conqueror—as agent of the Spanish crown.

At the same time, tales of travel assigned Old World values to New World spaces, attributing symbolic meaning derived from Christian belief systems to landscapes and peoples who had never known them. In the early literature of the Iberian-controlled Southern Hemisphere, as well as that of the Puritan colonies of the North, religious faith understood European conquest and settlement as proof of divine will. Cotton Mather's epically conceived *Magnalia Christi Americana* (*Christ's Great Works in America*) charted Christ's victories in the New World, while Puritan prose more generally described expansion as an ongoing battle against Satan, whose persistent attempts to tempt early settlers into wickedness and sin generated a set of lasting metaphoric associations in U.S. American literature: the forest, the night, the symbolism of color, the Indian devil, associations between love and death. Jorge Cañizares-Esguerra argues the case for Satan's equivalent playbook in Latin American writing, suggesting that attention to the hemispheric archive reveals Anglo and Latin American colonizations not as entirely distinct processes creating incompatible worlds but rooted in shared beliefs in Christian providence.

As compelling narratives of European meetings with the marvelous novelties of the Americas, much early travel writing is freighted with the predeterminations of a European logic of exploration in which expansion of trade and accumulation of wealth are inextricably embedded with the spread of Christianity. Travel writing thus insulated the practicalities of conquest against moral censure and limited scrutiny of the narrating subject by inventing the European traveler as an agent of religious and political progress. The historical tensions attending the colonial process were nonetheless quick to emerge in efforts to interpret the perceptions of American subjects for European readerships. Dominican friar Bartolomé de Las Casas's *Brevísima relación de la destrucción de las Indias* (*A Brief Account of the Destruction of the Indies* [1552]) paradoxically suggested both the need to ameliorate conditions for indigenous American peoples and the potential of enslaved African labor for Spain's Indies. Additional questions of narrative position present themselves in North American captivity narratives of the seventeenth century, in which the captive, normally a woman, rejects temptation while she awaits rescue, thereby establishing the captive body as a metaphor for Puritan purity and resolve. As Richard Slotkin writes, the captive's redemption confirms the promise of Christian salvation for the faithful among the readership, while "harrowing the hearts" of the as-yet unconverted.

The Politics of Prose

From its earliest days, writing about Atlantic travel was an explicitly politicized mixture of the secular and the religious, helping shape debates in American settlements as well as in European centers of power. The earliest travelogues, providing information on navigable sea routes, receptions by natives, and potential sources of riches, addressed themselves to wealthy patrons. Apparently little concerned with literary poetics, these texts took shape as private records, memoirs, or private correspondence. However, although literacy levels were generally low, the coincidental emergence of printing technology meant that private correspondence was sometimes destined for a wider public, as Columbus's announcement of his "discovery" in a letter to Luis de Sant Angel (1493) and the Venetian Pietro Pasqualigo's equivalent "Letter to his brothers" (1501), both published and circulated in pamphlet form, illustrate.

Print technology influenced travel writing by confirming the commercial value of adventure, as Elizabethan England turned its attention to the opportunities of the Atlantic. Tales of travel quickly showed their potential to earn money and fame for their writers, generating overlapping roles for the professional traveler and author. Walter Raleigh's *The Discovery of the Large, Rich and Bewtiful Empyre of Guiana* (1596), which detailed his search for "El Dorado" in northern South America, became a sensation when published in London. Meanwhile, commercial publications of travel compendia fed a growing public appetite for information and titillation. In an age of competition for sovereignty overseas, travel writing also proved useful in meeting the need for strategic forms of moral relativism—in establishing a distinction between Spanish piracy and English privateering, for example. Such was the imaginary purchase of travel that it soon became a vehicle for important works of philosophy and literature, including Thomas More's *Utopia* (1516), inflecting what Stephen Greenblatt calls "renaissance self fashioning" in English poetry. Most famously, William Shakespeare's *The Tempest* (1611) dramatized the fraught entanglements between European and American peoples, using a plot line that imagined the outcome of contact as tragedy.

Travelers' narratives of their voyages tended to adopt a more pragmatic tone. Typically the genre was shaped by the authorizing voice of the European male narrator, claiming to present disinterested observations of far-off people, places, practices, and things. Regardless of the fantastic nature of many early accounts, which regaled audiences with tales of cannibalism, fabulous riches, childlike natives, fearsome warlords, and innumerable intriguing women, these travel writings positioned themselves as conventionally realist, forwarding the fiction they presented as reliable, firsthand, eyewitness experiences. They relied on the proposition that narrative can bridge a gap in knowledge and experience between writer and reader. In this way travel writing establishes a form of pedagogic intimacy with its readers, who by learning from, become complicit in the ideological frameworks that inform the presentation of narrative and the cultural meanings superimposed on the information it contains.

Travel writing as reportage therefore appears deliberately to construct clear lines of generic separation from literary forms forwarding themselves explicitly as works of the imagination. Many texts are formally distinguished by the relationship they establish between the written word and visual imagery, by their overt correlation of narrative description and the testimonial function of the eye, in maps, frontispiece portraits, and other illustrations. Visual support for the truth claim of the narrative using increasingly intricate or technologically reliable visual detail characterizes much travel writing into the twenty-first century. In the context of the early-modern Atlantic, making visible what was far away and otherwise unknowable was a powerful means of creating, then controlling, the geohistorical record because it confirmed the literal status of narrative observation.

Stories of Atlantic travel sit in complex aesthetic relation to earlier forms of writing. On the one hand, they are part of the imaginary continuity of Western literature, aligning themselves with traditions predating the modern period, specifically with the Greek epics the *Iliad* and *Odyssey* (c. 800 BCE), which mapped the ancient world and in which themes of identity, exile, and home are prevalent; or with the medieval romance epic, in which the quest motif drives a story of high adventure including encounters with fabulous and potentially deadly foes while underwriting contemporary forms of gender identity and political hierarchy. On the other hand, Atlantic travel writing also carved a space for the quintessentially modern form of the novel. By blurring the boundaries of the factual, it suggested the literary value of prose fiction at a time when such validity typically accrued only to history. An early example in English, Aphra Behn's Restoration narrative *Oroonoko; or, the Royal Slave* (1688), drew on the currency accorded the travelers' tales of the period as well as on Behn's contestable personal experiences in Suriname. Positioning itself as witnessed fact, using a first-person narrator of markedly royalist sentiment, *Oroonoko* told a tragic tale of nobility, love, enslavement, and death. Although thematically more concerned with English rather than colonial politics, with kingship at home rather than slavery in the Americas, it is remarkable in its sympathetic presentation of Native Americans and of enslaved Africans as the focus of empathetic identification for readers. Written for commercial purposes, embedded in the colonial project and ris-

ing capitalist economy that drove the ever-increasing triangular trade in captive Africans, the work nonetheless provided an early counterpoint to trends in literary culture that increasingly characterized peoples of African or indigenous American descent as history-less and beyond the possibility of humanist representation.

Daniel Defoe's wildly popular fictional travelogue *Robinson Crusoe* (1719), for example, drew on these floating stereotypes of Native Americans (and Africans) as savage, childish, dangerous, and dependent in order to consolidate a model of European manhood as resilient, adaptable, inherently civilized, and possessed of natural leadership. The relationship between Crusoe and the man he rescues from the clutches of Carib tribesmen and renames "Friday" epitomizes how tropes of travel writing gradually came to underwrite the hegemony of white masculinity and to consolidate Atlantic hierarchies of race, gender, and labor. Further, not only did Defoe's work cast Crusoe ashore on an unpopulated island, suggesting land to be an available and uncontested resource, but—significantly in an age in which discussions of government became increasingly fraught—it also naturalized a racially based social contract between Crusoe and Friday, in which the latter is unquestioningly loyal and subservient and allows Crusoe to re-create him, through Christian conversion and the English language, into a darker, stranger, subject version of himself. Indeed, it was in the travel literature of Europeans and Euroamericans that "whiteness" was first invented in response to a need to rationalize the imposition of a racial hierarchy based on an increasingly institutionalized set of exploitative relationships imposed by colonial governments and continued in the independent American states that emerged from the late eighteenth century onward.

Atlantic travel writing, whether fictional or factual, then, served to confirm European historical agency, in part through attribution of essentialist "racial" characteristics that inscribed the symbolic as well as literal ascendency of whiteness in everwidening spheres of capitalism and militarism. Despite the prevalence of this political rationalization, ethical and moral doubts did find occasional expression in parodies of these travelers' tales. Jonathan Swift's *Gulliver's Travels* (1726) played with the slippage between artifice and fact, satirizing eighteenth-century British society, including the Grand Tour of Europe (and the Near East), a social ritual in the lives of young men of prospects since the seventeenth century.

The Grand Tour was an ideological exercise intended to "finish" young British men who had come down from Oxford or Cambridge. It allowed them to build on their formal educational experience by confirming exactly what history was and where culture might be found. Following a brief hiatus during the Napoleonic wars, the Grand Tour boomed when tourists, keen to prove their cultural credentials, flocked to a route designed not only for pleasure but also to authorize accounts of European expansion as a civilizing mission by correlating ancient and modern empires. By the end of the eighteenth century, the popularity, circulation, and lasting representative impact of travelogues and their fictional derivatives confirmed that what had begun as record keeping had blossomed into a set of conventions, genres, and subgenres that mapped and remapped the spaces, places, and subjectivities of the Atlantic in relation to contemporary political, ideological, and economic centers of power.

New literary forms weaving the mythology of the exotic or delineations of difference into the logic of expansion were not the only things to emerge from travel literature's transcription and encryption of America, Europe, and later Africa in the Western imagination. The turn of the nineteenth century witnessed the rise of the scientific traveler, less explicitly concerned with immediate commercial gain, the identification of available resources, or the possibilities of political expansion than with the purer motive of advancing scientific knowledge. Travel literature, although easily accused of departing from the factual or even the credible, contributed substantially to the development of knowledge accepted as geographical, geological, zoological, and botanical. In the nineteenth century, travel and travel writing in the guise of the scientific field journal became keystones in rationalist accounts of the natural world and in the development of scientific method in the biological and geographical sciences.

Scientific Expeditions

Of the scientific travel writing by individuals linked to the European societies and academies that flowered in this period, the most significant was that produced by Alexander von Humboldt. His *Le voyage aux régions équinoxiales du Nouveau Continent, fait en 1799–1804, par Alexandre de Humboldt et Aimé Bonpland* (1807) was a meticulous account of the geography, geology, and plants that he studied during his travels in South America, Cuba, and New Spain. Humboldt's detailed accounts of his observations greatly expanded stores of empirical data, providing the basis of "Humboldtian science" or quantitative method. As part of what Mary Louise Pratt calls "the reinvention of América," or the refraction of Latin America through the lens of German romanticism, Humboldt also conceptualized "nature" as an overwhelming and irrational force into which the intricacies of the region and its peoples could be collapsed. Stylistically, he also departed from the traditions of realism and reportage that characterized earlier work, using emotive description and suggestions of the numinous to generate an atmosphere of "otherness" that arguably prevails even in contemporary accounts of Latin America. Humboldt's discursive politics, in other words, reinforced the worldviews of European, North American, and Creole elites, including their attitudes toward indigenous and black populations.

The promise of scientific discovery reinvigorated travel writing. Gentleman naturalist Charles Darwin's first publication, the exciting memoir *Journal and Remarks, 1832–35* (first published in 1838 and commonly known as *Voyage of the Beagle*), based on an 1831–1836 expedition to South America, confirmed his reputation as a writer of popular literature as well as his stature as a scientist. Adventurous biographical detail therefore continued to produce personas amenable to public consumption, and through this personalism a form of commercial celebrity, even as it heralded a new era of European imperial activity based on technology and scientific knowledge. The memoir contains preliminary hints of Darwin's best-known contribution to science, the theory of evolution through natural selection, in the second edition of 1845, underlining the centrality of travel writing in the development of modern scientific knowledge.

Scientific travel writing reconfirmed the discursive capacity of the genre, which in its Atlantic years provided a vehicle for autobiography, populism, toadyism, cartographic record, celebrity, sensationalism, and scientific discourse, no less than for conventional fiction. As the mid-nineteenth century confirmed the success of the United States as a political entity, Alexis de Tocqueville's *Democracy in America* (*De la Démocratie en Amérique*, 1835) reinvented travel writing once again, this time as sociological authority. Tocqueville's work explained Jacksonian America's postcolonial social structures and democratic political order to a French audience in ways that acknowledged the parity of U.S. identity with that of republican France, thus marking a turning point in constructions of the European relationship with the Americas, at least for this one region. This literary handover of rights of self-representation to the new nation closed the historical circle begun by seventeenth-century Puritan migrants eager to build a city upon a hill. Subsequent travel writing about the United States departed from its counterparts for other regions of the hemisphere because, regardless of travelers' enthusiasm for the wildness of the West, or their sometime ambivalence to the repressions of the South, a level of social and cultural identification with the United States persisted, based on an understanding of its political space as modern, fundamentally progressive, and ultimately permitting a full flourishing of the Western political and literary personality.

Subaltern Travel

Black travel writing produced in the United States and the Caribbean resonated with a less triumphal appreciation of the American experience. Emerging from contexts requiring nuanced calibrations of literary form able to sidestep conventional racist exclusions, black travel writing repeatedly assumed hybrid generic forms that challenged the conventions they initially appeared to invoke. A centuries-long history of modern black Atlantic travel stretches from Leo Africanus's renaissance account of sub-Saharan Africa, *Della descrittione dell'Africa et delle cose notabili che iui sono, per Giovan Lioni Africano* (1550), republished in English in 1600 as *A Geographical Historie of Africa*. Africanus's account was exceptional in a period in which most of the African continent remained uncharted, even as the Portuguese were gaining initial impressions of its Atlantic coast. With the explosion of slaving in the eighteenth century, the schism of the Middle Passage informed later texts, through the pioneering narratives of Ukawsaw Grionniosaw (1772), John Marrant (1785), Ottobah Cugoano (1787),

and Olaudah Equiano (1789), whose legal and spiritual pilgrimages to freedom chart Western geographies of enslavement, subjectivity, and salvation in the Age of Enlightenment. Their writings demonstrated the ways in which writers less invested in legitimating extant transatlantic political and economic systems appropriated the trope of mobility to contrapuntal accounts of the triumphalist progress that the genre supported from Western pens. Cugoano's work is significant also in the history of Atlantic letters in forwarding what Henry Louis Gates, in his discussion of the writer's account of the last Inca emperor's (Ataualpa's) rejection of Western textuality in the face of Spanish emphasis on the authority of the written rather than spoken word, calls "the trope of the talking book." Raising questions about textuality within the text, Cuguano's work flagged the operations of Western historical method in producing as well as occluding the figure of the subaltern.

Indigenous American accounts of European arrival and indigenous displacements are few, limited to a scattering of illustrated codices of Mexican origin, although oral narratives that survived in the cultures of North America were written down in the twentieth century, including memorial accounts of the Trail of Tears of Cherokee people driven in the 1830s from Appalachia to Oklahoma. These bring the political force of Western travel writing sharply into focus by clarifying the partiality of the historical record, the artifice of writing, and the complicated role of memory in constructing narrative. Equally fraught questions on the inflections or omissions introduced in third-party mediations of oral narrative attend many non-European/Euroamerican accounts of travel. *History of Mary Prince, a West Indian Slave* (1831) is an account of Prince's experiences in the Caribbean and her subsequent journey to the United Kingdom. Transcribed and edited by white abolitionists, the text arguably tries to conscript her life history to their political interests, confirming the tensions attending the relationship between oral narrative and the power of amanuensis in cultural contexts privileging literacy.

By contrast, construction of the diasporan political subject in a context configured around the possibility of black freedom and sovereignty is evident in travel narratives exploring possible sites of settlement in Africa. The emigrationist movement encouraged "emigration" of formerly enslaved Afro-Europeans and later Afro-Americans to the purposely created states of Sierra Leone (U.K.) and Liberia (U.S.) in the early nineteenth century. Black writers turned convention on its head by imagining travel as a form of return or repatriation to an African "homeland," but they also hinted that their Western experience would help to civilize Africa. *Memoir of Captain Paul Cuffee: A Man of Colour* (1812) and *Journal of Daniel Coker, a Descendent of Africa* (1820) provide black European examples of the pursuit of political power and the triumph of Western culture that formed part of the fabric even of counternarratives of Atlantic travel. Travel writing produced by visitors to the West, however, was inflected inversely, presenting occidental culture as the curiosity to be narrated, mediated, and then digested by an eastern audience. The Egyptian Rifaʿa al-Tahtawi's *A Paris Profile* (1834) presents his account of Europe refracted through the lens of Islam, in one of the few displacements of Western civilizational hegemony or uses of an occidentalizing gaze that travel writing provides.

As the transatlantic antislavery movement gained political traction after 1845, slave narratives charting the journey from captivity in the South to freedom in North began to saturate Anglo-American literary markets. An ambivalence to imperial power can be detected in this black travel writing, particularly after the passage of the Fugitive Slave Act (1850) exposed those fleeing to freedom to recapture and the reverse journey back to slavery, thereby positioning the British Empire as the only unequivocally free soil. Conversely, British and French discussions of the morality and conditions of South Asians crossing the Kala Pani (Pacific Ocean) to become indentured servants in the Caribbean demonstrate travel writing's expressive adaptability to the challenges of emerging new economic and political realities. Indeed, for those able to marshal its generic power, the trope of mobility continued to frame the global politics of intercultural exchange in the century to come.

FIONNGHUALA SWEENEY

Bibliography

Africanus, Leo. *A Geographical Historie of Africa.* London: Eliot's Court Press, 1600.

Arana, Victoria, ed. "Black Travel Writing." Special edition *Sonia Sanchez Review* 9, no.1 (2003).

Aubin Codex, or "Manuscrito de 1576." Holdings of the British Museum.

Behn, Aphra. *Oroonoko; or, the Royal Slave.* London: Will Caning, 1688.

Cañizares-Esguerra, Jorge. *Puritan Conquistadores: Iberianizing the Atlantic, 1550–1700.* Stanford, CA: Stanford University Press, 2006.

Coker, Daniel. *Journal of Daniel Coker, a descendent of Africa, from the time of leaving New York, in the ship Elizabeth, Capt. Sebor, on a voyage for Sherbro, in Africa, in company with three agents, and about ninety persons of colour.* Baltimore, MD: Edward J. Coale, 1820.

Cuffee, Paul. *Memoir of Captain Paul Cuffee: A man of colour, to which is subjoined: The Epistle of the Society of Sierra Leone, in Africa.* York, UK: C. Peacock, 1812.

Darwin, Charles. *Journal and Remarks, 1832–35* [1838]. In *Narrative of the surveying voyages of His Majesty's ships Adventure and Beagle, between the years 1826 and 1836, describing their examination of the southern shores of South America, and the Beagle's circumnavigation of the globe,* edited by Robert Fitzroy. 3 vols. London: Henry Colburn, 1839.

Defoe, Daniel. *Life and Strange Adventures of Robinson Crusoe, of York, Mariner.* London: W. Taylor, 1719.

Diaz del Castillo, Bernal. *Historia verdadera de la conquista de la Nueva España.* Spain: n.p., 1632.

Douglass, Frederick. *Narrative of the Life of an American Slave, Written by Himself.* Boston, MA: Anti-slavery Office, 1845.

Gates, Henry Louis Jr. *The Signifying Monkey: A Theory of African-American Literary Criticism.* New York: Oxford University Press, 1988.

Gates, Henry Louis Jr., and William Andrews, eds. *Pioneers of the Black Atlantic: Five Slave Narratives, 1772–1815.* New York: Basic Civitas, 1998.

The Gentleman's Pocket Companion for Travelling into Foreign Parts. London: Thomas Taylor, 1722.

Hakluyt, Richard. *The Principal Navigations, Voiages, Traffiques and Discoueries of the English Nation.* London: G. Bishop, R. Newberie & R. Barker, 1589.

Humboldt, Alexander von. *Le voyage aux régions équinoxiales du Nouveau Continent, fait en 1799–1804, par Alexandre de Humboldt et Aimé Bonpland.* 30 vols. Paris: Chez F. Schoell, 1807.

Las Casas, Bartolomé de. *Brevísima relación de la destrucción de las Indias.* Spain: n.p., 1552.

Mather, Cotton. *Magnalia Christi Americana.* 2 vols. London: Thomas Parkhurst, 1702.

More, Thomas. *Utopia.* Leuven, Netherlands: Erasmus, 1516.

Pratt, Mary Louise. *Imperial Eyes: Travel Writing and Transculturation.* London and New York: Routledge, 1992.

Prince, Mary. *History of Mary Prince, a West Indian Slave. Related by herself. With a Supplement by the Editor. To which is added, the Narrative of Asa-Asa, A Captured African.* London: F. Westley and A. H. Davis, 1831.

Rowlandson, Mary. *Narrative of the Captivity and Restoration of Mrs. Mary Rowlandson,* Boston, MA: n.p., 1682.

Shakespeare, William. *The Tempest.* Entered by Edward Blount into the Stationers' Register 1623.

Slotkin, Richard. *Regeneration through Violence: The Myth of the American Frontier, 1600–1860,* Middletown, CT: Wesleyan University Press, 1973.

Swift, Jonathan. *Travels into Several Remote Nations of the World, in Four Parts. By Lemuel Gulliver, First a Surgeon, and then a Captain of Several Ships.* London: Benjamin Motte, 1726.

al-Tahtawi, Rifaʿa, *Takhlis al-Ibriz fi Talkhis Bariz [A Paris Profile].* Cairo: Bulaq Printing Press, 1834.

Tocqueville, Alexis de. *De la Démocratie en Amérique.* Bruxelles: L Hauman et Cie, 1835.

Young, Filson, and Windham Thomas Wyndham-Quin Dunraven. *Christopher Columbus and the New World of His Discovery.* Philadelphia: J. B. Lippincott, 1906.

Literary Genres: Utopias

See Utopias.

Livestock

If anyone kills unlawfully a slave or servant-girl belonging to someone else or a four-footed beast of the class of cattle, let him be condemned to pay the owner the highest value that the property had attained in the preceding year.
—*Digest.* 9. 2.2 (Justinian I, 530–533 CE)

Stock: 250 Negroes (12.500 £), 80 Steers (857£), and 60 Mules (1.200£)—£ 14,557 Sterling
—Bryan Edwards, on the expenditure of establishing a Jamaican estate (1790s)

Betty, Cynthia, Deborah, Eve, Joan, Marina, Mary, Bank, Roger, and Simon were some of the many names that slaves and cattle in the English Americas shared during the eighteenth century. That human beings and animals were given similar names and indeed were both considered livestock, as the opening quotes bear out, was a hallmark of work, economic production, and law in the Atlantic World.

European domestic animals had crossed the Atlantic in 1493 and within a brief period invaded a wide territory: first the Antilles and then Central and South America. By the nineteenth century, Atlantic trade had grown immensely and nourished a solid legal tradition of appropriating the lives and labor forces of Native Americans, African slaves, and domestic animals—all frequently treated similarly for legal purposes under the label "livestock." Ecological imperialism—Europeans prevailing in the Americas not only by force of arms but through the proliferation of and predations by the plants and animals they introduced, gradually destroying preexistent environment and cultures—and the growing prominence of livestock in Atlantic trade paralleled the development of international law, itself created to protect the enormous benefits of such exploitation.

A hundred years after the first pig landed on American soil there were more domestic livestock in the New World than any other mammals. Pigs provided food and tallow for lighting; mares and donkeys served in military campaigns and in mines; cows, sheep, and goats enriched conquerors and colonizers, who created an industry more profitable than mining from the animal power and slaughtered bodies of livestock, which had served as well to support the crucial mining itself. The transatlantic journeys of these animals were tragic for them and expensive for their owners: from a fourth to half of them died at sea.

European cattle reproduced in their new American environments to such an extent that by the 1510s the transatlantic trade involved mostly selected specimens for breeding. Regional markets started to grow after that, from the initial coastal settlements to new populations in mining areas, so that by the 1550s trade networks moved animals between the islands of the Caribbean, New Spain (Mexico), Tierra Firme (the isthmus of Panama), and Peru. The export of Castilian breeding and pastoral techniques, along with their stock, can also explain the fast development of the livestock industry in Spanish America. During the sixteenth century the general assembly (*concejo, mesta,* or *junta*) of the Honorable Council of Mesta Shepherds controlled transhumant herds—which grazed alternately on upland and lowland commons with the changing of the seasons—and production of wool, lamb, and hides in Castile, Andalusia, and Extremadura—where there was also a strong tradition of raising cows and pigs. In the New World, transhumant sheep wandered around Hispaniola first, and then in New Spain, where a comparable Mexican *mesta* controlled them. Castilian herding ecology involved seasonal movements of sheep between low wetlands and hilly uplands and local cattle ranching. As a consequence, the Mexican landscape suffered an ecocide—destruction of environments—which in turn resulted in an epistemicide—loss of centuries of Native American knowledge systems—despite legislation to protect native ecologies. By the seventeenth century, ranching had supplanted Native agriculture and destroyed rich agro-ecological knowledge.

Pigs multiplied first and faster than any other species, both in the Antilles and on the continent. The conquerors' military invasions of American lands owed their efficacy to the abundant animals in the supply trains in the rear guard to feed the armed men in the vanguard. After subduing Native inhabitants of conquered lands, the newcomers had to put the land they had invaded to uses profitable to the conquerors. Both Hernán Cortés (conqueror of Mexico in 1521) and his cousin Francisco Pizarro (who extended Castilian conquests to the south in the 1530s) transformed Veracruz and La Isla de las Flores (or Taboga) in Panama into centers of large-scale livestock exploitation. Herds were imported to the continent from the Antilles during the process of conquest, settlement, and opening mines; when the conquerors became officials of the crown and *encomenderos* in command of Indian labor forces, they also turned into great cattle barons, thanks to forced Native American labor and captured bodies, which they sometimes exchanged for cattle. Atlantic exports included pork, lard, tallow

for soap and candles (especially important in mines), and hides. Caravans leaving Potosí with silver en route to the ports in the Pacific traversed the mountains. On the return route, Indians working for Spanish merchants brought not only goods from Europe, Mexico, and the Philippines but also animals (sheep, llamas, pigs, and cattle) for feeding (meat and cheese), clothing, candles, transport, and as labor force (mainly llamas and mules). Until the second half of the seventeenth century, the ranches, called *estancias*, of Spanish *encomenderos* provided livestock raised by Indians to the mines; later the providers were the haciendas.

Hog breeding was extremely profitable in Mexico, Panama, Nicaragua, and Peru until the 1530s, particularly in mining towns. Later, pigs were so abundant that prices fell, and so did the value of investments in the industry. Cows, which provided beef, milk, tallow, and valuable hides, sheep, which provided wool, dairy products, and mutton, and horses became an essential link in the imperial economy. In the 1560s the transatlantic trade in hides and tallow trebled, increasing during the next decade, and these became a major export from the American colonies to Spain.

The rapid success of Spanish livestock raising was replicated in the Portuguese, French, Dutch, and English territories, and by the eighteenth century the touchstone of the Atlantic economy was livestock, either as traction for hauling or as raw materials to be transformed into commodities. In the case of the Portuguese colonies in Brazil, cattle raising on coastal plantations demanded increased imports of slaves used in export agriculture after the mid-seventeenth century, and in the south, mule raising helped to consolidate Brazil's southern frontier and provided taxes for the crown. In the British colonies, livestock raising was so extensive that by the middle of the seventeenth century meat and livestock from New England reached Newfoundland, Virginia, and the West Indies. During the eighteenth century, North American colonies exported cattle (from New Hampshire, Rhode Island, New York, and New Jersey), horses (from Delaware), and pork (from Georgia).

Atlantic livestock breeding was not an enterprise of Europeans alone. Native Americans cared for animals and were also consumers of their "products." At the end of the seventeenth century the Plains Indians seized runaway Spanish sheep, cattle, and horses from Santa Fe, and the Navajo Apaches, Ute, and Shoshone distributed these horses to the north through the Great Plains and to the Pacific Northwest. Horses became essential for southeastern Indians, especially for their deerskin trade.

Livestock raising and trade revolutionized Atlantic imperial economies, but such a profitable business required legitimization, and thus authorities in Europe created colonial laws and a fledgling international law, defining legal personhood and how "civilized" persons could appropriate nature to support their economic interests. Laws in Atlantic colonies—fashioned after metropolitan models, which in turn were based on Roman law—were grounded in principles of natural law. This set of principles considered a world made by God for humankind to use in common; under this conception, the "natural world" could be converted to personal property within a sovereign territory by mixing the subjects' labor with "natural" bounty. This legal argument was deployed not only to claim possession over "living stock," understood as a specific form of chattel (from which the term *cattle* derived) property but also to claim the rest of "nature" in the Americas, preeminently its lands. Livestock, therefore, which was understood as both domestic animals and enslaved humans, could be acquired by occupation (capture) or accession (taming or breeding). A corollary to this doctrine was that theft of either form of chattel property was a felony.

When a wild animal was captured or tamed, it was removed from the "state of nature," or wilderness, and became property of the taker. The offspring of female slaves or animals also became property of their owners. From 1492 until the formal abolition of slavery, Atlantic jurisprudence treated domesticated animals and human slaves alike, and so did their owners. In ranching colonies, such as Jamaica, "stock" meant both domesticated animals and slaves. Further, since both wild animals and "savage" Africans could be tamed, owners found eugenicist measures, such as chaining, whipping, or castrating them, appropriate. Thus, the concept was linked to a process of civilizing, domesticating, and commoditization of creatures as fungible personal property. Law transformed both humans and animals from potential persons—subjects of rights—into things—objects of rights—for the use and profit of their owners and their sovereigns.

From the late seventeenth century onward, a specific English concept of improvement through a nation's agriculture, farming, and commerce came to define civilization—and the accompanying rights of the "civilized" to appropriate "nature" in the Atlantic. Not raising animals as livestock involved being less civilized and having a lesser right to claim nature. This disabling distinction was applied to Native Americans but also occasionally to curtail English subjects' rights, on the grounds of their difficulties in controlling domestic livestock in open country. The mixture of "nature's bounty" with the subjects' work—agricultural or trade—justified the appropriation of "nature" (including animals) by their sovereign against such "less civilized nations" as Native Americans, or, according to the English crown, Spaniards. This conception of improvement of "nature" through its laborious taming gave rise to the Enlightenment theory of the four stages of civilization—hunting and gathering, nomadic pastoralism, agriculture, and finally commerce—and became the basis of the eighteenth-century law of nations, aimed to justify European appropriation of nature throughout the Atlantic World. This body of law—by defining civilization, humanity, and legal personhood according to financial interests—assured European and Neo-European (New World) rulers and investors the enormous benefits of exploiting livestock, humans, animals, and the rest of nature, all alike.

EVA BOTELLA-ORDINAS

Bibliography

Crosby, Alfred W. *Ecological Imperialism: The Biological Expansion of Europe, 900–1900.* Cambridge: Cambridge University Press, 1986.

Dayan, Colin. *The Law Is a White Dog: How Legal Rituals Make and Unmake Persons.* Princeton, NJ: Princeton University Press, 2011.

DeJohn Anderson, Virginia. *Creatures of Empire: How Domestic Animals Transformed Early America.* New York: Oxford University Press, 2001.

Del Río Moreno, Justo Luis, "Comercio trasatlántico y comercio regional ganadero en América (1492–1542)." *Trocadero: Revista de historia moderna y contemporánea* 6–7 (1994–1995): 231–248.

Morgan, Philip D. "Slaves and Livestock in Eighteenth-Century Jamaica: Vineyard Pen, 1750–1751." *The William and Mary Quarterly*, 3rd ser., 52, no. 1 (January 1995): 47–76.

Mami Wata

Mami Wata, pidgin English for "Water Mother" or "Water Mistress," is a deity worshipped by Africans in at least 50 cultures in more than 20 countries from Senegal to Tanzania. Her spirit "sisters" in the African Atlantic World—water deities such as, in Brazil, Yemanja/Odoya/Mãe d'Agua and Oxum, Watur Mama in Suriname, La Siren in Haiti, Mere or Maman d'Eau in the French Antilles, the Water Maids of Jamaica, and Santa Marta la Dominadora in the Dominican Republic—possess many of Mami Wata's attributes and share related manners of representation.

This essay traces Mami Wata's visual histories and cultures in the context of African Atlantic history from the latter part of the fifteenth to the twentieth century. It also explores, in particular, the creative use of circulating global images—mermaids, snake charmers, Hindu gods and goddesses, and Catholic saints—to represent her.

Mami as Mermaid

While knowledge concerning the early history of Mami Wata arts, beliefs, and practices remains conjectural, the momentous encounter between Europeans and Africans on the western Atlantic coast of Africa in the latter part of the fifteenth century may help fill in some details. In 1493 Christopher Columbus wrote in his journal that he had seen three mermaids in the Caribbean waters off the coast of Hispaniola (later Santo Domingo, today shared by Haiti and the Dominican Republic). At about the same time, Portuguese sailors and traders, exploring the Atlantic African coast near present day Sierra Leone, showed images of mermaids to Sapi sculptors, artists famous for carving stone and ivory, and commissioned them to carve salt cellars for the royal courts of Europe. Drawing on ancient and indigenous images of water divinities imagined as hybrid creatures (part human, part aquatic, and usually female), the ever-inventive Sapi sculptors immediately incorporated the European mermaid into their own cosmos by depicting her swimming with crocodiles, which symbolized water spirits to the Sapi and their neighbors (see figure 1). Thus began the visual history, beliefs, and practices surrounding the pan-Atlantic water deity, the composite that came to be known as Mami Wata—her name in the pidgin English created to facilitate cross-cultural communication and to "lubricate" trade. The mermaid became the major icon associated with her, until other supple global images added new representations, beliefs, and practices as new significant "others" entered the picture.

According to the accounts of early European travelers, Africans associated Europeans with the water—even as water spirits—a logical assumption given their arrival by sea in ships rising from below the marine horizon. More importantly, they associated the maritime sculptures that decorated the ships with representations of those spirits. Thus several ships' figureheads, including some depicting mermaids, have been documented in widely dispersed shrines for water spirits in Africa. As Africans' familiarity with European ways and mermaid lore increased, they interpreted, adapted, and transformed the image of the mermaid to create Mami Wata. What evolved was an elaborate belief system that, filtered through many cultural lenses, made her a significant transcultural, transoceanic religious phenomenon, an African and Afro-Atlantic expression of plurality and diversity.

In Africa and the African Atlantic World, people recognized the essential and sacred nature of water by honoring a host of aquatic spirits. The identities of these divinities were often as slippery and amorphous as water itself. And adding to the complexity of this history is a vast African pantheon of female and male water divinities that have come to be known as *mami* and *papi watas* (generic categories in the lower-case usage) who share many of Mami Wata's attributes but also have their own distinctive traits.

Figure 1. A salt cellar of the Sapi peoples adorned with a mermaid and crocodiles. Sherbro Island, late fifteenth century; ivory, 16 cm. The National Museum of Denmark, Copenhagen. Photograph © The National Museum of Denmark, Ethnographic Collection.

Mami Wata was at once beautiful, jealous, generous, seductive, and potentially deadly—and these characteristics are as alive today as they were in the Atlantic Era when Africans invented her to express their experiences of the contacts with strange foreigners. She could bring good fortune in the form of material wealth and money. As a kind of "proto-capitalist," her powers increased with the growing international trade between Africa and the rest of the world in the fifteenth to the twentieth centuries. However, Mami's powers extended far beyond the realm of personal economic gain. For some she bestowed good fortune and status through monetary fortune, but she was also essential for other forms of well-being and wealth, especially progeny. She helped with infertility, impotence, or infant mortality and was an irresistible seductive presence, one who offered the pleasures and powers that accompany devotion to a spiritual force. Yet she also represented danger, for a liaison with Mami Wata often required a substantial sacrifice, such as the life of a family member or celibacy in the realm of mortals. Despite this, she was thought to be capable of helping women and men negotiate their sexual desires and preferences. Mami also provided a spiritual and professional avenue for women to become powerful priestesses and healers of both psychospiritual and physical ailments and to assert female agency in generally male-dominated societies. She was personal ambition incarnate.

Mami Wata as Snake Charmer

The fluid adaptability that gave Mami Wata her eighteenth- and early nineteenth-century popularity lives on in more recent, better-documented times. Her more modern expressions similarly incorporate, and thus domesticate, the challenges posed by alien beings and their otherwise unaccountable ways for Africans and their descendants around the Atlantic.

One example was a transformation she underwent in the last two decades of the 1800s. In Africa sometime between 1885 and 1900, Mami Wata's mermaid representation was joined by another transoceanic, global image. A popular German chromolithograph poster of a female snake charmer that combined elements of the mermaid with allusions to indigenous African water serpent deities was printed in Hamburg circa 1885 and probably carried to Africa by African sailors from Hamburg. The print reached Nigeria, where by 1901 it had already inspired a sculpted image in a water spirit headdress at Bonny in the Niger River Delta. In 1955 the lithograph was sent by traders in Ghana to be reprinted in Bombay, India, where 12,000 copies were made and sent to Ghana for sale. Within a few years it became the primary icon for Mami Wata in the twentieth century (see figure 2), until the arrival of other images from across the Indian Ocean.

Mami as Hindu Goddess

Between the fifteenth and nineteenth centuries, the vast majority of foreigners from overseas seen by West Africans came from western Europe, but with colonial rule they were followed in the twentieth century by traders from Lebanon and India. Like their predecessors, they were associated with commerce—that is, mysteriously powerful wealth brought from overseas. Therefore, the same ambivalent combinations of the lures and costs of capitalism associated with mermaid images were extended to the more recent image of a snake charmer.

The independence of India in 1947 brought another new phase in popular representations of Mami Wata. The popularity of the Hamburg snake

Figure 2. The 1955 reprint (Bombay, India) of the original Hamburg chromolithograph shows a poster of a snake charmer, printed c. 1885 by the Adolph Friedlander Company. Twelve thousand copies were sent to Ghana and sold widely in West Africa. 35.6 x 25.4 cm. Private collection.

Figure 3. Inspired by an Indian print he had seen in 1977, the artist Joseph Kossivi Ahiator began dreaming of swimming with "The King of Mami Wata" and his queen "Na Krishna." Ahiator says those who see his painting would be able to "travel to India if they studied his painting well." Joseph Kossivi Ahiator (b. 1956, Aflao, Ghana); *Indian King of Mami Wata*, 2005; pigment on cloth, 225 x 267 cm. Fowler Museum x2005.5.1 Museum Purchase.

charmer chromolithograph (and its 1955 Indian reprint) and the presence of Indian merchants in West Africa led to a growing African interest in Indian prints of Hindu gods, goddesses, and spirits, which Africans interpreted as representations of a host of Mami Wata spirits (female *mami* and male *papi watas*) associated with specific bodies and levels of water and possessing specific attributes and powers. Africans used these prints as guides for rituals and for the preparation of altars known as "Mami Wata tables," expanding the pantheon of spirits and fostering a growing complexity in the worship of Mami Wata that included local elements as well as Christian, Hindu, Buddhist, astrological, and occult beliefs and practices (see figure 3).

Mami's Spirit Sisters in the African Atlantic World

The countless millions of Africans who were torn from their homeland and carried forcibly across the Atlantic between the sixteenth and nineteenth centuries brought with them beliefs and practices honoring ancestral deities, including Mami Wata. They revisualized, revitalized, and reestablished these spirits and deities in their radically novel circumstances in the Americas. They drew, with characteristic flexibility, on local as well as global images, arts, ideas, and actions, and interpreted them according to these local attributes. In doing so, they invested their spirits and deities with new meanings and then re-presented them in novel and dynamic ways to serve the believers' own specific—and continually changing—aesthetic, devotional, social, economic, and political aspirations.

Mami Wata, like other African cultural traditions, has been "commuting" back and forth across the Atlantic for hundreds of years. In the nineteenth century, Afro-Brazilians who were either exiled to Africa, due to their revolutionary activities in Brazil, or returned voluntarily, because they had been able to purchase their freedom, became intermediaries in the transatlantic trade. Among Afro-Brazilians who returned to Ouidah (modern Benin), Mami Wata was equated with the Yoruba river goddess Yemoja, who in Brazil became Yemanja, goddess of the sea. Both were often represented as mermaids and seen as fertile "mothers." Yemanja and Mami Wata have become "spirit sisters" whose sacred waters mingle local and Atlantic cultural currents from Africa, Portugal, and Afro-Brazil.

* * *

Not long after 1955, when Mami's snake-charmer chromolithograph reprinted in India was widely disseminated throughout West Africa, this new image of her crossed the Atlantic, probably to the Dominican Republic. There it soon acquired new meanings to serve the needs of believers in the Americas, as it had in Africa at the end of the nineteenth century. Contemporary African Pentecostal Christians, however, came to regard Mami Wata as evil and, ironically, in Catholic parts of the African Atlantic she has become a saint known as Santa Marta Dominadora. This contemporary malleability was at the core of her flexibility in expressing the many encounters in the Atlantic Era. Like the ocean itself, Mami Wata is a fluid, ever-changing, ubiquitous presence in the African Atlantic World.

HENRY JOHN DREWAL

Bibliography

Bastide, Roger. *The African Religions of Brazil: Toward a Sociology of the Interpretation of Civilizations.* Translated by Helen Sebba. Baltimore, MD: Johns Hopkins University Press, 1978.

Drewal, Henry John. *Mami Wata: Arts for Water Spirits in Africa and Its Diasporas.* Los Angeles: Fowler Museum of UCLA and University of Washington Press, 2008.

———, ed. *Sacred Waters: Arts for Mami Wata and Other Divinities in Africa and the Diaspora.* Bloomington: Indiana University Press, 2008.

Verger, Pierre. *Trade Relations between the Bight of Benin and Bahia, Seventeenth to Nineteenth Century.* Ibadan, Nigeria: Ibadan University Press, 1976.

Manumission

Manumission—from Latin, *manumittere*, "to let go from the hand," or release—is the liberation of slaves through institutional means provided for by law and accepted by society. The practice occurred in human history wherever slavery existed, and prominently—to varying degrees—in the Atlantic World. Throughout the duration of slave regimes, slaves were manumitted either out of the good graces of their masters, because they were their children or had provided good service, or because they had achieved sufficient means to buy their own release from enslavement.

A master could liberate a slave with or without conditions: if unconditional, the slave's liberation was immediate. Immediate release usually happened when the slave was the child of his master and was given her or his liberty while still a minor. Under conditional manumission, slaves would need to work for a given number of years, or until specified heirs of their master had died, in order to gain their liberty. Manumission could also be purchased in several ways, either through immediate payment, which could be made by the slave or through a third party, or in installments—which in Spanish was referred to as *coartación* (or *coartação* in Portuguese). Cases of *coartación* occurred more often in Spanish America than in Brazil, except in the region of Minas Gerais, where mining activity and the possibility of finding valuable precious stones increased the ability of slaves to purchase their liberty.

Formally, obtaining manumission involved various scenarios: receiving letters of liberty from one's owner; a provision in the owner's will and testament, which was sometimes motivated by religious beliefs, hoping that the release of a slave from bondage would bring salvation; or the baptism of the child of a slave mother. It was also common for manumission to be granted orally, in which case it was necessary for the slave to arrange witnesses to prove the granting of his or her freedom. Except for the freeing of infants or children through baptism, slaves most commonly gained their liberty by purchasing it.

It is difficult to estimate what proportions of the people enslaved in the Americas obtained manumission, because the act was often private, and—as a private matter between slave and master—few official statistics exist as testimony to the practice. Of course, the numbers varied according to times and places. More slaves were freed in Spanish America and Brazil than in the British Caribbean and North America, but the numbers of manumissions were small in all societies, probably liberating no more than one out of every five hundred slaves, such as in Virginia in 1790 (the year of the first U.S. federal census) and in some places and times, fewer than that. In Curaçao, in the same period, the ratio was 0.5 percent. In colonial Brazil before the 1820s, estimates suggest that at most, 2 percent of slaves were manumitted. The growing prospect of the end of the Atlantic slave trade in the first half of the nineteenth century generally contributed to reducing the numbers of manumissions as masters held on to human property they could no longer replace. As one slaving power after another abolished the trade, the average prices of slaves increased substantially in the countries that did not emancipate them: the United States, Brazil, and Cuba. In these three places, specifically, expanding plantations to grow cotton (the United States), sugar (Cuba), and coffee (Brazil) contributed further to reduce the chances of manumission.

In general, slaves who were more likely to achieve manumission were Creoles (slaves born in the Americas), those who lived in cities or worked as domestic servants or skilled artisans, or those who had close social relationships with their owner's family or with other slaves and freed men. Family ties among the liberated might result in spouses or parents paying the costs of manumission, especially for women and children.

Throughout the Americas women were liberated more than men, except in the United States, where the numbers of males and females were equivalent. The predominance of women among the manumitted was due to the greater opportunities they had for building emotional bonds with their owners or other free families. Many women manumitted in Brazil were Africans experienced in working in urban markets and more able to earn money to buy their liberation or to negotiate conditional manumission upon the deaths of their owners or their owners' immediate heirs. Young African men were least likely to achieve manumission.

However, even when the slave had the money needed to buy his or her manumission, the master was not obliged to grant it. The release originated from the master, which presupposed reciprocity on the part of the slave, who had to express gratitude and obedience to his or her former owner. In many cases, manumission could be abrogated if the freed person did not behave with proper deference. In practice, however, the withdrawal of manumission was a rather remote possibility and during the nineteenth century virtually ceased to exist.

Although manumission was formally a voluntary grant from a master, giving freedom cannot be attributed solely to their generosity or financial calculation. Every act of manumission was the outcome of negotiations between a slave and master. When these negotiations failed to produce agreement, slaves could anticipate their autonomy by petitioning a court to be sold by the master; they could also flee, or pursue liberation on specified legal grounds of cruelty or neglect. Those interventions of the royal judiciary—called *suits for liberty* (*ações de liberdade* in Portuguese and *procesos de libertad* in Spanish), in which slaves sued their masters in order to obtain liberty—occurred throughout the Americas. In Spanish America and Brazil, slaves even appealed for their release directly to the king. In these cases the slave might obtain liberty against the will of the owner.

Another, more widespread way to achieve freedom against the master's will was through military conscription or by enlisting in private militia forces. During the American Revolution and throughout the struggles for national independence in the French Empire, Spanish America, and Brazil, slaves were as much a part of the ranks of the English, French, Spanish, and Portuguese armies as they were in the ranks of the rebels, encouraged by promises of manumission made by both sides. Since the 1730s, Saint-Domingue's slaves commonly served as slave-catchers, gaining their own freedom in exchange for the maroons (fugitive former slaves) they turned in. For the same pursuit of liberty, slaves participated in armed conflicts in civil wars, such as the Farroupilha uprising (1835–1845), which took place in southern Brazil; the Paraguayan War (1865–1870) between Paraguay and the triple alliance of Brazil, Uruguay, and Argentina; and the American Civil War (1861–1865).

The various meanings of manumission as a strategy differed for slaves and their masters. For the masters, the promise of manumission was fundamental to the control they exercised over their slaves, enticing them into years of loyal service with the prospect of liberty in a remote and always conditional future. Other masters feared that manumissions, on larger scales, as in the British North American colonies and the United States in the decades immediately before and after independence, could undermine the foundations of the slave regime, leading to widespread freeings in the new nation. Manumission might have both of these meanings in differing times and places, strengthening or undermining the moral authority of the masters.

In these ways manumission, although a private act between master and slave, had social and political consequences. Even though the masters were responsible for their slaves, it was up to the state to set the terms of whatever liberties they acquired. Governments restricted manumissions when they thought that the emergence of communities of free blacks could weaken racial hierarchies. For this reason, from the mid-eighteenth century to the nineteenth century, colonies in the British and French Caribbean such as Jamaica and Saint-Domingue and several U.S. states enacted restrictive laws. In Saint-Domingue, even though the number of manumitted people was large compared with other American colonies throughout the eighteenth century, French colonial authorities virtually put the practice to an end by the close of the century. Ex-slaves and their descendants nonetheless became catalysts in the 1791–1804 violence that resulted in the free black nation of Haiti. Northern American states, such as Pennsylvania, New York, and New Jersey, required that masters pay taxes for freeing slaves and sustain the people they freed. In parts of the southern United States, freed people were forced to leave a state recognizing their freedom. Expulsions of freed people had occurred in South Carolina since the eighteenth century, but from the nineteenth century forward the practice spread to other states, such as Virginia. After 1852, the slaves freed in Louisiana had to leave the country entirely, and in 1860, Georgia, Mississippi, Alabama, and Louisiana banned any form of manumission whatsoever.

Although the growth of communities of free blacks also generated considerable concern in Spanish America and Brazil, it was not addressed by restricting manumission. Even though the populations of liberated Africans and their American descendants were considerable in the cities of these regions, such as Lima, Buenos Aires, Caracas, Rio de Janeiro, and Salvador (in Bahia, Brazil), many masters tried to maintain personal control of manumission until the eve of the abolition of slavery (which occurred at varying dates in the nineteenth century); employing this strategy allowed them to manipulate manumission in order to generate debts of gratitude that would result in the maintenance of personal obligations even after the end of legal slavery. For most slaves, though, manumission was no longer a concession from a master but rather—with the growth of the ideal of the participatory nation-state—recognition of their own inherent rights to personal freedom.

Even though manumissions occurred in every society that held human beings as slaves, in the Atlantic World the practice produced slaves with a public presence and presented a peril not apparent in the earlier practice of recognizing enslaved women as wives and mothers in large private households. Even when manumissions did not liberate large numbers of enslaved individuals, they were crucial to releasing the pressures of the massive numbers of enslaved peoples in the Americas. At the same time, the same authorities that structured practices of manumission also restricted them, fearing either that overly generous masters would lose control over their slaves or that growing communities of former slaves with political standing would become threats to control over the majorities remaining in slavery. Public regulation of manumission practices was thus peculiar to the Atlantic World, where enslaved populations had outgrown the household-centered practices of slaveholding in the Old World.

KEILA GRINBERG

Bibliography

Brana-Shute, Rosemary, and Randy Sparks, eds. *Paths to Freedom: Manumission in the Atlantic World.* Columbia: University of South Carolina Press, 2009.

Ghachem, Malick W. *The Old Regime and the Haitian Revolution.* Cambridge and New York: Cambridge University Press, 2012.

Hanger, Kimberly. *Bounded Lives, Bounded Places: Free Black Society in Colonial New Orleans, 1769–1803.* Durham, NC: Duke University Press, 1997.

Hunefeldt, Christine. *Paying the Price of Freedom: Family and Labor among Lima's Slaves, 1800–1854.* Berkeley: University of California Press, 1995.

Russell-Wood, A. J. R. *The Black Man in Slavery and Freedom in Colonial Brazil.* Oxford: Palgrave Macmillan, 1982.

Whitman, Stephen. *The Price of Freedom: Slavery and Manumission in Baltimore and Early National Maryland.* Lexington: University Press of Kentucky, 1997.

Marine Resources

Everyone around the rim of the Atlantic during the fifteenth century relied to varying degrees on marine resources, including fish, fur, flesh, hides, oil, ivory, feathers, eggs, shells, pearls, and salt. In the Senegambian and Gold Coast regions of West Africa, for example, near-shore fishermen and salt rakers plied their trades; in the Caribbean, Taino and Carib people harvested conch, spiny lobsters, and green turtles for food; in what are now Nova Scotia, New Brunswick, and eastern Maine, Mi'kmaq and Malecite hunter-gatherers derived as much as 90 percent of their annual caloric intake from the sea; and in western Europe, commercial and subsistence fisheries fed inland populations from southern Portugal to northern Norway. People shaped their lives around the marine resources of the Atlantic on which they depended, even as the harvesters also altered coastal marine ecosystems. From the sixteenth to the nineteenth centuries, as the Atlantic World became increasingly interconnected, other peoples' reliance on marine resources grew. Local access to certain species evaporated. Species previously ignored were targeted. New markets were created. Human impacts on the sea intensified dramatically.

Late-medieval western Europeans' desires for merchantable fish (primarily salted cod), along with the oil that could be rendered from whales and other marine mammals, contributed significantly to the creation of the Atlantic World. The Roman Catholic liturgical calendar, with its meatless holidays, promoted robust fisheries. Europe's coastal ecosystems had already been depleted by 1500, in the sense that harvesters could no longer secure the yields they desired of whales, salmon, sturgeon, cod, and other marine species with the technologies available. One impetus for Europeans' westward voyages across the North Atlantic was the paucity of accessible marine resources in home waters.

When once-productive fishing grounds off Norway failed during the early fifteenth century, probably on account of the Little Ice Age, English fishermen searched for cod as far out to sea as Iceland. By the early sixteenth century, English, Basque, Breton, French, and Portuguese mariners were regularly harvesting cod, whales, walrus, and seabirds (for bait) in the northern latitudes of North America that included modern Newfoundland, southern Labrador, eastern Nova Scotia, and New Brunswick. For a century prior to settlement in today's Atlantic Canada and New England, large numbers of European fishermen made voyages there each year. Catholic culture prompted, and commercial capitalism enabled, Old World people to eat regularly from New World ecosystems, spurring transfer of the biomass and energy of New World ecosystems to the Old World.

Meanwhile, Spanish soldiers, settlers, priests, and officials were making parallel inroads in the Caribbean, Mexico, and South America. While their initial intentions did not focus on marine resources, their settlements and conquests of indigenous peoples upset the balanced relationship between humans and the living sea in Latin American waters. Taino people, whose supreme deity, Yúcahu, was god of the sea and lord of the cassava, had long fished Caribbean waters using spears, nets, hooks, and botanically derived poisons. Under Spanish colonial domination, Taino conch divers were redirected to retrieve pearls from the sea bottom. Colonists also brought in enslaved Africans as adept divers and fishermen. As time passed, coastal Latin American and Caribbean people of European, African, and Native extraction hunted the large vertebrates—monk seals, manatees, and sea turtles—quite destructively, much more so than had been the norm before the Spaniards' arrival.

Christopher Columbus called the monk seals he saw near Santo Domingo "sea wolves." Their fur, flesh, and fat made them valuable, and extensive hunting followed, especially during the seventeenth and eighteenth centuries. Early twenty-first century scientists estimate that approximately one-quarter to one-third of a million monk seals lived in the Caribbean before the Europeans' arrival, meaning that at the birth of the Atlantic World coral reefs in the Caribbean supported populations of fish and invertebrates approximately six times larger than the biomass surviving today.

Vast numbers of green turtles in tropical American waters prior to the nineteenth century were extirpated as well. Unlike monk seals, green turtles are herbivores. Abundant bales of them grazed beds of tropical sea grass, keeping it short and healthy. Their removal from coastal ecosystems, while enriching some people and feeding others on land, depleted the healthy diversity of the sea. Uncropped sea grass shaded the bottom and reduced light penetration. It grew old and decomposed on site, feeding blooming microbial populations and promoting a substrate suitable for the slime molds that cause sea-grass wasting disease. Turtles had kept sea-grass beds healthy; without them the seas grew less rich in many other ways.

Scholars have known for some time how the creation of the Atlantic World wreaked havoc on the human ecology of the Americas. Less well known, and just being recognized, are the maritime aspects of the Atlantic World beyond ships and sailors traversing the surface of the sea: the radical depletion and restructuring of coastal ecosystems caused changes just as radical.

Damage appears to have been less pronounced on the coast of Africa than elsewhere before 1850. In the northwestern African region between the Senegal and Gambia rivers, local canoe men harvested fish for local consumption and trade before the arrival of Europeans, and thereafter as well. Fresh fish spoiled quickly in the tropical heat, so fish for interregional trade were dried or salted. Likewise, along the Gold Coast, in what today is Ghana, fishermen supplied local markets from dugout canoes. During the late seventeenth century, a Dutch trader noted that 500 to 600 canoes were fishing in the region around Elmina Castle alone. Angolan fishermen worked the rich upwellings of the cold Benguela Current from the protective waters of Luanda Bay, itself a celebrated source of a unique small mollusk, similar to the Indian Ocean cowrie, which served parts of West-Central Africa as a kind of prestige currency. None of these African regions, however, saw pressures on marine resources intensify to the degree that became normal

in the waters of North America, South America, and western Europe during the integration of the Atlantic World. Less large-scale commercial harvesting occurred in African coastal waters, but historical patterns of resource use changed to accommodate the vast growth in marine trade. Indian Ocean cowrie shells, regarded as hallowed because they originated in deep water, were imported by the thousands of tons for Dutch commercial agents in Amsterdam, particularly through Ouidah, in the area of western Africa known to Europeans as the Slave Coast. They were also being used extensively as currency in the Senegambian region by the end of the eighteenth century. A musket worth 0.55 pounds sterling in Europe in 1800, for instance, would sell in the Niger Valley for 12,000 cowrie shells.

The most commercially productive seas in the Atlantic World were cold North Atlantic waters ranging from the North Sea and the Norwegian Sea in the east to the Gulf of St. Lawrence and the Gulf of Maine in the west. Oceanographic conditions, including temperature, salinity, depth, and nutrient mixing made certain places there, such as Norway's Lofoten Islands and the Grand Banks of Newfoundland, teeming incubators of marine life. Commercially valuable species such as whales, walrus, seals, cod, haddock, mackerel, herring, salmon, and sturgeon thrived in those conditions, as did seabirds, lobsters, clams, and cockles.

European harvesters had plucked the low-hanging fruit from their coastal ecosystems by the end of the Middle Ages. Salmon, sturgeon, and other anadromous fish (species that lived in the ocean but conveniently returned each year to spawn in freshwater rivers or streams) had been hit especially hard in Europe, as had whales, seals, and walrus. Hunting pressure reduced the effective range of walrus, leaving herds only to the far north of Norway. Eiders, the most common sea ducks in European waters, were also overharvested for their meat and unsurpassed down. Unlike most seabirds, eiders molt their primary feathers all at once, meaning that every year for one month they are flightless and captured easily.

Coastal waters on the American shore from Massachusetts to Newfoundland supported species that were virtually identical to those found in northern European waters. Experienced early-modern mariners had a sense of "normal" levels of the populations of seals, seabirds, whales, and cod in European waters. Those mariners were flabbergasted by the abundance of these organisms in American seas. The difference, of course, was that American seas had not been extensively harvested before Europeans arrived. Native people certainly availed themselves of abundant marine resources, including fish, clams, eels, seabirds, seals, and eggs. But these aboriginal populations were sufficiently small in numbers that they rarely depleted their marine resources, other than by localized exhaustions of clam beds. Left fallow, clam beds rejuvenated.

Temperate American seas were harvested commercially beginning shortly after 1500, first by transient European mariners and then by settlers and their descendants. By 1850 the northwest Atlantic resembled temperate European seas in diminished estuarine productivity, extinctions and near-extinctions of species, range contractions of some of the survivors, and localized exhaustions. The 1850s are notable as the first decade in which fishermen on both sides of the Atlantic (in England, Norway, New England, and Atlantic Canada) begged their governments to do something about depleted fish stocks. They feared they were destroying the resource base on which they depended. Meanwhile, overharvesting had also significantly compromised the biological productivity even of what had been the richest Atlantic regions, such as Chesapeake Bay and the Caribbean Sea. Initial sixteenth-century low-investment, easy-entry strategies for extracting the rich marine resources of the Atlantic had become unsustainable at the vastly increased levels of commercial production that they had launched four centuries earlier.

W. JEFFREY BOLSTER

Bibliography

Bolster, W. Jeffrey. *The Mortal Sea: Fishing the Atlantic in the Age of Sail.* Cambridge, MA: Harvard University Press, 2012.

Curtin, Philip D. *Economic Change in Pre-colonial Africa: Senegambia in the Era of the Slave Trade.* Madison: University of Wisconsin Press, 1975.

Jackson, Jeremy B. C., et al. "Historical Overfishing and the Recent Collapse of Coastal Ecosystems." *Science* 293, no. 5330 (2001): 629–638.

Roberts, Callum. *The Unnatural History of the Sea.* Washington, DC: Island Press, 2007.

Maritime Populations

In 1400 the four continents of the Atlantic Basin were largely isolated from each other. By 1850 most of Europe, the Americas, and Africa were connected to each other in ways too varied and numerous to list. In this 450-year period, overseas European territorial claims were established, trade routes forged, and large-scale migrations undertaken. This dramatic integration of the Atlantic was possible, in large part, due to the skills of West Indian fishermen, West African Kru canoemen, *grumetes* (a Portuguese reference to an apprentice mariner or cabin boy) and *laptots* (derived from the Wolof word for sailor), European sailors, and North American coasting crews who hauled the sails and steered the vessels that moved the masses of peoples, goods, and ideas that characterized the Atlantic Era.

Success in this world of maritime mobility often depended upon recasting one's identity, forging new ties around novel interests shared with strangers. For sailors, migrants, and specialists in exploiting the marine resources of the Atlantic, vessels were sites of social transformation. Setting foot aboard the ships, vagrants became indentured servants, young boys became landsmen (that is, novice sailors), slave-ship captains became jailers, and enslaved people, who boarded as Cromanttees and Pawpaws (from Cormantin and Ouidah on the Gold and Slave coasts), became undifferentiated Africans. Whether free or enslaved, voluntary or impressed seamen, itinerant travelers or colonial officials, maritime populations regularly crossed the political, religious, and linguistic boundaries of their backgrounds. These maritime populations, like traders and merchants throughout the Atlantic, adapted to the environments through which they moved by learning languages, shifting political allegiances, adopting new religions, and changing clothes. As they traveled through the Atlantic they also introduced alien ideas challenging local powers. Sloop crews telling Bermudians of a slave conspiracy in New York and Spanish mariners bringing news of a new Haitian black republic to slaves elsewhere in the Caribbean were agents of potentially revolutionary change, and they were feared as such by officials.

Local authorities' anxieties about the maritime populations of the Atlantic were due, in part, to the not insignificant prominence among them of enslaved and free blacks. Ships' crews were generally more diverse than populations on land. During wars, when needs for mariners expanded significantly, ship captains—not least among them American-based privateers—often proved willing to hire blacks, resulting in hundreds of fugitives from slavery escaping into the Atlantic aboard ships. Atlantic black tars, as these African and African American seamen were called, grew significantly in numbers though this period; Royal Navy musters indicate that approximately 5 percent of its ships' crews in the eighteenth century were black, but it is estimated that by the early nineteenth century 18 percent of North America's 100,000 mariners were of African descent. Similar, if not greater, proportions of Africans and their American descendants manned the Brazil-based ships of the Portuguese Atlantic, including enslaved members of the crews of slavers.

The maritime skills, linguistic dexterity, and access to wide-ranging information that made maritime populations central to the integration of European systems in the Atlantic also often made them significant threats to claims of imperial sovereignty and to government control of commercial activities. As a result, monarchical authorities sought to exercise tight controls over the crews of ships flying their colors. Beyond official passports, such controls limited sailors' access to credit, restricted mariners' movements, and required imprisonment of free black tars during their ships' layovers in ports.

Governments had good cause to be concerned about Atlantic mariners' independence. At the same time as European governments were asserting control over maritime labor by such measures as British officials impressing seamen into both military and commercial service and French authorities registering the sailors aboard their ships, the members of these crews were seeking to improve their

lot. During wartime, privateering—or monarchy-sanctioned attacks by private vessels on enemy ships—offered both potential riches and release from the tight discipline of both naval and merchant ships. Seamen's resentment of the deprivations imposed on them led many to seek these attractions of privateering, with not inconsiderable prize moneys for those lucky enough to capture enemy vessels.

In contrast with the privateering authorized by European governments, piracy—unauthorized attacks on vessels sailing under authorized passports—operated in a more nebulous legal sphere. From the 1500s to the early 1700s, state-sanctioned plundering in times of peace was common, particularly by northern European ships preying on Iberian vessels and port cities. In remote Atlantic regions treated as beyond the limits of European sovereignty, such activities, which would have been considered piracy if practiced in waters considered European, were deemed acceptable, or at least beyond official redress. Francis Drake and other sixteenth-century Elizabethan buccaneers systematically attacked vessels in the western Atlantic flying other monarchs' colors. Crown-sanctioned piracy led to sizable pirate nests at Port Royal (Jamaica), Newport (Rhode Island), and Charleston (in the Carolina Lowcountry), where colonial officials and local merchants alike profited by supporting the pirates. Through the early 1700s, piracy made important contributions to otherwise struggling colonial economies, while at the same time relieving weak early governments of disturbers of the local peace by providing outlets for dissatisfied seamen to enlist and leave.

With the end of warfare, many mariners bristled at having to return to work under the harsh discipline of peacetime. As a result, particularly at the end of Queen Anne's War (1702–1713), considerable numbers of former privateers became pirates. However, the relatively democratic and egalitarian life of pirate ships was tempered by brutality, often by captains and also by members of the crew toward shipmates with less power, such as slaves and women. This last burst of piracy largely ended in Atlantic waters in the early 1720s, when European royal navies grew to the point of undertaking a concentrated effort to drive freebooting buccaneers from the Atlantic Ocean.

The Atlantic's capacious scale, as well as the high mortality on long voyages into the Pacific and Indian oceans, ensured that most mariners from Atlantic ports did not leave the ocean basin. The northern Atlantic's currents and trade winds favored a clockwise movement of ships around the ocean, which meant that few seamen from northern Atlantic ports ever crossed the Equator. While the counterclockwise circulation in the southern Atlantic brought Portuguese and Brazilian sailors more regularly into the Indian Ocean, the high mortality in travel to and from Asia meant that Britain, France, and the Netherlands manned their privately owned ships on voyages to India and farther east, where all had significant trading interests, with seamen native to the region, such as Lascars (locally recruited guards, soldiers, and sailors in the service of the trading companies operating there). Although the voyages of European- and American-based crews became longer by the nineteenth century, and some ventured into the Pacific and Indian oceans, Atlantic trade grew faster, and so the large majority of mariners remained in the Atlantic Basin. Whether sailing from Salem, Seville, Bahia, Bordeaux, or Scarborough (Yorkshire, England), most Atlantic seamen spent their lives within the Atlantic, where they helped to ensure that the ocean would become a maritime pathway connecting the diverse regions around its basin, rather than a barrier between the peoples of four continents.

CHARLES R. FOY

Bibliography

Bolster, W. Jeffrey. *Black Jacks: African American Seamen in the Age of Sail.* Cambridge, MA: Harvard University Press, 1997.

Jarvis, Michael. *In the Eye of All Trade: Bermuda, Bermudians, and the Maritime Atlantic World, 1680–1783.* Chapel Hill: University of North Carolina Press for Omohundro Institute of Early American History and Culture, 2010.

Klein, Herbert S. *Middle Passage: Comparative Studies in the Atlantic Slave Trade.* Princeton, NJ: Princeton University Press, 1978.

Rediker, Marcus. *Between the Devil and the Deep Blue Sea: Merchant Seamen, Pirates, and the Anglo-American Maritime World, 1700–1750.* Cambridge: Cambridge University Press, 1987.

Maroons

Communities formed by self-liberated slaves dotted the fringes of plantation America, from Brazil to the southeastern United States, from Peru to the American Southwest, for more than four centuries. Usually known in Spanish as *palenques* and in Portuguese as *quilombos* or *mocambos*, these new maroon societies ranged from tiny bands that survived less than a year to powerful states encompassing thousands of members that survived for generations or even centuries. (The English word *maroon* derives from Spanish *cimarrón*, itself based on a Taíno [Amerindian] root.) Today the descendants of these early maroons still form semi-independent enclaves in several parts of the hemisphere—Suriname and French Guiana, Jamaica, Brazil, Colombia, and Belize—remaining fiercely proud of their maroon origins and, in some cases at least, faithful to unique cultural traditions that their fugitive ancestors forged during the earliest days of African American history.

Marronage became a response to enslavement in Africa as well, in the wake of the internecine wars fostered by the Atlantic slave trade. Fugitives from the chaos and violence that dominated much of West-Central Africa, including runaways from slave coffles during the seventeenth- and eighteenth-century expansion of the trade, frequently founded maroon settlements in marginal areas. Some had populations of several hundred and lived by raiding more settled groups or even fought against their former masters. But all remained sufficiently caught up in the political ebb and flow of the era that they did not maintain separate maroon identities for more than a generation or two. During the eighteenth century, fugitives from the trade along the Upper Guinea coast also formed maroon communities, sometimes on islands just offshore, but mass recapture after months or years was the norm.

In the Americas, the meaning and attractiveness of *marronage* differed for enslaved people in different social positions, varying with their perceptions of themselves and their situations, which were influenced by such diverse factors as their countries of birth, the periods of time they had been in the New World, their task assignments as slaves, their family responsibilities, and the particular treatments they were receiving from overseers or masters. More general considerations were at play as well, such as the proportions of blacks to whites in the region, the proportions of freed people in the population, the natures of available terrains in which to establish communities, and the opportunities for manumission. Many maroons, particularly men, escaped during their first hours or days in the Americas. Enslaved Africans who had already spent some time in the New World seem to have been less prone to flight. But Creole slaves who were particularly acculturated, who had learned the ways of the plantation best, seem to have been highly represented among runaways, often escaping to urban areas where they could pass as free because of their independent skills and ability to speak the colonial language.

The large number of detailed newspaper advertisements for runaway slaves placed by masters attests to the high level of planter concern, while at the same time affording the critical historian an important set of sources for establishing the profiles of maroons, which varied significantly by historical period and country. Individual maroons fled not only to the hinterlands—many, especially skilled slaves, escaped to urban centers and successfully melted into the population of freed people, while others became maritime maroons, fleeing by fishing boat or other vessel across international borders. And in Haiti, maroons played a signal role as catalysts in the Haitian Revolution (1791), which created the first nation in the Americas in which all citizens were free.

Planters generally tolerated *petit marronage*—repetitive or periodic truancy with temporary goals such as visiting friends or lovers on neighboring plantations. But within the first decade of the existence of most slave-holding colonies in the Americas, the most brutal punishments—amputation of a leg, castration, suspension from a meathook through the ribs, slow roasting to death—had been reserved for long-term, recidivist maroons, and in many cases these draconian punishments were quickly written into law.

Marronage on the grand scale, with individual fugitives banding together in remote areas to create communities of their own, struck directly at the foundations of the plantation system, presenting military and economic threats that often taxed the colonists to their very limits. Maroon communities, whether hidden near the fringes of the plantations or deep in the forest, periodically raided plantations for firearms, tools, and women, often reuniting in freedom families that had formed during slavery. In a remarkable number of cases, the beleaguered colonists were eventually forced to sue their former slaves for peace. For example, in Brazil, Colombia, Cuba, Ecuador, Hispaniola, Jamaica, Mexico, and Suriname, they reluctantly offered treaties granting maroon communities their freedom, recognizing their territorial integrity, and making some provision for meeting their economic needs, in return for an end to hostilities toward the plantations and an agreement to return future runaways. Of course, many maroon societies never reached such acknowledged independence, being crushed by massive force of arms, and even when treaties were proposed they were sometimes refused or quickly violated. Nevertheless, new maroon communities seemed to appear almost as quickly as the old ones were exterminated, and for many plantation societies right up to final emancipation they remained, from a colonial perspective, a "chronic plague" and "gangrene."

To be viable, maroon communities had to be inaccessible, and villages were typically located in remote, inhospitable areas. In the southern United States, isolated swamps were a favorite setting, and maroons often became part of Native American communities. In Jamaica, some of the most famous maroon groups lived in the intricately accidented "cockpit country," where water and good soil are scarce but deep canyons and limestone sinkholes abound. And in the Guianas, seemingly impenetrable jungles provided maroons with a safe haven. Throughout the hemisphere, maroons developed extraordinary skills in guerrilla warfare. To the bewilderment of their colonial enemies, who attempted to employ rigid and conventional tactics learned on the open battlefields of Europe, these highly adaptable and mobile warriors took maximum advantage of confined environments, striking and withdrawing with great rapidity, making extensive use of ambushes to catch their adversaries in crossfire, fighting only when and where they chose, depending on reliable intelligence networks among nonmaroons (both slaves and white settlers), and often communicating by drums and horns.

The initial maroons in any New World colony hailed from a wide range of societies in West and West-Central Africa—at the outset, they shared

Figure 1. A 1599 painting by Andrés Sánchez Gallque of maroon leader Don Francisco de Arobe and his two sons, sent to Philip III of Spain. From the collections of the Museo de América, Madrid.

neither language nor other major aspects of culture. Their collective task, once off in the forests or mountains or swamplands, was nothing less than to create new communities and institutions, drawing on their diverse African heritages with added input from their European masters and new Amerindian neighbors. Scholars, mainly anthropologists, who have examined contemporary maroon life most closely seem to agree that such societies are often uncannily "African" in feeling but at the same time largely devoid of directly transplanted systems. However "African" in general character, no maroon social, political, religious, or aesthetic system can be reliably traced to a specific African ethnic provenience—they reveal rather their hybrid composition, forged in the early meeting of peoples bearing diverse African, European, and Amerindian cultures in the agonized and hence dynamic settings of the New World.

Some of the most famous maroon societies are Palmares (Brazil), Palenque de San Basilio (Colombia), the maroons of Esmeraldas (Ecuador), San Lorenzo de los Negros (Mexico), the maroons of Jamaica, and the Saamaka, Ndyuka, and other maroons of Suriname.

Palmares, in northeastern Brazil, flourished for a full century before its final defeat by a large Portu-

guese army in 1694–1695. A close-knit federation of villages, made up of some 11,000 people, it included, besides its largely Angolan-born Africans, Brazilian Indians, poor whites, and Portuguese deserters. During the seventeenth century, wave after wave of Dutch and then Portuguese armies were sent out against Palmares, which resisted with the help of its complex political and social organization, under the leadership of Ganga Zumba and, during its final years, the legendary Zumbi.

Palenque de San Basilio, still today a community near the Atlantic coast of Colombia, boasts a history stretching back to the seventeenth century. In recent years, historians, anthropologists, and linguists—working in collaboration with Palenqueros—have uncovered a great deal about continuities and changes in the life of these early Colombian freedom fighters, whose proud descendants still occupy the town today.

The maroon history of Esmeraldas, on the Pacific coast of Ecuador, began in the early sixteenth century, when Spanish ships carrying African slaves from Panama to Guayaquil and Lima were wrecked amid strong currents. A number of slave survivors sought freedom in the unconquered interior, where they allied with indigenous peoples. In the 1580s, having beaten back military expeditions sent to capture them, several maroon leaders traveled to Quito to make peace with the Spanish. In 1599, a portrait of one such leader, Don Francisco de Arobe, and his two sons, was commissioned and sent to Philip III of Spain to commemorate these negotiations (figure 1).

San Lorenzo de los Negros, in Veracruz on the Caribbean coast of Mexico, is probably the best known of the seventeenth-century maroon towns in Mexico. Under their leader Yanga, these maroons attempted to make peace as early as 1608, but it was not till 1630, after years of intermittent warfare, that the viceroy and the crown finally agreed to establish the town of free maroons.

The maroons of Jamaica, who continue to live in two main groups centered in Accompong (in the hills above Montego Bay) and in Moore Town (deep in the Blue Mountains), maintain strong traditions about their days as freedom fighters, when the former group was led by Cudjoe and the latter by the redoubtable woman warrior Nanny (whose likeness now graces the Jamaican 500 dollar bill). Two centuries of scholarship, some of it written by maroons themselves, offer diverse windows on the ways these men and women managed to build a vibrant culture within the confines of a relatively small island.

The maroons of Suriname now constitute the most fully documented case of how former slaves built new societies and cultures, under conditions of extreme deprivation, in the Americas—and how they developed and maintained semi-independent societies that persist in the present. From their late seventeenth-century origins and the details of their wars and treaty making to their current struggles with multinational mining and timber companies, much is now known about these peoples' achievements, in large part because of the extensive recent collaboration by Saamaka and Ndyuka maroons with anthropologists. Today, Suriname maroons—who number some 122,000 people—live in the interior of the country, in and around the capital Paramaribo, and in neighboring French Guiana as well as in the Netherlands.

Maroons and maroon societies hold a special place within the study of slavery. *Marronage* represented a major form of slave resistance, whether accomplished by lone individuals, by small groups, or in great collective rebellions. Throughout the Americas, maroon communities stood out as heroic

challenges to colonial authority, as the living proof of the existence of a slave consciousness that refused to be limited by the whites' manipulation of it. It is no accident that throughout the Caribbean today, the historical maroon—often mythologized into a larger-than-life figure—has become a touchstone of identity for the region's writers, artists, intellectuals, and politicians, the ultimate symbol of resistance to oppression and the fight for freedom.

RICHARD PRICE

Bibliography

Bilby, Kenneth M. *True-Born Maroons*. Gainesville: University Press of Florida, 2005.

Heuman, Gad, ed. *Out of the House of Bondage: Runaways, Resistance and Marronage in Africa and the New World*. London: Frank Cass, 1986.

Price, Richard, ed. *Maroon Societies: Rebel Slave Communities in the Americas*. 3rd ed. Baltimore, MD: Johns Hopkins University Press, 1996.

———. *Travels with Tooy: History, Memory, and the African American Imagination*. Chicago: University of Chicago Press, 2008.

Medicine

See Healing, African; Healing, African American; Healing, European; Healing, Native American.

Military Mobilization

In 1780, at the height of the War of American Independence, a German student ran away from his university studies at Leipzig only to be kidnapped by Hessian agents, who forced him into the service of King George III of England. Thousands, perhaps scores of thousands, of men had similar experiences, but rather few described them as artfully as Johann Gottfried Seume (1763–1810), who says in "Adventures of a Hessian Recruit":

> Here lay together in one berth, a nobleman of Brunswick, a postilion of Gotha, a Hessian lieutenant, and a bailiff of Meinungen; there a monk of Wurzberg, a French adju-

tant, a student from Jena, a game-keeper from Halberstadt, and a Viennese merchant; all in the past, that is, for now every one was *professor designatus* of the Hessian musket. (Seume, 6)

Seume's abduction, and the fates of the motley crew with whom he found himself armed and bedded down, were the result of long-standing struggles to recruit the manpower needed in the escalation of the scale of conflict that accompanied consolidation of military-fiscal monarchies in Europe. Though recruitment, training, and retention of men in uniform had long been a major concern for the military powers in Europe, military mobilization became even more pressing around 1500 with the opening of the Atlantic World. Newly formed monarchies such as Spain—forged from the combination of Aragon and Castile—and nations-in-the-making such as the Dutch Netherlands, as well as more formed countries such as England and France, all found themselves facing new demands for troops to occupy and defend their conquests as they engaged in the establishment of overseas colonies by force of arms. It was one thing to eliminate Native American regimes in Mexico and Peru, as was accomplished during the reign of Holy Roman emperor Charles V (r. 1520–1556) in Spain, but quite another to maintain the long lists of privates, sergeants, captains, and colonels necessary to patrol and defend these new domains. Perhaps it was merely coincidence that the emerging monarchies of maritime Europe also mobilized greater armies at home at the same time; scholars believe that the decade of the 1530s was critical in the development of larger forces whose loyalties were to an abstract sense of continuing collective interest—the root of modern nations—as opposed to earlier personal loyalties to king, queen, emperor, or local counts or dukes.

The emerging monarchies of Europe employed various methods, from outright coercion to appeals to self-interest, to get men out of the fields, factories, and drinking halls and into uniform. There were press-gangs, such as the one that seized Johann Seume in 1780, but there were also recruitment posters, signing bonuses, and all sorts of promises of the prestige and glories of life in the uniform of one's sovereign. The early Iberian conquests in Central and South America were carried out by aristocratic desperadoes, whom we now call conquistadors, and mostly volunteer bands of followers, but over time it became necessary to lure, persuade, and sometimes force men to "drink the King's shilling," an English expression that over time became synonymous with the fate of hundreds of thousands of men.

The peoples assaulted by the conquistadors had plenty of methods of their own with which to marshal warriors against the European intruders. The Aztecs and Incas mobilized far more warriors than their European foes, even though they were often derided when people spoke of the ease of the Spanish conquests. The fall of the Aztecs and Incas had little if anything to do with failures to mobilize defenders; rather, they succumbed to Spanish combinations of trickery, sleight-of-hand, and steel. Farther north, the Amerindians of North America similarly deployed hundreds, sometimes thousands of fighters. It took some persuading for Native American leaders such as Metacom (better known as King Philip), Popé, Pontiac, and Tecumseh to mount their effective resistance, but they compiled attackers in large numbers by combining the personal militialike followings of many chiefs. The major difference between European and Amerindian mobilizations lay in the lengths of time they served; American Indians agreed to fight for a single battle or a season's campaign at most, but they could not be forced into service for the duration of a war. Very likely, the fact that European soldiers were trained professionals *in uniform* made them subject to discipline and retention; the individually decorated Indian warrior was a freelancer, a part-time abandoner of family and fields, and therefore not as liable to compulsion from his superiors. European colonial authorities frequently recruited Indians for service in their ranks, for want of cooperating settlers and lack of support from monarchies in Europe; it is not coincidence that King Philip was killed by a fellow Indian, or that virtually all European forces in the Americas included Native spies in their ranks. But Europeans were rather shy of conscripting large numbers of Amerindians, since they distrusted Native fighters' effectiveness and loyalty against their own people.

Europeans in the Americas distrusted another large source of potential manpower even more. Africans were making the same transition from ad hoc local militia units to trained, standing armies as the continent militarized. Young men of fighting age in coastal Africa were being stolen, enslaved, and sold in massive numbers to plantation owners in the Americas. The early sugar barons in seventeenth-century Brazil, one of the principal destinations of the enslaved, dominated the politics of the region with bands of trained slave fighters; a celebrated black regiment, the Henriques, made critical contributions to the expulsion of the Dutch from Pernambuco in the 1650s. The Portuguese in Africa, particularly in their "conquest" of Angola, could not sustain soldiers of European origin in the tropical disease environments there, even after trying to populate regular units with condemned criminals from Portugal. Their African "conquests" relied largely on ad hoc mercenary alliances with the local authorities under their influence, the so-called *guerra preta* (or "black guard"). These intermittent, though not infrequent, mobilizations were indistinguishable in practice from opportunistic raiding for captives to enslave.

Governments in Europe and the Americas spurned the military capacities of the Africans they had enslaved, some of whom were experienced warriors. One of the few times that blacks were seen in the military forces of the northern Europeans was in November 1688, when the men and women of southern England saw 200 blacks from Dutch trading castles on the Gold Coast in the army of William of Orange. When William accomplished the Glorious Revolution, which transformed England into a much stronger military power, he may well have recognized the fighting potential of black manpower, but, if so, he would have been a man far ahead of his time. The red-coated British army remained lily-white.

The wars of western Europe increased in duration and intensity during the eighteenth century, commencing with the War of the Spanish Succession (1701–1713) and continuing in the War of the Austrian Succession (1744–1748) and the Seven Years' War, which raged from 1756 until 1763. This last conflict can truly be called a world war, in that men—and a few women—served on virtually all the oceans and practically all the continents (Australia remained an exception). The demand for military manpower was noticeable in every European society, but the methods of obtaining men for the ranks did not change very much. It took the advent of the War of American Independence (1775–1783) to alter significantly the means, methods, and techniques of military mobilization.

When the conflict commenced in 1775, George III and his ministers quickly determined that many of their subjects in the home islands did not wish to fight against their American cousins. Recruitment posters, sign-up bonuses, and generous doses of whiskey were needed to lure men into the ranks of the redcoats. The king also enlisted as many American Loyalists as he could and—not unlike the Portuguese authorities in Africa—recruited numerous Native American tribes as well. Perhaps most surprising of all, the British urged enslaved Africans and African Americans to flee their American masters and join the king's army. Perhaps 5,000 did so, and most—having little to attract them elsewhere—stayed with the British even after their cause was lost.

The king also simply purchased over 20,000 men from the landgrave (count) of Hesse, in the area of modern Frankfurt. That many of these recruits—mostly conscripted and unpaid—were less than exemplary soldiers can be seen in the story of Johann Seume, who described his own adventures in that company:

> We now began to drill. They had so advantageous an opinion of my personality as to entrust me with the high office of sergeant. You should have seen me when I had to teach others, how civilly I stood there, a young, beardless instructor in war, knowing nothing myself; and how most of our new officers understood even less than we and the recruits. (Seume, 7)

By an odd but fortuitous coincidence, 1780—the year that Seume was forced into the Hessian unit of the British army—was also the year that a famous caricature of the military process by Henry William Bunbury appeared in British newspapers. Entitled simply "The Recruits," it shows a British sergeant laying a stick across the front sides of three men he is attempting to muster into the army of George III. One is fat and stupid, another is lean and weak, and the third seems suspiciously shifty. The onlooker, who is clearly malnourished, appears to wonder if these rather sorry subjects are the fittest and finest John Bull could find.

By 1775, the year that the War of American Independence began, British, French, and Spanish colonists tended to be superior physically—on average, they were taller, stronger, and healthier than

Figure 1. Henry William Bunbury, *The Recruits*, 1780. Image courtesy of the Military & Historical Image Bank, www.historicalimagebank.com.

their Old World counterparts. Their superior physical fitness was especially noted in North America, where the high-protein diets of the colonists far exceeded what Europe fed the majority of its people.

There were other differences as well. With a handful of exceptions—dating back to the Thirty Years' War—the War of American Independence saw the first true citizens' army. When the war began, less than a score of men throughout the 13 colonies had any significant military experience. The inexperience among the officer corps was even more the case with the rank and file, most of whom truly did not know what they were headed into. The bravery, or foolhardiness, of many of the willing recruits staggers the modern imagination. Not only did many thousands of men volunteer, but so did a handful of women. The best-documented case, by far, is that of Deborah Sampson of Massachusetts, who deserted from her status as a bondswoman to enter the Continental Army. She served for two years, with some distinction, and her gender was discovered only after she was wounded. For the rest of a long life, she was proud of—and occasionally gave public talks on—the subject of her military service.

The Continental Army units were more effective than the British troops because the men in them had

sworn to serve for the duration of the war. Had the 13 colonies in North America been able to muster, say, 10 percent of their population, they could never have been conquered. But mobilization proved difficult for the rebellious colonists, too. George Washington, who had started his career as a major of militia, expressed great exasperation with the men who reported for duty in the Continental Army; when the British easily crossed from Brooklyn in 1776 to take Manhattan, he threw his cockade on the ground and exclaimed, "Are these the men with whom I am to save America?" (Greene, 216).

With the end of the War of American Independence in 1783, the Atlantic World reached a relative military balance between the monarchical powers in Europe, the newly independent United States, and the Central and South American countries still under Spanish rule. The Americans demobilized; the British did the same. It seemed that peace might prevail for some time. But the military triumph of the American popular forces helped to ignite the French Revolution of 1789 (as did the military debt incurred helping the United States win freedom). For the first two years, the French Revolution was a rather gentlemanly affair, with former nobles consorting with former subjects. But in 1792 the revolution turned radical and violent, and in 1793 the French king, Louis XVI, lost his head on the guillotine.

The Atlantic World then entered a new era of massive military mobilization. Turning again to the American example of a popular citizen army, the French revolutionaries announced the *levée en masse*, forced national service by every adult French man and woman. Young people served in the armies; their middle-aged parents made uniforms; and old men and women chanted patriotic songs in village squares. There had been armies serving institutionalized government before, and there had been a citizens' army in the North American colonies, but the French combined these two and added a third motivating consideration: their battle against the monarchical powers was one of fight and conquer, or perish.

Virtually every monarchical power in Europe mobilized for the ensuing decade (and more) of war against the violently explosive French Republic under General Napoleon Bonaparte. In the initial campaigns in 1793–1794, the French won, thanks to the enormous manpower they had mobilized.

That the Napoleonic Wars ended in disaster for France is explained more by the overweening ambition of a single military commander than by failures of mobilizing a national citizen army.

Even as the republican French enjoyed initial successes against their monarchical neighbors, they acted like oppressors toward their revolutionary counterparts in the Americas: the Haitians. The sugar-rich colony of Saint-Domingue had long been a source of revenue critical to France, and republican and then Napoleonic forces tried to stamp out the revolt that developed there among freed people. That they failed is evidenced by Saint-Domingue turning into the Republic of Haiti; that they had a deadly effect can be witnessed by modern Haiti being the poorest nation in the Western Hemisphere. North American observers took fright at the revolution in Haiti; they saw the possibility that black slave revolts would take place in Virginia, the Carolinas, and Georgia. Not surprisingly, these panics led to yet another feature of mobilization: the willingness of slave owners in the American South to muster militia to stamp out rebellions by the people they held in slavery.

The Haitian Revolution also brought a painful truth home to the European powers dispatching troops to the tropics: the necessity of fighting the diseases of low latitudes. The Napoleonic army sent to reduce Haiti lost 10,000 men to yellow fever in a single year's time, and subsequent deployments of British, French, and Spanish forces in Africa saw casualty figures of similarly devastating proportions. The European nations had progressed in strictly military terms beyond those they intended to colonize, but they—as yet—had no remedy for the fatal effects of tropical diseases on armies sent from the temperate climate of Europe.

By 1800, recruiting citizens to fight in the national armies and navies of the Atlantic World was significantly different from finding the mercenaries who had fought for European monarchs in 1600, or even 1700. The populations from which the recruits were drawn were more literate and sophisticated, and prospective soldiers had more prior experience on which to base comparisons. By that date, readers of German could listen to the words of Johann Seume's "Adventures of a Hessian Recruit," who had this to say: "Stay at home, and do not wander farther than to the shores of the Saale and the Elbe. It is far more comfortable to turn over the pages of a book of other people's adventures . . . than to go through the smallest part of them in person" (Seume, 2). Seume was, doubtless, luckier than many of his contemporaries in that he returned alive from service in North America. Many did not.

The Old World powers continued to face the difficulty of persuading men to remain in uniform. The shortages of manpower for military service would have proved insurmountable had new military technologies, such as the rifle, not multiplied the range and accuracy of the average soldier to degrees that allowed European nations to defeat opponents overseas without the massive investments of manpower in the earlier ages of siege warfare and musket volleys.

SAMUEL WILLARD CROMPTON

Bibliography

Barnett, Correlli. *Britain and Her Army, 1509–1970*. London: Penguin, 1970.

Greene, George W. *The Life of Nathanael Greene, Major-General in the Army of the Revolution*. 3 vols. New York: Putnam, 1867–1871. Reprinted Freeport, NY: Books for Libraries, 1972.

Parker, Geoffrey. *The Army of Flanders and the Spanish Road, 1567–1659*. New York: Cambridge University Press, 1972.

Reiss, Tom. *The Black Count: Glory, Revolution, Betrayal, and the Real Count of Monte Cristo*. New York: Crown, 2012.

Seume, Johann. "Adventures of a Hessian Recruit." Read to the Massachusetts Historical Society in November 1887, *Proceedings of the Massachusetts Historical Society*, Vol. IV, 2nd ser. (1887–1889).

Shy, John. *A People Numerous and Armed: Reflections on the Military Struggle for American Independence*. New York: Oxford University Press, 1976.

Young, Alfred F. *Masquerade: The Life and Times of Deborah Sampson, Continental Soldier*. New York: Alfred A. Knopf, 2005.

Military Technologies

As long as the mounted warrior and the armored foot soldier equipped with bows, arrows, spears, and lances remained the dominant technologies of military success, Europe—which regarded itself as

Christendom—was destined to be a minor player among the competing powers on the Eurasian continent, not necessarily even in the top three or four. When military technologies shifted after the fifteenth century to a combination of firearms, cannon, pikes, swords, and bayonets, the European powers gained a significant advantage, one that only increased as they made their way into the Atlantic World.

As late as 1400, the massive armies of the Mongols, Turks, and their allies were unbeatable in direct combat. Europe had been fortunate to survive the Mongol invasion of 1241, and Central Asian warriors equipped with composite bows remained the hallmark of military power for a long time. But when the next Central Asian invader, the Ottoman Turks, took Constantinople in 1453, their tactics and gunpowder weaponry introduced enormous innovations in military technologies. Constantinople had been besieged roughly 18 times over the centuries, falling only once, to its Latin Christian cousins in 1204. The Turks captured it in two months, primarily by using the massive siege cannon cast by their armories. Firepower, clearly, was an overwhelming new military technology.

When Ferdinand and Isabella of Aragon and Castile captured the citadel of Granada, the last Moorish holdout in Iberia, in January 1492, their troops were mounted on horses of the same type their great-great-grandsires had ridden a century earlier. They had added firearms to the mix, however, and although their harquebuses, the first shoulder-braced weaponry to be introduced, were crude, they struck fear into enemies who had never witnessed the fire and smoke of explosive propellants. The regally styled Ferdinand and Isabella, and their grandson Charles V, who ruled much of Europe between 1520 and 1556, looked like late-medieval monarchs, but their developing militaries gave them the power of a new age. It was during Charles's long reign that the Spaniards made their first conquests in the Americas, and the combination of trickery, horses, and Spanish steel that Hernán Cortés and Francisco Pizarro brought to warfare there resulted in vast increases of silver and gold at Spain's disposal. The Habsburg rulers spent lavishly on the newest of weaponry. By about 1580, they had remodeled the Spanish military system, with its soldiers using a combination of pikes, swords, sabers, and harquebuses. Other European powers resented the Spanish New World monopoly and began reorienting their military strategies, explorers for reconnaissance, sailors, and soldiers in the same direction.

The flintlock musket, pioneered around 1620, made possible the English, French, and Dutch incursions into North America; without that firepower, the Indians might well have destroyed the first colonists, especially once they recognized the insatiable European desire for land. The Europeans gained further technological advantage as they combated indigenous peoples in Africa, the Caribbean, and the Americas with the sword bayonet, which made its appearance during the Thirty Years' War (1618–1648). When the armies of King Louis XIV of France (r. 1643–1715) developed the socket bayonet, fastened firmly to the end of the musket barrel, the European powers appeared to have the requisite combination of fire, smoke, and steel to defeat practically all of their Atlantic opponents.

This sudden leap to weapons superiority did not mean the Christian European powers never suffered setbacks. In 1578, King Sebastian I of Portugal was killed and his army annihilated by the Moors of North Africa; it is not coincidental that Morocco was not colonized for another 250 years. Native Americans also occasionally had success against European colonizers. In 1675–1676, for instance, the Narragansett leader Metacom, whom the English called King Philip, used the settlers' muskets against them, and in 1680, an inspired prophet named Popé drove the Spanish out of far-northern New Spain (modern New Mexico). What the courageous indigenous fighters lacked, however, was iron, steel, and ready access to gunpowder, technological advantages that Europeans had been refining for 200 years.

In the European dynastic wars of the eighteenth century, military occupation of the mainland Americas was treated as a distant afterthought: the British and French were much more interested in the sugar-producing islands of the Caribbean, slave- and gold-yielding contacts in coastal Africa, and a great contest for territorial control in far-off India. The military technologies employed during the War of the Spanish Succession (1701–1714) and the War of the Austrian Succession (1744–1748) did not appear significantly different from those a hundred years earlier. What was different was the vastly greater size of the European armies in the field.

Thousands of men marched and countermarched across Europe, carrying muskets, rapiers, sabers, bayonets, and field cannon with them. Casualty lists grew in size, as did the collateral damage inflicted on civilians. These military depredations came at a time when Europe considered itself to be in its Age of Enlightenment, but it was difficult to see how the various armies and their generals had progressed significantly toward reasoned settlement of differences.

At the beginning of second half of the eighteenth century, European armed confrontations reached far beyond the confines of the region in what might be considered the first "world war": the Seven Years' War (1756–1763), which pitted Britain, Prussia, and Britain's overseas colonies against France, its Atlantic possessions, Austria, and Russia. During this momentous conflict, the superiority of the munitions of the European powers became undeniable. British, French, and Spanish warships had vast firepower, inflicting great damage and casualties on one another, and British, French, and Spanish infantries fought for the first time in North America and the Caribbean. The redcoated British soldier and his monkey-jacket-clad naval counterpart became the visible images of European military power. Although employing the same military technologies as in 1700, the British and Prussians defeated virtually all their enemies, making Britain into the great military, naval, and commercial power of the Atlantic World. By the time the Peace of Paris was signed in 1763, it seemed evident that European technologies were the best in the world, and that the British had topped all competitors in their deployment. Their lead only increased when some of their inventors turned to developing the rifle and the carronade, a smoothbore cannon effective at short ranges.

German gunsmiths had tinkered with the rifling of gun barrels as early as the sixteenth century, but it was in the German section of Pennsylvania that gunsmiths turned out the first true Kentucky rifle (though which state might claim the dubious honor remains a matter of dispute). By making spiral grooves in the barrel, gunsmiths were able to extend and control the trajectory of the projectiles it fired. The rifle was counterintuitive, in that one would imagine that the spinning bullet would fly out of control, when in fact its gyroscopic properties carried it much straighter to its target.

The British American colonists used the rifle first against Native Americans and then turned it on their British cousins during the War of American Independence (1775–1783). British analysts were astonished by the accuracy of the rifle fire of the colonials, and they put some of their best minds to work on coming up with a counter. Major Patrick Ferguson—who lost his life in 1780 at the Battle of King's Mountain in North Carolina—patented the first breech-loading rifle too late to make a difference in the war, but in 1800 Ezekiel Baker in London patented a much simpler and sturdier weapon, the Baker Rifle, which became the basis for British sharpshooting success.

But even as the solitary rifleman was making his appearance on the battlefield, political and military developments conspired to bring about a new version of the massed armed force. The French revolution (1789–1795) started as a moderate movement, aiming for a constitutional monarchy, but it became extreme and violent in 1793 when Louis XVI lost his head to the guillotine. As virtually all the monarchical powers of Europe attacked republican France, that nation's leaders pioneered the *levée en masse,* mobilizing about 850,000 men. When one side possessed such vast numbers, technologies of firepower seemed almost irrelevant, and between 1795 and 1808 the French beat back nearly all their foes.

Napoleon Bonaparte, who became emperor of France in 1804, then made two errors that spelled his doom and that foreshadowed the new military systems and technologies of the nineteenth century. When Napoleon invaded Russia in June 1812, French forces encountered a massive reservoir of Russian manpower. In fact, it was the first time in a long period that an Asian territorial power had been seen in such vast numbers in western Europe (some observers caustically referred to the Cossacks as the new version of the Huns). When Napoleon tried to keep his brother on the throne of Spain, he provoked the British to enter the conflict, and the sharpshooting British slowly but inexorably beat the best forces of France in the Peninsular War. The combination of factors in the confrontation was revealing. In Russia *and* in Spain Napoleon committed his troops to fight in areas with terrible roads, or no roads at all, which made it impossible to sustain his supply routes. In Russia and in Spain, Napoleon's brightly uniformed men made easy targets for guerrilla fighters. (The Spanish *guerrilla*, or warrior, entered the English language around this time). The difference between the Russian and Spanish fronts lay in the manners of defeat. In Russia, Napoleon was defeated by superior manpower; in Spain, inferior technology was his downfall.

Stubborn obsolescence was not the monopoly of the French. When the Duke of Wellington saw the first Congreve rockets—self-propelled missiles similar to rockets deployed in Mysore, India, in the 1790s—he said that he wished to be rid of the clumsy, inaccurate things. And neither the French nor the British appreciated the military advantage that could be derived from use of the hot-air balloon for reconnaissance: they remained purely a device for popular entertainment until the Crimean War, in the 1850s. However, by 1815—the year of Waterloo and the final defeat of Napoleon's forces—European powers had lifted their technological superiority over indigenous peoples to a ratio of at least four to one. The musket, rifle, bayonet, and cannon were more than enough to ensure European victories over all of their Atlantic foes, even with massive losses in manpower to yellow fever and other tropical pathogens and parasites. Two generations later, when the repeating rifle replaced its standard version and the Maxim (repeating machine) gun had appeared, European superiority would approach a factor of something greater than ten, or even twenty, to one.

Were the European peoples more clever—or just luckier—than Asians, Africans, and Americans? No one has yet explained fully how the land-based, slow-moving European military forces of 1415—the year of the Battle of Agincourt—turned into the fast-moving soldiers, sailors, and explorers who came to dominate the Americas, but who were defeated by diseases in Africa. It was entirely possible that another military power (Ottoman Turks, Safavid Persians, or some other Asian force) could have hit upon the same combination of firepower, mobility, and sharpshooting that characterized European military success. They would still have had to overcome a basic geographic challenge, however: mobility over an open ocean, which finally turned the Atlantic into the modern fulfillment of the Roman vision of *mare nostrum,* "our sea."

SAMUEL WILLARD CROMPTON

Bibliography

Black, Jeremy. *War and the World: Military Power and the Fate of Continents, 1450–2000.* New Haven, CT: Yale University Press, 1998.

Crompton, Samuel Willard. *The Repeating Rifle.* Philadelphia, PA: Chelsea House, 2004.

Diamond, Jared. *Guns, Germs, and Steel: The Fates of Human Societies.* New York: W. W. Norton, 1999.

Duffy, Christopher. *The Military Experience in the Age of Reason.* Oxford: Routledge, 1987.

Missionary Orders and Communities

The term *mission* is often used as a noun to describe a fixed space with substantial physical facilities centered around a Christian church. The stations established by seventeenth-century Jesuits in Paraguay might spring to mind, or one might think of the string of grand missions that Spanish Franciscans built in the eighteenth century along the Camino Real in Alta California.

Yet to understand the motivations for the transit of Christianity in the context of early-modern Atlantic history, *mission* is best understood as worldly action centered on a spiritual vocation. Early moderns who sought to live as missionaries did so with the express hope of achieving personal salvation in the afterlife as well as transforming the present world. Contemporary Christian discourse emphasized the fallen nature of pagans as sinners, yet missionaries' efforts to transform the lives of non-Christian "others" and to see to it that Spanish Catholic colonizers in the Americas maintained the integrity of their souls constituted the acts of charity necessary for the missionaries to become better Christians themselves. Conceived in this way, mission stations—and equally important, their urban churches, monasteries, and colleges—served as nodal points from which men (but also women, such as the French evangelical nun, Marie de l'Incarnation, 1599–1672) took missionary action in the name of salvation, which, in turn, expanded the presence of Catholicism in the Atlantic World. Especially among the mendicant orders, the new worlds revealed in the Americas sparked millenarian hopes that this opportunity to garner more souls for Christ would hasten end-times. This very high stakes and action-oriented relationship between "self" and "other" linked the Ultimate (salvation in the hereafter) with the penultimate (daily life and devout behavior in this world).

Sixteenth-century encounters with the world beyond Christian Europe were authorized by papal donations, committing the "most Christian" monarchs of Portugal and Spain to the proselytization and protection of the souls of their brethren rulers in Africa and Asia, with whom they traded, or the populations they inherited by right of military conquest in the Americas. Although the American context was decidedly new, the proselytizing techniques that missionaries brought to the challenge had been well honed over centuries of Christian evangelization in Europe. The monastic orders' outreach across the Atlantic in the immediate wake of military action has to be understood as an extension of their much earlier, systematic steps to integrate worldly activity into their spiritual vocations—in other words, the desire to cross the Atlantic was possible only because several centuries prior, monks had taken decisive steps to minister to their neighbors beyond the monastic walls.

Differing conceptions regarding the permeability of these walls shaped missionary corporate identities. Missionary orders distinguished themselves from one another in the ways they formalized the complex working out of the relationship between God, self, and neighbor. The mendicant orders, Franciscans (founded by St. Francis of Assisi, 1181–1209) and Dominicans (founded by St. Dominic de Guzmán, 1170–1221), also known as friars, had taken the first steps beyond the traditional isolation of Christian monasticism. The Franciscans, for example, were an order of brothers dedicated to lives of itinerant poverty in imitation of Christ's passion. Along with the Dominicans, a spiritual brotherhood dedicated to preaching, these mendicant orders had initiated the worldly trend in the thirteenth century by moving outside monastery walls into urban and rural spaces. In the early sixteenth century, the Society of Jesus (or the Jesuits) moved to tip the balance between contemplation and action in a decidedly worldly direction. The first generation of men who formed the Society of Jesus gathered around Ignatius of Loyola (1491–1556) and his Spiritual Exercises.

Their shared mission "to console souls" was expressed in these terms: "We are not monks! . . . the world is our [monastic] house" (O'Malley, 67–68). They called themselves "contemplatives in action."

These early-modern missionary orders worked in urban society, in both Europe and the large cosmopolitan cities of the Americas. The urban centers functioned as key points from which work in more distant locales (whether in rural Europe or in European holdings overseas) could be staged and, importantly, funded. Missionaries belonged to "orders" defined by precise regulations about comportment and devotional exercises. They sought the heavenly on earth by living together in convents and monasteries, or professed houses, with the orders differentiating themselves by the degrees to which they remained cloistered—that is, isolated from the profane world. Most orders founded their monasteries in the hearts of urban centers, both to facilitate access to the lay populace but also because these edifices and the men and women within them stood as exemplars of Christian piety for the lay public. Their prayers and devotional acts could inspire or prod lay Christians to lead more devout lives, demonstrating that the Christian promise of salvation could be attained through prayerful contemplation of the sufferings of Christ, his mother, and the communion of saints, whose dramatic devotional lives were exemplified in the awe-inspiring art that adorned Christian architecture.

Good works to alleviate the daily sufferings of one's "neighbors" constituted an important aspect of devotional life. Here, *neighbors* and *good works* referred to action taken on behalf of the local needy, but charitable action also fueled a sense of Catholic community that often had transatlantic dimensions. For example, the Mercederian order collected alms in the Americas in order to pay the ransoms of Christians kidnapped into slavery in Muslim North Africa. The "reform of self" motivated one to care for and/or reform one's neighbor: this has been the centerpiece of Christian motivations for expansion, honed over centuries and still operative today.

The Society of Jesus, formalized under direct papal authority, worked to counter the Protestant Reformation in northern Europe and to renew the devotional lives of Catholics in southern Europe. Late arrivals in the Americas, members of the Society of Jesus shared the goal of conversion in peripheral regions (northern Mexico and Paraguay) but also set themselves to the spiritual renewal, consolation, and, notably, education of Spaniards and *criollos* in urban locales. Similarly, the Theatines (established in 1524) forged corporate identities based upon worldly action, particularly among the Catholic communities on both sides of the Atlantic Ocean. European female orders such as the Ursulines (founded in 1535) also established missionary convents and schools to evangelize in New France, New Orleans, and Pondicherry, India. The Ursulines were greatly inspired by the Jesuits, whose formal *Constitutions* stated that they were an order of "pilgrims" and "apostles" dedicated to ministering to "the Turks or any other infidels, even those who live in the region called the Indies, or . . . any heretics whatever, or schismatics, or any of the faithful" (*Constitutions* of the Society of Jesus, approved by Papal Bull, September 1540).

The other mendicant orders differed among themselves, occupying a middle ground between the more worldly Jesuits and the pure monasticism of an order such as the Carthusians. Franciscans, for example, situated their monasteries in urban locales to facilitate access to the numerous lay populations of cities, but—and this was critical—the location of the monastery also enabled the friars' return to a stable locale to renew themselves as brothers (*frères*) and to express their primary dedication to communal life by singing the Divine Office. Bert Roest reminds historians not to get "carried away by the astounding development of the Franciscan order as a major pastoral taskforce," that is, as missionaries; to emphasize the mendicants' work in the world tells only half the story, "[f]or ultimately," Roest contends, "all 'worldly' activities (begging, handicrafts, teaching and probably even preaching) *had to be subservient to [contemplation]*" (Roest, 133). The mendicants placed a higher premium on being part of a prayerful community to counter worldly contamination.

Although missionary orders, once they traveled across the Atlantic Ocean, continued to differ over the right balance between contemplation and action, immediate transformations were required, particularly in the sixteenth-century Americas, as they had to grapple with the unprecedented circumstances of ministering to people who had no prior exposure to either Christianity or to European diseases. The combination of pervasive death and unsaved souls moved the missionaries into Indian communities during the first stages of evangelization. While sixteenth-century Spanish spiritual life was dominated by the practice of *recogimiento* (withdrawal), the Spanish Franciscans who traveled to the New World had to shake off attachments to contemplation and "hurry," as it was sometimes stated, toward the active life. Their anxiety to convert resulted in the architectural innovation of the open-air church, with walled outdoor courtyards that accommodated the large numbers who required baptism as well as providing ample space to attend mass. Native populations were recovering by the turn of the seventeenth century, and the open-air chapel was no longer required. Yet in the sixteenth century, as the numbers of Indians dwindled in the face of disease, the labors of administering the sacraments of catechism, baptism, marriage, and confession became even more difficult with the added necessity of administering last rites to the dying.

Initially, missionaries on both sides of the Atlantic utilized a top-down strategy to access souls, first converting community leaders. The Tlaxcalans in New Spain, who were key to Hernán Cortés's efforts to dismantle the Aztec Empire, offer a case in point, as their political alliance also entailed Christianization. The Tlaxcalan peoples well into the seventeenth century claimed rights and privileges from the crown by utilizing the status of "first converts." In South America, Guaraní leaders decided whether or not to live in the Jesuit Paraguayan missions. The Kongo regime in West-Central Africa adopted Catholicism in a similar manner, when Nzinga Mbemba, the political authority who had greeted the Portuguese, was baptized as Afonso and took leadership of what became a Christian Kongo aristocracy, aided by Capuchin missionaries. Later Kongo teachers and charismatics—most famously, Dona Beatriz (1684–1706), a spiritual healer and prophet who sought political power at the end of the seventeenth century—saw themselves as missionaries. Yet this strategy of top-down conversion was effective only in early stages of contact.

During the first half of the sixteenth century, missionaries expressed their sense of being overwhelmed by the urgency of the need to convert the inhabitants of the Americas. To facilitate conversion, missionaries established relationships with indigenous leaders, making use of *fiscales* (inspectors), intermediaries in charge of bringing community members to catechism and mass. They attempted to forge strong ties with the children of Native nobility in particular, who grew up in the shadow of the monasteries, as it were, as trained interpreters and practitioners of Christianity who would facilitate communication with their communities. Effective communication of Christian norms required the missionaries to acquire intimate knowledge of indigenous languages and practices. Most of the knowledge that modern scholars have about Native Americans before the sixteenth century was collected by the religious orders. Accordingly, mendicant missionaries wrote the first grammars and *vocabularios,* and, in the later sixteenth and early seventeenth centuries, the Society of Jesus added to the European intelligence about the people they meant to rule by converting them not only to a "faith" but also to a European way of life. The Jesuit colleges forged strong links with the Native communities, as they trained both the Spanish and Creole children who populated the administrative positions in the Church and colonial state and the children of Indian nobility with whom they worked.

By "knowing" the cultures of the indigenous peoples, missionary linguists and strategists aimed to eradicate "error and superstition" in order to establish the Catholic sacraments as the primary ritual markers of the Native Americans' life cycle—baptism and marriage, confession, reception of the Eucharist, and celebration of the feast days that marked the liturgical calendar, as well as last rites. Penitential practices established not only a more intimate relationship between priest and penitent but also a connection between the penitents and themselves, as believers were taught methods to examine their own consciences in order that they might better know and control their inner lives. Though the mendicants' primary goal was to establish Catholic sacramental life as central to the lives of their congregations, even as late as the eighteenth century friars in Mexico City balanced the needs of their flocks with the demands of their own dedication to lives of prayer. "Even though the work of this *convento grande* is so great,"

claimed a Mercedarian father, "and so greatly increased with many sung Masses, responses, burials, necessary attendances, and precious accomplishments, we sing terce and vespers every day with the required attendance of friars to the choir, except those who are legitimately unable" (Melquiades, 119).

Though personally dedicated to poverty, the missionary orders drew lavishly upon material culture as a medium for augmenting the relationship between heaven and earth. The orders funded paintings and distributed prints with images of the individual orders' most beloved saints or favored images of the Virgin. Prints and paintings were especially important evangelical instruments that missionaries utilized when conducting itinerant missions or evangelical revivals, during which missionaries would pass two to four weeks reanimating the spiritual lives of both Spanish and Indians who lived in communities distant from the large colonial urban centers. Many of the orders also struggled with communities to control the local shrines dedicated to miracles worked by Mary, Jesus, or patron saints. The proliferation of devotional literature in the form of these images and devotional guides printed in the Americas meant that the missionaries' reach extended well beyond their person-to-person contact in church, street, and confessional. Here we can see that missionaries aimed not only to convert but also to help all Christians orient their lives around Catholic sacramental life, and to that end they created permanent way markers in Church art and architecture.

Although the orders differed in their opinions on the proper ratio of contemplation to worldly action, in those early years of conversion all commitments to contemplation took a back seat to the tremendous labor of preaching, baptizing, and caring for the increasing numbers of indigenous Americans who were suffering warfare, dislocation, and—dramatically—the European pathogens against which they had no immunity. While early attempts at conversion targeted indigenous groups as a whole, wherever colonial powers developed strong urban societies centered on Christian norms, indigenous peoples were approached on an individual basis, souls to be saved one at a time.

MICHELLE MOLINA

Bibliography

Chatellier, Louis. *The Religion of the Poor: Rural Missions in Europe and the Formation of Modern Catholicism, c. 1500–c. 1800*. Translated by Brian Pearce. New York: Cambridge, 1997.

Clossey, Luke. *Salvation and Globalization in the Early Jesuit Missions*. Cambridge: Cambridge University Press, 2008

Klor de Alva, J. Jorge. "Colonizing Souls: The Failure of the Indian Inquisition and the Rise of Penitential Discipline." In *Cultural Encounters: The Impact of the Inquisition in Spain and the New World*, edited by Mary Elizabeth Perry and Anne J. Cruz, 3–22. Berkeley: University of California Press, 1991.

Martínez-Serna, J. Gabriel. "Procurators and the Making of the Jesuits' Atlantic Network." In *Soundings in Atlantic History: Latent Structures and Intellectual Currents, 1500–1830*, edited by Bernard Bailyn and Patricia L. Denault, 181–209. Cambridge, MA: Harvard University Press, 2009.

McAndrew, John. *The Open-Air Churches of Sixteenth-Century Mexico: Atrios, Posas, Open Chapels and Other Studies*. Cambridge, MA: Harvard University Press, 1965.

Melquiades, Andrés Martín. *Recogidos: Nueva visión de la mística española, 1500–1700*. Madrid: Seminario Suárez de la Fundación Universitaria Española, 1975.

Melvin, Karen. *Building Colonial Cities of God: Mendicant Orders and Urban Culture in New Spain*. Stanford, CA: Stanford University Press, 2012.

O'Malley, John W. *The First Jesuits*. Cambridge, MA: Harvard University Press, 1993.

———. "Was Ignatius a Church Reformer? How to Look at Early Modern Catholicism." *Catholic Historical Review* 77, no. 2 (1991): 177–293.

Osowski, Edward W. "Carriers of Saints: Traveling Alms Collectors and Nahua Gender Roles." In *Local Religion in Colonial Mexico*, edited by Martin Austin Nesvig, 155–186. Albuquerque: University of New Mexico Press, 2006.

Rapley, Elizabeth. *The Lord as Their Portion: The Story of the Religious Orders and How They Shaped Our World*. Grand Rapids, MI: Eerdmans, 2011.

Ricard, Robert. *The Spiritual Conquest of Mexico: An Essay on the Apostolate and the Evangelizing Methods of the Mendicant Orders in New Spain, 1523–1572*. Berkeley: University of California Press, 1982.

Roest, Bert. "The Discipline of the Heart: Pedagogies of Prayer in Medieval Franciscan Works of Religious Instruction." In *The Medieval Franciscans*, edited by T. J. Johnson, 414–448. Leiden: Brill, 2007.

Modernity

In human terms the Atlantic Ocean is intrinsically modern, a vast maritime space that has been routinely crossed only in the last five centuries. The Europeans' mastery of transatlantic navigation transformed the Western Ocean of their predecessors from a constraining boundary on the edge of their known world, a maelstrom seemingly capable of consuming civilized ventures, into a maritime highway to Africa and Asia, as well as to the entirely unanticipated riches of the Americas. Christopher Columbus's 1492 voyage, serving as a historical watershed dividing the medieval and modern eras, symbolizes European mastery of nature, from oceanic expanses to the intimate psychological spaces where human fears are incubated. The Europeans' dominance over depleted Native American populations and the Africans they held captive reinforced a conceit that their growing mastery of the physical environment was complemented by growing mastery of history itself, of the future. Africans and Amerindians, in contrast, seemed mired in unchanging traditional societies, while Asians were subject to despotic regimes intent on stalling, if not thwarting, progressive change. European access to ever-larger parts of the world, which they mistook for control, complemented the direction they also claimed over the future, over the emergence of modernity.

Despite transatlantic navigation marking the dawn of modernity, Atlantic developments are generally not given prominence in definitions of the concept, which usually focus—harmoniously enough—on scientific, industrial, secular, and political revolutions within Europe. In the European imagination, the Atlantic World offered spaces where people could escape the strictures of existing institutions, where the present and the future could elude undue homage to the past, where human potential for good could fulfill itself more freely than was possible in Europe. Conversely, those opportunities could produce deplorable excesses, countered by once-again productive criticism: the sixteenth-century Spanish debates over the murderous treatment of indigenous peoples by Spanish colonists in the New World and the progressive critiques among eighteenth- and nineteenth-century movements to abolish the Atlantic slave trade and American slavery are the leading examples. By Enlightenment standards, Euroamerican societies could be both exemplary and problematic, but correctable, examples of modernity's promise.

Recent reconsiderations of these Eurocentric biases tend to shorten the time frame of modernity's emergence, while expanding the geographic sweep of its manifestations. C. A. Bayly's globe-encircling examination of *The Birth of the Modern World, 1780–1914* (2004) exemplifies this tendency. Although his global approach highlights the multiple forms and expressions of modernity in the nineteenth century, it understates the developments in the Atlantic of the preceding three centuries and their contribution to the intellectual and financial platforms upon which later Europeans erected their vision of global modernity. This essay reconsiders the legacy of the earlier Atlantic, and how commercialization of labor and of land there and the intertwining of the languages of nature and modernity shaped modern European cultures, as well as African and Amerindian ones. Ironically, early-modern commentators increasingly described the growing commercialization of labor and land in and around the Atlantic as natural workings of trade, thereby obscuring how historically contingent those dramatic changes were. These Atlantic transformations were critical to an emerging European definition of modernity that emphasized the universality of humanity while simultaneously eviscerating the historical relevance of non-European cultures and their practices. African and Amerindian cultures, for their parts, charted courses that affirmed cultural difference, resisted Europeans' universalizing trends on their own very particular terms, and thereby maintained social heterogeneity in spite of Europeans' insistence on the universal value of their own modern ways.

The truism that Euroamerican societies, in contrast to European societies, were land rich and labor poor captures the assumption that labor is inherently mobile and that markets draw laborers to wherever they are employed most efficiently. This fundamental contention in neoclassical economic thought less often conveys the historical reality that Euroamerican economies were overwhelm-

ingly populated through coercion—of European indentured servants, African slaves, and Amerindian slaves and captives—and not by voluntary settlers. The people pulled into Atlantic labor markets found themselves physically alienated from their homelands and excluded from the economic returns from the American lands they plowed, planted, and harvested. Their presence and efforts, however, were critical to legitimize the competing territorial claims of European dynasties and the landed wealth of a small minority of European settlers.

At the level of diplomacy and emerging international law, English and French diplomats asserted territorial claims of European sovereigns against both the Native Americans and the Iberians' hegemonic claims of prior discovery, on the principle of investment of the labor of the monarchs' subjects—natural-born English and French settlers—in American land. John Locke, the English philosopher, articulated a variation on that idea in the *Second Treatise of Civil Government* (1690), arguing that individuals in a state of nature create a property claim in land by investing their labor, and that "in the beginning all the world was America" (Locke, 301). If natural-born subjects acted as proxies for the personal presence of European monarchs in establishing claims to sovereign land overseas, by a parallel logic slaves and indentured servants were proxies for legitimizing the property claims of private masters.

Millions of laborers, most working under some form of coercion and very few owning land, made the Atlantic economy operate, whether hoisting sails, planting tropical crops, curing fish, cutting logwood, or performing any of the myriad forms of manual labor in an age before fossil-fueled technologies. The ability of some landowners to amass dozens, if not hundreds, of enslaved Africans created productive capacity on modern scales, exceeding smaller European artisanal scales of operation. On the islands of the Caribbean, in particular, sugar plantations with their own boiling houses were among the first industrial-scale facilities built and owned by Europeans, requiring enormous investments of capital and large forces of anonymous labor to grow cane and produce sugar, virtually all of which was destined for unknown consumers in distant markets overseas. The monoculture of sugarcane on many Caribbean islands represented the modern characteristic of production sites separated widely from sites of consumption. Intensive concentration on foreign markets also distanced workers from the production of the food necessary for their own sustenance; plantation regimes imported food from distant growers. Even biological reproduction of the labor force was outsourced, mostly to Africa, and plantation labor forces were maintained only through purchases of additional captives.

By the late seventeenth century, the unfree labor forces of English and French Caribbean and North American enterprises, combined with the sailors who worked the transatlantic routes, were probably a majority of the population. Yet at approximately the same time, sex ratios in the English North American colonies were becoming balanced, birth rates began to exceed death rates, and the Euroamerican population began to grow naturally. By the mid-eighteenth century, the landowning settlers and their families in British North America numbered over 2 million, many of them descended from indentured servants who had survived their terms of service and acquired land. The numbers of African-descended slaves in both North America and the Caribbean and Atlantic islands was less than 1 million, even though far more Africans than Europeans had crossed the Atlantic to British colonies. The growth of landowning populations, particularly in temperate British North America, made the maturation of settler colonies seem a natural product of the growth of nations. The subsequent political independence of most colonial populations and the switch from monarchical to republican systems of government reinforced the conviction that this transition was the natural form of human development—of modernity.

Land ownership, particularly in British America, changed from a birthright to a purchase basis. Historically, European societies had restricted the ability of merchants to own land, either in their home societies or in foreign domains, reserving it for aristocratic families or military or religious orders. Such awards to established interests were an old European strategy to secure frontier regions, and the one that the Spanish and Portuguese used in claiming their territories overseas. In the late sixteenth and early seventeenth centuries, however, both the French and English monarchs delegated colonization to merchant enterprises. The access to land extended to French and English merchants was a striking novelty, and the French crown soon retreated from this strategy, instead adapting seigneurial grants to the Americas as well as delegating responsibilities for land and its occupants to Catholic orders. The English, however, continued colonization under the commercial terms established in charters, and the availability of land in full personal possession lured settlers, including foreign Protestants. British colonial assemblies passed private acts to naturalize foreigners, almost all of them Protestants, thereby giving them the right to own land under British sovereignty, pass it on to their heirs, or sell it. As well, British colonial governments and colonists in their private capacities alienated indigenous lands by making purchases, a practice quite foreign to Amerindians and subject to fraud and deception.

By the end of the eighteenth century in the Anglo-Atlantic World, mechanisms to allow foreign ownership of land had become normalized, and the British government was negotiating concessions for British subjects to own land in foreign places, such as Portuguese Madeira. By the nineteenth century, the British were exerting diplomatic pressure on other European sovereigns to end their restrictions on foreign ownership of land, particularly in places where British interests wished to invest, such as Latin America and the Ottoman domains. The right of individuals to own land anywhere in the world, regardless of citizenship in the nation-states then taking shape, and the right to dispose of it through commercial transactions, were increasingly treated in the Anglophone world as inherent in the natural functioning of trade. Older constraints on land use, ownership, and alienation were deemed unnatural. The intensified commercialization of land and naturalizing of the right of foreign ownership were critical mechanisms for introducing European modernity into the extra-European world, and they were two of the engines that drove nineteenth-century globalization. These fundamental aspects of modernity, however, had emerged over the prior two centuries in British America, where radical innovations gained the character of natural practices, justifying their being negotiated in, if not imposed on, the rest of the world.

Europeans' exploration, commercial investment, and military expansion overseas, combined with the empiricism of the scientific revolution, inspired in them the conceit that they could know nature better than nature knew itself. This confidence courted a claim to a worldly omniscience formerly attributed to the Christian God who had made the Earth, but it blended easily with Christian theologies that God had commanded humans to subdue the planet. Western Europeans' enhanced knowledge of nature, and their confidence in divine sanction for their overseas investments, allowed them to believe that the modernizing course on which their societies were moving was itself "natural." This complex of ideas was mutually reinforcing, so that inherent natural properties and processes operating independently of humankind could be invoked as rationales for complex historical developments without grappling with their inconsistencies, ironies, and often tragedies.

The European imperial impulse to enhance their knowledge of the natural world easily evolved into an imperial imperative to impose their naturalized vision of history on the extra-European world. This conflation of historical and natural processes made Europeans' rapidly changing societies seem more valid than those of any of the other communities around the world that they encountered. The European attribution of natural inferiority to Africans justified race-based slavery. The processes of so-called civilized development justified the ever-intensifying pressure placed on Amerindians to alienate their lands. Modernity itself became understood to be a "natural" process rather than a historical conceit and by extension the core of the universal human condition. Ironically, in this aberrant intellectual construction, the historical diversity of human societies could be interpreted only as aberrations. It was claimed that societies everywhere should naturally become more similar, along the paradigmatic lines of European societies, notwithstanding the historical evidence of rich variation among the peoples and polities of the world. By the mid-twentieth century, so convinced were Europeans of their spontaneous control of the world that they designed programs to modernize Africans, Asians, Latin Americans, and Pacific Islanders, confident that they alone knew how to accelerate the progress of these apparently retarded societies toward modernity, as though they were simply applying fertilizer to crops, merely enhancing natural processes.

Among the flaws in this European modernizing model was the belief that the historical processes they had generated over the previous centuries had changed most of the societies they encountered very little, if at all. This belief in the inherent passivity of everyone but themselves kept alive denials of the deep history of earlier, though less structured, European military and commercial intrusions. In the Atlantic World, Amerindian and African responses to these pressures were profound. In North America, as indigenous nations came to understand that many British practices were designed to dispossess them of their lands, they sought diplomatic protections, attempting to remove their lands from commercial buyouts. They became wary of Euroamerican investment, often choosing cultural preservation over material wealth, but with the result being economic impoverishment, at least in the increasingly material Euroamerican terms.

Africans, for their part, absorbed a growing range of commodities out of the Atlantic economy, whether American foodstuffs such as maize, Asian-made cottons, cowries from the Maldive Islands in the Indian Ocean, rum from Brazil and the Caribbean, and even the textiles and other commodities coming for centuries over caravan routes linked to the Mediterranean. For Africans, material goods conveyed the personage of their makers. Goods acquired through Atlantic trade carried the alienness, and potential dangers, of distant and unknown laborers. Africans therefore remade what they bought from the Atlantic to defuse its dangerous—because unknown—potential and domesticated it. They imported Venetian glass beads but melted and recast them. They unraveled cotton cloth from India and rewove the threads. They used embedded cowrie shells on masks and household furnishings. They covered guns with tacks of brass (their prestige metal), feathers, and other substances they knew to be empowering. Africans, unlike Europeans, did not see the human effort inhering in material objects as inert. On the other hand, the standardization of commodities, enhanced through the commercialization of anonymous labor, neutralized Europeans' awareness of foreign labor as diverse and personalized humanity. Among the successful strategies in the anti–slave trade and antislavery movements was a parallel effort to make the British public aware of enslaved laborers as "men and brothers"—imagery with which English china manufacturers marketed their wares thus reminded a nation of tea drinkers of the humanity behind sugar every time they tasted the sweetened tea in their cups.

At the dawn of the nineteenth century, most Africans and many Amerindians were far more different from Europeans than their ancestors had been in the sixteenth century, but not because Europeans had progressed and Africans and Amerindian societies remained unchanged. Rather, Africans and Amerindians had enhanced their own practices and production to make multiple modernities of their own. By resisting the arrogance of European universalist modernization, Amerindians and Africans made themselves integral parts of the story of Atlantic and eventually global modernity.

ELIZABETH MANCKE

Bibliography

"AHR Roundtable: Historians and the Question of Modernity." *American Historical Review* 116, no. 3 (2011): 631–751.

Bayly, C. A. *The Birth of the Modern World, 1780–1914: Global Connections and Comparisons.* Malden, MA : Blackwell, 2004.

Bowen, H. V., Elizabeth Mancke, and John G. Reid, eds. *Britain's Oceanic Empire: Atlantic and Indian Ocean Worlds, c. 1550–1850.* Cambridge: Cambridge University Press, 2012.

Goody, Jack. *The Theft of History.* Cambridge: Cambridge University Press, 2006.

Locke, John. *Two Treatises of Government.* Edited by Peter Laslett. Student Edition. Cambridge: Cambridge University Press, 1988.

Pagden, Anthony. *European Encounters with the New World: From Renaissance to Romanticism.* New Haven, CT: Yale University Press, 1993.

Monarchies and Agents

The consolidation of monarchies in Europe and inflows of resources from overseas were complementary processes in the Atlantic World, each defining and reinforcing the other. Early-modern European monarchies—increasingly contiguous territories ruled by a single recognized sovereign, usually hereditary—controlled more and more centralized administrations for the express purpose of developing extensive tax bases in order to extend the reach of monarchical law and engage in protracted warfare. Traditionally, a European monarch's legitimacy within the realm rested largely on longstanding cultural ties and semicontractual relations with residents of a territory, reinforced by the monarch's power to define and apply justice.

From this perspective—of territorial contiguity and contractual relations grounded in tradition and sovereign law—overseas territories were very nearly the opposite of kingdoms. They were recent creations of what Francisco Bethencourt has termed, in the Portuguese case, "distant, discontinuous, and fragmented territories" composed of varieties of peoples, many of whom did not share political, religious, or cultural values, even among European emigrants (Bethencourt, 197). The ruler delegated his or her sovereignty over these remote and diverse domains to a patchwork of subsidiary and often jurisdictionally overlapping private agents, primarily to develop overseas territories at least indirectly to benefit his or her war aims and philosophical ideals, but without committing the crown's own scarce capital. Only a small number of European dynasties eventually ruled overseas territories in this way. These five—Portugal, Spain (essentially created in 1469 by the union of Castile and Aragon), France, England (eventually encompassing the subsidiary kingdoms of Ireland and Scotland), and the ostensibly republican Netherlands (the United Provinces)—rimmed the open Atlantic, forming a distinct subcontinent, a "maritime" or "Atlantic" Europe.

Venturing Abroad to Consolidate Monarchy at Home

Defining the nature of the interaction between monarchy, the metropolitan political community, and the overseas territories has proven extremely difficult, for policy makers then and for historians since. From the late nineteenth century, scholars imbued with the nationalist ethos of that later time have supposed "an extraordinary devolution of authority outward from European centers to new American peripheries" (Greene, 12) to their Atlantic colonies, like seedlings transplanted to the Americas to grow into sturdy clones of mother nation-states. However, more nuanced recent scholarship, focusing more carefully on the worldviews of contemporaries at the time, have discerned a more dynamic and complex interplay of political realities informing actors on both sides of the Atlantic, a process Jack P. Greene has famously termed "negotiated authority." From the sixteenth century, Iberian monarchs and their closest advisors developed new forms and ideals of governance for both their home communities and overseas territories at the same time, centered on personal agents of royal sovereignty with experience on both sides of the Atlantic.

Through trial and error, monarchs and these agents merged internal and external forms of governance into integrated, functional administrations that became a quintessential feature of the "nation-states" that ensued in mid-eighteenth-century Europe. Royal bureaucracies, which grew in tandem with the increases in population and economic importance of overseas settlements, were composed of agents drawn from clerical orders and lower social groups, both at home and within the overseas territories, often creating a "two-tier" administration of royal agents—home and overseas—that increasingly triumphed over older landed and military aristocracies in Europe. The new monarchical agents were defined largely by a dynamically evolving maritime and especially naval culture. Whether via wide experience, through kinship and patronage networks that extended on both sides of the Atlantic, or by an intellectual grasp of a transoceanic perspective, these agents of royalty took the lead in redefining the administrative mechanisms of monarchy from personal lordships over home communities into secular, commercially alert, militarily expansive, and ideologically committed claimants to global power.

Late-medieval European monarchs had exercised their nominal sovereignty primarily as arbiters among relatively autonomous, rivalrous, regionally based aristocratic families, corporate bodies (artisan guilds, municipalities), and commoners or peasants, with the administrative and political support of the Church. The Church represented the only unifying pan-European institution, and the pope and clergy helped limit popular revolts within kingdoms and worked, at least in theory, to limit violence among them. As James Collins noted, medieval kings "discovered" God's law; this theological legitimation meant that the person of the monarch and his law formed an indissoluble whole, which

contemporaries viewed as mystically bonding him (or rarely, her) directly with each subject in mutual obligation for defense or service, as well as revenues, in times of need. Personnel capable of representing this sacred unity were few, tied closely to the person of the monarch by mutual claims of allegiance and loyalty; many were members of the extended royal family. These agents maintained civil peace and administered royal justice by embodying the monarch in their functions.

The development of institutions capable of representing monarchical authority in the early-modern Atlantic broke decisively with these medieval traditions of personified, sanctified sovereignty. Portuguese monarchs and their agents were the first to pioneer the basic features of monarch-agent relations overseas in the fifteenth century, and the other Atlantic European polities followed this pattern. Initially modeled on medieval military retainers during the Portuguese "Reconquista" of Iberia from its Moorish rulers in the fourteenth century, the crown created proprietary "captains" (*capitães*)—commissioned military agents to claim monarchical authority in the initial occupations of the islands of the eastern Atlantic and North African posts—who purchased their offices and held them as inheritable contracts, although always at the pleasure of the monarch. These captains generally received monopolies not only on trade but also on defense, regional diplomacy, justice, the founding of towns, and revenues from taxation. The crown later extended this proprietary system to Portuguese mercantile consortia or individual nobles to govern trade posts along the coasts of mainland West Africa and in northeastern Brazil. Key noble supporters of the monarch usually advocated expansion, which entrenched the legal position of the crown in accessing resources overseas. Prince Henry ("the Navigator," 1394–1460) subsidized and directed exploratory commercial voyages along the Atlantic coasts of West Africa, licensed private ventures through a House of Trade (the Casa da Guiné in Lisbon, 1443), and opened a school of open-ocean navigation. Italian, often Genoese, bankers underwrote Portuguese commercial ventures, and emigrants and soldiers might be drawn from a variety of European backgrounds, giving a more cosmopolitan tone to these early overseas ventures than prevailed among the monarchs' resident subjects.

Recruiting Agents

With the settlement of European populations in the Americas in the early sixteenth century, the Iberian monarchies experimented with more direct administrative relationships between the home country and their overseas enterprises. Within a generation of settlement, the Spanish Habsburg ruler Charles V (r. 1521–1556), as well as John III (r. 1521–1557) of Portugal, asserted personal control over law, commercial exchange, defense, and even the relations between their indigenous "subjects" and immigrating Europeans. The unleashing of freelancing sea-raiders and territorial conquerors added urgency to stabilizing the violent and chaotic impact of these predatory proprietary enterprises. The Portuguese and Spanish crowns acted mainly by attaching (or legally, reattaching) the territories directly to the monarch. In 1511 the Spanish revoked the wide-ranging private powers initially granted to Columbus and his heirs by establishing royal agents in a council (*audiencia*) with direct control over a royal judiciary in the Indies and the right to enact laws to govern powerful Europeans overseas. Charles V extended similar control within a generation or less over the freewheeling conquistadors who had run amok and destroyed the Aztec (1519–1521) and the Inca (1531–1533) and in effect placed the new territories under the direct control of the Habsburg monarch of Castile, as subsidiary kingdoms under American viceroys. This assertion of the person of the monarch not only ushered in a new range of royal agents (many of whom purchased their offices, in effect maintaining the nakedly commercial nature of the overseas enterprises) but also centralized control of legal, fiscal, and defense practices. For example, the Spanish crown attempted to strengthen royal authority over its new Native "subjects" in the Americas through the sweeping New Laws of 1542 by wresting the extensive *encomienda* labor grants from the heirs of conquistadors in New Spain, Central America, and Peru.

The Spanish crown reinforced its growing administrative control in 1544 by subdividing the expanding territories into *audiencias*, standardizing administrative, fiscal, and legal institutions, and—from 1574 especially—the appointment of clerics. In northeastern Brazil, the Portuguese crown appointed a governor-general (Tomé de Sousa, 1503–1579) to the new military captaincy of Salvador da Bahia in 1549 to create a model for direct royal administration of the earlier proprietary captaincies dispersed along Brazil's Atlantic coast. The monarchy in Lisbon filled out a hierarchical system in the last decades of the century, commissioning military officers and forming militia companies from the growing population of Portuguese subjects resident in Brazil and Angola and creating new posts in fiscal inspection and the courts by 1609, including a new colonial court of final appeal with the right to review royal ordinances. Both Iberian crowns asserted authority over the entirely novel human environments of the Atlantic through personal appointees to execute monarchical laws and administrative and fiscal procedures.

The northern Atlantic European monarchs—English, French, and Dutch—embarked on the high seas through the same pattern of unlicensed or clandestinely organized raiding, followed by more formal royal proprietary grants and eventually direct royal control. In 1624, the English crown revoked the Virginia Company's original charter of 1606, and by 1686 it canceled the Puritan charters of the New England settlements. In 1664 Louis XIV authorized his chief minister Jean-Baptiste Colbert (1619–1683) to reorganize a miscellaneous set of chartered private enterprises in New France, the French Caribbean settlements, and planned trading posts in West Africa into a massive, commercially integrated, and royally sponsored transatlantic monopoly modeled on the Dutch West India Company. Colbert placed the territories themselves directly in the monarch's possession and appointed royal agents, missionaries, and naval officers and soldiers to police, proselytize in, and protect the territories overseas.

By the era of the American Revolution, appointed staffs of all the European monarchies had grown by factors of three or even four over their mid-seventeenth-century levels. Officials handling overseas territorial and naval affairs on both sides of the Atlantic were better trained and employed in functionally defined offices, often by subdividing existing jurisdictions (ports or colonies) or limiting clerks to specific operations such as ordnance and supply, recruitment, or cartography. Monarchs authorized the refurbishing of existing naval bases and royal ports or the construction of new ones, from Ferrol in northern Spain (1726) to British Halifax (1749) to Point-à-Pitre on French Guadeloupe

(1764). Only the Dutch developed along paths extended from the powerful private interests in Europe rather than by extending royal authority through agents overseas. The Dutch West India Company, formed in 1621, had been organized expressly as a military arm of the Dutch Republic to attack Spanish convoys and to occupy the Portuguese settlements in Brazil, which it did from 1630 to 1654. In fact, the company's board of directors and military commanders were drawn largely from the same groups of wealthy and high-ranking families who held posts in the governing assembly of the Netherlands, the States-General. As the company's military operations decreased over the eighteenth century, so too did the size of its administration.

Otherwise, European crowns enlisted a wide variety of new collaborators in their home realms and, from the late seventeenth century, increasingly from the overseas territories they claimed, to create an array of new royal agents. The Catholic clergy constituted a more overt corps of royal agents during this period. Iberian monarchs assigned clerics to positions critical to cultivating alliances among indigenous peoples, collecting reconnaissance about overseas environments, and providing such basic training and charitable services as schools and hospitals for settlers and military personnel. Spanish monarchs included high-ranking clerics in the Council of the Indies, created in 1524, the first royal institution to advise on overseas affairs, and funded influential religious orders to organize and concentrate Native populations that survived the destruction of the major Mesoamerican and Andean political regimes in European-style *reducciones*, or Christian Native villages under crown control.

The French crown funded and assigned individual Jesuits, Dominicans, or, less often, Recollet priests to the lower Great Lakes and eastern woodland borderlands in North America to recruit indigenous allies and contest the incursions of British American traders and Protestant missionaries. In the Caribbean, the French crown supported proselytizing among enslaved Africans in order to increase their obedience on plantations, and—more realistically—used clerics to drive a wedge of royal authority into the otherwise legally unchallengeable power of the prospering planters over the Africans they owned as personal property. French regular clerics were instrumental in exploring, charting,

and compiling intelligence reports that royal ministers used to develop policies for overseas territories from Quebec to Senegal to Cayenne in South America.

The two major Protestant monarchies relied far less on religious agents as royal representatives, largely because clergy overseas confined themselves to ministering to European settlers already subjects of the crowns. Only from 1660 did the restored English monarchy make some inconsistent and local efforts to convert Native populations in New England into "praying towns," their own version of the Spanish *reducciones*. Later proselytizing by the Church of England through the Society for the Propagation of the Gospel (founded in 1701) proved ineffective. In contrast with the Catholic monarchies, religious dissidents such as the Quakers of early Pennsylvania were more successful in negotiating alliances with indigenous peoples than were missionaries supported by the crown.

Beyond recruiting clergy, all five Atlantic European monarchies further bypassed aristocratic rivals at home by awarding positions in crown service overseas to skilled commoners. The English monarchs as well as the Dutch directors of the West India Company, without strong religious allies, brokered alliances with indigenous peoples by drawing more widely than the Catholic monarchies on individuals with military experience, demonstrated cunning, familiarity with new environments (as by elevating ships' pilots from lowly positions into royal posts), or specialized linguistic and cultural knowledge. Some agents, such as William Johnson (1715–1774), combined all three of these qualifications. In New York's sensitive frontier marchland, Johnson used his personal charm and worked the connections of his Mohawk wife Degonwadonti (or Mary Brant, c. 1735–1796) with her kinfolk to forge a stable military alliance among the Iroquois nations, successfully defeating French attempts at similar alliances. The king not only honored Johnson with a baronetcy but also rewarded him with the critical—and profitable—position of superintendent of Indian Affairs (for the northern colonies). The French likewise promoted talented individuals from traditionally marginalized groups in Europe. Louis XIV's most famous naval commander, Jean Bart (1650–1702), for example, was the son of a Flemish fisherman. The French crown waived its own prohibitions against promoting nonnobles in the navy, and Bart ended his career as a celebrated admiral. The Dutch and Spanish recruited from among a broad range of personnel, including "nonnationals," albeit only for less lucrative posts. The first governor of Spanish Louisiana, Alesandro O'Reilly (1722–1794), had been born in Dublin.

Militarization and Monarchical Command

Militarization of the Atlantic from the late sixteenth century was specifically based on entirely new oceanic warfare. The medieval Christian kingdoms fringing the conflict-ridden Mediterranean, including France, Catalonia, and the Italian maritime cities, had maintained navies composed largely of rowed galleys. They had no need for expensive "blue-water" or long-distance sailing vessels, and ship-mounted cannon did not exist. When necessary, monarchs confiscated or chartered merchant vessels and modified them to ferry troops. From roughly the mid-sixteenth century, intensifying competition among Atlantic monarchies for the same sailing routes and access to prime tropical plantation lands took regional conflict "beyond the lines of amity." This fictional zone—imagined in the open Atlantic by European diplomats in the early seventeenth century—demarcated the area within which pan-European treaties held but beyond which warfare could rage without threatening peace among the dynasties in Europe.

To defend territorial and other royal claims in this vast maritime free-fire zone required precise coordination of the interior resources of a monarchy. These new demands included developing reliable supplies of naval stores both within and outside the kingdom, training and keeping registers of sailors, and reorganizing finances for long-term investments in military infrastructure, new harbor facilities, ordnance, and the ships themselves. In a sense, from the point of view of the monarchies, the entire Atlantic Basin consisted of strategic maritime resources. Nearly from the beginning, monarchs organized and even appropriated commercial initiatives to enhance defense. The Portuguese crown armed cargo vessels, as well as its first African commercial posts, with cannon, even as the Spanish crown integrated trade and military security with commercial/naval convoys, starting with the Spanish treasure fleet system (the *flota* and the *galleones*,

from the 1560s). The Dutch West India Company, formed by the States-General of the Netherlands to attack the shipping and settlements of the unified crowns of Spain and Portugal (during 1580–1640), was a similar state-armed private enterprise. In the occasional moments of peace "beyond the line," vessels of the royal navies reversed the medieval practice of seizing and arming commercial shipping to become merchant ships, carrying merchandise or people on the kings' accounts.

Militarization of the sea called for specialized knowledge of marine affairs by royal agents, who in turn had to think in broad, transatlantic terms. Aside from some elements of the diplomatic corps, the navy was the only administrative unit that encompassed the entire Atlantic Basin. These semiprofessionals established the functionally defined core institutions of maritime control—ordnance, finance, supply and provisioning, design and construction of warships, records, professional training, the recruiting (or more often kidnapping) of sailors, and the management of overseas territories—that emerged first in late seventeenth-century England and France and by the mid-eighteenth century became basic institutions in all five monarchies.

Much of this definitive turn toward professionalization focused on managing the heavy investment in long-term infrastructure—including expensive, highly crafted oceangoing ships that required skilled artisans to build, trained crews to sail, and competent commanders to ensure safety and success in war (or even trade). Efforts to professionalize maritime and naval resources also involved training and positioning dispersed networks of literate clerks both at home and overseas to handle the logistics of provisioning, repairs, munitions, ship's supplies, and cargoes, and to arrange for the transport of settlers and passengers. The extraordinary costs and coordination of maintaining naval forces required long-term financing, on a routine and continuing basis. In other words, blue-water navies fostered—indeed, paid for—a centralized bureaucracy based largely on competent management and long-term financing. Contemporary official reports also indicate that colonial agents applied metropolitan laws unevenly, if they did so at all, within and among the overseas royal jurisdictions, always with a view toward minimizing conflict with their charges, as well as maximizing self-enrichment.

The Portuguese created a rudimentary naval command (or admiralty) nearly a century before attempting the (successful) conquest of Ceuta in Morocco in 1415. Burgundian counts inaugurated a small navy in the mid-fifteenth century in what became the Netherlands. The Royal Navy of England dated from the 1540s, the era of Henry VIII, and the French entered the competition for maritime militarization at about the same time. In all cases, the formation of navies appeared to be linked in part to concurrent experiments in mounting heavy ordnance on seagoing vessels. However, none of these monarchies defined a permanent central naval administration until the mid-seventeenth century, when controlling resources on and around a vast ocean became a major challenge.

The subsequent growth and professionalization of navies brought experienced higher-echelon naval commanders formally into the institutions of monarchy. Naval experience and training enabled promotion by measured merit; very few ship commands could be purchased in any of the monarchies of Atlantic Europe, in contradistinction to army commissions purchased or awarded on the basis of family connections. Naval commanders also often exerted considerable influence in the royal courts and other metropolitan governing bodies. The Atlantic branch of the sixteenth-century French navy was largely Huguenot (Protestant) and energetically sponsored seaborne attacks and established bases to attack Catholic Spain, while its Mediterranean branch remained stoutly Catholic and closely concerned with promoting closer ties with other Catholic monarchies. As Great Britain's Royal Navy expanded during the eighteenth century, more than doubling in size and nearly quadrupling in cost, its senior officers, nearly all of whom had transatlantic experience, composed the largest and best-organized faction in Parliament.

Building a naval force effective on Atlantic scales required gathering together a variety of scattered offices and populating them with kin and clients. Jean-Baptiste Colbert (in)famously created a vast network to gather information and administer various parts of the kingdom, at one point himself personally controlling five key departments in addition to the navy; these networks were essential to exploiting systematically French-claimed territorial niches around the Atlantic Basin. In the early eigh-

teenth century, Don José Patiño (1666–1736) modernized Spain's navy by first gathering the offices of naval intendant, president of the Casa de la Contratación, and superintendent of Seville, the crown's major Atlantic port, into his hands, in order to coordinate efforts. When the Portuguese Marquis de Pombal (Sebastião José de Carvalho e Melo, 1699–1782) decided in the 1750s to place mineral-rich Brazil more firmly under control from Lisbon, he assigned his stepbrother as viceroy in Bahia to ensure that orders would be followed. Kinship and patronage ties among lower-echelon agents appear to have been crucial in creating a stable culture of service to the monarch.

Many of the same Dutch burghers who advised the provincial assemblies (or states), as well as the federate States-General, were also directors of the Dutch West India Company. British land-owning gentry and members of Parliament invested heavily in a variety of Atlantic trades or increasingly in the early manufacturing enterprises developed to tap Atlantic markets (including other Atlantic European states). Generations of French and French American clan groups, such as the Bégon, Bigot, and Vaudreuil families, defined service to the monarch, holding a variety of royal offices: managing Atlantic ports, financing and tax farming, staffing the provincial judiciary, serving as commanders in the army, or serving religious orders with overseas houses and investments. The intellectual exchange and practical sharing of expertise that such ties of kinship and patronage undoubtedly exerted on the formation of European overseas administrations remains understudied; teasing out the extent and nature of such networks will help in further understanding not only how royal agents cooperated in creating new ideologies of governance but also the considerable degree to which the strategies developed to create an integrated Atlantic World informed by state building in Europe.

Forming Atlantic Imperial Ideologies

Although historians conventionally equate the development of navies, overseas posts, and transatlantic trade with an ideology of "empire," it is not at all clear that contemporaries did so. For example, historians now routinely refer to a French overseas "empire," yet contemporary French officials on either side of the Atlantic (in comparison with their

Spanish and English counterparts) used the term rarely, and their official correspondence shows that they began to consider the disparate overseas territories as an integrated whole only on the eve of the Seven Years' War (1756–1763). As Thomas M. Fröschl noted, for many officials in the Catholic monarchies, there was a single empire and only one emperor, the Habsburg ruler of the Holy Roman Empire in the lands of central Europe. *Empire* connoted a universal domain, parallel to the universality of the Catholic church. This ideal of empire as land-based permeated even the writings of the Enlightenment philosophes.

Monarchies, in contrast, implied specific personal domains, and monarchs joined new, overseas lands to their own persons or to their dynastic heirs and administered them through personal agents. Portuguese monarchs described their overseas outposts as "enterprises"; the poet Luis Vaz de Camões in his poetic epic of exploration *The Lusiads*, written in the mid-sixteenth century to celebrate Portuguese audacity in the Indian Ocean, came closest to styling these ventures in imperial terms by comparing the voyage of Vasco da Gama—the first European to sail to India—favorably with the semi-mythical glories of imperial Rome; but he accorded Portuguese posts in Atlantic Africa only fleeting mention and gave none to Brazil.

Only the English and Spanish monarchs developed more formal theories of empire. Henry VIII first utilized the concept of "empire" in the 1530s, which underscored the temerity of his challenge to the papacy in Rome, and the term circulated at first as a response to Catholic claims to universality; only during the reign of Elizabeth I (1558–1603) did exponents of expansion employ "empire" to counter the universalist claims of the Iberians to overseas domains. Later English imperial ideology developed only after the growth of an ad hoc, unintegrated series of overseas posts and settlements; the ideology centered on commerce and liberty (both of trade and of the seas on which merchants sailed), and only more vaguely on ideals of a distinct, unified English community of interest. Only a few metropolitan officials with experience in the colonies, such as the alarmist Edward Randolph (1632–1703), who warned in the 1690s of New England's emerging trade competition with old England, appear to have systematically considered the advantages and disadvantages of claiming *imperium*

overseas. With the creation of a grander "Great Britain" in the 1707 Act of Union, which united England and Scotland, and maritime victories during the War of the Spanish Succession (1702–1713), British memorialists and colonial or naval officers began to analyze the benefits and challenges of a cohesive empire. The idea gained wide currency only in the euphoric aftermath of Britain's victory (1763) over France in the Seven Years' War. The defeat had the opposite impact in France, at first sparking disillusionment with overseas enterprises among French philosophes, which abated only with the clear and fast-growing importance of Saint-Domingue to French trade.

The Spanish monarchy presents a significant variation, in that the Spanish Habsburgs, with their own interests in the singular *imperium* of the Holy Roman Empire, initially rejected their own transatlantic mantle. It was the conqueror of the Aztecs, Hernán Cortés, who originally suggested that the then ruler Charles V style himself as a universal emperor. While it remains uncertain why Cortés suggested this ambitious claim, it is clear that embodying the all-but-sanctified authority of an Atlantic empire would elevate his own power as royal agent without alienating—rather, deeply flattering—the crown. Cortés's actions were the first of many similarly grandiose claims that agents overseas would make: the concept of an integrated transatlantic *imperium* was more likely to be advocated by monarchical agents abroad than by the monarchs themselves. At first Charles V and his advisors rejected use of the term; however, by the close of the sixteenth century, and, perhaps significantly, after the victories by rebellious Protestants in the Netherlands during the 1590s, the concept of a Spanish imperial domain came into more common usage in the court and among officials in the Spanish Americas.

The concept of a maritime *imperium* was global and not confined to the Atlantic. The "East Indies" appear to have been essential in defining English and French monarchical claims to universality, and future histories will undoubtedly explore connections between the Atlantic and Indian Ocean spheres. By linking the formation of large, integrated monarchical administrations in maritime Europe with the resources claimed through royal agents in the "distant, discontinuous, and fragmented territories," the early-modern European monarchy can be more clearly discerned as a creature born directly of the Atlantic World.

KENNETH J. BANKS

Bibliography

Bethencourt, Francisco. "Political Configurations and Local Powers." In *Portuguese Oceanic Expansion, 1400–1800*, edited by Francisco Bethencourt and Diogo Ramada Curto, 197–254. New York: Cambridge University Press, 2007.

Bowen, H. V., Elizabeth Mancke, and John G. Reid, eds. *Britain's Oceanic Empire: Atlantic and Indian Ocean Worlds, c. 1550–1850*. Cambridge: Cambridge University Press, 2012.

Burkholder, Mark, ed. *Administrators of Empire*. Aldershot, UK: Ashgate, 1998.

Collins, James B. *The State in Early Modern France*. Cambridge: Cambridge University Press, 1995.

Dull, Jonathan R. *The French Navy and the Seven Years' War*. Lincoln: University of Nebraska Press, 2005.

Elliott, Sir John H. *Empires of the Atlantic World: Britain and Spain in America, 1492–1800*. New Haven, CT: Yale University Press, 2006.

Fröschl, Thomas M. "American Empire–British Empire–Holy Roman Empire: The Meaning of Empire in Late Eighteenth-Century Political Discourse in the Atlantic World." *Nordamerikastudien* (Vienna: Verlag für Geschichte und Politik, 2000), 38–60.

Greene, Jack P. *Negotiated Authorities: Essays in Colonial Political and Constitutional History*. Charlottesville: University Press of Virginia, 1994.

McAlister, Lyle N. *Spain and Portugal in the New World, 1492–1700*. Minneapolis: University of Minnesota Press, 1984.

Prak, Maarten. *The Dutch Republic in the Seventeenth Century*. Translated by Diane Webb. Cambridge: Cambridge University Press, 2005.

Roper, Louis H., and Bertrand van Ruymbeke, eds. *Constructing Early Modern Empires: Proprietary Ventures in the Atlantic World, 1500–1750*. Leiden: Brill, 2007.

Muslims, African, in the Americas

Muslims were present in the Americas not long after "discovery" by Europeans. From these beginnings, Islam in the New World reflected political exigencies and cultural transformations taking place in the Old World, as an ascendant Europe accumulated the necessary financial resources, technological advantages, and seafaring experience to realize slowly but steadily its own economic interests. Muslims in conflict with Christian powers in Iberia, and at odds with indigenous polities in West Africa (and to a lesser extent, southeast Africa), gradually lost their struggle in Portugal and Spain in the fourteenth and fifteenth centuries, and those who were captured in war or imprisoned for infractions supplied a portion of the forced labor used in seafaring and construction in the Americas. These *forzados*, some of whom were North African, began arriving in the early sixteenth century in Spanish territories such as Hispaniola, which also began receiving captives from West Africa, some of whom were also Muslim.

In contrast with Islamic losses in Iberia, however, Muslims in West Africa were becoming increasingly powerful, their rise a consequence to some extent of slaving activities; Muslims organized initially to protect themselves, only later to participate in slaving. The first century or so of Portuguese slaving along western African coasts carried many captives to Portugal and Spain, most of them purchases from Muslim merchants, and some doubtless of the Islamic faith. With the expansion of plantation slavery in the Americas and growing transatlantic trade, West African Muslims enslaved their captives and were enslaved as well.

Of the 12 to 15 million Africans exported from Africa during the transatlantic slave trade, thousands, and probably tens of thousands, were Muslims, mostly from West Africa. Though these believers suffered the same ignominies as all others bound for the Americas in chains, their experiences of and responses to their enslavement distinguished them from other enslaved Africans. Indeed, the case of African Muslims in the Americas from the sixteenth through the nineteenth centuries suggests that, following separation from their communities of faith in Africa and integration into servile positions under non-Muslims across the Atlantic, ties to Africa, rather than diminishing, not only remained vibrant but on occasion were actually strengthened, as were bonds with coreligionists in the New World.

Muslims throughout the Americas gained notoriety for their self-reliance, independence of thought and action, dedication to their faith, and resistance to conditions they deemed inimical to their interests. Already in possession of a broad vision of community, globality, and sense of connectedness with fellow believers in other parts of the world, Muslims were uniquely positioned to withstand the vicissitudes of the plantation. Their sense of their own exceptionality, however, competed with simultaneously evolving notions of more encompassing African and racial identities, and on occasion complicated resistance movements demanding unity among the enslaved, to the degree that African Muslims and their descendants through the nineteenth century rarely made common cause with the larger enslaved population. In their very opposition to New World realities, Muslims could be remarkably conservative in their adherence to Old World values.

Of course, the notion of belonging in a single, worldwide Muslim community has been more theoretical or aspirational than actual since the fracturing, in the tenth century CE, of the Abbasid Caliphate in Baghdad, the last regime with a claim to comprehensive military authority over the Islamic world. Nor was West African Islam singular, having by the ninth century CE assumed its form as the religion of merchants along the West African Sahel who imported goods into the region via trans-Saharan routes. Islam would develop into the religion of ruling as well as trading elites, and by the fifteenth century Sahelian dynasties from the Atlantic coast to Lake Chad were nearly all Muslim.

What it meant to be a Muslim in West Africa soon resulted in reform efforts complete with jihads of the sword—Muslim scholars using the term to indicate armed struggle to preserve the faith—from the seventeenth through the nineteenth centuries. These military ventures were so coterminous with slaving activities that it is difficult to establish cause and effect. As a consequence, both Muslims and non-Muslims were caught in webs of capture and subsequent enslavement. Muslims were of varying cultures and ethnolinguistic backgrounds—Hausa, Fulbe, Mandinga, Soninke, Wolof, even Yoruba, all collective terms with varying meanings that shifted over time. Shared suffering under slavery in the New World, however, facilitated the fording of these differences and the rise of multiethnic confessional communities.

Having often come out of cosmopolitan milieus that could include Arab, Berber, and Tuareg populations protected by well-articulated central governments, many Muslims were literate in Arabic; some were descended from ruling families. In African societies stratified by social rank and occupational caste, these nobles were often themselves slaveholders. Thrust into the disorienting maelstrom of New World slavery, individuals sought to recover their Muslim sense of equilibrium and dignity. Thus, Senegambians brought into Hispaniola, Costa Rica, and Panama in the sixteenth and seventeenth centuries immediately engaged in subversion and revolt against their *kafir*, or unbelieving, masters. After the seventeenth century, the history of Muslims in any part of Spanish-claimed America becomes difficult to follow, but their memory is preserved in lore equating them with *brujería* (witchcraft) and powerful amulets known as *mandingas*. The masters' decidedly negative appraisal of Muslim Africans was certainly enhanced by their high profile in revolts and in *marronage*, or self-liberation in fugitive bands, but their ill repute was also shaped by the nearly 800-year struggle between Muslim and Christian forces in Iberia and the ongoing enslavement of Christians in North Africa.

If resistance against slavery, often armed and violent, characterized the Muslim experience in Spanish-claimed lands in the Americas through the seventeenth century, a different sort of "resisting" emerged during the eighteenth and nineteenth centuries in the anglophone Caribbean. Muslims in Jamaica and Trinidad were associated with stability and cooperation, while the stereotype of rebellion and sedition on Jamaica, as well as Antigua, fell to non-Muslim Akan speakers (from the Gold Coast) referred to as "Coromantee" or "Kromanti." In such places Muslims sought out one another, developed collaborative strategies to purchase one another's freedom, and pooled their resources to become landowners and slaveholders. They prayed together when possible and in Jamaica established their own structures of leadership under individuals like Abu Bakr (b. 1790) and Muhammad Kaba (b. 1756). With the Apprenticeship Act of 1834, through which the British sought to prepare an enslaved population for freedom, these Muslims petitioned the crown for repatriation to West Africa, some successfully, viewing the loss of their slaves and status as unacceptable.

The narrative of Islam in Brazil tends to be dominated by insurrectionary events attributed to Muslims in nineteenth-century Bahia. Comparing these Portuguese-claimed lands to Spanish America, where at least 25 percent of slaves imported came from African regions with significant Muslim populations, only 20 percent of the Africans reaching Brazil came from these. But slave importation into Brazil was 3.5 times that into Spanish America, so that the overall numbers of Muslims were greater. Muslims imported into Spanish America arrived much earlier than those brought to Brazil, who landed in significant numbers only in the nineteenth century and were concentrated in a lone state—Bahia. There, Muslims—largely Hausa and Yoruba—led a series of insurgencies from the early nineteenth century until 1835, when the celebrated Malê Revolt in the city of Salvador involving hundreds of participants was swiftly quelled. The ensuing investigation revealed a Muslim community under organized leadership intent upon the serious practice of Islam, with the insurrection itself influenced by the holy wars of the Sokoto Caliphate in what is now northern Nigeria. Before the nineteenth century, however, African Muslims in Brazil had also been viewed with grudging respect through the prism of the anti-Muslim conflict in fourteenth- and fifteenth-century Iberia. Slaveholders recognized that Muslims had been a formidable power with a respected culture and saw Muslims in Brazil as different from and superior to other Africans, a view that comported with phenotypical contrasts between lighter-appearing groups such as the Fulbe and Mandinga, who tended to be Muslim, and other, darker-complected African groups. Muslims enslaved in Brazil therefore tended to be placed in leadership positions, or given less physically grueling tasks, and Portuguese men found their women more sexually desirable than others. Following the 1835 revolt in Salvador, surviving Muslims assumed a much lower profile, but they maintained Muslim communities well into the second half of the nineteenth century, especially in urban centers like Rio de Janeiro.

The United States was also a major reception site for Muslims, with a relatively large proportion of captives (24 percent) arriving from Senegambia. As in Brazil, North American slaveholders favored Muslims over other Africans due to their lighter-complected phenotypes, their literacy, and their pastoral skills, and several achieved notoriety as leaders. Like their coreligionists in the anglophone Caribbean, they tended to be nonconfrontational toward the slavocracy, and they were often selected as plantation overseers. But they were not as well organized as Muslims in the Caribbean and Brazil; no evidence exists of religious leaders, corporate activities, pooling of resources, or efforts at transmitting their Islamic learning to others among the enslaved. In North America, Muslims stand out as individuals rather than as members of well-articulated communities, including such figures as Abd ar-Rahman (1762–1826), the celebrated "prince" and manager of a large cotton plantation in Mississippi, and Umar b. Said (1770–1864), the North Carolina writer in Arabic, who was also an autobiographer. Muslims in North America were acutely aware of their differences with others in the servile estate, from whom they maintained social and cultural distance.

The nineteenth century saw the decline of populations of African birth throughout the hemisphere, among them Muslims. The proper observation of Islam requires holy books, literacy, and sufficient security to perform prayer and other obligations of the faith, and while there was often cross-generational transmission of certain Muslim sensibilities—Muslim names, conservative dress, avoidance of pork, and so forth—the absence of supportive conditions meant that Muslims seldom passed on Islam as a coherent set of beliefs and practices to their American-born progeny. With the exception of places, such as Trinidad, where Muslims from the Indian subcontinent settled later in the nineteenth century, Islam would fade away in Spanish-speaking America as well as in the Caribbean with the dawn of the twentieth century.

MICHAEL A. GOMEZ

Bibliography

Alryyes, Ala. *A Muslim American Slave: The Life of Omar ibn Said.* Madison: University of Wisconsin Press, 2011.

N

Austin, Allan D. *African Muslims in Antebellum America: A Sourcebook.* New York: Garland, 1984.

Gomez, Michael A. *Black Crescent: The Experience and Legacy of African Muslims in the Americas.* New York: Cambridge University Press, 2005.

Reis, João José. *Slave Rebellion in Brazil: The Muslim Uprising of 1835 in Bahia.* Translated by Arthur Brakel. Baltimore, MD: Johns Hopkins University Press, 1993.

Nation

As a discipline, Atlantic history aims to go beyond the modern nation, projected into the past, as its main analytical framework. Yet, paradoxically, the field has given rise to multiple works that remain framed within the various "national Atlantics" of the Portuguese, Spanish, Dutch, French, and British, with most of the focus on the last. Nevertheless, the notion of this nationalized Atlantic has not been much discussed, despite the confusion of what historians subsume under the categories "British Atlantic" and "British Atlantic empire," for instance. It is all the more surprising that Atlantic dynamics made the nation "a continually contested terrain" and a major point of contention between the various Atlantic actors. The concept of *nation*, and the framework of analysis that goes with it, therefore, needs more aggressive interrogation: as an object of study to be historicized, that is, contextualized in the times under consideration. A much-needed political interpretation of the encounters among Europeans, Native Americans, and Africans would place the nation at the center of the Atlantic narrative, but as a way to connect nation with "empire" and "race," rather than as an object on its own. This interpretation would thus transcend the use of *nation* merely to anticipate how some American colonies later—during the Age of Revolutions—emerged as new nation-states.

A primary obstacle in correcting the misapplication of *nation* in Atlantic history is the tendency to conflate it with modern political nations, or nation-states, an interpretation not useful in analyzing the Atlantic World before the modern period. This conflation reduces the complexities of the concept's history, plotting a straight line from the rise of nationalisms in the eighteenth and nineteenth centuries, to the political transition from metropolitan monarchies and/or colonies to nation-states in revolutions and wars of independence, and finally to the process of filling in the boundaries of new politicized territories in the nineteenth century. These modern political nations did not exist before the Age of Revolutions proclaimed popular sovereignty and implemented political citizenship, with its principles of rights and responsibilities.

Administrators, missionaries, notaries, judges, settlers, and philosophers of European descent talked, wrote, and believed in the existence of "nations" as communities of people, related by (attributed) birth, rather than the modern politically and geographically defined states comprising many such "national" communities. For example, common usages included a "French nation" or an "English nation," neither to be confused with the larger and more diverse territorial claims of their monarchies; a "Basque nation," a "Welsh nation," a "Jewish nation," however dispersed geographically; a reconstituted "Bambara nation" among slaves in the Americas; an "Illinois nation"; and many others. Individuals of Native American or African descent also appropriated the category *nation* for themselves. In 1730, for instance, Francis Williams, a freeborn black Jamaican, invoked a British identity to claim the same privileges and liberties as the white British subjects of the Caribbean island. Hence the vernacular category of *nation* used by historical actors themselves, often in ambiguous ways, is distinct from the analytical category of *nation-state* as social scientists and some historians restrictively define it.

Nation varied in its uses across empires, territories, small communities, and ethnic groups, as well as over time. The term, which derives from the Latin *natio*, meaning "birth" or "people," was very similar in all the languages of the early-modern European imperial powers: *nación* in Spanish, *naçáo* in Portuguese, *natie* in Dutch, and *nation* in English and in French. It was ubiquitous especially in the documentation related to European territories overseas. In areas under European sovereignty, it was one of several much-used categories of identification and differentiation—alongside *class*, *gender*, and *race*—that simultaneously took several meanings: *diaspora* (including trading diaspora), *people*, *ethnicity*, *political community*, and others. If one believes that language has a performative function, not only reflecting but also producing difference, these usages testify that national identities defined the lines of struggles over power in the overseas territories, with multiple implications.

The main transformation in the conception of *nation* was its politicization within European empires from the early eighteenth century. From the late fifteenth century, the older ethnic conception of a nation as a people had been competing with a new definition as a territorialized political entity. Thus, for instance, in 1694 the *Dictionary of the French Academy* defined a nation as "all inhabitants from a same state, from a same country, who lived under the same laws and use the same language." Until the eighteenth century nations were taken as a fact of nature, and their existence was not questioned. England, France, Portugal, and even Germany and Italy, for instance, were unproblematically referred to as nations. It was only during the eighteenth century that a new conception of the nation appeared—as a political community constructed with government intervention. However, as Kathleen Wilson has underlined, "in the eighteenth century, nation as a political-territorial entity continued to compete with older Biblical and juridical concepts of nation as a people, located in a relatively fixed spatial and cultural terrain, that was conceived of geographically and ethnographically (as well as ethnocentrically)" (Wilson, 7).

Historians such as Linda Colley and David Bell have pointed to imperial rivalries as one important factor in this political redefinition of the nation. However, because those who have studied the politicization of the concept have focused chiefly on European metropoles, they have neglected the importance of other dynamics in Atlantic contexts. Besides imperial competition, the constraints on effective governance overseas, European emigration from multiethnic societies, the formation of multi-racial colonial societies, the slave trade, and the development of slavery and other forms of forced labor all contributed to give a new importance to the nation in the collective and individual representations. "Tensions of empires," to borrow an expression from Frederick Cooper and Ann Laura Stoler—that is, the conflicting relationships between metropole and colonies and among the various ethnic groups within colonial societies—turned American colonies into laboratories for the transformation of the concept of the nation.

The mixing of emigrants from various provinces and communities of European composite monarchies—along with the multiethnic societies in the American colonies and the Americans' shared confrontations with Indians and Africans—were instrumental in the development of new collective identities as "Spanish," "Portuguese," "British," or "French." For instance, while much of Iberia had been divided between the separate kingdoms of Castile and Aragon, a shared identity as Spanish began to emerge in the sixteenth and seventeenth centuries in the Spanish monarchy's overseas peripheries, where foreigners were prohibited from immigrating or trading. Imperial expansion was equally crucial in the development of a common identity—as British—among the subjects of the three formerly separate kingdoms of England, Scotland, and Wales and of Britain's overseas territories in the eighteenth century. The transfer of legal and social practices from the Iberian peninsula to Spanish colonies that distinguished Spaniards from foreigners and linked *vecindad* (local citizenship) closely with *naturaliza* (early-modern nationality) gave rise to discussions about what Spanish identity might be. In the British Atlantic World, too, tensions over royal grants of the privileges of subjects and later parliamentary naturalization in the English metropole paralleled political fights over naturalization, political representation, enfranchisement, and eligibility of foreign migrants in British American colonies.

At the same time, the openness of the Atlantic generated anxieties among European nations about their own identities as civilized and the possibility that life overseas, particularly miscegenation with people of Native or African descent, could drive them toward the savagery that they saw in these others. Debate about degeneracy in the New World started in the sixteenth century and had several revivals during the early-modern period. It raised doubts about the Spanishness, Englishness, or Frenchness of settlers of European or mixed descent born in the Americas. Settler communities reaffirmed their identities as European by purposefully confounding Spanish, British, or French identity with racialized identity as white. Their insistence on defining national identities by kinship and blood rather than by places of birth helped the colonists imagine that they remained equal to the descendants of their ancestors who had remained in Europe. However, this process of cultural differentiation would help metropolitan authorities legitimize downgrading colonial subjects to second-rate status during the Stamp Act crisis (1765) at the outset of the breakaway of the North American colonies from Britain or the exclusion of Saint-Domingue and other American territories of France from the new republican nation during the French Revolution.

Besides the merging of the new American national identities with whiteness, racialization of the territorial nation also developed around the issue of the political incorporation of resident Native Americans, slaves, and free people of color or *castas*: discussions about their legal status as local citizens and as royal subjects raised questions about what it meant to be Spanish, Portuguese, French, or English. Thus, in New France the 1627 charter of the Compagnie des Cent-Associés (Company of One Hundred Associates) recognized Christianized Native Americans as natural-born subjects of the French king, but when crown officials and Catholic missionaries in North America realized that they would not succeed in transforming them culturally into French men and women, the privileges attached to this status were progressively denied to them in practice. The failure of the initial policy of assimilation led officials and missionaries to establish a disjuncture between status as royal subject and membership in the corresponding national identity of French. Though not all non-European nations subject to European monarchical authority experienced the same degree of discrimination, European national identities everywhere became ethnicized and racialized as homogeneous. This redefinition fueled the intellectual debate about national characters and about nation, race, and history in the context of the eighteenth-century Enlightenment.

The reconceptualization of the nation as political and territorial, which arose in the early-modern colonial empires, did not obliterate the older ethnic groupings that the term had denoted: rather, the old and the new came into conflict with each other. From these tensions emerged the idea that political and juridical incorporation required cultural assimilation. With the racialization of both metropolitan and colonial societies, nation and empire could not merge: when European national identities started to coalesce around limited sets of characteristics, they correspondingly excluded all those who did not possess the selected markers of inclusion. What happened in the slave-trading outposts and colonies during the early-modern Atlantic period paved the way to modern conceptions of national identity, and corresponding citizenship, as homogeneous and exclusive.

CÉCILE VIDAL

Bibliography

Aubert, Guillaume. "Kinship, Blood, and the Emergence of the Racialized Nation in the French Atlantic World, 1600–1789." In *Blood and Kinship: Matter for Metaphor from Ancient Rome to the Present*, edited by Bernhard Jussen, Christopher H. Johnson, David Warren Sabean, and Simon Teuscher, 175–196. New York: Berghahn, 2013.

Bell, David A. *The Cult of the Nation in France: Inventing Nationalism, 1680–1800*. Cambridge, MA: Harvard University Press, 2003.

Cooper, Frederick, and Ann Laura Stoler. *Tensions of Empire: Colonial Cultures in a Bourgeois World*. Berkeley: University of California Press, 1997.

Havard, Gilles. "'Les forcer à devenir Citoyen': État, Sauvages et citoyenneté en Nouvelle-France (XVIIe–XVIIIe siècle)." *Annales H.S.S.* 64, no. 5 (2009): 985–1018.

Herzog, Tamar. *Defining Nations: Immigrants and Citizens in Early Modern Spain and Spanish America*. New Haven, CT: Yale University Press, 2003.

Newman, Brooke N. "Contesting 'Black Liberty' and Subjecthood in the Anglophone Caribbean, 1730s–1780s." *Slavery and Abolition* 32, no. 2 (2011): 169–183.

Sebastiani, Silvia. "Nations, Nationalism and National Characters." In *The Routledge Companion to Eigh-*

teenth Century Philosophy, edited by A. Garrett. New York: Routledge, 2012.

Wilson, Kathleen. *The Island Race: Englishness, Empire, and Gender in the Eighteenth Century.* New York: Routledge, 2003.

Native American Removals

American Indian removal in the United States is most commonly associated with the years surrounding the presidency of Andrew Jackson, who held office from 1829 to 1837. Jackson was a strong advocate of the relocation of Native peoples from their homelands near the eastern seaboard to the territories west of the Mississippi River, and in 1830 he signed into law what became known as the Indian Removal Act. Viewed within an Atlantic World context, however, this push for removal in North America must take into account historical conditions and events that laid the foundation for other forced relocations before the Jacksonian period and that produced similar removals in other parts of the Atlantic.

Focusing solely on the Jacksonian period, the struggle between the Cherokee Nation and the state of Georgia is a flash point in the removal of Native Americans and fits well into the historical confluence of several trends: the contemporaneous growth of cotton agriculture in the South, the expansion of voting rights throughout the new nation, and the debate over states' rights from the 1810s to the 1830s. The Cherokee role in that intently national narrative ends with passage of the Indian Removal Act in 1830, marking Congressional support for Georgia's position. The failure to enforce the 1832 Supreme Court decision in *Worcester v. Georgia*, which established federal authority over relations with Indian nations recognized as sovereign, illustrated that even a Cherokee legal victory against intrusion by a state lacked the power to halt the national push for removal. Three years after Senate ratification of the 1835 Treaty of New Echota, which empowered the national government to initiate removal of the Cherokee nation, federal soldiers rounded up over 12,000 Cherokee men, women, and children and forced them to move west of the Mississippi River along what became known as the Trail of Tears. The pressure for removal affected all Native communities from the Appalachian Mountains to the Mississippi River, not just the Cherokee. Over the course of the 1830s, as Creek, Choctaw, and Chickasaw were removed from the Southeast, federal, state, and local authorities also forcibly relocated thousands of Miami, Potawatomi, Shawnee, Delaware, Seneca, and Wyandot from their homes in the Great Lakes region. Despite the widespread removals of this era, the Cherokee struggle and the Trail of Tears remain its best-known component.

However, focusing on Cherokee removal and the Indian Removal Act downplays legacies of the early American republic. In the Southeast, for example, removals were connected with demands for more land—as well as with the development of slavery—earlier in the Colonial Era. While cotton cultivation sparked a period of tremendous land seizures in the Lower South in the first two decades of the nineteenth century, tobacco cultivation in Virginia in the seventeenth century had laid a foundation for the momentum of Indian dispossession. The rapid pace and expansive pattern of settlement in colonial New England had demonstrated that African slavery was not a necessary part of the pressure for removals: land hunger combined with the colonists' military efforts as early as the Pequot War (1634–1638) and King Philip's War (1675–1676) to erase Indian communities from the New England landscape. In addition, many of the prominent men in the nineteenth-century Native communities removed—from the Potawatomi in the Great Lakes region to the Creek in Alabama—were of mixed Native-English (and African) descent and thus physical legacies of the longer history of Atlantic encounters in North America. Descendants of the unions between European traders and Native women often led the negotiations that produced the removal treaties signed in the 1820s and 1830s.

Even as the nineteenth-century removals of Indians should be seen as results of prolonged events on Atlantic scales, the removals of indigenous peoples played a role in the broader development of the Atlantic World. The expansion of European trade and military control, by definition, involved displacements of indigenous peoples through treaties, warfare, and death from diseases. One clear example of the complexity of these multiple processes comes from the history of the Delaware, who occupied what is now New Jersey when Swedish, Dutch, and British colonists began to arrive in North America in the mid-seventeenth century. From then into the nineteenth century, the Delaware remained almost constantly on the move in response to the founding of Pennsylvania, the Walking Purchase agreement with the state's founders (the Penn family), the Seven Years' War, and the growth of the American republic. Some migrations were voluntary, in response to demographic losses, and others were forced through land seizures, warfare, and federal enactments. The Delawares' journey began on the Atlantic seaboard and continued through the fields and valleys of Pennsylvania, Ohio, Indiana, and Missouri. By the mid-nineteenth century their surviving descendants could be found in Ontario, the Kansas Territory, and Texas. Their dispersal illustrates the growing reach and influence of the Atlantic World over the course of three centuries.

Paralleling the removals of Native peoples in North America, English clearance of the populations of Highland Scotland in the last decades of the eighteenth century illustrates the broader connections between nineteenth-century Indian removals and the Atlantic World framework. Forced relocation, if not complete removal, of indigenous peoples is also reflected in the familiar story of European removals of Africans as slaves. The pan-Atlantic processes of these recurrent events reveal them to be integral to Europeans' consolidation of an Atlantic World, not an exceptional incident confined to a brief period, a single "trail of tears" in American history.

JOHN P. BOWES

Bibliography

Calloway, Colin G. *White People, Indians, and Highlanders: Tribal Peoples and Colonial Encounters in Scotland and America*. New York: Oxford University Press, 2008.

Carson, James Taylor. *Making an Atlantic World: Circles, Paths, and Stories from the Colonial South*. Knoxville: University of Tennessee Press, 2007.

Greene, Jack P., and Philip D. Morgan, eds. *Atlantic History: A Critical Appraisal*. New York: Oxford University Press, 2009.

Satz, Ronald N. *American Indian Policy in the Jacksonian Era*. Norman: University of Oklahoma Press, 2002.

Natural History

Natural history, developed in the Greco-Roman world by Aristotle (384–322 BCE) and Pliny the Elder (23–79 CE) and enriched in medieval Islam, refers to (1) the description of the three "kingdoms" of nature: plants, animals, and minerals; and (2) global taxonomies, or methods of classifying natural objects by classes, orders, genera, and species. Although ancient in origins, natural history exploded with the movements, mixing, and extinctions of peoples, plants, and animals that characterized the Atlantic World to become a major scientific and economic enterprise. Labeling the study of nature *natural history* privileges European science. However, expanding the definitions of natural history beyond the textual transmission of knowledge to include orally transmitted practices of cultivating, processing, and preparing plants and animals as foods and medicines highlights African and Amerindian specialized knowledge of flora and fauna and what these traditions also contributed to shaping the Atlantic World.

Rewriting European Natural History

Traditional scholarship links natural history with the rise of early-modern taxonomy, culminating in Carl Linnaeus's (1707–1778) *Systema naturae* (1735). Taxonomies strive to achieve global comprehensiveness. The goal is to provide a description and unique name for every organism (secured by a type specimen). Of all the categorizing subdisciplines of natural history in the early-modern period, botany was the most developed.

Many of Europe's leading naturalists of the era developed global networks to conduct large-scale trade in plants. Linnaeus, for example, sat at the center of a vast scientific empire where, in the comfort of his home and gardens in Uppsala, he received specimens and news of discoveries from some 570 correspondents in Sweden and around the world. Jan and Caspar Commelin similarly enjoyed a worldwide network through the gardens in Amsterdam, as did Paul Hermann and Herman Boerhaave in Leiden; the Jussieu brothers at the Jardin du Roi (now the Jardin des Plantes) in Paris; Mary Capell Somerset, duchess of Beaufort, at Badminton House; and Joseph Banks, eventually at Kew near London. From a European point of view, these various institutions became intellectual centers where the spoils of empire—plants, animals, and artifacts of all sorts from territories around the world—were transformed into the "science" of their times.

In recent years, scholars have rewritten this narrative to highlight how expertise in bioprospecting, plant identification, transport, and acclimatization accumulated to create natural history, but this newly wrought science also worked hand in hand with the expansion of western European economic and military might. Eighteenth-century political economists—from English and French mercantilists to German and Swedish cameralists—taught that exact knowledge of nature was key to amassing "wealth of nations," as Adam Smith put it, and hence power. If resources were not to be had domestically, they were to be obtained through conquest and colonization; such was especially the case for tropical plants that would not grow in cold European climates. Naturalists saw cacao, *ipecacuanha* (a Brazilian root used as an emetic), jalap (a Mexican vine used as a cathartic), and Peruvian bark (the source of quinine, a prophylactic against malaria) as moneymakers for king and country—and, often, for themselves. Peter Kalm, one of Linnaeus's students, writing from London in 1748, summed up this way of thinking: "Natural History is the base for all Economics, Commerce, and Manufacture" (Koerner, 104). Natural history was, by the eighteenth century, big science, to be sure, but it was also big business—an essential part of the projection of military might into the resource-rich Indies, East and West.

Atlantic World

Scholarship treating European natural history tends to see Europeans as agents of knowledge making. Broadening the focus of study to the Atlantic World reveals, by contrast, a robust mixing of and competition among African, Amerindian, and European knowledge traditions and highlights African and Amerindian expert knowledge of flora and fauna in lands unknown to Europeans. Amerindians, for example, moved plants from place to place in the Caribbean basin for hundreds of years prior to European contact. They were experts in the uses of plants as foods, medicines, and construction materials, for example, in canoes, hammocks, baskets, and other goods needed for daily life. Enslaved Africans, forced to abandon their homelands, were experts in tropical flora and carried with them plants and knowledge of their uses, especially to the Caribbean basin and to coastal regions and islands stretching from Jamestown, Virginia, to Bahia, Brazil.

Amerindians

When Christopher Columbus arrived in the "West Indies" in 1492, the islands were inhabited by peripatetic peoples, eventually classed as Arawaks, Taino, and Caribs, who had migrated into this area from South America sometime before 400 BCE. These peoples established gardens (called by Taino *conucos*) for the cultivation of their most prized foodstuffs and medicinal herbs. In his first Atlantic World encounter, Columbus collected fruits of these Amerindian natural-historical legacies, including tobacco, pineapples, and turkeys. Because indigenous populations of the Caribbean basin left no written documents, most of these Amerindian naturalists remain faceless and nameless, and knowledge of their extensive use of plants depends largely on European naturalists' very incomplete—though appreciative—accounts.

In the 1570s, Philip II of Spain sent Francisco Hernández (1515–1587) into New Spain (present-day Mexico) to study the region's peoples, fauna, and flora. Interviewing indigenous peoples through translators about the virtues and uses of plants, Hernández described, in Latin, more than 3,000 plants previously unknown in Europe. His manuscripts feature illustrations by three indigenous painters, baptized Pedro Vásquez, and Antón and Baltazar Elías, who were recognized in Hernández's will with a bequest of 60 ducats each. Hernández's 16-volume manuscript, presented to the king, perished in a fire. But selections from copies, some translated into Spanish and Nahuatl, were eventually published in Mexico in 1615 as *Quatro libros de la naturaleza, y virtudes de las plantas, y animales que estan recevidos en el uso de medicina en la Nueva España.*

Hernández celebrated indigenous peoples' domestication and cultivation of plants—including cacao, tomato, cassava, and many varieties of maize developed to thrive in different ecosystems throughout the Americas. Many of these plants in the wild—maize, for example—are inedible. Archaeologists have traced the oldest domesticated maize to the Oaxaca Valley, in southern Mexico, dating back some 6,200 years. Mexico is one of the world's centers for the development of agriculture. By the sixteenth century, these Amerindian cultivars were swept into the Atlantic economy and remade diets in both Africa and Europe.

Europeans of the early-modern period were also careful observers of Native American medicines. Hans Sloane (1660–1753), the future president of the Royal Society of London, traveled as a young man to Jamaica, where he collected information about plants previously unknown to him from "the Inhabitants, either Europeans, Indians or Blacks" (Schiebinger, 29). Jean-Baptiste-René Pouppé-Desportes (1704–1748), the French royal physician working in Cap Français, Saint-Domingue, also supplemented his European remedies with local "Carib simples." Because the first Europeans who came to the Americas, Pouppé-Desportes wrote, were afflicted by illnesses completely unknown to them, it was necessary to employ remedies used by "the naturals of the country whom one calls savages." In the third volume of his *Histoire des maladies de S. Domingue* (1770), Pouppé-Desportes presented what he called an "American pharmacopoeia," offering an extended list of Carib remedies for diseases. As was typical of works like his, he cross-referenced plant names in Latin, French, and the vernacular Carib. From 1732 until his death in 1748, Pouppé-Desportes collected and tested local remedies, which he then classified according to their medicinal properties.

European soldiers, planters, overseers, and physicians also learned much from the Amerindians whom they took as lovers, wives (perhaps in informal local marriages), and housekeepers. For example, early in the sixteenth century, according to Antonio Barrera-Osorio, the Spaniard Antonio de Villasante learned the virtues of plants in Hispaniola from his Christianized wife, Catalina de Ayahibx, a Taino chief, or *cacica*.

African Slaves

Judith Carney and Richard Rosomoff (2009) have discussed Africa's botanical legacy in the Atlantic World in detail. Shifting attention from European commodity crops from various parts of the world (sugar, coffee, cotton, and tobacco) and plantation economies of scale, Carney and Rosomoff examine African subsistence crops and the knowledge systems embedded in them. The African Diaspora, they emphasize, was one of plants as well as people.

Using shipping records, historical linguistics, and written documents, Carney and Rosomoff describe how enslaved Africans naturalized their Old World food staples in the American tropics—especially the Caribbean, where 40 percent of them landed. Successful Middle Passages required two meals per day for several months for several hundred slaves. Ships provisioned on the Guinea coast in Africa were often filled with unhusked, unmilled grains, such as rice and millet, which survivors planted in the Americas as seed for crops of their own. Ports of Caribbean plantations had all the ingredients needed for successful acclimatization of African crops in the Americas: seeds and people skilled in seed cultivation and processing, in addition to people with dietary preferences, who, without these resources of their own, often faced starvation at the hands of masters devoted single-mindedly to commercial agriculture.

Slaves planted these grains and other crops in gardens or provision grounds that they worked in the few hours allotted to them on Sundays and holidays. Altogether, Carney calculates, enslaved Africans acclimatized from Africa to tropical America 19 genera from 15 botanical families. These included species of rice, yam, millet, banana, groundnut, tamarind, guinea squash, hibiscus, sesame, okra (used as food and also combined with Amerindian plants to produce abortifacients), lablab (or hyacinth) bean, and sorghum. In this way, Carney states, "slaves Africanized the food system of plantation societies of the Americas" (Carney and Rosomoff, 2). African stewardship also served to adapt and thus perpetuate Amerindian plant usages even after their discoverers themselves were destroyed. The outcome, as slaves introduced Amerindian crops to their provision fields, was a fusion of two tropical farming systems: African and Amerindian.

Early-modern European physicians seeking to stave off the massive mortality Europeans faced in the tropics also learned a great deal about tropical medicine from the Africans they enslaved. With the decline of indigenous populations in the West Indies, slave medicines became increasingly important, even though in the first half of the eighteenth century Africans on the big sugar islands were no more native to the area than Europeans (at least 80 percent had been born in Africa). However, Africans, unlike Europeans, knew tropical diseases, their preventions, and cures. Nicolas Bourgeois (1710–1776), a long-time resident of French Saint-Domingue, appreciated slave medicines. Considering health a matter of importance to the welfare of the realm, he eulogized the "marvelous cures" abounding in the islands and remarked that *les nègres* were "almost the only ones who know how to use them"; they had, he wrote, more knowledge of these cures than the whites (*les blancs*) (Schiebinger, 80).

It is impossible to know with any precision how much herbal knowledge Africans transferred to the New World. The arriving slaves must have found familiar medicinal plants growing in the American tropics, and they must have discovered—through commerce with the Amerindians or their own trials and errors—plants with virtues similar to those they had used back home. They may also have found seeds of African medical plants on board slave ships. Bourgeois confirms that there were many "doctors" (*médecins*) among the enslaved Africans, who "brought their treatments from their own countries," though this exponent of European natural science did not discuss in detail the Africans' contributions to knowledge of the natural world.

Bourgeois also praised the skills of slave doctors. "I could see immediately," he wrote, "that the negroes were more ingenious than we in the art of procuring health. . . . Our colony possesses an infinity of negroes and negresses [*nègres & même des nègresses (sic)*] who practice medicine, and in whom many whites have much confidence. . . . The most dangerous [plant] poisons can be transformed into the most salubrious remedies when prepared by a skilled hand; I have seen cures that very much surprised me" (Schiebinger, 80).

*   *   *

Natural history, as systematic knowledge, strives to be a global science. In the early-modern period, much natural history was cultivated to enrich European commerce. The Dutch, English, and French, for example, had hundreds of gardens for accumulation and acclimatization of natural products stretched throughout their territorial holdings. Highly prized plants—nutmeg for example, used to perfume the streets of Rome for the coronation of the pope—would not grow in France but flourished in the western Indian Ocean in French colonial gardens in Isle de France (today's Mauritius). The Atlantic World, in particular, opened highways between Africa, the Americas, and Europe for the swift movement of plants and knowledge systems, and not only for Europeans. Africans brought to the Americas as slaves introduced and acclimatized African dietary staples in provision grounds. They also preserved Amerindian knowledge of plants in these gardens. The European-developed plantation complexes at the economic heart of the Atlantic World synthesized the diverse knowledge systems of Africans, Amerindians, and Europeans.

LONDA SCHIEBINGER

Bibliography

Barrera-Osorio, Antonio. *Experiencing Nature: The Spanish American Empire and the Early Scientific Revolution.* Austin: University of Texas Press, 2006.

Carney, Judith, and Richard Rosomoff. *In the Shadow of Slavery: Africa's Botanical Legacy in the Atlantic World.* Berkeley: University of California Press, 2009.

Kiple, Kenneth, and Kriemhild Coneè Ornelas. *The Cambridge World History of Food.* 2 vols. Cambridge: Cambridge University Press, 2000.

Koerner, Lisbet. *Linnaeus: Nature and Nation.* Cambridge, MA: Harvard University Press, 1999.

McCann, James. *Maize and Grace: Africa's Encounter with a New World Crop, 1500–2000.* Cambridge, MA: Harvard University Press, 2005.

Newsom, Lee A. "Caribbean Paleoethnobotany: Present Status and New Horizons." In *Crossing the Borders: New Methods and Techniques in the Study of Archaeological Materials from the Caribbean.* Tuscaloosa: University of Alabama Press, 2008.

Pouppé-Desportes, Jean-Baptiste-René. *Histoire des maladies de S. Domingue.* Vol. 3, *Traité ou Abrégé des plantes usuelles de S. Domingue.* Paris: Chez Lejay, 1770.

Schiebinger, Londa. *Plants and Empire: Colonial Bioprospecting in the Atlantic World.* Cambridge, MA: Harvard University Press, 2004.

Spary, E. C. *Utopia's Garden: French Natural History from Old Regime to Revolution.* Chicago: University of Chicago Press, 2000.

Varey, Simon, Rafael Chabrán, and Dora Weiner, eds. *Searching for the Secrets of Nature: The Life and Works of Dr. Francisco Hernández.* Stanford, CA: Stanford University Press, 2000.

Navies and Naval Arming

The royal dynasties in England, France, and Portugal led the way in developing navies in the fourteenth century. It was not coincidental that brass and iron cannon were deployed in maritime western Europe at the same time: certainly, gunpowder made the delivery of military force more feasible by sea. This expanded investment in naval power within the coastal waters of Europe provided the base from which these monarchies built maritime forces on Atlantic—and eventually global—scales unprecedented for terrestrial land-based political authorities. Naval warfare, and raising government revenues to support its equally unprecedented costs, were at the heart of the historical processes of integrating the Atlantic World.

A marked turn toward sea power characterizes the empires in northwest Europe in the fifteenth and sixteenth centuries, a trend noted most clearly in English (later British) maritime records, the most complete of such royal archives. Competitive escalations in naval development by France, Spain, and later Holland brought the mid- to late sixteenth century one of the most costly of arms races. The culminating Spanish Armada of 1588 is most familiar, but it followed a French armada, formed in 1545 with the same purpose, and numerous English provocations in attacks on French and Spanish ports. Overall, the late sixteenth century saw growing assaults by sea achieve a rough parity with conventional warfare on the land, and the expenses of heavy armed ships and cannon escalated for all sides involved.

Had the maritime European powers been limited to their own forests for timbers for this vast program of naval construction, they might have been forced to curtail maritime expansion. But the race for colonies in the New World coincided with the beginning of dynastic navies, and each of the major competitors looked to the Americas—as well as to Sweden, Norway, and Russia—for more trees with which to build larger and larger vessels of war.

Holland enjoyed a brief period at the top, when the Dutch West India Company (formed in 1621) dominated the Atlantic trade, and when her warships competed with England on an equal basis. It was not inevitable that England would eventually surpass Holland; its mercantile growth, marked by stylish consumer imports and lavish displays of wealth in the vibrantly successful Dutch Golden Age (roughly 1620–1660) may have diminished the devotion of the United Provinces (a name applied to the Dutch Republic in this era) to the arms race. It is not an uncommon pattern in the world's history for intruders to rely on violence and then turn to the economic means they have acquired to invest quietly in the domains of others, as later Dutch merchants did in the Atlantic.

The English raised the bar in maritime warfare in 1637, launching an unprecedentedly large and heavily armed warship, the HMS *Sovereign of the Seas*, with more than 100 brass and iron cannon. The French followed with *Le Roi Soleil* ("The Sun King," in honor of Louis XIV), and by 1690 both monarchies had a number of three-decker ships of the line, which were built to form a column across the wind and deliver the heaviest possible broadside against the opponent's ships; these massive vessels required on average crews of 500 men apiece. Holland kept pace at the midlevel of warships but did not compete at the three-decker level. Along with the costs of wood, pitch, tar, and cannon, a large human cost was involved: no one can say how many men drafted into the English, French, and Dutch navies might have contributed to productive aspects of civilian life. England pulled ahead of France after 1692—the year of the Battle of La Hogue off the north coast of France in the English Channel—and by 1700, over 80,000 men were operating the fleet of England's Royal Navy. The great age of naval competition had hardly begun.

In the increasingly maritime War of the Spanish Succession (1701–1714), Britain fought practically alone against France and Spain. The British achieved great success, capturing Gibraltar from

Figure 1. James E. Buttersworth, *HMS Sovereign of the Seas*. In the collection of the Old State House Museum in Boston.

Spain as well as winning a number of major fleet actions. France and Spain suffered from their geostrategic status as powers with major commitments on land as well as at sea. The Bourbon powers spent plenty on their fleets, but at war's end in 1714, they had little to show for it.

British naval dominance in the Atlantic truly began during a period of relatively prolonged peace—between 1712 and 1739, when the War of Jenkins' Ear broke out. Many agree that the long peace was instrumental in allowing investment in what later became "Lord Nelson's navy," under Horatio Viscount Nelson (1758–1805) in the Napoleonic Wars at the end of the eighteenth century. During the same period of peace, the British became adept at finding new sources of naval materials, especially white pine and oak from the northern

American colonies. The Royal Navy received larger budgets than before, while France, Spain, and Holland all fell behind in the building and arming of warships. When the War of Jenkins' Ear commenced, the British were ready for a major effort to sweep the Atlantic clean of opposition to their merchant fleet. And the war, for the first time, assumed a primarily maritime dimension, centered in the West Indies.

The War of the Austrian Succession (1744–1748), which emerged from the Jenkins' Ear conflict, confirmed the new British superiority. Britain had long possessed greater reservoirs of sailors; by the mid-eighteenth century it also had more ships and cannon than any two of its major competitors combined. Advances in gunnery, along with better sailors' diets, allowed the British to defeat all rivals.

A few short years of peace were followed by the Seven Years' War (1756–1763), which many historians consider the first armed conflict of true world proportions, its scale made possible by the mobility of the Royal Navy. Beginning in 1755, the British competed with France in the northern and southern Atlantic as well as in the Caribbean, Mediterranean, and Indian Ocean. The pattern, on the whole, was one of British triumph, with some close calls and even surprising French victories. In the "Miracle Year" of 1759, the British captured French Quebec, won important land battles, and smashed a potential French invasion fleet assembling in northwestern France, at Brittany's Quiberon Bay. Royal Navy expenditures soared, but the magnitude of the victories assuaged taxpayers. The Peace of Paris, in 1763, confirmed Britain's status as the world's great naval power, with no serious contenders.

Britain continued to build its colossal fleet. HMS *Victory*, rated at 100 guns, was launched in 1764. France attempted to keep pace, launching *Ville de Paris*, at 104 guns, in 1765. Spain also continued, launching *Santissima Trinidad*, the world's largest warship at 112 guns, in 1768. It is impossible to estimate what these ships cost in modern currencies; suffice it to say that the costs were enormous for their time. The new construction was needed for the great contest that began in 1775, with the rebellion of the British colonies in North America, and broadened into another pan-Atlantic war when France (1778), Spain (1779), and Holland (1780) entered the conflict.

The British dominated the North American coastline 90 percent of the time, but there were significant lapses, as when the French gained control of the Chesapeake Bay in 1781. Fighting off the European coasts was generally indecisive, although Britain beat back some spectacular attempts to take Gibraltar. The naval conflict in the Caribbean was also evenly matched until 1782, when the British won the Battle of the Saintes, near Dominica and Guadeloupe, over the same French fleet that had besieged their army at Yorktown, Virginia, effectively ending Britain's effort to retain control of its former colonies in North America. Though less stunning than the later iconic victories of Lord Nelson over the French, Saintes heralded a new era in destructive naval warfare: copper-sheathed vessels carrying carronades, a new cannon devastating at short ranges, were able to wreak great destruction. The Treaty of Paris (1783) confirmed American territorial independence, but the British Navy survived the storm and went on to support still grander maritime strategies of imperial consolidation of the nineteenth century.

The 1780s were the calm before the great Continental conflagration that followed the French Revolution. The British, French, and Spanish entered the French Revolutionary Wars (beginning in 1793) with substantially the same naval equipment as before. By 1800, Britain had about 120,000 sailors in the Royal Navy. France and Spain combined had about 100,000. All three nations made huge investments in their naval forces, culminating in the battles of the Nile (Britain against Napoleon's forces in Egypt, 1798), Copenhagen (where a Danish fleet challenged British ships enforcing the Continental Blockade, 1803), and Trafalgar (in the Atlantic, west of the Strait of Gibraltar, 1805). The last of these three has been overemphasized in the heroic literature devoted to the British admiral Nelson, who died in the battle, but the loss of 20 Franco-Spanish ships was a major blow to Napoleon. From 1805 on, the British taxpayer was given a break on naval expenses, as the theaters of Napoleon's wars shifted to land and the army received higher allocations of revenues. France did not give up the fight; Napoleon built new ships right up to the time of his first abdication in 1814.

A new combatant, meanwhile, entered the arena. The American colonists during their struggle against Britain built a navy based on privateers, that is, privately funded vessels of the sort that England and the Netherlands had used to challenge Spain in the sixteenth century (and that had in fact successfully defended England against Spain's Armada in 1588). The colonies also commenced building government frigates—smaller, more maneuverable, lighter-armed fighting ships—in 1794. None carried more than 50 guns, but they were built from American timbers and physically sound, and they carried heavier cannonballs than their opponents. The Americans beat the French in the undeclared Naval War of 1798–1800, bested the Tripolitan pirates in North Africa between 1801 and 1805, and gave the British some serious challenges during the War of 1812. The Tripolitan and Algerine pirates had been roaming the Mediterranean for centuries, but the Atlantic powers made a new, concerted effort to stamp out their activities in 1815, and by the next year the Atlantic entered a new era of relative maritime peace, leaving the British free to redeploy Royal Navy ships as the West Africa Squadron, dedicated to suppressing the transatlantic slave trading of the Portuguese, Brazilians, Spanish, and North Americans.

The dominant narrative of the Royal Navy's triumph in the Atlantic World tends to celebrate its violence and victories rather than trace the historical processes of how and why, perhaps because so many maritime historians have been English speaking. Such heroic fictional characters as Horatio Hornblower are much more accessible than their French, Spanish, Dutch, or Danish counterparts, and historians often echo the prescient Alexis de Tocqueville, who predicted in 1835 that the Americans would dominate the world's oceans as the Romans had once ruled on land. Economic and material considerations of Atlantic proportions, however, produced the historical processes supporting the heroic narrative.

England had—from 1400—more fishermen and merchant sailors than any other monarchy in Europe. It also had access to better timber from northern climes—whether homegrown or imported—than its Mediterranean rivals. Only the Dutch equaled the British in merchant shipping, and then for only a few decades, from 1650 to 1680. No other European monarchy had as much cash, as many sailors, or as many potential resources from its colonies. The establishment of the Bank of England (1694) and the financial strength it created enabled investments in marine armaments that allowed Britain to dominate the northern and southern Atlantic in the following generation. Although France and Spain continued to test the British fleet for another century, only the new United States had the territory and resources to challenge it as master of the seas, and the United States assumed that responsibility only after another century and a world war ruinously costly for its European antagonists.

Blessed with a longer coastline than Britain's, and possessing potential sailors in abundance, the United States was a major competitor on the Atlantic even before it began building ships of the line. As with Britain, material factors backed the human ones. The Americans could build more ships, at lower costs, than any other nation. After the War of

1812, they did not need a major navy, as no power other than the British could threaten them in any significant way. Perhaps through wisdom, possibly through neglect, the Americans did not build major warships until the Age of Steam arrived. When the USS *Constitution*, with only 44 guns but victorious in a series of naval engagements dating from the Barbary Wars, circled the globe in the 1840s, it was still one of the largest of all American war vessels.

Things could, of course, have gone differently. But given the preponderance of men, cannon, and timbers, it is not surprising that Britain "won" most conflicts during the Age of Sail as it played out in the Atlantic. Equally, it is unsurprising that the Americans built on British success and eventually stole most of their secrets, just as the English had formerly outdone the Dutch.

SAMUEL WILLARD CROMPTON

Bibliography

Hill, J. R., ed. *The Illustrated History of the Royal Navy*. New York: Oxford University Press, 1995.

Jardine, Lisa. *Going Dutch: How England Stole Holland's Glory*. New York: HarperCollins, 2009.

Padfield, Peter. *Maritime Supremacy and the Opening of the Western Mind*. New York: Overlook, 2001.

Roger, N. A. M. *The Wooden World: An Anatomy of the Georgian Navy*. London: William Collins, 1986.

Navigation and Nautical Sciences

In 1400, no one in what would become the Atlantic World knew much about deepwater navigation. Many coastal societies were well able to routinely sail moderate distances—between various islands in the Caribbean or different parts of Europe, or to islands near the African coast—but had little ability to go beyond the sight of land and, with the exception of deep-sea fishers, little reason. By 1800, travel across and around the Atlantic had become both lucrative and strategically important, and had spurred developments in ship design, cartography, and (most notably) the ability to determine the location of a ship at sea. These advances meant that by 1800 navigators had charts that correctly located most lands in terms of a grid of latitude and longitude and the ability to determine compass bearings and distances between any points in the seas. As most of the improvements in navigation benefited European countries—first the Portuguese, then the Spanish, then the French, English, and Dutch—navigation and nautical science were inextricably connected with the attempts to create or support integrated maritime connections.

At the beginning of the fifteenth century, the basic problems inhibiting deepwater navigation were threefold. First, captains of ships had to figure out what course to set, which required accurate charts showing both where the lands were in respect to one another and the locations of wind systems and currents to ride, as well as hazards to be avoided. This was the information that explorers were supposed to bring back. Second, they had to be able to maneuver the ship to follow the planned course, improving the technical capacities of the ship, and adjusting for winds and currents. Finally, they had to be able to figure out the location of the ship when out of sight of land (and so away from any landmarks), which required either the ability to measure speeds and account for currents and leeway (or slipping to the side of the plotted course) if traveling through dead reckoning, or the ability to use celestial phenomena to pinpoint location. Ideally, the locations as calculated would then be used to update charts, creating a cycle of improvements in both navigation and cartography.

For the initial explorers, the main challenges were safety—how not to run into land or run out of food or water—and reporting back accurately on where the ship had been. For those who followed, the problem was finding the same lands a second time, and—where possible—locating better ports, anchorages, and routes to make navigation safer and more reliable and efficient.

The early deep-sea navigators of the Atlantic World left few records beyond the remains of temporary settlements on the shores. In 1450 codfish were an important source of food in Europe and attracted large communities of fishers off the coasts of Iceland and Ireland. By the end of the century, fishing fleets out of various European ports competed for prime spots in Newfoundland, but little is known about the exact chronology or methods that they used to cross the ocean.

More is known about European explorations near the coast of Africa, from the Spanish conquest and colonization of the Canary Islands, which were then used as a jumping-off place for further voyages, to the Portuguese attempts to find a sailing route around Africa and on to the East Indies. These maritime explorers were the first sailors known to have experimented with celestial navigation in the Atlantic. They rode the strong Canary Current south and could return home only by tacking far out to sea to the northwest, with instructions to turn east toward Lisbon when the noonday sun or North Star was at the same height above the horizon as at their intended return destination. But navigation was primarily by dead reckoning, and sailors put the greatest efforts into trying to learn the currents and prevailing winds; few knew (or cared) how to use the stars.

Christopher Columbus was a part of this late fifteenth-century maritime tradition, relying primarily on experience, winds, and currents. The captains and navigators of other ships had extensive experience along the coast of Africa and used this experience, and the trust it inspired, to recruit crews. Columbus was himself suspect, not only for his unusually small estimate of the size of the earth but also for his plan to go with prevailing winds beyond the point of no return, counting on finding both hospitable lands to reprovision his ships and other winds favorable for the return journey. His fortuitous success, of course, began an intensive effort to chart not only the newly found lands but also the wind systems and currents of the Atlantic, so that ships could cross the ocean and return safely. At around the same time, the Portuguese found that swinging wide around Africa to the west brought them into better winds and currents and so to a faster—if much longer—route to the southern tip of Africa and on to the Indian Ocean. In the course of exploring this roundabout track, they blundered into the coast of Brazil, which they claimed, but their focus remained on the Indian Ocean and the East Indies. The open Atlantic, beyond their coasting south along the mainland of Africa in search of gold, was at best an afterthought.

Winds and currents remained the fundamental constraints of Atlantic navigation until the nineteenth century, when steamships broke free of these climatic propulsion systems. While sailing technologies improved greatly over the centuries, sailing ships remained fundamentally dependent on the reliable presence and direction of the winds. Increased maneuverability and better sail and hull designs allowed ships to sail closer to the wind, but they still could not sail against it, and, of course, remained vulnerable to being becalmed or destroyed in storms. These constraints made crossing the Atlantic fundamentally seasonal, to take the greatest advantage of wind patterns and to avoid the hurricane season, and encouraged most transatlantic traffic to sail within fairly narrow bands. While in theory navigators needed to be able to guide their ships anywhere in the trackless waters, in practice most ships followed similar routes, even though these predictable patterns greatly increased their vulnerability to pirates.

The task of navigators was to reproduce the routes initially surveyed by the explorers and make them routine. In this context, the Iberians took the lead, as first Portugal and then Spain created strict licensing systems for navigators and required classes and examinations to teach them celestial techniques. Regulators then created an institutional framework to make sure that the requisite charts, instruments, and nautical tables were readily available for purchase and reviewed for accuracy. Officials routinely questioned returning pilots about needed corrections. These training methods then spread to the rest of Europe, as the French built on the Portuguese model, and the British on the Spanish one, as governments and chartered companies designed systems to teach navigation and create and correct charts.

The basic methods of navigating in the Atlantic stayed largely the same, even as they increased enormously in accuracy. Every jurisdiction required navigators to be able to plot a course on a chart. In the fifteenth century, navigators used portolan charts based on techniques of sailing in the closed Mediterranean Sea, expanded to cover the Atlantic World. Portolans were based on webs of rhumb (straight) lines showing compass bearings between known ports and landmarks, overlaid with latitudes and, later, also longitudes.

This representation of the earth's surface accorded well with the primary methods of navigation, which relied first and foremost on compass bearings, and later on compass bearings corrected for magnetic variation. Navigators also needed to be able to calculate latitudes from the height of the noonday sun (at first generally using a mariner's astrolabe, then a backstaff, then a sextant) and from the North Star at night (generally using a cross-staff and later a sextant). They used measured latitudes to correct their estimates of the courses and distances their ships traveled.

Though the portolan charts were drawn without regard to formal projections, the distortions caused by depicting a round earth on a flat chart were minor compared to other sources of error, especially in the tropics where most initial overseas travel took place and the distortions were smallest. As knowledge of locations grew and precision in celestial navigation increased, cartographers searched for methods that would be both mathematically rigorous and useful to the navigators. Mercator projections, though unpopular when first introduced, eventually won out, since they allowed navigators to continue to use both compass bearings and latitudes. The distortions in representing distances (and thus sizes) were judged less important than bearings, given that distances at sea could not be measured with useful precision and errors could be corrected once in sight of recognizable land.

By the eighteenth century, the main unsolved technical problem was determining longitude. At first longitude had been a concern not of navigation but of claims to territories, since the 1494 treaty of Tordesillas set the boundary between the jurisdictions of Spain and Portugal as a nominal line of longitude 370 leagues (c. 1,275 miles) west of the Azores and of the islands of Cape Verde. This longitudinal formulation made the problem of interest to cartographers and sovereigns in Europe, even though few outside of Iberia recognized the rights thus bounded. The more practical problems associated with not being able to determine longitude at sea derived from the inability to measure distances accurately, hence the inability to estimate east-west progress and to know when to expect land. These imprecisions were much more dangerous in the world's other oceans and seas, since the Atlantic lacked the hidden reefs far from land and isolated islands common elsewhere. Nonetheless, those worried about the safety of navigation tended to test and implement new methods in the Atlantic, where journeys were short and relatively direct. Several European governments, spurred on by eager entrepreneurs promising new methods for determining usefully precise longitudes, offered substantial prizes for anyone who could find a practical way to determine the east-west component of ships'

P

positions at sea; the most famous was the British Longitude Prize created in 1714.

Determining longitude at sea was much more difficult than calculating latitudes. Latitudes could be found from the height of the sun at noon or from the height of the North Star; both methods allowed for easy and frequent observation and simple calculations, and both were in routine use from the early to mid-sixteenth century. But longitude relied either on infrequent occurrences, such as lunar eclipses, finicky observations (such as the moons of Jupiter, which were prohibitively difficult to observe accurately from a moving ship), or mathematical skill (since the first methods proposed for calculating longitude from lunar distances could take several hours of calculation). Furthermore, using the motions of the moon would require substantial improvements in available tables, prompting decades of astronomical observation and data gathering, culminating in such publications as the *Nautical Almanac*, first compiled in 1767. The main alternative was to build an extremely accurate clock, since differences in time were equivalent to differences in longitude. If a navigator could know simultaneously the time at his home port (kept by the clock) and the local time (calculated from the stars), then he could easily determine the difference between the two in longitude. But this method required timepieces far better than any available before John Harrison's (1693–1776) chronometers revolutionized the field in the middle of the eighteenth century.

By the early nineteenth century, navigators began to rely on being able to determine longitudes at sea. Most naval vessels were required to carry several chronometers, and most novice navigators were taught not only how to use these instruments but also how to calculate longitude using lunar distances. While exact measurement of longitudes was of greater practical importance outside of the Atlantic World, these devices contributed to the professionalization of navigation and the huge increase in the precision expected in navigation and cartography. With the ability to find longitudes at sea easily, and with increased use of steamships, navigators were freed from the constraints of winds and currents that had limited sailing routes since the fifteenth century and were able instead to plot new and more efficient courses.

In terms of blue-water navigation, the Atlantic was the easiest of the oceans to cross, since it was relatively small and had visible lands as points of reference and few hidden dangers. It was a relatively secure cradle for the infancy of European nautical sciences, which were nursed by its growing and changing commercial and strategic attractions.

ALISON SANDMAN

Bibliography

Andrewes, William J. H., ed. *The Quest for Longitude*. Proceedings of the Longitude Symposium, Harvard University, Cambridge, MA, November 4–6, 1993.

Howse, Derek. *Greenwich Time and the Discovery of the Longitude*. Oxford: Oxford University Press, 1980.

Smith, Roger C. *Vanguard of Empire: Ships of Exploration in the Age of Columbus*. Oxford: Oxford University Press, 1993.

Taylor, E. G. R. *The Haven-finding Art: A History of Navigation from Odysseus to Captain Cook*. New York: American Elsevier, 1971.

Woodward, David, ed. *The History of Cartography, Volume Three: Cartography in the European Renaissance*. Chicago: University of Chicago Press, 2007. See especially articles by Eric H. Ash, "Navigation Techniques and Practice in the Renaissance," 509–527, and John P. Snyder, "Map Projections in the Renaissance," 365–380.

Paramount Chiefdoms

The term *chiefdom* is a somewhat abstract term for a very real form of political organization that was ubiquitous among Native American societies at the time of contact with Europeans. It describes a multivillage entity with a clear social and political demarcation between commoners and elite lineages, from which a hereditary chief was drawn. A paramount chiefdom encompassed multiple chiefdoms owing tribute and some degree of obedience to a single, hereditary chief-of-chiefs who embodied spiritual, military, and economic power. Paramount chiefs were particularly interesting to Europeans because they resembled European monarchs and could wield a great deal of power. From the rain forests of Brazil through the Caribbean island of Hispaniola to the Chesapeake Bay homeland of the powerful leader Powhatan, the interactions of paramount chiefs and the European newcomers profoundly shaped the integration of the Americas into the Atlantic World.

What's in a Chiefdom?

Chiefdoms and paramount chiefdoms often emerged when a group felt a sustained need for defense against outsiders. One way of adapting to such shared threats was to coordinate efforts at defense and other external relations under a superior, and thus more hierarchical, authority. At the base of a paramount chiefdom were individual households, which typically clustered together in neighborhoods of a half-dozen hamlets and villages spaced a few miles apart. These villagers paid tribute to their local hereditary chief and supported the population of his town, which served as a capital and ceremonial center for the collectivity. In return chiefs maintained order within their communities and coordinated external relations through exchange, diplomacy, and war. Normally chiefs were at the apex of day-to-day local political integration, but in some cases they recognized a further level of authority on a larger scale: a paramount chief who coordinated relations among multiple chiefdoms that he (or occasionally she) had inherited, conquered, pressured, or negotiated with to cooperate on occasions of common concerns. Chiefs generally interfered little in the day-to-day affairs of the subordinate chiefdoms but played a strong role in coordinating their relations with outsiders.

Chiefs held their authority by virtue of their birth into a chiefly lineage. Individual charisma and accomplishments could help those who had been born into a ruling lineage to better exercise the authority conferred upon them by their ancestors, but such personal characteristics alone could not legitimize their use of power. Religious specialists reinforced the notion that the chief's hereditary powers were sanctioned by spiritual forces beyond the reach of rivals or common people. Ceremonies, architecture, and art all signaled the chief's access to power that potential challengers lacked, as did genealogies that rooted chiefly lineages in a universal spiritual order. Lesser, more specialized positions also carried with them authority independent of the personal achievements of the officeholders of the moment.

Collecting tribute and controlling long-distance exchange were central to the exercise of chiefly power. Networks of trade, tribute, and gifting tended to funnel spiritually potent goods into the hands of the elite lineages, chiefs, and paramount chiefs. Exotic things from faraway places (such as gold, rare feathers, shell beads, and captives) brought with them innate powers and were especially important in displaying and claiming the uniqueness that legitimated distinctive powers. Many such objects were believed to give their possessors privileged access to the spiritual sources from which all power ultimately came and thus often figured prominently in ceremonies performing and enacting the paramount's power.

Chiefs tried to monopolize the power that exotic goods conferred by limiting access to the outsiders who provided them. Food and trade goods circulating among ordinary people within the group were also subject to regular demands for tribute. Rather than amassing wealth, however, paramount chiefs strategically redistributed these same goods in conspicuous displays of largesse. The effect was to convert private wealth into political cohesiveness and collective power. By sharing goods acquired through trade or tribute, chiefs created loyalty and bonds of obligation on the recipients' parts. They would be expected to carry out the chief's decisions on behalf of the group and were also better able to carry out their duties because of the spiritual power inherent in these goods.

Chiefs were generalists. Unlike priests, war leaders, or political advisors with specialized areas of responsibility and competence, chiefs had powers covering the full range of religious, military, political, economic, and diplomatic affairs of the group as a whole. Thus they could usually outmaneuver officials whose sources of power were more narrowly defined. Yet each source of chiefly power—spiritual, military, and economic—could cut both ways. Local chiefs had access to spiritual power independent of their paramount chief's, the war leaders empowered to engage enemies could also turn against their own chief, and the flow of exotic prestige goods was impossible to control fully. Since no paramount chief could completely monopolize power, politics and diplomacy in paramount chiefdoms were complicated, fluid, and diverse.

An awareness of these broadly shared dynamics of paramount chiefdoms and chiefdoms, however, should not obscure their tremendously varying sizes, organizations, economies, gender and kinship norms, spiritual practices, and unique histories. Some anthropologists have treated chiefdoms as precursors to the state in a deterministic evolutionary scheme, which bears an uncomfortable resemblance to now-archaic Social Darwinism and other rationales for European colonialism in the name of progress. However, these types of ahistorical analysis can be countered by positioning individual paramount chiefdoms in their specific historical contexts. This historicized approach is particularly helpful for understanding Native American responses to the military and economic challenges Europeans posed for them after 1492.

American Chiefdoms in an Atlantic World

Recent, historically specific research has drawn attention to the process of chiefly cycling, the irregular but recurring rise and fall of chiefdoms owing to such internal structural dynamics as succession disputes or subordinate chiefs' abandonment of their paramounts and to such external pressures as environmental crises or military defeats in regional conflicts independent of Europeans. Chiefdoms often gained strength by picking up the pieces after their neighbors' collapses, only to succumb in due time to new paramount chiefdoms waxing under unusually able leaders. The paradoxical result was a high degree of regional stability as the rise, fall, growth, and collapse of specific polities canceled one another out and yielded a certain long-term continuity.

European newcomers often sought to understand at least the rudiments of the histories of the peoples they encountered. They had to, because their initial settlements were typically too small,

uninformed, and weak to progress without help from the more numerous and better-established indigenous polities around them. Thus they integrated themselves into the local configuration of indigenous diplomatic and trading dynamics. Since those configurations varied widely and changed constantly, Europeans needed in each case to understand the unique historical situation into which they had entered. On an Atlantic scale a pattern emerged: again and again the newcomers allied themselves with Native groups that needed external support against established (or rival) paramount chiefs too powerful for them to confront alone. Recognizing such opportunities enabled the newcomers to avert defeat at the outset, but once established they discarded their initial allies and either destroyed them or integrated them into the new colonial order.

The first Spanish settlement in America, for example, established in 1493 on the Caribbean island that the newcomers called Hispaniola, encountered the island's several paramount Taino chiefdoms at a turbulent moment in the island's indigenous history. Columbus's men adapted their strategies to this particular, complex situation, leveraging inter- and intrachiefdom rivalries to compensate for their own small numbers and gradually subordinating surviving chiefdoms to growing Spanish power. This strategy established patterns of manipulation that the Spanish then carried to other islands and eventually to the mainland itself. Similarly, in the Chesapeake Bay region the English needed to reckon with the power of the paramount chief Powhatan, which was on the rise when a small company of English settlers established Jamestown in 1607. There, too, a venture that was close to failing, as were other colonies in America, turned things around by exploiting rivalries and dissent within the paramountcy and reducing the surviving Native polities to dependent status. Not coincidentally, by 1650 the Virginia colony encompassed roughly the same territory as had Powhatan's chieftaincy.

Victorious colonists sometimes froze a paramount chiefdom in place, interrupting chiefly cycling by replacing the indigenous authorities with colonial officials while retaining core elements of the indigenous political system. When Spaniards first reached the central highlands of modern-day Colombia in 1537, for instance, they encountered two large paramount chiefdoms they called the "Zipa" and the "Zaque." For several generations the Zipa and the Zaque had been conquering and integrating successive subordinate chiefdoms, and increasingly they became regional rivals. As they had in Hispaniola and the Valley of Mexico, the Spanish took advantage of this rivalry, as well as the eagerness of reluctant, recently annexed subjects to see their new paramount chiefs toppled by the newcomers. By 1541 the Zaques' and Zipas' lines of succession had been broken. The two paramount chiefdoms were on their way to becoming constituent parts of Nuevo Reino de Granada, a key territory within the Viceroyalty of Peru in what was rapidly becoming a Spanish empire.

In other instances, engagement with the broader Atlantic World destroyed rather than coopted paramount chiefdoms. In much of the Amazon and Orinoco river basins in northern South America, for example, epidemic diseases, slave raiding, mining, and missions subjected paramount chiefdoms to pressures they were unable to withstand. The survivors splintered into small bands living in out-of-the-way places where, unlike other defeated chiefdoms, they could elude direct control by colonial governments. Ironically, these radically altered groups later came to be seen as exemplars of aboriginal ways untainted by the European presence that had in fact created them.

Indigenous paramount chiefdoms had long thrived on regional scales, where the larger polities were held together by a mixture of common interests and identities, ideology and ritual, mutual interest, pressure, and force. Paramount chiefs greeted the Europeans as if the strangers were operating within the same framework, drawing upon their accustomed sources of power to incorporate the newcomers as additions to their existing alliance systems. Rival chiefs and internal dissidents, no less eager than the Europeans to exploit the situation, recognized the newcomers as potential allies and used them to free themselves from the power of their paramount chiefs. Consequently, paramount chiefs and their opponents often inadvertently enabled the intruders to survive their initial weakness and to gather enough strength to overturn the established Native political order. Thus paramount chiefdoms, intended to concentrate power and deal effectively with outsiders, ironically proved uniquely vulnerable to European conquest—and

when they fell, they left significant power vacuums that Europeans were eager to exploit.

JAMES D. RICE

Bibliography

Barker, Alex W. "Chiefdoms." In *Handbook of Archaeological Theories*, edited by Christopher Chippindale, R. Alexander Bentley, and Herbert D. G. Maschner, 515–532. Lanham, MD: Alta Mira, 2008.

Earle, Timothy, ed. *Chiefdoms: Power, Economy, and Ideology.* New York: Cambridge University Press, 1991.

———. *How Chiefs Come to Power: The Political Economy in Prehistory.* Stanford, CA: Stanford University Press, 1997.

Redmond, Else M., ed. *Chiefdoms and Chieftaincy in the Americas.* Gainesville: University Press of Florida, 1998.

Patron-Client Networks

In the early-modern Atlantic World, to find oneself labeled a stranger (a foreigner or outsider) was to lack protective connections to kin, institutional support, or powerful patrons—which together spelled isolation and vulnerability. Interdependence and community belonging defined the societies of Europe, Africa, and the Americas. Less-powerful individuals and groups sought out connections to lords, patrons, landlords, or sponsors to enhance their social belonging, at times even to secure their survival. Dependency equaled protection. Beyond ordering local relations within the community, patronage was central to the expansion of long-distance commerce and to protecting it politically and militarily. For example, groups sharing language and cultural affinities within small-scale agricultural and hunter-gatherer Native American societies recognized leadership based on the ability to bring together clients from neighboring groups who provided complementary local products. Within the segmented polities of West Africa, newcomers sought out powerful landholding lineages (forming what are often referred to as *landlord-stranger relations*), both for logistical shelter and for protection of the associated ancestral and territorial spirits. In medieval Europe military lords legitimated as powerful dukes or kings gave protection to minor feudal landlords, who in turn took advantage of the personal and productive service of clients of their own and of serfs who depended on them for land and protection from the acquisitive designs of neighboring counterparts. Interdependence was both the ideal and the practice throughout the early Atlantic World.

In the dynasty building of the more powerful political regimes throughout the Atlantic World, similar densely interwoven family alliances among "noble classes" ideally contributed to stable continuities based on predictable hereditary succession, in which diplomacy and uncontestable rules of descent (such as primogeniture in Europe) countered the tendency toward warfare, both internally and among recognized and ranked dynasties. From the time of Charlemagne (emperor of the Franks in Europe, 800–814), ruling lineages in Europe formed ties of patronage with the prelates of the Catholic Church to promote naturalization of their power by "divine right" and its attendant hierarchies of patronage. Marriages between prominent patrons and aspiring clients created powerful partnerships. In the expansion of large dynasties and small-scale patronage networks alike, what some scholars have called a "trade in women" as wives or concubines served as one way to cement alliances. Among the paradigmatic instances in the Americas, Montezuma (Moctezuma, of the Aztecs, c. 1466–1520) offered several of his daughters as marriage partners to Hernán Cortés and his officers, and in the Chesapeake Powhatan (d. 1618) acceded to the union of his daughter Pocahontas with the Englishman John Rolfe (1585–1622). In both polygynous and matrilineal societies, the sexual and social comfort of a patron's daughters or enslaved concubines served as powerful inducements to friendly relations, whether to bring otherwise-unrelated men into the intimate space of the household or to plant spies within the encampments of suspect newcomers. The promise of marriage could also be used to transform outsiders from aliens to affines through blood ties, serving to bring clients into more affective and enduring bonds, transforming singular encounters defined only by competing benefits into extended collaborations that lasted beyond the current generation.

Patronage that crossed blood or ethnic lines was often based on trade, stimulated by the desire of wealthy individuals and dynasties to demonstrate and enhance their local status by displaying and distributing exotic luxury goods. Long-distance merchants provided the rare and distinguishing items—spices and foodstuffs; cloth and furs; stones, metals, or other items valued for adornment or ritual purposes; and slaves—in exchange for protection and local legitimacy. Among the Aztecs, a special class of traders called *pochteca* provided jade, plumage of the sacred quetzal, and slaves for patron aristocrats, who in turn obliged their merchant clients to serve as tax collectors and spies during their trading voyages. European nobility had always valued luxury goods imported from Asia, especially silks and spices, but after 1453 could access them only through the Ottoman-controlled Middle East, and at a disadvantage given Europe's lack of desired commodities or manufactures to sell. In Africa merchant-clients who had access to the most desired commodities could wield them to hold significant power, as rival elite groups competed to extend hospitality to them in anticipation of gifts, tax revenues, and profitable commercial alliances. North African Muslim traders trekked across the Sahara to connect with Mediterranean markets in search of gold from Timbuktu and Djenné to enhance their status in the eyes of their Ottoman patrons in Istanbul. In all three continents, slaves were among the most sought-after luxury purchases for patrons wishing to increase their economic power (taking advantage of slaves' productive labor) or their status (slaves became symbols of an owner's capacity to support a lavish household filled with exotic artisanry and other dependents).

Success in trade depended most on clients' and patrons' abilities to understand, even anticipate, one another's needs and desires in sometimes quite different social and cultural milieus. The most successful merchant-clients were those who, despite their outsider status, could divine their patrons' social power and adroitly adapt to local cultural rules regarding exchange. Likewise, the most influential patrons were those who could uphold their obligations to protect their clients and to honor those who brought something special to the exchange. Within the evolving Atlantic world of commerce, some merchant groups served as "go-betweens," greasing the wheels of patronage for profit and expansion. In the Andean highlands, the Incas sent colonists from a distinct ethnic group known as the *mitmaqkuna* to settle newly conquered territories and develop the region's agricultural produce, as well as to teach the new tributaries the imperial language (Quechua) and the fundamentals of Inca cosmology and politics. Sephardic Jews, marginalized in both the Christian and Muslim worlds, were forced into the distasteful but necessary role of moneylenders, becoming both patrons and clients of kings and kingmakers throughout the Mediterranean world. Multilingual children of mixed unions also served as go-betweens, whether the *métis* children of French fur trappers and Iroquoian women in North America, the *mamaluco* offspring of Portuguese settlers and indigenous women in Brazil, or the Eurafricans in various slaving posts in Africa, who served the interests of kin on both sides of the exchanges and became intermediaries in their own right as traders from Europe later sought entrée into this lucrative business.

Clients whose patrons sought benefits beyond those available through trade and diplomacy often turned to hostage taking and outright war, abandoning the voluntary and reciprocal ethos of patronage in favor of conquest and extraction, domination and victimization. Just as the fur trade brought Europeans into more intensely competitive relations with indigenous North American groups, so did slave trading in Africa; both created "raiding" mentalities in which the balance of exchange came to favor young male hunters or small bands of kidnapper-warriors whose prowess as predators gave them more capital to deploy in increasingly competitive commercial spheres. Although European slave traders along the West African seaboard in the fifteenth and sixteenth centuries had to operate under the constraints of their status as client-strangers, by the seventeenth century the Portuguese had become kingmakers in Central Africa, contracting mercenary Imbangala troops to intervene in other dynastic conflicts in Angola. By the nineteenth century the transatlantic slave trade had stimulated warfare and kidnapping in Africa to such heights that Europeans became influential patrons of new expansionist military regimes, such as Asante and Dahomey, through sales of weapons and gunpowder in exchange for captives taken in the wars they thus enabled. Similar intensification of warfare followed in the waves of European incur-

sions into North America—in the seventeenth century with coastal Algonquian societies, in the eighteenth with Iroquoian and Creek displacements, and throughout the nineteenth century with the most recalcitrant of Native Americans, whether Seminoles or Apache.

The corruption and privilege inherent in complex, large-scale patronage systems prompted periodic reform movements, often through groups that promoted competing rules for exchange based on religious mandates. To counteract the alienating impact of commercialization, religious groups—Sephardic Jews, Huguenots (French Calvinists), and Quakers in European colonial settlements and Muslim traders and scholars in West Africa—worked within trading diasporas created through in-group patronage and endogamous kinship, building strong transnational frameworks based on both standardized morality (religious law) and affective or family ties. The aggressive acquisitiveness of western Europe's centuries-old dynasties may have led to the downfall of colonial rule in the Americas, as European monarchies locked in a series of ostensibly dynastic wars (the War of the League of Augsburg [1688–1697], the War of the Spanish Succession [1701–1713], and the War of the Austrian Succession [1744–1748]) prompted Atlantic-wide economic and social disruptions (the War of the League of Augsburg in New England, or King William's War [1688–1697], the War of Jenkins' Ear [1739–1748], the Seven Years' War [1756–1763]), bankrupting European treasuries and prompting fiscal reforms that alienated elite American client-colonists. By the eighteenth century, Enlightenment philosophies of individual merit challenged the patronage arrangements of earlier generations, bringing a new political ethos in which patronage became synonymous with undeserved "privilege" and corruption, and its rituals of deference became humiliations to former clients who now deemed themselves "free." These liberal political impulses operated in tension with the continued reality of the need for traditional forms of patronage in building local and regional power networks. Patron-client systems thus both structured the integration of a commercial Atlantic World and provided the framework for periodic historical transformations.

KRISTEN BLOCK

Bibliography

Brooks, George E. *Landlords and Strangers: Ecology, Society, and Trade in Western Africa, 1000–1630.* Boulder, CO: Westview, 1994.

Brooks, James F. *Captives and Cousins: Slavery, Kinship and Community in the Southwest Borderlands.* Chapel Hill: University of North Carolina Press, 2002.

Herzog, Tamar. *Defining Nations: Immigrants and Citizens in Early Modern Spain and Spanish America.* New Haven, CT: Yale University Press, 2003.

Kettering, Sharon. *Patrons, Brokers, and Clients in Seventeenth-Century France.* New York: Oxford University Press, 1986.

Penal Transportation

Penal transportation—the forcing of convicts and other societal misfits into exile in remote territories—during the formative period of Atlantic history was a multifaceted strategy that the various European powers pursued for purposes of exploration, colonization, military staffing, punishment, and social control. Africans and Amerindians, while affected by the presence of, and their interactions with, European convicts, were largely outside these legal systems.

With its legal foundations in Roman law, penal transportation made its way into numerous early-modern European codes at a time when other punishment measures were few and consisted mostly of extended time in prisons, an expensive and unproductive alternative. The penalty of death was another possibility, but it, too, was unproductive since it assumed a large and potentially disposable population, such as those in France or Britain. Other forms of coerced labor, such as indentured service, the *mita* imposed on Native populations in Peru, or enslavement of Native Americans or Africans, contrasted sharply with penal transportation in the great masses of laborers they produced. The relative handful (perhaps 100,000 to 200,000) of European convicts pales in comparison with the millions of Africans trapped in slavery in the New World. Penal transportation was used concurrently with these other labor systems. In some arenas, such as Spanish military construction, convicts and slaves sometimes worked side by side. In such

areas as Portuguese São Tomé, convict laborers oversaw slaves. And in other areas, such as the frontier regions of Brazil, distinguishing convicts from free settlers was difficult. Penal transportation had a double utility in its applications: it removed political or social problems at home, and it remedied shortages of laborers or colonizers across the Atlantic.

Several European powers used penal transportation during this period, but the best-known system was an English one linking the British Isles with Maryland, Virginia, Barbados, and Jamaica. Less well known was French transportation of convicts to its New World colonies of New France (Quebec), Louisiana, and the West Indies. In the French case, most of the convicts transported served three-year indentures as servants. The French use of forced convict labor (*forçat*) in its New World holdings was modest at best, at least before 1700. The Spanish used penal labor to construct and staff fortifications in North Africa and the Caribbean. The Portuguese, though, more than any other power, used the practice widely in the Atlantic, from outposts in North and West Africa to island possessions, in coastal Angola, and in coastal Brazil. The Portuguese had been the first to staff overseas posts with exiled criminals, starting with pardoned convicts among the troops sent to their initial 1415 conquest of Ceuta in Morocco. The French would be the last to continue using it, closing their notorious penal colony in French Guiana only after World War II.

Punishment and Social Control

Penal transportation addressed religious, political, moral, and social-welfare issues in western Europe. Most of the convicts transported overseas had been judged guilty of either theft or murder. In some French and Portuguese colonies there was a preponderance of males, an imbalance addressed by the forced relocation of other undesirables—orphaned girls and prostitutes—who might offer the stability of marriage for the exiled males.

While penal transportation might be seen as relatively humane, since exile avoided corporal punishment—such as cutting off an ear—of the sort done during the Middle Ages, the psychological impact of dislocation and social control obtained through isolation in new and remote surroundings was powerful. It uprooted the convicts from their parishes, towns, friends, and families and left them to begin new lives alone in a distant and strange place. The threat of this punishment was constantly on the horizon in Europe, since ordinary people understood that forced relocation to a possibly dangerous, usually military outpost awaited those who broke society's norms. Members of religious and ethnic minorities, such as the Huguenots (Calvinists) from France, Quakers from England, and Jews and the Roma (Gypsies) from many European nations, all endured forced exile from Europe to the New World and Africa.

European Exploration and Colonization

Portuguese convicted of serious crimes during the fifteenth and sixteenth centuries often had their sentences commuted to exile along the newly explored coasts of Africa and Brazil. The rationale behind staffing small outposts with convicted criminals was that these outcasts would join local communities to survive, learn their local customs and languages, and thus be in positions to facilitate future interactions with the Portuguese. The most successful application of this policy involved the group of Afro-Portuguese merchant-traders it created in western Africa. On the western side of the Atlantic, several notable Portuguese convicts during the sixteenth century acted as critical linguistic and cultural intermediaries in the captaincies of Brazil. Caramuru (Diogo Álvares) was perhaps the best known of these, but several others rehabilitated themselves as go-betweens as well.

Convicts could provide the manpower in a given colony when other incentives failed to do so. Shortages of personnel could result when a given colony was little known in Europe or lay unsettled, as Barbados was when the English settled the island in the 1620s and 1630s: the colony's proprietors collected and sent prostitutes and convicts from London to provide an English presence in the West Indies. When a colony suffered a negative image, labor shortages could also result. In Louisiana, almost a century after it was settled by the French, colonial authorities had a very difficult time recruiting colonists to leave France for what many believed was a hot and humid land of giant man-eating lizards. In the 1720s the French Compagnie des Indes Occidentales sent convicts and prostitutes from French towns and cities to the struggling settlement of New Orleans. Perhaps the best-known case of the use of convicts to fill labor shortages was in Maryland and Virginia, for which convicts and indentured servants were often selected from the more desperate cohorts of the residents of England's seaports. The regularity of English shipping to the Chesapeake colonies made convict transport relatively easy and financially viable.

The Portuguese used convicts as colonizers in the fringe areas of its captaincies in Brazil, sending them to both the far north and the extreme south. Spain's larger population meant that it had many more potential émigrés than Portugal and thus could be more selective, not allowing similarly marginal figures to emigrate to the New World. In addition, the two major Spanish colonies of New Spain and Peru both had relatively large indigenous populations, further obviating the need for European convict labor.

European Military Staffing

Early-modern European armies and navies grew and diminished according to the current needs of the monarchies. Finding an adequate number of sailors, in particular, was a recurring problem for many early-modern regimes, given the dangers of life at sea and sailors' low social standing. Monarchs thus conscripted crews of naval forces through impressment, as well as by drawing upon convicts being held temporarily in jails.

The English (later the British) Royal Navy gained its leading role in the Atlantic through a long history of impressment for duty on board its vessels. The Portuguese sent numerous individuals to their military outposts along coastal western and southern Africa with the idea that they would join the military garrisons, who were nominally stationed there but infrequently and inadequately paid or equipped. This forced recruitment began during the early 1500s and continued into the nineteenth century. The Spanish developed a defense network of fortifications to protect the New World silver they were moving across the Atlantic to Europe. Building and operating these installations was a staggering financial challenge for the Spanish crown, met in part through transporting convicts—as well as buying slaves to build forts in Cuba, San Juan (Puerto Rico), and St. Augustine (Spanish Florida).

*　*　*

Some of the strategies of penal transportation European powers practiced in the Atlantic, such as colonization or military service, endured. Others were short-term responses to social or political upheavals, such as the mass transportation of Roma from Portugal to Brazil or the British Quakers sent in 1655 to Barbados. Detailed numbers of convicts and exiles are difficult to establish. Previous estimates have posited that the British sent around 50,000 convicts to American territories in the eighteenth century. The early-modern Portuguese forced another 50,000 convicts and "sinners" to relocate within the Portuguese Empire. Totals from the French and Spanish await additional research. In connecting the European homeland with its colonies in North and South America, the Atlantic islands, and the western and southern African coastlines, penal transportation was a significant strategy of recruiting personnel for the European frontiers of the Atlantic.

TIMOTHY J. COATES

Bibliography

Boucher, Philip P. *France and the American Tropics to 1700*. Baltimore, MD: Johns Hopkins University Press, 2008.

Coates, Timothy J. *Convicts and Orphans: Forced and State-Sponsored Colonizers in the Portuguese Empire, 1550–1755*. Stanford, CA: Stanford University Press, 2001.

Ekrich, A. Roger. *Bound for America: The Transportation of British Convicts to the Colonies, 1718–1775*. Oxford: Clarendon, 1987.

Metcalf, Alida C. *Go-betweens and the Colonization of Brazil, 1500–1600*. Austin: University of Texas Press, 2005.

Pike, Ruth. *Penal Servitude in Early Modern Spain*. Madison: University of Wisconsin Press, 1983.

Political Systems, African

Africans' politics during the Atlantic Era might be thought of as collective strategies, rather than collective identities. In their political dealings, Africans were inventive, borrowing well and often from one another and from beyond the continent. One major source of innovation was the world of Atlantic commerce, in the resources it offered expansive military autocrats, the wide-scale provision of desired goods, and the consequent permeation of debt in Africa. African polities in fact were far from political associations of primordial or natural simplicity—a mistaken characterization often propagated in popular, and even scholarly, literature: they were defined by complex and creative interactions within the multiplicities of the Atlantic World.

Prior to the fifteenth century, the lands of Africa along the continent's Atlantic seaboard were those most removed from long-distance trade. In contrast, the rice-producing Inland Niger Delta, centered on Jenne-Jeno, was an ecotone deeply engaged in commerce, a zone of contrasting ecologies and productive systems—with desert to the north, and woodlands and forests to the south. Thus the Bozo and Nono "peoples," really just farmers and fisherfolk speaking two trading dialects of Malinke, arose in this milieu; their mobile riverine operations carried high-value goods and gold, providing the tax-base for Mali, a massive military regime that, covering the valley of the upper river and beyond, reached its height in the century before the opening of the Atlantic coast.

For long afterwards, a succession of political collaborations drew on the memory of Mali and on its oral epic of a semilegendary hero, Sunjata, whose prestige was underwritten by the comprehensiveness of Mali's Islamic legacy. In the old center, the Inland Niger Delta, the Sunjata inheritance fell into oblivion, or never developed, but far to the west in the province of Casamance (modern Senegal), the legend was kept or revived, partly to serve the maintenance of "Mandinka" (i.e., Mande, the linguistic heritage of Mali), in the kingdom of Kaabu. Among these later political systems, engagement with the Atlantic World produced both instances of resistance and shrines devoted to the slave trade. Gonja, in the higher country in today's Burkina Faso, may not have been a polity in the Mande tradition of military rule but instead a balanced circuit of trading towns, each one serving in turn as market administrator in the consortium. Still the ruling stratum in Gonja traced its origins to "Malle" and ultimately to a hero similar to Sunjata.

Closter to the coasts, the forests in Senegal and the Gambia offered cover for people evading the larger Sudanic military regimes (Mali and those following it); they settled in ecological niches and often formed relationships of clientage with the dispersed residents of the surrounding hills. Some refugee regimes transcended the localism of their own communities by creating military or honorific networks or "castes" of specialists trained in generally useful skills: hunting, ceremonial performances, or ironworking. Others used Atlantic commercial resources to transform themselves. Wolof, originating in the lower valley of the Senegal River and once the lingo of mounted warrior-aristocrats as distinguished from the speech of the peasants below them, became the common speech of a vast hinterland electrified by the Atlantic economy.

The politicians of this African rim of Atlantic trade deployed its resources in infinitely varied ways and created correspondingly diverse political systems. However, all people did not have recourse to similar strategies, and many African persons were captured and claimed, in part or in whole, by others. In fact, the energizing effects of Atlantic commercial credit propelled many indebted borrowers, often heads of kin groups, into the Atlantic slave trade. These patriarchs in turn recruited labor and clients through the same commercial channels. Marginalized and frustrated, younger men in their networks sometimes mobilized to challenge the prevailing order. Some became slavers, others renegades and bandits. Thus, for instance, as slaving developed in sixteenth-century Upper Guinea, young men of diverse backgrounds, drawing on the Mande prestige born of Mali, gathered as "Mane" (the way Portuguese heard "Mande") and preyed on smaller dispersed populations in the forests of contemporary Sierra Leone.

The political positions from which Africans approached Atlantic resources had long been changing, some developing prior external commercial contacts in western Africa across the Sahara, or oriented toward the Indian Ocean in the east. Generally Africans maneuvered to incorporate *useful difference*, from new ideas in social organization, to new crops, to exotic and displayable imported goods, in order to distinguish themselves. Amid dynastic intrigues in Kongo in West-Central Africa, a line of rulers built their power by taking on the status of Christian papal protegés, relying on a resi-

dent Catholic monastic order as the network of specialists who represented their personal authority. These "kings" (in the perception of the Portuguese) sent warriors into a hinterland increasingly beset by violence, where they obtained captives to feed the slave trade. Long afterwards, the memory of a Christian Kongo remained as potent a mnemonic source of political unity as the Sunjata of the Mande in western Africa.

Irresponsible personal power, usually military, and the disruptions of slaving, especially when mingled with the disorders brought by recurring droughts, could bring violent reactions. Slaving increased in Central Africa in the second half of the sixteenth century and expelled the Christian political allies of the Portuguese in Kongo. Decades of severe drought exposed all the political systems of the Angola region to the south to more than a century of plundering by young warriors who terrified their victims by claiming to be superhuman "witches." These Imbangala, as they were called, seized refugees during the drought and sold them to Portuguese in the region, who understood their ideological posturing (in their own terms) as "cannibalism." Villagers, once linked through networks of specialists in the various skills of maintaining local communities—iron smelting, hunting, and communal ceremonial skills—clustered under the Imbangala to protect themselves from the pervasive conflicts engendered by expensively militarized warrior regimes. An aspiring seventeenth-century Angolan queen, Njinga, patterned her legitimacy after Kongo while mastering the performative codes of Imbangala ritual; a century later, another woman, Beatriz, claimed to be the incarnation of St. Anthony and tried to mobilize dispossessed people to restore the honored capital of the Kingdom of Kongo.

In the Calabar region east of the Niger River delta in the Gulf of Guinea, a series of families eked out small zones of control—which later analysts dignified as "city-states"—amid general political instability. They based their power on brokering trade from European merchants to African consumers inland from the coast. In what is today Ghana, to the west, the so-called Akan (the "because-of-war people") created an expansive military confederation (referred to as Asante) in the late 1600s, not by controlling the marketing of slaves, as was the strategy in many coastal city-states, but by buying and absorbing slaves from other parts of Africa. Akan pioneers mobilized slaves to clear tropical rain forest, permitting the early spread of Atlantic crops a century before the ascent of the Asante kingdom to its full military glory at the end of the 1700s. Other military regimes in western Africa, most notably Dahomey, inland from the lagoons that Europeans knew as the "Slave Coast," grew similarly by integrating captives.

Within almost all the political systems of West-Central Africa there were local communities of kin, affines (groups related by marriage), and clients. Political figures, sometimes prophetic in character, sometimes warlords, often combined force and ideological appeals. They did not eliminate local networks but overlaid them, creating political systems of a composite character, not units based on homogeneity or political equality. The growth of Atlantic interactions also strained some individuals' fealty to the local community, its unity, and constituent connections. For many decades in the eighteenth century, having developed the fiction of permanent kingly personhood, the Luba-Lunda "empire" in the center of Africa thrived and militarized by raiding adjacent populations and selling them to Atlantic traders from the south. By the middle of the nineteenth century, a group of enterprising men—beekeepers, blacksmiths, and gunsmiths by tradition—used these skills to corral the trade in imported firearms from the highlands of Angola, mainly by supplying wax and ivory to Atlantic commodity markets. They used their profits to marry into the villages and local hierarchies formerly within the Lunda ambit, claiming the women and minors for themselves, until—in hardly more than a generation—they had multiplied their numbers many times over and emerged as a new network. Later colonial ethnographers regarded their stockaded villages, with their iconic statues of ancestral warrior-kings, as of the Chokwe or Cokwe "tribe."

The Yoruba, now the great majority of people in southwestern Nigeria and adjacent regions of Benin, emerged as a similarly ethnicized political composite in the wake of decades of warfare among regional war leaders in the nineteenth century. Partisans of British imperial designs on the region, Brazilian intellectuals, and Christian African missionaries, who were recovered from enslavement and trained in Sierra Leone, created a unified front of political contention prominent today as the Yoruba ethnicity in Nigeria and elsewhere in the Atlantic World. Other seemingly "tribal" identities, for example Igbo and Tiv, also in Nigeria, were constructed around busy intersections with their commercial resources. Such was the case throughout Atlantic Africa.

The political creativity behind the growth of all these new configurations derived not from foreign influences, or even from Atlantic resources, but rather from their African contexts. To take one detailed example to the south of the Lunda-Luba, the Rozvi in Zimbabwe created themselves as a political community with home-grown strategies out of transregional and often transcontinental engagements with exterior—that is, Atlantic *and* Indian Ocean—resources. They were part of a wave of political and commercial reorganization that swept over present-day Zimbabwe and much of South Africa in the 1400s to 1600s, with its origins in a profitable confluence of Indian Ocean commercial credit and the vast herds of cattle on the inland plateaus, which had peaked around 1350 in a political structure centered on the stone enclosures now known as Great Zimbabwe.

The trained warrior regiments of a major successor regime, men called *vanyai*, struck out on their own under Dombo, a war-leader chief apparently of South African origin; they forged their unity in battling the Portuguese, until they controlled most of southern Zimbabwe and the valley of the middle Limpopo River. They called their authority "Rozvi." To the south, in what is today South Africa, *rozi dynasties—called "Rotse" or "Rootze-place" (or, as it was given in the nineteenth century, *harutse*) peoples—developed dominant chiefdoms by mobilizing and training (and co-circumcising) young men in highly effective age-grade militias. Kinship provided these rulers with a vocabulary of hierarchy and affiliation without overly constraining the ways in which they applied it. The realities of power are always more complex than its terminologies suggest.

In no case then should it be said that the Atlantic World brought hybridity to simpler precolonial modes of belonging. Rather, people's political strategies varied greatly, even where ethnicity came to matter (as in the Inland Niger Delta). Africans adapted external resources to temporary and varied circumstances, and wove overlapping networks and hierarchies around them. Some of the most militarized regimes—Mali, the Asante, Kongo, Yoruba, Cokwe, and the *vanyai* Rozvi—integrated followers into political communities through memory and ideology by retaining a sense of the past but innovating in dynamic ways. What is known in modern Africa as ethnicity is often only the imprint of the political strategies of the earlier Atlantic Era. Africans worked from the positions in which they found themselves. They were connected by what made them diverse: their facility for invention and adaptation in situations of novelty and crisis.

PAUL S. LANDAU

Bibliography

Boubacar, Barry. *Senegambia in the Era of the Slave Trade*. Cambridge: Cambridge University Press, 1998; first ed. (French) 1988.

Landau, Paul S. *Popular Politics in the History of South Africa, 1400–1948*. Cambridge: Cambridge University Press, 2010.

Matory, J. Lorand. *Black Atlantic Religion: Tradition, Transnationalism, and Matriarchy in the Afro-Brazilian Candomblé*. Princeton, NJ: Princeton University Press, 2005.

McCaskie, Thomas. *State and Society in Precolonial Asante*. Cambridge: Cambridge University Press, 2003.

McIntosh, Roderick. *Peoples of the Middle Niger: The Island of Gold*. New York: Wiley, 1998.

Miller, Joseph C. *Way of Death: Merchant Capitalism and the Angolan Slave Trade, 1730–1830*. Madison: University of Wisconsin Press, 1988.

Mudenge, S. I. G. *A Political History of the Munhumutapa, c. 1400–1902*. London: Curry, 1988.

Peel, J. D. Y. *The Religious Encounter and the Making of the Yoruba*. Bloomington: Indiana University Press, 2003.

Reader, John. *Africa: Biography of a Continent*. New York: Vintage, 1999.

Thornton, John K. *The Kongolese St. Anthony: Dona Beatriz Kimpa Vita and the Antonian Movement, 1684–1706*. Cambridge: Cambridge University Press, 1998.

Vansina, Jan. *How Societies Are Born: Governance in West Central Africa before 1600*. Charlottesville: University of Virginia Press, 2004.

Political Systems, Collective Consensual

Max Weber, the great sociologist of the early 1900s (1864–1920), defined the archetypical modern state based on the recent histories and ideological claims of the political systems of the modern Atlantic World. But the form of political organization that Weber described had not previously been preeminent or ubiquitous anywhere in the world. In the earlier Atlantic Era, the populations of Africa, the Native Americas, and (though to diminishing degrees) Europe had organized themselves in many other ways. To devotees of Weber, the political organizations that contrasted most glaringly with the core ideology of the modern nation-state—based on progress and competitive individualism—were largely invisible. They were therefore characterized in entirely negative terms, dismissed as "stateless," merely familial (based on kinship), or "religious." Such interpretations had strong overtones of political incapacity and primitivism, as well as a lack of the creative historical progress that Weber observed in Europe and the "civilization" that justified the global military imperialism of his era.

Cultural anthropologists in the Americas and colonial ethnographers in Africa questioned these dismissive characterizations from the very beginnings of firsthand European observation. Today, a half century of study since the 1960s allows historians to understand the systems invisible to Weberians in positive analytical terms of a politics based on community—rather than Weberian competitive individualism—and on multiplicities of diverse powers—rather than the monopoly of force in Weber's "state"—and thus operating by consensus rather than compulsion. The idea was politics without unilateral power, at least without the singularity Weber used to define it. These concepts of consensus and collectivity were only principles, of course, and in historical practice people in collective systems failed to live up to the theory no less often than politicians in Weber's "state" found ways around their own ideals. But whether or not the normative principles were always applied in practice, a plurality and diversity of powers indeed did underlay the strategies of—particularly—Africans and Native Americans in the early-modern Atlantic.

These political systems were based on preserving and aggregating small consensual communities. They reproduced the people in them, and thus accorded primacy to female fertility, centering their politics on controlling this vital force of life itself. Older males built continuity from the ancestors, to whom—by this reckoning—the living were indebted for their very lives and also accountable for ongoing collaboration. The living generations were responsible for passing the coherence of the group they had inherited on to children who would, accordingly, venerate them as ancestors in the future. At this primary level of reproducing socially the biologically reproducing community, the key political strategy centered on claiming the children born. The issue of allocating infants, of assigning them to the family of one parent or the other, arose because no reproducing group of kin was an island unto itself. By a universal rule prohibiting incest, sexual relations between males and females of the same family group were condemned and could not produce offspring recognized as legitimate. Thus every infant born had parents from different groups, both eager to claim the child for themselves. Success in their very purpose, reproduction, raised the specter of conflict that would divide the two groups joined in the marriage that produced the child.

An elegant rule of assigning unambiguous group affiliation to children resolved this potential dilemma. This principle, which ethnographers have termed *unilineal*, recognized kinship, and thus access to inheritance and belonging, through only one parent, either the mother (and her female relatives—that is, her sister and her daughters but not her brothers' children, who belonged to the matrilineal kin of their wives, their mothers) or the father (and his brothers and their sons, but not his sisters' offspring, who belonged to the kin groups of their husbands, their fathers). In these contexts of diversity, few—if any—historical communities allocated all resources according to one parent or the other, but they left no ambiguity about the proper allocations of the affiliations that they defined.

This obvious and unambiguous unilineality meant that all those included in a community shared the same, full set of kin through the generations. The enduring groups created by this principle contrasted with the bilateral systems of descent prevalent in the modern world, in which only full siblings share the same sets of relatives on the sides of both parents. Groups created through unilineal kinship became the operative frameworks for political strategies, since they endured through the generations, from ancestors in the remote past to the prospects of an indefinite future. The strong ethos of interpersonal commitment that prevailed within these multigenerational groups was a means of mobilizing for action. They acted collectively, particularly in relation to other similarly composed groups, presumably by internal consensus. The accord that they sought, and acted on when achieved, was attained through recognized procedures focused on persuading younger members of the accumulated wisdom of the senior generation. In practice, the more successful groups seized on historical contingencies—circumstances as they arose—to increase their numbers with unrelated clients, both individuals and groups, and incorporated individuals of alien origins through slaving.

The fundamental strategy of these reproducing groups centered on arranging legitimate mates for their marriageable youths. To maximize female reproductivity, elders married their females out to allied groups as soon as feasible after puberty, or as soon as proved advantageous. In matrilineal contexts—since matrilinearity assigned authority to males, the mothers' brothers or uncles, not to women—the young females whom these older men allocated were the daughters of their sisters. In patrilineal systems, elders allocated their own daughters and granddaughters (through sons). However, the responsibility for the external relations of the group allocated to senior males did not disable the females within their communities in the way that gender excludes women in modern states or in modern economies from access to key sources of individual fulfillment or "success," say, by voting or earning cash. Women, as the only reproducers in communities dedicated to reproduction, were respected, even feared. Individual circumstances varied enormously, of course, no less than in modern families, and isolated females acquired through slaving could fare much worse than legitimate wives backed by attentive communities of their own kin. But the communal ethos valued all contributions, however differentiated by biological sex, as well as along other dimensions, and this complementarity contrasted sharply with the exclusionary socially constructed gender of the modern world. The distinction between the two is clear: on the one hand, women in collective communities could aim to consolidate their valued positions within their group—even, if not particularly, for women acquired through slaving—and, on the other hand, women in a modern state could attempt to stand alone as rights-bearing individual citizens and compete for power or the resources of monetized wealth.

Elders (that is, the older males responsible for the community), whether uncles or fathers, succeeded politically by distributing their nieces or daughters widely through the groups living around them, receiving in return their reproductive young women as wives for themselves and their sons or nephews. In a pure form, giving a wife in one generation created a debt on the part of the wife takers, who repaid it by giving back a woman of their own in the generation following. However, groups in possession of material wealth, but lacking females, might offer a material substitute as a token, a pledge redeemable against a future female. Like any other system of exchange, these tokens of obligation were vulnerable to devaluation through inflation. And as they enabled wealthy males to bypass the slowness—even uncertainty—of bearing and raising girls to marriageable ages, these tokens often became generalized ways of acquiring women as wives. Amateur ethnographers described the resulting circulation of wives against standardized tokens in the irrelevant terms of modern economics as "bride-price."

In practice, authority within these kinship communities corrupted no less than personal power corrupts in the politics of the modern state, and the older men who managed these exchanges for their kin were tempted by the opportunity of hoarding for themselves the young wives whom the group could afford to acquire. Such polygynous senior males deprived younger male kin of the opportunity to marry, as the numbers of males and females in the population were, of course, roughly equal. Thus the age of marriage, and hence respectable adulthood, rose for males, sometimes into the thirties, while the marriage age of young women dropped into the low teens, and unborn female infants could be pledged generations before they would be born.

In these consensual communities, the elders' collective ability to deprive younger men of places

of respect did not constitute power in the modern sense of a personal, autonomous ability to compel others to act in conformity with one's wishes. Elderhood, or a concentration of authority in single "chiefs" to negotiate in limited spheres, was exercised more as a trusteeship on behalf of a collectivity, including ancestors. All members of these communities strived to distinguish their own capacities to contribute to the collective welfare. In a world in which humans saw themselves as organic parts of their environments, rather than standing apart from a "world of nature," power in the abstract was an ambient presence of unlimited potential and manifold manifestations and, in defined aspects, accessible to all with the skills or good fortune to realize it. It might appear anywhere, particularly in unusual or unexpected circumstances. By our modern reckoning this conception of power might be termed "historical," since it constituted effecting change (any departure from the ordinary or familiar) and, for the individual or group able to recognize the moment and seize it, offered the opportunity to direct this potential toward determined, immediate ends. Efficacious moments might be retrieved for subsequent use by exercising the proper techniques, which uninformed ethnographers diminished as "ritual," with overtones of routine repetition. But in the terms of this communal ethos these techniques were quite empirical, testable, and creative. They were methods of maintaining the coherence of the group and were readily discarded when they failed, in which case they might be replaced by new discoveries. They were anything but routinized, mindlessly repetitive, or "traditional." The human manifestations of power within communities thus were multiple, complementary, and engaging rather than singular, competitive, and excluding. Where consensus ruled, knowledge of the "secrets" of ambient power and collective belief in them, or consensus, constituted the efficacious strategies of politics. Among many such guardianships, representation of the group to outsiders was distinguishable analytically as "political" because it was the agency through which internal consensus was parlayed to other groups.

Communities turned pragmatically to knowledgeable manipulators of such power, according to the needs of the moment, as determined by consensus. Because groups were, by definition, enmeshed with other groups, they extended this strategy of mutual preservation, when and where circumstances merited it, to create larger-scale political composites. They mobilized these arrangements, of greater or lesser duration, according to advantages of the moment. By modern standards of "states" or other political institutions burdened by enormous fixed costs for infrastructure, these political composites appear "unstable." By the ad hoc standards of their creators, these networks were flexible: they were responsive to needs, spontaneously inclusive of the interested parties, and of minimal cost. No one wasted time or effort maintaining personnel or infrastructure that had no immediate use and were, in any case, products of the past and of no certain utility in the future. Simply put, they were consensual and efficient.

On these larger scales, politics assembled the differing—and thereby complementing—specializations of the component communities by respecting and preserving them. Since these composites were also special purpose, participants in them maintained as many such networks as might potentially become relevant. Like abstract ambient power, these composites represented an inventory of political potential, available to be mobilized depending on needs of the moment. In all these respects, they bore no resemblance to the costly institutionalized power that Weber defined as institutional "states." Because modern secularism, based on increasing devotion to progress and intensified by "separation of church and state," narrowed Weber's core definition of the "state" to a monopoly of violence, ethnographers marginalized such ad hoc political mobilization and strengthening of communities by defining it as "religious ritual," implicitly scorned as irrational relics from time immemorial.

On the eve of the transatlantic maritime contacts consolidated in the fifteenth and sixteenth centuries in sub-Saharan western Africa, militarization, with its costly infrastructure and its inherent tendency to escalate conflict, had recently become the dominating historical dynamic. Communities and composites there had reacted since the eighth century to the pressures of commercialization introduced by far-ranging Muslim merchants, and more intensively, since the thirteenth, imposed by mounted marauders from the desert. Personal centralized military power thus was imposed upon—but did not replace—these collaborative networks in northern and western Africa. These centralizing

effects, however, seldom lasted for long. Limited environmental resources, often reduced to desperate scarcities by droughts, usually stripped centralized initiatives of their potential for institutionalized permanence. In the meantime, the underlying communities adjusted flexibly and persisted.

In the Americas, the Inca and Aztec regimes exemplified a similar cyclical dynamic arising from the long-run unsustainability of consolidated militarized power. Maintaining warrior classes, with priestly acolytes and ever-greater displays of monumentality in stone, demanded conquest and plunder. But conquest and plunder mobilized opposition, and so militarization tended to escalate beyond sustainable levels. When it did, regimes grew overextended and collapsed, populations concentrated around their monumental centers dispersed, and stoneworks built for posterity fell into the ruin for which they are now celebrated—not without historical irony, and not without parallels among Europeans in the following centuries. Lacking horses, which the Spaniards introduced to the Americas only later, in the sixteenth century, the American warrior regimes plundered by assembling warriors from the relatively dense local populations of Meso- and Andean America. Similarly, the large political composites of North America—Kahokia in the middle Mississippi Valley, Iroquois in the northern Appalachian regions, Powhatan in the Chesapeake, and others later in New England—aggregated community militias. But, with fewer and more dispersed people to mobilize, they did so on a less sustained basis. Had diseases not depopulated these political composites and scattered the survivors, the component communities might well have continued; deaths and dispersals were lethal not only to their members but also to the composite collectives themselves.

From the seventeenth century, the political networks of Atlantic Africa—from the forests of the Upper Guinea Coast to the Cape of Good Hope—lacking horses, consolidated the military power that sustains centralization by drawing on commercial credit from the Atlantic and deploying the military capacities they built with it to capture people to sell to Europeans as slaves. Though Europeans along African coasts designated the chiefs entrusted with representing these collectivities as "kings," that is, sovereign authorities legally capable of negotiating within the emerging European law of nations, all such collectives—though to varying degrees—retained the underlying compound structure of the politics of consensus. The component communities of these political assemblages often appeared as "councils" advising the nominal "kings," who were in fact trustees charged with representing the composite externally. The councils, sometimes with power to dispose of their authorized delegates through ritual assassination, retained an effective veto internally. They exercised a controlling collective power also as holders of honorary titles designated by the central authority to recognize the communities in the composite, and then required to participate—or not—in elaborate performances of collective solidarity necessary to make decisions involving the whole. Their presence at these defining moments in the ongoing historical processes of these composite polities constituted consensus, without which the collectivity could not act officially. The courts of "kings" in medieval Europe—and the system of recognition by lords of lieges, marked as it was by similarly elaborate gradations—were hardly less complex, and recent scholarship has begun to emphasize the composite qualities of these early monarchies. More distinctively in Africa and the Americas, where polygynous marriages linked reproducing groups and where more, and more diverse, relationships enabled action, the larger polities were consolidated through the sometimes-numerous "wives" of the figureheads whom Europeans treated as "kings." They were not so much personally "powerful": rather, they were the channels through which the marriage alliances focused on the single figure at the polity's core. By channeling the polity's flows of reproduction through him, they embedded the compound energies of all the components in the whole. All these arrangements manifested the multiplicity and complementing diversity of human access to abstract power in the political systems of Africa and the Americas, even as they consolidated to engage the waves of militarization and commercialization on which Europeans sailed out over the Atlantic.

JOSEPH C. MILLER

Bibliography

Akyeampong, Emmanuel, and Pashington Obeng. "Spirituality, Gender and Power in Asante History." *International Journal of African Historical Studies* 28, no. 3 (1995): 481–508.

Guyer, Jane I., and S. M. E. Belinga. "Wealth in People as Wealth in Knowledge: Accumulation and Composition in Equatorial Africa." *Journal of African History* 36, no. 1 (1995): 91–120.

Miller, Joseph C. "The African Historical Dynamics of the Atlantic 'Age of Revolutions'." In *The Age of Revolutions in Global Context, c. 1760–1840*, edited by David Armitage and Sanjay Subrahmanyam, 101–124 (nn 246–250). New York: Palgrave Macmillan, 2010.

———. "Credit, Captives, Collateral, and Currencies: Debt, Slavery, and the Financing of the Atlantic World." In *Debt and Slavery in the Mediterranean and Atlantic Worlds*, edited by Gwyn Campbell and Alessandro Stanziani, 105–121 (nn 168–171). London: Pickering and Chatto, 2013.

Prophetic Movements

Prophetic movements in the early-modern Atlantic World unfolded as popular efforts to recover the sense of coherent communities that had eroded in the individuating dynamics of commercialization and colonialism. Led by charismatic figures, many of whom designated themselves prophets or special messengers from spiritual spheres, these movements—occurring in indigenous, plantation, and settler societies alike—sought access to integrating "higher powers" in order to restore order to troubled human affairs. Responding to disorder and divisions resulting from opportunistic individuals capitalizing on long-distance trade and cultural novelties, as well as from colonial military disruptions, these revitalization movements sought coherence in the form of cultural purity, political autonomy, and economic self-determination.

Native America

Indigenous American prophets fused elements of their own religions and European Christianity to indict European colonialism and to mobilize people to resist it. Prophets often responded to disease and dispossession by claiming direct revelations from forces beyond ordinary human ken, who reminded them that they and the Europeans were separate creations. They argued that the path to recovery of community vitality lay in rejecting observable lifeways identified with Europeans. These prophets urged instead the adoption of new or forgotten rituals that would purify Native communities from the contamination of Euroamerican influences, individual dissension, and the greed of material accumulation. These salvational messages did not need the medium of print to travel widely along indigenous social networks, and they often threatened not only colonial but also traditional structures of authority condemned as incapable of protecting their people.

In the 1560s, Quechua-speaking Andean people throughout the former Inca Empire, recently conquered by the Spanish and thus invalidated, flocked to a powerful prophetic movement called the Taki Onqoy, or the "Disease of the Dance." Its leaders accepted that the Christian god existed but insisted that he had created only the Spanish people and their homeland. Beings known as *huacas*, which inhabited sacred sites and were responsible for Andean creation, had been burned by the Spaniards, who considered them evil idols. Epidemic disease and Spanish military ascendancy were seen as evidence that the Christian god had weakened the power of the huacas. By rejecting trappings of Spanish religion and culture, Taki Onqoy promised, Andeans could assist the huacas in their reconquest of the Andean spiritual world. When the movement grew militant, the Spanish repressed it, but it remains an important memory in contemporary Andean national identity.

Andeans developed the Taki Onqoy within conquered territory, but indigenous prophets along the mid-eighteenth-century North American border between their own lands in the Ohio Valley and British seaboard settlements began articulating visions of pantribal unity against the colonists. In contrast with other indigenous strategies of negotiation and exchange with Euroamericans, these movements sought to separate the two groups. Drawing from dreams and other revelations, Native prophets defied and discredited Christianity's claim to universalism and taught that Indians and Europeans were distinct races. For them, revitalization of Native ways meant burying ancient rivalries among themselves in favor of unified opposition to Europeans. As much as they advocated a return to cultures free of European contamination, their calls

to unify departed radically from the past, threatening established Native authorities as well as Europeans. In 1763 and 1764, the teachings of the Delaware prophet Neolin animated an uprising against the British in the Great Lakes region, known as Pontiac's Rebellion. Pan-Indian resistance, motivated by a series of similar prophets, continued east of the Mississippi River into the early nineteenth century. These indigenous prophetic movements flourished primarily in geographic and temporal zones where the social and cultural effects of long-distance trade and disease were strong enough to seem threatening but where European (later, U.S.) military control was relatively weak.

West and West-Central Africa

Africans similarly responded to the social, political, and cultural ramifications of European commercialization, particularly the transatlantic slave trade, with a series of revitalization movements. In West and West-Central Africa, as in the Americas, European trade became significant by the late seventeenth century and provoked widespread warfare, political reorganization, and social changes. But the African context differed in the general absence before 1850 of a direct European military presence. In West Africa the political geography of revitalization movements reflected routes of long-distance trade and cultural exchange resulting from both coastal Atlantic trade and northern trans-Saharan networks.

The best-known movement with prophetic Christian elements developed in the early eighteenth century in the Kongo region of West-Central Africa and was reacting directly to the transatlantic slave trade. The Kongo crown had embraced the Roman Catholic Church early in the sixteenth century, and after almost 200 years of commercial, religious, and political interaction with the Portuguese the polity had become mired in a long-running civil war. In 1704, Dona Beatriz Kimpa Vita, a young noblewoman and spirit medium, declared that she had been possessed by the Catholic St. Anthony. He had revealed to her that Jesus, who was of Kongo origin, had been angered by the pervasive violence, dissension, and greed resulting from slaving to feed the Atlantic trade. After urging the king to end the violence and reunify his kingdom, she traveled widely in the war-ravaged land and developed a large following through her preaching and through the cures for sickness and infertility that she performed. She ultimately assembled a large crowd of devotees at the former capital city, which had been abandoned during a long-running civil war. Her challenge to both Kongo political authority and the Catholic Church resulted in her being condemned as a heretic and burned at the stake; thousands of her disciples were captured and enslaved.

The Islamic jihads that occurred in West Africa beginning in the late seventeenth century, although oriented across the Sahara rather than toward the Atlantic coast, also sought to combine spiritual renewal—purifying Islam of its local accretions—with social reform and political reorganization under the leadership of Muslim clerics. An early example was the revitalization movement in Senegambia in the 1670s led by the scholar Nasir al-Din. A series of further jihads in the eighteenth and nineteenth centuries succeeded in overthrowing ruling warrior elites across the West African savanna and Sahel. The victorious clerics then became involved in slaving themselves and reconfigured local social relations within Islamic frameworks. One of the most influential of these visionary leaders was Usman dan Fodio, a late-eighteenth-century clerical scholar in what is now northern Nigeria, who professed to have had a series of dreams in which he was visited by great Islamic scholars and even the prophet Muhammad. Although orthodox Islamic theology identifies Muhammad as the last of the prophets, dan Fodio assumed the ambitious mantle of Allah's "messenger." After a vision in which he was handed the Sword of Justice, dan Fodio also assumed the role of commander of the faithful (*amir al-muminin*) and beginning in 1802 organized a major jihad. His movement, and subsequent Islamic revivals that it inspired in the first half of the nineteenth century, reorganized politics across the West African Sahel under Muslim rulers.

While revitalization movements in both America and western Africa were responses to commercialization, and prophets on both continents similarly sought to unify the large and diverse groups trade brought into competitive contact, the movements on the opposite sides of the Atlantic often had strikingly different attitudes toward local spiritual beliefs. American revitalization movements typically sought to purify local traditions and to define European culture as "other"—even if in practice they included a good deal of cultural mixing. In the American context, Native communities faced shattering epidemics and had good reason to view European colonists as the alien root of their problems. In Africa, where neither Europeans nor North Africans posed an apparent threat of direct military control, broad-based movements embraced Christianity or Islam, both branches of the same Abrahamic spiritual tradition, drawing on the religions' evangelical drive for individual and absolute conversion and theological homogeneity. The enemies were the viable local communities who were divided by the competitive stresses of commerce and the violence of slaving, not the outsiders. Movements arising from both Islam and Christianity could thereby mobilize people from diverse local backgrounds into intensely focused groups unified around the earthly peace central to both of the monotheistic religions.

British North America and the Caribbean

In the settler and plantation societies of eighteenth-century British North America, commercially oriented communities, influenced by Enlightenment rationalism, turned increasingly skeptical eyes toward self-proclaimed prophets. As a result, some prophetic movements were tolerated, albeit with a measure of condescension, if their messages and practices did not seem unduly subversive, but movements that posed more profound challenges—such as to prevailing gender or labor regimes—were generally not. Here, the expansion of the United States inland from the Atlantic coast created for a time opportunities for groups facing suppression in the well-settled East to regroup, sometimes successfully, by migrating westward beyond the reach of authorities.

The Protestant tradition of direct personal revelation was at its most radical and subversive in its moral critique of the system of slavery, on which many in the most commercial regions depended. During the tumultuous transatlantic religious revival of the 1730s and 1740s known as the Great Awakening, antislavery visionaries were welcomed in places such as Pennsylvania, where established interests owned few slaves, but despised in places like South Carolina, where enslaved Africans composed two-thirds of the population and most of the assets of the wealthy. Around 1740, the South Carolina planter Hugh Bryant was "awakened" to a broad sense of human justice, or "born again," when it was revealed to him that slavery was un-Christian and that he was destined to become a prophet, an American Moses. But after failing to part the river through which he was hoping to lead local slaves to freedom, and almost drowning, he was forced to recant.

For the enslaved, the transformative potential of prophetic revitalization movements appeared in a series of revolts in the Caribbean—including Tacky's revolt in Jamaica in the 1760s. Tacky, an enslaved former leader in Africa's Gold Coast region, sought—in consultation with *obi* (or Obeah) practitioners (African spirit mediums and healers)—to create an independent African kingdom on the island. Enslaved people outnumbered free people in Jamaica by nine to one, and a temporary withdrawal of British troops from the island during the Seven Years' War (1756–1763) created an opening Tacky had perceived. But the revolt was crushed by an alliance of British authorities with the maroons, self-liberated former slaves, who controlled the island's mountainous interior. As the successful revolt in Haiti at the end of the eighteenth century showed, the extreme discipline of West Indian plantation societies fostered prophetic movements focused on revolt, not reform. In the 1830s in North America, where the ratio of enslaved to free people was much smaller than in the Caribbean, a series of apocalyptic visions inspired Nat Turner to organize what became one of the bloodiest, and subsequently iconic, slave revolts in U.S. history. Though it was quickly suppressed, lurid accounts of Turner's prophetic vision inspired waves of anxiety among white Southerners and a reaction more brutal than the rebellion itself, and it prompted new efforts to reinforce the hegemony of the slave system.

Among the radical prophetic movements of British settlers in North America that inspired withdrawals from colonial authority into political and military borderlands, the followers of Quaker prophet Jemima Wilkinson (1759–1812) left settled territory in Rhode Island in 1790 to form a new utopian community on colonial New York's border with the territories of the Iroquois. A host of other reform and utopian movements developed more or less separatist communities in the early nineteenth century, from the transcendentalist Fruitlands commune in Massachusetts in the 1840s to the Oneida, New York, community led by radical sex reformer John Humphrey Noyes (1811–1886). The most influential of these movements was the Latter Day Saints, or Mormons, established by the prophet Joseph Smith (1805–1844). Smith's revelations led him to proclaim theological tenets and social practices quite at odds with prevailing Christian norms, including monogamy. But instead of attempting to revolutionize the society from which he had come, Smith led his followers far into the American West. The thriving nationalist ideology of Manifest Destiny allowed the Eastern political establishment to tolerate the Mormons in the West only for a time. Conflicts developed and turned violent when other settlers in the region began asserting U.S. sovereignty and social norms. Over time, westward migration, the integration of transcontinental commercial networks, and the consolidation of American military power greatly diminished the ability of radical prophetic movements to find safe havens on isolated frontiers.

* * *

Prophetic movements developed throughout the Atlantic World in response to the disintegration of older communities created by European military conquests, to Atlantic commercial integration and growth, and particularly—in Africa and North America as well as in England—to the disruptions of transatlantic slaving. Among Native Americans, West Africans, the enslaved in American plantation societies, and social reformers elsewhere, prophetic movements often mobilized powerful followings by giving weakened or marginalized people the hope of restored coherence. Even among European settlers, Christian and Christian-derived prophetic messages inspired movements that fled to, and even flourished in, geopolitical borderlands. As disparate as these movements were in their expressions of human anxiety and hope, they remind us that peoples and places widely separated by geography and social position faced similar and often interconnected challenges and disruptions in the face of commercialization and its sequel, militarization, throughout the Atlantic World. As interconnected as the Atlantic World was, the diversity of prophetic movements among Native Americans, West African Muslims, rebellious slaves, and utopian religious communities developed from particular local contexts.

JOHN WOOD SWEET
JONATHAN TODD HANCOCK

Bibliography

Brooke, John L. *Refiner's Fire: The Making of Mormon Cosmology, 1644–1844.* New York: Cambridge University Press, 1994.

Dowd, Gregory Evans. *A Spirited Resistance: The North American Indian Struggle for Unity, 1745–1815.* Baltimore, MD: Johns Hopkins University Press, 1992.

Juster, Susan. *Doomsayers: Anglo-American Prophecy in the Age of Revolution.* Philadelphia: University of Pennsylvania Press, 2003.

Stern, Steve J. *Peru's Indian Peoples and the Challenge of Spanish Conquest: Huamanga to 1640.* Madison: University of Wisconsin Press, 1982.

Thornton, John. *The Kongolese Saint Anthony: Dona Beatriz Kimpa Vita and the Antonian Movement.* New York: Cambridge University Press, 1998.

Race

At the beginning of the fifteenth century, none of the peoples living around the Atlantic Basin explained variations among groups of humans by invoking inherent and essential collective differences that were immutable across generations. By the middle of the nineteenth century, a broad consensus had emerged among formally educated Europeans and European-descended people in the Americas that human beings could and should be divided into biologically defined groups whose members inherited standardized physical, intellectual, and moral attributes. A belief in racial difference, however, was not limited to elite whites. Parallel discourses of stereotyped difference had also emerged among many Indian peoples in the Americas and African peoples of the Diaspora. In short, the rise of racial thinking was a product of Atlantic encounters. The prevalent discourse of race underscores many scholars' belief that the creation of the Atlantic World in the wake of the Columbian Exchange was a crucible in which key contradictions of modernity were forged.

Before the European Age of Discovery, Europe was a relatively peripheral and isolated corner of Asia, according to the Islamic and Chinese perspectives prominent on a global scale at the time; it was dominated by Judaic and Christian monotheisms holding that all humans descended from a single divinely created couple. This theological unity did not prevent Christian aristocrats from thinking that peasants of their faith possessed unattractive qualities, nor did it stop people in one part of Europe from holding negative stereotypes about people from other places in it. Such elements of categorical thought about others, however, rarely degenerated into politicized beliefs that individuals of different backgrounds differed from one another in essential ways meriting inclusion or exclusion in specific social settings.

Ideas of structured biological difference began to emerge as Europeans engaged the Atlantic during the fifteenth century. The Spanish kingdoms of Aragon and Castile completed their centuries-long struggle to create a purely Christian Iberian Peninsula by expelling the last Muslim polities there in the same year that Columbus sailed across the Atlantic. Concerns about religious impurity in the local population lingered. Following the formal expulsion of Jewish and Muslim people from Spain after the "Reconquista," as the Christian reclamation of Iberian lands in Muslim hands became known, these concerns took the form of an ideological and legal insistence on untainted blood—*limpieza de sangre*—just when the discovery of new lands and deposits of precious metals in the Americas initiated a demand for labor that Iberian Christians could not supply.

Within a few decades plantation agriculture and sugar had crossed the Atlantic from the islands off the coast of Africa to Portuguese producers in Brazil, greatly increasing American demands for alien labor. Though the Portuguese first met this demand with coerced Indians, they increasingly turned to enslaved Africans. Well before the end of the sixteenth century, growing numbers of Indian and African people were assembled in a variety of oppressive labor systems, and the Spanish and Portuguese crowns were espousing policies regarding purity of Iberian Christian descent. This constellation of people from differing backgrounds under the control of an increasingly self-conscious immigrant minority did not immediately produce racialized politics, but it can be seen retrospectively to have formed the categorical differentiation that later would flourish as politicized modern conceptions of racial difference.

The forced-labor systems begun in the sixteenth century would grow as the Atlantic Era progressed. During the seventeenth century, the monarchies of northern Europe, especially those of present-day France and England, began to stake claims to territories in North America and the Caribbean, adapting and often intensifying the plantation complex while destroying or displacing Native peoples who might have stood in their way, replacing them with enslaved Africans. By early in the eighteenth century, European-controlled societies based on the labor of enslaved Africans dominated coastal Brazil, parts of the Caribbean coast of the southern mainland, the islands of the Caribbean, and the seaboard of southeastern North America. Indian laborers bound in various ways formed the economic foundation for the Spanish American mainland, including much of what is now Mexico and significant portions of the Andean highlands. Even regions such as New England and northern New France and the Río de la Plata—in which neither African slavery nor bound Indian labor played a major economic role—maintained color-based hierarchies that reflected the self-conscious differentiation among the populations of core colonial regions and anticipated the racial categories of nineteenth-century republics.

During the eighteenth century an array of similar, though not identical, ideologies of race took shape in Europe and the Americas. Europeans and European-descended people living in the Americas came to see Native Americans as physically weak and prone to illness, while elaborating long-standing stereotypes that Africans were constitutionally hardy and thus capable of withstanding the harsh work regimes of plantation slavery. Not coincidentally, these stereotypes justified colonizers' desires to seize Indian lands and exploit African labor. Seventeenth- and eighteenth-century developments in Europeans' understanding of the biological mechanisms governing heredity combined with Enlightenment desires to categorize and label living species of all types, humans as well as flora and fauna. This combination resulted in more powerful conceptual tools that helped to explain and harden the stereotypes Europeans had come to associate with African and American peoples.

By the end of the century the most "advanced" thinkers in western Europe were articulating the outlines of a full-blown biological theory of racialized differences among humans, effectively gaining traction against Christian traditions of human equality rooted in scriptural narratives of monogenesis, the theory that humankind was created once, resulting in a single species. Over the course of the first half of the nineteenth century, these social and natural-history discourses concerning race increasingly converged in a politicized faith that humankind was divided into three or more racial groups differing from one another in inherited, and therefore unalterable, ways: "whites" occupied the superior category, and "blacks" generally ranked as the least "advanced." By the end of the nineteenth century these theories of racial difference had infused Western thinking about physical evolution and extended to the new field of history, which itself was politicized, though a few rejected the depersonalization and absolute categorization of modern racial thinking.

Native Americans and Africans never reached as widely shared a consensus about the political importance and immutability of race as did Europeans. Given the horrible price they were paying for European racial exclusions, they started from a different point of view. Without overgeneralizing the many different indigenous societies and cultures of the Americas and Africa, it is safe to say that the peoples of the Americas and Africa most fundamentally defined themselves by their local and kin-based ties, more by collective than individual identities. Although of course large polities existed in both Africa and America, the profoundly local nature of African and American identities has been racialized since the Enlightenment by many monotheists and secular humanists as evidence that those societies had remained at earlier or more "primitive" stages of social and political development. However, most Europeans—as well as Africans and Native Americans—lived within constrained geographical horizons and conceived of themselves in local terms that centered on their home villages. That said, Africans and Americans prioritized their localisms in ways that monotheists and humanists did not. They understood human—meaning their own particular—origins not in universalist but in local terms, which had a spiritual dimension, as did their relationship to ancestors. The horrific dislocations that accompanied the growth of Atlantic commercial networks—for Native Americans primarily through war and disease and for Africans primarily through war and slaving—rent the social and metaphysical fabrics that gave meaning to the lives of these victims of European conquests and commercialized individuation.

Many of these isolated victims—those unlucky enough to experience dislocation but fortunate enough to survive it—strove to reconstitute meaningful lives of social belonging and cultural identity in a variety of ways. They elaborated new senses of "ethnic" or "tribal" identity up and down the Atlantic coast of Africa, as well as among the victims of slaving in different American societies. Native Americans created analogous processes of ethnogenesis, fueling the emergence of new polities or tribes from present-day Chile to Canada. By the beginning of the nineteenth century, Africans and their descendants in the Diaspora, and some Native Americans, began to develop counternarratives that rejected European racialized rankings of the different peoples of the world, though they did so largely within the biological premise that humans inherited differentiated moral, intellectual, and physical qualities.

Many Christians thought that God had different plans for different racial groups, though some insisted that the distinctive gifts of different groups were equivalent in worth; others accepted the principle of ranking but reversed Europeans' ordering of the differences. None of these varieties of categorizing and ranking humanity dominated African and Native American thinking to the overwhelming extent that racialized hierarchy dominated that of Europeans and their American descendants. Residents of nineteenth-century Africa and populations of African descent in much of Spanish and Portuguese America often felt primary allegiance to specific ethnic identities—for example, the neo-African groups created in Brazil, such as the Nago/Lucumi, Mina, and Congo. Most Native Americans saw membership in legally recognized "tribes" as more important than a racialized pan-Indian identity.

Whatever the alternatives to racial thinking among those excluded by it from the nation-states of the nineteenth century, the central story of race in the Atlantic World is that of the destructive triumph of an ideology of differentiated human abilities and disabilities rooted in appeals to mechanistic biological processes of reproduction. This highly prejudicial thinking used the unquestioned authority of science to enshrine European dominance rooted in conquests and dispersals of Native Americans and in the displacement of millions of Africans through the Atlantic slave trade. W. E. B. DuBois, one of the leading African American intellectuals of the twentieth century, proved prophetic in predicting that the primary social problem of his lifetime would be the color line drawn to exclude citizens from the civic and human rights guaranteed by modern states. He was right, in large part because of the asymmetrical mixing of differing human populations in the Atlantic Basin from 1500 to 1900.

JAMES SIDBURY

Bibliography

Gomez, Michael Angelo. *Exchanging Our Country Marks: The Transformation of African Identities in the Colonial and Antebellum South.* Chapel Hill: University of North Carolina Press, 1998.

Hannaford, Ivan. *Race: The History of an Idea in the West.* Washington, DC: Woodrow Wilson Center Press, and Baltimore, MD: Johns Hopkins University Press, 1996.

Jordan, Winthrop D. *White over Black: American Attitudes toward the Negro, 1550–1812.* Chapel Hill: University of North Carolina Press, 1968.

Sidbury, James, and Jorge Cañizares-Esguerra. "Mapping Ethnogenesis in the Early Modern Atlantic World." *William and Mary Quarterly*, 3rd ser., 68 (2011): 181–208.

Raiders

Returning from his third American voyage in 1498, Christopher Columbus faced French corsairs off Madeira. The Atlantic World he had helped open was already crawling with predators. Some, like the Spanish conquistadors, sought personal gain at others' expense on land, whereas others, like the French corsairs, sought their fortunes at sea. Outlaw raiders loomed large in the early-modern imagination, yet most raiders operated under legal cover, justifying aggressive quests for profit with royal papers. Indeed, much early-modern Atlantic raiding could be classified as the subcontracting or outsourcing of larceny for the aims of governments unprepared to act on their own on transoceanic scales. Only certain rebel groups, such as fugitive slaves and unconquerable Native Americans, raided to survive. However practiced, raiding revealed the limited reach of law in the Atlantic World.

Why was despoiling so common in the early Atlantic? Much aggression arose from competition for newly available resources among emerging monarchies and their increasingly restless subjects. Still, we may wonder at the intensity of the violence. Evidence shows that European raiders preyed upon Native Americans and Africans with what today seems like astonishing cruelty. Yet most Europeans, Native Americans, and Africans appear to have been no less cruel in their attacks on one another. Spain's enemies quickly claimed that sacking Spanish subjects was justified by the injustice of Spanish conquests and subsequent abuse of the conquered. Even without such pretexts, harsh attacks often prevailed over diplomacy, and only the prospect of military alliances, trade, and perhaps soul saving led to cooperation across political, ethnic, or racial lines.

Non-Europeans mostly raided in response to outside threats or to new opportunities to trade in stolen goods and bodies. Backlands slaving in both Africa and the Americas developed in these ways, soon reverberating far beyond the immediate zone of violent contact. Elsewhere, fugitives from colonial intrusion practiced petty banditry and rustled cattle, usually to subsist rather than to profit. Atlantic raiding, whatever its form, followed cycles linked to larger political or commercial developments, as well as to droughts, plagues, and other threats. How did raiding's victims respond? Sources suggest that most inhabitants of the early-modern Atlantic World expected to be preyed upon sooner or later. Suffering at the hands of raiders was one of life's many misfortunes, and the absence of authorities to administer justice encouraged what might be called epicycles of retribution or vengeance.

Despite their diversity, raiders shared some common aims and strategies. Atlantic raiders routinely seized commodities and human bodies, not land. Only for the Spanish conquistadors was land itself a significant, if tertiary, aim. Most raiders aimed to acquire and cash out any fungible wealth and then to move on—not to possess or produce anything. Precedents were numerous in the Mediterranean and northern Atlantic, but the range of opportunities for raiding grew exponentially with systematic European exploitation of the Americas. New European gunmaking and shipbuilding technologies were also key, although Europeans did not long monopolize them, as seen with the rise of North African corsairing after the Castilian conquest of Granada in 1492, and then a century later with the newly armed Moroccan sultan's invasion of the Songhai regime in western Africa.

Privately financed raiding spearheaded colonizing projects throughout the Atlantic Basin, and the new settlements in turn drew other raiders. Such European parasitical raiding often led to permanent territorial claims and shifts in political relations, eventually settling into colonial détente. The transformation of Jamaica in the later-seventeenth century from Caribbean pirate base to plantation colony was typical. In general, metropolitan support for Atlantic raiding, whether by Spaniards, Frenchmen, Dutchmen, or Englishmen, favored hardheaded reasons of state over utopian fantasies, although the two could be entwined. From one perspective, the French colonies in Florida and Brazil that the Spanish and Portuguese destroyed in the 1560s were Huguenot refuges; from another, they were nests of pirates.

The challenge for many Atlantic raiders was to sustain their parasitism on settled agricultural societies or established trade flows without killing their hosts. The victims of raiding in turn responded by shoring up their defenses and attempting to extend the rule of law—or, in this context, a government monopoly on legitimate violence—into the farthest reaches of the Atlantic Basin, to eliminate the contested "middle ground." By the early eighteenth century, alleged pirates were tried in the colonies and executed on the spot, hung from gibbets washed by the formerly lawless sea. When active defenses proved untenable or too expensive, the raiders' victims withdrew, as happened in western Hispaniola and elsewhere in the Spanish Caribbean. Either active or passive defense could end a raiding cycle or force major reconfiguration of colonial borders or trade patterns. Operating at the margins of, or outside, the law, Atlantic raiders were first and foremost opportunists. Some, like the Caribbean buccaneers, formed new if fleeting cultures.

Conquistadors

"The Spaniard does not settle or inhabit deserted lands, however healthy and rich they may be in gold and silver; he inhabits and settles where he finds Indians" (Vargas Machuca, 61). Thus did a late-arriving conquistador characterize Spanish raiding in the Americas up to about 1620. It is clear that most conquistadors raided Native communities not only for booty but also to seize and harness labor for the production of tribute. Conquest expeditions were almost entirely funded by private investors, and many were legalized only after the fact. Indeed, the Spanish conquest of the Americas resulted not from some grand imperial plan, but rather from a string of ad hoc, swashbuckling business enterprises, many of which failed.

In the Caribbean phase of Spanish expansion, slave raiding under the guise of punishing "Carib cannibals" was the principal means of accumulating capital. This early circum-Caribbean raiding also provided would-be Spanish conquerors of inland regimes with essential cultural knowledge and field experience. In these early sorties Spanish raiders learned to dupe indigenous hosts with promises of peaceful trade or an offer of military aid in order to gain access to chiefs, or *caciques*, whom they then captured and held for ransom—often only to murder them once it was paid. This pattern of "decapitating headmen" was duly repeated by Cortés in Mexico, by Francisco Pizarro in Peru, and by Gonzalo Jiménez de Quesada in New Granada (today's Colombia). The booty extorted in these raiding enterprises flooded into Spain and the rest of Europe, firing the imaginations of new generations of would-be conquistadors. The dream of lording over hundreds or even thousands of tribute-paying subjects was even more exciting for raiders inclined to knighthood. One such raider was Juan de Oñate, a Mexican-born Spaniard who led the brutal conquest of New Mexico beginning in 1598. The vast desert separating his native Zacatecas from remote Santa Fe became one of the Americas' many enduring raiding frontiers, as lawless and violent as any sea.

Pirates of the Seas

The term *pirate* was an epithet. Although the Spanish and Portuguese used it occasionally to refer to early French and later English and Dutch attackers, far more common, and respectable, was the word *corsair*. Corsairs were ostensibly engaged in acts of maritime reprisal, which is to say they carried licenses from a sovereign permitting them to seek redress for some past raid by means of a new attack on another vessel flying the same flag as the initial perpetrator—"an eye for an eye." Governments issued letters of marque and reprisal—authorizations to raid—in times of war as a means of sapping an enemy's strength in supplies, manpower, and money on the cheap.

Like the Spanish conquistadors, most early-modern corsairs pooled capital to organize raiding voyages, then shared out booty at the end. Corsairing, like conquest, was raiding as business, based on signed contracts that could hold up in court. From the perspective of its victims, however, corsairing felt just like illegal piracy—which in fact it often was. Corsairs routinely attacked "noncombatants" during peacetime or outside the bounds specified in their letters of marque and reprisal. The only real way to deal with such scofflaw Atlantic raiders was to arm oneself against them.

High-seas piracy, like most varieties of raiding, rose and fell in cycles. From Columbus's day until about 1560, French corsairs were the main scourge, both in the Americas and along the coast of Africa. After 1560 Elizabethan Englishmen such as Francis Drake epitomized the corsair as renaissance maverick. This daring, individualistic way of "singeing the king of Spain's beard" faded with the death of Elizabeth I in 1603, but the Dutch, since 1568 rebelling against Spain, were already replacing the English as the most belligerent seaborne raiders in the Atlantic. With the creation of the Dutch East and West India companies in the early seventeenth century, Dutch corsairing took on corporate as well as political dimensions, yielding the largest hauls of booty yet seen, especially silver, and ending with seizures of Spanish and Portuguese territories in the New World.

Dutch overreach after 1640 overlapped with the emergence in the Caribbean of a new variety of seaborne raider: the freelance buccaneer. Former indentured servants, military veterans, some runaway slaves and Native Americans, and others marginalized by the consolidation of Atlantic institutions joined forces to raid Spanish vessels in the Caribbean, at first to supplement their subsistence on feral cattle but soon also to seize treasure and captives for disposition at friendly ports. Slaves could be sold, and money bought alcohol, tobacco, firearms, and sex. Lax defenses enabled new cycles of mayhem.

Once again, the bullion-rich Spanish were the obvious target for organized raids, and French, Dutch, English, and even Danish outposts or merchant bazaars soon sprouted to fence stolen treasure. Port Royal, Jamaica, was for a time proud to be a pirate haven. As the buccaneers accumulated capital and renown, they expanded rapidly in the 1660s and grew more daring, culminating with Henry Morgan's 1671 sack of Panama City. As Alexander Exquemelin, a buccaneer veteran of this 1,800-man expedition, put it, "it is the same law among these people as with other pirates: *No prey, no pay*" (Antony, 65).

Spanish protests at the disorder prompted a general crackdown on Caribbean piracy. In response, the buccaneers scattered, many sailing off to raid in the Pacific and Indian oceans. Perennial wars between the European powers drew the buccaneers back to the Atlantic, where they engaged in "legal" corsairing—rerigged as privateering. The Spanish had turned to reprisal raiding as well, licensing mostly Basque vessels to seize enemy ships on their own accounts. Periodic wars muddied the legal waters still more, and in 1697 the French navy joined buccaneers to attack the key Spanish slave port of Cartagena de Indias. A number of veteran pirates, most of them English or Anglo-American, were drawn similarly into the War of the Spanish Succession after 1702. However, the buccaneers' age of anarchy was almost over.

The end of the War of the Spanish Succession in 1713 left Atlantic waters filled with naval veterans facing slim prospects for employment but with considerable skills in maritime raiding. Most, again, were from the British Isles or from English-speaking colonies. Some of these seamen found work on merchant vessels and others with the fledgling Royal Navy, but many chafed under the harsh discipline of the merchant marine and the navy and turned pirate. Their last gasp, and by some accounts the Golden Age of Atlantic piracy, lasted from 1713 to about 1725. The British had decided to take a hard line on piracy, declaring it a capital crime. Thanks to the Royal Navy, plus metropolitan and colonial authorities, such celebrated pirates as Edward "Blackbeard" Teach, Ann Bonny, and Mary Read were either killed or captured. The pirate's refrain, "A merry life and a short one," captured well the end of Atlantic buccaneering.

Bandits and Slave-Raiding Frontiers

The term *slaver* here refers to inland raiders who lived by capturing and enslaving others, although by the eighteenth century it usually referred to the transatlantic slave ships that carried captives to the Americas. More or less full-time kidnappers of similar sorts also ravaged the backlands of Spanish America and Brazil, and both indigenous raiders and Europeans practiced slaving in North America, although hunting humans there never approached the commercial scale of the African trade. European Christians, so-called white slaves, were not exempt from capture by North African Muslim regimes, but their raiding was mostly limited to Mediterranean shores, where they took captives, whom they typically held for ransom and forced to work in punitive or domestic tasks. The scale of this traffic was considerable—before the eighteenth century it was well in excess of the capture and sale of sub-Saharan Africans and Native Americans—but it was primarily a kidnapping and extortion racket with redemption for cash as the aim, rather than a slaving business transferring captives permanently for purposes of commercial production. The point was coins, not hands.

European slaving of the commercial sort began in the fifteenth century in the Canary Islands and in a few places along Africa's long Atlantic coast. Spanish raiding against Canary natives soon led to their extermination, but the Portuguese and their later European competitors on the mainland of Africa left the raiding almost entirely to African suppliers, merely purchasing the captives they were offered. Malaria and other tropical diseases made European survival and reproduction in sub-Saharan Africa extremely difficult, and the Europeans' weakness, together with the efficiencies of their African suppliers, largely excluded them from inland raiding. Demand for captive Africans grew with the creation of sugar plantations in the eastern Atlantic islands and then in the Americas. This growing market prompted several African societies to expand the captive-taking aspect of their wars, even making sale a central aim. Both small groups and military regimes of considerable scale took up slaving as their livelihood.

Bands of professional raiders, called Jagas or Imbangala, emerged in the late sixteenth century in the interior of Angola, the Portuguese *conquista* in West-Central Africa, for example. Moving swiftly through Angola's drought-stricken backlands to seize whole villages and liquidate their inhabitants, these bandit groups seem to have lived almost entirely from raiding. They allegedly sacrificed some of the captives they seized but sold most to the Portuguese, and briefly (in the 1640s) also to the Dutch. As long as Europeans wanted to purchase captives, bands such as the Imbangala were likely to thrive.

Backland slave raiding of a comparable type also appeared in Brazil, the major market for Angolan and other sub-Saharan African captives. Sugar and tobacco planters in northeastern Brazil lacked access to sedentary Native American tributaries like those conquered by the Spanish, so many sought indigenous hands by raiding for captives. Portuguese military men in Brazil, like the Spanish conquistadors, sought their fortunes by searching—desperately, as it turned out—for mineral wealth. Their expeditions, sometimes called *bandeiras* from the pennants that these raiders flew in quasi-military fashion, often had to settle for Native captives, some of them acquired in barter, others taken by kidnapping. These were sold to coastal planters or merchants, and the profits were pooled for capital to fund the next expedition. The *bandeirantes* at times added attacks on indigenous villages to their ostensible prospecting and bartering expeditions. Claiming these captives as the product of "just"

wars against dangerous and soulless savages, the raiders in effect became professional slavers. Raiding for captives to sell persisted into the nineteenth century.

Spanish American and Brazilian slavers hunted fugitives of African descent as well. Indeed, several late-arriving conquistadors cut their teeth trying to recapture runaway slaves or maroons (from the Spanish *cimarrón*) in Venezuela, Panama, Ecuador, and Mexico. Maroons and unconquerable Native Americans who preyed upon Spanish settlements were targeted both as rebels against crown authority and as criminal raiders or "highwaymen." Why did such groups rob Spanish travelers and pillage Spanish towns? In most cases it was to supplement their diets, to seize equipment and luxuries they could not manufacture, and occasionally to supplement their numbers. Unable in most instances to sell stolen booty or ransom captives, indigenous and maroon rebels were essentially subsistence raiders.

Communities that lived by raiding could also be found deep within Africa and North America, and runaways might disappear from European view into jungles, deserts, or mountains, but they lacked the Atlantic connections of the groups treated here as "rebels." Virtually all documented maroon communities, whether in Brazil, Suriname, Colombia, Jamaica, or Mexico, lived within raiding distance of European towns or plantations. Already themselves subject to "re-enslaving" raids, maroons responded by pilfering tools, weapons, and food—sometimes kidnapping other slaves or liberating family members. As a result, they went from being regarded as simple fugitives to being assaulted as chronic bandits. Crown authorities generally proved unwilling to fund expeditions against maroons, leading to increasingly violent reprisals led by private colonists and their auxiliaries, "neo-conquistadors" and *bandeirantes*. When these sorties failed, colonial authorities negotiated peace with the maroons, offering gifts—in effect, tribute or bribes—to buy off their raiding.

Indigenous rebels were far more common in the Americas and indeed could be found in any frontier region there. The Mapuche of southern Chile fought the Spanish throughout colonial times along a mutual raiding frontier. They adopted certain Spanish weapons, along with horses, and frequently took human captives to augment their numbers. Yet the Mapuche also retained many cultural practices of their own, presumably amplifying the importance of valiant raiding as an expression of manhood. Recent studies of the Comanche of North America have suggested that, like the Imbangala of greater Angola, they created a whole new political economy based on raiding, primarily for captives. They traded some of the people they seized, most of them Native rivals, to merchants serving markets as far away as New France or the Windward Islands of the Caribbean. These chronic Native American raiders sometimes attacked only periodically to supplement their own resources, while others raided on grand scales, depending on what they stole—or what they used their booty to buy.

Conclusion

The global scale of European investment in the early-modern period (c. 1450–1750), supported by new transportation and weapons technologies, whether cast as European expansion overseas, as the rise of global capitalism, or as creation of a world-system, propelled explosive growth in freelance raiding, both at sea and on land, along its uncontrollable interfaces with local communities. The violence of the slaving that wracked Africa was not different in its historical dynamic from much raiding in the Americas, such as that of the Spanish conquistadors, or from such English corsairs as Francis Drake. These European raiders bore the initial costs and risks of what became Europe-centered financial and military control of the Atlantic, and, like medieval knights, they expected to be rewarded with titles of nobility for their initiative, daring, and success in extending the realm. They provided the private financing behind what became imperial endeavors at a time when governments lacked resources to act in more controlled, costlier ways.

The violence they perfected became the basis for the strategies of later maritime raiding, such as that of the Caribbean buccaneers, as growing government infrastructure and investment provided targets for others to profit in the short term from their vulnerabilities. Monarchy-sponsored raiding and attacks that later monarchies criminalized were not mutually exclusive, and it could be said that private and government aims were in dialectical tension throughout early-modern times and in some places long afterward.

Although the flows of precious metals and valuable merchandise were clear objects of desire for Atlantic thieves, most organized raiders preyed on people in the regions only marginally integrated into these commercial flows, taking captives and selling them away into the increasingly labor-hungry capitalist enclaves, usually for plantation or mine work in the tropics or subtropics. Raiders used their access to ships, horses, guns, and information to extend the reach of mostly metropolitan European but occasionally African or Asian—or even American—investors into the remotest frontiers, beyond their physical presence and far ahead of any military control.

Raiders, as semiautonomous subcontractors of empire, proved as dangerous as they were useful to central authorities and wealthy financiers. They were Atlantic extensions of the mercenary troops late-medieval warlords had used to consolidate monarchical power in Europe. As with the early-modern pirates of the Caribbean, such well-informed and well-armed professionals in violence could prove uncontrollable in the vast, open spaces of an entire ocean, but replacing them with more formal aggressors such as armies and navies proved expensive. Raiders—European and others—were the low-cost cutting edge of integrating the Atlantic as a European-controlled economic and political domain.

KRIS LANE

Bibliography

Andrews, Kenneth R. *The Spanish Caribbean: Trade and Plunder, 1530–1630.* New Haven, CT: Yale University Press, 1978.

Antony, Robert, ed. *Pirates in the Age of Sail.* New York: W. W. Norton, 2007.

Benton, Lauren. *A Search for Sovereignty: Law and Geography in European Empires, 1400–1900.* New York: Cambridge University Press, 2010.

Bromley, J. S. *Corsairs and Navies, 1660–1760.* London: Hambledon, 1987.

Colás, Alejandro, and Bryan Mabee, eds. *Mercenaries, Pirates, Bandits, and Empires: Private Violence in Historical Context.* New York: Columbia University Press, 2010.

Davis, Robert C. *Christian Slaves, Muslim Masters: White Slavery in the Mediterranean, the Barbary Coast, and*

Italy, 1500–1800. New York: Palgrave Macmillan, 2003.

Earle, Peter. *The Pirate Wars.* London: Methuen, 2003.

Marley, David F. *Pirates and Privateers of the Americas.* Santa Barbara, CA: ABC-CLIO, 1994.

Miller, Joseph C. *Way of Death: Merchant Capitalism and the Angolan Slave Trade, 1730–1830.* Madison: University of Wisconsin Press, 1988.

Monteiro, John M. *Negros da terra: Índios e bandeirantes nas origens de São Paulo.* São Paulo, Brazil: Companhia das Letras, 1994.

Pennell, C. R., ed. *Bandits at Sea: A Pirates Reader.* New York: New York University Press, 2002.

Price, Richard, ed. *Maroon Societies: Rebel Slave Communities in the Americas.* 3rd ed. Baltimore, MD: Johns Hopkins University Press, 1996.

Rediker, Marcus. *Villains of All Nations.* Boston, MA: Beacon, 2004.

Restall, Matthew, and Felipe Fernandez-Armesto. *Conquistadors: A Very Short Introduction.* New York: Oxford University Press, 2012.

Thornton, John K. *Warfare in Atlantic Africa, 1500–1800.* New York: Routledge, 2000.

Vargas Machuca, Bernardo de. *Defending the Conquest: Bernardo de Vargas Machuca's Defense and Discourse of the Western Conquests.* University Park: Penn State University Press, 2010.

Religions

See Prophetic Movements; Religions, African; *specific religions*; *religions of specific regions*.

Religions, African

African religions, including Islam, contributed to new forms of "Atlantic" religion from the late fifteenth to the end of the nineteenth centuries, while at the same time the participants in the numerous religious systems in Africa changed their practices as they engaged this new form of "commerce," roughly corresponding to the period of Atlantic commerce. This analysis focuses on African religious history as recorded in the period, rather than attempting to project practices observed in twentieth-century ethnographies back to

earlier and very different times. The areas most integrated into the Atlantic World were within a few hundred miles of the coast, stretching from the Sahel of southern Mauritania to the savannas of southern Angola, in four broad regions from which most slaves were taken: Senegambia in far western Africa, the Upper Guinea Coast, the Slave Coast and the Bight of Biafra in Lower Guinea, and the Kongo-Angola area south of the equator.

As Africans first engaged Atlantic trade in the latter half of the fifteenth century, most adhered to religions created by particular communities or ethnic groups that expressed their senses of identity. Smaller groups of Muslims were concentrated in the Sahel and Sudanic regions of western Africa. Christians and Jews were limited to northern and northeastern Africa, as minorities amid the Muslim population dominant in those regions. Although Africans' indigenous religions were associated with particular communities, they flexibly adopted ritual practices or ideas of spirits from neighboring communities and did not share the zealous monotheistic sense that others' religious traditions were invalid.

Although these African religions, estimated to have numbered well over 1,000, were as diverse as the communities that created them, they shared common elements, some derived from their openness to borrowing from one another. Most African religions attributed the process of creation of the world and its living beings, as well as a number of different types of lesser spiritual forces or beings, to an ultimate presence. The prominence of this supreme being varied among different religious traditions and over time, but it was widely associated with the creation of life and the fates of human beings after death. In some cases, the supreme being communicated with humans through prophets, who could acquire considerable authority based on their privileged communications with ultimate power. More frequently, however, the supreme being communicated through spirit mediums or indirectly through lesser spirits. The lesser spirits ranged from highly anthropomorphic deities such as the Yoruba *orisha*, whose biographies were quite well known in their communities, to spiritualized ancestors who assisted their living descendants, to relatively impersonal types of particular spiritual powers. Trickster deities, who enjoyed chaos and disorder but were not forces of evil, served important roles in the explanation of uncertainty and misfortune.

The first Europeans who sailed along Africa's Atlantic coast were often unaware of these traditions, since they found none of the houses of worship or books of scripture that they defined as "religion." The Christian obligation to save "heathens" from their apparent lack of "religion" became an important justification for acquiring the people they and their successors transported in the Atlantic slave trade. Only rarely were the enslaved Africans able to bring material objects they associated with their religious traditions with them through the hardships of the Middle Passage, but they carried memories of their religious heritages and traditions of spirit possession that facilitated the movement of deities and spirits across the Atlantic, and their very bodies bore witness to rituals of scarification that in many areas of Atlantic Africa brought spiritualized protection on their journeys from childhood to adulthood.

In the far western Sudanic and Sahelian areas, from the mouth of the Gambia River to the southern reaches of the Sahara Desert and inland from the coast to the floodplain of the upper Niger, a number of hierarchically organized or caste-based communities, many of whom spoke Mande languages, gave kings the major ritual responsibilities for seeking rain and other necessities for community welfare. Although significant Muslim communities had coexisted with these indigenous religions since the tenth century, their faith remained strong in deities associated with agriculture, fertility of the land and of women, initiations of adolescent girls and boys into the responsibilities of adulthood, divination, blacksmithing, and other kinds of specialized knowledge.

Some communities may have affiliated themselves with Islam to avoid enslavement by the Islamic communities in the region or by Muslim slave raiders operating from the Mauritanian desert. The intensification of raiding and warfare associated with the Atlantic slave trade in the widespread Mande-speaking area may also have contributed to popular alienation from the indigenous religions of slave-raiding warlords and strengthened the appeal of Islam in rural areas. Many of the Islamic and Mande elements in the emerging religion systems of the Atlantic World originated in this region. Within African religious traditions, imports

of iron and the increasing frequency of war and disease—the latter associated with the former through the mobility of populations captured or fleeing—may have contributed to the growing importance of spirits associated with iron smithing, war, and healing. In the religions of the Africans in the Americas, these spiritual communities became associated with "houses" or "nations" of the Mandingas (Mande) or Siniga (Senegal).

In the region from the Gambia River south to the Liberian-Ivoirean (modern Côte d'Ivoire) border, the northern limits of the Guinean forest, most people lived in small kingdoms, township-republics, or acephalous societies (those without leaders, or chiefs). Their religious traditions focused on supreme beings and lesser spirits and on male and female secret-initiation societies. During the period of Atlantic slaving, many coastal communities used the authority of spirits, their cults and priests, to regulate participation in the trade, to prevent raiding within their communities, and to ensure that the personal wealth derived from raiding was distributed throughout the entire community. In spite of these efforts to preserve their relative egalitarianism, members of slave-trading elites invested their new wealth in religious offices and in status as elders in various religious societies, thus consolidating their personal control.

Iron, war, and healing shrines appear to have increased in this region, too. Though many of the people captured from the Upper Guinea coast show up as Felupes (Diola) and Brames (Manjaco) in sixteenth-century Spanish slave censuses from Peru to Argentina, because European slavers bought from Mande-speaking intermediaries, they often misidentified them as "Mandingas," and their contributions to religious practices in their transatlantic destinations may have been subsumed under that generic category.

The largest number of Africans transported to the Americas came from the eastward-running coast of western Africa known as Lower Guinea, especially the part of it referred to as the Slave Coast. This region stretched from modern Côte d'Ivoire (Ivory Coast) to the Cross Rivers area on the modern border between Nigeria and Cameroon. In this region, supreme beings were often perceived as having gendered characteristics. The supreme being of the Fon-Ewe areas (modern Togo and Benin, then Dahomey), Mawu-Lesa, was a composite, with the feminine aspect of Mawu preceding the masculine aspect. Fluid gendering—or perhaps a blend transcending this basic contrast in cultures based on reproduction—was also found among some Yoruba *orisha*, most notably Shango and Obatala, which remained important in the diaspora in these deities' association with female Catholic saints. Spirit possession and rich oral biographies of lesser gods were especially important in this region and facilitated the retention and revival of these Lower Guinea traditions in diasporic religious practices. However, some oracles of lesser spirits and priests of the supreme being exploited the growing demand for slaves for transatlantic markets, corrupting their traditions by expanding the range of offenses for which priests could condemn people for sale into slavery. Among the coastal peoples of Togo and Benin, memories of selling people—some of them friends and relatives—provoked survivors to create new forms of spirit cults to ease the sense of moral wrongdoing by supplicating the spirits of the victims of the trade.

Throughout the equatorial region of Atlantic Africa, stretching from the Cross River area to southern Angola, people speaking Bantu languages shared a concept of a supreme being, often known as Nzambi. Other foci of the religions of this region included ancestors, especially deceased kings and chiefs, and power objects known as *nkisi*. Consecrated *nkisi* could concentrate spiritualized power to heal the sick, settle disputes, and attain victory in warfare. This focus on power objects was one contribution of enslaved people from this region to the emerging religions of the African Diaspora in the Atlantic World. According to the Kongo philosopher Fu-kiau Bonseki, Kongo associated the Atlantic Ocean on their west with the body of water that separated the land of the living from the land of the dead. When people died, they followed the setting sun into this ocean (*kalunga*), where they were reborn into the world of ancestors. The Portuguese who arrived in Kongo in the late fifteenth century came from the west, and their pale features identified them with the whiteness of ancestors, an association that was reinforced by their greater comfort on water than on dry land.

Equatorial Africa's early and intense participation in the Atlantic slave trade led to great political instability and to religious movements that sought to restore order, gain control over the Atlantic trade,

and heal new forms of illness, both moral and physical, associated with commerce and population mobility. Among these cults was a shrine of affliction, known as Lemba, in which initiates underwent ritual therapies to cure them of their sufferings from greed. The enslaved, too, carried Lemba across the Atlantic, where it became important in diasporic religions. In Kongo, south of the mouth of the Congo River, an aristocracy adopted Christianity early in the sixteenth century to seek alliance with the pope through collaboration with local Catholic missionaries, and many people sought stability within the arms of the Church. Within this context, when the Christian aristocracy engaged in civil wars at the end of the seventeenth century, a woman fell gravely ill and claimed that she had died and been reborn with the spirit of St. Anthony of Padua, the patron saint of Portugal who was particularly associated with healing. She mobilized a large following to restore the integrity of ancient Kongo until she was captured by the Portuguese and burned at the stake. Kimpa Vita, or Dona Beatriz as she became known, was also celebrated as the Joan of Arc of the Kongo.

All four regions of Atlantic Africa contributed their spirits and cults to the religious traditions of Africans in the transatlantic world. Individual forms of resistance in the American South and collective revolts in northeastern Brazil drew inspiration from indigenous African religions and from African Islam. Enslaved people carried concepts of spirit possession and knowledge of power objects through the Middle Passage: these also facilitated the continued vitality of African forms of religious expression in the Americas. Long-standing patterns of openness to borrowing from other religious traditions and the absence of doctrines of exclusive revelation also facilitated the creation of the hybrid religions that became powerful among the African Diaspora in the Americas.

ROBERT M. BAUM

Bibliography

Baum, Robert M. *Shrines of the Slave Trade: Diola Religion and Society in Precolonial Senegambia.* New York: Oxford University Press, 1999.
Janzen, John. *Lemba, 1650–1930: A Drum of Affliction in Africa and the New World.* New York: Garland, 1982.
Janzen, John, and Wyatt MacGaffey, eds. *An Anthology of*

Kongo Religion. Lawrence: University of Kansas Press, 1974.

Mudimbe, Valentin. *The Invention of Africa: Gnosis, Philosophy and the Order of Knowledge.* Bloomington: Indiana University Press, 1988.

Rosenthal, Judy. *Possession, Ecstasy, and Law in Ewe Voodoo.* Charlottesville: University of Virginia Press, 1998.

Religions, African, Historiography of

For some years now, scholars have expressed increasing dissatisfaction with the concept of "African religion," some putting "religion" in ironic quotation marks, others pleading for an entirely new perspective. The main thrust of the critiques is that what we know as African religion is not so much African as it is a product of Christians' confrontations with Africans whom they wanted to convert. In this encounter missionaries identified as "religion" statements and practices that merely looked like religion to them. Scholars influenced by the epistemological structure of the modern world, in which religion, politics, and economics are separate activities associated with their own academic disciplines and reading publics, accepted this package as a discrete sector of African culture. Some of them, aware of the ethnocentrism and exoticizing effect of this vocabulary of religion, have nevertheless felt its use to be unavoidable, but some still confronted the historiographical issues directly. Paul Landau writes, "Once we do away with the anachronistic uses of 'religion' we are free to accept that all people act and react in the landscape of the real" (Landau, 21).

No word exists in indigenous African languages to denote the abstraction "religion," although in modern times older words have been bent to this new purpose. The etymology of the word is uncertain even in European languages; it came into general use only after Christians confronted systems of belief other than their own in the seventeenth century, not least in the unfamiliar worlds around their Atlantic, and began to consider the possibility of abandoning religious belief altogether. The three principal European models of African religion—fetishism, animism, and spirituality—were products of different phases in their long encounter with Af-ricans; they explain more about the self-conception of Europeans than about Africa.

For the philosophers of the eighteenth-century Enlightenment, predecessors of the nineteenth century's sociologists and anthropologists, Africans seemed to have no religion but instead exhibited the opposite of moral and rational thinking in the form of *fetish.* Portuguese sailors had found in the fifteenth century that the coastal peoples of West and Central Africa did not, as they expected, worship idols; instead they relied on what the Portuguese, adapting a medieval term for witchcraft, called *fetissos* (fetishes). At first *fetissos* were thought to be false versions of familiar objects of devotion, the crosses and rosaries that Catholic Christians carried. The arrival of Dutch rivals to the Portuguese in the seventeenth century modified the idea of *fetisso.* To the Dutch, Protestants who measured their prospects of salvation by material success, the false religious value of the fetish caused Africans to attribute false economic value to material things and to understand physical cause and effect wrongly as magic. Nevertheless, oaths sworn on fetishes functioned to sanction commercial contracts and regulate affairs; for centuries, in the intercultural spaces of the African coast, Europeans obliged to do business there on local terms relied on fetishes, having to admit that, as instruments of social control, fetishes worked.

Fetishism served in the eighteenth century as the iconic type of primordial, absolute irrationality, as W. Pietz shows. As nineteenth-century romanticism and relativism came to challenge the rationalist pretensions of the Enlightenment, anthropologists adopted a somewhat more charitable view of African culture. E. B. Tylor, in his foundational ethnographic study of *Primitive Culture* (1871), upheld "the psychic unity of mankind"; all people, he said, thought in the same way, and all were "animists," that is, they believed in spiritual beings; religion, serving to explain natural phenomena, was a kind of bad science. As cultural evolution progressed, he held, people became more discriminating and developed increasingly abstract and therefore "universal" beliefs; even Christianity, according to Tylor, was a refined animism. Still today, animism is widely used as an all-purpose label for any sort of African belief and practice that is not Christianity or Islam.

By the end of the nineteenth century, European powers had conquered most of Africa. Missionaries and anthropologists gained access to people living in the interior of the continent and began to write firsthand reports about them. What had been seen as African or "primitive" culture they saw as religion, identifying beliefs in spirits, the sacred, ritual, prayer, worship, priests, shrines, sacrifice and sin, or whatever they saw as the African equivalents of these Judeo-Christian basics. The Kongo word *nkisi*, for example, which meant what the Portuguese called *fetish*, was translated as "holy," and *sema*, which meant to renew a fetish after it had been invalidated, became "to create," as in the first verse of Genesis. Rosalind Shaw has called this appropriative process "translation from above." Meanwhile, as Europe itself was wracked by wars that seemed to threaten civilization, the idea gained ground, initially among artists, that Africans and other colonized people retained cultural values lost in the materialism of the modern. Africans, it was alleged, were naturally religious in this vague and comprehensive sense, possessing a spirituality superior to that of tired mainstream religions. Ultimately this effort to appreciate was a form of orientalism, an essentializing, or stereotyping, caricature that simply inverted the eighteenth-century view that Africans had no religion at all by making all of their lives "spiritual" while keeping in place the radical difference that the colonial era posited between "us" and "them."

The new anthropology of the twentieth century rejected the premise of social evolution behind this contrast as conjectural and adopted a politically liberal program intended to show that "primitive" societies, in their own fashion, "worked," that is, met the needs of their people. Beliefs and practices that were, on their face, embarrassing to the rational mind (or at least to the European common sense of the era), could be shown to have side-effects, such as promoting social solidarity and respect for authority. Magic, it could be argued, should not be understood as false instrumentality but as theater, an expression of desire. The seemingly absurd could be endowed with meaning by calling it symbolic of something else regarded as more "real," metaphorical rather than literal. In all this, scholars with no particular evangelical commitment retained the Christian translations, so that, for example, all killing of animals in other than obviously utilitarian contexts was taken to be "sacrifice." In anthropological practice "African religion" came to include any belief in forces Europeans deemed imaginary or, in relation to cause and effect, judged to be false in physical or chemical terms, with the result, as Landau says, that "most anything that Africans say or said about themselves became religious insofar as it stood in need of clarification."

Christian missionaries converted and educated large numbers of Africans under colonial rule; some of the world's largest congregations of both Catholics and Protestants today are African. As the independence of African countries loomed in the 1950s, churches sought ways to indigenize themselves, to seem less like alien imports. Catholics had long argued that all peoples must have some apprehension of the universal God; they looked for "steppingstones" to bridge the gap they perceived between African culture and Christianity and show that African values amounted to a proto-gospel. Critics called this approach intellectual smuggling. In 1954 Geoffrey Parrinder, a liberal Protestant, in his influential *African Traditional Religion*, conferred seeming respectability on what had been superstition and animism but implied that all Africans thought alike, thus reviving an implicitly evolutionary assumption. African Christian intellectuals were much more aggressive in asserting parity between African religious thought and "world religions." E. Bolaji Idowu, in *Olódùmarè: God in Yoruba Belief* and *African Traditional Religion*, argued that Africans were monotheists with a thoroughly developed sense of God; John Mbiti followed with a pluralistic version allowing for diversity in African religions but insisting that all African religious practices were implicitly directed towards monotheistic High Gods. Both of these writers, however, drew their idea of "the spiritual" from German Lutheran theologians. Since then, many African scholars have joined in, enriching both the arguments and the ethnography, but always retaining, as Shaw says, "the general template of Judeo-Christian forms and evaluations."

To abandon the Judeo-Christian template and the post-Enlightenment identification of religion with "belief" deemed irrational is at least to begin a move beyond ethnocentric constructions, instead situating all people in landscapes of what is real to them. People expect life to be normal and events to be generally predictable within the parameters of such landscapes, so that they can make plans and muster resources to pursue them. Most such landscapes contain enough validity that predictions based on them in fact come true, or may be made to seem so, but people are also aware that irregular events, favorable or unfavorable, also occur, produced by forces that by definition must be occult, since if they were not hidden they would be included in calculations of the evident and normal. All people therefore try to explain, predict, and control such mysterious intrusions, constructing theoretical spaces in which these invisible forces are imagined as operating. In Central Africa, "the land of the dead" is such a space, as are, in the modern world, "the unconscious" and "the market," all of them assumed to be included in the real, though not open to inspection by the uninitiated. Social practice always has its ideological dimension, some elements of which may strike the nonparticipant as mere "belief." It is difficult to say exactly what anyone believes, and still more difficult to show that his or her actions are motivated by such belief. People are usually vague about beliefs in the abstract but agree on a repertoire of standard practices in which they know what parts they should play. Shifting the focus of inquiry away from the uncertain content of belief to practice, social relationships, and individual goals brings beliefs marginalized as religion into proximity with politics and economics and makes them central to real life and amenable to historiography. This understanding of religion as experience is not to take African religion away from theology and give it to rational-choice theory but rather to focus on the boundary between the known and the suspected, an operational distinction of great interest to actors and observers alike, and often a topic of controversy. What is knowledge to me, to you may be error, superstition, or paranoia; on the whole, knowledge is cumulative, but in particular instances what was fact can become folklore, or the reverse.

This approach in terms of universal human experiences opens the way to a genuinely comparative anthropology that would seriously—that is, without ironic quotation marks—employ the language of "religion" in Africa to explain ourselves. Senator McCarthy's pursuit of suspected communists was a witch hunt, psychoanalysis is a cult of affliction, and Wall Street market predictions are divination. A dispassionately comparative anthropology does not now exist, because the implicit mission of anthropology has always been to defend the modern world from the possibility that in many respects we might also be exotic, even "primitive." But how real is the army of subversive agents? Is psychoanalysis a science or a cult? How reliable can any prediction of the future be? Such questions have been extensively debated in the United States, but only in an intellectual space, defined as modern, from which "Africa" is excluded. In the United States, as in Africa, the search for occult causes of unanticipated events and ways to avoid or control them is an aspect of life experience in general; in Africa, as in other "nonmodern" places, the same sort of response to experience is marginalized by outsiders as "religion."

The forces that Africans attempt to control through what we call divination, cults of affliction, fetishes, or appeals to ancestors are invisible and real but not supernatural; they are misrepresented by promiscuous use of such exoticizing terms as "worship," "spirits," and "sacred." The "witches" against whose malevolence one may seek protection are not spiritual either; they are jealous relatives or neighbors who have obtained skills known only to them and who make use of them to better themselves at the expense of others. The Ghanaian philosopher Kwasi Wiredu writes that "belief in countless 'mystical,' 'spiritual,' and 'supernatural' entities has been attributed to the African race [but in fact] these categories do not exist in Akan thought, for example; they would seem not to exist in the thought of many other African peoples." African "spirits" are very much of this world, and addressed as such; the experienced reality is true even of the land of the dead in Central Africa, which Kongo people thought of as a real place on the surface of the earth to which one could go, although only experts knew the route. The dead are usually immediately present, especially at night; their immanence is not surprising since, in societies in which one's "family" includes unnumbered cousins, uncles, and aunts, one's social position and possibilities are defined in the first place collectively and genealogically rather than by individual education or profession. "Ancestor worship," one of the few aspects of African culture to which missionaries extended approval, is simply the extension to dead elders, invisible (except in dreams) but still very much present as shared memories, of the kinds of respect offered to them in life. Elders are formidable figures, to be addressed with appropriate obeisance; offering a calabash of beer to a deceased elder is no more religious than offering it to a living one, argues Michael Singleton, a Catholic missionary anthropologist.

Kwasi Wiredu rightly invites us to formulate modern thought in African languages. I have been trying to formulate African thought in modern language and so to wipe away the lingering exoticism of nineteenth-century anthropology; of the Victorian novels in which G. A. Henty, John Buchan, Edgar Rice Burroughs, H. Rider Haggard, Rudyard Kipling, and many more celebrated the triumphs of their "rationality" over the "primitivism" of others; and of innumerable recent movies in the same vein. As James Kenneth Stephen hopefully wrote in 1891, we can look forward to the day when "the Rudyards cease from Kipling and the Haggards ride no more." Nothing about this appreciation of multiple realities would prevent us from recognizing spirituality, mysticism, theology, logic, or irrationality where they occur, but it eliminates "religion" as the defining feature of "Africans" or "African culture."

WYATT MACGAFFEY

Bibliography

Idowu, E. B. *African Traditional Religion: A Definition.* Maryknoll, NY: Orbis, 1973.

———. *Olódùmarè: God in Yoruba Belief.* London: Longmans, 1962.

Landau, P. "'Religion' and Christian Conversion in African History: A New Model." *Journal of Religious History* 23, no. 1 (1999): 8–30.

Mbiti, John S. *Introduction to African Religion.* Portsmouth, NH: Heinemann, 1975.

Pietz, W. "The Problem of the Fetish, I." *Res* 9 (1995): 5–17.

Shaw, R. "The Invention of African Traditional Religion." *Religion* 20 (1990), 339–353.

Singleton, M. "Speaking to the Ancestors: Religion as Interlocutory Interaction." *Anthropos* 104 (2009): 311–332.

Wiredu, K. "Formulating Modern Thought in African Languages." In *The Surreptitious Speech*, edited by V. Y. Mudimbe, 301–32. Chicago: Chicago University Press, 1992.

Religions, African, in the Americas

The domain of the religious long served as a touchstone for the study of the cultural interrelations between Africa and the Americas. Since the pioneering research of Raimundo Nina Rodrigues (1862–1906) in Brazil, Fernando Ortiz (1881–1969) in Cuba, Jean Price-Mars (1876–1969) in Haiti, and the North American anthropologist Melville J. Herskovits (1895–1963) in Suriname, Haiti, and Trinidad, practices understood as "survivals" of African religious traditions in New World societies have been assigned crucial status in investigations of cultural continuities between Africa and the Americas. These founders of African Americanist scholarship perceived religious practices to be particularly resistant to change, and thus of heightened importance in determining what—thanks to their efforts—became known as the African cultural heritage in the Americas. Such a legacy is nowadays beyond dispute. Yet not only has the methodological basis for its assessment by comparison of (often historically and sociologically ill-contextualized) ethnographic data from both sides of the Atlantic become subject to sustained critique; rather the conceptual apparatus for describing "traits" as they appear to outside observers, which once allowed for the seemingly unproblematic recognition of "African" forms of "religion" in the Americas, has also been called into question.

Such doubts about understanding contemporary social phenomena in the Americas as transplanted "African religions" have also arisen because the term *religion* represents all but a self-evident, universally valid designator of unambiguously delimitable aspects of human experience, thought, and/or behavior. Instead, conceptions of religion, as they consolidated in modern secularist liberal thought, carry a heavy ideological burden. This is because the modern use of "religion" to demarcate an institutional realm based on faith and separate from the domain of "rational" action is informed by both post-Reformation Christian notions of faith and transcendence and normative Western secularist presuppositions concerning the role that "religious belief" ought to play in civic life. To characterize forms of thought and action in other, and earlier, Atlantic contexts as "religious" thus opens the door to anachronistic or ethnocentric distortions of worlds in which "religion" simply did not exist as a realm of experience presumably separable from mundane (let alone secular) rationalities.

Obviously, enslaved Africans carried into the Diaspora views of the world that included propositions about deities, ancestral spirits, and forces with which humans reckoned in ritually regulated ways. The enslaved unquestionably tried, and at times managed (to varying degrees), to draw upon such notions in shaping the institutions that came to integrate the new worlds they created for themselves in the Americas. But while there certainly were exceptions (such as the large number of captive Muslims from western Africa, or some of the captives from the Congo basin who may have been subject to prior Catholic missionization), the majority of Africans who reached the Americas during more than 350 years of slave trading can hardly be said to have been practicing a "religion" in the modern sense of a domain distinguishable from other spheres of life. Instead, it was only in the course of their enslavement that their masters came to objectify certain of their practices as magic, witchcraft, or insubordination based on misguided superstition—either in accordance with laws regulating slave behavior or (particularly in Catholic colonies) in the context of forced Christianization. Whatever traditions of ritual praxis emerged and consolidated among enslaved Africans and their descendants in the New World should be viewed as products of contexts in which alien and oppressive legal and ecclesiastical regimes sought to repress what they construed as dangerous signs of African agency and creativity.

Masters in the British West Indies thus construed Obeah within colonial laws designed to suppress forms of slave resistance they supposed to be "supernaturally inspired," well before the congeries of actual practices it came to circumscribe attained the sense of "assault sorcery" that the term tends now to carry in the region. Likewise, it is clear that the ritual complexes that Haitians, Cubans, or Brazilians had come to designate as Sevi Loa, Regla de Ocha, or Candomblé by the end of the nineteenth century were anything but mechanically transmitted "survivals" of once-coherent and continuing West African "religious traditions." Instead, what early ethnographers in the Americas came to describe as remnants of such imagined traditions were in fact products of struggles on the part of—sometimes identifiable—enslaved or free ritual experts and organic intellectuals to defend practices inherited (or sometimes invented) by them against persecution. That successes in building new communities in the Americas increasingly came to involve "legitimate religion" should not surprise us.

This process of redefining ritualized collective experiences as "religion" in the modern sense of a separate domain of "spirituality" is particularly evident in the case of the Jamaican Rastafari movement, which, from its inception in the 1930s, modeled itself on Christian templates, while violently rejecting locally dominant versions as the "religion of the oppressor." Here we find the explicit foregrounding of an ultimately modern, Western sense of "the religious" that practitioners of some of the historically older "African-derived" ritual complexes in, for example, Haiti, Cuba, or Brazil began to embrace only in the second half of the twentieth century.

What we face in the latter cases is not the degeneration of formerly coherent "African religions" into New World "cultism" or "magic" under the impact of slavery and Western modernity, as Roger Bastide (1898–1974) and others had once argued. Instead, they are ritual traditions that their adherents, by the middle of the twentieth century, had begun self-consciously to rationalize in light of the legitimacy and security the label "religion" afforded in the political cultures of modern nation-states. A striking illustration of the protection that practices deemed "religious" are granted under modern secular law can be seen in the 1993 U.S. Supreme Court victory of the Cuban-American obá oriaté (ritual specialist in Regla de Ocha) Ernesto Pichardo, which legalized animal sacrifice for his officially incorporated Church of the Lukumí Babalu Ayé. But similar processes also underlay Brazil's 1984 recognition of the Federação Nacional do Culto Afro-Brasileiro (National Federation of Afro-Brazilian Religion, an umbrella organization uniting different Afro-Brazilian cult houses), or the more recent acknowledgment of Obeah in Guyana and Shango in Trinidad as parts of the official cultural heritages of these modern nation-states. In all these cases, what started out as slave resistance and turned into crime or infringement of public order in the post-emancipation period has now attained legal protection as "religion," even national religion.

But the relativity of the idea of "religion" is not the only problem in a historical understanding of the phrase "African religions." In recent years the modifier *African* has also come under scrutiny. Scholars seem increasingly wary of applying this adjective to New World phenomena without qualifications (thus, "African-derived" or even "African-inspired"), aiming to forestall attribution of an inherent, essential character to people marginalized by what might be seen as racist logic. Once applied to human culture and sociality, *African* can hardly be said to enjoy the self-evidence of, for example, designations of geographical entities such as the Rift Valley or Mount Cameroon. Instead, it reveals itself as problematic when one considers the arbitrariness of geohistorical definitions (as when North African societies are considered part of the "Middle East"). Yet the fundamentally *historical*—and so both changing and contestable—nature of *African* becomes obvious in conditions when it might meaningfully apply to, for example, Afrikaners (and their Dutch Calvinist religion) in South Africa or to American Episcopalians who broke away from the Anglican Church in protest over the ordination of gay priests and aligned themselves with African primates who condemn the practice, and who tend to extol Africa's mission in the renewal of Christianity in the West.

The question whether a version of Christianity espoused by African theologians can be regarded as an "African religion" merely inverts questions that have long plagued Christian missionaries and Islamic clerics concerned with the indigenization in Africa of the notionally universal religions of outsiders: Where to set a limit on local adaptations, beyond which their results would have to be branded as "too African" (syncretically localized) and therefore unacceptably heterodox? If the "Africanness" of religious praxis and belief is an issue germane *in* Africa, then attribution of "Africanness" to phenomena *outside* the continent is even more problematic. Who, for one, ought to be granted the authority to decide what is or is not "African" about practices or conceptions observable in the Americas? What might be the criteria for such judgments? On what grounds might they be ratified or contested? Today we know that Herskovits's famous "scale of intensity of New World Africanisms" did not merely rest on ahistorical and essentialist presuppositions: it also betrayed what David Scott has

called an epistemologically dubious and politically problematic "verificationist" agenda that left "such questions as whether or not or to what extent [contemporary African American cultures] are authentically African" to anthropologists and other observing outsiders (Scott, 108). Contemporary scholarship that continues to rely on the comparison of descriptive data from both sides of the Atlantic has become far more sensitive to historical context in Africa and the Americas. Yet it still can be argued that such attribution sidesteps a number of issues of self-definition that, if anything, have gained—rather than lost—poignancy in the early twenty-first century.

Forms of religious identification that emphasize origins as "African" can no longer be seen as standing in an unmediated relationship to specific historical antecedents on the continent—to wit the already mentioned Rastafari movement, which is Jamaican and not Ethiopian, or Kwanzaa celebrations, which claim vaguely East African inspirations and now are enshrined as a national holiday in the United States. Both were born not from any historical transatlantic cultural transfer but rather from fundamentally modern American visions of Africa. But these are merely particularly obvious examples along a spectrum of ways in which adherents of New World ritual traditions have variously imagined and projected their practices into "African pasts." Thus while some practitioners of Cuban Regla de Ocha have since the 1930s actively sought ethnographic ratification of the "Yoruba-origins" of their traditions, members of the Cuban male esoteric sodality *abakuá* have, at least until recently, expressed little interest in patently similar associations in the Bight of Biafra. In Brazil, a transatlantic mobile elite of entrepreneurial Candomblé priests exerted a formative influence on the emergence of what in Nigeria eventually became known as "Yoruba religion"—thus giving the descendants in the Diaspora a hand in the "making," as J. Lorand Matory puts it, of its own "African baseline." Finally, as Paul C. Johnson has demonstrated for the Garifuna communities living on the Caribbean coast of Honduras, what he calls the "diasporic horizons" of New World religious practices can shift over time. Thus Honduran Garifuna emigrants to the United States who came under the influence of the North American Yoruba Movement have begun to relocate the focus of their ancestor cult from the site of the Garifunas' eighteenth-century historical ethno-genesis in St. Vincent to not just Africa in general but Yorubaland in particular.

Current research on transatlantic flows of people and information has unsettled a scholarly imagination that defined "Africanity" as resulting from transmissions of African religious traditions across the Atlantic to the Americas through the slave trade, and their subsequent transformation under slavery in the context of Christianity and Western modernity. This picture of mechanical movement of abstracted "cultures" is now in patent need of revision—especially since web-based resources have placed forms of "religious Africanity" at the disposal of pretty much anyone, anywhere, who cares to deploy them in acts of self-fashioning. Afro-Cuban cult houses, Candomblé *terreiros*, Rastafari yards, and Vodou temples are now no longer restricted to their sites of origin in Cuba, Brazil, Jamaica, and Haiti but have been documented not only across the Americas but in Europe and Asia as well, where they have increasingly merged with local New Age sensibilities. Jacob Olupona and Terry Rey thus speak of forms of "Yoruba-derived orisha-worship" as an incipient world religion.

While this claim of potential universalism may be rash (given the lack of central authority among the adherents of the many local traditions lumped under the label), the irony could not be more obvious. We may have come full circle: from persecution of the ways in which Africans aimed to forge new communities under the conditions of their New World enslavement, to initial recognition of African cultural transfers to the New World, to their incorporation into local and national cultural projects, and now to increasing globalization as part and parcel of contemporary migratory processes and through the web-based spread of forms of *spirituality* marked as *African*—whatever these terms might be taken to mean.

STEPHAN PALMIÉ

Bibliography

Herskovits, Melville J. *The Myth of the Negro Past*. New York: Harpers, 1941.

Johnson, Paul C. *Diaspora Conversion: Black Carib Religion and the Recovery of Africa*. Berkeley: University of California Press, 2007.

Matory, J. Lorand. *Black Atlantic Religion*. Princeton, NJ: Princeton University Press, 2005.

Mintz, Sidney W., and Richard Price. *The Birth of African American Culture: An Anthropological Approach*. Boston, MA: Beacon, 1992.

Olupona, Jacob K., and Terry Rey. "Introduction." In *Òrìṣà Devotion as World Religion: The Globalization of Yorùbá Religious Culture*, edited by Jacob K. Olupona and Terry Rey, 3–28. Madison: University of Wisconsin Press, 2008.

Palmié, Stephan, ed. *Africas of the Americas: Beyond the Search for Origins in the Study of Afro-Atlantic Religions*. Leiden: Brill, 2008.

Paton, Diana, and Maarit Forde, eds. *Obeah and Other Powers: The Politics of Caribbean Religion and Healing*. Durham, NC: Duke University Press, 2012.

Price, Richard, and Sally Price. *The Root of Roots: Or, How Afro-American Anthropology Got Its Start*. Chicago: Prickly Paradigm, 2003.

Scott, David. *Refashioning Futures: Criticism after Postcoloniality*. Princeton, NJ: Princeton University Press, 1999.

Representative Government

See Government, Representative

Revolts, Slave

Many layers and forms of revolt punctuated the history of Atlantic slavery. Resistance ran the gamut from daily refusal of the arbitrary terms of the slaves' relationships to particular masters to outright and violent resistance against the system as such. In the life of any particular enslaved person, or any community of the enslaved, these differing forms often coexisted with or followed one another. The challenge in understanding the more spectacular revolts that form the focus of this essay is to look at them historically, as specific events embedded in this larger context. That context was not just the economic and social condition of slavery itself but also the broader history of the political philosophy and vision of the enslaved, for whom open revolt was a way of expressing projects for alternative futures that the enslaved nurtured over time.

Seeing revolts as calculated strategies, of course, runs counter to established narratives of violence as fundamental and inevitable in the context of the oppression of slavery. Yet, ironically, this ennobling reading also has the risk of rendering the enslaved themselves as flat, indeed mute, almost automata within a history controlled by others, their oppressors. If resistance is everywhere, then in a sense it is also nowhere as a considered historical plan, and certainly it becomes difficult to write a history of revolt as a contingency that changed over time and was situated in, and defined by, particular contexts. Alternatively, interpreting slave revolts, as some scholars have also done, mainly in relationship to structural circumstances of varying sorts—food crises, decreases in troop deployments, particularly harsh treatment by a particularly brutal master—is also limiting in its determinism. While it is certainly useful to think through the ways in which the enslaved interpreted and took advantage of opportunities as they imagined, planned, and occasionally carried out revolts, the key is to avoid a mechanical linkage of cause and effect. Instead, this essay foregrounds a dynamic and grounded interpretation of particular events of revolt.

Slave revolts are as old as slavery itself: whether in Rome, in Islamic palaces, in West and Central Africa, or in the Atlantic World, many stories of revolt are told. But slave societies in the Americas also generated distinct occasions for and forms of revolt. The racialization of Atlantic slavery could create solidarities that shaped revolts around ideological and social patterns created among the enslaved, and between them and communities of free people who suffered continuing marginalization based on color they were seen to share with the enslaved. Probably more important, however, was that the enslaved were majorities in several New World populations, notably in Haiti and Jamaica, and also in other regions. The enslaved sometimes composed nine-tenths of these populations—an overwhelming proportion far above their numbers in any prior slave society. Black majorities generated levels of paranoia approaching panic among their masters, and brutal public discipline and torture became consistent features of American plantation societies, which only strengthened motivations for the enslaved to retaliate with violence.

Historians chronicled slave revolts. In the eighteenth century, the various editions of the Abbé Raynal's frequently banned but widely read *Histoire philosophique et politique des Deux Indes* (1770) included discussions of the Jamaican maroons and other slave resisters. It went so far as to include a famous and rousing passage (cribbed largely from Louis Sebastien's work of utopian imagining, *The Year 2440*) evoking the inevitable and necessary coming of a "Black Spartacus" who would lead the enslaved into a thoroughly bloody and apocalyptic revolt and be lionized for his daring. The figure of the slave rebel was already frightening and enthralling theatergoers in London and Paris, and fascinating readers of literature. By the time the Haitian independence struggle began in 1791, a set of narratives about slave rebels was already current in European society. The French general Etienne Laveaux, in charge of the army sent to quell the islandwide revolt, hailed Toussaint L'Ouverture, general of the rebel forces, as the predicted "Black Spartacus" himself. Some claimed that the former slave turned rebel leader, then turned general had been inspired by reading Raynal.

The interplay between imagined representation and experienced reality continues even now to shape the possible stories about slave revolts. These are, perhaps justifiably, usually tragic, and in two different forms. In one—the narrative that dominates in the United States—slave rebels conspire, and occasionally begin to act, but are always defeated either by traitors within or by the overwhelming force of their masters' power. This makes reasonably good sense when applied to Gabriel's planned uprising in Richmond in 1800 and Nat Turner's famous (and still much debated) conspiracy in Southside Virginia in 1831. Yet the history of slavery in the United States in fact includes two significant episodes of slave revolt that can be counted as successes. In the Stono Rebellion (1739, in South Carolina) a group of slaves escaped to freedom in Spanish Florida. More broadly, the history of the Civil War, stretching from John Brown's attack on the arsenal at Harper's Ferry (Virginia) in 1859, which helped trigger the conflict, to the broad and active participation of the enslaved in shaping its course and terms, was a triumph.

Elsewhere in the Americas slave rebels are often depicted as heroic precursors to emancipation, as prophets who suffered for being ahead of their time. The maroon communities in Jamaica, Suriname, and Brazil offer something more, as their rebellions created communities that continue to this day, enclaves of quasi autonomy within the boundaries of governments against which they often struggle, sometimes violently. Rebel leaders in the British Caribbean, from Tacky in Jamaica (1760) to Bussa in Barbados (1816), also serve among the heirs to slavery as reminders of a constant struggle to maintain dignity and fight for freedom. In the French Caribbean, slave rebels of various epochs have been monumentalized, including Solitude, an evanescent figure in a revolt in Guadeloupe in 1802 who became the subject of a novel and now boasts a monument in Pointe-à-Pitre. The contemporary musical group Akiyo, whose parades of hundreds of members are a powerful part of carnival in Guadeloupe, sing an anthem that declares, "It's not Victor Schoelcher [the French abolitionist] who liberated us / It's the Maroons who liberated us." In Patrick Chamoiseau's epic novel *Texaco*, the slave rebel takes the shape of the mysterious figure of the Mentoh, who lives on the plantation but always refuses slavery and ultimately inspires revolt.

Haiti, as the sole independent country created by slave revolt, has profoundly shaped the ways in which the story of rebellion is imagined and told. The story of the nation's birth is also often told as a tragedy, of the promise of revolution devolving into two centuries of war, tyranny, and poverty. But that telling reflects a history of ideological pressure and limited imagination. Haiti's story starts with a slave revolt but continues through successive stages, first forming a powerful new political and military movement, then securing local abolition that was ratified and expanded into French empire-wide emancipation, then successfully defending that emancipation when the French government threatened it. A former field slave, Jean-Jacques Dessalines (1768–1806), who some scholars now believe was African-born, became the founder of a nation and its first emperor. He was one among many who, in the course of just a few years, rose from their obscure circumstances and harsh reality to transform the Atlantic World politically and economically. One of them, Jean-Baptiste Belley, born in Africa and manumitted before the revolution, ended as a representative from Saint-Domingue in the revolutionary French National Convention, where he became the subject of a striking portrait

by Anne-Louis Girodet that remains one of the most powerful visual meditations on the possibility of revolt and social and personal transformation ever created.

Haiti's political success, the foundational tale of revolt of the enslaved, is also often folded into a larger tragedy about the limits, indeed impossibility, of contemplating violent social transformation. As Michel-Rolph Trouillot argued in his book *Silencing the Past* (1996), many found and others still find the reality of the Haitian Revolution—the fact that the enslaved carried out a revolution predicated on intellectual, political, and social transformation of a kind rarely seen in history—simply unthinkable, impossible to square with narratives of progress and history built on the order and profitability of slavery. The hostile reaction to the Haitian Revolution by powerful nations and empires around Haiti limited the revolt's impact and, combined with fissures and conflicts over the meanings of freedom within Haitian society, led to ongoing political conflict and social division. The Martinican poet and political leader Aimé Césaire (1913–2008) in a play about Henri Christophe (1767–1820), who at one point in the Haitian Revolution declared himself "king," made the story of this man a tragedy, seeing irony in the ways in which former slaves could become corrupt and tyrannical oppressors of their own people. But such accounts of human frailty tend to obscure the story of Haitians who, following their slave revolt, in fact produced a quite viable and solid economic and social system in the nineteenth century, securing themselves a degree of autonomy and a quality of life significantly better than that of people of African descent anywhere else in the Americas. The initial fulfillment of the promise of revolt Haitians themselves sometimes forget, though the figure of Dessalines—the ultimate slave rebel—serves as a constant source of pride, as well as a reminder of all that has been betrayed and all that still needs to be accomplished in Haiti and beyond.

Historians in these societies have long debated, and will certainly continue to try to discern, precisely what slave revolts contributed to the history of the Atlantic. Did they set the stage for abolition and emancipation, or did they sometimes also delay freedom? Did they improve the lot of the slaves or instead lead only to harsher repression? Though the answers vary in particular cases, no history of the Atlantic can be written without giving serious attention to the revolts of the enslaved.

LAURENT DUBOIS

Bibliography

Aptheker, Herbert. *American Negro Slave Revolts*. New York and London: Columbia University Press and P. S. King & Staples, Ltd, 1943.

Bilby, Kenneth M. *True-Born Maroons*. Gainesville: University Press of Florida, 2005.

Césaire, Aimé. *The Tragedy of the Roi Christophe*. Translated by Ralph Manheim. New York: Grove, 1970.

Chamoiseau, Patrick. *Texaco*. Translated by Rose-Myriam Réjouis and Val Vinokurov. New York: Pantheon, 1997.

Dubois, Laurent. *Avengers of the New World*. Cambridge, MA: Harvard University Press, 2004.

———. *Haiti: The Aftershocks of History*. New York: Metropolitan Books, 2012.

Sidbury, James. *Ploughshares into Swords: Race, Rebellion, and Identity in Gabriel's Virginia, 1730–1810*. New York: Cambridge University Press, 1997.

Trouillot, Michel-Rolph. *Silencing the Past: Power and the Production of History*. Boston, MA: Beacon, 1996.

Viotti da Costa, Emília. *Crowns of Glory, Tears of Blood: The Demerara Slave Rebellion of 1823*. New York: Oxford University Press, 1994.

Revolutions, National: France

In July of 1789, the newly constituted French National Assembly gave the Marquis de Lafayette, best known as a hero of the War of American Independence, a task for which he seemed eminently suited. That task was to draft a type of document very much in vogue in the northern Atlantic World of the late eighteenth century: a "declaration of rights." Following a century of international rumination about the nature of selves and justice, as well as a growing association of the legitimate exercise of power with written texts, the delegates to this new representative body quickly became convinced of the need for such a statement as a prerequisite for all future political action. And for both practi-

cal guidance and symbolic effect, they not only looked to earlier North American examples, such as the preambles to the state constitutions of the 1770s and 1780s. They also entrusted the most celebrated French veteran of British America's struggle against colonial rule with jump-starting the process—a project for which Lafayette very publically sought the counsel of Thomas Jefferson, then living in Paris as ambassador of the new United States.

From the start, the lawyers, merchants, and liberal nobles and clerics who led the way in 1789 saw their project as nation building. Their aim was to transform French subjects, long accustomed to thinking themselves members of corporate bodies organized roughly along feudal lines, into legally equal citizens who would collectively reimagine themselves as an indivisible, sovereign nation. But the delegates to the National Assembly also made it clear that they envisioned this turn from absolutist to constitutional rule as a global event. That expansive ambition meant insisting that the principles they were articulating were equally valid for all peoples. Moreover, it meant reminding authorities everywhere that history—as recent events in North America had already made clear—was on the National Assembly's side. In the mythology of the leaders of 1789, the chief ideas associated with the Declaration of the Rights of Man and the Citizen, not to mention their chief exponents, were destined to repeatedly traverse the vast waters of the Atlantic Ocean.

Ironically, though, the main causal link between the late eighteenth-century political upheavals on the western and eastern shores of the North Atlantic was not initially ideological. It was economic. We cannot forget that by 1789, the hexagonally shaped area of Europe called France was itself the commercial and administrative hub of a large network of trade and military outposts. The French monarchy competed with other imperial states clustered around the Atlantic Basin, foremost among them Great Britain, over control of territory and resources in the Americas and over an extensive transoceanic trade in people and other commodities, including food, cloth, even printed texts such as "declarations," whose circulation formed the centerpiece of what we now consider the transatlantic Enlightenment. When, in 1778, French troops came to the aid of British North American settlers in their revolt against the growing financial demands of the British crown, the rationale on the part of Louis XVI (r. 1774–1793) was power directed toward profit: advancing French trade at the expense of the British. For the French in the last decades of the eighteenth century, the Americas were a space of political imagination. But even more, they were a space of economic opportunity.

Accordingly, for France, the key impact of the "patriot" victory in the War of American Independence was financial. The only surprise, perhaps, is just how little the French state benefited from the 1783 Treaty of Paris that ended Britain's efforts to hold onto its North American territories. What the monarchy seated at Versailles had won was an enormous war debt that it had no means to pay down. The rising costs of maintaining a powerful court, with its expanding military, commercial, technological, and, increasingly, imperial ambitions, had become a pressing issue among Europe's maritime monarchies. Parallel intensifying competition in eighteenth-century Africa suggests a pan-Atlantic phenomenon. In the case of the French crown, extensive international borrowing to finance its role in, first, the Seven Years' War and then the War of American Independence—coupled with the limited legal ability of either Louis XV (r. 1715–1774) or Louis XVI to draw any significant revenue out of the privileged classes in France—created a fiscal crisis in the 1770s and 1780s. It was this fiscal disaster, specifically the bankrupting of the royal treasury once it became impossible to borrow further, that triggered the process that led to the creation of the National Assembly and, ultimately, the composition of the Declaration of the Rights of Man and the Citizen in the summer of 1789. This foundational text articulating the principles of a new sociopolitical order cannot be disassociated from a variety of long-term geopolitical and economic processes taking place across the Atlantic World over the previous century, including the expansion of the state's domain, the growth of claims to overseas territories as sources of commercial profit, and new connections among remote regions that would trigger a series of multicontinental wars and the growing conundrum (as Great Britain's George III discovered first in the 1760s) of how to pay for them.

Indeed, as the summer of 1789 wore on, the notion of a close conceptual kinship between the earlier North American demand for "liberty" and recent events in France began to fray, the victim of distinctive on-the-ground anxieties in the two very different Atlantic locations. Already by early August, some deputies to the National Assembly had started to insist that profound divergences in culture, religion, political formation, and the social order itself made North America—still widely imagined as something close to a natural state, albeit one that had inscribed natural rights in constitutionalism—a very poor example for the tradition-laden French. The version of the Declaration of the Rights of Man and the Citizen finally adopted in a moment of rushed compromise moved farther from U.S. precedents than had Lafayette's first, American-inspired draft; the French took significantly different positions both on the sources of rights (nature versus the social contract) and on the role of the state in guaranteeing those rights. But those who looked to the English parliamentary system for models to imitate found themselves equally frustrated—and increasingly branded as reactionaries. The particular course by which the French Revolution unfolded starting in the fall of 1789 was largely the result of specific national and at times even local factors: the failures of the monarchy in its previous reform efforts; centuries of fraught church-state relations as well as recent internecine struggles within the Catholic Church; the endurance of French nobles' claims to various ancient privileges; the divergent economic as well as political ambitions of different sectors of the Third Estate (as ordinary citizens were traditionally known); the flourishing of radical ideas in an extensive black market for print; the rise of new affective and gender norms that rendered the past "decadent" by comparison; a recent history of popular protest, much of it focused on economic exploitation; and the situation of Paris, with its concentration of economic, political, and intellectual power, at the very center. The Anglo-American Tom Paine's lack of any real political success in a culture that he never seemed to grasp despite his desire to be a vehicle of international revolution is emblematic of this divide. His great political tract *Common Sense* (1776) was, like many key American revolutionary texts, republished in 1789 in French—but with the unanticipated consequence that the very idea of the people's "common sense" would shortly thereafter become associated primarily with counterrevolutionary reaction.

What, then, of the so-called Reign of Terror that characterized the Year II (as 1793–1794 was known according to the new revolutionary calendar)? How can the radical turn of the French Revolution be illuminated by an Atlantic perspective? In a second irony, only with the declaration of war on Austria in April 1792, followed by the advent of what is generally taken to be the most distinctive phase of the French Revolution—the creation of a kingless republic followed by an emergency government that temporarily made terror "the order of the day"—did the Atlantic context once again become crucial. But this intrusion of transoceanic events occurred largely by accident rather than by design. For just as the French were hoping to export their emancipatory creed of "wars of peoples against kings" to the east, unanticipated developments in Saint-Domingue, the single most profitable of all eighteenth-century New World possessions, drew the French into a new battle on the western side of the Atlantic.

Questions about the rights of white colonial subjects and the rights of free people of color surfaced almost immediately in the Caribbean and then in France, responses to competing demands for representation in the new National Assembly as well as the liberal rhetoric of the moment. Determining the nature of the people who could claim to be citizens and the geographic spaces in which citizenship could be exercised proved contentious from the start of the French Revolution. But the emergence of the question of the future of slavery—a backburner issue before 1792 for all but a small handful of "enlightened" elites—was to send the revolution in new directions both militarily and conceptually. For at the same moment as the French army was attempting to export novel notions of liberty, citizenship, and nationhood through conquest and expansion within Europe, the issue of slave labor (as a matter of both individual property rights and the "rights of man") started to create new political cleavages both within metropolitan France and in its Atlantic colonies. Eventually, the confrontation with the institution of chattel slavery would also revolutionize the French Revolution, extending the meanings of all three key revolutionary terms—liberty, citizenship, and nationhood—in ways feared both by self-proclaimed American "revolutionaries" and by most of their counterparts in France.

News of a massive revolt of enslaved men and women in part of Saint-Domingue, itself precipitated partially by local instabilities brought on by turbulence in the metropole, made its way back to Paris in late October 1791. There, loss of revenues from the disruption of sugar production had the immediate effect of worsening France's continuing domestic economic crisis. For many French revolutionary leaders, the obvious answer was to call on the army to intervene on behalf of Caribbean planters and to restore stability, coupled with notions of the sanctity of private property; investments tied to Saint-Domingue were a significant source of income for many deputies to the various revolutionary assemblies. But as popular pressure for more comprehensive forms of "equality" as well as "liberty" grew within France, and as the outlawing of skin color as a barrier to citizenship finally dissolved any natural explanation for the enslaved condition of people of African descent (as many in France had warned it would), the argument for the French Revolution requiring an end to chattel slavery gained ground in radical circles. By winter 1792, crowds enraged about the high price of sugar attacked shops in Paris, succeeding—as so often in this revolutionary moment—in melding cries of economic distress with ideology. Soon the French military would find itself fighting on the side of liberation (or so revolutionary leaders repeatedly claimed) within and against most of continental Europe. It would also, in the Caribbean, find itself battling, sequentially, in defense of slave owners and then in partnership with former slaves, as the Spanish and British monarchies, seizing an opportunity, also intervened militarily in this international power struggle. Moreover, once refugees from the violence in Saint-Domingue began arriving in North America, this conflict exacerbated tensions between France and the United States, turning France's erstwhile partner in revolution into a potential political rival.

This is not the place to retell the story of the Haitian independence movement or of the waves of circum-Atlantic emigration triggered by the European and Caribbean wars of revolutionary France. For France, the most significant consequence of these events on the other side of the Atlantic was that they eventually forced the hand of the Jacobin-led Convention in a radical new direction. At the height of the Terror, some rights (i.e., divorce, social welfare, suffrage) were expanded—to the horror of many American *and* British observers—far beyond the boundaries of the War of American Independence. Other rights (i.e., freedom of press and association, due process) were curtailed in a reversal of the principles of both 1776 and 1789. In this emergency context, France became, in 1794, the first colonial power in Europe to abolish slavery formally in all its overseas possessions. It also became the first such state to grant full political rights to people of African descent, whether or not formerly enslaved. Jean-Baptiste Belley, an ex-slave, ceremoniously became the inaugural black deputy to be seated in a European legislative body. Despite the fact that the Convention had been forced into this ruling by circumstances at the imperial periphery and by "men" of the very kind that the authors of the Declaration of Rights had attempted to ignore, the First Republic was able to proclaim the end of "aristocracy of the skin" alongside "aristocracy of birth" as one of the great victories of the French Revolution, an achievement that marked a profound difference in terms of inclusiveness from the American struggle for independence eleven years earlier.

Soon thereafter, of course, Napoleon Bonaparte would reverse many of the gains as well as horrors of the most radical phase of the French Revolution. In France's New World colonies, though not in Saint-Domingue (renamed Haiti in 1804 to mark its independence from France), Napoleon restored the institution of slavery. But with the 1803 sale of Louisiana, which, from his perspective, the loss of Saint-Domingue had made dispensable, Napoleon gave up on his ambitions for a French empire in North America and turned his ambitions eastward to imagine an imperial republic extending across continental Europe all the way to Russia. It was left to Jefferson—the only man to have had a hand in crafting both the American Declaration of Independence and the French Declaration of the Rights of Man and the Citizen—to extend the push of Atlantic commerce and conquest to the west.

We should not, however, disregard the role of ideas derived from the French Revolution in shaping the post-revolutionary Atlantic World. The French Revolution left its intellectual mark in two distinct ways. In yet another irony, a transatlantic discourse emerged before the revolution was even over that stressed the value of hierarchy, organic growth, and especially, local tradition and culture—in contrast to the egalitarian and universalizing language of the Declaration of the Rights of Man and the Citizen. This counterrevolutionary ideology, a self-conscious defense of the old order, became the basis of modern conservative thought in Europe and the Americas alike. But the French Revolution, in combination with the Haitian wars and the North American struggle for independence, would also produce a symbolic repertory that remained ripe for use well into the nineteenth century not just in furthering liberal colonialism but also in inspiring slave insurrections, independence movements, and other forms of political protest directed *against* established powers. The history of subsequent movements for political autonomy often looks, paradoxically, like a history of demands for nationhood free from European political dominance but framed according to a set of concepts and emblems derived from the French Revolution. This is, perhaps, the legacy of a series of tensions—between citizenship bounded by the nation and notions of universal rights, between internal nation-state building and expansionism abroad, between liberty of property and liberty of persons, and between equality before the law and equality of means—that were part of this extraordinary upheaval from the start.

The story of the French Revolution has not always been told in this paradoxical, transatlantic vein. For most of the time since the 1790s, the French Revolution has had to be distinguished from the War of American Independence precisely because they anchored two different myths of national origins. Their singularities were understood to stem, in both cases, from particular, local circumstances—a tradition of self-governance in New England, for example, or the genius of the philosophes in France. Moreover, these two examples of eighteenth-century Atlantic revolution came to have very different values for later political theorists and actors. Over the 200 years that followed 1789, leftists of all kinds, in France and around the globe, touted the French Revolution as the very model of revolutionary progress. In Marx's telling, the events of 1789–1794 constituted an essential step towards the realization of true equality and a promise of a better world to come. The American story, by contrast, was not traditionally accorded a similarly global stature. But to this day, conservative thinkers have been equally eager to acknowledge the difference between an ostensibly mild-mannered, liberty-infused revolt that produced the United States and the bloody social upheaval and experiment in extreme egalitarianism orchestrated by the French. In this version, the Americans alone (literally) kept their head. Even in the twentieth century, insurgents in all parts of the world have often felt compelled to make a choice—to opt either for an American-style template in efforts to achieve independence (despite the fact that the North American revolt left most of the British Empire, including the imperial center, intact) or for the more radical style of change ostensibly favored by the French (which also failed to stem a colonizing impulse).

However, in very recent years, we have become collectively enamored of the idea of a wave of closely related eighteenth- and early nineteenth-century uprisings stretching across the Atlantic from Amsterdam to Cap Français to Lima. This quest for connections is driven perhaps by our desire to find the roots of the contemporary economic phenomenon known as "globalization," perhaps by our disenchantment with both nationalism and universal socialism as political models, or perhaps simply by an eagerness to overcome long-standing assumptions about what Sanjay Subrahmanyam and David Armitage call the "primacy of Europe as the matrix of revolution." In this new narrative, Paris has been retrofitted as but one (albeit important) node in a bigger network—much as it was in the 1950s and early 1960s for R. R. Palmer and Jacques Godechot, who first bucked the trend against national distinctiveness and reinvigorated Tom Paine's old idea of an "age of revolutions" in which influences flowed in multiple directions around the Atlantic World.

Yet the story of the Age of Atlantic Revolutions is currently being narrated in ways that break rather substantially with this mid-twentieth-century, celebratory scholarship, too. It is not only a question of expanding geography, of adding in the Caribbean, Central and South America, and western Africa. Where Palmer and Godechot emphasized democracy—that is, the spreading challenge, in theory and in practice, to monarchical and aristocratic rule—the story line is now more likely to emphasize the violent expansionism of nation-states and their elites in competition over resources

on the one hand, and the internal divisions of race, ethnicity, religion, and other forms of identity and difference on the other. Ideas, including those embedded in political discourse, have started to become superstructural once again. Local phenomena that do not easily fit a transnational Atlantic paradigm—people who did not move, for example—run the risk of being obscured. The challenge for the next wave of historians will thus be twofold: first, to integrate the transoceanic with the national and even local dimensions of the French Revolution and, second, to make clear the links between these complex, large-scale developments and the precise ideas articulated in the Declaration of the Rights of Man and the Citizen and other key revolutionary texts.

SOPHIA ROSENFELD

Bibliography

Albertone, Manuela, and Antonino de Francesco, eds. *Rethinking the Atlantic World: Europe and America in the Age of Democratic Revolutions.* Basingstoke, UK: Palgrave Macmillan, 2009.

Armitage, David, and Sanjay Subrahmanyam, eds. *The Age of Revolutions in Global Context, c. 1760–1840.* Basingstoke, UK: Palgrave Macmillan, 2010.

Cheney, Paul. *Revolutionary Commerce: Globalization and the French Monarchy.* Cambridge, MA: Harvard University Press, 2010.

Desan, Suzanne, Lynn Hunt, and William Nelson, eds. *The French Revolution in Global Perspective.* Ithaca, NY: Cornell University Press, 2013.

Gaspar, David, and David Geggus, eds. *A Turbulent Time: The French Revolution and the Greater Caribbean.* Bloomington: Indiana University Press, 2003.

Godechot, Jacques. *France and the Atlantic Revolution of the Eighteenth Century, 1770–1799.* Translated by Herbert H. Rowen. New York: Free Press, 1965 [1963].

Jourdan, Annie. *La Révolution, une exception française?* Paris: Flammarion, 2004.

Kaiser, Thomas, and Dale Van Kley, eds. *From Deficit to Deluge: The Origins of the French Revolution.* Stanford, CA: Stanford University Press, 2010.

Klaits, Joseph, and Michael H. Haltzel, eds. *The Global Ramifications of the French Revolution.* Cambridge: Cambridge University Press, 1994.

Klooster, Wim. *Revolutions in the Atlantic World: A Com-

parative History. New York: New York University Press, 2009.

Popkin, Jeremy. *You Are All Free: The Haitian Revolution and the Abolition of Slavery*. Cambridge: Cambridge University Press, 2010.

Rosenfeld, Sophia. *Common Sense: A Political History*. Cambridge, MA: Harvard University Press, 2011.

Van Kley, Dale, ed. *The French Idea of Freedom: The Old Regime and the Declaration of Rights of 1789*. Stanford, CA: Stanford University Press, 1994.

River Systems

The extensive river systems that emptied into the Atlantic provided access far into the interiors of the continents surrounding the sea. Along the largest rivers, and thriving off the fish and wildlife resources of riverine wetlands, were some of the most densely populated societies to appear before modern times. Rivers provided Europeans with access to human and material resources, thus encouraging agricultural development and the production of commodities for trade with the Atlantic World.

In considering the relationship between the Atlantic Ocean and the river systems of the four continents that border it, Europe is exceptional. Of the world's fifteen largest river systems, six empty directly into the Atlantic Ocean, none of them European. (A seventh, the Nile, flows into the Atlantic by way of the Mediterranean Sea.) Together, these systems drain most of North America, South America, and Africa—all continents that tilt toward the Atlantic Ocean. In contrast, no large river systems in Europe empty into the Atlantic; indeed, the Eurasian continent tilts away from the Atlantic and toward the Arctic, Indian, and Pacific oceans. Thus, in the formative years of European expansion, only the nations that bordered the Atlantic had easy access to it, but they found vast river systems offering gateways leading far into the interiors of the other three Atlantic continents. In some cases, Europeans took control of river systems and used them as ties to bind their claims to territory. In other cases, indigenous populations remained firmly in control of river systems and kept Europeans dependent on them for access to upriver human and material resources. Thus rivers were arteries of access to territory and trade around

the Atlantic, the avenues along which moved commodities and people—furs, agricultural products, minerals, explorers, settlers, armies, slaves—and European nations contested with one another and with Native peoples for access to and control over them.

The European governments most active in the Atlantic World—Spain, Portugal, France, the Netherlands, and Great Britain—all bordered the ocean. While they established important port cities, including Rotterdam, London, Nantes, Lisbon, and Seville, on rivers that offered safe mooring for oceangoing vessels, those rivers provided limited access—none, in the case of the Thames—to the interior of Europe. The Rhine, at 800 miles the longest in western Europe, rises in the Swiss Alps and gathers water from 65,000 square miles in parts of Austria, Liechtenstein, eastern France, western Germany, and the Netherlands before emptying into the North Sea. The Elbe, which has its headwaters in the present-day Czech Republic, although it flows most of its way through Germany, is smaller than the Rhine and until the nineteenth century was contained entirely within the Holy Roman Empire. The Tagus, which begins in Spain and ends in Portugal, drains only half as much area as the Rhine. The other primary European rivers with mouths on the Atlantic—the Loire and Seine in France, the Thames in England, the Guadalquivir in Spain—are smaller still and have been contained within single political domains since before the time of Columbus.

In contrast, the rivers of the Americas and Africa reach thousands of miles into their relatively flat continents, much farther than the rivers of Europe. The Amazon of South America drains an area more than forty times greater than the watershed of the Rhine. The systems of the Mississippi of North America and the Congo of Africa also flow from regions many times larger than any of the river systems of western Europe. If the Atlantic region is taken to include the rivers that feed the ocean, then the geographical parameters of Atlantic history reach across North America to the Rocky Mountains, west into South America to the Andean highlands within a few hundred miles of the Pacific Coast, and eastward across Africa into the western part of Tanzania, whose coastline faces the Indian Ocean. In contrast, only the extreme western edge of the Eurasian continent, the area north of Italy and west of Poland, lies within the geophysical limits of Atlantic history.

Initially, the river mouths of Africa and the Americas offered European sailors fresh water and safe harbors from storms as they charted coastlines unfamiliar to them. The Portuguese worked their way south around Africa through a chain of settlements starting at the mouth of the Senegal, the first stream of any sort south of the Sahara Desert. They established their gold-buying station of Elmina on the River Benya and by 1482 contacted political authorities in Kongo through Mpinda, at the Congo's mouth. They established their military and trading post of Luanda in 1575 on the first open bay north of the sand-barred mouth of the Kwanza and used that river as the axis of their slave-raiding and trading in western Central Africa.

Coastal explorers interpreted large flows of fresh water as beckoning signs of large landmasses. Columbus correctly understood that the fresh water at the mouth of the Orinoco indicated that he had encountered not another island but a large continent. Alonso Álvarez de Pineda drew a similar conclusion about a river mouth he encountered in 1519 as he charted the northern rim of the Gulf of Mexico, although historians still debate whether he found the Mississippi or the Mobile. Spanish and other European mariners spent years testing every promisingly large stream for a water passage through the continents that they could never quite believe blocked the sea route to Asia that Columbus had sought. The dream of finding a water route through the continent—shared by Jacques Cartier on the St. Lawrence and Henry Hudson on the river that now bears his name—persisted for centuries and in part inspired the late eighteenth-century expeditions of Peter Pond and Alexander MacKenzie on the Saskatchewan, which flowed from the western watershed of Hudson Bay, and of Lewis and Clark on the Missouri River in 1804–1806.

Europeans often found heavily populated territories as they ventured into these rivers. Many of the river systems of the Americas and Africa were home to large, sometimes powerful political systems, including the Mississippian and Plaquemine chiefdoms of the lower Mississippi Valley, the hierarchical and well-populated Marajoara and Omagua societies of the Amazon Valley, the Kongo and its provinces along the Congo, and the Mali and Songhai "empires" of the middle and upper basins of the Niger. The representatives of these powerful military and political networks challenged European intruders. For example, in 1541–1542 the Plaquemine villages ruled by a chief the Spanish called Quigualtam chased the survivors of Hernando de Soto's army out of the Mississippi River Valley. (Soto himself died before he could confront Quigualtam directly.) When Réne-Robert Cavalier, Sieur de la Salle claimed the Mississippi Valley for France nearly a century and a half later, the French had to contend with the Natchez chiefdom on the banks of the river in what is now Mississippi. In 1729, the Natchez rose up in war against the French and very nearly wiped them out. Although the French ultimately prevailed, the government in Paris scaled back its plans for and investments in the Mississippi River Valley and looked instead to the vast region of the Great Lakes, accessible through the St. Lawrence, and to island holdings in the Antilles. Similarly, the Omagua, Machiparo, and other Native Americans contested the Portuguese presence in the Amazon River Valley.

The politically integrated populations of Africa, protected by the geography of the continent, which blocked every accessible river with rapids at only short distances inland, provided even greater obstacles to European intrusion. In 1483, Diogo Cão (or Cam) sailed a short way up the Congo and encountered representatives of the Kongo polity, but it was another three centuries before Europeans ventured past the great falls that dammed the stream below Malebo Pool, which became the commercial hub of the vast interior network of streams. Portuguese mariners arrived at the delta of the Niger in the 1470s but could not penetrate its maze of marshes.

The inaccessibility of African river systems restricted Europeans to the continent's Atlantic coastline, further encouraging them to venture up the rivers of the American continents instead. Native American opposition, often initially quite fierce, weakened when populations there succumbed to the Old World diseases that the Europeans carried. The river systems, because they were avenues of human movement and interaction, became vectors of these deadly diseases. A good example of the speed with which diseases could travel along river systems comes from the accounts of Hernando de Soto's arrival at the upper Wateree and Catawba rivers of South Carolina; he found many largely deserted

Cofitachequi villages that had suffered an unidentified plague, probably malaria, conveyed upriver by Native traders who had encountered Europeans on the Atlantic coast. In 1535, people in the small village of Stadacona (today, Quebec City) on the St. Lawrence began to die in the presence of French visitors, probably from diseases the French carried. The village of Stadacona—as well as the village of Hochelaga, its upriver neighbor (today, Montreal)—was entirely gone within 68 years. By the start of the sixteenth century, European diseases had reached the Ojibwa bands of the Lake Superior region, where no European had yet set foot. Within a century of European arrival in the Americas disease had greatly reduced the substantial populations of the Mississippi and Amazon valleys, as well as the populations of the Paraná and Río de la Plata region, who had numbered perhaps 1.5 million when the Spanish first encountered them.

The riverine environments in the tropical Americas and Africa provided suitable habitats for protozoa and insect vectors of other diseases to which Europeans were vulnerable, malaria and yellow fever foremost among them. Malaria, which may have originated in West Africa and which was endemic to floodplain environments in much of Africa and Asia (and southern Europe) at the time of Columbus, was quickly transferred to the Americas. American river systems from the St. Lawrence to the Paraná were home to indigenous species of mosquitoes that, like their Old World cousins, proved to be superb carriers of the deadly disease, and malaria plagued populations along the lower James River region of Virginia, along the Edisto, Altamaha, and other slow-moving rivers of South Carolina and Georgia, and in the lower Mississippi Valley. Europeans in both North and South America worsened the problem of malaria as they cleared wetlands to construct fields, simultaneously expanding mosquito breeding habitats and destroying habitats for birds and amphibious reptiles that fed on the insects.

Europeans brought no new diseases to the populations of Africa, with the possible exception of syphilis and yaws, but the rivers descending to the Atlantic from the African interior channeled European ideas and goods. The Portuguese, working through scattered missionaries supported through settlements in the vicinity of the Congo, succeeded in converting many communities in the region to Roman Catholicism in the sixteenth century. Many of the Central Africans who were forced across the Atlantic as slaves were already familiar with European materials, languages, culture, and religion. It is probable that the first enslaved Africans brought in 1619 to the English settlement of Jamestown, on the James River, came from this region in Africa and that their familiarity with Europeans and their ways enabled them to blend into the early English community in Virginia, although subsequent generations of English systematically excluded their more numerous successors.

Few other African river systems were vectors of European culture, but many were conveyors of the captives taken off into the slave trade. From the Senegal in western Africa to the Kwanza south of the mouth of the Congo, enslaved peoples, most of them captives of war, were passed down rivers, through networks of trade and military alliances, to Europeans waiting on the coast. Significant numbers of the people shipped out of Africa originated from the inland upper Niger Valley, from where they were passed down the Senegal and Gambia or carried overland to bays and inlets to the south. The Congo became a major artery of the slave trade in the early nineteenth century. Europeans contested access to the mouths of these streams. In Upper Guinea, the British and French settled for a division of access to the slave-yielding interior via the Senegal and Gambia, respectively. The mouth of the Congo in Central Africa divided the Portuguese-controlled coasts to the south from Dutch, British, and French slavers approaching the area from the north, and after 1811 the lower river became a haven from Brazilian, Spanish, and other evaders of British efforts to suppress Atlantic slaving.

In the American continents, river systems defined the boundaries of European territorial ambitions. The French pushed into the Great Lakes region via the St. Lawrence, and from there continued down the Mississippi to the Gulf of Mexico. With New Orleans at one end of a chain of settlements and Quebec at the other, a relatively small number of French held a vast portion of inland North America connected by this extensive network of natural waterways. Meanwhile, the English on the Atlantic seaboard found no comparable river system and so remained hemmed in along the coast. There they settled at the mouths of the available rivers, some quite minor: Boston on the Charles,

New York (originally the Dutch colony of New Amsterdam) on the Hudson, Philadelphia on the Delaware, Jamestown on the James, Charles Town (Charleston) on the Ashley and Cooper. They then moved inland as far as the fall lines, the points at which waterfalls or rapids blocked navigation from the coast. Fall-line settlements such as Lowell in Massachusetts, Georgetown on the Potomac, Richmond in Virginia, and Augusta in Georgia became important warehousing and milling centers and eventually sites of early industrialization, as well as of the eventual national capital.

It was not until completion of the Erie Canal along the Mohawk, a tributary of the Hudson, in 1825 that a North American Atlantic port city finally gained riverine access to the interior of the continent. This artificial waterway linked the Atlantic port of New York with the Great Lakes and eventually with the Ohio Valley. Lack of access to the continental interior had forced New York merchants in the eighteenth century, like their counterparts in other British colonial ports, to develop a thriving Atlantic commerce. This positioned them to take maximum advantage of the sudden access to the interior provided by the canal. New York City quickly grew to become the cultural and commercial center of North America, rivaling London in the Atlantic World, and bringing the vast forests and plains north and west of Chicago into the watershed of the Atlantic. The Welland Canal, which bypassed Niagara Falls between Lake Erie and the St. Lawrence River, completed the integration of the Great Lakes region into the maritime commerce of the Atlantic when it opened in 1830.

Both these water routes tapped the vast plains that the Louisiana Purchase had in 1803 brought into the territorial United States. The U.S. government had used the larger western tributaries of the Mississippi system to assess the economic potential of the region. The Missouri expedition led by Lewis and Clark is the best known, but there were others. In 1806 Zebulon Pike led a party up the Osage, Arkansas, and Platte, eventually reaching the high plains of what is now Colorado. In the same year Thomas Freeman and Peter Custis undertook a more strictly scientific exploration of the Red River into what is now northern Texas. The primary purposes of these expeditions were to extend U.S. authority and commerce into the Far West. Explorers noted potential agricultural and mineral resources and identified potential trading partners from among the many Native Americans resident along these rivers. While the hoped-for resources were indeed up the rivers, at their headwaters in the Rocky Mountains and in the fertile grasslands that bordered them, conducting commerce by water ultimately proved impractical. The streams became too shallow for deep-draft commercial vessels not far upriver from their mouths on the Mississippi. Most westward travelers journeyed by water to western Missouri and from there ventured overland along trails that often followed the broad valleys of shallow rivers. Not until the second half of the nineteenth century, after the construction of several transcontinental railroads, was the eastern water network linked to the Pacific Coast. Chicago, flourishing at the western end of the Great Lakes–Erie Canal waterway, emerged by 1880 as the nation's central railroad hub.

The commodity trades of the Americas moved down river systems to the Atlantic. The St. Lawrence was the primary avenue of the French fur trade until the British succeeded in redirecting much of it north to their posts on Hudson Bay. The Mississippi was, for a period, an important secondary route for the fur trade, as well as the source of deerskins that French traders tapped. But it was the spread of cotton plantations up the Mississippi in the early nineteenth century that turned the river into a thriving commercial channel. Trade in agricultural commodities had begun along the Mississippi River in the late eighteenth century, when French landowners successfully planted rice, indigo, and sugar. Anglo-Americans who moved into the region during the early years of American independence added tobacco to the mix. By the early nineteenth century, however, it was clear that cotton was destined to be king in the Mississippi Valley. The Ohio, a tributary, was also used to transport tens of thousands of slaves from the eastern seaboard into the emerging Cotton Kingdom of the Deep South. By 1850 these trades, facilitated by the numerous steamboats that by that time worked the river, had transformed New Orleans from a struggling outpost of the Spanish and French into the fifth-largest seaport in North America.

The Amazon proved much more difficult to turn to European advantage than did the Mississippi. The Spaniard Vicente Yáñez Pinzón encountered it in 1500. In 1541–1542, the same year that Hernando de Soto arrived at the Mississippi River, Francisco de Orellana navigated from east of Quito in present-day Ecuador down the Amazon to the Atlantic. The first ascent of the river was made by Pedro Teixeira for the Portuguese in 1637–1647. Settlement and development of the vast tropical forests the Amazon drained came much more slowly. Several large chiefdoms in its valley and on the island of Marajú at its mouth blocked European intrusion. As late as the 1830s, the Native peoples of the forests were organizing rebellions against the authorities of Pará, the Brazilian state at the mouth of the river. Not until the 1850s did steamboats begin to ply the river, by which time about 300,000 people lived in the entire Amazon Basin (175,000 whites, 25,000 slaves, and 100,000 Native people). The economy of Pará, as in the Mississippi Valley, was based on slaves cultivating agricultural staples, including sugar, cotton, and rice, as well as coffee, for export across the Atlantic.

Some rivers provided access to valuable mineral resources in the mountains. To the geographically naive first explorers, who were in many ways operating as prospectors, rivers meant mountains, and mountains offered the prospect of gold and silver. In Senegambia the Portuguese and others tapped the centuries-old gold trade from the upper Niger region across the Sahara Desert, but elsewhere Europeans' dreams of cities of gold were illusory, particularly where the streams drained vast, agriculturally rich, and populous plains, as in North America. The Portuguese attempted to occupy Angola militarily in pursuit of "mountains of silver," which were in fact the rocky western faces of the plateaus visible above the lower Kwanza, glistening in the setting sun after afternoon rains. La Salle hoped that western tributaries of the Mississippi would provide French access to the silver mines of Spanish New Mexico; he was wrong.

The Spaniards and Portuguese in South America had better luck. The Paraná and São Francisco systems in Brazil provided back-door access to the gold mines of Minas Gerais, otherwise monopolized by nearby Rio de Janeiro and the port of Santos, for slavers in São Salvador (Bahia) in the north and through the Río de la Plata in the south. The name of this large marine estuary, the "river of silver," designated its primary value to Europeans throughout the Atlantic Era, as it offered another riverine back door for Atlantic traders hoping to intrude on the Spanish networks carrying the silver of Potosí, high in the Bolivian Andes, circuitously north through Lima, the Pacific, and the Isthmus of Panama to Cartagena on the Caribbean coast of South America (and the Spanish viceroyalty of New Granada).

Ultimately, the river systems at the hearts of these colonial economies in the Americas delineated the outlines of the nation-states that emerged from them by the early nineteenth century. A portion of the St. Lawrence system, including the Great Lakes, became the boundary between Canada and the United States, much as it had separated the French and British colonial territories, and the Iroquois and Huron confederacies and their allies before then. In 1763, at the end of the Seven Years' War, the western border between the North American seaboard territories of Great Britain and the interior territories of Spain was drawn along the Mississippi. In the decades following, and as the colonies won independence and formed republics, the boundary steadily hopped from river valley to river valley in the Southwest, to the Sabine, to the Nueces, and finally to the Rio Grande (Rio Bravo). In South America, new nations formed to encompass river systems. The Portuguese pushed their claims from the Brazilian coast up the Amazon and its headwaters into Andean territories that the Spanish claimed in Peru and Colombia. Border treaties were regularly contested into the twentieth century, when Brazil, Peru, and Bolivia all competed for rubber-tree forests in the upper Amazon. The border, however, strayed little from the eighteenth-century line drawn along the Javary and the Guaporé, both tributaries of the Amazon. Today, most of the Amazon system is contained within Brazil. In the early nineteenth century, the Orinoco system defined the Atlantic half of the short-lived republic of Gran Colombia. Today, the system falls for the most part within Venezuela, although its upper length forms the international border with Colombia. Borders firmed up only much later did not follow the contours of river systems so neatly, as is the case for the Paraná and Uruguay river area, and for the states of the Congo and Niger river regions in Africa.

CHRISTOPHER MORRIS

Bibliography

Aron, Stephen. *American Confluence: The Missouri Frontier from Borderland to Border State.* Bloomington: Indiana University Press, 2006.

Eltis, David. *The Rise of African Slavery in the Americas.* Cambridge: Cambridge University Press, 2000.

Ethridge, Robbie, and Charles Hudson, eds. *The Transformation of the Southeastern Indians, 1540–1760.* Jackson: University Press of Mississippi, 2002.

Ganson, Barbara. *The Guaraní under Spanish Rule in the Río de la Plata.* Stanford, CA: Stanford University Press, 2005.

Johnson, Walter. *River of Dark Dreams: Slavery and Empire in the Cotton Kingdom.* Cambridge, MA: Harvard University Press, 2013.

Morris, Christopher. *The Big Muddy: An Environmental History of the Mississippi and Its Peoples from Hernando de Soto to Hurricane Katrina.* New York: Oxford University Press, 2012.

Salomon, Frank, and Stuart B. Schwartz, eds. *The Cambridge History of the Native Peoples of the Americas, Volume 3, South America.* Cambridge: Cambridge University Press, 1999.

Sheriff, Carol. *The Artificial River: The Erie Canal and the Paradox of Progress, 1817–1862.* New York: Hill and Wang, 1996.

Trigger, Bruce G., and Wilcomb E. Washburn, eds. *The Cambridge History of the Native Peoples of the Americas, Volume 1, North America.* Cambridge: Cambridge University Press, 1996.

Yalcindag, Erhan, et al. "Multiple Independent Introductions of *Plasmodium falciparum* in South America." *Proceedings of the National Academy of Sciences* 109 (2012): 511–516.

Science

See Natural History; Navigation and Nautical Sciences.

Seven Years' War

Europeans and their descendants in the Americas engaged in and endured war—with one another, with indigenous Americans, and with enslaved Africans and their descendants—on a regular basis. Expansion of territory, competition for resources and influence, prestige, and the retention of political control all motivated these armed conflicts in both hemispheres. Turmoil could also erupt when dynastic and diplomatic relations broke down in Europe, and the European powers with Atlantic empires—Spain, Portugal, the Dutch Republic, France, and Britain—increasingly drew their American colonies into these conflicts in the metropoles. Before the eighteenth century, an implicit agreement between the European monarchies ensured that these rivalries would be contained and could not be used to justify war in Europe. The Seven Years' War, known in North America as the French and Indian War, ruptured this principle of "no peace beyond the line." This most transformative event of the eighteenth-century Atlantic World started in the Americas and spilled back into Europe.

The roots of the war lay in unresolved tensions from prior Atlantic conflicts dating back to the end of the War of the Spanish Succession (1701–1713). Disputes over Britain's lucrative monopoly contract (*asiento*) to supply enslaved Africans to Spanish America (the War of Jenkins' Ear/*Guerra del Asiento*) were subsumed into the War of the Austrian Succession (1744–1748). This conflict spanned the Atlantic, where Anglo-American colonists designated their experience of the violence as "King George's War," after the monarch they saw as having disrupted their peace. While the 1748 Treaty of Aix-la-Chapelle resolved continental European disputes, it failed to end their territorial, commercial, and naval rivalries in the Atlantic, and nurtured lingering grievances that soon bore fruit as the Seven Years' War.

The conflict exploded first in the Ohio River Valley, as Shawnee, Delaware, Mingos, Britain, and France competed over the region. In 1754 the agents of the two European powers, accompanied by Native peoples, engaged in a battle at Fort Necessity, in the great meadows in western Pennsylvania south of the Monongahela River. George Washington, then a colonel in the Virginia militia, lost and signed terms of capitulation offered by Louis Coulon de Villiers that acknowledged both France's right to the Ohio Country and Washington's complicity in the earlier murder of a French envoy, Joseph Coulon de Jumonville (who happened to be Villiers's brother). This outcome sparked an international scandal and pushed Europeans and Americans into preparations for another war, which for the first time shifted large metropolitan armies from other military theaters into the Americas.

The British defeat at Fort Necessity attested to the influence that American Indians wielded in instigating the Seven Years' War and then in prosecuting the conflict. Jumonville's alleged death at Washington's hands sparked the European propaganda campaigns that led to war, but it is most likely that the killer was a Mingo named Tanaghrisson. Wary of both French and British pretensions to Native-claimed territory, Tanaghrisson hoped that igniting tensions between the two European intruders in the borderlands would favor indigenous interests. The mobilization of European troops that started in 1755 and continued for years achieved the Mingos' goal to a certain degree, at least in the short run. The upheaval put Indians in a position to manipulate Europeans in North America and in the Caribbean to their own advantage, and many different Native nations played critical roles in aiding (or frustrating) the ambitions of the overextended European forces. Most importantly, Indians fought for their own sovereignty and to limit European ambitions in American lands.

The Anglo-American name for the Seven Years' War, the "French and Indian War," is a misnomer that obfuscates the complexity of Native participation, but it at least acknowledges the importance of the indigenous presence. Equally critical, but less recognized, were the contributions to the conflict of enslaved and free people of color. For example, the military support provided by individuals of African descent played a crucial role during the successful 1762 British siege of Havana, in the war's Caribbean theater. The war also provided enslaved people with opportunities to obtain freedom as a reward for loyal service to European armies, in either defensive or offensive campaigns. In times of imperial war, slaveholders' fears of arming the subjugated became a lesser consideration than mobilizing every able-bodied man to defend valuable sugar plantations, strategically important citadels, and civilian populations. Free and enslaved people of color, and Indians, moved around the Atlantic as well during interimperial war, serving on naval vessels (like Olaudah Equiano, a freed slave and later prominent autobiographer and abolitionist in Britain), with invading forces (like the Stockbridge Indians from Massachusetts with British forces attacking Martinique), or as fugitives, fleeing from territory claimed by one contender to liberation in that of another.

References to the conflict as the Seven Years' War are also misleading temporally, focusing exclusively on 1756 to 1763, Continental Europe's official dates for this conflict. For the French in Canada, the conflict lasted from 1744 to 1760 and was remembered as *La Guerre de la Conquête*, the War of Conquest, reflecting the resulting cession of New France to Britain. The name "French and Indian War" (1754–1763) and the "war of independence" waged by Algonquian-speaking peoples of the Great Lakes and Ohio Valley (1763–1765) might imply separate events, but they are not, thus making the midcentury conflict in North America over a decade in duration. The Spanish Atlantic remained relatively insulated from the violence until 1761, when France's Louis XV successfully pressed his Bourbon cousin Charles III, on the throne in Spain, to enter the war. Spain's two-year intervention was disastrous, as it quickly led to humiliating losses, not only of Havana but also of Manila, in the Philippines, to Britain.

The least-studied theater of the war was on the coasts of Atlantic Africa, where historians barely note the gains and losses among the European slave-buying posts there. While western and central Africans watched the ravages of the transatlantic slave trade grow steadily throughout the 1700s, the limited conflicts of the Seven Years' War along these coasts not only spared most Africans from this war's violence but also provided new opportunities for coastal polities. British and French struggles over Gorée and Île Saint-Louis, just off Cape Verde in

Senegambia, allowed West African political authorities, cities, and individual commercial suppliers to negotiate the terms of trade for the enslaved individuals, gum Arabic, hides, and gold they sold.

The greater effect of the war in Africa was its disruption of the thriving Atlantic trade in captives for the American territories that were the focus of the conflict. The majority of the engagements in the Seven Years' War raged in the northern Atlantic, and Brazil evaded outright conflict thanks to Portuguese neutrality and the Braganza dynasty's close alliance with Britain. But this greatest consumer of African lives in the Atlantic, and the sugar islands of the Caribbean, watched the war's naval disputes diminish the volume and reliability of slaving voyages and thus threaten plantation and mining productivity. In a southern Atlantic context, disruptions of maritime trade revealed Brazil's, and especially Spanish America's, high degree of dependency on third-party suppliers. This recognition in turn inspired both Iberian monarchies to new interests in Africa. Almost 300 years after the Treaty of Tordesillas (1494) had granted the eastern Atlantic to Portugal and the western shores to Spain, in the 1760s and 1770s Spain sought for the first time to secure continuous access to human labor by establishing its own slave-trading posts off the West African coast. Portugal, under the dynamic first minister the Marquis de Pombal (Sebastião José de Carvalho e Melo, 1750–1777), chartered two Lisbon-based commercial companies to develop its captaincies in northeastern Brazil and to bring the Brazil-based slaving business in Angola similarly under control from Lisbon.

At the Treaty of Paris, which ended the conflict in 1763, European diplomats thoroughly redrew the lines of European authority in the Atlantic. France, with a ruined navy and large swaths of its overseas territories lost to Britain, abandoned its claims in South Asia and North America. Versailles formally ceded New France (Canada) to Britain in order to regain the sugar-rich Caribbean islands of Guadeloupe and Martinique and the slave-buying posts in Senegambia that supplied labor to them. The terms of the treaty also protected France's lucrative North Atlantic fisheries, but the looming war debt and the sting of defeat fueled the demands of the French public for explanations and scapegoats. From 1761 to 1766, the *Affaire du Canada* and the *Affaire Lally-Tollendal* put the colonial administrators who had surrendered French imperial claims to Britain in Canada and India on trial for corruption. The convicted Canadians suffered fines and exiles; the Comte de Lally, commander of the losing French army in India, paid for his failure with his life. While the war proved a national setback, France still managed to deny Britain its Louisiana colony in North America, secretly transferring the territory to Spain in 1762. As early as 1763, the French government began undertaking new imperial schemes in Guyana, in the Îles Malouines (Falklands), and in Gorée and Angola in Africa, Madagascar and Réunion in the Indian Ocean, and Tahiti in the Pacific.

In Paris, Spain regained Havana and Manila but lost Florida to Britain. Its devastating Atlantic losses in the war further extended the sweeping Bourbon Reforms (after 1778), designed in Madrid to reinvigorate the commerce of the Spanish territories in the Americas and to exert metropolitan influence in the Atlantic regions that had become a growing focus of European warfare. Contradictorily, the reforms were also meant to pare down the rising, and unbearable, expenses of maintaining claims to vast American lands under the conditions of escalating military conflict on Atlantic scales. The rhetoric of returning Spain to the glory of its seventeenth-century dominance of the Atlantic took no account of how high British militarization had raised the bar for warfare on an oceanic, incipiently global scale.

In the Northern Hemisphere of the Atlantic World, the Treaty of Paris appeared to cement British dominance, by leaving London with territories that stretched from the Gulf of St. Lawrence to the Gulf of Mexico. But jubilation there and in British North America dissipated within months of the conclusion of the peace. Sovereign Native nations inhabited most of "New France," but their presence and perspectives had received no consideration at the Paris peace talks. Irate Native peoples throughout the North American interior rejected the ambitious attempts of the new British authorities in Canada and the thirteen colonies to subjugate them and continued their wars against both Britons and Anglo-Americans, maintaining an uneasy armed stalemate until 1815.

The unprecedented costs of prolonged pan-Atlantic, even global, warfare seriously depleted the financial resources of the European monarchies.

Britain reversed its anemic military fortunes of 1755–1758 only after prime minister William Pitt the Elder enacted a program of unlimited spending for the British military and dispatched thousands of redcoats to North America, Europe, the Caribbean, Africa, and India. Government debt grew precipitously as a result. Even after the Treaty of Paris, alliances with, or wars against, American Indians incurred exorbitant expenditures. Parliament's attempts to pay down these debts and make Britain's subjects in North America bear the cost of their own military occupation, through such acts as the Stamp Tax (1765), induced the breakdown between the colonists and the metropole and ultimately spurred the American war for political independence.

The Seven Years' War also stretched the royal treasuries in France and Spain to their breaking points. Both monarchies needed to reassert control over their military costs in the Atlantic and began exploring fiscally conservative policies, like Spain's Bourbon Reforms, which ultimately proved no less self-defeating than Britain's attempted taxation of North Americans. France, despite the immense wealth generated by sugar production in Saint-Domingue and the French Antilles, could not escape the crushing debt of the Seven Years' War and also cast about for new sources of revenue. The finances of the *ancien régime* at Versailles never recovered and, when coupled with France's support of the North American rebellions against Britain 20 years later, contributed to the grievances that destroyed the Bourbon monarchy after 1789.

The regional conflicts gathered under the umbrella term *Seven Years' War* reshaped the Atlantic World from the 1750s forward. Though local experiences varied tremendously in Africa, throughout the Americas, and at sea, the resources that the European authorities invested in the war afforded thousands of individuals in militaries and other services previously unimaginable opportunities to experience the physical and intellectual diversity of empire. Men and women traveled in the service of, or as a result of, imperial ambitions among locations throughout the Atlantic; Olaudah Equiano, for example, grew up in Africa and visited Barbados, the Miskito Coast of Central America, North America, Quebec, the Arctic, and London. Civilian populations saw the Atlantic war infiltrate their homes directly. Individuals in Lisbon, New York, Gorée, London, or Montreal heard of the sieges of Fort William Henry in North America, and of Havana in Cuba. Public and government imaginations magnified Atlantic triumphs more than any others in this global war through images like the *Scenographia Americana* (1768) that introduced Britons to their new American possessions. Ironically, just as the Seven Years' War promoted new and more coherent imperial ambitions in Europe, the crushing cost of the military competition in the Atlantic led directly to the loss of the territories in the Americas that dynasties in Europe had fought it to retain.

CHRISTIAN AYNE CROUCH

Bibliography

Anderson, Fred. *Crucible of War: The Seven Years' War and the Fate of Empire in British North America, 1754–1766*. New York: Vintage, 2000.

Calloway, Colin. *The Scratch of a Pen: 1763 and the Transformation of North America*. Oxford: Oxford University Press, 2006.

Furstenberg, François. "The Significance of the Trans-Appalachian Frontier in Atlantic History, c. 1754–1815." *American Historical Review* 113, no. 3 (2008): 647–677.

Pares, Richard. *War and Trade in the West Indies, 1739–1763*. Oxford: Clarendon, 1936.

Slavery, U.S.

Slave labor in the United States underwrote national prosperity, contributed to the Industrial Revolution in Britain, and was part of the development of a capitalist world-system. Yet U.S. slavery differed from slaveries in other areas of the Atlantic World for several key reasons, including the national prohibition on slave importation beginning in 1808 and the growth of a large, African-descended enslaved population through reproduction.

Colonial British North America was a collection of settler societies at the margins of a booming Atlantic complex, and enslavers used bound laborers to produce commodities marketed through an imperial framework. Following independence, slavery in North America grew in the twin contexts of capitalist development and expansion of the republic's continental empire. By the mid-nineteenth century, the United States contained the largest number of enslaved people in any country in the Americas. That expansion caused a constitutional crisis that resulted in civil war ending chattel slavery in 1865.

English colonization of the eastern seaboard of North America was part of its geostrategic competition with European continental powers, including Iberian and French monarchies and the Dutch Republic. But Native Americans controlled the terms of trade and settlement. English colonists gained a foothold on the continent in the seventeenth century, demanded captives from the Indian populations, and bound them as laborers. European traders' demands for captives initially overlapped with those of indigenous slaving networks, mainly for women and children. As Europeans introduced more trade goods and settlers and then aggressively defended settlements, northeastern Indians intensified wars to take captives in order to repopulate, take revenge, and ensure political viability. The southeastern mainland became a shatter zone, and Indian polities reformed as defensive confederations.

Where bound labor on the colonial eastern seaboard was marginal, the people enslaved secured limited but significant privileges. In 1625 the Dutch West India Company established a trading fort at the southern tip of Manhattan Island. By the time England conquered New Netherland in 1664, the settlement was the site of the largest population of enslaved people of African descent in North America. Most farmed or performed craft or domestic work.

African-descended slaves held in seventeenth-century English North America tended to be polyglot and not unfamiliar with the broader Atlantic contexts of bondage to Europeans, yet visible African descent became a marker of exclusion. By the late seventeenth century, colonial legislatures made permanent slave status inherited through the maternal line and forbade marriages with Euroamericans. However, most bound laborers in the Chesapeake throughout the seventeenth century were English. South Carolina was a net exporter of captives before the Yamasee War (1715–1717). Following it, planters cultivating rice demanded African

captives, who soon made up a majority of the population.

The eastern seaboard became the marginal northern rim of the Caribbean commodity-production complex in the eighteenth century, importing captive Africans to cultivate tobacco and rice, the poorer cousins of the sugar grown on the islands. As Virginia and South Carolina planters demanded more bound laborers from Africa, violence against bondspersons intensified, and plantations grew larger and more numerous. As in the Caribbean, financing plantations brought slaveholders into the dependency of debt to merchant-creditors in the British Isles. Planters used their property in human beings as collateral for loans as well as to cultivate the staple crops they sold to cover what they owed. Slave children became increasingly important to North American slavery because they sustained the population of enslaved people without incurring further debt to suppliers. Slave women's labor took on the dual significance of agricultural production and childbirth. Slave populations began to reproduce in Virginia in the 1720s and in South Carolina by midcentury. Growing families among the enslaved convinced Virginia planters to buy more females, mostly from the Bight of Biafra; there were heavily male sex ratios in every other branch of the Atlantic slave trade.

As the Chesapeake and Carolina Lowcountry became more and more reliant on enslaved laborers, slavery attenuated in the Middle Atlantic colonies and in New England. It was also marginal in the upland southern interior. French plans to colonize the lower Mississippi Valley early in the eighteenth century faltered, and Louisiana instead became a minor provisioning ground for the sugar islands of the Caribbean. Enslaved people performed a variety of work and demanded such privileges as *coartación*, a limited continuing form of bondage while a slave worked to buy manumission in installments, especially after Louisiana reverted to Spain following the Seven Years' War (1756–1763).

The War of American Independence elaborated a language of political freedom that was partly the result of the British colonies' history of racial slavery: civil liberties for Euroamericans were conditioned by, if not premised on, bondage for residents of African descent. The War of American Independence (1775–1783) disrupted trade with the West Indies and Britain, resulting in the decline of tobacco cultivation in Virginia. Several of the independent states in the Middle Atlantic and New England passed abolition measures. The eventual federal republic embedded these contrasting economic contexts in the Northern and Southern states at the core of a single legal system. The republican framework of the Federal Constitution protected the property interests of slaveholders, with slaves becoming arguably the major class of assets in North America.

Political independence from Britain did not relieve Americans of economic dependence. Southern prosperity remained based on British markets and capital. British manufacturers demanded cotton, which grew well in the southern interior. Planters in the Lower South competed with counterparts in northeastern Brazil. British commercial paper traveled west across the Atlantic and circulated through commercial hubs such as New York to finance slave-grown products in the states. A transatlantic chain of credit connected Northern commercial interests with Southern planters, and textile manufacturers in New England prospered on slave-grown cotton. Sterling bills of exchange returned to England to pay for British manufactured goods. Technological refinements such as the cotton gin created efficiencies after about 1800 that boosted productivity, but slaveholders had to pay high proportions of their costs up front to buy their labor forces, which required significant initial investments, financed ultimately by foreign bankers and secured by human capital, and pushed planters to the edge of their borrowing capacity. The enslaved laborers paid the costs by working under relentless drivers with minimal housing or provisions, other than what they could create for themselves after long days in the sun.

The War of 1812 (1812–1815) disrupted trade with Britain, but when it resumed, cotton production expanded, and Americans surged westward into the river valleys of the interior South, overwhelming and extirpating the Indians living there. Because the United States banned importation of captives after 1808, the slaveholders building the Lower South in following decades migrated there with slaves or bought bondspeople from Chesapeake and Carolina sellers, who owned slaves in greater numbers than stagnant agricultural sectors could profitably employ. Between 1790 and 1860 the ensuing forced migration carried over a million African-descended, American-born slaves across state lines.

Waves of resettlement swept from tidewater to piedmont, piedmont to interior south, and interior south to trans-Mississippi West, tearing generation from generation in enslaved families, as the political union through which they were moved grew westward according to the designs of slaveholders sending commodities across the Atlantic to cosmopolitan markets. The Chesapeake and Carolina Lowcountry, the one place in the Americas where the enslaved population reproduced in abundance, was also the place where they were prevented from maintaining family ties and with continuity. The Atlantic seaboard saw intergenerational theft, as slave traders separated young workers from their families. Re-isolation on frontier plantations rendered many of them dependent on slaveholders' contexts and connections rather than able to rely on intergenerational support and cultural continuity.

As the early federal republic expanded into a continental empire, the extensions of slavery at its core exacerbated the regional divisions at the heart of the Constitution. Citizens in nonslaveholding areas opposed slaveholders' arrogation of power yet accepted political concessions, such as the Missouri Compromise of 1820, that gave slaveholding interests a preponderance of power at the federal level. By the 1840s, aggressive territorial expansion beyond the Mississippi raised these tensions to the threshold of disunion. Political divisions over slavery in the trans-Mississippi West in the 1850s culminated in political realignment along sectional lines. In 1860–1861, the states of the Lower South dissolved their ties with the Union and formed a separate Confederacy. The geopolitics of slavery under the Constitution dissolved into the Civil War (1861–1865), and by 1863 the Lincoln administration extended its military strategies to disable the Confederacy by offering emancipation to its slaves. Despite the minor nuance of compensated emancipation in the District of Columbia, slavery was ended by force of arms and, finally, by constitutional amendment in the newly re-United States. Emancipation extinguished the nation's second most valuable form of property, after land itself.

In the broader Atlantic context, slavery in the United States grew from a minor appendage of the

British West Indian economy into a vital component of the national economy and of industrial development in Britain. The labor and reproductive energies of African-descended families were key to the development of the political economy of the South. The U.S. political context, a constituted republic, led to a uniquely formal legal and public definition of slavery, one that identified servitude with African descent, limited citizenship to those of identified European ancestry, and obscured the complex historical development of the institution in North America.

By the mid-nineteenth century, pro- and antislavery writers had invented a shared narrative of U.S. slavery as dramas of masters and slaves set on plantation tableaux, the main difference being that proslavery apologists viewed the arrangement as organic and benign, while opponents claimed that slavery violated the fundamental rights of African-descended people. Abolitionists defined slavery as an artificial institution capable of legal termination, with the emancipated capable of taking their deserved places in a republic. Following emancipation, however, former slaves in many areas of the South were compelled to exercise their new freedom of contract to resume growing cotton for former owners, or else sink into debt peonage on their own.

CALVIN SCHERMERHORN

Bibliography

Berlin, Ira. *Generations of Captivity: A History of African-American Slaves*. Cambridge, MA: Harvard University Press, 2003.

Blackburn, Robin. *The American Crucible: Slavery, Emancipation and Human Rights*. New York: Verso, 2011.

Gallay, Alan. *The Indian Slave: The Rise of the English Empire in the American South, 1670–1717*. New Haven, CT: Yale University Press, 2001.

Miller, Joseph C. *The Problem of Slavery as History: A Global Approach*. New Haven, CT: Yale University Press, 2012.

Schermerhorn, Calvin. *Money over Mastery, Family over Freedom: Slavery in the Antebellum Upper South*. Baltimore, MD: Johns Hopkins University Press, 2011.

Van Cleve, George William. *A Slaveholders' Union: Slavery, Politics, and the Constitution in the Early American Republic*. Chicago: University of Chicago Press, 2010.

Slave Trade, Suppression of Atlantic

The campaign to abolish the transatlantic slave trade spanned four continents—Europe, Africa, and North and South America—and involved colonial powers and colonies in the Americas and Africa, as well as recently independent nations in the Americas. It was conducted through a combination of complex diplomatic treaties and costly and logistically challenging naval operations. It lasted several decades, from the end of the British slave trade in 1807 to the departure of the last slave ship from Africa to Cuba in 1867.

The broad contours of suppressing the shipping of Africans across the Atlantic as slaves are well known. In regions under British influence, exports of slaves ended after Parliament declared the trade illegal in 1807. A West Africa Squadron of the Royal Navy was then deployed to enforce Britain's growing series of treaty agreements with Portugal, Spain, and Brazil to eliminate slaving by vessels sailing under their flags, mostly north of the Equator. The Iberian slavers did not enforce these agreements, and so the ships of the West Africa Squadron seized them and diverted them to "treaty" ports—Havana, Rio de Janeiro, Luanda, and, most of all, Britain's "colony of freedom" in Africa at Freetown, Sierra Leone—where they were released as liberated "recaptives," or *libertos*, in Angola, Brazil, and Cuba, to very uncertain fates under local authorities.

Scholars disagree on how exactly this process of suppressing an obviously economically viable labor-supply system developed. One school argues that British naval operations largely failed to increase the costs of slaving in West Africa and thus to reduce the volume of the trade. Others, though, have demonstrated that naval suppression had an immediate impact in reducing exports of slaves from certain parts of the African coast. Another equally important analysis holds that, even when naval operations were not sufficient to end shipments of slaves completely, they allowed for continuation of the trade by prompting sufficient organizational changes in it to circumvent diplomatic and naval strategies of suppression in the short term. Naval pressure contributed to the eventual demise of the trade by creating conditions that increased costs and risks associated with shipments of slaves.

By far the most sustained challenge to Britain's surveillance and suppression of maritime slaving came in the southern Atlantic, particularly in Angola and Brazil, two Portuguese colonies (until 1822, in Brazil's case) that constituted the two most important axes of the slave trade in the Atlantic World. Brazil, easily the largest single destination of the trade in the Americas, was deeply dependent on it for the continuous replenishing of its plantation labor forces. Slavery permeated several levels of Brazilian economy and society, from sugar plantations in the northeast to gold mining in southern Minas Gerais to the urban economies and societies of Rio de Janeiro, Salvador, and Recife. As Brazil also became a large producer of coffee in the nineteenth century, dependence on enslaved labor increased. Not surprisingly, this trade ended, in 1850, only after Brazil's protracted evasion of British diplomatic pressure over two decades and routine violations of the 1831 law that had first banned the entry of slaves into Brazil. As a result, the almost 1 million Africans taken as captives to Brazil after 1831, as well as their descendants, were held in slavery illegally under international law until the emancipation in 1888.

Another significant obstacle to ending the slave trade in the southern Atlantic derived from the close connections between Brazil and Angola. By the time Britain moved to suppress the trade in the nineteenth century, these two Portuguese colonies had for centuries interacted with one another in complex and intense ways that, though primarily based on slaving, also involved tight social and cultural ties. Owing to these connections, the slave trade in the southern Atlantic was formidably resistant to British abolitionism. Shipments continued in spite of increasing British diplomatic and naval pressures. Brazil's declaration of independence from Portuguese rule in 1822 complicated these efforts at suppression, and even when Portugal outlawed shipments of slaves from its African colonies in 1836, Brazilians continued, and even intensified, their slaving. During this illegal phase of the trade, this southern Atlantic component became highly

international, with networks of investment and operations that linked not only Angola and Brazil but also southeastern Africa (Mozambique), Cuba, Spain, Portugal, and the United States. After Brazil ended imports of captives in 1850, these systems continued shipping slaves to Cuba from Angola and Kongo until the 1860s.

In seeking to understand the impact of the suppression of the maritime Atlantic trade, scholars have mostly focused on such macrostructural issues as the transition from the slave trade to "legitimate" commerce in Africa, which would replace exports of human beings. British abolitionists used this high-sounding expression, "legitimate commerce," to highlight the trades in commodity exports—ivory, beeswax, and vegetable oils such as palm oil and peanut oil—that they argued would bring prosperity to Africa, as well as to themselves, and thus justify their naval interventions on the high seas. Many see the aggressive investment that followed as a link between abolitionism in the 1830s and the onset of European colonialism in Africa in the 1870s and 1880s. Arguments emphasizing that the anti–slave trade movements laid the groundwork for the rise of European colonialism in Africa focus on western Africa north of the Equator but ignore Angola and Kongo, the regions that provided the majority of the captives taken across the Atlantic in the nineteenth century.

British efforts to suppress the slave trade to Brazil occurred when the country was already independent from Portugal (1822), and the political establishment there mostly favored continuing imports of captives. However, two factors eventually forced the imperial government of Brazil to abolish the trade in 1850. First, in 1835, the Malê revolt, led mostly by Muslim slaves recently arrived from the Bight of Benin, disrupted the second-largest city in Brazil (Salvador, Bahia). Although crushed by authorities, this revolt showed in stark relief the destabilizing consequences of large numbers of enslaved Africans imported into Brazil. Second, amid the institutional instability produced by political revolts in several provinces of Brazil that sought to challenge Rio de Janeiro's central power as capital of the empire (1822), Brazilian authorities decided to end imports of slaves so as to eliminate British diplomatic manipulation in the cause of abolitionism as an additional source of institutional instability.

The demise of the slave trade in 1850 effectively marked the start of the slow ending of slavery in Brazil 38 years later.

The first attempt to end exports of slaves from Angola, still a colony of Portugal, came in the wake of an 1831 law in Brazil to prevent the entry of captives there. The fact that a law that applied to independent Brazil reverberated across the Atlantic in Portuguese Angola, leading to a decline in shipments of slaves in Luanda, illustrates the tightness of the ties between Angola and Brazil, regardless of the nominally separate diplomatic standings of the two countries. This law did not end the trade but instead dispersed loadings of slaves to regions such as Cabinda and Ambriz, to the north of the capital city Luanda, beyond the narrow limits of effective Portuguese sovereignty in the region. These ports, where anti–slave trade measures could not be enforced, continued well into the 1860s as significant sources of exports of captives. British naval suppression, together with active diplomacy in Lisbon and Luanda, forced the Portuguese government to take concrete steps against the slave trade, since they feared that the British might use the moral cause of abolitionism as a pretext to stake territorial claims over territories that the Portuguese regarded as their own in Angola and Kongo. But Portugal's weak effort to suppress slaving did not prevent the return of shipments of slaves from its own ports in Luanda and Benguela, the two largest slave-embarkation points south of the Equator. Yet, as elsewhere in Africa, British naval pressure contributed to the eventual ending of slave trading by increasing the shippers' risks and costs.

Beyond British pressures, Portugal was motivated to end Angola's reliance on slaving by its geopolitical strategy of developing the African colony to replace the American riches lost in Brazil. Production of agricultural commodities in Africa, though based on enslaved and forced labor, would compensate. Even before Portugal had turned against the slave trade, Portuguese intellectuals had argued that strengthening economic and institutional ties between Angola and Portugal would necessitate the end of exports of slaves. Slaving deprived the African colony of labor needed locally, while also promoting the economic welfare of its rebellious former colony in South America. Portugal's abolitionism was deeply compromised by the weakness of its colonial administration and by the strong political lobby of slave dealers in Angola. By the mid-1840s, however, the Portuguese government had begun to enact laws against the slave trade as part of a broader project to develop Angola's economic potential and to establish Portuguese military and administrative control over such regions close to Luanda as the slaving port at Ambriz. Whatever the possible connection of British slave-trade suppression policies with colonialism in western Africa, Portuguese military and administrative occupation in the southern Atlantic was an integral part of the complicated politics of abolishing Atlantic slaving.

ROQUINALDO FERREIRA

Bibliography

Eltis, David. *Economic Growth and the Ending of the Transatlantic Slave Trade.* New York: Oxford University Press, 1987.

Marques, João Pedro. *The Sounds of Silence: Nineteenth-Century Portugal and the Abolition of the Slave Trade.* New York: Berghahn, 2006.

Paquette, Gabriel. *Imperial Portugal in the Age of Atlantic Revolutions: The Luso-Brazilian World, c. 1770–1850.* New York: Cambridge University Press, 2013.

Parron, Tâmis. *A política da escravidão no Império do Brasil, 1826–1865.* Rio de Janeiro: Civilização Brasileira, 2011.

Slaving, in Africa

Slaving denotes a congeries of strategies for creating, valuing, moving, and utilizing human captives. Entrepreneurial women and men deployed slaving strategies in Africa, as elsewhere in the world, for their own economic and political advancement. Slaving was a risk-taking business activity that often used distant connections to create value and generate economic growth. Because slaving activities involved human beings as both captors and investors, they inevitably triggered wide-ranging social changes. Activities of slave trading and slaving in Africa intersected but were not synonymous. The distinction is one between part and whole, between means and ends; it is analytically significant because of the dissimilar ways in which slave trading and slaving cast light on the history of entrepreneurship in Africa.

Slave trading designates transportation of captives and the financial and organizational networks employed to move them. Slaving, on the other hand, is a practice much broader in scope and significance that encompasses what historians have traditionally called "slavery in Africa" and a good bit more, with an emphasis on entrepreneurship in changing and challenging circumstances. Slaving implies a historical-analytical emphasis on the methods, motives, and achievements of Africans who created and utilized captives, as well as on the socioeconomic meanings and consequences of their actions. As entrepreneurs who often trespassed on social norms by prying individuals loose from family and political networks and moving them forcibly from one labor and social context to another, slavers represented a small but influential minority in African and world history. Their entrepreneurial activities remain poorly understood, often ignored, frequently denied, and sometimes disputed by scholars.

Atlantic studies have had an ambiguous relationship with understanding slaving in Africa, both productive and inhibiting. On the positive side, scholarship on slaving and slave trading in Africa has emerged as an extension of research in Atlantic history. Viewing the Americas as a "plantation complex" that consumed captive Africans, historian Philip Curtin a half century ago initiated the practice of rigorously counting the number of African slaves who passed westward across the Atlantic. The Transatlantic Slave Trade Database, compiled and refined over the last few decades in the spirit of Curtin's early work, has allowed historians to refine their estimates of the regions of Africa that supplied captives to the Americas and the timing of their departures and patterns of their destinations. On the downside, Atlantic history, focused as it has been primarily on the Americas and Europe, has tended to distort the study of slaving activities within Africa by focusing more on the captives sold by traders into the ocean than on those retained by slavers within Africa, sometimes leaving the impression that Atlantic-oriented slaving was of greater geographical spread and significance in Africa than it actually was.

In Atlantic history, slavers—European, African, or mixed-race—typically appear as morally questionable figures who accumulated riches for narcissistic and unproductive ends. Yet in African economies, slavers represented a progressive force in that they generally transformed social, economic, and labor systems to produce growth, and sometimes even development, from which they also personally gained. One could think of slaving there in a very general way as an African historical equivalent of Europe's Industrial Revolution. Though fundamentally different in character, the one powered by fossil fuel and the other by the human hand and back, the two were linked in numerous ways.

On the Congo River of West-Central Africa, merchants who coalesced around canoe transportation on the river and came to identify themselves as Bobangi eliminated their competition on the river's central waterways to procure and ferry captives downstream, some of them for sale to Europeans on the coast. Their commercial success spurred production of food along the river, fueled the process of Bobangi ethnogenesis, and increased the use and varieties of captives around Malebo Pool (the downstream terminus of the system, today the region of modern Brazzaville and Kinshasa). Pressed by British-led abolition on the Atlantic in the early nineteenth century, West African slavers also transformed the region's economies from exporting humans to exporting such commodities as peanuts and palm oil produced by captives and their descendants. Slaving activities increased in the African interior during this transition, as sales of captives abroad declined. Because slaving was one of Africa's most widespread forms of commercial activity between the seventeenth and early twentieth centuries, as calculated by the value of its "output," slavers rank among the most significant of Africa's movers and shakers.

As such, slavers were often, if not always, at the leading edges of socioeconomic innovation. They frequently employed violence in pursuit of their goals and acted with the most callous of attitudes toward their victims but also engaged in creative types of transactions requiring imagination and planning before implementation. Slavers were key players in linking disparate regions of the continent with one another, as well as to places outside of the continent. The ways in which slaving was financed and organized varied dramatically from

Senegambia in Africa's northwest, to the Upper Guinea Coast, the Bight of Benin, the Niger River Delta, the Cameroon rivers, and Luanda and Benguela, to name only the principal Atlantic coastal regions.

A significant method for creating captives was direct violence in organized warfare and systematic raiding. Many scholars have estimated that warfare produced the majority of captives, at least those sold as slaves to Europeans. These conclusions are based primarily on the origins of individuals entering the transatlantic slave trade rather than on patterns of slaving within Africa more generally, and therefore must be taken with a good pinch of salt. What is more important for understanding African implications of slaving than the methods of capturing the people sold, however, are the ways in which martial leaders assembled the armies and paramilitary raiders and the precedents they broke in the process of conducting their violent activities. In Madagascar, the nineteenth-century empire of Antananarivo financed a professional standing army of some 35,000 men, in part by capturing and selling any who resisted its military expansion. That army, in turn, deeply eroded the control of elders over their male children, who found greater possibilities of advancement through merit in the army than through the ranks of seniority at home or through civilian service to aristocratic government. The slaving army and its bureaucracy also overthrew royal aristocracies who had formed them and advanced Christianity and literacy through a system of schools. Both Evangelical Protestantism and military rule in Madagascar built on an economic foundation of slaving.

Another force for change flowing from African slaving related to the economic uses of the captives retained. Strategies for setting captives *apart* as labor coerced for the benefit of their captors, whether in households and villages of slave families or in gangs of headbearers or canoe men or builders, were common. Another method for employing captives was to *incorporate* them into the communities or other assemblages of their captors as retainers or as soldiers, eventually providing them the base from which to claim prerogatives enjoyed by those born into the society, though sometimes this took generations of struggle and intermarriage. Zulu military regiments in nineteenth-century southeastern Africa, by contrast, actively and quickly incorporated massive numbers of the people they captured as wives and warriors. Imitators of the Zulu military slaving system carried the strategy north and west over vast portions of southern and Central Africa.

Household slaving, common across the continent, absorbed captured and purchased women as wives and children as dependents. This strategy of mobilizing labor and skills could turn the children of the natally alienated captives into quasi-kin. Many commercial firms built by slaving offered their captives opportunities for rapid advancement in the organizations that had enslaved them, a phenomenon found from the Zambezi valley of Mozambique to the Congo River of West-Central Africa, and especially within Saharan regions. In the last, some of the enslaved resident agents learned to conduct correspondence in Arabic with their master-patrons regarding business conditions for slaving in the far-flung locations where they lived, and to keep accounts. Saharan literacy, as in Madagascar, was closely linked to the business of slaving, and monotheistic Christianity and Islam both provided religious community for isolated captives far from their homes.

While slavers typically engaged in slaving activities to advance their personal interests or those of their extended kin, what might have motivated their searches for advancement at such extreme social cost to their victims is difficult to discern. One theory holds that slavers were typically persons marginal to more powerful and dominant social groups, such as younger males in lineages dominated by elders or merchants subordinated to the dynastic aristocracies that ruled Africa's large military polities and regulated business within them. Marginal groups employed slaving, the argument goes, to catapult themselves by violence into positions of power or to the forefront of economic advantage, at the expense of the beneficiaries of the older forms of economic and political organization that excluded them. This pattern may have held in certain places and times, but elites often turned to the business of slaving to meet marginal challengers on their own ground, employing revenue-generating activities in slaving to maintain a precarious dominance. There was no single pattern of who tended to engage in slaving, or how, or why.

In whatever way slavers came to the business, they dealt creatively in effecting meaningful and imaginative configurations of linkages, in trust and debt, in diverse commodities and currencies, and in moving captives across different communities and value systems. If trust was critical to the conduct of slaving as a business, slaves themselves were often generated by breaking trust or disregarding guarantees of personal and collective security. Trade goods ranging from Arabic-language books of the southern and eastern Mediterranean to minted tea imported from China were integral to slaving in northwestern Africa. Horses and salt entered West Africa from the Sahara, both paid for by slaving and both assuming lives of their own in the kitchens and armies of the West African savannas. In several parts of Africa, ivory flowed in tandem with captives as a side investment for slavers hedging their bets, making it a key export into the Indian and Atlantic Oceans. Ivory was tied, in turn, to mobile hunting parties in the interior that enriched the local authorities on whose lands elephants were felled. Across much of Africa, too, imported textiles of various origins and qualities were critical to slaving, linking the entrepreneurial activities of African slavers to those of counterpart artisans and industrialists from Bombay to Bordeaux and from Bristol to Boston.

Debt and the imported goods flowed through different African economies of meaning and consumption. Africans sold captives abroad largely for textiles. The textiles of varying colors and patterns that slaving brought to Africa found fashion markets as fickle and ever-changing as those in Paris, London, and New York. These imported cloths assumed novel meanings and uses, as Africans processed them further into apparel or employed them in varying ways as local currencies and in ritual life.

In parts of Indian Ocean Africa, including greater Ethiopia and Madagascar, silver Maria Theresa *thalers*, Spanish pieces of eight, and French five-franc coins (all designated as "dollars"), mined in South America and minted in the Americas and Europe, served as the basis for new, though restricted, silver currency zones. Slaving typically meant juggling and exchanging multiple currencies across the margins of the pervasive discontinuities of African currency and value systems, few of them extensive in geographical reach. Textiles taken on credit might be transformed into metal currencies such as iron hoes, and these again transformed into

cowrie shells or bars of salt. Discontinuities between currency and value could ruin a business—or bring abundant value to the sagacious manipulator. Financial currencies, or currencies of account, held varying social significance and prestige. Silver, gold, cowrie shells, and bars of salt were more liquid; livestock, textiles, and liquor circulated among restricted circles with greater social status. Successful slavers developed versatile entrepreneurial skills and approached these constraints as opportunities to expand their fields of business and their social visibility.

The strategies and logic of African slaving thus exploited the specific social and intellectual contexts in which slavers operated and, as a result, are poorly accessed by the quantitative abstractions of liberal economics. At the Dahomean and Asante courts in West Africa, slavers delivered captives to be ceremonially beheaded in terrifying expressions of the rulers' violent power over human life. These and other ceremonies that amounted to the planned sacrifice of captive lives were linked to broader ideas about the prosperity of kingdoms. They make little sense in terms of slavery in the Americas, where captives were usually set to laboring activities to produce monetary returns and where to destroy a slave demolished value and undermined prestige rather than increasing either. Balanta-speaking farmers in coastal Upper Guinea captured and moved captives in a sustained but carefully controlled flow to buy iron from European suppliers for the heavy agricultural implements they needed to cultivate their waterlogged soils. Slaving, for them, was a form of investment in agricultural productivity and a speculation in security.

Slavers thrived especially in Africa's growing cities. Urban growth everywhere lures human capital, and cities have been places conducive to slaving and the investment of slaving gains. Until World War I, African cities were often filled with captives. In Lagos city (now Nigeria), slavers ferried in captives until, by the early nineteenth century, slaves had become the majority of the city's residents. Entrepreneurs sank profits earned from slaving into urban real estate to diversify their incomes by seeking rents, sometimes from their own slaves. Later, capital amassed in slaving and real estate underwrote intensive investments in production and processing of palm oil in the region.

The dramatically varying logics of slaving in Africa can be understood only through engagement in language, philosophy, and religion. The slave-trading databases that have so enriched Atlantic history have enabled historians to extrapolate only the strategies of Europeans and the experiences of captives aboard ships, but the limited extent of these projections has done little more than raise questions about slaving activities within Africa. Most notably, slaving emphasizes Africans as initiators of slaving systems and as consumers of the imports they gained from international connections—as entrepreneurs and business people—while slave trading has typically focused on Africans as enslaved victims. It might be said that slave trading with Europeans has been about Africa's margins and its human dispersions, while African slaving is more about its internal and international connections built by moving people. Both were integral to Africa's history of human captivity, but slaving represents a more holistic and critical approach to the consequences and aftermath of enslavement for parts of the African continent and their many internal and external connections.

While key to Atlantic history, African slaving was not principally Atlantic oriented, nor can it be well understood in Atlantic terms. Only a portion, perhaps relatively few, of Africa's captives crossed the Atlantic. Multiple centers of slaving activity within Africa transformed captives into laborers, wives, kin, or military buddies, and disseminated the commodities exchanged for them. Slaving occupied significant sectors of African economies and societies, particularly during the eighteenth and nineteenth centuries. In these centuries, captives were concentrated in great numbers at centers within the continent, such as in the Futa Jallon highlands; along the Middle Niger River; within Hausaland, Unyamwezi, and Buganda; around Lake Malawi and the basin of the Ruvuma River in eastern Africa; around the confluence of the White and Blue Niles; in the cities of Egypt and the Maghreb; in various Saharan oases; and in certain parts of the Angolan and Ethiopian highlands. It is therefore important not to conflate African slaving with the sector of these activities that sustained the slave trade across the Atlantic. These internal centers also fed captives into the Mediterranean and Indian Ocean trades. Recent published estimates of the total of Africa's many slave trades suggest Atlantic slaving accounted for roughly a quarter or less of the captives generated within the continent.

PIER M. LARSON

Bibliography

Eltis, David, David Richardson, Stephen D. Behrendt, and Manolo Florentino. The Transatlantic Slave Trade Database, http://www.slavevoyages.org. 2007.

Harms, Robert. River of Wealth, River of Sorrow: The Central Zaire Basin in the Era of the Slave and Ivory Trade, 1500–1891. New Haven, CT: Yale University Press, 1981.

Lydon, Ghislaine. On Trans-Saharan Trails: Islamic Law, Trade Networks, and Cross-Cultural Exchange in Nineteenth-Century Western Africa. Cambridge: Cambridge University Press, 2009.

Mann, Kristin. Slavery and the Birth of an African City: Lagos, 1760–1900. Bloomington: Indiana University Press, 2007.

Miller, Joseph C. The Problem of Slavery as History: A Global Approach. New Haven, CT: Yale University Press, 2012.

Nwokeji, G. Ugo. The Slave Trade and Culture in the Bight of Biafra: An African Society in the Atlantic World. Cambridge: Cambridge University Press, 2010.

Peterson, Brian J. Islamization from Below: The Making of Muslim Communities in Rural French Sudan, 1880–1960. New Haven, CT: Yale University Press, 2011.

Piot, Charles. "Of Slaves and the Gift: Kabre Sale of Kin during the Era of the Slave Trade." Journal of African History 37, no. 1 (1996), 31–49.

Prestholdt, Jeremy. Domesticating the World: African Consumerism and the Genealogies of Globalization. Berkeley: University of California Press, 2008.

Slaving, European, from Africa

Free and coerced migrations from Europe and Africa were vital in repeopling the Americas following the demographic collapse of the Native populations that accompanied European colonization. Many Europeans migrated under various forms of contract, some more liberal than others, but only Africans arrived as chattel slaves, without consent or contract. Why Africans were deemed enslaveable while Europeans, for the most part, were not remains a hotly debated question. Cultural factors, such as the morality of pan-European Christianity, rather than simple economic calculations, provide the most likely explanation.

Whatever the reasons, between the sixteenth and eighteenth centuries there was a striking "blackening" of migration to the Americas; modest annual flows of up to 6,000 enslaved Africans across the Atlantic in the early period increased continually until reaching an apex in the second half of the eighteenth century, when some 80,000 or more captives landed every year. Continuing beyond the Atlantic Era, it is now estimated that between 1500 and 1867 at least 12.5 million Africans were put on board ships bound for the Americas. The eighteenth-century surge in this coerced migration, which accounted for almost half that total, swamped the continuing flow of European emigrants to the New World. This repopulating of the Americas also transformed Atlantic Africa, where the enslaved boarded ships owned by Europeans and by their colonial cousins, into the principal zone of cross-cultural exchange in early-modern Atlantic, or even early-modern global, history.

European contact with Africa and with enslaved Africans long predated colonization of the Americas. For more than a millennium, enslaved Africans had crossed the Sahara to be sold in Christian as well as Muslim markets in the Mediterranean basin. That trans-Saharan flow would continue until almost the dawn of the twentieth century. Moreover, when Portuguese voyagers began in the fifteenth century to explore the Atlantic coast of Africa, they returned with not only such commodities as gold and ivory but also enslaved Africans, whom they sold in Iberian and other markets in Europe. A modest traffic in captives from Africa into Europe via the eastern Atlantic continued well beyond the sixteenth century. But colonization of the Americas under the Portuguese and Spanish and, more specifically, efforts on the parts of both to exploit the mineral and agricultural potential of the New World, encouraged Iberian traders, with support from their political masters, to redirect their slaving activities in the eastern Atlantic toward creating a controllable labor force of enslaved Africans in Brazil and New Spain.

The Portuguese largely monopolized European slaving from Africa over the sixteenth century, trading—and sometimes also raiding—in Upper Guinea, notably Senegambia, and Angola, south of the Congo River. Ships dispatched from Lisbon and other Iberian ports took captives from Angola to markets in Spanish America, often under royal license (the *asiento*). Brazil became increasingly important from the last third of the sixteenth century, as ships from Recife and Salvador da Bahia in northeastern Brazil and finally also from Rio de Janeiro entered the trade. By 1600, therefore, two circuits of European slaving from Africa had begun to emerge: one was the famous triangular circuit, largely north of the equator, operating out of Europe to Africa and then across the Atlantic and back; the other a bilateral trade across the South Atlantic linking Brazil and Angola. Though never wholly separate, these two patterns became increasingly organized over time and persisted—with modifications—until well into the nineteenth century. Guided in the Age of Sail by the different gyres of winds and ocean currents of the Northern and Southern hemispheres, the distinct geographical contours of the two trading circuits were reinforced by northern European entrants into Atlantic slaving.

Beginning in the early seventeenth century, the newly independent Dutch, together with the English and the French, broke the Iberian powers' near stranglehold over colonization in the Americas and, in doing so, necessarily also entered systematically into slaving from Africa. The colonizing effort of the northwest European powers centered not on South America but on the Caribbean and mainland North America. From the second half of the seventeenth century, the English in particular emerged as serious challengers to the Portuguese in slaving from Africa. Central to the rise of the English challenge and ultimately the strong presence of northwest European ports generally in the Atlantic slave trade was the sugar revolution that began in Barbados in the 1640s and over the following two centuries spread throughout the Caribbean Basin. Slaving thus fed a growing appetite in Europe and other parts of the Atlantic World for sugar and its derivatives, molasses and rum.

The sugar-slavery axis, firmly established first in Brazil in the mid-sixteenth century, drove the rapid growth of the Atlantic slave trade from the 1670s.

Production of American plantation crops other than sugar, such as tobacco, rice, coffee, and cotton, also became closely identified with enslaved Africans. The mining of precious metals in Brazil—though less so in Spanish territories—after the 1690s depended on African slave labor as well. But estimates suggest that up to 80 percent of the 10.7 million Africans who survived the Atlantic crossing were destined to work in the cane fields of Brazil and the Caribbean, where some were used to expand production of crops, but many replaced predecessors who had died prematurely in the unforgiving conditions of producing plantation sugar. Replacement demand for slaves became a major component of total demand for the same in the Americas, as captive populations in sugar colonies commonly failed to sustain their numbers through natural reproduction. Since British Jamaica and French Saint-Domingue were the major eighteenth-century Caribbean producers of sugar, it is hardly surprising that Bristol, Liverpool, London, and Nantes joined Pernambuco, Salvador da Bahia, and Rio de Janeiro in Brazil as the major ports of origin for the voyages to Africa that then carried captives across the Atlantic. Overall, the Portuguese, British, and French—in that order—accounted collectively for close to 85 percent of the slaves crossing the Atlantic. Sugar cultivation in Suriname and, after 1789, also in Cuba ensured that Dutch and Spanish traders, many of the latter based at Havana, controlled much of the rest. The numbers of enslaved Africans entering mainland North America were comparatively small, less than 5 percent of the total Atlantic trade. From this relatively small proportion of trafficked Africans would emerge the huge slave population of the U.S. antebellum South.

These American demands for enslaved laborers largely dictated the rhythms of European slaving. The significance of demand is underlined by data that show a direct relationship between rising real slave prices (that is, nominal slave prices deflated by sugar prices) and slave-labor productivity in the Caribbean and growing deliveries of enslaved Africans between 1670 and 1807. The growth in the trade also depended on the responsiveness of African slave supply systems to American market demand for captives and on the capacity of traders of European descent to build efficient and sustainable commercial relations with African dealers along the Atlantic seaboard. African supply-side responses—and the Afro-European commercial and financial networks that were integral parts of them—accelerated the emergence of slaving as Africa's primary mode of integration into the Atlantic World.

African responses to American demand for slaves increased exports from Senegambia and Angola, the two principal sources of captives before 1650, as well as opening new sources of captives along the coasts of Atlantic Africa and ultimately along the Indian Ocean coast of southeast Africa. Of the two original supply regions, Angola south of the Congo River mouth exhibited the greater long-term growth, providing a large proportion of all captive Africans sent to Brazil. This bilateral Angola-Brazil link accounted for Portuguese and Brazilian shippers' leading position among the European slavers throughout the history of the Atlantic trade.

Of the new sources of captives in Africa, the stretch of coastline from modern-day Ghana to the Congo River, which encompassed the regions Europeans knew as the Gold Coast, the Slave Coast (or Bight of Benin), the Bight of Biafra (east of the delta of the Niger River), and the Loango Coast to the south as far as the mouth of the Congo River, proved to be the most substantial and consistent. By contrast, the coastline west and north of Ghana, comprising regions known as Sierra Leone and the Windward Coast, became a major source of captives only in the second half of the eighteenth century, contributing to the height of the trade. The contribution of southeast Africa to Atlantic slaving was largely confined to the period from the 1780s onward. Most major adjustments in the sources of slaves in Atlantic Africa after 1650 were related to the entry of northern European merchants, who tended to concentrate their activities at undeveloped points of access to African suppliers anywhere between the Senegal and Congo rivers, eventually intruding even on claimed Portuguese territories south to the Kalahari Desert. These added locations, in turn, expanded the number of African communities victimized by European slaving, while the dominance of specific European trading groups at selected African embarkation centers ensured uneven distributions by ethnicity in the Americas of African survivors of the Middle Passage. The extent to which the resulting concentrations of Africans of specific origins in specific destinations allowed or fostered reconstitutions of African groups of similar cultural backgrounds in the Americas has been and remains a hotly debated issue.

Although almost every part of Atlantic Africa between the Sahara and the Kalahari—from Senegal in the north to Angola in the south—ended up supplying slaves to Europeans, European slavers concentrated their transactions at only 10 major points of embarkation. Together these leading ports accounted for almost two-thirds of the captives (those whose places of embarkation have been documented). They were the African counterparts of the comparably prominent slave ports in Europe and the Americas, such as Liverpool and Rio de Janeiro. From north to south the leading African centers of the slave trade included Anomabu on the Gold Coast, Ouidah on the Slave Coast, Bonny and Old Calabar in the Bight of Biafra, Malembo and Cabinda on the Loango Coast, and Luanda and Benguela in Angola. Most of these ports shipped between 500,000 and 750,000 captives over varying periods, but Ouidah is estimated to have embarked over 1 million, mostly in the eighteenth century, and Luanda over 2.8 million between the 1570s and the 1840s. The long and continuous trade from Luanda made it alone responsible for dispatching more than one in five of all Africans entering the Atlantic slave trade. Together with Ouidah, the two accounted for around three in ten. Such degrees of concentration match those among the ports in America and Europe outfitting slave ships for Africa.

Local suppliers at some of these African ports were wholly African, whereas in others they included immigrant Europeans and their Eurafrican descendants, often based at European factories or forts. One European group or another tended to dominate slave exports at some ports, such as the Portuguese and Brazilians at Luanda and Benguela, the English at Bonny and Old Calabar, or the French in Senegal. Along the Gold Coast, a half dozen European monarchies built some 40 coastal fortifications (the famous "slave castles" of modern Ghana), often within sight of one another, in attempts to exclude rivals. At others, several European trading communities might buy captives at the same time; Ouidah (in modern Benin) owed its large numbers of exports to the

competition it fostered among Brazilian, French, and English slavers.

Regardless of the Europeans involved, each port, together with second-tier ports in some cases, provided brokering and provisioning services vital to the functioning of Afro-European exchange. For Europeans these local traders were gateways to African consumers of the trade goods they bartered for slaves; for Africans who controlled local and regional slave supply networks, the coastal brokers provided access to European shippers of slaves and through them to slave markets in the Americas. Some of these supply networks reached deep into the African interior. The leading African slave ports, like their counterparts in Europe, provided knowledge about local commercial practices and the trust and social capital vital to efficiency in any sort of business transaction. They performed with considerable efficiency. For example, trends in coastal slave prices closely shadowed those in transatlantic markets; the ages, sexes, and ethnic compositions of the slaves sold reflected the preferences for captives among American purchasers; and the duration of costly turnarounds of European ships in African slave ports matched those at ports elsewhere in the Atlantic. By these measures, all varied in their performances across time and space, indicating some market imperfections within what, by any standards, were highly competitive, geographically extended, and financially complex and risky business operations. However, overall improvements in the efficiency of coastal slaving transactions in Atlantic Africa linked to specific locations of activity were evident. These growing efficiencies imply that without African economic skills European slaving in the Atlantic was unlikely to have attained the scale it did.

European slaving from Africa came under moral and political scrutiny in the late eighteenth century, at the very time its volume attained unprecedented heights. The causes and timing of efforts to suppress an efficient and, to some minds, essential economic enterprise have attracted intense historical debate. In seeking to understand this apparent economic paradox, we should not ignore the increased costs caused by efforts of captives on board slave ships to resist their captors, or the widespread publicity in the contemporary media given to brutal suppression of shipboard and other rebellions, as well as other forms of violence that captains used toward their captives. Such publicity was particularly evident in Britain, where antislavery thought became ingrained in popular politics from the 1780s onward. In the final analysis, however, it was lawmakers in Europe who gradually proscribed legal European participation in Atlantic slaving—beginning with Denmark in 1803, followed by Great Britain and the United States in 1807—and who also sanctioned, in Britain's case especially, the use of naval power and diplomatic pressure to suppress Atlantic slaving after 1815. Although all the participating European powers, as well as the United States and Brazil, formally outlawed involvement in the Atlantic slave trade by their nationals by 1836, Brazilian, Spanish, and some U.S. ships continued to traffic enslaved Africans across the Atlantic for another 30 years, carrying about a million additional captives into slavery in the Americas. The continuing voyages were testimony to the relative efficiency of slavery as a labor system throughout much of the Americas at the time, to consequent continuing demand for enslaved Africans, and to the efficiency of the slaving operations in Africa that Europeans, in tandem with African slave suppliers, had created during the previous three centuries. It was only after the American Civil War, when chattel slavery itself was perceived to be close to formal extinction throughout the Americas, that these incentives to pursue transatlantic slaving were finally ended.

—DAVID RICHARDSON

Bibliography

Behrendt, Stephen D., David Eltis, and David Richardson. "The Costs of Coercion: African Agency in the Pre-Modern Atlantic World." *Economic History Review*, 2nd ser., 54, no. 3 (2001): 454–476.

Eltis, David. *The Rise of African Slavery in the Americas*. New York: Cambridge University Press, 1999.

Eltis, David, and David Richardson. *Atlas of the Transatlantic Slave Trade*. New Haven, CT: Yale University Press, 2010.

Eltis, David, David Richardson, Stephen D. Behrendt, and Manolo Florentino. *The Transatlantic Slave Trade Database*, http://www.slavevoyages.org. 2007.

Law, Robin. *Ouidah: The Social History of a West African Slaving "Port," 1727–1892*. Athens: Ohio University Press, 2004.

Lovejoy, Paul E., and David Richardson. "Trust, Pawnship and Atlantic History: The Institutional Foundations of the Old Calabar Slave Trade." *American Historical Review* 104, no. 2 (1999): 333–355.

Miller, Joseph C. *Way of Death: Merchant Capitalism and the Angolan Slave Trade, 1730–1830*. Madison: University of Wisconsin Press, 1988.

Richardson, David. "Cultures of Exchange: Atlantic Africa during the Era of Slave Trade." *Transactions of the Royal Historical Society*, 6th ser., 19 (2009): 151–179.

Thornton, John. *Africa and Africans in the Making of the Atlantic World, 1400–1800*, 2nd edition. New York: Cambridge University Press, 1998.

Slaving, European, of Native Americans

The dominant historical paradigm of New World slavery holds that initial enslavement of Indians disappeared as European diseases took their toll. The losses of Native populations then led Europeans to enslave Africans, who were biologically more resistant to disease and who made better workers because they were already acculturated to obeying "big men" in Africa, as opposed to Native Americans, who were so independent that they preferred death to enslavement. This picture is wrong on several counts. Africans were not peculiarly suited to enslavement, either biologically or culturally. They suffered horribly from New World diseases, just as did Europeans who had also left their natal communities and familiar disease environments and moved to the Americas or Africa. On Atlantic scales, Europeans and Indians also were enslaved in large numbers: however much they presumably loved their individual freedom, when deprived of it they too made excellent slaves. Millions of European Christians in the early-modern era, in fact, spent their lives as slaves in Muslim North Africa (and under the Ottomans in Asia), and over 400 years, from 1492 until the end of the nineteenth century, millions of Indians spent their lives as slaves of the Europeans in the Americas. The enslavement of Africans came to predominate in the

New World, largely because of their availability for enslavement, but in many areas unfree Native American (and European) labor was also employed.

Iberian Indian Slave Systems

Christopher Columbus, familiar with Iberian and Italian slave markets of the late fifteenth century, was the first European to trade in Native American slaves: he shipped over 1,500 Indians from the Caribbean to Spain to help cover the costs of his New World voyages. (His brother, Bartolomé, also became a significant slaver.) The initial market for Indian slaves in Spain was soon superseded by local demands in the Caribbean. The horrific death rate of Hispaniola's Native population from overwork and disease led the Spanish to pursue replacement laborers in gold mines and on early plantations. As their influence spread through the West Indies and then to the American mainland, the Spanish aggressively captured Indians and removed them, as slaves, from their homelands to Spanish enterprises. Juan Ponce de León, governor of Puerto Rico in the 1510s, for instance, scoured Cuba for Indians to enslave and almost depopulated the Bahamas by taking almost 40,000 of the inhabitants of that archipelago. Though mythology has him in Florida seeking the Fountain of Youth, in actuality he explored the peninsula in search of more slaves. By the middle of the sixteenth century, Spanish slaving expeditions had captured and removed Indians from their natal communities on many of the islands off the coast of South America, including Curaçao, Trinidad, and Aruba. They then moved on to the Central American mainland in modern-day Nicaragua, Costa Rica, and Honduras. In less than 40 years after Columbus's arrival in Hispaniola, they had enslaved approximately 1 million American Indians.

Some Spaniards opposed the rampant enslavement of Indians. Queen Isabella and others expressed concerns for the souls of American people and whether God would approve of Spain's New World claims to dominion unless they brought the indigenes to Christ. Although the queen failed to stop the slaving, Spaniards began to divide the Indian populations into those perceived as capable of conversion and incorporation into their declared *república de indios* and others labeled Caribs, or cannibals, who allegedly were incapable of being civilized and should therefore, under prevailing papal bulls, be enslaved or killed. In actuality, they often labeled Indians who merely opposed Spanish sovereignty as cannibals and enslaved them, while they also forced many deemed Christians or potential Christians to toil under a variety of other unfree labor systems. These systems included *yanaconajo*, which tied Indians to particular lands awarded to Spanish owners, and *encomienda*, which consigned Indians to specific individuals for the purposes of labor or tribute paying. Another system of forced labor combined with tribute, *repartimiento*, was used widely in Spanish America to compel Indians to work for varying periods of time for minimal wages on public-works projects, in the mines, and in many other ways for the state, Church, and colonists. In addition, millions of Indians throughout Spanish America lived under debt peonage and other regional systems of compulsory labor.

Though Spain outlawed Indian slavery in 1542 in the famous New Laws, hundreds of thousands of Native people remained slaves under their many exceptions. For example, the Spanish could legally purchase and own Indians initially enslaved by non-Spanish subjects, the Portuguese, or other Indians. Spanish enslavement of Indians remained common in Chile and Peru until the end of the seventeenth century and in New Mexico and Texas into the nineteenth century. Some Spanish systems of bondage for American Indians lasted into the 1820s and later in places as diverse as Florida and Ecuador, Colombia and Bolivia.

Even with the increasing availability of African laborers brought to the Americas in the slave trade, Europeans pursued unfree Indian laborers. The bulk of the enslaved Africans were shipped to the wealthy sugar plantation areas of the West Indies and Brazil, where masters could pay top prices for large numbers of workers, while Indians tended to be enslaved and retained in frontier regions. The Portuguese, however, enslaved large numbers of Indians for plantation work in marginal regions in Brazil, while they simultaneously imported Africans in others. The Portuguese barred Indian slavery in a series of laws issued from the late 1570s to 1609, but planters in Brazil nonetheless continued to enslave Indians well into the eighteenth century. One slave-hunting expedition alone, in 1628, yielded around 60,000 captives, many of them put to work in support services for the plantation system, such as production of food.

Europeans enslaved Indians wherever and whenever they could because it was a relatively easy and quick way to obtain capital. When the German Wesler Company colonized Venezuela in the late 1520s under Spanish licensing, their failed attempt at mining led them to recover financial solvency by capturing Indians for sale to the West Indies. In North America, a long-term overland route in the eighteenth and nineteenth centuries carried Indians from Utah and Colorado to northern Mexico, where enslavement of local Indian populations was illegal. Simple human mobility facilitated the movement of Indians over long-distance land routes: they could be forced to walk hundreds, or even thousands, of miles to buyers, and they could carry supplies and goods as they moved. Spanish use of *tamemes*—Indian slave bearers in overland expeditions—had begun with the conquistadors, but slave traders of later centuries enhanced their profits by selling their slaves after delivery of the cargoes they carried.

English and French Slavers

English and French colonists had even less compunction in enslaving Indians than the Iberians, as their monarchical sponsors paid virtually no attention to the souls of the Indian populations in the territories they claimed, and few voices condemning Native slavery could be heard from English and French churches. Indians captured in wars in French North America were enslaved. French traders also purchased the captives of their Indian allies as they ranged widely in the northern woodlands and drove them to French settlements in maritime Canada, the Illinois Country, and Louisiana. French officials in Louisiana intended to model their economy on the example of contemporaneous South Carolina in its early years, before the 1720s, by capturing Indians to sell to the West Indies in exchange for African slaves to work on plantations. The system never succeeded as envisioned because the English and English-allied Indians preyed on so many Native populations of the region that the French in Louisiana chose for diplomatic reasons to ally with the victimized groups against the English rather than to capture them. The French in Louisiana nonetheless continued to enslave other Indians, directing their procurement toward more distant areas, such as the Missouri Country and Texas and shipping some to the West Indies.

The English enslaved Indians in all of their mainland colonies. The planters of the English West Indies readily purchased the captives they shipped. Indian war captives in seventeenth-century New England were enslaved and shipped in such large numbers to the West Indies and to Spain that a few Puritan merchants specialized as brokers in the trade. Even Roger Williams, the famed founder of Rhode Island and a man of high conscience where Indians were concerned, dropped his initial opposition to Indian slavery and conducted an auction of captive Native Americans. After most of the New England colonies outlawed enslaving Indians in the early eighteenth century, authorities continued to punish Indians for minor crimes with bondage for periods of years to purchasers, who frequently shipped the condemned out of the region, ending any possibility of their return to their home communities.

Relatively few Indians were enslaved in the colonies of Pennsylvania and New York, though less out of principle than out of practicality. The nearby and powerful Iroquois assimilated many of the captives they seized, and the English colonies had no military capability to capture Native Americans who lived too far from the European areas to raid. Residents of both colonies instead purchased Indian captives from other colonies, and records exist of free Indians in Pennsylvania complaining to authorities over the enslavement of their people.

Virginia and Maryland settlers enslaved Indians almost from the beginning of colonization in the Chesapeake. Tobacco farmers and planters desired more cheap labor than English indentured servants provided, and so colonists enslaved Indians in times of both war and peace. After the middle of the seventeenth century, Virginia traders supplied the Westo Indians of the area around what is now Savannah, Georgia, with guns and European goods to bring Indian captives to the colony. This overland trade extended all the way to the Florida coast and west of the Appalachian Mountains. Bacon's Rebellion in Virginia (1676) arose largely out of an attempt by colonists without slaves to enslave the colony's "friendly" Indian allies. Despite laws passed in the eighteenth century against enslavement of

Indians in the Old Dominion, many Native peoples in Virginia remained in slavery, as government authorities legalized their captivity by reclassifying them as Negroes.

The founding of the Carolina colony in 1670 increased the scale of Indian slaving in North America many times over. Traders operating out of Charles Town (modern-day Charleston, South Carolina) took over the Westo trade from the Virginians and began supplying Native allies with trade goods to send slaving expeditions of their own against other Native groups. They thus enabled a frenzy of slaving by Native raiders that overtook the entire Southeast, from the Carolinas to the Florida Keys and west to Texas: for a half century until the 1720s, more Indians were exported from the region than Africans imported to it. The governor of South Carolina, James Moore (1700–1703), for instance, organized a major expedition in 1702 to take St. Augustine, Florida, from the Spanish. Although this failed in its strategic goals, it was a fiscal success, returning with numerous Indian captives. Two years later Moore joined with Native allies to mount a second expedition into Florida, this time against the Spaniards' chief Native ally there, the Apalachee. This English-Yamasee-Creek army, in what is now coastal and central Georgia, returned with over 4,000 Indians, most of whom were sold into slavery in the West Indies. A few years later another English-Creek army went far west into modern-day Alabama and Mississippi to bring back Choctaw slaves. The expedition largely failed, but even its critics in South Carolina noted that the stated purpose of reducing French power in the region by attacking Indians friendly to them was a specious argument; it would have been easier to destroy the small French settlements. The real purpose of these expeditions, and others at the time, was to obtain slaves.

The slaving frenzy in the Southeast continued until about 1717. Over 100 South Carolina traders lived in the towns of allied Indians and armed them to capture other Indians to enslave. After the devastation of the Apalachee in these raids, English slavers joined Yamasee and Creek expeditions that swept into Florida, eventually as far south as the Keys, effectively emptying the peninsula of most of its Native populations. The British were so proud of these slave raids that several widely published maps documented the systematic way that the Carolin-

ians and their Indian allies depopulated the peninsula. Indians allied to the English devastated groups along the Mississippi River, on the coast of the Gulf of Mexico, and west into Arkansas, Louisiana, and Texas. The English had no political reason for engineering these attacks; their sole goal was to obtain slaves. Most of the victims were marched to Charles Town, put on ships, and sent to the West Indies, Virginia, New England, and the Middle Colonies. These slaves worked in agriculture in the plantation colonies of the South, and in the northern port cities as domestics or in trades.

In 1715 Carolina's initial Indian allies united and turned *against* the English in what became known as the Yamasee War. When English authorities ignored the growing complaints of the Indians that their own people were being enslaved and that the traders had foisted unbearable debt on them, Indians who had been doing the bidding of the English killed dozens of the traders living among them. This war ended the large-scale expeditions to obtain slaves in the coastal region. Enslavement of Indians continued in the South on a much smaller scale but mostly shifted to the West. Through the eighteenth and nineteenth centuries, the ongoing capturing of Indians in North America took place west of the Mississippi, all the way to California. Indians there enslaved other Indians for sale to the French in Louisiana, Illinois, and Canada, and then to the British after France lost its North American claims in the Seven Years' War (1756–1763). Many others were sold to the Spanish in New Mexico, Texas, and northern Mexico. Sometimes the Spanish undertook their own slaving expeditions, especially victimizing the Apache in the Southwest. In these borderlands Indians were sold at annual trade fairs in numbers so large that some described the month in which they occurred as the "month of slaves." Not until the end of the American Civil War did the U.S. government send federal troops to put an end to Indian slavery in these territories, and even then Native slaving persisted in areas of California into the late nineteenth century.

* * *

The Europeans' main object in capturing Indians was to obtain labor at minimal expense. Indians had enslaved Indians before Columbus reached America, though mostly in small numbers for ceremonial purposes, as individual punishments, and sometimes for personnel to replace population losses. Indians had rarely enslaved people with whom they had no previous contact before the arrival of European buyers. But the European drive for virtually unlimited numbers of unpaid workers to produce commercial profits motivated the tremendous growth in slaving in the sixteenth and seventeenth centuries. After the arrival of the Europeans, they and the Indians enslaved anonymous victims whom neither had encountered previously to satisfy the almost insatiable desire of Atlantic commercial markets for labor.

Enslaving Indians had expanded from a range of local affairs to an international business. Europeans introduced the means to move captives thousands of miles by sea or overland to distant Atlantic markets. In absolute numbers, the European trade in enslaved Indians never approached the approximately 12 million Africans moved to the Americas, but its consequences were just as disastrous for millions of individuals and hundreds of communities. Relative to the populations raided, it was at least as large and contributed much more to depopulation in the Americas than slaving in Africa reduced populations there. For Europeans enslaving Indians was a low-cost initial strategy for staffing the explosive growth in an Atlantic economy built around commodity production in the Americas, enabling otherwise marginal commercial interests to participate, and setting a competitive pace that later only much more massive enslavements of Africans could sustain.

ALAN GALLAY

Bibliography

Floyd, Troy S. *The Columbus Dynasty in the Caribbean, 1492–1526.* Albuquerque: University of New Mexico Press, 1973.

Gallay, Alan, ed. *Indian Slavery in Colonial America.* Lincoln: University of Nebraska Press, 2009.

———. *The Indian Slave Trade: The Rise of the English Empire in the American South, 1670–1717.* New Haven, CT: Yale University Press, 2002.

Newson, Linda A. *The Cost of Conquest: Indian Decline in Honduras under Spanish Rule.* Boulder, CO: Westview, 1986.

Sherman, William L. *Forced Labor in Sixteenth-Century Central America.* Lincoln: University of Nebraska Press, 1979.

Villamarin, Juan A., and Judith E. Villamarin. *Indian Labor in Mainland Spanish America.* Newark: University of Delaware Press, 1975.

Slaving, Muslim, of Christians

The fall of Constantinople to the Muslim Ottomans in 1453 was followed by the surrender of Muslim Granada to the Catholic monarchs of Spain in 1492 and the expulsion of the Moriscos (converted Moors) between 1609 and 1614 from the Iberian Peninsula. These events meant that the Islamic world and the Christian West (including the newly discovered Americas) were destined to fight out their differences on the Mediterranean and its Atlantic extension, since both were highways for global trade. The Christian nations of Europe had to contend with the Ottoman Empire and its regencies along the North African coast (Algiers, Tunis, and Tripoli), as well as with Morocco, whose main corsair outpost, Salé (home of the Sallee Rovers), was on the Atlantic shore of that kingdom. Known as the Barbary States, these four cities, though increasingly falling behind much of western Europe, were still treated as equals and even, at times, allies against fellow Europeans.

For much of the early-modern period, the Barbary States were seen as complex places. They were a menace to European safety. But these cities were far more cosmopolitan than one could find in most of Europe. It has been estimated that of the 100,000 inhabitants of Algiers in the early seventeenth century, up to a full third, whether captives or renegades, were Christian. Such religious and ethnic diversity would have been impossible to find in any European city. Not surprisingly, many sailors—young, poor, uneducated, and without many prospects at home—turned renegade to seek opportunities in Algiers, Tunis, or Marrakech in Morocco. Even those with good skills felt no compunction switching sides and fighting against their former coreligionists.

From the seventeenth to the first half of the nineteenth century, European and, for a brief time, American merchant vessels were attacked by Muslim corsairs—many led by Christian renegades—and their crews held captive in *bagnios* or slave prisons that have been compared to Nazi or Soviet concentration camps. For populations like those of Spain and England, the number of captives ran into the tens of thousands during the seventeenth and eighteenth centuries. Some 20,000 Britons were held captive in those two centuries, whereas 15,000 Spaniards had to be redeemed in the seventeenth century alone. (Malta, on the other hand, housed some 10,000 Muslim captives in 1720.) Mutual captivity was such a regular way of life that Catholic orders dedicated to the redemption of Christian slaves had been established many centuries before. Also, it is quite possible that the large number of British captives may have contributed to the study of Arabic at Oxford and to new translations of the Qur'ān, and may even have precipitated the English Civil War of 1642. Similarly, one doubts whether we would have had the novel *Don Quixote* if its author, Miguel de Cervantes, had not been imprisoned in Algiers in the late sixteenth century.

As Cervantes's case suggests, being taken captive was not an unusual fate at this time. Until the eighteenth century, many Europeans, although engaged in the transatlantic trade, thought that slavery was something that could happen to them, too. It was simply the cost of doing business. For Britain, the volume of trade in the Mediterranean and southern Europe was equal to its trade with the rest of the world, including North America and India. Despite its powerful Royal Navy, it simply did not have enough resources or manpower to protect its island, let alone defend every small merchant vessel at sea. It is not for no reason that until the middle of the eighteenth century Britain housed more troops in its Mediterranean possessions of Gibraltar and Minorca than it did in all of North America. Unlike the Native peoples of the Americas, Muslims were taken seriously: they were considered heirs to a great civilization.

The Europeans who flocked to North America in the seventeenth century carried with them such views. After all, the emblematic *Mayflower* had traded in the Muslim Mediterranean before taking European "pilgrims" to the New World. Like their countrymen back in England, colonial settlers raised money in churches to free captives in Barbary and used these fundraising occasions to de-

nounce Islam as a fraudulent religion invented by a deranged prophet. Such views have persisted in one way or another to our own time, although by the time of the American Revolution, in the late eighteenth century, the focus had shifted from theology to culture and politics. Islam, to members of the revolutionary generation, fostered tyranny and thus was as profoundly anti-American as it had been to their colonial ancestors.

No sooner had Americans freed themselves from the despotism of George III than they found themselves ensnared by the same centuries-old culture of privateering in the broader Mediterranean region. Just as for Britain, trade in that divided sea was vital to the new republic. Americans could ill afford to bypass the corsairs' trap. However, America's losses were relatively small—only about 700 American sailors suffered the pain of captivity in the Barbary States. Like the European nations, the United States was forced to pay tribute for safe passage and to ransom its captives. But it also negotiated a historic treaty with Morocco in order to secure the Atlantic and concentrate on the more aggressive Ottoman regencies.

Although miles away from North Africa, Americans—like Europeans—read the narratives of a few captives who published their tales of misfortune in Muslim lands. Their travails and suffering renewed their readers' faith in their nation and solidified American patriotism. To the Americans who were proud of their newly acquired freedom, being captured and enduring conditions of slavery was a shocking affront to the principles for which so many had sacrificed. They did pay tribute, but they also fought back and built a navy that eventually allowed them to force Tripoli and Algiers to agree to terms of peace in 1805.

American captivity narratives were more than denunciations of Islamic despotism, however; they also provided useful information about North African Muslim societies and, at times, praised their more humane treatment of slaves. British and American abolitionists used the plight of Western captives to highlight the West's double standard toward the issue of slavery, while no less a leader than Abraham Lincoln was influenced by the tale of a Moroccan trader who saved the lives of Americans shipwrecked on the Atlantic coast of the Sahara. In the end, the enslavement of Christians in Muslim lands was played out against a complex history that is with us still.

ANOUAR MAJID

Bibliography

Allison, Robert J. *The Crescent Obscured: The United States and the Muslim World, 1776–1815*. New York: Oxford University Press, 1995.

Colley, Linda. *Captives*. New York: Pantheon, 2002.

Sovereignty

The creation of the European Atlantic World can in many ways be seen as the extension and consequence of contests over sovereignty—who and what held final jurisdiction over any given set of people, places, and resources—among various claimants to power within the world of medieval and early-modern Christendom. In turn, the increasing maritime contact with the Atlantic, coastal Africa, and the Indian Ocean beginning with late fifteenth-century navigators sponsored by the Spanish and Portuguese crowns—most notably Christopher Columbus, Bartolomeu Dias, and Vasco da Gama—raised many questions about the nature of European legal authority in the rest of the world, both with respect to indigenous peoples and among the European powers themselves.

Attempting to resolve these issues, Pope Alexander VI's bull (decree or charter) Inter Caetera of 1493 and its subsequent clarification in the Luso-Spanish Treaty of Tordesillas (1494) established a longitudinal line of demarcation west of the Azores, delegating responsibility for European expansion to the east exclusively to Portugal and to the west to Spain. Though prompted by the new circumstances of maritime expansion, the bull was the culmination of a century of papal interest in overseas expansion. It was also a fairly traditional and familiar instrument, which followed from a long history of the papacy's attempts to claim a strong role in determining European dynastic politics, calling on its spiritual authority as the head of the Church and as nominal successor to the ostensibly universal empire of ancient Rome. At the same time, this spiritual "donation" became the basis for the claims of the two Iberian monarchies, especially after they were united under a single crown (1580–1640), to the exclusive authority among European maritime powers to spread Christianity to—and thus military, commercial, and political jurisdiction in—the non-Christian world.

Other Catholic monarchies, particularly France, pushed back against such an expansive notion of both papal and Iberian sovereignty in Europe and abroad. However, the greatest challenge to such claims came in the early sixteenth century, as the Protestant Reformation prompted new and at times radical articulations of regional and imperial autonomy, perhaps most notoriously embodied in the English Parliament's bold declaration under Henry VIII in 1533 that England had become an "empire," independent from any appeals to papal dominion or Church law. The language of empire—derived from the Latin concept of *imperium*, or sovereignty—embodied in this claim to independence from the papacy would in retrospect set the ideological and discursive possibilities for the idea of extending forms of European sovereignty abroad, into the Atlantic. At the same time, the split from Rome in many ways laid the groundwork for the European dynastic and strategic rivalries, as well as the political, martial, and legal framework that propelled European upstarts such as the English and Dutch to break into the Spanish-dominated Atlantic. For example, the objection by King Philip II (r. 1556–1598) of Spain to the succession of the Protestant Queen Elizabeth (r. 1558–1603) to the English crown—justified both by his support for her Catholic cousin and rival, Queen Mary of Scotland, and by his own claims to the English throne through his marriage to her predecessor, Queen Mary—not only prompted the attempted Spanish invasions of England (the "Armada" of 1588) and Ireland (1601) but also inspired a flood of English pirates and privateers in the Spanish Caribbean in the closing decades of the sixteenth century. Elizabethan support for the "Dutch revolt" in the Spanish Netherlands from the 1560s onward only exacerbated those tensions, while the new Calvinist, republican United Provinces that emerged from it also began to establish itself as a power in Europe, in part by extending commercial and military influence into the Atlantic.

By the later seventeenth century, the Atlantic had become a full-fledged theater for intra-European conflicts over dynastic succession and attempts to consolidate inchoate early-modern fiscal-military regimes, even among coreligionists; these included three Anglo-Dutch maritime wars from the 1650s to the 1670s. The French pretension to preeminence in Europe was supported by transatlantic commerce and plantations at the northern borders of Spanish America. Scottish attempts after the Glorious Revolution (1688) to defend their sovereignty within the British multiple monarchy prompted the so-called Darien scheme, an attempt by the newly created Company of Scotland Trading to Africa and the Indies to break into both the Spanish Atlantic and the English and Dutch East Indian trades with an ill-fated colonial venture in New Caledonia, in current-day Panama, in 1695.

If this Atlantic expansion was marked by the ambitions of established as well as emergent powers in Europe, it also mirrored the complexity embedded in the European political order. Despite the rhetorical and ideological claims by some to absolute—at times even divine—monarchy, juridical and political authority in Europe was pluralistic and layered in nature. Physical borders between monarchical domains were fuzzy. Civil, common, natural, and canon law systems all coexisted and overlapped within the supposedly sovereign domains of royal dynasties, and the boundaries of authority among various governing agents—monarchs, consultative legislatures, courts, and localities—were matters of constant renegotiation. Thus, while the Atlantic World was a place into which European interdynastic and diplomatic disputes could be projected, it served as a relatively malleable venue in which to work out the jurisdictional tensions within these evolving polities as well.

For example, the competing regional political dynamics within the federal United Provinces of the Netherlands were clearly evident behind the scenes of such supposedly national enterprises as the Dutch West India Company. Similarly, authority abroad was never absolute or singular. Rather, it was marked by a cacophony of overlapping and intersecting forms of governance: metropolitan officials—such as royal governors, inspectors, and surveyors—as well as colonial proprietors, corporations, merchant guilds, municipalities, pueblos, colonial councils, judicatures, trading companies, and other local communities. Moreover, the disputes over sovereignty themselves took place over a patchwork of geographical spaces of varied shapes, not so much large swaths of homogeneous territory as the passageways, routes, and thoroughfares that connected them: roads, rivers, littorals, sea lanes, and the like. And early-modern European conceptions of sovereignty were often less concerned with the entirety of landmasses than with specific resources and the labor to make profitable use of them.

The legal instruments, alongside treatises, maps, and various other sources that promoted and justified European legal order abroad, offered competing visions of imperial and colonial sovereignty. On the one hand, European monarchs, parliaments, judicial authorities, and the theorists who supported them often articulated a concept of complete sovereignty over their subjects abroad. For example, English colonial charters to proprietors and corporations formulaically reserved ultimate sovereignty to the crown and set specific borders to colonial spaces. In reality, however, legal practice in the Atlantic was far more fragmented and hybrid in nature. Many of the charters, patents, decrees, and other instruments that ostensibly bound those various enterprises to sovereign monarchies and republics back home drew upon legal traditions and formulae—papal bulls, medieval corporate charters, grants of feudal land tenure—that extended the traditionally pluralistic European political order overseas. Political and legal practices mirrored such jurisdictional diversity. For example, the Spanish principle and practice of *obedezco pero no cumplo* ("I obey but do not comply") allowed the crown to retain titular sovereignty while authorities on the ground ignored or resisted laws and orders from home that they felt did not apply to local exigencies. Likewise, though English charters consistently demanded laws made overseas not be "repugnant" to English law, in practice laws differed dramatically not only from colony to colony but even within any given colony, affecting every domain from probate to religious toleration.

Colonies constantly sparred over the boundaries of their authority, both with one another and with royal officials sent from Europe. Meanwhile, individuals traveled fairly fluidly among the competing jurisdictional spaces, as the Atlantic enterprise itself moved so many people from such varied origins—

Native Americans, enslaved Africans, foreign merchant communities—in and out of these ill-defined jurisdictions. This fluidity meant that European legal and political regimes were malleable works-in-progress, regularly borrowing from and negotiating among various traditions. These legal assemblages were especially heterogeneous in spaces that changed hands among the rival European powers or in border zones where sovereignty constantly shifted through either diplomacy or war. Even legal authorities in Europe could not agree which laws, courts, agencies, and institutions prevailed abroad; in England, such contests extended from fine points of disagreement between the civil and common lawyers and judges to the conflict between the monarchy and Parliament that led to such epochal events as the Civil War (1640s) and the Glorious Revolution at the end (1688) of the seventeenth century.

Thus, the great pretensions among European sovereigns about the possibilities for *imperium* over their subjects abroad belied the fragmented nature of effective authority in Europe and the Atlantic alike. In due course the relatively rapid and ad hoc expansion into the Atlantic raised vibrant disputes among European statesmen, theorists, and jurists. Rival powers, particularly in England, France, and the Netherlands, sought new definitions of property, authority, just war, and sovereignty to legitimate their presence in the world beyond Europe against Iberian claims to exclusive dominion.

Of course, such arguments about possession and occupation of territory overseas did not arise only as Europeans jockeyed for position; they also were parts of an extensive European debate about the legal framing of engagements with the inhabitants of these previously unknown lands as well as with the other immigrants, free and unfree, all of whom brought with them divergent and competing ideas about sovereignty. The most immediate ambiguity to resolve centered on how Europeans might interpret the local forms of political authority that they encountered in the Americas and Africa. European thinkers divided on the question of whether non-Christian indigenes possessed authority to wage just war, and thus to make legitimate treaties and agreements of peace, to hold property, or even to govern themselves and thus claim the fruits of their own labor. The ensuing debates raised new questions about the nature of political authority (*impe-rium*) and private ownership (*dominium*) of property that ultimately transformed European thought about sovereignty and the law of nations (the forerunner of international law) at home and abroad.

In West Africa, European agents tended to understand local rulers as sovereign "kings" or "princes," which in turn allowed for commercial exchange—particularly in slaves—as well as negotiations and treaties for independent or semi-independent settlements and enclaves within coastal trading ports, such as Cape Coast Castle on the Gold Coast. At the same time, European theorists and courts increasingly expressed assertive forms of sovereignty, especially in declaring their legal rights to enslave African peoples, transport them across the Atlantic, and sell them as property in markets in the Americas. In the western Atlantic, explorers, colonial promoters, settlers, and theorists often represented lands as largely unpeopled and untrammeled. If they were not uninhabited at first, the very real and rapid depopulation of island and coastal America—whether through disease or displacement—and the at times radically discordant understandings of the nature of ownership and sovereignty gave urgency to defining ways of thinking about fundamental questions of territorial possession. One solution was to imagine much of the western Atlantic littoral as *res* or *terra nullius*—that is, newly discovered land treated legally as unoccupied. Initial Spanish claims to sovereignty in the Atlantic rested on this notion of first discovery, as well as—contradictorily—the authority of the pope's dispensation of the responsibility to minister to non-Christian souls.

At the same time, critics of Spanish colonial policy—certainly its other European rivals, but many within the Spanish world as well—mobilized a variety of arguments that relied on alternative definitions of sovereignty overseas. Theorists, statesmen, and historians such as Richard Hakluyt (c. 1552–1616), Samuel Purchas (c. 1577–1626), Hugo Grotius (1583–1645), and later John Locke (1632–1704) found particular recourse to, among other sources, the ideas and languages of humanism, which drew upon the intellectual traditions of the ancient Roman republic as well as of the early-modern Italian city-states, in developing new understandings of natural law, personal property, and the relationship between civic obligation and political authority. One of the most crucial ideas to arise out of these animated debates was the notion that one could claim rights only to something that one actually *possessed*; possession—especially in the case of territory—in turn required actual maintenance, occupation, and for some, also, the active improvement, plantation, and cultivation of what was claimed. The emphasis on active investment in "natural" resources effectively overrode both Iberian pretensions to vast unoccupied portions of the hemisphere by donation or discovery, as well as most indigenous claims to sovereignty—given the overwhelming sense among Europeans that Native Americans, even where acknowledged as present on the land, had failed to exploit it in a manner Europeans recognized as productive.

This principle—that land had to be occupied and improved to be claimed—resolved in many ways the apparent contradiction between the legal framing of the Americas as *terra nullius* and the fact that Europeans in practice found it necessary to recognize at least limited forms of Native sovereignty. This recognition made it possible to make treaties and commercial agreements with indigenous peoples, both against European rivals and for acquisition of land. Those wishing to secure a European legal presence in the Americas developed strategies to obviate such acknowledged authority, such as the infamous Spanish *requerimiento*, a legal decree that "required" indigenous Americans to convert to Christianity; their failure to do so (after having been duly informed by a public reading of this decree—in Spanish, of course) supposedly constituted forfeiture of their rights to sovereignty over their territories and even their own persons.

Such manipulative legalities were deeply controversial within the Spanish Empire. Yet what had originated as a defense of the rights of indigenous Americans amid Spanish debates over the proper nature of European authority—most notably from authors like Bartolomé de Las Casas (1484–1566) and the Salamanca-school theorist Francisco de Vitoria (1483–1546)—by the seventeenth and eighteenth centuries became yet another argument among various European theorists for erosion of those very same rights, if European colonists could argue that Native American "princes" had failed to live up to the responsibilities of sovereign powers. European legal discourse allowed for more and more conditions under which Native sovereignty could thus disappear or be challenged, by arguing indigenous powers had left land vacant or unculti-

vated, had violated the terms of treaties of peace and commerce, or were simply bestial, barbarous, or otherwise less than human (through accusations of cannibalism and other practices of savagery). In conjunction with the principle in the emergent European law of nations that all sovereigns were obliged to provide free passage and protection for "peaceful" merchants, arguments admitting to Native sovereignty ironically formed a foundation for legitimating war against, dispossession of, and conquest of Native peoples.

The ideas that shaped European approaches to sovereignty in the Atlantic World drew upon extant legal traditions and both ancient and recent history. Biblical exegesis played a central role in European law. The Muslim Mediterranean world also loomed large in this European Atlantic imaginary, as the Spanish applied lessons they had drawn from their own "Reconquista" of the Iberian peninsula to conceptions of indigenous American sovereignty, or as the English read Native American politics in the light of their previous experiences with the "Turk," that is, the Ottoman regime in the eastern Mediterranean and North Africa. Even Spain and Portugal's Protestant rivals, despite their ostensible hostility to Iberian empire and Catholic universalism, consistently drew upon canon law and mimicked the language and aspirations of the papal bulls in their own charters and dispensations to proprietors and corporate bodies, who they insisted were implementing monarchical sovereignty overseas. They also framed their estimations of the legitimacy of indigenous polities in negotiating on questions of war, peace, and property in the language of rights and responsibilities of "infidels" in canon- and natural-law traditions. These competing theoretical claims to sovereignty translated into a variety of symbolic acts, ceremonies, and documentary practices on the ground as well: drawing and publishing maps, naming places and bodies of water, building fences, planting crosses, and performing familiar legal or religious rites (like the *requerimiento*), many of which were incomprehensible or at best opaque to indigenous powers as well as disputed by European rivals.

Many of these disputes centered on alleged rights to territory and the labor of its inhabitants, but European contacts around the Atlantic World prompted a perhaps even more complicated and vexing controversy over whether, or to what extent, a power could claim sovereignty over uninhabited oceanic space itself. Spanish and Portuguese claims to exclusive jurisdiction abroad implied the rights to command and control Europeans on the seas. Hugo Grotius's anonymously published *Mare Liberum* (*The Free Sea*, 1609)—which was rooted in Dutch conflicts with the Portuguese over the East Indies—suggested that the sea, unlike land or coastal waters adjacent to sovereign territory, could not be occupied, let alone improved, in the way required to establish sovereignty over habitable territory; the open seas thus could not be closed to outsiders under any particular sovereignty. European concerns thus fed into debates over sovereign power on the oceans, the extent to which polities could claim exclusive rights in littoral, or "territorial," waters, and the policing power of individuals, corporate groups, and polities with respect to one another as well as against forms of maritime violence such as piracy.

Disputes over sovereignty touched any range of European activities in the Atlantic, from fishing rights on Newfoundland's Grand Banks to Iberian claims of monopolistic dominion over territories and peoples overseas. Moreover, the question of jurisdiction beyond the seas extended outside rivalries among sovereign powers in Europe to the limits of the authority of these regimes over their own subjects abroad. The English Navigation Acts, for example, first promulgated in 1651 but revised and reissued periodically through the seventeenth and eighteenth centuries, placed restrictions on English shipping in the Atlantic, established political authority over its crews, and regulated its ports of call; such laws were clearly novel sorts of claims—at various points quite controversial ones—to express the sovereignty of, first, the English Republic (the Commonwealth, 1649–1660) and then the restored monarchy (Charles II, 1661) and its successors over the sea lanes of the Atlantic. The Spanish *asiento*, which licensed exclusive rights to supply enslaved Africans to Spanish territories in the Americas, and the British abolition of the slave trade in 1807, implied similar legal capacities to control transnational commerce, again asserting rival definitions of sovereignty over the sea that continue to inform debates on international law today.

The unique problems created by dynastic, and later territorial, competition in the legally ambiguous spaces of the Atlantic, both on the ocean and the lands encircling it, fundamentally transformed—some have argued even themselves constituted—early-modern European notions of particular, as distinct from universal, sovereignty. They gave shape to the "law of nations" needed to regulate the competition created by derogation of an inherently singular final authority (such as the pope) to territorially limited, and thus multiple, claimants. No single definition of sovereignty emerged from these contests. Ambiguities endured into the eighteenth century, when subjects of the European monarchies began to amplify their own claims to sovereignty, eventually forcefully. The so-called Age of Revolutions in the late eighteenth century can be seen as preoccupied with resolving the contradictions inherent in the various European claims to sovereignty in the Atlantic. Over the course of the "long" eighteenth century, interimperial conflicts transformed from extensions of European dynastic conflicts into the Atlantic zone—the Nine Years' War (1689–1697), War of the Spanish Succession (1702–1713), and War of the Austrian Succession (1739–1748)—to wars driven themselves by contests over territories in the Atlantic World itself—beginning with the Seven Years' War (1756–1763) and followed by others, including the War of American Independence (1775–1783) and the French Revolutionary and Napoleonic Wars after 1789. These conflicts in the end loosened the Spanish grip on its initial claim to absolute sovereignty in the Indies, which in any event had been waning since the late seventeenth century, and gave rise to the great eighteenth-century Anglo-French maritime and territorial contests for colonial sovereignty.

The great costs of eighteenth-century warfare also forced European ministries to make increasingly bold claims to exercise sovereignty over their overseas subjects. In the case of the expanding fiscal-military power of the British crown and Parliament, this assertion led to even more aggressive taxes, surveillance, and restrictions on colonial trade. These trends led, in turn, to a wave of rebellions and revolutions across the Atlantic World by the late eighteenth and early nineteenth centuries. Yet the independent polities that emerged in the Americas by the early nineteenth century out of rebellions against European sovereignty—the United States, Haiti, and a wave of republics in Central and South America—hardly made a firm break with the complex competing claims to territorial sovereignty worked out over centuries of extending European legal frameworks into the Atlantic. Instead, the new "national" states modified, extended, and codified this legal heritage into the nineteenth and twentieth centuries, continuing to confront many of the same issues about the rights and autonomy of indigenous communities, political and economic autonomy among these American states, neutrality and sovereignty at sea, and the creation of new claims to sovereignty, made especially by the United States, over both the great expanses of the American continents and territories overseas.

PHILIP J. STERN

Bibliography

Adelman, Jeremy. *Sovereignty and Revolution in the Iberian Atlantic.* Princeton, NJ: Princeton University Press, 2006.

Armitage, David. *The Ideological Origins of the British Empire.* Cambridge: Cambridge University Press, 2000.

Benton, Lauren. *Law and Colonial Cultures: Legal Regimes in World History, 1400–1900.* Cambridge: Cambridge University Press, 2002.

———. *A Search for Sovereignty: Law and Geography in European Empires, 1400–1900.* Cambridge: Cambridge University Press, 2009.

Bilder, Mary Sarah. *The Transatlantic Constitution: Colonial Legal Culture and the Empire.* Cambridge, MA: Harvard University Press, 2004.

Fitzmaurice, Andrew. *Humanism and America: An Intellectual History of English Colonization, 1500–1625.* Cambridge: Cambridge University Press, 2003.

Hseuh, Vicki. *Hybrid Constitutions: Challenging Legacies of Law, Privilege, and Culture in Colonial America.* Durham, NC: Duke University Press, 2010.

Macmillan, Ken. *Sovereignty and Possession in the English New World: The Legal Foundations of Empire, 1576–1640.* Cambridge: Cambridge University Press, 2006.

Muldoon, James. *Empire and Order: The Concept of Empire, 800–1800.* New York: Palgrave, 1999.

Pagden, Anthony. *Lords of All the World: Ideologies of Empire in Spain, Britain, and France, c. 1500–c. 1800.* New Haven, CT: Yale University Press, 1995.

Seed, Patricia. *Ceremonies of Possession in Europe's Conquest of the New World.* Cambridge: Cambridge University Press, 1995.

Tomlins, Christopher. *Freedom Bound: Law, Labor, and Civic Identity in Colonizing English America, 1580–1865.* Cambridge: Cambridge University Press, 2010.

Tomlins, Christopher L., and Bruce H. Mann, eds. *The Many Legalities of Early America.* Chapel Hill: University of North Carolina Press, 2001.

Tuck, Richard. *The Rights of War and Peace: Political Thought and the International Order from Grotius to Kant.* Oxford: Oxford University Press, 1999.

White, Richard. *The Middle Ground: Indians, Empires, and Republics in the Great Lakes Region, 1650–1815.* Cambridge: Cambridge University Press, 1991.

Specie

One of the more prominent motivations propelling Portugal and subsequently Spain into the Atlantic was a centuries-long "bullion famine" across Christian Europe. During the Crusades of the twelfth and thirteenth centuries, Italian merchants had introduced Europe to a plethora of riches via the eastern Mediterranean—intricately woven rugs from Persia, silks and porcelain from China, and spices from around the Indian Ocean. But Europeans had few products of their own to offer in return, other than specie—payment in cash. The general paucity of silver and gold within Europe that could be mobilized for the acquisition of Asian luxuries was one of the principal lures that drew the Portuguese toward the Niger River goldfields of sub-Saharan Africa in the early fifteenth century.

Within Europe, limited stocks of bullion encouraged the development of credit instruments to finance long-distance trade, such as merchants' paper bills of exchange. But paper notes and credit did not mobilize armies of soldiers or mercenaries or day laborers paid in coin. African gold was the initial specie lubricant for the wheels of commerce when Prince Henry the Navigator of Portugal financed the maritime exploration of the northwest shores of Africa, opening the Atlantic World and drawing Europe into an ever-expanding trade in sugar and other commodities, as well as slaves. The fall of Constantinople in 1453 to the Ottomans, however, disrupted the outflow of bullion through the Mediterranean to the Silk Road across Central Asia to China, setting the stage for Spain to send

Columbus sailing west across the Atlantic in search of a more direct, and less costly, route to China and Japan. With the silver produced from his inadvertent discovery of America, the Spanish monarchy would become the most powerful military power in Europe within half a century, as specie mobilized mercenaries and markets.

However, on the eve of the conquest of the last Muslim stronghold at Granada in 1492, which would end the Christian reconquest of Iberia, Spain lacked both the agricultural output of her French neighbor and the easily navigable waterways of central and northern Europe. Her population was divided against itself into religious factions, speaking numerous languages and regional dialects. Myriad legal and economic traditions separated artisan guilds, the Mesta sheep ranchers of Castile, and Catholic churchmen into privileged classes. In combination with a general want of natural endowments, these obstacles to innovation and economic development meant that Spain was far from prosperity. Nonetheless, in 1513, only two decades after Columbus sailed, Niccolò Machiavelli could rightly observe, "We have in our days Ferdinand, king of Aragon, the present king of Spain, who may, not improperly, be called a new prince, since he has transformed from a small and weak king into the greatest monarch in Christendom" (*The Prince*, chapter XXI). What was the cause of this sudden renaissance?

The initial forays of the Spanish into the Caribbean secured the bases that would propel Cortés to Mexico (1519–1521) and Pizarro to Peru (1530–1533), where conquests of the Aztec and Inca military regimes opened the way for Spanish exploitation of the vast silver deposits of the Cerro Rico at Potosí and Zacatecas in northern Mexico, launching the initial phase of New World bullion production. As the conquistadors shifted from pillaging native societies to mobilizing Africans and Amerindians with sizable investments in mining, annual imports of specie at Seville increased more than a hundredfold in a century, from some 300,000 ounces of gold and silver in 1500, rising to 5 million by 1540, 12 million by 1570, 30 million by 1590 and 40 million by 1600. Annual production hovered around 30 million through the 1610s, faltered in the 1620s, and fell precipitously until the 1650s to a nadir of 5 to 7 million, marking the end of Potosí's global importance. A second phase shifted the center of Latin American silver production permanently to Mexico, with a long, slow-but-steady rise over the eighteenth century, peaking at 23 million ounces annually in the 1790s. Shipped largely as coin, these *pesos de ocho* (the proverbial "pieces of eight") weighed roughly an ounce and were of 85 to 90 percent fineness. They would eventually become the model of the U.S. silver dollar. So great was the volume of silver mined that even Spain's Ottoman rivals benefited, creating a new fiscal category—*riyals*—to track the hundreds of thousands of Spanish American *reales* passing through the Levant.

For Spain, the result was more than a century of unequaled wealth and power, both military and commercial. Charles I (r. 1516–1556) used some of this bounty of specie to purchase the prestigious title of Holy Roman Emperor and then led his Habsburg progeny into a series of costly and generally disastrous imperial and religious conflicts, terminating with the Peace of Westphalia (1648) and the reign of his great-grandson, Philip IV (r. 1621–1655). New World bullion largely paid for the enormous military mobilization on all sides in Europe during this period. So important to militarization were gold and silver that interruption of even a single year's shipment could bring about a temporary truce. Yet at the height of the Thirty Years' War (1618–1648), American treasure seldom reached the Spanish mainland, as agents of Spain's bankers took possession of the arriving silver at the coastal port town of Sanlucar, rather than risk diversion of the credits owed farther up the Guadalquivir River at Seville. The transfer of troops and supplies from Italy through central Europe to German-speaking principalities and the Netherlands at midcentury was, like the Spanish Armada of the 1580s, facilitated by merchant-banking houses such as the Fuggers and Welsers, who in turn spread American silver widely through the military budgets of the warrior-aristocrats across Europe and the Mediterranean, transforming commercial letters of exchange into presumably more secure instruments of government debt in specie.

In commerce, demand among Iberian or New World Spaniards for fine European textiles, Chinese silks and porcelain, and the spices of the Indian Ocean channeled the precious metals of Mexico and Peru to the merchants of greater Europe. Though the Americas produced tens of millions of ounces of bullion, little of it remained for long in the Western Hemisphere. Taxes such as the *quinto real*, import and export duties, and numerous monopolies—on items from cockfights to ice and tobacco—delivered an ever-larger share of the bounteous specie into royal hands. The remainder was exported to acquire the exotic luxuries of the Asian world, frequently leaving the Iberian colonies without sufficient coin to carry out local transactions like buying a loaf of bread or a piece of meat. Just as scarcity of monetary metals across Europe forced a resort to bills of exchange, emigration of silver coin from the mining colonies in trade with Europe likewise propelled the dissemination of credit and commercial paper back across the Atlantic. Spanish coin and Continental credit equally lubricated the engines of international war and global trade, with transcontinental flows of specie bringing parity in rice prices between Europe and Japan by the 1660s, as well as in the bimetallic ratio of gold and silver between Europe and China by the 1690s, and between Europe and India by the end of the eighteenth century.

Looking back on the impact of Spain's silver-based "Golden Age," Alfonso Nuñez de Castro remarked in 1669, "Let London manufacture those fine fabrics of hers to her heart's content; let Holland her chambrays; Florence her cloth; the Indies [Americas] their beaver and vicuna; Milan her brocade, Italy and Flanders their linens . . . so long as our capital can enjoy them; the only thing it proves is that all nations train their journeymen for Madrid, and that Madrid is the queen of Parliaments, for all the world serves her and she serves nobody" (Vives, 127). Thus silver secured the two cornerstones of Europe's industrial and industrious revolutions: supply *and* demand, built on the liquidity of American silver.

This initial phase of American bullion production and commercial liquidity was not without its costs. First, the reexport of specie from Spain to greater Europe contributed to a massive inflationary trend known to economic historians as the Price Revolution of the sixteenth and seventeenth centuries. Real wages fell or stagnated just as Europe's population began to rise rapidly. The result was more job seekers at a time when those in possession of bullion were diverting it to pay for wars or luxury imports. The slowing economy pushed both urban and rural laborers increasingly to emigrate from Europe in pursuit of land and self-sufficiency in farming and away from the cold realities of early-modern markets imbalanced by the influx of silver.

At the same time, the spectacular flood of specie into pre-1650 Europe captured the imaginations of contemporary observers, politicians, merchants and philosophers alike—the Dutch, French, and English mercantilists. Sitting on the margins of the Spanish commercial-military nexus, the merchant-investors of Amsterdam, followed by those of Paris and London—each lacking its own native or American supplies of bullion—came to depend on investment in production, or economic development, and the positive balance of payments that sales of goods and services to attract specie would return. As Adam Smith later remarked in *The Wealth of Nations* (1776), "The value of a free-stone quarry, for example, will necessarily increase with the increasing improvement and population of the country round about it, especially if it should be the only one in the neighborhood. But the value of a silver mine, even though there should not be another within a thousand miles of it, will not necessarily increase with the improvement of the country in which it is situated" (Smith, 220). Put another way, the lack of bullion forced the more culturally open and tolerant societies of Holland, England, and France, with notable émigré Calvinist and Jewish merchant communities and an increasingly cosmopolitan leaning, to innovate economically. The growing profits and power from manufacturing productivity in northern Europe came at the expense of Spain. Thus, though greater Europe toiled at the behest of Madrid during the 1600s, it grew wealthy doing so, while the latter languished economically, and eventually also militarily, politically, and culturally. For many contemporary observers like Nuñez de Castro, all that was visible was Spanish wealth and power. For mercantilists such as the English merchant Thomas Mun (1571–1641), however, the tons of silver arriving from Spanish America represented power and opportunity via industry, industriousness, and favorable balances of payments vis-à-vis passive, inefficient, and unproductive *rentiers* like Spain.

The Calvinist Dutch acquired specie through commerce and funneled it, in part, toward war with Catholic Spain, first in defense of religious liberties and later in pursuit of political independence. But how to mobilize the limited supplies of bullion to support two agendas simultaneously, toward trade *and* war? From 1609 credit and commerce concentrated the value of monetary metals in the Wisselbank, which leveraged its holdings of specie via issues of stock and bills of exchange, the financial tools of the Dutch East India and West India companies, founded in 1602 and 1621, respectively. These financial strategies funded construction of a merchant fleet that by 1650 controlled 90 percent of Europe's trade with the wider world, backed by maritime military capacity to protect the global interests of Dutch merchants and bankers. The Dutch steadily supplanted the Portuguese around the world, still moving African gold east around the Cape to Asia and slaves west across the Atlantic, while the Spanish found themselves on the losing side of the Thirty Years' War (1618–1648).

The English and French emerged to challenge the Spanish and Dutch during the 1600s, in Europe and around the Atlantic, first piratically in pursuit of bullion and later in search of territory for extraction of natural resources and cultivation. Monetary policy and its capacity to fund economic development were other aspects of specie important for the integration of the Atlantic World around investment and production rather than raiding and piracy.

A comparative analysis of England and France, taken in combination with the expanding reliance on credit and paper, illustrates the financial power of specie. Currency reform under Elizabeth I and Sir Thomas Gresham (1519–1579), primary financier to the later Tudor dynasty, raised the esteem of English coin in international markets following the debasements (minting coins with less bullion content) of the first Tudors, attracting foreign bullion to finance trade. Similarly, under the Valois in France, with Jean Bodin (1530–1596) and Jean de Malestroit (d. 1578) revealing the mechanisms of the silver-induced inflation of the era, crown policy favored greater regularity in standards of coinage. At the same time, Spain turned increasingly to copper and debasement to stretch its American specie even further, yet—in effect—mining one's own money to manufacture more coin became a further impediment to imperial Spain.

Monetary policies in England and France diverged markedly during the seventeenth century, as the latter followed Spain and embarked upon a series of debasements that drove the value of its coins steadily down, accelerated by manufacture of increasing volumes of coin, especially copper. In other words, like Spain, France raised revenue via inflation, and the result was economic stagnation. England, by contrast, was so rigid in maintaining the value of its specie that it alternately overvalued either gold or silver, precipitating outflows of each metal from the country, further fueling their mercantilists' preoccupation with bullion and the ensuing domestic shortages of gold and silver.

Monetary policy had shifted markedly away from bullionism by the end of the seventeenth century, during the reigns of Louis XIV in France (1643–1715) and William III in England (1689–1702). To the unenlightened observer of the splendid displays of wealth at the royal courts, France and Louis were rich, like the earlier Iberian Habsburgs, while England under the Stuarts and William of Orange was poor; but neither yet enjoyed the regular access to bullion that Spain's American empire continued to provide. While French fiscal policy eventually proved even more chaotic than Spain's a century earlier, England developed paper alternatives to single-minded pursuit of metallic wealth, surpassing in creativity even the inspired credit instruments of the Dutch merchants and the Wisselbank.

While bills of exchange originated in late-medieval Europe as a means of facilitating long-distance trade, throughout the 1600s institutions like the Dutch Wisselbank extended their utility. The growing assets of commercial houses backed discounted bills and consigned paper as acceptable mediums of exchange, or even as capital, in lieu of coin. As commercial credit expanded from the sixteenth century into the seventeenth, the relative reliance on specie to fund investment declined. Critics of the bullion-stimulated Price Revolution could point with considerable justification to the contributions of credit to the price fluctuations of agricultural commodities in England and France. The leverage available through issuing shares of stock, merchant commercial paper, and bank notes had mobilized economic growth that eventually outstripped the economic stimulus of all the silver the Americas had yielded for Spain.

The market in paper credit instruments, in lieu of increasingly scarce specie, likewise financed English colonial formation via joint-stock companies, from the Virginia Company (1606–1624) onward. The dredging of English rivers to facilitate inland transportation, the early operations of the British in Africa's slave trade, and numerous canal projects all relied on debt subscriptions to overcome limited domestic supplies of bullion. Whether originating in the need to move agricultural commodities to market and to underwrite purchasing power for the commodities delivered, or in a market for English government debt to cover the expensive seventeenth-century wars with the Dutch for commercial control in the Atlantic, English banking almost from its beginnings combined currency exchange, credit for local and long-distance trade, capital for internal improvements, and government financing. And the aftermarket in, or further circulation of, paper-based credit originating from these and other ventures moved English monetary stocks through the economy faster, offsetting the persistent shortage in bullion that was a hallmark of economic life in an expanding early-modern Europe. With regard to the larger question of capital formation for investment in industrial plants and equipment, the English found themselves with seemingly boundless financial resources from the end of the seventeenth century and a growing advantage over their less-liquid French, Dutch, and Spanish rivals.

The disastrous loss of warships in the English Channel at Beachy Head in 1690, in the Nine Years' War (1688–1697) that pitted a pan-European alliance against the forces of Louis XIV, was the moment that precipitated England's ultimate financial revolution. Already struggling to raise revenue for even basic government functions, let alone the ongoing war in Ireland, William III was suddenly faced with need for even more money to rebuild the Royal Navy and turned to London's merchants in a grand bargain. William chartered the Bank of England as a private entity empowered to serve as repository for government funds, thus creating a pool of specie to anchor an ever-expanding web of credit by means of a paper currency (which became the pound—backed by sterling silver), and a terminus to connect the agricultural producers and cottage manufacturers of the English countryside with the

wider world via London merchants and the domestic credit instruments that they issued. The fortuitous discovery of large quantities of gold at Minas Gerais in Brazil the year before the Bank of England was chartered, combined with the growing intimacy of England and Portugal in the ensuing century, brought critical additional specie support to the English for their emerging systems of paper credit. Accordingly, the new central bank raised subscriptions for William's £1.2 million loan in only twelve days, and England's public national debt was born.

However, in contrast with earlier borrowing by military monarchs—Habsburg Spain, Bourbon France, or even Tudor England—the administration of William III and its eighteenth-century successors paid their bills. Where sovereign debt had previously brought only ruin for European speculators, holding England's obligations became a source of strength, undergirding annuities and insurance schemes, enabling rural development projects, and interconnecting the activities of country banking while providing start-up capital for innumerable industrial ventures, beginning with construction of the greatest of Europe's merchant marines and military fleets.

Advancing into the final eighteenth-century phase of intense competition in the Atlantic among the European mercantilist powers, the Dutch, albeit holding wider interests around the globe, could not match England's largest unified market in central or western Europe. France attempted to follow England's successful venture into credit and banking via financial adviser and investor John Law (1671–1729), but royal bankruptcy and repudiation of debts remained an easier alternative than fiscal reform, setting the stage for eventual revolution. In contrast to their cousins in Versailles, the French Bourbons, on the Spanish throne after the War of the Spanish Succession ended in 1713, undertook fiscal reforms after 1763—unleashing anew the productive power of the silver that flowed from their American territories. So great was the subsequent expansion of mining in Mexico that it largely funded a naval arms race with England during the last decades of the eighteenth century. With naval construction mobilized by Mexican silver at El Ferrol in far northwestern Spain and La Habana in Cuba, Spain's military fleet came even with the

Royal Navy by 1800, possessing five of the nine largest warships in the world. But the Battle of Trafalgar, fought in 1805 off the Strait of Gibraltar, would reveal that Spain's efforts had been all for naught. Bills and banknotes had mastered bullion. For all its silver, Spain fell into decline and succumbed to the Bonapartes, while England's primacy in the industrial age of the nineteenth century was all but assured.

DAVID WEILAND

Bibliography

Brewer, John. *The Sinews of Power: War, Money and the English State, 1688–1783*. Cambridge, MA: Harvard University Press, 1990.

De Vries, Jan, and Ad van der Woude. *The First Modern Economy: Success, Failure, and Perseverance of the Dutch Economy, 1500–1815*. Cambridge: Cambridge University Press, 1997.

Flynn, Dennis Owen, Arturo Giráldez, and Richard Von Glahn, eds. *Global Connections and Monetary History, 1470–1800*. Aldershot, UK: Ashgate, 2003.

Morineau, Michel. *Incroyables gazetters et fabuleaux metaux: Les retours des trésors américains d'après les gazettes hollandaises (XVIe–XVIIIe siècles)*. London: Cambridge University Press, 1985.

Perez Herrero, Pedro. *Plata y libranzas: La articulación comercial del Mexico borbonico*. Mexico City: Centro de Estudios Historicos/Colegio de Mexico, 1988.

Pressnell, L. S. *Country Banking in the Industrial Revolution*. Oxford: Clarendon, 1956.

Richards, J. F., ed. *Precious Metals in the Later Medieval and Early Modern Worlds*. Durham, NC: Carolina Academic Press, 1983.

Smith, Adam. *An inquiry into the nature and causes of the wealth of nations: By Adam Smith, . . . In two volumes*. London: printed for W. Strahan and T. Cadell, 1776.

Spooner, Frank C. *The International Economy and Monetary Movements in France, 1493–1725*. Cambridge, MA: Harvard University Press, 1972.

Stein, Stanley J., and Barbara Stein. *Silver, Trade and War: Spain and America in the Making of Early Modern Europe*. Baltimore, MD: Johns Hopkins University Press, 2000.

Vives, Jaime Vicens. "The Decline of Spain in the Seventeenth Century." In *The Economic Decline of Empires*, edited by Carlo M. Cipolla (Reprint, Abingdon, UK: Routledge, 2006), 121–167.

Technologies, African

In the mid-eighteenth century, the Scottish philosopher David Hume wrote that Africans had never had "symptoms of ingenuity." The continent, he continued, had "no arts . . . no indigenous manufactures." European intellectuals would debate the legitimacy of such disdain for much time to come. But by the mid-nineteenth century, dismissals such as Hume's were widely accepted. From the vantage point of a rapidly industrializing Europe, Africa was condemned as "backward," its peoples' "crude" technologies a sure sign of their "inferiority." Thus, no one would question British geographer Richard Burton when in 1864 he described African technology as consisting of nothing more than cutting canoes, weaving basketry, making "rude weapons," and in scattered places "practicing rough metallurgy" (Adas, 110, 154).

Of course Burton, like Hume before him, failed to understand African technologies in their local social, cultural, and political contexts. Technologies become commonplace because they are useful in achieving outcomes desired by their creators. For this reason, any consideration of technology in Atlantic Africa from 1400 to 1850 should focus not on what Europeans had done, but rather on what Africans wanted, the constraints within which they—like any historical actors—worked, and how they went about achieving their goals. Beyond the basic elements necessary for survival, human desires have not been constant over time or in all places. Culture shapes desires and channels ways of fulfilling them. Politics both makes possible and limits technologies used to attain outcomes desired. The historical contingency of technologies can be illustrated in Africa through an analysis of transportation, food production, and warfare.

In Hume's Europe, a variety of factors compelled capitalists and politicians to look overseas for markets. Meeting their desires required a reliable way to navigate oceans to reach distant ports. In Hume's day, sailing ships took traders to Africa, and most of the traders were interested in acquiring human captives. In the eyes of many, large and complex ships were symbols of European technological superiority over "backward" savages. But sailing ships could not navigate inland, where most Africans lived, since rapids blocked navigation on most rivers at only short distances from the ocean. Inland, the canoe was the most useful, accessible, and flexible means of travel on water. It was, as it remains in many places today, the best way to move people and goods to where Africans most wanted to move them, which was from point to point along the riverbanks, where they lived. Europeans and Africans had different desires, different ecologies with which to contend, and, it follows, different technologies.

A similar contrast and parallel contextual explanations can be seen in Africans' approaches to transportation by land. From 1400 to 1850, West Africans transported vast quantities of Atlantic imports, as well as their own products, almost exclusively by head porterage—long lines of men carrying packed loads weighing 60 pounds or so on their heads. Despite the fact that Europeans repeatedly introduced wheeled vehicles, West Africans found no significant use for these large, heavy conveyances. The reason was simple. Draft animals needed to pull the enormous bulk of these machines could not survive in most West African disease environments. Hence, into the early twentieth century even European colonial regimes used head porters to transport goods overland, until they could finance railroads. Africans' shunning of wheeled transport was not a sign of technological "backwardness." Head porters were useful, flexible, and available. Wheeled vehicles were not.

Another example of a seemingly elementary, but in reality useful, technology is the hoe—the agricultural implement of choice in West Africa from 1400 to 1850. Though European explorers thought the hoe a primitive tool, in tropical Africa it was in fact superior to the plow, which Europeans considered "more advanced." In tropical Africa, heavy seasonal rains and year-round elevated temperatures combined to leave hard-baked laterite soils rela-

tively poor in quality. Farmers therefore practiced swidden (or "slash-and-burn") agriculture, which involved cutting brush, felling trees, and burning the dead vegetation. The procedure left a thin layer of ash on the soil, which served as fertilizer. Cultivators, usually women, used hoes to work the ash into the top layer of soil. Plows were of no use, since they dug deeply and turned up soils with few or no nutrients. Moreover, plowing causes moisture to leach from the exposed earth, which African farmers conserved by using hoes to make small mounds and plant in them. The hoe, then, had greater utility in Africa than the plow.

Hoes and other existing agricultural technologies proved adaptable after 1500, when Africans transformed their food supplies by adapting cultigens from the Americas. Most important in supplying calories were maize and cassava (or manioc), which by the mid-seventeenth century were becoming central to diets in Atlantic Africa. However, the sheer availability of these crops did not dictate the embrace of new agricultural technologies; they were not inherently superior. In some areas existing cereals allowed African societies to achieve their desired outcomes, even under severe pressure from the violence of slaving.

Even with the historical viability of these African technologies, and even in contexts of pervasive change between 1400 and 1850, Africans did not shun new technologies that they found useful. In some regions, African smelters had produced high-quality iron for more than a millennium before the European caravels arrived in the fifteenth century. But long histories of smelting meant that supplies of the hard woods needed to make charcoal to attain high temperatures for smelting were depleted in many places. In other regions of Africa, ore and the purchasing power to acquire manufactured iron had always been lacking, so iron tools had never been commonplace. Atlantic merchants supplied bars of smelted iron to regions where it was needed, at first primarily in exchange for commodities extractable from remaining forests and later primarily for slaves. With iron, African smiths shaped hoes and knives that cultivators used to clear fields and harvest their crops. Farmers along Africa's Upper Guinea coast seeking refuge from slaving spreading from the interior used this iron to make tools to cut deeply into mangrove swamps along the shore, dam their waters, and produce bountiful quantities of rice on fertile soils that had previously been too overgrown to cultivate. Until the advent of mechanical mills in the Americas, these Upper Guineans were the most productive rice growers on the Atlantic rim. They achieved this leading position by exploiting imported raw material to augment old technologies in new ways of getting what they desired.

As the violence of slaving grew from 1400 to 1850, West Africans similarly extended old military technologies. Where large hooved domestic livestock could survive Africa's disease environments, imported horses gave enormous advantages over locally mobilized infantries in mobile hit-and-run raiding. Imported, muzzle-loading muskets also reshaped military strategies after the late seventeenth century, not least because their range made them effective in combating cavalry. They were not, however, particularly effective in confronting opposing warriors moving rapidly in loose formations through thick vegetation. These cheap guns fired only a short distance and were inaccurate and slow to reload. For these reasons, Africans often used firearms as supplements to, and not substitutes for, their own military technologies—spears and bows and arrows.

Europeans had adopted firearms largely because cannonballs had great penetrative power, effective in assaulting the massive stone defense works built to keep out the armored foot soldiers of an earlier era. But military tactics in Africa centered on mobility, not on besieging stationary positions. African warriors did not wear much armor, and the penetrating power of their weaponry was unimportant. Lightweight spears and arrows, often made more effective with the addition of iron tips, were more useful for fighting at a distance. At close range, swords and spears prevailed, particularly when they had iron edges and points, which African smiths crafted both with Atlantic imports and by domestic smelting. The use of horses in suitable areas, the application of gun technologies in situations where they gave an advantage, and the addition of iron tips to arrows and spears from 1400 to 1850 helped powerful men solidify control over local populations and establish new military regimes, with economies dependent on slaving.

If Africans embraced new technologies pragmatically, choosing some because of their usefulness and rejecting others, politics and cultures also shaped these choices. Powerful and wealthy elites are able to finance and even compel widespread use of new technologies. Innovation is not cheap, and existing technologies represent heavy fixed investments in equipment and training. Direct financial support is often necessary to invest in change, and so, too, is indirect support. Railroads, for example, would not have been possible without nineteenth-century governments making land available for rights-of-way and without the growing sophistication of financial instruments to amass the capital necessary even with government subsidies. Often it is only critical military threats to collective survival that concentrate the investment necessary for technological change. Africans did not have modern comprehensive armed political regimes capable of undertaking these costs, not least because accelerating militarization and growing financial capacities in the Atlantic left Africa increasingly indebted to Europe. Hence, Africans did not often direct the powerful and complex governing institutions on the continent toward advancing technological capacities.

The outcomes people desire *and* the ways they see as acceptable in achieving them are shared collective inheritances and hard for individual innovators to change. Between 1400 and 1850, Africans viewed people as the sources of the physical power that we have displaced using nonhuman energy sources that we appropriate through technology. People were Africa's sources of productivity, and Africans devoted enormous ingenuity and effort to assembling them in efficacious groups. In Africa, land was not owned, since it was abundant, and rights to occupy it came by belonging to communities, not by individual possession. Individuated stores of material wealth, like cattle, could vanish with drought and disease, but relationships in communities enabled materially impoverished individuals to survive. Social units were wealthy if they comprised many people, both kin born and slaves brought into them. Communities celebrated and enforced selfless dedication to the collective. Material accumulation, which is at the foundations of modern ideologies and which is advanced through technologies, was seen in Africa as an abomination. In Africa, greed was not good. Selfishness and personal accumulation were thought to be destructive of mutually supportive community. Technologies that concentrated wealth in the hands of a few were tools of witches, abominations to be rejected.

It is for this reason that many African communities, such as those of the rice-growing Balanta on Africa's Upper Guinea coast, shun modern machinery even today. Balanta think that working together with handcrafted, long-handled hoes in lowland mangrove marshes defines, as it long has, responsible citizens, and personhood itself. Balanta are not ignorant of technologies that Europeans see as "more advanced." However, as a community, they have other desires and perpetuate long-standing loyalties that, in their position marginal to the commercial wealth of the modern world, they cannot afford to abandon. For them, the viable option is their ethos of shared suffering and equal distribution of the resources they have among male household heads, who qualify by excelling with the collective technology.

In a continent of rich cultural diversity, this ideal of self-realization by contributing to the collectivity has never been embraced by everyone. But culture, politics, and ecology have combined in place after place in Africa to shape how people have chosen to adapt technologies, as others the world over have also done. Africans transformed old and invented new ways of doing things as they engaged with Atlantic merchants from 1400 to 1850. They also retained time-tested methods of achieving desired outcomes. Other existing technologies they adopted because their indebtedness to Atlantic commerce left them with no means to invest in costly imported alternatives.

WALTER HAWTHORNE

Bibliography

Adas, Michael. *Machines as the Measure of Men: Science, Technology, and Ideologies of Western Dominance.* Ithaca, NY: Cornell University Press, 1989.

Austen, Ralph A., and Danie Headrick. "The Role of Technology in the African Past." *African Studies Review* 26 (1983): 163–184.

Hawthorne, Walter. *Planting Rice and Harvesting Slaves: Transformations along the Guinea-Bissau Coast, 1400–1900.* Portsmouth, UK: Heinemann, 2003.

Miller, Joseph C. *Way of Death: Merchant Capitalism and the Angolan Slave Trade, 1730–1830.* Madison: University of Wisconsin Press, 1988.

Thornton, John K. *Warfare in Atlantic Africa, 1500–1800.* London: UCL Press, 1999.

Technology

See Military Technologies; Navigation and Nautical Sciences; Technologies, African.

Trading Companies

While early-modern European monarchs and republics certainly took great political and financial interest in Atlantic commerce and plantations from their very beginnings, the actual business of financing and administering European trade and settlement around the Atlantic was quite frequently the work of chartered corporations, firms, partnerships, and other forms of mercantile and colonial companies. Political authorities in Europe, still very much inchoate and in formation, often lacked the resources, infrastructure, and even political vision to undertake such enterprises on their own. Especially for the Dutch, English, and French following in the wake of Spanish expansion in the Atlantic, with its vast territories and great reserves of American silver, it frequently fell to merchants to provide the impetus, investment, and leadership for such ventures and to persuade others, including traditional social and political elites, of their potential value. Companies—with their unique legal privileges, wealthy directorships, networks of patronage, and labyrinthine political and financial connections—underwrote almost every aspect of overseas expansion, from managing European wharfs and docks and insuring and victualing ships to governing cities and provinces in the Americas, and they were thus critical in the shaping of the Atlantic World.

The legal and organizational structures of Atlantic companies varied across time and space and even within particular national and legal traditions, ranging from firms under single proprietorship and simple partnerships to guilds and so-called regulated companies (guildlike institutions that maintained and policed common chartered rights among a consortia of individual traders under a single legal identity). By the seventeenth century, however, Atlantic ventures increasingly took the relatively novel form of joint-stock companies, which pooled funds from shareholders in a separately constituted, but commonly directed, enterprise. Generally, joint-stock companies were more centralized in their governing structures and could raise far greater amounts of capital than other forms of collaboration, sometimes even more than European monarchies and republics. Since anyone, in theory, could own stock, they also had the potential to create wider coalitions and constituencies among merchants, gentry, nobility, other elites, and in some cases foreigners, *investing* them financially, politically, and socially in colonial ventures.

The scope and size of Atlantic companies varied. In some cases, European governments granted companies monopolies over all or most of the colonial projects in the Atlantic writ large, such as the Dutch West India Company (chartered first in 1621 and again in 1674–1791) or the more short-lived Portuguese Brazil Company (Companhia Geral do Comércio do Brasil, 1649–1664). The French experience was somewhat more compartmentalized. The Compagnie des Îles d'Amérique (1635–1664) first administered a number of colonial possessions in the Caribbean but was ultimately dissolved and succeeded by the Compagnie des Indes Occidentales (1664–1674). Quebec was similarly settled in the early seventeenth century by a series of court-company partnerships, culminating in the Company of New France (1627–1663), while Louisiana's legal standing in the late seventeenth and early eighteenth centuries also morphed through a rotation of corporate manifestations: the Mississippi Company (1684–1717), the Company of the West (1717–1720), and finally the Company of the Indies. Despite some early failed projects for an English West India Company and the initially wide brief of the Virginia Company (1607), which extended to most of the English claims in North America, the English Atlantic was divided into a mosaic of distinct individual and corporate enterprises, each of which governed over a far smaller parcel of the Atlantic littoral: Newfoundland, Plymouth, Providence (an island near what is today Nicaragua), Guinea, Guiana, the Northwest Passage, Somers Island (Bermuda), New England, Massachusetts Bay (1629–1684), and Hudson Bay (1670), among others. There were also multiple attempts at companies to trade in West Africa and

from there to the Americas, culminating in the Royal African Company in 1672. If French, Dutch, and British Atlantic companies had initially been intended to compete with the Spanish, by the eighteenth century they had demonstrated such efficacy in mobilizing new capital that the Iberians themselves belatedly began to charter private companies of their own, modeled on those efforts. The Spanish, for example, established the Guipúzcoa Company in Bilbao in 1728 to govern the Venezuelan trade, while Portugal, under the ambitious leadership of the Marquis of Pombal (Sebastião José de Carvalho e Melo, 1750–1777), created two trading companies to attempt to revitalize its faltering economic presence in Brazil and to extend its claims to territories in Africa.

By their very nature as extensions of sovereign authority in Europe, these Atlantic companies did far more than trade. In some sense, all companies were first and foremost communities, which produced or cemented social relations, political connections, collective bonds, institutional cultures, and political or religious missions and identities. After all, the very word—*company*—was rooted in notions of association and sociability; the idea that a company was also a "fellowship," a "brotherhood," and a "body politic" was often reflected in the charters and even the names of Atlantic ventures, such as William Penn's grant to a "Free Society of Traders in Pennsylvania" or the French Compagnie des Cent-Associés (Company of 100 Associates). Moreover, the Atlantic was also populated with a number of noneconomic bodies that were nonetheless called *companies*—either generically (for example, militia companies, ubiquitous at the level of towns and other communities) or specifically, as in the Company or Society of Jesus (the Jesuits) or Philadelphia's Library Company, a subscription library and quasi learned society founded in 1731 by Benjamin Franklin, among others.

Companies were part of a collage of legal entities—including royal governors, individual proprietors, religious orders, and the like—delegated to govern European claims throughout the Atlantic World. These bodies appointed governors, engaged servants, and encouraged settlers to come to overseas colonies, and they were of course largely responsible for the financing and facilitating of the trade in enslaved Africans to the Americas. They conducted diplomacy and war with both African and indigenous American polities, planted cities and built forts, established and administered laws, collected taxes, and much more. Many thus promoted themselves not merely as profit-making enterprises but also—even primarily—as ventures with great political, religious, and even civilizational missions.

For example, in the wake of the Dutch revolt against Spain in the late sixteenth and early seventeenth centuries, advocates for the Dutch West India Company stressed its central role in redeeming both the Calvinist Low Countries and Native Americans from Spanish Catholic tyranny. Any number of English ventures, notably the Virginia Company, drew liberally on humanist ideals of civic virtue and on notions of Protestant providentialism in conceptualizing their colonial callings. The English Providence Island Company (1630–1641) similarly envisioned its colony off the Nicaraguan coast as a haven for Puritan expatriates, a font of commercial wealth, and a launching point for challenges to Spanish control in the area. Similarly, the Company of Scotland Trading to Africa and the Indies (also known as the "Darien Company," chartered in 1695) envisioned its ill-fated colony of New Caledonia (Darien), on the eastern end of the isthmus of Panama, as a way to enter Scotland in the race for East Indies trade, a means to bottleneck Spanish power in the Atlantic, and a free port that could remake the European balance of power—all at the same time.

The leading roles that companies played in European trade and settlement in the Atlantic reveals just how blurry the lines between "public" and "private" enterprise were in the early-modern world. Companies clearly depended upon the political support of European governments to preserve monopoly rights over potential competitors as well as to secure their privileges from foreign companies and governments alike. They employed European diplomats and legal systems to combat interlopers, confront rival companies, and settle boundary disputes, even with their own compatriots. In turn, European governments depended no less upon these Atlantic ventures. Companies extended European dynastic struggles into the Americas and provided a good portion of the ships, seamen, and commodities that fueled those conflicts at home and abroad, particularly at sea. While some made

handsome profits supplying the needs of European navies, from timber to rum, they were also ripe for plunder from their royal sponsors; Spain's Royal Havana Company, for example, was required to provide the Spanish navy with warships and Seville with tobacco near, at, or sometimes below cost. Atlantic companies also served as a financial backbone for these growing European states, through customs and excise taxes as well as credit. For example, the English South Sea Company—along with two other corporations, the East India Company and the Bank of England—was a principal financier of the vast eighteenth-century expansion of the British national debt.

Many companies were thus tethered to the fate of their chartering regimes, to their foreign policies, and even to the whims of particular monarchs and ministers. For example, the ambitions of some in England in the early 1620s for a West India Company, as well as the Scottish Darien Company in the 1690s, were scuttled largely by the crown's fears of upsetting tenuous diplomatic relations with the Iberians. The Virginia Company charter was granted in 1607 only to be revoked in 1624; the crown claimed the business of governing Virginia had become too important to be "committed to any Company or Corporation, to whom it may be proper to trust matters of trade and commerce, but cannot be fit or safe to communicate the ordering of State affairs." The rapid turnover of French Atlantic companies can similarly be credited, at least in part, to the ambitions and frequent interventions of some of the crown's most powerful advisors, such as Cardinal Richelieu (principal minister, 1624–1642), Jean-Baptiste Colbert (minister of finances, 1665–1683), and John Law (controller general, 1715–1720).

Yet as much as trading companies were tied to their "home" governments, their directors, investors, and administrators did not necessarily share the ambitions or policies of the politicians. The Spanish companies in Venezuela and Cuba both enjoyed government-enforced monopoly rights in the Atlantic but ultimately helped to empower local colonial investors in governance. In any number of cases, such as the Dutch West India Company's mid-seventeenth-century seizure of Portuguese Brazil, companies' actions were directly at odds with the foreign-policy goals of European capitals. Some could even be outright defiant. For the better part of the seventeenth century, the English Massachusetts Bay Company famously resisted the English crown's attempts to recall its charter, even going so far as to remove the charter itself physically to New England.

Companies thus exemplified the complexity and pluralism of attempting to govern European claims to distant corners and unfamiliar challenges of a circum-Atlantic World. Their prominence raised philosophical dilemmas about the natures of both European and indigenous sovereignties and figured prominently in debates over the early-modern "law of nations" (the forerunner of nineteenth-century international law) as well as, of course, the prolific writings of seventeenth-century theorists on the nature of wealth, money, and credit in a commercializing economy. Conversely, the successes and failures of companies, however they might be judged, fueled a good deal of the critique of the so-called mercantilist constraints on trade that transformed political economy in the eighteenth century. The notion that chartered monopolies were both economically regressive and politically despotic underscored Adam Smith's arguments in *The Wealth of Nations,* while the French economist François Quesnay (1694–1774) explicitly criticized the constitution of a *"colonie des compagnies,"* in which commerce and politics were so intertwined that the former tended to determine the latter. Such assessments were only accentuated by the fact that the most devastating and scandalous financial crises of the eighteenth century—the notorious 1720 stock-market crashes (or "bubbles") in both England and France—were linked directly to Atlantic enterprises: the South Sea and Mississippi Companies, respectively.

The growing assault on exclusive rights chartered to companies was central also to the political theory and rhetoric of the Atlantic "Age of Revolutions" at the end of the eighteenth century; political rebels from Boston to Buenos Aires frequently cited monopolies as emblematic of the corruption inherent in the nexus of court patronage, corporate privilege, and colonization. Seen from another angle, however, such accusations of "corruption" and pleas against private interest on behalf of "public good" were integral to the ambitions of both expanding European polities and newer American ones to exploit colonial resources more directly and to impose a semblance of order on the patchwork these companies had established in the early-modern Atlantic.

In a sense, it was precisely the success of early-modern trading companies, among others, in establishing Atlantic colonies and networks and prodding European governments to become so effective at mobilizing resources, law, and ideology on their behalf that laid the groundwork for their demise. By the nineteenth century, chartered monopoly corporations had come to be widely derided as relics of a bygone "mercantilist" age. Ironically, however, it was under this banner of free trade and a state-dominated international system that the Atlantic World witnessed an explosion in new joint-stock companies, partnerships, and firms deeply dependent upon the expansion of European and American power around the globe. Such companies continued to shape those regimes, whether through "informal empires" (characterized by the dominance of foreign markets enforced by both state- and corporate-sponsored military power) or, much like their forebears—companies such as the United Fruit Company in Central America, the British South Africa Company, and Royal Niger Companies—through continued intimate and direct involvement in colonial politics, infrastructure, and governance.

PHILIP J. STERN

Bibliography

Andrews, Kenneth. *Trade, Plunder, and Settlement: Maritime Enterprise and the Genesis of the British Empire, 1480–1630.* Cambridge: Cambridge University Press, 1984.

Cheney, Paul. *Revolutionary Commerce: Globalization and the French Monarchy.* Cambridge, MA: Harvard University Press, 2010.

Fitzmaurice, Andrew. *Humanism and America: An Intellectual History of English Colonisation, 1500–1625.* Cambridge and New York: Cambridge University Press, 2003.

Koot, Christian J. *Empire at the Periphery: British Colonists, Anglo-Dutch Trade, and the Development of the British Atlantic, 1621–1713.* New York: New York University Press, 2010.

Kupperman, Karen. *Providence Island, 1630–1641: The Other Puritan Colony.* Cambridge: Cambridge University Press, 1993.

Liss, Peggy K., and Franklin W. Knight, eds. *Atlantic Port Cities: Economy, Culture, and Society in the Atlantic.* Knoxville: University of Tennessee Press, 1991.

Schmidt, Benjamin. *Innocence Abroad: The Dutch Imagination and the New World, 1570–1670.* Cambridge: Cambridge University Press, 2001.

Withington, Philip. *Society in Early Modern England: The Vernacular Origins of Some Powerful Ideas.* Cambridge: Polity Press, 2010.

Zahedieh, Nuala. *The Capital and the Colonies: London and the Atlantic Economy, 1660–1700.* Cambridge: Cambridge University Press, 2010.

Trading Diasporas

Cross-cultural Atlantic commerce is the legacy of trading diasporas—communities of merchants and itinerant traders dispersed from their homelands to engage in commerce outside their own economic and legal domains—that flourished in the sixteenth, seventeenth, and eighteenth centuries. In an early-modern trading diaspora, merchants from one community, having left either voluntarily or forcibly, lived as aliens in the port towns of another, learning the languages, customs, and commercial practices of their hosts. Members of these diasporic groups were united by distinctive ethnic, linguistic, religious, and kinship ties. The most prominent trading diasporas in the early-modern Atlantic economy—the subjects of this essay—were those of the Sephardic and New Christian Jews, Dutch, French Huguenots, Irish, and British North Americans.

The definition of an Atlantic trading diaspora might easily be expanded to include all British, French, Spanish, and Portuguese overseas traders doing business in the Atlantic within the legal frameworks defined by the monarchs to whom they owed allegiance and from whom they expected protection. However, most of these loyal subjects were involved only marginally in diasporic trade in the cross-cultural sense that the academic literature often invokes: unlike the French *coureurs de bois* in North America, for example, who lived with, and often married into, the Native communities from whom they bought beaver pelts and skins, they remained ensconced in the domains defined by the monarchies they served. And members of sub-groups—such as the Scots or Quakers within the British commercial system—though widely dispersed and internally cohesive—traded for the most part in conformity with the rules that governed their home economies.

Each of these trading diasporas accelerated the development—even the integration—of the Atlantic economy, but their prominence and efficacy are sometimes obscured by historiography that emphasizes the great maritime military powers and reduces the significance of the people who thrived on and across the margins of empire. Cross-cultural trading diasporas, although alien and to some degree ancillary, offered significant benefits to their hosts, including access to foreign markets, financial services, and legal redress—all unavailable within their imperial trading structures. Diasporic communities also bridged the political, cultural, and religious divides that otherwise confined the flows of goods and services in the early-modern Atlantic.

Alien traders had to meet high standards of credit, trust, and agency in their transactions to gain acceptance into the commercial life of their host societies. Acceptance also required resilience, accommodation, and the capacity to nurture their own cultural ties within the contexts of others. Over time, intermarriage with their hosts and other strategies of integration reduced the distinctiveness of diasporic traders, with the notable exception of the Sephardic Jews. By the end of the eighteenth century, the diasporic trading communities discussed here had been largely absorbed into the societies in which they had settled.

Communities of Sephardic Jews, New Christians, and Crypto-Jews

The expulsion of the Jews from Spain in 1492 set off a chain of events that led to formation of the first, and perhaps most significant, trading diaspora in the Atlantic World. During the sixteenth century—working primarily within the context of Portuguese outposts in western Africa, the islands of the eastern Atlantic, and Brazil—Sephardic, New Christian, and crypto-Jewish, or hidden-Jewish, traders were instrumental in establishing the model for sugar production and slave labor that became the underlying core of the Atlantic economy.

As many as 100,000 Spanish Jews sought refuge after 1492 in Portugal. Their sanctuary was short-lived, however. In January 1496 the Portuguese monarch, Manuel I, decreed the expulsion of all Jews from Portugal by October 1497. Realizing the dire economic consequences resulting from the departure of most of his realm's commercial community, the king reversed course, prohibiting their exit but requiring that all Jews in his kingdom accept Christianity—by force, if necessary. Those resisting faced harsh treatment, and many devout Jews fled the Iberian Peninsula to become Sephardim (a Hebrew reference to Spain, the land where they had originated). Among the Jews who remained behind, most (referred to as New Christians) adopted Roman Catholicism. However, many of the New Christians chose the dangerous course of adhering secretly to Jewish ritual while living outwardly as Catholics. They are known as crypto-Jews.

Well before the 1490s, a significant number of Sephardic Jews had escaped Spanish persecution by reestablishing themselves in North African and eastern Mediterranean territories controlled by the Ottoman Turks. The Sephardim were welcomed as cross-cultural brokers with Europe at the time the Turks were pushing Venetian Catholic traders out of the eastern Mediterranean. Sephardic Jews became expert at bridging religions and cultures and doing business in an Islamic society that encouraged multicultural transactions. In the process, Sephardic merchants, as aliens, learned negotiating skills that gave them a distinctive advantage in the even less familiar transatlantic and colonial trading environments in Africa and the Americas.

In addition to the New Christians situated within the Portuguese Atlantic territories, enclaves of New Christians—many of them crypto-Jews—appeared in northern European ports that were tolerant of organized Jewish life. Those who settled in Bordeaux, Bayonne, and other French ports, for example, presented themselves at first as Christians. But in France, unlike on the Iberian peninsula, no Inquisition persecuted them, and eventually New Christians dropped the pretense of adherence to Roman Catholicism and lived openly according to Jewish norms. The same reclaiming of ancestral traditions was under way elsewhere, notably at Antwerp, then at the peak of its dominance of European commerce. As New Christians dispersed through Atlantic Europe, they laid the foundation for a diasporic community distinct from—but intimately connected to—that of the Sephardic Jews overseas.

The rising demand for sugar brought these two communities prosperously together, with New Christians living privately as crypto-Jews and normative Sephardic Jews speaking the same languages, deriving from the same Iberian background, and often having shared family ties. Sugar production was originally established in the Portuguese Atlantic islands off western Africa but spread to São Tomé, another African island colony of Portugal on the equator, and then in the 1550s, on a much larger scale, across the Atlantic to Brazil.

New Christians were present in the sugar trade—and its symbiotic partner, the Atlantic slave trade—from the outset. Portuguese New Christians had been instrumental in forging the slave trade in the eastern Atlantic islands and to Iberia that predated the emergence of sugar as the driver of the Atlantic economy. In the middle decades of the sixteenth century, the Brazilian sugar trade cemented the relationship between Portuguese New Christians, whether living in the Old World or in Brazil, and the increasingly influential Sephardic Diaspora in northwestern Europe. These developments were accelerated by the dynastic union of the Spanish and Portuguese crowns in 1580, an event that expanded the reach of New Christians in the Iberian Atlantic.

In Amsterdam—the largest of the new European centers of Jewish life—Sephardic Jews had by the 1690s become prominent in all aspects of the city's commerce. The most important of the links maintained by the Sephardim of Amsterdam were to New Christian communities in Lisbon and Oporto in Portugal and throughout the Portuguese Atlantic. New Christian wealth grew rapidly as they gained access to markets in northern Europe, but their legal standing was always precarious. The spread of the Inquisition to the New World had led New Christians in Brazil—and their coreligionists in Amsterdam—to welcome the Dutch West India Company's attempts to conquer Brazil in the seventeenth century. The Dutch were successful, and in 1630 they established a Jewish enclave at Recife, capital of the captaincy of Pernambuco, where Jews could practice their religion free from harassment. But an uprising in 1654 led to Portuguese reoccupation of Dutch Brazil and to expulsion of the Jews.

The majority of the Jewish community at Recife returned to Amsterdam, and the rest put down roots throughout the western Atlantic wherever they could. A few settled in New Amsterdam (later New York), where they established the first synagogue in North America; others made their way to Newport, Rhode Island, where they were joined by Jews from Europe. By the 1660s Jewish settlements grew in the Caribbean at Cayenne, Suriname, Essequibo, Barbados, Jamaica, and Curaçao.

Unlike the French Huguenots, who were Calvinists, a generation later in Protestant countries, the Sephardic Jews and New Christians could not count on the sympathy of host peoples; the best they could expect was a grudging toleration. The Iberians presented the greatest threat. The spread of the Inquisition to Peru in the 1630s and to New Spain (Mexico and Central America) and New Granada (northern South America) in the 1640s weakened crypto-Jewish networks in the Spanish possessions. The restoration of the Portuguese monarchy and dissolution of the dynastic union between Portugal and Spain in 1640 led to a long and bitter war lasting until 1668, which fragmented the networks of Spanish and Portuguese New Christians hitherto integrated across both shores of the Atlantic. The organized Sephardic communities in the New World thereafter lived and traded independently.

The Sephardim in Amsterdam and Dutch Curaçao became crucial intermediaries between Spanish America and Great Britain and France, the emerging economic powers in the Atlantic economy by the end of the seventeenth century. A short-lived (1693–1720) Sephardic settlement at Tucacas, on the northwest coast of Venezuela, for example, served as the center of a smuggling network that reached deep into the interior of the Spanish Empire, linking Curaçao with cities as far away as Santa Fe de Bogotá and Quito (in modern Colombia and Ecuador). However, mercantilist regulations were increasingly confining Atlantic trade within growing monarchical domains and had the effect of fragmenting the once tightly knit community of Jewish traders dispersed throughout the Atlantic.

Nonetheless, the Sephardic diaspora remained a significant feature of the Atlantic economy until the outbreak of the wars of the French revolution in 1793. Family ties and religious sympathies provided a framework for interdependency and interaction, all richly illustrated in the Atlantic commerce of Aaron Lopez of Newport, Rhode Island, one of that port's great figures in the years before the War of American Independence. This cultural coherence had long given intersecting networks of Sephardic Jews, New Christians, and crypto-Jews a remarkable degree of flexibility and the capacity to cross other religious, political, and cultural divides.

Dutch Communities

The Dutch trading diaspora took the lead in undermining Iberian dominance of Atlantic commerce during Amsterdam's "Golden Age" (1585–1672). The city became the staple market for the world, even though the Dutch Republic was—in terms of territory, population, and natural resources—the smallest of the major European powers of the era. In the sixteenth century, the Dutch had built this commercial prosperity on the efficiency of Amsterdam's bulk carrying trade from western Europe to the Baltic region. By the turn of the seventeenth century, however, Dutch seaborne commerce had evolved into a sophisticated entrepôt trade, transshipping commodities to and from markets worldwide.

Though strongly Calvinist, the Dutch Republic thrived also because it welcomed traders of all religions and monarchical loyalties, attracting business across territorial boundaries and legal domains. Amsterdam's phenomenal success as a commercial center rested upon an abundance of shipping, the rational exploitation of markets, and financial institutions capable of funding trading ventures at low rates of interest. The Atlantic component of Dutch commerce was largely in the hands of a trading diaspora of resident and itinerant Dutch merchants in nearly every Atlantic port.

Dutch ships had entered the western Atlantic in the 1580s to harass Spanish shipping and to challenge the authority of Catholic Spain during the Protestant Dutch Republic's long struggle for independence. Well-armed Dutch traders—able to draw upon the unparalleled commercial and financial resources of Amsterdam—established a flourishing interloping commerce in territories nominally under the control of the Spanish king.

Later, during the first half of the seventeenth century, merchants from the Dutch Republic took up residence in the newly acquired English and French islands in the Caribbean, as well as on the mainland of North America. On Barbados, St. Christopher, Montserrat, Nevis, Martinique, and Guadeloupe, as well as in Tidewater Virginia and Massachusetts Bay, Dutch traders played critical roles in the early stages of economic development by providing access to capital, credit, and markets. Drawing on its wide commercial reach, the Dutch trading diaspora offered an astonishing array of goods at prices that undersold the competition. Dutch merchants delivered on time, made credit available at rates unmatched in London or the French Atlantic ports, and provided affordable and reliable marine insurance.

Mercantilists in England and France recognized the Dutch threat to their policies of limiting Atlantic commerce to traders from their own ports. In 1651 the government in London enacted the first of a series of statutes—collectively known as the Acts of Trade and Navigation—designed to expel the Dutch from English-Atlantic trade. In the following decade, the French minister of the marine, Jean-Baptiste Colbert, began construction of an even more restrictive commercial system with the same goal of protecting local merchants. Exclusions targeted at Dutch commerce and the Dutch trading diaspora were among the causes of the recurrent Anglo-Dutch wars of the seventeenth century (1652–1654, 1665–1667, and 1672–1674) and the Franco-Dutch War (1672–1678).

The significance of the Dutch trading diaspora in the Atlantic diminished as a result of losses during these wars and the growing efficiency of English maritime commerce. Even so, in the eighteenth century thinly disguised branch offices of Dutch merchant houses in Great Britain, Ireland, and France continued to finance, freight, and insure Atlantic voyages across the hardening lines of monarchical jurisdictional claims. Off the Venezuelan coast, for example, the Dutch island of Curaçao defied Madrid's pretensions of a self-sufficient Iberian Atlantic and served as northern Europe's offshore entry point into the Spanish Main, as Spain's mainland territories were known. In British America, merchants with Dutch roots—such as Philip Cuyler of New York—channeled a well-established pattern of smuggling known as the Dutch trade through Amsterdam and Rotterdam. And the tiny island of St. Eustatius in the eastern Caribbean—the point of articulation between the Dutch and North American trading diasporas—remained the very embodiment of Atlantic transnational commerce until late in the War of American Independence.

French Huguenot Communities

A trading diaspora of French Huguenots—members of the Calvinistic or Reformed communion of France—facilitated the flow of economic resources out of Catholic France into the Protestant Atlantic, and vice versa. By the time that Louis XIV's revocation of the Edict of Nantes (1685) deprived French Protestants of all religious and civil liberties, Huguenots had been gathering for more than a century in the Dutch Republic, England, Ireland, Denmark, and Switzerland. The outflow turned into a flood after 1685 as Huguenot traders settled in the maritime ports and overseas colonies of Protestant Europe. The refugees cultivated commercial relationships in Protestant trading centers situated to benefit from the expanding Atlantic economy, notably in Amsterdam and London.

In France, the Huguenot community had included members of the mercantile elite with significant financial resources and years of experience in Atlantic commerce. They had, as well, close ties to regions in France that produced the exports—such as brandy and wine—sought after in French America. And French Calvinists had taken the lead in developing Bordeaux, La Rochelle, and other French Atlantic ports in the middle decades of the seventeenth century. They freighted ships, settled sons and nephews abroad, and nurtured the formation of continental markets for colonial staples—principally sugar.

The overseas Huguenot community included many who had left their homeland voluntarily to seek opportunities abroad, and a significant number of Huguenot traders remained behind. And even though historians may have exaggerated the damage to the French economy from the flight of the Huguenots, the exodus alarmed and frustrated French officials. But whether or not the expatriates left France willingly and whether or not the French economy suffered extensively, much of the success of the Huguenot trading diaspora depended upon continuing relationships with kin and business associates in France. Well endowed with contacts,

Huguenots in France—and throughout the Atlantic—became skilled at facilitating capital flows and providing banking services across borders.

Among Huguenots—especially after 1685—bonds of religion and family were stronger than the bond of loyalty to the line of kings in Paris then integrating the maritime fringes of France under the central monarchy. Although French Huguenots arrived at their hosts' doorsteps as linguistic and culturally distinct aliens, their Atlantic commerce flourished in an atmosphere of personal trust based on carefully nurtured relationships among scattered families sharing a common religion.

Mercantile families such as the Faneuils of La Rochelle—well established in London, Rotterdam, Boston, and New York by the middle decades of the eighteenth century—were both connected internationally and integrated into their host societies. And when opportunistic, they did business outside the confines of the Protestant Atlantic. The Faneuils of New England, for example, cooperated with family members in Quebec and La Rochelle to expedite the clandestine shipment of French Canadian furs through Huguenot agents in Albany to markets in Great Britain and Ireland.

Irish Communities

Only the Irish and Jewish trading diasporas did business in all of the Atlantic territories controlled by European monarchies. Although a constituent part of the English (later British) Empire, Ireland's potential as a competitor in Atlantic trade led the English Parliament to pass the Staple Act of 1663, the first of a string of statutes that restricted Irish participation in colonial commerce. However, entrepreneurial Irishmen from Galway, Cork, Waterford, and Dublin—many associated with the salted-provisions trade—had long since put down roots on the European continent and in the emerging English and French Caribbean. By the time the Staple Act went into effect, Irish merchants were well experienced at cultivating relationships across imperial boundaries.

Ireland's commercial presence on the European continent was strongest in Spain, Portugal, France, and the Catholic ports of the Low Countries, all places that had welcomed Roman Catholic refugees in the wake of Ireland's ethnic and sectarian struggles of the seventeenth century. By the turn of the eighteenth century, Irish trading houses in Protestant Amsterdam and Rotterdam were transshipping thousands of barrels of Irish beef, pork, and butter to the "foreign" Caribbean. This trade grew considerably when British involvement in the dynastic wars of Europe—increasingly waged on the Atlantic—disrupted the flow of Irish produce to France or Spain or to their overseas territories. The expatriate Irish community at Bordeaux, in addition to its involvement in the provisions trade, figured prominently in the production and export of the region's famed wines and brandies, some of which found their way across the Atlantic.

In the Dutch and Danish West Indies, trading houses with ties to both Ireland and Irish interests on the European continent were an important presence, and firms such as McCarty & Company in Saint-Domingue did a large salted-provisions business in the French West Indies. Much of the Irish beef destined for the French Caribbean was intended for enslaved Africans, who were required by a royal edict to have meat included in their regular diet. In addition to the Irish merchants resident in the French, Dutch, and Danish West Indies, Irish trading houses were active on nearly every British island in the Caribbean.

By the 1720s linen had displaced salted provisions as Ireland's leading export. And in 1731, a change in the British Acts of Trade and Navigation permitted Ireland to import certain "unenumerated" goods directly from North America. Within a decade, the Irish linen industry was wholly dependent upon flaxseed imported from North America, some 450,000 bushels per year. Irish flaxseed merchants in New York and Philadelphia—ambitious, aggressive, and well connected to the Irish trading diaspora—became adept at circumventing British restrictions on Irish and colonial trade.

In the middle decades of the eighteenth century, much of the wealth generated in the provisions and linen business flowed back into the Irish trading diaspora through the agency of London's Irish merchant community, an enclave of over 50 firms in the 1760s—several with branch operations in the French, Spanish, and Portuguese domains. Irish trading houses at home, on the European continent, and in the British and "foreign" Caribbean benefited, both directly and indirectly, from the financial and marketing services provided by Irish intermediaries in London.

British North American and American Communities

The North American trading diaspora—the only one of the five discussed here to face east—served primarily to evade London's efforts to contain the commerce of mainland British America within the British mercantilist system. Because governments in London, Paris, and Madrid alike lacked the administrative apparatus necessary to enforce the commercial restrictions they had established, North American provisions, building materials, and a wide array of other goods flowed largely unimpeded into Caribbean markets, where French and Spanish buyers purchased them on terms favorable to British North American traders. Until the outbreak of the Seven Years' War (1756–1763), lax customs enforcement throughout the region and Great Britain's tacit policy of "benign neglect" of its subjects' business in French sugar and Spanish silver fostered frequent exchanges across the nominal boundaries of empire.

Beginning in the 1680s, North American merchants and mariners—with the tacit cooperation of the Dutch and the Danes—took on an increasing share of the West Indian carrying trade. The North American presence on St. Eustatius through much of the eighteenth century expedited cross-border exchanges with Guadeloupe, Martinique, and other markets in the eastern Caribbean. And beginning in the late seventeenth century, an enclave of New Yorkers on Curaçao facilitated an illicit trade with New Spain that became a key feature of economic life in the western Caribbean. Curaçao and St. Eustatius, as well as Suriname, were open to the trades of all nations, and the resident Americans who did business there fit comfortably into the polyglot, free-trading milieu fostered by their Dutch hosts. The Danish West Indian islands of St. Croix, St. Thomas, and St. John likewise welcomed British North American traders in the 1750s, some of whom settled and became naturalized subjects of the Danish crown. Access to French produce through the Dutch and Danish islands allowed North American merchants to undercut their bitter rivals—the British West Indians—and make inroads into the continental European markets for sugar, coffee, indigo, and other semitropical goods.

The North American presence in the "foreign" Caribbean grew dramatically during the Anglo-French wars of the middle decades of the eighteenth century, when British warships and privateers disrupted the flow of commerce between France and its West Indian colonies. Merchants from New England and the Middle Atlantic colonies, seizing on the opportunity to exchange desperately needed provisions and "warlike stores" for cheap French sugar, established themselves in neutral ports within easy striking distance of the French Islands—and occasionally in the French West Indian ports themselves. The most important of these enclaves was that at Monte Cristi Bay in Spanish Santo Domingo (today's Dominican Republic), on the north coast of Hispaniola just a few miles east of the border with French Saint-Domingue (today's Haiti). Resident "Mount merchants"—such as Richard Mercer of New York—managed the trade of hundreds of North American vessels until 1762, when Spain entered the Anglo-French conflict.

In response to these violations of mercantilist restrictions, Great Britain tightened its grip on colonial commerce at the close of the Seven Years' War. The French West Indies—at the same time—were becoming more hospitable to North American traders, in spite of stern directives from Versailles to the contrary. As a consequence, Mole Saint-Nicolas, a town at the far western tip of Saint-Domingue, became one of the busiest shipping points in the Caribbean in the decade before the War of American Independence. Well represented among the North American traders at "the Mole" were merchants from Newport, Rhode Island, and New London, Connecticut, ports with notoriously lax customs enforcement and a long history of defiance of British efforts to discipline the merchants of its North American ports.

The North Americans' brazen flouting of the Acts of Trade and Navigation was driven by a persistent trade imbalance, exacerbated by these very acts, that characterized Anglo-American commerce in New England and the Middle Atlantic colonies, regions with growing populations, rising incomes, and a seemingly insatiable demand for imported manufactured goods. Often, the best—and most accessible—markets for the exports of New England and the Middle Atlantic colonies were those beyond imperial boundaries. The vitality of colonial America's illicit trade at the Mole, at Suriname, and elsewhere in the "foreign" Caribbean contributed to rising British American tensions in the run-up to what became the War of American Independence.

A variant of this North American trading diaspora played a small but significant part in the War of American Independence (1776–1783). In concert with the Continental Congress's Secret Committee of Trade—and working under the umbrella of French support after 1778 for the Patriot cause—American traders at Nantes, Bordeaux, and Le Havre purchased weapons, clothing, and other military supplies for George Washington's beleaguered army. While in Europe, these representatives of military contractors in the United States began to establish business contacts that would later support the overseas commerce of the new American state. The high-risk trade conducted by the Patriot side during the War of American Independence was dependent upon neutral shipping and resident American merchants in the neutral islands, particularly at St. Eustatius—"the Golden Rock"—the critical link in the American supply chain until the island was sacked by the British military in 1781.

The Significance of Trading Diasporas in the Atlantic World

Early-modern trading diasporas operated across the borders, as well as in the interstices, of the great imperial commercial systems. Trade and exchange across cultural lines and monarchical claims were among the most important stimuli in the formation and integration of the Atlantic economy. The Atlantic trading diasporas grew in significance because they linked markets that the monarchs of Europe had created—to a striking degree—by excluding their rivals. As a consequence, goods and resources flowed across the lines of territorial sovereignty, and with them traveled political news and a multiplicity of cultural perspectives. Each of the Atlantic trading diasporas—those of the New Christian and Sephardic Jews, Dutch, Huguenots, Irish, and North Americans—provided its hosts access to capital, credit, and marine insurance, as well as an array of services, which enabled long-distance traders to expand the range and scope of their operations. Without these trading diasporas, the rapid economic development that distinguished the early-modern Atlantic World would have been much slower, and the eventual European dominance of the world economy less likely.

THOMAS M. TRUXES

Bibliography

Bernardini, Paolo, and Norman Fiering, eds. *The Jews and the Expansion of Europe to the West, 1450–1800*. New York: Berghahn, 2001.

Bosher, J. F. "Huguenot Merchants and the Protestant International in the Seventeenth Century." *The William and Mary Quarterly* 52 (January 1995): 77–102.

Cullen, L. M. *Economy, Trade, and Irish Merchants at Home and Abroad, 1600–1988*. Dublin: Four Courts Press, 2012.

Curtin, Philip D. *Cross-Cultural Trade in World History*. Cambridge: Cambridge University Press, 1984.

Enthoven, Victor. "'That Abominable Nest of Pirates': St. Eustatius and the North Americans, 1680–1780." *Early American Studies: An Interdisciplinary Journal* 10 (spring 2012): 227–301.

Green, Toby. *The Rise of the Trans-Atlantic Slave Trade in Western Africa, 1300–1589*. Cambridge: Cambridge University Press, 2012.

Israel, Jonathan I. *Diasporas within a Diaspora: Jews, Crypto-Jews, and the World of Maritime Empires, 1540–1740*. Leiden: Brill, 2002.

———. *Dutch Primacy in World Trade, 1585–1740*. Oxford: Clarendon, 1990.

Kagan, Richard L., and Philip D. Morgan, eds. *Atlantic Diasporas: Jews, Conversos, and Crypto-Jews in the Age of Mercantilism, 1500–1800*. Baltimore, MD: Johns Hopkins University Press, 2009.

Klooster, Wim. *Illicit Riches: Dutch Trade in the Caribbean, 1648–1795*. Leiden: KITLV, 1998.

Koot, Christian J. *Empire at the Periphery: British Colonists, Anglo-Dutch Trade, and the Development of the British Atlantic, 1621–1713*. New York: New York University Press, 2011.

Scoville, Warren C. *The Persecution of Huguenots and French Economic Development, 1680–1720*. Berkeley: University of California Press, 1960.

Truxes, Thomas M. *Defying Empire: Trading with the Enemy in Colonial New York*. New Haven, CT: Yale University Press, 2008.

———. "Dutch-Irish Cooperation in the Mid-Eighteenth-Century Wartime Atlantic." *Early American Studies: An Interdisciplinary Journal* 10 (spring 2012): 302–334.

Van Ruymbeke, Bertrand, and Randy J. Sparks, eds. *Memory and Identity: The Huguenots in France and the Atlantic Diaspora*. Columbia: University of South Carolina Press, 2003.

Underdevelopment

A coherent body of scholarship aimed at explaining persisting income inequalities among the world's regions—"underdevelopment"—arose in the 1960s in reaction to the then-prevalent socioeconomic concept of modernization, or development theory. According to that optimistic modeling of the future, wealthier, or economically developed, countries played a largely positive role by acting as mentors to, and investors in, third-world countries—understood as inherently less developed—in the attempts of the latter, many of them newly independent nations, to follow them on the path to modernity on the model of material plenty, or at least adequacy, and democratic political institutions.

This exemplary definition of modernity obviously saw development and underdevelopment from the perspective of the more "advanced" northern Atlantic regions of the United States and western Europe. In contrast, the new generation of scholars who challenged this view and its assumptions—first, significantly, in the southern Atlantic region of Latin America—elaborated a theory of dependency that did not take "underdevelopment" as a natural state but sought to explain it as a disabling process imposed from Europe and the United States—that is, the twentieth-century heirs to the Atlantic economy of the early-modern era. These scholars assigned responsibility for the impoverishment of the rest of the world, which they saw as growing, in a sharp critique of the capitalist policies of industrialized countries—such as, and especially, the United States—as exploitative drains on the wealth of the rest of the world. Even though subsequently challenged and criticized as an ideological relic, especially because of its strong Marxian overtones, dependency theory—or the structural-historical theory of underdevelopment as a global process—can still provide a critical analysis of unequal exchanges in provoking differences in the allocation of the world's wealth. The theory is especially powerful in understanding the historical divide in the Atlantic World between North America and Latin America.

Andre Gunder-Frank and His Critics

Even though elaborated by a number of Latin American scholars (*dependentistas*) all informed by Marxist structural theory, dependency theory had its iconic intellectual in German-born economist Andre Gunder Frank (1929–2005). Following in the footsteps of crucial Marxist thinkers in the 1960s, Frank looked at the historical trajectory of global capitalism as a process of inherently uneven development enforced through the military domination of imperialism and colonialism. He synthesized his argument in the phrase "the development of underdevelopment," which described "the results of the policies of large corporations, major states in the core zones, and interstate agencies which promoted 'free trade' in the world-economy" (Wallerstein, 12). Thus, to Frank, development in the North Atlantic and underdevelopment in the rest of the world—especially in Africa and South America—were the two sides of a single zero-sum coin: the gains of one came significantly at the expense of the others.

Developed core countries kept peripheries underdeveloped by incorporating them into a global system of capitalist trade and investment originating during the colonial period and by appropriating surpluses produced beyond the core. They then used these surpluses to fuel their own development, leaving underdevelopment in the peripheral regions. A corollary of this theory was that underdeveloped regions with weaker ties to the industrialized metropole were less underdeveloped and therefore remained within the range of development and modernity. Frank thought that he had glimpsed some hope specifically in Latin America, when a brief period of isolation from the modern West in the 1920s and 1930s had seen significant steps forward, particularly in terms of industrialization.

By the 1970s, dependency theory had undergone harsh criticism, especially because it seemed to be limited by a strict economic determinism, clearly derived from orthodox Marxism; the criticism also homed in on a seeming neglect of political, cultural, and other historical circumstances. Further, even though dependency theory criticized the singular model of modernization put forward in development theory on the grounds that other roads might lead to material prosperity and respect for human rights, the assumption remained that third-world countries were underdeveloped in relation to the supposed standard of development represented by western Europe and the United States. Dependency theory was incorporated within Immanuel Wallerstein's "world-systems" analysis. At the same time, Wallerstein converted Frank's original model of the "West draining the Rest" economically to a historical model of the development of world capitalism beginning with European engagement with the Atlantic in the sixteenth century. In this historical model he attempted to avoid the mechanistic determinism of the one-way drain of the North Atlantic through a more complex dialectic between cores and what he called peripheries and semi-peripheries as the components of a capitalist "world-economy."

In the 1990s Edwin Hoffman Rhyne added a particularly sharp critique of dependency theory, arguing in favor of discarding it altogether: to him it appeared unuseful in studying third-world countries. To Rhyne, the main tenets of dependency theory could not be proven in any meaningful way: as he listed them, "(1) the unchallenged omnipotence of the North Atlantic metropole throughout the world; (2) the neglect of indigenous variables as possible explanations of development; and (3) the implied assumption that growth and development are the normal state of affairs" (Rhyne, 370). To be sure, Rhyne has been only the latest scholar to voice more nuanced concerns over a theory that many now see as an ideological relic—a Marxist vision of unilateral causation—of what may prove to have been a two-century-long phase of global differentiation growing out of the commercial integration of the Atlantic Era.

Yet dependency theory remains one of the more coherent and organic explanations of the structural factors that have created the economic differentials of the modern world. As a model of the global expansion and diversification of a capitalist system of accumulation, it can still offer important insights into underdevelopment in the recent past, especially in the work of Björn Hettne. In several studies, Hettne has stressed the ability of dependency theory to create, for the first time, a school of socioeconomic thought that was not Western-centric. As it sought to understand economic inequality by focusing on the regional circumstances contributing to the slowness of the world's peripheral regions to develop, it offered an alternative to the European model of development. Dependency theory also placed development and underdevelopment equally for the first time within the historical trajectory of the world economy as a whole.

In this connection, Hettne has also alerted scholars to the fact that, especially in Wallerstein's modified "world-systems" version, dependency theory has led to identification of reasons for the underdevelopment of the world's peripheral regions in conditions related to the historical development of world capitalism—specifically the division between core and peripheral areas that characterizes the capitalist world-economy—and in the consequent international division of labor. He rejects the notion that the reasons lie in factors internal to those countries—that is, in the absence of capital or of entrepreneurs.

Atlantic Aspects of Underdevelopment Theory

The dependency theory of underdevelopment originated in an Atlantic setting for particular reasons. To begin with, the earliest and strongest advocates of dependency theory were Latin American *dependentistas* seeking an explanation for the obvious divide in wealth and resources between the Northern and Southern hemispheres in the New World. They reacted to North American and Eurocentric models of historical development as capitalist-led modernization. The best current scholarship on Atlantic history also integrated the north and south in the Atlantic World. Despite their best intentions, though, *dependentistas* ended up creating a paradigm that in practice "imputed causal primacy to the North Atlantic metropole" (Rhyne, 375). Therefore, in the words of Ramon Grosfoguel, effectively they "were caught up in developmentalist assumptions similar to intellectual currents they attempted to criticize" (Grosfoguel, 372). Scholarship in Atlantic history, to escape the Eurocentric limitations of dependency theory, must account for the historical development of contrasting wealth and poverty in the Atlantic World through arguments that take fully into account Rhyne's emphasis on local and regional circumstances and treat the massive economic growth and integration of the Atlantic Era as the passing phase in world history that it was.

ENRICO DAL LAGO

Bibliography

Frank, Andre Gunder. *Capitalism and Underdevelopment in Latin America.* New York: Monthly Review Press, 1967.

Grosfoguel, Ramon. "Developmentalism, Modernity, and Dependency Theory in Latin America." *Nepantla: Views from South* 1 (2000): 347–374.

Hettne, Björn. *Development Theory and the Three Worlds: Towards an International Political Economy of Development.* London: Longman, 1995.

Rhyne, Edwin Hoffman. "Dependency Theory: Requiescat in Pace?" *Sociological Inquiry* 60 (November 1990): 370–385.

Wallerstein, Immanuel. *World-Systems Analysis: An Introduction.* Durham, NC: Duke University Press, 2004.

Utopias

The concept of the utopia in social planning emerged in Europe with the unique openness of the Atlantic, which seemed to offer opportunities for fresh starts. Begun as a literary genre with Thomas More's *Utopia* (1516) and applied in different ways in the early Atlantic period in the Americas, utopian expressions in literature—and utopian ideals in philosophy and political thinking—not only motivated movements for social amelioration across the world, but also laid the base for European visions of historical progress that marked their militarized campaigns to "civilize" newfound places and peoples.

The Origins of a Genre

Thomas More's *Utopia* was a seminal work in the development of what we now consider a literary form. But for More, a humanist lawyer and not yet a knight or sainted martyr, Utopia was a place, not a genre. Its name, derived from Greek, could be translated as "no place," suggesting its fictional character. More's cunning little book asked if it was also a good place, a *eutopia*, and if its austere way of life and reliance on community of property represented the best possible form of society. As readers ever after have been aware, the answers are ambiguous.

More was hardly the first author to invent a commonwealth. Plato had long before anticipated him, not only in *The Republic* and *The Laws* but also in imagining the lost island of Atlantis, larger than Libya (Mediterranean Africa) and Asia together, which once had existed in the Atlantic Ocean but was destroyed by a massive earthquake. Nor can More be said to have invented the feigned travel narrative in this work. That honor arguably belongs to Lucian of Samosata, the second-century Greek rhetorician and satirist, who was among More's favorite writers and whose *True History* is sometimes said to be the first science-fiction story. Nevertheless, by adding materials drawn from accounts of actual but hitherto unknown places and peoples to this imaginative literary tradition, More's Latin text, published in 1516, whose full title translated into English is *Of the Best State of a Commonwealth and the New Isle of Utopia*, gave the tale the appearance of a traveler's account to an actual place, permanently altering the travel-narrative genre, in effect inventing utopian literature.

In More's text, Hythlodaeus, the traveler, began the journey on which he encountered the new isle of Utopia from the coast of what is now Brazil but made it back to Europe via Calicut, in Madras, after a stopover at Taprobane (the ancient name for Sri Lanka). So his "No Place" could just as easily have been a site in the Atlantic as in the Indian Ocean— or even in the Pacific Ocean. We face a somewhat similar geographical puzzle about the location of Caliban and Prospero's island in Shakespeare's *The Tempest* (c. 1611), which drew on the genre. Although the plot derives in large measure from William Strachey's account of the Atlantic hurricane and shipwreck that had stranded a group of Virginia settlers in Bermuda in 1609, the play implies that the island must be in the Mediterranean. The important point, however, is not where the island might be found, but, as emphasized by Gonzalo in imagining it in the play as a possible utopia, that it seemed to lack a social order and was therefore a blank slate on which it was possible to inscribe an ideal polity.

According to Sir Philip Sidney, for whom fiction was philosophy teaching by example, the fictional character of More's book made it especially useful to what he called "the most excellent determination of goodness" (Sidney, 220–224). In his view, however, the principal examples of teaching by fiction were works like Virgil's *Aeneid* that portrayed the virtuous deeds of particular individuals. More's *Utopia* was different, as Sidney says, since it represents the complete "patterning of a commonwealth" (Sidney, 222–223). Its utility comes from describing the island as a functioning social system in which each element reinforces the others in promoting virtuous actions and good citizenship. More's image of a newly made land—a land on which one could inscribe one's most deeply held values and perfect the building of society from first foundations—therefore represents one reason, perhaps the most important, why the model of utopia played so prominent a role among early-modern Europeans as they came to terms with the new discoveries in the Atlantic World.

Atlantic Expressions

More did not think a utopian form of society could be established in Europe: "common opinion" and the wealth and power of the privileged would prevent it (More, 201–202). Nevertheless, with a leap of the imagination, it was possible to believe that a New Utopia—a society functioning without private property—might be built in the vast and seemingly underdeveloped territories of the Americas. Whether More himself thought the new isle of Utopia actually represented "the best form of a commonwealth" is left ambiguous in his work. But his fiction kept open the possibility that the hindrances that would prevent the establishment of a society without property in Europe need not hold in a newfound land.

By the standards of the day, More's *Utopia* was a best seller, reaching the Americas almost at once; a copy of a 1518 Latin edition was among the items in the library of Friar Juan de Zumárraga, who became the first bishop of Mexico in 1528. It is heavily annotated in Zumárraga's hand. Almost from the outset, other authors began to draw on More's model for their own purposes. Many followed Plato's precedent in his *Republic* in creating what the humanist statesman Sir Thomas Smith called, in *De Republica Anglorum*, published in 1583, "feigned commonwealths, such as never was nor never shall be" the products, he said, of their "vain imaginations" (Smith, 144).

One of the first figures to experiment with common property in practice was Vasco de Quiroga, a close reader of More's writings in Spain as well as a canon lawyer and student of theology. In 1531 he traveled to New Spain, where he served until 1535 as a judge in the second Audiencia, the body that governed the region. Subsequently he became the first bishop of Michoacán in Mexico. Writing in 1535, Quiroga explained that America's people and "almost everything in it" displayed the virtues that had been found "in the first and golden age" of ancient legend, something he hoped to preserve (Quiroga, 7). Because, as Quiroga put it, the "fertility" of Mexican soil freely provided sustenance to its Native peoples "almost without labour care or seeking on their part," they seemed to have "the same customs and manners" as had prevailed, according to the ancient descriptions, in the ancient kingdom of Saturn. His idyllic description, which parallels the same travel narratives on which More himself had drawn, suggests that Quiroga believed the Native peoples' way of life strongly resembled that of More's Utopians.

Even though, to Quiroga, European life was "already one of iron and steel," he feared that the Native people of New Spain would mistakenly regard it as the true "golden world" and seek to emulate it (Quiroga, 8). As a judge in New Spain, therefore, he proposed to the Council of the Indies in Spain to regulate the Native peoples' lives to protect them from this temptation. His plan, derived from More's work, was to form a series of rationally ordered city-utopias, in each of which 6,000 households composed of between 10 and 16 couples would live together as single families. A strict and hierarchical order of rule would prevail, and the method for choosing the magistrates was copied directly from *Utopia*. Although his plan did not find a favorable hearing in Spain's royal council, he was not prevented from using his own resources to found two hospital villages based on his model. Their most distinctive features were the common ownership of property, the elimination of luxuries, and the distribution of the products of the villagers' common labor according to need. These villages were still thriving well after Quiroga's death in 1565.

The elimination of private property is utopia's paradigmatic mark. The founders of Plymouth Plantation in Massachusetts imposed it in 1620 when the settlers arrived in New England, declaring themselves "knit together as a body in a most strict and sacred bond and covenant with the Lord"; they were "tied," they said, "to all care of each others good, and of the whole by every one and so mutually" (Bradford, 1:76). Accordingly, they initiated a common economic course, equated with Plato's, laboring together on lands belonging to the collectivity, and receiving sustenance from a common stock.

By 1623, however, the Plymouth colonists, faced with severe food shortages and no prospect of supply, abandoned the propertyless regime. Instead of producing social peace and economic productivity, Plymouth's communism resulted in the opposite. The young men complained that they spent their strength working for other men's families, the strong that they received the same food and clothing as those less able, and the "aged and graver men" that they were "equalized in labors" and supplies "with the meaner and younger sort." Although the colony was to continue "the general way" in other things, every man was now to "set corn . . . for his own particular and in that regard [to] trust to themselves." According to William Bradford, sometime governor of the colony, the change almost immediately "made all hands very industrious" (Bradford, 1:302–303).

In *Utopia*, More, speaking as a character in the dialogue and resting his case in part on his understanding of the power of sin in human affairs, had offered similar criticisms of its propertyless regime. Bradford, however, argued at first that "men's corruption" represented only a partial hindrance to the scheme. The communal economic regime itself, he said, was also to blame (Bradford, 1:303). However, in a note he added later to his history, he poignantly lamented the fate of the "sacred bond" on which

the pilgrims initially had based their settlement. Over time, he said, the "subtle serpent" had "slyly wound himself under fair pretenses of necessity and the like, to untwist [its] sacred bonds . . . and as it were insensibly by degrees to dissolve, or in great measure to weaken, the same." When their "fidelity decayed . . . their ruin approached" and their "sweet communion" dissolved into the tradesmen's modes of personal acquisition they had sought to leave behind when they departed from "the hard, and continual labor" they were living in Leiden (Bradford, 1:40, 76n). Maintaining a utopian form of community in Plymouth proved impossible.

Although in coming from the Old World to New England the Plymouth settlers hoped they would find "a better, and easier place of living" where they "might have liberty and live comfortably," they discovered, as would most other early migrants to the Americas, that their newfound land was not very different from the world they had left behind (Bradford, 1:53). To quote the title of Bishop Joseph Hall's 1605 parody of the genre, the colony turned out to be *A New World and Yet the Same*. This outcome most likely would have been no surprise to More, who in his book had acknowledged that the best aspects of Utopia were things we "may rather wish for than hope after" (More, 202).

Dystopia and utopia are siblings, the former born only a short time after the latter. Rabelais's satiric *Pantagruel* (1532) provides one of the first literary allusions to More's imagined community and also offers one of the earliest examples of its antithesis. Toward its end, the tale imagines a community just like our own, in which good and bad are inextricably mixed, and all but the very rich must earn their bread by the sweat of their brows. The eponymous Pantagruel is a giant large enough to hold an entire community in his mouth. In the thirty-second chapter, Alcofribas, the narrator, climbs into this cavernous space, where he sees great mountain ranges (the giant's teeth) and "great plains, great forests and big strong cities." The first person he meets is a man planting cabbages. In amazement, Alcofribas asks him what he is doing. " 'I'm planting cabbages,' he said. 'And how and what for?' said I. 'Ah, sir,' came the response, 'not everyone can have balls as heavy as a mortar, and we can't all be rich. I earn my living this way, and I take them to sell in the market, in the city that is behind in here.' 'Jesus,' said I, 'then there's a new world

V

here?' 'To be sure,' said he, 'it's hardly new, but they do indeed say that outside of here there's a new earth, where they have both sun and moon, and all sorts of fine carryings-on; but this one is older'" (Rabelais, 239). Later, having enjoyed the pleasures of a four-month sojourn in a lovely valley "full of delights," he is robbed by brigands. "At this point," he says, "I began to think that it is very true what they say, that half the world doesn't know how the other half lives" (Rabelais, 240).

Alcofribas's final thought was already a proverb by the time Rabelais employed it and has remained so into the present day, referring to the distance separating the rich from the poor in everyday society. In Rabelais's work, however, it also alludes to the fact that half the world was hidden from the other half until the European discovery of the Americas. When the veil was lifted, the "New World" at first seemed to some Europeans a place where human beings lived as close to perfection as was possible on this earth. To others it appeared possible to establish such a place of perfection there. But from the very outset of Atlantic history there were skeptics. Although the New World of America was no utopia in ethical and ontological terms, it remained "pregnant with all possibilities," open to "every experiment"—a place where one might hope to "begin the world over again," as Thomas Paine later would put it (Paine, 113).

DAVID HARRIS SACKS

Bibliography

Auerbach, Erich. "The World in Pantagruel's Mouth." In *Mimesis: The Representation of Reality in Western Literature*. Translated by Willard Trask. Princeton, NJ: Princeton University Press, 1953.

Bradford, William. *The History of Plymouth Plantation,* *1620–1647*. Edited by Chauncey Ford. 2 vols. Boston: Massachusetts Historical Society, 1912.

More, Thomas. *Utopia by Sir Thomas More, Translated by Ralph Robynson, 1556*. Edited by David Harris Sacks. Boston and New York: Bedford/St. Martin's, 1999.

Paine, Thomas, *Common Sense*. In Thomas Paine, *Common Sense and Related Writings*, edited by Thomas P. Slaughter. Boston and New York: Bedford/St. Martin's, 2001.

Quiroga, Vasco de. *Información en Derecho* (1535), originally published in *Colección de Documentos Inéditos del Archivi de Indias* (Madrid, 1864–1889), x. 363; as cited in Silvio Zavala, *Sir Thomas More in New Spain: A Utopian Adventure of the Renaissance*. London: The Hispanic & Luso Brazilian Councils, 1955.

Sidney, Philip. *The Defence of Poesy*. In *The Oxford Authors: Sir Philip Sidney*. Edited by Katherine Duncan-Jones. Oxford and New York: Oxford University Press, 1989.

Smith, Sir Thomas. *De Republica Anglorum*. Edited by Mary Dewar. Cambridge: Cambridge University Press, 1982.

Visual Representations

To take up the matter of "visual representation" in the making and transformation of the Atlantic World from the sugar plantations of the Caribbean to the heartlands of Europe is to confront a diverse array of genres and media from natural-history illustration and tables of inventories to plantation diagrams and devices of cartography, to name only a few examples of visual efforts to comprehend the novelties encountered in, and hence challenges of controlling, the Atlantic. These techniques of ordering, classification, and view making attempted to manage unstable regimes of power as well as enact and contest the Atlantic as a historical space of the world-scaping flows of people, plants, machines, and mass-produced artifacts that made the plantation and the cargo ship (or the slave ship) as much the laboratories of modernity as the European metropolis.

Visual representations of the Atlantic—from survey maps and plans to diagrams to land- and seascapes—did more than just visually reproduce a world wrought by colonization, trade, and slave la-

Figure 1. Jean Baptiste Du Tertre, *Histoire générale des Antilles habitées par les François*, 1667, volumes 3–4, intaglio print, 1 plate folded. Courtesy of General Collection, Beinecke Rare Book and Manuscript Library, Yale University.

bor. Such images also functioned as key components of enacting, comprehending, and contesting social, cultural, and political practice. They circulated along networks of exchange, collecting, performance, and display that attest to the ways in which power was, and still is, negotiated through the visual field. Visual representations operated as shaping agents in their own right, participating actively in the making—and also the contestation and transformation—of contacts and intimacies among four continents.

We might take the printed diagram and the system of colonial visuality within which it operated as a paradigmatic example (figure 1). In Jean-Baptiste Du Tertre's *Histoire générale des Antilles habitées par les François* (1667), the look, the visual attitude, and the surveilling gaze of the idealized figure of the elegant overseer, balanced on an exaggeratedly large cane and standing in the center of the image, may be read as the crucial motor of the indigo plantation over which he looms as its head. In such working diagrams for production, it is not just indigo being produced; the images also rein-

force the technology of colonial oversight that drove the plantation machine.

While working diagrams of the plantation participated in the imposition of a colonial order of things, the abstract design of the visual inventory of the printed table transmuted the vagaries and particularities of living animals, plants, and human bodies into the rationalized generalities of numerical quantities charted and tabulated in precise regimenting columns. Figure 2 shows the standardized large-format table printed in Jacques-François Dutrône de la Couture's treatise on the cultivation of sugarcane, the *Précis sur la canne* (1791). The abstracting grid of a logic of equivalence that is at once discriminatory—in the development of a modern visual and corporeal surface schema for distinguishing races, sexes, and species, for example—and reductive to a leveling sameness was not exclusive to the inventory or table. The conventions of the arts of mapmaking converted unruly and diverse tracts of land, bodies of surging waters, and the diverse vitality of human bodies to allegorical coupled male-female pairs that extended a regime

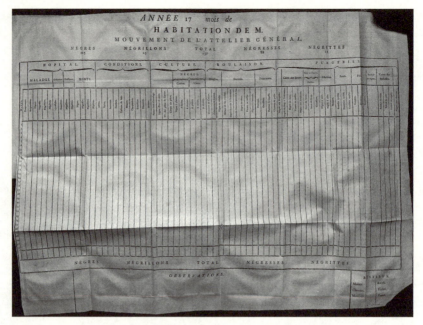

Figure 2. Table, engraving, in Jacques-François Dutrône de la Couture, *Précis sur la canne* (Paris, 1791). Courtesy of Special Collections, University of Wisconsin-Madison.

of male-female domesticity along the grid of commercial navigation, enwrapping the globe in a heteroreproductivity universalized as an order of nature.

Art and its aesthetic technologies as means of visual governance also structured the *Ports of France* (1753–1765), a series of 15 epic land- and seascape paintings that composed the only major French colonial state commission in the eighteenth century (figure 3). Produced by Joseph Vernet during the Seven Years' War (1756–1763), the *Ports of France* orchestrated the art of empire making and its technologies of plantation and transplantation as an aesthetic spectacle of the order that criticism of the time analogized baldly as "populating the colonies" and "governing the world." With their welter of human detail on the ground subsumed into the far greater expanse of the sky of imperial grandeur, the paintings of land and sea in the *Ports of France* do more than represent the Atlantic potential onto which they opened. The privileging of a view from above sustains the illusion of what Mary Louise Pratt has characterized as the perspective of the "Master-of-All-I-Survey." What is consumed as an aesthetic order serves the economic and political

function of providing ostensibly justifiable administration of a system of power through oversight: the political task of the "arts" of empire.

Yet the abstractions of maps, views, and charts did not subsume the material excesses of colonial botanizing and natural-history specimen collecting that transported exotic matter into the cabinets, collections, and archives that exhibited, for example, a Taino *zemi* (a magical object that houses a spirit) in an early-modern collection in Rome and a magic lantern (an early-modern philosophical instrument demonstrating the way in which the eye was supposed to work by casting an image) in Sor Juana de la Cruz's (1651–1695) study in colonial Mexico. The attempted imposition of a monoculture, such as the exclusive cultivation of sugarcane on estates in the Caribbean, also involved negotiating the processes of hybridization, that is, comprehending the diversity of the Atlantic World (and beyond), which diagramming, inventorying, mapping, view making, and collecting for display attempted to manage through their devices of order. The coconut palm and vaunted sugarcane now iconic of the New World plantation, both colonial transplants from the Old World, hybridized the

Figure 3. Joseph Vernet, *First View of Bordeaux*, 1758, oil on canvas, Musée de la Marine, Paris. Copyright Réunion des Musées Nationaux/Art Resource, New York.

tropical Americas themselves. Such arts of attempted imperial imposition and transposition from one part of the world to another did not go unchallenged by revolt and revolution, even from within the frame of the oversight and machinery of the imperial landscape of the Atlantic World. In addition, many complex practices—for example, slaves cultivating exotic transplants in their gardens (the small and marginal parts of the masters' estates set aside for their own use), the building and maintenance of maroon fugitive communities, and the deployment of indigenous knowledge of plants— give us a picture of creative and expressive landscaping to set alongside other everyday aesthetic tactics of survival. The rituals of lived religions of the enslaved (Vodou and Obeah), their performances of Carnival, and their cultivation of modes of dress and grooming such as the erotic display attributed to the lavishly costumed figure of the Mulatta in fantasy scenes of eighteenth-century Barbados and Saint-Domingue (figure 4) and the black dandyism of Mungo Macaroni in the streets of eighteenth-century London (figure 5) served as more than just a means of survival; they produced living cultures, or countercultures, of modernity.

Figure 4. *The Barbadoes Mulatto Girl*, 1779, engraved print from painting by Agostino Brunias, Yale Center for British Art.

Figure 5. *A Mungo Macaroni by M. Darly*, 1772, etching. © Trustees of the British Museum.

Figure 6. Francis Bacon, *Novum Organum Scientiarium* (intended as part of *Instauratio Magna*), 1620, title page. © Trustees of the British Museum.

The flowing waters of the Atlantic World constituted a powerful, but also contested, picture of the beginnings of the global capitalist system. Premised on uncontrollable movements, the Atlantic immediately presents us with the problem of perspective. The aesthetic question of the world picture of the Atlantic from above, below, or somewhere in between is a concern with social and political stakes; it has an imperial genealogy. The Atlantic as a composite of contested and multiple perspectives appeared in the frontispiece to Francis Bacon's *The Great Instauration* (1620) as the classical myth of Hercules battling the many-headed hydra. The contestation and complexity may appear resolved by the frontispiece's restaging of the story as the triumphant return of the ship of science, discovery, and state power, surging safely through the framing pillars of Hercules (figure 6). However, one may also imagine within the unseen interior of the cargo hold, tossed by the energetically rendered waves, the pressure of the unrepresented, the not-so-easily tamed, many-headed hydra of insurgencies, of a history from below wrought by the often anony-

mous and motley crews (sailors, slaves, pirates, indentured servants, market women, indigenous peoples) who also made history in the Atlantic.

The agency of the Atlantic as a visual and materializing concept is inseparable from the still-potent figures of slave and cargo ships that traversed the ocean currents connecting Europe, Africa, Asia, and the Americas along the disputed circuits of trade, exploration, collection, and missionizing. In mobilizing literary critic Mikhail Bakhtin's concept of the chronotope, that device by which time and history are formed spatially and geopolitically, sociologist Paul Gilroy has demonstrated that the slave ship in such emblematic works as British romantic painter J. M. W. Turner's *Slavers Throwing Overboard the Dead and Dying—Typhoon Coming On* (1840) does far more than lend roiling aesthetic form to the emergence of modernity as bound up

Figure 7. Joseph Mallord William Turner (English, 1775–1851), *Slave Ship (Slavers Throwing Overboard the Dead and Dying, Typhoon Coming On)*, 1840, oil on canvas, 90.8 x 122.6 cm (35 3/4 x 48 1/4 in.), Museum of Fine Arts, Boston.

with the violence and deaths of slavery (figure 7). The famous printed diagrams and wooden models of the slave ship *Brookes* (figure 8), produced as part of the transatlantic movement for the abolition of the slave trade, opened the hold of the ship to inspection and its demonstration as only a tomb. In a radical denial of even the possibility of agency, these models convert the enslaved into the abstract, regimented rows of inert, factory-stamped, identical and lifeless merchandise.

The ship was also a vehicle of sexual fantasy and desire inseparable from the erotic economies and gendering dynamics of power in the wake of colonization. Thomas Stothard's *The Voyage of the Sable Venus, from Angola to the West Indies*, a copper engraving reproduced in Bryan Edwards's *History, Civil and Commercial, of the British Colonies in the West Indies* (1793) (figure 9) recasts the Middle Pas-

sage as a rococo fantasy of British empire submitting at the feet of a blackened goddess of love, cruising and ruling the waves on the ship as half-shell. The complex chronotope of the ship condenses a history of abstracting reduction, stereotyping, and fetishization in the political economy of the conversion of humans into things.

Looking back at the heritage of these far-from-finished processes of encounter, aesthetic survival, cultural crossings, and invention, the rogue ship of many potentialities across the charted waters of the ocean as chronotope for modernity continues to be a site of reinvention for contemporary artistic intervention precisely because of its unsettled and unsettling mixture. In the twenty-first century, the world picture of the global reveals other ways to open the hold of the ship. The tidal turn to the view of the Atlantic from the vantage of the

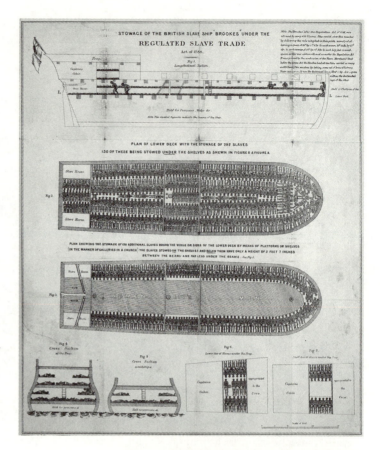

Figure 8. "Stowage of the British Slave Ship 'Brookes' under the Regulated Slave Trade, Act of 1788," Plan of the British Slave Ship *Brookes*, 1789, Albert and Shirley Small Special Collections Library, University of Virginia.

Figure 9. W. Grainger after Thomas Stothard, *The Voyage of the Sable Venus from Angola to the West Indies*, 1794, engraving, in Bryan Edwards, *The History, Civil and Commercial, of the British Colonies in the West Indies, 1794*, vol. 2, facing page 32. Courtesy of Special Collections, University of Wisconsin-Madison.

Figure 10. María Magdalena Campos-Pons, *Elevata*, 2002, 20 x 24 Polaroid print, Composition of 16 Polacolor #6 24-by-20 Polaroid prints, 243.8 x 203.2 cm (96 x 80 in.) installed, Harvard Art Museums/Fogg Museum. Purchased through the generosity of Susan H. Edwards; Dorothy Heath; Saundra Lane; Richard and Ronay Menschel Fund for the Acquisition of Photographs; The Widgeon Point Charitable Foundation; Melvin R. Seiden; Dr. Daniel Tassel; Caroline Cunningham Young; and Alice Sachs Zimet, P2004.11. Copyright: © 2001 Maria M. Campos-Pons; Photo Katya Kallsen © President and Fellows of Harvard College.

watery deep in Cuban Diaspora artist María Magdalena Campos-Pons's *Elevata* (Elevated, 2002) (figure 10) maps the Atlantic through the portals of sixteen large-format Polaroid prints arranged in an extension of the navigational lines of longitude and latitude, a semblance of the grid of the rationalizing organizational system of centralized time-space. In *Elevata*, the Atlantic as world picture of the global is turned on its head, repositioning the sea of history as a matter of orientation and perspective. Through the grid, the globe appears awash in the sea of space, deep in the ocean of the Middle Passage, which might also be up in the blue sky where a divided and suspended orb floats amid the encircling tendrils of the extended ropes of braided hair from a body that, upside down, appears to rise to the surface or top of the plane even as it is also submerged. A dynamic and compounded vehicle of history, the slave ship shaped the Atlantic World not only as a vessel of loss in the Middle Passage but also as a rolling microcosm of transculturating energies.

JILL H. CASID

W

Bibliography

Bleichmar, Daniela. *Visible Empire: Botanical Expeditions and Visual Culture in the Hispanic Enlightenment.* Chicago: University of Chicago Press, 2012.

Casid, Jill H. *Sowing Empire: Landscape and Colonization.* Minneapolis: University of Minnesota Press, 2005.

Gilroy, Paul. *The Black Atlantic: Modernity and Double Consciousness.* Cambridge, MA: Harvard University Press, 1993.

Kriz, Kay Dian. *Slavery, Sugar, and the Culture of Refinement: Picturing the British West Indies, 1700–1840.* New Haven, CT: Yale University Press, 2008.

Linebaugh, Peter, and Marcus Rediker. *The Many-Headed Hydra: Sailors, Slaves, Commoners, and the Hidden History of the Revolutionary Atlantic.* Boston, MA: Beacon, 2000.

Miller, Monica L. *Black Dandyism and the Styling of Black Diasporic Identity.* Durham, NC: Duke University Press, 2009.

Mirzoeff, Nicholas. *The Right to Look: A Counterhistory of Visuality.* Durham, NC: Duke University Press, 2011.

Quilley, Geoff, and Kay Dian Kriz, eds. *An Economy of Colour: Visual Culture and the North Atlantic World, 1660–1830.* Manchester, UK: Manchester University Press, 2003.

Roach, Joseph. *Cities of the Dead: Circum-Atlantic Performance.* New York: Columbia University Press, 1996.

Traub, Valerie. "Mapping the Global Body." In *Early Modern Visual Culture: Representation, Race, and Empire in Renaissance England.* Edited by Peter Erickson and Clark Hulse. Philadelphia: University of Pennsylvania Press, 2000.

Wood, Marcus. *Blind Memory: Visual Representations of Slavery in England and America, 1780–1865.* London: Routledge, 2000.

War, Seven Years'

See Seven Years' War

Wars, African: Slaving and Other

War in western Africa before the arrival of Europeans ranged from raids on small communities to large set-piece encounters in which expansionist states established control over large areas. The taking of prisoners, their use, and their sale were always important objectives. Conflicts large and small fed captives into two linked slaving systems with different geographical orientations, one involving the western African latitudes just south of the Sahara and providing slaves to the Mediterranean, the other from inland along the Atlantic coast channeling slaves into the European trade. Many captives of these wars were also kept and used as slaves within Africa.

When the Portuguese first sailed along Africa's Atlantic coasts in the fifteenth century, most people in the regions they contacted lived in relatively decentralized societies with no chiefs or in small polities with limited chiefly authority. Warfare probably consisted mostly of occasional raiding between neighbors. These conflicts likely focused on land, access to water resources, and remedying food shortages. Early states probably emerged from the ability of some communities to impose themselves on others for such purposes. Conflict was also often fed by the desire of young men to prove their bravery. With populations limited in Africa, control of people was more important than land. Thus, raiding often consisted of the taking of slaves, particularly women and children. In the open grassland savanna, weapons consisted largely of spears, javelins, and bows and arrows. In the forest, where fighting often involved ambushes and engagements in narrow spaces, weapons were usually swords, knives, and clubs.

Increasing political complexity and scale did not necessarily involve serious warfare. Thus, an integrated economy and society emerged around the inland delta of the upper Niger River that was marked by cities, long-distance trade, and occupational specialization. There is no indication in the archeological record of defensive walls, hierarchical political structures, or sustained warfare. Farther north, small states emerged where population growth and desiccation in areas south of the Sahara led to conflict over diminishing habitable territory. With the coming of horse-mounted warriors in the middle of the first millennium BCE, these communities were preyed upon and often retreated to secure defensive locations, but while horses were facilitating wars, camels were making long-distance trade easier. In the long run, the cavalry-based polities found it more advantageous to tax the trade or serve as bases for it, although conflict was constant between raiders from the desert and agriculture-based states in the savanna. Horses could not operate in forested areas of Central Africa and were never introduced in the savanna areas south of the Congo rain forest. Wars in Central Africa were fought by infantry, generally in large set-piece battles. Most armies were lightly armed with lances and bows, but elite corps sometimes fought with shields, swords, and—beginning in the sixteenth century—firearms.

In the latter part of the first millennium CE, the first of a series of imperial states emerged in the western Sudan: Ghana, Mali, and then Songhai followed between about 800 and 1600. Kanem and its successor state, Bornu, emerged over the same centuries in the Chad Basin. The three western empires profited from sending gold to North Africa, but all of these desert-side states also shipped slaves north into and across the Sahara, and all tried to control the profitable regional trade between pastoralists and agriculturalists. Most were also raiders of surrounding populations and large-scale users of the slaves they captured. The slaves were soldiers, servants, farmers, and workers. All these regimes maintained cavalry, though none ever had enough horses for their military. Despite the difficulty of maintaining horses in tropical latitudes, cavalry were able to sweep through large areas inhabited by smaller-scale, less-centralized societies that found it difficult to mobilize the numbers needed to defend themselves against raiders on horses.

Islam became useful to the desert-side warriors as a justification for enslaving populations deemed heathen or unbelievers, who often ignored Islamic law limiting enslavement to a role in legal jihads to convert non-Muslims. Slave raids did not meet this requirement of the Prophet. A series of non-Muslim societies also took up the horse and the technology of cavalry warfare. The Mossi, based in what is now Burkina Faso, raided the desert-side societies in the valley of the bend of the Niger River and in the late fifteenth century sacked Timbuktu, but the Songhai military eventually beat them back. In the Middle Belt of what is now Nigeria, there were other non-Muslim, warlike societies. The savanna and southern desert were thus dominated by large, aggressive military regimes that used cavalry to rule extensive areas and raided regions beyond for slaves. There was a southward-moving, slave-raiding frontier that was linked to commercial penetration of more forested areas to the south. The horsemen who defended these trade routes often played central roles in developing states in these wetter latitudes.

When the Portuguese first came to West Africa in the second half of the fifteenth century, they were more interested in gold than slaves. In fact, Europeans acquired many commodities, but from the beginning, slaves were the most profitable trade. In the fifteenth and sixteenth centuries, these slaves came mostly from local networks. They were available because slaves were often moved away from their areas of origin, where they might escape back to their former homes. There thus was a market for slaves, but in most areas only for local captives. Some people, of course, resisted the possibility of profiting from the sale of human beings. However, a few large kingdoms became important sources of captives. The most important was the Kongo kingdom in West-Central Africa, where the Portuguese developed a slave trade from the early sixteenth century.

Europeans in Africa had very limited military capacity. They controlled the seas, but once their ships moved into river estuaries, this hegemony was conscribed. African boatmen could surround a large sailing vessel, inhibit its operations, and even capture it if they had enough men. On land, Africans either prevented Europeans from building forts or castles or, where they allowed castles to be built, made the Europeans subject to African authority. Only in Angola in the middle of the seventeenth century did the Portuguese manage to conquer significant territory, and that with great difficulty. Even there, to get the slaves they wanted they were forced to work through African military partners.

During the sixteenth and seventeenth centuries, African warrior regimes pushed a slaving frontier far into the interior, similar to the desert-side frontier in West Africa, sometimes profiting from the organizational capacities of inland populations, who developed political networks oriented toward the coast in order to access Atlantic trade. A key variable was that potential victims learned to defend themselves effectively, often by enslaving others. African communities also quickly learned to protect themselves in compact villages surrounded by stockades, in which attackers who managed to get inside the walls found themselves in a maze of narrow alleyways where defenders could trap and capture them. Villages also sometimes moved into more easily defended locations on mountaintops or in marshes.

The slave trade increased slowly until the mid-seventeenth century, when growing European demand for sugar fueled a rise in prices for slaves to work in the plantations of the West Indies. The subsequent expansion of Atlantic slaving led to the rise of a series of powerful slaving states in the late seventeenth and early eighteenth centuries. States such as Oyo, west of the middle Niger River, and Segu, in the upper Niger valley, used cavalry. In the forests of Lower Guinea, Asante and Dahomey were infantry regimes. Most of these states used slave soldiers and dispatched annual military campaigns, sometimes targeting areas that had resisted their authority but often also going after regions where they could take prisoners most easily. In many areas, warriors were also encouraged to raid. The Portuguese had introduced muskets in sixteenth-century Central Africa, but in West Africa guns became important only from the late seventeenth century.

In 1808, both Britain and the United States ended their Atlantic trade in slaves, but the military pursuit of captives in Africa only increased, as prisoners of war were increasingly directed to producing commodities within Africa for both regional African and European markets. Militarization intensified further in the 1860s in a weapons revolution that began when breech-loading rifles replaced flintlock muskets. Rifles had tooled barrels that

spun the bullets they fired more accurately and with ranges twice that of the muskets they replaced. Breech-loading rifles were charged within the reach of the rifleman and could be loaded and fired from the cover of a prostrate position. Within a decade, most such rifles were repeaters, in which a magazine loaded with bullets was inserted into the rifle, for witheringly rapid fire.

As better weapons developed in Europe, arms manufacturers often sold off the previous generation of obsolete weaponry abroad, including to Africa. Some African war leaders also managed to obtain late-model rifles. A few were even able to obtain one or two pieces of field artillery, but none acquired machine guns, the breakthrough weapon of the day in terms of killing power. During the last third of the nineteenth century, modern rifles made possible the emergence of a series of warlords able to deploy small, disciplined forces armed with late-model weapons to very destructive effect. The one limitation of these forces was that, without artillery, they could not seize well-fortified positions. One effect of four centuries of slavery-based warfare was that African population densities remained low, leaving people more valuable than land.

MARTIN A. KLEIN

Bibliography

Lamphear, John. *African Military History*. London: Ashgate, 2007.

Reid, Richard J. *Warfare in African History*. New York: Cambridge University Press, 2012.

Roberts, Richard. *Warriors, Merchants and Slaves: The State and the Economy in the Middle Niger, 1700–1914*. Stanford, CA: Stanford University Press, 1987.

Smith, Robert S. *Warfare and Diplomacy in Pre-colonial West Africa*. London: Methuen, 1977.

Thornton, John K. *Warfare in Atlantic Africa, 1500–1800*. London: Routledge, 1999.

Wars, Napoleonic

The French Revolutionary and Napoleonic wars were a series of draining conflicts between France and shifting alliances of other European powers between 1792 and 1815. These struggles changed the political face of Europe, transforming the dynastic states of the Old Regime and laying the foundation for the modern nation-states of the Continent. Although usually envisioned as a European conflict, the Napoleonic Wars—in memories of participants and observers, as the Great War of their generation—unfolded, perhaps determinatively, also in the Atlantic World. The Caribbean Basin and Latin America served as important sources of revenues and resources for European powers struggling to bear the costs of the most extensive wars in European history. Militarily, both North and South America and the islands of the Caribbean became important theaters for maritime conflicts over colonies. Diverse colonial populations throughout the Americas seized the moment of the distractions of war in Europe to launch sometimes violent confrontations over their political futures.

Never before had European governments resorted to mobilization of civilian and military resources to the extent they did during this period, which left a legacy of civilian participation, fundamental to the subsequent growth of popular nationalism, in the political communities and armies in question. The initial French wars were undertaken to defend and then to disseminate the republican populism of the 1789 revolution in Paris. With Napoleon Bonaparte's seizure of power in 1799, France's war aims reverted to more traditional territorial military conquest and influence over the other powers on the Continent.

The Atlantic Basin became an important theater of this showdown in 1805–1815, a new phase of what some historians describe as the "Second Hundred Years War" waged by France and England (later, Britain) since 1689. The long-standing Franco-British conflicts over colonies in the Caribbean were complicated by slave uprisings inspired by the French Revolution. The French Declaration of the Rights of Man and of the Citizen (1789) raised high expectations in the French colonies, especially in Saint-Domingue (later Haiti), where wealthy white planters hoped to be freed from French commercial restrictions and free men of color (*gens de couleur*) desired to gain the political rights affirmed in the document. Ongoing political turmoil between aggrieved white planters and inspired *gens de couleur* stirred slaves in the densely settled plains and hills of Saint-Domingue's northern province to rise up against their masters in August 1791. The slave revolt quickly spread throughout the French portion of the island, with the militia of the free coloreds providing an important military force against the slave rebels. In gratitude, the French revolutionary government in April 1792 extended citizenship to all free men of color and, two years later, abolished slavery altogether. The violence and victory in Saint-Domingue served as a powerful example for many poorer Spanish, French, and Portuguese colonials seeking greater political and economic freedoms.

By the late eighteenth century, naval control of the seas and the international trade lanes became a central strategic element of the rivalries among the great powers in Europe. But a powerful navy was not as essential to the survival of France during these wars as it was to Britain. Attacked from almost all sides, France concentrated on building up its land forces, and the expectations placed upon the French fleet were drastically less demanding than those of the British, with significant consequences for the battle for the Atlantic.

Economic, administrative, and technical innovations in the Royal Navy, as well as turmoil in the French navy, gave Britain a distinct military superiority at sea as compared with French and Spanish rivals. Britain had a far larger ocean trade than these principal enemies, which gave it a larger reserve of professional seamen to man its warships. British commanders, especially Horatio Nelson, adopted bold methods in confronting their enemies; their repeated victories laid the foundation for the British naval hegemony over the Atlantic and Mediterranean basins.

Although France could do little about events in Haiti or other islands in the Caribbean while at war against Britain, first consul Napoleon Bonaparte nonetheless made the decision to reassert French authority over former French colonies in the Americas. With the Treaty of San Ildefonso (1800), France gained the vast Louisiana territory on the North American continent from Spain. Bonaparte perceived rebellious Saint-Domingue as a vital strategic point to secure these French interests in North America. He sent an expeditionary force to the island in 1802, but the armed blacks and mulattoes, united under Jean-Jacques Dessalines, fought off the French army. By 1803, the costs of France's renewed war with Britain required selling the Louisiana Territory to the United States, leaving Haiti no longer vital to French interests. Without further support or supplies, the French withdrew in November 1803 from Cap Français (now Cap Haïtien).

In fall 1805, the British triumph at sea off the coast of Trafalgar in the Atlantic, just west of the Strait of Gibraltar, offset French military victories on the Continent. Throughout the previous spring and summer, the French fleet had eluded the British blockade of the Atlantic port of Toulon, rendezvoused with a Spanish fleet, and sailed for the West Indies. Napoleon wanted to use these maneuvers as a diversion to draw off British squadrons from the eastern Atlantic and Mediterranean so that his forces could secure control of European waters and move the French army across the English Channel to invade Britain. The plan failed. British admiral Horatio Nelson pursued the French fleet to the West Indies and then back to Europe. By then, Napoleon, with his original plan in shambles and Austria and Russia already confronting him from the east, had already broken up his camps at Boulogne, overlooking the English Channel, and begun the march to the Danube. He ordered his Atlantic fleet and the Spanish fleet to set a course for the Mediterranean in order to provide protection for the French forces in Italy.

As the combined Franco–Spanish fleet approached Spain, Nelson confronted it on October 21 near Cape Trafalgar. For five hours the battle raged. Nelson himself was killed by a musket ball. Yet the result was one of the most decisive and consequential naval victories in history. The British fleet captured seventeen Franco–Spanish ships and destroyed one, without losing a single vessel of their own. The loss at Trafalgar left France no longer able to contest British control of the seas, allowing Britain to project its naval power throughout the Atlantic World.

France's efforts to rebuild its empire in the Atlantic World ended with the sale of Louisiana to the United States in 1803 and the defeats in Haiti and at Trafalgar. The British Royal Navy conducted naval operations to seize the remaining French possessions in the Caribbean, while the weakened French fleets failed to achieve any significant objectives. The British government chose to exploit its naval supremacy to prevail in this protracted war, and in May 1806 it began enacting Orders in Council that blockaded the European coast, rivers, and ports

from the Elbe (Prussia) to the port of Brest (France's northern Atlantic coast). The combination of these decrees and Britain's policy of searching American ships for deserters led the United States to enact the Embargo Act of 1807, which prohibited American ships from engaging in trade with the European belligerents. In response, Napoleon issued a series of decrees that declared the British islands to be in a state of blockade, imprisoned British subjects on the Continent, and prohibited all commerce and correspondence with them.

The collective result of all these acts was the Continental Blockade, which had profound political, military, and economic consequences. Britain found itself in strategic isolation and focused its military strategy on containing French gains in Europe while expanding British overseas interests. As an island nation with a long tradition of maritime trade and a powerful navy, Britain naturally pursued a maritime strategy in which control of the seas (especially the Atlantic Ocean) was a substantial priority. Of crucial importance for British maritime power was protecting the Atlantic trade that sustained the war effort by securing sources of raw material (iron, tar, timber, pitch, tallow, and so on) for its naval stores.

Although focused on Europe, the Continental blockade disrupted trade in the Atlantic World generally. It produced a serious economic downturn in the United States, which could no longer send its staple exports (such as cotton and tobacco) to European markets. The British navy began targeting American merchants conducting business with France; by 1812 the British had seized some 400 ships. Furthermore, hard pressed for seamen for the expanding naval forces required to blockade an entire continent, the British also instituted a policy of stopping American ships and impressing American seamen, who they claimed were British subjects liable to conscription. Reports of British impressments caused an explosion of American outrage and eventually contributed to the outbreak of the 1812 war between Britain and the United States.

Relations between France and the United States were strained as well. Napoleon found the Americans troublesome or worse. To start with, he was annoyed by the American entrepreneurs who delivered weapons and ammunition to rebels in Saint-Domingue, over which France still claimed sovereignty. He resented the fact that American merchants, often in collusion with the British, continually penetrated the Continental blockade and served as principal suppliers of the British forces in Spain and Portugal. France also criticized the U.S. answer to the British embargo, the Non-Intercourse Act (1809), which effectively cut off U.S. traffic with France but did little to hinder American trade with Britain. Shortly before the United States declared war on Britain in June 1812, the U.S. Senate fell just two votes shy of declaring war on France.

The blockade also caused a disastrous decline in the economies of Spanish and French colonies in the Caribbean. Thus, at Martinique, the British trade embargo meant, in the words of a local French official, that "not one barrel of flour, salted meats, or cod" had reached the island from North America: "the roads [of the ports] are empty." The dearth of commercial activity was in a sharp contrast with the bustling trade before the blockade, when nearly 740 ships had visited Martinique's ports in the first half of 1806 alone. The naval stores on the islands were quickly exhausted, further constraining French ability to protect interests in the region. Consequently Martinique, the last major French colony, fell to a British invasion in 1809.

By then, Napoleon had already turned away from his consistent losses throughout the Atlantic World and concentrated on expanding French control of the European continent. In 1807, Napoleon occupied Portugal in a bid to enforce his own blockade against Britain, forcing the Portuguese royal family and court to flee, escorted by British ships, to refuge in Brazil. The arrival of the king, Prince João, and the royal court at Rio de Janeiro transfused fresh and vigorous life into the vast American domain, where over the next few years banks, printing presses, libraries, and newspapers were established. In December 1815, the colony was elevated in status to a "kingdom" co-equal with Portugal. The roughly 15,000 Portuguese immigrants accompanying the court, however, sharpened existing tensions with native-born Brazilians; when the Portuguese king and court returned in 1822 to Portugal in the wake of Napoleon's defeat, native-born Brazilians backed the crown prince in a declaration of Brazil's political independence as an empire.

The Spanish colonies' break with Spain was a much more tumultuous process. In 1804 Napoleon had forced Spain to support his struggle against Britain. Spain's alliance with Napoleon in his European wars, beyond the devastating naval defeat at Trafalgar, gave Britain the pretext it had been seeking to challenge Spanish hegemony in the Western Hemisphere. The British made two attempts to force their way into Spanish American markets in 1806–1807, dispatching expeditions to Buenos Aires, the capital of the Viceroyalty of La Plata (modern Argentina) and the Atlantic gateway to the silver of the high Andes. Local militia forces successfully repelled these expeditions, without any support from Spain. Like the victories of the rebel army in North America three decades earlier, these military successes of local forces reinvigorated calls for secession from the monarchy in Iberia.

Such sentiments only grew in 1808, when Napoleon removed Charles IV of Spain and his son Ferdinand from power in Madrid and named his own brother, Joseph Bonaparte, as king of Spain. Absent what they perceived to be a legitimate monarch, pro-independence leaders in Central and Latin America saw an opportunity to move toward their goal. Loyalty to the Bourbon dynasty meant opposition to the French-imposed regime in Madrid, mobilizing local monarchist elites throughout Spanish Latin America to join in creating juntas (groups of local interests) to assert local rule. In 1809–1810, juntas in the colonial capitals of Montevideo, Caracas, Quito, La Paz, Buenos Aires, and Santiago organized popular demonstrations that forced Spanish officials to cede their authority.

The question remained whether these juntas were temporary organizations to be disbanded when the legitimate Bourbon monarchy returned to Spain or precursors to a permanent transfer of power from Madrid to the Americas. Royalists made the former argument, while pro-independence republicans saw the chance to win complete independence from Spain. Tensions between these groups quickly escalated into fighting even before the British restored Ferdinand VII to the throne in 1813. Ferdinand dispatched Spanish troops to the Americas in an effort to put down the anti-Spanish rebellions, but after a decade of war, Spain's American colonies, from Mexico in the north to Chile and Argentina in the south, emerged independent.

The eventual successes of these South American wars of independence rested on the achievements of two accomplished military leaders, Simón Bolívar, a wealthy Venezuelan Creole, and José de San Martín, a military officer in Argentina who had pursued a career in the Spanish army and fought in the Peninsular War against the French. When Venezuela declared its independence from Spain in 1811, the regime became embroiled in prolonged conflict between royalists and republicans. In 1813 Bolívar expelled the royalist forces and consolidated the forces in favor of independence. But this success proved short lived, and over the next two years Bolívar twice had to flee into exile.

He nonetheless persevered in his fight for independence, and a turning point came in the summer of 1819, when Bolívar led over 2,000 soldiers on a daring march through the seemingly impassable Andes Mountains into what is now Colombia. Surprising the Spanish royalist army in Bogotá, he scored a decisive victory over royalist forces at Boyacá. By 1821, after consolidating his gains in Venezuela and Colombia, Bolívar marched south into Ecuador, where he finally met José de San Martín, who had led pro-independence military forces in southeastern Latin America. Paraguay had proclaimed independence in 1811, followed by the rebels in Buenos Aires, who joined in establishing the United Provinces of the Río de la Plata in 1816. In 1817, San Martín led an army on a grueling march west across the southern Andes to link up with the rebel army of Bernardo O'Higgins in Chile and defeat royalist forces there and in Peru. In 1822, Bolívar and San Martín met at Guayaquil (Ecuador), where together they decided the future of the revolutionary movements in Hispanic America.

Meanwhile, with the distraction of Spanish forces in Napoleon's wars in Europe, political and social discontent also reached a climax in Mexico. Distraught by widespread poverty and hardship, a priest in the small village of Dolores, Padre Miguel de Hidalgo y Costilla, took the first step toward independence when he delivered the famed Grito de Dolores (the "Cry of Dolores," or "sorrows"), a call for rebellion against Spanish rule. In the fall of 1810, he led tens of thousands of poor farmers and other supporters toward Mexico City but was defeated by the Spanish army; Hidalgo himself was captured and executed. The rebels then rallied around another strong leader, Padre José María Morelos, who led the military rebellion for four more years before suffering a decisive defeat. Events in Mexico took yet another turn in 1820, when a revolution in Spain brought liberals to power there.

Remarkably, Mexico's independence was achieved finally when conservative forces in the viceroyalty attempted to seize the moment to rise up against this fleeting liberal regime in the homeland and were defeated.

The initial British effort to contain the military forces of continental France in the 1790s in defense of the principle of monarchical rule—already challenged successfully by North Americans, with critical French military assistance—combined with the terrifying chaos of slave revolt in Saint-Domingue to make the Atlantic a decisive theater of the global military struggle usually known by the name of the ambitious and audacious French first consul, Napoleon Bonaparte. The Royal Navy's military control of the seas contained Napoleon's military strategy within continental Europe. Nevertheless, an indirect but profound effect of Napoleon's European conquests was a decisive weakening of the European combatants' presence in the Americas. This loosening of these transatlantic ties manifested itself in two different processes: an almost bloodless dissolution of Portugal's colonial presence in Brazil and a violent disintegration of Spain's authority in its mainland territories. Settler elites, like their English counterparts in North America, seized upon this moment of military weakness to declare political regimes of their own, independent of European control.

The costs of the French war effort led Napoleon to sell the entire Mississippi River watershed to the new United States, which was emboldened in the Atlantic also by the profits of blockade running and resentment of British retaliation in seizing seamen on U.S.-registered ships. Britain won more than two decades of military struggles in Europe, confirmed by the Treaty of Vienna in 1815, by controlling the Atlantic. In this assertion of maritime power, Britain gained economic entrée to the weak new nations of the Americas left in the wake of the titanic struggles, but the principle of monarchy for which the country had stood steadfast, at unprecedented costs in men, materiel, and money, had been lost. The political and economic realignments emerging from the Napoleonic Wars expanded the subsequent history of the nineteenth century to global proportions, ending the Atlantic Era of intra-European struggles from which they had emerged.

—ALEXANDER MIKABERIDZE

Bibliography

Belaubre, Christophe, Jordana Dym, and John Savage. *Napoleon's Atlantic: The Impact of Napoleonic Empire in the Atlantic World.* Leiden: Brill, 2010.

Dubois, Laurent. *Avengers of the New World: The Story of the Haitian Revolution.* Cambridge: Harvard University Press, 2004.

Geggus, David Patrick. *The Impact of the Haitian Revolution in the Atlantic World.* Columbia: University of South Carolina Press, 2001.

Ocampo, Emilio. *The Emperor's Last Campaign: A Napoleonic Empire in America.* Tuscaloosa: University of Alabama Press, 2009.

Robson, Martin. *Britain, Portugal and South America in the Napoleonic Wars: Alliances and Diplomacy in Economic Maritime Conflict.* London: I. B. Tauris, 2011.

Wars of Conquest

In 1519 Hernán Cortés, leading some 500 Spanish soldiers, seized control of the Aztec Empire in the great valley of present-day Mexico. The conquest was amazing, even to the conquerors. Since the sixteenth century a legend has circulated that the Aztec emperor Montezuma, along with his followers, was dazzled into submission. Upon seeing pale, bearded men riding horses and wielding unfamiliar weaponry of unimaginable power, he concluded that the newcomers were gods and dared not oppose them. A twentieth-century variant of this story of effortless conquest emphasizes illnesses; the Spanish brought an array of contagious diseases with them, and thousands of indigenous Mexicans, lacking immunities to Old World germs, died of fevers. The Aztecs were simultaneously debilitated and impressed by the Spanish soldiers' immunity to the plagues, and they succumbed almost instantaneously to a sense of their own inferiority. This interpretation of the Spanish conquest of New Spain as overwhelming has recently faced scholarly criticism, in part because it fails to credit the strategic choices made by the thousands of Mesoamericans who enabled Cortés, by joining forces with him, to overthrow Montezuma. They believed that Cortés could be a useful ally in their own opposition to Aztec rule. Within days of his arrival, they recognized the value of European firearms, and as

the Spanish encroachment continued, they also appreciated the advantages the Spanish secured through their horses, construction of roads, and the maintenance of supply lines to their forces in the field.

From the time of Columbus onward, the military ascendancy in the Americas of all the European monarchies depended similarly on their abilities to transport and deploy large numbers of soldiers while keeping their men clothed, fed, healthy, and well armed. The indigenous responses to European military technology, however, varied. Upon confronting well-supplied European armies, some capitulated or sided with the newcomers, while others resisted by adopting new, peculiarly American ways of fighting. In North America, Iroquois fighters had had long experience with palisades and siege warfare by the early seventeenth century, and their first reaction to the Europeans' iron weaponry was to redouble their efforts to maintain effective fortifications. In offensive operations against colonists and Native American foes alike, they massed their forces for coordinated assaults. Only in the second half of the seventeenth century did they adopt the guerrilla-like tactics popularly associated with "Indian warfare," scattering their warriors and relying on ambushes. In the medium term their adoption of the "skulking way of war" was effective in securing a measure of autonomy from the European powers. It also allowed the Iroquois to intimidate other Native American groups and thereby expand their reach geographically and economically. In the long term, however, the nearly constant low-level conflict perpetuated animosities and provoked reprisals, so that among the Iroquois warfare rivaled infectious disease as a cause of demographic decline.

While Native Americans responded in a great variety of ways to the European invasion of the Americas and the arrival of new military technology, the indigenous responses nearly everywhere in North America entailed an escalation in captive taking. Some, like the Iroquois, seized prisoners from other Native American communities in order to adopt them and thus maintain their own numbers in the face of severe demographic decline. Others, including several tribes in the Southeast, sold Native prisoners to French and British trading partners, in effect feeding a slave trade.

Slave trading in Africa and in the Americas illustrates the fundamental importance of Native warfare in shaping the dynamics of European territorial claims. According to the immediate precedent, common throughout Europe in the Middle Ages but surviving in the early-modern era only in the Mediterranean, soldiers captured in a just war against enemies of the Christian God could be disposed of as slaves. By fighting on the wrong side and losing, captured combatants forfeited their lives. Enslavement was understood to be an expression of mercy; in fact, the legal term for it was *redemption*. European slave traders operating on the coasts of Africa or in the Americas sometimes argued that the people they purchased had lost their claims to freedom by losing in unjustified wars.

They argued more generally that Native American and African cultures were characterized by relentless, merciless conflicts. The peoples of those continents were continuously and culpably violent. This morally loaded assertion vilified all members of the societies of Africa and the Americas, not just the warriors. Irrationally brutal people deserved subjugation, and indeed they could be improved through it. Conquests thus could serve the interests of the conquered, and indeed even enslavement could operate to the slaves' benefit, because European supremacy in effect liberated Africans and Native Americans from the persistent violence they otherwise suffered.

The bitter irony embedded in this argument, of course, was that Europeans promoted, participated in, and intensified indigenous warfare in Africa and the Americas. By providing a market for slaves, colonial traders encouraged slave raids, and by demonizing "natives" the Europeans invited dehumanizing conflicts. Events in the eighteenth and early nineteenth centuries in the Minas Gerais region of south-central Brazil illustrate dynamics that operated in many places during the period of European conquests in the Americas. In an effort to control the spread of territorial claims in a region rich in gold and diamonds, Portuguese authorities designated most of the area "forbidden land," warning settlers that it was inhabited by wild people who engaged in constant warfare. That forbidding description did not keep prospectors out; it only inspired the colonists who entered to prepare for the worst and anticipate savagery. The resulting escalation of violence culminated in a futile attempt to enslave, slaughter, or expel the Native peoples blamed for it. Throughout the Americas, designat-

ing a people "savage" exposed them to violence unhindered by the rules of war and simultaneously expanded the vulnerable populations by blurring or eliminating any distinction between warrior and civilian.

In the British imperial context, these brutalizing effects are clearly seen in scalp-bounty proclamations issued by colonial authorities and by the British army in the seventeenth and eighteenth centuries—which routinely offered prizes for the scalps of men, women, and children. In 1749 in Nova Scotia, Governor Edward Cornwallis, within days of his arrival from Britain, initiated such a policy. As he did so, he explained that he was following "the custom of America." Although a tradition of gift exchange involving scalps had ancient Native American origins, his bounty transformed the practice into a clumsy, ineffective instrument of genocide. Cornwallis declared that he wanted to destroy all the Mi'kmaq in Nova Scotia, but he never came close, because his soldiers were ill equipped to fight the Mi'kmaq on their own ground, and he had no Native American allies.

Britain's mid-eighteenth-century campaigns in the Canadian Maritime Provinces, from the founding of Halifax in 1749 through the seizure of French Louisbourg in 1758, stand out in the history of European colonization in North America because they proceeded without the aid of any indigenous groups. Elsewhere, from the time of Cortés onward, colonial leaders reasoned that they needed Native allies in order to succeed. Despite many colonists' misgivings about arming neighbors defined as untrustworthy, a powerful logic justified the enlistment of indigenous military aid. Colonists constituted only small minorities within the regions they intended to occupy. Furthermore, they knew that they would be operating on unfamiliar terrain if hostilities arose. They feared that they would be facing adversaries who not only knew the land better than they did but fought in ways appropriate to the challenges of the local environments. The problem of navigating unfamiliar swamps and woods seemed almost to dictate reliance on locals and their specialized military tactics.

Native American warriors fought in support of European campaigns in recognition of the reality of the European presence in the Americas, and they were also encouraged by a combination of threats and positive inducements. They contributed in a variety of capacities. Some enlisted in specialized ranger companies and took orders from colonial officers who directed them to fight "like Indians." Others, maintaining a measure of political coherence, entered imperial wars as allies of rival European armies. Even in times of formal peace between the monarchies in Europe, Native Americans offered military aid to the colonial regimes, for example supporting plantation slavery by capturing fleeing Africans and helping to suppress slave uprisings. Indigenous warriors played a critical role in the military defeat of a large-scale, yearlong revolt among Dutch Guiana's enslaved Africans in 1763 and 1764.

The maintenance of chattel slavery as a labor system sparked a relentless cycle of warfare on the margins of the American colonies. The notorious brutality of wars involving escaped slaves—with men, women, and children targeted indifferently, homes and fields destroyed, captured enemies decapitated or burned alive, and corpses placed on display for weeks or months—reflected the desperation of both the runaways and the plantation owners. Slaveholders in the British Caribbean denigrated fugitive maroons as traitors, murderers, and savages reverting to the vicious culture they attributed to Africans. The British disdained negotiations with them, but on the few occasions when maroon communities acquired enough strength to endure, most notably on Jamaica, colonial authorities had little choice but to accept the limits of their own power and agree at least temporarily to terms. Colonial officials faced similar dilemmas near many other slaveholding societies in the Caribbean and on the American mainland.

When imperial authorities designated some areas "forbidden land," sponsored the military tactics they condemned as "savage," recruited Native allies, or negotiated with maroons, they were acknowledging their own inability to effect conquest of all the territories they claimed in the Americas. Though some imperial promoters may have dreamed of a more thoroughly controlled future for these colonies, in the short term most of those with experience in the Western Hemisphere believed that life in America would be distinguished by perpetual, low-level conflict. This expectation was written into the emerging law of nations of the time. As early as 1559, European diplomats began to insert provisions into their peace treaties declaring that the Americas were exceptional. Though the dynasties involved vowed to maintain peace in Europe, they acknowledged that they could not guarantee peace on other side of the Atlantic, "beyond the line." This admission of limits to their control informed European diplomacy through most of the seventeenth century. It is noteworthy that Europe's diplomats did not identify America's indigenous populations as the principal obstacles to the maintenance of peace. Nor did they think that the numerous slaves were the problem. The intractable difficulty they recognized was the incompatibility of the Spanish monarchy's claim to most of the hemisphere with their own territorial pretensions.

Theoretical discussions and popular perceptions of the distinctiveness of early American ways of war have generally focused on the clash of military cultures that occurred when Native Americans battled Europeans. But concentrating excessively on the violence associated with these encounters runs the risk of distracting us from the pain that the Europeans and colonists inflicted on one another in the American wars of conquest. The Christian conquest of Iberia in the fourteenth and fifteenth centuries and the English occupation of Ireland in the second half of the sixteenth century featured large-scale slaughter and spectacular violence. In order to effect and secure their conquests, European armies threatened to uproot and displace noncombatants on both sides of the ocean, but after the sixteenth century they were more likely to do so on the American side, with the aim of consolidating their control of the colonies they had claimed.

On some occasions, as when the Protestant English Empire conquered Protestant New Netherland and when the British Empire took the populous French colony of Canada, they left the local colonial populations in place. But on others, as in Jamaica, St. Kitts, Newfoundland, Nova Scotia, Cape Breton Island, and Florida, mass evacuations followed successful military campaigns. In the seventeenth and eighteenth centuries, colonial populations were relocated more often, more systematically, more efficiently, and more thoroughly than Native groups. This is not to say that Indians were treated more lightly. Colonists often had places to go, as well as positive inducements to emigrate. Indeed, settlers with experience in the Americas constituted a highly valued source of labor, and defeated colonial regimes usually wanted their subjects back. Conquered colonists were therefore frequently shipped around the Atlantic World. Native Americans, by contrast, frequently faced slaughter.

Considering the process of wars of conquest in broad terms, several features make the early-modern Atlantic World unique. The first involves the extended duration of conflict. Columbus used force against the indigenous peoples of the Caribbean islands in the 1490s, and resistance followed. Across the Americas, fighting between settlers and Native Americans would continue intermittently for the next 400 years. Wars continued because of the enormous size of the continents, the large numbers of Europeans and Africans who crossed the ocean, and the persistence of Native peoples who refused to be integrated, or were never invited, into the colonial polities. When the worst of the fighting ended in the late nineteenth century, vast regions in the Arctic and Amazon Basin remained unconquered.

Similarly, the resilient populations of Africa and tropical diseases lethal to troops from temperate-latitude backgrounds defeated European settlements there and limited wars of conquest before the end of the nineteenth century. Africans also provided the gold, ivory, and other commodities, as well as captives European traders sought, without involving military occupation. The principal exception was that the Portuguese claimed to have conquered the kingdom of Angola, in West-Central Africa, and retained a weak military presence in its coastal regions only through alliances with local groups. The nominal conquest was supposed to have involved a just war that, like conquests in the Americas, established legal authority for the pervasive slaving that persisted until the period of effective European military occupation at the end of the nineteenth century.

At the temperate southern tip of Africa, the Dutch East India Company established a provisioning settlement at Cape Town in 1652 but did not confront resistance that required military conquest. The Khoikhoi herders of the area dispersed in the wake of a devastating epidemic of smallpox in 1714, and their survivors joined a growing population of enslaved Asians and other Africans on Dutch wheat farms and vineyards. The dynamics of this commercial form of slavery were no less fraught than the tensions in its American counterparts, and

a ring of autonomous maroonlike communities of fugitives—Griqua, "Bastaards," and others mixing with larger African populations to the north—grew up in the eighteenth century on the margins of the Dutch settlement at the Cape. Systematic wars of conquest in southern Africa ensued only after the Dutch settlers at the Cape fled British emancipation of their slaves in the 1830s and tried—not always successfully—to take the lands of the Africans to the north.

A final characteristic that distinguishes the wars of imperial conquest in the Americas from European engagements with the rest of the world was chattel slavery. Captive taking and prisoner exchanges had long been accepted components of African, European, and Native American military and diplomatic traditions. The commercialization of the slave trade, however, increased the frequency of captive taking, degraded the status of captives, and necessitated the erection of new, violent institutions to maintain discipline, prevent escapes, and suppress insurrections. Under these circumstances, many territorial conquests remained insecure.

GEOFFREY PLANK

Bibliography

Gould, Eliga H. "Zones of Law, Zones of Violence: The Legal Geography of the British Atlantic, c. 1772." *William and Mary Quarterly* 3rd ser., 60 (2003): 471–510.

Keener, Craig S. "An Ethnohistorical Analysis of Iroquois Assault Tactics Used against Fortified Settlements of the Northeast in the Seventeenth Century." *Ethnohistory* 46 (1999): 777–807.

Langfur, Hal. *The Forbidden Lands: Colonial Identity, Frontier Violence, and the Persistence of Brazil's Eastern Indians.* Stanford, CA: Stanford University Press, 2006.

Lee, Wayne E., ed. *Empires and Indigenes: Intercultural Alliance, Imperial Expansion, and Warfare in the Early Modern World.* New York: New York University Press, 2011.

Plank, Geoffrey. *An Unsettled Conquest: The British Campaign against the Peoples of Acadia.* Philadelphia: University of Pennsylvania Press, 2000.

Townsend, Camilla. "Burying the White Gods: New Perspectives on the Conquest of Mexico." *American Historical Review* 108 (2003): 659–687.

Wars of Independence, American

A series of interrelated wars splintered empires and left multiple, mostly republican nation-states throughout the Americas from the 1770s through the 1830s. The legacy of these wars, including the war for independence in the future United States and those waged by Simón Bolívar and José de San Martín in Spanish America, was more than independence. Often quite long and excessively violent, they decisively shaped the institutions and issues that would preoccupy the peoples who lived within the hotly contested national borders they produced from the Atlantic Era that preceded them.

Many popular uprisings in the Americas did not lead to independent republics because that was never their goal. (Some of these are considered in other essays in this collection.) And recent scholars have noted that the term *wars of independence* tends to conflate all insurgencies under a rubric of national movements modeled on European nations. But the indigenous or mixed-race peoples who joined rebellions led by Pontiac (1763–1766) and Tecumseh (1811–1813), for instance, in eastern North America and Túpac Amaru II in Peru (1780), or insurgencies, such as the one in Mexico led by Miguel Hidalgo y Castilla (1808–1811), were generally motivated by local issues, such as changes in commercial practices or access to land rights. Though Haiti was an important exception, indigenous peoples and enslaved Africans almost never imagined the creation of a nation-state.

The Seven Years' War and Its Effects

The entangled histories of Atlantic wars for independence that are the focus of this essay begin with the Atlantic-wide Seven Years' War, or the Great War for Empire (1756–1763). That war was the climax of a series of European conflicts, almost all of which pitted France and its allies against Great Britain and its allies. Decades of these inconclusive struggles had prompted a military revolution in Europe, defined by especially costly intensifications in weapons and tactics. The monarchies of Europe had developed fiscal-military states that could manage and support long campaigns of warfare on

increasingly Atlantic scales. Perhaps the most far-reaching strains on politics in this regard were in Great Britain. Georgian monarchs in London—weakened by a lack of money, civil war, and the failure of their Stuart predecessors Charles II (r. 1660–1685) and James II (r. 1685–1689) to emulate the growing power and grandiose style of Louis XIV of France (r. 1643–1715)—had to go to Parliament regularly to win consent for taxes that would support the escalating militarization of dynastic politics in Europe. Great Britain decisively defeated France in North America and Asia in 1763, in part because of its consolidation of a constitutional fiscal-military state capable of raising money and deploying naval power all over the world. Spanish fears of French and especially British intrusion into the Pacific had led Madrid initially to opt for neutrality in these struggles. When the Spanish, concluding that Britain was the more serious threat, finally joined the French in 1761, they were too late. The British captured Spain's only outpost in Asia, at Manila, in 1762 and acquired the Philippine archipelago in the 1763 Treaty of Paris, which officially confirmed the British victory in the war.

Britain's global triumph provoked reforms throughout all of the European territories in the Atlantic. In Great Britain, Parliament passed new regulations on trade and migration intended to raise revenues to cover the enormous debt left by the war, including a Stamp Act designed to make the administration of its North American colonies self-supporting. In Spain, defeat produced the Bourbon Reforms, a concerted attempt at making a vast American empire more efficient. In Portugal, Sebastião José de Carvalho e Melo, Marquess of Pombal and prime minister (1750–1777) under King João I, pushed through a similar set of administrative reforms, although as much out of admiration for, as concern about, the British. All these reforms raised the issue of the extent to which colonists of European ancestry—called *créoles* in the French Empire and *criollos* in the Spanish Empire—were entitled to the rights and privileges of their fellow subjects born in England and Castile.

This tension often played out within local militias, the key military units in all European colonies, as the regular armed forces of Europe's monarchies were fully deployed in conflicts on the Continent. The colonial militia units usually reflected local social structures and power hierarchies. In New England, the civilian militia units had a well-honed sense of their right to consent (through consultation) to decisions about length of their service, compensation, and general treatment. During and after the Seven Years' War, this assertive attitude put them at odds with officers in the British army who demanded absolute obedience. Within the Spanish Empire, all members of colonial militia—including *castas* (populations of mixed backgrounds in Spanish cities), *pardos* (a racialized term for freed former slaves, often with European parentage), poor men of Indian and mixed-race backgrounds—eventually enjoyed a special status, referred to as *fueromilitar*, that included the right to trial by their military peers rather than by civilian authorities. Controversy produced by planned limitations of the *fueromilitar* manifested a divergence between imperial and colonial assumptions about the responsibilities of subjects in the colonies. As metropolitan and local gentries fell out with each other and began to engage in civil war, suddenly many peoples, regardless of class, race, or gender, were demanding their natural rights rather than privileges granted by the monarchs, often on the grounds of their participation in military campaigns.

Global wars between the European monarchies laid bare serious tensions within colonies as well as among the various components of consolidating empires. Throughout the Americas, service as a soldier equated with a claim to participation in the politics of the realm. Having fought for their king in the 1750s and 1760s, Euroamericans expected their monarchs to treat them well, to reward rather than marginalize them. Disappointed by the attitude of metropolitan governments, many British Americans sought a new political standing in which they would be citizens—that is, active participants in their governance, rather than subjects. When they mobilized as the Continental Army, under George Washington, to assert their rights through armed rebellion, a long war united disparate mainland colonies from New Hampshire to Georgia. It also solidified the attachment of those in Canada and the Caribbean islands who chose to remain loyal to the British Empire.

A French and Spanish alliance with the United States in 1778 transformed the war into a general European conflict. But in regions south of Pennsylvania the numbers of enslaved Africans and descendants of Africans held in slavery, indigenous peoples, and *castas* usually dwarfed those born in Europe or to European parents. There the outbreak of war brought questions of race into conflict with the idea that local military rank equated with membership in the independent polity that might result. Were all men, of whatever backgrounds, who fought for independence entitled to the rights and responsibilities of citizenship? Would the European monarchies reward loyalist slaves with freedom? The French Revolution (1789) in Europe complicated matters, as it spawned new ideas and policies on political rights. Republican France abolished slavery in its overseas territories in 1794, and the Spanish Constitution of 1812, when Spain still retained claim to all of its territories in the Americas, recognized as citizens all free or freed people (except those of African ancestry) born, naturalized, or residing in Spanish territories for at least ten years. This inclusivity went well beyond the bounds of what most *créoles* or *criollos* were willing to countenance, even for members of militia units who had faithfully served the empire.

Questions of membership in these increasingly participatory polities often transcended all other considerations, turning incipient wars for independence into civil wars defined by race or inhibiting their development altogether. In Virginia in 1775 the royal governor granted freedom to enslaved Africans who fought for King George; this consequently drove many British subjects in the colony into support for the rebellion against the crown. Black men brandishing arms in Haiti in the revolt there in 1791 and winning their independence in 1804 constituted the most threatening image of the social implications of wars that might yield independence, as observers saw that these wars might leave masters relatively defenseless against the people they held in slavery. In Mexico, an insurgent movement (1810–1815) of tens of thousands of *castas* and mestizos (people of mixed Indian and Spanish descent, who were the majority in Mexico) led by Hidalgo and later by José Maria Morelos raised the specter of violent social revolution.

Throughout the Atlantic World, *criollos* were most reluctant to fight for their independence in regions where they were most outnumbered. Support for independence was anemic at best in the West Indies beyond Haiti, while the strongest movements were in the United States and Chile. In the Spanish and Portuguese colonies, talk of independence was initially little more than an effort to fill a vacuum created by the collapse of imperial authority in the destruction of Napoleon's invasion of Iberia. It was this 1808 occupation of Spain by his armies that prompted the creation of revolutionary juntas in major urban areas throughout the empire. Pro-independence forces fared relatively well until 1814, the time at which the Napoleonic armies were expelled from Iberia, but fared badly thereafter, when the metropolitan government could focus on defense of the Americas. More often than not, Spanish forces had the support of large numbers of *criollos*.

Both in Europe and in the wealthiest parts of the Americas, propertied interests restored monarchy. The vast majority of *criollos* in Mexico not only failed to respond to Hidalgo's 1810 Grito de Dolores (El Grito de Independencia), Mexico's Declaration of Independence, but also participated in the royal troops' brutal suppression of the rebels. Hidalgo was captured and executed in 1811, and Morelos in 1815. Mexican *criollos* chose independence only in 1820, when officers in the Spanish army preparing to embark for the Americas forced Ferdinand VII to restore the Constitution of 1812: they proclaimed a monarchy of their own rather than risk a republic. A similar move to adopt the seeming security of monarchy developed in Brazil. A liberal constitutional revolution in Portugal in 1821 provoked a violent war for independence in Brazil, ending with creation of an American empire that lasted until 1889.

Military Intensification, Social Conflicts, and Intra-Regional Discord

As internal tensions among politicized and racialized parties in the Americas transformed imperial civil conflicts into regional civil wars, struggles for independence became total wars. The Anglo-American war for independence, a nasty enough affair during the 1776–1777 campaign in New Jersey, became a war of terror and destruction in the Carolinas in 1780–1781. Guerrilla raids, massive destruction of civilian property, and murder of noncombatants were commonplace. In some areas, the war became an excuse to engage in ethnic cleansing against indigenous peoples who had chosen neutrality or sided with the British. In late 1779, George Washington authorized a campaign in upstate New York that burned Iroquois villages and destroyed food that was to have fed people during the winter. Similar atrocities grew out of the chaos in Spanish America, especially in borderlands.

But the violence in the United States was relatively restrained compared with the brutality and destruction in the rest of the Americas. Although specific numbers are notoriously difficult to confirm, well over 100,000 people in Haiti died between 1792 and 1807 in racialized slaughters. In the Spanish Empire, wars often consisted of raids by bandits and insurgents, broad movements of untrained marauders, and counterinsurgency by Spanish and Creole officers and officials. Leaders equipped with professional soldiers and driven by ruthless determination were frequently willing to deploy terror. Among the most successful was Félix Calleja, a royalist general who had lived in New Spain since 1789 and who used his military experience, talent, and a well-equipped and disciplined army to defeat insurgents in Mexico. In the wake of victory, Calleja made few distinctions between insurgents and noncombatants, destroying villages and food, corralling people into barricaded towns, and executing soldiers and civilians without ceremony. Not only did his men inflict tens of thousands of casualties, they also severely disrupted the economic foundations of New Spain, including haciendas and mines. It would take decades for Mexico to recover.

Many rebel leaders sought to imitate the tactics and strategy of European armies, right down to modeling their dress and behavior on figures such as Napoleon Bonaparte. Despite their disadvantages in weapons, especially artillery, and in training, they engaged in pitched battles in broad daylight that amounted to duels of honor on a grand scale. Only a few succeeded in fighting better-trained and better-equipped royalist forces on their own tactical grounds, and usually in regions where the *criollo* population felt relatively secure. Most notable was José de San Martín, who in early 1817 led a well-trained army in a famous march over the Andes to liberate Chile. In the United States, George Washington had learned quickly that he could not defeat the British in pitched battles and had turned to a guerrilla strategy of avoiding major engagements and harassing the enemy until they finally grew tired of the costs and went home. Creole leaders, eager to distance themselves from *castas*, and distrustful of what they considered to be unreliable and unruly militia, were horrified by the huge numbers of people of color swarming to ill-defined calls for independence. Indeed, a marker of *criollos'* sense of themselves as a distinctively civilized people, alone entitled to lead new nations, was their insistence on playing by European rules, although they also engaged in tactical alliances with men of color—especially in South America.

The career of Simón Bolívar (1783–1830) illustrates the tensions common in these wars. Born in Caracas, Bolívar was educated in a Spanish military academy and traveled in Europe, where he became a great admirer of Napoleon Bonaparte. In 1813, he became a leader of independence forces in New Granada, centered on modern Colombia and Venezuela, and issued a Decreto de Guerra a Muerte (Declaration of War to the Death). Bolívar soon realized that he could not succeed without alliances with people of color, including Haitians—independent since 1804—some of whom joined to fight with him in Venezuela in 1817. To outlast imperial armies, supporters of independence not only had to form coalitions with *castas* and mestizos but also to promise a degree of equality and internal autonomy. Supporters of European authority had to make similar concessions. By 1820, only 10 to 15 percent of the Spanish army in Venezuela was white; the rest were *castas* and Indians. Of the roughly 10,000 to 12,000 royalist troops engaged in the climactic Battle of Ayacucho in 1824, fewer than 1 percent were European-born. The warfare among the various regions grouped together as Gran Colombia (1819–1830) also highlighted the degree to which local loyalties challenged efforts to form federations on the not-untroubled model of the United States. Bolívar's considerable political skills and personal charisma proved unable to overcome centrifugal tendencies that eventually divided Gran Colombia into Colombia, Venezuela, Ecuador, and Peru.

Outcomes

The Atlantic character of the wars fought in the Americas was reflected in their outcomes as well as in their origins. North American rebels failed to expand their confederation of colonial militias into Canada or the Caribbean, either in the 1775–1783 conflict in North America or in the ensuing war of 1812–1815, thereby leaving the British with strong outposts in the Americas. The expensive and ultimately ineffective 1802 French invasion of Haiti prompted Napoleon to sell his claims to western North America to the United States in the Louisiana Purchase of 1803. The divisive and regional character of the Spanish Wars for Independence permanently broke up the major imperial entity in the Americas into multiple republics. The officer corps who had led these wars exercised disproportionate influence on the contours of new republics, starting with the United States. George Washington was only the first of the successful military leaders to become a political leader of a new nation. These officers were often key supporters of strong central governments, in no small part because they were acutely aware of the challenges of coordinating and implementing policies to deal with well-entrenched regional rivalries across long distances, with inadequate means of transportation and communication, with few or weak fiscal institutions to support operations, and with unclear or overlapping lines of power.

To a significant extent, the military mobilization of independence movements tended to foreshadow the institutional development of the nations they created. The Continental Army in the United States was the first truly national institution, bringing together men from all over eastern North America. Washington's success at managing a motley collection of militia and Continental troops was his chief qualification for the presidency in 1789. By contrast, the difficulties faced by Spanish American leaders such as Bolívar—especially after the Haitian war—in building workable coalitions among vastly diverse groups of people who mistrusted one another presaged the military coups d'état common in nineteenth-century republics in South America. The legacy of these wars included intense conflict between supporters of strong central governments, the Roman Catholic Church, and social hierarchy on the one hand, and various liberal groups who wanted local autonomy, free trade, and a degree of political equality on the other. In the United States in the nineteenth century, the war for independence passed into popular memory as one of the foundations of American nationalism, less a protracted civil war than a consensual defense of human rights. Citizens of South American republics, on the other hand, tended to perpetuate the unresolved conflicts of the independence era in struggles, often armed, over who their true leaders might be and the extent of their contributions to independence, and whether the wars had divided citizens along class and racial lines more than uniting them in strong nation-states.

ANDREW CAYTON

Bibliography

Adelman, Jeremy. *Sovereignty and Revolution in the Iberian Atlantic*. Princeton, NJ: Princeton University Press, 2009.

Anderson, Fred, and Andrew Cayton. *The Dominion of War: Empire and Liberty in North America, 1500–2000*. New York: Viking, 2005.

Anna, Timothy. *Spain and the Loss of America*. Lincoln: University of Nebraska Press, 1983.

Archer, Christon I., ed. *The Wars of Independence in Spanish America*. Wilmington, DE: Scholarly Resources, 2000.

Fischer, David Hackett. *Washington's Crossing*. New York: Oxford University Press, 2006.

Lee, Wayne. *Barbarians and Brothers: Atrocity and Restraint in Anglo-American Warfare, 1500–1865*. New York: Oxford University Press, 2011.

Lynch, John. *Simón Bolívar, A Life*. New Haven, CT: Yale University Press, 2007.

Mapp, Paul. *The Elusive West and the Contest for Empire, 1713–1763*. Chapel Hill: University of North Carolina Press for the Omohundro Institute of Early American History and Culture, 2011.

McKenzie, S. P. *Revolutionary Armies in the Modern Era: A Revisionist Approach*. London: Routledge, 1997.

Popkin, Jeremy D. *You Are All Free: The Haitian Revolution and the Abolition of Slavery*. Cambridge: Cambridge University Press, 2010.

Wasserman, Mark. *Everyday Life and Politics in Nineteenth-Century Mexico: Men, Women, and War*. Albuquerque: University of New Mexico Press, 2000.

Young, Eric Van. *The Other Rebellion: Popular Violence, Ideology, and the Mexican Struggle for Independence, 1810–1821*. Stanford, CA: Stanford University Press, 2002.

Weapons of the Weak

Historians have puzzled over why, given the brutal exploitation of so many people in the early-modern Atlantic World, so few seem to have chosen to rebel against their oppressors. The anthropologist James C. Scott theorized "everyday forms of resistance" as the most viable strategy for exploited people whose open rebellion would have been crushed by overwhelming violence. Vulnerable people used "weapons of the weak" by quietly manipulating the very powers that dominated them, achieving small victories unnoticed by their oppressors. Confrontational resistance rarely brought as much meaningful change as did the small gains that accrued day by day. In the Atlantic arena, enslaved people of African descent and Native American laborers in New Spain, two populations traditionally associated with weapons of the weak, manipulated the economic, intellectual, and religious tools that their exploiters inadvertently provided them.

Stealing Time

When forced laborers recognized their economic value to their oppressors, they took control of key aspects of their work. In many agricultural regions of the Americas, enslaved Africans who believed they were overworked or mistreated simply threatened to absent themselves. Many followed through on their threats by hiding out during crucial harvest seasons when every hand was needed. Some sought new, less demanding masters in neighboring regions or joined communities of runaway slaves in remote places accessible to them but hard for their owners to reach. These strategies leveraged the high value of slaves to masters who relied on them to generate revenue or to avoid defaulting on European debts. A master might then tolerate a short-term absence if the runaway returned at a moment of peak labor scarcity or possessed a skill essential to productive operations. But most agricultural workers avoided retribution by choosing less-confrontational ways of subverting production. Many limited their workloads by feigning or exaggerating illness. Others asserted that their assignments required more time than allotted and proved their point by working less vigorously whenever unobserved. Workers who wished to ease their labor less directly destroyed equipment or set fire to essential buildings.

Native Americans in New Spain, exploited without being enslaved, also used their oppressors' economic dependence on them to moderate their working conditions. European immigrants, whose access to Spanish territories was tightly restricted, failed to meet the labor needs of plantations, textile workshops, and mining operations there. Managers turned to state-sanctioned labor drafts from nearby Indian towns but found that forced laborers combated these requirements by feigning incomprehension and slowing down work. A growing class of displaced individuals from the large indigenous population filled the void by agreeing to work for pay, using the labor shortage to bargain for better conditions and advance wages. Those laborers who were most willing to move—usually young, male, and Spanish-speaking—could shift from unsatisfactory jobs to others with more promise, effectively forcing employers to compete for their labor. Mining commanded the highest wages, but hired workers even in textiles and commercial agriculture used mobility and linguistic ability to strengthen their positions.

Enslaved people of African descent in many places lessened their material deprivations by using the hours left to them to grow extra food and earn money. In South Carolina, instead of using "gang system" working groups for set numbers of hours, managers switched to a "task system" that assigned jobs (measured in bushels, rows, or acres) and promised that, upon completion, the day's remaining hours would belong to the slaves. Those extra hours could be key to survival in certain regions, such as Jamaica and South Carolina, where masters in fact depended on slaves to cultivate their own provisions in garden plots. Some produced more food than they could eat, selling it at Sunday markets. Others "stole" from their masters whatever they believed rightly to be theirs. Either way, even a little extra money furnished significant comforts to people at the margins.

Turning the Tables

Coerced laborers also turned their masters' own ideologies of control and justice against them.

Christian ideals motivated European authorities' involvements in the Americas and justified domination of indigenous groups and the perpetual enslavement of Africans. Yet these laborers and their advocates used these religious principles to argue for improvements in their conditions. Masters could not compel slaves to work on Sundays, ceding those precious hours for community building and personal economic activity. In fact, the threat of eternal damnation induced at least some masters to govern their slaves with a semblance of Christian charity. In Anglophone regions, an ideology of patriarchalism demanded obedience from dependents but also promised a reciprocal responsibility to care for and protect them. Slaves who understood these ethical commitments petitioned masters for holidays and gifts, cast-off clothing, and reduced work assignments. Near the end of the eighteenth century, growing transatlantic cultures that celebrated humanitarianism, familial affection, and individualism softened this ideology into a paternalism that emphasized consensual relations, strengthening further the bargaining power of the enslaved. For example, masters honored requests not to disperse families by selling individuals to new owners. A petitioner who emphasized love for and faithful service to a master invoked paternalistic responsibilities, if not also sentiments, that could threaten a master with dishonor, resulting in a certificate of manumission.

Catholicism provided Indians and Africans in New Spain with similar opportunities to turn its sacraments against their masters and Spanish authorities. When it was decided that Indians, as Christian neophytes, deserved exemption from inquisitions, individuals whose behavior attracted the attention of inquisitors identified themselves as Indian even if in other situations they self-identified as mestizo (of mixed Indian and European backgrounds). Royal and religious authorities each competed to defend the indigenous population from the abuses of the other, and Indians played crown and church against each other to obtain relief from grievances. Civil authorities could be counted on to act against ecclesiastical abuses, while religious authorities tended to take up Indian causes that undermined their secular counterparts. Each body granted Indians access to its courts, and indigenous litigants cannily moved lawsuits from one court to the other when they saw advantage that way. People of African descent who were dragged before courts, but who were familiar with the dominant language and legal culture, similarly invoked European values and appealed to the sense of duty of officials who were, after all, entrusted with the application of their own laws. Those who understood legal procedures and standards of evidence could steer their trials away from the worst outcomes.

At times, oppressed people could also take advantage of a conflict between two monarchical regimes that were competing for their collaboration. Political boundaries in the Americas took on new legal importance as the kingdoms of Spain and England (later Great Britain) pursued possessions overseas. Slaves crossed the asserted boundaries to leverage their value, as laborers and as potential soldiers, to bargain for greater autonomy. Many crossed from British South Carolina to Spanish Florida, from Jamaica to Cuba, and from the Leeward Islands to Puerto Rico. Spanish authorities recognized the geopolitical gains of depopulating economic regions critical to the British, while reinforcing their own fighting populations. They therefore granted freedom to runaway slaves who converted to Catholicism, and in some instances organized them into formidable militias. During the American Revolution, some slaves of rebellious colonists capitalized on British military commanders' offers of this opportunity. These chances for freedom and political membership, however, came only to individuals willing to leave behind families or communities. Most found that price too high.

Strength in Numbers

Perhaps the most powerful weapons for "the weak" were relationships that promoted social cohesion, mutual responsibility, and group support in times of individual need. People formed these ethical bonds not only from natural human impulses but also as strategic responses to the vulnerability of being alone. Captors used social isolation to control workers recruited for local projects by bringing them in from distant places. But workers did not allow their isolation to last. Displaced Africans formed enduring connections even while on the Middle Passage; years after arrival, they recognized and respected former "shipmates."

English colonial law did not recognize marriages for the enslaved, but in practice slaveholders acknowledged these attachments and sometimes honored them. As patriarchalism softened into paternalism, masters informally recognized slave families, especially when abolitionism threatened further imports at the end of the eighteenth century, and amelioration of slaves' domestic conditions seemed the best way to maintain workforces. Those who did not respect the ties of family risked losing a slave's labor, at least temporarily while he took flight to visit his wife and children. The greatest motivation for running away was not freedom in a legal sense, but rather the opportunity to visit relatives. In Spanish America, the powerful Catholic Church ensured that slaves' marriages would be protected legally as sacraments. In fact, couples separated through sale of one spouse or the other could petition for Church intervention to reunite their families. The Church ordered masters to give leave for a husband to visit his wife one working day per week, and it forced masters to arrange propitious sales, on threat of excommunication. The enslaved often invoked the sacrament of marriage to trump the property rights of masters.

Forced laborers who were congregated in large numbers created power structures of their own, largely undetected by masters blinded by their dehumanizing ideologies of slavery. Slaves in British America elevated men respected in local communities, bestowed titles on those who accrued material wealth, and chose leaders on "election days" that paralleled the political contests of their enfranchised European counterparts. These artifacts of self-governance were the visible tips of vast submerged structures of power among the enslaved. Religious practitioners also provided leadership and cohesion for groups of displaced laborers. In Brazil diviners used skills learned in Africa to adjudicate disputes, identify thieves, and explain illnesses seen as having interpersonal origins. More often than not they reinforced the cohesion of the group by fingering outsiders as causes of crime or misfortune among their people. Diviners evoked religious, medical, and judicial rituals with cognates in several regions of Africa to create hybrid communities, with themselves at the center. In other heavily Africanized regions of the Americas, Obeah (in the British West Indies) and Vodou (in the French Antilles) provided similar social cohesion for groups that the enslaved formed well below the radar of their masters' surveillance.

Diviners grew especially powerful when they attracted the business of white masters looking to augment failed Christian remedies. They sold their services to masters by promising to remedy the human problems slavery itself had created: they identified thieves, healed overworked laborers, and provided advice about how to handle people whom masters viewed through only the narrowest of exploitive lenses. Because diviners established the "truth" of a situation for anyone who accepted their spiritual authority, those who convinced masters of their abilities gained temporary access to masters' coercive power. For example, one practitioner who was enlisted to identify a thief told his master that he needed to release several people from jail in order to do so. Other diviners identified suspected culprits as their masters' friends and relatives. All the while, they collected fees for their seeming insights. Some convinced their masters to hire them out as healers, winning themselves mobility, autonomy, lighter work, and perhaps some extra cash. Their greatest service, though, was in controlling information on which masters based decisions and, especially, in providing a focal point for displaced Africans to gather around.

Christianity provided ready-made institutionalized venues and mechanisms that Africans isolated by enslavement used to form communities of their own. It is unclear to what degree they understood Christian dogma as European believers did. Africans in the Americas gave Christianity myriad forms of their own, but universally they used it to assemble for reasons that their captors could not easily reject. Even in Anglo America, where masters usually overpowered religious organizations in favor of their own secular governments, missionaries from marginal sects provided venues for activities that enslaved African Americans used to strengthen their communities. By the end of the eighteenth century, an African Methodist Episcopal Church emerged as a social center and political space for black Americans.

Exploited laborers in Mexico and Brazil created political communities by embracing the Old World institution of the lay brotherhood of worshippers in a Catholic parish. The Church hoped that the religious brotherhoods would provide a way for newly arrived Africans to internalize Catholicism. Enslaved Africans readily occupied the officially sanctioned meeting space, but not for orthodox Catholic purposes. They practiced their own hybridized religions, whether African or Afro-Christian, and they performed customary feast-day processions with their own singing and dancing. Many of the brotherhoods became enclaves for people who identified with certain ethnic communities or worked in particular skilled trades, enabling those segments of the enslaved population to mobilize to protect their interests. These organizations also gave monetary assistance to the needy and to slaves who needed cash to purchase their freedom, further knitting their communities together.

These communities of the weak strengthened other weapons against the strong by passing on knowledge on how to manipulate masters and ecclesiastical courts or by shielding thieves and arsonists from detection. As in any community, of course, exploited laborers competed with one another, harbored resentments, and pursued rivalries. These tensions, if kept stable or resolved productively, potentially deepened community ties. In societies of exploitation, however, dominant powers sometimes used these divisions to control the weak. In Brazil and Mexico, inquisitors relied on a victim's neighbors and acquaintances for evidence of sinful living. In British America, masters rewarded slaves who reported on the crimes of others. Potential constant surveillance made it difficult to create new bonds of trust. Yet, for all of the grim legal proceedings that compose the historical record, much more social solidarity went unrecorded by authorities who could not see it or did not care.

Local Goals, Atlantic Weapons

Unprotected people defended themselves by manipulating their local positions in broader processes that occurred on Atlantic scales. They understood the value of their labor in chronically underpopulated places and recognized their indebted masters' economic vulnerability to interruptions in their work. In complex encounters in Europe, Africa, and the Americas they pleaded for better treatment by appropriating the cultural and religious assumptions of their oppressors. They took advantage of conflicts between powerful colonizers in disputed regions to bargain for recognition of their rights, and they found shelter under the umbrella of colonial institutions intended to enlist them spiritually. Day by day, displaced and vulnerable people created new communities that they hoped would sustain them in the face of adversity. Weapons of the weak were not intended to turn worlds upside down. Unprotected people found more value in personal autonomy and communal continuity than in violent political revolution. Most of them preferred low-risk, high-reward strategies that won human-scale victories by turning the strengths of their oppressors against them.

JASON T. SHARPLES

Bibliography

Bennett, Herman L. *Africans in Colonial Mexico: Absolutism, Christianity, and Afro-Creole Consciousness, 1570–1640.* Bloomington: Indiana University Press, 2003.

Benton, Lauren A. *Law and Colonial Cultures: Legal Regimes in World History, 1400–1900.* New York: Cambridge University Press, 2001.

Morgan, Philip D. *Slave Counterpoint: Black Culture in the Eighteenth-Century Chesapeake and Lowcountry.* Chapel Hill: University of North Carolina Press for the Omohundro Institute of Early American History and Culture, 1998.

Scott, James C. *Weapons of the Weak: Everyday Forms of Peasant Resistance.* New Haven, CT: Yale University Press, 1985.

Sweet, James H. *Recreating Africa: Culture, Kinship, and Religion in the African-Portuguese World, 1441–1770.* Chapel Hill: University of North Carolina Press, 2006.

Van Young, Eric. *Hacienda and Market in Eighteenth-Century Mexico: The Rural Economy of the Guadalajara Region, 1675–1820.* Berkeley: University of California Press, 1981.

World/Global History

During the past few decades, world history and other approaches to understanding human affairs on planetary scales, including global history, have grown into a highly diversified research field that is entangled with branches of Atlantic history. Many practitioners of world/global history have become highly critical of Eurocentric and nation-centered perspectives. Even so, the sociologies of world history and Atlantic history continue to privilege Western scholarly communities.

Contours of a Field

Atlantic history in its present shape is far from constituting a single, coherent academic field. Rather, a wide variety of research initiatives based in different regional frameworks contribute either explicitly or implicitly to the history of the "Atlantic." Only a small fraction of the academic literature that has been ascribed to "Atlantic history" offers the compound, inclusive narrative of the Atlantic that is inherent to the concept. Quite to the contrary, most of the relevant literature ranges from studies covering small regions to projects operating on transnational or even larger, macroscopic scales. In fact, many publications that are highly relevant for "Atlantic history" do not even cover that ocean in an immediate sense.

Similarly, the terms *world history* and *global history* do not point to unified research fields. Even a quick glance at important forums such as the *Journal of World History* or the *Journal of Global History* suggests that only a small proportion of the projects commonly considered to be relevant really covers genuinely worldwide or "global" topics and problems. Rather than investigating the entire planet, the majority of contributions to world history mainly investigate much smaller regions. What they usually have in common is a quest to draw connections among different local experiences. This impulse is particularly significant for an academic discipline such as history, which has long been dominated by nation-centered and other, similarly constrained, perspectives.

In that sense it is certainly not the case that world/global history represents no more than a receptacle for all the currents of historical research: it is far less—and at the same time much more—than the entirety of historiography in its present state. Nevertheless, the apparent lack of clear disciplinary contours poses a definitional problem. For instance, particularly during the 1990s and early 2000s, much ink was spilled in debates about possible field designations and their relationship with each other. For instance, prominent advocates of the term *global history* argued that the much older expression *world history* was too tainted by its own heritage of narratives based on assumptions of European religious and, later, civilizational or even racial supremacy. They proposed *global history* as an alternative less laden with the presumed virtues of "Western (Christian) civilization."

However, as many other scholars responded, world historians as a research community have grown widely critical of teleological and Eurocentric perspectives presenting the "rise of the West" as the culminating moment in the history of the globe. In addition, in the United States and many other countries, world history has become a research field in the sense that its primary products are no longer textbooks and trade books offering seemingly comprehensive accounts of the history of humankind. The field has evolved into a rather diverse landscape of more concrete themes and projects, the majority of which are based primarily on source work and, by implication, also operate on far more modest, albeit transnational geographical scales. World history seen from this broad, research-based perspective can include, for example, a project on postwar cartoons in Japan and the United States, as well as a study of pan-African networks linking Los Angeles and Addis Ababa in Ethiopia.

This multifaceted research landscape makes it impossible to distinguish world history categorically from other branches of historiography, such as social history, cultural history, environmental history, or—in the present context—Atlantic history. Thus, as world history has grown far beyond its Eurocentric heritage, it is also not feasible to differentiate this field from global history. The same overlapping characterizes a whole range of terminological alternatives, such as *transnational history* or *translocal history*, that have come to enjoy a certain prominence in recent years. In fact, most researchers do not insist on using any particular field designation.

So it is certainly appropriate to operate with *world/global history*, the heading for this essay, or similarly combined expressions. Whether in "world," "global," or "transnational" history, increasing numbers of historians have become involved in tackling the political and intellectual regimes of territoriality that for so long have dominated historiography. For instance, important historiographical trends have explored alternatives to the idea of the nation as the main container of the past. In addition, more and more scholars have become critical of the "myth of continents" bceause it insinuates that such vast and diverse spaces as "Asia" or "Africa" share a cultural

or a common past. In that sense also, the "area studies," as they were founded during the Cold War period, at least implicitly provided a rather distorted vision of the past, for research on entire world regions was compartmentalized into different research communities. Such institutional structures, often built around particular linguistic skills, had the overall effect that different regional experts faced hurdles in attempting to collaborate with one another on global scales. In addition to these problems intrinsic to research on regions outside of the West, the historiography of Europe and North America was for a long time regionally isolated and developed only a few engagements with scholarship focusing on other parts of the world.

World history, or global history, thus stands for the quest to experiment with conceptions of space that deliberately transgress the mental and institutional maps that have defined historiography since its inception as a modern field of research and teaching. Similarly, as part of a search for alternatives to Western-centric worldviews and hegemonic storylines, many scholars have come to challenge the idea of Europe as a coherent, self-enveloping civilization. Certainly, not all the new work in world history has sought to abandon the normative lenses that have dominated world-history writing. Nevertheless, critiques of narratives based on the assumption of Western-led progress have become rather common among the scholarly communities working on world/global and transnational history. The main question is how to find convincing alternatives to Eurocentric perspectives.

Agency in World History

While most scholars in world history certainly do not want to write nations out of the human experience, they typically do not want to see them as objectively given ways of organizing and understanding the past. Hence it is small wonder that concepts like flows, webs, connections, entanglements, and mutual influences have moved to the center of historians' areas of inquiry. Taking the multitude of recent approaches together, the globe emerges as a kaleidoscopic realm of overlapping, entangled, and interacting spaces.

This integrative approach ought not to be misunderstood as a collective craze about boundless webs projected from the global present backward into the past. Among other themes, recent scholarship in the field of world/global history has added new facets to the study of hierarchical relations across social, cultural, and geographical boundaries. For example, economic historians have come to focus on how transnational flows in the trade of such key commodities as sugar or cotton transformed entire communities by integrating them into systems of unequal relations. Other scholars have started applying transnational or even global-historical perspectives to the history of Eurocentrism. For example, they study how certain ideologies, notions of modernity as well as ideas about advancement and backwardness, came to be spread across many cultures and societies around the world. For instance, in many colonial societies ideas of Western-led progress had a heavy impact on political and intellectual life.

Generally speaking, world/global history has grown very critical of approaches juxtaposing an expansionist, dynamic West with a purely reactive "rest." In a growing number of historical portraits, European colonial powers no longer figure as the unmoved movers of the rest of the globe. Quite to the contrary, many research projects now consider how colonial encounters and other global entanglements affected European societies. In addition, there is a trend to break down the presumed contrasts between colonizing (European) and colonized (other) societies by focusing on the parallels in the experiences of specific social groups within these two conventional frameworks. Hybridization and creolization have emerged as two of the key concepts that are guiding a growing number of studies. Hence, as a general trend, world history has been characterized by a growing readiness to grant more narrative space and historical agency to the world outside of the West.

Atlantic History and World/Global History

Since world/global history can be defined only loosely as a field that overlaps with a large number of other research areas, it is also impossible to draw a clear dividing line with Atlantic history. The historical study of maritime spaces, like the Atlantic, is a good example of historians' growing interest in conceiving of space beyond the conventional nation-state framework. After all, the topographies of oceans and seas do not match the boundaries of single nations or continents—rather, their openness to movements invites the historical observer to take alternate routes around nation-centered thinking.

Among the world's oceanic rims, the history of the Atlantic is being studied most widely. In a development synchronic with world/global history, Atlantic history has grown into a vibrant field characterized by detailed research projects taking—at least as a general tendency—increasingly critical attitudes toward both nation-centered and Eurocentric approaches. Maritime historians have come to investigate a wealth of topics from translocal perspectives. Examples range from trading communities and exchanges among cultures of nautical and other technologies to the specific mechanisms behind, and limits of, ideologies of imperial expansion and dominance. Also analogous to the developments in world history, Atlantic history has come to be characterized by efforts to critically reconsider older concepts of historical agents. This has been, for example, the case with the black Atlantic literature that helped to move the study of Atlantic history even further from Western-centric and elite-centered perspectives.

As with world history, the growing importance of Atlantic histories has contributed to challenging the idea of Europe as a coherent historical unit. For instance, during the past few centuries the social histories of Britain, Ireland, and other countries were more closely connected with North America than with much of eastern Europe. Even within working-class milieus, a larger number of families maintained close ties between the eastern and the western shores of the Atlantic. In that sense, the study of transatlantic family connection shows the necessity of transcending national perspectives and, at the same time, the inadequacy of replacing them with the history of continents like "Europe."

Atlantic history has also been an arena generating challenges to the idea that home-grown European inventions changed the world. For instance, detailed studies have added much substance to the argument that modern national revolutions emerged in a complex Atlantic nexus rather than emanating from an inspired European epicenter. An example is the Atlantic scholarship on the consequences of the Haitian revolution, fought by African-descended persons, many enslaved, for freedom from French rule. These groups need to be seen as important forces that contributed to applying human-rights discourses to people outside of the Western context. It is obvious that the implications of such studies go further than viewing the Atlantic as a system of regional interaction. Rather, they invite scholars to further reconsider some major world-historical narratives.

Such broad scholarly initiatives hold out the promise of opening up more connections of Atlantic history with other aspects of the world's past. For instance, the currently largely separate scholarly communities studying the Atlantic, Indian, and Pacific oceans will gain individually and collectively from dialogues with one another. New questions and paradigms necessarily arise from lowering the communication barriers between separate academic circles working on compatible themes. In recent decades, both world history and Atlantic history have provided opportunities for scholars representing a variety of disciplinary backgrounds and areas to collaborate with one another. In many of these projects, the boundaries between world and Atlantic history have already become blurred.

While both Atlantic history and world history have created new ways of understanding the past, they still remain dominated by Anglo-American scholarship, which—despite all efforts to overcome Eurocentric perspectives—perpetuates the academic hierarchies they seek to break down. For example, U.S.-based scholars can typically afford to ignore relevant scholarship produced in Africa and Latin America, but the opposite is far from being the case. If we understand world history and Atlantic history as fields seeking to produce new balanced and integrative perspectives, we need to make their respective research communities more inclusive. The historiography of the Atlantic and the world will inevitably fall short of its potential for dialogue and diversity if the communication barriers between privileged and underprivileged scholarly communities across the Atlantic and around the world remain as high as they have been in the past.

DOMINIC M. SACHSENMAIER

Bibliography

Iriye, Akira, and Pierre-Yves Saunier, eds. *The Palgrave Dictionary of Transnational History: From the Mid-nineteenth Century to the Present Day*. New York: Palgrave Macmillan, 2009.

Manning, Patrick. *Navigating World History: Historians Create a Global Past*. New York: Palgrave Macmillan, 2003.

Osterhammel, Jürgen, and Niels P. Petersson. *Globalization: A Short History*. Princeton, NJ: Princeton University Press, 2005.

Sachsenmaier, Dominic. *Global Perspectives on Global History: Theories and Approaches in a Connected World*. Cambridge: Cambridge University Press, 2011.

Wigen, Kären E., and Martin W. Lewis. "A Maritime Response to the Crisis in Area Studies." *Geographical Review* 89, no. 2 (1999): 161–168.

World-Systems Theory

World-systems theory originated in the 1970s as a methodological approach that combines theoretical nuances both from history's focus on change and from sociology's search for general patterns. Its author and main proponent has been Immanuel Wallerstein, a prominent historical sociologist who has drawn, on one hand, from Marxist theories of the evolutionary development of world capitalism and, on the other hand, from Fernand Braudel's approach to world history as operating over multiple time-scales, including a basic dynamic of very long—even millennial—duration. World-systems theory, now hailed as a forerunner of current theories of globalization, responded to the unidimensional and unidirectional model of development-as-progress in vogue in post–World War II theories of economic and social modernization. It sought to reconfigure the "wealth of [the modern] nations" that Adam Smith had anticipated in 1776 in what was, effectively, the first analysis of the political economy of the early-modern Atlantic, as the result of a complex historical process of a "capitalist world-economy" that had originated and expanded by subordinating different regions of the world to a concentration of capital in a western European core.

The starting point of this process related to the making of an integrated Atlantic World through exploration of the Americas, and the consequent interoceanic exchange of goods, from c. 1500 onward. In *The Modern World-System*—a four-volume socioeconomic and political history of the world from the sixteenth to the twentieth centuries, with two further volumes planned—Wallerstein explained in detail both the theoretical underpinnings of his model and his views on the historical development of the modern capitalist world-economy. His work has attracted a great deal of criticism, proportionate to its profound influence on thinking about history on Atlantic scales and beyond, but it has also remained resilient through his and others' refinements of his watershed approach to world history and to the history of capitalism.

Wallerstein's World-Systems Theory and Its Critics

Essentially, in the words of William I. Robinson, a historical sociologist, "world-systems theory as elaborated by Wallerstein starts with the proposition that the appropriate unit of analysis for macrosocial inquiry in the modern world is neither class, nor state/society, nor country, but the larger historical system in which those categories are located" (Robinson, 727). Thus, rejecting the once-orthodox view that history should investigate the rise of states and nations, Wallerstein defined the comparably coherent units of analysis as all the global regions, including countries and societies subsumed in them, of a "world-system" with significant—in the sense of enabling change—mutual relationships with one another. According to Wallerstein, world-systems took two forms over the long course of the history of the world: world-empires and world-economies. World-empires were the large, self-contained socioeconomic spheres of historical engagement dominant until the sixteenth century, highly centralized and diverse political systems operating mostly through tribute within territorial boundaries; typical examples were the empires of the Romans and Han (Chinese, 206 BCE–220 CE).

Since about 1500 CE, the start of the Atlantic Era, the world has witnessed the emergence of a different, modern type of world-system, a world-economy based on capitalist investment in production and trade extended out to the rest of the globe from western Europe. Unlike the earlier world-empires, as Wallerstein's theory goes, the modern world-economy did not operate within a single political entity with a fixed boundary, but rather incorporated different political centers and differing social and political institutions. The growing number of regions of the world linked in this single world-economic system were integrated in three different, complementing ways. The so-called core regions—western Europe and eventually North America—were the most economically advanced, through incipient and then full-scale industrial capitalism, accompanied by wage labor and military power. Effectively, these were the regions that accumulated the wealth generated by the entire capitalist world-system. The most powerful countries in them, all located in the northern Atlantic, succeeded one another in a series of periods of world-economic hegemony. The Netherlands had been the core region in the seventeenth century, followed by England in the eighteenth century, and by the twentieth century the core region was firmly located in the United States. Complementing these processes, but not to their advantage, the less economically advanced regions supplied raw materials—essentially agricultural commodities—to the economically developed core and were accordingly termed *peripheries*. In these regions, forms of unfree agricultural labor, from slavery to serfdom, were the norm. Another group of regions were termed by Wallerstein *semi-peripheries*; they were either former core areas no longer at the cutting edge of capitalist development or former peripheries on their way to becoming regions of the core. Beyond the fringes of this modern world-system lay seemingly inert regions like Africa.

Criticism of Wallerstein's world-system approach to history appeared soon after publication of the first volume of *The Modern World-System* in 1974. It charged the author with creating a teleological approach to world history, or even a Eurocentric view of it, that subordinated the semiautonomous histories of many regions elsewhere to the larger dynamics of his "world-system." Critics also saw this systemic approach as giving too much weight to economic structures that made little or no allowance for human agency or creativity. This effective dehumanization of history was initially driven home by orthodox Marxist historians, such as Robert Brenner, who thought that Wallerstein's market determinism had led him to neglect the crucial importance of class struggle in making world history.

William Robinson has specifically questioned the usefulness of the long-term time framework adopted by this theory in accounting for recent dispersions of financial power in the global world-economy. In particular, Robinson has argued that these economic changes of the late twentieth and early twenty-first centuries have led to the making of "an integrated global financial system" which, since the 1970s, "has replaced the national-bank dominated systems of earlier periods." According to Robinson, this recent phase of global economic integration is incompatible with Wallerstein's view of a world-economy "broken down into distinct and competing national economies," all assigned their particular places in the capitalist world-system as either cores, peripheries, or semi-peripheries (Robinson, 17).

In 1976, Wallerstein founded the Fernand Braudel Center for the Study of Economies, Historical Systems, and Civilizations at the State University of New York at Binghamton. This center has published a prestigious scholarly journal called *Review*, in the pages of which historians who embrace Wallerstein's world-systems theory have debated its methodological issues. One of the most important outcomes of these debates in world-historical terms has been to apply world-systems analysis to earlier periods, both in antiquity and in the medieval world, as well as to such other parts of the globe as the Indian Ocean and the South China Sea. Thus, Christopher Chase-Dunn has compared world-systems throughout history and argued that preagrarian societies were already "multicultural world-systems with their own complex networks of exchange" (Robinson, 160). Chase-Dunn, Janet Abu-Lughod, and partly Giovanni Arrighi have also traced the European capitalist world-system further back in time than Wallerstein's date of c. 1500, and specifically to the twelfth- and thirteenth-century Mediterranean. Jason Moore has extended study of the historical expansion of the capitalist world-economy to investigate environmental changes in what he has called "commodity frontiers"—that is, seeing the areas that Wallerstein called peripheries in terms of exploitation not only of mostly unfree labor but also of environmental depletion to meet the core's continuously increasing demand for specific raw materials.

An Atlantic World-System?

World-systems theory has provided a global model in which the creation of an integrated Atlantic World has become part of a world-historical narrative of the development of capitalism in Europe. Even though Atlantic historians, like other critics, have criticized Wallerstein's model for its Eurocentrism and emphasis on economics, they have all welcomed his inclusion of all the regions of the Atlantic World in the historical narrative that explained the rise of the modern world-economy centered in Europe.

Systematic applications of the world-systems approach have also illuminated Atlantic history, particularly Dale Tomich and Michael Zeuske's focus on slavery in the Americas. They have argued that a type of exploitative, capitalist-oriented "second slavery" emerged at the end of the eighteenth century in the U.S. South, Cuba, and Brazil following a first slavery, which had characterized the colonial Americas. This second slavery structurally advanced the Atlantic to a central position among the peripheries of the world-economy through the "mass concentration of slave labourers devoted to staple production and the creation of new productive spaces in order to meet growing world market demand for tropical and semi-tropical plantation staples generated by industrialization and urbanization" (Tomich and Zeuske, 92). In other words, from the 1790s, the growing demand for cotton, sugar, and coffee generated by the industrializing and industrialized North Atlantic regions—mainly Britain and the northeastern United States—led to the comparably massive slave-based production of those three crops in plantations in the southern United States, Cuba, and Brazil.

Scholars are currently in the process of analyzing further how the idea of a "second slavery" in the nineteenth century, ultimately traceable to Wallerstein's approach, can reconcile the capitalist, or corelike, characteristics of these highly profitable and exploitative systems of unfree labor characteristic of peripheral regions: the cotton-based plantation slavery in North America for industrial production in Britain and the sugar-based and coffee-based production for consumer markets in the plantation slavery predominant in Cuba and Brazil. This updated version of the "world-systems" perspective thus promises to differentiate among contrasting components of a region formerly considered only as an undifferentiated periphery, thus allowing scholars to define the contributions of distinct regions within the Atlantic World as well as the Atlantic as a whole in the historical development of the capitalist world-economy.

ENRICO DAL LAGO

Bibliography

Moore, Jason W. "Sugar and the Expansion of the Early Modern World-Economy: Commodity Frontiers, Ecological Transformations, and Industrialization." *Review* (Fernand Braudel Center) 23, no. 3 (2000): 409–433.

Robinson, William I. "Globalization and the Sociology of Immanuel Wallerstein: Critical Appraisal." *International Sociology* 26, no. 4 (2011): 723–745.

Tomich, Dale, and Michael Zeuske. "Introduction: The Second Slavery: Mass Slavery, World-Economy, and Comparative Microhistories." *Review* (Fernand Braudel Center) 31 (2008): 91–100.

Wallerstein, Immanuel. *The Modern World-System.* 4 vols. Berkeley: University of California Press, 2011 (first three volumes originally published in 1974–1989).

———. *World-Systems Analysis: An Introduction.* Durham, NC: Duke University Press, 2004.

Index

Abd ar-Rahman, 353
Abdul-Rahman Ibn Sori, 261
Aboab da Fonseca, Isaac, 268
abolition, of slavery, 44, 47–49, 179, 181, 212–13, 256, 422;
    and plantations, 165, 178; Muslim clerics and, 262; slave re-
    volts and, 406
abolition, of the slave trade, 47–49, **57–59**, 181, 423–25; and
    captivity narratives, 306; connection to political transforma-
    tions of, ix, 255; and economic changes, 157, 158; images
    produced for, 473; Muslim clerics and, 262; and planta-
    tions, 178; and sovereignty, 443
abolitionists and abolitionism: and American captivity narra-
    tives, 438; inspired by Haitian revolt, 249; and "legitimate"
    African trade, 156; Olaudah Equiano, 41, 418; and recogni-
    tion of slave families, 493; suppression of, 287; and usurpa-
    tion of narratives, 311–12. *See also* antislavery movements
Abu Bakr, 352
Abu-Lughod, Janet, 500
Academy of Linceans, 34
Academy of Sciences, 34
Acemoglu, D., 176
Acosta de, José, *The Natural and Moral History of the Indies,*
    272
Act for the Liberties of the People, 297
Act of Union, 228, 350
Acts of Trade and Navigation, 39, 459, 460, 461
Adams, Herbert Baxter, 83
Addis Ababa, 499
Adelman, Jeremy, 214
Adriatic Sea, 6
Affaire du Canada, 419
Affaire Lally-Tollendal, 419
Afonso I, 20; Christianity and, 19, 20, 88, 95, 97, 338
Africa: agriculture in, 155; Catholicism in, 15, 16, 65–66, 67,
    90, 93, 94–97, 195–96, 271, 319, 338, 377, 384–85, 397,
    398, 399, 402, 414; Christians and Christianity in, 15, 16,
    20, 30, 48, 66, 69, 88, 90, 93–97, 124, 129, 266, 377, 378,
    384–85, 386–87, 395, 396, 397, 398, 399, 403; diasporas
    in and from, 132, 195, 207, 360, 397; diseases in, 68, 94,
    95, 128, 135, 136, 139, 151, 167–68, 190, 191, 232, 233,
    234, 235, 238, 331, 336, 337, 361, 393, 396, 414, 433,
    450, 451, 486; drought in, 8, 9, 23, 24, 25, 31, 37, 73, 75,
    105–6, 206, 377, 382, 393, 451; economies (economic

strategies) of, **139–44**, 155–58, 426, 428, 429, 432; Euro-
    peans in (Europe and), ix, 9, 12, 14, 15, 23, 25, 29, 48, 49,
    59, 74, 103, 107, 135, 147, 235, 239, 241, 258, 272, 334,
    385, 424, 484; foods of, 27, 34, 63, 64, 108, 109–10, 132,
    140, 157, 168, 191, 205, 206–7, 343, 360, 361, 376, 450;
    gold from, viii–ix, 4, 8, 9, 10, 14, 16, 19, 21, 26, 29, 39,
    40, 68, 72–73, 113, 114, 124, 132, 143, 155, 156, 158,
    211, 258, 282, 334, 366, 372, 376, 413, 416, 419, 428,
    430, 444, 447, 477, 486; healing practices from, 85–86, 95,
    96, 128, 140, 230–32, 396, 397; languages of, 15–16, 29,
    66, 125, 142, 231, 269, 271, 272, 398, 401; Mami Wata
    and, 316–19; Muslims and Islam in, 8, 9, 10, 26, 29, 47,
    94, 133, 140, 233, 257–62, 266, 352, 376, 385, 395, 396,
    397, 398, 403, 427, 477; political systems (military regimes)
    of, ix, 16, 20, 48, 69, 157, 258, 261, 273, 373, 376–79,
    419, 427, 451, 477; Portuguese in, 9, 10, 14, 15–16, 19,
    20, 21, 23, 24–25, 26, 72–73, 77, 86, 88, 93, 94–95, 96,
    113, 124, 132, 145, 156, 178, 182, 186, 235, 271, 282,
    331, 348, 350, 351, 378, 413, 414, 416; religions and reli-
    gious practices of, 95, 97, 395–97, 398–404; revitalization
    movements in, 384–85; the slave trade and, 36, 37–38, 46,
    48, 49, 57, 58, 59, 62, 64, 67, 68, 70, 96, 103, 110, 126,
    128, 136, 140, 141, 142, 143, 156, 157, 160, 188, 191,
    206, 221, 226, 233, 240–41, 253, 254, 259–60, 261, 291,
    326, 351, 373, 376, 377, 384, 389, 396, 397, 404, 418,
    423–25, 426, 429, 432, 434, 484; technologies and, 449–
    52; wars and, 42, 44, 286, 419. *See also* Afro-Asiatic lan-
    guages; Afro-Brazilians; Afro-Creoles; Afro-Eurasia; Afro-
    Europeans; Eurafricans; Luso-Africans
African Americans, 44, 126, 127, 271, 389, 401, 403, 494; as
    "Atlantic black tars," 325; Christianity and, 96–99; death
    and burial practices of, 128, 129; enslaved, promised their
    freedom for siding with the British, 254, 256, 331; enslave-
    ment of, 50, 167, 168, 254, 331; healing practices of, 233–
    34; literary and visual expressions of, 299–304; as maroons,
    126, 325; slave narratives of, 300, 301, 302, 304, 306, 309
Africanus, Leo, *A Geographical Historie of Africa,* 311
Afro-Americans, 312
Afro-Asiatic languages, 270
Afro-Brazilians, 97, 276, 318–19, 402
Afro-Creoles, 164, 222
Afro-Eurasia, 3, 11, 134
Afro-Europeans, 136, 312, 431, 432

UNIVERSITY OF WINCHESTER
LIBRARY